Indiana
Rules of Court

Volume II – Federal

2016

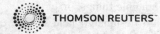
THOMSON REUTERS

Mat#41608337

PREFACE

Designed for use in the office or courtroom, this pamphlet contains Indiana federal rules.

WHAT'S NEW

Indiana Rules of Court, Volume II – Federal, 2015, includes rules and associated material governing practice before the Indiana federal courts. It is current with amendments received through November 1, 2015.

CONTACT US

For additional information or research assistance, call the West reference attorneys at 1-800-REF-ATTY (1-800-733-2889). Contact West's editorial department directly with your questions and suggestions by e-mail at editors.us-legal@thomsonreuters.com.

Thank you for subscribing to this product. Should you have any questions regarding this product please contact Customer Service at 1-800-328-4880 or by fax at 1-800-340-9378. If you would like to inquire about related publications, or to place an order, please contact us at 1-800-344-5009 or visit us online.

THE PUBLISHER

December 2015

THOMSON REUTERS PROVIEW™

This title is one of many now available on your tablet as an eBook.

Take your research mobile. Powered by the Thomson Reuters ProView™ app, our eBooks deliver the same trusted content as your print resources, but in a compact, on-the-go format.

ProView eBooks are designed for the way you work. You can add your own notes and highlights to the text, and all of your annotations will transfer electronically to every new edition of your eBook.

You can also instantly verify primary authority with built-in links to WestlawNext® and KeyCite®, so you can be confident that you're accessing the most current and accurate information.

To find out more about ProView eBooks and available discounts, call 1-800-344-5009.

TABLE OF CONTENTS

FEDERAL
RULES OF CIVIL PROCEDURE
FOR THE
UNITED STATES DISTRICT COURTS

Including Amendments Effective December 1, 2015, Absent Contrary Congressional Action

---

TITLE I. SCOPE OF RULES; FORM OF ACTION

RULE 1. SCOPE AND PURPOSE

[Text of Rule 1 effective until December 1, 2015, absent contrary Congressional action.]

These rules govern the procedure in all civil actions and proceedings in the United States district courts, except as stated in Rule 81. They should be construed and administered to secure the just, speedy, and inexpensive determination of every action and proceeding.

[Text of Rule 1 effective December 1, 2015, absent contrary Congressional action.]

These rules govern the procedure in all civil actions and proceedings in the United States district courts, except as stated in Rule 81. They should be construed, administered, and employed by the court and the parties to secure the just, speedy, and inexpensive determination of every action and proceeding.

(Amended December 29, 1948, effective October 20, 1949; February 28, 1966, effective July 1, 1966; April 22, 1993, effective December 1, 1993; April 30, 2007, effective December 1, 2007; April 29, 2015, effective December 1, 2015, absent contrary Congressional action.)

RULE 2. ONE FORM OF ACTION

There is one form of action—the civil action.

(Amended April 30, 2007, effective December 1, 2007.)

TITLE II. COMMENCING AN ACTION; SERVICE OF PROCESS, PLEADINGS, MOTIONS, AND ORDERS

RULE 3. COMMENCING AN ACTION

A civil action is commenced by filing a complaint with the court.

(Amended April 30, 2007, effective December 1, 2007.)

RULE 4. SUMMONS

(a) Contents; Amendments.

(1) *Contents.* A summons must:

(A) name the court and the parties;

(B) be directed to the defendant;

(C) state the name and address of the plaintiff's attorney or—if unrepresented—of the plaintiff;

(D) state the time within which the defendant must appear and defend;

(E) notify the defendant that a failure to appear and defend will result in a default judgment against the defendant for the relief demanded in the complaint;

(F) be signed by the clerk; and

(G) bear the court's seal.

(2) *Amendments.* The court may permit a summons to be amended.

(b) Issuance. On or after filing the complaint, the plaintiff may present a summons to the clerk for signature and seal. If the summons is properly completed, the clerk must sign, seal, and issue it to the plaintiff for service on the defendant. A summons—or a copy of a summons that is addressed to multiple defendants—must be issued for each defendant to be served.

(c) Service.

(1) *In General.* A summons must be served with a copy of the complaint. The plaintiff is responsible for having the summons and complaint served within the time allowed by Rule 4(m) and must furnish the necessary copies to the person who makes service.

(2) *By Whom.* Any person who is at least 18 years old and not a party may serve a summons and complaint.

(3) *By a Marshal or Someone Specially Appointed.* At the plaintiff's request, the court may order that service be made by a United States marshal or deputy marshal or by a person specially appointed by the court. The court must so order if the plaintiff is authorized to proceed in forma pauperis under 28 U.S.C. § 1915 or as a seaman under 28 U.S.C. § 1916.

[Text of subdivision (d) effective until December 1, 2015, absent contrary Congressional action.]

(d) Waiving Service.

(1) *Requesting a Waiver.* An individual, corporation, or association that is subject to service under Rule 4(e), (f), or (h) has a duty to avoid unnecessary expenses of serving the summons. The plaintiff may notify such a defendant that an action has been commenced and request that the defendant waive service of a summons. The notice and request must:

3

(A) be in writing and be addressed:

 (i) to the individual defendant; or

 (ii) for a defendant subject to service under Rule 4(h), to an officer, a managing or general agent, or any other agent authorized by appointment or by law to receive service of process;

(B) name the court where the complaint was filed;

(C) be accompanied by a copy of the complaint, two copies of a waiver form, and a prepaid means for returning the form;

(D) inform the defendant, using text prescribed in Form 5, of the consequences of waiving and not waiving service;

(E) state the date when the request is sent;

(F) give the defendant a reasonable time of at least 30 days after the request was sent—or at least 60 days if sent to the defendant outside any judicial district of the United States—to return the waiver; and

(G) be sent by first-class mail or other reliable means.

(2) *Failure to Waive.* If a defendant located within the United States fails, without good cause, to sign and return a waiver requested by a plaintiff located within the United States, the court must impose on the defendant:

(A) the expenses later incurred in making service; and

(B) the reasonable expenses, including attorney's fees, of any motion required to collect those service expenses.

(3) *Time to Answer After a Waiver.* A defendant who, before being served with process, timely returns a waiver need not serve an answer to the complaint until 60 days after the request was sent—or until 90 days after it was sent to the defendant outside any judicial district of the United States.

(4) *Results of Filing a Waiver.* When the plaintiff files a waiver, proof of service is not required and these rules apply as if a summons and complaint had been served at the time of filing the waiver.

(5) *Jurisdiction and Venue Not Waived.* Waiving service of a summons does not waive any objection to personal jurisdiction or to venue.

[Text of subdivision (d) effective December 1, 2015, absent contrary Congressional action.]

(d) Waiving Service.

(1) *Requesting a Waiver.* An individual, corporation, or association that is subject to service under Rule 4(e), (f), or (h) has a duty to avoid unnecessary expenses of serving the summons. The plaintiff may notify such a defendant that an action has been commenced and request that the defendant waive service of a summons. The notice and request must:

(A) be in writing and be addressed:

 (i) to the individual defendant; or

 (ii) for a defendant subject to service under Rule 4(h), to an officer, a managing or general agent, or any other agent authorized by appointment or by law to receive service of process;

(B) name the court where the complaint was filed;

(C) be accompanied by a copy of the complaint, 2 copies of the waiver form appended to this Rule 4, and a prepaid means for returning the form;

(D) inform the defendant, using the form appended to this Rule 4, of the consequences of waiving and not waiving service;

(E) state the date when the request is sent;

(F) give the defendant a reasonable time of at least 30 days after the request was sent—or at least 60 days if sent to the defendant outside any judicial district of the United States—to return the waiver; and

(G) be sent by first-class mail or other reliable means.

(2) *Failure to Waive.* If a defendant located within the United States fails, without good cause, to sign and return a waiver requested by a plaintiff located within the United States, the court must impose on the defendant:

(A) the expenses later incurred in making service; and

(B) the reasonable expenses, including attorney's fees, of any motion required to collect those service expenses.

(3) *Time to Answer After a Waiver.* A defendant who, before being served with process, timely returns a waiver need not serve an answer to the complaint until 60 days after the request was sent—or until 90 days after it was sent to the defendant outside any judicial district of the United States.

(4) *Results of Filing a Waiver.* When the plaintiff files a waiver, proof of service is not required and these rules apply as if a summons and complaint had been served at the time of filing the waiver.

(5) *Jurisdiction and Venue Not Waived.* Waiving service of a summons does not waive any objection to personal jurisdiction or to venue.

(e) Serving an Individual Within a Judicial District of the United States. Unless federal law provides otherwise, an individual—other than a minor, an incompetent person, or a person whose waiver has been filed—may be served in a judicial district of the United States by:

(1) following state law for serving a summons in an action brought in courts of general jurisdiction in the state where the district court is located or where service is made; or

(2) doing any of the following:

   (A) delivering a copy of the summons and of the complaint to the individual personally;

   (B) leaving a copy of each at the individual's dwelling or usual place of abode with someone of suitable age and discretion who resides there; or

   (C) delivering a copy of each to an agent authorized by appointment or by law to receive service of process.

(f) Serving an Individual in a Foreign Country. Unless federal law provides otherwise, an individual—other than a minor, an incompetent person, or a person whose waiver has been filed—may be served at a place not within any judicial district of the United States:

(1) by any internationally agreed means of service that is reasonably calculated to give notice, such as those authorized by the Hague Convention on the Service Abroad of Judicial and Extrajudicial Documents;

(2) if there is no internationally agreed means, or if an international agreement allows but does not specify other means, by a method that is reasonably calculated to give notice:

   (A) as prescribed by the foreign country's law for service in that country in an action in its courts of general jurisdiction;

   (B) as the foreign authority directs in response to a letter rogatory or letter of request; or

   (C) unless prohibited by the foreign country's law, by:

     (i) delivering a copy of the summons and of the complaint to the individual personally; or

     (ii) using any form of mail that the clerk addresses and sends to the individual and that requires a signed receipt; or

(3) by other means not prohibited by international agreement, as the court orders.

(g) Serving a Minor or an Incompetent Person. A minor or an incompetent person in a judicial district of the United States must be served by following state law for serving a summons or like process on such a defendant in an action brought in the courts of general jurisdiction of the state where service is made. A minor or an incompetent person who is not within any judicial district of the United States must be served in the manner prescribed by Rule 4(f)(2)(A), (f)(2)(B), or (f)(3).

(h) Serving a Corporation, Partnership, or Association. Unless federal law provides otherwise or the defendant's waiver has been filed, a domestic or foreign corporation, or a partnership or other unincorporated association that is subject to suit under a common name, must be served:

(1) in a judicial district of the United States:

   (A) in the manner prescribed by Rule 4(e)(1) for serving an individual; or

   (B) by delivering a copy of the summons and of the complaint to an officer, a managing or general agent, or any other agent authorized by appointment or by law to receive service of process and—if the agent is one authorized by statute and the statute so requires—by also mailing a copy of each to the defendant; or

(2) at a place not within any judicial district of the United States, in any manner prescribed by Rule 4(f) for serving an individual, except personal delivery under (f)(2)(C)(i).

(i) Serving the United States and Its Agencies, Corporations, Officers, or Employees.

(1) *United States.* To serve the United States, a party must:

   (A)(i) deliver a copy of the summons and of the complaint to the United States attorney for the district where the action is brought—or to an assistant United States attorney or clerical employee whom the United States attorney designates in a writing filed with the court clerk—or

     (ii) send a copy of each by registered or certified mail to the civil-process clerk at the United States attorney's office;

   (B) send a copy of each by registered or certified mail to the Attorney General of the United States at Washington, D.C.; and

   (C) if the action challenges an order of a nonparty agency or officer of the United States, send a copy of each by registered or certified mail to the agency or officer.

(2) *Agency; Corporation; Officer or Employee Sued in an Official Capacity.* To serve a United States agency or corporation, or a United States officer or employee sued only in an official capacity, a party must serve the United States and also send a copy of the summons and of the complaint by registered or certified mail to the agency, corporation, officer, or employee.

(3) Officer or Employee Sued Individually. To serve a United States officer or employee sued in an individual capacity for an act or omission occurring in connection with duties performed on the United States' behalf (whether or not the officer or employee is also sued in an official capacity), a party must serve the United States and also serve the officer or employee under Rule 4(e), (f), or (g).

(4) Extending Time. The court must allow a party a reasonable time to cure its failure to:

    (A) serve a person required to be served under Rule 4(i)(2), if the party has served either the United States attorney or the Attorney General of the United States; or

    (B) serve the United States under Rule 4(i)(3), if the party has served the United States officer or employee.

(j) Serving a Foreign, State, or Local Government.

(1) Foreign State. A foreign state or its political subdivision, agency, or instrumentality must be served in accordance with 28 U.S.C. § 1608.

(2) State or Local Government. A state, a municipal corporation, or any other state-created governmental organization that is subject to suit must be served by:

    (A) delivering a copy of the summons and of the complaint to its chief executive officer; or

    (B) serving a copy of each in the manner prescribed by that state's law for serving a summons or like process on such a defendant.

(k) Territorial Limits of Effective Service.

(1) In General. Serving a summons or filing a waiver of service establishes personal jurisdiction over a defendant:

    (A) who is subject to the jurisdiction of a court of general jurisdiction in the state where the district court is located;

    (B) who is a party joined under Rule 14 or 19 and is served within a judicial district of the United States and not more than 100 miles from where the summons was issued; or

    (C) when authorized by a federal statute.

(2) Federal Claim Outside State–Court Jurisdiction. For a claim that arises under federal law, serving a summons or filing a waiver of service establishes personal jurisdiction over a defendant if:

    (A) the defendant is not subject to jurisdiction in any state's courts of general jurisdiction; and

    (B) exercising jurisdiction is consistent with the United States Constitution and laws.

(l) Proving Service.

(1) Affidavit Required. Unless service is waived, proof of service must be made to the court. Except for service by a United States marshal or deputy marshal, proof must be by the server's affidavit.

(2) Service Outside the United States. Service not within any judicial district of the United States must be proved as follows:

    (A) if made under Rule 4(f)(1), as provided in the applicable treaty or convention; or

    (B) if made under Rule 4(f)(2) or (f)(3), by a receipt signed by the addressee, or by other evidence satisfying the court that the summons and complaint were delivered to the addressee.

(3) Validity of Service; Amending Proof. Failure to prove service does not affect the validity of service. The court may permit proof of service to be amended.

[Text of subdivision (m) effective until December 1, 2015, absent contrary Congressional action.]

(m) Time Limit for Service. If a defendant is not served within 120 days after the complaint is filed, the court—on motion or on its own after notice to the plaintiff—must dismiss the action without prejudice against that defendant or order that service be made within a specified time. But if the plaintiff shows good cause for the failure, the court must extend the time for service for an appropriate period. This subdivision (m) does not apply to service in a foreign country under Rule 4(f) or 4(j)(1).

[Text of subdivision (m) effective December 1, 2015, absent contrary Congressional action.]

(m) Time Limit for Service. If a defendant is not served within 90 days after the complaint is filed, the court — on motion or on its own after notice to the plaintiff — must dismiss the action without prejudice against that defendant or order that service be made within a specified time. But if the plaintiff shows good cause for the failure, the court must extend the time for service for an appropriate period. This subdivision (m) does not apply to service in a foreign country under Rule 4(f) or 4(j)(1) or to service of a notice under Rule 71.1(d)(3)(A).

(n) Asserting Jurisdiction over Property or Assets.

(1) Federal Law. The court may assert jurisdiction over property if authorized by a federal statute. Notice to claimants of the property must be given as provided in the statute or by serving a summons under this rule.

6

(2) **State Law.** On a showing that personal jurisdiction over a defendant cannot be obtained in the district where the action is brought by reasonable efforts to serve a summons under this rule, the court may assert jurisdiction over the defendant's assets found in the district. Jurisdiction is acquired by seizing the assets under the circumstances and in the manner provided by state law in that district.

[Text of former Form 5 effective December 1, 2015, absent contrary Congressional action.]

Rule 4   Notice of a Lawsuit and Request to Waive Service of Summons.

(Caption)

To (*name the defendant or — if the defendant is a corporation, partnership, or association — name an officer or agent authorized to receive service*):

Why are you getting this?

A lawsuit has been filed against you, or the entity you represent, in this court under the number shown above. A copy of the complaint is attached.

This is not a summons, or an official notice from the court. It is a request that, to avoid expenses, you waive formal service of a summons by signing and returning the enclosed waiver. To avoid these expenses, you must return the signed waiver within (*give at least 30 days or at least 60 days if the defendant is outside any judicial district of the United States*) from the date shown below, which is the date this notice was sent. Two copies of the waiver form are enclosed, along with a stamped, self-addressed envelope or other prepaid means for returning one copy. You may keep the other copy.

What happens next?

If you return the signed waiver, I will file it with the court. The action will then proceed as if you had been served on the date the waiver is filed, but no summons will be served on you and you will have 60 days from the date this notice is sent (see the date below) to answer the complaint (or 90 days if this notice is sent to you outside any judicial district of the United States).

If you do not return the signed waiver within the time indicated, I will arrange to have the summons and complaint served on you. And I will ask the court to require you, or the entity you represent, to pay the expenses of making service.

Please read the enclosed statement about the duty to avoid unnecessary expenses.

I certify that this request is being sent to you on the date below.

Date: _____

_____
(Signature of the attorney
or unrepresented party)

_____
(Printed name)

_____
(Address)

_____
(E–mail address)

_____
(Telephone number)

[Text of former Form 6 effective December 1, 2015, absent contrary Congressional action.]

Rule 4   Waiver of the Service of Summons.

(Caption)

To (*name the plaintiff's attorney or the unrepresented plaintiff*):

I have received your request to waive service of a summons in this action along with a copy of the complaint, two copies of this waiver form, and a prepaid means of returning one signed copy of the form to you.

I, or the entity I represent, agree to save the expense of serving a summons and complaint in this case.

I understand that I, or the entity I represent, will keep all defenses or objections to the lawsuit, the court's jurisdiction, and the venue of the action, but that I waive any objections to the absence of a summons or of service.

I also understand that I, or the entity I represent, must file and serve an answer or a motion under Rule 12 within 60 days from _____, the date when this request was sent (or 90 days if it was sent outside the United States). If I fail to do so, a default judgment will be entered against me or the entity I represent.

Date: _____

_____
(Signature of the attorney
or unrepresented party)

_____
(Printed name)

_____
(Address)

_____
(E–mail address)

_____
(Telephone number)

(Attach the following)

Duty to Avoid Unnecessary Expenses of Serving a Summons

Rule 4 of the Federal Rules of Civil Procedure requires certain defendants to cooperate in saving unnecessary expenses of serving a summons and complaint. A defendant who is located in the United States and who fails to return a signed waiver of service requested by a plaintiff located in the United States will be required to pay the expenses of service, unless the defendant shows good cause for the failure.

"Good cause" does not include a belief that the lawsuit is groundless, or that it has been brought in an improper venue, or that the court has no jurisdiction over this matter or over the defendant or the defendant's property.

If the waiver is signed and returned, you can still make these and all other defenses and objections, but you cannot object to the absence of a summons or of service.

If you waive service, then you must, within the time specified on the waiver form, serve an answer or a motion under Rule 12 on the plaintiff and file a copy with the court. By signing and returning the waiver form, you are allowed more time to respond than if a summons had been served.

(Amended January 21, 1963, effective July 1, 1963; February 28, 1966, effective July 1, 1966; April 29, 1980, effective August 1, 1980; amended by Pub.L. 97-462, § 2, January 12, 1983, 96 Stat. 2527, effective 45 days after January 12, 1983; amended March 2, 1987, effective August 1, 1987; April 22, 1993, effective December 1, 1993; April 17, 2000, effective December 1, 2000; April 30, 2007, effective December 1, 2007; April 29, 2015, effective December 1, 2015, absent contrary Congressional action.)

RULE 4.1　SERVING OTHER PROCESS

(a) **In General.** Process—other than a summons under Rule 4 or a subpoena under Rule 45—must be served by a United States marshal or deputy marshal or by a person specially appointed for that purpose. It may be served anywhere within the territorial limits of the state where the district court is located and, if authorized by a federal statute, beyond those limits. Proof of service must be made under Rule 4(*l*).

(b) **Enforcing Orders: Committing for Civil Contempt.** An order committing a person for civil contempt of a decree or injunction issued to enforce federal law may be served and enforced in any district. Any other order in a civil-contempt proceeding may be served only in the state where the issuing court is located or elsewhere in the United States within 100 miles from where the order was issued.

(Adopted April 22, 1993, effective December 1, 1993; amended April 30, 2007, effective December 1, 2007.)

RULE 5.　SERVING AND FILING PLEADINGS AND OTHER PAPERS

(a) **Service: When Required.**

(1) *In General.* Unless these rules provide otherwise, each of the following papers must be served on every party:

(A) an order stating that service is required;

(B) a pleading filed after the original complaint, unless the court orders otherwise under Rule 5(c) because there are numerous defendants;

(C) a discovery paper required to be served on a party, unless the court orders otherwise;

(D) a written motion, except one that may be heard ex parte; and

(E) a written notice, appearance, demand, or offer of judgment, or any similar paper.

(2) *If a Party Fails to Appear.* No service is required on a party who is in default for failing to appear. But a pleading that asserts a new claim for relief against such a party must be served on that party under Rule 4.

(3) *Seizing Property.* If an action is begun by seizing property and no person is or need be named as a defendant, any service required before the filing of an appearance, answer, or claim must be made on the person who had custody or possession of the property when it was seized.

(b) **Service: How Made.**

(1) *Serving an Attorney.* If a party is represented by an attorney, service under this rule must be made on the attorney unless the court orders service on the party.

(2) *Service in General.* A paper is served under this rule by:

(A) handing it to the person;

(B) leaving it:

(i) at the person's office with a clerk or other person in charge or, if no one is in charge, in a conspicuous place in the office; or

(ii) if the person has no office or the office is closed, at the person's dwelling or usual place of abode with someone of suitable age and discretion who resides there;

(C) mailing it to the person's last known address—in which event service is complete upon mailing;

(D) leaving it with the court clerk if the person has no known address;

(E) sending it by electronic means if the person consented in writing—in which event service is complete upon transmission, but is not effective if the serving party learns that it did not reach the person to be served; or

(F) delivering it by any other means that the person consented to in writing—in which event service is complete when the person making service delivers it to the agency designated to make delivery.

(3) *Using Court Facilities.* If a local rule so authorizes, a party may use the court's transmission facilities to make service under Rule 5(b)(2)(E).

(c) Serving Numerous Defendants.

(1) *In General.* If an action involves an unusually large number of defendants, the court may, on motion or on its own, order that:

(A) defendants' pleadings and replies to them need not be served on other defendants;

(B) any crossclaim, counterclaim, avoidance, or affirmative defense in those pleadings and replies to them will be treated as denied or avoided by all other parties; and

(C) filing any such pleading and serving it on the plaintiff constitutes notice of the pleading to all parties.

(2) *Notifying Parties.* A copy of every such order must be served on the parties as the court directs.

(d) Filing.

(1) *Required Filings; Certificate of Service.* Any paper after the complaint that is required to be served—together with a certificate of service—must be filed within a reasonable time after service. But disclosures under Rule 26(a)(1) or (2) and the following discovery requests and responses must not be filed until they are used in the proceeding or the court orders filing: depositions, interrogatories, requests for documents or tangible things or to permit entry onto land, and requests for admission.

(2) *How Filing Is Made—In General.* A paper is filed by delivering it:

(A) to the clerk; or

(B) to a judge who agrees to accept it for filing, and who must then note the filing date on the paper and promptly send it to the clerk.

(3) *Electronic Filing, Signing, or Verification.* A court may, by local rule, allow papers to be filed, signed, or verified by electronic means that are consistent with any technical standards established by the Judicial Conference of the United States. A local rule may require electronic filing only if reasonable exceptions are allowed. A paper filed electronically in compliance with a local rule is a written paper for purposes of these rules.

(4) *Acceptance by the Clerk.* The clerk must not refuse to file a paper solely because it is not in the form prescribed by these rules or by a local rule or practice.

(Amended January 21, 1963, effective July 1, 1963; March 30, 1970, effective July 1, 1970; April 29, 1980, effective August 1, 1980; March 2, 1987, effective August 1, 1987; April 30, 1991, effective December 1, 1991; April 22, 1993, effective December 1, 1993; April 23, 1996, effective December 1, 1996; April 17, 2000, effective December 1, 2000; April 23, 2001, effective December 1, 2001; April 12, 2006, effective December 1, 2006; April 30, 2007, effective December 1, 2007.)

RULE 5.1 CONSTITUTIONAL CHALLENGE TO A STATUTE—NOTICE, CERTIFICATION, AND INTERVENTION

(a) Notice by a Party. A party that files a pleading, written motion, or other paper drawing into question the constitutionality of a federal or state statute must promptly:

(1) file a notice of constitutional question stating the question and identifying the paper that raises it, if:

(A) a federal statute is questioned and the parties do not include the United States, one of its agencies, or one of its officers or employees in an official capacity; or

(B) a state statute is questioned and the parties do not include the state, one of its agencies, or one of its officers or employees in an official capacity; and

(2) serve the notice and paper on the Attorney General of the United States if a federal statute is questioned—or on the state attorney general if a state statute is questioned—either by certified or registered mail or by sending it to an electronic address designated by the attorney general for this purpose.

(b) Certification by the Court. The court must, under 28 U.S.C. § 2403, certify to the appropriate attorney general that a statute has been questioned.

(c) Intervention; Final Decision on the Merits. Unless the court sets a later time, the attorney general may intervene within 60 days after the notice is filed or after the court certifies the challenge, whichever is earlier. Before the time to intervene expires, the court may reject the constitutional challenge, but may not enter a final judgment holding the statute unconstitutional.

(d) **No Forfeiture.** A party's failure to file and serve the notice, or the court's failure to certify, does not forfeit a constitutional claim or defense that is otherwise timely asserted.

(Adopted April 12, 2006, effective December 1, 2006; amended April 30, 2007, effective December 1, 2007.)

RULE 5.2 PRIVACY PROTECTION FOR FILINGS MADE WITH THE COURT

(a) **Redacted Filings.** Unless the court orders otherwise, in an electronic or paper filing with the court that contains an individual's social-security number, taxpayer-identification number, or birth date, the name of an individual known to be a minor, or a financial-account number, a party or nonparty making the filing may include only:

(1) the last four digits of the social-security number and taxpayer-identification number;

(2) the year of the individual's birth;

(3) the minor's initials; and

(4) the last four digits of the financial-account number.

(b) **Exemptions from the Redaction Requirement.** The redaction requirement does not apply to the following:

(1) a financial-account number that identifies the property allegedly subject to forfeiture in a forfeiture proceeding;

(2) the record of an administrative or agency proceeding;

(3) the official record of a state-court proceeding;

(4) the record of a court or tribunal, if that record was not subject to the redaction requirement when originally filed;

(5) a filing covered by Rule 5.2(c) or (d); and

(6) a pro se filing in an action brought under 28 U.S.C. §§ 2241, 2254, or 2255.

(c) **Limitations on Remote Access to Electronic Files; Social–Security Appeals and Immigration Cases.** Unless the court orders otherwise, in an action for benefits under the Social Security Act, and in an action or proceeding relating to an order of removal, to relief from removal, or to immigration benefits or detention, access to an electronic file is authorized as follows:

(1) the parties and their attorneys may have remote electronic access to any part of the case file, including the administrative record;

(2) any other person may have electronic access to the full record at the courthouse, but may have remote electronic access only to:

(A) the docket maintained by the court; and

(B) an opinion, order, judgment, or other disposition of the court, but not any other part of the case file or the administrative record.

(d) **Filings Made Under Seal.** The court may order that a filing be made under seal without redaction. The court may later unseal the filing or order the person who made the filing to file a redacted version for the public record.

(e) **Protective Orders.** For good cause, the court may by order in a case:

(1) require redaction of additional information; or

(2) limit or prohibit a nonparty's remote electronic access to a document filed with the court.

(f) **Option for Additional Unredacted Filing Under Seal.** A person making a redacted filing may also file an unredacted copy under seal. The court must retain the unredacted copy as part of the record.

(g) **Option for Filing a Reference List.** A filing that contains redacted information may be filed together with a reference list that identifies each item of redacted information and specifies an appropriate identifier that uniquely corresponds to each item listed. The list must be filed under seal and may be amended as of right. Any reference in the case to a listed identifier will be construed to refer to the corresponding item of information.

(h) **Waiver of Protection of Identifiers.** A person waives the protection of Rule 5.2(a) as to the person's own information by filing it without redaction and not under seal.

(Adopted April 30, 2007, effective December 1, 2007.)

RULE 6. COMPUTING AND EXTENDING TIME; TIME FOR MOTION PAPERS

(a) **Computing Time.** The following rules apply in computing any time period specified in these rules, in any local rule or court order, or in any statute that does not specify a method of computing time.

(1) *Period Stated in Days or a Longer Unit.* When the period is stated in days or a longer unit of time:

(A) exclude the day of the event that triggers the period;

(B) count every day, including intermediate Saturdays, Sundays, and legal holidays; and

(C) include the last day of the period, but if the last day is a Saturday, Sunday, or legal holiday, the period continues to run until the end of the next day that is not a Saturday, Sunday, or legal holiday.

(2) *Period Stated in Hours.* When the period is stated in hours:

(A) begin counting immediately on the occurrence of the event that triggers the period;

(B) count every hour, including hours during intermediate Saturdays, Sundays, and legal holidays; and

(C) if the period would end on a Saturday, Sunday, or legal holiday, the period continues to run until the same time on the next day that is not a Saturday, Sunday, or legal holiday.

(3) *Inaccessibility of the Clerk's Office.* Unless the court orders otherwise, if the clerk's office is inaccessible:

(A) on the last day for filing under Rule 6(a)(1), then the time for filing is extended to the first accessible day that is not a Saturday, Sunday, or legal holiday; or

(B) during the last hour for filing under Rule 6(a)(2), then the time for filing is extended to the same time on the first accessible day that is not a Saturday, Sunday, or legal holiday.

(4) *"Last Day" Defined.* Unless a different time is set by a statute, local rule, or court order, the last day ends:

(A) for electronic filing, at midnight in the court's time zone; and

(B) for filing by other means, when the clerk's office is scheduled to close.

(5) *"Next Day" Defined.* The "next day" is determined by continuing to count forward when the period is measured after an event and backward when measured before an event.

(6) *"Legal Holiday" Defined.* "Legal holiday" means:

(A) the day set aside by statute for observing New Year's Day, Martin Luther King Jr.'s Birthday, Washington's Birthday, Memorial Day, Independence Day, Labor Day, Columbus Day, Veterans' Day, Thanksgiving Day, or Christmas Day;

(B) any day declared a holiday by the President or Congress; and

(C) for periods that are measured after an event, any other day declared a holiday by the state where the district court is located.

(b) **Extending Time.**

(1) *In General.* When an act may or must be done within a specified time, the court may, for good cause, extend the time:

(A) with or without motion or notice if the court acts, or if a request is made, before the original time or its extension expires; or

(B) on motion made after the time has expired if the party failed to act because of excusable neglect.

(2) *Exceptions.* A court must not extend the time to act under Rules 50(b) and (d), 52(b), 59(b), (d), and (e), and 60(b).

(c) **Motions, Notices of Hearing, and Affidavits.**

(1) *In General.* A written motion and notice of the hearing must be served at least 14 days before the time specified for the hearing, with the following exceptions:

(A) when the motion may be heard ex parte;

(B) when these rules set a different time; or

(C) when a court order—which a party may, for good cause, apply for ex parte—sets a different time.

(2) *Supporting Affidavit.* Any affidavit supporting a motion must be served with the motion. Except as Rule 59(c) provides otherwise, any opposing affidavit must be served at least 7 days before the hearing, unless the court permits service at another time.

(d) **Additional Time After Certain Kinds of Service.** When a party may or must act within a specified time after service and service is made under Rule 5(b)(2)(C), (D), (E), or (F), 3 days are added after the period would otherwise expire under Rule 6(a).

(Amended December 27, 1946, effective March 19, 1948; January 21, 1963, effective July 1, 1963; February 28, 1966, effective July 1, 1966; December 4, 1967, effective July 1, 1968; March 1, 1971, effective July 1, 1971; April 28, 1983, effective August 1, 1983; April 29, 1985, effective August 1, 1985; March 2, 1987, effective August 1, 1987; April 29, 1999, effective December 1, 1999; April 23, 2001, effective December 1, 2001; April 25, 2005, effective December 1, 2005; April 30, 2007, effective December 1, 2007; March 26, 2009, effective December 1, 2009.)

TITLE III. PLEADINGS AND MOTIONS

RULE 7. PLEADINGS ALLOWED; FORM OF MOTIONS AND OTHER PAPERS

(a) **Pleadings.** Only these pleadings are allowed:

(1) a complaint;

(2) an answer to a complaint;

(3) an answer to a counterclaim designated as a counterclaim;

(4) an answer to a crossclaim;

(5) a third-party complaint;

(6) an answer to a third-party complaint; and

(7) if the court orders one, a reply to an answer.

(b) Motions and Other Papers.

    (1) *In General.* A request for a court order must be made by motion. The motion must:

        (A) be in writing unless made during a hearing or trial;

        (B) state with particularity the grounds for seeking the order; and

        (C) state the relief sought.

    (2) *Form.* The rules governing captions and other matters of form in pleadings apply to motions and other papers.

(Amended December 27, 1946, effective March 19, 1948; January 21, 1963, effective July 1, 1963; April 28, 1983, effective August 1, 1983; April 30, 2007, effective December 1, 2007.)

RULE 7.1 DISCLOSURE STATEMENT

(a) Who Must File; Contents. A nongovernmental corporate party must file 2 copies of a disclosure statement that:

    (1) identifies any parent corporation and any publicly held corporation owning 10% or more of its stock; or

    (2) states that there is no such corporation.

(b) Time to File; Supplemental Filing. A party must:

    (1) file the disclosure statement with its first appearance, pleading, petition, motion, response, or other request addressed to the court; and

    (2) promptly file a supplemental statement if any required information changes.

(Adopted April 29, 2002, effective December 1, 2002; April 30, 2007, effective December 1, 2007.)

RULE 8. GENERAL RULES OF PLEADING

(a) Claim for Relief. A pleading that states a claim for relief must contain:

    (1) a short and plain statement of the grounds for the court's jurisdiction, unless the court already has jurisdiction and the claim needs no new jurisdictional support;

    (2) a short and plain statement of the claim showing that the pleader is entitled to relief; and

    (3) a demand for the relief sought, which may include relief in the alternative or different types of relief.

(b) Defenses; Admissions and Denials.

    (1) *In General.* In responding to a pleading, a party must:

        (A) state in short and plain terms its defenses to each claim asserted against it; and

        (B) admit or deny the allegations asserted against it by an opposing party.

    (2) *Denials—Responding to the Substance.* A denial must fairly respond to the substance of the allegation.

    (3) *General and Specific Denials.* A party that intends in good faith to deny all the allegations of a pleading—including the jurisdictional grounds—may do so by a general denial. A party that does not intend to deny all the allegations must either specifically deny designated allegations or generally deny all except those specifically admitted.

    (4) *Denying Part of an Allegation.* A party that intends in good faith to deny only part of an allegation must admit the part that is true and deny the rest.

    (5) *Lacking Knowledge or Information.* A party that lacks knowledge or information sufficient to form a belief about the truth of an allegation must so state, and the statement has the effect of a denial.

    (6) *Effect of Failing to Deny.* An allegation—other than one relating to the amount of damages—is admitted if a responsive pleading is required and the allegation is not denied. If a responsive pleading is not required, an allegation is considered denied or avoided.

(c) Affirmative Defenses.

    (1) *In General.* In responding to a pleading, a party must affirmatively state any avoidance or affirmative defense, including:

- accord and satisfaction;
- arbitration and award;
- assumption of risk;
- contributory negligence;
- duress;
- estoppel;
- failure of consideration;
- fraud;
- illegality;
- injury by fellow servant;
- laches;
- license;
- payment;
- release;
- res judicata;
- statute of frauds;
- statute of limitations; and
- waiver.

    (2) *Mistaken Designation.* If a party mistakenly designates a defense as a counterclaim, or a counterclaim as a defense, the court must, if justice requires, treat the pleading as though it were correctly designated, and may impose terms for doing so.

(d) Pleading to Be Concise and Direct; Alternative Statements; Inconsistency.

   (1) *In General.* Each allegation must be simple, concise, and direct. No technical form is required.

   (2) *Alternative Statements of a Claim or Defense.* A party may set out 2 or more statements of a claim or defense alternatively or hypothetically, either in a single count or defense or in separate ones. If a party makes alternative statements, the pleading is sufficient if any one of them is sufficient.

   (3) *Inconsistent Claims or Defenses.* A party may state as many separate claims or defenses as it has, regardless of consistency.

(e) Construing Pleadings. Pleadings must be construed so as to do justice.

(Amended February 28, 1966, effective July 1, 1966; March 2, 1987, effective August 1, 1987; April 30, 2007, effective December 1, 2007; April 28, 2010, effective December 1, 2010.)

RULE 9. PLEADING SPECIAL MATTERS

(a) Capacity or Authority to Sue; Legal Existence.

   (1) *In General.* Except when required to show that the court has jurisdiction, a pleading need not allege:

     (A) a party's capacity to sue or be sued;

     (B) a party's authority to sue or be sued in a representative capacity; or

     (C) the legal existence of an organized association of persons that is made a party.

   (2) *Raising Those Issues.* To raise any of those issues, a party must do so by a specific denial, which must state any supporting facts that are peculiarly within the party's knowledge.

(b) Fraud or Mistake; Conditions of Mind. In alleging fraud or mistake, a party must state with particularity the circumstances constituting fraud or mistake. Malice, intent, knowledge, and other conditions of a person's mind may be alleged generally.

(c) Conditions Precedent. In pleading conditions precedent, it suffices to allege generally that all conditions precedent have occurred or been performed. But when denying that a condition precedent has occurred or been performed, a party must do so with particularity.

(d) Official Document or Act. In pleading an official document or official act, it suffices to allege that the document was legally issued or the act legally done.

(e) Judgment. In pleading a judgment or decision of a domestic or foreign court, a judicial or quasi-judicial tribunal, or a board or officer, it suffices to plead the judgment or decision without showing jurisdiction to render it.

(f) Time and Place. An allegation of time or place is material when testing the sufficiency of a pleading.

(g) Special Damages. If an item of special damage is claimed, it must be specifically stated.

(h) Admiralty or Maritime Claim.

   (1) *How Designated.* If a claim for relief is within the admiralty or maritime jurisdiction and also within the court's subject-matter jurisdiction on some other ground, the pleading may designate the claim as an admiralty or maritime claim for purposes of Rules 14(c), 38(e), and 82 and the Supplemental Rules for Admiralty or Maritime Claims and Asset Forfeiture Actions. A claim cognizable only in the admiralty or maritime jurisdiction is an admiralty or maritime claim for those purposes, whether or not so designated.

   (2) *Designation for Appeal.* A case that includes an admiralty or maritime claim within this subdivision (h) is an admiralty case within 28 U.S.C. § 1292(a)(3).

(Amended February 28, 1966, effective July 1, 1966; December 4, 1967, effective July 1, 1968; March 30, 1970, effective July 1, 1970; March 2, 1987, effective August 1, 1987; April 11, 1997, effective December 1, 1997; April 12, 2006, effective December 1, 2006; April 30, 2007, effective December 1, 2007.)

RULE 10. FORM OF PLEADINGS

(a) Caption; Names of Parties. Every pleading must have a caption with the court's name, a title, a file number, and a Rule 7(a) designation. The title of the complaint must name all the parties; the title of other pleadings, after naming the first party on each side, may refer generally to other parties.

(b) Paragraphs; Separate Statements. A party must state its claims or defenses in numbered paragraphs, each limited as far as practicable to a single set of circumstances. A later pleading may refer by number to a paragraph in an earlier pleading. If doing so would promote clarity, each claim founded on a separate transaction or occurrence—and each defense other than a denial— must be stated in a separate count or defense.

(c) Adoption by Reference; Exhibits. A statement in a pleading may be adopted by reference elsewhere in the same pleading or in any other pleading or motion. A copy of a written instrument that is an exhibit to a pleading is a part of the pleading for all purposes.

(Amended April 30, 2007, effective December 1, 2007.)

RULE 11. SIGNING PLEADINGS, MOTIONS, AND OTHER PAPERS; REPRESENTATIONS TO THE COURT; SANCTIONS

(a) **Signature.** Every pleading, written motion, and other paper must be signed by at least one attorney of record in the attorney's name—or by a party personally if the party is unrepresented. The paper must state the signer's address, e-mail address, and telephone number. Unless a rule or statute specifically states otherwise, a pleading need not be verified or accompanied by an affidavit. The court must strike an unsigned paper unless the omission is promptly corrected after being called to the attorney's or party's attention.

(b) **Representations to the Court.** By presenting to the court a pleading, written motion, or other paper—whether by signing, filing, submitting, or later advocating it—an attorney or unrepresented party certifies that to the best of the person's knowledge, information, and belief, formed after an inquiry reasonable under the circumstances:

(1) it is not being presented for any improper purpose, such as to harass, cause unnecessary delay, or needlessly increase the cost of litigation;

(2) the claims, defenses, and other legal contentions are warranted by existing law or by a nonfrivolous argument for extending, modifying, or reversing existing law or for establishing new law;

(3) the factual contentions have evidentiary support or, if specifically so identified, will likely have evidentiary support after a reasonable opportunity for further investigation or discovery; and

(4) the denials of factual contentions are warranted on the evidence or, if specifically so identified, are reasonably based on belief or a lack of information.

(c) **Sanctions.**

(1) *In General.* If, after notice and a reasonable opportunity to respond, the court determines that Rule 11(b) has been violated, the court may impose an appropriate sanction on any attorney, law firm, or party that violated the rule or is responsible for the violation. Absent exceptional circumstances, a law firm must be held jointly responsible for a violation committed by its partner, associate, or employee.

(2) *Motion for Sanctions.* A motion for sanctions must be made separately from any other motion and must describe the specific conduct that allegedly violates Rule 11(b). The motion must

be served under Rule 5, but it must not be filed or be presented to the court if the challenged paper, claim, defense, contention, or denial is withdrawn or appropriately corrected within 21 days after service or within another time the court sets. If warranted, the court may award to the prevailing party the reasonable expenses, including attorney's fees, incurred for the motion.

(3) *On the Court's Initiative.* On its own, the court may order an attorney, law firm, or party to show cause why conduct specifically described in the order has not violated Rule 11(b).

(4) *Nature of a Sanction.* A sanction imposed under this rule must be limited to what suffices to deter repetition of the conduct or comparable conduct by others similarly situated. The sanction may include nonmonetary directives; an order to pay a penalty into court; or, if imposed on motion and warranted for effective deterrence, an order directing payment to the movant of part or all of the reasonable attorney's fees and other expenses directly resulting from the violation.

(5) *Limitations on Monetary Sanctions.* The court must not impose a monetary sanction:

(A) against a represented party for violating Rule 11(b)(2); or

(B) on its own, unless it issued the show-cause order under Rule 11(c)(3) before voluntary dismissal or settlement of the claims made by or against the party that is, or whose attorneys are, to be sanctioned.

(6) *Requirements for an Order.* An order imposing a sanction must describe the sanctioned conduct and explain the basis for the sanction.

(d) **Inapplicability to Discovery.** This rule does not apply to disclosures and discovery requests, responses, objections, and motions under Rules 26 through 37.

(Amended April 28, 1983, effective August 1, 1983; March 2, 1987, effective August 1, 1987; April 22, 1993, effective December 1, 1993; April 30, 2007, effective December 1, 2007.)

RULE 12. DEFENSES AND OBJECTIONS: WHEN AND HOW PRESENTED; MOTION FOR JUDGMENT ON THE PLEADINGS; CONSOLIDATING MOTIONS; WAIVING DEFENSES; PRETRIAL HEARING

(a) **Time to Serve a Responsive Pleading.**

(1) *In General.* Unless another time is specified by this rule or a federal statute, the time for serving a responsive pleading is as follows:

(A) A defendant must serve an answer:

   (i) within 21 days after being served with the summons and complaint; or

   (ii) if it has timely waived service under Rule 4(d), within 60 days after the request for a waiver was sent, or within 90 days after it was sent to the defendant outside any judicial district of the United States.

(B) A party must serve an answer to a counterclaim or crossclaim within 21 days after being served with the pleading that states the counterclaim or crossclaim.

(C) A party must serve a reply to an answer within 21 days after being served with an order to reply, unless the order specifies a different time.

(2) *United States and Its Agencies, Officers, or Employees Sued in an Official Capacity.* The United States, a United States agency, or a United States officer or employee sued only in an official capacity must serve an answer to a complaint, counterclaim, or crossclaim within 60 days after service on the United States attorney.

(3) *United States Officers or Employees Sued in an Individual Capacity.* A United States officer or employee sued in an individual capacity for an act or omission occurring in connection with duties performed on the United States' behalf must serve an answer to a complaint, counterclaim, or crossclaim within 60 days after service on the officer or employee or service on the United States attorney, whichever is later.

(4) *Effect of a Motion.* Unless the court sets a different time, serving a motion under this rule alters these periods as follows:

(A) if the court denies the motion or postpones its disposition until trial, the responsive pleading must be served within 14 days after notice of the court's action; or

(B) if the court grants a motion for a more definite statement, the responsive pleading must be served within 14 days after the more definite statement is served.

(b) How to Present Defenses. Every defense to a claim for relief in any pleading must be asserted in the responsive pleading if one is required. But a party may assert the following defenses by motion:

(1) lack of subject-matter jurisdiction;

(2) lack of personal jurisdiction;

(3) improper venue;

(4) insufficient process;

(5) insufficient service of process;

(6) failure to state a claim upon which relief can be granted; and

(7) failure to join a party under Rule 19.

A motion asserting any of these defenses must be made before pleading if a responsive pleading is allowed. If a pleading sets out a claim for relief that does not require a responsive pleading, an opposing party may assert at trial any defense to that claim. No defense or objection is waived by joining it with one or more other defenses or objections in a responsive pleading or in a motion.

(c) Motion for Judgment on the Pleadings. After the pleadings are closed—but early enough not to delay trial—a party may move for judgment on the pleadings.

(d) Result of Presenting Matters Outside the Pleadings. If, on a motion under Rule 12(b)(6) or 12(c), matters outside the pleadings are presented to and not excluded by the court, the motion must be treated as one for summary judgment under Rule 56. All parties must be given a reasonable opportunity to present all the material that is pertinent to the motion.

(e) Motion for a More Definite Statement. A party may move for a more definite statement of a pleading to which a responsive pleading is allowed but which is so vague or ambiguous that the party cannot reasonably prepare a response. The motion must be made before filing a responsive pleading and must point out the defects complained of and the details desired. If the court orders a more definite statement and the order is not obeyed within 14 days after notice of the order or within the time the court sets, the court may strike the pleading or issue any other appropriate order.

(f) Motion to Strike. The court may strike from a pleading an insufficient defense or any redundant, immaterial, impertinent, or scandalous matter. The court may act:

(1) on its own; or

(2) on motion made by a party either before responding to the pleading or, if a response is not allowed, within 21 days after being served with the pleading.

(g) Joining Motions.

(1) *Right to Join.* A motion under this rule may be joined with any other motion allowed by this rule.

(2) *Limitation on Further Motions.* Except as provided in Rule 12(h)(2) or (3), a party that makes a motion under this rule must not make another motion under this rule raising a defense or objection that was available to the party but omitted from its earlier motion.

(h) Waiving and Preserving Certain Defenses.

(1) *When Some Are Waived.* A party waives any defense listed in Rule 12(b)(2)-(5) by:

(A) omitting it from a motion in the circumstances described in Rule 12(g)(2); or

(B) failing to either:

(i) make it by motion under this rule; or

(ii) include it in a responsive pleading or in an amendment allowed by Rule 15(a)(1) as a matter of course.

(2) *When to Raise Others.* Failure to state a claim upon which relief can be granted, to join a person required by Rule 19(b), or to state a legal defense to a claim may be raised:

(A) in any pleading allowed or ordered under Rule 7(a);

(B) by a motion under Rule 12(c); or

(C) at trial.

(3) *Lack of Subject–Matter Jurisdiction.* If the court determines at any time that it lacks subject-matter jurisdiction, the court must dismiss the action.

(i) Hearing Before Trial. If a party so moves, any defense listed in Rule 12(b)(1)-(7)—whether made in a pleading or by motion—and a motion under Rule 12(c) must be heard and decided before trial unless the court orders a deferral until trial.

(Amended December 27, 1946, effective March 19, 1948; January 21, 1963, effective July 1, 1963; February 28, 1966, effective July 1, 1966; March 2, 1987, effective August 1, 1987; April 22, 1993, effective December 1, 1993; April 17, 2000, effective December 1, 2000; April 30, 2007, effective December 1, 2007; March 26, 2009, effective December 1, 2009.)

RULE 13.   COUNTERCLAIM AND CROSSCLAIM

(a) Compulsory Counterclaim.

(1) *In General.* A pleading must state as a counterclaim any claim that—at the time of its service—the pleader has against an opposing party if the claim:

(A) arises out of the transaction or occurrence that is the subject matter of the opposing party's claim; and

(B) does not require adding another party over whom the court cannot acquire jurisdiction.

(2) *Exceptions.* The pleader need not state the claim if:

(A) when the action was commenced, the claim was the subject of another pending action; or

(B) the opposing party sued on its claim by attachment or other process that did not establish personal jurisdiction over the plead-

er on that claim, and the pleader does not assert any counterclaim under this rule.

(b) Permissive Counterclaim. A pleading may state as a counterclaim against an opposing party any claim that is not compulsory.

(c) Relief Sought in a Counterclaim. A counterclaim need not diminish or defeat the recovery sought by the opposing party. It may request relief that exceeds in amount or differs in kind from the relief sought by the opposing party.

(d) Counterclaim Against the United States. These rules do not expand the right to assert a counterclaim—or to claim a credit—against the United States or a United States officer or agency.

(e) Counterclaim Maturing or Acquired After Pleading. The court may permit a party to file a supplemental pleading asserting a counterclaim that matured or was acquired by the party after serving an earlier pleading.

(f) [Abrogated]

(g) Crossclaim Against a Coparty. A pleading may state as a crossclaim any claim by one party against a coparty if the claim arises out of the transaction or occurrence that is the subject matter of the original action or of a counterclaim, or if the claim relates to any property that is the subject matter of the original action. The crossclaim may include a claim that the coparty is or may be liable to the cross-claimant for all or part of a claim asserted in the action against the crossclaimant.

(h) Joining Additional Parties. Rules 19 and 20 govern the addition of a person as a party to a counterclaim or crossclaim.

(i) Separate Trials; Separate Judgments. If the court orders separate trials under Rule 42(b), it may enter judgment on a counterclaim or crossclaim under Rule 54(b) when it has jurisdiction to do so, even if the opposing party's claims have been dismissed or otherwise resolved.

(Amended December 27, 1946, effective March 19, 1948; January 21, 1963, effective July 1, 1963; February 28, 1966, effective July 1, 1966; March 2, 1987, effective August 1, 1987; April 30, 2007, effective December 1, 2007; March 26, 2009, effective December 1, 2009.)

RULE 14.   THIRD–PARTY PRACTICE

(a) When a Defending Party May Bring in a Third Party.

(1) *Timing of the Summons and Complaint.* A defending party may, as third-party plaintiff, serve a summons and complaint on a nonparty who is or may be liable to it for all or part of the claim against it. But the third-party plaintiff must, by motion, obtain the court's leave if it

files the third-party complaint more than 14 days after serving its original answer.

(2) **Third–Party Defendant's Claims and Defenses.** The person served with the summons and third-party complaint—the "third-party defendant":

    (A) must assert any defense against the third-party plaintiff's claim under Rule 12;

    (B) must assert any counterclaim against the third-party plaintiff under Rule 13(a), and may assert any counterclaim against the third-party plaintiff under Rule 13(b) or any crossclaim against another third-party defendant under Rule 13(g);

    (C) may assert against the plaintiff any defense that the third-party plaintiff has to the plaintiff's claim; and

    (D) may also assert against the plaintiff any claim arising out of the transaction or occurrence that is the subject matter of the plaintiff's claim against the third-party plaintiff.

(3) **Plaintiff's Claims Against a Third–Party Defendant.** The plaintiff may assert against the third-party defendant any claim arising out of the transaction or occurrence that is the subject matter of the plaintiff's claim against the third-party plaintiff. The third-party defendant must then assert any defense under Rule 12 and any counterclaim under Rule 13(a), and may assert any counterclaim under Rule 13(b) or any crossclaim under Rule 13(g).

(4) **Motion to Strike, Sever, or Try Separately.** Any party may move to strike the third-party claim, to sever it, or to try it separately.

(5) **Third–Party Defendant's Claim Against a Nonparty.** A third-party defendant may proceed under this rule against a nonparty who is or may be liable to the third-party defendant for all or part of any claim against it.

(6) **Third–Party Complaint In Rem.** If it is within the admiralty or maritime jurisdiction, a third-party complaint may be in rem. In that event, a reference in this rule to the "summons" includes the warrant of arrest, and a reference to the defendant or third-party plaintiff includes, when appropriate, a person who asserts a right under Supplemental Rule C(6)(a)(i) in the property arrested.

(b) **When a Plaintiff May Bring in a Third Party.** When a claim is asserted against a plaintiff, the plaintiff may bring in a third party if this rule would allow a defendant to do so.

(c) **Admiralty or Maritime Claim.**

(1) **Scope of Impleader.** If a plaintiff asserts an admiralty or maritime claim under Rule 9(h), the defendant or a person who asserts a right under Supplemental Rule C(6)(a)(i) may, as a third-party plaintiff, bring in a third-party defendant who may be wholly or partly liable—either to the plaintiff or to the third-party plaintiff—for remedy over, contribution, or otherwise on account of the same transaction, occurrence, or series of transactions or occurrences.

(2) **Defending Against a Demand for Judgment for the Plaintiff.** The third-party plaintiff may demand judgment in the plaintiff's favor against the third-party defendant. In that event, the third-party defendant must defend under Rule 12 against the plaintiff's claim as well as the third-party plaintiff's claim; and the action proceeds as if the plaintiff had sued both the third-party defendant and the third-party plaintiff.

(Amended December 27, 1946, effective March 19, 1948; January 21, 1963, effective July 1, 1963; February 28, 1966, effective July 1, 1966; March 2, 1987, effective August 1, 1987; April 17, 2000, effective December 1, 2000; April 12, 2006, effective December 1, 2006; April 30, 2007, effective December 1, 2007; March 26, 2009, effective December 1, 2009.)

RULE 15. AMENDED AND SUPPLEMENTAL PLEADINGS

(a) **Amendments Before Trial.**

(1) **Amending as a Matter of Course.** A party may amend its pleading once as a matter of course within:

    (A) 21 days after serving it, or

    (B) if the pleading is one to which a responsive pleading is required, 21 days after service of a responsive pleading or 21 days after service of a motion under Rule 12(b), (e), or (f), whichever is earlier.

(2) **Other Amendments.** In all other cases, a party may amend its pleading only with the opposing party's written consent or the court's leave. The court should freely give leave when justice so requires.

(3) **Time to Respond.** Unless the court orders otherwise, any required response to an amended pleading must be made within the time remaining to respond to the original pleading or within 14 days after service of the amended pleading, whichever is later.

(b) **Amendments During and After Trial.**

(1) **Based on an Objection at Trial.** If, at trial, a party objects that evidence is not within the issues raised in the pleadings, the court may permit the pleadings to be amended. The court should freely permit an amendment when doing so will aid in presenting the merits and the objecting party fails to satisfy the court that the

evidence would prejudice that party's action or defense on the merits. The court may grant a continuance to enable the objecting party to meet the evidence.

(2) *For Issues Tried by Consent.* When an issue not raised by the pleadings is tried by the parties' express or implied consent, it must be treated in all respects as if raised in the pleadings. A party may move—at any time, even after judgment—to amend the pleadings to conform them to the evidence and to raise an unpleaded issue. But failure to amend does not affect the result of the trial of that issue.

(c) **Relation Back of Amendments.**

(1) *When an Amendment Relates Back.* An amendment to a pleading relates back to the date of the original pleading when:

(A) the law that provides the applicable statute of limitations allows relation back;

(B) the amendment asserts a claim or defense that arose out of the conduct, transaction, or occurrence set out—or attempted to be set out—in the original pleading; or

(C) the amendment changes the party or the naming of the party against whom a claim is asserted, if Rule 15(c)(1)(B) is satisfied and if, within the period provided by Rule 4(m) for serving the summons and complaint, the party to be brought in by amendment:

(i) received such notice of the action that it will not be prejudiced in defending on the merits; and

(ii) knew or should have known that the action would have been brought against it, but for a mistake concerning the proper party's identity.

(2) *Notice to the United States.* When the United States or a United States officer or agency is added as a defendant by amendment, the notice requirements of Rule 15(c)(1)(C)(i) and (ii) are satisfied if, during the stated period, process was delivered or mailed to the United States attorney or the United States attorney's designee, to the Attorney General of the United States, or to the officer or agency.

(d) **Supplemental Pleadings.** On motion and reasonable notice, the court may, on just terms, permit a party to serve a supplemental pleading setting out any transaction, occurrence, or event that happened after the date of the pleading to be supplemented. The court may permit supplementation even though the original pleading is defective in stating a claim or defense. The court may order

that the opposing party plead to the supplemental pleading within a specified time.

(Amended January 21, 1963, effective July 1, 1963; February 28, 1966, effective July 1, 1966; March 2, 1987, effective August 1, 1987; April 30, 1991, effective December 1, 1991; amended by Pub.L. 102–198, § 11, December 9, 1991, 105 Stat. 1626; amended April 22, 1993, effective December 1, 1993; April 30, 2007, effective December 1, 2007; March 26, 2009, effective December 1, 2009.)

RULE 16. PRETRIAL CONFERENCES; SCHEDULING; MANAGEMENT

(a) **Purposes of a Pretrial Conference.** In any action, the court may order the attorneys and any unrepresented parties to appear for one or more pretrial conferences for such purposes as:

(1) expediting disposition of the action;

(2) establishing early and continuing control so that the case will not be protracted because of lack of management;

(3) discouraging wasteful pretrial activities;

(4) improving the quality of the trial through more thorough preparation; and

(5) facilitating settlement.

[Text of subdivision (b) effective until December 1, 2015, absent contrary Congressional action.]

(b) **Scheduling.**

(1) *Scheduling Order.* Except in categories of actions exempted by local rule, the district judge—or a magistrate judge when authorized by local rule—must issue a scheduling order:

(A) after receiving the parties' report under Rule 26(f); or

(B) after consulting with the parties' attorneys and any unrepresented parties at a scheduling conference or by telephone, mail, or other means.

(2) *Time to Issue.* The judge must issue the scheduling order as soon as practicable, but in any event within the earlier of 120 days after any defendant has been served with the complaint or 90 days after any defendant has appeared.

(3) *Contents of the Order.*

(A) *Required Contents.* The scheduling order must limit the time to join other parties, amend the pleadings, complete discovery, and file motions.

(B) *Permitted Contents.* The scheduling order may:

(i) modify the timing of disclosures under Rules 26(a) and 26(e)(1);

(ii) modify the extent of discovery;

    (iii) provide for disclosure or discovery of electronically stored information;

    (iv) include any agreements the parties reach for asserting claims of privilege or of protection as trial-preparation material after information is produced;

    (v) set dates for pretrial conferences and for trial; and

    (vi) include other appropriate matters.

  (4) *Modifying a Schedule.* A schedule may be modified only for good cause and with the judge's consent.

[Text of subdivision (b) effective December 1, 2015, absent contrary Congressional action.]

(b) Scheduling.

  (1) *Scheduling Order.* Except in categories of actions exempted by local rule, the district judge—or a magistrate judge when authorized by local rule—must issue a scheduling order:

    (A) after receiving the parties' report under Rule 26(f); or

    (B) after consulting with the parties' attorneys and any unrepresented parties at a scheduling conference.

  (2) *Time to Issue.* The judge must issue the scheduling order as soon as practicable, but unless the judge finds good cause for delay, the judge must issue it within the earlier of 90 days after any defendant has been served with the complaint or 60 days after any defendant has appeared.

  (3) *Contents of the Order.*

    (A) *Required Contents.* The scheduling order must limit the time to join other parties, amend the pleadings, complete discovery, and file motions.

    (B) *Permitted Contents.* The scheduling order may:

    (i) modify the timing of disclosures under Rules 26(a) and 26(e)(1);

    (ii) modify the extent of discovery;

    (iii) provide for disclosure, discovery, or preservation of electronically stored information;

    (iv) include any agreements the parties reach for asserting claims of privilege or of protection as trial-preparation material after information is produced, including agreements reached under Federal Rule of Evidence 502;

    (v) direct that before moving for an order relating to discovery, the movant must request a conference with the court;

    (vi) set dates for pretrial conferences and for trial; and

    (vii) include other appropriate matters.

  (4) *Modifying a Schedule.* A schedule may be modified only for good cause and with the judge's consent.

(c) Attendance and Matters for Consideration at a Pretrial Conference.

  (1) *Attendance.* A represented party must authorize at least one of its attorneys to make stipulations and admissions about all matters that can reasonably be anticipated for discussion at a pretrial conference. If appropriate, the court may require that a party or its representative be present or reasonably available by other means to consider possible settlement.

  (2) *Matters for Consideration.* At any pretrial conference, the court may consider and take appropriate action on the following matters:

    (A) formulating and simplifying the issues, and eliminating frivolous claims or defenses;

    (B) amending the pleadings if necessary or desirable;

    (C) obtaining admissions and stipulations about facts and documents to avoid unnecessary proof, and ruling in advance on the admissibility of evidence;

    (D) avoiding unnecessary proof and cumulative evidence, and limiting the use of testimony under Federal Rule of Evidence 702;

    (E) determining the appropriateness and timing of summary adjudication under Rule 56;

    (F) controlling and scheduling discovery, including orders affecting disclosures and discovery under Rule 26 and Rules 29 through 37;

    (G) identifying witnesses and documents, scheduling the filing and exchange of any pretrial briefs, and setting dates for further conferences and for trial;

    (H) referring matters to a magistrate judge or a master;

    (I) settling the case and using special procedures to assist in resolving the dispute when authorized by statute or local rule;

    (J) determining the form and content of the pretrial order;

    (K) disposing of pending motions;

    (L) adopting special procedures for managing potentially difficult or protracted actions that may involve complex issues, multiple parties, difficult legal questions, or unusual proof problems;

   (M) ordering a separate trial under Rule 42(b) of a claim, counterclaim, crossclaim, third-party claim, or particular issue;

   (N) ordering the presentation of evidence early in the trial on a manageable issue that might, on the evidence, be the basis for a judgment as a matter of law under Rule 50(a) or a judgment on partial findings under Rule 52(c);

   (O) establishing a reasonable limit on the time allowed to present evidence; and

   (P) facilitating in other ways the just, speedy, and inexpensive disposition of the action.

(d) Pretrial Orders. After any conference under this rule, the court should issue an order reciting the action taken. This order controls the course of the action unless the court modifies it.

(e) Final Pretrial Conference and Orders. The court may hold a final pretrial conference to formulate a trial plan, including a plan to facilitate the admission of evidence. The conference must be held as close to the start of trial as is reasonable, and must be attended by at least one attorney who will conduct the trial for each party and by any unrepresented party. The court may modify the order issued after a final pretrial conference only to prevent manifest injustice.

(f) Sanctions.

   (1) *In General.* On motion or on its own, the court may issue any just orders, including those authorized by Rule 37(b)(2)(A)(ii)-(vii), if a party or its attorney:

      (A) fails to appear at a scheduling or other pretrial conference;

      (B) is substantially unprepared to participate— or does not participate in good faith—in the conference; or

      (C) fails to obey a scheduling or other pretrial order.

   (2) *Imposing Fees and Costs.* Instead of or in addition to any other sanction, the court must order the party, its attorney, or both to pay the reasonable expenses—including attorney's fees—incurred because of any noncompliance with this rule, unless the noncompliance was substantially justified or other circumstances make an award of expenses unjust.

(Amended April 28, 1983, effective August 1, 1983; March 2, 1987, effective August 1, 1987; April 22, 1993, effective December 1, 1993; April 12, 2006, effective December 1, 2006; April 30, 2007, effective December 1, 2007; April 29, 2015, effective December 1, 2015, absent contrary Congressional action.)

TITLE IV. PARTIES

RULE 17. PLAINTIFF AND DEFENDANT; CAPACITY; PUBLIC OFFICERS

(a) Real Party in Interest.

   (1) *Designation in General.* An action must be prosecuted in the name of the real party in interest. The following may sue in their own names without joining the person for whose benefit the action is brought:

      (A) an executor;

      (B) an administrator;

      (C) a guardian;

      (D) a bailee;

      (E) a trustee of an express trust;

      (F) a party with whom or in whose name a contract has been made for another's benefit; and

      (G) a party authorized by statute.

   (2) *Action in the Name of the United States for Another's Use or Benefit.* When a federal statute so provides, an action for another's use or benefit must be brought in the name of the United States.

   (3) *Joinder of the Real Party in Interest.* The court may not dismiss an action for failure to prosecute in the name of the real party in interest until, after an objection, a reasonable time has been allowed for the real party in interest to ratify, join, or be substituted into the action. After ratification, joinder, or substitution, the action proceeds as if it had been originally commenced by the real party in interest.

(b) Capacity to Sue or Be Sued. Capacity to sue or be sued is determined as follows:

   (1) for an individual who is not acting in a representative capacity, by the law of the individual's domicile;

   (2) for a corporation, by the law under which it was organized; and

   (3) for all other parties, by the law of the state where the court is located, except that:

      (A) a partnership or other unincorporated association with no such capacity under that state's law may sue or be sued in its common name to enforce a substantive right existing under the United States Constitution or laws; and

(B) 28 U.S.C. §§ 754 and 959(a) govern the capacity of a receiver appointed by a United States court to sue or be sued in a United States court.

(c) Minor or Incompetent Person.

(1) *With a Representative.* The following representatives may sue or defend on behalf of a minor or an incompetent person:

(A) a general guardian;

(B) a committee;

(C) a conservator; or

(D) a like fiduciary.

(2) *Without a Representative.* A minor or an incompetent person who does not have a duly appointed representative may sue by a next friend or by a guardian ad litem. The court must appoint a guardian ad litem—or issue another appropriate order—to protect a minor or incompetent person who is unrepresented in an action.

(d) Public Officer's Title and Name. A public officer who sues or is sued in an official capacity may be designated by official title rather than by name, but the court may order that the officer's name be added.

(Amended December 27, 1946, effective March 19, 1948; December 29, 1948, effective October 20, 1949; February 28, 1966, effective July 1, 1966; March 2, 1987, effective August 1, 1987; April 25, 1988, effective August 1, 1988; amended by Pub.L. 100–690, Title VII, § 7049, November 18, 1988, 102 Stat. 4401 (although amendment by Pub.L. 100–690 could not be executed due to prior amendment by Court order which made the same change effective August 1, 1988); April 30, 2007, effective December 1, 2007.)

RULE 18.   JOINDER OF CLAIMS

(a) In General. A party asserting a claim, counterclaim, crossclaim, or third-party claim may join, as independent or alternative claims, as many claims as it has against an opposing party.

(b) Joinder of Contingent Claims. A party may join two claims even though one of them is contingent on the disposition of the other; but the court may grant relief only in accordance with the parties' relative substantive rights. In particular, a plaintiff may state a claim for money and a claim to set aside a conveyance that is fraudulent as to that plaintiff, without first obtaining a judgment for the money.

(Amended February 28, 1966, effective July 1, 1966; March 2, 1987, effective August 1, 1987; April 30, 2007, effective December 1, 2007.)

RULE 19.   REQUIRED JOINDER OF PARTIES

(a) Persons Required to Be Joined if Feasible.

(1) *Required Party.* A person who is subject to service of process and whose joinder will not deprive the court of subject-matter jurisdiction must be joined as a party if:

(A) in that person's absence, the court cannot accord complete relief among existing parties; or

(B) that person claims an interest relating to the subject of the action and is so situated that disposing of the action in the person's absence may:

(i) as a practical matter impair or impede the person's ability to protect the interest; or

(ii) leave an existing party subject to a substantial risk of incurring double, multiple, or otherwise inconsistent obligations because of the interest.

(2) *Joinder by Court Order.* If a person has not been joined as required, the court must order that the person be made a party. A person who refuses to join as a plaintiff may be made either a defendant or, in a proper case, an involuntary plaintiff.

(3) *Venue.* If a joined party objects to venue and the joinder would make venue improper, the court must dismiss that party.

(b) When Joinder Is Not Feasible. If a person who is required to be joined if feasible cannot be joined, the court must determine whether, in equity and good conscience, the action should proceed among the existing parties or should be dismissed. The factors for the court to consider include:

(1) the extent to which a judgment rendered in the person's absence might prejudice that person or the existing parties;

(2) the extent to which any prejudice could be lessened or avoided by:

(A) protective provisions in the judgment;

(B) shaping the relief; or

(C) other measures;

(3) whether a judgment rendered in the person's absence would be adequate; and

(4) whether the plaintiff would have an adequate remedy if the action were dismissed for nonjoinder.

(c) Pleading the Reasons for Nonjoinder. When asserting a claim for relief, a party must state:

(1) the name, if known, of any person who is required to be joined if feasible but is not joined; and

(2) the reasons for not joining that person.

(d) Exception for Class Actions. This rule is subject to Rule 23.

(Amended February 28, 1966, effective July 1, 1966; March 2, 1987, effective August 1, 1987; April 30, 2007, effective December 1, 2007.)

RULE 20. PERMISSIVE JOINDER OF PARTIES

(a) Persons Who May Join or Be Joined.

(1) *Plaintiffs.* Persons may join in one action as plaintiffs if:

(A) they assert any right to relief jointly, severally, or in the alternative with respect to or arising out of the same transaction, occurrence, or series of transactions or occurrences; and

(B) any question of law or fact common to all plaintiffs will arise in the action.

(2) *Defendants.* Persons—as well as a vessel, cargo, or other property subject to admiralty process in rem—may be joined in one action as defendants if:

(A) any right to relief is asserted against them jointly, severally, or in the alternative with respect to or arising out of the same transaction, occurrence, or series of transactions or occurrences; and

(B) any question of law or fact common to all defendants will arise in the action.

(3) *Extent of Relief.* Neither a plaintiff nor a defendant need be interested in obtaining or defending against all the relief demanded. The court may grant judgment to one or more plaintiffs according to their rights, and against one or more defendants according to their liabilities.

(b) Protective Measures. The court may issue orders—including an order for separate trials—to protect a party against embarrassment, delay, expense, or other prejudice that arises from including a person against whom the party asserts no claim and who asserts no claim against the party.

(Amended February 28, 1966, effective July 1, 1966; March 2, 1987, effective August 1, 1987; April 30, 2007, effective December 1, 2007.)

RULE 21. MISJOINDER AND NONJOINDER OF PARTIES

Misjoinder of parties is not a ground for dismissing an action. On motion or on its own, the court may at any time, on just terms, add or drop a party. The court may also sever any claim against a party.

(Amended April 30, 2007, effective December 1, 2007.)

RULE 22. INTERPLEADER

(a) Grounds.

(1) *By a Plaintiff.* Persons with claims that may expose a plaintiff to double or multiple liability may be joined as defendants and required to interplead. Joinder for interpleader is proper even though:

(A) the claims of the several claimants, or the titles on which their claims depend, lack a common origin or are adverse and independent rather than identical; or

(B) the plaintiff denies liability in whole or in part to any or all of the claimants.

(2) *By a Defendant.* A defendant exposed to similar liability may seek interpleader through a crossclaim or counterclaim.

(b) Relation to Other Rules and Statutes. This rule supplements—and does not limit—the joinder of parties allowed by Rule 20. The remedy this rule provides is in addition to—and does not supersede or limit—the remedy provided by 28 U.S.C. §§ 1335, 1397, and 2361. An action under those statutes must be conducted under these rules.

(Amended December 29, 1948, effective October 20, 1949; March 2, 1987, effective August 1, 1987; April 30, 2007, effective December 1, 2007.)

RULE 23. CLASS ACTIONS

(a) Prerequisites. One or more members of a class may sue or be sued as representative parties on behalf of all members only if:

(1) the class is so numerous that joinder of all members is impracticable;

(2) there are questions of law or fact common to the class;

(3) the claims or defenses of the representative parties are typical of the claims or defenses of the class; and

(4) the representative parties will fairly and adequately protect the interests of the class.

(b) Types of Class Actions. A class action may be maintained if Rule 23(a) is satisfied and if:

(1) prosecuting separate actions by or against individual class members would create a risk of:

(A) inconsistent or varying adjudications with respect to individual class members that would establish incompatible standards of conduct for the party opposing the class; or

(B) adjudications with respect to individual class members that, as a practical matter, would be dispositive of the interests of the other members not parties to the individual adjudications or would substantially impair or impede their ability to protect their interests;

(2) the party opposing the class has acted or refused to act on grounds that apply generally to the class, so that final injunctive relief or corresponding declaratory relief is appropriate respecting the class as a whole; or

(3) the court finds that the questions of law or fact common to class members predominate over any questions affecting only individual members, and that a class action is superior to other available methods for fairly and efficiently adjudicating the controversy. The matters pertinent to these findings include:

(A) the class members' interests in individually controlling the prosecution or defense of separate actions;

(B) the extent and nature of any litigation concerning the controversy already begun by or against class members;

(C) the desirability or undesirability of concentrating the litigation of the claims in the particular forum; and

(D) the likely difficulties in managing a class action.

(c) Certification Order; Notice to Class Members; Judgment; Issues Classes; Subclasses.

(1) *Certification Order.*

(A) *Time to Issue.* At an early practicable time after a person sues or is sued as a class representative, the court must determine by order whether to certify the action as a class action.

(B) *Defining the Class; Appointing Class Counsel.* An order that certifies a class action must define the class and the class claims, issues, or defenses, and must appoint class counsel under Rule 23(g).

(C) *Altering or Amending the Order.* An order that grants or denies class certification may be altered or amended before final judgment.

(2) *Notice.*

(A) *For (b)(1) or (b)(2) Classes.* For any class certified under Rule 23(b)(1) or (b)(2), the court may direct appropriate notice to the class.

(B) *For (b)(3) Classes.* For any class certified under Rule 23(b)(3), the court must direct to class members the best notice that is practicable under the circumstances, including individual notice to all members who can be identified through reasonable effort. The notice must clearly and concisely state in plain, easily understood language:

(i) the nature of the action;

(ii) the definition of the class certified;

(iii) the class claims, issues, or defenses;

(iv) that a class member may enter an appearance through an attorney if the member so desires;

(v) that the court will exclude from the class any member who requests exclusion;

(vi) the time and manner for requesting exclusion; and

(vii) the binding effect of a class judgment on members under Rule 23(c)(3).

(3) *Judgment.* Whether or not favorable to the class, the judgment in a class action must:

(A) for any class certified under Rule 23(b)(1) or (b)(2), include and describe those whom the court finds to be class members; and

(B) for any class certified under Rule 23(b)(3), include and specify or describe those to whom the Rule 23(c)(2) notice was directed, who have not requested exclusion, and whom the court finds to be class members.

(4) *Particular Issues.* When appropriate, an action may be brought or maintained as a class action with respect to particular issues.

(5) *Subclasses.* When appropriate, a class may be divided into subclasses that are each treated as a class under this rule.

(d) Conducting the Action.

(1) *In General.* In conducting an action under this rule, the court may issue orders that:

(A) determine the course of proceedings or prescribe measures to prevent undue repetition or complication in presenting evidence or argument;

(B) require—to protect class members and fairly conduct the action—giving appropriate notice to some or all class members of:

(i) any step in the action;

(ii) the proposed extent of the judgment; or

(iii) the members' opportunity to signify whether they consider the representation fair and adequate, to intervene and present claims or defenses, or to otherwise come into the action;

(C) impose conditions on the representative parties or on intervenors;

(D) require that the pleadings be amended to eliminate allegations about representation of absent persons and that the action proceed accordingly; or

(E) deal with similar procedural matters.

(2) *Combining and Amending Orders.* An order under Rule 23(d)(1) may be altered or amended from time to time and may be combined with an order under Rule 16.

(e) Settlement, Voluntary Dismissal, or Compromise. The claims, issues, or defenses of a certified class may be settled, voluntarily dismissed, or compromised only with the court's approval. The following procedures apply to a proposed settlement, voluntary dismissal, or compromise:

(1) The court must direct notice in a reasonable manner to all class members who would be bound by the proposal.

(2) If the proposal would bind class members, the court may approve it only after a hearing and on finding that it is fair, reasonable, and adequate.

(3) The parties seeking approval must file a statement identifying any agreement made in connection with the proposal.

(4) If the class action was previously certified under Rule 23(b)(3), the court may refuse to approve a settlement unless it affords a new opportunity to request exclusion to individual class members who had an earlier opportunity to request exclusion but did not do so.

(5) Any class member may object to the proposal if it requires court approval under this subdivision (e); the objection may be withdrawn only with the court's approval.

(f) Appeals. A court of appeals may permit an appeal from an order granting or denying class-action certification under this rule if a petition for permission to appeal is filed with the circuit clerk within 14 days after the order is entered. An appeal does not stay proceedings in the district court unless the district judge or the court of appeals so orders.

(g) Class Counsel.

(1) *Appointing Class Counsel.* Unless a statute provides otherwise, a court that certifies a class must appoint class counsel. In appointing class counsel, the court:

(A) must consider:

(i) the work counsel has done in identifying or investigating potential claims in the action;

(ii) counsel's experience in handling class actions, other complex litigation, and the types of claims asserted in the action;

(iii) counsel's knowledge of the applicable law; and

(iv) the resources that counsel will commit to representing the class;

(B) may consider any other matter pertinent to counsel's ability to fairly and adequately represent the interests of the class;

(C) may order potential class counsel to provide information on any subject pertinent to the appointment and to propose terms for attorney's fees and nontaxable costs;

(D) may include in the appointing order provisions about the award of attorney's fees or nontaxable costs under Rule 23(h); and

(E) may make further orders in connection with the appointment.

(2) *Standard for Appointing Class Counsel.* When one applicant seeks appointment as class counsel, the court may appoint that applicant only if the applicant is adequate under Rule 23(g)(1) and (4). If more than one adequate applicant seeks appointment, the court must appoint the applicant best able to represent the interests of the class.

(3) *Interim Counsel.* The court may designate interim counsel to act on behalf of a putative class before determining whether to certify the action as a class action.

(4) *Duty of Class Counsel.* Class counsel must fairly and adequately represent the interests of the class.

(h) Attorney's Fees and Nontaxable Costs. In a certified class action, the court may award reasonable attorney's fees and nontaxable costs that are authorized by law or by the parties' agreement. The following procedures apply:

(1) A claim for an award must be made by motion under Rule 54(d)(2), subject to the provisions of this subdivision (h), at a time the court sets. Notice of the motion must be served on all parties and, for motions by class counsel, directed to class members in a reasonable manner.

(2) A class member, or a party from whom payment is sought, may object to the motion.

(3) The court may hold a hearing and must find the facts and state its legal conclusions under Rule 52(a).

(4) The court may refer issues related to the amount of the award to a special master or a magistrate judge, as provided in Rule 54(d)(2)(D).

(Amended February 28, 1966, effective July 1, 1966; March 2, 1987, effective August 1, 1987; April 24, 1998, effective December 1, 1998; March 27, 2003, effective December 1, 2003; April 30, 2007, effective December 1, 2007; March 26, 2009, effective December 1, 2009.)

RULE 23.1   DERIVATIVE ACTIONS

(a) Prerequisites. This rule applies when one or more shareholders or members of a corporation or an unincorporated association bring a derivative action to enforce a right that the corporation or association may properly assert but has failed to enforce. The derivative action may not be maintained if it appears that the plaintiff does not fairly and adequately represent the interests of shareholders or members who are similarly situated in enforcing the right of the corporation or association.

(b) Pleading Requirements. The complaint must be verified and must:

  (1) allege that the plaintiff was a shareholder or member at the time of the transaction complained of, or that the plaintiff's share or membership later devolved on it by operation of law;

  (2) allege that the action is not a collusive one to confer jurisdiction that the court would otherwise lack; and

  (3) state with particularity:

    (A) any effort by the plaintiff to obtain the desired action from the directors or comparable authority and, if necessary, from the shareholders or members; and

    (B) the reasons for not obtaining the action or not making the effort.

(c) Settlement, Dismissal, and Compromise. A derivative action may be settled, voluntarily dismissed, or compromised only with the court's approval. Notice of a proposed settlement, voluntary dismissal, or compromise must be given to shareholders or members in the manner that the court orders.

(Adopted February 28, 1966, effective July 1, 1966; amended March 2, 1987, effective August 1, 1987; April 30, 2007, effective December 1, 2007.)

RULE 23.2   ACTIONS RELATING TO UNINCORPORATED ASSOCIATIONS

This rule applies to an action brought by or against the members of an unincorporated association as a class by naming certain members as representative parties. The action may be maintained only if it appears that those parties will fairly and adequately protect the interests of the association and its members. In conducting the action, the court may issue any appropriate orders corresponding with those in Rule 23(d), and the procedure for settlement, volun-

tary dismissal, or compromise must correspond with the procedure in Rule 23(e).

(Adopted February 28, 1966, effective July 1, 1966; amended April 30, 2007, effective December 1, 2007.)

RULE 24.   INTERVENTION

(a) Intervention of Right. On timely motion, the court must permit anyone to intervene who:

  (1) is given an unconditional right to intervene by a federal statute; or

  (2) claims an interest relating to the property or transaction that is the subject of the action, and is so situated that disposing of the action may as a practical matter impair or impede the movant's ability to protect its interest, unless existing parties adequately represent that interest.

(b) Permissive Intervention.

  (1) *In General.* On timely motion, the court may permit anyone to intervene who:

    (A) is given a conditional right to intervene by a federal statute; or

    (B) has a claim or defense that shares with the main action a common question of law or fact.

  (2) *By a Government Officer or Agency.* On timely motion, the court may permit a federal or state governmental officer or agency to intervene if a party's claim or defense is based on:

    (A) a statute or executive order administered by the officer or agency; or

    (B) any regulation, order, requirement, or agreement issued or made under the statute or executive order.

  (3) *Delay or Prejudice.* In exercising its discretion, the court must consider whether the intervention will unduly delay or prejudice the adjudication of the original parties' rights.

(c) Notice and Pleading Required. A motion to intervene must be served on the parties as provided in Rule 5. The motion must state the grounds for intervention and be accompanied by a pleading that sets out the claim or defense for which intervention is sought.

(Amended December 27, 1946, effective March 19, 1948; December 29, 1948, effective October 20, 1949; January 21, 1963, effective July 1, 1963; February 28, 1966, effective July 1, 1966; March 2, 1987, effective August 1, 1987; April 30, 1991, effective December 1, 1991; April 12, 2006, effective December 1, 2006; April 30, 2007, effective December 1, 2007.)

RULE 25. SUBSTITUTION OF PARTIES

(a) Death.

(1) *Substitution if the Claim Is Not Extinguished.* If a party dies and the claim is not extinguished, the court may order substitution of the proper party. A motion for substitution may be made by any party or by the decedent's successor or representative. If the motion is not made within 90 days after service of a statement noting the death, the action by or against the decedent must be dismissed.

(2) *Continuation Among the Remaining Parties.* After a party's death, if the right sought to be enforced survives only to or against the remaining parties, the action does not abate, but proceeds in favor of or against the remaining parties. The death should be noted on the record.

(3) *Service.* A motion to substitute, together with a notice of hearing, must be served on the parties as provided in Rule 5 and on nonparties as provided in Rule 4. A statement noting death must be served in the same manner. Service may be made in any judicial district.

(b) Incompetency. If a party becomes incompetent, the court may, on motion, permit the action to be continued by or against the party's representative. The motion must be served as provided in Rule 25(a)(3).

(c) Transfer of Interest. If an interest is transferred, the action may be continued by or against the original party unless the court, on motion, orders the transferee to be substituted in the action or joined with the original party. The motion must be served as provided in Rule 25(a)(3).

(d) Public Officers; Death or Separation from Office. An action does not abate when a public officer who is a party in an official capacity dies, resigns, or otherwise ceases to hold office while the action is pending. The officer's successor is automatically substituted as a party. Later proceedings should be in the substituted party's name, but any misnomer not affecting the parties' substantial rights must be disregarded. The court may order substitution at any time, but the absence of such an order does not affect the substitution.

(Amended December 29, 1948, effective October 20, 1949; April 17, 1961, effective July 19, 1961; January 21, 1963, effective July 1, 1963; March 2, 1987, effective August 1, 1987; April 30, 2007, effective December 1, 2007.)

TITLE V. DISCLOSURES AND DISCOVERY

RULE 26. DUTY TO DISCLOSE; GENERAL PROVISIONS GOVERNING DISCOVERY

(a) Required Disclosures.

(1) *Initial Disclosure.*

(A) *In General.* Except as exempted by Rule 26(a)(1)(B) or as otherwise stipulated or ordered by the court, a party must, without awaiting a discovery request, provide to the other parties:

(i) the name and, if known, the address and telephone number of each individual likely to have discoverable information—along with the subjects of that information—that the disclosing party may use to support its claims or defenses, unless the use would be solely for impeachment;

(ii) a copy—or a description by category and location—of all documents, electronically stored information, and tangible things that the disclosing party has in its possession, custody, or control and may use to support its claims or defenses, unless the use would be solely for impeachment;

(iii) a computation of each category of damages claimed by the disclosing party—who must also make available for inspection and copying as under Rule 34 the documents or other evidentiary material, unless privileged or protected from disclosure, on which each computation is based, including materials bearing on the nature and extent of injuries suffered; and

(iv) for inspection and copying as under Rule 34, any insurance agreement under which an insurance business may be liable to satisfy all or part of a possible judgment in the action or to indemnify or reimburse for payments made to satisfy the judgment.

(B) *Proceedings Exempt from Initial Disclosure.* The following proceedings are exempt from initial disclosure:

(i) an action for review on an administrative record;

(ii) a forfeiture action in rem arising from a federal statute;

(iii) a petition for habeas corpus or any other proceeding to challenge a criminal conviction or sentence;

(iv) an action brought without an attorney by a person in the custody of the United States, a state, or a state subdivision;

(v) an action to enforce or quash an administrative summons or subpoena;

(vi) an action by the United States to recover benefit payments;

(vii) an action by the United States to collect on a student loan guaranteed by the United States;

(viii) a proceeding ancillary to a proceeding in another court; and

(ix) an action to enforce an arbitration award.

(C) *Time for Initial Disclosures—In General.* A party must make the initial disclosures at or within 14 days after the parties' Rule 26(f) conference unless a different time is set by stipulation or court order, or unless a party objects during the conference that initial disclosures are not appropriate in this action and states the objection in the proposed discovery plan. In ruling on the objection, the court must determine what disclosures, if any, are to be made and must set the time for disclosure.

(D) *Time for Initial Disclosures—For Parties Served or Joined Later.* A party that is first served or otherwise joined after the Rule 26(f) conference must make the initial disclosures within 30 days after being served or joined, unless a different time is set by stipulation or court order.

(E) *Basis for Initial Disclosure; Unacceptable Excuses.* A party must make its initial disclosures based on the information then reasonably available to it. A party is not excused from making its disclosures because it has not fully investigated the case or because it challenges the sufficiency of another party's disclosures or because another party has not made its disclosures.

(2) *Disclosure of Expert Testimony.*

(A) *In General.* In addition to the disclosures required by Rule 26(a)(1), a party must disclose to the other parties the identity of any witness it may use at trial to present evidence under Federal Rule of Evidence 702, 703, or 705.

(B) *Witnesses Who Must Provide a Written Report.* Unless otherwise stipulated or ordered by the court, this disclosure must be accompanied by a written report—prepared and signed by the witness—if the witness is one retained or specially employed to provide expert testimony in the case or one whose duties as the party's employee regularly involve giving expert testimony. The report must contain:

(i) a complete statement of all opinions the witness will express and the basis and reasons for them;

(ii) the facts or data considered by the witness in forming them;

(iii) any exhibits that will be used to summarize or support them;

(iv) the witness's qualifications, including a list of all publications authored in the previous 10 years;

(v) a list of all other cases in which, during the previous 4 years, the witness testified as an expert at trial or by deposition; and

(vi) a statement of the compensation to be paid for the study and testimony in the case.

(C) *Witnesses Who Do Not Provide a Written Report.* Unless otherwise stipulated or ordered by the court, if the witness is not required to provide a written report, this disclosure must state:

(i) the subject matter on which the witness is expected to present evidence under Federal Rule of Evidence 702, 703, or 705; and

(ii) a summary of the facts and opinions to which the witness is expected to testify.

(D) *Time to Disclose Expert Testimony.* A party must make these disclosures at the times and in the sequence that the court orders. Absent a stipulation or a court order, the disclosures must be made:

(i) at least 90 days before the date set for trial or for the case to be ready for trial; or

(ii) if the evidence is intended solely to contradict or rebut evidence on the same subject matter identified by another party under Rule 26(a)(2)(B) or (C), within 30 days after the other party's disclosure.

(E) *Supplementing the Disclosure.* The parties must supplement these disclosures when required under Rule 26(e).

(3) *Pretrial Disclosures.*

(A) *In General.* In addition to the disclosures required by Rule 26(a)(1) and (2), a party must provide to the other parties and promptly file the following information about the evidence that it may present at trial other than solely for impeachment:

(i) the name and, if not previously provided, the address and telephone number of each witness—separately identifying those the party expects to present and those it may call if the need arises;

(ii) the designation of those witnesses whose testimony the party expects to present by deposition and, if not taken stenographically, a transcript of the pertinent parts of the deposition; and

    (iii) an identification of each document or other exhibit, including summaries of other evidence—separately identifying those items the party expects to offer and those it may offer if the need arises.

(B) *Time for Pretrial Disclosures; Objections.* Unless the court orders otherwise, these disclosures must be made at least 30 days before trial. Within 14 days after they are made, unless the court sets a different time, a party may serve and promptly file a list of the following objections: any objections to the use under Rule 32(a) of a deposition designated by another party under Rule 26(a)(3)(A)(ii); and any objection, together with the grounds for it, that may be made to the admissibility of materials identified under Rule 26(a)(3)(A)(iii). An objection not so made—except for one under Federal Rule of Evidence 402 or 403—is waived unless excused by the court for good cause.

(4) *Form of Disclosures.* Unless the court orders otherwise, all disclosures under Rule 26(a) must be in writing, signed, and served.

[Text of subdivision (b) effective until December 1, 2015, absent contrary Congressional action.]

(b) Discovery Scope and Limits.

(1) *Scope in General.* Unless otherwise limited by court order, the scope of discovery is as follows: Parties may obtain discovery regarding any nonprivileged matter that is relevant to any party's claim or defense—including the existence, description, nature, custody, condition, and location of any documents or other tangible things and the identity and location of persons who know of any discoverable matter. For good cause, the court may order discovery of any matter relevant to the subject matter involved in the action. Relevant information need not be admissible at the trial if the discovery appears reasonably calculated to lead to the discovery of admissible evidence. All discovery is subject to the limitations imposed by Rule 26(b)(2)(C).

(2) *Limitations on Frequency and Extent.*

    (A) *When Permitted.* By order, the court may alter the limits in these rules on the number of depositions and interrogatories or on the length of depositions under Rule 30. By order or local rule, the court may also limit the number of requests under Rule 36.

    (B) *Specific Limitations on Electronically Stored Information.* A party need not provide discovery of electronically stored information from sources that the party identifies as not reasonably accessible because of undue burden or cost. On motion to compel discovery or for a protective order, the party from whom discovery is sought must show that the information is not reasonably accessible because of undue burden or cost. If that showing is made, the court may nonetheless order discovery from such sources if the requesting party shows good cause, considering the limitations of Rule 26(b)(2)(C). The court may specify conditions for the discovery.

    (C) *When Required.* On motion or on its own, the court must limit the frequency or extent of discovery otherwise allowed by these rules or by local rule if it determines that:

    (i) the discovery sought is unreasonably cumulative or duplicative, or can be obtained from some other source that is more convenient, less burdensome, or less expensive;

    (ii) the party seeking discovery has had ample opportunity to obtain the information by discovery in the action; or

    (iii) the burden or expense of the proposed discovery outweighs its likely benefit, considering the needs of the case, the amount in controversy, the parties' resources, the importance of the issues at stake in the action, and the importance of the discovery in resolving the issues.

(3) *Trial Preparation: Materials.*

    (A) *Documents and Tangible Things.* Ordinarily, a party may not discover documents and tangible things that are prepared in anticipation of litigation or for trial by or for another party or its representative (including the other party's attorney, consultant, surety, indemnitor, insurer, or agent). But, subject to Rule 26(b)(4), those materials may be discovered if:

    (i) they are otherwise discoverable under Rule 26(b)(1); and

    (ii) the party shows that it has substantial need for the materials to prepare its case and cannot, without undue hardship, obtain their substantial equivalent by other means.

    (B) *Protection Against Disclosure.* If the court orders discovery of those materials, it must protect against disclosure of the mental impressions, conclusions, opinions, or legal theories of a party's attorney or other representative concerning the litigation.

    (C) *Previous Statement.* Any party or other person may, on request and without the re-

quired showing, obtain the person's own previous statement about the action or its subject matter. If the request is refused, the
person may move for a court order, and Rule
37(a)(5) applies to the award of expenses. A
previous statement is either:

(i) a written statement that the person has
signed or otherwise adopted or approved;
or

(ii) a contemporaneous stenographic, mechanical, electrical, or other recording—or a
transcription of it—that recites substantially verbatim the person's oral statement.

(4) *Trial Preparation: Experts.*

(A) *Deposition of an Expert Who May Testify.*
A party may depose any person who has
been identified as an expert whose opinions
may be presented at trial. If Rule
26(a)(2)(B) requires a report from the expert,
the deposition may be conducted only after
the report is provided.

(B) *Trial–Preparation Protection for Draft Reports or Disclosures.* Rules 26(b)(3)(A) and
(B) protect drafts of any report or disclosure
required under Rule 26(a)(2), regardless of
the form in which the draft is recorded.

(C) *Trial–Preparation Protection for Communications Between a Party's Attorney and Expert Witnesses.* Rules 26(b)(3)(A) and (B)
protect communications between the party's
attorney and any witness required to provide
a report under Rule 26(a)(2)(B), regardless of
the form of the communications, except to
the extent that the communications:

(i) relate to compensation for the expert's
study or testimony;

(ii) identify facts or data that the party's attorney provided and that the expert considered in forming the opinions to be expressed; or

(iii) identify assumptions that the party's attorney provided and that the expert relied
on in forming the opinions to be expressed.

(D) *Expert Employed Only for Trial Preparation.* Ordinarily, a party may not, by interrogatories or deposition, discover facts
known or opinions held by an expert who has
been retained or specially employed by another party in anticipation of litigation or to
prepare for trial and who is not expected to
be called as a witness at trial. But a party
may do so only:

(i) as provided in Rule 35(b); or

(ii) on showing exceptional circumstances under which it is impracticable for the party
to obtain facts or opinions on the same
subject by other means.

(E) *Payment.* Unless manifest injustice would
result, the court must require that the party
seeking discovery:

(i) pay the expert a reasonable fee for time
spent in responding to discovery under
Rule 26(b)(4)(A) or (D); and

(ii) for discovery under (D), also pay the other
party a fair portion of the fees and expenses it reasonably incurred in obtaining
the expert's facts and opinions.

(5) *Claiming Privilege or Protecting Trial-Preparation Materials.*

(A) *Information Withheld.* When a party withholds information otherwise discoverable by
claiming that the information is privileged or
subject to protection as trial-preparation material, the party must:

(i) expressly make the claim; and

(ii) describe the nature of the documents, communications, or tangible things not produced or disclosed—and do so in a manner
that, without revealing information itself
privileged or protected, will enable other
parties to assess the claim.

(B) *Information Produced.* If information produced in discovery is subject to a claim of
privilege or of protection as trial-preparation
material, the party making the claim may
notify any party that received the information of the claim and the basis for it. After
being notified, a party must promptly return,
sequester, or destroy the specified information and any copies it has; must not use or
disclose the information until the claim is
resolved; must take reasonable steps to retrieve the information if the party disclosed
it before being notified; and may promptly
present the information to the court under
seal for a determination of the claim. The
producing party must preserve the information until the claim is resolved.

*[Text of subdivision (b) effective December 1, 2015,
absent contrary Congressional action.]*

(b) Discovery Scope and Limits.

(1) *Scope in General.* Unless otherwise limited by
court order, the scope of discovery is as follows:
Parties may obtain discovery regarding any
nonprivileged matter that is relevant to any
party's claim or defense and proportional to the

needs of the case, considering the importance of the issues at stake in the action, the amount in controversy, the parties' relative access to relevant information, the parties' resources, the importance of the discovery in resolving the issues, and whether the burden or expense of the proposed discovery outweighs its likely benefit. Information within this scope of discovery need not be admissible in evidence to be discoverable.

(2) *Limitations on Frequency and Extent.*

  (A) *When Permitted.* By order, the court may alter the limits in these rules on the number of depositions and interrogatories or on the length of depositions under Rule 30. By order or local rule, the court may also limit the number of requests under Rule 36.

  (B) *Specific Limitations on Electronically Stored Information.* A party need not provide discovery of electronically stored information from sources that the party identifies as not reasonably accessible because of undue burden or cost. On motion to compel discovery or for a protective order, the party from whom discovery is sought must show that the information is not reasonably accessible because of undue burden or cost. If that showing is made, the court may nonetheless order discovery from such sources if the requesting party shows good cause, considering the limitations of Rule 26(b)(2)(C). The court may specify conditions for the discovery.

  (C) *When Required.* On motion or on its own, the court must limit the frequency or extent of discovery otherwise allowed by these rules or by local rule if it determines that:

    (i) the discovery sought is unreasonably cumulative or duplicative, or can be obtained from some other source that is more convenient, less burdensome, or less expensive;

    (ii) the party seeking discovery has had ample opportunity to obtain the information by discovery in the action; or

    (iii) the proposed discovery is outside the scope permitted by Rule 26(b)(1).

(3) *Trial Preparation: Materials.*

  (A) *Documents and Tangible Things.* Ordinarily, a party may not discover documents and tangible things that are prepared in anticipation of litigation or for trial by or for another party or its representative (including the other party's attorney, consultant, surety, indemnitor, insurer, or agent). But, subject to Rule 26(b)(4), those materials may be discovered if:

    (i) they are otherwise discoverable under Rule 26(b)(1); and

    (ii) the party shows that it has substantial need for the materials to prepare its case and cannot, without undue hardship, obtain their substantial equivalent by other means.

  (B) *Protection Against Disclosure.* If the court orders discovery of those materials, it must protect against disclosure of the mental impressions, conclusions, opinions, or legal theories of a party's attorney or other representative concerning the litigation.

  (C) *Previous Statement.* Any party or other person may, on request and without the required showing, obtain the person's own previous statement about the action or its subject matter. If the request is refused, the person may move for a court order, and Rule 37(a)(5) applies to the award of expenses. A previous statement is either:

    (i) a written statement that the person has signed or otherwise adopted or approved; or

    (ii) a contemporaneous stenographic, mechanical, electrical, or other recording—or a transcription of it—that recites substantially verbatim the person's oral statement.

(4) *Trial Preparation: Experts.*

  (A) *Deposition of an Expert Who May Testify.* A party may depose any person who has been identified as an expert whose opinions may be presented at trial. If Rule 26(a)(2)(B) requires a report from the expert, the deposition may be conducted only after the report is provided.

  (B) *Trial–Preparation Protection for Draft Reports or Disclosures.* Rules 26(b)(3)(A) and (B) protect drafts of any report or disclosure required under Rule 26(a)(2), regardless of the form in which the draft is recorded.

  (C) *Trial–Preparation Protection for Communications Between a Party's Attorney and Expert Witnesses.* Rules 26(b)(3)(A) and (B) protect communications between the party's attorney and any witness required to provide a report under Rule 26(a)(2)(B), regardless of the form of the communications, except to the extent that the communications:

    (i) relate to compensation for the expert's study or testimony;

    (ii) identify facts or data that the party's attorney provided and that the expert considered in forming the opinions to be expressed; or

(iii) identify assumptions that the party's attorney provided and that the expert relied on in forming the opinions to be expressed.

(D) *Expert Employed Only for Trial Preparation.* Ordinarily, a party may not, by interrogatories or deposition, discover facts known or opinions held by an expert who has been retained or specially employed by another party in anticipation of litigation or to prepare for trial and who is not expected to be called as a witness at trial. But a party may do so only:

(i) as provided in Rule 35(b); or

(ii) on showing exceptional circumstances under which it is impracticable for the party to obtain facts or opinions on the same subject by other means.

(E) *Payment.* Unless manifest injustice would result, the court must require that the party seeking discovery:

(i) pay the expert a reasonable fee for time spent in responding to discovery under Rule 26(b)(4)(A) or (D); and

(ii) for discovery under (D), also pay the other party a fair portion of the fees and expenses it reasonably incurred in obtaining the expert's facts and opinions.

(5) *Claiming Privilege or Protecting Trial-Preparation Materials.*

(A) *Information Withheld.* When a party withholds information otherwise discoverable by claiming that the information is privileged or subject to protection as trial-preparation material, the party must:

(i) expressly make the claim; and

(ii) describe the nature of the documents, communications, or tangible things not produced or disclosed—and do so in a manner that, without revealing information itself privileged or protected, will enable other parties to assess the claim.

(B) *Information Produced.* If information produced in discovery is subject to a claim of privilege or of protection as trial-preparation material, the party making the claim may notify any party that received the information of the claim and the basis for it. After being notified, a party must promptly return, sequester, or destroy the specified information and any copies it has; must not use or disclose the information until the claim is resolved; must take reasonable steps to retrieve the information if the party disclosed it before being notified; and may promptly

present the information to the court under seal for a determination of the claim. The producing party must preserve the information until the claim is resolved.

[Text of subdivision (c) effective until December 1, 2015, absent contrary Congressional action.]

(c) Protective Orders.

(1) *In General.* A party or any person from whom discovery is sought may move for a protective order in the court where the action is pending— or as an alternative on matters relating to a deposition, in the court for the district where the deposition will be taken. The motion must include a certification that the movant has in good faith conferred or attempted to confer with other affected parties in an effort to resolve the dispute without court action. The court may, for good cause, issue an order to protect a party or person from annoyance, embarrassment, oppression, or undue burden or expense, including one or more of the following:

(A) forbidding the disclosure or discovery;

(B) specifying terms, including time and place, for the disclosure or discovery;

(C) prescribing a discovery method other than the one selected by the party seeking discovery;

(D) forbidding inquiry into certain matters, or limiting the scope of disclosure or discovery to certain matters;

(E) designating the persons who may be present while the discovery is conducted;

(F) requiring that a deposition be sealed and opened only on court order;

(G) requiring that a trade secret or other confidential research, development, or commercial information not be revealed or be revealed only in a specified way; and

(H) requiring that the parties simultaneously file specified documents or information in sealed envelopes, to be opened as the court directs.

(2) *Ordering Discovery.* If a motion for a protective order is wholly or partly denied, the court may, on just terms, order that any party or person provide or permit discovery.

(3) *Awarding Expenses.* Rule 37(a)(5) applies to the award of expenses.

[Text of subdivision (c) effective December 1, 2015, absent contrary Congressional action.]

(c) Protective Orders.

(1) *In General.* A party or any person from whom discovery is sought may move for a protective order in the court where the action is pending — or as an alternative on matters relating to a deposition, in the court for the district where the deposition will be taken. The motion must include a certification that the movant has in good faith conferred or attempted to confer with other affected parties in an effort to resolve the dispute without court action. The court may, for good cause, issue an order to protect a party or person from annoyance, embarrassment, oppression, or undue burden or expense, including one or more of the following:

(A) forbidding the disclosure or discovery;

(B) specifying terms, including time and place or the allocation of expenses, for the disclosure or discovery;

(C) prescribing a discovery method other than the one selected by the party seeking discovery;

(D) forbidding inquiry into certain matters, or limiting the scope of disclosure or discovery to certain matters;

(E) designating the persons who may be present while the discovery is conducted;

(F) requiring that a deposition be sealed and opened only on court order;

(G) requiring that a trade secret or other confidential research, development, or commercial information not be revealed or be revealed only in a specified way; and

(H) requiring that the parties simultaneously file specified documents or information in sealed envelopes, to be opened as the court directs.

(2) *Ordering Discovery.* If a motion for a protective order is wholly or partly denied, the court may, on just terms, order that any party or person provide or permit discovery.

(3) *Awarding Expenses.* Rule 37(a)(5) applies to the award of expenses.

[Text of subdivision (d) effective until December 1, 2015, absent contrary Congressional action.]

(d) Timing and Sequence of Discovery.

(1) *Timing.* A party may not seek discovery from any source before the parties have conferred as required by Rule 26(f), except in a proceeding exempted from initial disclosure under Rule 26(a)(1)(B), or when authorized by these rules, by stipulation, or by court order.

(2) *Sequence.* Unless, on motion, the court orders otherwise for the parties' and witnesses' convenience and in the interests of justice:

(A) methods of discovery may be used in any sequence; and

(B) discovery by one party does not require any other party to delay its discovery.

[Text of subdivision (d) effective December 1, 2015, absent contrary Congressional action.]

(d) Timing and Sequence of Discovery.

(1) *Timing.* A party may not seek discovery from any source before the parties have conferred as required by Rule 26(f), except in a proceeding exempted from initial disclosure under Rule 26(a)(1)(B), or when authorized by these rules, by stipulation, or by court order.

(2) *Early Rule 34 Requests.*

(A) *Time to Deliver.* More than 21 days after the summons and complaint are served on a party, a request under Rule 34 may be delivered:

(i) to that party by any other party, and

(ii) by that party to any plaintiff or to any other party that has been served.

(B) *When Considered Served.* The request is considered to have been served at the first Rule 26(f) conference.

(3) *Sequence.* Unless the parties stipulate or the court orders otherwise for the parties' and witnesses' convenience and in the interests of justice:

(A) methods of discovery may be used in any sequence; and

(B) discovery by one party does not require any other party to delay its discovery.

(e) Supplementing Disclosures and Responses.

(1) *In General.* A party who has made a disclosure under Rule 26(a)—or who has responded to an interrogatory, request for production, or request for admission—must supplement or correct its disclosure or response:

(A) in a timely manner if the party learns that in some material respect the disclosure or response is incomplete or incorrect, and if the additional or corrective information has not otherwise been made known to the other parties during the discovery process or in writing; or

(B) as ordered by the court.

(2) *Expert Witness.* For an expert whose report must be disclosed under Rule 26(a)(2)(B), the party's duty to supplement extends both to information included in the report and to information given during the expert's deposition. Any additions or changes to this information must be disclosed by the time the party's pretrial disclosures under Rule 26(a)(3) are due.

[Text of subdivision (f) effective until December 1, 2015, absent contrary Congressional action.]

(f) Conference of the Parties; Planning for Discovery.

(1) *Conference Timing.* Except in a proceeding exempted from initial disclosure under Rule 26(a)(1)(B) or when the court orders otherwise, the parties must confer as soon as practicable—and in any event at least 21 days before a scheduling conference is to be held or a scheduling order is due under Rule 16(b).

(2) *Conference Content; Parties' Responsibilities.* In conferring, the parties must consider the nature and basis of their claims and defenses and the possibilities for promptly settling or resolving the case; make or arrange for the disclosures required by Rule 26(a)(1); discuss any issues about preserving discoverable information; and develop a proposed discovery plan. The attorneys of record and all unrepresented parties that have appeared in the case are jointly responsible for arranging the conference, for attempting in good faith to agree on the proposed discovery plan, and for submitting to the court within 14 days after the conference a written report outlining the plan. The court may order the parties or attorneys to attend the conference in person.

(3) *Discovery Plan.* A discovery plan must state the parties' views and proposals on:

(A) what changes should be made in the timing, form, or requirement for disclosures under Rule 26(a), including a statement of when initial disclosures were made or will be made;

(B) the subjects on which discovery may be needed, when discovery should be completed, and whether discovery should be conducted in phases or be limited to or focused on particular issues;

(C) any issues about disclosure or discovery of electronically stored information, including the form or forms in which it should be produced;

(D) any issues about claims of privilege or of protection as trial-preparation materials, including—if the parties agree on a procedure to assert these claims after production—whether to ask the court to include their agreement in an order;

(E) what changes should be made in the limitations on discovery imposed under these rules or by local rule, and what other limitations should be imposed; and

(F) any other orders that the court should issue under Rule 26(c) or under Rule 16(b) and (c).

(4) *Expedited Schedule.* If necessary to comply with its expedited schedule for Rule 16(b) conferences, a court may by local rule:

(A) require the parties' conference to occur less than 21 days before the scheduling conference is held or a scheduling order is due under Rule 16(b); and

(B) require the written report outlining the discovery plan to be filed less than 14 days after the parties' conference, or excuse the parties from submitting a written report and permit them to report orally on their discovery plan at the Rule 16(b) conference.

[Text of subdivision (f) effective December 1, 2015, absent contrary Congressional action.]

(f) Conference of the Parties; Planning for Discovery.

(1) *Conference Timing.* Except in a proceeding exempted from initial disclosure under Rule 26(a)(1)(B) or when the court orders otherwise, the parties must confer as soon as practicable—and in any event at least 21 days before a scheduling conference is to be held or a scheduling order is due under Rule 16(b).

(2) *Conference Content; Parties' Responsibilities.* In conferring, the parties must consider the nature and basis of their claims and defenses and the possibilities for promptly settling or resolving the case; make or arrange for the disclosures required by Rule 26(a)(1); discuss any issues about preserving discoverable information; and develop a proposed discovery plan. The attorneys of record and all unrepresented parties that have appeared in the case are jointly responsible for arranging the conference, for attempting in good faith to agree on the proposed discovery plan, and for submitting to the court within 14 days after the conference a written report outlining the plan. The court may order the parties or attorneys to attend the conference in person.

(3) *Discovery Plan.* A discovery plan must state the parties' views and proposals on:

(A) what changes should be made in the timing, form, or requirement for disclosures under Rule 26(a), including a statement of when initial disclosures were made or will be made;

(B) the subjects on which discovery may be needed, when discovery should be completed, and whether discovery should be conducted in phases or be limited to or focused on particular issues;

(C) any issues about disclosure, discovery, or preservation of electronically stored information, including the form or forms in which it should be produced;

(D) any issues about claims of privilege or of protection as trial-preparation materials, including — if the parties agree on a procedure to assert these claims after production — whether to ask the court to include their agreement in an order under Federal Rule of Evidence 502;

(E) what changes should be made in the limitations on discovery imposed under these rules or by local rule, and what other limitations should be imposed; and

(F) any other orders that the court should issue under Rule 26(c) or under Rule 16(b) and (c).

(4) *Expedited Schedule.* If necessary to comply with its expedited schedule for Rule 16(b) conferences, a court may by local rule:

(A) require the parties' conference to occur less than 21 days before the scheduling conference is held or a scheduling order is due under Rule 16(b); and

(B) require the written report outlining the discovery plan to be filed less than 14 days after the parties' conference, or excuse the parties from submitting a written report and permit them to report orally on their discovery plan at the Rule 16(b) conference.

(g) Signing Disclosures and Discovery Requests, Responses, and Objections.

(1) *Signature Required; Effect of Signature.* Every disclosure under Rule 26(a)(1) or (a)(3) and every discovery request, response, or objection must be signed by at least one attorney of record in the attorney's own name—or by the party personally, if unrepresented—and must state the signer's address, e-mail address, and telephone number. By signing, an attorney or party certifies that to the best of the person's knowledge, information, and belief formed after a reasonable inquiry:

(A) with respect to a disclosure, it is complete and correct as of the time it is made; and

(B) with respect to a discovery request, response, or objection, it is:

(i) consistent with these rules and warranted by existing law or by a nonfrivolous argument for extending, modifying, or reversing existing law, or for establishing new law;

(ii) not interposed for any improper purpose, such as to harass, cause unnecessary delay, or needlessly increase the cost of litigation; and

(iii) neither unreasonable nor unduly burdensome or expensive, considering the needs

of the case, prior discovery in the case, the amount in controversy, and the importance of the issues at stake in the action.

(2) *Failure to Sign.* Other parties have no duty to act on an unsigned disclosure, request, response, or objection until it is signed, and the court must strike it unless a signature is promptly supplied after the omission is called to the attorney's or party's attention.

(3) *Sanction for Improper Certification.* If a certification violates this rule without substantial justification, the court, on motion or on its own, must impose an appropriate sanction on the signer, the party on whose behalf the signer was acting, or both. The sanction may include an order to pay the reasonable expenses, including attorney's fees, caused by the violation.

(Amended December 27, 1946, effective March 19, 1948; January 21, 1963, effective July 1, 1963; February 28, 1966, effective July 1, 1966; March 30, 1970, effective July 1, 1970; April 29, 1980, effective August 1, 1980; April 28, 1983, effective August 1, 1983; March 2, 1987, effective August 1, 1987; April 22, 1993, effective December 1, 1993; April 17, 2000, effective December 1, 2000; April 12, 2006, effective December 1, 2006; April 30, 2007, effective December 1, 2007; April 28, 2010, effective December 1, 2010; April 29, 2015, effective December 1, 2015, absent contrary Congressional action.)

RULE 27. DEPOSITIONS TO PERPETUATE TESTIMONY

(a) Before an Action Is Filed.

(1) *Petition.* A person who wants to perpetuate testimony about any matter cognizable in a United States court may file a verified petition in the district court for the district where any expected adverse party resides. The petition must ask for an order authorizing the petitioner to depose the named persons in order to perpetuate their testimony. The petition must be titled in the petitioner's name and must show:

(A) that the petitioner expects to be a party to an action cognizable in a United States court but cannot presently bring it or cause it to be brought;

(B) the subject matter of the expected action and the petitioner's interest;

(C) the facts that the petitioner wants to establish by the proposed testimony and the reasons to perpetuate it;

(D) the names or a description of the persons whom the petitioner expects to be adverse parties and their addresses, so far as known; and

(E) the name, address, and expected substance of the testimony of each deponent.

(2) *Notice and Service.* At least 21 days before the hearing date, the petitioner must serve each expected adverse party with a copy of the petition and a notice stating the time and place of the hearing. The notice may be served either inside or outside the district or state in the manner provided in Rule 4. If that service cannot be made with reasonable diligence on an expected adverse party, the court may order service by publication or otherwise. The court must appoint an attorney to represent persons not served in the manner provided in Rule 4 and to cross-examine the deponent if an unserved person is not otherwise represented. If any expected adverse party is a minor or is incompetent, Rule 17(c) applies.

(3) *Order and Examination.* If satisfied that perpetuating the testimony may prevent a failure or delay of justice, the court must issue an order that designates or describes the persons whose depositions may be taken, specifies the subject matter of the examinations, and states whether the depositions will be taken orally or by written interrogatories. The depositions may then be taken under these rules, and the court may issue orders like those authorized by Rules 34 and 35. A reference in these rules to the court where an action is pending means, for purposes of this rule, the court where the petition for the deposition was filed.

(4) *Using the Deposition.* A deposition to perpetuate testimony may be used under Rule 32(a) in any later-filed district-court action involving the same subject matter if the deposition either was taken under these rules or, although not so taken, would be admissible in evidence in the courts of the state where it was taken.

(b) Pending Appeal.

(1) *In General.* The court where a judgment has been rendered may, if an appeal has been taken or may still be taken, permit a party to depose witnesses to perpetuate their testimony for use in the event of further proceedings in that court.

(2) *Motion.* The party who wants to perpetuate testimony may move for leave to take the depositions, on the same notice and service as if the action were pending in the district court. The motion must show:

  (A) the name, address, and expected substance of the testimony of each deponent; and

  (B) the reasons for perpetuating the testimony.

(3) *Court Order.* If the court finds that perpetuating the testimony may prevent a failure or delay of justice, the court may permit the depositions to be taken and may issue orders like those authorized by Rules 34 and 35. The depositions may be taken and used as any other deposition taken in a pending district-court action.

(c) Perpetuation by an Action. This rule does not limit a court's power to entertain an action to perpetuate testimony.

(Amended December 27, 1946, effective March 19, 1948; December 29, 1948, effective October 20, 1949; March 1, 1971, effective July 1, 1971; March 2, 1987, effective August 1, 1987; April 25, 2005, effective December 1, 2005; April 30, 2007, effective December 1, 2007; March 26, 2009, effective December 1, 2009.)

RULE 28. PERSONS BEFORE WHOM DEPOSITIONS MAY BE TAKEN

(a) Within the United States.

(1) *In General.* Within the United States or a territory or insular possession subject to United States jurisdiction, a deposition must be taken before:

  (A) an officer authorized to administer oaths either by federal law or by the law in the place of examination; or

  (B) a person appointed by the court where the action is pending to administer oaths and take testimony.

(2) *Definition of "Officer".* The term "officer" in Rules 30, 31, and 32 includes a person appointed by the court under this rule or designated by the parties under Rule 29(a).

(b) In a Foreign Country.

(1) *In General.* A deposition may be taken in a foreign country:

  (A) under an applicable treaty or convention;

  (B) under a letter of request, whether or not captioned a "letter rogatory";

  (C) on notice, before a person authorized to administer oaths either by federal law or by the law in the place of examination; or

  (D) before a person commissioned by the court to administer any necessary oath and take testimony.

(2) *Issuing a Letter of Request or a Commission.* A letter of request, a commission, or both may be issued:

  (A) on appropriate terms after an application and notice of it; and

  (B) without a showing that taking the deposition in another manner is impracticable or inconvenient.

(3) *Form of a Request, Notice, or Commission.* When a letter of request or any other device is used according to a treaty or convention, it must be captioned in the form prescribed by that treaty or convention. A letter of request

may be addressed "To the Appropriate Authority in [name of country]." A deposition notice or a commission must designate by name or descriptive title the person before whom the deposition is to be taken.

(4) Letter of Request—Admitting Evidence. Evidence obtained in response to a letter of request need not be excluded merely because it is not a verbatim transcript, because the testimony was not taken under oath, or because of any similar departure from the requirements for depositions taken within the United States.

(c) Disqualification. A deposition must not be taken before a person who is any party's relative, employee, or attorney; who is related to or employed by any party's attorney; or who is financially interested in the action.

(Amended December 27, 1946, effective March 19, 1948; January 21, 1963, effective July 1, 1963; April 29, 1980, effective August 1, 1980; March 2, 1987, effective August 1, 1987; April 22, 1993, effective December 1, 1993; April 30, 2007, effective December 1, 2007.)

RULE 29. STIPULATIONS ABOUT DISCOVERY PROCEDURE

Unless the court orders otherwise, the parties may stipulate that:

(a) a deposition may be taken before any person, at any time or place, on any notice, and in the manner specified—in which event it may be used in the same way as any other deposition; and

(b) other procedures governing or limiting discovery be modified—but a stipulation extending the time for any form of discovery must have court approval if it would interfere with the time set for completing discovery, for hearing a motion, or for trial.

(Amended March 30, 1970, effective July 1, 1970; April 22, 1993, effective December 1, 1993; April 30, 2007, effective December 1, 2007.)

RULE 30. DEPOSITIONS BY ORAL EXAMINATION

[Text of subdivision (a) effective until December 1, 2015, absent contrary Congressional action.]

(a) When a Deposition May Be Taken.

(1) Without Leave. A party may, by oral questions, depose any person, including a party, without leave of court except as provided in Rule 30(a)(2). The deponent's attendance may be compelled by subpoena under Rule 45.

(2) With Leave. A party must obtain leave of court, and the court must grant leave to the extent consistent with Rule 26(b)(2):

(A) if the parties have not stipulated to the deposition and:

(i) the deposition would result in more than 10 depositions being taken under this rule or Rule 31 by the plaintiffs, or by the defendants, or by the third-party defendants;

(ii) the deponent has already been deposed in the case; or

(iii) the party seeks to take the deposition before the time specified in Rule 26(d), unless the party certifies in the notice, with supporting facts, that the deponent is expected to leave the United States and be unavailable for examination in this country after that time; or

(B) if the deponent is confined in prison.

[Text of subdivision (a) effective December 1, 2015, absent contrary Congressional action.]

(a) When a Deposition May Be Taken.

(1) Without Leave. A party may, by oral questions, depose any person, including a party, without leave of court except as provided in Rule 30(a)(2). The deponent's attendance may be compelled by subpoena under Rule 45.

(2) With Leave. A party must obtain leave of court, and the court must grant leave to the extent consistent with Rule 26(b)(1) and (2):

(A) if the parties have not stipulated to the deposition and:

(i) the deposition would result in more than 10 depositions being taken under this rule or Rule 31 by the plaintiffs, or by the defendants, or by the third-party defendants;

(ii) the deponent has already been deposed in the case; or

(iii) the party seeks to take the deposition before the time specified in Rule 26(d), unless the party certifies in the notice, with supporting facts, that the deponent is expected to leave the United States and be unavailable for examination in this country after that time; or

(B) if the deponent is confined in prison.

(b) Notice of the Deposition; Other Formal Requirements.

(1) Notice in General. A party who wants to depose a person by oral questions must give reasonable written notice to every other party. The notice must state the time and place of the deposition and, if known, the deponent's name and address. If the name is unknown, the notice must provide a general description sufficient to identify the person or the particular class or group to which the person belongs.

(2) Producing Documents. If a subpoena duces tecum is to be served on the deponent, the materials designated for production, as set out in the subpoena, must be listed in the notice or in an attachment. The notice to a party deponent may be accompanied by a request under Rule 34 to produce documents and tangible things at the deposition.

(3) Method of Recording.

(A) *Method Stated in the Notice.* The party who notices the deposition must state in the notice the method for recording the testimony. Unless the court orders otherwise, testimony may be recorded by audio, audiovisual, or stenographic means. The noticing party bears the recording costs. Any party may arrange to transcribe a deposition.

(B) *Additional Method.* With prior notice to the deponent and other parties, any party may designate another method for recording the testimony in addition to that specified in the original notice. That party bears the expense of the additional record or transcript unless the court orders otherwise.

(4) By Remote Means. The parties may stipulate— or the court may on motion order—that a deposition be taken by telephone or other remote means. For the purpose of this rule and Rules 28(a), 37(a)(2), and 37(b)(1), the deposition takes place where the deponent answers the questions.

(5) Officer's Duties.

(A) *Before the Deposition.* Unless the parties stipulate otherwise, a deposition must be conducted before an officer appointed or designated under Rule 28. The officer must begin the deposition with an on-the-record statement that includes:

(i) the officer's name and business address;

(ii) the date, time, and place of the deposition;

(iii) the deponent's name;

(iv) the officer's administration of the oath or affirmation to the deponent; and

(v) the identity of all persons present.

(B) *Conducting the Deposition; Avoiding Distortion.* If the deposition is recorded non-stenographically, the officer must repeat the items in Rule 30(b)(5)(A)(i)-(iii) at the beginning of each unit of the recording medium. The deponent's and attorneys' appearance or demeanor must not be distorted through recording techniques.

(C) *After the Deposition.* At the end of a deposition, the officer must state on the record that the deposition is complete and must set out any stipulations made by the attorneys about custody of the transcript or recording and of the exhibits, or about any other pertinent matters.

(6) Notice or Subpoena Directed to an Organization. In its notice or subpoena, a party may name as the deponent a public or private corporation, a partnership, an association, a governmental agency, or other entity and must describe with reasonable particularity the matters for examination. The named organization must then designate one or more officers, directors, or managing agents, or designate other persons who consent to testify on its behalf; and it may set out the matters on which each person designated will testify. A subpoena must advise a nonparty organization of its duty to make this designation. The persons designated must testify about information known or reasonably available to the organization. This paragraph (6) does not preclude a deposition by any other procedure allowed by these rules.

(c) Examination and Cross–Examination; Record of the Examination; Objections; Written Questions.

(1) Examination and Cross–Examination. The examination and cross-examination of a deponent proceed as they would at trial under the Federal Rules of Evidence, except Rules 103 and 615. After putting the deponent under oath or affirmation, the officer must record the testimony by the method designated under Rule 30(b)(3)(A). The testimony must be recorded by the officer personally or by a person acting in the presence and under the direction of the officer.

(2) Objections. An objection at the time of the examination—whether to evidence, to a party's conduct, to the officer's qualifications, to the manner of taking the deposition, or to any other aspect of the deposition—must be noted on the record, but the examination still proceeds; the testimony is taken subject to any objection. An objection must be stated concisely in a nonargumentative and nonsuggestive manner. A person may instruct a deponent not to answer only when necessary to preserve a privilege, to enforce a limitation ordered by the court, or to present a motion under Rule 30(d)(3).

(3) Participating Through Written Questions. Instead of participating in the oral examination, a party may serve written questions in a sealed envelope on the party noticing the deposition, who must deliver them to the officer. The officer must ask the deponent those questions and record the answers verbatim.

[Text of subdivision (d) effective until December 1, 2015, absent contrary Congressional action.]

(d) Duration; Sanction; Motion to Terminate or Limit.

(1) *Duration.* Unless otherwise stipulated or ordered by the court, a deposition is limited to 1 day of 7 hours. The court must allow additional time consistent with Rule 26(b)(2) if needed to fairly examine the deponent or if the deponent, another person, or any other circumstance impedes or delays the examination.

(2) *Sanction.* The court may impose an appropriate sanction—including the reasonable expenses and attorney's fees incurred by any party—on a person who impedes, delays, or frustrates the fair examination of the deponent.

(3) *Motion to Terminate or Limit.*

(A) *Grounds.* At any time during a deposition, the deponent or a party may move to terminate or limit it on the ground that it is being conducted in bad faith or in a manner that unreasonably annoys, embarrasses, or oppresses the deponent or party. The motion may be filed in the court where the action is pending or the deposition is being taken. If the objecting deponent or party so demands, the deposition must be suspended for the time necessary to obtain an order.

(B) *Order.* The court may order that the deposition be terminated or may limit its scope and manner as provided in Rule 26(c). If terminated, the deposition may be resumed only by order of the court where the action is pending.

(C) *Award of Expenses.* Rule 37(a)(5) applies to the award of expenses.

[Text of subdivision (d) effective December 1, 2015, absent contrary Congressional action.]

(d) Duration; Sanction; Motion to Terminate or Limit.

(1) *Duration.* Unless otherwise stipulated or ordered by the court, a deposition is limited to one day of 7 hours. The court must allow additional time consistent with Rule 26(b)(1) and (2) if needed to fairly examine the deponent or if the deponent, another person, or any other circumstance impedes or delays the examination.

(2) *Sanction.* The court may impose an appropriate sanction—including the reasonable expenses

and attorney's fees incurred by any party—on a person who impedes, delays, or frustrates the fair examination of the deponent.

(3) *Motion to Terminate or Limit.*

(A) *Grounds.* At any time during a deposition, the deponent or a party may move to terminate or limit it on the ground that it is being conducted in bad faith or in a manner that unreasonably annoys, embarrasses, or oppresses the deponent or party. The motion may be filed in the court where the action is pending or the deposition is being taken. If the objecting deponent or party so demands, the deposition must be suspended for the time necessary to obtain an order.

(B) *Order.* The court may order that the deposition be terminated or may limit its scope and manner as provided in Rule 26(c). If terminated, the deposition may be resumed only by order of the court where the action is pending.

(C) *Award of Expenses.* Rule 37(a)(5) applies to the award of expenses.

(e) Review by the Witness; Changes.

(1) *Review; Statement of Changes.* On request by the deponent or a party before the deposition is completed, the deponent must be allowed 30 days after being notified by the officer that the transcript or recording is available in which:

(A) to review the transcript or recording; and

(B) if there are changes in form or substance, to sign a statement listing the changes and the reasons for making them.

(2) *Changes Indicated in the Officer's Certificate.* The officer must note in the certificate prescribed by Rule 30(f)(1) whether a review was requested and, if so, must attach any changes the deponent makes during the 30-day period.

(f) Certification and Delivery; Exhibits; Copies of the Transcript or Recording; Filing.

(1) *Certification and Delivery.* The officer must certify in writing that the witness was duly sworn and that the deposition accurately records the witness's testimony. The certificate must accompany the record of the deposition. Unless the court orders otherwise, the officer must seal the deposition in an envelope or package bearing the title of the action and marked "Deposition of [witness's name]" and must promptly send it to the attorney who arranged for the transcript or recording. The attorney must store it under conditions that will protect it against loss, destruction, tampering, or deterioration.

(2) *Documents and Tangible Things.*

(A) *Originals and Copies.* Documents and tangible things produced for inspection during a deposition must, on a party's request, be marked for identification and attached to the deposition. Any party may inspect and copy them. But if the person who produced them wants to keep the originals, the person may:

(i) offer copies to be marked, attached to the deposition, and then used as originals—after giving all parties a fair opportunity to verify the copies by comparing them with the originals; or

(ii) give all parties a fair opportunity to inspect and copy the originals after they are marked—in which event the originals may be used as if attached to the deposition.

(B) *Order Regarding the Originals.* Any party may move for an order that the originals be attached to the deposition pending final disposition of the case.

(3) *Copies of the Transcript or Recording.* Unless otherwise stipulated or ordered by the court, the officer must retain the stenographic notes of a deposition taken stenographically or a copy of the recording of a deposition taken by another method. When paid reasonable charges, the officer must furnish a copy of the transcript or recording to any party or the deponent.

(4) *Notice of Filing.* A party who files the deposition must promptly notify all other parties of the filing.

(g) Failure to Attend a Deposition or Serve a Subpoena; Expenses. A party who, expecting a deposition to be taken, attends in person or by an attorney may recover reasonable expenses for attending, including attorney's fees, if the noticing party failed to:

(1) attend and proceed with the deposition; or

(2) serve a subpoena on a nonparty deponent, who consequently did not attend.

(Amended January 21, 1963, effective July 1, 1963; March 30, 1970, effective July 1, 1970; March 1, 1971, effective July 1, 1971; November 20, 1972, effective July 1, 1975; April 29, 1980, effective August 1, 1980; March 2, 1987, effective August 1, 1987; April 22, 1993, effective December 1, 1993; April 17, 2000, effective December 1, 2000; April 30, 2007, effective December 1, 2007; April 29, 2015, effective December 1, 2015, absent contrary Congressional action.)

RULE 31. DEPOSITIONS BY WRITTEN QUESTIONS

[Text of subdivision (a) effective until December 1, 2015, absent contrary Congressional action.]

(a) When a Deposition May Be Taken.

(1) *Without Leave.* A party may, by written questions, depose any person, including a party, without leave of court except as provided in Rule 31(a)(2). The deponent's attendance may be compelled by subpoena under Rule 45.

(2) *With Leave.* A party must obtain leave of court, and the court must grant leave to the extent consistent with Rule 26(b)(2):

(A) if the parties have not stipulated to the deposition and:

(i) the deposition would result in more than 10 depositions being taken under this rule or Rule 30 by the plaintiffs, or by the defendants, or by the third-party defendants;

(ii) the deponent has already been deposed in the case; or

(iii) the party seeks to take a deposition before the time specified in Rule 26(d); or

(B) if the deponent is confined in prison.

(3) *Service; Required Notice.* A party who wants to depose a person by written questions must serve them on every other party, with a notice stating, if known, the deponent's name and address. If the name is unknown, the notice must provide a general description sufficient to identify the person or the particular class or group to which the person belongs. The notice must also state the name or descriptive title and the address of the officer before whom the deposition will be taken.

(4) *Questions Directed to an Organization.* A public or private corporation, a partnership, an association, or a governmental agency may be deposed by written questions in accordance with Rule 30(b)(6).

(5) *Questions from Other Parties.* Any questions to the deponent from other parties must be served on all parties as follows: cross-questions, within 14 days after being served with the notice and direct questions; redirect questions, within 7 days after being served with cross-questions; and recross-questions, within 7 days after being served with redirect questions. The court may, for good cause, extend or shorten these times.

[Text of subdivision (a) effective December 1, 2015, absent contrary Congressional action.]

(a) When a Deposition May Be Taken.

(1) *Without Leave.* A party may, by written questions, depose any person, including a party, without leave of court except as provided in Rule 31(a)(2). The deponent's attendance may be compelled by subpoena under Rule 45.

(2) **With Leave.** A party must obtain leave of court, and the court must grant leave to the extent consistent with Rule 26(b)(1) and (2):

   (A) if the parties have not stipulated to the deposition and:

   (i) the deposition would result in more than 10 depositions being taken under this rule or Rule 30 by the plaintiffs, or by the defendants, or by the third-party defendants;

   (ii) the deponent has already been deposed in the case; or

   (iii) the party seeks to take a deposition before the time specified in Rule 26(d); or

   (B) if the deponent is confined in prison.

(3) **Service; Required Notice.** A party who wants to depose a person by written questions must serve them on every other party, with a notice stating, if known, the deponent's name and address. If the name is unknown, the notice must provide a general description sufficient to identify the person or the particular class or group to which the person belongs. The notice must also state the name or descriptive title and the address of the officer before whom the deposition will be taken.

(4) **Questions Directed to an Organization.** A public or private corporation, a partnership, an association, or a governmental agency may be deposed by written questions in accordance with Rule 30(b)(6).

(5) **Questions from Other Parties.** Any questions to the deponent from other parties must be served on all parties as follows: cross-questions, within 14 days after being served with the notice and direct questions; redirect questions, within 7 days after being served with cross-questions; and recross-questions, within 7 days after being served with redirect questions. The court may, for good cause, extend or shorten these times.

(b) **Delivery to the Officer; Officer's Duties.** The party who noticed the deposition must deliver to the officer a copy of all the questions served and of the notice. The officer must promptly proceed in the manner provided in Rule 30(c), (e), and (f) to:

(1) take the deponent's testimony in response to the questions;

(2) prepare and certify the deposition; and

(3) send it to the party, attaching a copy of the questions and of the notice.

(c) **Notice of Completion or Filing.**

(1) **Completion.** The party who noticed the deposition must notify all other parties when it is completed.

(2) **Filing.** A party who files the deposition must promptly notify all other parties of the filing.

(Amended March 30, 1970, effective July 1, 1970; March 2, 1987, effective August 1, 1987; April 22, 1993, effective December 1, 1993; April 30, 2007, effective December 1, 2007; April 29, 2015, effective December 1, 2015, absent contrary Congressional action.)

RULE 32.　USING DEPOSITIONS IN COURT PROCEEDINGS

(a) **Using Depositions.**

(1) **In General.** At a hearing or trial, all or part of a deposition may be used against a party on these conditions:

   (A) the party was present or represented at the taking of the deposition or had reasonable notice of it;

   (B) it is used to the extent it would be admissible under the Federal Rules of Evidence if the deponent were present and testifying; and

   (C) the use is allowed by Rule 32(a)(2) through (8).

(2) **Impeachment and Other Uses.** Any party may use a deposition to contradict or impeach the testimony given by the deponent as a witness, or for any other purpose allowed by the Federal Rules of Evidence.

(3) **Deposition of Party, Agent, or Designee.** An adverse party may use for any purpose the deposition of a party or anyone who, when deposed, was the party's officer, director, managing agent, or designee under Rule 30(b)(6) or 31(a)(4).

(4) **Unavailable Witness.** A party may use for any purpose the deposition of a witness, whether or not a party, if the court finds:

   (A) that the witness is dead;

   (B) that the witness is more than 100 miles from the place of hearing or trial or is outside the United States, unless it appears that the witness's absence was procured by the party offering the deposition;

   (C) that the witness cannot attend or testify because of age, illness, infirmity, or imprisonment;

   (D) that the party offering the deposition could not procure the witness's attendance by subpoena; or

   (E) on motion and notice, that exceptional circumstances make it desirable—in the interest of justice and with due regard to the importance of live testimony in open court—to permit the deposition to be used.

(5) *Limitations on Use.*

(A) *Deposition Taken on Short Notice.* A deposition must not be used against a party who, having received less than 14 days' notice of the deposition, promptly moved for a protective order under Rule 26(c)(1)(B) requesting that it not be taken or be taken at a different time or place—and this motion was still pending when the deposition was taken.

(B) *Unavailable Deponent; Party Could Not Obtain an Attorney.* A deposition taken without leave of court under the unavailability provision of Rule 30(a)(2)(A)(iii) must not be used against a party who shows that, when served with the notice, it could not, despite diligent efforts, obtain an attorney to represent it at the deposition.

(6) *Using Part of a Deposition.* If a party offers in evidence only part of a deposition, an adverse party may require the offeror to introduce other parts that in fairness should be considered with the part introduced, and any party may itself introduce any other parts.

(7) *Substituting a Party.* Substituting a party under Rule 25 does not affect the right to use a deposition previously taken.

(8) *Deposition Taken in an Earlier Action.* A deposition lawfully taken and, if required, filed in any federal- or state-court action may be used in a later action involving the same subject matter between the same parties, or their representatives or successors in interest, to the same extent as if taken in the later action. A deposition previously taken may also be used as allowed by the Federal Rules of Evidence.

(b) **Objections to Admissibility.** Subject to Rules 28(b) and 32(d)(3), an objection may be made at a hearing or trial to the admission of any deposition testimony that would be inadmissible if the witness were present and testifying.

(c) **Form of Presentation.** Unless the court orders otherwise, a party must provide a transcript of any deposition testimony the party offers, but may provide the court with the testimony in nontranscript form as well. On any party's request, deposition testimony offered in a jury trial for any purpose other than impeachment must be presented in nontranscript form, if available, unless the court for good cause orders otherwise.

(d) **Waiver of Objections.**

(1) *To the Notice.* An objection to an error or irregularity in a deposition notice is waived unless promptly served in writing on the party giving the notice.

(2) *To the Officer's Qualification.* An objection based on disqualification of the officer before whom a deposition is to be taken is waived if not made:

(A) before the deposition begins; or

(B) promptly after the basis for disqualification becomes known or, with reasonable diligence, could have been known.

(3) *To the Taking of the Deposition.*

(A) *Objection to Competence, Relevance, or Materiality.* An objection to a deponent's competence—or to the competence, relevance, or materiality of testimony—is not waived by a failure to make the objection before or during the deposition, unless the ground for it might have been corrected at that time.

(B) *Objection to an Error or Irregularity.* An objection to an error or irregularity at an oral examination is waived if:

(i) it relates to the manner of taking the deposition, the form of a question or answer, the oath or affirmation, a party's conduct, or other matters that might have been corrected at that time; and

(ii) it is not timely made during the deposition.

(C) *Objection to a Written Question.* An objection to the form of a written question under Rule 31 is waived if not served in writing on the party submitting the question within the time for serving responsive questions or, if the question is a recross-question, within 7 days after being served with it.

(4) *To Completing and Returning the Deposition.* An objection to how the officer transcribed the testimony—or prepared, signed, certified, sealed, endorsed, sent, or otherwise dealt with the deposition—is waived unless a motion to suppress is made promptly after the error or irregularity becomes known or, with reasonable diligence, could have been known.

(Amended March 30, 1970, effective July 1, 1970; November 20, 1972, effective July 1, 1975; April 29, 1980, effective August 1, 1980; March 2, 1987, effective August 1, 1987; April 22, 1993, effective December 1, 1993; April 30, 2007, effective December 1, 2007; March 26, 2009, effective December 1, 2009.)

RULE 33. INTERROGATORIES TO PARTIES

[Text of subdivision (a) effective until December 1, 2015, absent contrary Congressional action.]

(a) **In General.**

(1) *Number.* Unless otherwise stipulated or ordered by the court, a party may serve on any other party no more than 25 written interrogatories, including all discrete subparts. Leave to serve additional interrogatories may be granted to the extent consistent with Rule 26(b)(2).

(2) Scope. An interrogatory may relate to any matter that may be inquired into under Rule 26(b). An interrogatory is not objectionable merely because it asks for an opinion or contention that relates to fact or the application of law to fact, but the court may order that the interrogatory need not be answered until designated discovery is complete, or until a pretrial conference or some other time.

[Text of subdivision (a) effective December 1, 2015, absent contrary Congressional action.]

(a) In General.

(1) Number. Unless otherwise stipulated or ordered by the court, a party may serve on any other party no more than 25 written interrogatories, including all discrete subparts. Leave to serve additional interrogatories may be granted to the extent consistent with Rule 26(b)(1) and (2).

(2) Scope. An interrogatory may relate to any matter that may be inquired into under Rule 26(b). An interrogatory is not objectionable merely because it asks for an opinion or contention that relates to fact or the application of law to fact, but the court may order that the interrogatory need not be answered until designated discovery is complete, or until a pretrial conference or some other time.

(b) Answers and Objections.

(1) Responding Party. The interrogatories must be answered:

(A) by the party to whom they are directed; or

(B) if that party is a public or private corporation, a partnership, an association, or a governmental agency, by any officer or agent, who must furnish the information available to the party.

(2) Time to Respond. The responding party must serve its answers and any objections within 30 days after being served with the interrogatories. A shorter or longer time may be stipulated to under Rule 29 or be ordered by the court.

(3) Answering Each Interrogatory. Each interrogatory must, to the extent it is not objected to, be answered separately and fully in writing under oath.

(4) Objections. The grounds for objecting to an interrogatory must be stated with specificity. Any ground not stated in a timely objection is waived unless the court, for good cause, excuses the failure.

(5) Signature. The person who makes the answers must sign them, and the attorney who objects must sign any objections.

(c) Use. An answer to an interrogatory may be used to the extent allowed by the Federal Rules of Evidence.

(d) Option to Produce Business Records. If the answer to an interrogatory may be determined by examining, auditing, compiling, abstracting, or summarizing a party's business records (including electronically stored information), and if the burden of deriving or ascertaining the answer will be substantially the same for either party, the responding party may answer by:

(1) specifying the records that must be reviewed, in sufficient detail to enable the interrogating party to locate and identify them as readily as the responding party could; and

(2) giving the interrogating party a reasonable opportunity to examine and audit the records and to make copies, compilations, abstracts, or summaries.

(Amended December 27, 1946, effective March 19, 1948; March 30, 1970, effective July 1, 1970; April 29, 1980, effective August 1, 1980; April 22, 1993, effective December 1, 1993; April 12, 2006, effective December 1, 2006; April 30, 2007, effective December 1, 2007; April 29, 2015, effective December 1, 2015, absent contrary Congressional action.)

RULE 34. PRODUCING DOCUMENTS, ELECTRONICALLY STORED INFORMATION, AND TANGIBLE THINGS, OR ENTERING ONTO LAND, FOR INSPECTION AND OTHER PURPOSES

(a) In General. A party may serve on any other party a request within the scope of Rule 26(b):

(1) to produce and permit the requesting party or its representative to inspect, copy, test, or sample the following items in the responding party's possession, custody, or control:

(A) any designated documents or electronically stored information—including writings, drawings, graphs, charts, photographs, sound recordings, images, and other data or data compilations—stored in any medium from which information can be obtained either directly or, if necessary, after translation by the responding party into a reasonably usable form; or

(B) any designated tangible things; or

(2) to permit entry onto designated land or other property possessed or controlled by the responding party, so that the requesting party may inspect, measure, survey, photograph, test, or sample the property or any designated object or operation on it.

[Text of subdivision (b) effective until December 1, 2015, absent contrary Congressional action.]

(b) Procedure.

  (1) *Contents of the Request.* The request:

    (A) must describe with reasonable particularity each item or category of items to be inspected;

    (B) must specify a reasonable time, place, and manner for the inspection and for performing the related acts; and

    (C) may specify the form or forms in which electronically stored information is to be produced.

  (2) *Responses and Objections.*

    (A) *Time to Respond.* The party to whom the request is directed must respond in writing within 30 days after being served. A shorter or longer time may be stipulated to under Rule 29 or be ordered by the court.

    (B) *Responding to Each Item.* For each item or category, the response must either state that inspection and related activities will be permitted as requested or state an objection to the request, including the reasons.

    (C) *Objections.* An objection to part of a request must specify the part and permit inspection of the rest.

    (D) *Responding to a Request for Production of Electronically Stored Information.* The response may state an objection to a requested form for producing electronically stored information. If the responding party objects to a requested form—or if no form was specified in the request—the party must state the form or forms it intends to use.

    (E) *Producing the Documents or Electronically Stored Information.* Unless otherwise stipulated or ordered by the court, these procedures apply to producing documents or electronically stored information:

      (i) A party must produce documents as they are kept in the usual course of business or must organize and label them to correspond to the categories in the request;

      (ii) If a request does not specify a form for producing electronically stored information, a party must produce it in a form or forms in which it is ordinarily maintained or in a reasonably usable form or forms; and

      (iii) A party need not produce the same electronically stored information in more than one form.

[Text of subdivision (b) effective December 1, 2015, absent contrary Congressional action.]

(b) Procedure.

  (1) *Contents of the Request.* The request:

    (A) must describe with reasonable particularity each item or category of items to be inspected;

    (B) must specify a reasonable time, place, and manner for the inspection and for performing the related acts; and

    (C) may specify the form or forms in which electronically stored information is to be produced.

  (2) *Responses and Objections.*

    (A) *Time to Respond.* The party to whom the request is directed must respond in writing within 30 days after being served or — if the request was delivered under Rule 26(d)(2) — within 30 days after the parties' first Rule 26(f) conference. A shorter or longer time may be stipulated to under Rule 29 or be ordered by the court.

    (B) *Responding to Each Item.* For each item or category, the response must either state that inspection and related activities will be permitted as requested or state with specificity the grounds for objecting to the request, including the reasons. The responding party may state that it will produce copies of documents or of electronically stored information instead of permitting inspection. The production must then be completed no later than the time for inspection specified in the request or another reasonable time specified in the response.

    (C) *Objections.* An objection must state whether any responsive materials are being withheld on the basis of that objection. An objection to part of a request must specify the part and permit inspection of the rest.

    (D) *Responding to a Request for Production of Electronically Stored Information.* The response may state an objection to a requested form for producing electronically stored information. If the responding party objects to a requested form—or if no form was specified in the request—the party must state the form or forms it intends to use.

    (E) *Producing the Documents or Electronically Stored Information.* Unless otherwise stipulated or ordered by the court, these procedures apply to producing documents or electronically stored information:

    (i) A party must produce documents as they are kept in the usual course of business or must organize and label them to correspond to the categories in the request;

    (ii) If a request does not specify a form for producing electronically stored information, a party must produce it in a form or forms in which it is ordinarily maintained or in a reasonably usable form or forms; and

    (iii) A party need not produce the same electronically stored information in more than one form.

(c) Nonparties. As provided in Rule 45, a nonparty may be compelled to produce documents and tangible things or to permit an inspection.

(Amended December 27, 1946, effective March 19, 1948; March 30, 1970, effective July 1, 1970; April 29, 1980, effective August 1, 1980; March 2, 1987, effective August 1, 1987; April 30, 1991, effective December 1, 1991; April 22, 1993, effective December 1, 1993; April 12, 2006, effective December 1, 2006; April 30, 2007, effective December 1, 2007; April 29, 2015, effective December 1, 2015, absent contrary Congressional action.)

RULE 35. PHYSICAL AND MENTAL EXAMINATIONS

(a) Order for an Examination.

    (1) *In General.* The court where the action is pending may order a party whose mental or physical condition—including blood group—is in controversy to submit to a physical or mental examination by a suitably licensed or certified examiner. The court has the same authority to order a party to produce for examination a person who is in its custody or under its legal control.

    (2) *Motion and Notice; Contents of the Order.* The order:

    (A) may be made only on motion for good cause and on notice to all parties and the person to be examined; and

    (B) must specify the time, place, manner, conditions, and scope of the examination, as well as the person or persons who will perform it.

(b) Examiner's Report.

    (1) *Request by the Party or Person Examined.* The party who moved for the examination must, on request, deliver to the requester a copy of the examiner's report, together with like reports of all earlier examinations of the same condition. The request may be made by the party against whom the examination order was issued or by the person examined.

    (2) *Contents.* The examiner's report must be in writing and must set out in detail the examiner's findings, including diagnoses, conclusions, and the results of any tests.

    (3) *Request by the Moving Party.* After delivering the reports, the party who moved for the examination may request—and is entitled to receive—from the party against whom the examination order was issued like reports of all earlier or later examinations of the same condition. But those reports need not be delivered by the party with custody or control of the person examined if the party shows that it could not obtain them.

    (4) *Waiver of Privilege.* By requesting and obtaining the examiner's report, or by deposing the examiner, the party examined waives any privilege it may have—in that action or any other action involving the same controversy—concerning testimony about all examinations of the same condition.

    (5) *Failure to Deliver a Report.* The court on motion may order—on just terms—that a party deliver the report of an examination. If the report is not provided, the court may exclude the examiner's testimony at trial.

    (6) *Scope.* This subdivision (b) applies also to an examination made by the parties' agreement, unless the agreement states otherwise. This subdivision does not preclude obtaining an examiner's report or deposing an examiner under other rules.

(Amended March 30, 1970, effective July 1, 1970; March 2, 1987, effective August 1, 1987; amended by Pub.L. 100–690, Title VII, § 7047(b), November 18, 1988, 102 Stat. 4401; amended April 30, 1991, effective December 1, 1991; April 30, 2007, effective December 1, 2007.)

RULE 36. REQUESTS FOR ADMISSION

(a) Scope and Procedure.

    (1) *Scope.* A party may serve on any other party a written request to admit, for purposes of the pending action only, the truth of any matters within the scope of Rule 26(b)(1) relating to:

    (A) facts, the application of law to fact, or opinions about either; and

    (B) the genuineness of any described documents.

    (2) *Form; Copy of a Document.* Each matter must be separately stated. A request to admit the genuineness of a document must be accompanied by a copy of the document unless it is, or has been, otherwise furnished or made available for inspection and copying.

    (3) *Time to Respond; Effect of Not Responding.* A matter is admitted unless, within 30 days after being served, the party to whom the request is directed serves on the requesting party a written answer or objection addressed to the matter and signed by the party or its attorney. A shorter or longer time for responding may be stipulated to under Rule 29 or be ordered by the court.

(4) *Answer.* If a matter is not admitted, the answer must specifically deny it or state in detail why the answering party cannot truthfully admit or deny it. A denial must fairly respond to the substance of the matter; and when good faith requires that a party qualify an answer or deny only a part of a matter, the answer must specify the part admitted and qualify or deny the rest. The answering party may assert lack of knowledge or information as a reason for failing to admit or deny only if the party states that it has made reasonable inquiry and that the information it knows or can readily obtain is insufficient to enable it to admit or deny.

(5) *Objections.* The grounds for objecting to a request must be stated. A party must not object solely on the ground that the request presents a genuine issue for trial.

(6) *Motion Regarding the Sufficiency of an Answer or Objection.* The requesting party may move to determine the sufficiency of an answer or objection. Unless the court finds an objection justified, it must order that an answer be served. On finding that an answer does not comply with this rule, the court may order either that the matter is admitted or that an amended answer be served. The court may defer its final decision until a pretrial conference or a specified time before trial. Rule 37(a)(5) applies to an award of expenses.

(b) Effect of an Admission; Withdrawing or Amending It. A matter admitted under this rule is conclusively established unless the court, on motion, permits the admission to be withdrawn or amended. Subject to Rule 16(e), the court may permit withdrawal or amendment if it would promote the presentation of the merits of the action and if the court is not persuaded that it would prejudice the requesting party in maintaining or defending the action on the merits. An admission under this rule is not an admission for any other purpose and cannot be used against the party in any other proceeding.

(Amended December 27, 1946, effective March 19, 1948; March 30, 1970, effective July 1, 1970; March 2, 1987, effective August 1, 1987; April 22, 1993, effective December 1, 1993; April 30, 2007, effective December 1, 2007.)

RULE 37. FAILURE TO MAKE DISCLOSURES OR TO COOPERATE IN DISCOVERY; SANCTIONS

[Text of subdivision (a) effective until December 1, 2015, absent contrary Congressional action.]

(a) Motion for an Order Compelling Disclosure or Discovery.

(1) *In General.* On notice to other parties and all affected persons, a party may move for an order compelling disclosure or discovery. The motion must include a certification that the movant has in good faith conferred or attempted to confer with the person or party failing to make disclosure or discovery in an effort to obtain it without court action.

(2) *Appropriate Court.* A motion for an order to a party must be made in the court where the action is pending. A motion for an order to a nonparty must be made in the court where the discovery is or will be taken.

(3) *Specific Motions.*

(A) *To Compel Disclosure.* If a party fails to make a disclosure required by Rule 26(a), any other party may move to compel disclosure and for appropriate sanctions.

(B) *To Compel a Discovery Response.* A party seeking discovery may move for an order compelling an answer, designation, production, or inspection. This motion may be made if:

(i) a deponent fails to answer a question asked under Rule 30 or 31;

(ii) a corporation or other entity fails to make a designation under Rule 30(b)(6) or 31(a)(4);

(iii) a party fails to answer an interrogatory submitted under Rule 33; or

(iv) a party fails to respond that inspection will be permitted—or fails to permit inspection—as requested under Rule 34.

(C) *Related to a Deposition.* When taking an oral deposition, the party asking a question may complete or adjourn the examination before moving for an order.

(4) *Evasive or Incomplete Disclosure, Answer, or Response.* For purposes of this subdivision (a), an evasive or incomplete disclosure, answer, or response must be treated as a failure to disclose, answer, or respond.

(5) *Payment of Expenses; Protective Orders.*

(A) *If the Motion Is Granted (or Disclosure or Discovery Is Provided After Filing).* If the motion is granted—or if the disclosure or requested discovery is provided after the motion was filed—the court must, after giving an opportunity to be heard, require the party or deponent whose conduct necessitated the motion, the party or attorney advising that conduct, or both to pay the movant's reasonable expenses incurred in making the motion, including attorney's fees. But the court must not order this payment if:

(i) the movant filed the motion before attempting in good faith to obtain the disclosure or discovery without court action;

(ii) the opposing party's nondisclosure, response, or objection was substantially justified; or

(iii) other circumstances make an award of expenses unjust.

(B) *If the Motion Is Denied.* If the motion is denied, the court may issue any protective order authorized under Rule 26(c) and must, after giving an opportunity to be heard, require the movant, the attorney filing the motion, or both to pay the party or deponent who opposed the motion its reasonable expenses incurred in opposing the motion, including attorney's fees. But the court must not order this payment if the motion was substantially justified or other circumstances make an award of expenses unjust.

(C) *If the Motion Is Granted in Part and Denied in Part.* If the motion is granted in part and denied in part, the court may issue any protective order authorized under Rule 26(c) and may, after giving an opportunity to be heard, apportion the reasonable expenses for the motion.

[Text of subdivision (a) effective December 1, 2015, absent contrary Congressional action.]

(a) Motion for an Order Compelling Disclosure or Discovery.

(1) *In General.* On notice to other parties and all affected persons, a party may move for an order compelling disclosure or discovery. The motion must include a certification that the movant has in good faith conferred or attempted to confer with the person or party failing to make disclosure or discovery in an effort to obtain it without court action.

(2) *Appropriate Court.* A motion for an order to a party must be made in the court where the action is pending. A motion for an order to a nonparty must be made in the court where the discovery is or will be taken.

(3) *Specific Motions.*

(A) *To Compel Disclosure.* If a party fails to make a disclosure required by Rule 26(a), any other party may move to compel disclosure and for appropriate sanctions.

(B) *To Compel a Discovery Response.* A party seeking discovery may move for an order compelling an answer, designation, production, or inspection. This motion may be made if:

(i) a deponent fails to answer a question asked under Rule 30 or 31;

(ii) a corporation or other entity fails to make a designation under Rule 30(b)(6) or 31(a)(4);

(iii) a party fails to answer an interrogatory submitted under Rule 33; or

(iv) a party fails to produce documents or fails to respond that inspection will be permitted — or fails to permit inspection — as requested under Rule 34.

(C) *Related to a Deposition.* When taking an oral deposition, the party asking a question may complete or adjourn the examination before moving for an order.

(4) **Evasive or Incomplete Disclosure, Answer, or Response.** For purposes of this subdivision (a), an evasive or incomplete disclosure, answer, or response must be treated as a failure to disclose, answer, or respond.

(5) **Payment of Expenses; Protective Orders.**

(A) *If the Motion Is Granted (or Disclosure or Discovery Is Provided After Filing).* If the motion is granted—or if the disclosure or requested discovery is provided after the motion was filed—the court must, after giving an opportunity to be heard, require the party or deponent whose conduct necessitated the motion, the party or attorney advising that conduct, or both to pay the movant's reasonable expenses incurred in making the motion, including attorney's fees. But the court must not order this payment if:

(i) the movant filed the motion before attempting in good faith to obtain the disclosure or discovery without court action;

(ii) the opposing party's nondisclosure, response, or objection was substantially justified; or

(iii) other circumstances make an award of expenses unjust.

(B) *If the Motion Is Denied.* If the motion is denied, the court may issue any protective order authorized under Rule 26(c) and must, after giving an opportunity to be heard, require the movant, the attorney filing the motion, or both to pay the party or deponent who opposed the motion its reasonable expenses incurred in opposing the motion, including attorney's fees. But the court must not order this payment if the motion was substantially justified or other circumstances make an award of expenses unjust.

(C) *If the Motion Is Granted in Part and Denied in Part.* If the motion is granted in part and denied in part, the court may issue any protective order authorized under Rule 26(c) and may, after giving an opportunity to be heard, apportion the reasonable expenses for the motion.

(b) Failure to Comply with a Court Order.

(1) *Sanctions Sought in the District Where the Deposition Is Taken.* If the court where the discovery is taken orders a deponent to be sworn or to answer a question and the deponent fails to obey, the failure may be treated as contempt of court. If a deposition-related motion is transferred to the court where the action is pending, and that court orders a deponent to be sworn or to answer a question and the deponent fails to obey, the failure may be treated as contempt of either the court where the discovery is taken or the court where the action is pending.

(2) *Sanctions Sought in the District Where the Action Is Pending.*

(A) *For Not Obeying a Discovery Order.* If a party or a party's officer, director, or managing agent—or a witness designated under Rule 30(b)(6) or 31(a)(4)—fails to obey an order to provide or permit discovery, including an order under Rule 26(f), 35, or 37(a), the court where the action is pending may issue further just orders. They may include the following:

(i) directing that the matters embraced in the order or other designated facts be taken as established for purposes of the action, as the prevailing party claims;

(ii) prohibiting the disobedient party from supporting or opposing designated claims or defenses, or from introducing designated matters in evidence;

(iii) striking pleadings in whole or in part;

(iv) staying further proceedings until the order is obeyed;

(v) dismissing the action or proceeding in whole or in part;

(vi) rendering a default judgment against the disobedient party; or

(vii) treating as contempt of court the failure to obey any order except an order to submit to a physical or mental examination.

(B) *For Not Producing a Person for Examination.* If a party fails to comply with an order under Rule 35(a) requiring it to produce another person for examination, the court may issue any of the orders listed in Rule 37(b)(2)(A)(i)-(vi), unless the disobedient par-

ty shows that it cannot produce the other person.

(C) *Payment of Expenses.* Instead of or in addition to the orders above, the court must order the disobedient party, the attorney advising that party, or both to pay the reasonable expenses, including attorney's fees, caused by the failure, unless the failure was substantially justified or other circumstances make an award of expenses unjust.

(c) Failure to Disclose, to Supplement an Earlier Response, or to Admit.

(1) *Failure to Disclose or Supplement.* If a party fails to provide information or identify a witness as required by Rule 26(a) or (e), the party is not allowed to use that information or witness to supply evidence on a motion, at a hearing, or at a trial, unless the failure was substantially justified or is harmless. In addition to or instead of this sanction, the court, on motion and after giving an opportunity to be heard:

(A) may order payment of the reasonable expenses, including attorney's fees, caused by the failure;

(B) may inform the jury of the party's failure; and

(C) may impose other appropriate sanctions, including any of the orders listed in Rule 37(b)(2)(A)(i)-(vi).

(2) *Failure to Admit.* If a party fails to admit what is requested under Rule 36 and if the requesting party later proves a document to be genuine or the matter true, the requesting party may move that the party who failed to admit pay the reasonable expenses, including attorney's fees, incurred in making that proof. The court must so order unless:

(A) the request was held objectionable under Rule 36(a);

(B) the admission sought was of no substantial importance;

(C) the party failing to admit had a reasonable ground to believe that it might prevail on the matter; or

(D) there was other good reason for the failure to admit.

(d) Party's Failure to Attend Its Own Deposition, Serve Answers to Interrogatories, or Respond to a Request for Inspection.

(1) *In General.*

(A) *Motion; Grounds for Sanctions.* The court where the action is pending may, on motion, order sanctions if:

(i) a party or a party's officer, director, or managing agent—or a person designated under Rule 30(b)(6) or 31(a)(4)—fails, after being served with proper notice, to appear for that person's deposition; or

  (ii) a party, after being properly served with interrogatories under Rule 33 or a request for inspection under Rule 34, fails to serve its answers, objections, or written response.

(B) *Certification.* A motion for sanctions for failing to answer or respond must include a certification that the movant has in good faith conferred or attempted to confer with the party failing to act in an effort to obtain the answer or response without court action.

(2) *Unacceptable Excuse for Failing to Act.* A failure described in Rule 37(d)(1)(A) is not excused on the ground that the discovery sought was objectionable, unless the party failing to act has a pending motion for a protective order under Rule 26(c).

(3) *Types of Sanctions.* Sanctions may include any of the orders listed in Rule 37(b)(2)(A)(i)-(vi). Instead of or in addition to these sanctions, the court must require the party failing to act, the attorney advising that party, or both to pay the reasonable expenses, including attorney's fees, caused by the failure, unless the failure was substantially justified or other circumstances make an award of expenses unjust.

[Text of subdivision (e) effective until December 1, 2015, absent contrary Congressional action.]

(e) Failure to Provide Electronically Stored Information. Absent exceptional circumstances, a court may not impose sanctions under these rules on a party for failing to provide electronically stored information lost as a result of the routine, good-faith operation of an electronic information system.

[Text of subdivision (e) effective December 1, 2015, absent contrary Congressional action.]

(e) Failure to Preserve Electronically Stored Information. If electronically stored information that should have been preserved in the anticipation or conduct of litigation is lost because a party failed to take reasonable steps to preserve it, and it cannot be restored or replaced through additional discovery, the court:

(1) upon finding prejudice to another party from loss of the information, may order measures no greater than necessary to cure the prejudice; or

(2) only upon finding that the party acted with the intent to deprive another party of the information's use in the litigation may:

  (A) presume that the lost information was unfavorable to the party;

  (B) instruct the jury that it may or must presume the information was unfavorable to the party; or

  (C) dismiss the action or enter a default judgment.

(f) Failure to Participate in Framing a Discovery Plan. If a party or its attorney fails to participate in good faith in developing and submitting a proposed discovery plan as required by Rule 26(f), the court may, after giving an opportunity to be heard, require that party or attorney to pay to any other party the reasonable expenses, including attorney's fees, caused by the failure.

(Amended December 29, 1948, effective October 20, 1949; March 30, 1970, effective July 1, 1970; April 29, 1980, effective August 1, 1980; amended by Pub.L. 96–481, Title II, § 205(a), October 21, 1980, 94 Stat. 2330, effective October 1, 1981; amended March 2, 1987, effective August 1, 1987; April 22, 1993, effective December 1, 1993; April 17, 2000, effective December 1, 2000; April 12, 2006, effective December 1, 2006; April 30, 2007, effective December 1, 2007; April 16, 2013, effective December 1, 2013; April 29, 2015, effective December 1, 2015, absent contrary Congressional action.)

TITLE VI.   TRIALS

RULE 38.   RIGHT TO A JURY TRIAL; DEMAND

(a) Right Preserved. The right of trial by jury as declared by the Seventh Amendment to the Constitution—or as provided by a federal statute—is preserved to the parties inviolate.

(b) Demand. On any issue triable of right by a jury, a party may demand a jury trial by:

(1) serving the other parties with a written demand—which may be included in a pleading—

no later than 14 days after the last pleading directed to the issue is served; and

(2) filing the demand in accordance with Rule 5(d).

(c) Specifying Issues. In its demand, a party may specify the issues that it wishes to have tried by a jury; otherwise, it is considered to have demanded a jury trial on all the issues so triable. If the party has demanded a jury trial on only some issues, any other party may—within 14 days after being served with the demand or within a shorter time ordered by the court—serve a demand for a jury trial on any other or all factual issues triable by jury.

(d) Waiver; Withdrawal. A party waives a jury trial unless its demand is properly served and filed. A proper demand may be withdrawn only if the parties consent.

(e) Admiralty and Maritime Claims. These rules do not create a right to a jury trial on issues in a claim that is an admiralty or maritime claim under Rule 9(h).

(Amended February 28, 1966, effective July 1, 1966; March 2, 1987, effective August 1, 1987; April 22, 1993, effective December 1, 1993; April 30, 2007, effective December 1, 2007; March 26, 2009, effective December 1, 2009.)

RULE 39. TRIAL BY JURY OR BY THE COURT

(a) When a Demand Is Made. When a jury trial has been demanded under Rule 38, the action must be designated on the docket as a jury action. The trial on all issues so demanded must be by jury unless:

(1) the parties or their attorneys file a stipulation to a nonjury trial or so stipulate on the record; or

(2) the court, on motion or on its own, finds that on some or all of those issues there is no federal right to a jury trial.

(b) When No Demand Is Made. Issues on which a jury trial is not properly demanded are to be tried by the court. But the court may, on motion, order a jury trial on any issue for which a jury might have been demanded.

(c) Advisory Jury; Jury Trial by Consent. In an action not triable of right by a jury, the court, on motion or on its own:

(1) may try any issue with an advisory jury; or

(2) may, with the parties' consent, try any issue by a jury whose verdict has the same effect as if a jury trial had been a matter of right, unless the action is against the United States and a federal statute provides for a nonjury trial.

(Amended April 30, 2007, effective December 1, 2007.)

RULE 40. SCHEDULING CASES FOR TRIAL

Each court must provide by rule for scheduling trials. The court must give priority to actions entitled to priority by a federal statute.

(Amended April 30, 2007, effective December 1, 2007.)

RULE 41. DISMISSAL OF ACTIONS

(a) Voluntary Dismissal.

(1) *By the Plaintiff.*

(A) *Without a Court Order.* Subject to Rules 23(e), 23.1(c), 23.2, and 66 and any applicable federal statute, the plaintiff may dismiss an action without a court order by filing:

(i) a notice of dismissal before the opposing party serves either an answer or a motion for summary judgment; or

(ii) a stipulation of dismissal signed by all parties who have appeared.

(B) *Effect.* Unless the notice or stipulation states otherwise, the dismissal is without prejudice. But if the plaintiff previously dismissed any federal- or state-court action based on or including the same claim, a notice of dismissal operates as an adjudication on the merits.

(2) *By Court Order; Effect.* Except as provided in Rule 41(a)(1), an action may be dismissed at the plaintiff's request only by court order, on terms that the court considers proper. If a defendant has pleaded a counterclaim before being served with the plaintiff's motion to dismiss, the action may be dismissed over the defendant's objection only if the counterclaim can remain pending for independent adjudication. Unless the order states otherwise, a dismissal under this paragraph (2) is without prejudice.

(b) Involuntary Dismissal; Effect. If the plaintiff fails to prosecute or to comply with these rules or a court order, a defendant may move to dismiss the action or any claim against it. Unless the dismissal order states otherwise, a dismissal under this subdivision (b) and any dismissal not under this rule—except one for lack of jurisdiction, improper venue, or failure to join a party under Rule 19—operates as an adjudication on the merits.

(c) Dismissing a Counterclaim, Crossclaim, or Third–Party Claim. This rule applies to a dismissal of any counterclaim, crossclaim, or third-party claim. A claimant's voluntary dismissal under Rule 41(a)(1)(A)(i) must be made:

(1) before a responsive pleading is served; or

(2) if there is no responsive pleading, before evidence is introduced at a hearing or trial.

(d) Costs of a Previously Dismissed Action. If a plaintiff who previously dismissed an action in any court files an action based on or including the same claim against the same defendant, the court:

(1) may order the plaintiff to pay all or part of the costs of that previous action; and

(2) may stay the proceedings until the plaintiff has complied.

(Amended December 27, 1946, effective March 19, 1948; January 21, 1963, effective July 1, 1963; February 28, 1966, effective July 1, 1966; December 4, 1967, effective July 1, 1968; March 2, 1987, effective August 1, 1987; April 30, 1991, effective December 1, 1991; April 30, 2007, effective December 1, 2007.)

RULE 42. CONSOLIDATION; SEPARATE TRIALS

(a) Consolidation. If actions before the court involve a common question of law or fact, the court may:

(1) join for hearing or trial any or all matters at issue in the actions;

(2) consolidate the actions; or

(3) issue any other orders to avoid unnecessary cost or delay.

(b) Separate Trials. For convenience, to avoid prejudice, or to expedite and economize, the court may order a separate trial of one or more separate issues, claims, crossclaims, counterclaims, or third-party claims. When ordering a separate trial, the court must preserve any federal right to a jury trial.

(Amended February 28, 1966, effective July 1, 1966; April 30, 2007, effective December 1, 2007.)

RULE 43. TAKING TESTIMONY

(a) In Open Court. At trial, the witnesses' testimony must be taken in open court unless a federal statute, the Federal Rules of Evidence, these rules, or other rules adopted by the Supreme Court provide otherwise. For good cause in compelling circumstances and with appropriate safeguards, the court may permit testimony in open court by contemporaneous transmission from a different location.

(b) Affirmation Instead of an Oath. When these rules require an oath, a solemn affirmation suffices.

(c) Evidence on a Motion. When a motion relies on facts outside the record, the court may hear the matter on affidavits or may hear it wholly or partly on oral testimony or on depositions.

(d) Interpreter. The court may appoint an interpreter of its choosing; fix reasonable compensation to be paid from funds provided by law or by one or more parties; and tax the compensation as costs.

(Amended February 28, 1966, effective July 1, 1966; November 20, 1972, and December 18, 1972, effective July 1, 1975; March 2, 1987, effective August 1, 1987; April 23, 1996, effective December 1, 1996; April 30, 2007, effective December 1, 2007.)

RULE 44. PROVING AN OFFICIAL RECORD

(a) Means of Proving.

(1) *Domestic Record.* Each of the following evidences an official record—or an entry in it—that is otherwise admissible and is kept within the United States, any state, district, or commonwealth, or any territory subject to the administrative or judicial jurisdiction of the United States:

(A) an official publication of the record; or

(B) a copy attested by the officer with legal custody of the record—or by the officer's deputy—and accompanied by a certificate that the officer has custody. The certificate must be made under seal:

(i) by a judge of a court of record in the district or political subdivision where the record is kept; or

(ii) by any public officer with a seal of office and with official duties in the district or political subdivision where the record is kept.

(2) *Foreign Record.*

(A) *In General.* Each of the following evidences a foreign official record—or an entry in it—that is otherwise admissible:

(i) an official publication of the record; or

(ii) the record—or a copy—that is attested by an authorized person and is accompanied either by a final certification of genuineness or by a certification under a treaty or convention to which the United States and the country where the record is located are parties.

(B) *Final Certification of Genuineness.* A final certification must certify the genuineness of the signature and official position of the attester or of any foreign official whose certificate of genuineness relates to the attestation or is in a chain of certificates of genuineness relating to the attestation. A final certification may be made by a secretary of a United States embassy or legation; by a consul general, vice consul, or consular agent of the United States; or by a diplomatic or consular official of the foreign country assigned or accredited to the United States.

(C) *Other Means of Proof.* If all parties have had a reasonable opportunity to investigate a foreign record's authenticity and accuracy, the court may, for good cause, either:

(i) admit an attested copy without final certification; or

(ii) permit the record to be evidenced by an attested summary with or without a final certification.

(b) Lack of a Record. A written statement that a diligent search of designated records revealed no record or entry of a specified tenor is admissible as evidence that the records contain no such record or entry. For domestic records, the statement must be authenticated under Rule 44(a)(1). For foreign records, the statement must comply with (a)(2)(C)(ii).

(c) Other Proof. A party may prove an official record—or an entry or lack of an entry in it—by any other method authorized by law.

(Amended February 28, 1966, effective July 1, 1966; March 2, 1987, effective August 1, 1987; April 30, 1991, effective December 1, 1991; April 30, 2007, effective December 1, 2007.)

RULE 44.1 DETERMINING FOREIGN LAW

A party who intends to raise an issue about a foreign country's law must give notice by a pleading or other writing. In determining foreign law, the court may consider any relevant material or source, including testimony, whether or not submitted by a party or admissible under the Federal Rules of Evidence. The court's determination must be treated as a ruling on a question of law.

(Adopted February 28, 1966, effective July 1, 1966; amended November 20, 1972, effective July 1, 1975; March 2, 1987, effective August 1, 1987; April 30, 2007, effective December 1, 2007.)

RULE 45. SUBPOENA

(a) In General.

(1) *Form and Contents.*

(A) *Requirements—In General.* Every subpoena must:

(i) state the court from which it issued;

(ii) state the title of the action and its civil-action number;

(iii) command each person to whom it is directed to do the following at a specified time and place: attend and testify; produce designated documents, electronically stored information, or tangible things in that person's possession, custody, or control; or permit the inspection of premises; and

(iv) set out the text of Rule 45(d) and (e).

(B) *Command to Attend a Deposition—Notice of the Recording Method.* A subpoena commanding attendance at a deposition must state the method for recording the testimony.

(C) *Combining or Separating a Command to Produce or to Permit Inspection; Specifying the Form for Electronically Stored Information.* A command to produce documents, electronically stored information, or tangible things or to permit the inspection of premises may be included in a subpoena commanding attendance at a deposition, hearing, or trial, or may be set out in a separate subpoena. A subpoena may specify the form or forms in which electronically stored information is to be produced.

(D) *Command to Produce; Included Obligations.* A command in a subpoena to produce documents, electronically stored information, or tangible things requires the responding person to permit inspection, copying, testing, or sampling of the materials.

(2) *Issuing Court.* A subpoena must issue from the court where the action is pending.

(3) *Issued by Whom.* The clerk must issue a subpoena, signed but otherwise in blank, to a party who requests it. That party must complete it before service. An attorney also may issue and sign a subpoena if the attorney is authorized to practice in the issuing court.

(4) *Notice to Other Parties Before Service.* If the subpoena commands the production of documents, electronically stored information, or tangible things or the inspection of premises before trial, then before it is served on the person to whom it is directed, a notice and a copy of the subpoena must be served on each party.

(b) Service.

(1) *By Whom and How; Tendering Fees.* Any person who is at least 18 years old and not a party may serve a subpoena. Serving a subpoena requires delivering a copy to the named person and, if the subpoena requires that person's attendance, tendering the fees for 1 day's attendance and the mileage allowed by law. Fees and mileage need not be tendered when the subpoena issues on behalf of the United States or any of its officers or agencies.

(2) *Service in the United States.* A subpoena may be served at any place within the United States.

(3) *Service in a Foreign Country.* 28 U.S.C. § 1783 governs issuing and serving a subpoena directed to a United States national or resident who is in a foreign country.

(4) *Proof of Service.* Proving service, when necessary, requires filing with the issuing court a statement showing the date and manner of service and the names of the persons served. The statement must be certified by the server.

(c) Place of Compliance.

(1) *For a Trial, Hearing, or Deposition.* A subpoena may command a person to attend a trial, hearing, or deposition only as follows:

(A) within 100 miles of where the person resides, is employed, or regularly transacts business in person; or

(B) within the state where the person resides, is employed, or regularly transacts business in person, if the person

(i) is a party or a party's officer; or

(ii) is commanded to attend a trial and would not incur substantial expense.

(2) *For Other Discovery.* A subpoena may command:

(A) production of documents, electronically stored information, or tangible things at a place within 100 miles of where the person resides, is employed, or regularly transacts business in person; and

(B) inspection of premises at the premises to be inspected.

(d) Protecting a Person Subject to a Subpoena; Enforcement.

(1) *Avoiding Undue Burden or Expense; Sanctions.* A party or attorney responsible for issuing and serving a subpoena must take reasonable steps to avoid imposing undue burden or expense on a person subject to the subpoena. The court for the district where compliance is required must enforce this duty and impose an appropriate sanction—which may include lost earnings and reasonable attorney's fees—on a party or attorney who fails to comply.

(2) *Command to Produce Materials or Permit Inspection.*

(A) *Appearance Not Required.* A person commanded to produce documents, electronically stored information, or tangible things, or to permit the inspection of premises, need not appear in person at the place of production or inspection unless also commanded to appear for a deposition, hearing, or trial.

(B) *Objections.* A person commanded to produce documents or tangible things or to permit inspection may serve on the party or attorney designated in the subpoena a written objection to inspecting, copying, testing, or sampling any or all of the materials or to inspecting the premises—or to producing electronically stored information in the form or forms requested. The objection must be

served before the earlier of the time specified for compliance or 14 days after the subpoena is served. If an objection is made, the following rules apply:

(i) At any time, on notice to the commanded person, the serving party may move the court for the district where compliance is required for an order compelling production or inspection.

(ii) These acts may be required only as directed in the order, and the order must protect a person who is neither a party nor a party's officer from significant expense resulting from compliance.

(3) *Quashing or Modifying a Subpoena.*

(A) *When Required.* On timely motion, the court for the district where compliance is required must quash or modify a subpoena that:

(i) fails to allow a reasonable time to comply;

(ii) requires a person to comply beyond the geographical limits specified in Rule 45(c);

(iii) requires disclosure of privileged or other protected matter, if no exception or waiver applies; or

(iv) subjects a person to undue burden.

(B) *When Permitted.* To protect a person subject to or affected by a subpoena, the court for the district where compliance is required may, on motion, quash or modify the subpoena if it requires:

(i) disclosing a trade secret or other confidential research, development, or commercial information; or

(ii) disclosing an unretained expert's opinion or information that does not describe specific occurrences in dispute and results from the expert's study that was not requested by a party.

(C) *Specifying Conditions as an Alternative.* In the circumstances described in Rule 45(d)(3)(B), the court may, instead of quashing or modifying a subpoena, order appearance or production under specified conditions if the serving party:

(i) shows a substantial need for the testimony or material that cannot be otherwise met without undue hardship; and

(ii) ensures that the subpoenaed person will be reasonably compensated.

(e) Duties in Responding to a Subpoena.

(1) *Producing Documents or Electronically Stored Information.* These procedures apply to producing documents or electronically stored information:

(A) *Documents.* A person responding to a subpoena to produce documents must produce them as they are kept in the ordinary course of business or must organize and label them to correspond to the categories in the demand.

(B) *Form for Producing Electronically Stored Information Not Specified.* If a subpoena does not specify a form for producing electronically stored information, the person responding must produce it in a form or forms in which it is ordinarily maintained or in a reasonably usable form or forms.

(C) *Electronically Stored Information Produced in Only One Form.* The person responding need not produce the same electronically stored information in more than one form.

(D) *Inaccessible Electronically Stored Information.* The person responding need not provide discovery of electronically stored information from sources that the person identifies as not reasonably accessible because of undue burden or cost. On motion to compel discovery or for a protective order, the person responding must show that the information is not reasonably accessible because of undue burden or cost. If that showing is made, the court may nonetheless order discovery from such sources if the requesting party shows good cause, considering the limitations of Rule 26(b)(2)(C). The court may specify conditions for the discovery.

(2) *Claiming Privilege or Protection.*

(A) *Information Withheld.* A person withholding subpoenaed information under a claim that it is privileged or subject to protection as trial-preparation material must:

  (i) expressly make the claim; and

  (ii) describe the nature of the withheld documents, communications, or tangible things in a manner that, without revealing information itself privileged or protected, will enable the parties to assess the claim.

(B) *Information Produced.* If information produced in response to a subpoena is subject to a claim of privilege or of protection as trial-preparation material, the person making the claim may notify any party that received the information of the claim and the basis for it. After being notified, a party must promptly return, sequester, or destroy the specified information and any copies it has; must not use or disclose the information until the claim is resolved; must take reasonable

steps to retrieve the information if the party disclosed it before being notified; and may promptly present the information under seal to the court for the district where compliance is required for a determination of the claim. The person who produced the information must preserve the information until the claim is resolved.

(f) Transferring a Subpoena–Related Motion. When the court where compliance is required did not issue the subpoena, it may transfer a motion under this rule to the issuing court if the person subject to the subpoena consents or if the court finds exceptional circumstances. Then, if the attorney for a person subject to a subpoena is authorized to practice in the court where the motion was made, the attorney may file papers and appear on the motion as an officer of the issuing court. To enforce its order, the issuing court may transfer the order to the court where the motion was made.

(g) Contempt. The court for the district where compliance is required—and also, after a motion is transferred, the issuing court—may hold in contempt a person who, having been served, fails without adequate excuse to obey the subpoena or an order related to it.

(Amended December 27, 1946, effective March 19, 1948; December 29, 1948, effective October 20, 1949; March 30, 1970, effective July 1, 1970; April 29, 1980, effective August 1, 1980; April 29, 1985, effective August 1, 1985; March 2, 1987, effective August 1, 1987; April 30, 1991, effective December 1, 1991; April 25, 2005, effective December 1, 2005; April 12, 2006, effective December 1, 2006; April 30, 2007, effective December 1, 2007; April 16, 2013, effective December 1, 2013.)

RULE 46. OBJECTING TO A RULING OR ORDER

A formal exception to a ruling or order is unnecessary. When the ruling or order is requested or made, a party need only state the action that it wants the court to take or objects to, along with the grounds for the request or objection. Failing to object does not prejudice a party who had no opportunity to do so when the ruling or order was made.

(Amended March 2, 1987, effective August 1, 1987; April 30, 2007, effective December 1, 2007.)

RULE 47. SELECTING JURORS

(a) Examining Jurors. The court may permit the parties or their attorneys to examine prospective jurors or may itself do so. If the court examines the jurors, it must permit the parties or their attorneys to make any further inquiry it considers proper, or must itself ask any of their additional questions it considers proper.

(b) Peremptory Challenges. The court must allow the number of peremptory challenges provided by 28 U.S.C. § 1870.

(c) Excusing a Juror. During trial or deliberation, the court may excuse a juror for good cause.

(Amended February 28, 1966, effective July 1, 1966; April 30, 1991, effective December 1, 1991; April 30, 2007, effective December 1, 2007.)

RULE 48. NUMBER OF JURORS; VERDICT; POLLING

(a) Number of Jurors. A jury must begin with at least 6 and no more than 12 members, and each juror must participate in the verdict unless excused under Rule 47(c).

(b) Verdict. Unless the parties stipulate otherwise, the verdict must be unanimous and must be returned by a jury of at least 6 members.

(c) Polling. After a verdict is returned but before the jury is discharged, the court must on a party's request, or may on its own, poll the jurors individually. If the poll reveals a lack of unanimity or lack of assent by the number of jurors that the parties stipulated to, the court may direct the jury to deliberate further or may order a new trial.

(Amended April 30, 1991, effective December 1, 1991; April 30, 2007, effective December 1, 2007; March 26, 2009, effective December 1, 2009.)

RULE 49. SPECIAL VERDICT; GENERAL VERDICT AND QUESTIONS

(a) Special Verdict.

   (1) *In General.* The court may require a jury to return only a special verdict in the form of a special written finding on each issue of fact. The court may do so by:

      (A) submitting written questions susceptible of a categorical or other brief answer;

      (B) submitting written forms of the special findings that might properly be made under the pleadings and evidence; or

      (C) using any other method that the court considers appropriate.

   (2) *Instructions.* The court must give the instructions and explanations necessary to enable the jury to make its findings on each submitted issue.

   (3) *Issues Not Submitted.* A party waives the right to a jury trial on any issue of fact raised by the pleadings or evidence but not submitted to the jury unless, before the jury retires, the party demands its submission to the jury. If the party does not demand submission, the court may make a finding on the issue. If the court makes no finding, it is considered to have made a finding consistent with its judgment on the special verdict.

(b) General Verdict with Answers to Written Questions.

   (1) *In General.* The court may submit to the jury forms for a general verdict, together with written questions on one or more issues of fact that the jury must decide. The court must give the instructions and explanations necessary to enable the jury to render a general verdict and answer the questions in writing, and must direct the jury to do both.

   (2) *Verdict and Answers Consistent.* When the general verdict and the answers are consistent, the court must approve, for entry under Rule 58, an appropriate judgment on the verdict and answers.

   (3) *Answers Inconsistent with the Verdict.* When the answers are consistent with each other but one or more is inconsistent with the general verdict, the court may:

      (A) approve, for entry under Rule 58, an appropriate judgment according to the answers, notwithstanding the general verdict;

      (B) direct the jury to further consider its answers and verdict; or

      (C) order a new trial.

   (4) *Answers Inconsistent with Each Other and the Verdict.* When the answers are inconsistent with each other and one or more is also inconsistent with the general verdict, judgment must not be entered; instead, the court must direct the jury to further consider its answers and verdict, or must order a new trial.

(Amended January 21, 1963, effective July 1, 1963; March 2, 1987, effective August 1, 1987; April 30, 2007, effective December 1, 2007.)

RULE 50. JUDGMENT AS A MATTER OF LAW IN A JURY TRIAL; RELATED MOTION FOR A NEW TRIAL; CONDITIONAL RULING

(a) Judgment as a Matter of Law.

   (1) *In General.* If a party has been fully heard on an issue during a jury trial and the court finds that a reasonable jury would not have a legally sufficient evidentiary basis to find for the party on that issue, the court may:

      (A) resolve the issue against the party; and

      (B) grant a motion for judgment as a matter of law against the party on a claim or defense that, under the controlling law, can be maintained or defeated only with a favorable finding on that issue.

(2) *Motion.* A motion for judgment as a matter of law may be made at any time before the case is submitted to the jury. The motion must specify the judgment sought and the law and facts that entitle the movant to the judgment.

(b) Renewing the Motion After Trial; Alternative Motion for a New Trial. If the court does not grant a motion for judgment as a matter of law made under Rule 50(a), the court is considered to have submitted the action to the jury subject to the court's later deciding the legal questions raised by the motion. No later than 28 days after the entry of judgment—or if the motion addresses a jury issue not decided by a verdict, no later than 28 days after the jury was discharged—the movant may file a renewed motion for judgment as a matter of law and may include an alternative or joint request for a new trial under Rule 59. In ruling on the renewed motion, the court may:

(1) allow judgment on the verdict, if the jury returned a verdict;

(2) order a new trial; or

(3) direct the entry of judgment as a matter of law.

(c) Granting the Renewed Motion; Conditional Ruling on a Motion for a New Trial.

(1) *In General.* If the court grants a renewed motion for judgment as a matter of law, it must also conditionally rule on any motion for a new trial by determining whether a new trial should be granted if the judgment is later vacated or reversed. The court must state the grounds for conditionally granting or denying the motion for a new trial.

(2) *Effect of a Conditional Ruling.* Conditionally granting the motion for a new trial does not affect the judgment's finality; if the judgment is reversed, the new trial must proceed unless the appellate court orders otherwise. If the motion for a new trial is conditionally denied, the appellee may assert error in that denial; if the judgment is reversed, the case must proceed as the appellate court orders.

(d) Time for a Losing Party's New-Trial Motion. Any motion for a new trial under Rule 59 by a party against whom judgment as a matter of law is rendered must be filed no later than 28 days after the entry of the judgment.

(e) Denying the Motion for Judgment as a Matter of Law; Reversal on Appeal. If the court denies the motion for judgment as a matter of law, the prevailing party may, as appellee, assert grounds entitling it to a new trial should the appellate court conclude that the trial court erred in denying the motion. If the appellate court reverses the judgment, it may order a new trial, direct the trial court to determine whether a new trial should be granted, or direct the entry of judgment.

(Amended January 21, 1963, effective July 1, 1963; March 2, 1987, effective August 1, 1987; April 30, 1991, effective December 1, 1991; April 22, 1993, effective December 1, 1993; April 27, 1995, effective December 1, 1995; April 12, 2006, effective December 1, 2006; April 30, 2007, effective December 1, 2007; March 26, 2009, effective December 1, 2009.)

RULE 51. INSTRUCTIONS TO THE JURY; OBJECTIONS; PRESERVING A CLAIM OF ERROR

(a) Requests.

(1) *Before or at the Close of the Evidence.* At the close of the evidence or at any earlier reasonable time that the court orders, a party may file and furnish to every other party written requests for the jury instructions it wants the court to give.

(2) *After the Close of the Evidence.* After the close of the evidence, a party may:

(A) file requests for instructions on issues that could not reasonably have been anticipated by an earlier time that the court set for requests; and

(B) with the court's permission, file untimely requests for instructions on any issue.

(b) Instructions. The court:

(1) must inform the parties of its proposed instructions and proposed action on the requests before instructing the jury and before final jury arguments;

(2) must give the parties an opportunity to object on the record and out of the jury's hearing before the instructions and arguments are delivered; and

(3) may instruct the jury at any time before the jury is discharged.

(c) Objections.

(1) *How to Make.* A party who objects to an instruction or the failure to give an instruction must do so on the record, stating distinctly the matter objected to and the grounds for the objection.

(2) *When to Make.* An objection is timely if:

(A) a party objects at the opportunity provided under Rule 51(b)(2); or

(B) a party was not informed of an instruction or action on a request before that opportunity to object, and the party objects promptly after learning that the instruction or request will be, or has been, given or refused.

(d) Assigning Error; Plain Error.

　(1) *Assigning Error.* A party may assign as error:

　　(A) an error in an instruction actually given, if that party properly objected; or

　　(B) a failure to give an instruction, if that party properly requested it and—unless the court rejected the request in a definitive ruling on the record—also properly objected.

　(2) *Plain Error.* A court may consider a plain error in the instructions that has not been preserved as required by Rule 51(d)(1) if the error affects substantial rights.

(Amended March 2, 1987, effective August 1, 1987; March 27, 2003, effective December 1, 2003; April 30, 2007, effective December 1, 2007.)

RULE 52.　FINDINGS AND CONCLUSIONS BY THE COURT; JUDGMENT ON PARTIAL FINDINGS

(a) Findings and Conclusions.

　(1) *In General.* In an action tried on the facts without a jury or with an advisory jury, the court must find the facts specially and state its conclusions of law separately. The findings and conclusions may be stated on the record after the close of the evidence or may appear in an opinion or a memorandum of decision filed by the court. Judgment must be entered under Rule 58.

　(2) *For an Interlocutory Injunction.* In granting or refusing an interlocutory injunction, the court must similarly state the findings and conclusions that support its action.

　(3) *For a Motion.* The court is not required to state findings or conclusions when ruling on a motion under Rule 12 or 56 or, unless these rules provide otherwise, on any other motion.

　(4) *Effect of a Master's Findings.* A master's findings, to the extent adopted by the court, must be considered the court's findings.

　(5) *Questioning the Evidentiary Support.* A party may later question the sufficiency of the evidence supporting the findings, whether or not the party requested findings, objected to them, moved to amend them, or moved for partial findings.

　(6) *Setting Aside the Findings.* Findings of fact, whether based on oral or other evidence, must not be set aside unless clearly erroneous, and the reviewing court must give due regard to the trial court's opportunity to judge the witnesses' credibility.

(b) Amended or Additional Findings. On a party's motion filed no later than 28 days after the entry of judgment, the court may amend its findings—or make additional findings—and may amend the judgment accordingly. The motion may accompany a motion for a new trial under Rule 59.

(c) Judgment on Partial Findings. If a party has been fully heard on an issue during a nonjury trial and the court finds against the party on that issue, the court may enter judgment against the party on a claim or defense that, under the controlling law, can be maintained or defeated only with a favorable finding on that issue. The court may, however, decline to render any judgment until the close of the evidence. A judgment on partial findings must be supported by findings of fact and conclusions of law as required by Rule 52(a).

(Amended December 27, 1946, effective March 19, 1948; January 21, 1963, effective July 1, 1963; April 28, 1983, effective August 1, 1983; April 29, 1985, effective August 1, 1985; April 30, 1991, effective December 1, 1991; April 22, 1993, effective December 1, 1993; April 27, 1995, effective December 1, 1995; April 30, 2007, effective December 1, 2007; March 26, 2009, effective December 1, 2009.)

RULE 53.　MASTERS

(a) Appointment.

　(1) *Scope.* Unless a statute provides otherwise, a court may appoint a master only to:

　　(A) perform duties consented to by the parties;

　　(B) hold trial proceedings and make or recommend findings of fact on issues to be decided without a jury if appointment is warranted by:

　　　(i) some exceptional condition; or

　　　(ii) the need to perform an accounting or resolve a difficult computation of damages; or

　　(C) address pretrial and posttrial matters that cannot be effectively and timely addressed by an available district judge or magistrate judge of the district.

　(2) *Disqualification.* A master must not have a relationship to the parties, attorneys, action, or court that would require disqualification of a judge under 28 U.S.C. § 455, unless the parties, with the court's approval, consent to the appointment after the master discloses any potential grounds for disqualification.

　(3) *Possible Expense or Delay.* In appointing a master, the court must consider the fairness of imposing the likely expenses on the parties and must protect against unreasonable expense or delay.

(b) Order Appointing a Master.

　(1) *Notice.* Before appointing a master, the court must give the parties notice and an opportunity to be heard. Any party may suggest candidates for appointment.

(2) *Contents.* The appointing order must direct the master to proceed with all reasonable diligence and must state:

   (A) the master's duties, including any investigation or enforcement duties, and any limits on the master's authority under Rule 53(c);

   (B) the circumstances, if any, in which the master may communicate ex parte with the court or a party;

   (C) the nature of the materials to be preserved and filed as the record of the master's activities;

   (D) the time limits, method of filing the record, other procedures, and standards for reviewing the master's orders, findings, and recommendations; and

   (E) the basis, terms, and procedure for fixing the master's compensation under Rule 53(g).

(3) *Issuing.* The court may issue the order only after:

   (A) the master files an affidavit disclosing whether there is any ground for disqualification under 28 U.S.C. § 455; and

   (B) if a ground is disclosed, the parties, with the court's approval, waive the disqualification.

(4) *Amending.* The order may be amended at any time after notice to the parties and an opportunity to be heard.

(c) Master's Authority.

(1) *In General.* Unless the appointing order directs otherwise, a master may:

   (A) regulate all proceedings;

   (B) take all appropriate measures to perform the assigned duties fairly and efficiently; and

   (C) if conducting an evidentiary hearing, exercise the appointing court's power to compel, take, and record evidence.

(2) *Sanctions.* The master may by order impose on a party any noncontempt sanction provided by Rule 37 or 45, and may recommend a contempt sanction against a party and sanctions against a nonparty.

(d) Master's Orders. A master who issues an order must file it and promptly serve a copy on each party. The clerk must enter the order on the docket.

(e) Master's Reports. A master must report to the court as required by the appointing order. The master must file the report and promptly serve a copy on each party, unless the court orders otherwise.

(f) Action on the Master's Order, Report, or Recommendations.

(1) *Opportunity for a Hearing; Action in General.* In acting on a master's order, report, or recommendations, the court must give the parties notice and an opportunity to be heard; may receive evidence; and may adopt or affirm, modify, wholly or partly reject or reverse, or resubmit to the master with instructions.

(2) *Time to Object or Move to Adopt or Modify.* A party may file objections to—or a motion to adopt or modify—the master's order, report, or recommendations no later than 21 days after a copy is served, unless the court sets a different time.

(3) *Reviewing Factual Findings.* The court must decide de novo all objections to findings of fact made or recommended by a master, unless the parties, with the court's approval, stipulate that:

   (A) the findings will be reviewed for clear error; or

   (B) the findings of a master appointed under Rule 53(a)(1)(A) or (C) will be final.

(4) *Reviewing Legal Conclusions.* The court must decide de novo all objections to conclusions of law made or recommended by a master.

(5) *Reviewing Procedural Matters.* Unless the appointing order establishes a different standard of review, the court may set aside a master's ruling on a procedural matter only for an abuse of discretion.

(g) Compensation.

(1) *Fixing Compensation.* Before or after judgment, the court must fix the master's compensation on the basis and terms stated in the appointing order, but the court may set a new basis and terms after giving notice and an opportunity to be heard.

(2) *Payment.* The compensation must be paid either:

   (A) by a party or parties; or

   (B) from a fund or subject matter of the action within the court's control.

(3) *Allocating Payment.* The court must allocate payment among the parties after considering the nature and amount of the controversy, the parties' means, and the extent to which any party is more responsible than other parties for the reference to a master. An interim allocation may be amended to reflect a decision on the merits.

(h) Appointing a Magistrate Judge. A magistrate judge is subject to this rule only when the order referring a matter to the magistrate judge states that the reference is made under this rule.

(Amended February 28, 1966, effective July 1, 1966; April 28, 1983, effective August 1, 1983; March 2, 1987, effective August 1, 1987; April 30, 1991, effective December 1, 1991; April 22, 1993, effective December 1, 1993; March 27, 2003, effective December 1, 2003; April 30, 2007, effective December 1, 2007; March 26, 2009, effective December 1, 2009.)

TITLE VII. JUDGMENT

RULE 54. JUDGMENT; COSTS

(a) Definition; Form. "Judgment" as used in these rules includes a decree and any order from which an appeal lies. A judgment should not include recitals of pleadings, a master's report, or a record of prior proceedings.

(b) Judgment on Multiple Claims or Involving Multiple Parties. When an action presents more than one claim for relief—whether as a claim, counterclaim, crossclaim, or third-party claim—or when multiple parties are involved, the court may direct entry of a final judgment as to one or more, but fewer than all, claims or parties only if the court expressly determines that there is no just reason for delay. Otherwise, any order or other decision, however designated, that adjudicates fewer than all the claims or the rights and liabilities of fewer than all the parties does not end the action as to any of the claims or parties and may be revised at any time before the entry of a judgment adjudicating all the claims and all the parties' rights and liabilities.

(c) Demand for Judgment; Relief to Be Granted. A default judgment must not differ in kind from, or exceed in amount, what is demanded in the pleadings. Every other final judgment should grant the relief to which each party is entitled, even if the party has not demanded that relief in its pleadings.

(d) Costs; Attorney's Fees.

  (1) *Costs Other Than Attorney's Fees.* Unless a federal statute, these rules, or a court order provides otherwise, costs—other than attorney's fees—should be allowed to the prevailing party. But costs against the United States, its officers, and its agencies may be imposed only to the extent allowed by law. The clerk may tax costs on 14 days' notice. On motion served within the next 7 days, the court may review the clerk's action.

  (2) *Attorney's Fees.*

    (A) *Claim to Be by Motion.* A claim for attorney's fees and related nontaxable expenses must be made by motion unless the substantive law requires those fees to be proved at trial as an element of damages.

    (B) *Timing and Contents of the Motion.* Unless a statute or a court order provides otherwise, the motion must:

      (i) be filed no later than 14 days after the entry of judgment;

      (ii) specify the judgment and the statute, rule, or other grounds entitling the movant to the award;

      (iii) state the amount sought or provide a fair estimate of it; and

      (iv) disclose, if the court so orders, the terms of any agreement about fees for the services for which the claim is made.

    (C) *Proceedings.* Subject to Rule 23(h), the court must, on a party's request, give an opportunity for adversary submissions on the motion in accordance with Rule 43(c) or 78. The court may decide issues of liability for fees before receiving submissions on the value of services. The court must find the facts and state its conclusions of law as provided in Rule 52(a).

    (D) *Special Procedures by Local Rule; Reference to a Master or a Magistrate Judge.* By local rule, the court may establish special procedures to resolve fee-related issues without extensive evidentiary hearings. Also, the court may refer issues concerning the value of services to a special master under Rule 53 without regard to the limitations of Rule 53(a)(1), and may refer a motion for attorney's fees to a magistrate judge under Rule 72(b) as if it were a dispositive pretrial matter.

    (E) *Exceptions.* Subparagraphs (A)-(D) do not apply to claims for fees and expenses as sanctions for violating these rules or as sanctions under 28 U.S.C. § 1927.

(Amended December 27, 1946, effective March 19, 1948; April 17, 1961, effective July 19, 1961; March 2, 1987, effective August 1, 1987; April 22, 1993, effective December 1, 1993; April 29, 2002, effective December 1, 2002; March 27, 2003, effective December 1, 2003; April 30, 2007, effective December 1, 2007; March 26, 2009, effective December 1, 2009.)

RULE 55. DEFAULT; DEFAULT JUDGMENT

(a) Entering a Default. When a party against whom a judgment for affirmative relief is sought has failed to plead or otherwise defend, and that failure is shown by affidavit or otherwise, the clerk must enter the party's default.

(b) Entering a Default Judgment.

(1) *By the Clerk.* If the plaintiff's claim is for a sum certain or a sum that can be made certain by computation, the clerk—on the plaintiff's request, with an affidavit showing the amount due—must enter judgment for that amount and costs against a defendant who has been defaulted for not appearing and who is neither a minor nor an incompetent person.

(2) *By the Court.* In all other cases, the party must apply to the court for a default judgment. A default judgment may be entered against a minor or incompetent person only if represented by a general guardian, conservator, or other like fiduciary who has appeared. If the party against whom a default judgment is sought has appeared personally or by a representative, that party or its representative must be served with written notice of the application at least 7 days before the hearing. The court may conduct hearings or make referrals—preserving any federal statutory right to a jury trial—when, to enter or effectuate judgment, it needs to:

(A) conduct an accounting;

(B) determine the amount of damages;

(C) establish the truth of any allegation by evidence; or

(D) investigate any other matter.

[Text of subdivision (c) effective until December 1, 2015, absent contrary Congressional action.]

(c) Setting Aside a Default or a Default Judgment. The court may set aside an entry of default for good cause, and it may set aside a default judgment under Rule 60(b).

[Text of subdivision (c) effective December 1, 2015, absent contrary Congressional action.]

(c) Setting Aside a Default or a Default Judgment. The court may set aside an entry of default for good cause, and it may set aside a final default judgment under Rule 60(b).

(d) Judgment Against the United States. A default judgment may be entered against the United States, its officers, or its agencies only if the claimant establishes a claim or right to relief by evidence that satisfies the court.

(Amended March 2, 1987, effective August 1, 1987; April 30, 2007, effective December 1, 2007; March 26, 2009, effective December 1, 2009; April 29, 2015, effective December 1, 2015, absent contrary Congressional action.)

RULE 56. SUMMARY JUDGMENT

(a) Motion for Summary Judgment or Partial Summary Judgment. A party may move for summary judgment, identifying each claim or defense—or the part of each claim or defense—on which summary judgment is sought. The court shall grant summary judgment if the movant shows that there is no genuine dispute as to any material fact and the movant is entitled to judgment as a matter of law. The court should state on the record the reasons for granting or denying the motion.

(b) Time to File a Motion. Unless a different time is set by local rule or the court orders otherwise, a party may file a motion for summary judgment at any time until 30 days after the close of all discovery.

(c) Procedures.

(1) *Supporting Factual Positions.* A party asserting that a fact cannot be or is genuinely disputed must support the assertion by:

(A) citing to particular parts of materials in the record, including depositions, documents, electronically stored information, affidavits or declarations, stipulations (including those made for purposes of the motion only), admissions, interrogatory answers, or other materials; or

(B) showing that the materials cited do not establish the absence or presence of a genuine dispute, or that an adverse party cannot produce admissible evidence to support the fact.

(2) *Objection That a Fact Is Not Supported by Admissible Evidence.* A party may object that the material cited to support or dispute a fact cannot be presented in a form that would be admissible in evidence.

(3) *Materials Not Cited.* The court need consider only the cited materials, but it may consider other materials in the record.

(4) *Affidavits or Declarations.* An affidavit or declaration used to support or oppose a motion must be made on personal knowledge, set out facts that would be admissible in evidence, and show that the affiant or declarant is competent to testify on the matters stated.

(d) When Facts Are Unavailable to the Nonmovant. If a nonmovant shows by affidavit or declaration that, for specified reasons, it cannot present facts essential to justify its opposition, the court may:

(1) defer considering the motion or deny it;

(2) allow time to obtain affidavits or declarations or to take discovery; or

(3) issue any other appropriate order.

(e) **Failing to Properly Support or Address a Fact.** If a party fails to properly support an assertion of fact or fails to properly address another party's assertion of fact as required by Rule 56(c), the court may:

(1) give an opportunity to properly support or address the fact;

(2) consider the fact undisputed for purposes of the motion;

(3) grant summary judgment if the motion and supporting materials—including the facts considered undisputed—show that the movant is entitled to it; or

(4) issue any other appropriate order.

(f) **Judgment Independent of the Motion.** After giving notice and a reasonable time to respond, the court may:

(1) grant summary judgment for a nonmovant;

(2) grant the motion on grounds not raised by a party; or

(3) consider summary judgment on its own after identifying for the parties material facts that may not be genuinely in dispute.

(g) **Failing to Grant All the Requested Relief.** If the court does not grant all the relief requested by the motion, it may enter an order stating any material fact—including an item of damages or other relief—that is not genuinely in dispute and treating the fact as established in the case.

(h) **Affidavit or Declaration Submitted in Bad Faith.** If satisfied that an affidavit or declaration under this rule is submitted in bad faith or solely for delay, the court—after notice and a reasonable time to respond—may order the submitting party to pay the other party the reasonable expenses, including attorney's fees, it incurred as a result. An offending party or attorney may also be held in contempt or subjected to other appropriate sanctions.

(Amended December 27, 1946, effective March 19, 1948; January 21, 1963, effective July 1, 1963; March 2, 1987, effective August 1, 1987; April 30, 2007, effective December 1, 2007; March 26, 2009, effective December 1, 2009; April 28, 2010, effective December 1, 2010.)

RULE 57. DECLARATORY JUDGMENT

These rules govern the procedure for obtaining a declaratory judgment under 28 U.S.C. § 2201. Rules 38 and 39 govern a demand for a jury trial. The existence of another adequate remedy does not preclude a declaratory judgment that is otherwise appropriate. The court may order a speedy hearing of a declaratory-judgment action.

(Amended December 29, 1948, effective October 20, 1949; April 30, 2007, effective December 1, 2007.)

RULE 58. ENTERING JUDGMENT

(a) **Separate Document.** Every judgment and amended judgment must be set out in a separate document, but a separate document is not required for an order disposing of a motion:

(1) for judgment under Rule 50(b);

(2) to amend or make additional findings under Rule 52(b);

(3) for attorney's fees under Rule 54;

(4) for a new trial, or to alter or amend the judgment, under Rule 59; or

(5) for relief under Rule 60.

(b) **Entering Judgment.**

(1) *Without the Court's Direction.* Subject to Rule 54(b) and unless the court orders otherwise, the clerk must, without awaiting the court's direction, promptly prepare, sign, and enter the judgment when:

(A) the jury returns a general verdict;

(B) the court awards only costs or a sum certain; or

(C) the court denies all relief.

(2) *Court's Approval Required.* Subject to Rule 54(b), the court must promptly approve the form of the judgment, which the clerk must promptly enter, when:

(A) the jury returns a special verdict or a general verdict with answers to written questions; or

(B) the court grants other relief not described in this subdivision (b).

(c) **Time of Entry.** For purposes of these rules, judgment is entered at the following times:

(1) if a separate document is not required, when the judgment is entered in the civil docket under Rule 79(a); or

(2) if a separate document is required, when the judgment is entered in the civil docket under Rule 79(a) and the earlier of these events occurs:

(A) it is set out in a separate document; or

(B) 150 days have run from the entry in the civil docket.

(d) Request for Entry. A party may request that judgment be set out in a separate document as required by Rule 58(a).

(e) Cost or Fee Awards. Ordinarily, the entry of judgment may not be delayed, nor the time for appeal extended, in order to tax costs or award fees. But if a timely motion for attorney's fees is made under Rule 54(d)(2), the court may act before a notice of appeal has been filed and become effective to order that the motion have the same effect under Federal Rule of Appellate Procedure 4(a)(4) as a timely motion under Rule 59.

(Amended December 27, 1946, effective March 19, 1948; January 21, 1963, effective July 1, 1963; April 22, 1993, effective December 1, 1993; April 29, 2002, effective December 1, 2002; April 30, 2007, effective December 1, 2007.)

RULE 59. NEW TRIAL; ALTERING OR AMENDING A JUDGMENT

(a) In General.

(1) *Grounds for New Trial.* The court may, on motion, grant a new trial on all or some of the issues—and to any party—as follows:

(A) after a jury trial, for any reason for which a new trial has heretofore been granted in an action at law in federal court; or

(B) after a nonjury trial, for any reason for which a rehearing has heretofore been granted in a suit in equity in federal court.

(2) *Further Action After a Nonjury Trial.* After a nonjury trial, the court may, on motion for a new trial, open the judgment if one has been entered, take additional testimony, amend findings of fact and conclusions of law or make new ones, and direct the entry of a new judgment.

(b) Time to File a Motion for a New Trial. A motion for a new trial must be filed no later than 28 days after the entry of judgment.

(c) Time to Serve Affidavits. When a motion for a new trial is based on affidavits, they must be filed with the motion. The opposing party has 14 days after being served to file opposing affidavits. The court may permit reply affidavits.

(d) New Trial on the Court's Initiative or for Reasons Not in the Motion. No later than 28 days after the entry of judgment, the court, on its own, may order a new trial for any reason that would justify granting one on a party's motion. After giving the parties notice and an opportunity to be heard, the court may grant a timely motion for a new trial for a reason not stated in the motion. In either event, the court must specify the reasons in its order.

(e) Motion to Alter or Amend a Judgment. A motion to alter or amend a judgment must be filed no later than 28 days after the entry of the judgment.

(Amended December 27, 1946, effective March 19, 1948; February 28, 1966, effective July 1, 1966; April 27, 1995, effective December 1, 1995; April 30, 2007, effective December 1, 2007; March 26, 2009, effective December 1, 2009.)

RULE 60. RELIEF FROM A JUDGMENT OR ORDER

(a) Corrections Based on Clerical Mistakes; Oversights and Omissions. The court may correct a clerical mistake or a mistake arising from oversight or omission whenever one is found in a judgment, order, or other part of the record. The court may do so on motion or on its own, with or without notice. But after an appeal has been docketed in the appellate court and while it is pending, such a mistake may be corrected only with the appellate court's leave.

(b) Grounds for Relief from a Final Judgment, Order, or Proceeding. On motion and just terms, the court may relieve a party or its legal representative from a final judgment, order, or proceeding for the following reasons:

(1) mistake, inadvertence, surprise, or excusable neglect;

(2) newly discovered evidence that, with reasonable diligence, could not have been discovered in time to move for a new trial under Rule 59(b);

(3) fraud (whether previously called intrinsic or extrinsic), misrepresentation, or misconduct by an opposing party;

(4) the judgment is void;

(5) the judgment has been satisfied, released or discharged; it is based on an earlier judgment that has been reversed or vacated; or applying it prospectively is no longer equitable; or

(6) any other reason that justifies relief.

(c) Timing and Effect of the Motion.

(1) *Timing.* A motion under Rule 60(b) must be made within a reasonable time—and for reasons (1), (2), and (3) no more than a year after the entry of the judgment or order or the date of the proceeding.

(2) *Effect on Finality.* The motion does not affect the judgment's finality or suspend its operation.

(d) Other Powers to Grant Relief. This rule does not limit a court's power to:

(1) entertain an independent action to relieve a party from a judgment, order, or proceeding;

(2) grant relief under 28 U.S.C. § 1655 to a defendant who was not personally notified of the action; or

(3) set aside a judgment for fraud on the court.

(e) Bills and Writs Abolished. The following are abolished: bills of review, bills in the nature of bills of review, and writs of coram nobis, coram vobis, and audita querela.

(Amended December 27, 1946, effective March 19, 1948; December 29, 1948, effective October 20, 1949; March 2, 1987, effective August 1, 1987; April 30, 2007, effective December 1, 2007.)

RULE 61. HARMLESS ERROR

Unless justice requires otherwise, no error in admitting or excluding evidence—or any other error by the court or a party—is ground for granting a new trial, for setting aside a verdict, or for vacating, modifying, or otherwise disturbing a judgment or order. At every stage of the proceeding, the court must disregard all errors and defects that do not affect any party's substantial rights.

(Amended April 30, 2007, effective December 1, 2007.)

RULE 62. STAY OF PROCEEDINGS TO ENFORCE A JUDGMENT

(a) Automatic Stay; Exceptions for Injunctions, Receiverships, and Patent Accountings. Except as stated in this rule, no execution may issue on a judgment, nor may proceedings be taken to enforce it, until 14 days have passed after its entry. But unless the court orders otherwise, the following are not stayed after being entered, even if an appeal is taken:

(1) an interlocutory or final judgment in an action for an injunction or a receivership; or

(2) a judgment or order that directs an accounting in an action for patent infringement.

(b) Stay Pending the Disposition of a Motion. On appropriate terms for the opposing party's security, the court may stay the execution of a judgment—or any proceedings to enforce it—pending disposition of any of the following motions:

(1) under Rule 50, for judgment as a matter of law;

(2) under Rule 52(b), to amend the findings or for additional findings;

(3) under Rule 59, for a new trial or to alter or amend a judgment; or

(4) under Rule 60, for relief from a judgment or order.

(c) Injunction Pending an Appeal. While an appeal is pending from an interlocutory order or final judgment that grants, dissolves, or denies an injunction, the court may suspend, modify, restore, or grant an injunction on terms for bond or other terms that secure the opposing party's rights. If the judgment appealed from is rendered by a statutory three-judge district court, the order must be made either:

(1) by that court sitting in open session; or

(2) by the assent of all its judges, as evidenced by their signatures.

(d) Stay with Bond on Appeal. If an appeal is taken, the appellant may obtain a stay by supersedeas bond, except in an action described in Rule 62(a)(1) or (2). The bond may be given upon or after filing the notice of appeal or after obtaining the order allowing the appeal. The stay takes effect when the court approves the bond.

(e) Stay Without Bond on an Appeal by the United States, Its Officers, or Its Agencies. The court must not require a bond, obligation, or other security from the appellant when granting a stay on an appeal by the United States, its officers, or its agencies or on an appeal directed by a department of the federal government.

(f) Stay in Favor of a Judgment Debtor Under State Law. If a judgment is a lien on the judgment debtor's property under the law of the state where the court is located, the judgment debtor is entitled to the same stay of execution the state court would give.

(g) Appellate Court's Power Not Limited. This rule does not limit the power of the appellate court or one of its judges or justices:

(1) to stay proceedings—or suspend, modify, restore, or grant an injunction—while an appeal is pending; or

(2) to issue an order to preserve the status quo or the effectiveness of the judgment to be entered.

(h) Stay with Multiple Claims or Parties. A court may stay the enforcement of a final judgment entered under Rule 54(b) until it enters a later judgment or judgments, and may prescribe terms necessary to secure the benefit of the stayed judgment for the party in whose favor it was entered.

(Amended December 27, 1946, effective March 19, 1948; December 29, 1948, effective October 20, 1949; April 17, 1961, effective July 19, 1961; March 2, 1987, effective August 1, 1987; April 30, 2007, effective December 1, 2007; March 26, 2009, effective December 1, 2009.)

RULE 62.1 INDICATIVE RULING ON A MOTION FOR RELIEF THAT IS BARRED BY A PENDING APPEAL

(a) Relief Pending Appeal. If a timely motion is made for relief that the court lacks authority to grant because of an appeal that has been docketed and is pending, the court may:

(1) defer considering the motion;

(2) deny the motion; or

(3) state either that it would grant the motion if the court of appeals remands for that purpose or that the motion raises a substantial issue.

(b) **Notice to the Court of Appeals.** The movant must promptly notify the circuit clerk under Federal Rule of Appellate Procedure 12.1 if the district court states that it would grant the motion or that the motion raises a substantial issue.

(c) **Remand.** The district court may decide the motion if the court of appeals remands for that purpose.

(Added March 26, 2009, effective December 1, 2009.)

RULE 63. JUDGE'S INABILITY TO PROCEED

If a judge conducting a hearing or trial is unable to proceed, any other judge may proceed upon certifying familiarity with the record and determining that the case may be completed without prejudice to the parties. In a hearing or a nonjury trial, the successor judge must, at a party's request, recall any witness whose testimony is material and disputed and who is available to testify again without undue burden. The successor judge may also recall any other witness.

(Amended March 2, 1987, effective August 1, 1987; April 30, 1991, effective December 1, 1991; April 30, 2007, effective December 1, 2007.)

TITLE VIII. PROVISIONAL AND FINAL REMEDIES

RULE 64. SEIZING A PERSON OR PROPERTY

(a) **Remedies Under State Law—In General.** At the commencement of and throughout an action, every remedy is available that, under the law of the state where the court is located, provides for seizing a person or property to secure satisfaction of the potential judgment. But a federal statute governs to the extent it applies.

(b) **Specific Kinds of Remedies.** The remedies available under this rule include the following—however er designated and regardless of whether state procedure requires an independent action:

- arrest;
- attachment;
- garnishment;
- replevin;
- sequestration; and
- other corresponding or equivalent remedies.

(Amended April 30, 2007, effective December 1, 2007.)

RULE 65. INJUNCTIONS AND RESTRAINING ORDERS

(a) **Preliminary Injunction.**

(1) *Notice.* The court may issue a preliminary injunction only on notice to the adverse party.

(2) *Consolidating the Hearing with the Trial on the Merits.* Before or after beginning the hearing on a motion for a preliminary injunction, the court may advance the trial on the merits and consolidate it with the hearing. Even when consolidation is not ordered, evidence that is received on the motion and that would be admissible at trial becomes part of the trial record and

need not be repeated at trial. But the court must preserve any party's right to a jury trial.

(b) **Temporary Restraining Order.**

(1) *Issuing Without Notice.* The court may issue a temporary restraining order without written or oral notice to the adverse party or its attorney only if:

(A) specific facts in an affidavit or a verified complaint clearly show that immediate and irreparable injury, loss, or damage will result to the movant before the adverse party can be heard in opposition; and

(B) the movant's attorney certifies in writing any efforts made to give notice and the reasons why it should not be required.

(2) *Contents; Expiration.* Every temporary restraining order issued without notice must state the date and hour it was issued; describe the injury and state why it is irreparable; state why the order was issued without notice; and be promptly filed in the clerk's office and entered in the record. The order expires at the time after entry—not to exceed 14 days—that the court sets, unless before that time the court, for good cause, extends it for a like period or the adverse party consents to a longer extension. The reasons for an extension must be entered in the record.

(3) *Expediting the Preliminary–Injunction Hearing.* If the order is issued without notice, the motion for a preliminary injunction must be set for hearing at the earliest possible time, taking precedence over all other matters except hearings on older matters of the same character. At the hearing, the party who obtained the order must proceed with the motion; if the party does not, the court must dissolve the order.

(4) **Motion to Dissolve.** On 2 days' notice to the party who obtained the order without notice—or on shorter notice set by the court—the adverse party may appear and move to dissolve or modify the order. The court must then hear and decide the motion as promptly as justice requires.

(c) **Security.** The court may issue a preliminary injunction or a temporary restraining order only if the movant gives security in an amount that the court considers proper to pay the costs and damages sustained by any party found to have been wrongfully enjoined or restrained. The United States, its officers, and its agencies are not required to give security.

(d) **Contents and Scope of Every Injunction and Restraining Order.**

(1) **Contents.** Every order granting an injunction and every restraining order must:

(A) state the reasons why it issued;

(B) state its terms specifically; and

(C) describe in reasonable detail—and not by referring to the complaint or other document—the act or acts restrained or required.

(2) **Persons Bound.** The order binds only the following who receive actual notice of it by personal service or otherwise:

(A) the parties;

(B) the parties' officers, agents, servants, employees, and attorneys; and

(C) other persons who are in active concert or participation with anyone described in Rule 65(d)(2)(A) or (B).

(e) **Other Laws Not Modified.** These rules do not modify the following:

(1) any federal statute relating to temporary restraining orders or preliminary injunctions in actions affecting employer and employee;

(2) 28 U.S.C. § 2361, which relates to preliminary injunctions in actions of interpleader or in the nature of interpleader; or

(3) 28 U.S.C. § 2284, which relates to actions that must be heard and decided by a three-judge district court.

(f) **Copyright Impoundment.** This rule applies to copyright-impoundment proceedings.

(Amended December 27, 1946, effective March 19, 1948; December 29, 1948, effective October 20, 1949; February 28, 1966, effective July 1, 1966; March 2, 1987, effective August 1, 1987; April 23, 2001, effective December 1, 2001; April 30, 2007, effective December 1, 2007; March 26, 2009, effective December 1, 2009.)

RULE 65.1   PROCEEDINGS AGAINST A SURETY

Whenever these rules (including the Supplemental Rules for Admiralty or Maritime Claims and Asset Forfeiture Actions) require or allow a party to give security, and security is given through a bond or other undertaking with one or more sureties, each surety submits to the court's jurisdiction and irrevocably appoints the court clerk as its agent for receiving service of any papers that affect its liability on the bond or undertaking. The surety's liability may be enforced on motion without an independent action. The motion and any notice that the court orders may be served on the court clerk, who must promptly mail a copy of each to every surety whose address is known.

(Adopted February 28, 1966, effective July 1, 1966; amended March 2, 1987, effective August 1, 1987; April 12, 2006, effective December 1, 2006; April 30, 2007, effective December 1, 2007.)

RULE 66.   RECEIVERS

These rules govern an action in which the appointment of a receiver is sought or a receiver sues or is sued. But the practice in administering an estate by a receiver or a similar court-appointed officer must accord with the historical practice in federal courts or with a local rule. An action in which a receiver has been appointed may be dismissed only by court order.

(Amended December 27, 1946, effective March 19, 1948; December 29, 1948, effective October 20, 1949; April 30, 2007, effective December 1, 2007.)

RULE 67.   DEPOSIT INTO COURT

(a) **Depositing Property.** If any part of the relief sought is a money judgment or the disposition of a sum of money or some other deliverable thing, a party—on notice to every other party and by leave of court—may deposit with the court all or part of the money or thing, whether or not that party claims any of it. The depositing party must deliver to the clerk a copy of the order permitting deposit.

(b) **Investing and Withdrawing Funds.** Money paid into court under this rule must be deposited and withdrawn in accordance with 28 U.S.C. §§ 2041 and 2042 and any like statute. The money must be deposited in an interest-bearing account or invested in a court-approved, interest-bearing instrument.

(Amended December 29, 1948, effective October 20, 1949; April 28, 1983, effective August 1, 1983; April 30, 2007, effective December 1, 2007.)

RULE 68.   OFFER OF JUDGMENT

(a) Making an Offer; Judgment on an Accepted Offer. At least 14 days before the date set for trial, a party defending against a claim may serve on an opposing party an offer to allow judgment on specified terms, with the costs then accrued. If, within 14 days after being served, the opposing party serves written notice accepting the offer, either party may then file the offer and notice of acceptance, plus proof of service. The clerk must then enter judgment.

(b) Unaccepted Offer. An unaccepted offer is considered withdrawn, but it does not preclude a later offer. Evidence of an unaccepted offer is not admissible except in a proceeding to determine costs.

(c) Offer After Liability is Determined. When one party's liability to another has been determined but the extent of liability remains to be determined by further proceedings, the party held liable may make an offer of judgment. It must be served within a reasonable time—but at least 14 days—before the date set for a hearing to determine the extent of liability.

(d) Paying Costs After an Unaccepted Offer. If the judgment that the offeree finally obtains is not more favorable than the unaccepted offer, the offeree must pay the costs incurred after the offer was made.

(Amended December 27, 1946, effective March 19, 1948; February 28, 1966, effective July 1, 1966; March 2, 1987, effective August 1, 1987; April 30, 2007, effective December 1, 2007; March 26, 2009, effective December 1, 2009.)

RULE 69.   EXECUTION

(a) In General.

(1) *Money Judgment; Applicable Procedure.* A money judgment is enforced by a writ of execution, unless the court directs otherwise. The procedure on execution—and in proceedings supplementary to and in aid of judgment or execution—must accord with the procedure of the state where the court is located, but a federal statute governs to the extent it applies.

(2) *Obtaining Discovery.* In aid of the judgment or execution, the judgment creditor or a successor in interest whose interest appears of record may obtain discovery from any person—including the judgment debtor—as provided in these rules or by the procedure of the state where the court is located.

(b) Against Certain Public Officers. When a judgment has been entered against a revenue officer in the circumstances stated in 28 U.S.C. § 2006, or against an officer of Congress in the circumstances stated in 2 U.S.C. § 118, the judgment must be satisfied as those statutes provide.

(Amended December 29, 1948, effective October 20, 1949; March 30, 1970, effective July 1, 1970; March 2, 1987 effective August 1, 1987; April 30, 2007, effective December 1, 2007.)

RULE 70.   ENFORCING A JUDGMENT FOR A SPECIFIC ACT

(a) Party's Failure to Act; Ordering Another to Act. If a judgment requires a party to convey land, to deliver a deed or other document, or to perform any other specific act and the party fails to comply within the time specified, the court may order the act to be done—at the disobedient party's expense—by another person appointed by the court. When done, the act has the same effect as if done by the party.

(b) Vesting Title. If the real or personal property is within the district, the court—instead of ordering a conveyance—may enter a judgment divesting any party's title and vesting it in others. That judgment has the effect of a legally executed conveyance.

(c) Obtaining a Writ of Attachment or Sequestration. On application by a party entitled to performance of an act, the clerk must issue a writ of attachment or sequestration against the disobedient party's property to compel obedience.

(d) Obtaining a Writ of Execution or Assistance. On application by a party who obtains a judgment or order for possession, the clerk must issue a writ of execution or assistance.

(e) Holding in Contempt. The court may also hold the disobedient party in contempt.

(Amended April 30, 2007, effective December 1, 2007.)

RULE 71.   ENFORCING RELIEF FOR OR AGAINST A NONPARTY

When an order grants relief for a nonparty or may be enforced against a nonparty, the procedure for enforcing the order is the same as for a party.

(Amended March 2, 1987, effective August 1, 1987; April 30, 2007, effective December 1, 2007.)

TITLE IX. SPECIAL PROCEEDINGS

RULE 71.1 CONDEMNING REAL OR PERSONAL PROPERTY

(a) Applicability of Other Rules. These rules govern proceedings to condemn real and personal property by eminent domain, except as this rule provides otherwise.

(b) Joinder of Properties. The plaintiff may join separate pieces of property in a single action, no matter whether they are owned by the same persons or sought for the same use.

(c) Complaint.

(1) *Caption.* The complaint must contain a caption as provided in Rule 10(a). The plaintiff must, however, name as defendants both the property—designated generally by kind, quantity, and location—and at least one owner of some part of or interest in the property.

(2) *Contents.* The complaint must contain a short and plain statement of the following:

  (A) the authority for the taking;

  (B) the uses for which the property is to be taken;

  (C) a description sufficient to identify the property;

  (D) the interests to be acquired; and

  (E) for each piece of property, a designation of each defendant who has been joined as an owner or owner of an interest in it.

(3) *Parties.* When the action commences, the plaintiff need join as defendants only those persons who have or claim an interest in the property and whose names are then known. But before any hearing on compensation, the plaintiff must add as defendants all those persons who have or claim an interest and whose names have become known or can be found by a reasonably diligent search of the records, considering both the property's character and value and the interests to be acquired. All others may be made defendants under the designation "Unknown Owners."

(4) *Procedure.* Notice must be served on all defendants as provided in Rule 71.1(d), whether they were named as defendants when the action commenced or were added later. A defendant may answer as provided in Rule 71.1(e). The court, meanwhile, may order any distribution of a deposit that the facts warrant.

(5) *Filing; Additional Copies.* In addition to filing the complaint, the plaintiff must give the clerk at least one copy for the defendants' use and additional copies at the request of the clerk or a defendant.

(d) Process.

(1) *Delivering Notice to the Clerk.* On filing a complaint, the plaintiff must promptly deliver to the clerk joint or several notices directed to the named defendants. When adding defendants, the plaintiff must deliver to the clerk additional notices directed to the new defendants.

(2) *Contents of the Notice.*

  (A) *Main Contents.* Each notice must name the court, the title of the action, and the defendant to whom it is directed. It must describe the property sufficiently to identify it, but need not describe any property other than that to be taken from the named defendant. The notice must also state:

    (i) that the action is to condemn property;

    (ii) the interest to be taken;

    (iii) the authority for the taking;

    (iv) the uses for which the property is to be taken;

    (v) that the defendant may serve an answer on the plaintiff's attorney within 21 days after being served with the notice;

    (vi) that the failure to so serve an answer constitutes consent to the taking and to the court's authority to proceed with the action and fix the compensation; and

    (vii) that a defendant who does not serve an answer may file a notice of appearance.

  (B) *Conclusion.* The notice must conclude with the name, telephone number, and e-mail address of the plaintiff's attorney and an address within the district in which the action is brought where the attorney may be served.

(3) *Serving the Notice.*

  (A) *Personal Service.* When a defendant whose address is known resides within the United States or a territory subject to the administrative or judicial jurisdiction of the United States, personal service of the notice (without a copy of the complaint) must be made in accordance with Rule 4.

  (B) *Service by Publication.*

    (i) A defendant may be served by publication only when the plaintiff's attorney files a certificate stating that the attorney believes the defendant cannot be personally served, because after diligent inquiry within the state where the complaint is filed, the defendant's place of residence is still unknown or, if known, that it is beyond the territorial limits of personal service. Service is then made by publishing the notice—once a week for at least 3 successive weeks—in a newspaper published in the county where the property is located or, if there is no such newspaper, in a newspaper with general circulation where the property is located. Before the last publication, a copy of the notice must also be mailed to every defendant who cannot be personally served but whose place of residence is then known. Unknown owners may be served by publication in the same manner by a notice addressed to "Unknown Owners."

    (ii) Service by publication is complete on the date of the last publication. The plaintiff's attorney must prove publication and mailing by a certificate, attach a printed copy of the published notice, and mark on the copy the newspaper's name and the dates of publication.

(4) *Effect of Delivery and Service.* Delivering the notice to the clerk and serving it have the same effect as serving a summons under Rule 4.

(5) *Amending the Notice; Proof of Service and Amending the Proof.* Rule 4(a)(2) governs amending the notice. Rule 4(*l*) governs proof of service and amending it.

(e) **Appearance or Answer.**

(1) *Notice of Appearance.* A defendant that has no objection or defense to the taking of its property may serve a notice of appearance designating the property in which it claims an interest. The defendant must then be given notice of all later proceedings affecting the defendant.

(2) *Answer.* A defendant that has an objection or defense to the taking must serve an answer within 21 days after being served with the notice. The answer must:

    (A) identify the property in which the defendant claims an interest;

    (B) state the nature and extent of the interest; and

    (C) state all the defendant's objections and defenses to the taking.

(3) *Waiver of Other Objections and Defenses; Evidence on Compensation.* A defendant waives all objections and defenses not stated in its answer. No other pleading or motion asserting an additional objection or defense is allowed. But at the trial on compensation, a defendant—whether or not it has previously appeared or answered—may present evidence on the amount of compensation to be paid and may share in the award.

(f) **Amending Pleadings.** Without leave of court, the plaintiff may—as often as it wants—amend the complaint at any time before the trial on compensation. But no amendment may be made if it would result in a dismissal inconsistent with Rule 71.1(i)(1) or (2). The plaintiff need not serve a copy of an amendment, but must serve notice of the filing, as provided in Rule 5(b), on every affected party who has appeared and, as provided in Rule 71.1(d), on every affected party who has not appeared. In addition, the plaintiff must give the clerk at least one copy of each amendment for the defendants' use, and additional copies at the request of the clerk or a defendant. A defendant may appear or answer in the time and manner and with the same effect as provided in Rule 71.1(e).

(g) **Substituting Parties.** If a defendant dies, becomes incompetent, or transfers an interest after being joined, the court may, on motion and notice of hearing, order that the proper party be substituted. Service of the motion and notice on a nonparty must be made as provided in Rule 71.1(d)(3).

(h) **Trial of the Issues.**

(1) *Issues Other Than Compensation; Compensation.* In an action involving eminent domain under federal law, the court tries all issues, including compensation, except when compensation must be determined:

    (A) by any tribunal specially constituted by a federal statute to determine compensation; or

    (B) if there is no such tribunal, by a jury when a party demands one within the time to answer or within any additional time the court sets, unless the court appoints a commission.

(2) *Appointing a Commission; Commission's Powers and Report.*

    (A) *Reasons for Appointing.* If a party has demanded a jury, the court may instead appoint a three-person commission to determine compensation because of the character, location, or quantity of the property to be condemned or for other just reasons.

    (B) *Alternate Commissioners.* The court may appoint up to two additional persons to serve as alternate commissioners to hear the case and replace commissioners who, before a decision is filed, the court finds unable or disqualified to perform their duties. Once the commission renders its final decision, the court must discharge any alternate who has not replaced a commissioner.

    (C) *Examining the Prospective Commissioners.* Before making its appointments, the court must advise the parties of the identity and qualifications of each prospective commissioner and alternate, and may permit the parties to examine them. The parties may not suggest appointees, but for good cause may object to a prospective commissioner or alternate.

(D) *Commission's Powers and Report.* A commission has the powers of a master under Rule 53(c). Its action and report are determined by a majority. Rule 53(d), (e), and (f) apply to its action and report.

(i) Dismissal of the Action or a Defendant.

(1) *Dismissing the Action.*

(A) *By the Plaintiff.* If no compensation hearing on a piece of property has begun, and if the plaintiff has not acquired title or a lesser interest or taken possession, the plaintiff may, without a court order, dismiss the action as to that property by filing a notice of dismissal briefly describing the property.

(B) *By Stipulation.* Before a judgment is entered vesting the plaintiff with title or a lesser interest in or possession of property, the plaintiff and affected defendants may, without a court order, dismiss the action in whole or in part by filing a stipulation of dismissal. And if the parties so stipulate, the court may vacate a judgment already entered.

(C) *By Court Order.* At any time before compensation has been determined and paid, the court may, after a motion and hearing, dismiss the action as to a piece of property. But if the plaintiff has already taken title, a lesser interest, or possession as to any part of it, the court must award compensation for the title, lesser interest, or possession taken.

(2) *Dismissing a Defendant.* The court may at any time dismiss a defendant who was unnecessarily or improperly joined.

(3) *Effect.* A dismissal is without prejudice unless otherwise stated in the notice, stipulation, or court order.

(j) Deposit and Its Distribution.

(1) *Deposit.* The plaintiff must deposit with the court any money required by law as a condition to the exercise of eminent domain and may make a deposit when allowed by statute.

(2) *Distribution; Adjusting Distribution.* After a deposit, the court and attorneys must expedite the proceedings so as to distribute the deposit and to determine and pay compensation. If the compensation finally awarded to a defendant exceeds the amount distributed to that defendant, the court must enter judgment against the plaintiff for the deficiency. If the compensation awarded to a defendant is less than the amount distributed to that defendant, the court must enter judgment against that defendant for the overpayment.

(k) Condemnation Under a State's Power of Eminent Domain. This rule governs an action involving eminent domain under state law. But if state law provides for trying an issue by jury—or for trying the issue of compensation by jury or commission or both—that law governs.

(*l*) Costs. Costs are not subject to Rule 54(d).

(Adopted April 30, 1951, effective August 1, 1951; amended January 21, 1963, effective July 1, 1963; April 29, 1985, effective August 1, 1985; March 2, 1987, effective August 1, 1987; April 25, 1988, effective August 1, 1988; amended by Pub.L. 100–690, Title VII, § 7050, November 18, 1988, 102 Stat. 4401 (although amendment by Pub.L. 100–690 could not be executed due to prior amendment by Court order which made the same change effective August 1, 1988); amended April 22, 1993, effective December 1, 1993; March 27, 2003, effective December 1, 2003; April 30, 2007, effective December 1, 2007; March 26, 2009, effective December 1, 2009.)

RULE 72. MAGISTRATE JUDGES: PRETRIAL ORDER

(a) Nondispositive Matters. When a pretrial matter not dispositive of a party's claim or defense is referred to a magistrate judge to hear and decide, the magistrate judge must promptly conduct the required proceedings and, when appropriate, issue a written order stating the decision. A party may serve and file objections to the order within 14 days after being served with a copy. A party may not assign as error a defect in the order not timely objected to. The district judge in the case must consider timely objections and modify or set aside any part of the order that is clearly erroneous or is contrary to law.

(b) Dispositive Motions and Prisoner Petitions.

(1) *Findings and Recommendations.* A magistrate judge must promptly conduct the required proceedings when assigned, without the parties' consent, to hear a pretrial matter dispositive of a claim or defense or a prisoner petition challenging the conditions of confinement. A record must be made of all evidentiary proceedings and may, at the magistrate judge's discretion, be made of any other proceedings. The magistrate judge must enter a recommended disposition, including, if appropriate, proposed findings of fact. The clerk must promptly mail a copy to each party.

(2) *Objections.* Within 14 days after being served with a copy of the recommended disposition, a party may serve and file specific written objections to the proposed findings and recommendations. A party may respond to another party's objections within 14 days after being served with a copy. Unless the district judge orders

otherwise, the objecting party must promptly arrange for transcribing the record, or whatever portions of it the parties agree to or the magistrate judge considers sufficient.

(3) *Resolving Objections.* The district judge must determine de novo any part of the magistrate judge's disposition that has been properly objected to. The district judge may accept, reject, or modify the recommended disposition; receive further evidence; or return the matter to the magistrate judge with instructions.

(Former Rule 72 abrogated December 4, 1967, effective July 1, 1968; new Rule 72 adopted April 28, 1983, effective August 1, 1983; amended April 30, 1991, effective December 1, 1991; April 22, 1993, effective December 1, 1993; April 30, 2007, effective December 1, 2007; March 26, 2009, effective December 1, 2009.)

RULE 73. MAGISTRATE JUDGES: TRIAL BY CONSENT; APPEAL

(a) **Trial by Consent.** When authorized under 28 U.S.C. § 636(c), a magistrate judge may, if all parties consent, conduct a civil action or proceeding, including a jury or nonjury trial. A record must be made in accordance with 28 U.S.C. § 636(c)(5).

(b) **Consent Procedure.**

(1) *In General.* When a magistrate judge has been designated to conduct civil actions or proceedings, the clerk must give the parties written notice of their opportunity to consent under 28 U.S.C. § 636(c). To signify their consent, the parties must jointly or separately file a statement consenting to the referral. A district judge or magistrate judge may be informed of a party's response to the clerk's notice only if all parties have consented to the referral.

(2) *Reminding the Parties About Consenting.* A district judge, magistrate judge, or other court official may remind the parties of the magistrate judge's availability, but must also advise them that they are free to withhold consent without adverse substantive consequences.

(3) *Vacating a Referral.* On its own for good cause—or when a party shows extraordinary circumstances—the district judge may vacate a referral to a magistrate judge under this rule.

(c) **Appealing a Judgment.** In accordance with 28 U.S.C. § 636(c)(3), an appeal from a judgment entered at a magistrate judge's direction may be taken to the court of appeals as would any other appeal from a district-court judgment.

(Former Rule 73 abrogated December 4, 1967, effective July 1, 1968; new Rule 73 adopted April 28, 1983, effective August 1, 1983; amended March 2, 1987, effective August 1, 1987; April 22, 1993, effective December 1, 1993; April 11, 1997, effective December 1, 1997; April 30, 2007, effective December 1, 2007.)

RULE 74. METHOD OF APPEAL FROM MAGISTRATE JUDGE TO DISTRICT JUDGE UNDER TITLE 28, U.S.C. § 636(c)(4) AND RULE 73(d) [ABROGATED]

(Former Rule 74 abrogated December 4, 1967, effective July 1, 1968; new Rule 74 adopted April 28, 1983, effective August 1, 1983; amended April 22, 1993, effective December 1, 1993; abrogated April 11, 1997, effective December 1, 1997; April 30, 2007, effective December 1, 2007.)

RULE 75. PROCEEDINGS ON APPEAL FROM MAGISTRATE JUDGE TO DISTRICT JUDGE UNDER RULE 73(d) [ABROGATED]

(Former Rule 75 abrogated December 4, 1967, effective July 1, 1968; new Rule 75 adopted April 28, 1983, effective August 1, 1983; amended March 2, 1987, effective August 1, 1987; April 22, 1993, effective December 1, 1993; abrogated April 11, 1997, effective December 1, 1997; April 30, 2007, effective December 1, 2007.)

TITLE X. DISTRICT COURTS AND CLERKS: CONDUCTING BUSINESS; ISSUING ORDERS

RULE 77. CONDUCTING BUSINESS; CLERK'S AUTHORITY; NOTICE OF AN ORDER OR JUDGMENT

(a) **When Court Is Open.** Every district court is considered always open for filing any paper, issuing and returning process, making a motion, or entering an order.

(b) **Place for Trial and Other Proceedings.** Every trial on the merits must be conducted in open court and, so far as convenient, in a regular courtroom. Any other act or proceeding may be done or conducted by a judge in chambers, without the attendance of the clerk or other court official, and anywhere inside or outside the district. But no hearing—other than one ex parte— may be conducted outside the district unless all the affected parties consent.

(c) Clerk's Office Hours; Clerk's Orders.

(1) *Hours.* The clerk's office—with a clerk or deputy on duty—must be open during business hours every day except Saturdays, Sundays, and legal holidays. But a court may, by local rule or order, require that the office be open for specified hours on Saturday or a particular legal holiday other than one listed in Rule 6(a)(6)(A).

(2) *Orders.* Subject to the court's power to suspend, alter, or rescind the clerk's action for good cause, the clerk may:

(A) issue process;

(B) enter a default;

(C) enter a default judgment under Rule 55(b)(1); and

(D) act on any other matter that does not require the court's action.

(d) Serving Notice of an Order or Judgment.

(1) *Service.* Immediately after entering an order or judgment, the clerk must serve notice of the entry, as provided in Rule 5(b), on each party who is not in default for failing to appear. The clerk must record the service on the docket. A party also may serve notice of the entry as provided in Rule 5(b).

(2) *Time to Appeal Not Affected by Lack of Notice.* Lack of notice of the entry does not affect the time for appeal or relieve—or authorize the court to relieve—a party for failing to appeal within the time allowed, except as allowed by Federal Rule of Appellate Procedure (4)(a).

(Amended December 27, 1946, effective March 19, 1948; January 21, 1963, effective July 1, 1963; December 4, 1967, effective July 1, 1968; March 1, 1971, effective July 1, 1971; March 2, 1987, effective August 1, 1987; April 30, 1991, effective December 1, 1991; April 23, 2001, effective December 1, 2001; April 30, 2007, effective December 1, 2007; April 25, 2014, effective December 1, 2014.)

RULE 78. HEARING MOTIONS; SUBMISSION ON BRIEFS

(a) Providing a Regular Schedule for Oral Hearings. A court may establish regular times and places for oral hearings on motions.

(b) Providing for Submission on Briefs. By rule or order, the court may provide for submitting and determining motions on briefs, without oral hearings.

(Amended March 2, 1987, effective August 1, 1987; April 30, 2007, effective December 1, 2007.)

RULE 79. RECORDS KEPT BY THE CLERK

(a) Civil Docket.

(1) *In General.* The clerk must keep a record known as the "civil docket" in the form and manner prescribed by the Director of the Administrative Office of the United States Courts with the approval of the Judicial Conference of the United States. The clerk must enter each civil action in the docket. Actions must be assigned consecutive file numbers, which must be noted in the docket where the first entry of the action is made.

(2) *Items to be Entered.* The following items must be marked with the file number and entered chronologically in the docket:

(A) papers filed with the clerk;

(B) process issued, and proofs of service or other returns showing execution; and

(C) appearances, orders, verdicts, and judgments.

(3) *Contents of Entries; Jury Trial Demanded.* Each entry must briefly show the nature of the paper filed or writ issued, the substance of each proof of service or other return, and the substance and date of entry of each order and judgment. When a jury trial has been properly demanded or ordered, the clerk must enter the word "jury" in the docket.

(b) Civil Judgments and Orders. The clerk must keep a copy of every final judgment and appealable order; of every order affecting title to or a lien on real or personal property; and of any other order that the court directs to be kept. The clerk must keep these in the form and manner prescribed by the Director of the Administrative Office of the United States Courts with the approval of the Judicial Conference of the United States.

(c) Indexes; Calendars. Under the court's direction, the clerk must:

(1) keep indexes of the docket and of the judgments and orders described in Rule 79(b); and

(2) prepare calendars of all actions ready for trial, distinguishing jury trials from nonjury trials.

(d) Other Records. The clerk must keep any other records required by the Director of the Administrative Office of the United States Courts with the approval of the Judicial Conference of the United States.

(Amended December 27, 1946, effective March 19, 1948; December 29, 1948, effective October 20, 1949; January 21, 1963, effective July 1, 1963; April 30, 2007, effective December 1, 2007.)

RULE 80. STENOGRAPHIC TRANSCRIPT AS EVIDENCE

If stenographically reported testimony at a hearing or trial is admissible in evidence at a later trial, the testimony may be proved by a transcript certified by the person who reported it.

(Amended December 27, 1946, effective March 19, 1948; April 30, 2007, effective December 1, 2007.)

TITLE XI. GENERAL PROVISIONS

RULE 81. APPLICABILITY OF THE RULES IN GENERAL; REMOVED ACTIONS

(a) Applicability to Particular Proceedings.

(1) *Prize Proceedings.* These rules do not apply to prize proceedings in admiralty governed by 10 U.S.C. §§ 7651–7681.

(2) *Bankruptcy.* These rules apply to bankruptcy proceedings to the extent provided by the Federal Rules of Bankruptcy Procedure.

(3) *Citizenship.* These rules apply to proceedings for admission to citizenship to the extent that the practice in those proceedings is not specified in federal statutes and has previously conformed to the practice in civil actions. The provisions of 8 U.S.C. § 1451 for service by publication and for answer apply in proceedings to cancel citizenship certificates.

(4) *Special Writs.* These rules apply to proceedings for habeas corpus and for quo warranto to the extent that the practice in those proceedings:

(A) is not specified in a federal statute, the Rules Governing Section 2254 Cases, or the Rules Governing Section 2255 Cases; and

(B) has previously conformed to the practice in civil actions.

(5) *Proceedings Involving a Subpoena.* These rules apply to proceedings to compel testimony or the production of documents through a subpoena issued by a United States officer or agency under a federal statute, except as otherwise provided by statute, by local rule, or by court order in the proceedings.

(6) *Other Proceedings.* These rules, to the extent applicable, govern proceedings under the following laws, except as these laws provide other procedures:

(A) 7 U.S.C. §§ 292, 499g(c), for reviewing an order of the Secretary of Agriculture;

(B) 9 U.S.C., relating to arbitration;

(C) 15 U.S.C. § 522, for reviewing an order of the Secretary of the Interior;

(D) 15 U.S.C. § 715d(c), for reviewing an order denying a certificate of clearance;

(E) 29 U.S.C. §§ 159, 160, for enforcing an order of the National Labor Relations Board;

(F) 33 U.S.C. §§ 918, 921, for enforcing or reviewing a compensation order under the Longshore and Harbor Workers' Compensation Act; and

(G) 45 U.S.C. § 159, for reviewing an arbitration award in a railway-labor dispute.

(b) Scire Facias and Mandamus. The writs of scire facias and mandamus are abolished. Relief previously available through them may be obtained by appropriate action or motion under these rules.

(c) Removed Actions.

(1) *Applicability.* These rules apply to a civil action after it is removed from a state court.

(2) *Further Pleading.* After removal, repleading is unnecessary unless the court orders it. A defendant who did not answer before removal must answer or present other defenses or objections under these rules within the longest of these periods:

(A) 21 days after receiving—through service or otherwise—a copy of the initial pleading stating the claim for relief;

(B) 21 days after being served with the summons for an initial pleading on file at the time of service; or

(C) 7 days after the notice of removal is filed.

(3) *Demand for a Jury Trial.*

(A) *As Affected by State Law.* A party who, before removal, expressly demanded a jury trial in accordance with state law need not renew the demand after removal. If the state law did not require an express demand for a jury trial, a party need not make one after removal unless the court orders the parties to do so within a specified time. The court must so order at a party's request and may so order on its own. A party who fails to make a demand when so ordered waives a jury trial.

(B) *Under Rule 38.* If all necessary pleadings have been served at the time of removal, a party entitled to a jury trial under Rule 38 must be given one if the party serves a demand within 14 days after:

(i) it files a notice of removal; or

(ii) it is served with a notice of removal filed by another party.

(d) Law Applicable.

(1) *"State Law" Defined.* When these rules refer to state law, the term "law" includes the state's statutes and the state's judicial decisions.

(2) *"State" Defined.* The term "state" includes, where appropriate, the District of Columbia and any United States commonwealth or territory.

(3) *"Federal Statute" Defined in the District of Columbia.* In the United States District Court for the District of Columbia, the term "federal statute" includes any Act of Congress that applies locally to the District.

(Amended December 28, 1939, effective April 3, 1941; December 27, 1946, effective March 19, 1948; December 29, 1948, effective October 20, 1949; April 30, 1951, effective August 1, 1951; January 21, 1963, effective July 1, 1963; February 28, 1966, effective July 1, 1966; December 4, 1967, effective July 1, 1968; March 1, 1971, effective July 1, 1971; March 2, 1987, effective August 1, 1987; April 23, 2001, effective December 1, 2001; April 29, 2002, effective December 1, 2002; April 30, 2007, effective December 1, 2007; March 26, 2009, effective December 1, 2009.)

RULE 82. JURISDICTION AND VENUE UNAFFECTED

These rules do not extend or limit the jurisdiction of the district courts or the venue of actions in those courts. An admiralty or maritime claim under Rule 9(h) is not a civil action for purposes of 28 U.S.C. §§ 1391–1392.

(Amended December 29, 1948, effective October 20, 1949; February 28, 1966, effective July 1, 1966; April 23, 2001, effective December 1, 2001; April 30, 2007, effective December 1, 2007.)

RULE 83. RULES BY DISTRICT COURTS; JUDGE'S DIRECTIVES

(a) Local Rules.

(1) *In General.* After giving public notice and an opportunity for comment, a district court, acting by a majority of its district judges, may adopt and amend rules governing its practice. A local rule must be consistent with—but not duplicate—federal statutes and rules adopted under 28 U.S.C. §§ 2072 and 2075, and must conform to any uniform numbering system prescribed by the Judicial Conference of the United States. A local rule takes effect on the date specified by the district court and remains in effect unless amended by the court or abrogated by the judicial council of the circuit. Copies of rules and amendments must, on their adoption, be furnished to the judicial council and the Administrative Office of the United States Courts and be made available to the public.

(2) *Requirement of Form.* A local rule imposing a requirement of form must not be enforced in a way that causes a party to lose any right because of a nonwillful failure to comply.

(b) Procedure When There Is No Controlling Law. A judge may regulate practice in any manner consistent with federal law, rules adopted under 28 U.S.C. §§ 2072 and 2075, and the district's local rules. No sanction or other disadvantage may be imposed for noncompliance with any requirement not in federal law, federal rules, or the local rules unless the alleged violator has been furnished in the particular case with actual notice of the requirement.

(Amended April 29, 1985, effective August 1, 1985; April 27, 1995, effective December 1, 1995; April 30, 2007, effective December 1, 2007.)

RULE 84. FORMS

[Text of Rule 84 effective until December 1, 2015, absent contrary Congressional action.]

The forms in the Appendix suffice under these rules and illustrate the simplicity and brevity that these rules contemplate.

[Text of Rule 84 effective December 1, 2015, absent contrary Congressional action.]

[Abrogated (Apr. ___, 2015, eff. Dec. 1, 2015).]

(Amended December 27, 1946, effective March 19, 1948; April 30, 2007, effective December 1, 2007; April 29, 2015, effective December 1, 2015, absent contrary Congressional action.)

RULE 85. TITLE

These rules may be cited as the Federal Rules of Civil Procedure.

(Amended April 30, 2007, effective December 1, 2007.)

RULE 86. EFFECTIVE DATES

(a) In General. These rules and any amendments take effect at the time specified by the Supreme Court, subject to 28 U.S.C. § 2074. They govern:

(1) proceedings in an action commenced after their effective date; and

(2) proceedings after that date in an action then pending unless:

(A) the Supreme Court specifies otherwise; or

(B) the court determines that applying them in a particular action would be infeasible or work an injustice.

(b) December 1, 2007 Amendments. If any provision in Rules 1–5.1, 6–73, or 77–86 conflicts with another law, priority in time for the purpose of 28 U.S.C. § 2072(b) is not affected by the amendments taking effect on December 1, 2007.

(Amended December 27, 1946, effective March 19, 1948; December 29, 1948, effective October 20, 1949; April 17, 1961, effective July 19, 1961; January 21, 1963, and March 18, 1963, effective July 1, 1963; April 30, 2007, effective December 1, 2007.)

APPENDIX OF FORMS

(See Rule 84)

FORM 1. CAPTION

*[Absent contrary Congressional action, Form 1 will
be abrogated effective December 1, 2015.]*

(Use on every summons, complaint, answer, motion, or other document.)

United States District Court
for the
———— District of ————

A B, Plaintiff	)
	)
v.	)
	) Civil Action No. ————
C D, Defendant	)
	)
v.	)
	)
E F, Third–Party Defendant	)
(Use if needed.)	)

(Name of Document)

(Added Apr. 30, 2007, eff. Dec. 1, 2007. Abrogated eff. Dec. 1, 2015, absent contrary Congressional action.)

FORM 2. DATE, SIGNATURE, ADDRESS, E–MAIL ADDRESS, AND TELEPHONE NUMBER

[Absent contrary Congressional action, Form 2 will be abrogated effective December 1, 2015.]

(Use at the conclusion of pleadings and other papers that require a signature.)

Date _____

_____

(Signature of the attorney or unrepresented party)

_____

(Printed name)

_____

(Address)

_____

(E-mail address)

_____

(Telephone number)

(Added Apr. 30, 2007, eff. Dec. 1, 2007. Abrogated eff. Dec. 1, 2015, absent contrary Congressional action.)

FORM 3.   SUMMONS

*[Absent contrary Congressional action, Form 3 will
be abrogated effective December 1, 2015.]*

(Caption—See Form 1.)

To *name the defendant*:

A lawsuit has been filed against you.

Within 21 days after service of this summons on you (not counting the day you received it), you must serve on the plaintiff an answer to the attached complaint or a motion under Rule 12 of the Federal Rules of Civil Procedure. The answer or motion must be served on the plaintiff's attorney, _____, whose address is _____. If you fail to do so, judgment by default will be entered against you for the relief demanded in the complaint. You also must file your answer or motion with the court.

Date _____

_____

Clerk of Court

(Court Seal)

(Use 60 days if the defendant is the United States or a United States agency, or is an officer or employee of the United States allowed 60 days by Rule 12(a)(3).)

(Added Apr. 30, 2007, eff. Dec. 1, 2007; amended Mar. 26, 2009, eff. Dec. 1, 2009. Abrogated eff. Dec. 1, 2015, absent contrary Congressional action.)

FORM 4. SUMMONS ON A THIRD-PARTY COMPLAINT

*[Absent contrary Congressional action, Form 4 will
be abrogated effective December 1, 2015.]*

(Caption—See Form 1.)

To *name the third-party defendant*:

A lawsuit has been filed against defendant _____, who as third-party plaintiff is making this claim against you to pay part or all of what [he] may owe to the plaintiff _____.

Within 21 days after service of this summons on you (not counting the day you received it), you must serve on the plaintiff and on the defendant an answer to the attached third-party complaint or a motion under Rule 12 of the Federal Rules of Civil Procedure. The answer or motion must be served on the defendant's attorney, _____, whose address is, _____, and also on the plaintiff's attorney, _____, whose address is, _____. If you fail to do so, judgment by default will be entered against you for the relief demanded in the third-party complaint. You also must file the answer or motion with the court and serve it on any other parties.

A copy of the plaintiff's complaint is also attached. You may—but are not required to—respond to it.

Date _____

_____

Clerk of Court

(Court Seal)

(Added Apr. 30, 2007, eff. Dec. 1, 2007; amended Mar. 26, 2009, eff. Dec. 1, 2009. Abrogated eff. Dec. 1, 2015, absent contrary Congressional action.)

FORM 5. NOTICE OF A LAWSUIT AND REQUEST TO WAIVE SERVICE OF A SUMMONS

[Absent contrary Congressional action, Form 5 will be abrogated effective December 1, 2015 and the text of the form will be directly incorporated into Rule 4.]

(Caption—See Form 1.)

To *(name the defendant—or if the defendant is a corporation, partnership, or association name an officer or agent authorized to receive service)*:

Why are you getting this?

A lawsuit has been filed against you, or the entity you represent, in this court under the number shown above. A copy of the complaint is attached.

This is not a summons, or an official notice from the court. It is a request that, to avoid expenses, you waive formal service of a summons by signing and returning the enclosed waiver. To avoid these expenses, you must return the signed waiver within *(give at least 30 days or at least 60 days if the defendant is outside any judicial district of the United States)* from the date shown below, which is the date this notice was sent. Two copies of the waiver form are enclosed, along with a stamped, self-addressed envelope or other prepaid means for returning one copy. You may keep the other copy.

What happens next?

If you return the signed waiver, I will file it with the court. The action will then proceed as if you had been served on the date the waiver is filed, but no summons will be served on you and you will have 60 days from the date this notice is sent (see the date below) to answer the complaint (or 90 days if this notice is sent to you outside any judicial district of the United States).

If you do not return the signed waiver within the time indicated, I will arrange to have the summons and complaint served on you. And I will ask the court to require you, or the entity you represent, to pay the expenses of making service.

Please read the enclosed statement about the duty to avoid unnecessary expenses.

I certify that this request is being sent to you on the date below.

(Date and sign—See Form 2.)

(Added Apr. 30, 2007, eff. Dec. 1, 2007. Abrogated eff. Dec. 1, 2015, absent contrary Congressional action.)

FORM 6. WAIVER OF THE SERVICE OF SUMMONS

[Absent contrary Congressional action, Form 6 will be abrogated effective December 1, 2015 and the text of the form will be directly incorporated into Rule 4.]

(Caption—See Form 1.)

To *name the plaintiff's attorney or the unrepresented plaintiff*:

I have received your request to waive service of a summons in this action along with a copy of the complaint, two copies of this waiver form, and a prepaid means of returning one signed copy of the form to you.

I, or the entity I represent, agree to save the expense of serving a summons and complaint in this case.

I understand that I, or the entity I represent, will keep all defenses or objections to the lawsuit, the court's jurisdiction, and the venue of the action, but that I waive any objections to the absence of a summons or of service.

I also understand that I, or the entity I represent, must file and serve an answer or a motion under Rule 12 within 60 days from _____, the date when this request was sent (or 90 days if it was sent outside the United States). If I fail to do so, a default judgment will be entered against me or the entity I represent.

(Date and sign—See Form 2.)

(Attach the following to Form 6.)

Duty to Avoid Unnecessary Expenses of Serving a Summons

Rule 4 of the Federal Rules of Civil Procedure requires certain defendants to cooperate in saving unnecessary expenses of serving a summons and complaint. A defendant who is located in the United States and who fails to return a signed waiver of service requested by a plaintiff located in the United States will be required to pay the expenses of service, unless the defendant shows good cause for the failure.

"Good cause" does *not* include a belief that the lawsuit is groundless, or that it has been brought in an improper venue, or that the court has no jurisdiction over this matter or over the defendant or the defendant's property.

If the waiver is signed and returned, you can still make these and all other defenses and objections, but you cannot object to the absence of a summons or of service.

If you waive service, then you must, within the time specified on the waiver form, serve an answer or a motion under Rule 12 on the plaintiff and file a copy with the court. By signing and returning the waiver form, you are allowed more time to respond than if a summons had been served.

(Added Apr. 30, 2007, eff. Dec. 1, 2007. Abrogated eff. Dec. 1, 2015, absent contrary Congressional action.)

FORM 7. STATEMENT OF JURISDICTION

*[Absent contrary Congressional action, Form 7 will
be abrogated effective December 1, 2015.]*

a.   *(For diversity-of-citizenship jurisdiction.)* The plaintiff is [a citizen of *Michigan*] [a corporation incorporated under the laws of *Michigan* with its principal place of business in *Michigan*]. The defendant is [a citizen of *New York*] [a corporation incorporated under the laws of *New York* with its principal place of business in *New York*]. The amount in controversy, without interest and costs, exceeds the sum or value specified by 28 U.S.C. § 1332.

b.   *(For federal-question jurisdiction.)* This action arises under [the United States Constitution, *specify the article or amendment and the section*] [a United States treaty *specify*] [a federal statute, ___ U.S.C. § ___].

c.   *(For a claim in the admiralty or maritime jurisdiction.)* This is a case of admiralty or maritime jurisdiction. *(To invoke admiralty status under Rule 9(h) use the following:* This is an admiralty or maritime claim within the meaning of Rule 9(h).)

(Added Apr. 30, 2007, eff. Dec. 1, 2007. Abrogated eff. Dec. 1, 2015, absent contrary Congressional action.)

FORM 8. STATEMENT OF REASONS FOR OMITTING A PARTY

*[Absent contrary Congressional action, Form 8 will
be abrogated effective December 1, 2015.]*

*(If a person who ought to be made a party under Rule 19(a) is not named, include
this statement in accordance with Rule 19(c).)*

This complaint does not join as a party *name* who [is not subject to this court's personal jurisdiction] [cannot be made a party without depriving this court of subject-matter jurisdiction] because *state the reason.*

(Added Apr. 30, 2007, eff. Dec. 1, 2007. Abrogated eff. Dec. 1, 2015, absent contrary Congressional action.)

FORM 9. STATEMENT NOTING A PARTY'S DEATH

*[Absent contrary Congressional action, Form 9 will
be abrogated effective December 1, 2015.]*

(Caption—See Form 1.)

In accordance with Rule 25(a) *name the person,* who is [a party to this action] [a representative of or successor to the deceased party] notes the death during the pendency of this action of *name,* [*describe as party* in this action].

(Date and sign—See Form 2.)

(Added Apr. 30, 2007, eff. Dec. 1, 2007. Abrogated eff. Dec. 1, 2015, absent contrary Congressional action.)

FORM 10. COMPLAINT TO RECOVER A SUM CERTAIN

*[Absent contrary Congressional action, Form 10 will
be abrogated effective December 1, 2015.]*

(Caption—See Form 1.)

1. (Statement of Jurisdiction—See Form 7.)

(Use one or more of the following as appropriate and include a demand for judgment.)

(a) On a Promissory Note

2. On *date,* the defendant executed and delivered a note promising to pay the plaintiff on *date* the sum of $_____ with interest at the rate of ___ percent. A copy of the note [is attached as Exhibit A] [is summarized as follows: _____.]

3. The defendant has not paid the amount owed.

(b) On an Account

2. The defendant owes the plaintiff $_____ according to the account set out in Exhibit A.

(c) For Goods Sold and Delivered

2. The defendant owes the plaintiff $_____ for goods sold and delivered by the plaintiff to the defendant from *date* to *date*.

(d) For Money Lent

2. The defendant owes the plaintiff $_____ for money lent by the plaintiff to the defendant on *date*.

(e) For Money Paid by Mistake

2. The defendant owes the plaintiff $_____ for money paid by mistake to the defendant on *date* under these circumstances: *describe with particularity in accordance with Rule 9(b).*

(f) For Money Had and Received

2. The defendant owes the plaintiff $_____ for money that was received from *name* on *date* to be paid by the defendant to the plaintiff.

Demand for Judgment

Therefore, the plaintiff demands judgment against the defendant for $_____, plus interest and costs.

(Date and sign—See Form 2.)

(Added Apr. 30, 2007, eff. Dec. 1, 2007. Abrogated eff. Dec. 1, 2015, absent contrary Congressional action.)

FORM 11. COMPLAINT FOR NEGLIGENCE

*[Absent contrary Congressional action, Form 11 will
be abrogated effective December 1, 2015.]*

(Caption—See Form 1.)

1. (Statement of Jurisdiction—See Form 7.)

2. On *date*, at *place*, the defendant negligently drove a motor vehicle against the plaintiff.

3. As a result, the plaintiff was physically injured, lost wages or income, suffered physical and mental pain, and incurred medical expenses of $_____.

Therefore, the plaintiff demands judgment against the defendant for $_____, plus costs.

(Date and sign—See Form 2).

(Added Apr. 30, 2007, eff. Dec. 1, 2007. Abrogated eff. Dec. 1, 2015, absent contrary Congressional action.)

FORM 12.   COMPLAINT FOR NEGLIGENCE WHEN THE PLAINTIFF DOES NOT KNOW WHO IS RESPONSIBLE

[Absent contrary Congressional action, Form 12 will be abrogated effective December 1, 2015.]

(Caption—See Form 1.)

1.   (Statement of Jurisdiction—See Form 7.)

2.   On *date*, at *place*, defendant *name* or defendant *name* or both of them willfully or recklessly or negligently drove, or caused to be driven, a motor vehicle against the plaintiff.

3.   As a result, the plaintiff was physically injured, lost wages or income, suffered mental and physical pain, and incurred medical expenses of $_____.

Therefore, the plaintiff demands judgment against one or both defendants for $_____, plus costs.

(Date and sign—See Form 2.)

(Added Apr. 30, 2007, eff. Dec. 1, 2007.   Abrogated eff. Dec. 1, 2015, absent contrary Congressional action.)

FORM 13. COMPLAINT FOR NEGLIGENCE UNDER THE FEDERAL EMPLOYERS' LIABILITY ACT

[Absent contrary Congressional action, Form 13 will be abrogated effective December 1, 2015.]

(Caption—See Form 1.)

1. (Statement of Jurisdiction—See Form 7.)

2. At the times below, the defendant owned and operated in interstate commerce a railroad line that passed through a tunnel located at _____.

3. On *date*, the plaintiff was working to repair and enlarge the tunnel to make it convenient and safe for use in interstate commerce.

4. During this work, the defendant, as the employer, negligently put the plaintiff to work in a section of the tunnel that the defendant had left unprotected and unsupported.

5. The defendant's negligence caused the plaintiff to be injured by a rock that fell from an unsupported portion of the tunnel.

6. As a result, the plaintiff was physically injured, lost wages or income, suffered mental and physical pain, and incurred medical expenses of $_____.

Therefore, the plaintiff demands judgment against the defendant for $_____, and costs.

(Date and sign—See Form 2.)

(Added Apr. 30, 2007, eff. Dec. 1, 2007. Abrogated eff. Dec. 1, 2015, absent contrary Congressional action.)

FORM 14. COMPLAINT FOR DAMAGES UNDER THE MERCHANT MARINE ACT

[Absent contrary Congressional action, Form 14 will be abrogated effective December 1, 2015.]

(Caption—See Form 1.)

1. (Statement of Jurisdiction—See Form 7.)

2. At the times below, the defendant owned and operated the vessel *name* and used it to transport cargo for hire by water in interstate and foreign commerce.

3. On *date*, at *place*, the defendant hired the plaintiff under seamen's articles of customary form for a voyage from _____ to _____ and return at a wage of $_____ a month and found, which is equal to a shore worker's wage of $_____ a month.

4. On *date*, the vessel was at sea on the return voyage. (*Describe the weather and the condition of the vessel.*)

5. (*Describe as in Form 11 the defendant's negligent conduct.*)

6. As a result of the defendant's negligent conduct and the unseaworthiness of the vessel, the plaintiff was physically injured, has been incapable of any gainful activity, suffered mental and physical pain, and has incurred medical expenses of $_____.

Therefore, the plaintiff demands judgment against the defendant for $_____, plus costs.

(Date and sign—See Form 2.)

(Added Apr. 30, 2007, eff. Dec. 1, 2007. Abrogated eff. Dec. 1, 2015, absent contrary Congressional action.)

FORM 15. COMPLAINT FOR THE CONVERSION OF PROPERTY

*[Absent contrary Congressional action, Form 15 will
be abrogated effective December 1, 2015.]*

(Caption—See Form 1.)

1. (Statement of Jurisdiction—See Form 7.)

2. On *date*, at *place*, the defendant converted to the defendant's own use property owned by the plaintiff. The property converted consists of *describe*.

3. The property is worth $_____.

Therefore, the plaintiff demands judgment against the defendant for $_____, plus costs.

(Date and sign—See Form 2.)

(Added Apr. 30, 2007, eff. Dec. 1, 2007. Abrogated eff. Dec. 1, 2015, absent contrary Congressional action.)

FORM 16. THIRD–PARTY COMPLAINT

*[Absent contrary Congressional action, Form 16 will
be abrogated effective December 1, 2015.]*

(Caption—See Form 1.)

1. Plaintiff *name* has filed against defendant *name* a complaint, a copy of which
    is attached.

2. *(State grounds entitling defendant's name to recover from third-party defen-
    dant's name for (all or an identified share) of any judgment for plaintiff's
    name against defendant's name.)*

Therefore, the defendant demands judgment against *third-party defendant's
name* for *all or an identified share* of sums that may be adjudged against the
defendant in the plaintiff's favor.

(Date and sign—See Form 2.)

(Added Apr. 30, 2007, eff. Dec. 1, 2007. Abrogated eff. Dec. 1, 2015, absent contrary
Congressional action.)

FORM 17. COMPLAINT FOR SPECIFIC PERFORMANCE OF A CONTRACT TO CONVEY LAND

*[Absent contrary Congressional action, Form 17 will
be abrogated effective December 1, 2015.]*

(Caption—See Form 1.)

1. (Statement of Jurisdiction—See Form 7.)

2. On *date*, the parties agreed to the contract [attached as Exhibit A][summarize the contract].

3. As agreed, the plaintiff tendered the purchase price and requested a conveyance of the land, but the defendant refused to accept the money or make a conveyance.

4. The plaintiff now offers to pay the purchase price.

Therefore, the plaintiff demands that:

    (a) the defendant be required to specifically perform the agreement and pay damages of $_____, plus interest and costs, or

    (b) if specific performance is not ordered, the defendant be required to pay damages of $_____, plus interest and costs.

(Date and sign—See Form 2.)

(Added Apr. 30, 2007, eff. Dec. 1, 2007. Abrogated eff. Dec. 1, 2015, absent contrary Congressional action.)

FORM 18. COMPLAINT FOR PATENT INFRINGEMENT

*[Absent contrary Congressional action, Form 18 will
be abrogated effective December 1, 2015.]*

(Caption—See Form 1.)

1. (Statement of Jurisdiction—See Form 7.)

2. On *date*, United States Letters Patent No. _____ were issued to the plaintiff for an invention in an *electric motor*. The plaintiff owned the patent throughout the period of the defendant's infringing acts and still owns the patent.

3. The defendant has infringed and is still infringing the Letters Patent by making, selling, and using *electric motors* that embody the patented invention, and the defendant will continue to do so unless enjoined by this court.

4. The plaintiff has complied with the statutory requirement of placing a notice of the Letters Patent on all *electric motors* it manufactures and sells and has given the defendant written notice of the infringement.

Therefore, the plaintiff demands:

   (a) a preliminary and final injunction against the continuing infringement;

   (b) an accounting for damages; and

   (c) interest and costs.

(Date and sign—See Form 2.)

(Added Apr. 30, 2007, eff. Dec. 1, 2007. Abrogated eff. Dec. 1, 2015, absent contrary Congressional action.)

FORM 19.　COMPLAINT FOR COPYRIGHT INFRINGEMENT AND UNFAIR COMPETITION

[Absent contrary Congressional action, Form 19 will be abrogated effective December 1, 2015.]

(Caption—See Form 1.)

1. (Statement of Jurisdiction—See Form 7.)

2. Before *date*, the plaintiff, a United States citizen, wrote a book entitled _____.

3. The book is an original work that may be copyrighted under United States law. A copy of the book is attached as Exhibit A.

4. Between *date* and *date*, the plaintiff applied to the copyright office and received a certificate of registration dated _____ and identified as *date, class, number*.

5. Since *date*, the plaintiff has either published or licensed for publication all copies of the book in compliance with the copyright laws and has remained the sole owner of the copyright.

6. After the copyright was issued, the defendant infringed the copyright by publishing and selling a book entitled _____, which was copied largely from the plaintiff's book. A copy of the defendant's book is attached as Exhibit B.

7. The plaintiff has notified the defendant in writing of the infringement.

8. The defendant continues to infringe the copyright by continuing to publish and sell the infringing book in violation of the copyright, and further has engaged in unfair trade practices and unfair competition in connection with its publication and sale of the infringing book, thus causing irreparable damage.

Therefore, the plaintiff demands that:

(a) until this case is decided the defendant and the defendant's agents be enjoined from disposing of any copies of the defendant's book by sale or otherwise;

(b) the defendant account for and pay as damages to the plaintiff all profits and advantages gained from unfair trade practices and unfair competition in selling the defendant's book, and all profits and advantages gained from infringing the plaintiff's copyright (but no less than the statutory minimum);

(c) the defendant deliver for impoundment all copies of the book in the defendant's possession or control and deliver for destruction all infringing copies and all plates, molds, and other materials for making infringing copies;

(d) the defendant pay the plaintiff interest, costs, and reasonable attorney's fees; and

(e) the plaintiff be awarded any other just relief.

(Date and sign—See Form 2.)

(Added Apr. 30, 2007, eff. Dec. 1, 2007. Abrogated eff. Dec. 1, 2015, absent contrary Congressional action.)

FORM 20. COMPLAINT FOR INTERPLEADER AND DECLARATORY RELIEF

[Absent contrary Congressional action, Form 20 will be abrogated effective December 1, 2015.]

(Caption—See Form 1.)

1. (Statement of Jurisdiction—See Form 7.)

2. On *date*, the plaintiff issued a life insurance policy on the life of *name* with *name* as the named beneficiary.

3. As a condition for keeping the policy in force, the policy required payment of a premium during the first year and then annually.

4. The premium due on *date* was never paid, and the policy lapsed after that date.

5. On *date*, after the policy had lapsed, both the insured and the named beneficiary died in an automobile collision.

6. Defendant *name* claims to be the beneficiary in place of *name* and has filed a claim to be paid the policy's full amount.

7. The other two defendants are representatives of the deceased persons' estates. Each defendant has filed a claim on behalf of each estate to receive payment of the policy's full amount.

8. If the policy was in force at the time of death, the plaintiff is in doubt about who should be paid.

Therefore, the plaintiff demands that:

(a) each defendant be restrained from commencing any action against the plaintiff on the policy;

(b) a judgment be entered that no defendant is entitled to the proceeds of the policy or any part of it, but if the court determines that the policy was in effect at the time of the insured's death, that the defendants be required to interplead and settle among themselves their rights to the proceeds, and that the plaintiff be discharged from all liability except to the defendant determined to be entitled to the proceeds; and

(c) the plaintiff recover its costs.

(Date and sign—See Form 2.)

(Added Apr. 30, 2007, eff. Dec. 1, 2007. Abrogated eff. Dec. 1, 2015, absent contrary Congressional action.)

FORM 21. COMPLAINT ON A CLAIM FOR A DEBT AND TO SET ASIDE A FRAUDULENT CONVEYANCE UNDER RULE 18(b)

[Absent contrary Congressional action, Form 21 will be abrogated effective December 1, 2015.]

(Caption—See Form 1.)

1. (Statement of Jurisdiction—See Form 7.)

2. On *date*, defendant *name* signed a note promising to pay to the plaintiff on *date* the sum of $_____ with interest at the rate of ___ percent. [The pleader may, but need not, attach a copy or plead the note verbatim.]

3. Defendant *name* owes the plaintiff the amount of the note and interest.

4. On *date*, defendant *name* conveyed all defendant's real and personal property *if less than all, describe it fully* to defendant *name* for the purpose of defrauding the plaintiff and hindering or delaying the collection of the debt.

Therefore, the plaintiff demands that:

    (a) judgment for $_____, plus costs, be entered against defendant(s) *name(s)*; and

    (b) the conveyance to defendant *name* be declared void and any judgment granted be made a lien on the property.

(Date and sign—See Form 2.)

(Added Apr. 30, 2007, eff. Dec. 1, 2007. Abrogated eff. Dec. 1, 2015, absent contrary Congressional action.)

FORM 30.   ANSWER PRESENTING DEFENSES UNDER RULE 12(b)

*[Absent contrary Congressional action, Form 30 will
be abrogated effective December 1, 2015.]*

(Caption—See Form 1.)

Responding to Allegations in the Complaint

1. Defendant admits the allegations in paragraphs _____.

2. Defendant lacks knowledge or information sufficient to form a belief about the truth of the allegations in paragraphs _____.

3. Defendant admits *identify part of the allegation* in paragraph _____ and denies or lacks knowledge or information sufficient to form a belief about the truth of the rest of the paragraph.

Failure to State a Claim

4. The complaint fails to state a claim upon which relief can be granted.

Failure to Join a Required Party

5. If there is a debt, it is owed jointly by the defendant and *name* who is a citizen of _____. This person can be made a party without depriving this court of jurisdiction over the existing parties.

Affirmative Defense—Statute of Limitations

6. The plaintiff's claim is barred by the statute of limitations because it arose more than _____ years before this action was commenced.

Counterclaim

7. *(Set forth any counterclaim in the same way a claim is pleaded in a complaint. Include a further statement of jurisdiction if needed.)*

Crossclaim

8. *(Set forth a crossclaim against a coparty in the same way a claim is pleaded in a complaint. Include a further statement of jurisdiction if needed.)*

(Date and sign—See Form 2.)

(Added Apr. 30, 2007, eff. Dec. 1, 2007. Abrogated eff. Dec. 1, 2015, absent contrary Congressional action.)

FORM 31. ANSWER TO A COMPLAINT FOR MONEY HAD AND RECEIVED WITH A COUNTERCLAIM FOR INTERPLEADER

[Absent contrary Congressional action, Form 31 will be abrogated effective December 1, 2015.]

(Caption—See Form 1.)

Response to the Allegations in the Complaint
(See Form 30.)

Counterclaim for Interpleader

1. The defendant received from *name* a deposit of $_____.

2. The plaintiff demands payment of the deposit because of a purported assignment from *name*, who has notified the defendant that the assignment is not valid and who continues to hold the defendant responsible for the deposit.

Therefore, the defendant demands that:

   (a) *name* be made a party to this action;

   (b) the plaintiff and *name* be required to interplead their respective claims;

   (c) the court decide whether the plaintiff or *name* or either of them is entitled to the deposit and discharge the defendant of any liability except to the person entitled to the deposit; and

   (d) the defendant recover costs and attorney's fees.

(Date and sign—See Form 2.)

(Added Apr. 30, 2007, eff. Dec. 1, 2007. Abrogated eff. Dec. 1, 2015, absent contrary Congressional action.)

FORM 40.   MOTION TO DISMISS UNDER RULE 12(b) FOR LACK OF JURISDICTION, IMPROPER VENUE, INSUFFICIENT SERVICE OF PROCESS, OR FAILURE TO STATE A CLAIM

[Absent contrary Congressional action, Form 40 will be abrogated effective December 1, 2015.]

(Caption—See Form 1.)

The defendant moves to dismiss the action because:

1. the amount in controversy is less than the sum or value specified by 28 U.S.C. § 1332;

2. the defendant is not subject to the personal jurisdiction of this court;

3. venue is improper (this defendant does not reside in this district and no part of the events or omissions giving rise to the claim occurred in the district);

4. the defendant has not been properly served, as shown by the attached affidavits of _____; or

5. the complaint fails to state a claim upon which relief can be granted.

(Date and sign—See Form 2.)

(Added Apr. 30, 2007, eff. Dec. 1, 2007. Abrogated eff. Dec. 1, 2015, absent contrary Congressional action.)

FORM 41. MOTION TO BRING IN A THIRD–PARTY DEFENDANT

*[Absent contrary Congressional action, Form 41 will
be abrogated effective December 1, 2015.]*

(Caption—See Form 1.)

The defendant, as third-party plaintiff, moves for leave to serve on <u>name</u> a summons and third-party complaint, copies of which are attached.

(Date and sign—See Form 2.)

(Added Apr. 30, 2007, eff. Dec. 1, 2007. Abrogated eff. Dec. 1, 2015, absent contrary Congressional action.)

FORM 42. MOTION TO INTERVENE AS A DEFENDANT UNDER RULE 24

[Absent contrary Congressional action, Form 42 will be abrogated effective December 1, 2015.]

(Caption—See Form 1.)

1. <u>name</u> moves for leave to intervene as a defendant in this action and to file the attached answer.

(State grounds under Rule 24(a) or (b).)

2. The plaintiff alleges patent infringement. We manufacture and sell to the defendant the articles involved, and we have a defense to the plaintiff's claim.

3. Our defense presents questions of law and fact that are common to this action.

(Date and sign—See Form 2.)

[An Intervener's Answer must be attached. See Form 30.]

(Added Apr. 30, 2007, eff. Dec. 1, 2007. Abrogated eff. Dec. 1, 2015, absent contrary Congressional action.)

FORM 50.   REQUEST TO PRODUCE DOCUMENTS AND TANGIBLE THINGS, OR TO ENTER ONTO LAND UNDER RULE 34

[Absent contrary Congressional action, Form 50 will be abrogated effective December 1, 2015.]

(Caption—See Form 1.)

The plaintiff *name* requests that the defendant *name* respond within _____ days to the following requests:

1. To produce and permit the plaintiff to inspect and copy and to test or sample the following documents, including electronically stored information:

    (Describe each document and the electronically stored information, either individually or by category.)

    (State the time, place, and manner of the inspection and any related acts.)

2. To produce and permit the plaintiff to inspect and copy—and to test or sample—the following tangible things:

    (Describe each thing, either individually or by category.)

    (State the time, place, and manner of the inspection and any related acts.)

3. To permit the plaintiff to enter onto the following land to inspect, photograph, test, or sample the property or an object or operation on the property.

    (Describe the property and each object or operation.)

    (State the time and manner of the inspection and any related acts.)

    (Date and sign—See Form 2.)

(Added Apr. 30, 2007, eff. Dec. 1, 2007. Abrogated eff. Dec. 1, 2015, absent contrary Congressional action.)

FORM 51.   REQUEST FOR ADMISSIONS UNDER RULE 36

*[Absent contrary Congressional action, Form 51 will
be abrogated effective December 1, 2015.]*

(Caption—See Form 1.)

The plaintiff *name* asks the defendant *name* to respond within 30 days to these requests by admitting, for purposes of this action only and subject to objections to admissibility at trial:

1. The genuineness of the following documents, copies of which [are attached] [are or have been furnished or made available for inspection and copying].

(List each document.)

2. The truth of each of the following statements:

(List each statement.)

(Date and sign—See Form 2.)

(Added Apr. 30, 2007, eff. Dec. 1, 2007. Abrogated eff. Dec. 1, 2015, absent contrary Congressional action.)

FORM 52. REPORT OF THE PARTIES' PLANNING MEETING

*[Absent contrary Congressional action, Form 52 will
be abrogated effective December 1, 2015.]*

(Caption—See Form 1.)

1. The following persons participated in a Rule 26(f) conference on   *date*   by *state the method of conferring* :

2. Initial Disclosures. The parties [have completed] [will complete by   *date*] the initial disclosures required by Rule 26(a)(1).

3. Discovery Plan. The parties propose this discovery plan:

    (Use separate paragraphs or subparagraphs if the parties disagree.)

    (a) Discovery will be needed on these subjects: *(describe)*

    (b) Disclosure or discovery of electronically stored information should be handled as follows: *(briefly describe the parties' proposals, including the form or forms for production.)*

    (c) The parties have agreed to an order regarding claims of privilege or of protection as trial-preparation material asserted after production, as follows: *(briefly describe the provisions of the proposed order.)*

    (d) (Dates for commencing and completing discovery, including discovery to be commenced or completed before other discovery.)

    (e) (Maximum number of interrogatories by each party to another party, along with dates the answers are due.)

    (f) (Maximum number of requests for admission, along with the dates responses are due.)

    (g) (Maximum number of depositions for each party.)

    (h) (Limits on the length of depositions, in hours.)

    (i) (Dates for exchanging reports of expert witnesses.)

    (j) (Dates for supplementations under Rule 26(e).)

4. Other Items:

    (a) (A date if the parties ask to meet with the court before a scheduling order.)

    (b) (Requested dates for pretrial conferences.)

    (c) (Final dates for the plaintiff to amend pleadings or to join parties.)

    (d) (Final dates for the defendant to amend pleadings or to join parties.)

    (e) (Final dates to file dispositive motions.)

    (f) (State the prospects for settlement.)

    (g) (Identify any alternative dispute resolution procedure that may enhance settlement prospects.)

    (h) (Final dates for submitting Rule 26(a)(3) witness lists, designations of witnesses whose testimony will be presented by deposition, and exhibit lists.)

(i) (Final dates to file objections under Rule 26(a)(3).)

(j) (Suggested trial date and estimate of trial length.)

(k) (Other matters.)

(Date and sign—see Form 2.)

(Added Apr. 30, 2007, eff. Dec. 1, 2007. As amended Apr. 28, 2010, eff. Dec. 1, 2010. Abrogated eff. Dec. 1, 2015, absent contrary Congressional action.)

FORM 60. NOTICE OF CONDEMNATION

*[Absent contrary Congressional action, Form 60 will
be abrogated effective December 1, 2015.]*

(Caption—See Form 1.)

To *name the defendant*.

1. A complaint in condemnation has been filed in the United States District Court for the _____District of _____, to take property to use for *purpose*. The interest to be taken is *describe*. The court is located in the United States courthouse at this address: _____.

2. The property to be taken is described below. You have or claim an interest in it.

(Describe the property.)

3. The authority for taking this property is *cite*.

4. If you want to object or present any defense to the taking you must serve an answer on the plaintiff's attorney within 21 days [after being served with this notice][from *(insert the date of the last publication of notice)*]. Send your answer to this address: _____.

5. Your answer must identify the property in which you claim an interest, state the nature and extent of that interest, and state all your objections and defenses to the taking. Objections and defenses not presented are waived.

6. If you fail to answer you consent to the taking and the court will enter a judgment that takes your described property interest.

7. Instead of answering, you may serve on the plaintiff's attorney a notice of appearance that designates the property in which you claim an interest. After you do that, you will receive a notice of any proceedings that affect you. Whether or not you have previously appeared or answered, you may present evidence at a trial to determine compensation for the property and share in the overall award.

(Date and sign—See Form 2.)

(Added Apr. 30, 2007, eff. Dec. 1, 2007; amended Mar. 26, 2009, eff. Dec. 1, 2009. Abrogated eff. Dec. 1, 2015, absent contrary Congressional action.)

FORM 61. COMPLAINT FOR CONDEMNATION

*[Absent contrary Congressional action, Form 61 will
be abrogated effective December 1, 2015.]*

(Caption—See Form 1; name as defendants the property and at least one owner.)

1. (Statement of Jurisdiction—See Form 7.)

2. This is an action to take property under the power of eminent domain and to determine just compensation to be paid to the owners and parties in interest.

3. The authority for the taking is _____.

4. The property is to be used for _____.

5. The property to be taken is (*describe in enough detail for identification—or attach the description and state "is described in Exhibit A, attached."*)

6. The interest to be acquired is _____.

7. The persons known to the plaintiff to have or claim an interest in the property are: _____. (*For each person include the interest claimed.*)

8. There may be other persons who have or claim an interest in the property and whose names could not be found after a reasonably diligent search. They are made parties under the designation "Unknown Owners."

Therefore, the plaintiff demands judgment:

(a) condemning the property;

(b) determining and awarding just compensation; and

(c) granting any other lawful and proper relief.

(Date and sign—See Form 2.)

(Added Apr. 30, 2007, eff. Dec. 1, 2007. Abrogated eff. Dec. 1, 2015, absent contrary Congressional action.)

FORM 70. JUDGMENT ON A JURY VERDICT

*[Absent contrary Congressional action, Form 70 will
be abrogated effective December 1, 2015.]*

(Caption—See Form 1.)

This action was tried by a jury with Judge _____ presiding, and the jury has rendered a verdict.

It is ordered that:

[the plaintiff *name* recover from the defendant *name* the amount of $_____ with interest at the rate of ___%, along with costs.]

[the plaintiff recover nothing, the action be dismissed on the merits, and the defendant *name* recover costs from the plaintiff *name.*]

Date _____

_____

Clerk of Court

(Added Apr. 30, 2007, eff. Dec. 1, 2007. Abrogated eff. Dec. 1, 2015, absent contrary Congressional action.)

FORM 71. JUDGMENT BY THE COURT WITHOUT A JURY

*[Absent contrary Congressional action, Form 71 will
be abrogated effective December 1, 2015.]*

(Caption—See Form 1.)

This action was tried by Judge _____ without a jury and the following decision was reached:

It is ordered that [the plaintiff *name* recover from the defendant *name* the amount of $_____, with prejudgment interest at the rate of ___%, postjudgment interest at the rate of ___%, along with costs.] [the plaintiff recover nothing, the action be dismissed on the merits, and the defendant *name* recover costs from the plaintiff *name*.]

Date_____

_____

Clerk of Court

(Added Apr. 30, 2007, eff. Dec. 1, 2007.   Abrogated eff. Dec. 1, 2015, absent contrary Congressional action.)

FORM 80. NOTICE OF A MAGISTRATE JUDGE'S AVAILABILITY

*[Absent contrary Congressional action, Form 80 will
be abrogated effective December 1, 2015.]*

1. A magistrate judge is available under title 28 U.S.C. § 636(c) to conduct the proceedings in this case, including a jury or nonjury trial and the entry of final judgment. But a magistrate judge can be assigned only if all parties voluntarily consent.

2. You may withhold your consent without adverse substantive consequences. The identity of any party consenting or withholding consent will not be disclosed to the judge to whom the case is assigned or to any magistrate judge.

3. If a magistrate judge does hear your case, you may appeal directly to a United States court of appeals as you would if a district judge heard it.

A form called *Consent to an Assignment to a United States Magistrate Judge* is available from the court clerk's office.

(Added Apr. 30, 2007, eff. Dec. 1, 2007. Abrogated eff. Dec. 1, 2015, absent contrary Congressional action.)

FORM 81.   CONSENT TO AN ASSIGNMENT TO A MAGISTRATE JUDGE

[Absent contrary Congressional action, Form 81 will be abrogated effective December 1, 2015.]

(Caption—See Form 1.)

I voluntarily consent to have a United States magistrate judge conduct all further proceedings in this case, including a trial, and order the entry of final judgment. (Return this form to the court clerk—not to a judge or magistrate judge.)

Date_____

_____

Signature of the Party

(Added Apr. 30, 2007, eff. Dec. 1, 2007.   Abrogated eff. Dec. 1, 2015, absent contrary Congressional action.)

FORM 82. ORDER OF ASSIGNMENT TO A MAGISTRATE JUDGE

*[Absent contrary Congressional action, Form 82 will
be abrogated effective December 1, 2015.]*

(Caption—See Form 1.)

With the parties' consent it is ordered that this case be assigned to United States Magistrate Judge _____ of this district to conduct all proceedings and enter final judgment in accordance with 28 U.S.C. § 636(c).

Date _____

_____

United States District Judge

(Added Apr. 30, 2007, eff. Dec. 1, 2007. Abrogated eff. Dec. 1, 2015, absent contrary Congressional action.)

SUPPLEMENTAL RULES FOR ADMIRALTY OR MARITIME CLAIMS AND ASSET FORFEITURE ACTIONS

RULE A. SCOPE OF RULES

(1) These Supplemental Rules apply to:

(A) the procedure in admiralty and maritime claims within the meaning of Rule 9(h) with respect to the following remedies:

(i) maritime attachment and garnishment,

(ii) actions in rem,

(iii) possessory, petitory, and partition actions, and

(iv) actions for exoneration from or limitation of liability;

(B) forfeiture actions in rem arising from a federal statute; and

(C) the procedure in statutory condemnation proceedings analogous to maritime actions in rem, whether within the admiralty and maritime jurisdiction or not. Except as otherwise provided, references in these Supplemental Rules to actions in rem include such analogous statutory condemnation proceedings.

(2) The Federal Rules of Civil Procedure also apply to the foregoing proceedings except to the extent that they are inconsistent with these Supplemental Rules.

(Added Feb. 28, 1966, eff. July 1, 1966; amended Apr. 12, 2006, eff. Dec. 1, 2006.)

RULE B. IN PERSONAM ACTIONS: ATTACHMENT AND GARNISHMENT

(1) **When Available; Complaint, Affidavit, Judicial Authorization, and Process.** In an in personam action:

(a) If a defendant is not found within the district when a verified complaint praying for attachment and the affidavit required by Rule B(1)(b) are filed, a verified complaint may contain a prayer for process to attach the defendant's tangible or intangible personal property—up to the amount sued for—in the hands of garnishees named in the process.

(b) The plaintiff or the plaintiff's attorney must sign and file with the complaint an affidavit stating that, to the affiant's knowledge, or on information and belief, the defendant cannot be found within the district. The court must review the complaint and affidavit and, if the conditions of this Rule B appear to exist, enter an order so stating and authorizing process of attachment and garnishment. The clerk may issue supplemental process enforcing the court's order upon application without further court order.

(c) If the plaintiff or the plaintiff's attorney certifies that exigent circumstances make court review impracticable, the clerk must issue the summons and process of attachment and garnishment. The plaintiff has the burden in any post-attachment hearing under Rule E(4)(f) to show that exigent circumstances existed.

(d)(i) If the property is a vessel or tangible property on board a vessel, the summons, process, and any supplemental process must be delivered to the marshal for service.

(ii) If the property is other tangible or intangible property, the summons, process, and any supplemental process must be delivered to a person or organization authorized to serve it, who may be (A) a marshal; (B) someone under contract with the United States; (C) someone specially appointed by the court for that purpose; or, (D) in an action brought by the United States, any officer or employee of the United States.

(e) The plaintiff may invoke state-law remedies under Rule 64 for seizure of person or property for the purpose of securing satisfaction of the judgment.

(2) **Notice to Defendant.** No default judgment may be entered except upon proof—which may be by affidavit—that:

(a) the complaint, summons, and process of attachment or garnishment have been served on the defendant in a manner authorized by Rule 4;

(b) the plaintiff or the garnishee has mailed to the defendant the complaint, summons, and process of attachment or garnishment, using any form of mail requiring a return receipt; or

(c) the plaintiff or the garnishee has tried diligently to give notice of the action to the defendant but could not do so.

(3) **Answer.**

(a) **By Garnishee.** The garnishee shall serve an answer, together with answers to any interrogatories served with the complaint, within 21 days after service of process upon the garnishee. Interrogatories to the garnishee may be served with the complaint without leave of court. If the garnishee refuses or neglects to answer on oath as to the debts, credits, or effects of the defendant in the garnishee's hands, or any interrogatories concerning such debts, credits, and effects that may be propounded by the plaintiff, the court may award compulsory process against the garnishee. If the garnishee admits any debts, credits, or effects, they shall be held in the garnishee's hands or paid into the registry of the court, and shall be held in either case subject to the further order of the court.

(b) By Defendant. The defendant shall serve an answer within 30 days after process has been executed, whether by attachment of property or service on the garnishee.

(Added Feb. 28, 1966, eff. July 1, 1966; amended Apr. 29, 1985, eff. Aug. 1, 1985; Mar. 2, 1987, eff. Aug. 1, 1987; Apr. 17, 2000, eff. Dec. 1, 2000; Apr. 25, 2005, eff. Dec. 1, 2005; Mar. 26, 2009, eff. Dec. 1, 2009.)

RULE C. IN REM ACTIONS: SPECIAL PROVISIONS

(1) When Available. An action in rem may be brought:

(a) To enforce any maritime lien;

(b) Whenever a statute of the United States provides for a maritime action in rem or a proceeding analogous thereto.

Except as otherwise provided by law a party who may proceed in rem may also, or in the alternative, proceed in personam against any person who may be liable.

Statutory provisions exempting vessels or other property owned or possessed by or operated by or for the United States from arrest or seizure are not affected by this rule. When a statute so provides, an action against the United States or an instrumentality thereof may proceed on in rem principles.

(2) Complaint. In an action in rem the complaint must:

(a) be verified;

(b) describe with reasonable particularity the property that is the subject of the action; and

(c) state that the property is within the district or will be within the district while the action is pending.

(3) Judicial Authorization and Process.

(a) Arrest Warrant.

(i) The court must review the complaint and any supporting papers. If the conditions for an in rem action appear to exist, the court must issue an order directing the clerk to issue a warrant for the arrest of the vessel or other property that is the subject of the action.

(ii) If the plaintiff or the plaintiff's attorney certifies that exigent circumstances make court review impracticable, the clerk must promptly issue a summons and a warrant for the arrest of the vessel or other property that is the subject of the action. The plaintiff has the burden in any post-arrest hearing under Rule E(4)(f) to show that exigent circumstances existed.

(b) Service.

(i) If the property that is the subject of the action is a vessel or tangible property on board a vessel, the warrant and any supplemental process must be delivered to the marshal for service.

(ii) If the property that is the subject of the action is other property, tangible or intangible, the warrant and any supplemental process must be delivered to a person or organization authorized to enforce it, who may be: (A) a marshal; (B) someone under contract with the United States; (C) someone specially appointed by the court for that purpose; or, (D) in an action brought by the United States, any officer or employee of the United States.

(c) Deposit in Court. If the property that is the subject of the action consists in whole or in part of freight, the proceeds of property sold, or other intangible property, the clerk must issue—in addition to the warrant—a summons directing any person controlling the property to show cause why it should not be deposited in court to abide the judgment.

(d) Supplemental Process. The clerk may upon application issue supplemental process to enforce the court's order without further court order.

(4) Notice. No notice other than execution of process is required when the property that is the subject of the action has been released under Rule E(5). If the property is not released within 14 days after execution, the plaintiff must promptly—or within the time that the court allows—give public notice of the action and arrest in a newspaper designated by court order and having general circulation in the district, but publication may be terminated if the property is released before publication is completed. The notice must specify the time under Rule C(6) to file a statement of interest in or right against the seized property and to answer. This rule does not affect the notice requirements in an action to foreclose a preferred ship mortgage under 46 U.S.C. §§ 31301 et seq., as amended.

(5) Ancillary Process. In any action in rem in which process has been served as provided by this rule, if any part of the property that is the subject of the action has not been brought within the control of the court because it has been removed or sold, or because it is intangible property in the hands of a person who has not been served with process, the court may, on motion, order any person having possession or control of such property or its proceeds to show cause why it should not be delivered into the custody of the marshal or other person or organization having a warrant for the arrest of the property, or paid into court to abide the judgment; and, after hearing, the court may enter such judgment as law and justice may require.

(6) Responsive Pleading; Interrogatories.

(a) Statement of Interest; Answer. In an action in rem:

(i) a person who asserts a right of possession or any ownership interest in the property that is the subject of the action must file a verified statement of right or interest:

(A) within 14 days after the execution of process, or

(B) within the time that the court allows;

(ii) the statement of right or interest must describe the interest in the property that supports the person's demand for its restitution or right to defend the action;

(iii) an agent, bailee, or attorney must state the authority to file a statement of right or interest on behalf of another; and

(iv) a person who asserts a right of possession or any ownership interest must serve an answer within 21 days after filing the statement of interest or right.

(b) Interrogatories. Interrogatories may be served with the complaint in an in rem action without leave of court. Answers to the interrogatories must be served with the answer to the complaint.

(Added Feb. 28, 1966, eff. July 1, 1966; amended Apr. 29, 1985, eff. Aug. 1, 1985; Mar. 2, 1987, eff. Aug. 1, 1987; Apr. 30, 1991, eff. Dec. 1, 1991; Apr. 17, 2000, eff. Dec. 1, 2000; Apr. 29, 2002, eff. Dec. 1, 2002; Apr. 25, 2005, eff. Dec. 1, 2005; Apr. 12, 2006, eff. Dec. 1, 2006; Apr. 23, 2008, eff. Dec. 1, 2008; Mar. 26, 2009, eff. Dec. 1, 2009.)

RULE D. POSSESSORY, PETITORY, AND PARTITION ACTIONS

In all actions for possession, partition, and to try title maintainable according to the course of the admiralty practice with respect to a vessel, in all actions so maintainable with respect to the possession of cargo or other maritime property, and in all actions by one or more part owners against the others to obtain security for the return of the vessel from any voyage undertaken without their consent, or by one or more part owners against the others to obtain possession of the vessel for any voyage on giving security for its safe return, the process shall be by a warrant of arrest of the vessel, cargo, or other property, and by

notice in the manner provided by Rule B(2) to the adverse party or parties.

(Added Feb. 28, 1966, eff. July 1, 1966.)

RULE E. ACTIONS IN REM AND QUASI IN REM: GENERAL PROVISIONS

(1) Applicability. Except as otherwise provided, this rule applies to actions in personam with process of maritime attachment and garnishment, actions in rem, and petitory, possessory, and partition actions, supplementing Rules B, C, and D.

(2) Complaint; Security.

(a) Complaint. In actions to which this rule is applicable the complaint shall state the circumstances from which the claim arises with such particularity that the defendant or claimant will be able, without moving for a more definite statement, to commence an investigation of the facts and to frame a responsive pleading.

(b) Security for Costs. Subject to the provisions of Rule 54(d) and of relevant statutes, the court may, on the filing of the complaint or on the appearance of any defendant, claimant, or any other party, or at any later time, require the plaintiff, defendant, claimant, or other party to give security, or additional security, in such sum as the court shall direct to pay all costs and expenses that shall be awarded against the party by any interlocutory order or by the final judgment, or on appeal by any appellate court.

(3) Process.

(a) In admiralty and maritime proceedings process in rem or of maritime attachment and garnishment may be served only within the district.

(b) Issuance and Delivery. Issuance and delivery of process in rem, or of maritime attachment and garnishment, shall be held in abeyance if the plaintiff so requests.

(4) Execution of Process; Marshal's Return; Custody of Property; Procedures for Release.

(a) In General. Upon issuance and delivery of the process, or, in the case of summons with process of attachment and garnishment, when it appears that the defendant cannot be found within the district, the marshal or other person or organization having a warrant shall forthwith execute the process in accordance with this subdivision (4), making due and prompt return.

(b) Tangible Property. If tangible property is to be attached or arrested, the marshal or other person or organization having the warrant shall take it into the marshal's possession for safe custody. If the character or situation of the property is such that the taking of actual possession is impracticable, the marshal or other person executing the process shall affix a copy thereof to the property in a conspicuous place and leave a copy of the complaint and process with the person having possession or the person's agent. In furtherance of the marshal's custody of any vessel the marshal is authorized to make a written request to the collector of customs not to grant clearance to such vessel until notified by the marshal or deputy marshal or by the clerk that the vessel has been released in accordance with these rules.

(c) Intangible Property. If intangible property is to be attached or arrested the marshal or other person or organization having the warrant shall execute the process by leaving with the garnishee or other obligor a copy of the complaint and process requiring the garnishee or other obligor to answer as provided in Rules B(3)(a) and C(6); or the marshal may accept for payment into the registry of the court the amount owed to the extent of the amount claimed by the plaintiff with interest and costs, in which event the garnishee or other obligor shall not be required to answer unless alias process shall be served.

(d) Directions With Respect to Property in Custody. The marshal or other person or organization having the warrant may at any time apply to the court for directions with respect to property that has been attached or arrested, and shall give notice of such application to any or all of the parties as the court may direct.

(e) Expenses of Seizing and Keeping Property; Deposit. These rules do not alter the provisions of Title 28, U.S.C., § 1921, as amended, relative to the expenses of seizing and keeping property attached or arrested and to the requirement of deposits to cover such expenses.

(f) Procedure for Release From Arrest or Attachment. Whenever property is arrested or attached, any person claiming an interest in it shall be entitled to a prompt hearing at which the plaintiff shall be required to show why the arrest or attachment should not be vacated or other relief granted consistent with these rules. This subdivision shall have no application to suits for seamen's wages when process is issued upon a certification of sufficient cause filed pursuant to Title 46, U.S.C. §§ 603 and 604 or to actions by the United States for forfeitures for violation of any statute of the United States.

(5) Release of Property.

(a) Special Bond. Whenever process of maritime attachment and garnishment or process in rem is issued the execution of such process shall be stayed, or the property released, on the giving of security, to be approved by the court or clerk, or by stipulation of the parties, conditioned to answer the judgment of the court or of any appellate court.

The parties may stipulate the amount and nature of such security. In the event of the inability or refusal of the parties so to stipulate the court shall fix the principal sum of the bond or stipulation at an amount sufficient to cover the amount of the plaintiff's claim fairly stated with accrued interest and costs; but the principal sum shall in no event exceed (i) twice the amount of the plaintiff's claim or (ii) the value of the property on due appraisement, whichever is smaller. The bond or stipulation shall be conditioned for the payment of the principal sum and interest thereon at 6 per cent per annum.

(b) General Bond. The owner of any vessel may file a general bond or stipulation, with sufficient surety, to be approved by the court, conditioned to answer the judgment of such court in all or any actions that may be brought thereafter in such court in which the vessel is attached or arrested. Thereupon the execution of all such process against such vessel shall be stayed so long as the amount secured by such bond or stipulation is at least double the aggregate amount claimed by plaintiffs in all actions begun and pending in which such vessel has been attached or arrested. Judgments and remedies may be had on such bond or stipulation as if a special bond or stipulation had been filed in each of such actions. The district court may make necessary orders to carry this rule into effect, particularly as to the giving of proper notice of any action against or attachment of a vessel for which a general bond has been filed. Such bond or stipulation shall be indorsed by the clerk with a minute of the actions wherein process is so stayed. Further security may be required by the court at any time.

If a special bond or stipulation is given in a particular case, the liability on the general bond or stipulation shall cease as to that case.

(c) Release by Consent or Stipulation; Order of Court or Clerk; Costs. Any vessel, cargo, or other property in the custody of the marshal or other person or organization having the warrant may be released forthwith upon the marshal's acceptance and approval of a stipulation, bond, or other security, signed by the party on whose behalf the property is detained or the party's attorney and expressly authorizing such release, if all costs and charges of the court and its officers shall have first been paid. Otherwise no property in the custody of the marshal, other person or organization having the warrant, or other officer of the court shall be released without an order of the court; but such order may be entered as of course by the clerk, upon the giving of approved security as provided by law and these rules, or upon the dismissal or discontinuance of the action; but the marshal or other person or organization having the warrant shall not deliver any property so released until the costs and charges of the officers of the court shall first have been paid.

(d) Possessory, Petitory, and Partition Actions. The foregoing provisions of this subdivision (5) do not apply to petitory, possessory, and partition actions. In such cases the property arrested shall be released only by order of the court, on such terms and conditions and on the giving of such security as the court may require.

(6) Reduction or Impairment of Security. Whenever security is taken the court may, on motion and hearing, for good cause shown, reduce the amount of security given; and if the surety shall be or become insufficient, new or additional sureties may be required on motion and hearing.

(7) Security on Counterclaim.

(a) When a person who has given security for damages in the original action asserts a counterclaim that arises from the transaction or occurrence that is the subject of the original action, a plaintiff for whose benefit the security has been given must give security for damages demanded in the counterclaim unless the court for cause shown, directs otherwise. Proceedings on the original claim must be stayed until this security is given unless the court directs otherwise.

(b) The plaintiff is required to give security under Rule E(7)(a) when the United States or its corporate instrumentality counterclaims and would have been required to give security to respond in damages if a private party but is relieved by law from giving security.

(8) Restricted Appearance. An appearance to defend against an admiralty and maritime claim with respect to which there has issued process in rem, or process of attachment and garnishment, may be expressly restricted to the defense of such claim, and in that event is not an appearance for the purposes of any other claim with respect to which such process is not available or has not been served.

(9) Disposition of Property; Sales.

(a) Interlocutory Sales; Delivery.

(i) On application of a party, the marshal, or other person having custody of the property, the court may order all or part of the property sold—with the sales proceeds, or as much of them as will satisfy the judgment, paid into court to await further orders of the court—if:

(A) the attached or arrested property is perishable, or liable to deterioration, decay, or injury by being detained in custody pending the action;

(B) the expense of keeping the property is excessive or disproportionate; or

(C) there is an unreasonable delay in securing release of the property.

(ii) In the circumstances described in Rule E(9)(a)(i), the court, on motion by a defendant or a person filing a statement of interest or right under Rule C(6), may order that the property, rather than being sold, be delivered to the movant upon giving security under these rules.

(b) Sales; Proceeds. All sales of property shall be made by the marshal or a deputy marshal, or by other person or organization having the warrant, or by any other person assigned by the court where the marshal or other person or organization having the warrant is a party in interest; and the proceeds of sale shall be forthwith paid into the registry of the court to be disposed of according to law.

(10) Preservation of Property. When the owner or another person remains in possession of property attached or arrested under the provisions of Rule E(4)(b) that permit execution of process without taking actual possession, the court, on a party's motion or on its own, may enter any order necessary to preserve the property and to prevent its removal.

(Added Feb. 28, 1966, eff. July 1, 1966; amended Apr. 29, 1985, eff. Aug. 1, 1985; Mar. 2, 1987, eff. Aug. 1, 1987; Apr. 30, 1991, eff. Dec. 1, 1991; Apr. 17, 2000, eff. Dec. 1, 2000; Apr. 12, 2006, eff. Dec. 1, 2006.)

RULE F. LIMITATION OF LIABILITY

(1) Time for Filing Complaint; Security. Not later than six months after receipt of a claim in writing, any vessel owner may file a complaint in the appropriate district court, as provided in subdivision (9) of this rule, for limitation of liability pursuant to statute. The owner (a) shall deposit with the court, for the benefit of claimants, a sum equal to the amount or value of the owner's interest in the vessel and pending freight, or approved security therefor, and in addition such sums, or approved security therefor, as the court may from time to time fix as necessary to carry out the provisions of the statutes as amended; or (b) at the owner's option shall transfer to a trustee to be appointed by the court, for the benefit of claimants, the owner's interest in the vessel and pending freight, together with such sums, or approved security therefor, as the court may from time to time fix as necessary to carry out the provisions of the statutes as amended. The plaintiff shall also give security for costs and, if the plaintiff elects to give security, for interest at the rate of 6 percent per annum from the date of the security.

(2) Complaint. The complaint shall set forth the facts on the basis of which the right to limit liability is asserted and all facts necessary to enable the court to determine the amount to which the owner's liability shall be limited. The complaint may demand exoneration from as well as limitation of liability. It shall state the voyage if any, on which the demands sought to be limited arose, with the date and place of its termination; the amount of all demands including all unsatisfied liens or claims of lien, in contract or in tort or otherwise, arising on that voyage, so far as known to the plaintiff, and what actions and proceedings, if any, are pending thereon; whether the vessel was damaged, lost, or abandoned, and, if so, when and where; the value of the vessel at the close of the voyage or, in case of wreck, the value of her wreckage, strippings, or proceeds, if any, and where and in whose possession they are; and the amount of any pending freight recovered or recoverable. If the plaintiff elects to transfer the plaintiff's interest in the vessel to a trustee, the complaint must further show any prior paramount liens thereon, and what voyages or trips, if any, she has made since the voyage or trip on which the claims sought to be limited arose, and any existing liens arising upon any such subsequent voyage or trip, with the amounts and causes thereof, and the names and addresses of the lienors, so far as known; and whether the vessel sustained any injury upon or by reason of such subsequent voyage or trip.

(3) Claims Against Owner; Injunction. Upon compliance by the owner with the requirements of subdivision (1) of this rule all claims and proceedings against the owner or the owner's property with respect to the matter in question shall cease. On application of the plaintiff the court shall enjoin the further prosecution of any action or proceeding against the plaintiff or the plaintiff's property with respect to any claim subject to limitation in the action.

(4) Notice to Claimants. Upon the owner's compliance with subdivision (1) of this rule the court shall issue a notice to all persons asserting claims with respect to which the complaint seeks limitation, admonishing them to file their respective claims with the clerk of the court and to serve on the attorneys for the plaintiff a copy thereof on or before a date to be named in the notice. The date so fixed shall not be less than 30 days after issuance of the notice. For cause shown, the court may enlarge the time within which claims may be filed. The notice shall be published in such newspaper or newspapers as the court may direct once a week for four successive weeks prior to the date fixed for the filing of claims. The plaintiff not later than the day of second publication shall also mail a copy of the notice to every person known to have made any claim against the vessel or the plaintiff arising out of the voyage or trip on which the claims sought to be limited arose. In cases involving death a copy of such notice shall be mailed to the decedent at the decedent's last known address, and also to any person who shall be known to have made any claim on account of such death.

(5) Claims and Answer. Claims shall be filed and served on or before the date specified in the notice provided for in subdivision (4) of this rule. Each claim shall specify the facts upon which the claimant relies in support of the claim, the items thereof, and the dates on which the same accrued. If a claimant desires to contest either the right to exoneration from or the right to limitation of liability the claimant shall file and serve an answer to the complaint unless the claim has included an answer.

(6) Information to be Given Claimants. Within 30 days after the date specified in the notice for filing claims, or within such time as the court thereafter may allow, the plaintiff shall mail to the attorney for each claimant (or if the claimant has no attorney to the claimant) a list setting forth (a) the name of each claimant, (b) the name and address of the claimant's attorney (if the claimant is known to have one), (c) the nature of the claim, i.e., whether property loss, property damage, death, personal injury etc., and (d) the amount thereof.

(7) Insufficiency of Fund or Security. Any claimant may by motion demand that the funds deposited in court or the security given by the plaintiff be increased on the ground that they are less than the value of the plaintiff's interest in the vessel and pending freight. Thereupon the court shall cause due appraisement to be made of the value of the plaintiff's interest in the vessel and pending freight; and if the court finds that the deposit or security is either insufficient or excessive it shall order its increase or reduction. In like manner any claimant may demand that the deposit or security be increased on the ground that it is insufficient to carry out the provisions of the statutes relating to claims in respect of loss of life or bodily injury; and, after notice and hearing, the court may similarly order that the deposit or security be increased or reduced.

(8) Objections to Claims: Distribution of Fund. Any interested party may question or controvert any claim without filing an objection thereto. Upon determination of liability the fund deposited or secured, or the proceeds of the vessel and pending freight, shall be divided pro rata, subject to all relevant provisions of law, among the several claimants in proportion to the amounts of their respective claims, duly proved, saving, however, to all parties any priority to which they may be legally entitled.

(9) Venue; Transfer. The complaint shall be filed in any district in which the vessel has been attached or arrested to answer for any claim with respect to which the plaintiff seeks to limit liability; or, if the vessel has not been attached or arrested, then in any district in which the owner has been sued with respect to any such claim. When the vessel has not been attached or arrested to answer the matters aforesaid, and suit has not been commenced against the owner, the proceedings may be had in the district in which the vessel may be, but if the vessel is not within any district and no suit has been commenced in any district, then the complaint may be filed in any district. For the convenience of parties and witnesses, in the interest of justice, the court may transfer the action to any district; if venue is wrongly laid the court shall dismiss or, if it be in the interest of justice, transfer the action to any district in which it could have been brought. If the vessel shall have been sold, the proceeds shall represent the vessel for the purposes of these rules.

(Added Feb. 28, 1966, eff. July 1, 1966; amended Mar. 2, 1987, eff. Aug. 1, 1987.)

RULE G. FORFEITURE
ACTIONS IN REM

(1) **Scope.** This rule governs a forfeiture action in rem arising from a federal statute. To the extent that this rule does not address an issue, Supplemental Rules C and E and the Federal Rules of Civil Procedure also apply.

(2) **Complaint.** The complaint must:

(a) be verified;

(b) state the grounds for subject-matter jurisdiction, in rem jurisdiction over the defendant property, and venue;

(c) describe the property with reasonable particularity;

(d) if the property is tangible, state its location when any seizure occurred and—if different—its location when the action is filed;

(e) identify the statute under which the forfeiture action is brought; and

(f) state sufficiently detailed facts to support a reasonable belief that the government will be able to meet its burden of proof at trial.

(3) **Judicial Authorization and Process.**

(a) **Real Property.** If the defendant is real property, the government must proceed under 18 U.S.C. § 985.

(b) **Other Property; Arrest Warrant.** If the defendant is not real property:

(i) the clerk must issue a warrant to arrest the property if it is in the government's possession, custody, or control;

(ii) the court—on finding probable cause—must issue a warrant to arrest the property if it is not in the government's possession, custody, or control and is not subject to a judicial restraining order; and

(iii) a warrant is not necessary if the property is subject to a judicial restraining order.

(c) **Execution of Process.**

(i) The warrant and any supplemental process must be delivered to a person or organization authorized to execute it, who may be: (A) a marshal or any other United States officer or employee; (B) someone under contract with the United States; or (C) someone specially appointed by the court for that purpose.

(ii) The authorized person or organization must execute the warrant and any supplemental process on property in the United States as soon as practicable unless:

(A) the property is in the government's possession, custody, or control; or

(B) the court orders a different time when the complaint is under seal, the action is stayed before the warrant and supplemental process are executed, or the court finds other good cause.

(iii) The warrant and any supplemental process may be executed within the district or, when authorized by statute, outside the district.

(iv) If executing a warrant on property outside the United States is required, the warrant may be transmitted to an appropriate authority for serving process where the property is located.

(4) **Notice.**

(a) **Notice by Publication.**

(i) **When Publication Is Required.** A judgment of forfeiture may be entered only if the government has published notice of the action within a reasonable time after filing the complaint or at a time the court orders. But notice need not be published if:

(A) the defendant property is worth less than $1,000 and direct notice is sent under Rule G(4)(b) to every person the government can reasonably identify as a potential claimant; or

(B) the court finds that the cost of publication exceeds the property's value and that other means of notice would satisfy due process.

(ii) **Content of the Notice.** Unless the court orders otherwise, the notice must:

(A) describe the property with reasonable particularity;

(B) state the times under Rule G(5) to file a claim and to answer; and

(C) name the government attorney to be served with the claim and answer.

(iii) **Frequency of Publication.** Published notice must appear:

(A) once a week for three consecutive weeks; or

(B) only once if, before the action was filed, notice of nonjudicial forfeiture of the same property was published on an official internet government forfeiture site for at least 30 consecutive days, or in a newspaper of general circulation for three consecutive weeks in a district where publication is authorized under Rule G(4)(a)(iv).

(iv) Means of Publication. The government should select from the following options a means of publication reasonably calculated to notify potential claimants of the action:

(A) if the property is in the United States, publication in a newspaper generally circulated in the district where the action is filed, where the property was seized, or where property that was not seized is located;

(B) if the property is outside the United States, publication in a newspaper generally circulated in a district where the action is filed, in a newspaper generally circulated in the country where the property is located, or in legal notices published and generally circulated in the country where the property is located; or

(C) instead of (A) or (B), posting a notice on an official internet government forfeiture site for at least 30 consecutive days.

(b) Notice to Known Potential Claimants.

(i) Direct Notice Required. The government must send notice of the action and a copy of the complaint to any person who reasonably appears to be a potential claimant on the facts known to the government before the end of the time for filing a claim under Rule G(5)(a)(ii)(B).

(ii) Content of the Notice. The notice must state:

(A) the date when the notice is sent;

(B) a deadline for filing a claim, at least 35 days after the notice is sent;

(C) that an answer or a motion under Rule 12 must be filed no later than 21 days after filing the claim; and

(D) the name of the government attorney to be served with the claim and answer.

(iii) Sending Notice.

(A) The notice must be sent by means reasonably calculated to reach the potential claimant.

(B) Notice may be sent to the potential claimant or to the attorney representing the potential claimant with respect to the seizure of the property or in a related investigation, administrative forfeiture proceeding, or criminal case.

(C) Notice sent to a potential claimant who is incarcerated must be sent to the place of incarceration.

(D) Notice to a person arrested in connection with an offense giving rise to the forfeiture who is not incarcerated when notice is sent may be sent

to the address that person last gave to the agency that arrested or released the person.

(E) Notice to a person from whom the property was seized who is not incarcerated when notice is sent may be sent to the last address that person gave to the agency that seized the property.

(iv) When Notice Is Sent. Notice by the following means is sent on the date when it is placed in the mail, delivered to a commercial carrier, or sent by electronic mail.

(v) Actual Notice. A potential claimant who had actual notice of a forfeiture action may not oppose or seek relief from forfeiture because of the government's failure to send the required notice.

(5) Responsive Pleadings.

(a) Filing a Claim.

(i) A person who asserts an interest in the defendant property may contest the forfeiture by filing a claim in the court where the action is pending. The claim must:

(A) identify the specific property claimed;

(B) identify the claimant and state the claimant's interest in the property;

(C) be signed by the claimant under penalty of perjury; and

(D) be served on the government attorney designated under Rule G(4)(a)(ii)(C) or (b)(ii)(D).

(ii) Unless the court for good cause sets a different time, the claim must be filed:

(A) by the time stated in a direct notice sent under Rule G(4)(b);

(B) if notice was published but direct notice was not sent to the claimant or the claimant's attorney, no later than 30 days after final publication of newspaper notice or legal notice under Rule G(4)(a) or no later than 60 days after the first day of publication on an official internet government forfeiture site; or

(C) if notice was not published and direct notice was not sent to the claimant or the claimant's attorney:

(1) if the property was in the government's possession, custody, or control when the complaint was filed, no later than 60 days after the filing, not counting any time when the complaint was under seal or when the action was stayed before execution of a warrant issued under Rule G(3)(b); or

(2) if the property was not in the government's possession, custody, or control when the complaint was filed, no later than 60 days after the government complied with 18 U.S.C. § 985(c) as to real property, or 60 days after process was executed on the property under Rule G(3).

(iii) A claim filed by a person asserting an interest as a bailee must identify the bailor, and if filed on the bailor's behalf must state the authority to do so.

(b) Answer. A claimant must serve and file an answer to the complaint or a motion under Rule 12 within 21 days after filing the claim. A claimant waives an objection to in rem jurisdiction or to venue if the objection is not made by motion or stated in the answer.

(6) Special Interrogatories.

(a) Time and Scope. The government may serve special interrogatories limited to the claimant's identity and relationship to the defendant property without the court's leave at any time after the claim is filed and before discovery is closed. But if the claimant serves a motion to dismiss the action, the government must serve the interrogatories within 21 days after the motion is served.

(b) Answers or Objections. Answers or objections to these interrogatories must be served within 21 days after the interrogatories are served.

(c) Government's Response Deferred. The government need not respond to a claimant's motion to dismiss the action under Rule G(8)(b) until 21 days after the claimant has answered these interrogatories.

(7) Preserving, Preventing Criminal Use, and Disposing of Property; Sales.

(a) Preserving and Preventing Criminal Use of Property. When the government does not have actual possession of the defendant property the court, on motion or on its own, may enter any order necessary to preserve the property, to prevent its removal or encumbrance, or to prevent its use in a criminal offense.

(b) Interlocutory Sale or Delivery.

(i) Order to Sell. On motion by a party or a person having custody of the property, the court may order all or part of the property sold if:

(A) the property is perishable or at risk of deterioration, decay, or injury by being detained in custody pending the action;

(B) the expense of keeping the property is excessive or is disproportionate to its fair market value;

(C) the property is subject to a mortgage or to taxes on which the owner is in default; or

(D) the court finds other good cause.

(ii) Who Makes the Sale. A sale must be made by a United States agency that has authority to sell the property, by the agency's contractor, or by any person the court designates.

(iii) Sale Procedures. The sale is governed by 28 U.S.C. §§ 2001, 2002, and 2004, unless all parties, with the court's approval, agree to the sale, aspects of the sale, or different procedures.

(iv) Sale Proceeds. Sale proceeds are a substitute res subject to forfeiture in place of the property that was sold. The proceeds must be held in an interest-bearing account maintained by the United States pending the conclusion of the forfeiture action.

(v) Delivery on a Claimant's Motion. The court may order that the property be delivered to the claimant pending the conclusion of the action if the claimant shows circumstances that would permit sale under Rule G(7)(b)(i) and gives security under these rules.

(c) Disposing of Forfeited Property. Upon entry of a forfeiture judgment, the property or proceeds from selling the property must be disposed of as provided by law.

(8) Motions.

(a) Motion To Suppress Use of the Property as Evidence. If the defendant property was seized, a party with standing to contest the lawfulness of the seizure may move to suppress use of the property as evidence. Suppression does not affect forfeiture of the property based on independently derived evidence.

(b) Motion To Dismiss the Action.

(i) A claimant who establishes standing to contest forfeiture may move to dismiss the action under Rule 12(b).

(ii) In an action governed by 18 U.S.C. § 983(a)(3)(D) the complaint may not be dismissed on the ground that the government did not have adequate evidence at the time the complaint was filed to establish the forfeitability of the property. The sufficiency of the complaint is governed by Rule G(2).

(c) Motion To Strike a Claim or Answer.

(i) At any time before trial, the government may move to strike a claim or answer:

(A) for failing to comply with Rule G(5) or (6), or

(B) because the claimant lacks standing.

(ii) The motion:

(A) must be decided before any motion by the claimant to dismiss the action; and

(B) may be presented as a motion for judgment on the pleadings or as a motion to determine after a hearing or by summary judgment whether the claimant can carry the burden of establishing standing by a preponderance of the evidence.

(d) Petition To Release Property.

(i) If a United States agency or an agency's contractor holds property for judicial or nonjudicial forfeiture under a statute governed by 18 U.S.C. § 983(f), a person who has filed a claim to the property may petition for its release under § 983(f).

(ii) If a petition for release is filed before a judicial forfeiture action is filed against the property, the petition may be filed either in the district where the property was seized or in the district where a warrant to seize the property issued. If a judicial forfeiture action against the property is later filed in another district—or if the government shows that the action will be filed in another district—the petition may be transferred to that district under 28 U.S.C. § 1404.

(e) Excessive Fines. A claimant may seek to mitigate a forfeiture under the Excessive Fines Clause of the Eighth Amendment by motion for summary judgment or by motion made after entry of a forfeiture judgment if:

(i) the claimant has pleaded the defense under Rule 8; and

(ii) the parties have had the opportunity to conduct civil discovery on the defense.

(9) Trial. Trial is to the court unless any party demands trial by jury under Rule 38.

(Added Apr. 12, 2006, eff. Dec. 1, 2006; amended Mar. 26, 2009, eff. Dec. 1, 2009.)

INDEX TO
FEDERAL RULES OF CIVIL PROCEDURE

FEDERAL RULES OF EVIDENCE

Including Amendments Effective December 1, 2014

ARTICLE I. GENERAL PROVISIONS

RULE 101. SCOPE; DEFINITIONS

(a) Scope. These rules apply to proceedings in United States courts. The specific courts and proceedings to which the rules apply, along with exceptions, are set out in Rule 1101.

(b) Definitions. In these rules:

(1) "civil case" means a civil action or proceeding;

(2) "criminal case" includes a criminal proceeding;

(3) "public office" includes a public agency;

(4) "record" includes a memorandum, report, or data compilation;

(5) a "rule prescribed by the Supreme Court" means a rule adopted by the Supreme Court under statutory authority; and

(6) a reference to any kind of written material or any other medium includes electronically stored information.

(Pub.L. 93–595, § 1, Jan. 2, 1975, 88 Stat. 1929; Mar. 2, 1987, eff. Oct. 1, 1987; Apr. 25, 1988, eff. Nov. 1, 1988; Apr. 22, 1993, eff. Dec. 1, 1993; Apr. 26, 2011, eff. Dec. 1, 2011.)

RULE 102. PURPOSE

These rules should be construed so as to administer every proceeding fairly, eliminate unjustifiable expense and delay, and promote the development of evidence law, to the end of ascertaining the truth and securing a just determination.

(Pub.L. 93–595, § 1, Jan. 2, 1975, 88 Stat.1929; Apr. 26, 2011, eff. Dec. 1, 2011.)

RULE 103. RULINGS ON EVIDENCE

(a) Preserving a Claim of Error. A party may claim error in a ruling to admit or exclude evidence only if the error affects a substantial right of the party and:

(1) if the ruling admits evidence, a party, on the record:

(A) timely objects or moves to strike; and

(B) states the specific ground, unless it was apparent from the context; or

(2) if the ruling excludes evidence, a party informs the court of its substance by an offer of proof, unless the substance was apparent from the context.

(b) Not Needing to Renew an Objection or Offer of Proof. Once the court rules definitively on the record—either before or at trial—a party need not renew an objection or offer of proof to preserve a claim of error for appeal.

(c) Court's Statement About the Ruling; Directing an Offer of Proof. The court may make any statement about the character or form of the evidence, the objection made, and the ruling. The court may direct that an offer of proof be made in question-and-answer form.

(d) Preventing the Jury from Hearing Inadmissible Evidence. To the extent practicable, the court must conduct a jury trial so that inadmissible evidence is not suggested to the jury by any means.

(e) Taking Notice of Plain Error. A court may take notice of a plain error affecting a substantial right, even if the claim of error was not properly preserved.

(Pub.L. 93–595, § 1, Jan. 2, 1975, 88 Stat. 1929; Apr. 17, 2000, eff. Dec. 1, 2000; Apr. 26, 2011, eff. Dec. 1, 2011.)

RULE 104. PRELIMINARY QUESTIONS

(a) In General. The court must decide any preliminary question about whether a witness is qualified, a privilege exists, or evidence is admissible. In so deciding, the court is not bound by evidence rules, except those on privilege.

(b) Relevance That Depends on a Fact. When the relevance of evidence depends on whether a fact exists, proof must be introduced sufficient to support a finding that the fact does exist. The court may admit the proposed evidence on the condition that the proof be introduced later.

(c) Conducting a Hearing So That the Jury Cannot Hear It. The court must conduct any hearing on a preliminary question so that the jury cannot hear it if:

(1) the hearing involves the admissibility of a confession;

(2) a defendant in a criminal case is a witness and so requests; or

(3) justice so requires.

(d) Cross–Examining a Defendant in a Criminal Case. By testifying on a preliminary question, a defendant in a criminal case does not become subject to cross-examination on other issues in the case.

(e) Evidence Relevant to Weight and Credibility. This rule does not limit a party's right to introduce before the jury evidence that is relevant to the weight or credibility of other evidence.

(Pub.L. 93–595, § 1, Jan. 2, 1975, 88 Stat.1930; Mar. 2, 1987, eff. Oct. 1, 1987; Apr. 26, 2011, eff. Dec. 1, 2011.)

RULE 105. LIMITING EVIDENCE THAT IS NOT ADMISSIBLE AGAINST OTHER PARTIES OR FOR OTHER PURPOSES

If the court admits evidence that is admissible against a party or for a purpose—but not against another party or for another purpose—the court, on timely request, must restrict the evidence to its proper scope and instruct the jury accordingly.

(Pub.L. 93–595, § 1, Jan. 2, 1975, 88 Stat. 1930; Apr. 26, 2011, eff. Dec. 1, 2011.)

RULE 106. REMAINDER OF OR RELATED WRITINGS OR RECORDED STATEMENTS

If a party introduces all or part of a writing or recorded statement, an adverse party may require the introduction, at that time, of any other part—or any other writing or recorded statement—that in fairness ought to be considered at the same time.

(Pub.L. 93–595, § 1, Jan. 2, 1975, 88 Stat. 1930; Mar. 2, 1987, eff. Oct. 1, 1987; Apr. 26, 2011, eff. Dec. 1, 2011.)

ARTICLE II. JUDICIAL NOTICE

RULE 201. JUDICIAL NOTICE OF ADJUDICATIVE FACTS

(a) Scope. This rule governs judicial notice of an adjudicative fact only, not a legislative fact.

(b) Kinds of Facts That May Be Judicially Noticed. The court may judicially notice a fact that is not subject to reasonable dispute because it:

(1) is generally known within the trial court's territorial jurisdiction; or

(2) can be accurately and readily determined from sources whose accuracy cannot reasonably be questioned.

(c) Taking Notice. The court:

(1) may take judicial notice on its own; or

(2) must take judicial notice if a party requests it and the court is supplied with the necessary information.

(d) Timing. The court may take judicial notice at any stage of the proceeding.

(e) Opportunity to Be Heard. On timely request, a party is entitled to be heard on the propriety of taking judicial notice and the nature of the fact to be noticed. If the court takes judicial notice before notifying a party, the party, on request, is still entitled to be heard.

(f) Instructing the Jury. In a civil case, the court must instruct the jury to accept the noticed fact as conclusive. In a criminal case, the court must instruct the jury that it may or may not accept the noticed fact as conclusive.

(Pub.L. 93–595, § 1, Jan. 2, 1975, 88 Stat. 1930; Apr. 26, 2011, eff. Dec. 1, 2011.)

ARTICLE III. PRESUMPTIONS IN CIVIL CASES

RULE 301. PRESUMPTIONS IN CIVIL CASES GENERALLY

In a civil case, unless a federal statute or these rules provide otherwise, the party against whom a presumption is directed has the burden of producing evidence to rebut the presumption. But this rule does not shift the burden of persuasion, which remains on the party who had it originally.

(Pub.L. 93–595, § 1, Jan. 2, 1975, 88 Stat. 1931; Apr. 26, 2011, eff. Dec. 1, 2011.)

RULE 302. APPLYING STATE LAW TO PRESUMPTIONS IN CIVIL CASES

In a civil case, state law governs the effect of a presumption regarding a claim or defense for which state law supplies the rule of decision.

(Pub.L. 93–595, § 1, Jan. 2, 1975, 88 Stat. 1931; Apr. 26, 2011, eff. Dec. 1, 2011.)

ARTICLE IV. RELEVANCE AND ITS LIMITS

RULE 401. TEST FOR RELEVANT EVIDENCE

Evidence is relevant if:

(a) it has any tendency to make a fact more or less probable than it would be without the evidence; and

(b) the fact is of consequence in determining the action.

(Pub.L. 93–595, § 1, Jan. 2, 1975, 88 Stat.1931; Apr. 26, 2011, eff. Dec. 1, 2011.)

RULE 402. GENERAL ADMISSIBILITY OF RELEVANT EVIDENCE

Relevant evidence is admissible unless any of the following provides otherwise:

- the United States Constitution;
- a federal statute;
- these rules; or
- other rules prescribed by the Supreme Court.

Irrelevant evidence is not admissible.

(Pub.L. 93–595, § 1, Jan. 2, 1975, 88 Stat. 1931; Apr. 26, 2011, eff. Dec. 1, 2011.)

RULE 403. EXCLUDING RELEVANT EVIDENCE FOR PREJUDICE, CONFUSION, WASTE OF TIME, OR OTHER REASONS

The court may exclude relevant evidence if its probative value is substantially outweighed by a danger of one or more of the following: unfair prejudice, confusing the issues, misleading the jury, undue delay, wasting time, or needlessly presenting cumulative evidence.

(Pub.L. 93–595, § 1, Jan. 2, 1975, 88 Stat. 1932; Apr. 26, 2011, eff. Dec. 1, 2011.)

RULE 404. CHARACTER EVIDENCE; CRIMES OR OTHER ACTS

(a) Character Evidence.

(1) Prohibited Uses. Evidence of a person's character or character trait is not admissible to prove that on a particular occasion the person acted in accordance with the character or trait.

(2) Exceptions for a Defendant or Victim in a Criminal Case. The following exceptions apply in a criminal case:

(A) a defendant may offer evidence of the defendant's pertinent trait, and if the evidence is admitted, the prosecutor may offer evidence to rebut it;

(B) subject to the limitations in Rule 412, a defendant may offer evidence of an alleged victim's pertinent trait, and if the evidence is admitted, the prosecutor may:

(i) offer evidence to rebut it; and

(ii) offer evidence of the defendant's same trait; and

(C) in a homicide case, the prosecutor may offer evidence of the alleged victim's trait of peacefulness to rebut evidence that the victim was the first aggressor.

(3) Exceptions for a Witness. Evidence of a witness's character may be admitted under Rules 607, 608, and 609.

(b) Crimes, Wrongs, or Other Acts.

(1) Prohibited Uses. Evidence of a crime, wrong, or other act is not admissible to prove a person's character in order to show that on a particular occasion the person acted in accordance with the character.

(2) Permitted Uses; Notice in a Criminal Case. This evidence may be admissible for another purpose, such as proving motive, opportunity, intent, preparation, plan, knowledge, identity, absence of mistake, or lack of accident. On request by a defendant in a criminal case, the prosecutor must:

(A) provide reasonable notice of the general nature of any such evidence that the prosecutor intends to offer at trial; and

(B) do so before trial—or during trial if the court, for good cause, excuses lack of pretrial notice.

(Pub.L. 93–595, § 1, Jan. 2, 1975, 88 Stat.1932; Mar. 2, 1987, eff. Oct. 1, 1987; Apr. 30, 1991, eff. Dec. 1, 1991; Apr. 17, 2000, eff. Dec. 1, 2000; Apr. 12, 2006, eff. Dec. 1, 2006; Apr. 26, 2011, eff. Dec. 1, 2011.)

RULE 405. METHODS OF PROVING CHARACTER

(a) By Reputation or Opinion. When evidence of a person's character or character trait is admissible, it may be proved by testimony about the person's reputation or by testimony in the form of an opinion. On cross-examination of the character witness, the court may allow an inquiry into relevant specific instances of the person's conduct.

(b) By Specific Instances of Conduct. When a person's character or character trait is an essential element of a charge, claim, or defense, the character or trait may also be proved by relevant specific instances of the person's conduct.

(Pub.L. 93–595, § 1, Jan. 2, 1975, 88 Stat. 1932; Mar. 2, 1987, eff. Oct. 1, 1987; Apr. 26, 2011, eff. Dec. 1, 2011.)

RULE 406. HABIT; ROUTINE PRACTICE

Evidence of a person's habit or an organization's routine practice may be admitted to prove that on a particular occasion the person or organization acted in accordance with the habit or routine practice. The court may admit this evidence regardless of whether it is corroborated or whether there was an eyewitness.

(Pub.L. 93–595, § 1, Jan. 2, 1975, 88 Stat. 1932; Apr. 26, 2011, eff. Dec. 1, 2011.)

RULE 407. SUBSEQUENT REMEDIAL MEASURES

When measures are taken that would have made an earlier injury or harm less likely to occur, evidence of the subsequent measures is not admissible to prove:

- negligence;
- culpable conduct;
- a defect in a product or its design; or
- a need for a warning or instruction.

But the court may admit this evidence for another purpose, such as impeachment or—if disputed—proving ownership, control, or the feasibility of precautionary measures.

(Pub.L. 93–595, § 1, Jan. 2, 1975, 88 Stat. 1932; Apr. 11, 1997, eff. Dec. 1, 1997; Apr. 26, 2011, eff. Dec. 1, 2011.)

RULE 408. COMPROMISE OFFERS AND NEGOTIATIONS

(a) Prohibited Uses. Evidence of the following is not admissible—on behalf of any party—either to prove or disprove the validity or amount of a disputed claim or to impeach by a prior inconsistent statement or a contradiction:

(1) furnishing, promising, or offering—or accepting, promising to accept, or offering to accept—a valuable consideration in compromising or attempting to compromise the claim; and

(2) conduct or a statement made during compromise negotiations about the claim—except when offered in a criminal case and when the negotiations related to a claim by a public office in the exercise of its regulatory, investigative, or enforcement authority.

(b) Exceptions. The court may admit this evidence for another purpose, such as proving a witness's bias or prejudice, negating a contention of undue

delay, or proving an effort to obstruct a criminal investigation or prosecution.

(Pub.L. 93–595, § 1, Jan. 2, 1975, 88 Stat. 1933; Apr. 12, 2006, eff. Dec. 1, 2006; Apr. 26, 2011, eff. Dec. 1, 2011.)

RULE 409. OFFERS TO PAY MEDICAL AND SIMILAR EXPENSES

Evidence of furnishing, promising to pay, or offering to pay medical, hospital, or similar expenses resulting from an injury is not admissible to prove liability for the injury.

(Pub.L. 93–595, § 1, Jan. 2, 1975, 88 Stat.1933; Apr. 26, 2011, eff. Dec. 1, 2011.)

RULE 410. PLEAS, PLEA DISCUSSIONS, AND RELATED STATEMENTS

(a) Prohibited Uses. In a civil or criminal case, evidence of the following is not admissible against the defendant who made the plea or participated in the plea discussions:

(1) a guilty plea that was later withdrawn;

(2) a nolo contendere plea;

(3) a statement made during a proceeding on either of those pleas under Federal Rule of Criminal Procedure 11 or a comparable state procedure; or

(4) a statement made during plea discussions with an attorney for the prosecuting authority if the discussions did not result in a guilty plea or they resulted in a later-withdrawn guilty plea.

(b) Exceptions. The court may admit a statement described in Rule 410(a)(3) or (4):

(1) in any proceeding in which another statement made during the same plea or plea discussions has been introduced, if in fairness the statements ought to be considered together; or

(2) in a criminal proceeding for perjury or false statement, if the defendant made the statement under oath, on the record, and with counsel present.

(Pub.L. 93–595, § 1, Jan. 2, 1975, 88 Stat. 1933; Pub.L. 94–149, § 1(9), Dec. 12, 1975, 89 Stat. 805; Apr. 30, 1979, eff. Dec. 1, 1980; Apr. 26, 2011, eff. Dec. 1, 2011.)

RULE 411. LIABILITY INSURANCE

Evidence that a person was or was not insured against liability is not admissible to prove whether the person acted negligently or otherwise wrongfully. But the court may admit this evidence for another purpose, such as proving a witness's bias or prejudice or proving agency, ownership, or control.

(Pub.L. 93–595, § 1, Jan. 2, 1975, 88 Stat.1933; Mar. 2, 1987, eff. Oct. 1, 1987; Apr. 26, 2011, eff. Dec. 1, 2011.)

RULE 412. SEX–OFFENSE CASES: THE VICTIM'S SEXUAL BEHAVIOR OR PREDISPOSITION

(a) Prohibited Uses. The following evidence is not admissible in a civil or criminal proceeding involving alleged sexual misconduct:

(1) evidence offered to prove that a victim engaged in other sexual behavior; or

(2) evidence offered to prove a victim's sexual predisposition.

(b) Exceptions.

(1) Criminal Cases. The court may admit the following evidence in a criminal case:

(A) evidence of specific instances of a victim's sexual behavior, if offered to prove that someone other than the defendant was the source of semen, injury, or other physical evidence;

(B) evidence of specific instances of a victim's sexual behavior with respect to the person accused of the sexual misconduct, if offered by the defendant to prove consent or if offered by the prosecutor; and

(C) evidence whose exclusion would violate the defendant's constitutional rights.

(2) Civil Cases. In a civil case, the court may admit evidence offered to prove a victim's sexual behavior or sexual predisposition if its probative value substantially outweighs the danger of harm to any victim and of unfair prejudice to any party. The court may admit evidence of a victim's reputation only if the victim has placed it in controversy.

(c) Procedure to Determine Admissibility.

(1) Motion. If a party intends to offer evidence under Rule 412(b), the party must:

(A) file a motion that specifically describes the evidence and states the purpose for which it is to be offered;

(B) do so at least 14 days before trial unless the court, for good cause, sets a different time;

(C) serve the motion on all parties; and

(D) notify the victim or, when appropriate, the victim's guardian or representative.

(2) Hearing. Before admitting evidence under this rule, the court must conduct an in camera hearing and give the victim and parties a right to attend and be heard. Unless the court orders otherwise, the motion, related materials, and the record of the hearing must be and remain sealed.

(d) Definition of "Victim." In this rule, "victim" includes an alleged victim.

(Added Pub.L. 95–540, § 2(a), Oct. 28, 1978, 92 Stat. 2046; amended Pub.L. 100–690, Title VII, § 7046(a), Nov. 18, 1988, 102 Stat. 4400; Apr. 29, 1994, eff. Dec. 1, 1994; Pub.L. 103–322, Title IV, § 40141(b), Sept. 13, 1994, 108 Stat. 1919; Apr. 26, 2011, eff. Dec. 1, 2011.)

RULE 413. SIMILAR CRIMES IN SEXUAL–ASSAULT CASES

(a) Permitted Uses. In a criminal case in which a defendant is accused of a sexual assault, the court may admit evidence that the defendant committed any other sexual assault. The evidence may be considered on any matter to which it is relevant.

(b) Disclosure to the Defendant. If the prosecutor intends to offer this evidence, the prosecutor must disclose it to the defendant, including witnesses' statements or a summary of the expected testimony. The prosecutor must do so at least 15 days before trial or at a later time that the court allows for good cause.

(c) Effect on Other Rules. This rule does not limit the admission or consideration of evidence under any other rule.

(d) Definition of "Sexual Assault." In this rule and Rule 415, "sexual assault" means a crime under federal law or under state law (as "state" is defined in 18 U.S.C. § 513) involving:

(1) any conduct prohibited by 18 U.S.C. chapter 109A;

(2) contact, without consent, between any part of the defendant's body—or an object—and another person's genitals or anus;

(3) contact, without consent, between the defendant's genitals or anus and any part of another person's body;

(4) deriving sexual pleasure or gratification from inflicting death, bodily injury, or physical pain on another person; or

(5) an attempt or conspiracy to engage in conduct described in subparagraphs (1)–(4).

(Added Pub.L. 103–322, Title XXXII, § 320935(a), Sept. 13, 1994, 108 Stat. 2136; Apr. 26, 2011, eff. Dec. 1, 2011.)

RULE 414. SIMILAR CRIMES IN CHILD–MOLESTATION CASES

(a) Permitted Uses. In a criminal case in which a defendant is accused of child molestation, the court may admit evidence that the defendant committed any other child molestation. The evidence may be considered on any matter to which it is relevant.

(b) Disclosure to the Defendant. If the prosecutor intends to offer this evidence, the prosecutor must disclose it to the defendant, including witnesses' statements or a summary of the expected testimony. The prosecutor must do so at least 15 days before trial or at a later time that the court allows for good cause.

(c) Effect on Other Rules. This rule does not limit the admission or consideration of evidence under any other rule.

(d) Definition of "Child" and "Child Molestation." In this rule and Rule 415:

(1) "child" means a person below the age of 14; and

(2) "child molestation" means a crime under federal law or under state law (as "state" is defined in 18 U.S.C. § 513) involving:

(A) any conduct prohibited by 18 U.S.C. chapter 109A and committed with a child;

(B) any conduct prohibited by 18 U.S.C. chapter 110;

(C) contact between any part of the defendant's body—or an object—and a child's genitals or anus;

(D) contact between the defendant's genitals or anus and any part of a child's body;

(E) deriving sexual pleasure or gratification from inflicting death, bodily injury, or physical pain on a child; or

(F) an attempt or conspiracy to engage in conduct described in subparagraphs (A)–(E).

(Added Pub.L. 103–322, Title XXXII, § 320935(a), Sept. 13, 1994, 108 Stat. 2135; Apr. 26, 2011, eff. Dec. 1, 2011.)

RULE 415. SIMILAR ACTS IN CIVIL CASES INVOLVING SEXUAL ASSAULT OR CHILD MOLESTATION

(a) Permitted Uses. In a civil case involving a claim for relief based on a party's alleged sexual assault or child molestation, the court may admit evidence that the party committed any other sexual assault or child molestation. The evidence may be considered as provided in Rules 413 and 414.

(b) Disclosure to the Opponent. If a party intends to offer this evidence, the party must disclose it to the party against whom it will be offered, including witnesses' statements or a summary of the expected testimony. The party must do so at least 15 days before trial or at a later time that the court allows for good cause.

(c) Effect on Other Rules. This rule does not limit the admission or consideration of evidence under any other rule.

(Added Pub.L. 103–322, Title XXXII, § 320935(a), Sept. 13, 1994, 108 Stat. 2137; Apr. 26, 2011, eff. Dec. 1, 2011.)

ARTICLE V. PRIVILEGES

RULE 501. PRIVILEGE IN GENERAL

The common law—as interpreted by United States courts in the light of reason and experience—governs a claim of privilege unless any of the following provides otherwise:

- the United States Constitution;
- a federal statute; or
- rules prescribed by the Supreme Court.

But in a civil case, state law governs privilege regarding a claim or defense for which state law supplies the rule of decision.

(Pub.L. 93–595, § 1, Jan. 2, 1975, 88 Stat. 1933; Apr. 26, 2011, eff. Dec. 1, 2011.)

RULE 502. ATTORNEY–CLIENT PRIVILEGE AND WORK PRODUCT; LIMITATIONS ON WAIVER

The following provisions apply, in the circumstances set out, to disclosure of a communication or information covered by the attorney-client privilege or work-product protection.

(a) Disclosure Made in a Federal Proceeding or to a Federal Office or Agency; Scope of a Waiver.

When the disclosure is made in a federal proceeding or to a federal office or agency and waives the attorney-client privilege or work-product protection, the waiver extends to an undisclosed communication or information in a federal or state proceeding only if:

(1) the waiver is intentional;

(2) the disclosed and undisclosed communications or information concern the same subject matter; and

(3) they ought in fairness to be considered together.

(b) Inadvertent Disclosure. When made in a federal proceeding or to a federal office or agency, the disclosure does not operate as a waiver in a federal or state proceeding if:

(1) the disclosure is inadvertent;

(2) the holder of the privilege or protection took reasonable steps to prevent disclosure; and

(3) the holder promptly took reasonable steps to rectify the error, including (if applicable) following Federal Rule of Civil Procedure 26(b)(5)(B).

(c) Disclosure Made in a State Proceeding. When the disclosure is made in a state proceeding and is not the subject of a state-court order concerning waiver, the disclosure does not operate as a waiver in a federal proceeding if the disclosure:

(1) would not be a waiver under this rule if it had been made in a federal proceeding; or

(2) is not a waiver under the law of the state where the disclosure occurred.

(d) Controlling Effect of a Court Order. A federal court may order that the privilege or protection is not waived by disclosure connected with the litigation pending before the court—in which event the disclosure is also not a waiver in any other federal or state proceeding.

(e) Controlling Effect of a Party Agreement. An agreement on the effect of disclosure in a federal proceeding is binding only on the parties to the agreement, unless it is incorporated into a court order.

(f) Controlling Effect of This Rule. Notwithstanding Rules 101 and 1101, this rule applies to state proceedings and to federal court-annexed and federal court-mandated arbitration proceedings, in the circumstances set out in the rule. And notwithstanding Rule 501, this rule applies even if state law provides the rule of decision.

(g) Definitions. In this rule:

(1) "attorney-client privilege" means the protection that applicable law provides for confidential attorney-client communications; and

(2) "work-product protection" means the protection that applicable law provides for tangible material (or its intangible equivalent) prepared in anticipation of litigation or for trial.

(Pub.L. 110–322, § 1(a), Sept. 19, 2008, 122 Stat. 3537; Apr. 26, 2011, eff. Dec. 1, 2011.)

ARTICLE VI. WITNESSES

RULE 601. COMPETENCY TO TESTIFY IN GENERAL

Every person is competent to be a witness unless these rules provide otherwise. But in a civil case, state law governs the witness's competency regarding a claim or defense for which state law supplies the rule of decision.

(Pub.L. 93–595, § 1, Jan. 2, 1975, 88 Stat.1934; Apr. 26, 2011, eff. Dec. 1, 2011.)

RULE 602. NEED FOR PERSONAL KNOWLEDGE

A witness may testify to a matter only if evidence is introduced sufficient to support a finding that the witness has personal knowledge of the matter. Evidence to prove personal knowledge may consist of the witness's own testimony. This rule does not apply to a witness's expert testimony under Rule 703.

(Pub.L. 93–595, § 1, Jan. 2, 1975, 88 Stat. 1934; Mar. 2, 1987, eff. Oct. 1, 1987; Apr. 25, 1988, eff. Nov. 1, 1988; Apr. 26, 2011, eff. Dec. 1, 2011.)

RULE 603. OATH OR AFFIRMATION TO TESTIFY TRUTHFULLY

Before testifying, a witness must give an oath or affirmation to testify truthfully. It must be in a form designed to impress that duty on the witness's conscience.

(Pub.L. 93–595, § 1, Jan. 2, 1975, 88 Stat. 1934; Mar. 2, 1987, eff. Oct. 1, 1987; Apr. 26, 2011, eff. Dec. 1, 2011.)

RULE 604. INTERPRETER

An interpreter must be qualified and must give an oath or affirmation to make a true translation.

(Pub.L. 93–595, § 1, Jan. 2, 1975, 88 Stat. 1934; Mar. 2, 1987, eff. Oct. 1, 1987; Apr. 26, 2011, eff. Dec. 1, 2011.)

RULE 605. JUDGE'S COMPETENCY AS A WITNESS

The presiding judge may not testify as a witness at the trial. A party need not object to preserve the issue.

(Pub.L. 93–595, § 1, Jan. 2, 1975, 88 Stat. 1934; Apr. 26, 2011, eff. Dec. 1, 2011.)

RULE 606. JUROR'S COMPETENCY AS A WITNESS

(a) At the Trial. A juror may not testify as a witness before the other jurors at the trial. If a juror is called to testify, the court must give a party an opportunity to object outside the jury's presence.

(b) During an Inquiry Into the Validity of a Verdict or Indictment.

(1) **Prohibited Testimony or Other Evidence.** During an inquiry into the validity of a verdict or indictment, a juror may not testify about any statement made or incident that occurred during the jury's deliberations; the effect of anything on that juror's or another juror's vote; or any juror's mental processes concerning the verdict or indictment. The court may not receive a juror's affidavit or evidence of a juror's statement on these matters.

(2) **Exceptions.** A juror may testify about whether:

(A) extraneous prejudicial information was improperly brought to the jury's attention;

(B) an outside influence was improperly brought to bear on any juror; or

(C) a mistake was made in entering the verdict on the verdict form.

(Pub.L. 93–595, § 1, Jan. 2, 1975, 88 Stat. 1934; Pub.L. 94–149, § 1(10), Dec. 12, 1975, 89 Stat. 805; Mar. 2, 1987, eff. Oct. 1, 1987; Apr. 12, 2006, eff. Dec. 1, 2006; Apr. 26, 2011, eff. Dec. 1, 2011.)

RULE 607. WHO MAY IMPEACH A WITNESS

Any party, including the party that called the witness, may attack the witness's credibility.

(Pub.L. 93–595, § 1, Jan. 2, 1975, 88 Stat.1934; Mar. 2, 1987, eff. Oct. 1, 1987; Apr. 26, 2011, eff. Dec. 1, 2011.)

RULE 608. A WITNESS'S CHARACTER FOR TRUTHFULNESS OR UNTRUTHFULNESS

(a) Reputation or Opinion Evidence. A witness's credibility may be attacked or supported by testimony about the witness's reputation for having a character for truthfulness or untruthfulness, or by testimony in the form of an opinion about that character. But evidence of truthful character is admissible only after the witness's character for truthfulness has been attacked.

(b) Specific Instances of Conduct. Except for a criminal conviction under Rule 609, extrinsic evidence is not admissible to prove specific instances of a witness's conduct in order to attack or support the witness's character for truthfulness. But the court may, on cross-examination, allow them to be inquired into if they are probative of the character for truthfulness or untruthfulness of:

(1) the witness; or

(2) another witness whose character the witness being cross-examined has testified about.

By testifying on another matter, a witness does not waive any privilege against self-incrimination for testimony that relates only to the witness's character for truthfulness.

(Pub.L. 93–595, § 1, Jan. 2, 1975, 88 Stat.1935; Mar. 2, 1987, eff. Oct. 1, 1987; Apr. 25, 1988, eff. Nov. 1, 1988; Mar. 27, 2003, eff. Dec. 1, 2003; Apr. 26, 2011, eff. Dec. 1, 2011.)

RULE 609. IMPEACHMENT BY EVIDENCE OF A CRIMINAL CONVICTION

(a) In General. The following rules apply to attacking a witness's character for truthfulness by evidence of a criminal conviction:

(1) for a crime that, in the convicting jurisdiction, was punishable by death or by imprisonment for more than one year, the evidence:

(A) must be admitted, subject to Rule 403, in a civil case or in a criminal case in which the witness is not a defendant; and

(B) must be admitted in a criminal case in which the witness is a defendant, if the probative value of the evidence outweighs its prejudicial effect to that defendant; and

(2) for any crime regardless of the punishment, the evidence must be admitted if the court can readily determine that establishing the elements of the crime required proving—or the witness's admitting—a dishonest act or false statement.

(b) Limit on Using the Evidence After 10 Years. This subdivision (b) applies if more than 10 years have passed since the witness's conviction or release from confinement for it, whichever is later. Evidence of the conviction is admissible only if:

(1) its probative value, supported by specific facts and circumstances, substantially outweighs its prejudicial effect; and

(2) the proponent gives an adverse party reasonable written notice of the intent to use it so that the party has a fair opportunity to contest its use.

(c) Effect of a Pardon, Annulment, or Certificate of Rehabilitation. Evidence of a conviction is not admissible if:

(1) the conviction has been the subject of a pardon, annulment, certificate of rehabilitation, or other equivalent procedure based on a finding that the person has been rehabilitated, and the person has not been convicted of a later crime punishable by death or by imprisonment for more than one year; or

(2) the conviction has been the subject of a pardon, annulment, or other equivalent procedure based on a finding of innocence.

(d) Juvenile Adjudications. Evidence of a juvenile adjudication is admissible under this rule only if:

(1) it is offered in a criminal case;

(2) the adjudication was of a witness other than the defendant;

(3) an adult's conviction for that offense would be admissible to attack the adult's credibility; and

(4) admitting the evidence is necessary to fairly determine guilt or innocence.

(e) Pendency of an Appeal. A conviction that satisfies this rule is admissible even if an appeal is pending. Evidence of the pendency is also admissible.

(Pub.L. 93–595, § 1, Jan. 2, 1975, 88 Stat.1935; Mar. 2, 1987, eff. Oct. 1, 1987; Jan. 26, 1990, eff. Dec. 1, 1990; Apr. 12, 2006, eff. Dec. 1, 2006; Apr. 26, 2011, eff. Dec. 1, 2011.)

RULE 610. RELIGIOUS BELIEFS OR OPINIONS

Evidence of a witness's religious beliefs or opinions is not admissible to attack or support the witness's credibility.

(Pub.L. 93–595, § 1, Jan. 2, 1975, 88 Stat.1936; Mar. 2, 1987, eff. Oct. 1, 1987; Apr. 26, 2011, eff. Dec. 1, 2011.)

RULE 611. MODE AND ORDER OF EXAMINING WITNESSES AND PRESENTING EVIDENCE

(a) Control by the Court; Purposes. The court should exercise reasonable control over the mode and order of examining witnesses and presenting evidence so as to:

(1) make those procedures effective for determining the truth;

(2) avoid wasting time; and

(3) protect witnesses from harassment or undue embarrassment.

(b) Scope of Cross–Examination. Cross-examination should not go beyond the subject matter of the direct examination and matters affecting the witness's credibility. The court may allow inquiry into additional matters as if on direct examination.

(c) Leading Questions. Leading questions should not be used on direct examination except as necessary to develop the witness's testimony. Ordinarily, the court should allow leading questions:

(1) on cross-examination; and

(2) when a party calls a hostile witness, an adverse party, or a witness identified with an adverse party.

(Pub.L. 93–595, § 1, Jan. 2, 1975, 88 Stat. 1936; Mar. 2, 1987, eff. Oct. 1, 1987; Apr. 26, 2011, eff. Dec. 1, 2011.)

RULE 612. WRITING USED TO REFRESH A WITNESS'S MEMORY

(a) Scope. This rule gives an adverse party certain options when a witness uses a writing to refresh memory:

(1) while testifying; or

(2) before testifying, if the court decides that justice requires the party to have those options.

(b) Adverse Party's Options; Deleting Unrelated Matter. Unless 18 U.S.C. § 3500 provides otherwise in a criminal case, an adverse party is entitled to have the writing produced at the hearing, to inspect it, to cross-examine the witness about it, and to introduce in evidence any portion that relates to the witness's testimony. If the producing party claims that the writing includes unrelated matter, the court must examine the writing in camera, delete any unrelated portion, and order that the rest be delivered to the adverse party. Any portion deleted over objection must be preserved for the record.

(c) Failure to Produce or Deliver the Writing. If a writing is not produced or is not delivered as ordered, the court may issue any appropriate order. But if the prosecution does not comply in a criminal case, the court must strike the witness's testimony or—if justice so requires—declare a mistrial.

(Pub.L. 93–595, § 1, Jan. 2, 1975, 88 Stat. 1936; Mar. 2, 1987, eff. Oct. 1, 1987; Apr. 26, 2011, eff. Dec. 1, 2011.)

RULE 613. WITNESS'S PRIOR STATEMENT

(a) Showing or Disclosing the Statement During Examination. When examining a witness about the witness's prior statement, a party need not show it or disclose its contents to the witness. But the party must, on request, show it or disclose its contents to an adverse party's attorney.

(b) Extrinsic Evidence of a Prior Inconsistent Statement. Extrinsic evidence of a witness's prior inconsistent statement is admissible only if the witness is given an opportunity to explain or deny the statement and an adverse party is given an opportunity to examine the witness about it, or if justice so requires. This subdivision (b) does not apply to an opposing party's statement under Rule 801(d)(2).

(Pub.L. 93–595, § 1, Jan. 2, 1975, 88 Stat.1936; Mar. 2, 1987, eff. Oct. 1, 1987; Apr. 25, 1988, eff. Nov. 1, 1988; Apr. 26, 2011, eff. Dec. 1, 2011.)

RULE 614. COURT'S CALLING OR EXAMINING A WITNESS

(a) Calling. The court may call a witness on its own or at a party's request. Each party is entitled to cross-examine the witness.

(b) Examining. The court may examine a witness regardless of who calls the witness.

(c) Objections. A party may object to the court's calling or examining a witness either at that time or at the next opportunity when the jury is not present.

(Pub.L. 93–595, § 1, Jan. 2, 1975, 88 Stat.1937; Apr. 26, 2011, eff. Dec. 1, 2011.)

RULE 615. EXCLUDING WITNESSES

At a party's request, the court must order witnesses excluded so that they cannot hear other witnesses' testimony. Or the court may do so on its own. But this rule does not authorize excluding:

(a) a party who is a natural person;

(b) an officer or employee of a party that is not a natural person, after being designated as the party's representative by its attorney;

(c) a person whose presence a party shows to be essential to presenting the party's claim or defense; or

(d) a person authorized by statute to be present.

(Pub.L. 93–595, § 1, Jan. 2, 1975, 88 Stat.1937; Mar. 2, 1987, eff. Oct. 1, 1987; Apr. 25, 1988, eff. Nov. 1, 1988; Pub.L. 100–690, Nov. 18, 1988, Title VII, § 7075(a), 102 Stat. 4405; Apr. 24, 1998, eff. Dec. 1, 1998; Apr. 26, 2011, eff. Dec. 1, 2011.)

ARTICLE VII. OPINIONS AND EXPERT TESTIMONY

RULE 701. OPINION TESTIMONY BY LAY WITNESSES

If a witness is not testifying as an expert, testimony in the form of an opinion is limited to one that is:

(a) rationally based on the witness's perception;

(b) helpful to clearly understanding the witness's testimony or to determining a fact in issue; and

(c) not based on scientific, technical, or other specialized knowledge within the scope of Rule 702.

(Pub.L. 93–595, § 1, Jan. 2, 1975, 88 Stat.1937; Mar. 2, 1987, eff. Oct. 1, 1987; Apr. 17, 2000, eff. Dec. 1, 2000; Apr. 26, 2011, eff. Dec. 1, 2011.)

RULE 702. TESTIMONY BY EXPERT WITNESSES

A witness who is qualified as an expert by knowledge, skill, experience, training, or education may testify in the form of an opinion or otherwise if:

(a) the expert's scientific, technical, or other specialized knowledge will help the trier of fact to understand the evidence or to determine a fact in issue;

(b) the testimony is based on sufficient facts or data;

(c) the testimony is the product of reliable principles and methods; and

(d) the expert has reliably applied the principles and methods to the facts of the case.

(Pub.L. 93–595, § 1, Jan. 2, 1975, 88 Stat. 1937; Apr. 17, 2000, eff. Dec. 1, 2000; Apr. 26, 2011, eff. Dec. 1, 2011.)

RULE 703. BASES OF AN EXPERT'S OPINION TESTIMONY

An expert may base an opinion on facts or data in the case that the expert has been made aware of or personally observed. If experts in the particular field would reasonably rely on those kinds of facts or data in forming an opinion on the subject, they need not be admissible for the opinion to be admitted. But if the facts or data would otherwise be inadmissible, the proponent of the opinion may disclose them to the jury only if their probative value in helping the jury

evaluate the opinion substantially outweighs their prejudicial effect.

(Pub.L. 93–595, § 1, Jan. 2, 1975, 88 Stat.1937; Mar. 2, 1987, eff. Oct. 1, 1987; Apr. 17, 2000, eff. Dec. 1, 2000; Apr. 26, 2011, eff. Dec. 1, 2011.)

RULE 704. OPINION ON AN ULTIMATE ISSUE

(a) In General—Not Automatically Objectionable. An opinion is not objectionable just because it embraces an ultimate issue.

(b) Exception. In a criminal case, an expert witness must not state an opinion about whether the defendant did or did not have a mental state or condition that constitutes an element of the crime charged or of a defense. Those matters are for the trier of fact alone.

(Pub.L. 93–595, § 1, Jan. 2, 1975, 88 Stat. 1937; Pub.L. 98–473, Title IV, § 406, Oct. 12, 1984, 98 Stat. 2067; Apr. 26, 2011, eff. Dec. 1, 2011.)

RULE 705. DISCLOSING THE FACTS OR DATA UNDERLYING AN EXPERT'S OPINION

Unless the court orders otherwise, an expert may state an opinion—and give the reasons for it—without first testifying to the underlying facts or data. But the expert may be required to disclose those facts or data on cross-examination.

(Pub.L. 93–595, § 1, Jan. 2, 1975, 88 Stat. 1938; Mar. 2, 1987, eff. Oct. 1, 1987; Apr. 22, 1993, eff. Dec. 1, 1993; Apr. 26, 2011, eff. Dec. 1, 2011.)

RULE 706. COURT–APPOINTED EXPERT WITNESSES

(a) Appointment Process. On a party's motion or on its own, the court may order the parties to show cause why expert witnesses should not be appointed and may ask the parties to submit nominations. The court may appoint any expert that the parties agree on and any of its own choosing. But the court may only appoint someone who consents to act.

(b) Expert's Role. The court must inform the expert of the expert's duties. The court may do so in writing and have a copy filed with the clerk or may do so orally at a conference in which the parties have an opportunity to participate. The expert:

    (1) must advise the parties of any findings the expert makes;

    (2) may be deposed by any party;

    (3) may be called to testify by the court or any party; and

    (4) may be cross-examined by any party, including the party that called the expert.

(c) Compensation. The expert is entitled to a reasonable compensation, as set by the court. The compensation is payable as follows:

    (1) in a criminal case or in a civil case involving just compensation under the Fifth Amendment, from any funds that are provided by law; and

    (2) in any other civil case, by the parties in the proportion and at the time that the court directs—and the compensation is then charged like other costs.

(d) Disclosing the Appointment to the Jury. The court may authorize disclosure to the jury that the court appointed the expert.

(e) Parties' Choice of Their Own Experts. This rule does not limit a party in calling its own experts.

(Pub.L. 93–595, § 1, Jan. 2, 1975, 88 Stat.1938; Mar. 2, 1987, eff. Oct. 1, 1987; Apr. 26, 2011, eff. Dec. 1, 2011.)

ARTICLE VIII. HEARSAY

RULE 801. DEFINITIONS THAT APPLY TO THIS ARTICLE; EXCLUSIONS FROM HEARSAY

(a) Statement. "Statement" means a person's oral assertion, written assertion, or nonverbal conduct, if the person intended it as an assertion.

(b) Declarant. "Declarant" means the person who made the statement.

(c) Hearsay. "Hearsay" means a statement that:

    (1) the declarant does not make while testifying at the current trial or hearing; and

    (2) a party offers in evidence to prove the truth of the matter asserted in the statement.

(d) Statements That Are Not Hearsay. A statement that meets the following conditions is not hearsay:

    (1) A Declarant–Witness's Prior Statement. The declarant testifies and is subject to cross-examination about a prior statement, and the statement:

        (A) is inconsistent with the declarant's testimony and was given under penalty of perjury at a trial, hearing, or other proceeding or in a deposition;

        (B) is consistent with the declarant's testimony and is offered:

        (i) to rebut an express or implied charge that the declarant recently fabricated it or acted from a recent improper influence or motive in so testifying; or

        (ii) to rehabilitate the declarant's credibility as a witness when attacked on another ground; or

        (C) identifies a person as someone the declarant perceived earlier.

    (2) An Opposing Party's Statement. The statement is offered against an opposing party and:

        (A) was made by the party in an individual or representative capacity;

        (B) is one the party manifested that it adopted or believed to be true;

        (C) was made by a person whom the party authorized to make a statement on the subject;

        (D) was made by the party's agent or employee on a matter within the scope of that relationship and while it existed; or

        (E) was made by the party's coconspirator during and in furtherance of the conspiracy.

The statement must be considered but does not by itself establish the declarant's authority under (C); the existence or scope of the relationship under (D); or the existence of the conspiracy or participation in it under (E).

(Pub.L. 93–595, § 1, Jan. 2, 1975, 88 Stat.1938; Pub.L. 94–113, § 1, Oct. 16, 1975, 89 Stat. 576; Mar. 2, 1987, eff. Oct. 1, 1987; Apr. 11, 1997, eff. Dec. 1, 1997; Apr. 26, 2011, eff. Dec. 1, 2011; Apr. 25, 2014, eff. Dec. 1, 2014.)

RULE 802. THE RULE AGAINST HEARSAY

Hearsay is not admissible unless any of the following provides otherwise:

- a federal statute;
- these rules; or
- other rules prescribed by the Supreme Court.

(Pub.L. 93–595, § 1, Jan. 2, 1975, 88 Stat. 1939; Apr. 26, 2011, eff. Dec. 1, 2011.)

RULE 803. EXCEPTIONS TO THE RULE AGAINST HEARSAY—REGARDLESS OF WHETHER THE DECLARANT IS AVAILABLE AS A WITNESS

The following are not excluded by the rule against hearsay, regardless of whether the declarant is available as a witness:

(1) Present Sense Impression. A statement describing or explaining an event or condition, made while or immediately after the declarant perceived it.

(2) Excited Utterance. A statement relating to a startling event or condition, made while the declarant was under the stress of excitement that it caused.

(3) Then–Existing Mental, Emotional, or Physical Condition. A statement of the declarant's then-existing state of mind (such as motive, intent, or plan) or emotional, sensory, or physical condition (such as mental feeling, pain, or bodily health), but not including a statement of memory or belief to prove the fact remembered or believed unless it relates to the validity or terms of the declarant's will.

(4) Statement Made for Medical Diagnosis or Treatment. A statement that:

    (A) is made for—and is reasonably pertinent to—medical diagnosis or treatment; and

    (B) describes medical history; past or present symptoms or sensations; their inception; or their general cause.

(5) Recorded Recollection. A record that:

    (A) is on a matter the witness once knew about but now cannot recall well enough to testify fully and accurately;

    (B) was made or adopted by the witness when the matter was fresh in the witness's memory; and

    (C) accurately reflects the witness's knowledge.

If admitted, the record may be read into evidence but may be received as an exhibit only if offered by an adverse party.

(6) Records of a Regularly Conducted Activity. A record of an act, event, condition, opinion, or diagnosis if:

    (A) the record was made at or near the time by—or from information transmitted by—someone with knowledge;

    (B) the record was kept in the course of a regularly conducted activity of a business, organization, occupation, or calling, whether or not for profit;

    (C) making the record was a regular practice of that activity;

    (D) all these conditions are shown by the testimony of the custodian or another qualified witness, or by a certification that complies with Rule 902(11) or (12) or with a statute permitting certification; and

    (E) the opponent does not show that the source of information or the method or circumstances of preparation indicate a lack of trustworthiness.

(7) Absence of a Record of a Regularly Conducted Activity. Evidence that a matter is not included in a record described in paragraph (6) if:

    (A) the evidence is admitted to prove that the matter did not occur or exist;

    (B) a record was regularly kept for a matter of that kind; and

    (C) the opponent does not show that the possible source of the information or other circumstances indicate a lack of trustworthiness.

(8) Public Records. A record or statement of a public office if:

    (A) it sets out:

        (i) the office's activities;

        (ii) a matter observed while under a legal duty to report, but not including, in a criminal case, a matter observed by law-enforcement personnel; or

        (iii) in a civil case or against the government in a criminal case, factual findings from a legally authorized investigation; and

    (B) the opponent does not show that the source of information or other circumstances indicate a lack of trustworthiness.

(9) Public Records of Vital Statistics. A record of a birth, death, or marriage, if reported to a public office in accordance with a legal duty.

(10) Absence of a Public Record. Testimony—or a certification under Rule 902—that a diligent search failed to disclose a public record or statement if:

    (A) the testimony or certification is admitted to prove that

        (i) the record or statement does not exist; or

        (ii) a matter did not occur or exist, if a public office regularly kept a record or statement for a matter of that kind; and

    (B) in a criminal case, a prosecutor who intends to offer a certification provides written notice of that intent at least 14 days before trial, and the defendant does not object in writing within 7 days of receiving the notice—unless the court sets a different time for the notice or the objection.

(11) Records of Religious Organizations Concerning Personal or Family History. A statement of birth, legitimacy, ancestry, marriage, divorce, death, relationship by blood or marriage, or similar facts of personal or family history, contained in a regularly kept record of a religious organization.

(12) Certificates of Marriage, Baptism, and Similar Ceremonies. A statement of fact contained in a certificate:

(A) made by a person who is authorized by a religious organization or by law to perform the act certified;

(B) attesting that the person performed a marriage or similar ceremony or administered a sacrament; and

(C) purporting to have been issued at the time of the act or within a reasonable time after it.

(13) Family Records. A statement of fact about personal or family history contained in a family record, such as a Bible, genealogy, chart, engraving on a ring, inscription on a portrait, or engraving on an urn or burial marker.

(14) Records of Documents That Affect an Interest in Property. The record of a document that purports to establish or affect an interest in property if:

(A) the record is admitted to prove the content of the original recorded document, along with its signing and its delivery by each person who purports to have signed it;

(B) the record is kept in a public office; and

(C) a statute authorizes recording documents of that kind in that office.

(15) Statements in Documents That Affect an Interest in Property. A statement contained in a document that purports to establish or affect an interest in property if the matter stated was relevant to the document's purpose—unless later dealings with the property are inconsistent with the truth of the statement or the purport of the document.

(16) Statements in Ancient Documents. A statement in a document that is at least 20 years old and whose authenticity is established.

(17) Market Reports and Similar Commercial Publications. Market quotations, lists, directories, or other compilations that are generally relied on by the public or by persons in particular occupations.

(18) Statements in Learned Treatises, Periodicals, or Pamphlets. A statement contained in a treatise, periodical, or pamphlet if:

(A) the statement is called to the attention of an expert witness on cross-examination or relied on by the expert on direct examination; and

(B) the publication is established as a reliable authority by the expert's admission or testimony, by another expert's testimony, or by judicial notice.

If admitted, the statement may be read into evidence but not received as an exhibit.

(19) Reputation Concerning Personal or Family History. A reputation among a person's family by blood, adoption, or marriage—or among a person's associates or in the community—concerning the person's birth, adoption, legitimacy, ancestry, marriage, divorce, death, relationship by blood, adoption, or marriage, or similar facts of personal or family history.

(20) Reputation Concerning Boundaries or General History. A reputation in a community—arising before the controversy—concerning boundaries of land in the community or customs that affect the land, or concerning general historical events important to that community, state, or nation.

(21) Reputation Concerning Character. A reputation among a person's associates or in the community concerning the person's character.

(22) Judgment of a Previous Conviction. Evidence of a final judgment of conviction if:

(A) the judgment was entered after a trial or guilty plea, but not a nolo contendere plea;

(B) the conviction was for a crime punishable by death or by imprisonment for more than a year;

(C) the evidence is admitted to prove any fact essential to the judgment; and

(D) when offered by the prosecutor in a criminal case for a purpose other than impeachment, the judgment was against the defendant.

The pendency of an appeal may be shown but does not affect admissibility.

(23) Judgments Involving Personal, Family, or General History, or a Boundary. A judgment that is admitted to prove a matter of personal, family, or general history, or boundaries, if the matter:

(A) was essential to the judgment; and

(B) could be proved by evidence of reputation.

(24) **[Other Exceptions.]** [Transferred to Rule 807.]

(Pub.L. 93–595, § 1, Jan. 2, 1975, 88 Stat. 1939; Pub.L. 94–149, § 1(11), Dec. 12, 1975, 89 Stat. 805; Mar. 2, 1987, eff. Oct. 1, 1987; Apr. 11, 1997, eff. Dec. 1, 1997; Apr. 17, 2000, eff. Dec. 1, 2000; Apr. 26, 2011, eff. Dec. 1, 2011; Apr. 16, 2013, eff. Dec. 1, 2013; Apr. 25, 2014, eff. Dec. 1, 2014.)

RULE 804. EXCEPTIONS TO THE RULE AGAINST HEARSAY—WHEN THE DECLARANT IS UNAVAILABLE AS A WITNESS

(a) Criteria for Being Unavailable. A declarant is considered to be unavailable as a witness if the declarant:

(1) is exempted from testifying about the subject matter of the declarant's statement because the court rules that a privilege applies;

(2) refuses to testify about the subject matter despite a court order to do so;

(3) testifies to not remembering the subject matter;

(4) cannot be present or testify at the trial or hearing because of death or a then-existing infirmity, physical illness, or mental illness; or

(5) is absent from the trial or hearing and the statement's proponent has not been able, by process or other reasonable means, to procure:

(A) the declarant's attendance, in the case of a hearsay exception under Rule 804(b)(1) or (6); or

(B) the declarant's attendance or testimony, in the case of a hearsay exception under Rule 804(b)(2), (3), or (4).

But this subdivision (a) does not apply if the statement's proponent procured or wrongfully caused the declarant's unavailability as a witness in order to prevent the declarant from attending or testifying.

(b) The Exceptions. The following are not excluded by the rule against hearsay if the declarant is unavailable as a witness:

(1) **Former Testimony.** Testimony that:

(A) was given as a witness at a trial, hearing, or lawful deposition, whether given during the current proceeding or a different one; and

(B) is now offered against a party who had—or, in a civil case, whose predecessor in interest had—an opportunity and similar motive to develop it by direct, cross-, or redirect examination.

(2) **Statement Under the Belief of Imminent Death.** In a prosecution for homicide or in a civil case, a statement that the declarant, while believing the declarant's death to be imminent, made about its cause or circumstances.

(3) **Statement Against Interest.** A statement that:

(A) a reasonable person in the declarant's position would have made only if the person believed it to be true because, when made, it was so contrary to the declarant's proprietary or pecuniary interest or had so great a tendency to invalidate the declarant's claim against someone else or to expose the declarant to civil or criminal liability; and

(B) is supported by corroborating circumstances that clearly indicate its trustworthiness, if it is offered in a criminal case as one that tends to expose the declarant to criminal liability.

(4) **Statement of Personal or Family History.** A statement about:

(A) the declarant's own birth, adoption, legitimacy, ancestry, marriage, divorce, relationship by blood, adoption, or marriage, or similar facts of personal or family history, even though the declarant had no way of acquiring personal knowledge about that fact; or

(B) another person concerning any of these facts, as well as death, if the declarant was related to the person by blood, adoption, or marriage or was so intimately associated with the person's family that the declarant's information is likely to be accurate.

(5) **[Other Exceptions.]** [Transferred to Rule 807.]

(6) **Statement Offered Against a Party That Wrongfully Caused the Declarant's Unavailability.** A statement offered against a party that wrongfully caused—or acquiesced in wrongfully causing—the declarant's unavailability as a witness, and did so intending that result.

(Pub.L. 93–595, § 1, Jan. 2, 1975, 88 Stat. 1942; Pub.L. 94–149, § 1(12), (13), Dec. 12, 1975, 89 Stat. 806; Mar. 2, 1987, eff. Oct. 1, 1987; Pub.L. 100–690, Title VII, § 7075(b), Nov. 18, 1988, 102 Stat. 4405; Apr. 11, 1997, eff. Dec. 1, 1997; Apr. 28, 2010, eff. Dec. 1, 2010; Apr. 26, 2011, eff. Dec. 1, 2011.)

RULE 805. HEARSAY WITHIN HEARSAY

Hearsay within hearsay is not excluded by the rule against hearsay if each part of the combined statements conforms with an exception to the rule.

(Pub.L. 93–595, § 1, Jan. 2, 1975, 88 Stat. 1943; Apr. 26, 2011, eff. Dec. 1, 2011.)

RULE 806. ATTACKING AND SUPPORTING THE DECLARANT'S CREDIBILITY

When a hearsay statement—or a statement described in Rule 801(d)(2)(C), (D), or (E)—has been admitted in evidence, the declarant's credibility may be attacked, and then supported, by any evidence that would be admissible for those purposes if the declarant had testified as a witness. The court may admit evidence of the declarant's inconsistent statement or conduct, regardless of when it occurred or whether the declarant had an opportunity to explain or deny it. If the party against whom the statement was admitted calls the declarant as a witness, the party may examine the declarant on the statement as if on cross-examination.

(Pub.L. 93–595, § 1, Jan. 2, 1975, 88 Stat. 1943; Mar. 2, 1987, eff. Oct. 1, 1987; Apr. 11, 1997, eff. Dec. 1, 1997; Apr. 26, 2011, eff. Dec. 1, 2011.)

RULE 807. RESIDUAL EXCEPTION

(a) In General. Under the following circumstances, a hearsay statement is not excluded by the rule against hearsay even if the statement is not specifically covered by a hearsay exception in Rule 803 or 804:

(1) the statement has equivalent circumstantial guarantees of trustworthiness;

(2) it is offered as evidence of a material fact;

(3) it is more probative on the point for which it is offered than any other evidence that the proponent can obtain through reasonable efforts; and

(4) admitting it will best serve the purposes of these rules and the interests of justice.

(b) Notice. The statement is admissible only if, before the trial or hearing, the proponent gives an adverse party reasonable notice of the intent to offer the statement and its particulars, including the declarant's name and address, so that the party has a fair opportunity to meet it.

(Added Apr. 11, 1997, eff. Dec. 1, 1997; Apr. 26, 2011, eff. Dec. 1, 2011.)

ARTICLE IX. AUTHENTICATION AND IDENTIFICATION

RULE 901. AUTHENTICATING OR IDENTIFYING EVIDENCE

(a) In General. To satisfy the requirement of authenticating or identifying an item of evidence, the proponent must produce evidence sufficient to support a finding that the item is what the proponent claims it is.

(b) Examples. The following are examples only—not a complete list—of evidence that satisfies the requirement:

(1) **Testimony of a Witness with Knowledge.** Testimony that an item is what it is claimed to be.

(2) **Nonexpert Opinion About Handwriting.** A nonexpert's opinion that handwriting is genuine, based on a familiarity with it that was not acquired for the current litigation.

(3) **Comparison by an Expert Witness or the Trier of Fact.** A comparison with an authenticated specimen by an expert witness or the trier of fact.

(4) **Distinctive Characteristics and the Like.** The appearance, contents, substance, internal patterns, or other distinctive characteristics of the item, taken together with all the circumstances.

(5) **Opinion About a Voice.** An opinion identifying a person's voice—whether heard firsthand or through mechanical or electronic transmission or recording—based on hearing the voice at any time under circumstances that connect it with the alleged speaker.

(6) **Evidence About a Telephone Conversation.** For a telephone conversation, evidence that a call was made to the number assigned at the time to:

(A) a particular person, if circumstances, including self-identification, show that the person answering was the one called; or

(B) a particular business, if the call was made to a business and the call related to business reasonably transacted over the telephone.

(7) **Evidence About Public Records.** Evidence that:

(A) a document was recorded or filed in a public office as authorized by law; or

(B) a purported public record or statement is from the office where items of this kind are kept.

(8) **Evidence About Ancient Documents or Data Compilations.** For a document or data compilation, evidence that it:

(A) is in a condition that creates no suspicion about its authenticity;

(B) was in a place where, if authentic, it would likely be; and

(C) is at least 20 years old when offered.

(9) **Evidence About a Process or System.** Evidence describing a process or system and showing that it produces an accurate result.

(10) Methods Provided by a Statute or Rule. Any method of authentication or identification allowed by a federal statute or a rule prescribed by the Supreme Court.

(Pub.L. 93–595, § 1, Jan. 2, 1975, 88 Stat.1943; Apr. 26, 2011, eff. Dec. 1, 2011.)

RULE 902. EVIDENCE THAT IS SELF–AUTHENTICATING

The following items of evidence are self-authenticating; they require no extrinsic evidence of authenticity in order to be admitted:

(1) Domestic Public Documents That Are Sealed and Signed. A document that bears:

(A) a seal purporting to be that of the United States; any state, district, commonwealth, territory, or insular possession of the United States; the former Panama Canal Zone; the Trust Territory of the Pacific Islands; a political subdivision of any of these entities; or a department, agency, or officer of any entity named above; and

(B) a signature purporting to be an execution or attestation.

(2) Domestic Public Documents That Are Not Sealed but Are Signed and Certified. A document that bears no seal if:

(A) it bears the signature of an officer or employee of an entity named in Rule 902(1)(A); and

(B) another public officer who has a seal and official duties within that same entity certifies under seal—or its equivalent—that the signer has the official capacity and that the signature is genuine.

(3) Foreign Public Documents. A document that purports to be signed or attested by a person who is authorized by a foreign country's law to do so. The document must be accompanied by a final certification that certifies the genuineness of the signature and official position of the signer or attester—or of any foreign official whose certificate of genuineness relates to the signature or attestation or is in a chain of certificates of genuineness relating to the signature or attestation. The certification may be made by a secretary of a United States embassy or legation; by a consul general, vice consul, or consular agent of the United States; or by a diplomatic or consular official of the foreign country assigned or accredited to the United States. If all parties have been given a reasonable opportunity to investigate the document's authenticity and accuracy, the court may, for good cause, either:

(A) order that it be treated as presumptively authentic without final certification; or

(B) allow it to be evidenced by an attested summary with or without final certification.

(4) Certified Copies of Public Records. A copy of an official record—or a copy of a document that was recorded or filed in a public office as authorized by law—if the copy is certified as correct by:

(A) the custodian or another person authorized to make the certification; or

(B) a certificate that complies with Rule 902(1), (2), or (3), a federal statute, or a rule prescribed by the Supreme Court.

(5) Official Publications. A book, pamphlet, or other publication purporting to be issued by a public authority.

(6) Newspapers and Periodicals. Printed material purporting to be a newspaper or periodical.

(7) Trade Inscriptions and the Like. An inscription, sign, tag, or label purporting to have been affixed in the course of business and indicating origin, ownership, or control.

(8) Acknowledged Documents. A document accompanied by a certificate of acknowledgment that is lawfully executed by a notary public or another officer who is authorized to take acknowledgments.

(9) Commercial Paper and Related Documents. Commercial paper, a signature on it, and related documents, to the extent allowed by general commercial law.

(10) Presumptions Under a Federal Statute. A signature, document, or anything else that a federal statute declares to be presumptively or prima facie genuine or authentic.

(11) Certified Domestic Records of a Regularly Conducted Activity. The original or a copy of a domestic record that meets the requirements of Rule 803(6)(A)–(C), as shown by a certification of the custodian or another qualified person that complies with a federal statute or a rule prescribed by the Supreme Court. Before the trial or hearing, the proponent must give an adverse party reasonable written notice of the intent to offer the record—and must make the record and certification available for inspection—so that the party has a fair opportunity to challenge them.

(12) Certified Foreign Records of a Regularly Conducted Activity. In a civil case, the original or a copy of a foreign record that meets the requirements of Rule 902(11), modified as follows: the certification, rather than complying with a federal statute or Supreme Court rule, must be signed in a manner that, if falsely made, would subject the maker to a criminal penalty in the country where the certification is signed. The proponent must also meet the notice requirements of Rule 902(11).

(Pub.L. 93–595, § 1, Jan. 2, 1975, 88 Stat. 1944; Mar. 2, 1987, eff. Oct. 1, 1987; Apr. 25, 1988, eff. Nov. 1, 1988; Apr. 17, 2000, eff. Dec. 1, 2000; Apr. 26, 2011, eff. Dec. 1, 2011.)

RULE 903. SUBSCRIBING WITNESS'S TESTIMONY

A subscribing witness's testimony is necessary to authenticate a writing only if required by the law of the jurisdiction that governs its validity.

(Pub.L. 93–595, § 1, Jan. 2, 1975, 88 Stat.1945; Apr. 26, 2011, eff. Dec. 1, 2011.)

ARTICLE X. CONTENTS OF WRITINGS, RECORDINGS, AND PHOTOGRAPHS

RULE 1001. DEFINITIONS THAT APPLY TO THIS ARTICLE

In this article:

(a) A "writing" consists of letters, words, numbers, or their equivalent set down in any form.

(b) A "recording" consists of letters, words, numbers, or their equivalent recorded in any manner.

(c) A "photograph" means a photographic image or its equivalent stored in any form.

(d) An "original" of a writing or recording means the writing or recording itself or any counterpart intended to have the same effect by the person who executed or issued it. For electronically stored information, "original" means any printout—or other output readable by sight—if it accurately reflects the information. An "original" of a photograph includes the negative or a print from it.

(e) A "duplicate" means a counterpart produced by a mechanical, photographic, chemical, electronic, or other equivalent process or technique that accurately reproduces the original.

(Pub.L. 93–595, § 1, Jan. 2, 1975, 88 Stat. 1945; Apr. 26, 2011, eff. Dec. 1, 2011.)

RULE 1002. REQUIREMENT OF THE ORIGINAL

An original writing, recording, or photograph is required in order to prove its content unless these rules or a federal statute provides otherwise.

(Pub.L. 93–595, § 1, Jan. 2, 1975, 88 Stat. 1946; Apr. 26, 2011, eff. Dec. 1, 2011.)

RULE 1003. ADMISSIBILITY OF DUPLICATES

A duplicate is admissible to the same extent as the original unless a genuine question is raised about the original's authenticity or the circumstances make it unfair to admit the duplicate.

(Pub.L. 93–595, § 1, Jan. 2, 1975, 88 Stat. 1946; Apr. 26, 2011, eff. Dec. 1, 2011.)

RULE 1004. ADMISSIBILITY OF OTHER EVIDENCE OF CONTENT

An original is not required and other evidence of the content of a writing, recording, or photograph is admissible if:

(a) all the originals are lost or destroyed, and not by the proponent acting in bad faith;

(b) an original cannot be obtained by any available judicial process;

(c) the party against whom the original would be offered had control of the original; was at that time put on notice, by pleadings or otherwise, that the original would be a subject of proof at the trial or hearing; and fails to produce it at the trial or hearing; or

(d) the writing, recording, or photograph is not closely related to a controlling issue.

(Pub.L. 93–595, § 1, Jan. 2, 1975, 88 Stat. 1946; Mar. 2, 1987, eff. Oct. 1, 1987; Apr. 26, 2011, eff. Dec. 1, 2011.)

RULE 1005. COPIES OF PUBLIC RECORDS TO PROVE CONTENT

The proponent may use a copy to prove the content of an official record—or of a document that was recorded or filed in a public office as authorized by law—if these conditions are met: the record or document is otherwise admissible; and the copy is certified as correct in accordance with Rule 902(4) or is testified to be correct by a witness who has compared it with the original. If no such copy can be obtained by reasonable diligence, then the proponent may use other evidence to prove the content.

(Pub.L. 93–595, § 1, Jan. 2, 1975, 88 Stat. 1946; Apr. 26, 2011, eff. Dec. 1, 2011.)

RULE 1006. SUMMARIES TO PROVE CONTENT

The proponent may use a summary, chart, or calculation to prove the content of voluminous writings, recordings, or photographs that cannot be conveniently examined in court. The proponent must make the originals or duplicates available for examination or copying, or both, by other parties at a reasonable time and place. And the court may order the proponent to produce them in court.

(Pub.L. 93–595, § 1, Jan. 2, 1975, 88 Stat. 1946; Apr. 26, 2011, eff. Dec. 1, 2011.)

RULE 1007. TESTIMONY OR STATEMENT OF A PARTY TO PROVE CONTENT

The proponent may prove the content of a writing, recording, or photograph by the testimony, deposition, or written statement of the party against whom the evidence is offered. The proponent need not account for the original.

(Pub.L. 93–595, § 1, Jan. 2, 1975, 88 Stat. 1947; Mar. 2, 1987, eff. Oct. 1, 1987; Apr. 26, 2011, eff. Dec. 1, 2011.)

RULE 1008. FUNCTIONS OF THE COURT AND JURY

Ordinarily, the court determines whether the proponent has fulfilled the factual conditions for admitting other evidence of the content of a writing, recording, or photograph under Rule 1004 or 1005. But in a jury trial, the jury determines—in accordance with Rule 104(b)—any issue about whether:

(a) an asserted writing, recording, or photograph ever existed;

(b) another one produced at the trial or hearing is the original; or

(c) other evidence of content accurately reflects the content.

(Pub.L. 93–595, § 1, Jan. 2, 1975, 88 Stat. 1947; Apr. 26, 2011, eff. Dec. 1, 2011.)

ARTICLE XI.   MISCELLANEOUS RULES

RULE 1101. APPLICABILITY OF THE RULES

(a) To Courts and Judges. These rules apply to proceedings before:

- United States district courts;
- United States bankruptcy and magistrate judges;
- United States courts of appeals;
- the United States Court of Federal Claims; and
- the district courts of Guam, the Virgin Islands, and the Northern Mariana Islands.

(b) To Cases and Proceedings. These rules apply in:

- civil cases and proceedings, including bankruptcy, admiralty, and maritime cases;
- criminal cases and proceedings; and
- contempt proceedings, except those in which the court may act summarily.

(c) Rules on Privilege. The rules on privilege apply to all stages of a case or proceeding.

(d) Exceptions. These rules—except for those on privilege—do not apply to the following:

(1) the court's determination, under Rule 104(a), on a preliminary question of fact governing admissibility;

(2) grand-jury proceedings; and

(3) miscellaneous proceedings such as:

- extradition or rendition;

- issuing an arrest warrant, criminal summons, or search warrant;
- a preliminary examination in a criminal case;
- sentencing;
- granting or revoking probation or supervised release; and
- considering whether to release on bail or otherwise.

(e) Other Statutes and Rules. A federal statute or a rule prescribed by the Supreme Court may provide for admitting or excluding evidence independently from these rules.

(Pub.L. 93–595, § 1, Jan. 2, 1975, 88 Stat. 1947; Pub.L. 94–149, § 1(14), Dec. 12, 1975, 89 Stat. 806; Pub.L. 95–598, Title II, § 251, Nov. 6, 1978, 92 Stat. 2673; Pub.L. 97–164, Title I, § 142, Apr. 2, 1982, 96 Stat. 45; Mar. 2, 1987, eff. Oct. 1, 1987; Apr. 25, 1988, eff. Nov. 1, 1988; Pub.L. 100–690, Title VII, § 7075(c), Nov. 18, 1988, 102 Stat. 4405; Apr. 22, 1993, eff. Dec. 1, 1993; Apr. 26, 2011, eff. Dec. 1, 2011.)

RULE 1102. AMENDMENTS

These rules may be amended as provided in 28 U.S.C. § 2072.

(Pub.L. 93–595, § 1, Jan. 2, 1975, 88 Stat.1948; Apr. 30, 1991, eff. Dec. 1, 1991; Apr. 26, 2011, eff. Dec. 1, 2011.)

RULE 1103. TITLE

These rules may be cited as the Federal Rules of Evidence.

(Pub.L. 93–595, § 1, Jan. 2, 1975, 88 Stat.1948; Apr. 26, 2011, eff. Dec. 1, 2011.)

INDEX TO
FEDERAL RULES OF EVIDENCE

FEDERAL RULES OF APPELLATE PROCEDURE

Including Amendments Effective December 1, 2014

TITLE I. APPLICABILITY OF RULES

RULE 1. SCOPE OF RULES; DEFINITION; TITLE

(a) Scope of Rules.

(1) These rules govern procedure in the United States courts of appeals.

(2) When these rules provide for filing a motion or other document in the district court, the procedure must comply with the practice of the district court.

(b) Definition. In these rules, "state" includes the District of Columbia and any United States commonwealth or territory.

(c) Title. These rules are to be known as the Federal Rules of Appellate Procedure.

(As amended Apr. 30, 1979, eff. Aug. 1, 1979; Apr. 25, 1989, eff. Dec. 1, 1989; Apr. 29, 1994, eff. Dec. 1, 1994; Apr. 24, 1998, eff. Dec. 1, 1998; Apr. 29, 2002, eff. Dec. 1, 2002; Apr. 28, 2010, eff. Dec. 1, 2010.)

RULE 2. SUSPENSION OF RULES

On its own or a party's motion, a court of appeals may—to expedite its decision or for other good cause—suspend any provision of these rules in a particular case and order proceedings as it directs, except as otherwise provided in Rule 26(b).

(As amended Apr. 24, 1998, eff. Dec. 1, 1998.)

TITLE II. APPEAL FROM A JUDGMENT OR ORDER OF A DISTRICT COURT

RULE 3. APPEAL AS OF RIGHT— HOW TAKEN

(a) Filing the Notice of Appeal.

(1) An appeal permitted by law as of right from a district court to a court of appeals may be taken only by filing a notice of appeal with the district clerk within the time allowed by Rule 4. At the time of filing, the appellant must furnish the clerk with enough copies of the notice to enable the clerk to comply with Rule 3(d).

(2) An appellant's failure to take any step other than the timely filing of a notice of appeal does not affect the validity of the appeal, but is ground only for the court of appeals to act as it considers appropriate, including dismissing the appeal.

(3) An appeal from a judgment by a magistrate judge in a civil case is taken in the same way as an appeal from any other district court judgment.

(4) An appeal by permission under 28 U.S.C. § 1292(b) or an appeal in a bankruptcy case may be taken only in the manner prescribed by Rules 5 and 6, respectively.

(b) Joint or Consolidated Appeals.

(1) When two or more parties are entitled to appeal from a district-court judgment or order, and their interests make joinder practicable, they may file a joint notice of appeal. They may then proceed on appeal as a single appellant.

(2) When the parties have filed separate timely notices of appeal, the appeals may be joined or consolidated by the court of appeals.

(c) Contents of the Notice of Appeal.

(1) The notice of appeal must:

(A) specify the party or parties taking the appeal by naming each one in the caption or body of the notice, but an attorney representing more than one party may describe those parties with such terms as "all plaintiffs," "the defendants," "the plaintiffs A, B, et al.," or "all defendants except X";

(B) designate the judgment, order, or part thereof being appealed; and

(C) name the court to which the appeal is taken.

(2) A pro se notice of appeal is considered filed on behalf of the signer and the signer's spouse and minor children (if they are parties), unless the notice clearly indicates otherwise.

(3) In a class action, whether or not the class has been certified, the notice of appeal is sufficient if it names one person qualified to bring the appeal as representative of the class.

(4) An appeal must not be dismissed for informality of form or title of the notice of appeal, or for failure to name a party whose intent to appeal is otherwise clear from the notice.

(5) Form 1 in the Appendix of Forms is a suggested form of a notice of appeal.

(d) Serving the Notice of Appeal.

(1) The district clerk must serve notice of the filing of a notice of appeal by mailing a copy to each party's counsel of record—excluding the appellant's—or, if a party is proceeding pro se, to the party's last known address. When a defendant in a criminal case appeals, the clerk must also serve a copy of the notice of appeal on the defendant, either by personal service or by mail addressed to the defendant. The clerk must promptly send a copy of the notice of appeal and of the docket entries—and any later docket entries—to the clerk of the court of appeals named in the notice. The district clerk must note, on each copy, the date when the notice of appeal was filed.

(2) If an inmate confined in an institution files a notice of appeal in the manner provided by Rule 4(c), the district clerk must also note the date when the clerk docketed the notice.

(3) The district clerk's failure to serve notice does not affect the validity of the appeal. The clerk must note on the docket the names of the parties to whom the clerk mails copies, with the date of mailing. Service is sufficient despite the death of a party or the party's counsel.

(e) Payment of Fees. Upon filing a notice of appeal, the appellant must pay the district clerk all required fees. The district clerk receives the appellate docket fee on behalf of the court of appeals.

(As amended Apr. 30, 1979, eff. Aug. 1, 1979; Mar. 10, 1986, eff. July 1, 1986; Apr. 25, 1989, eff. Dec. 1, 1989; Apr. 22, 1993, eff. Dec. 1, 1993; Apr. 29, 1994, eff. Dec. 1, 1994; Apr. 24, 1998, eff. Dec. 1, 1998.)

[RULE 3.1 APPEAL FROM A JUDGMENT OF A MAGISTRATE JUDGE IN A CIVIL CASE (ABROGATED APR. 24, 1998, EFF. DEC. 1, 1998)]

RULE 4. APPEAL AS OF RIGHT— WHEN TAKEN

(a) Appeal in a Civil Case.

(1) Time for Filing a Notice of Appeal.

(A) In a civil case, except as provided in Rules 4(a)(1)(B), 4(a)(4), and 4(c), the notice of appeal required by Rule 3 must be filed with the district clerk within 30 days after entry of the judgment or order appealed from.

(B) The notice of appeal may be filed by any party within 60 days after entry of the judgment or order appealed from if one of the parties is:

    (i) the United States;

    (ii) a United States agency;

    (iii) a United States officer or employee sued in an official capacity; or

    (iv) a current or former United States officer or employee sued in an individual capacity for an act or omission occurring in connection with duties performed on the United States' behalf—including all instances in which the United States represents that person when the judgment or order is entered or files the appeal for that person.

(C) An appeal from an order granting or denying an application for a writ of error coram nobis is an appeal in a civil case for purposes of Rule 4(a).

(2) Filing Before Entry of Judgment. A notice of appeal filed after the court announces a decision or order—but before the entry of the judgment or order—is treated as filed on the date of and after the entry.

(3) Multiple Appeals. If one party timely files a notice of appeal, any other party may file a notice of appeal within 14 days after the date when the first notice was filed, or within the time otherwise prescribed by this Rule 4(a), whichever period ends later.

(4) Effect of a Motion on a Notice of Appeal.

(A) If a party timely files in the district court any of the following motions under the Federal Rules of Civil Procedure, the time to file an appeal runs for all parties from the entry of the order disposing of the last such remaining motion:

    (i) for judgment under Rule 50(b);

    (ii) to amend or make additional factual findings under Rule 52(b), whether or not granting the motion would alter the judgment;

    (iii) for attorney's fees under Rule 54 if the district court extends the time to appeal under Rule 58;

    (iv) to alter or amend the judgment under Rule 59;

    (v) for a new trial under Rule 59; or

    (vi) for relief under Rule 60 if the motion is filed no later than 28 days after the judgment is entered.

(B)(i) If a party files a notice of appeal after the court announces or enters a judgment—but before it disposes of any motion listed in Rule 4(a)(4)(A)—the notice becomes effective to appeal a judgment or order, in whole or in part, when the order disposing of the last such remaining motion is entered.

    (ii) A party intending to challenge an order disposing of any motion listed in Rule 4(a)(4)(A), or a judgment's alteration or amendment upon such a motion, must file a notice of appeal, or an amended notice of appeal—in compliance with Rule 3(c)—within the time prescribed by this Rule measured from the entry of the order disposing of the last such remaining motion.

(iii) No additional fee is required to file an amended notice.

(5) Motion for Extension of Time.

(A) The district court may extend the time to file a notice of appeal if:

(i) a party so moves no later than 30 days after the time prescribed by this Rule 4(a) expires; and

(ii) regardless of whether its motion is filed before or during the 30 days after the time prescribed by this Rule 4(a) expires, that party shows excusable neglect or good cause.

(B) A motion filed before the expiration of the time prescribed in Rule 4(a)(1) or (3) may be ex parte unless the court requires otherwise. If the motion is filed after the expiration of the prescribed time, notice must be given to the other parties in accordance with local rules.

(C) No extension under this Rule 4(a)(5) may exceed 30 days after the prescribed time or 14 days after the date when the order granting the motion is entered, whichever is later.

(6) Reopening the Time to File an Appeal. The district court may reopen the time to file an appeal for a period of 14 days after the date when its order to reopen is entered, but only if all the following conditions are satisfied:

(A) the court finds that the moving party did not receive notice under Federal Rule of Civil Procedure 77(d) of the entry of the judgment or order sought to be appealed within 21 days after entry;

(B) the motion is filed within 180 days after the judgment or order is entered or within 14 days after the moving party receives notice under Federal Rule of Civil Procedure 77(d) of the entry, whichever is earlier; and

(C) the court finds that no party would be prejudiced.

(7) Entry Defined.

(A) A judgment or order is entered for purposes of this Rule 4(a):

(i) if Federal Rule of Civil Procedure 58(a) does not require a separate document, when the judgment or order is entered in the civil docket under Federal Rule of Civil Procedure 79(a); or

(ii) if Federal Rule of Civil Procedure 58(a) requires a separate document, when the judg-

ment or order is entered in the civil docket under Federal Rule of Civil Procedure 79(a) and when the earlier of these events occurs:

● the judgment or order is set forth on a separate document, or

● 150 days have run from entry of the judgment or order in the civil docket under Federal Rule of Civil Procedure 79(a).

(B) A failure to set forth a judgment or order on a separate document when required by Federal Rule of Civil Procedure 58(a) does not affect the validity of an appeal from that judgment or order.

(b) Appeal in a Criminal Case.

(1) Time for Filing a Notice of Appeal.

(A) In a criminal case, a defendant's notice of appeal must be filed in the district court within 14 days after the later of:

(i) the entry of either the judgment or the order being appealed; or

(ii) the filing of the government's notice of appeal.

(B) When the government is entitled to appeal, its notice of appeal must be filed in the district court within 30 days after the later of:

(i) the entry of the judgment or order being appealed; or

(ii) the filing of a notice of appeal by any defendant.

(2) Filing Before Entry of Judgment. A notice of appeal filed after the court announces a decision, sentence, or order—but before the entry of the judgment or order—is treated as filed on the date of and after the entry.

(3) Effect of a Motion on a Notice of Appeal.

(A) If a defendant timely makes any of the following motions under the Federal Rules of Criminal Procedure, the notice of appeal from a judgment of conviction must be filed within 14 days after the entry of the order disposing of the last such remaining motion, or within 14 days after the entry of the judgment of conviction, whichever period ends later. This provision applies to a timely motion:

(i) for judgment of acquittal under Rule 29;

(ii) for a new trial under Rule 33, but if based on newly discovered evidence, only if the motion is made no later than 14 days after the entry of the judgment; or

(iii) for arrest of judgment under Rule 34.

(B) A notice of appeal filed after the court announces a decision, sentence, or order—but before it disposes of any of the motions referred to in Rule 4(b)(3)(A)—becomes effective upon the later of the following:

(i) the entry of the order disposing of the last such remaining motion; or

(ii) the entry of the judgment of conviction.

(C) A valid notice of appeal is effective—without amendment—to appeal from an order disposing of any of the motions referred to in Rule 4(b)(3)(A).

(4) **Motion for Extension of Time.** Upon a finding of excusable neglect or good cause, the district court may—before or after the time has expired, with or without motion and notice—extend the time to file a notice of appeal for a period not to exceed 30 days from the expiration of the time otherwise prescribed by this Rule 4(b).

(5) **Jurisdiction.** The filing of a notice of appeal under this Rule 4(b) does not divest a district court of jurisdiction to correct a sentence under Federal Rule of Criminal Procedure 35(a), nor does the filing of a motion under 35(a) affect the validity of a notice of appeal filed before entry of the order disposing of the motion. The filing of a motion under Federal Rule of Criminal Procedure 35(a) does not suspend the time for filing a notice of appeal from a judgment of conviction.

(6) **Entry Defined.** A judgment or order is entered for purposes of this Rule 4(b) when it is entered on the criminal docket.

(c) **Appeal by an Inmate Confined in an Institution.**

(1) If an inmate confined in an institution files a notice of appeal in either a civil or a criminal case, the notice is timely if it is deposited in the institution's internal mail system on or before the last day for filing. If an institution has a system designed for legal mail, the inmate must use that system to receive the benefit of this rule. Timely filing may be shown by a declaration in compliance with 28 U.S.C. § 1746 or by a notarized statement, either of which must set forth the date of deposit and state that first-class postage has been prepaid.

(2) If an inmate files the first notice of appeal in a civil case under this Rule 4(c), the 14–day period provided in Rule 4(a)(3) for another party to file a notice of appeal runs from the date when the district court dockets the first notice.

(3) When a defendant in a criminal case files a notice of appeal under this Rule 4(c), the 30–day period for the government to file its notice of appeal runs from the entry of the judgment or order appealed from or from the district court's docketing of the defendant's notice of appeal, whichever is later.

(d) **Mistaken Filing in the Court of Appeals.** If a notice of appeal in either a civil or a criminal case is mistakenly filed in the court of appeals, the clerk of that court must note on the notice the date when it was received and send it to the district clerk. The notice is then considered filed in the district court on the date so noted.

(As amended Apr. 30, 1979, eff. Aug. 1, 1979; Nov. 18, 1988, Pub.L. 100–690, Title VII, § 7111, 102 Stat. 4419; Apr. 30, 1991, eff. Dec. 1, 1991; Apr. 22, 1993, eff. Dec. 1, 1993; Apr. 27, 1995, eff. Dec. 1, 1995; Apr. 24, 1998, eff. Dec. 1, 1998; Apr. 29, 2002, eff. Dec. 1, 2002; Apr. 25, 2005, eff. Dec. 1, 2005; Mar. 26, 2009, eff. Dec. 1, 2009; Apr. 28, 2010, eff. Dec. 1, 2010; Apr. 26, 2011, eff. Dec. 1, 2011.)

RULE 5. APPEAL BY PERMISSION

(a) **Petition for Permission to Appeal.**

(1) To request permission to appeal when an appeal is within the court of appeals' discretion, a party must file a petition for permission to appeal. The petition must be filed with the circuit clerk with proof of service on all other parties to the district-court action.

(2) The petition must be filed within the time specified by the statute or rule authorizing the appeal or, if no such time is specified, within the time provided by Rule 4(a) for filing a notice of appeal.

(3) If a party cannot petition for appeal unless the district court first enters an order granting permission to do so or stating that the necessary conditions are met, the district court may amend its order, either on its own or in response to a party's motion, to include the required permission or statement. In that event, the time to petition runs from entry of the amended order.

(b) **Contents of the Petition; Answer or Cross–Petition; Oral Argument.**

(1) The petition must include the following:

(A) the facts necessary to understand the question presented;

(B) the question itself;

(C) the relief sought;

(D) the reasons why the appeal should be allowed and is authorized by a statute or rule; and

(E) an attached copy of:

(i) the order, decree, or judgment complained of and any related opinion or memorandum, and

(ii) any order stating the district court's permission to appeal or finding that the necessary conditions are met.

(2) A party may file an answer in opposition or a cross-petition within 10 days after the petition is served.

(3) The petition and answer will be submitted without oral argument unless the court of appeals orders otherwise.

(c) Form of Papers; Number of Copies. All papers must conform to Rule 32(c)(2). Except by the court's permission, a paper must not exceed 20 pages, exclusive of the disclosure statement, the proof of service, and the accompanying documents required by Rule 5(b)(1)(E). An original and 3 copies must be filed unless the court requires a different number by local rule or by order in a particular case.

(d) Grant of Permission; Fees; Cost Bond; Filing the Record.

(1) Within 14 days after the entry of the order granting permission to appeal, the appellant must:

(A) pay the district clerk all required fees; and

(B) file a cost bond if required under Rule 7.

(2) A notice of appeal need not be filed. The date when the order granting permission to appeal is entered serves as the date of the notice of appeal for calculating time under these rules.

(3) The district clerk must notify the circuit clerk once the petitioner has paid the fees. Upon receiving this notice, the circuit clerk must enter the appeal on the docket. The record must be forwarded and filed in accordance with Rules 11 and 12(c).

(As amended Apr. 30, 1979, eff. Aug. 1, 1979; Apr. 29, 1994, eff. Dec. 1, 1994; Apr. 24, 1998, eff. Dec. 1, 1998; Apr. 29, 2002, eff. Dec. 1, 2002; Mar. 26, 2009, eff. Dec. 1, 2009.)

[RULE 5.1 APPEAL BY LEAVE UNDER 28 U.S.C. § 636(C)(5) (ABROGATED APR. 24, 1998, EFF. DEC. 1, 1998)]

RULE 6. APPEAL IN A BANKRUPTCY CASE

(a) Appeal From a Judgment, Order, or Decree of a District Court Exercising Original Jurisdiction in a Bankruptcy Case. An appeal to a court of appeals from a final judgment, order, or decree of a district court exercising jurisdiction under 28 U.S.C. § 1334 is taken as any other civil appeal under these rules.

(b) Appeal From a Judgment, Order, or Decree of a District Court or Bankruptcy Appellate Panel Exercising Appellate Jurisdiction in a Bankruptcy Case.

(1) **Applicability of Other Rules.** These rules apply to an appeal to a court of appeals under 28 U.S.C. § 158(d)(1) from a final judgment, order, or decree of a district court or bankruptcy appellate panel exercising appellate jurisdiction under 28 U.S.C. § 158(a) or (b), but with these qualifications:

(A) Rules 4(a)(4), 4(b), 9, 10, 11, 12(c), 13–20, 22–23, and 24(b) do not apply;

(B) the reference in Rule 3(c) to "Form 1 in the Appendix of Forms" must be read as a reference to Form 5;

(C) when the appeal is from a bankruptcy appellate panel, "district court," as used in any applicable rule, means "appellate panel"; and

(D) in Rule 12.1, "district court" includes a bankruptcy court or bankruptcy appellate panel.

(2) **Additional Rules.** In addition to the rules made applicable by Rule 6(b)(1), the following rules apply:

(A) Motion for Rehearing.

(i) If a timely motion for rehearing under Bankruptcy Rule 8022 is filed, the time to appeal for all parties runs from the entry of the order disposing of the motion. A notice of appeal filed after the district court or bankruptcy appellate panel announces or enters a judgment, order, or decree—but before disposition of the motion for rehearing—becomes effective when the order disposing of the motion for rehearing is entered.

(ii) If a party intends to challenge the order disposing of the motion—or the alteration or amendment of a judgment, order, or decree upon the motion—then the party, in compliance with Rules 3(c) and 6(b)(1)(B), must file a notice of appeal or amended notice of appeal. The notice or amended notice must be filed within the time prescribed by Rule 4—excluding Rules 4(a)(4) and 4(b)—measured from the entry of the order disposing of the motion.

(iii) No additional fee is required to file an amended notice.

(B) The Record on Appeal.

(i) Within 14 days after filing the notice of appeal, the appellant must file with the clerk possessing the record assembled in accordance with Bankruptcy Rule 8009—and serve on the appellee—a statement of the issues to be presented on appeal and a designation of the record to be certified and made available to the circuit clerk.

(ii) An appellee who believes that other parts of the record are necessary must, within 14 days after being served with the appellant's designation, file with the clerk and serve on the appellant a designation of additional parts to be included.

(iii) The record on appeal consists of:

• the redesignated record as provided above;

• the proceedings in the district court or bankruptcy appellate panel; and

- a certified copy of the docket entries prepared by the clerk under Rule 3(d).

(C) Making the Record Available.

(i) When the record is complete, the district clerk or bankruptcy-appellate-panel clerk must number the documents constituting the record and promptly make it available to the circuit clerk. If the clerk makes the record available in paper form, the clerk will not send documents of unusual bulk or weight, physical exhibits other than documents, or other parts of the record designated for omission by local rule of the court of appeals, unless directed to do so by a party or the circuit clerk. If unusually bulky or heavy exhibits are to be made available in paper form, a party must arrange with the clerks in advance for their transportation and receipt.

(ii) All parties must do whatever else is necessary to enable the clerk to assemble the record and make it available. When the record is made available in paper form, the court of appeals may provide by rule or order that a certified copy of the docket entries be made available in place of the redesignated record. But any party may request at any time during the pendency of the appeal that the redesignated record be made available.

(D) Filing the Record. When the district clerk or bankruptcy-appellate-panel clerk has made the record available, the circuit clerk must note that fact on the docket. The date noted on the docket serves as the filing date of the record. The circuit clerk must immediately notify all parties of the filing date.

(c) Direct Review by Permission Under 28 U.S.C. § 158(d)(2).

(1) Applicability of Other Rules. These rules apply to a direct appeal by permission under 28 U.S.C. § 158(d)(2), but with these qualifications:

(A) Rules 3–4, 5(a)(3), 6(a), 6(b), 8(a), 8(c), 9–12, 13–20, 22–23, and 24(b) do not apply;

(B) as used in any applicable rule, "district court" or "district clerk" includes—to the extent appropriate—a bankruptcy court or bankruptcy appellate panel or its clerk; and

(C) the reference to "Rules 11 and 12(c)" in Rule 5(d)(3) must be read as a reference to Rules 6(c)(2)(B) and (C).

(2) Additional Rules. In addition, the following rules apply:

(A) The Record on Appeal. Bankruptcy Rule 8009 governs the record on appeal.

(B) Making the Record Available. Bankruptcy Rule 8010 governs completing the record and making it available.

(C) Stays Pending Appeal. Bankruptcy Rule 8007 applies to stays pending appeal.

(D) Duties of the Circuit Clerk. When the bankruptcy clerk has made the record available, the circuit clerk must note that fact on the docket. The date noted on the docket serves as the filing date of the record. The circuit clerk must immediately notify all parties of the filing date.

(E) Filing a Representation Statement. Unless the court of appeals designates another time, within 14 days after entry of the order granting permission to appeal, the attorney who sought permission must file a statement with the circuit clerk naming the parties that the attorney represents on appeal.

(Added Apr. 25, 1989, eff. Dec. 1, 1989; amended Apr. 30, 1991, eff. Dec. 1, 1991; Apr. 22, 1993, eff. Dec. 1, 1993; Apr. 24, 1998, eff. Dec. 1, 1998; Mar. 26, 2009, eff. Dec. 1, 2009; Apr. 25, 2014, eff. Dec. 1, 2014.)

RULE 7. BOND FOR COSTS ON APPEAL IN A CIVIL CASE

In a civil case, the district court may require an appellant to file a bond or provide other security in any form and amount necessary to ensure payment of costs on appeal. Rule 8(b) applies to a surety on a bond given under this rule.

(As amended Apr. 30, 1979, eff. Aug. 1, 1979; Apr. 24, 1998, eff. Dec. 1, 1998.)

RULE 8. STAY OR INJUNCTION PENDING APPEAL

(a) Motion for Stay.

(1) Initial Motion in the District Court. A party must ordinarily move first in the district court for the following relief:

(A) a stay of the judgment or order of a district court pending appeal;

(B) approval of a supersedeas bond; or

(C) an order suspending, modifying, restoring, or granting an injunction while an appeal is pending.

(2) Motion in the Court of Appeals; Conditions on Relief. A motion for the relief mentioned in Rule 8(a)(1) may be made to the court of appeals or to one of its judges.

(A) The motion must:

(i) show that moving first in the district court would be impracticable; or

(ii) state that, a motion having been made, the district court denied the motion or failed to afford the relief requested and state any reasons given by the district court for its action.

(B) The motion must also include:

(i) the reasons for granting the relief requested and the facts relied on;

(ii) originals or copies of affidavits or other sworn statements supporting facts subject to dispute; and

(iii) relevant parts of the record.

(C) The moving party must give reasonable notice of the motion to all parties.

(D) A motion under this Rule 8(a)(2) must be filed with the circuit clerk and normally will be considered by a panel of the court. But in an exceptional case in which time requirements make that procedure impracticable, the motion may be made to and considered by a single judge.

(E) The court may condition relief on a party's filing a bond or other appropriate security in the district court.

(b) Proceeding Against a Surety. If a party gives security in the form of a bond or stipulation or other undertaking with one or more sureties, each surety submits to the jurisdiction of the district court and irrevocably appoints the district clerk as the surety's agent on whom any papers affecting the surety's liability on the bond or undertaking may be served. On motion, a surety's liability may be enforced in the district court without the necessity of an independent action. The motion and any notice that the district court prescribes may be served on the district clerk, who must promptly mail a copy to each surety whose address is known.

(c) Stay in a Criminal Case. Rule 38 of the Federal Rules of Criminal Procedure governs a stay in a criminal case.

(As amended Mar. 10, 1986, eff. July 1, 1986; Apr. 27, 1995, eff. Dec. 1, 1995; Apr. 24, 1998, eff. Dec. 1, 1998.)

RULE 9. RELEASE IN A CRIMINAL CASE

(a) Release Before Judgment of Conviction.

(1) The district court must state in writing, or orally on the record, the reasons for an order regarding the release or detention of a defendant in a criminal case. A party appealing from the order must file with the court of appeals a copy of the district court's order and the court's statement of reasons as soon as practicable after filing the notice of appeal. An appellant who questions the factual basis for the district court's order must file a transcript of the release proceedings or an explanation of why a transcript was not obtained.

(2) After reasonable notice to the appellee, the court of appeals must promptly determine the appeal on the basis of the papers, affidavits, and parts of the record that the parties present or the court requires. Unless the court so orders, briefs need not be filed.

(3) The court of appeals or one of its judges may order the defendant's release pending the disposition of the appeal.

(b) Release After Judgment of Conviction. A party entitled to do so may obtain review of a district-court order regarding release after a judgment of conviction by filing a notice of appeal from that order in the district court, or by filing a motion in the court of appeals if the party has already filed a notice of appeal from the judgment of conviction. Both the order and the review are subject to Rule 9(a). The papers filed by the party seeking review must include a copy of the judgment of conviction.

(c) Criteria for Release. The court must make its decision regarding release in accordance with the applicable provisions of 18 U.S.C. §§ 3142, 3143, and 3145(c).

(As amended Apr. 24, 1972, eff. Oct. 1, 1972; Oct. 12, 1984, Pub.L. 98–473, Title II, § 210, 98 Stat. 1987; Apr. 29, 1994, eff. Dec. 1, 1994; Apr. 24, 1998, eff. Dec. 1, 1998.)

RULE 10. THE RECORD ON APPEAL

(a) Composition of the Record on Appeal. The following items constitute the record on appeal:

(1) the original papers and exhibits filed in the district court;

(2) the transcript of proceedings, if any; and

(3) a certified copy of the docket entries prepared by the district clerk.

(b) The Transcript of Proceedings.

(1) Appellant's Duty to Order. Within 14 days after filing the notice of appeal or entry of an order disposing of the last timely remaining motion of a type specified in Rule 4(a)(4)(A), whichever is later, the appellant must do either of the following:

(A) order from the reporter a transcript of such parts of the proceedings not already on file as the appellant considers necessary, subject to a local rule of the court of appeals and with the following qualifications:

(i) the order must be in writing;

(ii) if the cost of the transcript is to be paid by the United States under the Criminal Justice Act, the order must so state; and

(iii) the appellant must, within the same period, file a copy of the order with the district clerk; or

(B) file a certificate stating that no transcript will be ordered.

(2) Unsupported Finding or Conclusion. If the appellant intends to urge on appeal that a finding or conclusion is unsupported by the evidence or is contrary to the evidence, the appellant must include in the record a transcript of all evidence relevant to that finding or conclusion.

(3) Partial Transcript. Unless the entire transcript is ordered:

(A) the appellant must—within the 14 days provided in Rule 10(b)(1)—file a statement of the issues that the appellant intends to present on the appeal and must serve on the appellee a copy of both the order or certificate and the statement;

(B) if the appellee considers it necessary to have a transcript of other parts of the proceedings, the appellee must, within 14 days after the service of the order or certificate and the statement of the issues, file and serve on the appellant a designation of additional parts to be ordered; and

(C) unless within 14 days after service of that designation the appellant has ordered all such parts, and has so notified the appellee, the appellee may within the following 14 days either order the parts or move in the district court for an order requiring the appellant to do so.

(4) Payment. At the time of ordering, a party must make satisfactory arrangements with the reporter for paying the cost of the transcript.

(c) Statement of the Evidence When the Proceedings Were Not Recorded or When a Transcript Is Unavailable. If the transcript of a hearing or trial is unavailable, the appellant may prepare a statement of the evidence or proceedings from the best available means, including the appellant's recollection. The statement must be served on the appellee, who may serve objections or proposed amendments within 14 days after being served. The statement and any objections or proposed amendments must then be submitted to the district court for settlement and approval. As settled and approved, the statement must be included by the district clerk in the record on appeal.

(d) Agreed Statement as the Record on Appeal. In place of the record on appeal as defined in Rule 10(a), the parties may prepare, sign, and submit to the district court a statement of the case showing how the issues presented by the appeal arose and were decided in the district court. The statement must set forth only those facts averred and proved or sought to be proved that are essential to the court's resolution of the issues. If the statement is truthful, it—together with any additions that the district court may consider necessary to a full presentation of the issues on appeal—must be approved by the district court and must then be certified to the court of appeals as the record on appeal. The district clerk must then send it to the circuit clerk within the time provided by Rule 11. A copy of the agreed statement may be filed in place of the appendix required by Rule 30.

(e) Correction or Modification of the Record.

(1) If any difference arises about whether the record truly discloses what occurred in the district court, the difference must be submitted to and settled by that court and the record conformed accordingly.

(2) If anything material to either party is omitted from or misstated in the record by error or accident, the omission or misstatement may be corrected and a supplemental record may be certified and forwarded:

(A) on stipulation of the parties;

(B) by the district court before or after the record has been forwarded; or

(C) by the court of appeals.

(3) All other questions as to the form and content of the record must be presented to the court of appeals.

(As amended Apr. 30, 1979, eff. Aug. 1, 1979; Mar. 10, 1986, eff. July 1, 1986; Apr. 30, 1991, eff. Dec. 1, 1991; Apr. 22, 1993, eff. Dec. 1, 1993; Apr. 27, 1995, eff. Dec. 1, 1995; Apr. 24, 1998, eff. Dec. 1, 1998; Mar. 26, 2009, eff. Dec. 1, 2009.)

RULE 11.   FORWARDING THE RECORD

(a) Appellant's Duty. An appellant filing a notice of appeal must comply with Rule 10(b) and must do whatever else is necessary to enable the clerk to assemble and forward the record. If there are multiple appeals from a judgment or order, the clerk must forward a single record.

(b) Duties of Reporter and District Clerk.

(1) Reporter's Duty to Prepare and File a Transcript. The reporter must prepare and file a transcript as follows:

(A) Upon receiving an order for a transcript, the reporter must enter at the foot of the order the date of its receipt and the expected completion date and send a copy, so endorsed, to the circuit clerk.

(B) If the transcript cannot be completed within 30 days of the reporter's receipt of the order, the reporter may request the circuit clerk to grant additional time to complete it. The clerk must note on the docket the action taken and notify the parties.

(C) When a transcript is complete, the reporter must file it with the district clerk and notify the circuit clerk of the filing.

(D) If the reporter fails to file the transcript on time, the circuit clerk must notify the district judge and do whatever else the court of appeals directs.

(2) District Clerk's Duty to Forward. When the record is complete, the district clerk must number the documents constituting the record and send them promptly to the circuit clerk together with a list of the documents correspondingly numbered and reasonably identified. Unless directed to do so by a party or the circuit clerk, the district clerk will not send to the court of appeals documents of unusual bulk or weight, physical exhibits other than documents, or other parts of the record designated for omission by local rule of the court of appeals. If the exhibits are unusually bulky or heavy, a party must arrange with the clerks in advance for their transportation and receipt.

(c) Retaining the Record Temporarily in the District Court for Use in Preparing the Appeal. The parties may stipulate, or the district court on motion may order, that the district clerk retain the record temporarily for the parties to use in preparing the papers on appeal. In that event the district clerk must certify to the circuit clerk that the record on appeal is complete. Upon receipt of the appellee's brief, or earlier if the court orders or the parties agree, the appellant must request the district clerk to forward the record.

(d) [Abrogated.]

(e) Retaining the Record by Court Order.

(1) The court of appeals may, by order or local rule, provide that a certified copy of the docket entries be forwarded instead of the entire record. But a party may at any time during the appeal request that designated parts of the record be forwarded.

(2) The district court may order the record or some part of it retained if the court needs it while the appeal is pending, subject, however, to call by the court of appeals.

(3) If part or all of the record is ordered retained, the district clerk must send to the court of appeals a copy of the order and the docket entries together with the parts of the original record allowed by the district court and copies of any parts of the record designated by the parties.

(f) Retaining Parts of the Record in the District Court by Stipulation of the Parties. The parties may agree by written stipulation filed in the district court that designated parts of the record be retained in the district court subject to call by the court of appeals or request by a party. The parts of the record so designated remain a part of the record on appeal.

(g) Record for a Preliminary Motion in the Court of Appeals. If, before the record is forwarded, a party makes any of the following motions in the court of appeals:

- for dismissal;
- for release;
- for a stay pending appeal;
- for additional security on the bond on appeal or on a supersedeas bond; or
- for any other intermediate order—

the district clerk must send the court of appeals any parts of the record designated by any party.

(As amended Apr. 30, 1979, eff. Aug. 1, 1979; Mar. 10, 1986, eff. July 1, 1986; Apr. 24, 1998, eff. Dec. 1, 1998.)

RULE 12. DOCKETING THE APPEAL; FILING A REPRESENTATION STATEMENT; FILING THE RECORD

(a) Docketing the Appeal. Upon receiving the copy of the notice of appeal and the docket entries from the district clerk under Rule 3(d), the circuit clerk must docket the appeal under the title of the district-court action and must identify the appellant, adding the appellant's name if necessary.

(b) Filing a Representation Statement. Unless the court of appeals designates another time, the attorney who filed the notice of appeal must, within 14 days after filing the notice, file a statement with the circuit clerk naming the parties that the attorney represents on appeal.

(c) Filing the Record, Partial Record, or Certificate. Upon receiving the record, partial record, or district clerk's certificate as provided in Rule 11, the circuit clerk must file it and immediately notify all parties of the filing date.

(As amended Apr. 30, 1979, eff. Aug. 1, 1979; Mar. 10, 1986, eff. July 1, 1986; Apr. 22, 1993, eff. Dec. 1, 1993; Apr. 24, 1998, eff. Dec. 1, 1998; Mar. 26, 2009, eff. Dec. 1, 2009.)

RULE 12.1 REMAND AFTER AN INDICATIVE RULING BY THE DISTRICT COURT ON A MOTION FOR RELIEF THAT IS BARRED BY A PENDING APPEAL

(a) Notice to the Court of Appeals. If a timely motion is made in the district court for relief that it lacks authority to grant because of an appeal that has been docketed and is pending, the movant must promptly notify the circuit clerk if the district court states either that it would grant the motion or that the motion raises a substantial issue.

(b) Remand After an Indicative Ruling. If the district court states that it would grant the motion or that the motion raises a substantial issue, the court of appeals may remand for further proceedings but retains jurisdiction unless it expressly dismisses the appeal. If the court of appeals remands but retains jurisdiction, the parties must promptly notify the circuit clerk when the district court has decided the motion on remand.

(Added Mar. 26, 2009, eff. Dec. 1, 2009.)

TITLE III. APPEALS FROM THE UNITED STATES TAX COURT

RULE 13. APPEALS FROM THE TAX COURT

(a) Appeal as of Right.

(1) How Obtained; Time for Filing a Notice of Appeal.

(A) An appeal as of right from the United States Tax Court is commenced by filing a notice of appeal with the Tax Court clerk within 90 days after the entry of the Tax Court's decision. At the time of filing, the appellant must furnish the clerk with enough copies of the notice to enable the clerk to comply with Rule 3(d). If one party files a timely notice of appeal, any other party may file a notice of appeal within 120 days after the Tax Court's decision is entered.

(B) If, under Tax Court rules, a party makes a timely motion to vacate or revise the Tax Court's decision, the time to file a notice of appeal runs from the entry of the order disposing of the motion or from the entry of a new decision, whichever is later.

(2) Notice of Appeal; How Filed. The notice of appeal may be filed either at the Tax Court clerk's office in the District of Columbia or by mail addressed to the clerk. If sent by mail the notice is considered filed on the postmark date, subject to § 7502 of the Internal Revenue Code, as amended, and the applicable regulations.

(3) Contents of the Notice of Appeal; Service; Effect of Filing and Service. Rule 3 prescribes the contents of a notice of appeal, the manner of service, and the effect of its filing and service.

Form 2 in the Appendix of Forms is a suggested form of a notice of appeal.

(4) The Record on Appeal; Forwarding; Filing.

(A) Except as otherwise provided under Tax Court rules for the transcript of proceedings, the appeal is governed by the parts of Rules 10, 11, and 12 regarding the record on appeal from a district court, the time and manner of forwarding and filing, and the docketing in the court of appeals.

(B) If an appeal is taken to more than one court of appeals, the original record must be sent to the court named in the first notice of appeal filed. In an appeal to any other court of appeals, the appellant must apply to that other court to make provision for the record.

(b) Appeal by Permission. An appeal by permission is governed by Rule 5.

(As amended Apr. 30, 1979, eff. Aug. 1, 1979; Apr. 29, 1994, eff. Dec. 1, 1994; Apr. 24, 1998, eff. Dec. 1, 1998; Apr. 16, 2013, eff. Dec. 1, 2013.)

RULE 14. APPLICABILITY OF OTHER RULES TO APPEALS FROM THE TAX COURT

All provisions of these rules, except Rules 4, 6–9, 15–20, and 22–23, apply to appeals from the Tax Court. References in any applicable rule (other than Rule 24(a)) to the district court and district clerk are to be read as referring to the Tax Court and its clerk.

(As amended Apr. 24, 1998, eff. Dec. 1, 1998; Apr. 16, 2013, eff. Dec. 1, 2013.)

TITLE IV. REVIEW OR ENFORCEMENT OF AN ORDER OF AN ADMINISTRATIVE AGENCY, BOARD, COMMISSION, OR OFFICER

RULE 15. REVIEW OR ENFORCEMENT OF AN AGENCY ORDER—HOW OBTAINED; INTERVENTION

(a) Petition for Review; Joint Petition.

(1) Review of an agency order is commenced by filing, within the time prescribed by law, a petition for review with the clerk of a court of appeals authorized to review the agency order. If their interests make joinder practicable, two or more

persons may join in a petition to the same court to review the same order.

(2) The petition must:

(A) name each party seeking review either in the caption or the body of the petition—using such terms as "et al.," "petitioners," or "respondents" does not effectively name the parties;

(B) name the agency as a respondent (even though not named in the petition, the United States is a respondent if required by statute); and

(C) specify the order or part thereof to be reviewed.

(3) Form 3 in the Appendix of Forms is a suggested form of a petition for review.

(4) In this rule "agency" includes an agency, board, commission, or officer; "petition for review" includes a petition to enjoin, suspend, modify, or otherwise review, or a notice of appeal, whichever form is indicated by the applicable statute.

(b) Application or Cross–Application to Enforce an Order; Answer; Default.

(1) An application to enforce an agency order must be filed with the clerk of a court of appeals authorized to enforce the order. If a petition is filed to review an agency order that the court may enforce, a party opposing the petition may file a cross-application for enforcement.

(2) Within 21 days after the application for enforcement is filed, the respondent must serve on the applicant an answer to the application and file it with the clerk. If the respondent fails to answer in time, the court will enter judgment for the relief requested.

(3) The application must contain a concise statement of the proceedings in which the order was entered, the facts upon which venue is based, and the relief requested.

(c) Service of the Petition or Application. The circuit clerk must serve a copy of the petition for review, or an application or cross-application to enforce an agency order, on each respondent as prescribed by Rule 3(d), unless a different manner of service is prescribed by statute. At the time of filing, the petitioner must:

(1) serve, or have served, a copy on each party admitted to participate in the agency proceedings, except for the respondents;

(2) file with the clerk a list of those so served; and

(3) give the clerk enough copies of the petition or application to serve each respondent.

(d) Intervention. Unless a statute provides another method, a person who wants to intervene in a proceeding under this rule must file a motion for leave to intervene with the circuit clerk and serve a copy on all parties. The motion—or other notice of intervention authorized by statute—must be filed within 30 days after the petition for review is filed and must contain a concise statement of the interest of the moving party and the grounds for intervention.

(e) Payment of Fees. When filing any separate or joint petition for review in a court of appeals, the petitioner must pay the circuit clerk all required fees.

(As amended Apr. 22, 1993, eff. Dec. 1, 1993; Apr. 24, 1998, eff. Dec. 1, 1998; Mar. 26, 2009, eff. Dec. 1, 2009.)

RULE 15.1   BRIEFS AND ORAL ARGUMENT IN A NATIONAL LABOR RELATIONS BOARD PROCEEDING

In either an enforcement or a review proceeding, a party adverse to the National Labor Relations Board proceeds first on briefing and at oral argument, unless the court orders otherwise.

(Added Mar. 10, 1986, eff. July 1, 1986; amended Apr. 24, 1998, eff. Dec. 1, 1998.)

RULE 16.   THE RECORD ON REVIEW OR ENFORCEMENT

(a) Composition of the Record. The record on review or enforcement of an agency order consists of:

(1) the order involved;

(2) any findings or report on which it is based; and

(3) the pleadings, evidence, and other parts of the proceedings before the agency.

(b) Omissions From or Misstatements in the Record. The parties may at any time, by stipulation, supply any omission from the record or correct a misstatement, or the court may so direct. If necessary, the court may direct that a supplemental record be prepared and filed.

(As amended Apr. 24, 1998, eff. Dec. 1, 1998.)

RULE 17.   FILING THE RECORD

(a) Agency to File; Time for Filing; Notice of Filing. The agency must file the record with the circuit clerk within 40 days after being served with a petition for review, unless the statute authorizing review provides otherwise, or within 40 days after it files an application for enforcement unless the respondent fails to answer or the court orders otherwise. The court may shorten or extend the time to file the record. The clerk must notify all parties of the date when the record is filed.

(b) Filing—What Constitutes.

(1) The agency must file:

(A) the original or a certified copy of the entire record or parts designated by the parties; or

(B) a certified list adequately describing all documents, transcripts of testimony, exhibits, and other material constituting the record, or describing those parts designated by the parties.

(2) The parties may stipulate in writing that no record or certified list be filed. The date when the stipulation is filed with the circuit clerk is treated as the date when the record is filed.

(3) The agency must retain any portion of the record not filed with the clerk. All parts of the record retained by the agency are a part of the record on review for all purposes and, if the court or a party so requests, must be sent to the court regardless of any prior stipulation.

(As amended Apr. 24, 1998, eff. Dec. 1, 1998.)

RULE 18.   STAY PENDING REVIEW

(a) Motion for a Stay.

(1) Initial Motion Before the Agency. A petitioner must ordinarily move first before the agency for a stay pending review of its decision or order.

(2) Motion in the Court of Appeals. A motion for a stay may be made to the court of appeals or one of its judges.

(A) The motion must:

(i) show that moving first before the agency would be impracticable; or

(ii) state that, a motion having been made, the agency denied the motion or failed to afford the relief requested and state any reasons given by the agency for its action.

(B) The motion must also include:

(i) the reasons for granting the relief requested and the facts relied on;

(ii) originals or copies of affidavits or other sworn statements supporting facts subject to dispute; and

(iii) relevant parts of the record.

(C) The moving party must give reasonable notice of the motion to all parties.

(D) The motion must be filed with the circuit clerk and normally will be considered by a panel of the court. But in an exceptional case in which time requirements make that procedure impracticable, the motion may be made to and considered by a single judge.

(b) Bond. The court may condition relief on the filing of a bond or other appropriate security.

(As amended Apr. 24, 1998, eff. Dec. 1, 1998.)

RULE 19.   SETTLEMENT OF A JUDGMENT ENFORCING AN AGENCY ORDER IN PART

When the court files an opinion directing entry of judgment enforcing the agency's order in part, the agency must within 14 days file with the clerk and serve on each other party a proposed judgment conforming to the opinion. A party who disagrees with the agency's proposed judgment must within 10 days file with the clerk and serve the agency with a proposed judgment that the party believes conforms to the opinion. The court will settle the judgment and direct entry without further hearing or argument.

(As amended Mar. 10, 1986, eff. July 1, 1986; Apr. 24, 1998, eff. Dec. 1, 1998; Mar. 26, 2009, eff. Dec. 1, 2009.)

RULE 20.   APPLICABILITY OF RULES TO THE REVIEW OR ENFORCEMENT OF AN AGENCY ORDER

All provisions of these rules, except Rules 3–14 and 22–23, apply to the review or enforcement of an agency order. In these rules, "appellant" includes a petitioner or applicant, and "appellee" includes a respondent.

(As amended Apr. 24, 1998, eff. Dec. 1, 1998.)

TITLE V.   EXTRAORDINARY WRITS

RULE 21.   WRITS OF MANDAMUS AND PROHIBITION, AND OTHER EXTRAORDINARY WRITS

(a) Mandamus or Prohibition to a Court: Petition, Filing, Service, and Docketing.

(1) A party petitioning for a writ of mandamus or prohibition directed to a court must file a petition with the circuit clerk with proof of service on all parties to the proceeding in the trial court. The party must also provide a copy to the trial-court judge. All parties to the proceeding in the trial court other than the petitioner are respondents for all purposes.

(2)(A) The petition must be titled "In re [name of petitioner]."

(B) The petition must state:

(i) the relief sought;

(ii) the issues presented;

(iii) the facts necessary to understand the issue presented by the petition; and

(iv) the reasons why the writ should issue.

(C) The petition must include a copy of any order or opinion or parts of the record that may be essential to understand the matters set forth in the petition.

(3) Upon receiving the prescribed docket fee, the clerk must docket the petition and submit it to the court.

(b) Denial; Order Directing Answer; Briefs; Precedence.

(1) The court may deny the petition without an answer. Otherwise, it must order the respondent, if any, to answer within a fixed time.

(2) The clerk must serve the order to respond on all persons directed to respond.

(3) Two or more respondents may answer jointly.

(4) The court of appeals may invite or order the trial-court judge to address the petition or may invite an amicus curiae to do so. The trial-court judge may request permission to address the petition but may not do so unless invited or ordered to do so by the court of appeals.

(5) If briefing or oral argument is required, the clerk must advise the parties, and when appropriate, the trial-court judge or amicus curiae.

(6) The proceeding must be given preference over ordinary civil cases.

(7) The circuit clerk must send a copy of the final disposition to the trial-court judge.

(c) Other Extraordinary Writs. An application for an extraordinary writ other than one provided for in Rule 21(a) must be made by filing a petition with the circuit clerk with proof of service on the respondents. Proceedings on the application must conform, so far as is practicable, to the procedures prescribed in Rule 21(a) and (b).

(d) Form of Papers; Number of Copies. All papers must conform to Rule 32(c)(2). Except by the court's permission, a paper must not exceed 30 pages, exclusive of the disclosure statement, the proof of service, and the accompanying documents required by Rule 21(a)(2)(C). An original and 3 copies must be filed unless the court requires the filing of a different number by local rule or by order in a particular case.

(As amended Apr. 29, 1994, eff. Dec. 1, 1994; Apr. 23, 1996, eff. Dec. 1, 1996; Apr. 24, 1998, eff. Dec. 1, 1998; Apr. 29, 2002, eff. Dec. 1, 2002.)

TITLE VI. HABEAS CORPUS; PROCEEDINGS IN FORMA PAUPERIS

RULE 22. HABEAS CORPUS AND SECTION 2255 PROCEEDINGS

(a) Application for the Original Writ. An application for a writ of habeas corpus must be made to the appropriate district court. If made to a circuit judge, the application must be transferred to the appropriate district court. If a district court denies an application made or transferred to it, renewal of the application before a circuit judge is not permitted. The applicant may, under 28 U.S.C. § 2253, appeal to the court of appeals from the district court's order denying the application.

(b) Certificate of Appealability.

(1) In a habeas corpus proceeding in which the detention complained of arises from process issued by a state court, or in a 28 U.S.C. § 2255 proceeding, the applicant cannot take an appeal unless a circuit justice or a circuit or district judge issues a certificate of appealability under 28 U.S.C. § 2253(c). If an applicant files a notice of appeal, the district clerk must send to the court of appeals the certificate (if any) and the statement described in Rule 11(a) of the Rules Governing Proceedings Under 28 U.S.C. § 2254 or § 2255 (if any), along with the notice of appeal and the file of the district-court proceedings. If the district judge has denied

the certificate, the applicant may request a circuit judge to issue it.

(2) A request addressed to the court of appeals may be considered by a circuit judge or judges, as the court prescribes. If no express request for a certificate is filed, the notice of appeal constitutes a request addressed to the judges of the court of appeals.

(3) A certificate of appealability is not required when a state or its representative or the United States or its representative appeals.

(As amended Pub.L. 104–132, Title I, § 103, Apr. 24, 1996, 110 Stat. 1218; Apr. 24, 1998, eff. Dec. 1, 1998; Mar. 26, 2009, eff. Dec. 1, 2009.)

RULE 23. CUSTODY OR RELEASE OF A PRISONER IN A HABEAS CORPUS PROCEEDING

(a) Transfer of Custody Pending Review. Pending review of a decision in a habeas corpus proceeding commenced before a court, justice, or judge of the United States for the release of a prisoner, the person having custody of the prisoner must not transfer custody to another unless a transfer is directed in accordance with this rule. When, upon application, a custodian shows the need for a transfer, the court, justice, or judge rendering the decision under review may authorize the transfer and substitute the successor custodian as a party.

(b) Detention or Release Pending Review of Decision Not to Release. While a decision not to release a prisoner is under review, the court or judge rendering the decision, or the court of appeals, or the Supreme Court, or a judge or justice of either court, may order that the prisoner be:

    (1) detained in the custody from which release is sought;

    (2) detained in other appropriate custody; or

    (3) released on personal recognizance, with or without surety.

(c) Release Pending Review of Decision Ordering Release. While a decision ordering the release of a prisoner is under review, the prisoner must—unless the court or judge rendering the decision, or the court of appeals, or the Supreme Court, or a judge or justice of either court orders otherwise—be released on personal recognizance, with or without surety.

(d) Modification of the Initial Order on Custody. An initial order governing the prisoner's custody or release, including any recognizance or surety, continues in effect pending review unless for special reasons shown to the court of appeals or the Supreme Court, or to a judge or justice of either court, the order is modified or an independent order regarding custody, release, or surety is issued.

(As amended Mar. 10, 1986, eff. July 1, 1986; Apr. 24, 1998, eff. Dec. 1, 1998.)

RULE 24. PROCEEDING IN FORMA PAUPERIS

(a) Leave to Proceed In Forma Pauperis.

    (1) Motion in the District Court. Except as stated in Rule 24(a)(3), a party to a district-court action who desires to appeal in forma pauperis must file a motion in the district court. The party must attach an affidavit that:

        (A) shows in the detail prescribed by Form 4 of the Appendix of Forms the party's inability to pay or to give security for fees and costs;

        (B) claims an entitlement to redress; and

        (C) states the issues that the party intends to present on appeal.

    (2) Action on the Motion. If the district court grants the motion, the party may proceed on appeal without prepaying or giving security for fees and costs, unless a statute provides otherwise. If the

district court denies the motion, it must state its reasons in writing.

    (3) Prior Approval. A party who was permitted to proceed in forma pauperis in the district-court action, or who was determined to be financially unable to obtain an adequate defense in a criminal case, may proceed on appeal in forma pauperis without further authorization, unless:

        (A) the district court—before or after the notice of appeal is filed—certifies that the appeal is not taken in good faith or finds that the party is not otherwise entitled to proceed in forma pauperis and states in writing its reasons for the certification or finding; or

        (B) a statute provides otherwise.

    (4) Notice of District Court's Denial. The district clerk must immediately notify the parties and the court of appeals when the district court does any of the following:

        (A) denies a motion to proceed on appeal in forma pauperis;

        (B) certifies that the appeal is not taken in good faith; or

        (C) finds that the party is not otherwise entitled to proceed in forma pauperis.

    (5) Motion in the Court of Appeals. A party may file a motion to proceed on appeal in forma pauperis in the court of appeals within 30 days after service of the notice prescribed in Rule 24(a)(4). The motion must include a copy of the affidavit filed in the district court and the district court's statement of reasons for its action. If no affidavit was filed in the district court, the party must include the affidavit prescribed by Rule 24(a)(1).

(b) Leave to Proceed In Forma Pauperis on Appeal from the United States Tax Court or on Appeal or Review of an Administrative–Agency Proceeding. A party may file in the court of appeals a motion for leave to proceed on appeal in forma pauperis with an affidavit prescribed by Rule 24(a)(1):

    (1) in an appeal from the United States Tax Court; and

    (2) when an appeal or review of a proceeding before an administrative agency, board, commission, or officer proceeds directly in the court of appeals.

(c) Leave to Use Original Record. A party allowed to proceed on appeal in forma pauperis may request that the appeal be heard on the original record without reproducing any part.

(As amended Apr. 30, 1979, eff. Aug. 1, 1979; Mar. 10, 1986, eff. July 1, 1986; Apr. 24, 1998, eff. Dec. 1, 1998; Apr. 29, 2002, eff. Dec. 1, 2002; Apr. 16, 2013, eff. Dec. 1, 2013.)

TITLE VII. GENERAL PROVISIONS

RULE 25. FILING AND SERVICE

(a) Filing.

(1) **Filing with the Clerk.** A paper required or permitted to be filed in a court of appeals must be filed with the clerk.

(2) **Filing: Method and Timeliness.**

(A) **In general.** Filing may be accomplished by mail addressed to the clerk, but filing is not timely unless the clerk receives the papers within the time fixed for filing.

(B) **A brief or appendix.** A brief or appendix is timely filed, however, if on or before the last day for filing, it is:

(i) mailed to the clerk by First–Class Mail, or other class of mail that is at least as expeditious, postage prepaid; or

(ii) dispatched to a third-party commercial carrier for delivery to the clerk within 3 days.

(C) **Inmate filing.** A paper filed by an inmate confined in an institution is timely if deposited in the institution's internal mailing system on or before the last day for filing. If an institution has a system designed for legal mail, the inmate must use that system to receive the benefit of this rule. Timely filing may be shown by a declaration in compliance with 28 U.S.C. § 1746 or by a notarized statement, either of which must set forth the date of deposit and state that first-class postage has been prepaid.

(D) **Electronic filing.** A court of appeals may by local rule permit or require papers to be filed, signed, or verified by electronic means that are consistent with technical standards, if any, that the Judicial Conference of the United States establishes. A local rule may require filing by electronic means only if reasonable exceptions are allowed. A paper filed by electronic means in compliance with a local rule constitutes a written paper for the purpose of applying these rules.

(3) **Filing a Motion with a Judge.** If a motion requests relief that may be granted by a single judge, the judge may permit the motion to be filed with the judge; the judge must note the filing date on the motion and give it to the clerk.

(4) **Clerk's Refusal of Documents.** The clerk must not refuse to accept for filing any paper presented for that purpose solely because it is not presented in proper form as required by these rules or by any local rule or practice.

(5) **Privacy Protection.** An appeal in a case whose privacy protection was governed by Federal Rule of Bankruptcy Procedure 9037, Federal Rule of Civil Procedure 5.2, or Federal Rule of Criminal Procedure 49.1 is governed by the same rule on appeal. In all other proceedings, privacy protection is governed by Federal Rule of Civil Procedure 5.2, except that Federal Rule of Criminal Procedure 49.1 governs when an extraordinary writ is sought in a criminal case.

(b) Service of All Papers Required. Unless a rule requires service by the clerk, a party must, at or before the time of filing a paper, serve a copy on the other parties to the appeal or review. Service on a party represented by counsel must be made on the party's counsel.

(c) Manner of Service.

(1) Service may be any of the following:

(A) personal, including delivery to a responsible person at the office of counsel;

(B) by mail;

(C) by third-party commercial carrier for delivery within 3 days; or

(D) by electronic means, if the party being served consents in writing.

(2) If authorized by local rule, a party may use the court's transmission equipment to make electronic service under Rule 25(c)(1)(D).

(3) When reasonable considering such factors as the immediacy of the relief sought, distance, and cost, service on a party must be by a manner at least as expeditious as the manner used to file the paper with the court.

(4) Service by mail or by commercial carrier is complete on mailing or delivery to the carrier. Service by electronic means is complete on transmission, unless the party making service is notified that the paper was not received by the party served.

(d) Proof of Service.

(1) A paper presented for filing must contain either of the following:

(A) an acknowledgment of service by the person served; or

(B) proof of service consisting of a statement by the person who made service certifying:

(i) the date and manner of service;

(ii) the names of the persons served; and

(iii) their mail or electronic addresses, facsimile numbers, or the addresses of the places of delivery, as appropriate for the manner of service.

(2) When a brief or appendix is filed by mailing or dispatch in accordance with Rule 25(a)(2)(B), the proof of service must also state the date and man-

ner by which the document was mailed or dispatched to the clerk.

(3) Proof of service may appear on or be affixed to the papers filed.

(e) Number of Copies. When these rules require the filing or furnishing of a number of copies, a court may require a different number by local rule or by order in a particular case.

(As amended Mar. 10, 1986, eff. July 1, 1986; Apr. 30, 1991, eff. Dec. 1, 1991; Apr. 22, 1993, eff. Dec. 1, 1993; Apr. 29, 1994, eff. Dec. 1, 1994; Apr. 23, 1996, eff. Dec. 1, 1996; Apr. 24, 1998, eff. Dec. 1, 1998; Apr. 29, 2002, eff. Dec. 1, 2002; Apr. 12, 2006, eff. Dec. 1, 2006; Apr. 30, 2007, eff. Dec. 1, 2007; Mar. 26, 2009, eff. Dec. 1, 2009.)

RULE 26. COMPUTING AND EXTENDING TIME

(a) Computing Time. The following rules apply in computing any time period specified in these rules, in any local rule or court order, or in any statute that does not specify a method of computing time.

(1) Period Stated in Days or a Longer Unit. When the period is stated in days or a longer unit of time:

(A) exclude the day of the event that triggers the period;

(B) count every day, including intermediate Saturdays, Sundays, and legal holidays; and

(C) include the last day of the period, but if the last day is a Saturday, Sunday, or legal holiday, the period continues to run until the end of the next day that is not a Saturday, Sunday, or legal holiday.

(2) Period Stated in Hours. When the period is stated in hours:

(A) begin counting immediately on the occurrence of the event that triggers the period;

(B) count every hour, including hours during intermediate Saturdays, Sundays, and legal holidays; and

(C) if the period would end on a Saturday, Sunday, or legal holiday, the period continues to run until the same time on the next day that is not a Saturday, Sunday, or legal holiday.

(3) Inaccessibility of the Clerk's Office. Unless the court orders otherwise, if the clerk's office is inaccessible:

(A) on the last day for filing under Rule 26(a)(1), then the time for filing is extended to the first accessible day that is not a Saturday, Sunday, or legal holiday; or

(B) during the last hour for filing under Rule 26(a)(2), then the time for filing is extended to the

same time on the first accessible day that is not a Saturday, Sunday, or legal holiday.

(4) "Last Day" Defined. Unless a different time is set by a statute, local rule, or court order, the last day ends:

(A) for electronic filing in the district court, at midnight in the court's time zone;

(B) for electronic filing in the court of appeals, at midnight in the time zone of the circuit clerk's principal office;

(C) for filing under Rules 4(c)(1), 25(a)(2)(B), and 25(a)(2)(C)—and filing by mail under Rule 13(b)—at the latest time for the method chosen for delivery to the post office, third-party commercial carrier, or prison mailing system; and

(D) for filing by other means, when the clerk's office is scheduled to close.

(5) "Next Day" Defined. The "next day" is determined by continuing to count forward when the period is measured after an event and backward when measured before an event.

(6) "Legal Holiday" Defined. "Legal holiday" means:

(A) the day set aside by statute for observing New Year's Day, Martin Luther King Jr.'s Birthday, Washington's Birthday, Memorial Day, Independence Day, Labor Day, Columbus Day, Veterans' Day, Thanksgiving Day, or Christmas Day;

(B) any day declared a holiday by the President or Congress; and

(C) for periods that are measured after an event, any other day declared a holiday by the state where either of the following is located: the district court that rendered the challenged judgment or order, or the circuit clerk's principal office.

(b) Extending Time. For good cause, the court may extend the time prescribed by these rules or by its order to perform any act, or may permit an act to be done after that time expires. But the court may not extend the time to file:

(1) a notice of appeal (except as authorized in Rule 4) or a petition for permission to appeal; or

(2) a notice of appeal from or a petition to enjoin, set aside, suspend, modify, enforce, or otherwise review an order of an administrative agency, board, commission, or officer of the United States, unless specifically authorized by law.

(c) Additional Time after Service. When a party may or must act within a specified time after service, 3 days are added after the period would otherwise expire under Rule 26(a), unless the paper is delivered on the date of service stated in the proof of service. For purposes of this Rule 26(c), a paper that is served electronically is not treated as delivered on the date of service stated in the proof of service.

(As amended Mar. 1, 1971, eff. July 1, 1971; Mar. 10, 1986, eff. July 1, 1986; Apr. 25, 1989, eff. Dec. 1, 1989; Apr. 30, 1991, eff. Dec. 1, 1991; Apr. 23, 1996, eff. Dec. 1, 1996; Apr. 24, 1998, eff. Dec. 1, 1998; Apr. 29, 2002, eff. Dec. 1, 2002; Apr. 25, 2005, eff. Dec. 1, 2005; Mar. 26, 2009, eff. Dec. 1, 2009.)

RULE 26.1 CORPORATE DISCLOSURE STATEMENT

(a) Who Must File. Any nongovernmental corporate party to a proceeding in a court of appeals must file a statement that identifies any parent corporation and any publicly held corporation that owns 10% or more of its stock or states that there is no such corporation.

(b) Time for Filing; Supplemental Filing. A party must file the Rule 26.1(a) statement with the principal brief or upon filing a motion, response, petition, or answer in the court of appeals, whichever occurs first, unless a local rule requires earlier filing. Even if the statement has already been filed, the party's principal brief must include the statement before the table of contents. A party must supplement its statement whenever the information that must be disclosed under Rule 26.1(a) changes.

(c) Number of Copies. If the Rule 26.1(a) statement is filed before the principal brief, or if a supplemental statement is filed, the party must file an original and 3 copies unless the court requires a different number by local rule or by order in a particular case.

(Added Apr. 25, 1989, eff. Dec. 1, 1989; amended Apr. 30, 1991, eff. Dec. 1, 1991; Apr. 29, 1994, eff. Dec. 1, 1994; Apr. 24, 1998, eff. Dec. 1, 1998; Apr. 29, 2002, eff. Dec. 1, 2002.)

RULE 27. MOTIONS

(a) In General.

(1) Application for Relief. An application for an order or other relief is made by motion unless these rules prescribe another form. A motion must be in writing unless the court permits otherwise.

(2) Contents of a Motion.

(A) Grounds and relief sought. A motion must state with particularity the grounds for the motion, the relief sought, and the legal argument necessary to support it.

(B) Accompanying documents.

(i) Any affidavit or other paper necessary to support a motion must be served and filed with the motion.

(ii) An affidavit must contain only factual information, not legal argument.

(iii) A motion seeking substantive relief must include a copy of the trial court's opinion or agency's decision as a separate exhibit.

(C) Documents barred or not required.

(i) A separate brief supporting or responding to a motion must not be filed.

(ii) A notice of motion is not required.

(iii) A proposed order is not required.

(3) Response.

(A) Time to file. Any party may file a response to a motion; Rule 27(a)(2) governs its contents. The response must be filed within 10 days after service of the motion unless the court shortens or extends the time. A motion authorized by Rules 8, 9, 18, or 41 may be granted before the 10-day period runs only if the court gives reasonable notice to the parties that it intends to act sooner.

(B) Request for affirmative relief. A response may include a motion for affirmative relief. The time to respond to the new motion, and to reply to that response, are governed by Rule 27(a)(3)(A) and (a)(4). The title of the response must alert the court to the request for relief.

(4) Reply to Response. Any reply to a response must be filed within 7 days after service of the response. A reply must not present matters that do not relate to the response.

(b) Disposition of a Motion for a Procedural Order. The court may act on a motion for a procedural order—including a motion under Rule 26(b)—at any time without awaiting a response, and may, by rule or by order in a particular case, authorize its clerk to act on specified types of procedural motions. A party adversely affected by the court's, or the clerk's, action may file a motion to reconsider, vacate, or modify that action. Timely opposition filed after the motion is granted in whole or in part does not constitute a request to reconsider, vacate, or modify the disposition; a motion requesting that relief must be filed.

(c) Power of a Single Judge to Entertain a Motion. A circuit judge may act alone on any motion, but may not dismiss or otherwise determine an appeal or other proceeding. A court of appeals may provide by rule or by order in a particular case that only the court may act on any motion or class of motions. The court may review the action of a single judge.

(d) Form of Papers; Page Limits; and Number of Copies.

(1) Format.

(A) Reproduction. A motion, response, or reply may be reproduced by any process that yields a clear black image on light paper. The paper must be opaque and unglazed. Only one side of the paper may be used.

(B) Cover. A cover is not required, but there must be a caption that includes the case number, the name of the court, the title of the case, and a brief descriptive title indicating the purpose of the motion and identifying the party or parties for whom it is filed. If a cover is used, it must be white.

(C) Binding. The document must be bound in any manner that is secure, does not obscure the text, and permits the document to lie reasonably flat when open.

(D) Paper size, line spacing, and margins. The document must be on 8½ by 11 inch paper. The text must be double-spaced, but quotations more than two lines long may be indented and single-spaced. Headings and footnotes may be single-spaced. Margins must be at least one inch on all four sides. Page numbers may be placed in the margins, but no text may appear there.

(E) Typeface and type styles. The document must comply with the typeface requirements of Rule 32(a)(5) and the type-style requirements of Rule 32(a)(6).

(2) Page Limits. A motion or a response to a motion must not exceed 20 pages, exclusive of the corporate disclosure statement and accompanying documents authorized by Rule 27(a)(2)(B), unless the court permits or directs otherwise. A reply to a response must not exceed 10 pages.

(3) Number of Copies. An original and 3 copies must be filed unless the court requires a different number by local rule or by order in a particular case.

(e) Oral Argument. A motion will be decided without oral argument unless the court orders otherwise.

(As amended Apr. 30, 1979, eff. Aug. 1, 1979; Apr. 25, 1989, eff. Dec. 1, 1989; Apr. 29, 1994, eff. Dec. 1, 1994; Apr. 24, 1998, eff. Dec. 1, 1998; Apr. 29, 2002, eff. Dec. 1, 2002; Apr. 25, 2005, eff. Dec. 1, 2005; Mar. 26, 2009, eff. Dec. 1, 2009.)

RULE 28. BRIEFS

(a) Appellant's Brief. The appellant's brief must contain, under appropriate headings and in the order indicated:

(1) a corporate disclosure statement if required by Rule 26.1;

(2) a table of contents, with page references;

(3) a table of authorities—cases (alphabetically arranged), statutes, and other authorities—with references to the pages of the brief where they are cited;

(4) a jurisdictional statement, including:

(A) the basis for the district court's or agency's subject-matter jurisdiction, with citations to applicable statutory provisions and stating relevant facts establishing jurisdiction;

(B) the basis for the court of appeals' jurisdiction, with citations to applicable statutory provisions and stating relevant facts establishing jurisdiction;

(C) the filing dates establishing the timeliness of the appeal or petition for review; and

(D) an assertion that the appeal is from a final order or judgment that disposes of all parties' claims, or information establishing the court of appeals' jurisdiction on some other basis;

(5) a statement of the issues presented for review;

(6) a concise statement of the case setting out the facts relevant to the issues submitted for review, describing the relevant procedural history, and identifying the rulings presented for review, with appropriate references to the record (see Rule 28(e));

(7) a summary of the argument, which must contain a succinct, clear, and accurate statement of the arguments made in the body of the brief, and which must not merely repeat the argument headings;

(8) the argument, which must contain:

(A) appellant's contentions and the reasons for them, with citations to the authorities and parts of the record on which the appellant relies; and

(B) for each issue, a concise statement of the applicable standard of review (which may appear in the discussion of the issue or under a separate heading placed before the discussion of the issues);

(9) a short conclusion stating the precise relief sought; and

(10) the certificate of compliance, if required by Rule 32(a)(7).

(b) Appellee's Brief. The appellee's brief must conform to the requirements of Rule 28(a)(1)–(8) and (10), except that none of the following need appear unless the appellee is dissatisfied with the appellant's statement:

(1) the jurisdictional statement;

(2) the statement of the issues;

(3) the statement of the case; and

(4) the statement of the standard of review.

(c) Reply Brief. The appellant may file a brief in reply to the appellee's brief. Unless the court permits, no further briefs may be filed. A reply brief must contain a table of contents, with page references, and a table of authorities—cases (alphabetically arranged), statutes, and other authorities—with references to the pages of the reply brief where they are cited.

(d) References to Parties. In briefs and at oral argument, counsel should minimize use of the terms "appellant" and "appellee." To make briefs clear, counsel should use the parties' actual names or the designations used in the lower court or agency proceeding, or such descriptive terms as "the employee," "the injured person," "the taxpayer," "the ship," "the stevedore."

(e) References to the Record. References to the parts of the record contained in the appendix filed with the appellant's brief must be to the pages of the appendix. If the appendix is prepared after the briefs are filed, a party referring to the record must follow one of the methods detailed in Rule 30(c). If the original record is used under Rule 30(f) and is not consecutively paginated, or if the brief refers to an unreproduced part of the record, any reference must be to the page of the original document. For example:

- Answer p. 7;
- Motion for Judgment p. 2;
- Transcript p. 231.

Only clear abbreviations may be used. A party referring to evidence whose admissibility is in controversy must cite the pages of the appendix or of the transcript at which the evidence was identified, offered, and received or rejected.

(f) Reproduction of Statutes, Rules, Regulations, etc. If the court's determination of the issues presented requires the study of statutes, rules, regulations, etc., the relevant parts must be set out in the brief or in an addendum at the end, or may be supplied to the court in pamphlet form.

(g) [Reserved]

(h) [Reserved]

(i) Briefs in a Case Involving Multiple Appellants or Appellees. In a case involving more than one appellant or appellee, including consolidated cases, any number of appellants or appellees may join in a brief, and any party may adopt by reference a part of another's brief. Parties may also join in reply briefs.

(j) Citation of Supplemental Authorities. If pertinent and significant authorities come to a party's attention after the party's brief has been filed—or after oral argument but before decision—a party may promptly advise the circuit clerk by letter, with a copy to all other parties, setting forth the citations. The letter must state the reasons for the supplemental citations, referring either to the page of the brief or to a point argued orally. The body of the letter must not

exceed 350 words. Any response must be made promptly and must be similarly limited.

(As amended Apr. 30, 1979, eff. Aug. 1, 1979; Mar. 10, 1986, eff. July 1, 1986; Apr. 25, 1989, eff. Dec. 1, 1989; Apr. 30, 1991, eff. Dec. 1, 1991; Apr. 22, 1993, eff. Dec. 1, 1993; Apr. 29, 1994, eff. Dec. 1, 1994; Apr. 24, 1998, eff. Dec. 1, 1998; Apr. 29, 2002, eff. Dec. 1, 2002; Apr. 25, 2005, eff. Dec. 1, 2005; Apr. 16, 2013, eff. Dec. 1, 2013.)

RULE 28.1 CROSS–APPEALS

(a) Applicability. This rule applies to a case in which a cross-appeal is filed. Rules 28(a)-(c), 31(a)(1), 32(a)(2), and 32(a)(7)(A)-(B) do not apply to such a case, except as otherwise provided in this rule.

(b) Designation of Appellant. The party who files a notice of appeal first is the appellant for the purposes of this rule and Rules 30 and 34. If notices are filed on the same day, the plaintiff in the proceeding below is the appellant. These designations may be modified by the parties' agreement or by court order.

(c) Briefs. In a case involving a cross-appeal:

(1) Appellant's Principal Brief. The appellant must file a principal brief in the appeal. That brief must comply with Rule 28(a).

(2) Appellee's Principal and Response Brief. The appellee must file a principal brief in the cross-appeal and must, in the same brief, respond to the principal brief in the appeal. That appellee's brief must comply with Rule 28(a), except that the brief need not include a statement of the case unless the appellee is dissatisfied with the appellant's statement.

(3) Appellant's Response and Reply Brief. The appellant must file a brief that responds to the principal brief in the cross-appeal and may, in the same brief, reply to the response in the appeal. That brief must comply with Rule 28(a)(2)–(8) and (10), except that none of the following need appear unless the appellant is dissatisfied with the appellee's statement in the cross-appeal:

(A) the jurisdictional statement;

(B) the statement of the issues;

(C) the statement of the case; and

(D) the statement of the standard of review.

(4) Appellee's Reply Brief. The appellee may file a brief in reply to the response in the cross-appeal. That brief must comply with Rule 28(a)(2)–(3) and (10) and must be limited to the issues presented by the cross-appeal.

(5) No Further Briefs. Unless the court permits, no further briefs may be filed in a case involving a cross-appeal.

(d) Cover. Except for filings by unrepresented parties, the cover of the appellant's principal brief must be blue; the appellee's principal and response brief, red; the appellant's response and reply brief, yellow; the appellee's reply brief, gray; an intervenor's or amicus curiae's brief, green; and any supplemental brief, tan. The front cover of a brief must contain the information required by Rule 32(a)(2).

(e) Length.

(1) Page Limitation. Unless it complies with Rule 28.1(e)(2) and (3), the appellant's principal brief must not exceed 30 pages; the appellee's principal and response brief, 35 pages; the appellant's response and reply brief, 30 pages; and the appellee's reply brief, 15 pages.

(2) Type-Volume Limitation.

(A) The appellant's principal brief or the appellant's response and reply brief is acceptable if:

(i) it contains no more than 14,000 words; or

(ii) it uses a monospaced face and contains no more than 1,300 lines of text.

(B) The appellee's principal and response brief is acceptable if:

(i) it contains no more than 16,500 words; or

(ii) it uses a monospaced face and contains no more than 1,500 lines of text.

(C) The appellee's reply brief is acceptable if it contains no more than half of the type volume specified in Rule 28.1(e)(2)(A).

(3) Certificate of Compliance. A brief submitted under Rule 28.1(e)(2) must comply with Rule 32(a)(7)(C).

(f) Time to Serve and File a Brief. Briefs must be served and filed as follows:

(1) the appellant's principal brief, within 40 days after the record is filed;

(2) the appellee's principal and response brief, within 30 days after the appellant's principal brief is served;

(3) the appellant's response and reply brief, within 30 days after the appellee's principal and response brief is served; and

(4) the appellee's reply brief, within 14 days after the appellant's response and reply brief is served, but at least 7 days before argument unless the court, for good cause, allows a later filing.

(As added April 25, 2005, eff. Dec. 1, 2005; amended Mar. 26, 2009, eff. Dec. 1, 2009; Apr. 16, 2013, eff. Dec. 1, 2013.)

RULE 29. BRIEF OF AN AMICUS CURIAE

(a) When Permitted. The United States or its officer or agency or a state may file an amicus-curiae brief without the consent of the parties or leave of court. Any other amicus curiae may file a brief only by leave of court or if the brief states that all parties have consented to its filing.

(b) Motion for Leave to File. The motion must be accompanied by the proposed brief and state:

(1) the movant's interest; and

(2) the reason why an amicus brief is desirable and why the matters asserted are relevant to the disposition of the case.

(c) Contents and Form. An amicus brief must comply with Rule 32. In addition to the requirements of Rule 32, the cover must identify the party or parties supported and indicate whether the brief supports affirmance or reversal. An amicus brief need not comply with Rule 28, but must include the following:

(1) if the amicus curiae is a corporation, a disclosure statement like that required of parties by Rule 26.1;

(2) a table of contents, with page references;

(3) a table of authorities—cases (alphabetically arranged), statutes, and other authorities—with references to the pages of the brief where they are cited;

(4) a concise statement of the identity of the amicus curiae, its interest in the case, and the source of its authority to file;

(5) unless the amicus curiae is one listed in the first sentence of Rule 29(a), a statement that indicates whether:

(A) a party's counsel authored the brief in whole or in part;

(B) a party or a party's counsel contributed money that was intended to fund preparing or submitting the brief; and

(C) a person—other than the amicus curiae, its members, or its counsel—contributed money that was intended to fund preparing or submitting the brief and, if so, identifies each such person;

(6) an argument, which may be preceded by a summary and which need not include a statement of the applicable standard of review; and

(7) a certificate of compliance, if required by Rule 32(a)(7).

(d) Length. Except by the court's permission, an amicus brief may be no more than one-half the maximum length authorized by these rules for a party's principal brief. If the court grants a party permission to file a longer brief, that extension does not affect the length of an amicus brief.

(e) Time for Filing. An amicus curiae must file its brief, accompanied by a motion for filing when necessary, no later than 7 days after the principal brief of the party being supported is filed. An amicus curiae that does not support either party must file its brief no later than 7 days after the appellant's or petitioner's principal brief is filed. A court may grant leave for later filing, specifying the time within which an opposing party may answer.

(f) Reply Brief. Except by the court's permission, an amicus curiae may not file a reply brief.

(g) Oral Argument. An amicus curiae may participate in oral argument only with the court's permission.

(As amended Apr. 24, 1998, eff. Dec. 1, 1998; Apr. 28, 2010, eff. Dec. 1, 2010.)

RULE 30.   APPENDIX TO THE BRIEFS

(a) Appellant's Responsibility.

(1) Contents of the Appendix. The appellant must prepare and file an appendix to the briefs containing:

(A) the relevant docket entries in the proceeding below;

(B) the relevant portions of the pleadings, charge, findings, or opinion;

(C) the judgment, order, or decision in question; and

(D) other parts of the record to which the parties wish to direct the court's attention.

(2) Excluded Material. Memoranda of law in the district court should not be included in the appendix unless they have independent relevance. Parts of the record may be relied on by the court or the parties even though not included in the appendix.

(3) Time to File; Number of Copies. Unless filing is deferred under Rule 30(c), the appellant must file 10 copies of the appendix with the brief and must serve one copy on counsel for each party separately represented. An unrepresented party proceeding in forma pauperis must file 4 legible copies with the clerk, and one copy must be served on counsel for each separately represented party. The court may by local rule or by order in a particular case require the filing or service of a different number.

(b) All Parties' Responsibilities.

(1) Determining the Contents of the Appendix. The parties are encouraged to agree on the contents of the appendix. In the absence of an agreement, the appellant must, within 14 days after the record is filed, serve on the appellee a designation of the parts of the record the appellant intends to include in the appendix and a statement of the issues the appellant intends to present for review. The appellee may, within 14 days after receiving the designa-

tion, serve on the appellant a designation of additional parts to which it wishes to direct the court's attention. The appellant must include the designated parts in the appendix. The parties must not engage in unnecessary designation of parts of the record, because the entire record is available to the court. This paragraph applies also to a cross-appellant and a cross-appellee.

(2) Costs of Appendix. Unless the parties agree otherwise, the appellant must pay the cost of the appendix. If the appellant considers parts of the record designated by the appellee to be unnecessary, the appellant may advise the appellee, who must then advance the cost of including those parts. The cost of the appendix is a taxable cost. But if any party causes unnecessary parts of the record to be included in the appendix, the court may impose the cost of those parts on that party. Each circuit must, by local rule, provide for sanctions against attorneys who unreasonably and vexatiously increase litigation costs by including unnecessary material in the appendix.

(c) Deferred Appendix.

(1) Deferral Until After Briefs Are Filed. The court may provide by rule for classes of cases or by order in a particular case that preparation of the appendix may be deferred until after the briefs have been filed and that the appendix may be filed 21 days after the appellee's brief is served. Even though the filing of the appendix may be deferred, Rule 30(b) applies; except that a party must designate the parts of the record it wants included in the appendix when it serves its brief, and need not include a statement of the issues presented.

(2) References to the Record.

(A) If the deferred appendix is used, the parties may cite in their briefs the pertinent pages of the record. When the appendix is prepared, the record pages cited in the briefs must be indicated by inserting record page numbers, in brackets, at places in the appendix where those pages of the record appear.

(B) A party who wants to refer directly to pages of the appendix may serve and file copies of the brief within the time required by Rule 31(a), containing appropriate references to pertinent pages of the record. In that event, within 14 days after the appendix is filed, the party must serve and file copies of the brief, containing references to the pages of the appendix in place of or in addition to the references to the pertinent pages of the record. Except for the correction of typographical errors, no other changes may be made to the brief.

(d) Format of the Appendix. The appendix must begin with a table of contents identifying the page at which each part begins. The relevant docket entries must follow the table of contents. Other parts of the record must follow chronologically. When pages from the transcript of proceedings are placed in the appendix, the transcript page numbers must be shown in brackets immediately before the included pages. Omissions in the text of papers or of the transcript must be indicated by asterisks. Immaterial formal matters (captions, subscriptions, acknowledgments, etc.) should be omitted.

(e) Reproduction of Exhibits. Exhibits designated for inclusion in the appendix may be reproduced in a separate volume, or volumes, suitably indexed. Four copies must be filed with the appendix, and one copy must be served on counsel for each separately represented party. If a transcript of a proceeding before an administrative agency, board, commission, or officer was used in a district-court action and has been designated for inclusion in the appendix, the transcript must be placed in the appendix as an exhibit.

(f) Appeal on the Original Record Without an Appendix. The court may, either by rule for all cases or classes of cases or by order in a particular case, dispense with the appendix and permit an appeal to proceed on the original record with any copies of the record, or relevant parts, that the court may order the parties to file.

(As amended Mar. 30, 1970, eff. July 1, 1970; Mar. 10, 1986, eff. July 1, 1986; Apr. 30, 1991, eff. Dec. 1, 1991; Apr. 29, 1994, eff. Dec. 1, 1994; Apr. 24, 1998, eff. Dec. 1, 1998; Mar. 26, 2009, eff. Dec. 1, 2009.)

RULE 31. SERVING AND FILING BRIEFS

(a) Time to Serve and File a Brief.

(1) The appellant must serve and file a brief within 40 days after the record is filed. The appellee must serve and file a brief within 30 days after the appellant's brief is served. The appellant may serve and file a reply brief within 14 days after service of the appellee's brief but a reply brief must be filed at least 7 days before argument, unless the court, for good cause, allows a later filing.

(2) A court of appeals that routinely considers cases on the merits promptly after the briefs are filed may shorten the time to serve and file briefs, either by local rule or by order in a particular case.

(b) Number of Copies. Twenty-five copies of each brief must be filed with the clerk and 2 copies must be served on each unrepresented party and on counsel for each separately represented party. An unrepresented party proceeding in forma pauperis must file 4 legible copies with the clerk, and one copy must be served on each unrepresented party and on counsel for each separately represented party. The court may

by local rule or by order in a particular case require the filing or service of a different number.

(c) Consequence of Failure to File. If an appellant fails to file a brief within the time provided by this rule, or within an extended time, an appellee may move to dismiss the appeal. An appellee who fails to file a brief will not be heard at oral argument unless the court grants permission.

(As amended Mar. 30, 1970, eff. July 1, 1970; Mar. 10, 1986, eff. July 1, 1986; Apr. 29, 1994, eff. Dec. 1, 1994; Apr. 24, 1998, eff. Dec. 1, 1998; Apr. 29, 2002, eff. Dec. 1, 2002; Mar. 26, 2009, eff. Dec. 1, 2009.)

RULE 32. FORM OF BRIEFS, APPENDICES, AND OTHER PAPERS

(a) Form of a Brief.

(1) Reproduction.

(A) A brief may be reproduced by any process that yields a clear black image on light paper. The paper must be opaque and unglazed. Only one side of the paper may be used.

(B) Text must be reproduced with a clarity that equals or exceeds the output of a laser printer.

(C) Photographs, illustrations, and tables may be reproduced by any method that results in a good copy of the original; a glossy finish is acceptable if the original is glossy.

(2) Cover. Except for filings by unrepresented parties, the cover of the appellant's brief must be blue; the appellee's, red; an intervenor's or amicus curiae's, green; any reply brief, gray; and any supplemental brief, tan. The front cover of a brief must contain:

(A) the number of the case centered at the top;

(B) the name of the court;

(C) the title of the case (see Rule 12(a));

(D) the nature of the proceeding (e.g., Appeal, Petition for Review) and the name of the court, agency, or board below;

(E) the title of the brief, identifying the party or parties for whom the brief is filed; and

(F) the name, office address, and telephone number of counsel representing the party for whom the brief is filed.

(3) Binding. The brief must be bound in any manner that is secure, does not obscure the text, and permits the brief to lie reasonably flat when open.

(4) Paper Size, Line Spacing, and Margins. The brief must be on 8½ by 11 inch paper. The text must be double-spaced, but quotations more than two lines long may be indented and single-spaced. Headings and footnotes may be single-spaced. Margins must be at least one inch on all four sides. Page numbers may be placed in the margins, but no text may appear there.

(5) Typeface. Either a proportionally spaced or a monospaced face may be used.

(A) A proportionally spaced face must include serifs, but sans-serif type may be used in headings and captions. A proportionally spaced face must be 14–point or larger.

(B) A monospaced face may not contain more than 10½ characters per inch.

(6) Type Styles. A brief must be set in a plain, roman style, although italics or boldface may be used for emphasis. Case names must be italicized or underlined.

(7) Length.

(A) Page limitation. A principal brief may not exceed 30 pages, or a reply brief 15 pages, unless it complies with Rule 32(a)(7)(B) and (C).

(B) Type-volume limitation.

(i) A principal brief is acceptable if:

● it contains no more than 14,000 words; or

● it uses a monospaced face and contains no more than 1,300 lines of text.

(ii) A reply brief is acceptable if it contains no more than half of the type volume specified in Rule 32(a)(7)(B)(i).

(iii) Headings, footnotes, and quotations count toward the word and line limitations. The corporate disclosure statement, table of contents, table of citations, statement with respect to oral argument, any addendum containing statutes, rules or regulations, and any certificates of counsel do not count toward the limitation.

(C) Certificate of compliance.

(i) A brief submitted under Rules 28.1(e)(2) or 32(a)(7)(B) must include a certificate by the attorney, or an unrepresented party, that the brief complies with the type-volume limitation. The person preparing the certificate may rely on the word or line count of the word-processing system used to prepare the brief. The certificate must state either:

● the number of words in the brief; or

● the number of lines of monospaced type in the brief.

(ii) Form 6 in the Appendix of Forms is a suggested form of a certificate of compliance. Use of Form 6 must be regarded as sufficient to meet

the requirements of Rules 28.1(e)(3) and 32(a)(7)(C)(i).

(b) Form of an Appendix. An appendix must comply with Rule 32(a)(1), (2), (3), and (4), with the following exceptions:

(1) The cover of a separately bound appendix must be white.

(2) An appendix may include a legible photocopy of any document found in the record or of a printed judicial or agency decision.

(3) When necessary to facilitate inclusion of odd-sized documents such as technical drawings, an appendix may be a size other than 8½ by 11 inches, and need not lie reasonably flat when opened.

(c) Form of Other Papers.

(1) Motion. The form of a motion is governed by Rule 27(d).

(2) Other Papers. Any other paper, including a petition for panel rehearing and a petition for hearing or rehearing en banc, and any response to such a petition, must be reproduced in the manner prescribed by Rule 32(a), with the following exceptions:

(A) A cover is not necessary if the caption and signature page of the paper together contain the information required by Rule 32(a)(2). If a cover is used, it must be white.

(B) Rule 32(a)(7) does not apply.

(d) Signature. Every brief, motion, or other paper filed with the court must be signed by the party filing the paper or, if the party is represented, by one of the party's attorneys.

(e) Local Variation. Every court of appeals must accept documents that comply with the form requirements of this rule. By local rule or order in a particular case a court of appeals may accept documents that do not meet all of the form requirements of this rule.

(As amended Apr. 24, 1998, eff. Dec. 1, 1998; Apr. 29, 2002, eff. Dec. 1, 2002; Apr. 25, 2005, eff. Dec. 1, 2005.)

RULE 32.1   CITING JUDICIAL DISPOSITIONS

(a) Citation Permitted. A court may not prohibit or restrict the citation of federal judicial opinions, orders, judgments, or other written dispositions that have been:

(i) designated as "unpublished," "not for publication," "non-precedential," "not precedent," or the like; and

(ii) issued on or after January 1, 2007.

(b) Copies Required. If a party cites a federal judicial opinion, order, judgment, or other written disposition that is not available in a publicly accessible electronic database, the party must file and serve a copy of that opinion, order, judgment, or disposition with the brief or other paper in which it is cited.

(Added Apr. 12, 2006, eff. Dec. 1, 2006.)

RULE 33. APPEAL CONFERENCES

The court may direct the attorneys—and, when appropriate, the parties—to participate in one or more conferences to address any matter that may aid in disposing of the proceedings, including simplifying the issues and discussing settlement. A judge or other person designated by the court may preside over the conference, which may be conducted in person or by telephone. Before a settlement conference, the attorneys must consult with their clients and obtain as much authority as feasible to settle the case. The court may, as a result of the conference, enter an order controlling the course of the proceedings or implementing any settlement agreement.

(As amended Apr. 29, 1994, eff. Dec. 1, 1994; Apr. 24, 1998, eff. Dec. 1, 1998.)

RULE 34. ORAL ARGUMENT

(a) In General.

(1) Party's Statement. Any party may file, or a court may require by local rule, a statement explaining why oral argument should, or need not, be permitted.

(2) Standards. Oral argument must be allowed in every case unless a panel of three judges who have examined the briefs and record unanimously agrees that oral argument is unnecessary for any of the following reasons:

(A) the appeal is frivolous;

(B) the dispositive issue or issues have been authoritatively decided; or

(C) the facts and legal arguments are adequately presented in the briefs and record, and the decisional process would not be significantly aided by oral argument.

(b) Notice of Argument; Postponement. The clerk must advise all parties whether oral argument will be scheduled, and, if so, the date, time, and place for it, and the time allowed for each side. A motion to postpone the argument or to allow longer argument must be filed reasonably in advance of the hearing date.

(c) Order and Contents of Argument. The appellant opens and concludes the argument. Counsel must not read at length from briefs, records, or authorities.

(d) Cross-Appeals and Separate Appeals. If there is a cross-appeal, Rule 28.1(b) determines which party is the appellant and which is the appellee for purposes of oral argument. Unless the court directs otherwise, a cross-appeal or separate appeal must be argued when the initial appeal is argued. Separate parties should avoid duplicative argument.

(e) Nonappearance of a Party. If the appellee fails to appear for argument, the court must hear appellant's argument. If the appellant fails to appear for argument, the court may hear the appellee's argument. If neither party appears, the case will be decided on the briefs, unless the court orders otherwise.

(f) Submission on Briefs. The parties may agree to submit a case for decision on the briefs, but the court may direct that the case be argued.

(g) Use of Physical Exhibits at Argument; Removal. Counsel intending to use physical exhibits other than documents at the argument must arrange to place them in the courtroom on the day of the argument before the court convenes. After the argument, counsel must remove the exhibits from the courtroom, unless the court directs otherwise. The clerk may destroy or dispose of the exhibits if counsel does not reclaim them within a reasonable time after the clerk gives notice to remove them.

(As amended Apr. 30, 1979, eff. Aug. 1, 1979; Mar. 10, 1986, eff. July 1, 1986; Apr. 30, 1991, eff. Dec. 1, 1991; Apr. 22, 1993, eff. Dec. 1, 1993; Apr. 24, 1998, eff. Dec. 1, 1998; Apr. 25, 2005, eff. Dec. 1, 2005.)

RULE 35. EN BANC DETERMINATION

(a) When Hearing or Rehearing En Banc May Be Ordered. A majority of the circuit judges who are in regular active service and who are not disqualified may order that an appeal or other proceeding be heard or reheard by the court of appeals en banc. An en banc hearing or rehearing is not favored and ordinarily will not be ordered unless:

(1) en banc consideration is necessary to secure or maintain uniformity of the court's decisions; or

(2) the proceeding involves a question of exceptional importance.

(b) Petition for Hearing or Rehearing En Banc. A party may petition for a hearing or rehearing en banc.

(1) The petition must begin with a statement that either:

(A) the panel decision conflicts with a decision of the United States Supreme Court or of the court to which the petition is addressed (with citation to the conflicting case or cases) and consideration by the full court is therefore necessary to secure and maintain uniformity of the court's decisions; or

(B) the proceeding involves one or more questions of exceptional importance, each of which must be concisely stated; for example, a petition may assert that a proceeding presents a question of exceptional importance if it involves an issue on which the panel decision conflicts with the authoritative decisions of other United States Courts of Appeals that have addressed the issue.

(2) Except by the court's permission, a petition for an en banc hearing or rehearing must not exceed 15 pages, excluding material not counted under Rule 32.

(3) For purposes of the page limit in Rule 35(b)(2), if a party files both a petition for panel rehearing and a petition for rehearing en banc, they are considered a single document even if they are filed separately, unless separate filing is required by local rule.

(c) Time for Petition for Hearing or Rehearing En Banc. A petition that an appeal be heard initially en banc must be filed by the date when the appellee's brief is due. A petition for a rehearing en banc must be filed within the time prescribed by Rule 40 for filing a petition for rehearing.

(d) Number of Copies. The number of copies to be filed must be prescribed by local rule and may be altered by order in a particular case.

(e) Response. No response may be filed to a petition for an en banc consideration unless the court orders a response.

(f) Call for a Vote. A vote need not be taken to determine whether the case will be heard or reheard en banc unless a judge calls for a vote.

(As amended Apr. 30, 1979, eff. Aug. 1, 1979; Apr. 29, 1994, eff. Dec. 1, 1994; Apr. 24, 1998, eff. Dec. 1, 1998; Apr. 25, 2005, eff. Dec. 1, 2005.)

RULE 36. ENTRY OF JUDGMENT; NOTICE

(a) Entry. A judgment is entered when it is noted on the docket. The clerk must prepare, sign, and enter the judgment:

(1) after receiving the court's opinion—but if settlement of the judgment's form is required, after final settlement; or

(2) if a judgment is rendered without an opinion, as the court instructs.

(b) Notice. On the date when judgment is entered, the clerk must serve on all parties a copy of the opinion—or the judgment, if no opinion was written—and a notice of the date when the judgment was entered.

(As amended Apr. 24, 1998, eff. Dec. 1, 1998; Apr. 29, 2002, eff. Dec. 1, 2002.)

RULE 37. INTEREST ON JUDGMENT

(a) When the Court Affirms. Unless the law provides otherwise, if a money judgment in a civil case is affirmed, whatever interest is allowed by law is payable from the date when the district court's judgment was entered.

(b) When the Court Reverses. If the court modifies or reverses a judgment with a direction that a money judgment be entered in the district court, the mandate must contain instructions about the allowance of interest.

(As amended Apr. 24, 1998, eff. Dec. 1, 1998.)

RULE 38. FRIVOLOUS APPEAL— DAMAGES AND COSTS

If a court of appeals determines that an appeal is frivolous, it may, after a separately filed motion or notice from the court and reasonable opportunity to respond, award just damages and single or double costs to the appellee.

(As amended Apr. 29, 1994, eff. Dec. 1, 1994; Apr. 24, 1998, eff. Dec. 1, 1998.)

RULE 39. COSTS

(a) Against Whom Assessed. The following rules apply unless the law provides or the court orders otherwise:

(1) if an appeal is dismissed, costs are taxed against the appellant, unless the parties agree otherwise;

(2) if a judgment is affirmed, costs are taxed against the appellant;

(3) if a judgment is reversed, costs are taxed against the appellee;

(4) if a judgment is affirmed in part, reversed in part, modified, or vacated, costs are taxed only as the court orders.

(b) Costs For and Against the United States. Costs for or against the United States, its agency, or officer will be assessed under Rule 39(a) only if authorized by law.

(c) Costs of Copies. Each court of appeals must, by local rule, fix the maximum rate for taxing the cost of producing necessary copies of a brief or appendix, or copies of records authorized by Rule 30(f). The rate must not exceed that generally charged for such work in the area where the clerk's office is located and should encourage economical methods of copying.

(d) Bill of Costs: Objections; Insertion in Mandate.

(1) A party who wants costs taxed must—within 14 days after entry of judgment—file with the cir-

cuit clerk, with proof of service, an itemized and verified bill of costs.

(2) Objections must be filed within 14 days after service of the bill of costs, unless the court extends the time.

(3) The clerk must prepare and certify an itemized statement of costs for insertion in the mandate, but issuance of the mandate must not be delayed for taxing costs. If the mandate issues before costs are finally determined, the district clerk must—upon the circuit clerk's request—add the statement of costs, or any amendment of it, to the mandate.

(e) Costs on Appeal Taxable in the District Court. The following costs on appeal are taxable in the district court for the benefit of the party entitled to costs under this rule:

(1) the preparation and transmission of the record;

(2) the reporter's transcript, if needed to determine the appeal;

(3) premiums paid for a supersedeas bond or other bond to preserve rights pending appeal; and

(4) the fee for filing the notice of appeal.

(As amended Apr. 30, 1979, eff. Aug. 1, 1979; Mar. 10, 1986, eff. July 1, 1986; Apr. 24, 1998, eff. Dec. 1, 1998; Mar. 26, 2009, eff. Dec. 1, 2009.)

RULE 40. PETITION FOR PANEL REHEARING

(a) Time to File; Contents; Answer; Action by the Court if Granted.

(1) Time. Unless the time is shortened or extended by order or local rule, a petition for panel rehearing may be filed within 14 days after entry of judgment. But in a civil case, unless an order shortens or extends the time, the petition may be filed by any party within 45 days after entry of judgment if one of the parties is:

(A) the United States;

(B) a United States agency;

(C) a United States officer or employee sued in an official capacity; or

(D) a current or former United States officer or employee sued in an individual capacity for an act or omission occurring in connection with duties performed on the United States' behalf—including all instances in which the United States represents that person when the court of appeals' judgment is entered or files the petition for that person.

(2) Contents. The petition must state with particularity each point of law or fact that the petitioner believes the court has overlooked or misapprehended and must argue in support of the petition. Oral argument is not permitted.

(3) Answer. Unless the court requests, no answer to a petition for panel rehearing is permitted. But ordinarily rehearing will not be granted in the absence of such a request.

(4) Action by the Court. If a petition for panel rehearing is granted, the court may do any of the following:

(A) make a final disposition of the case without reargument;

(B) restore the case to the calendar for reargument or resubmission; or

(C) issue any other appropriate order.

(b) Form of Petition; Length. The petition must comply in form with Rule 32. Copies must be served and filed as Rule 31 prescribes. Unless the court permits or a local rule provides otherwise, a petition for panel rehearing must not exceed 15 pages.

(As amended Apr. 30, 1979, eff. Aug. 1, 1979; Apr. 29, 1994, eff. Dec. 1, 1994; Apr. 24, 1998, eff. Dec. 1, 1998; Apr. 26, 2011, eff. Dec. 1, 2011.)

RULE 41. MANDATE: CONTENTS; ISSUANCE AND EFFECTIVE DATE; STAY

(a) Contents. Unless the court directs that a formal mandate issue, the mandate consists of a certified copy of the judgment, a copy of the court's opinion, if any, and any direction about costs.

(b) When Issued. The court's mandate must issue 7 days after the time to file a petition for rehearing expires, or 7 days after entry of an order denying a timely petition for panel rehearing, petition for rehearing en banc, or motion for stay of mandate, whichever is later. The court may shorten or extend the time.

(c) Effective Date. The mandate is effective when issued.

(d) Staying the Mandate.

(1) On Petition for Rehearing or Motion. The timely filing of a petition for panel rehearing, petition for rehearing en banc, or motion for stay of mandate, stays the mandate until disposition of the petition or motion, unless the court orders otherwise.

(2) Pending Petition for Certiorari.

(A) A party may move to stay the mandate pending the filing of a petition for a writ of certiorari in the Supreme Court. The motion must be served on all parties and must show that the certiorari petition would present a substantial question and that there is good cause for a stay.

(B) The stay must not exceed 90 days, unless the period is extended for good cause or unless the party who obtained the stay files a petition for the writ and so notifies the circuit clerk in writing within the period of the stay. In that case, the stay continues until the Supreme Court's final disposition.

(C) The court may require a bond or other security as a condition to granting or continuing a stay of the mandate.

(D) The court of appeals must issue the mandate immediately when a copy of a Supreme Court order denying the petition for writ of certiorari is filed.

(As amended Apr. 29, 1994, eff. Dec. 1, 1994; Apr. 24, 1998, eff. Dec. 1, 1998; Apr. 29, 2002, eff. Dec. 1, 2002; Mar. 26, 2009, eff. Dec. 1, 2009.)

RULE 42. VOLUNTARY DISMISSAL

(a) Dismissal in the District Court. Before an appeal has been docketed by the circuit clerk, the district court may dismiss the appeal on the filing of a stipulation signed by all parties or on the appellant's motion with notice to all parties.

(b) Dismissal in the Court of Appeals. The circuit clerk may dismiss a docketed appeal if the parties file a signed dismissal agreement specifying how costs are to be paid and pay any fees that are due. But no mandate or other process may issue without a court order. An appeal may be dismissed on the appellant's motion on terms agreed to by the parties or fixed by the court.

(As amended Apr. 24, 1998, eff. Dec. 1, 1998.)

RULE 43. SUBSTITUTION OF PARTIES

(a) Death of a Party.

(1) After Notice of Appeal Is Filed. If a party dies after a notice of appeal has been filed or while a proceeding is pending in the court of appeals, the decedent's personal representative may be substituted as a party on motion filed with the circuit clerk by the representative or by any party. A party's motion must be served on the representative in accordance with Rule 25. If the decedent has no representative, any party may suggest the death on the record, and the court of appeals may then direct appropriate proceedings.

(2) Before Notice of Appeal Is Filed—Potential Appellant. If a party entitled to appeal dies before filing a notice of appeal, the decedent's personal representative—or, if there is no personal representative, the decedent's attorney of record—may file a notice of appeal within the time prescribed by these rules. After the notice of appeal is filed, substitution must be in accordance with Rule 43(a)(1).

(3) Before Notice of Appeal Is Filed—Potential Appellee. If a party against whom an appeal may be taken dies after entry of a judgment or order in the district court, but before a notice of appeal is filed, an appellant may proceed as if the death had not occurred. After the notice of appeal is filed, substitution must be in accordance with Rule 43(a)(1).

(b) Substitution for a Reason Other Than Death. If a party needs to be substituted for any reason other than death, the procedure prescribed in Rule 43(a) applies.

(c) Public Officer: Identification; Substitution.

(1) Identification of Party. A public officer who is a party to an appeal or other proceeding in an official capacity may be described as a party by the public officer's official title rather than by name. But the court may require the public officer's name to be added.

(2) Automatic Substitution of Officeholder. When a public officer who is a party to an appeal or other proceeding in an official capacity dies, resigns, or otherwise ceases to hold office, the action does not abate. The public officer's successor is automatically substituted as a party. Proceedings following the substitution are to be in the name of the substituted party, but any misnomer that does not affect the substantial rights of the parties may be disregarded. An order of substitution may be entered at any time, but failure to enter an order does not affect the substitution.

(As amended Mar. 10, 1986, eff. July 1, 1986; Apr. 24, 1998, eff. Dec. 1, 1998.)

RULE 44. CASE INVOLVING A CONSTITUTIONAL QUESTION WHEN THE UNITED STATES OR THE RELEVANT STATE IS NOT A PARTY

(a) Constitutional Challenge to Federal Statute. If a party questions the constitutionality of an Act of Congress in a proceeding in which the United States or its agency, officer, or employee is not a party in an official capacity, the questioning party must give written notice to the circuit clerk immediately upon the filing of the record or as soon as the question is raised in the court of appeals. The clerk must then certify that fact to the Attorney General.

(b) Constitutional Challenge to State Statute. If a party questions the constitutionality of a statute of a State in a proceeding in which that State or its agency, officer, or employee is not a party in an official capacity, the questioning party must give written notice to the circuit clerk immediately upon the filing of the record or as soon as the question is raised in the court of appeals. The clerk must then certify that fact to the attorney general of the State.

(As amended Apr. 24, 1998, eff. Dec. 1, 1998; Apr. 29, 2002, eff. Dec. 1, 2002.)

RULE 45. CLERK'S DUTIES

(a) General Provisions.

(1) **Qualifications.** The circuit clerk must take the oath and post any bond required by law. Neither the clerk nor any deputy clerk may practice as an attorney or counselor in any court while in office.

(2) **When Court Is Open**. The court of appeals is always open for filing any paper, issuing and returning process, making a motion, and entering an order. The clerk's office with the clerk or a deputy in attendance must be open during business hours on all days except Saturdays, Sundays, and legal holidays. A court may provide by local rule or by order that the clerk's office be open for specified hours on Saturdays or on legal holidays other than New Year's Day, Martin Luther King, Jr.'s Birthday, Washington's Birthday, Memorial Day, Independence Day, Labor Day, Columbus Day, Veterans' Day, Thanksgiving Day, and Christmas Day.

(b) Records.

(1) **The Docket.** The circuit clerk must maintain a docket and an index of all docketed cases in the manner prescribed by the Director of the Administrative Office of the United States Courts. The clerk must record all papers filed with the clerk and all process, orders, and judgments.

(2) **Calendar.** Under the court's direction, the clerk must prepare a calendar of cases awaiting argument. In placing cases on the calendar for argument, the clerk must give preference to appeals in criminal cases and to other proceedings and appeals entitled to preference by law.

(3) **Other Records.** The clerk must keep other books and records required by the Director of the Administrative Office of the United States Courts, with the approval of the Judicial Conference of the United States, or by the court.

(c) Notice of an Order or Judgment.

Upon the entry of an order or judgment, the circuit clerk must immediately serve a notice of entry on each party, with a copy of any opinion, and must note the date of service on the docket. Service on a party represented by counsel must be made on counsel.

(d) Custody of Records and Papers.

The circuit clerk has custody of the court's records and papers. Unless the court orders or instructs otherwise, the clerk must not permit an original record or paper to be taken from the clerk's office. Upon disposition of the case, original papers constituting the record on appeal or review must be returned to the court or agency from which they were received. The clerk must preserve a copy of any brief, appendix, or other paper that has been filed.

(As amended Mar. 1, 1971, eff. July 1, 1971; Mar. 10, 1986, eff. July 1, 1986; Apr. 24, 1998, eff. Dec. 1, 1998; Apr. 29, 2002, eff. Dec. 1, 2002; Apr. 25, 2005, eff. Dec. 1, 2005.)

RULE 46. ATTORNEYS

(a) Admission to the Bar.

(1) **Eligibility.** An attorney is eligible for admission to the bar of a court of appeals if that attorney is of good moral and professional character and is admitted to practice before the Supreme Court of the United States, the highest court of a state, another United States court of appeals, or a United States district court (including the district courts for Guam, the Northern Mariana Islands, and the Virgin Islands).

(2) **Application.** An applicant must file an application for admission, on a form approved by the court that contains the applicant's personal statement showing eligibility for membership. The applicant must subscribe to the following oath or affirmation:

"I, _____, do solemnly swear [or affirm] that I will conduct myself as an attorney and counselor of this court, uprightly and according to law; and that I will support the Constitution of the United States."

(3) **Admission Procedures.** On written or oral motion of a member of the court's bar, the court will act on the application. An applicant may be admitted by oral motion in open court. But, unless the court orders otherwise, an applicant need not appear before the court to be admitted. Upon admission, an applicant must pay the clerk the fee prescribed by local rule or court order.

(b) Suspension or Disbarment.

(1) **Standard.** A member of the court's bar is subject to suspension or disbarment by the court if the member:

(A) has been suspended or disbarred from practice in any other court; or

(B) is guilty of conduct unbecoming a member of the court's bar.

(2) **Procedure.** The member must be given an opportunity to show good cause, within the time prescribed by the court, why the member should not be suspended or disbarred.

(3) **Order.** The court must enter an appropriate order after the member responds and a hearing is held, if requested, or after the time prescribed for a response expires, if no response is made.

(c) Discipline. A court of appeals may discipline an attorney who practices before it for conduct unbecoming a member of the bar or for failure to comply with any court rule. First, however, the court must afford the attorney reasonable notice, an opportunity to show cause to the contrary, and, if requested, a hearing.

(As amended Mar. 10, 1986, eff. July 1, 1986; Apr. 24, 1998, eff. Dec. 1, 1998.)

RULE 47. LOCAL RULES BY COURTS OF APPEALS

(a) Local Rules.

(1) Each court of appeals acting by a majority of its judges in regular active service may, after giving appropriate public notice and opportunity for comment, make and amend rules governing its practice. A generally applicable direction to parties or lawyers regarding practice before a court must be in a local rule rather than an internal operating procedure or standing order. A local rule must be consistent with—but not duplicative of—Acts of Congress and rules adopted under 28 U.S.C. § 2072 and must conform to any uniform numbering system prescribed by the Judicial Conference of the United States. Each circuit clerk must send the Administrative Office of the United States Courts a copy of each local rule and internal operating procedure when it is promulgated or amended.

(2) A local rule imposing a requirement of form must not be enforced in a manner that causes a party to lose rights because of a nonwillful failure to comply with the requirement.

(b) Procedure When There Is No Controlling Law. A court of appeals may regulate practice in a particular case in any manner consistent with federal law, these rules, and local rules of the circuit. No sanction or other disadvantage may be imposed for noncompliance with any requirement not in federal law, federal rules, or the local circuit rules unless the alleged violator has been furnished in the particular case with actual notice of the requirement.

(As amended Apr. 27, 1995, eff. Dec. 1, 1995; Apr. 24, 1998, eff. Dec. 1, 1998.)

RULE 48. MASTERS

(a) Appointment; Powers. A court of appeals may appoint a special master to hold hearings, if necessary, and to recommend factual findings and disposition in matters ancillary to proceedings in the court. Unless the order referring a matter to a master specifies or limits the master's powers, those powers include, but are not limited to, the following:

(1) regulating all aspects of a hearing;

(2) taking all appropriate action for the efficient performance of the master's duties under the order;

(3) requiring the production of evidence on all matters embraced in the reference; and

(4) administering oaths and examining witnesses and parties.

(b) Compensation. If the master is not a judge or court employee, the court must determine the master's compensation and whether the cost is to be charged to any party.

(As amended Apr. 29, 1994, eff. Dec. 1, 1994; Apr. 24, 1998, eff. Dec. 1, 1998.)

APPENDIX OF FORMS

FORM 1. NOTICE OF APPEAL TO A COURT OF APPEALS FROM A JUDGMENT OR ORDER OF A DISTRICT COURT

United States District Court for the _____
District of _____
File Number _____

A.B., Plaintiff	)
	)
v.	) *Notice of Appeal*
	)
C.D., Defendant	)

Notice is hereby given that [____(here name all parties taking the appeal)____, (plaintiffs) (defendants) in the above named case,[1]] hereby appeal to the United States Court of Appeals for the _____ Circuit (from the final judgment) (from an order (describing it)) entered in this action on the _____ day of _____, 20___.

(s) _____

Attorney for [_____]
[Address:_____]

(As amended Apr. 22, 1993, eff. Dec. 1, 1993; Mar. 27, 2003, eff. Dec. 1, 2003.)

[1] See Rule 3(c) for permissible ways of identifying appellants.

FORM 2. NOTICE OF APPEAL TO A COURT OF APPEALS FROM A DECISION OF THE UNITED STATES TAX COURT

UNITED STATES TAX COURT

Washington, D.C.

A.B., Petitioner	)	
	)	
v.	)	Docket No. _____
	)	
Commissioner of Internal	)	
Revenue, Respondent	)	

Notice of Appeal

Notice is hereby given that [____ here name all parties taking the appeal [1]   ], hereby appeals to the United States Court of Appeals for the _____ Circuit from (that part of) the decision of this court entered in the above captioned proceeding on the _____ day of _____, 20___ (relating to _____).

(s)   _____

Counsel for [_____]

[Address:_____]

(As amended Apr. 22, 1993, eff. Dec. 1, 1993; Mar. 27, 2003, eff. Dec. 1, 2003.)

[1] See Rule 3(c) for permissible ways of identifying appellants.

FORM 3.   PETITION FOR REVIEW OF ORDER OF AN AGENCY, BOARD, COMMISSION OR OFFICER

United States Court of Appeals for the _____ Circuit

A.B., Petitioner)
)
v.   )   Petition for Review
XYZ Commission, Respondent   )

[____ (here name all parties bringing the petition[1])____] hereby petitions the court for review of the Order of the XYZ Commission (describe the order) entered on _____, 20___.

[(s)] _____
Attorney for Petitioners
Address:_____

(As amended Apr. 22, 1993, eff. Dec. 1, 1993; Mar. 27, 2003, eff. Dec. 1, 2003.)

[1] See Rule 15.

FORM 4. AFFIDAVIT ACCOMPANYING MOTION FOR PERMISSION TO APPEAL IN FORMA PAUPERIS

UNITED STATES DISTRICT COURT
for the
<_____> DISTRICT OF <_____>

<Name(s) of plaintiff(s)>,
 	
        Plaintiff(s)
 	
v.
 	
<Name(s) of defendant(s)>,
 	
        Defendant(s)
	)
	)
	)
	)
	)
	) Case No. <Number>
	)
	)
	)
	)

Affidavit in Support of Motion

I swear or affirm under penalty of perjury that, because of my poverty, I cannot prepay the docket fees of my appeal or post a bond for them. I believe I am entitled to redress. I swear or affirm under penalty of perjury under United States laws that my answers on this form are true and correct. (28 U.S.C. § 1746; 18 U.S.C. § 1621.)

Signed: _____

Instructions

Complete all questions in this application and then sign it. Do not leave any blanks: if the answer to a question is "0," "none," or "not applicable (N/A)," write in that response. If you need more space to answer a question or to explain your answer, attach a separate sheet of paper identified with your name, your case's docket number, and the question number.

Date: _____

My issues on appeal are:

1. *For both you and your spouse estimate the average amount of money received from each of the following sources during the past 12 months. Adjust any amount that was received weekly, biweekly, quarterly, semiannually, or annually to show the monthly rate. Use gross amounts, that is, amounts before any deductions for taxes or otherwise.*

Income source	Average monthly amount during the past 12 months		Amount expected next month	
	You	Spouse	You	Spouse
Employment	$_____	$_____	$_____	$_____
Self-employment	$_____	$_____	$_____	$_____
Income from real property (such as rental income)	$_____	$_____	$_____	$_____
Interest and dividends	$_____	$_____	$_____	$_____
Gifts	$_____	$_____	$_____	$_____
Alimony	$_____	$_____	$_____	$_____
Child support	$_____	$_____	$_____	$_____
Retirement (such as social security, pensions, annuities, insurance)	$_____	$_____	$_____	$_____
Disability (such as social security, insurance payments)	$_____	$_____	$_____	$_____
Unemployment payments	$_____	$_____	$_____	$_____

Public-assistance (such as
   welfare) $_____ $_____ $_____ $_____
Other (specify): _____ $_____ $_____ $_____ $_____
          **Total monthly
            income:** $_____ $_____ $_____ $_____

2. *List your employment history for the past two years, most recent employer first. (Gross monthly pay is before taxes or other deductions.)*

Employer	Address	Dates of employment	Gross monthly pay
_____	_____	_____	_____
_____	_____	_____	_____
_____	_____	_____	_____

3. *List your spouse's employment history for the past two years, most recent employer first. (Gross monthly pay is before taxes or other deductions.)*

Employer	Address	Dates of employment	Gross monthly pay
_____	_____	_____	_____
_____	_____	_____	_____
_____	_____	_____	_____

4. *How much cash do you and your spouse have? $_____*
Below, state any money you or your spouse have in bank accounts or in any other financial institution.

Financial institution	Type of account	Amount you have	Amount your spouse has
_____	_____	$_____	$_____
_____	_____	$_____	$_____
_____	_____	$_____	$_____

If you are a prisoner seeking to appeal a judgment in a civil action or proceeding, you must attach a statement certified by the appropriate institutional officer showing all receipts, expenditures, and balances during the last six months in your institutional accounts. If you have multiple accounts, perhaps because you have been in multiple institutions, attach one certified statement of each account.

5. *List the assets, and their values, which you own or your spouse owns. Do not list clothing and ordinary household furnishings.*

Home (Value)	**Other real estate** (Value)	**Motor vehicle #1** (Value)
_____	_____	Make & year: _____
_____	_____	Model: _____
		Registration #: _____

Motor vehicle #2 (Value)	**Other assets** (Value)	**Other assets** (Value)
Make & year: _____	_____	_____
Model: _____	_____	_____
Registration #: _____	_____	_____

6. *State every person, business, or organization owing you or your spouse money, and the amount owed.*

Person owing you or your spouse money	Amount owed to you	Amount owed to your spouse
_____	_____	_____
_____	_____	_____
_____	_____	_____

7. *State the persons who rely on you or your spouse for support.*

Name [or, if under 18, initials only]	Relationship	Age
_____	_____	_____
_____	_____	_____
_____	_____	_____

8. *Estimate the average monthly expenses of you and your family. Show separately the amounts paid by your spouse. Adjust any payments that are made weekly, biweekly, quarterly, semiannually, or annually to show the monthly rate.*

	You	**Your Spouse**
Rent or home-mortgage payment (include lot rented for mobile home)	$_____	$_____
Are real-estate taxes included? ☐ Yes ☐ No		
Is property insurance included? ☐ Yes ☐ No		
Utilities (electricity, heating fuel, water, sewer, and Telephone)	$_____	$_____
Home maintenance (repairs and upkeep)	$_____	$_____
Food	$_____	$_____
Clothing	$_____	$_____
Laundry and dry-cleaning	$_____	$_____
Medical and dental expenses	$_____	$_____
Transportation (not including motor vehicle payments)	$_____	$_____
Recreation, entertainment, newspapers, magazines, etc.	$_____	$_____
Insurance (not deducted from wages or included in mortgage payments)		
Homeowner's or renter's:	$_____	$_____
Life:	$_____	$_____
Health:	$_____	$_____
Motor Vehicle:	$_____	$_____
Other: _____	$_____	$_____
Taxes (not deducted from wages or included in mortgage payments) (specify): __	$_____	$_____
Installment payments		
Motor Vehicle:	$_____	$_____
Credit card (name): _____	$_____	$_____
Department store (name): _____	$_____	$_____
Other: _____	$_____	$_____
Alimony, maintenance, and support paid to others	$_____	$_____
Regular expenses for operation of business, profession, or farm (attach detailed statement)	$_____	$_____
Other (specify): _____	$_____	$_____
Total monthly expenses:	$_____	$_____

9. *Do you expect any major changes to your monthly income or expenses or in your assets or liabilities during the next 12 months?*
☐ Yes ☐ No   If yes, describe on an attached sheet.

10. *Have you spent—or will you be spending—any money for expenses or attorney fees in connection with this lawsuit?* ☐ Yes ☐ No
If yes, how much? $_____

11. *Provide any other information that will help explain why you cannot pay the docket fees for your appeal.*

12. *State the city and state of your legal residence.*

Your daytime phone number: (___) _____
Your age: _____ *Your years of schooling:* _____
Last four digits of your social-security number: _____

(As amended Apr. 24, 1998, eff. Dec. 1, 1998; Apr. 28, 2010, eff. Dec. 1, 2010; Apr. 16, 2013, eff. Dec. 1, 2013.)

FORM 5. NOTICE OF APPEAL TO A COURT OF APPEALS FROM A JUDGMENT OR ORDER OF A DISTRICT COURT OR A BANKRUPTCY APPELLATE PANEL

United States District Court for the ....
District of ....

In re   )

....................................,   )
          Debtor   )   File No..........

....................................,   )
         Plaintiff   )

          v.   )

....................................,   )
        Defendant   )

Notice of Appeal to
United States Court of Appeals
for the .... Circuit

......................·...., the plaintiff [or defendant or other party] appeals to the United States Court of Appeals for the .... Circuit from the final judgment [or order or decree] of the district court for the district of ....
[or bankruptcy appellate panel of the .... circuit], entered in this case on ...., 20.... [here describe the judgment, order, or decree] ....

     The parties to the judgment [or order or decree] appealed from and the names and addresses of their respective attorneys are as follows:

Dated ....

Signed ....

                       Attorney for Appellant

Address: ....
....

(Added Apr. 25, 1989, eff. Dec. 1, 1989; Mar. 27, 2003, eff. Dec. 1, 2003.)

FORM 6. CERTIFICATE OF COMPLIANCE WITH RULE 32(A)

Certificate of Compliance With Type-Volume Limitation, Typeface
Requirements, and Type Style Requirements

1. This brief complies with the type-volume limitation of Fed. R. App. P.
32(a)(7)(B) because:

☐ this brief contains [*state the number of*] words, excluding the parts of the brief
exempted by Fed. R. App. P. 32(a)(7)(B)(iii), *or*

☐ this brief uses a monospaced typeface and contains [*state the number of*] lines
of text, excluding the parts of the brief exempted by Fed. R. App. P.
32(a)(7)(B)(iii).

2. This brief complies with the typeface requirements of Fed. R. App. P. 32(a)(5)
and the type style requirements of Fed. R. App. P. 32(a)(6) because:

☐ this brief has been prepared in a proportionally spaced typeface using [*state
name and version of word processing program*] in [*state font size and name of
type style*], *or*

☐ this brief has been prepared in a monospaced typeface using [*state name and
version of word processing program*] with [*state number of characters per inch
and name of type style*].

(s)_____

Attorney for _____

Dated: _____

(Added Apr. 29, 2002, eff. Dec. 1, 2002.)

INDEX TO
FEDERAL RULES OF APPELLATE PROCEDURE

UNITED STATES COURT OF APPEALS
FOR THE
SEVENTH CIRCUIT

Including Amendments Received Through
November 1, 2015

TITLE I.   APPLICABILITY OF RULES

FRAP 1.   SCOPE OF RULES; TITLE

[For text of rule, see the Federal Rules of Appellate Procedure]

RULE 1.   SCOPE OF RULES

These rules govern procedure in the United States Court of Appeals for the Seventh Circuit. They are to be known as the Circuit Rules of the United States Court of Appeals for the Seventh Circuit.
[Amended effective December 1, 1997.]

FRAP 2.   SUSPENSION OF RULES

[For text of rule, see the Federal Rules of Appellate Procedure]

RULE 2.   SUSPENSION OF CIRCUIT RULES

In the interest of expediting decision or for other good cause, the court may suspend the requirements of these Circuit Rules.

TITLE II.   APPEAL FROM A JUDGMENT OR ORDER OF A DISTRICT COURT

FRAP 3.   APPEAL AS OF RIGHT— HOW TAKEN

[For text of rule, see the Federal Rules of Appellate Procedure]

RULE 3.   NOTICE OF APPEAL, DOCKETING FEE, DOCKETING STATEMENT, AND DESIGNATION OF COUNSEL OF RECORD

(a) Forwarding Copy of Notice of Appeal. When the clerk of the district court transmits to the clerk of this court a copy of the notice of appeal, the district court clerk shall include any docketing statement. In civil cases the clerk of the district court shall include the judgments or orders under review, any tran-scribed oral statement of reasons, opinion, memorandum of decision, findings of fact, and conclusions of law.

(b) Dismissal of Appeal for Failure to Pay Docketing Fee. If a proceeding is docketed without prepayment of the docketing fee, the appellant shall pay the fee within 14 days after docketing. If the appellant fails to do so, the clerk is authorized to dismiss the appeal.

(c)(1) *Docketing Statement.* The appellant must serve on all parties a docketing statement and file it with the clerk of the district court at the time of the filing of the notice of appeal or with the clerk of this court within seven days of filing the notice of appeal. The docketing statement must comply with the requirements of Circuit Rule 28(a). If there have been prior or related appellate proceedings in the case, or if the party believes that the earlier appellate proceedings are sufficiently related to the new appeal, the statement must identify these proceedings by caption and number. The statement also must describe any prior litigation in the district court that, although not appealed, (a) arises out of the same criminal conviction, or (b) has been designated by the district court as satisfying the criteria of 28 U.S.C. § 1915(g). If any of the parties to the litigation appears in an official capacity, the statement must identify the current occupant of the office. The docketing statement in a collateral attack on a criminal conviction must identify the prisoner's current place of confinement and its current warden; if the prisoner has been released, the statement must describe the nature of any ongoing custody (such as supervised release) and identify the custodian. If the docketing statement is not complete and correct, the appellee must provide a complete one to the court of appeals clerk within 14 days after the date of the filing of the appellant's docketing statement.

(2) Failure to file the docketing statement within 14 days of the filing of the notice of appeal will lead to the imposition of a $100 fine on counsel. Failure to file the statement within 28 days of the filing of the notice of appeal will be treated as abandonment of the appeal, and the appeal will be dismissed. When the appeal is docketed, the court will remind the litigants of these provisions.

(d) **Counsel of Record.** The attorney whose name appears on the docketing statement or other document first filed by that party in this court will be deemed counsel of record, and a separate notice of appearance need not be filed. If the name of more than one attorney is shown, the attorney who is counsel of record must be clearly identified. (There can be only one counsel of record.) If no attorney is so identified, the court will treat the first listed as counsel of record. The court will send documents only to the counsel of record for each party, who is responsible for transmitting them to other lawyers for the same party. The docketing statement or other document must provide the post office address, email address and telephone number of counsel of record. The names of other members of the Bar of this Court and, if desired, their post office and email addresses, may be added but counsel of record must be clearly identified. An attorney representing a party who will not be filing a document shall enter a separate notice of appearance as counsel of record indicating the name of the party represented. Counsel of record may not withdraw, without consent of the court, unless another counsel of record is simultaneously substituted.

[Amended effective February 1, 1992; June 1, 1995; January 1, 1997; December 1, 1997; December 1, 1998; December 1, 2014.]

FRAP 3.1 APPEAL FROM A JUDGMENT OF A MAGISTRATE JUDGE IN A CIVIL CASE [ABROGATED]

[For text of rule, see the Federal Rules of Appellate Procedure]

FRAP 4. APPEAL AS OF RIGHT— WHEN TAKEN

[For text of rule, see the Federal Rules of Appellate Procedure]

FRAP 5. APPEAL BY PERMISSION

[For text of rule, see the Federal Rules of Appellate Procedure]

FRAP 6. APPEAL IN A BANKRUPTCY CASE FROM A FINAL JUDGMENT, ORDER, OR DECREE OF A DISTRICT COURT OR BANKRUPTCY APPELLATE PANEL

[For text of rule, see the Federal Rules of Appellate Procedure]

FRAP 7. BOND FOR COSTS ON APPEAL IN A CIVIL CASE

[For text of rule, see the Federal Rules of Appellate Procedure]

FRAP 8. STAY OR INJUNCTION PENDING APPEAL

[For text of rule, see the Federal Rules of Appellate Procedure]

RULE 8. MOTIONS FOR STAYS AND INJUNCTIONS PENDING APPEAL

Counsel's obligation under Fed. R. App. P. 8(a) to provide this court with the reasons the district judge gave for denying relief includes an obligation to supply any statement of reasons by a magistrate judge or bankruptcy judge. Filing with the motion a copy of the order or memorandum of decision in which the reasons were stated, or if they were stated orally in open court, a copy of the transcript of proceedings is preferred; but, in an emergency, if such a copy is not available, counsel's statement of the reasons given by the district or bankruptcy court will suffice.

[Amended effective December 1, 1997.]

FRAP 9. RELEASE IN A CRIMINAL CASE

[For text of rule, see the Federal Rules of Appellate Procedure]

RULE 9. MOTIONS CONCERNING CUSTODY PENDING TRIAL OR APPEAL

(a) All requests for release from custody pending trial shall be by motion. The defendant shall file a notice of appeal followed by a motion.

(b) All requests to reverse orders granting bail or enlargement pending trial or appeal shall be by motion. The government shall file a notice of appeal followed by a motion.

(c) All requests for release from custody after sentencing and pending the disposition of the appeal shall be by motion in the main case. There is no need for a separate notice of appeal.

(d) Any motion filed under this rule shall be accompanied by a memorandum of law.

[Amended effective February 1, 1992.]

FRAP 10. THE RECORD ON APPEAL

[For text of rule, see the Federal Rules of Appellate Procedure]

RULE 10. PREPARATION OF RECORD IN DISTRICT COURT APPEALS

(a) Record Preparation Duties. The clerk of the district court shall prepare within 14 days of filing the notice of appeal the original papers, transcripts filed in the district court, and exhibits received or offered in evidence (with the exceptions listed below). The transcript of a deposition is "filed" within the meaning of this rule, and an exhibit is "received or offered," to the extent that it is tendered to the district court in support of a brief or motion, whether or not the rules of the district court treat deposition transcripts or exhibits as part of the record. These materials may be designated as part of the record on appeal without the need for a motion under Fed. R. App. P. 10(e). Counsel must ensure that exhibits and transcripts to be included in the record which are not in the possession of the district court clerk are furnished to the clerk within fourteen days after the filing of the notice of appeal. The following items will not be included in a record unless specifically requested by a party by item and date of filing within fourteen days after the

notice of appeal is filed or unless specifically ordered by this court:

> briefs and memoranda,
>
> notices of filings,
>
> subpoenas,
>
> summonses,
>
> motions to extend time,
>
> affidavits and admissions of service and mailing,
>
> notices of settings,
>
> depositions and notices, and
>
> jury lists.

(b) Correction or Modification of Record. A motion to correct or modify the record pursuant to Rule 10(e), Fed. R. App. P., or a motion to strike matter from the record on the ground that it is not properly a part thereof shall be presented first to the district court. That court's order ruling on the motion will be transmitted to this court as part of the record.

(c) Order or Certification with Regard to Transcript. Counsel and court reporters are to utilize the form prescribed by this court when ordering transcripts or certifying that none will be ordered. For specific requirements, see Rules 10(b) and 11(b), Fed. R. App. P.

(d) Ordering Transcripts in Criminal Cases.

(1) *Transcripts in Criminal Justice Act Cases.* At the time of the return of a verdict of guilty or, in the case of a bench trial, an adjudication of guilt in a criminal case in which the defendant is represented by counsel appointed under the Criminal Justice Act (C.J.A.), counsel for the defendant shall request a transcript of testimony and other relevant proceedings by completing a C.J.A. Form No. 24 and giving it to the district judge. If the district judge believes an appeal is probable, the judge shall order transcribed so much of the proceedings as the judge believes necessary for an appeal. The transcript shall be filed with the clerk of the district court within 40 days after the return of a verdict of guilty or, in the case of a bench trial, the adjudication of guilt or within seven days after sentencing, whichever occurs later. If the district judge decides not to order the transcript at that time, the judge shall retain the C.J.A. Form No. 24 without ruling. If a notice of appeal is filed later, appointed counsel or counsel for a defendant allowed after trial to proceed on appeal in forma pauperis shall immediately notify the district judge of the filing of a notice of appeal and file or renew the request made on C.J.A. Form No. 24 for a free transcript.

(2) *Transcripts in Other Criminal Cases.* Within 14 days after filing the notice of appeal in other criminal cases, the appellant or appellant's counsel shall deposit with the court reporter the estimated cost of the transcript ordered pursuant to Rule 10(b), Fed. R. App. P., unless the district court orders that the transcript be paid for by the United States. A non-indigent appellant must pay a pro rata share of the cost of a transcript prepared at the request of an indigent co-defendant under the Criminal Justice Act unless the district court determines that fairness requires a different division of the cost. Failure to comply with this paragraph will be cause for dismissal of the appeal.

(e) Indexing of Transcript. The transcript of proceedings to be transmitted to this court as part of the record on appeal (and any copies prepared for the use of the court or counsel in the case on appeal) shall be produced by the reporter in a volume or volumes, with the pages consecutively numbered throughout all volumes. The transcript of proceedings, or the first volume thereof, shall contain a suitable index, which shall refer to the number of the volume as well as the page, shall be cumulative for all volumes, and shall include the following information:

(1) An alphabetical list of witnesses, giving the pages on which the direct and each other examination of each witness begins.

(2) A list of exhibits by number, with a brief description of each exhibit indicating the nature of its contents, and with a reference to the pages of the transcript where each exhibit has been identified, offered, and received or rejected.

(3) A list of other significant portions of the trial such as opening statements, arguments to the jury, and instructions, with a reference to the page where each begins.

When the record includes transcripts of more than one trial or other distinct proceeding, and it would be cumbersome to apply this paragraph to all the transcripts taken together as one, the rule may be applied separately to each transcript of one trial or other distinct proceeding.

(f) Presentence Reports. The presentence report is part of the record on appeal in every criminal case. The district court should transmit this report under seal, unless it has already been placed in the public record in the district court. If the report is transmitted under seal, the report may not be included in the appendix to the brief or the separate appendix under Fed. R. App. P. 30 and Circuit Rule 30. Counsel of record may review the presentence report at the clerk's office but may not review the probation offi-

cer's written comments and any other portion submitted in camera to the trial judge.

(g) Effect of Omissions from the Record on Appeal. When a party's argument is countered by a contention of waiver for failure to raise the point in the trial court or before an agency, the party opposing the waiver contention must give the record cite where the point was asserted and also ensure that the record before the court of appeals contains the relevant document or transcript.

[Amended effective February 1, 1992; June 1, 1995; January 1, 1996; December 1, 2009; December 1, 2014.]

FRAP 11.   FORWARDING THE RECORD

[For text of rule, see the Federal Rules of Appellate Procedure]

RULE 11.   RECORD ON APPEAL

(a) Record Transmission. When the appeal is ready for scheduling for oral argument or submission, the clerk of the court of appeals will notify the district court clerk to transmit the record to the court of appeals. The parties may agree or the court of appeals may order that the record be sent to the clerk of the court of appeals at an earlier time. But in no event shall the clerk of the district court transmit bulky items, currency, securities, liquids, drugs, weapons, or similar items without a specific order of this court.

(b) Transcript and Other Supplemental Transmissions. When trial or hearing transcripts, or other parts of the record, are filed with the clerk of the district court (or exhibits that have been retained in the district court for use in preparation of the transcript are returned to the clerk) after initial transmission of the record, they shall be immediately transmitted to this court and filed as a supplemental record without the requirement of this court's order. This immediate transmission meets the requirements of Rule 11(b), Fed. R. App. P., that the court reporter notify the clerk of the court of appeals that the transcript has been filed with the clerk of the district court.

(c) Extension of Time.

(1) *Requests for Extension to be Addressed to Court of Appeals.* All requests for extension of time for filing the record or parts thereof shall be addressed to the court of appeals.

(2) *Extension of Time for Preparation of Transcript.* Any request by a court reporter for an exten-

sion of time longer than 30 days from the date the transcript was first ordered must be filed with the clerk of this court on a form prescribed by the court. The request must include the date the transcript was ordered, the reasons for both that request, and any previous requests for extensions of time, and a certificate that all parties or their counsel have been sent a copy of the request. If the request is for an extension of time longer than 60 days from the date the transcript was first ordered, it must include a statement from the district judge who tried the case or the chief judge of the district court that the request has been brought to that judge's attention and that steps are being taken to insure that all ordered transcripts will be promptly prepared.

(d) Withdrawal of Record. During the time allowed for the preparation and filing of a brief, an attorney for a party or a party acting pro se may withdraw any record not in electronic format upon giving a receipt to the clerk who has physical custody of the record. Once a panel of judges is assigned, a non-electronic record may not be withdrawn without an order of the court. Original exhibits may not be withdrawn but may be examined only in the clerk's office. The party who has withdrawn a non-electronic record may not file a brief or petition for rehearing until the record has been returned to the clerk's office from which it was withdrawn. Except as provided above, non-electronic records shall not be taken from a clerk's office without leave of this court on written motion. Failure of a party to return non-electronic records to the clerk may be treated as contempt of this court. When the party withdrawing the record is incarcerated, the clerk who has physical custody of the record, on order of this court, will send the record to the warden of the institution with the request that the record be made available to the party under super-

vised conditions and be returned to the respective clerk before a specified date.

[Amended effective February 1, 1992; December 1, 2014.]

FRAP 12. DOCKETING THE APPEAL; FILING A REPRESENTATION STATEMENT; FILING THE RECORD

[For text of rule, see the Federal Rules of Appellate Procedure]

RULE 12. DOCKETING THE APPEAL

(a) Docketing. The clerk will notify counsel and parties acting pro se of the date the appeal is docketed.

(b) Caption. The parties on appeal shall be designated in the title of the cause in court as they appeared in the district court, with the addition of identification of appellant and appellee, for example, John Smith, Plaintiff–Appellee v. William Jones, Defendant–Appellant. Actions seeking habeas corpus shall be designated "Petitioner v. Custodian" and not "United States ex rel. Petitioner v. Custodian".

[Amended effective January 1, 1990; February 1, 1992; December 1, 1997.]

FRAP 12.1 REMAND AFTER AN INDICATIVE RULING BY THE DISTRICT COURT ON A MOTION FOR RELIEF THAT IS BARRED BY A PENDING APPEAL

[For text of rule, see the Federal Rules of Appellate Procedure]

TITLE III. APPEALS FROM THE UNITED STATES TAX COURT

FRAP 13. APPEALS FROM THE TAX COURT

[For text of rule, see the Federal Rules of Appellate Procedure]

FRAP 14. APPLICABILITY OF OTHER RULES TO APPEALS FROM THE TAX COURT

[For text of rule, see the Federal Rules of Appellate Procedure]

TITLE IV.   REVIEW OR ENFORCEMENT OF AN ORDER OF AN ADMINISTRATIVE AGENCY, BOARD, COMMISSION, OR OFFICER

FRAP 15.   REVIEW OR ENFORCEMENT OF AN AGENCY ORDER—HOW OBTAINED; INTERVENTION

[For text of rule, see the Federal Rules of Appellate Procedure]

FRAP 15.1   BRIEFS AND ORAL ARGUMENT IN A NATIONAL LABOR RELATIONS BOARD PROCEEDING

[For text of rule, see the Federal Rules of Appellate Procedure]

FRAP 16.   THE RECORD ON REVIEW OR ENFORCEMENT

[For text of rule, see the Federal Rules of Appellate Procedure]

FRAP 17.   FILING THE RECORD

[For text of rule, see the Federal Rules of Appellate Procedure]

FRAP 18.   STAY PENDING REVIEW

[For text of rule, see the Federal Rules of Appellate Procedure]

FRAP 19.   SETTLEMENT OF A JUDGMENT ENFORCING AN AGENCY ORDER IN PART

[For text of rule, see the Federal Rules of Appellate Procedure]

FRAP 20.   APPLICABILITY OF RULES TO THE REVIEW OR ENFORCEMENT OF AN AGENCY ORDER

[For text of rule, see the Federal Rules of Appellate Procedure]

TITLE V.   EXTRAORDINARY WRITS

FRAP 21. WRITS OF MANDAMUS AND PROHIBITION, AND OTHER EXTRAORDINARY WRITS

[For text of rule, see the Federal Rules of Appellate Procedure]

TITLE VI.   HABEAS CORPUS; PROCEEDINGS IN FORMA PAUPERIS

FRAP 22.   HABEAS CORPUS AND SECTION 2255 PROCEEDINGS

[For text of rule, see the Federal Rules of Appellate Procedure]

RULE 22.   DEATH PENALTY CASES

(a) Operation and Scope.

(1) This rule applies to all cases involving persons under sentence of capital punishment.

(2) Cases within the scope of this rule will be assigned to a panel as soon as the appeal is docketed. The panel to which a case is assigned will handle all substantial matters pertaining to the case, including certificates of appealability, stays of execution, consideration of the merits, second or successive petitions, remands from the Supreme Court of the United States, and associated procedural matters. If a judge on the panel is unavailable to participate, another judge may be substituted.

(3) Pursuant to 18 U.S.C. § 3006A, and 18 U.S.C. § 3599, 28 U.S.C. § 2254(h), and 28 U.S.C. § 2255(g), appellate counsel shall be appointed for any person under a sentence of death who is financially unable to obtain representation, requests that counsel be appointed, and does not already have counsel appointed by a state under 28 U.S.C. § 2261.

(4) The panel to which a case is assigned may make changes in procedure and scheduling in any case when justice so requires.

(b) Notice of Appeal and Required Documents.

(1) The district court clerk must notify the clerk of this court by telephone immediately upon the filing of a notice of appeal of a case within the scope of this rule. In all cases within the scope of this rule, the district court clerk must immediately transmit the record to the court of appeals. A supplemental record may be sent later if items are not currently available.

(2) Upon receipt of the record from the district court clerk, or any petition, application or motion invoking the jurisdiction of this court, the clerk of this court shall docket the appeal. The panel will be immediately notified.

(3) Upon filing a notice of appeal, the appellant shall immediately transmit to the court a copy of, or a citation to, each state or federal court opinion, memorandum decision, order, transcript of oral statement of reasons, or judgment involving an issue to be presented on appeal to this court. If a document or transcript is needed and is not immediately available, appellant shall submit an affidavit as to the decision and reasons given by the court. Appellant shall file the document or transcript as soon as it is available.

(c) Briefs.

(1) Unless the court sets another schedule, the following time limitations apply.

(A) On direct appeal in a federal criminal prosecution, the appellant shall serve and file a brief within 63 days after the date on which the appeal is docketed. The appellee shall serve and file a brief within 49 days after service of the brief by the appellant. The appellant may serve and file a reply brief within 21 days after service of the brief by the appellee.

(B) In all other cases within the scope of this rule the appellant will have 28 days from the date on which the notice of appeal is filed to file and serve a brief. The appellee then will have 21 days from the service of the brief to file and serve a brief. Within seven days after service of the appellee's brief, appellant may file and serve a reply brief.

(2) If an issue is raised that was not presented at a prior stage of the litigation (for example, in the district court, the appropriate state court, or this court on a prior appeal), the party raising the issue must state why the issue was not raised and why relief should nonetheless be granted.

(d) Submission and Oral Argument.

(1) The court will hear oral argument in every direct appeal in a federal criminal prosecution and in every appeal from the decision concerning an initial petition under 28 U.S.C. § 2254 in a state case. In

any other case, a request for oral argument will be evaluated under the standards of Fed. R. App. P. 34(a).

(2) Oral argument will be held expeditiously after the filing of the reply brief.

(3) The merits of an appeal may be decided summarily if the panel decides that an appeal is frivolous. In such a case, the panel may issue a single opinion deciding both the merits of the appeal and the motion for a stay of execution.

(e) Opinion or Order.

(1) The panel's decision shall be made without undue delay. In cases to which 28 U.S.C. § 2266 applies, the panel's decision will be issued no later than 120 days after the date the reply brief was filed.

(2) In cases in which an execution date has been set and not stayed, the panel will release the decision with dispatch to allow the losing party time to ask for rehearing or consideration by the Supreme Court.

(f) Panel or En Banc Rehearing.

(1) Any active judge of the court may, within 14 days after filing of the opinion, notify the panel and the clerk to hold issuance of the mandate and poll the court for en banc consideration. If the mandate has already issued, it may be recalled by the panel or by the en banc court. All judges are to vote within 14 days after the request for the vote on en banc consideration. A judge unable by reason of illness or absence to act within the time allowed by this rule may extend the time to act for a reasonable period upon written notice to the other judges. Unless within 30 days after the petition for rehearing, or the answer to the petition (if one has been requested), is filed, a majority of the panel, or of the judges in active service, has voted to grant rehearing or rehearing en banc, the court will enter an order denying the petition.

(2) If the court decides to rehear an appeal en banc, the appeal will be scheduled for oral argument expeditiously and decided within the time allowed by 28 U.S.C. § 2266(c).

(g) Second or Successive Petitions or Appeals. A second or successive petition or appeal will be assigned to the panel that handled the first appeal, motion for stay of execution, application for certificate of appealability or other prayer for relief. A motion for leave to commence a second or successive case is governed by Circuit Rule 22.2 and likewise will be assigned to the original panel.

(h) Stay of Execution.

(1) A stay of execution is granted automatically (A) on direct appeal in a federal criminal prosecution by Fed. R. Crim. P. 38(a), and (B) in some state cases by 28 U.S.C. § 2262(a). A stay of execution is forbidden in some state cases by 28 U.S.C. § 2262(b) and (c). All requests with respect to stays of execution over which the court possesses discretion, or in which any party contends that § 2262 or Rule 38(a) has not been followed, must be made by motion under this rule.

(2) An appellant may not file a motion to stay execution or to vacate a stay of execution unless there is an appeal accompanied by a certificate of appealability or a request that this court issue a certificate of appealability together with a copy of the district judge's statement as to why the certificate should not issue. The request for a certificate of appealability and the motion to stay execution shall be decided together.

(3) The movant shall file the motion and shall immediately notify opposing counsel by telephone. If the following documents have not yet been filed with this court as part of the record, a copy of each shall be filed with each copy of the motion:

(i) certificate of appealability;

(ii) the complaint, petition or motion seeking relief in the district court and the response thereto;

(iii) the district court decision on the merits;

(iv) the motion in the district court to stay execution or vacate stay of execution and the response thereto; and

(v) the district court decision on the motion to stay execution or vacate stay of execution.

If any required document cannot be filed, the movant shall state the reason for the omission.

(4) If an issue is raised that was not presented at a prior stage of the litigation (for example, in the district court, the appropriate state court, or this court on a prior appeal), the party raising the issue must state why the issue was not raised and why relief should nonetheless be granted.

(5) If the attorney for the government has no objection to the motion for stay, the court shall enter an order staying the execution.

(6) Parties shall endeavor to file motions with the clerk during normal business hours. Parties having emergency motions during nonbusiness hours shall call the clerk's telephone number for recorded instructions. The clerk shall promptly notify, by telephone, the designated representatives of the appropriate governmental body or counsel for petitioner of any such motions or other communications received by the clerk during nonbusiness hours. Each side must keep the clerk informed of the home and office telephone

number and email address of one attorney who will serve as emergency representative.

(7) An order of the panel granting or denying a motion to issue or vacate a stay of execution shall set forth the reasons for its decision.

(i) Clerk's List of Cases. The clerk shall maintain a list by jurisdiction of cases within the scope of this rule.

(j) Notification of State Supreme Court Clerk. The clerk shall send to the state supreme court a copy of the final decision in any habeas corpus case within the scope of this rule.

[Amended effective January 1, 1990; February 1, 1992; June 1, 1995; May 30, 1996; January 1, 1997; December 1, 2009; December 1, 2014.]

RULE 22.2 SUCCESSIVE PETITIONS FOR COLLATERAL REVIEW

(a) A request under 28 U.S.C. § 2244(b) or the final paragraph of 28 U.S.C. § 2255 for leave to file a second or successive petition must include the following information and attachments, in this order:

(1) A disclosure statement, if required by Circuit Rule 26.1.

(2) A short narrative statement of all claims the person wishes to present for decision. This statement must disclose whether any of these claims has been presented previously to any state or federal court and, if it was, how each court to which it was presented resolved it. If the claim has not previously been presented to a federal court, the applicant must state either:

(A) That the claim depends on a new rule of constitutional law, made retroactive to cases on collateral review by the Supreme Court; or

(B) That the factual predicate for the claim could not have been discovered previously through the exercise of due diligence and that the facts, if proven and viewed in light of the evidence as a whole, would be sufficient to establish by clear and convincing evidence that no reasonable fact-finder would have found the applicant guilty of the crime, had there been no constitutional error.

(3) A short narrative statement explaining how the person proposes to establish the requirements mentioned above. An applicant who relies on a new rule of constitutional law must identify the new rule, the

case that establishes that rule, and the decision of the Supreme Court that holds this new rule applicable to cases on collateral review.

(4) Copies of all opinions rendered by any state or federal court previously rendered in the criminal prosecution, any appeal, and any collateral attack.

(5) Copies of all prior petitions or motions for collateral review.

(b) A copy of the application, together with all attachments, must be served on the attorney for the appropriate government agency at the same time as the application is filed with the court. The application must include a certificate stating who was served, by what means, and when. If the application is made by a prisoner who is not represented by counsel, filing and service may be made under the terms of Fed. R. App. P. 4(c).

(c) Except in capital cases in which execution is imminent, the attorney for the custodian (in state cases) or the United States Attorney (in federal cases) may file a response within 14 days. When an execution is imminent, the court will not wait for a response. A response must include copies of any petitions or opinions that the applicant omitted from the papers.

(d) The applicant may file a reply memorandum within 14 days of the response, after which the request will be submitted to a panel of the court for decision.

(e) An applicant's failure to supply the information and documents required by this rule will lead the court to dismiss the application, but without prejudice to its renewal in proper form.

[Adopted effective May 30, 1996. Amended December 1, 2001; December 1, 2009.]

FRAP 23. CUSTODY OR RELEASE OF A PRISONER IN A HABEAS CORPUS PROCEEDING

[For text of rule, see the Federal Rules of Appellate Procedure]

FRAP 24. PROCEEDING IN FORMA PAUPERIS

[For text of rule, see the Federal Rules of Appellate Procedure]

TITLE VII. GENERAL PROVISIONS

FRAP 25. FILING AND SERVICE

*[For text of rule, see the Federal Rules
of Appellate Procedure]*

RULE 25. ELECTRONIC FILING

(a) All documents must be filed and served electronically.

(b) Subsection (a) does not apply to documents submitted by unrepresented litigants who are not themselves lawyers. Nor may documents be served electronically on unrepresented parties who are not lawyers. Filing by, and service on, these unrepresented litigants must be accomplished by paper copies in compliance with national and circuit rules other than this Rule 25.

(c) Any party may request by motion an exemption from this rule. The motion, which need not be filed or served electronically, must provide a good reason. A motion for exemption must be filed at least seven days before the brief, petition, or other document is due.

(d) Electronic filing is accomplished via the court's website, www.ca7.uscourts.gov. The procedures for filing are specified on the website, and paper copies of the procedures may be obtained from the Clerk. Paper copies of documents are required (and will be accepted) only to the extent provided in these e-filing procedures.

[Amended effective May 1, 2011.]

FRAP 26. COMPUTING AND EXTENDING TIME

*[For text of rule, see the Federal Rules
of Appellate Procedure]*

RULE 26. EXTENSIONS OF TIME TO FILE BRIEFS

Extensions of time to file briefs are not favored. A request for an extension of time shall be in the form of a motion supported by affidavit. The date the brief is due shall be stated in the motion. The affidavit must disclose facts which establish to the satisfaction of the court that with due diligence, and giving priority to the preparation of the brief, it will not be possible to file the brief on time.

In addition, if the time for filing the brief has been previously extended, the affidavit shall set forth the filing date of any prior motions and the court's ruling thereon. All factual statements required by this rule shall be set forth with specificity. Generalities, such as that the purpose of the motion is not for delay, or that counsel is too busy will not be sufficient.

Grounds that may merit consideration are:

(1) Engagement in other litigation, provided such litigation is identified by caption, number, and court, and there is set forth (a) a description of action taken on a request for continuance or deferment of other litigation; (b) an explanation of the reasons why other litigation should receive priority over the case in which the petition is filed; and (c) other relevant circumstances including why other associated counsel cannot either prepare the brief for filing or, in the alternative, relieve the movant's counsel of the other litigation claimed as a ground for extension.

(2) The matter under appeal is so complex that an adequate brief cannot reasonably be prepared by the date the brief is due, provided that the complexity is factually demonstrated in the affidavit.

(3) Extreme hardship to counsel will result unless an extension is granted, in which event the nature of the hardship must be set forth in detail.

The motion shall be filed at least seven days before the brief is due, unless it is made to appear in the motion that the facts which are the basis of the motion did not exist earlier or were not, or with due diligence could not have been, known earlier to the movant's counsel. Notice of the fact that an extension will be sought must be given to the opposing counsel together with a copy of the motion prior to the filing thereof.

In criminal cases, or in other cases in which a party may be in custody (including military service), a statement must be set forth in the affidavit as to the custodial status of the party, including the conditions of the party's bail, if any.

[Amended December 1, 2009.]

FRAP 26.1 CORPORATE DISCLOSURE STATEMENT

*[For text of rule, see the Federal Rules
of Appellate Procedure]*

RULE 26.1 DISCLOSURE STATEMENT

(a) Who Must File. Each attorney for a nongovernmental party or amicus curiae, and each private attorney representing a governmental party, must file a separate statement under this rule. A party or amicus required to file a corporate disclosure statement under Fed. R. App. P. 26.1 may combine the information required by subsection (b) of this rule with the statement required by the national rule. A disclosure statement constitutes an attorney's appearance. An attorney filing a disclosure statement need not file a representation statement under Fed. R. App. P. 12(b).

(b) Contents of Statement. The statement must disclose the names of all law firms whose partners or associates have appeared for the party or amicus in the case (including proceedings in the district court or before an administrative agency) or are expected to appear in this court. If any litigant is using a pseudonym, the statement must disclose the litigant's true name. A disclosure required by the preceding sentence will be kept under seal. Attorneys are encouraged to use the disclosure statement form posted on the Court of Appeals' website.

(c) Time for Filing. The statement under this rule and Fed. R. App. P. 26.1 must be filed no later than 21 days after docketing the appeal, with a party's first motion or response to an adversary's motion, or when directed by the court, whichever time is earliest. A disclosure statement for each attorney for a non-governmental party or amicus curiae, and each private attorney representing a governmental party, also must accompany any petition for permission to appeal under Fed. R. App. P. 5 and must be included with a second or successive petition for collateral review, an appellant's brief, an appellee's brief, a brief of amicus curiae, and any petition for rehearing en banc. See Cir. R. 22.2(a)(1); Fed. R. App. P. 28(a)(1), (b); Fed. R. App. P. 29(c)(1); Cir. R. 35.

(d) Duty to Update. Counsel must file updated disclosure statements under this rule and Fed. R. App. P. 26.1 within 14 days of any change in the information required to be disclosed.

[Adopted effective March 23, 1999. Amended effective December 1, 2001; December 1, 2014.]

FRAP 27. MOTIONS

[For text of rule, see the Federal Rules of Appellate Procedure]

RULE 27. EMERGENCY FILINGS

Counsel who anticipate the need for emergency action while the Clerk's office is closed should alert the Clerk's office during business hours, and at the earliest possible time. Although documents seeking emergency relief must be filed in compliance with Circuit Rule 25, failure to provide advance notice may delay action by the court. Counsel should not expect that electronic filings will be read and acted on outside business hours, unless arrangements for the emergency filing have been made in advance.

[Amended effective May 1, 2011.]

FRAP 28. BRIEFS

[For text of rule, see the Federal Rules of Appellate Procedure]

RULE 28. BRIEFS

Briefs must conform to Fed. R. App. P. 28 and the additional provisions in Circuit Rules 12(b), 30 and 52.

The following requirements supplement those in the corresponding provisions of Fed. R. App. P. 28:

(a) Appellant's Jurisdictional Statement. The jurisdictional statement in appellant's brief, see Fed. R. App. P. 28(a)(4), must contain the following details:

(1) The statement concerning the district court's jurisdiction shall identify the provision of the constitution or federal statute involved if jurisdiction is based on the existence of a federal question. If jurisdiction depends on diversity of citizenship, the statement shall identify the jurisdictional amount and the citizenship of each party to the litigation. If any party is a corporation, the statement shall identify both the state of incorporation and the state in which the corporation has its principal place of business. If any party is an unincorporated association or partnership the statement shall identify the citizenship of all members. The statement shall supply similar details concerning the invocation of supplemental jurisdiction or other sources of jurisdiction.

(2) The statement concerning appellate jurisdiction shall identify the statutory provision believed to confer jurisdiction on this court and the following particulars:

(i) The date of entry of the judgment or decree sought to be reviewed.

(ii) The filing date of any motion for a new trial or alteration of the judgment or any other motion claimed to toll the time within which to appeal.

(iii) The disposition of such a motion and the date of its entry.

(iv) The filing date of the notice of appeal (together with information about an extension of time if one was granted).

(v) If the case is a direct appeal from the decision of a magistrate judge, the dates on which each party consented in writing to the entry of final judgment by the magistrate judge.

(3) If the appeal is from an order other than a final judgment which adjudicates all of the claims with respect to all parties, counsel shall provide the information necessary to enable the court to determine whether the order is immediately appealable. Elaboration will be necessary in the following cases although the list is illustrative rather than exhaustive:

(i) If any claims or parties remain for disposition in the district court, identify the nature of these claims and the ground on which an appeal may be taken in advance of the final judgment. If there has been a certificate under Fed. R. Civ. P. 54(b) or if this is an appeal by permission under 28 U.S.C. § 1292(b), give the particulars and describe the relation between the claims or parties subject to the appeal and the claims or parties remaining in the district court.

(ii) If the ground of jurisdiction is the "collateral order doctrine," describe how the order meets each of the criteria of that doctrine: finality, separability from the merits of the underlying action, and practical unreviewability on appeal from a final judgment. Cite pertinent cases establishing the appealability of orders of the character involved.

(iii) If the order sought to be reviewed remands a case to a bankruptcy judge or administrative agency, explain what needs to be done on remand and why the order is nonetheless "final."

(iv) Whenever some issues or parties remain before the district court, give enough information to enable the court to determine whether the order is appealable. Appeals from orders granting or staying arbitration or abstaining from decision as well as appeals from the grant or denial of injunctions require careful exposition of jurisdictional factors.

(b) Appellee's Jurisdictional Statement. The appellee's brief shall state explicitly whether or not the jurisdictional summary in the appellant's brief is complete and correct. If it is not, the appellee shall provide a complete jurisdictional summary.

(c) [Deleted]

(d) Briefs in Multiple Appeals.

(1) If a cross-appeal is filed, the clerk will designate which party will file the opening brief, and will set a briefing schedule in accordance with Fed. R. App. P. 28.1.

(2) The court will entertain motions for realignment of the briefing schedule and enlargement of the number of pages when the norm established by this rule proves inappropriate. Because it is improper to take a cross-appeal in order to advance additional arguments in support of a judgment, the court will not grant motions under this subsection by cross-appellants that do not seek to enlarge their rights under the judgment.

(3) Captions of Briefs in Multiple Appeals. When two or more parties file cross-appeals or other separate but related appeals, the briefs shall bear the appellate case numbers and captions of all related appeals.

(e) Citation of Supplemental Authority. Counsel shall file the original letter and ten copies of supplemental authorities drawn to the court's attention under Fed. R. App. P. 28(j).

(f) Citation to the United States Reports. Citation to the opinions of the Supreme Court of the United States must include the Volume and page of the United States Reports, once the citation is available.

[Amended effective February 1, 1992; June 1, 1995; December 1, 1997; December 1, 1998; December 1, 2014.]

FRAP 28.1   CROSS–APPEALS

[For text of rule, see the Federal Rules of Appellate Procedure]

FRAP 29.   BRIEF OF AN AMICUS CURIAE

[For text of rule, see the Federal Rules of Appellate Procedure]

FRAP 30.   APPENDIX TO THE BRIEFS

[For text of rule, see the Federal Rules of Appellate Procedure]

RULE 30.   APPENDICES

(a) Contents. The appellant shall submit, bound with the main brief, an appendix containing the judgment or order under review and any opinion, memorandum of decision, findings of fact and conclusions of law, or oral statement of reasons delivered by the trial court or administrative agency upon the rendering of that judgment, decree, or order.

(b) Additional Contents. The appellant shall also include in an appendix:

(1) Copies of any other opinions, orders, or oral rulings in the case that address the issues sought to be raised. If the appellant's brief challenges any oral ruling, the portion of the transcript containing the judge's rationale for that ruling must be included in the appendix.

(2) Copies of any opinions or orders in the case rendered by magistrate judges or bankruptcy judges that address the issues sought to be raised.

(3) Copies of all opinions, orders, findings of fact and conclusions of law rendered in the case by administrative agencies (including their administrative law judges and adjudicative officers such as administrative appeals judges, immigration judges, members of boards and commissions, and others who serve functionally similar roles). This requirement applies whether the original review of the administrative decision is in this court or was conducted by the district court.

(4) If this is a collateral attack on a criminal conviction, then the appendix also must include copies of all opinions by any federal court or state appellate court previously rendered in the criminal prosecution, any appeal, and any earlier collateral attack.

(5) An order concerning a motion for new trial, alteration or amendment of the judgment, rehearing, and other relief sought under Rules 52(a) or 59, Fed. R. Civ. P.

(6) Any other short excerpts from the record, such as essential portions of the pleading or charge, disput-

ed provisions of a contract, pertinent pictures, or brief portions of the transcript, that are important to a consideration of the issues raised on appeal.

(7) The documents in (b) may also be placed in the appendix bound with the brief if these documents when added to the required appendix in (a) do not exceed fifty pages.

(c) Appendix to the brief of a Cross–Appellant. The brief of a cross-appellant must comply with this rule, but it need not include materials contained in the appendix of the appellant.

(d) Statement That All Required Materials Are in Appendix. The appendix to each appellant's brief shall contain a statement that all of the materials required by parts (a) and (b) of this rule are included. If there are no materials within the scope of parts (a) and (b) of this rule, counsel shall so certify.

(e) Stipulated Joint Appendix and Supplemental Appendices. The parties may file a stipulated joint appendix. A supplemental appendix, containing material not included in an appendix previously filed, may be filed with the appellee's brief. An appendix should not be lengthy, and costs for a lengthy appendix will not be awarded.

(f) Indexing of Appendix. If a party elects to file an appendix containing portions of the transcript of proceedings, it shall contain an index of the portions of the transcript contained therein in the form and detail described in Circuit Rule 10(e) as well as a complete table of contents.

[Amended effective December 1, 1997; December 1, 1998.]

FRAP 31. SERVING AND FILING BRIEFS

[For text of rule, see the Federal Rules of Appellate Procedure]

RULE 31. FILING OF BRIEFS AND FAILURE TO TIMELY FILE BRIEFS

(a) Time for Filing Briefs. Except in agency cases, the time for filing briefs shall run from the date the appeal is docketed, regardless of the completeness of the record at the time of docketing, unless the court orders otherwise.

(b) Number of Briefs Required. The clerk of this court is authorized to accept 15 copies of briefs as substantial compliance with Rule 31(b), Fed. R. App. P. Appointed counsel shall also file 15 copies.

(c) Failure of Appellant to File Brief. When an appellant's original brief is not filed when it is due, the procedure shall be as follows:

(1) *All Criminal Cases in Which the Defendant Has Counsel and Civil Cases With Court–Appointed Counsel.* The clerk shall enter an order directing counsel to show cause within 14 days why disciplinary action should not be taken. The court will then take appropriate action.

(2) *All Other Cases.* The clerk shall enter an order directing counsel, or a pro se appellant, to show cause why the appeal should not be dismissed. The court will then take appropriate action.

(d) Failure of Appellee to File Brief. When an appellee's brief is not filed on time, the clerk shall enter an order requiring the appellee to show cause within 14 days why the case should not be treated as ready for oral argument or submission and the appellee denied oral argument. The court will then take appropriate action.

(e) [Rescinded]

[Amended effective February 1, 1992; January 1, 1997; December 1, 2001; May 1, 2011.]

FRAP 32. FORM OF BRIEFS, APPENDICES, AND OTHER PAPERS

[For text of rule, see the Federal Rules of Appellate Procedure]

RULE 32. FORM OF A BRIEF

(a) A brief need not comply with the portion of Fed. R. App. P. 32(a)(3) requiring it to "lie reasonably flat when open." A brief's binding is acceptable if it is secure and does not obscure the text.

(b) A brief need not comply with the 14–point–type requirement in Fed. R. App. P. 32(a)(5)(A). A brief is acceptable if proportionally spaced type is 12 points or larger in the body of the brief, and 11 points or larger in footnotes.

[Amended effective January 1, 1990; February 1, 1992; January 1, 1996; January 1, 1997; June, 1997; December 1, 1997; December 1, 1998; December 1, 2001.]

FRAP 32.1 CITING JUDICIAL DISPOSITIONS

[For text of rule, see the Federal Rules of Appellate Procedure]

RULE 32.1 PUBLICATION OF OPINIONS

(a) Policy. It is the policy of the circuit to avoid issuing unnecessary opinions.

(b) Publication. The court may dispose of an appeal by an opinion or an order. Opinions, which may be signed or per curiam, are released in printed form, are published in the Federal Reporter, and constitute the law of the circuit. Orders, which are unsigned, are released in photocopied form, are not published in the Federal Reporter, and are not treated as precedents. Every order bears the legend: "Nonprecedential disposition. To be cited only in accordance with Fed. R. App. P. 32.1."

(c) Motion to Change Status. Any person may request by motion that an order be reissued as an opinion. The motion should state why this change would be appropriate.

(d) Citation of Older Orders. No order of this court issued before January 1, 2007, may be cited except to support a claim of preclusion (res judicata or collateral estoppel) or to establish the law of the case from an earlier appeal in the same proceeding.

[Effective January 1, 2007.]

FRAP 33.   APPEAL CONFERENCES

[For text of rule, see the Federal Rules of Appellate Procedure]

RULE 33.   PREHEARING CONFERENCE

At the conference the court may, among other things, examine its jurisdiction, simplify and define issues, consolidate cases, establish the briefing schedule, set limitations on the length of briefs, and explore the possibility of settlement.

[Amended effective February 1, 1992.]

FRAP 34.   ORAL ARGUMENT

[For text of rule, see the Federal Rules of Appellate Procedure]

RULE 34.   ORAL ARGUMENT

(a) Notice to Clerk. The names of counsel intending to argue orally shall be furnished to the clerk not later than five business days before the argument.

(b) Calendar.

(1) The calendar for a particular day will generally consist of six appeals scheduled for oral argument at 9:30 a.m. The amount of time allotted for oral argument will be set based on the nature of the case. The clerk will notify counsel of the allocation approximately 21 days before the argument. The types of cases listed below are to be given priority, though the sequence of listing here is not intended to indicate relative priority among the types of cases.

(i) Appeal from an order of confinement after refusal of an immunized witness to testify before the grand jury. (These appeals must be decided within 30 days.) 28 U.S.C. § 1826.

(ii) Criminal Appeals. Rule 45(b), Fed. R. App. P.

(iii) Appeals from orders refusing or imposing conditions of release, which will be heard without the necessity of briefs. Rule 9, Fed. R. App. P.

(iv) Appeals involving issues of public importance.

(v) Habeas corpus and 28 U.S.C. § 2255 appeals.

(vi) Appeals from the granting, denying, or modifying of injunctions.

(vii) Petitions for writs of mandamus and prohibition and other extraordinary writs. Rule 21(b) and (c), Fed. R. App. P.

(viii) "Any other action if good cause therefore is shown. For purposes of this subsection, 'good cause' is shown if a right under the Constitution of the United States or a Federal Statute (including rights under section 552 of Title 5) would be maintained in a factual context that indicates that a request for expedited consideration has merit." 28 U.S.C. § 1657.

(2) Consideration will be given to requests addressed to the clerk by out-of-town counsel to schedule more than one appeal for oral argument the same day in order to minimize travel time and expenses.

(3) Requests by counsel, made in advance of the scheduling of an appeal for oral argument, that the court avoid scheduling the oral argument for a particular day or week will be respected, if possible.

(4) Once an appeal has been scheduled for oral argument, the court will not ordinarily reschedule it. Requests under subparagraphs (2) and (3) of this paragraph should therefore be made as early as possible. Counsel should have in mind that, when practicable, criminal appeals are scheduled for oral argument shortly after the appellant's brief is filed and civil appeals shortly after the appellee's brief is filed.

(c) Divided Argument Not Favored. Divided arguments on behalf of a single party or multiple parties with the same interests are not favored by the court. When such arguments are nevertheless divided or when more than one counsel argues on the same side for parties with differing interests, the time allowed shall be apportioned between such counsel in their own discretion. If counsel are unable to agree, the court will allocate the time.

(d) Preparation. In preparing for oral arguments, counsel should be mindful that this court follows the practice of reading briefs prior to oral argument.

(e) Waiver or Postponement. Any request for waiver or postponement of a scheduled oral argument must be made by formal motion, with proof of service on all other counsel or parties. Postponements will be granted only in extraordinary circumstances.

(f) Statement Concerning Oral Argument. A party may include, as part of a principal brief, a short statement explaining why oral argument is (or is not) appropriate under the criteria of Fed. R. App. P. 34(a).

(g) Citation of Authorities at Oral Argument. Counsel may not cite or discuss a case at oral argument unless the case has been cited in one of the briefs or drawn to the attention of the court and opposing counsel by a filing under Fed R. App. P. 28(j). The filing may be made on the day of oral argument, if absolutely necessary, but should be made sooner.

(h) Argument by Law Student. The court may permit a law student to present oral argument under supervision of a member of this court's bar, with the client's written approval, if the representation is part of a program of an accredited law school. The supervising attorney's motion must be filed at least 14 days before the date on which argument is to be held and must state the reasons why presentation of argument by a law student is appropriate.

[Amended effective January 1, 1996; December 1, 1997; December 1, 2001; December 1, 2009; December 1, 2014.]

FRAP 35. EN BANC DETERMINATION

[For text of rule, see the Federal Rules of Appellate Procedure]

RULE 35. PETITIONS FOR REHEARING EN BANC

Every petition for rehearing en banc, and every brief of an amicus curiae supporting or opposing a petition for rehearing en banc, must include a statement providing the information required by Fed. R. App. P. 26.1 and Circuit Rule 26.1 as of the date the petition is filed.

[Adopted effective June 1, 1995. Amended effective January 1, 1996; December 1, 1998; March 23, 1999.]

FRAP 36. ENTRY OF JUDGMENT; NOTICE

[For text of rule, see the Federal Rules of Appellate Procedure]

RULE 36. REASSIGNMENT OF REMANDED CASES

Whenever a case tried in a district court is remanded by this court for a new trial, it shall be reassigned by the district court for trial before a judge other than the judge who heard the prior trial unless the remand order directs or all parties request that the same judge retry the case. In appeals which are not subject to this rule by its terms, this court may nevertheless direct in its opinion or order that this rule shall apply on remand.

FRAP 37. INTEREST ON JUDGMENTS

[For text of rule, see the Federal Rules of Appellate Procedure]

FRAP 38. FRIVOLOUS APPEALS— DAMAGES AND COSTS

[For text of rule, see the Federal Rules of Appellate Procedure]

FRAP 39. COSTS

[For text of rule, see the Federal Rules of Appellate Procedure]

RULE 39. COSTS OF PRINTING BRIEFS AND APPENDICES

The cost of printing or otherwise producing copies of briefs and appendices shall not exceed the maximum rate per page as established by the clerk of the court of appeals. If a commercial printing process has been used, a copy of the bill must be attached to the itemized and verified bill of costs filed and served by the party.

FRAP 40. PETITION FOR PANEL REHEARING

[For text of rule, see the Federal Rules of Appellate Procedure]

RULE 40. PETITIONS FOR REHEARING

(a) Table of Contents. The petition for rehearing shall include a table of contents with page references and a table of cases (alphabetically arranged), statutes and other authorities cited, with reference to the pages of the brief where they are cited.

(b) Number of Copies. Fifteen copies of a petition for rehearing shall be filed, except that 30 shall be filed if the petitioner suggests rehearing en banc.

(c) Time for Filing After Decision in Agency Case. The date on which this court enters a final order or files a dispositive opinion is the date of the "entry of judgment" for the purpose of commencing the period for filing a petition for rehearing in accordance with Fed. R. App. P. 40, notwithstanding the fact that a formal detailed judgment is entered at a later date.

(d) Time for Filing After Decision From the Bench. The time limit for filing a petition for rehearing shall run from the date of this court's written order following a decision from the bench.

(e) Rehearing Sua Sponte Before Decision. A proposed opinion approved by a panel of this court adopting a position which would overrule a prior decision of this court or create a conflict between or among circuits shall not be published unless it is first circulated among the active members of this court and a majority of them do not vote to rehear en banc the issue of whether the position should be adopted. In the discretion of the panel, a proposed opinion which would establish a new rule or procedure may be similarly circulated before it is issued. When the position is adopted by the panel after compliance with this procedure, the opinion, when published, shall contain a footnote worded, depending on the circumstances, in substance as follows:

This opinion has been circulated among all judges of this court in regular active service. (No judge favored, or, A majority did not favor) a rehearing en banc on the question of (e.g., overruling *Doe v. Roe*).

[Amended effective June 1, 1995; January 1, 1996; January 1, 1997; December 1, 1997.]

FRAP 41. MANDATE: CONTENTS; ISSUANCE AND EFFECTIVE DATE; STAY

[For text of rule, see the Federal Rules of Appellate Procedure]

RULE 41. IMMEDIATE ISSUANCE OF MANDATE AFTER CERTAIN DISPOSITIONS

The mandate will issue immediately when an appeal is dismissed (1) voluntarily, (2) for failure to pay the docket fee, (3) for failure to file the docketing statement under Circuit Rule 3(c), or (4) for failure by the appellant to file a brief.

[Amended effective February 1, 1992; June 1, 1995; December 1, 1998.]

FRAP 42. VOLUNTARY DISMISSAL

[For text of rule, see the Federal Rules of Appellate Procedure]

FRAP 43. SUBSTITUTION OF PARTIES

[For text of rule, see the Federal Rules of Appellate Procedure]

RULE 43. CHANGE IN PUBLIC OFFICES

Whenever any of the parties to the litigation appears in an official capacity and there is a change in the occupant of the office after the filing of the Rule 3(c)(1) docketing statement, the official-capacity litigant (other than a member of the Cabinet) must notify the court of the identity of the new occupant of the office. Similarly, in collateral attacks on confinement,

the parties must notify the court of any change in custodian or custodial status.

[Adopted effective June 1, 1995.]

FRAP 44. CASE INVOLVING A CONSTITUTIONAL QUESTION WHERE UNITED STATES IS NOT A PARTY

[For text of rule, see the Federal Rules of Appellate Procedure]

FRAP 45. CLERK'S DUTIES

[For text of rule, see the Federal Rules of Appellate Procedure]

RULE 45. FEES

(a) Fees To Be Collected by the Clerk. All fees collected by the clerk shall be in accordance with the Court of Appeals Miscellaneous Fee Schedule established by the Judicial Conference of the United States under 28 U.S.C. § 1913. No other fees for miscellaneous services than those prescribed by the Judicial Conference of the United States shall be charged or collected by any clerk of court.

(b) Fees To Be Paid in Advance. The clerk shall not be required to docket any proceeding or perform any other service until all fees due to the clerk have been paid, except at the direction of a judge of this court or at the instance of a party who is entitled to proceed without prepayment of fees.

[Amended effective November 1, 2003; December 1, 2014.]

FRAP 46. ATTORNEYS

[For text of rule, see the Federal Rules of Appellate Procedure]

RULE 46. ATTORNEYS

(a) Admission. The lead attorney for all parties represented by counsel in this court must be admitted to practice in this court. Counsel have thirty days from docketing of the matter in this court to comply. In addition, any attorney who orally argues an appeal must be admitted to practice in this court. An applicant for admission to the bar of this court shall file with the clerk an application on the form furnished by the clerk. The oath or affirmation thereon may be taken before any officer authorized by federal or state law to administer an oath. When an appropriate application and motion have been filed and fee tendered, if a fee be required, the clerk shall present the papers to an active or senior circuit judge for action in chambers unless the applicant requests admission in open court. If admission is in open court, the applicant must appear in person and the sponsor shall make an oral motion in support of the written application. If admission is in chambers, the applicant and sponsor need not appear.

(b) Admission Fees. The prescribed fee for admission is a $15.00 local fee* plus a national fee prescribed by the Court of Appeals Miscellaneous Fee Schedule, except that attorneys who have been appointed by the district court or this court to represent a party on appeal in forma pauperis, law clerks to judges of this court or the district courts, and attorneys employed by the United States or any agency thereof need not pay the fee. The clerk shall receive the $15.00 local fee as trustee of the lawyers fund and shall deposit it in a bank designated by the court. Payments from the fund shall be made for the purchase of law books, for library conveniences, or other court purposes, by checks duly signed by the clerk as trustee and countersigned by two judges of this court.

(c) Government Attorneys. Attorneys for any federal, state or local government office or agency may appear before this court in connection with their official duties without being formally admitted to practice before the court.

(d) Striking a Name From the Roll of Attorneys. Whenever it is shown to this court that any members of its bar have been disbarred or suspended from practice, or their names have been stricken from the roll of attorneys, in any state, or the District of Columbia, they will be forthwith suspended from practice before this court. They will thereupon be afforded the opportunity to show cause, within 30 days, why their names should not be stricken from the roll of attorneys admitted to practice before this court. Upon the attorney's response to the rule to show cause, or upon the expiration of the 30 days if no response is made, this court will enter an appropriate order.

[Amended effective January 1, 1991; December 1, 2014.]

* [**Publisher's Note:** For the most current admission fee charged by the Court, contact the Clerk's Office. *See also* the Federal Courts Miscellaneous Fee Schedules, *post.*]

FRAP 47. LOCAL RULES BY COURTS OF APPEALS

[For text of rule, see the Federal Rules of Appellate Procedure]

RULE 47. ADVISORY COMMITTEE

The court shall appoint an Advisory Committee to provide a forum for continuing study of the procedures of the court and to serve as a conduit between members of the bar who have suggestions for change and the court, which retains ultimate responsibility for effectuating change. The committee shall consist of one district judge, one law school professor, and two attorneys from each state of the circuit, Illinois, Indiana, and Wisconsin, and, as ex officio members,

the President and First Vice–President of the Seventh Circuit Bar Association, the Circuit Executive, the Senior Staff Attorney, and the Clerk of this court. The district judges, attorneys, and law school professors on the committee shall serve three-year terms with the appointments being staggered.

The court shall appoint a chairman from the membership of the committee to serve for a two-year term. The advisory committee shall promulgate its own rules, and call its own meetings. The advisory committee shall arrange for notice of proposed rule changes and shall consider comments received. From time to time, as it deems necessary or advisable, it shall make recommendations to the circuit council or to the court. Suggestions for consideration by the advisory committee may be filed with the clerk of this court.

[Amended effective February 1, 1992.]

FRAP 48. MASTERS

[For text of rule, see the Federal Rules of Appellate Procedure]

RULE 50. JUDGES TO GIVE REASONS WHEN DISMISSING A CLAIM, GRANTING SUMMARY JUDGMENT, OR ENTERING AN APPEALABLE ORDER

Whenever a district court resolves any claim or counterclaim on the merits, terminates the litigation in its court (as by remanding or transferring the case, or denying leave to proceed in forma pauperis with or without prejudice), or enters an interlocutory order that may be appealed to the court of appeals, the judge shall give his or her reasons, either orally on the record or by written statement. The court urges the parties to bring to this court's attention as soon as possible any failure to comply with this rule.

[Amended effective May 1, 1993; June 1, 1995.]

RULE 51. SUMMARY DISPOSITION OF CERTAIN APPEALS BY CONVICTED PERSONS; WAIVER OF APPEAL

(a) Duties of Criminal Trial Counsel. Trial counsel in a criminal case, whether retained or appointed by the district court, is responsible for the continued representation of the client desiring to appeal unless specifically relieved by the court of appeals upon a motion to withdraw. Such relief shall be freely granted. If trial counsel was appointed by the district court and a notice of appeal has been filed, trial counsel will be appointed as appellate counsel without further proof of the client's eligibility for appointed counsel. If the client was not found to be eligible for Criminal Justice Act representation in the district court but appears to qualify on appeal, trial counsel must immediately assist the client in filing in the district court a motion to proceed as one who is financially unable to obtain an adequate defense in a criminal case. This motion must be accompanied by an affidavit containing substantially the same information as contained in Form 4 of the Appendix to the Federal Rules of Appellate Procedure. If the motion is granted, the court of appeals will appoint trial counsel as appellate counsel unless the district court informs the court of appeals that new counsel should be appointed. If the motion is denied by the district court, trial counsel may file a similar motion in the court of appeals. Counsel may have additional duties under Part V of the Circuit's Plan implementing the Criminal Justice Act of 1964.

(b) Withdrawal of Court–Appointed Counsel in a Criminal Case. When representing a convicted person in a proceeding to review the conviction, court-appointed counsel who files a brief characterizing an appeal as frivolous and moves to withdraw (see *Anders v. California*, 386 U.S. 738 (1967); *United States v. Edwards*, 777 F.2d 364 (7th Cir. 1985)) shall file with the brief a proof of service which also indicates the current address of the client. Except as provided in paragraph (g) of this rule, the clerk shall then send to the client by certified mail, return receipt requested, a copy of the brief and motion, with a notice in substantially the form set out in Appendix I to these rules. The same procedures shall be followed by court-appointed counsel and the clerk when a motion to dismiss the appeal has been filed by the appellee and the appellant's counsel believes that any argument that could be made in opposition to the motion would be frivolous.

(c) Time for Filing Motion to Withdraw in a Criminal Case. Any motion to withdraw for good cause (other than the frivolousness of an appeal) must be filed in the court of appeals within 14 days of the notice of appeal. The court of appeals will make all appellate appointments.

(d) Notice of Motion to Dismiss Pro Se Appeal. When a convicted person appears pro se in a proceeding to review the conviction, and the government moves to dismiss the appeal for a reason other than failure to file a brief on time, the clerk shall, unless paragraph (e) of this rule applies, send to the convicted person by certified mail, return receipt requested, a copy of the motion with a notice in substantially the form set out in Appendix II to these rules.

(e) Dismissal if No Response. If no response to a notice under paragraph (a) or (b) of this rule is received within 30 days after the mailing, the appeal may be dismissed.

(f) Voluntary Waiver of Appeal. Notwithstanding the preceding paragraphs, if the convicted person consents to dismissal of the appeal after consultation with appellate counsel, the appeal may be dismissed upon the filing of a motion accompanied by an executed acknowledgment and consent in substantially the form set out in Appendix III to these rules. See Rule 42(b), Fed. R. App. P.

(g) Incompetent Appellant. If, in a case in which paragraph (a) or (b) of this rule would otherwise be applicable, the convicted person has been found incompetent or there is reason to believe that person is incompetent, the motion shall so state and the matter shall be referred directly to the court by the clerk for such action as law and justice may require.

[Former Circuit Rule 4 redesignated Circuit Rule 51(a) and (c) and amended effective December 1, 1997. Amended December 1, 1998; December 1, 2009.]

RULE 52. CERTIFICATION OF QUESTIONS OF STATE LAW

(a) When the rules of the highest court of a state provide for certification to that court by a federal court of questions arising under the laws of that state which will control the outcome of a case pending in the federal court, this court, sua sponte or on motion of a party, may certify such a question to the state court in accordance with the rules of that court, and may stay the case in this court to await the state court's decision of the question certified. The certification will be made after the briefs are filed in this court. A motion for certification shall be included in the moving party's brief.

(b) If the state court decides the certified issue, then within 21 days after the issuance of its opinion the parties must file in this court statements of their positions about what action this court should take to complete the resolution of the appeal.

[Amended December 1, 1998.]

RULE 53. PLAN FOR PUBLICATION OF OPINIONS OF THE SEVENTH CIRCUIT PROMULGATED PURSUANT TO RESOLUTION OF THE JUDICIAL CONFERENCE OF THE UNITED STATES [RESCINDED DEC. 27, 2006, EFF. JAN. 1, 2007. SEE, NOW, LOCAL RULE 32.1]

RULE 54. REMANDS FROM SUPREME COURT

When the Supreme Court remands a case to this court for further proceedings, counsel for the parties shall, within 21 days after the issuance of a certified copy of the Supreme Court's judgment pursuant to its Rule 45.3, file statements of their positions as to the action which ought to be taken by this court on remand.

[Amended effective December 1, 1997.]

RULE 55. PROHIBITION OF PHOTOGRAPHS AND BROADCASTS

The taking of photographs in, or radio or television broadcasting from the courtroom or any other place on the 27th floor or judges' chambers or corridors adjacent thereto on the 26th floor of the Federal Courthouse located at 219 South Dearborn Street, Chicago, Illinois, without permission of the court, is prohibited.

RULE 56. OPPORTUNITY TO OBJECT AND MAKE PROPOSALS ON THE RECORD

(a) Opportunity to State Objections and Their Rationale. Whenever a rule of court requires concrete proposals or objections and reasons in order to preserve a claim for appeal (e.g., Fed. R. Civ. P. 51, Fed. R. Crim. P. 30, Fed R. Evid. 103(a)), the judge must ensure that parties have an adequate opportunity to put their proposals, objections, and reasons on the record. When the judge entertains proposals or objections off the record (for example, a sidebar conference or a jury instruction conference in chambers), as soon as practicable the judge must offer an opportunity to summarize on the record the proposal or objection discussed, and the reasons for the proposal or objection. The judge then must state the ruling made.

(b) Waiver. Parties offered an opportunity to make a record under part (a) of this rule must use it in order to preserve a position for appeal. No proposal, objection, or reason may be urged as a ground of appeal unless placed on the record. A lawyer who believes that he or she has not been given an adequate opportunity to make a record under this rule must so state on the record. This rule does not alter any obligation imposed by any other rule to make concrete proposals or to state objections and reasons in order to preserve a claim for appeal.

[Adopted effective June 1, 1995.]

RULE 57. REMANDS FOR REVISION OF JUDGMENT

A party who during the pendency of an appeal has filed a motion under Fed. R. Civ. P. 60(a) or 60(b), Fed. R. Crim. P. 35(b), or any other rule that permits the modification of a final judgment, should request the district court to indicate whether it is inclined to grant the motion. If the district court so indicates, this court will remand the case for the purpose of modifying the judgment. Any party dissatisfied with the judgment as modified must file a fresh notice of appeal.

[Adopted effective January 1, 1996.]

RULE 60. SEVENTH CIRCUIT JUDICIAL CONFERENCE

(a) Purpose of the Conference. Each year the Chief Judge shall call a circuit judicial conference in accordance with 28 U.S.C. § 333 for the purpose of considering the business of courts and advising means of improving the administration of justice within the circuit. The Chief Judge shall designate the location of the conference and either preside at it or designate officers of the Seventh Circuit Bar Association, or others, to preside.

(b) Members of the Conference. Each active Circuit, District, Bankruptcy, and Magistrate Judge of the Circuit shall be a member of the conference. The following shall be members of the conference and are encouraged to attend: (1) Senior Circuit, District and Bankruptcy Judges; (2) Circuit Executive, Deputy Circuit Executive, Senior Staff Attorney for the Seventh Circuit, staff attorneys and law clerks to all Circuit, District, Bankruptcy, and Magistrate Judges; (3) Clerks of the Court of Appeals, District Courts and Bankruptcy Courts in the Circuit; (4) United States Attorneys in the Circuit and their legal staffs; (5) Federal Defenders in the Circuit and their legal staffs; (6) Members of the Seventh Circuit Bar Association; (7) Special guests invited by the Chief Judge or by the President of the Seventh Circuit Bar Association with the approval of the Chief Judge; (8) United States Trustees in the Circuit and their legal staffs.

(c) Planning of the Conference. The Judicial Conference shall be planned by a committee composed of eight persons, four judges appointed annually by the Chief Judge from the active judges in the Circuit and four members of the Seventh Circuit Bar Association appointed annually by the President of the Bar Association. The Chief Judge, after consultation with the President of the Bar Association, shall designate one of the members to chair the committee.

(d) Executive Session. All or part of one day of the conference shall be designated by the Chief Judge as an executive session to be attended only by active Circuit, District and Bankruptcy Judges, Magistrate Judges and other court personnel.

(e) Record of the Conference. The Clerk of the Court of Appeals shall make and preserve a record of the proceedings at the Judicial Conference.

[Amended effective January 1, 1990; December 1, 1997; December 1, 2003.]

APPENDICES

APPENDIX OF FORMS TO FEDERAL RULES OF APPELLATE PROCEDURE

FORM 1.   NOTICE OF APPEAL TO A COURT OF APPEALS FROM A JUDGMENT OR ORDER OF A DISTRICT COURT

[For text of form, see the Federal Rules of Appellate Procedure]

FORM 2.   NOTICE OF APPEAL TO A COURT OF APPEALS FROM A DECISION OF THE UNITED STATES TAX COURT

[For text of form, see the Federal Rules of Appellate Procedure]

FORM 3.   PETITION FOR REVIEW OF ORDER OF AN AGENCY, BOARD, COMMISSION OR OFFICER

[For text of form, see the Federal Rules of Appellate Procedure]

FORM 4.   AFFIDAVIT ACCOMPANYING MOTION FOR PERMISSION TO APPEAL IN FORMA PAUPERIS

[For text of form, see the Federal Rules of Appellate Procedure]

FORM 5.   NOTICE OF APPEAL TO A COURT OF APPEALS FROM A JUDGMENT OR ORDER OF A DISTRICT COURT OR A BANKRUPTCY APPELLATE PANEL

[For text of form, see the Federal Rules of Appellate Procedure]

FORM 6.   CERTIFICATE OF COMPLIANCE WITH RULE 32(a)

[For text of form, see the Federal Rules of Appellate Procedure]

APPENDIX OF FORMS TO THE CIRCUIT RULES

APPENDIX I. NOTICE RE: DEFENDANT COUNSEL'S MOTION FOR LEAVE TO WITHDRAW UNDER CIRCUIT RULE 51(b)

To: _____
                              (Name)

_____
    (Street Address or Prison Box)

_____
         (City, State, Zip Code)

You are the appellant in a case now pending in this court:

Case No. _____

_____

                                    v.

_____

Your attorney filed a brief on _____, 20___, stating a belief that your appeal is frivolous and requesting permission to withdraw from the case. Please be advised as follows:

1) You have 30 days from the date this notice was mailed in which to raise any points that you choose which show why your conviction should be set aside.

2) If you do not respond within the 30 days, the court may affirm or dismiss your appeal. An affirmance or dismissal would mean that your case would be finally decided against you.

3) If you want to make a showing why the court should not affirm or dismiss your appeal and believe that there is a very good reason why you will not be able to file your objections with the court within the 30–day limit, you should *immediately* write to the court and ask for additional time up to 30 days. If additional time is granted, you must file your reasons why the court should not affirm or dismiss your appeal before your additional time expires.

4) You do not have a right to another attorney unless this court finds that your showing requires that your case be further briefed or argued. If the court finds that your case should be further briefed or argued, an attorney will be appointed for you who will argue your appeal.

If you want to write to this court, you should address your letter to:

Clerk of the Court
United States Court of Appeals
219 South Dearborn Street
Chicago, Illinois 60604

Be sure, when writing, to show clearly the name and number of your case.

Notice mailed _____, 20___

_____
Deputy Clerk, U.S. Court of Appeals

Attorney for appellant
_____
(Name)
_____
(Street Address)
_____
(City, State, Zip Code)
_____
(Area Code and Telephone Number)

APPENDIX II. FORM OF NOTICE FOR MOTION FOR DISMISSAL UNDER CIRCUIT RULE 51(d)

To: _____

(Name)

_____

(Street Address or Prison Box)

_____

(City, State, Zip Code)

You are the appellant in a case now pending in this court:

Case No. _____

_____

v.

_____

A motion was filed by the opposing party on _____, 20___, which asks the court to dismiss your appeal. You have 30 days in which to answer the motion. Please be advised as follows:

1) You have a right to answer. You can either agree to the requested dismissal or object to the motion.

2) If you object, you should explain your objections carefully and show why you contend the court should hear your case.

3) If you agree that your case should be dismissed, you should write the court immediately that you agree.

4) If you do not respond within 30 days after this notice was mailed, the court may affirm or dismiss your appeal. An affirmance or dismissal would mean that your case would be finally decided against you.

5) If you want to file objections and feel that there is a very good reason why you will not be able to file your objections with the court within the 30–day limit, you should *immediately* write to the court and ask for additional time up to 30 days. If additional time is granted, you must file your objections before your additional time expires.

6) If you are appealing from a conviction and upon receiving notice of motion for dismissal of your appeal you desire an attorney, you should immediately

    (a) employ an attorney if you can afford one; or

    (b) request this court to appoint an attorney for you if you cannot afford one.

The court will appoint an attorney if it concludes that your appeal is not frivolous.

If you want to write to this court, you should address your letter to:

Clerk of the Court

United States Court of Appeals

219 South Dearborn Street

Chicago, Illinois 60604

Be sure, when writing, to show clearly the name and number of your case.

Notice mailed _____, 20____.

_____

Deputy Clerk, U.S. Court of Appeals

Attorney for appellant

_____

(Name)

_____

(Street Address)

_____

(City, State, Zip Code)

_____

(Area Code and Telephone Number)

APPENDIX III. FORM OF ACKNOWLEDGMENT OF ATTORNEY'S MOTION FOR DISMISSAL AND CONSENT TO THE DISMISSAL OF THE APPEAL

Case No. _____

_____

v.

_____

To: Clerk of the Court
      United States Court of Appeals
      219 South Dearborn Street
      Chicago, Illinois 60604

I have been informed of my attorney's intention to move to dismiss my appeal.

I concur in my attorney's decision and hereby waive all rights to object or raise any points on appeal.

_____
(Name)

_____
(Street Address or Prison Box)

_____
(City, State, Zip Code)

OPERATING PROCEDURES

INTRODUCTION

These are procedures for the court's internal operations. The court may dispense with their use in particular cases. Litigants acquire no rights under these procedures.

IOP 1. MOTIONS

(a) Number of Judges Necessary to Determine Motions.

(1) *Ordinary Practice.* At least two judges shall act on requests for bail, denials of certificates of appealability, and denials of leave to proceed on appeal in forma pauperis. Ordinarily three judges shall act to dismiss or otherwise finally determine an appeal or other proceeding, unless the dismissal is by stipulation or is for procedural reasons. Three judges shall also act to deny a motion to expedite an appeal when the denial may result in the mooting of the appeal. All other motions shall be entertained by a single judge in accordance with the practice set forth in paragraph (c). In the interest of expediting a decision or for other good cause, a fewer number of judges than provided in these procedures may decide any motion.

(2) *En Banc Requests.* If en banc consideration of a motion is requested, no more than the normal number of judges required for such a motion need act on it. If en banc reconsideration of the decision on a motion is requested, the motion will be considered by the same judge or judges who acted on the motion originally and, if and to the extent necessary to constitute a panel of three, one or more members of the motions panel. A judge may request that any motion be considered by the court en banc.

(b) Selection of Judges to Determine Motions.

The responsibility to handle motions shall be rotated among the judges. If a single judge to whom a motion is presented orders a response, the motion and response will ordinarily be presented to the same judge for ruling.

(c) Motion Practice.

(1) *Motions That May Require Immediate Action.* A staff attorney will read upon filing the following motions (whether labeled emergency or not): (i) for bond; (ii) for injunction; (iii) for stay of injunction; (iv) for stay of an agency order; (v) to dismiss appeals not by agreement; (vi) for leave to appeal from an interlocutory order pursuant to 28 U.S.C. § 1292(b); (vii) to stay or recall the mandate; (viii) to supplement the record; and (ix) all other emergency motions. If the motion requires immediate action, it will be taken to the motions judge and, if necessary, a panel. If it does not require immediate action, the staff attorney will wait up to fourteen days for a response to be filed before taking the motion to the motions judge or panel.

(2) *Routine Motions.* Routine motions (see subparagraph (7)) will be given to court staff who will read the motion and any affidavit in support thereof as well as any response to the motion. The designated staff member is then authorized, acting pursuant to such general directions and criteria as the court prescribes, to prepare an order in the name of the court either granting or denying the motion or requesting a response to the motion. If the designated staff member has any questions about what action should be taken, the motions judge will be consulted. Once a panel has been assigned for the oral argument or submission of an appeal, or after an appeal has actually been orally argued or submitted for decision without oral argument, the court staff should consult the presiding judge on motions that would otherwise be considered routine.

(3) *Nonroutine Motions.* A staff attorney shall read each nonroutine motion (see subparagraph (7)) and then present it to the motions judge and, if necessary, the motions panel. The judge or panel will then advise the staff attorney as to the decision and direct that an order be prepared accordingly. The staff attorney will then prepare the order. If the order states detailed reasons for the decision, the staff attorney will take the original of the order to the motions judge or one of the judges on the motions panel to read and approve. The same procedure will be followed whenever a judge asks to see the prepared order before it is released.

(4) *Duties of Clerk of Court.* When an order is in final form and ready for release, copies of the order will be reproduced and mailed to the litigants and to any other persons who are affected by the order, such as the district court clerk, the district judge, the United States Marshal, *et al.* The clerk will make certain that the language of the order is technically proper.

(5) *Automatic Reconsideration When Response Filed After Ruling.* If a response to a motion is properly filed after the court has ruled on the motion adversely to the respondent, the motion and response will be reconsidered and a new order stating this fact and ruling on the motion shall be issued.

(6) *Record Keeping.* The clerk shall keep a record of all orders by date of entry and also place a copy of each order in the file folder of the appeal.

(7) *Classification of Motions and Actions by Court.* Motions and actions of the court are classified for purposes of this paragraph as follows:

Type	Classification
To extend time or to file instanter	Routine
To consolidate appeals	Routine
To hold briefing in abeyance	Routine
To expedite or schedule briefing (But see 1(a) supra.)	Routine
To intervene as of right	Routine
To withdraw exhibits for preparation of a brief by counsel of record or party appearing pro se prior to case being scheduled for oral argument	Routine
To listen to tapes of oral argument under supervision of the clerk's office	Routine
To withdraw as counsel in criminal cases when other counsel has filed or is simultaneously filing an appearance	Routine
To withdraw as counsel in civil cases	Routine
To correct error in the caption of a case	Routine
To withdraw a previously filed motion before the court has acted upon it	Routine
To file a deferred appendix (generally denied)	Routine
To dismiss by agreement (except in cases to which panels have already been assigned)	Routine
To supplement record (if no objection)	Routine
(with an item before district court)	Routine
(with item not clearly before district court)	Routine
(to deny with leave to renew after moving to correct record in district court pursuant to Fed. R. App. P.10(e))	Routine
For leave to appeal in forma pauperis (if denied without prejudice to renewal after district court denial)	Routine
(if denied for any other reason)	Nonroutine
(if granted)	Nonroutine
For leave to file brief amicus curiae	Nonroutine
For leave to file oversized brief	Nonroutine
To stay or recall mandate	Nonroutine
For appointment of counsel	Nonroutine
To postpone oral argument	Nonroutine
For certificate of appealability (if denied)	Nonroutine
(if granted)	Nonroutine
For leave to commence second or successive collateral attack	Nonroutine
To dismiss, not by agreement	Nonroutine
For bond, injunction, or stay of injunction	Nonroutine
To reconsider any order of court (other than pursuant to subparagraph (5))	Nonroutine
For leave to appeal from interlocutory order, pursuant to 28 U.S.C. § 1292(b)	Nonroutine
All other motions	Nonroutine

The following actions by the court shall be handled similarly to the stated procedures for routine or nonroutine motions:

Issuance of orders to show cause pursuant to Circuit Rule 31(c) and (d)	Routine
Discharge of rules to show cause under Fed. R. App.P. 31(c) and Circuit Rule 31(c) and (d) (granting discharge)	Routine
(denying discharge)	Nonroutine

Type	Classification
Orders pursuant to Fed. R. App. P. 34	Nonroutine

(8) The clerk is authorized to reject repetitious motions to reconsider.

[Amended effective December 1, 2009.]

IOP 2.   TITLES AND PRECEDENCE OF JUDGES

(a) Except to the extent required by law, the court does not distinguish between judges in regular active service and senior judges with respect to title, precedence, and eligibility to participate in the court's decisions.

(b) Judges hold precedence in this sequence for the purpose of presiding at a session of the court: (1) Circuit Justice; (2) the Chief Judge of the circuit; (3) the judge of this circuit in regular active service with the greatest seniority according to the terms of 28 U.S.C. § 45(b). Every panel includes at least one circuit judge in regular active service, so no further provision for the selection of a presiding judge is necessary.

(c) Subject to part (b) of this rule, judges have precedence and are listed on opinions in the following order: (1) Circuit Justice; (2) Chief Judge of the circuit; (3) Associate Justice (Retired); (4) Circuit Judges by seniority of commission (without distinction between judges of this and other circuits); (5) District Judges by seniority of commission.

(d) Clerk's office personnel will ensure that all orders and opinions comply with this rule. The Clerk's office also will ensure that the description of the panel is consistent and conforms to the appropriate model: "X, Chief Judge, and Y and Z, Circuit Judges"; "X, Y, and Z, Circuit Judges"; "X and Y, Circuit Judges, and Z, District Judge."

IOP 3.   ISSUANCE OF OPINIONS

(a) When an opinion is ready for release, the author will send the opinion (together with any concurring or dissenting opinions) to the printer immediately.

(b) The Clerk's office will provide each writing judge with page proofs of the opinion. Each judge will review the proofs promptly. If within three business days the Clerk's office has not received a response, the Clerk will call to inquire about the status of the opinion.

(c) The Clerk's office will release the opinion immediately after receipt of the printed copies, unless the writing judge has asked the clerk to delay release to permit the judge to check the corrected proofs against the printed opinion.

IOP 4.   INCLUSION OF COSTS [ABROGATED]

[Abrogated effective October 22, 1996]

IOP 5.   HEARINGS AND REHEARINGS EN BANC

(a) **Request for Answer and Subsequent Request for Vote.** If a petition for rehearing en banc is filed, a request for an answer (which may be made by any Seventh Circuit judge in regular active service or by any member of the panel that rendered the decision sought to be reheard) must be made within 14 days after the electronic filing of the en banc petition. If an answer is requested, the clerk shall notify the prevailing party that an answer be filed within 14 days from the date of the court's request. Within 10 days of the electronic filing of the answer, any judge entitled to request an answer, may request a vote on the petition for rehearing en banc.

(b) **Request for Vote When No Answer Requested.** Ordinarily an answer will be requested prior to a request for a vote. A request for a vote on the petition (which may be made by any judge entitled to request an answer) must be made within 14 days from the electronic filing of the petition. If a vote is so requested, the clerk shall notify the prevailing party that an answer to the petition is due within 14 days.

(c) **Notification to File Answer.** The judge who requests an answer pursuant to paragraph (a) or who requests a vote pursuant to paragraph (b) shall be responsible for having the clerk notify the prevailing party to file an answer to the petition.

(d) **Voting.**

(1) *Majority.* A simple majority of the voting active judges is required to grant a rehearing en banc.

(2) *Time for Voting.* Judges are expected to vote within 14 days of the request for a vote or within 14 days of the filing of the answer pursuant to the request for a vote, whichever is later.

(e) **Preparation of Order.** After the vote is completed, the authoring judge, or the presiding judge of the panel if the author is a visiting judge, will prepare and send to the clerk an appropriate order. Minority positions will be noted in the denial of a petition for rehearing en banc or the denial of a petition for rehearing unless the judges in the minority request otherwise. Minority positions will not be noted in orders granting a rehearing or rehearing en banc unless so requested by the minority judge. An order granting rehearing en banc should specifically state that the original panel's decision is thereby vacated.

(f) Participants in Rehearings En Banc. Only Seventh Circuit active judges and any Seventh Circuit senior judge who was a member of the original panel may participate in rehearings en banc.

(g) Similar Procedures for Hearings En Banc. Similar voting procedures and time limits shall apply for requests for hearings en banc except that a staff attorney may circulate such a request.

(h) Distribution of Petitions. Petitions for rehearing that do not suggest rehearing en banc are distributed only to the panel. Petitions for rehearing en banc are distributed to all judges entitled to vote on the petition.

[Amended effective December 1, 2009.]

IOP 6. PANEL ASSIGNMENTS IN CERTAIN CASES

(a) Remands From the Supreme Court. A case remanded by the Supreme Court to this court for further proceedings will ordinarily be reassigned to the same panel that heard the case previously. If a member of that panel was a visiting judge and it is inconvenient for the visitor to participate further, that judge may be replaced by designation or by lot, as the chief judge directs.

(b) Successive Appeals. Briefs in a subsequent appeal in a case in which the court has heard an earlier appeal will be sent to the panel that heard the prior appeal. That panel will decide the successive appeal on the merits unless there is no overlap in the issues presented. When the subsequent appeal presents different issues but involves the same essential facts as the earlier appeal, the panel will decide the subsequent appeal unless it concludes that considerations of judicial economy do not support retaining the case. If the panel elects not to decide the new appeal, it will return the case for reassignment at random. If the original panel retains the successive appeal, it will notify the circuit executive whether oral argument is necessary. If oral argument is scheduled, any visiting judge will be replaced by a member of this court designated by lot. Cases that have been heard by the court en banc are outside the scope of this procedure, and successive appeals will be assigned at random unless the en banc court directs otherwise.

(c) Successive Collateral Attacks. An application for leave to file a second or successive petition under 28 U.S.C. § 2254 or § 2255 (see also 28 U.S.C. § 2244(b) and Circuit Rule 22.2) will be assigned to the panel that heard the prior appeal. If there was no appeal in the prior case, the application will be assigned to the current motions panel.

(d) Certain Cases Before Motion Panels. When a motion panel decides that a motion or petition should be set for oral argument or the appeal expedited, it may recommend to the chief judge that the matter be assigned for argument and decision to the same panel. In the absence of such a recommendation, the matter will ordinarily be assigned in the same manner as other appeals.

IOP 7. ROUTINE ACTION BY THE CLERK

(a) Dismissal for Failure to Prosecute. Statutes and rules of court call for the parties to take specified steps at particular times, and the court treats failure to take some of these steps as failure to prosecute, leading to dismissal. Failure to pay the docket fee, failure to file the docketing statement required by Circuit Rule 3(c), and failure by the appellant or petitioner to file a brief, amount to abandonment of the appeal.

(1) Seven days after the docket fee, docketing statement, or brief is due, the Clerk will send a notice, by certified mail, reminding the party of the obligation. The notice will inform the party about the consequence of continued delay in satisfying the obligation.

(2) If the party or counsel does not respond within 21 days of the date of the notice, the Clerk will enter an order dismissing the appeal for want of prosecution. In a criminal appeal with appointed counsel, however, the Clerk will not dismiss the appeal but will instead discharge the lawyer and appoint new counsel. When counsel is discharged under this procedure, the Clerk also will enter an order requiring the lawyer to show cause why abandonment of the client should not lead to disbarment.

(3) If the party responds within 21 days but does not comply with the obligation, or if the Clerk has not received a receipt showing delivery of the notice, a staff attorney will present the papers to the motions panel for decision.

(b) Removal From the List of Attorneys Authorized to Practice. States within the jurisdiction of this circuit send the court lists of attorneys who have been suspended from practice, disbarred, or resigned to prevent consideration of a pending ethical complaint. As a rule, these attorneys have had ample opportunity to contest that adverse action and do not oppose parallel action by other jurisdictions, leading to routine handling in this court.

(1) Promptly after learning that a member of this court's bar has been suspended for a year or more, has been disbarred, or has resigned from the bar of a jurisdiction in which the attorney is authorized to practice, the Clerk will send a notice, by certified mail, directing the lawyer to explain within 30 days why this court should not strike him from the roll of attorneys authorized to practice.

(2) If the lawyer does not respond within 30 days, or if the lawyer consents to the proposed disposition, the Clerk will enter an order removing the lawyer

from the roll of attorneys authorized to practice in this court.

(3) If the lawyer responds within 30 days but does not consent to the proposed disposition, or if within that time the Clerk has not received a receipt showing delivery of the notice, a staff attorney will present the papers to the motions panel for decision.

(c) **Review of the Clerk's Action.** A petition for rehearing contesting the entry of a routine order under this operating procedure will be treated as a motion and referred to the motions panel. An order by the motions panel permitting the appeal to continue has the effect of reinstating the appeal, and the Clerk will reset the briefing schedule accordingly.

IOP 8. MULTIPLE APPEALS

When multiple parties to the same case have taken appeals, the court's senior staff attorney will review the docketing statements filed under Circuit Rule 3 and issue a scheduling order governing the filing of briefs.

When multiple appellants have the same or a closely related interest in the appeal, the senior staff attorney ordinarily will provide for the filing of a joint opening brief, with provision in appropriate cases for separate individual briefs to present points that do not concern all appellants. When the parties have filed cross appeals, the scheduling order usually will call on the party principally aggrieved by the judgment to file the opening brief. For example, when the judgment holds the defendant liable and the plaintiff's cross appeal concerns the amount of damages or an award of attorney's fees, the defendant normally will file the opening brief.

IOP 9. PRESUMPTIVE TIMES FOR ACTION

Expeditious preparation and release of opinions and orders is important not only to litigants ("Justice delayed is justice denied") but also to the operation of the court. Delay in the preparation of or response to opinions means that other judges must reread the briefs and re-study the record in order to act conscientiously on their colleagues' drafts. Dispatch in circulating drafts and responding to a colleague's circulations therefore reduces duplicative work and improves the quality of justice. With these considerations in mind, the court establishes the following presumptive times for action, anticipating that in most cases judges will take less time but understanding that circumstances may make it imprudent to adhere to these norms mechanically. Every judge should, and may, take the time required for adequate study and reflection.

(a) A judge assigned to write a draft after a case has been identified at conference as suitable for dispo-

sition by a brief unpublished order should circulate the draft to the other members of the panel within 21 days of the date the case was argued or submitted.

(b) A judge assigned to write a published opinion should circulate the draft to the other members of the panel within 90 days of the date the case was argued or submitted. When the case is unusually complex, extended research is required, or other special circumstances apply, however, the writing judge may extend this time to 180 days by giving appropriate notice to the other members of the panel.

(c) Responding to drafts circulated by other judges is the first order of business. Every judge should respond by approval, memorandum suggesting changes, or notice that a separate opinion is under active consideration within 14 days of the circulation of a draft.

(d) As a rule, writing separate concurring or dissenting opinions takes precedence over all business other than initial responses to newly circulated drafts. Separate opinions should be circulated to the panel within 28 days after the initial response described in part (c) of this procedure.

(e) Once the opinion has issued, judges should act promptly on any further motions. In particular, members of the panel should vote within 14 days on any petition for rehearing. Under Operating Procedure 5, judges have 14 days to request a response to a petition for rehearing en banc, and 14 days to call for a vote on the petition once the response has been received. Once a judge has called for a vote, all other judges should register their votes within 14 days. Once this time (including extensions described below) has passed, and sufficient votes have been received to grant or deny the petition for rehearing or petition for rehearing en banc, the court will enter an order to that effect without waiting for additional responses.

(f) Each judge should establish a tickler system designed to ensure adherence to these norms. When one chambers does not receive a draft, vote or response within the time presumptively established, secretaries or law clerks should inquire. This step not only catches communications lost in transmission but also serves as a backup reminder system.

(g) A judge who believes that additional time is required to permit full consideration should notify the other members of the panel to that effect. If the judge believes that more than 30 days (in the case of opinions) or 14 days (in the case of other actions), in addition to the time presumptively established by this procedure, is essential, the judge also should notify the chief judge of the delay and the reasons for it.

(h) The presiding judge of a panel should reassign the case if the judge initially assigned to draft the order or opinion has not circulated the draft within the time provided by parts (a) and (b) of this procedure, plus the extra time allowed by part (g), unless in consultation with the assigned author and the chief judge the presiding judge decides that reassignment would delay disposition still further.

(i) If two members of the panel have agreed on an opinion, and the third member does not respond within the time provided by part (c), or does not complete a separate opinion within the time presumptively established by parts (d) and (g), the writing judge should inquire of the third member whether a response is imminent. If further delay is anticipated, the majority should issue the opinion with a notation that the third judge reserves the right to file a separate opinion later.

(j) When the presumptive time for action established by this procedure is 14 days, the time may be extended on notice that a judge is unavailable to act on judicial business. The time specified by this notice is added to the time presumptively established by this procedure.

[Amended effective December 1, 2009.]

IOP 10. SEALING PORTIONS OF THE RECORD

(a) Requirement of Judicial Approval. Except to the extent portions of the record are required to be sealed by statute (e.g., 18 U.S.C. § 3509(d)) or a rule of procedure (e.g., Fed. R. Crim. P. 6(e), Circuit Rule 26.1(b)), every document filed in or by this court (whether or not the document was sealed in the district court) is in the public record unless a judge of this court orders it to be sealed.

(b) Delay in Disclosure. Documents sealed in the district court will be maintained under seal in this court for 14 days, to afford time to request the approval required by section (a) of this procedure.

THE PLAN OF THE UNITED STATES COURT OF APPEALS FOR THE SEVENTH CIRCUIT TO SUPPLEMENT THE PLANS OF THE SEVERAL UNITED STATES DISTRICT COURTS WITHIN THE SEVENTH CIRCUIT

INTRODUCTION

Pursuant to the approval of the Judicial Council of the Seventh Circuit, the United States Court of Appeals for the Seventh Circuit adopts the following Plan for furnishing representation for persons financially unable to obtain adequate representation in the cases and situations defined in the Criminal Justice Act of 1964, as amended, 18 U.S.C. § 3006A ("Act"), and 21 U.S.C. § 848(q), and the *Guidelines for the Administration of the Criminal Justice Act*, Volume VII, *Guide to Judiciary Policies and Procedures* ("CJA Guidelines"). This Plan supplements the plans heretofore adopted by the several United States District Courts within the Seventh Circuit and approved in final form by the Judicial Council of the Seventh Circuit.

Representation shall include counsel and investigative, expert, and other services necessary for an adequate defense.

I. STATEMENT OF POLICY

The Judicial Council recognizes that the successful operation of this plan will require the active and continual cooperation of members of the bar, appropriate bar associations and legal aid agencies. In particular, it is expected that the advice and assistance of the Seventh Circuit Bar Association will contribute greatly to the successful working of this Plan.

The judges, circuit executive, clerk, all federal public defender organizations and community defender organizations, and private attorneys appointed under the CJA should comply with the *CJA Guidelines* approved by the Judicial Conference of the United States and/or its Committee on Defender Services and with the Plan.

The payment of compensation to counsel under the Act, in most cases, probably will be something less than compensatory. Service of counsel by appointment under the Act will continue to require a substantial measure of dedication and public service. The responsibility of members of the bar to accept appointments and to serve in these cases is the same as it traditionally has been in the past and is in no way lessened by the passage of the Act. We have complete confidence in the professional integrity of the bar to fulfill this responsibility.

In the administration of this Plan, the Court will be particularly careful to safeguard against the opportunity for any charges of fiscal laxity, favoritism or other abuse which may cast a shadow on the general judicial system. The public funds involved will be expended with characteristic judicial responsibility.

It is deemed advisable at all times to coordinate efficiently the operation of this Plan with the several state courts to the end that there be a proper cooperation between the federal and state judicial systems.

The Court will welcome any proper and approved plan of cooperation whereby the services of advanced law school students may be made available to provide legal research assistance to appointed counsel, thereby to furnish such assistance to appointed counsel who may find it helpful and to broaden the interest and capabilities of law school students in the field of criminal law.

Finally, and most important, the Plan shall be administered so that those accused of crime will not, because they are financially unable to pay for adequate representation, be deprived of any element of representation necessary to enable them to have a fair opportunity to be heard on appeal in this Court.

II. PREPARATION OF PANEL OF ATTORNEYS

1. The Clerk of this Court, under the direction and supervision and with approval of the Court, shall forthwith prepare and maintain a panel of practicing attorneys, or attorneys from a bar association, legal aid agency, or defender organization furnishing representation pursuant to the Plan, in areas of the principal places of holding district court within the Seventh Circuit, who are deemed competent to provide adequate representation on appeal for persons qualifying under the Act. The Clerk of this Court shall reexamine the panel of attorneys annually to assure that it is kept current at all times.

2. Attorneys for the panel shall be selected without regard to race, color, creed, or membership in any organized bar association.

3. The Clerk shall solicit the assistance of the Seventh Circuit Bar Association, law schools, and any other appropriate bar association, in the preparation and maintenance of the panel of attorneys.

4. Additions to and removals from the panel of attorneys may be made at any time by the Court or any active member thereof.

5. The clerk of court shall provide each appointed attorney a copy of this Plan upon the attorney's first appointment under the CJA or designation as a mem-

ber of the panel and shall also make available to them a current copy of the *Guidelines*.

III. DETERMINATION OF NEED FOR APPOINTMENT OF COUNSEL

1. In all cases where the defendant was found by the district court to be financially unable to obtain adequate representation, the Court may accept this finding and appoint an attorney without further proof. *But see* Fed. R. App. P. 24(a).

2. At any time before or after the appointment of counsel, the Court may examine or reexamine the financial status of the defendant. If the Court finds upon such inquiry that the defendant is financially able to employ counsel or make partial payment for his representation, then the Court may make an order appropriate under the circumstances denying or terminating such appointment pursuant to subsection (c) of the Act, or requiring such partial payment to be made pursuant to subsection (f) of the Act, as the interests of justice may dictate.

3. In determining the need for appointment of counsel under the Act, the Courts shall not be governed by a requirement of indigence on the part of the defendant, but rather by his financial inability to employ counsel, in harmony with Congressional intent in formulating this program of assistance to those found to be in need within the spirit and purpose of the Act.

IV. APPOINTMENT OF COUNSEL

1. Counsel furnishing representation under the Plan shall be selected from a panel of attorneys designated or approved by the Court, or from a bar association, legal aid agency, or defender organization furnishing representation pursuant to the Plan. When the Court determines that the appointment of an attorney who is not a member of the panel is in the interest of justice, judicial economy, or continuity of representation, or there is some other exceptional circumstance warranting his or her appointment, the attorney may be admitted to the panel and appointed to represent the individual. Agreeable with the directives of the Judicial Conference of the United States, at least 25% of all such appointments shall be assigned to members of the private bar. Such order of appointment of counsel may be entered by the current motion judge or by any active member of the Court.

2. In all cases on appeal where the defendant was represented in the district court by court appointed counsel, such counsel shall continue to represent the defendant on appeal, unless and until relieved by order of this Court. The Court may, in appropriate cases, designate such counsel to continue on appeal.

3. At the time such appeals are docketed in this Court, the Clerk shall notify defendant's court appointed trial counsel that he shall continue such representation of defendant in this Court unless and until relieved by order of this Court, and shall request such trial counsel to advise the Court whether he desires to continue such representation throughout the appeal.

4. In appeals under the Act involving more than one defendant, if the Court finds the need, because of conflicting interests of certain defendants or where circumstances otherwise warrant, separate counsel may be appointed for any one or more of the defendants as may be required for their adequate representation.

5. The Court may, in its discretion, at any stage of the proceedings on appeal, substitute one appointed attorney for another.

6. If, at any stage of the proceedings on appeal, the Court finds the defendant is financially unable to pay counsel whom he has retained, the Court may appoint counsel as provided in subsection (b) of the Act and authorize payment as provided in subsection (d) of the Act and the *CJA Guidelines*, pursuant to subsection (c) of the Act.

7. More than one attorney may be appointed in any case determined by the Court to be extremely difficult. In a capital case, at least two attorneys should be appointed. Except as provided by section 848(q)(7) of title 21, U.S.C., at least one attorney appointed in a capital case shall meet the experience qualifications required by section 848(q)(6) of title 21, U.S.C. Pursuant to section 848(q)(7), the presiding judicial officer, for good cause, may appoint an attorney who may not qualify under section 848(q)(6), but who has the background, knowledge, and experience necessary to represent the defendant properly in a capital case, giving due consideration to the seriousness of the possible penalty and to the unique and complex nature of the litigation.

8. The selection of counsel to represent any person under the Act shall remain the sole and exclusive responsibility of the Court.

V. DUTIES OF APPOINTED COUNSEL

1. The services to be rendered a defendant by counsel appointed under the Act shall be reasonably commensurate with those rendered if counsel were privately employed, having regard for the circumstances of each case and as the interests of justice may require.

2. If, at any stage of the proceedings on appeal, appointed counsel obtains information that a client is financially able to make payment, in whole or in part, for legal or other services in connection with his or her representation, and the source of the attorney's information is not protected as a privileged communication, counsel shall advise the Court.

3. After an adverse decision on appeal by this Court, appointed counsel shall advise the defendant in writing of his right to seek review of such decision by the Supreme Court of the United States. If, after consultation (by correspondence, or otherwise), the represented person requests it and there are reasonable grounds for counsel properly to do so, the appointed attorney must prepare and file a petition for writ of certiorari and other necessary and appropriate documents and must continue to represent the defendant until relieved by the Supreme Court. Counsel who conclude that reasonable grounds for filing a petition for writ of certiorari do not exist must promptly inform the defendant, who may by motion request this Court to direct counsel to seek certiorari.

4. Attorneys appointed pursuant to any provisions of the Act shall conform to the highest standards of professional conduct, including but not limited to the provisions of the American Bar Association's Model Rules of Professional Conduct.

5. Appointed appellate attorneys have a duty to continue to represent their clients after remand to the district court. An attorney appointed for the appeal who is unable to continue at the trial level should move in the district court for withdrawal and appointment of trial counsel.

6. Attorneys appointed in a federal death penalty case, unless replaced by similarly qualified counsel upon the attorney's own motion or upon motion of the defendant, shall represent the defendant throughout every stage of the available judicial proceedings, including all available post-conviction process, together with applications for stays of execution and other appropriate motions and procedures, and shall also represent the defendant in proceedings for executive or other clemency as may be available to the defendant.

VI. PAYMENT OF CLAIMS FOR COMPENSATION AND EXPENSES

1. An attorney, bar association, legal aid agency, or community defender organization appointed by the Court pursuant to the Plan shall be compensated for their services and reimbursed for their expenses reasonably incurred within the limitations and subject to the conditions of subsection (d) of the Act.

2. The hourly rates of compensation fixed by the Act are designated and intended to be maximum rates only and shall be treated as such.

3. No appointed representative under the Plan shall accept a payment from or on behalf of the person represented in this Court without prior authorization by a United States circuit judge on the form provided for such purpose. All such authorized payments shall be received subject to the directions contained in such

order and pursuant to the provisions of subsection (f) of the Act.

4. Each appointed representative under the Plan shall be entitled to reimbursement for expenses reasonably incurred for travel and out-of-pocket expenditures. Travel by privately owned automobile should be claimed at the rate per mile set forth in the *Travel and Transportation* regulations, Volume I, *Guide to Judiciary Policies and Procedures*, plus parking fees and tolls. Transportation other than by privately owned automobile should be claimed on an actual cost basis. Per diem in lieu of subsistence is not allowable. Meals and lodging expenses, which are reasonably incurred based upon the prevailing limitations placed upon travel and subsistence expenses of federal judiciary employees in accordance with existing travel regulations, as well as telephone toll calls, telegrams and copying (except printing), are reimbursable. Non-reimbursable items include general office overhead, personal items for the person represented, filing fees, and printing. (A person represented under the Act is not required to pay filing fees.)

5. An appointed attorney or other authorized legal entity shall not incur any expense subject to claim for reimbursement in excess of $300 except for necessary travel and maintenance to and from this Court for hearing on oral argument, without prior Court approval. In the event it is deemed necessary to provide an appendix of the record on appeal of more than 50 pages, they shall first petition the Court for authority to incur such expense and obtain approval therefor.

6. All claims for compensation and reimbursement for expenses reasonably incurred shall be itemized and prepared on prescribed forms and filed with the Clerk of this Court. All such claims should be filed promptly and in any event not more than 30 days after the conclusion of such services.

7. A panel of judges hearing an appeal, or any active member of the Court if designated by such panel, shall, in each instance, fix the compensation and allow the reimbursement for expenses to be paid to the appointed representative as provided in the Act. After such approval, the Clerk of this Court shall forthwith forward such claims to the Director of the Administrative Office of the United States Courts for payment.

8. Counsel's time and expenses involved in the preparation of a petition for a writ of certiorari shall be considered as applicable to the case before this Court, and should be vouchered as such.

VII. MISCELLANEOUS

1. The United States Court of Appeals shall submit a report of the appointment of counsel to the Administrative Office of the United States Courts in such form and at such times as the Judicial Confer-

ence of the United States may direct, and otherwise comply with such rules, regulations, and guidelines governing the operation of Plans formulated by the Judicial Conference of the United States, pursuant to subsection (h) of the Act.

2. Where standard forms have been prescribed and distributed by the Director of the Administrative Office of the United States Courts, such forms shall be used, where applicable, in all proceedings under this Plan.

3. Amendments to the Plan may be made from time to time by the Judicial Council of this circuit, and such amendments shall be forwarded immediately to the Administrative Office of the United States Courts.

VIII. EFFECTIVE DATE

This Plan shall become effective January 1, 1991. Approved and adopted by the Seventh Circuit Judicial Council on December 3, 1990. As amended January 1, 1996.

STANDARDS FOR PROFESSIONAL CONDUCT WITHIN THE SEVENTH FEDERAL JUDICIAL CIRCUIT

Adopted December 14, 1992

Preamble

A lawyer's conduct should be characterized at all times by personal courtesy and professional integrity in the fullest sense of those terms. In fulfilling our duty to represent a client vigorously as lawyers, we will be mindful of our obligations to the administration of justice, which is a truth-seeking process designed to resolve human and societal problems in a rational, peaceful, and efficient manner.

A judge's conduct should be characterized at all times by courtesy and patience toward all participants. As judges we owe to all participants in a legal proceeding respect, diligence, punctuality, and protection against unjust and improper criticism or attack.

Conduct that may be characterized as uncivil, abrasive, abusive, hostile, or obstructive impedes the fundamental goal of resolving disputes rationally, peacefully, and efficiently. Such conduct tends to delay and often to deny justice.

The following standards are designed to encourage us, judges and lawyers, to meet our obligations to each other, to litigants and to the system of justice, and thereby achieve the twin goals of civility and professionalism, both of which are hallmarks of a learned profession dedicated to public service.

We expect judges and lawyers will make a mutual and firm commitment to these standards. Voluntary adherence is expected as part of a commitment by all participants to improve the administration of justice throughout this Circuit.

These standards shall not be used as a basis for litigation or for sanctions or penalties. Nothing in these standards supersedes or detracts from existing disciplinary codes or alters existing standards of conduct against which lawyer negligence may be determined.

These standards should be reviewed and followed by all judges and lawyers participating in any proceeding, in this Circuit. Copies may be made available to clients to reinforce our obligation to maintain and foster these standards.

LAWYERS' DUTIES TO OTHER COUNSEL

1. We will practice our profession with a continuing awareness that our role is to advance the legitimate interests of our clients. In our dealings with others we will not reflect the ill feelings of our clients. We will treat all other counsel, parties, and witnesses in a civil and courteous manner, not only in court, but also in all other written and oral communications.

2. We will not, even when called upon by a client to do so, abuse or indulge in offensive conduct directed to other counsel, parties, or witnesses. We will abstain from disparaging personal remarks or acrimony toward other counsel, parties, or witnesses. We will treat adverse witnesses and parties with fair consideration.

3. We will not encourage or knowingly authorize any person under our control to engage in conduct that would be improper if we were to engage in such conduct.

4. We will not, absent good cause, attribute bad motives or improper conduct to other counsel or bring the profession into disrepute by unfounded accusations of impropriety.

5. We will not seek court sanctions without first conducting a reasonable investigation and unless fully justified by the circumstances and necessary to protect our client's lawful interests.

6. We will adhere to all express promises and to agreements with other counsel, whether oral or in writing, and will adhere in good faith to all agreements implied by the circumstances or local customs.

7. When we reach an oral understanding on a proposed agreement or a stipulation and decide to commit it to writing, the drafter will endeavor in good faith to state the oral understanding accurately and completely. The drafter will provide the opportunity for review of the writing to other counsel. As drafts are exchanged between or among counsel, changes from prior drafts will be identified in the draft or otherwise explicitly brought to the attention of other counsel. We will not include in a draft matters to which there has been no agreement without explicitly advising other counsel in writing of the addition.

8. We will endeavor to confer early with other counsel to assess settlement possibilities. We will not falsely hold out the possibility of settlement as a means to adjourn discovery or to delay trial.

9. In civil actions, we will stipulate to relevant matters if they are undisputed and if no good faith advocacy basis exists for not stipulating.

10. We will not use any form of discovery or discovery scheduling as a means of harassment.

11. We will make good faith efforts to resolve by agreement our objections to matters contained in pleadings and discovery requests and objections.

12. We will not time the filing or service of motions or pleadings in any way that unfairly limits another party's opportunity to respond.

13. We will not request an extension of time solely for the purpose of unjustified delay or to obtain a tactical advantage.

14. We will consult other counsel regarding scheduling matters in a good faith effort to avoid scheduling conflicts.

15. We will endeavor to accommodate previously scheduled dates for hearings, depositions, meetings, conferences, vacations, seminars, or other functions that produce good faith calendar conflicts on the part of other counsel. If we have been given an accommodation because of a calendar conflict, we will notify those who have accommodated us as soon as the conflict has been removed.

16. We will notify other counsel and, if appropriate, the court or other persons, at the earliest possible time when hearings, depositions, meetings, or conferences are to be canceled or postponed. Early notice avoids unnecessary travel and expense of counsel and may enable the court to use the previously reserved time for other matters.

17. We will agree to reasonable requests for extensions of time and for waiver of procedural formalities, provided our clients' legitimate rights will not be materially or adversely affected.

18. We will not cause any default or dismissal to be entered without first notifying opposing counsel, when we know his or her identity.

19. We will take depositions only when actually needed to ascertain facts or information or to perpetuate testimony. We will not take depositions for the purposes of harassment or to increase litigation expenses.

20. We will not engage in any conduct during a deposition that would not be appropriate in the presence of a judge.

21. We will not obstruct questioning during a deposition or object to deposition questions unless necessary under the applicable rules to preserve an objection or privilege for resolution by the court.

22. During depositions we will ask only those questions we reasonably believe are necessary for the prosecution or defense of an action.

23. We will carefully craft document production requests so they are limited to those documents we reasonably believe are necessary for the prosecution or defense of an action. We will not design production requests to place an undue burden or expense on a party.

24. We will respond to document requests reasonably and not strain to interpret the request in an artificially restrictive manner to avoid disclosure of relevant and non-privileged documents. We will not produce documents in a manner designed to hide or obscure the existence of particular documents.

25. We will carefully craft interrogatories so they are limited to those matters we reasonably believe are necessary for the prosecution or defense of an action, and we will not design them to place an expense or undue burden or expense on a party.

26. We will respond to interrogatories reasonably and will not strain to interpret them in an artificially restrictive manner to avoid disclosure of relevant and non-privileged information.

27. We will base our discovery objections on a good faith belief in their merit and will not object solely for the purpose of withholding or delaying the disclosure of relevant information.

28. When a draft order is to be prepared by counsel to reflect a court ruling, we will draft an order that accurately and completely reflects the court's ruling. We will promptly prepare and submit a proposed order to other counsel and attempt to reconcile any differences before the draft order is presented to the court.

29. We will not ascribe a position to another counsel that counsel has not taken or otherwise seek to create an unjustified inference based on counsel's statements or conduct.

30. Unless specifically permitted or invited by the court, we will not send copies of correspondence between counsel to the court.

LAWYERS' DUTIES TO THE COURT

1. We will speak and write civilly and respectfully in all communications with the court.

2. We will be punctual and prepared for all court appearances so that all hearings, conferences, and trials may commence on time; if delayed, we will notify the court and counsel, if possible.

3. We will be considerate of the time constraints and pressures on the court and court staff inherent in their efforts to administer justice.

4. We will not engage in any conduct that brings disorder or disruption to the courtroom. We will advise our clients and witnesses appearing in court of the proper conduct expected and required there and, to the best of our ability, prevent our clients and witnesses from creating disorder or disruption.

5. We will not knowingly misrepresent, mischaracterize, misquote, or miscite facts or authorities in any oral or written communication to the court.

6. We will not write letters to the court in connection with a pending action, unless invited or permitted by the court.

7. Before dates for hearings or trials are set, or if that is not feasible, immediately after such date has been set, we will attempt to verify the availability of necessary participants and witnesses so we can promptly notify the court of any likely problems.

8. We will act and speak civilly to court marshals, clerks, court reporters, secretaries, and law clerks with an awareness that they, too, are an integral part of the judicial system.

COURTS' DUTIES TO LAWYERS

1. We will be courteous, respectful, and civil to lawyers, parties, and witnesses. We will maintain control of the proceedings, recognizing that judges have both the obligation and the authority to insure that all litigation proceedings are conducted in a civil manner.

2. We will not employ hostile, demeaning, or humiliating words in opinions or in written or oral communications with lawyers, parties, or witnesses.

3. We will be punctual in convening all hearings, meetings, and conferences; if delayed, we will notify counsel, if possible.

4. In scheduling all hearings, meetings and conferences we will be considerate of time schedules of lawyers, parties, and witnesses.

5. We will make all reasonable efforts to decide promptly all matters presented to us for decision.

6. We will give the issues in controversy deliberate, impartial, and studied analysis and consideration.

7. While endeavoring to resolve disputes efficiently, we will be considerate of the time constraints and pressures imposed on lawyers by the exigencies of litigation practice.

8. We recognize that a lawyer has a right and a duty to present a cause fully and properly, and that a litigant has a right to a fair and impartial hearing. Within the practical limits of time, we will allow lawyers to present proper arguments and to make a complete and accurate record.

9. We will not impugn the integrity or professionalism of any lawyer on the basis of the clients whom or the causes which a lawyer represents.

10. We will do our best to insure that court personnel act civilly toward lawyers, parties, and witnesses.

11. We will not adopt procedures that needlessly increase litigation expense.

12. We will bring to lawyers' attention uncivil conduct which we observe.

JUDGES' DUTIES TO EACH OTHER

1. We will be courteous, respectful, and civil in opinions, ever mindful that a position articulated by another judge is the result of that judge's earnest effort to interpret the law and the facts correctly.

2. In all written and oral communications, we will be abstain from disparaging personal remarks or criticisms, or sarcastic or demeaning comments about another judge.

3. We will endeavor to work with other judges in an effort to foster a spirit of cooperation in our mutual goal of enhancing the administration of justice.

ELECTRONIC CASE FILING

(a) Scope of Electronic Filing.

(1) The court has adopted a Case Management/Electronic Case Filing (CM/ECF) system. The system enables the filing of documents submitted, signed or verified by electronic means that comply with procedures established by the court. Participation is mandatory for attorneys practicing in this court.

(2) Except as otherwise prescribed by local rule or order, all cases are assigned to the court's electronic filing system.

(3) Except as otherwise prescribed by local rule or court order, all briefs, appendices, motions, petitions for rehearing, and other documents filed in any case with the court by an Attorney Filing User registered as set forth under Circuit Rules/Electronic Case Filing (ECF) procedures, must be filed electronically using the electronic filing system.

(4) Paper copies are required for briefs, appendices and petitions for rehearing as provided in Paragraph (h)(2) of these procedures, but not for other pleadings unless specifically requested by the Court.

(5) Upon the court's request, an Attorney Filing User must promptly provide the Clerk, in a format designated by the court, an identical electronic version of any paper document previously filed in the same case by that Attorney Filing User.

(b) Eligibility, Registration, Passwords.

(1) Attorneys who intend to practice in this court, including those regularly admitted or admitted pro hac vice to the bar of the court and attorneys authorized to represent the United States without being admitted to the bar of this court, must register as Attorney Filing Users of the court's electronic filing system.

(2) Registration requirements are defined in the Electronic Case Filing (ECF) User Manual.

(3) Registration as an Attorney Filing User constitutes consent to electronic service of all documents as provided in these ECF Procedures and the Federal Rules of Appellate Procedure.

(4) Attorney Filing Users agree to protect the security of their passwords and immediately notify the PACER Service Center and the Clerk if they learn that their password has been compromised. Attorney Filing Users may be sanctioned for failure to comply with this provision.

(5) The court may terminate or sanction an Attorney Filing User's electronic filing privileges for abusing the system by an inordinate number of filings, filings of excessive size, or other failures to comply with the electronic filing procedures and standards.

(c) Implications of Electronic Filing.

(1) Electronic transmission of a document to the electronic filing system consistent with these procedures, together with the transmission of a Notice of Docket Activity from the court, constitutes filing of the document under the Federal Rules of Appellate Procedure and the local rules of this court, and constitutes entry of the document on the docket kept by the Clerk under Fed. R. App. P. 36 and 45(b).

(2) If the court requires a party to file a motion for leave to file, both the motion and document at issue should be submitted electronically. The underlying document should be tendered as an attachment to the motion and will be filed if the court so directs.

(3) Electronic documents must be in Portable Document Format (PDF). All documents must be generated by printing to PDF from the original word processing file, so that the text of the digital document is searchable. PDF images created by scanning paper documents are not searchable and may be used only for appendix or reference materials not available in PDF format.

(4) When a document has been filed electronically, the official record is the electronic document stored by the court, and the filing party is bound by the document as filed. Except in the case of documents first filed in paper form and subsequently submitted electronically under these procedures, a document filed electronically is deemed filed at the date and time stated on the Notice of Docket Activity from the court. Filing must be completed before midnight, Central Time, to be considered timely filed, unless otherwise ordered by the court.

(d) Service of Documents by Electronic Means.

(1) The Notice of Docket Activity that is generated by the court's electronic filing system constitutes service of the filed document on all Attorney Filing Users. Parties who are not Attorney Filing Users must be served with a copy of any document filed electronically in accordance with the Federal Rules of Appellate Procedure and the local rules. If the document is not available electronically, the filer must use an alternative method of service.

(2) The Notice of Docket Activity generated by the court's electronic filing system does not replace the certificate of service required by Fed. R. App. P. 25.

(e) Entry of Court–Issued Documents.

(1) Except as otherwise provided by local rule or court order, all orders, decrees, judgments, and proceedings of the court relating to cases filed and maintained in the CM/ECF system will be filed in accordance with these procedures, which will constitute

entry on the docket kept by the Clerk under Fed. R. App. P. 36 and 45(b).

(2) Any order or other court-issued document filed electronically without the original signature of a judge or authorized court personnel has the same force and effect as if a judge or the Clerk had signed a paper copy of the order.

(3) Orders also may be issued as "text-only" entries on the docket, without an attached document. Such orders are official and binding.

(f) Attachments and Exhibits to Motions and Original Proceedings.

(1) Attorney Filing Users must submit all documents referenced as exhibits or attachments in electronic form within any file size limits the Clerk may prescribe, as well as any paper copies the Clerk specifies. See ECF User Manual for specifics.

(2) An Attorney Filing User must submit as exhibits or attachments only those excerpts of the referenced documents that are directly germane to the matter under consideration by the court. Excerpted material must be clearly and prominently identified as such.

(3) The court may require parties to file additional excerpts or the complete document.

(g) Sealed Documents.

(1) A motion to file documents under seal must be filed electronically unless prohibited by law, local rule, or court order.

(2) Proposed sealed materials must be filed electronically by following the directions provided with the electronic filing system. Failure to follow these directions will result in public disclosure of sensitive material. Attorney Filing Users are responsible for ensuring that sealed materials are filed appropriately.

(3) If the court grants the motion, the order of the court authorizing the filing of documents under seal may be filed electronically unless prohibited by law.

(4) Documents ordered placed under seal may be filed traditionally in paper or electronically, as authorized by the court. If filed traditionally, a paper copy of the authorizing order must be attached to the documents under seal and delivered to the Clerk.

(h) Briefs, Appendices and Petitions for Rehearing.

(1) A brief, appendix and petition for rehearing (and any answer filed thereto) will be considered timely once it is submitted to the court's electronic filing system. It will be considered filed on the court's docket only after a review for compliance with applicable rules, acceptance by the Clerk, and issuance of a Notice of Docket Activity.

(2) Filers are also required to submit the necessary number of duplicate paper copies of briefs, appendices and petitions for rehearing, in accordance with Fed. R. App. P. 30(a)(3) and Circuit Rules 31(b) and 40(b). Duplicate paper copies must be received by the Clerk within seven days of the Notice of Docket Activity generated upon acceptance of the electronic brief or appendices. Duplicate paper copies of petitions for rehearing must be submitted within three days of the Notice of Docket Activity.

(i) Signatures.

(1) The user log-in and password required to submit documents to the electronic filing system serve as the Attorney Filing User's signature on all electronic documents filed with the court. They also serve as a signature for purposes of the Federal Rules of Appellate Procedure, the local rules of this court, and any other purpose for which a signature is required in connection with proceedings before this court.

(2) The name of the Attorney Filing User under whose log-in and password the document is submitted must be preceded by an "s/" and typed in the space where the signature would otherwise appear.

(3) No Attorney Filing User or other person may knowingly permit or cause to permit an Attorney Filing User's log-in and password to be used by anyone other than an authorized agent of the Attorney Filing User.

(4) Documents requiring signatures of more than one party must be electronically filed either by: (A) submitting a scanned document containing all necessary signatures; (B) representing the consent of the other parties on the document; (C) identifying on the document the parties whose signatures are required and submitting a notice of endorsement by the other parties no later than three business days after filing; or (D) in any other manner approved by the court.

(5) Electronically represented signatures of all parties and Attorney Filing Users as described above are presumed to be valid signatures. If any party, counsel of record, or Attorney Filing User objects to the representation of his or her signature on an electronic document as described above, he or she must, within 14 days, file a notice setting forth the basis of the objection.

(j) Notice of Court Orders and Judgments.

(1) Immediately upon the entry of an order or judgment in a case assigned to the electronic filing system, the Clerk will electronically transmit a Notice of Docket Activity to Attorney Filing Users in the case.

(2) Electronic transmission of the Notice of Docket Activity constitutes the notice and service of the opinion or order required by Fed. R. App. P. 36(b) and 45(c).

(3) The Clerk must give notice in paper form to a person who has not consented to electronic service in accordance with the Federal Rules of Appellate Procedure.

(k) Technical Failures. An Attorney Filing User whose filing is made untimely as the result of a technical failure may seek appropriate relief from the court by filing a motion.

(*l*) Public Access.

(1) Parties must refrain from including, or must partially redact where inclusion is necessary, the following personal data identifiers from all documents filed with the court, including exhibits thereto, whether filed electronically or in paper, unless otherwise ordered by the court:

(A) Social Security Numbers. If an individual's Social Security number must be included, only the last four digits of that number should be used.

(B) Names of Minor Children. If the involvement of a minor child must be mentioned, only the initials of that child should be used.

(C) Dates of Birth. If an individual's date of birth must be included, only the year should be used.

(D) Financial Account Numbers. If financial account numbers are relevant, only the last four digits of these numbers should be used.

(E) Home Addresses. In criminal cases, if a home address must be included, only the city and state should be listed.

(2) In compliance with the E–Government Act of 2002, a party wishing to file a document containing the personal data identifiers listed above may:

(A) File an un-redacted version of the document under seal, or

(B) File a reference list under seal.

(i) The reference list must contain the complete personal data identifier(s) and the redacted identifier(s) used in its(their) place in the filing.

(ii) All references in the case to the redacted identifiers included in the reference list will be construed to refer to the corresponding complete personal data identifier.

(iii) The reference list must be filed under seal, and may be amended as of right.

(3) The un-redacted version of the document or the reference list must be retained by the court as part of the record. The court may, however, still require the party to file a redacted copy for the public file.

(4) The responsibility for redacting these personal identifiers rests solely with counsel and the parties. The Clerk will not review each pleading for compliance with this rule.

(m) Hyperlinks.

(1) Electronically filed documents may contain the following types of hyperlinks:

(A) Hyperlinks to other portions of the same document; and

(B) Hyperlinks to a location on the Internet that contains a source document for a citation.

(2) Hyperlinks to cited authority may not replace standard citation format. Complete citations must be included in the text of the filed document. A hyperlink, or any site to which it refers, will not be considered part of the record. Hyperlinks are simply convenient mechanisms for accessing material cited in a filed document.

(3) The court accepts no responsibility for, and does not endorse, any product, organization, or content at any hyperlinked site, or at any site to which that site might be linked. The court accepts no responsibility for the availability or functionality of any hyperlink.

[Amended effective May 24, 2011.]

RULES FOR JUDICIAL–CONDUCT AND JUDICIAL–DISABILITY PROCEEDINGS

PREFACE

These Rules were promulgated by the Judicial Conference of the United States, after public comment, pursuant to 28 U.S.C. §§ 331 and 358, to establish standards and procedures for addressing complaints filed by complainants or identified by chief judges, under the Judicial Conduct and Disability Act, 28 U.S.C. §§ 351–364.

ARTICLE I. GENERAL PROVISIONS

RULE 1. SCOPE

These Rules govern proceedings under the Judicial Conduct and Disability Act, 28 U.S.C. §§ 351–364 (the Act), to determine whether a covered judge has engaged in conduct prejudicial to the effective and expeditious administration of the business of the courts or is unable to discharge the duties of office because of mental or physical disability.

[Adopted March 11, 2008, effective April 10, 2008.]

Commentary on Rule 1

In September 2006, the Judicial Conduct and Disability Act Study Committee, appointed in 2004 by Chief Justice Rehnquist and known as the "Breyer Committee," presented a report, known as the "Breyer Committee Report," 239 F.R.D. 116 (Sept. 2006), to Chief Justice Roberts that evaluated implementation of the Judicial Conduct and Disability Act of 1980, 28 U.S.C. §§ 351–364. The Breyer Committee had been formed in response to criticism from the public and the Congress regarding the effectiveness of the Act's implementation. The Executive Committee of the Judicial Conference directed the Judicial Conference Committee on Judicial Conduct and Disability to consider the recommendations made by the Breyer Committee and to report on their implementation to the Conference.

The Breyer Committee found that it could not evaluate implementation of the Act without establishing interpretive standards, Breyer Committee Report, 239 F.R.D. at 132, and that a major problem faced by chief judges in implementing the Act was the lack of authoritative interpretive standards. Id. at 212–15. The Breyer Committee then established standards to guide its evaluation, some of which were new formulations and some of which were taken from the "Illustrative Rules Governing Complaints of Judicial Misconduct and Disability," discussed below. The principal standards used by the Breyer Committee are in Appendix E of its Report. Id. at 238.

Based on the findings of the Breyer Committee, the Judicial Conference Committee on Judicial Conduct and Disability concluded that there was a need for the Judicial Conference to exercise its power under Section 358 of the Act to fashion standards guiding the various officers and bodies who must exercise responsibility under the Act. To that end, the Judicial Conference Committee proposed rules that were based largely on Appendix E of the Breyer Committee Report and the Illustrative Rules.

The Illustrative Rules were originally prepared in 1986 by the Special Committee of the Conference of Chief Judges of the United States Courts of Appeals, and were subsequently revised and amended, most recently in 2000, by the predecessor to the Committee on Judicial Conduct and Disability. The Illustrative Rules were adopted, with minor variations, by circuit judicial councils, to govern complaints under the Judicial Conduct and Disability Act.

After being submitted for public comment pursuant to 28 U.S.C. § 358(c), the present Rules were promulgated by the Judicial Conference on March 11, 2008.

RULE 2. EFFECT AND CONSTRUCTION

(a) Generally. These Rules are mandatory; they supersede any conflicting judicial-council rules. Judicial councils may promulgate additional rules to implement the Act as long as those rules do not conflict with these Rules.

(b) Exception. A Rule will not apply if, when performing duties authorized by the Act, a chief judge, a special committee, a judicial council, the Judicial Conference Committee on Judicial Conduct and Disability, or the Judicial Conference of the United States expressly finds that exceptional circumstances render application of that Rule in a particular proceeding manifestly unjust or contrary to the purposes of the Act or these Rules.

[Adopted March 11, 2008, effective April 10, 2008.]

Commentary on Rule 2

Unlike the Illustrative Rules, these Rules provide mandatory and nationally uniform provisions governing the substantive and procedural aspects of misconduct and disability proceedings under the Act. The mandatory nature of these Rules is authorized by 28 U.S.C. § 358(a) and (c). Judicial councils retain the power to promulgate rules consistent with these Rules. For example, a local rule may authorize the electronic distribution of materials pursuant to Rule 8(b).

Rule 2(b) recognizes that unforeseen and exceptional circumstances may call for a different approach in particular cases.

RULE 3. DEFINITIONS

(a) Chief Judge. "Chief judge" means the chief judge of a United States Court of Appeals, of the United States Court of International Trade, or of the United States Court of Federal Claims.

(b) Circuit Clerk. "Circuit clerk" means a clerk of a United States court of appeals, the clerk of the United States Court of International Trade, the clerk of the United States Court of Federal Claims, or the circuit executive of the United States Court of Appeals for the Federal Circuit.

(c) Complaint. A complaint is:

(1) a document that, in accordance with Rule 6, is filed by any person in his or her individual capacity or on behalf of a professional organization; or

(2) information from any source, other than a document described in (c) (1), that gives a chief judge probable cause to believe that a covered judge, as defined in Rule 4, has engaged in misconduct or may have a disability, whether or not the information is framed as or is intended to be an allegation of misconduct or disability.

(d) Court of Appeals, District Court, and District Judge. "Courts of appeals," "district court," and "district judge," where appropriate, include the United States Court of Federal Claims, the United States Court of International Trade, and the judges thereof.

(e) Disability. "Disability" is a temporary or permanent condition rendering a judge unable to discharge the duties of the particular judicial office. Examples of disability include substance abuse, the inability to stay awake during court proceedings, or a severe impairment of cognitive abilities.

(f) Judicial Council and Circuit. "Judicial council" and "circuit," where appropriate, include any courts designated in 28 U.S.C. § 363.

(g) Magistrate Judge. "Magistrate judge," where appropriate, includes a special master appointed by the Court of Federal Claims under 42 U.S.C. § 300aa–12(c).

(h) Misconduct. Cognizable misconduct:

(1) is conduct prejudicial to the effective and expeditious administration of the business of the courts. Misconduct includes, but is not limited to:

(A) using the judge's office to obtain special treatment for friends or relatives;

(B) accepting bribes, gifts, or other personal favors related to the judicial office;

(C) having improper discussions with parties or counsel for one side in a case;

(D) treating litigants or attorneys in a demonstrably egregious and hostile manner;

(E) engaging in partisan political activity or making inappropriately partisan statements;

(F) soliciting funds for organizations; or

(G) violating other specific, mandatory standards of judicial conduct, such as those pertaining to

restrictions on outside income and requirements for financial disclosure.

(2) is conduct occurring outside the performance of official duties if the conduct might have a prejudicial effect on the administration of the business of the courts, including a substantial and widespread lowering of public confidence in the courts among reasonable people.

(3) does not include:

(A) an allegation that is directly related to the merits of a decision or procedural ruling. An allegation that calls into question the correctness of a judge's ruling, including a failure to recuse, without more, is merits-related. If the decision or ruling is alleged to be the result of an improper motive, e.g., a bribe, ex parte contact, racial or ethnic bias, or improper conduct in rendering a decision or ruling, such as personally derogatory remarks irrelevant to the issues, the complaint is not cognizable to the extent that it attacks the merits.

(B) an allegation about delay in rendering a decision or ruling, unless the allegation concerns an improper motive in delaying a particular decision or habitual delay in a significant number of unrelated cases.

(i) Subject Judge. "Subject judge" means any judge described in Rule 4 who is the subject of a complaint.

[Adopted March 11, 2008, effective April 10, 2008.]

Commentary on Rule 3

Rule 3 is derived and adapted from the Breyer Committee Report and the Illustrative Rules.

Unless otherwise specified or the context otherwise indicates, the term "complaint" is used in these Rules to refer both to complaints identified by a chief judge under Rule 5 and to complaints filed by complainants under Rule 6.

Under the Act, a "complaint" may be filed by "any person" or "identified" by a chief judge. See 28 U.S.C. § 351(a) and (b). Under Rule 3(c)(1), complaints may be submitted by a person, in his or her individual capacity, or by a professional organization. Generally, the word "complaint" brings to mind the commencement of an adversary proceeding in which the contending parties are left to present the evidence and legal arguments, and judges play the role of an essentially passive arbiter. The Act, however, establishes an administrative, inquisitorial process. For example, even absent a complaint under Rule 6, chief judges are expected in some circumstances to trigger the process—"identify a complaint," see 28 U.S.C. § 351(b) and Rule 5—and conduct an investigation without becoming a party. See 28 U.S.C. § 352(a); Breyer Committee Report, 239 F.R.D. at 214; Illustrative Rule 2(j). Even when a complaint is filed by someone other than the chief judge, the complainant lacks many rights that a litigant would have, and the chief judge, instead of being limited to the "four corners of the complaint," must, under Rule 11, proceed as though misconduct or disability has been alleged where the complainant reveals information of misconduct or disability but does not claim it as such. See Breyer Committee Report, 239 F.R.D. at 183–84.

An allegation of misconduct or disability filed under Rule 6 is a "complaint," and the Rule so provides in subsection (c)(1). However, both the nature of the process and the use of the term "identify" suggest that the word "complaint" covers more than a document formally triggering the process. The process relies on chief judges considering known information and triggering the process when appropriate. "Identifying" a "complaint," therefore, is best understood as the chief judge's concluding that information known to the judge constitutes probable cause to believe that misconduct occurred or a disability exists, whether or not the information is framed as, or intended to be an accusation. This definition is codified in (c)(2).

Rule 3(e) relates to disability and provides only the most general definition, recognizing that a fact-specific approach is the only one available.

The phrase "prejudicial to the effective and expeditious administration of the business of the courts" is not subject to precise definition, and subsection (h)(1) therefore provides some specific examples. Although the Code of Conduct for United States Judges may be informative, its main precepts are highly general; the Code is in many potential applications aspirational rather than a set of disciplinary rules. Ultimately, the responsibility for determining what constitutes misconduct under the statute is the province of the judicial council of the circuit subject to such review and limitations as are ordained by the statute and by these Rules.

Even where specific, mandatory rules exist—for example, governing the receipt of gifts by judges, outside earned income, and financial disclosure obligations—the distinction between the misconduct statute and the specific, mandatory rules must be borne in mind. For example, an inadvertent, minor violation of any one of these Rules, promptly remedied when called to the attention of the judge, might still be a violation but might not rise to the level of misconduct under the statute. By contrast, a pattern of such violations of the Code might well rise to the level of misconduct.

An allegation can meet the statutory standard even though the judge's alleged conduct did not occur in the course of the performance of official duties. The Code of Conduct for United States Judges expressly covers a wide range of extra-official activities, and some of these activities may constitute misconduct. For example, allegations that a judge solicited funds for a charity or participated in a partisan political event are cognizable under the Act.

On the other hand, judges are entitled to some leeway in extra-official activities. For example, misconduct may not include a judge being repeatedly and publicly discourteous to a spouse (not including physical abuse) even though this might cause some reasonable people to have diminished confidence in the courts. Rule 3(h)(2) states that conduct of this sort is covered, for example, when it might lead to a "substantial and widespread" lowering of such confidence.

Rule 3(h)(3)(A) tracks the Act, 28 U.S.C. § 352(b)(1)(A)(ii), in excluding from the definition of misconduct allegations "[d]irectly related to the merits of a decision or procedural ruling." This exclusion preserves the independence of judges in the exercise of judicial power by ensuring that the complaint procedure is not used to collaterally attack the substance of a judge's ruling. Any allegation that calls into question the correctness of an official action of a judge—

without more—is merits-related. The phrase "decision or procedural ruling" is not limited to rulings issued in deciding Article III cases or controversies. Thus, a complaint challenging the correctness of a chief judge's determination to dismiss a prior misconduct complaint would be properly dismissed as merits-related—in other words, as challenging the substance of the judge's administrative determination to dismiss the complaint—even though it does not concern the judge's rulings in Article III litigation. Similarly, an allegation that a judge had incorrectly declined to approve a Criminal Justice Act voucher is merits-related under this standard.

Conversely, an allegation—however unsupported—that a judge conspired with a prosecutor to make a particular ruling is not merits-related, even though it "relates" to a ruling in a colloquial sense. Such an allegation attacks the propriety of conspiring with the prosecutor and goes beyond a challenge to the correctness—"the merits"—of the ruling itself. An allegation that a judge ruled against the complainant because the complainant is a member of a particular racial or ethnic group, or because the judge dislikes the complainant personally, is also not merits-related. Such an allegation attacks the propriety of arriving at rulings with an illicit or improper motive. Similarly, an allegation that a judge used an inappropriate term to refer to a class of people is not merits-related even if the judge used it on the bench or in an opinion; the correctness of the judge's rulings is not at stake. An allegation that a judge treated litigants or attorneys in a demonstrably egregious and hostile manner while on the bench is also not merits-related.

The existence of an appellate remedy is usually irrelevant to whether an allegation is merits-related. The merits-related ground for dismissal exists to protect judges' independence in making rulings, not to protect or promote the appellate process. A complaint alleging an incorrect ruling is merits-related even though the complainant has no recourse from that ruling. By the same token, an allegation that is otherwise cognizable under the Act should not be dismissed merely because an appellate remedy appears to exist (for example, vacating a ruling that resulted from an improper ex parte communication). However, there may be occasions when appellate and misconduct proceedings overlap, and consideration and disposition of a complaint under these Rules may be properly deferred by a chief judge until the appellate proceedings are concluded in order to avoid, inter alia, inconsistent decisions.

Because of the special need to protect judges' independence in deciding what to say in an opinion or ruling, a somewhat different standard applies to determine the merits-relatedness of a non-frivolous allegation that a judge's language in a ruling reflected an improper motive. If the judge's language was relevant to the case at hand—for example a statement that a claim is legally or factually "frivolous"—then the judge's choice of language is presumptively merits-related and excluded, absent evidence apart from the ruling itself suggesting an improper motive. If, on the other hand, the challenged language does not seem relevant on its face, then an additional inquiry under Rule 11 is necessary.

With regard to Rule 3(h)(3)(B), a complaint of delay in a single case is excluded as merits-related. Such an allegation may be said to challenge the correctness of an official action of the judge—in other words, assigning a low priority to deciding the particular case. But, by the same token, an allegation of a habitual pattern of delay in a significant number of unrelated cases, or an allegation of deliberate delay in a single case arising out of an illicit motive, is not merits-related.

The remaining subsections of Rule 3 provide technical definitions clarifying the application of the Rules to the various kinds of courts covered.

RULE 4. COVERED JUDGES

A complaint under these Rules may concern the actions or capacity only of judges of United States courts of appeals, judges of United States district courts, judges of United States bankruptcy courts, United States magistrate judges, and judges of the courts specified in 28 U.S.C. § 363.

[Adopted March 11, 2008, effective April 10, 2008.]

Commentary on Rule 4

This Rule tracks the Act. Rule 8(c) and (d) contain provisions as to the handling of complaints against persons not covered by the Act, such as other court personnel, or against both covered judges and noncovered persons.

ARTICLE II. INITIATION OF A COMPLAINT

RULE 5. IDENTIFICATION OF A COMPLAINT

(a) **Identification.** When a chief judge has information constituting reasonable grounds for inquiry into whether a covered judge has engaged in misconduct or has a disability, the chief judge may conduct an inquiry, as he or she deems appropriate, into the accuracy of the information even if no related complaint has been filed. A chief judge who finds probable cause to believe that misconduct has occurred or that a disability exists may seek an informal resolution that he or she finds satisfactory. If no informal resolution is achieved or is feasible, the chief judge may identify a complaint and, by written order stating the reasons, begin the review provided in Rule 11. If the evidence of misconduct is clear and convincing and no informal resolution is achieved or is feasible, the chief judge must identify a complaint. A chief judge must not decline to identify a complaint merely because the person making the allegation has not filed a complaint under Rule 6. This Rule is subject to Rule 7.

(b) **Noncompliance With Rule 6(d).** Rule 6 complaints that do not comply with the requirements of Rule 6(d) must be considered under this Rule.

[Adopted March 11, 2008, effective April 10, 2008.]

Commentary on Rule 5

This Rule is adapted from the Breyer Committee Report, 239 F.R.D. at 245–46.

The Act authorizes the chief judge, by written order stating reasons, to identify a complaint and thereby dispense with the filing of a written complaint. See 28 U.S.C. § 351(b). Under Rule 5, when a chief judge becomes aware of information constituting reasonable grounds to inquire into possible misconduct or disability on the part of a covered judge, and no formal complaint has been filed, the chief judge has the power in his or her discretion to begin an appropriate inquiry. A chief judge's decision whether to informally seek a resolution and/or to identify a complaint is guided by the results of that inquiry. If the chief judge concludes that there is probable cause to believe that misconduct has occurred or a disability exists, the chief judge may seek an informal resolution, if feasible, and if failing in that, may identify a complaint. Discretion is accorded largely for the reasons police officers and prosecutors have discretion in making arrests or bringing charges. The matter may be trivial and isolated, based on marginal evidence, or otherwise highly unlikely to lead to a misconduct or disability finding. On the other hand, if the inquiry leads the chief judge to conclude that there is clear and convincing evidence of misconduct or a disability, and no satisfactory informal resolution has been achieved or is feasible, the chief judge is required to identify a complaint.

An informal resolution is one agreed to by the subject judge and found satisfactory by the chief judge. Because an informal resolution under Rule 5 reached before a complaint is filed under Rule 6 will generally cause a subsequent Rule 6 complaint alleging the identical matter to be concluded, see Rule 11(d), the chief judge must be sure that the resolution is fully appropriate before endorsing it. In doing so, the chief judge must balance the seriousness of the matter against the particular judge's alacrity in addressing the issue. The availability of this procedure should encourage attempts at swift remedial action before a formal complaint is filed.

When a complaint is identified, a written order stating the reasons for the identification must be provided; this begins the process articulated in Rule 11. Rule 11 provides that once the chief judge has identified a complaint, the chief judge, subject to the disqualification provisions of Rule 25, will perform, with respect to that complaint, all functions assigned to the chief judge for the determination of complaints filed by a complainant.

In high-visibility situations, it may be desirable for the chief judge to identify a complaint without first seeking an informal resolution (and then, if the circumstances warrant, dismiss or conclude the identified complaint without appointment of a special committee) in order to assure the public that the allegations have not been ignored.

A chief judge's decision not to identify a complaint under Rule 5 is not appealable and is subject to Rule 3(h)(3)(A), which excludes merits-related complaints from the definition of misconduct.

A chief judge may not decline to identify a complaint solely on the basis that the unfiled allegations could be raised by one or more persons in a filed complaint, but none of these persons has opted to do so.

Subsection (a) concludes by stating that this Rule is "subject to Rule 7." This is intended to establish that only: (i) the chief judge of the home circuit of a potential subject judge, or (ii) the chief judge of a circuit in which misconduct is alleged to have occurred in the course of official business while the potential subject judge was sitting by designation, shall have the power or a duty under this Rule to identify a complaint.

Subsection (b) provides that complaints filed under Rule 6 that do not comply with the requirements of Rule 6(d), must be considered under this Rule. For instance, if a complaint has been filed but the form submitted is unsigned, or the truth of the statements therein are not verified in writing under penalty of perjury, then a chief judge must nevertheless consider the allegations as known information, and proceed to follow the process described in Rule 5(a).

RULE 6.   FILING A COMPLAINT

(a) Form. A complainant may use the form reproduced in the appendix to these Rules or a form designated by the rules of the judicial council in the circuit in which the complaint is filed. A complaint form is also available on each court of appeals' website or may be obtained from the circuit clerk or any district court or bankruptcy court within the circuit. A form is not necessary to file a complaint, but the complaint must be written and must include the information described in (b).

(b) Brief Statement of Facts. A complaint must contain a concise statement that details the specific facts on which the claim of misconduct or disability is based. The statement of facts should include a description of:

(1) what happened;

(2) when and where the relevant events happened;

(3) any information that would help an investigator check the facts; and

(4) for an allegation of disability, any additional facts that form the basis of that allegation.

(c) Legibility. A complaint should be typewritten if possible. If not typewritten, it must be legible. An illegible complaint will be returned to the complainant with a request to resubmit it in legible form. If a resubmitted complaint is still illegible, it will not be accepted for filing.

(d) Complainant's Address and Signature; Verification. The complainant must provide a contact address and sign the complaint. The truth of the statements made in the complaint must be verified in writing under penalty of perjury. If any of these requirements are not met, the complaint will be accepted for filing, but it will be reviewed under only Rule 5(b).

(e) Number of Copies; Envelope Marking. The complainant shall provide the number of copies of the complaint required by local rule. Each copy should be in an envelope marked "Complaint of Misconduct" or "Complaint of Disability." The envelope must not show the name of any subject judge.

[Adopted March 11, 2008, effective April 10, 2008.]

Commentary on Rule 6

The Rule is adapted from the Illustrative Rules and is self-explanatory.

RULE 7.   WHERE TO INITIATE COMPLAINTS

(a) Where to File. Except as provided in (b),

(1) a complaint against a judge of a United States court of appeals, a United States district court, a United States bankruptcy court, or a United States magistrate judge must be filed with the circuit clerk in the jurisdiction in which the subject judge holds office.

(2) a complaint against a judge of the United States Court of International Trade or the United States Court of Federal Claims must be filed with the respective clerk of that court.

(3) a complaint against a judge of the United States Court of Appeals for the Federal Circuit must be filed with the circuit executive of that court.

(b) Misconduct in Another Circuit; Transfer. If a complaint alleges misconduct in the course of official business while the subject judge was sitting on a court by designation under 28 U.S.C. §§ 291–293 and 294(d), the complaint may be filed or identified with the circuit clerk of that circuit or of the subject judge's home circuit. The proceeding will continue in the circuit of the first-filed or first-identified complaint. The judicial council of the circuit where the complaint was first filed or first identified may transfer the complaint to the subject judge's home circuit or to the circuit where the alleged misconduct occurred, as the case may be.

[Adopted March 11, 2008, effective April 10, 2008.]

Commentary on Rule 7

Title 28 U.S.C. § 351 states that complaints are to be filed with "the clerk of the court of appeals for the circuit." However, in many circuits, this role is filled by circuit executives. Accordingly, the term "circuit clerk," as defined in Rule 3(b) and used throughout these Rules, applies to circuit executives.

Section 351 uses the term "the circuit" in a way that suggests that either the home circuit of the subject judge or the circuit in which misconduct is alleged to have occurred is the proper venue for complaints. With an exception for judges sitting by designation, the Rule requires the identifying or filing of a misconduct or disability complaint in the circuit in which the judge holds office, largely based on the administrative perspective of the Act. Given the Act's emphasis on the future conduct of the business of the courts, the circuit in which the judge holds office is the appropriate forum because that circuit is likely best able to influence a judge's future behavior in constructive ways.

However, when judges sit by designation, the non-home circuit has a strong interest in redressing misconduct in the course of official business, and where allegations also involve a member of the bar—ex parte contact between an attorney and a judge, for example—it may often be desirable to have the judicial and bar misconduct proceedings take place in the same venue. Rule 7(b), therefore, allows transfer to, or filing or identification of a complaint in, the non-home circuit. The proceeding may be transferred by the judicial council of the filing or identified circuit to the other circuit.

RULE 8. ACTION BY CLERK

(a) Receipt of Complaint. Upon receiving a complaint against a judge filed under Rule 5 or 6, the circuit clerk must open a file, assign a docket number according to a uniform numbering scheme promulgated by the Judicial Conference Committee on Judicial Conduct and Disability, and acknowledge the complaint's receipt.

(b) Distribution of Copies. The clerk must promptly send copies of a complaint filed under Rule 6 to the chief judge or the judge authorized to act as chief judge under Rule 25(f), and copies of complaints filed under Rule 5 or 6 to each subject judge. The clerk must retain the original complaint. Any further distribution should be as provided by local rule.

(c) Complaints Against Noncovered Persons. If the clerk receives a complaint about a person not holding an office described in Rule 4, the clerk must not accept the complaint for filing under these Rules.

(d) Receipt of Complaint About a Judge and Another Noncovered Person. If a complaint is received about a judge described in Rule 4 and a person not holding an office described in Rule 4, the clerk must accept the complaint for filing under these Rules only with regard to the judge and must inform the complainant of the limitation.

[Adopted March 11, 2008, effective April 10, 2008.]

Commentary on Rule 8

This Rule is adapted from the Illustrative Rules and is largely self-explanatory.

The uniform docketing scheme described in subsection (a) should take into account potential problems associated with a complaint that names multiple judges. One solution may be to provide separate docket numbers for each subject judge. Separate docket numbers would help avoid difficulties in tracking cases, particularly if a complaint is dismissed with respect to some, but not all of the named judges.

Complaints against noncovered persons are not to be accepted for processing under these Rules but may, of course, be accepted under other circuit rules or procedures for grievances.

RULE 9. TIME FOR FILING OR IDENTIFYING A COMPLAINT

A complaint may be filed or identified at any time. If the passage of time has made an accurate and fair investigation of a complaint impractical, the complaint must be dismissed under Rule 11(c)(1)(E).

[Adopted March 11, 2008, effective April 10, 2008.]

Commentary on Rule 9

This Rule is adapted from the Act, 28 U.S.C. §§ 351, 352(b)(1)(A)(iii), and the Illustrative Rules.

RULE 10. ABUSE OF THE COMPLAINT PROCEDURE

(a) Abusive Complaints. A complainant who has filed repetitive, harassing, or frivolous complaints, or has otherwise abused the complaint procedure, may be restricted from filing further complaints. After giving the complainant an opportunity to show cause in writing why his or her right to file further complaints should not be limited, a judicial council may prohibit, restrict, or impose conditions on the complainant's use of the complaint procedure. Upon written request of the complainant, the judicial council may revise or withdraw any prohibition, restriction, or condition previously imposed.

(b) Orchestrated Complaints. When many essentially identical complaints from different complainants are received and appear to be part of an orchestrated campaign, the chief judge may recommend that the judicial council issue a written order instructing the circuit clerk to accept only a certain number of such complaints for filing and to refuse to accept further ones. The clerk must send a copy of any such order to anyone whose complaint was not accepted.

[Adopted March 11, 2008, effective April 10, 2008.]

Commentary on Rule 10

This Rule is adapted from the Illustrative Rules.

Rule 10(a) provides a mechanism for a judicial council to restrict the filing of further complaints by a single complainant who has abused the complaint procedure. In some instances, however, the complaint procedure may be abused in a manner for which the remedy provided in Rule 10(a) may not be appropriate. For example, some circuits have been inundated with submissions of dozens or hundreds of essentially identical complaints against the same judge or judges, all submitted by different complainants. In many of these instances, persons with grievances against a particular judge or judges used the Internet or other technology to orchestrate mass complaint-filing campaigns against them. If each complaint submitted as part of such a campaign were accepted for filing and processed according to these Rules, there would be a serious drain on court resources without any benefit to the adjudication of the underlying merits.

A judicial council may, therefore, respond to such mass filings under Rule 10(b) by declining to accept repetitive complaints for filing, regardless of the fact that the complaints are nominally submitted by different complainants. When the first complaint or complaints have been dismissed on the merits, and when further, essentially identical submissions follow, the judicial council may issue a second order noting that these are identical or repetitive complaints, directing the circuit clerk not to accept these complaints or any further such complaints for filing, and directing the clerk to send each putative complainant copies of both orders.

ARTICLE III. REVIEW OF A COMPLAINT BY THE CHIEF JUDGE

RULE 11. REVIEW BY THE CHIEF JUDGE

(a) Purpose of Chief Judge's Review. When a complaint is identified by the chief judge or is filed, the chief judge must review it unless the chief judge is disqualified under Rule 25. If the complaint contains information constituting evidence of misconduct or disability, but the complainant does not claim it as such, the chief judge must treat the complaint as if it did allege misconduct or disability and give notice to the subject judge. After reviewing the complaint, the chief judge must determine whether it should be:

(1) dismissed;

(2) concluded on the ground that voluntary corrective action has been taken;

(3) concluded because intervening events have made action on the complaint no longer necessary; or

(4) referred to a special committee.

(b) Inquiry by Chief Judge. In determining what action to take under Rule 11(a), the chief judge may conduct a limited inquiry. The chief judge, or a designee, may communicate orally or in writing with the complainant, the subject judge, and any others who may have knowledge of the matter, and may review transcripts or other relevant documents. In conducting the inquiry, the chief judge must not determine any reasonably disputed issue.

(c) Dismissal.

(1) *Allowable Grounds.* A complaint must be dismissed in whole or in part to the extent that the chief judge concludes that the complaint:

(A) alleges conduct that, even if true, is not prejudicial to the effective and expeditious administration of the business of the courts and does not indicate a mental or physical disability resulting in inability to discharge the duties of judicial office;

(B) is directly related to the merits of a decision or procedural ruling;

(C) is frivolous;

(D) is based on allegations lacking sufficient evidence to raise an inference that misconduct has occurred or that a disability exists;

(E) is based on allegations which are incapable of being established through investigation;

(F) has been filed in the wrong circuit under Rule 7; or

(G) is otherwise not appropriate for consideration under the Act.

(2) *Disallowed Grounds.* A complaint must not be dismissed solely because it repeats allegations of a previously dismissed complaint if it also contains material information not previously considered and does not constitute harassment of the subject judge.

(d) Corrective Action. The chief judge may conclude the complaint proceeding in whole or in part if:

(1) an informal resolution under Rule 5 satisfactory to the chief judge was reached before the complaint was filed under Rule 6, or

(2) the chief judge determines that the subject judge has taken appropriate voluntary corrective action that acknowledges and remedies the problems raised by the complaint.

(e) Intervening Events. The chief judge may conclude the complaint proceeding in whole or in part upon determining that intervening events render some or all of the allegations moot or make remedial action impossible.

(f) Appointment of Special Committee. If some or all of the complaint is not dismissed or concluded, the chief judge must promptly appoint a special committee to investigate the complaint or any relevant portion of it and to make recommendations to the judicial council. Before appointing a special committee, the chief judge must invite the subject judge to respond to the complaint either orally or in writing if the judge was not given an opportunity during the limited inquiry. In the chief judge's discretion, separate complaints may be joined and assigned to a single special committee. Similarly, a single complaint about more than one judge may be severed and more than one special committee appointed.

(g) Notice of Chief Judge's Action; Petitions for Review.

(1) *When Special Committee Is Appointed.* If a special committee is appointed, the chief judge must notify the complainant and the subject judge that the matter has been referred to a special committee and identify the members of the committee. A copy of the order appointing the special committee must be sent to the Judicial Conference Committee on Judicial Conduct and Disability.

(2) *When Chief Judge Disposes of Complaint Without Appointing Special Committee.* If the chief judge disposes of the complaint under Rule 11(c), (d), or (e), the chief judge must prepare a supporting memorandum that sets forth the reasons for the disposition. Except as authorized by 28 U.S.C. § 360, the memorandum must not include the name of the complainant or of the subject judge. The order and the supporting memorandum, which may be one document, must be provided to the complainant, the subject judge, and the Judicial Conference Committee on Judicial Conduct and Disability.

(3) *Right of Petition for Review.* If the chief judge disposes of a complaint under Rule 11(c), (d), or (e), the complainant and subject judge must be notified of the right to petition the judicial council for review of the disposition, as provided in Rule 18. If a petition for review is filed, the chief judge must promptly transmit all materials obtained in connection with the inquiry under Rule 11(b) to the circuit clerk for transmittal to the judicial council.

(h) Public Availability of Chief Judge's Decision. The chief judge's decision must be made public to the extent, at the time, and in the manner provided in Rule 24.

[Adopted March 11, 2008, effective April 10, 2008.]

Commentary on Rule 11

Subsection (a) lists the actions available to a chief judge in reviewing a complaint. This subsection provides that where a complaint has been filed under Rule 6, the ordinary doctrines of waiver do not apply. A chief judge must identify as a complaint any misconduct or disability issues raised by the factual allegations of the complaint even if the complainant makes no such claim with regard to those issues. For example, an allegation limited to misconduct in fact-finding that mentions periods during a trial when the judge was asleep must be treated as a complaint regarding disability. Some formal order giving notice of the expanded scope of the proceeding must be given to the subject judge.

Subsection (b) describes the nature of the chief judge's inquiry. It is based largely on the Breyer Committee Report, 239 F.R.D. at 243–45. The Act states that dismissal is appropriate "when a limited inquiry ... demonstrates that the allegations in the complaint lack any factual foundation or are conclusively refuted by objective evidence." 28 U.S.C. § 352(b)(1)(B). At the same time, however, Section 352(a) states that "[t]he chief judge shall not undertake to make findings of fact about any matter that is reasonably in dispute." These two statutory standards should be read together, so that a matter is not "reasonably" in dispute if a limited inquiry shows that the allegations do not constitute misconduct or disability, that they lack any reliable factual foundation, or that they are conclusively refuted by objective evidence.

In conducting a limited inquiry under subsection (b), the chief judge must avoid determinations of reasonably disputed issues, including reasonably disputed issues as to whether the facts alleged constitute misconduct or disability, which are ordinarily left to a special committee and the judicial council. An allegation of fact is ordinarily not "refuted" simply because the subject judge denies it. The limited inquiry must reveal something more in the way of refutation before it is appropriate to dismiss a complaint that is otherwise cognizable. If it is the complainant's word against the subject judge's—in other words, there is simply no other significant evidence of what happened or of the complainant's unreliability—then there must be a special-committee investigation. Such a credibility issue is a matter "reasonably in dispute" within the meaning of the Act.

However, dismissal following a limited inquiry may occur when the complaint refers to transcripts or to witnesses and the chief judge determines that the transcripts and witnesses all support the subject judge. Breyer Committee Report, 239 F.R.D. at 243. For example, consider a complaint alleging that the subject judge said X, and the complaint mentions, or it is independently clear, that five people may have heard what the judge said. Id. The chief judge is told by the subject judge and one witness that the judge did not say X, and the chief judge dismisses the complaint without questioning the other four possible witnesses. Id. In this example, the matter remains reasonably in dispute. If all five witnesses say the judge did not say X, dismissal is appropriate, but if potential witnesses who are reasonably accessible have not been questioned, then the matter remains reasonably in dispute. Id.

Similarly, under (c)(1)(A), if it is clear that the conduct or disability alleged, even if true, is not cognizable under these Rules, the complaint should be dismissed. If that issue is reasonably in dispute, however, dismissal under (c)(1)(A) is inappropriate.

Essentially, the standard articulated in subsection (b) is that used to decide motions for summary judgment pursuant to Fed. R. Civ. P. 56. Genuine issues of material fact are not resolved at the summary judgment stage. A material fact is one that "might affect the outcome of the suit under the governing law," and a dispute is "genuine" if "the evidence is such that a reasonable jury could return a verdict for the nonmoving party." *Anderson v. Liberty Lobby*, 477 U.S. 242, 248 (1986). Similarly, the chief judge may not resolve a genuine issue concerning a material fact or the existence of misconduct or a disability when conducting a limited inquiry pursuant to subsection (b).

Subsection (c) describes the grounds on which a complaint may be dismissed. These are adapted from the Act, 28 U.S.C. § 352(b), and the Breyer Committee Report, 239 F.R.D. at 239–45. Subsection (c)(1)(A) permits dismissal of an allegation that, even if true, does not constitute misconduct or disability under the statutory standard. The proper standards are set out in Rule 3 and discussed in the Commentary on that Rule. Subsection (c)(1)(B) permits dismissal of complaints related to the merits of a decision by a subject judge; this standard is also governed by Rule 3 and its accompanying Commentary.

Subsections (c)(1)(C)–(E) implement the statute by allowing dismissal of complaints that are "frivolous, lacking sufficient evidence to raise an inference that misconduct has occurred, or containing allegations which are incapable of being established through investigation." 28 U.S.C. § 352(b)(1)(A)(iii).

Dismissal of a complaint as "frivolous," under Rule 11(c)(1)(C), will generally occur without any inquiry beyond the face of the complaint. For instance, when the allegations are facially incredible or so lacking in indicia of reliability that no further inquiry is warranted, dismissal under this subsection is appropriate.

A complaint warranting dismissal under Rule 11(c)(1)(D) is illustrated by the following example. Consider a complainant who alleges an impropriety and asserts that he knows of it because it was observed and reported to him by a person who is identified. The judge denies that the event occurred. When contacted, the source also denies it. In such a case, the chief judge's proper course of action may turn on whether the source had any role in the allegedly improper conduct. If the complaint was based on a lawyer's statement that he or she had an improper ex parte contact with a judge, the lawyer's denial of the impropriety might not be taken as wholly persuasive, and it would be appropriate to conclude that a real factual issue is raised. On the other hand, if the complaint quoted a disinterested third party and that disinterested party denied that the statement had been made, there would be no value in opening a formal investigation. In such a case, it would be appropriate to dismiss the complaint under Rule 11(c)(1)(D).

Rule 11(c)(1)(E) is intended, among other things, to cover situations when no evidence is offered or identified, or when the only identified source is unavailable. Breyer Committee Report, 239 F.R.D. at 243. For example, a complaint alleges that an unnamed attorney told the complainant that the judge did X. Id. The subject judge denies it. The chief judge requests that the complainant (who does not purport to have observed the judge do X) identify the unnamed witness, or that the unnamed witness come forward so that the chief judge can learn the unnamed witness's account. Id. The complainant responds that he has spoken with the unnamed witness, that the unnamed witness is an attorney who practices in federal court, and that the unnamed witness is unwilling to be identified or to come forward. Id. at 243–44. The allegation is then properly dismissed as containing allegations that are incapable of being established through investigation. Id.

If, however, the situation involves a reasonable dispute over credibility, the matter should proceed. For example, the complainant alleges an impropriety and alleges that he or she observed it and that there were no other witnesses; the subject judge denies that the event occurred. Unless the complainant's allegations are facially incredible or so lacking indicia of reliability warranting dismissal under Rule 11(c)(1)(C), a special committee must be appointed because there is a material factual question that is reasonably in dispute.

Dismissal is also appropriate when a complaint is filed so long after an alleged event that memory loss, death, or changes to unknown residences prevent a proper investigation.

Subsection (c)(2) indicates that the investigative nature of the process prevents the application of claim preclusion principles where new and material evidence becomes available. However, it also recognizes that at some point a renewed investigation may constitute harassment of the subject judge and should be foregone, depending of course on the seriousness of the issues and the weight of the new evidence.

Rule 11(d) implements the Act's provision for dismissal if voluntary appropriate corrective action has been taken. It is largely adapted from the Breyer Committee Report, 239

F.R.D. 244–45. The Act authorizes the chief judge to conclude the proceedings if "appropriate corrective action has been taken." 28 U.S.C. § 352(b)(2). Under the Rule, action taken after the complaint is filed is "appropriate" when it acknowledges and remedies the problem raised by the complaint. Breyer Committee Report, 239 F.R.D. at 244. Because the Act deals with the conduct of judges, the emphasis is on correction of the judicial conduct that was the subject of the complaint. Id. Terminating a complaint based on corrective action is premised on the implicit understanding that voluntary self-correction or redress of misconduct or a disability is preferable to sanctions. Id. The chief judge may facilitate this process by giving the subject judge an objective view of the appearance of the judicial conduct in question and by suggesting appropriate corrective measures. Id. Moreover, when corrective action is taken under Rule 5 satisfactory to the chief judge before a complaint is filed, that informal resolution will be sufficient to conclude a subsequent complaint based on the identical conduct.

"Corrective action" must be voluntary action taken by the subject judge. Breyer Committee Report, 239 F.R.D. at 244. A remedial action directed by the chief judge or by an appellate court without the participation of the subject judge in formulating the directive or without the subject judge's subsequent agreement to such action does not constitute the requisite voluntary corrective action. Id. Neither the chief judge nor an appellate court has authority under the Act to impose a formal remedy or sanction; only the judicial council can impose a formal remedy or sanction under 28 U.S.C. § 354(a)(2). Id. Compliance with a previous council order may serve as corrective action allowing conclusion of a later complaint about the same behavior. Id.

Where a judge's conduct has resulted in identifiable, particularized harm to the complainant or another individual, appropriate corrective action should include steps taken by that judge to acknowledge and redress the harm, if possible, such as by an apology, recusal from a case, or a pledge to refrain from similar conduct in the future. Id. While the Act is generally forward-looking, any corrective action should, to the extent possible, serve to correct a specific harm to an individual, if such harm can reasonably be remedied. Id. In some cases, corrective action may not be "appropriate" to justify conclusion of a complaint unless the complainant or other individual harmed is meaningfully apprised of the nature of the corrective action in the chief judge's order, in a direct communication from the subject judge, or otherwise. Id.

Voluntary corrective action should be proportionate to any plausible allegations of misconduct in the complaint. The form of corrective action should also be proportionate to any sanctions that a judicial council might impose under Rule 20(b), such as a private or public reprimand or a change in case assignments. Breyer Committee Report, 239 F.R.D at 244–45. In other words, minor corrective action will not suffice to dispose of a serious matter. Id.

Rule 11(e) implements Section 352(b)(2) of the Act, which permits the chief judge to "conclude the proceeding," if "action on the complaint is no longer necessary because of intervening events," such as a resignation from judicial office. Ordinarily, however, stepping down from an administrative post such as chief judge, judicial-council member, or court-committee chair does not constitute an event rendering unnecessary any further action on a complaint alleging judicial misconduct. Breyer Committee Report, 239 F.R.D. at 245.

As long as the subject of the complaint performs judicial duties, a complaint alleging judicial misconduct must be addressed. Id.

If a complaint is not disposed of pursuant to Rule 11(c), (d), or (e), a special committee must be appointed. Rule 11(f) states that a subject judge must be invited to respond to the complaint before a special committee is appointed, if no earlier response was invited.

Subject judges, of course, receive copies of complaints at the same time that they are referred to the chief judge, and they are free to volunteer responses to them. Under Rule 11(b), the chief judge may request a response if it is thought necessary. However, many complaints are clear candidates for dismissal even if their allegations are accepted as true, and there is no need for the subject judge to devote time to a defense.

The Act requires that the order dismissing a complaint or concluding the proceeding contain a statement of reasons and that a copy of the order be sent to the complainant. 28 U.S.C. § 352(b). Rule 24, dealing with availability of information to the public, contemplates that the order will be made public, usually without disclosing the names of the complainant or the subject judge. If desired for administrative purposes, more identifying information can be included in a non-public version of the order.

When complaints are disposed of by chief judges, the statutory purposes are best served by providing the complainant with a full, particularized, but concise explanation, giving reasons for the conclusions reached. See also Commentary on Rule 24, dealing with public availability.

Rule 11(g) provides that the complainant and subject judge must be notified, in the case of a disposition by the chief judge, of the right to petition the judicial council for review. A copy of a chief judge's order and memorandum, which may be one document, disposing of a complaint must be sent by the circuit clerk to the Judicial Conference Committee on Judicial Conduct and Disability.

ARTICLE IV. INVESTIGATION AND REPORT BY SPECIAL COMMITTEE

RULE 12. COMPOSITION OF SPECIAL COMMITTEE

(a) Membership. Except as provided in (e), a special committee appointed under Rule 11(f) must consist of the chief judge and equal numbers of circuit and district judges. If the complaint is about a district judge, bankruptcy judge, or magistrate judge, then, when possible, the district-judge members of the committee must be from districts other than the district of the subject judge. For the courts named in 28 U.S.C. § 363, the committee must be selected from the judges serving on the subject judge's court.

(b) Presiding Officer. When appointing the committee, the chief judge may serve as the presiding officer or else must designate a committee member as the presiding officer.

(c) Bankruptcy Judge or Magistrate Judge as Adviser. If the subject judge is a bankruptcy judge or magistrate judge, he or she may, within 14 days after being notified of the committee's appointment, ask the chief judge to designate as a committee adviser another bankruptcy judge or magistrate judge, as the case may be. The chief judge must grant such a request but may otherwise use discretion in naming the adviser. Unless the adviser is a Court of Federal Claims special master appointed under 42 U.S.C. § 300aa–12(c), the adviser must be from a district other than the district of the subject bankruptcy judge or subject magistrate judge. The adviser cannot vote but has the other privileges of a committee member.

(d) Provision of Documents. The chief judge must certify to each other member of the committee and to any adviser copies of the complaint and statement of facts in whole or relevant part, and any other relevant documents on file.

(e) Continuing Qualification of Committee Members. A member of a special committee who was qualified to serve when appointed may continue to serve on the committee even though the member relinquishes the position of chief judge, active circuit judge, or active district judge, as the case may be, but only if the member continues to hold office under Article III, Section 1, of the Constitution of the United States, or under 28 U.S.C. § 171.

(f) Inability of Committee Member to Complete Service. If a member of a special committee can no longer serve because of death, disability, disqualification, resignation, retirement from office, or other reason, the chief judge must decide whether to appoint a replacement member, either a circuit or district judge as needed under (a). No special committee appointed under these Rules may function with only a single member, and the votes of a two-member committee must be unanimous.

(g) Voting. All actions by a committee must be by vote of a majority of all members of the committee.

[Adopted March 11, 2008, effective April 10, 2008.]

Commentary on Rule 12

This Rule is adapted from the Act and the Illustrative Rules.

Rule 12 leaves the size of a special committee flexible, to be determined on a case-by-case basis. The question of committee size is one that should be weighed with care in view of the potential for consuming the members' time; a large committee should be appointed only if there is a special reason to do so.

Although the Act requires that the chief judge be a member of each special committee, 28 U.S.C. § 353(a)(1), it does not require that the chief judge preside. Accordingly, Rule 12(b) provides that if the chief judge does not preside, he or she must designate another committee member as the presiding officer.

Rule 12(c) provides that the chief judge must appoint a bankruptcy judge or magistrate judge as an adviser to a special committee at the request of a bankruptcy or magistrate subject judge.

Subsection (c) also provides that the adviser will have all the privileges of a committee member except a vote. The adviser, therefore, may participate in all deliberations of the committee, question witnesses at hearings, and write a separate statement to accompany the special committee's report to the judicial council.

Rule 12(e) provides that a member of a special committee who remains an Article III judge may continue to serve on the committee even though the member's status otherwise changes. Thus, a committee that originally consisted of the chief judge and an equal number of circuit and district judges, as required by the law, may continue to function even though changes of status alter that composition. This provision reflects the belief that stability of membership will contribute to the quality of the work of such committees.

Stability of membership is also the principal concern animating Rule 12(f), which deals with the case in which a special committee loses a member before its work is complete. The Rule permits the chief judge to determine whether a replacement member should be appointed. Generally, appointment of a replacement member is desirable in these situations unless the committee has conducted evidentiary hearings before the vacancy occurs. However, cases may arise in which a committee is in the late stages of its work, and in which it would be difficult for a new member to play a meaningful role. The Rule also preserves the collegial character of the committee process by prohibiting a single surviving member from serving as a committee and by providing that a committee of two surviving members will, in essence, operate under a unanimity rule.

Rule 12(g) provides that actions of a special committee must be by vote of a majority of all the members. All the members of a committee should participate in committee decisions. In that circumstance, it seems reasonable to require that committee decisions be made by a majority of the membership, rather than a majority of some smaller quorum.

RULE 13. CONDUCT OF AN INVESTIGATION

(a) Extent and Methods of Special–Committee Investigation. Each special committee must determine the appropriate extent and methods of the investigation in light of the allegations of the complaint. If, in the course of the investigation, the committee has cause to believe that the subject judge may have engaged in misconduct or has a disability that is beyond the scope of the complaint, the committee must refer the new matter to the chief judge for action under Rule 5 or Rule 11.

(b) Criminal Conduct. If the committee's investigation concerns conduct that may be a crime, the committee must consult with the appropriate prosecutorial authorities to the extent permitted by the Act to avoid compromising any criminal investigation. The committee has final authority over the timing and extent of its investigation and the formulation of its recommendations.

(c) Staff. The committee may arrange for staff assistance to conduct the investigation. It may use existing staff of the judicial branch or may hire special staff through the Director of the Administrative Office of the United States Courts.

(d) Delegation of Subpoena Power; Contempt. The chief judge may delegate the authority to exercise the committee's subpoena powers. The judicial council or special committee may institute a contempt proceeding under 28 U.S.C. § 332(d) against anyone who fails to comply with a subpoena.

[Adopted March 11, 2008, effective April 10, 2008.]

Commentary on Rule 13

This Rule is adapted from the Illustrative Rules.

Rule 13, as well as Rules 14, 15, and 16, are concerned with the way in which a special committee carries out its mission. They reflect the view that a special committee has two roles that are separated in ordinary litigation. First, the committee has an investigative role of the kind that is characteristically left to executive branch agencies or discovery by civil litigants. 28 U.S.C. § 353(c). Second, it has a formalized fact-finding and recommendation-of-disposition role that is characteristically left to juries, judges, or arbitrators. Id. Rule 13 generally governs the investigative stage. Even though the same body has responsibility for both roles under the Act, it is important to distinguish between them in order to ensure that appropriate rights are afforded at appropriate times to the subject judge.

One of the difficult questions that can arise is the relationship between proceedings under the Act and criminal investigations. Rule 13(b) assigns responsibility for coordination to the special committee in cases in which criminal conduct is suspected, but gives the committee the authority to determine the appropriate pace of its activity in light of any criminal investigation.

Title 28 U.S.C. § 356(a) provides that a special committee will have full subpoena powers as provided in 28 U.S.C. § 332(d). Section 332(d)(1) provides that subpoenas will be issued on behalf of judicial councils by the circuit clerk "at the direction of the chief judge of the circuit or his designee." Rule 13(d) contemplates that, where the chief judge designates someone else as presiding officer of a special committee, the presiding officer also be delegated the authority to direct the circuit clerk to issue subpoenas related to committee proceedings. That is not intended to imply, however, that the decision to use the subpoena power is exercisable by the presiding officer alone. See Rule 12(g).

RULE 14. CONDUCT OF HEARINGS BY SPECIAL COMMITTEE

(a) Purpose of Hearings. The committee may hold hearings to take testimony and receive other evidence, to hear argument, or both. If the committee is investigating allegations against more than one judge, it may hold joint or separate hearings.

(b) Committee Evidence. Subject to Rule 15, the committee must obtain material, nonredundant evidence in the form it considers appropriate. In the committee's discretion, evidence may be obtained by committee members, staff, or both. Witnesses offering testimonial evidence may include the complainant and the subject judge.

(c) Counsel for Witnesses. The subject judge has the right to counsel. The special committee has discretion to decide whether other witnesses may have counsel present when they testify.

(d) Witness Fees. Witness fees must be paid as provided in 28 U.S.C. § 1821.

(e) Oath. All testimony taken at a hearing must be given under oath or affirmation.

(f) Rules of Evidence. The Federal Rules of Evidence do not apply to special-committee hearings.

(g) Record and Transcript. A record and transcript must be made of all hearings.

[Adopted March 11, 2008, effective April 10, 2008.]

Commentary on Rule 14

This Rule is adapted from Section 353 of the Act and the Illustrative Rules.

Rule 14 is concerned with the conduct of fact-finding hearings. Special-committee hearings will normally be held only after the investigative work has been completed and the committee has concluded that there is sufficient evidence to warrant a formal fact-finding proceeding. Special-committee proceedings are primarily inquisitorial rather than adversarial. Accordingly, the Federal Rules of Evidence do not apply to such hearings. Inevitably, a hearing will have something of an adversary character. Nevertheless, that tendency should be moderated to the extent possible. Even though a proceeding will commonly have investigative and hearing stages, committee members should not regard themselves as prosecutors one day and judges the next. Their duty—and that of their staff—is at all times to be impartial seekers of the truth.

Rule 14(b) contemplates that material evidence will be obtained by the committee and presented in the form of affidavits, live testimony, etc. Staff or others who are organizing the hearings should regard it as their role to present evidence representing the entire picture. With respect to testimonial evidence, the subject judge should normally be called as a committee witness. Cases may arise in which the judge will not testify voluntarily. In such cases, subpoena powers are available, subject to the normal testimonial privileges. Although Rule 15(c) recognizes the subject judge's statutory right to call witnesses on his or her own behalf, exercise of this right should not usually be necessary.

RULE 15. RIGHTS OF SUBJECT JUDGE

(a) Notice.

(1) *Generally.* The subject judge must receive written notice of:

(A) the appointment of a special committee under Rule 11(f);

(B) the expansion of the scope of an investigation under Rule 13(a);

(C) any hearing under Rule 14, including its purposes, the names of any witnesses the committee intends to call, and the text of any statements that have been taken from those witnesses.

(2) *Suggestion of Additional Witnesses.* The subject judge may suggest additional witnesses to the committee.

(b) Report of the Special Committee. The subject judge must be sent a copy of the special committee's report when it is filed with the judicial council.

(c) Presentation of Evidence. At any hearing held under Rule 14, the subject judge has the right to present evidence, to compel the attendance of witnesses, and to compel the production of documents. At the request of the subject judge, the chief judge or the judge's designee must direct the circuit clerk to issue a subpoena to a witness under 28 U.S.C. § 332(d)(1). The subject judge must be given the opportunity to cross-examine committee witnesses, in person or by counsel.

(d) Presentation of Argument. The subject judge may submit written argument to the special committee and must be given a reasonable opportunity to present oral argument at an appropriate stage of the investigation.

(e) Attendance at Hearings. The subject judge has the right to attend any hearing held under Rule 14 and to receive copies of the transcript, of any documents introduced, and of any written arguments submitted by the complainant to the committee.

(f) Representation by Counsel. The subject judge may choose to be represented by counsel in the exercise of any right enumerated in this Rule. As provided in Rule 20(e), the United States may bear the costs of the representation.

[Adopted March 11, 2008, effective April 10, 2008.]

Commentary on Rule 15

This Rule is adapted from the Act and the Illustrative Rules.

The Act states that these Rules must contain provisions requiring that "the judge whose conduct is the subject of a complaint ... be afforded an opportunity to appear (in person or by counsel) at proceedings conducted by the investigating panel, to present oral and documentary evidence, to compel the attendance of witnesses or the production of documents, to cross-examine witnesses, and to present argument orally or in writing." 28 U.S.C. § 358(b)(2). To implement this provision, Rule 15(e) gives the judge the right to attend any hearing held for the purpose of receiving evidence of record or hearing argument under Rule 14.

The Act does not require that the subject judge be permitted to attend all proceedings of the special committee. Accordingly, the Rules do not give a right to attend other proceedings—for example, meetings at which the committee is engaged in investigative activity, such as interviewing persons to learn whether they ought to be called as witnesses or examining for relevance purposes documents delivered pursuant to a subpoena duces tecum, or meetings in which the committee is deliberating on the evidence or its recommendations.

RULE 16.   RIGHTS OF COMPLAINANT IN INVESTIGATION

(a) Notice. The complainant must receive written notice of the investigation as provided in Rule 11(g)(1). When the special committee's report to the judicial council is filed, the complainant must be notified of the filing. The judicial council may, in its discretion, provide a copy of the report of a special committee to the complainant.

(b) Opportunity to Provide Evidence. If the committee determines that the complainant may have evidence that does not already exist in writing, a representative of the committee must interview the complainant.

(c) Presentation of Argument. The complainant may submit written argument to the special committee. In its discretion, the special committee may permit the complainant to offer oral argument.

(d) Representation by Counsel. A complainant may submit written argument through counsel and, if permitted to offer oral argument, may do so through counsel.

(e) Cooperation. In exercising its discretion under this Rule, a special committee may take into account the degree of the complainant's cooperation in preserving the confidentiality of the proceedings, including the identity of the subject judge.

[Adopted March 11, 2008, effective April 10, 2008.]

Commentary on Rule 16

This Rule is adapted from the Act and the Illustrative Rules.

In accordance with the view of the process as fundamentally administrative and inquisitorial, these Rules do not give the complainant the rights of a party to litigation, and leave the complainant's role largely to the discretion of the special committee. However, Rule 16(b) provides that, where a special committee has been appointed and it determines that the complainant may have additional evidence, the complainant must be interviewed by a representative of the committee. Such an interview may be in person or by telephone, and the representative of the committee may be either a member or staff.

Rule 16 does not contemplate that the complainant will ordinarily be permitted to attend proceedings of the special committee except when testifying or presenting oral argument. A special committee may exercise its discretion to permit the complainant to be present at its proceedings, or to permit the complainant, individually or through counsel, to participate in the examination or cross-examination of witnesses.

The Act authorizes an exception to the normal confidentiality provisions where the judicial council in its discretion provides a copy of the report of the special committee to the complainant and to the subject judge. 28 U.S.C. § 360(a)(1). However, the Rules do not entitle the complainant to a copy of the special committee's report.

In exercising their discretion regarding the role of the complainant, the special committee and the judicial council should protect the confidentiality of the complaint process. As a consequence, subsection (e) provides that a special committee may consider the degree to which a complainant has cooperated in preserving the confidentiality of the proceedings in determining what role beyond the minimum required by these Rules should be given to that complainant.

RULE 17.   SPECIAL–COMMITTEE REPORT

The committee must file with the judicial council a comprehensive report of its investigation, including findings and recommendations for council action. The report must be accompanied by a statement of the vote by which it was adopted, any separate or dissenting statements of committee members, and the record of any hearings held under Rule 14. A copy of the report and accompanying statement must be sent to the Judicial Conference Committee on Judicial Conduct and Disability.

[Adopted March 11, 2008, effective April 10, 2008.]

Commentary on Rule 17

This Rule is adapted from the Illustrative Rules and is self-explanatory. The provision for sending a copy of the special-committee report and accompanying statement to the Judicial Conference Committee is new.

ARTICLE V. JUDICIAL–COUNCIL REVIEW

RULE 18. PETITIONS FOR REVIEW OF CHIEF JUDGE DISPOSITIONS UNDER RULE 11(C), (D), OR (E)

(a) Petitions for Review. After the chief judge issues an order under Rule 11(c), (d), or (e), a complainant or subject judge may petition the judicial council of the circuit to review the order. By rules promulgated under 28 U.S.C. § 358, the judicial council may refer a petition for review filed under this Rule to a panel of no fewer than five members of the council, at least two of whom must be district judges.

(b) When to File; Form; Where to File. A petition for review must be filed in the office of the circuit clerk within 35 days of the date on the clerk's letter informing the parties of the chief judge's order. The petition should be in letter form, addressed to the circuit clerk, and in an envelope marked "Misconduct Petition" or "Disability Petition." The name of the subject judge must not be shown on the envelope. The letter should be typewritten or otherwise legible. It should begin with "I hereby petition the judicial council for review of . . ." and state the reasons why the petition should be granted. It must be signed.

(c) Receipt and Distribution of Petition. A circuit clerk who receives a petition for review filed within the time allowed and in proper form must:

(1) acknowledge its receipt and send a copy to the complainant or subject judge, as the case may be;

(2) promptly distribute to each member of the judicial council, or its relevant panel, except for any member disqualified under Rule 25, or make available in the manner provided by local rule, the following materials:

   (A) copies of the complaint;

   (B) all materials obtained by the chief judge in connection with the inquiry;

   (C) the chief judge's order disposing of the complaint;

   (D) any memorandum in support of the chief judge's order;

   (E) the petition for review; and

   (F) an appropriate ballot;

(3) send the petition for review to the Judicial Conference Committee on Judicial Conduct and Disability. Unless the Judicial Conference Committee requests them, the clerk will not send copies of the materials obtained by the chief judge.

(d) Untimely Petition. The clerk must refuse to accept a petition that is received after the deadline in (b).

(e) Timely Petition Not in Proper Form. When the clerk receives a petition filed within the time allowed but in a form that is improper to a degree that would substantially impair its consideration by the judicial council—such as a document that is ambiguous about whether it is intended to be a petition for review—the clerk must acknowledge its receipt, call the filer's attention to the deficiencies, and give the filer the opportunity to correct the deficiencies within 21 days of the date of the clerk's letter about the deficiencies or within the original deadline for filing the petition, whichever is later. If the deficiencies are corrected within the time allowed, the clerk will proceed according to paragraphs (a) and (c) of this Rule. If the deficiencies are not corrected, the clerk must reject the petition.

[Adopted March 11, 2008, effective April 10, 2008.]

Commentary on Rule 18

Rule 18 is adapted largely from the Illustrative Rules.

Subsection (a) permits a subject judge, as well as the complainant, to petition for review of a chief judge's order dismissing a complaint under Rule 11(c), or concluding that appropriate corrective action or intervening events have remedied or mooted the problems raised by the complaint pursuant to Rule 11(d) or (e). Although the subject judge may ostensibly be vindicated by the dismissal or conclusion of a complaint, a chief judge's order may include language disagreeable to the subject judge. For example, an order may dismiss a complaint, but state that the subject judge did in fact engage in misconduct. Accordingly, a subject judge may wish to object to the content of the order and is given the opportunity to petition the judicial council of the circuit for review.

Subsection (b) contains a time limit of thirty-five days to file a petition for review. It is important to establish a time limit on petitions for review of chief judges' dispositions in order to provide finality to the process. If the complaint requires an investigation, the investigation should proceed; if it does not, the subject judge should know that the matter is closed.

The standards for timely filing under the Federal Rules of Appellate Procedure should be applied to petitions for review. See Fed. R. App. P. 25(a)(2)(A) and (C).

Rule 18(e) provides for an automatic extension of the time limit imposed under subsection (b) if a person files a petition that is rejected for failure to comply with formal requirements.

RULE 19. JUDICIAL–COUNCIL DISPOSITION OF PETITIONS FOR REVIEW

(a) Rights of Subject Judge. At any time after a complainant files a petition for review, the subject judge may file a written response with the circuit clerk. The clerk must promptly distribute copies of the response to each member of the judicial council or of the relevant panel, unless that member is disqualified under Rule 25. Copies must also be distributed to the chief judge, to the complainant, and to the Judicial Conference Committee on Judicial Conduct and Disability. The subject judge must not otherwise communicate with individual council members about the matter. The subject judge must be given copies of any communications to the judicial council from the complainant.

(b) Judicial–Council Action. After considering a petition for review and the materials before it, a judicial council may:

(1) affirm the chief judge's disposition by denying the petition;

(2) return the matter to the chief judge with directions to conduct a further inquiry under Rule 11(b) or to identify a complaint under Rule 5;

(3) return the matter to the chief judge with directions to appoint a special committee under Rule 11(f); or

(4) in exceptional circumstances, take other appropriate action.

(c) Notice of Council Decision. Copies of the judicial council's order, together with any accompanying memorandum in support of the order or separate concurring or dissenting statements, must be given to the complainant, the subject judge, and the Judicial Conference Committee on Judicial Conduct and Disability.

(d) Memorandum of Council Decision. If the council's order affirms the chief judge's disposition, a supporting memorandum must be prepared only if the judicial council concludes that there is a need to supplement the chief judge's explanation. A memorandum supporting a council order must not include the name of the complainant or the subject judge.

(e) Review of Judicial–Council Decision. If the judicial council's decision is adverse to the petitioner, and if no member of the council dissented on the ground that a special committee should be appointed under Rule 11(f), the complainant must be notified that he or she has no right to seek review of the decision. If there was a dissent, the petitioner must be informed that he or she can file a petition for review under Rule 21(b) solely on the issue of whether a special committee should be appointed.

(f) Public Availability of Judicial–Council Decision. Materials related to the council's decision must be made public to the extent, at the time, and in the manner set forth in Rule 24.

[Adopted March 11, 2008, effective April 10, 2008.]

Commentary on Rule 19

This Rule is largely adapted from the Act and is self-explanatory.

The council should ordinarily review the decision of the chief judge on the merits, treating the petition for review for all practical purposes as an appeal. The judicial council may respond to a petition by affirming the chief judge's order, remanding the matter, or, in exceptional cases, taking other appropriate action.

RULE 20. JUDICIAL–COUNCIL CONSIDERATION OF REPORTS AND RECOMMENDATIONS OF SPECIAL COMMITTEES

(a) Rights of Subject Judge. Within 21 days after the filing of the report of a special committee, the subject judge may send a written response to the members of the judicial council. The judge must also be given an opportunity to present argument through counsel, written or oral, as determined by the council. The judge must not otherwise communicate with council members about the matter.

(b) Judicial–Council Action.

(1) *Discretionary Actions.* Subject to the judge's rights set forth in subsection (a), the judicial council may:

(A) dismiss the complaint because:

(i) even if the claim is true, the claimed conduct is not conduct prejudicial to the effective and expeditious administration of the business of the courts and does not indicate a mental or physical disability resulting in inability to discharge the duties of office;

(ii) the complaint is directly related to the merits of a decision or procedural ruling;

(iii) the facts on which the complaint is based have not been established; or

(iv) the complaint is otherwise not appropriate for consideration under 28 U.S.C. §§ 351–364.

(B) conclude the proceeding because appropriate corrective action has been taken or intervening events have made the proceeding unnecessary.

(C) refer the complaint to the Judicial Conference of the United States with the council's recommendations for action.

(D) take remedial action to ensure the effective and expeditious administration of the business of the courts, including:

(i) censuring or reprimanding the subject judge, either by private communication or by public announcement;

(ii) ordering that no new cases be assigned to the subject judge for a limited, fixed period;

(iii) in the case of a magistrate judge, ordering the chief judge of the district court to take action specified by the council, including the initiation of removal proceedings under 28 U.S.C. § 631(i) or 42 U.S.C. § 300aa–12(c)(2);

(iv) in the case of a bankruptcy judge, removing the judge from office under 28 U.S.C. § 152(e);

(v) in the case of a circuit or district judge, requesting the judge to retire voluntarily with the provision (if necessary) that ordinary length-of-service requirements will be waived; and

(vi) in the case of a circuit or district judge who is eligible to retire but does not do so, certifying the disability of the judge under 28 U.S.C. § 372(b) so that an additional judge may be appointed.

(E) take any combination of actions described in (b)(1)(A)–(D) of this Rule that is within its power.

(2) *Mandatory Actions.* A judicial council must refer a complaint to the Judicial Conference if the council determines that a circuit judge or district judge may have engaged in conduct that:

(A) might constitute ground for impeachment; or

(B) in the interest of justice, is not amenable to resolution by the judicial council.

(c) Inadequate Basis for Decision. If the judicial council finds that a special committee's report, recommendations, and record provide an inadequate basis for decision, it may return the matter to the committee for further investigation and a new report, or it may conduct further investigation. If the judicial council decides to conduct further investigation, the subject judge must be given adequate prior notice in writing of that decision and of the general scope and purpose of the additional investigation. The judicial council's conduct of the additional investigation must generally accord with the procedures and powers set forth in Rules 13 through 16 for the conduct of an investigation by a special committee.

(d) Council Vote. Council action must be taken by a majority of those members of the council who are not disqualified. A decision to remove a bankruptcy judge from office requires a majority vote of all the members of the council.

(e) Recommendation for Fee Reimbursement. If the complaint has been finally dismissed or concluded under (b)(1)(A) or (B) of this Rule, and if the subject judge so requests, the judicial council may recommend that the Director of the Administrative Office of the United States Courts use funds appropriated to the Judiciary to reimburse the judge for reasonable expenses incurred during the investigation, when those expenses would not have been incurred but for the requirements of the Act and these Rules. Reasonable expenses include attorneys' fees and expenses related to a successful defense or prosecution of a proceeding under Rule 21(a) or (b).

(f) Council Action. Council action must be by written order. Unless the council finds that extraordinary reasons would make it contrary to the interests of justice, the order must be accompanied by a memorandum setting forth the factual determinations on which it is based and the reasons for the council action. The order and the supporting memorandum must be provided to the complainant, the subject judge, and the Judicial Conference Committee on Judicial Conduct and Disability. The complainant and the subject judge must be notified of any right to review of the judicial council's decision as provided in Rule 21(b).

[Adopted March 11, 2008, effective April 10, 2008.]

Commentary on Rule 20

This Rule is largely adapted from the Illustrative Rules.

Rule 20(a) provides that within twenty-one days after the filing of the report of a special committee, the subject judge may address a written response to all of the members of the judicial council. The subject judge must also be given an opportunity to present oral argument to the council, personally or through counsel. The subject judge may not otherwise communicate with council members about the matter.

Rule 20(c) provides that if the judicial council decides to conduct an additional investigation, the subject judge must be given adequate prior notice in writing of that decision and of the general scope and purpose of the additional investigation. The conduct of the investigation will be generally in accordance with the procedures set forth in Rules 13 through 16 for the conduct of an investigation by a special committee. However, if hearings are held, the council may limit testimony or the presentation of evidence to avoid unnecessary repetition of testimony and evidence before the special committee.

Rule 20(d) provides that council action must be taken by a majority of those members of the council who are not disqualified, except that a decision to remove a bankruptcy judge from office requires a majority of all the members of the council as required by 28 U.S.C. § 152(e). However, it is inappropriate to apply a similar rule to the less severe actions that a judicial council may take under the Act. If some members of the council are disqualified in the matter, their disqualification should not be given the effect of a vote against council action.

With regard to Rule 20(e), the judicial council, on the request of the subject judge, may recommend to the Director of the Administrative Office of the United States Courts that the subject judge be reimbursed for reasonable expenses, including attorneys' fees, incurred. The judicial council has the authority to recommend such reimbursement where, after investigation by a special committee, the complaint has been finally dismissed or concluded under subsection (b)(1)(A) or (B) of this Rule. It is contemplated that such reimbursement may be provided for the successful prosecution or defense of a proceeding under Rule 21(a) or (b), in other words, one that results in a Rule 20(b)(1)(A) or (B) dismissal or conclusion.

Rule 20(f) requires that council action normally be supported with a memorandum of factual determinations and reasons and that notice of the action be given to the complainant and the subject judge. Rule 20(f) also requires that the notification to the complainant and the subject judge include notice of any right to petition for review of the council's decision under Rule 21(b).

ARTICLE VI. REVIEW BY JUDICIAL CONFERENCE COMMITTEE ON CONDUCT AND DISABILITY

RULE 21. COMMITTEE ON JUDICIAL CONDUCT AND DISABILITY

(a) Review by Committee. The Committee on Judicial Conduct and Disability, consisting of seven members, considers and disposes of all petitions for review under (b) of this Rule, in conformity with the Committee's jurisdictional statement. Its disposition of petitions for review is ordinarily final. The Judicial Conference of the United States may, in its sole discretion, review any such Committee decision, but a complainant or subject judge does not have a right to this review.

(b) Reviewable Matters.

(1) *Upon Petition.* A complainant or subject judge may petition the Committee for review of a judicial-council order entered in accordance with:

(A) Rule 20(b)(1)(A), (B), (D), or (E); or

(B) Rule 19(b)(1) or (4) if one or more members of the judicial council dissented from the order on the ground that a special committee should be appointed under Rule 11(f); in that event, the Committee's review will be limited to the issue of whether a special committee should be appointed.

(2) *Upon Committee's Initiative.* At its initiative and in its sole discretion, the Committee may review any judicial-council order entered under Rule 19(b)(1) or (4), but only to determine whether a special committee should be appointed. Before undertaking the review, the Committee must invite that judicial council to explain why it believes the appointment of a special committee is unnecessary, unless the reasons are clearly stated in the judicial council's order denying the petition for review. If the Committee believes that it would benefit from a submission by the subject judge, it may issue an appropriate request. If the Committee determines that a special committee should be appointed, the Committee must issue a written decision giving its reasons.

(c) Committee Vote. Any member of the Committee from the same circuit as the subject judge is disqualified from considering or voting on a petition for review. Committee decisions under (b) of this Rule must be by majority vote of the qualified Committee members. If only six members are qualified to vote on a petition for review, the decision must be made by a majority of a panel of five members drawn from a randomly selected list that rotates after each decision by a panel drawn from the list. The mem-

bers who will determine the petition must be selected based on committee membership as of the date on which the petition is received. Those members selected to hear the petition should serve in that capacity until final disposition of the petition, whether or not their term of committee membership has ended. If only four members are qualified to vote, the Chief Justice must appoint, if available, an ex-member of the Committee or, if not, another United States judge to consider the petition.

(d) Additional Investigation. Except in extraordinary circumstances, the Committee will not conduct an additional investigation. The Committee may return the matter to the judicial council with directions to undertake an additional investigation. If the Committee conducts an additional investigation, it will exercise the powers of the Judicial Conference under 28 U.S.C. § 331.

(e) Oral Argument; Personal Appearance. There is ordinarily no oral argument or personal appearance before the Committee. In its discretion, the Committee may permit written submissions from the complainant or subject judge.

(f) Committee Decisions. Committee decisions under this Rule must be transmitted promptly to the Judicial Conference of the United States. Other distribution will be by the Administrative Office at the direction of the Committee chair.

(g) Finality. All orders of the Judicial Conference or of the Committee (when the Conference does not exercise its power of review) are final.

[Adopted March 11, 2008, effective April 10, 2008.]

Commentary on Rule 21

This Rule is largely self-explanatory.

Rule 21(a) is intended to clarify that the delegation of power to the Judicial Conference Committee on Judicial Conduct and Disability to dispose of petitions does not preclude review of such dispositions by the Conference. However, there is no right to such review in any party.

Rules 21(b)(1)(B) and (b)(2) are intended to fill a jurisdictional gap as to review of dismissals or conclusions of complaints under Rule 19(b)(1) or (4). Where one or more members of a judicial council reviewing a petition have dissented on the ground that a special committee should have been appointed, the complainant or subject judge has the right to petition for review by the Committee but only as to that issue. Under Rule 21(b)(2), the Judicial Conference Committee on Judicial Conduct and Disability may review such a dismissal or conclusion in its sole discretion, whether or not such a dissent occurred, and only as to the appointment of a special committee. No party has a right to such review, and such review will be rare.

Rule 21(c) provides for review only by Committee members from circuits other than that of the subject judge. To avoid tie votes, the Committee will decide petitions for review by rotating panels of five when only six members are qualified. If only four members are qualified, the Chief Justice must appoint an additional judge to consider that petition for review.

Under this Rule, all Committee decisions are final in that they are unreviewable unless the Judicial Conference, in its discretion, decides to review a decision. Committee decisions, however, do not necessarily constitute final action on a complaint for purposes of Rule 24.

RULE 22. PROCEDURES FOR REVIEW

(a) Filing a Petition for Review. A petition for review of a judicial-council decision may be filed by sending a brief written statement to the Judicial Conference Committee on Judicial Conduct and Disability, addressed to:

> Judicial Conference Committee on Judicial Conduct and Disability
>
> Attn: Office of General Counsel
>
> Administrative Office of the United States Courts
>
> One Columbus Circle, NE
>
> Washington, D.C. 20544

The Administrative Office will send a copy of the petition to the complainant or subject judge, as the case may be.

(b) Form and Contents of Petition for Review. No particular form is required. The petition must contain a short statement of the basic facts underlying the complaint, the history of its consideration before the appropriate judicial council, a copy of the judicial council's decision, and the grounds on which the petitioner seeks review. The petition for review must specify the date and docket number of the judicial-council order for which review is sought. The petitioner may attach any documents or correspondence arising in the course of the proceeding before the judicial council or its special committee. A petition should not normally exceed 20 pages plus necessary attachments.

(c) Time. A petition must be submitted within 63 days of the date of the order for which review is sought.

(d) Copies. Seven copies of the petition for review must be submitted, at least one of which must be signed by the petitioner or his or her attorney. If the petitioner submits a signed declaration of inability to pay the expense of duplicating the petition, the Administrative Office must accept the original petition and must reproduce copies at its expense.

(e) Action on Receipt of Petition for Review. The Administrative Office must acknowledge receipt of a petition for review submitted under this Rule, notify the chair of the Judicial Conference Committee on Judicial Conduct and Disability, and distribute the petition to the members of the Committee for their deliberation.

[Adopted March 11, 2008, effective April 10, 2008.]

Commentary on Rule 22

Rule 22 is self-explanatory.

ARTICLE VII. MISCELLANEOUS RULES

RULE 23. CONFIDENTIALITY

(a) General Rule. The consideration of a complaint by the chief judge, a special committee, the judicial council, or the Judicial Conference Committee on Judicial Conduct and Disability is confidential. Information about this consideration must not be disclosed by any judge or employee of the judicial branch or by any person who records or transcribes testimony except as allowed by these Rules. In extraordinary circumstances, a chief judge may disclose the existence of a proceeding under these Rules when necessary to maintain public confidence in the federal judiciary's ability to redress misconduct or disability.

(b) Files. All files related to complaints must be separately maintained with appropriate security precautions to ensure confidentiality.

(c) Disclosure in Decisions. Except as otherwise provided in Rule 24, written decisions of the chief judge, the judicial council, or the Judicial Conference Committee on Judicial Conduct and Disability, and dissenting opinions or separate statements of members of the council or Committee may contain information and exhibits that the authors consider appropriate for inclusion, and the information and exhibits may be made public.

(d) Availability to Judicial Conference. On request of the Judicial Conference or its Committee on Judicial Conduct and Disability, the circuit clerk must furnish any requested records related to a complaint. For auditing purposes, the circuit clerk must provide access to the Committee to records of proceedings under the Act at the site where the records are kept.

(e) Availability to District Court. If the judicial council directs the initiation of proceedings for removal of a magistrate judge under Rule 20(b)(1)(D)(iii), the circuit clerk must provide to the chief judge of the district court copies of the report of the special committee and any other documents and records that were before the judicial council at the time of its decision. On request of the chief judge of the district court, the judicial council may authorize release to that chief judge of any other records relating to the investigation.

(f) Impeachment Proceedings. If the Judicial Conference determines that consideration of impeachment may be warranted, it must transmit the record of all relevant proceedings to the Speaker of the House of Representatives.

(g) Subject Judge's Consent. If both the subject judge and the chief judge consent in writing, any materials from the files may be disclosed to any person. In any such disclosure, the chief judge may require that the identity of the complainant, or of witnesses in an investigation conducted by a chief judge, a special committee, or the judicial council, not be revealed.

(h) Disclosure in Special Circumstances. The Judicial Conference, its Committee on Judicial Conduct and Disability, or a judicial council may authorize disclosure of information about the consideration of a complaint, including the papers, documents, and transcripts relating to the investigation, to the extent that disclosure is justified by special circumstances and is not prohibited by the Act. Disclosure may be made to judicial researchers engaged in the study or evaluation of experience under the Act and related modes of judicial discipline, but only where the study or evaluation has been specifically approved by the Judicial Conference or by the Judicial Conference Committee on Judicial Conduct and Disability. Appropriate steps must be taken to protect the identities of the subject judge, the complainant, and witnesses from public disclosure. Other appropriate safeguards to protect against the dissemination of confidential information may be imposed.

(i) Disclosure of Identity by Subject Judge. Nothing in this Rule precludes the subject judge from acknowledging that he or she is the judge referred to in documents made public under Rule 24.

(j) Assistance and Consultation. Nothing in this Rule precludes the chief judge or judicial council acting on a complaint filed under the Act from seeking the help of qualified staff or from consulting other judges who may be helpful in the disposition of the complaint.

[Adopted March 11, 2008, effective April 10, 2008.]

Commentary on Rule 23

Rule 23 was adapted from the Illustrative Rules.

The Act applies a rule of confidentiality to "papers, documents, and records of proceedings related to investigations conducted under this chapter" and states that they may not be disclosed "by any person in any proceeding," with enu-

merated exceptions. 28 U.S.C. § 360(a). Three questions arise: Who is bound by the confidentiality rule, what proceedings are subject to the rule, and who is within the circle of people who may have access to information without breaching the rule?

With regard to the first question, Rule 23(a) provides that judges, employees of the judicial branch, and those persons involved in recording proceedings and preparing transcripts are obliged to respect the confidentiality requirement. This of course includes subject judges who do not consent to identification under Rule 23(i).

With regard to the second question, Rule 23(a) applies the rule of confidentiality broadly to consideration of a complaint at any stage.

With regard to the third question, there is no barrier of confidentiality among a chief judge, judicial council, the Judicial Conference, and the Judicial Conference Committee on Judicial Conduct and Disability. Each may have access to any of the confidential records for use in their consideration of a referred matter, a petition for review, or monitoring the administration of the Act. A district court may have similar access if the judicial council orders the district court to initiate proceedings to remove a magistrate judge from office, and Rule 23(e) so provides.

In extraordinary circumstances, a chief judge may disclose the existence of a proceeding under these Rules. The disclosure of such information in high-visibility or controversial cases is to reassure the public that the federal judiciary is capable of redressing judicial misconduct or disability. Moreover, the confidentiality requirement does not prevent the chief judge from "communicat[ing] orally or in writing with . . . [persons] who may have knowledge of the matter," as part of a limited inquiry conducted by the chief judge under Rule 11(b).

Rule 23 recognizes that there must be some exceptions to the Act's confidentiality requirement. For example, the Act requires that certain orders and the reasons for them must be made public. 28 U.S.C. § 360(b). Rule 23(c) makes it explicit that memoranda supporting chief judge and council orders, as well as dissenting opinions and separate statements, may contain references to information that would otherwise be confidential and that such information may be made public. However, subsection (c) is subject to Rule 24(a) which provides the general rule regarding the public availability of decisions. For example, the name of a subject judge cannot be made public in a decision if disclosure of the name is prohibited by that Rule.

The Act makes clear that there is a barrier of confidentiality between the judicial branch and the legislative. It provides that material may be disclosed to Congress only if it is believed necessary to an impeachment investigation or trial of a judge. 28 U.S.C. § 360(a)(2). Accordingly, Section 355(b) of the Act requires the Judicial Conference to transmit the record of the proceeding to the House of Representatives if the Conference believes that impeachment of a subject judge may be appropriate. Rule 23(f) implements this requirement.

The Act provides that confidential materials may be disclosed if authorized in writing by the subject judge and by the chief judge. 28 U.S.C. § 360(a)(3). Rule 23(g) implements this requirement. Once the subject judge has consented to the disclosure of confidential materials related to a complaint, the chief judge ordinarily will refuse consent only to the extent necessary to protect the confidentiality interests of the complainant or of witnesses who have testified in investigatory proceedings or who have provided information in response to a limited inquiry undertaken pursuant to Rule 11. It will generally be necessary, therefore, for the chief judge to require that the identities of the complainant or of such witnesses, as well as any identifying information, be shielded in any materials disclosed, except insofar as the chief judge has secured the consent of the complainant or of a particular witness to disclosure, or there is a demonstrated need for disclosure of the information that, in the judgment of the chief judge, outweighs the confidentiality interest of the complainant or of a particular witness (as may be the case where the complainant is delusional or where the complainant or a particular witness has already demonstrated a lack of concern about maintaining the confidentiality of the proceedings).

Rule 23(h) permits disclosure of additional information in circumstances not enumerated. For example, disclosure may be appropriate to permit a prosecution for perjury based on testimony given before a special committee. Another example might involve evidence of criminal conduct by a judge discovered by a special committee.

Subsection (h) also permits the authorization of disclosure of information about the consideration of a complaint, including the papers, documents, and transcripts relating to the investigation, to judicial researchers engaged in the study or evaluation of experience under the Act and related modes of judicial discipline. The Rule envisions disclosure of information from the official record of complaint proceedings to a limited category of persons for appropriately authorized research purposes only, and with appropriate safeguards to protect individual identities in any published research results that ensue. In authorizing disclosure, the judicial council may refuse to release particular materials when such release would be contrary to the interests of justice, or that constitute purely internal communications. The Rule does not envision disclosure of purely internal communications between judges and their colleagues and staff.

Under Rule 23(j), chief judges and judicial councils may seek staff assistance or consult with other judges who may be helpful in the process of complaint disposition; the confidentiality requirement does not preclude this. The chief judge, for example, may properly seek the advice and assistance of another judge who the chief judge deems to be in the best position to communicate with the subject judge in an attempt to bring about corrective action. As another example, a new chief judge may wish to confer with a predecessor to learn how similar complaints have been handled. In consulting with other judges, of course, the chief judge should disclose information regarding the complaint only to the extent the chief judge deems necessary under the circumstances.

RULE 24. PUBLIC AVAILABILITY OF DECISIONS

(a) **General Rule; Specific Cases.** When final action has been taken on a complaint and it is no longer subject to review, all orders entered by the chief judge and judicial council, including any supporting memoranda and any dissenting opinions or separate statements by members of the judicial council, must be made public, with the following exceptions:

(1) if the complaint is finally dismissed under Rule 11(c) without the appointment of a special committee, or if it is concluded under Rule 11(d) because of voluntary corrective action, the publicly available materials must not disclose the name of the subject judge without his or her consent.

(2) if the complaint is concluded because of intervening events, or dismissed at any time after a special committee is appointed, the judicial council must determine whether the name of the subject judge should be disclosed.

(3) if the complaint is finally disposed of by a privately communicated censure or reprimand, the publicly available materials must not disclose either the name of the subject judge or the text of the reprimand.

(4) if the complaint is finally disposed of under Rule 20(b)(1)(D) by any action other than private censure or reprimand, the text of the dispositive order must be included in the materials made public, and the name of the subject judge must be disclosed.

(5) the name of the complainant must not be disclosed in materials made public under this Rule unless the chief judge orders disclosure.

(b) **Manner of Making Public.** The orders described in (a) must be made public by placing them in a publicly accessible file in the office of the circuit clerk or by placing the orders on the court's public website. If the orders appear to have precedential value, the chief judge may cause them to be published. In addition, the Judicial Conference Committee on Judicial Conduct and Disability will make available on the Federal Judiciary's website, www.uscourts.gov, selected illustrative orders described in paragraph (a), appropriately redacted, to provide additional information to the public on how complaints are addressed under the Act.

(c) **Orders of Judicial Conference Committee.** Orders of this Committee constituting final action in a complaint proceeding arising from a particular circuit will be made available to the public in the office of the clerk of the relevant court of appeals. The Committee will also make such orders available on the Federal Judiciary's website, www.uscourts.gov. When authorized by the Committee, other orders related to complaint proceedings will similarly be made available.

(d) **Complaints Referred to the Judicial Conference of the United States.** If a complaint is referred to the Judicial Conference under Rule 20(b)(1)(C) or 20(b)(2), materials relating to the complaint will be made public only if ordered by the Judicial Conference.

[Adopted March 11, 2008, effective April 10, 2008.]

Commentary on Rule 24

Rule 24 is adapted from the Illustrative Rules and the recommendations of the Breyer Committee.

The Act requires the circuits to make available only written orders of a judicial council or the Judicial Conference imposing some form of sanction. 28 U.S.C. § 360(b). The Judicial Conference, however, has long recognized the desirability of public availability of a broader range of orders and other materials. In 1994, the Judicial Conference "urge[d] all circuits and courts covered by the Act to submit to the West Publishing Company, for publication in Federal Reporter 3d, and to Lexis all orders issued pursuant to [the Act] that are deemed by the issuing circuit or court to have significant precedential value to other circuits and courts covered by the Act." Report of the Proceedings of the Judicial Conference of the United States, Mar. 1994, at 28. Following this recommendation, the 2000 revision of the Illustrative Rules contained a public availability provision very similar to Rule 24. In 2002, the Judicial Conference again voted to encourage the circuits "to submit non-routine public orders disposing of complaints of judicial misconduct or disability for publication by on-line and print services." Report of the Proceedings of the Judicial Conference of the United States, Sept. 2002, at 58. The Breyer Committee Report further emphasized that "[p]osting such orders on the judicial branch's public website would not only benefit judges directly, it would also encourage scholarly commentary and analysis of the orders." Breyer Committee Report, 239 F.R.D. at 216. With these considerations in mind, Rule 24 provides for public availability of a wide range of materials.

Rule 24 provides for public availability of orders of the chief judge, the judicial council, and the Judicial Conference Committee on Judicial Conduct and Disability and the texts of any memoranda supporting their orders, together with any dissenting opinions or separate statements by members of the judicial council. However, these orders and memoranda are to be made public only when final action on the complaint has been taken and any right of review has been exhausted. The provision that decisions will be made public only after final action has been taken is designed in part to avoid public disclosure of the existence of pending proceedings. Whether the name of the subject judge is disclosed will then depend on the nature of the final action. If the final action is an order predicated on a finding of misconduct or disability (other than a privately communicated censure or reprimand) the name of the judge must be made public. If the final action is dismissal of the complaint, the name of the subject judge must not be disclosed. Rule 24(a)(1) provides that where a proceeding is concluded under Rule 11(d) by the chief judge on the basis of voluntary corrective action, the name of the subject judge must not be disclosed. Shielding the name of the subject judge in this circumstance should encourage informal disposition.

If a complaint is dismissed as moot, or because intervening events have made action on the complaint unnecessary, after appointment of a special committee, Rule 24(a)(2) allows the judicial council to determine whether the subject judge will be identified. In such a case, no final decision has been rendered on the merits, but it may be in the public interest—particularly if a judicial officer resigns in the course of an investigation—to make the identity of the judge known.

Once a special committee has been appointed, and a proceeding is concluded by the full council on the basis of a remedial order of the council, Rule 24(a)(4) provides for disclosure of the name of the subject judge.

Finally, Rule 24(a)(5) provides that the identity of the complainant will be disclosed only if the chief judge so orders. Identifying the complainant when the subject judge is not identified would increase the likelihood that the identity of the subject judge would become publicly known, thus circumventing the policy of nondisclosure. It may not always be practicable to shield the complainant's identity while making public disclosure of the judicial council's order and supporting memoranda; in some circumstances, moreover, the complainant may consent to public identification.

RULE 25. DISQUALIFICATION

(a) General Rule. Any judge is disqualified from participating in any proceeding under these Rules if the judge, in his or her discretion, concludes that circumstances warrant disqualification. If the complaint is filed by a judge, that judge is disqualified from participating in any consideration of the complaint except to the extent that these Rules provide for a complainant's participation. A chief judge who has identified a complaint under Rule 5 is not automatically disqualified from considering the complaint.

(b) Subject Judge. A subject judge is disqualified from considering the complaint except to the extent that these Rules provide for participation by a subject judge.

(c) Chief Judge Not Disqualified From Considering a Petition for Review of a Chief Judge's Order. If a petition for review of a chief judge's order entered under Rule 11(c), (d), or (e) is filed with the judicial council in accordance with Rule 18, the chief judge is not disqualified from participating in the council's consideration of the petition.

(d) Member of Special Committee Not Disqualified. A member of the judicial council who serves on a special committee, including the chief judge, is not disqualified from participating in council consideration of the committee's report.

(e) Subject Judge's Disqualification After Appointment of a Special Committee. Upon appointment of a special committee, the subject judge is automatically disqualified from participating in any proceeding arising under the Act or these Rules as a member of any special committee, the judicial council of the circuit, the Judicial Conference of the United States, and the Judicial Conference Committee on Judicial Conduct and Disability. The disqualification continues until all proceedings on the complaint against the subject judge are finally terminated with no further right of review.

(f) Substitute for Disqualified Chief Judge. If the chief judge is disqualified from participating in consideration of the complaint, the duties and responsibilities of the chief judge under these Rules must be assigned to the most-senior active circuit judge not disqualified. If all circuit judges in regular active service are disqualified, the judicial council may determine whether to request a transfer under Rule 26, or, in the interest of sound judicial administration, to permit the chief judge to dispose of the complaint on the merits. Members of the judicial council who are named in the complaint may participate in this determination if necessary to obtain a quorum of the judicial council.

(g) Judicial–Council Action When Multiple Judges Are Disqualified. Notwithstanding any other provision in these Rules to the contrary,

(1) a member of the judicial council who is a subject judge may participate in its disposition if:

(A) participation by one or more subject judges is necessary to obtain a quorum of the judicial council;

(B) the judicial council finds that the lack of a quorum is due to the naming of one or more judges in the complaint for the purpose of disqualifying that judge or judges, or to the naming of one or more judges based on their participation in a decision excluded from the definition of misconduct under Rule 3(h)(3); and

(C) the judicial council votes that it is necessary, appropriate, and in the interest of sound judicial administration that one or more subject judges be eligible to act.

(2) otherwise disqualified members may participate in votes taken under (g)(1)(B) and (g)(1)(C).

(h) Disqualification of Members of the Judicial Conference Committee. No member of the Judicial Conference Committee on Judicial Conduct and Disability is disqualified from participating in any proceeding under the Act or these Rules because of consultations with a chief judge, a member of a special committee, or a member of a judicial council about the interpretation or application of the Act or these Rules, unless the member believes that the consultation would prevent fair-minded participation.

[Adopted March 11, 2008, effective April 10, 2008.]

Commentary on Rule 25

Rule 25 is adapted from the Illustrative Rules.

Subsection (a) provides the general rule for disqualification. Of course, a judge is not disqualified simply because the subject judge is on the same court. However, this subsection recognizes that there may be cases in which an appearance of bias or prejudice is created by circumstances other than an association with the subject judge as a colleague. For example, a judge may have a familial relationship with a complainant or subject judge. When such circumstances exist, a judge may, in his or her discretion, conclude that disqualification is warranted.

Subsection (e) makes it clear that the disqualification of the subject judge relates only to the subject judge's participation in any proceeding arising under the Act or these Rules as a member of a special committee, judicial council,

Judicial Conference, or the Judicial Conference Committee. The Illustrative Rule, based on Section 359(a) of the Act, is ambiguous and could be read to disqualify a subject judge from service of any kind on each of the bodies mentioned. This is undoubtedly not the intent of the Act; such a disqualification would be anomalous in light of the Act's allowing a subject judge to continue to decide cases and to continue to exercise the powers of chief circuit or district judge. It would also create a substantial deterrence to the appointment of special committees, particularly where a special committee is needed solely because the chief judge may not decide matters of credibility in his or her review under Rule 11.

While a subject judge is barred by Rule 25(b) from participating in the disposition of the complaint in which he or she is named, Rule 25(e) recognizes that participation in proceedings arising under the Act or these Rules by a judge who is the subject of a special committee investigation may lead to an appearance of self-interest in creating substantive and procedural precedents governing such proceedings; Rule 25(e) bars such participation.

Under the Act, a complaint against the chief judge is to be handled by "that circuit judge in regular active service next senior in date of commission." 28 U.S.C. § 351(c). Rule 25(f) provides that seniority among judges other than the chief judge is to be determined by date of commission, with the result that complaints against the chief judge may be routed to a former chief judge or other judge who was appointed earlier than the chief judge. The Rules do not purport to prescribe who is to preside over meetings of the judicial council. Consequently, where the presiding member of the judicial council is disqualified from participating under these Rules, the order of precedence prescribed by Rule 25(f) for performing "the duties and responsibilities of the chief circuit judge under these Rules" does not apply to determine the acting presiding member of the judicial council. That is a matter left to the internal rules or operating practices of each judicial council. In most cases the most senior active circuit judge who is a member of the judicial council and who is not disqualified will preside.

Sometimes a single complaint is filed against a large group of judges. If the normal disqualification rules are observed in such a case, no court of appeals judge can serve as acting chief judge of the circuit, and the judicial council will be without appellate members. Where the complaint is against all circuit and district judges, under normal rules no member of the judicial council can perform the duties assigned to the council under the statute.

A similar problem is created by successive complaints arising out of the same underlying grievance. For example, a complainant files a complaint against a district judge based on alleged misconduct, and the complaint is dismissed by the chief judge under the statute. The complainant may then file a complaint against the chief judge for dismissing the first complaint, and when that complaint is dismissed by the next senior judge, still a third complaint may be filed. The threat is that the complainant will bump down the seniority ladder until, once again, there is no member of the court of appeals who can serve as acting chief judge for the purpose of the next complaint. Similarly, complaints involving the merits of litigation may involve a series of decisions in which many judges participated or in which a rehearing en banc was denied by the court of appeals, and the complaint may name a majority of the judicial council as subject judges.

In recognition that these multiple-judge complaints are virtually always meritless, the judicial council is given discretion to determine: (1) whether it is necessary, appropriate, and in the interest of sound judicial administration to permit the chief judge to dispose of a complaint where it would otherwise be impossible for any active circuit judge in the circuit to act, and (2) whether it is necessary, appropriate, and in the interest of sound judicial administration, after appropriate findings as to need and justification are made, to permit subject judges of the judicial council to participate in the disposition of a petition for review where it would otherwise be impossible to obtain a quorum.

Applying a rule of necessity in these situations is consistent with the appearance of justice. See, e.g., In re Complaint of Doe, 2 F.3d 308 (8th Cir. Jud. Council 1993) (invoking the rule of necessity); In re Complaint of Judicial Misconduct, No. 91–80464 (9th Cir. Jud. Council 1992) (same). There is no unfairness in permitting the chief judge to dispose of a patently insubstantial complaint that names all active circuit judges in the circuit.

Similarly, there is no unfairness in permitting subject judges, in these circumstances, to participate in the review of a chief judge's dismissal of an insubstantial complaint. The remaining option is to assign the matter to another body. Among other alternatives, the council may request a transfer of the petition under Rule 26. Given the administrative inconvenience and delay involved in these alternatives, it is desirable to request a transfer only if the judicial council determines that the petition is substantial enough to warrant such action.

In the unlikely event that a quorum of the judicial council cannot be obtained to consider the report of a special committee, it would normally be necessary to request a transfer under Rule 26.

Rule 25(h) recognizes that the jurisdictional statement of the Judicial Conference Committee contemplates consultation between members of the Committee and judicial participants in proceedings under the Act and these Rules. Such consultation should not automatically preclude participation by a member in that proceeding.

RULE 26. TRANSFER TO ANOTHER JUDICIAL COUNCIL

In exceptional circumstances, a chief judge or a judicial council may ask the Chief Justice to transfer a proceeding based on a complaint identified under Rule 5 or filed under Rule 6 to the judicial council of another circuit. The request for a transfer may be made at any stage of the proceeding before a reference to the Judicial Conference under Rule 20(b)(1)(C) or 20(b)(2) or a petition for review is filed under Rule 22. Upon receiving such a request, the Chief Justice may refuse the request or select the transferee judicial council, which may then exercise the powers of a judicial council under these Rules.

[Adopted March 11, 2008, effective April 10, 2008.]

Commentary on Rule 26

Rule 26 is new; it implements the Breyer Committee's recommended use of transfers. Breyer Committee Report, 239 F.R.D. at 214–15.

Rule 26 authorizes the transfer of a complaint proceeding to another judicial council selected by the Chief Justice. Such transfers may be appropriate, for example, in the case of a serious complaint where there are multiple disqualifications among the original council, where the issues are highly visible and a local disposition may weaken public confidence in the process, where internal tensions arising in the council as a result of the complaint render disposition by a less involved council appropriate, or where a complaint calls into question policies or governance of the home court of appeals. The power to effect a transfer is lodged in the Chief Justice to avoid disputes in a council over where to transfer a sensitive matter and to ensure that the transferee council accepts the matter.

Upon receipt of a transferred proceeding, the transferee council shall determine the proper stage at which to begin consideration of the complaint—for example, reference to the transferee chief judge, appointment of a special committee, etc.

RULE 27. WITHDRAWAL OF COMPLAINTS AND PETITIONS FOR REVIEW

(a) **Complaint Pending Before Chief Judge.** With the chief judge's consent, a complainant may withdraw a complaint that is before the chief judge for a decision under Rule 11. The withdrawal of a complaint will not prevent a chief judge from identifying or having to identify a complaint under Rule 5 based on the withdrawn complaint.

(b) **Complaint Pending Before Special Committee or Judicial Council.** After a complaint has been referred to a special committee for investigation and before the committee files its report, the complainant may withdraw the complaint only with the consent of both the subject judge and either the special committee or the judicial council.

(c) **Petition for Review.** A petition for review addressed to a judicial council under Rule 18, or the Judicial Conference Committee on Judicial Conduct and Disability under Rule 22 may be withdrawn if no action on the petition has been taken.

[Adopted March 11, 2008, effective April 10, 2008.]

Commentary on Rule 27

Rule 27 is adapted from the Illustrative Rules and treats the complaint proceeding, once begun, as a matter of public business rather than as the property of the complainant. Accordingly, the chief judge or the judicial council remains responsible for addressing any complaint under the Act, even a complaint that has been formally withdrawn by the complainant.

Under subsection 27(a), a complaint pending before the chief judge may be withdrawn if the chief judge consents. Where the complaint clearly lacked merit, the chief judge may accordingly be saved the burden of preparing a formal order and supporting memorandum. However, the chief judge may, or be obligated under Rule 5, to identify a complaint based on allegations in a withdrawn complaint.

If the chief judge appoints a special committee, Rule 27(b) provides that the complaint may be withdrawn only with the consent of both the body before which it is pending (the special committee or the judicial council) and the subject judge. Once a complaint has reached the stage of appointment of a special committee, a resolution of the issues may be necessary to preserve public confidence. Moreover, the subject judge is given the right to insist that the matter be resolved on the merits, thereby eliminating any ambiguity that might remain if the proceeding were terminated by withdrawal of the complaint.

With regard to all petitions for review, Rule 27(c) grants the petitioner unrestricted authority to withdraw the petition. It is thought that the public's interest in the proceeding is adequately protected, because there will necessarily have been a decision by the chief judge and often by the judicial council as well in such a case.

RULE 28.   AVAILABILITY OF RULES AND FORMS

These Rules and copies of the complaint form as provided in Rule 6(a) must be available without charge in the office of the clerk of each court of appeals, district court, bankruptcy court, or other federal court whose judges are subject to the Act. Each court must also make these Rules and the complaint form available on the court's website, or provide an Internet link to the Rules and complaint form that are available on the appropriate court of appeals' website.

[Adopted March 11, 2008, effective April 10, 2008.]

RULE 29.   EFFECTIVE DATE

These Rules will become effective 30 days after promulgation by the Judicial Conference of the United States.

[Adopted March 11, 2008, effective April 10, 2008.]

APPENDIX

COMPLAINT FORM

Judicial Council of the _____ Circuit

COMPLAINT OF JUDICIAL MISCONDUCT OR DISABILITY

To begin the complaint process, complete this form and prepare the brief statement of facts described in item 5 (below). The RULES FOR JUDICIAL-CONDUCT AND JUDICIAL-DISABILITY PROCEEDINGS, adopted by the Judicial Conference of the United States, contain information on what to include in a complaint (Rule 6), where to file a complaint (Rule 7), and other important matters. The rules are available in federal court clerks' offices, on individual federal courts' Web sites, and on www.uscourts. gov.

Your complaint (this form and the statement of facts) should be typewritten and must be legible. For the number of copies to file, consult the local rules or clerk's office of the court in which your complaint is required to be filed. Enclose each copy of the complaint in an envelope marked "COMPLAINT OF MISCONDUCT" or "COMPLAINT OF DISABILITY" and submit it to the appropriate clerk of court. **Do not put the name of any judge on the envelope.**

1. Name of Complainant: _____
    Contact Address: _____
    _____

    Daytime telephone: (____) _____

2. Name(s) of Judge(s): _____
    Court: _____

3. Does this complaint concern the behavior of the judge(s) in a particular lawsuit or lawsuits?
    [ ] Yes   [ ] No
    If "yes," give the following information about each lawsuit:
    Court: _____
    Case Number: _____
    Docket number of any appeal to the _____ Circuit: _____
    Are (were) you a party or lawyer in the lawsuit?
    [ ] Party   [ ] Lawyer   [ ] Neither

    If you are (were) a party and have (had) a lawyer, give the lawyer's name, address, and telephone number:
    _____
    _____
    _____

4. Have you filed any lawsuits against the judge?
    [ ] Yes   [ ] No
    If "yes," give the following information about each such lawsuit:
    Court: _____
    Case Number: _____
    Present status of lawsuit: _____
    Name, address, and telephone number of your lawyer for the lawsuit against the judge:
    _____
    _____
    _____

    Court to which any appeal has been taken in the lawsuit against the judge:
    _____

    Docket number of the appeal: _____
    Present status of the appeal: _____

5.   **Brief Statement of Facts.** Attach a brief statement of the specific facts on which the claim of judicial misconduct or disability is based. Include what happened, when and where it happened, and any information that would help an investigator check the facts. If the complaint alleges judicial disability, also include any additional facts that form the basis of that allegation.

6.   **Declaration and signature:**

    I declare under penalty of perjury that the statements made in this complaint are true and correct to the best of my knowledge.

    (Signature)_____   (Date)_____

[Adopted March 11, 2008, effective April 10, 2008.]

INDEX TO UNITED STATES COURTS OF APPEALS
FOR THE SEVENTH CIRCUIT

UNITED STATES DISTRICT COURT FOR THE NORTHERN DISTRICT OF INDIANA

Including Amendments Received Through
November 1, 2015

2005–4.	In re: Privacy and Public Access to Criminal Electronic Case Files.

SELECTED GENERAL ORDERS

1996–6.	In the Matter of a United States District Court Library and Court Administration Fund.
2001–1.	In re: Presentence Procedures.
2003–21.	In re: A General Order of the Court [Alternative Dispute Resolution].
2007–2.	In re: Utilization of United States Magistrate in Ancillary Proceedings.
2007–5.	In re: Referral of Proceedings Supplemental.
2007–9.	In re: Release of Pretrial Service Reports to Attorneys.
2007–10.	In re: Utilization of United States Magistrate Judges.

2008–7.	In re: Cell Phone Policy for the United States Courthouses in the Northern District of Indiana.
2009–2.	In re: Application for Admission to Practice and Application for Admission to Practice Pro Hac Vice.
2010–8.	In re: Additional Presentence Procedures.
2011–13.	In re: The Establishment of Maximum Rates per Page for Transcripts.
2012–8.	In re: Rules for Filing Documents Under Seal in Criminal Cases.
2012–12.	In re: Fee Payment Via Pay.Gov.
2015–8.	In re: Deposit and Investment of Registry Funds.

JURY SELECTION PLAN

CRIMINAL JUSTICE ACT PLAN

LOCAL CIVIL RULES

N.D. IND. L.R. 1–1. CITATION AND SCOPE OF THE RULES

(a) Citation.

(1) *Civil Rules.* The local civil rules of the United States District Court for the Northern District of Indiana may be cited as "N.D. Ind. L.R."

(2) *Criminal Rules.* The local criminal rules of the United States District Court for the Northern District of Indiana may be cited as "N.D. Ind. L. Cr. R."

(3) *Patent Rules.* The local patent rules of the United States District Court for the Northern District of Indiana may be cited as "N.D. Ind. L.P.R."

(b) Effective Date and Scope of Rules. These rules, as amended, take effect on August 14, 2015. They govern all civil and criminal cases on or after that date. But in cases pending when the rules take effect, the court may apply the former local rules if it finds that applying these rules would not be feasible or would be unjust.

(c) Modification or Suspension of Rules. The court may, on its own motion or at the request of a party, suspend or modify any rule in a particular case in the interest of justice.

[Effective January 1, 2012. Amended effective January 1, 2013; August 14, 2015.]

N.D. IND. L.R. 1–2. AVAILABILITY AND AMENDMENTS

(a) Availability. These rules and appendices may be purchased from the clerk's office or accessed for free on the court's web site at www.innd.uscourts.gov.

(b) Amendments. These rules may not be amended without public notice and an opportunity for public comment. Notice of proposed amendments:

(1) must be submitted for publication in Res Gestae, the Indiana State Bar Association's monthly publication; and

(2) may also be published elsewhere.

[Effective January 1, 2012.]

N.D. IND. L.R. 1–3. SANCTIONS FOR FORMATTING ERRORS

(a) Non–Compliance. If a person files a paper that does not comply with the rules governing the format of papers filed with the court, the court may:

(1) strike the paper from the record; or

(2) fine the person up to $1,000.

(b) Notice. Before sanctioning a person under subdivision (a)(2), the court must:

(1) notify the person that the paper is noncompliant; and

(2) give the person the opportunity either to be heard or to revise the paper.

[Effective January 1, 2012.]

N.D. IND. L.R. 5–1. ELECTRONIC FILING REQUIRED

Papers must be filed, signed, and verified electronically unless excepted by the court's *CM/ECF Civil and Criminal User Manual.*

[Effective January 1, 2012. Amended effective August 14, 2015.]

N.D. IND. L.R. 5–2. ELECTRONIC SERVICE

(a) Electronic Service Permitted. Electronically filed papers may be served electronically if service is consistent with the *CM/ECF User Manual*.

(b) When Electronic Service is Deemed Completed. A person registered to use the court's electronic-filing system is served with an electronically filed paper when a "Notice of Electronic Filing" is transmitted to that person through the court's electronic filing-system.

(c) Serving Non–Registered Persons. A person who has not registered to use the court's electronic-filing system but who is entitled to service of a paper must be served according to these rules and the Federal Rules of Civil or Criminal Procedure.

[Effective January 1, 2012.]

N.D. IND. L.R. 5–3. FILING UNDER SEAL OR EX PARTE

(a) General Rule. The clerk may not maintain a filing under seal unless authorized to do so by statute, court rule, or court order.

(b) Filing Cases Under Seal.

(1) *Papers Required.* To seal a case, a party must:

(A) simultaneously file directly with the clerk:

(i) the initial pleadings;

(ii) a motion requesting that the court seal the case;

(iii) a proposed order; and

(B) otherwise comply with the *CM/ECF User Manual*.

(2) *Treatment of Case Pending Ruling.* When the clerk receives a new case with a motion to seal it, the clerk must seal the case pending a ruling on the motion.

(3) *If Motion Is Denied.* If the court denies the motion, the clerk must immediately unseal the case and may do so without first notifying the filing party.

(c) Ex Parte and Sealed Filings.

(1) *In a Civil Case.* To file a sealed document (other than an initial filing) or a document ex parte in a civil case, a party must file it electronically as required by the *CM/ECF User Manual*.

(2) *In a Criminal Case.*

(A) The following documents may be filed under seal without motion or further order of the court provided counsel has a good faith belief that sealing is required to ensure the safety, privacy or cooperation of a person or entity, or to otherwise protect a substantial public interest:

(i) Documents filed pre-indictment;

(ii) Documents filed in a sealed case post-indictment and prior to the first defendant being arrested;

(iii) Requests for search warrants, including warrants for tracking devices;

(iv) Requests for interception of communications pursuant to 18 U.S.C. § 2516;

(v) Requests for phone record information pursuant to 18 U.S.C. § 2703;

(vi) Requests for tax return information pursuant to 26 U.S.C. § 6103;

(vii) Motions for sentence variance or reduction based on substantial assistance pursuant to Fed. R. Crim. P. 35 or U.S.S.G. § 5K1.1, including supporting documents; and

(viii) Motions for competency exam.

(B) When the documents identified above are filed under seal pursuant to this Rule, the filing party must place the words "under seal" below the case number on the document.

(C) Other than the documents identified above, documents may be sealed if and only if they are subject to a prior protective order or are accompanied by a contemporaneous motion to seal, which motions may be filed under seal if necessary, by using the following procedure:

(i) electronically file a "Notice of Manual Filing;"

(ii) affix the Notice of Electronic Filing (NEF) of Notice of Manual Filing to the envelope's exterior. The contents of the envelope should include:

(a) a motion for leave to file the document under seal;

(b) a proposed form of Order for the motion for leave to file the document under seal; and

(c) the motion or document to be filed under seal.

(iii) deliver the document to the clerk in an envelope without folding it;

(iv) counsel must provide an original for the clerk's office and a copy for the judge of each of the documents contained within the envelope.

[Effective January 1, 2012. Amended effective January 1, 2013.]

N.D. IND. L.R. 5–4. FORMAT OF PAPERS

(a) Generally. Any pleading, motion, brief, affidavit, notice, or proposed order, whether filed electronically or by delivering it to the clerk, must:

(1) be plainly typewritten, printed, or prepared by a clearly legible copying process;

(2) use 8.5″ × 11″ pages;

(3) have at least 1–inch margins;

(4) use at least 12–point type in the body and at least 10–point type in footnotes;

(5) be double spaced (except for headings, footnotes, and quoted material);

(6) have consecutively numbered pages;

(7) include a title on the first page;

(8) include a separate index identifying and briefly describing each exhibit if there are more than four exhibits; and

(9) except in proposed orders and affidavits, include the filer's name, address, telephone number, fax number (where available), and e-mail address (where available).

(b) Manual Filings.

(1) *Form, Style, and Size of Papers.* Papers delivered to the clerk for filing must:

    (A) be flat, unfolded, and on good-quality, white paper;

    (B) not have a cover or a back; and

    (C) include the filer's original signature.

(2) *Rubber–Stamped and Faxed Signatures.* An original paper with a rubber-stamped or faxed signature is unsigned for purposes of Fed. R. Civ. P. 11 and 26(g).

(3) *Affidavits.* Only the affiant need sign an affidavit.

(4) *Filing with Clerk Required.* Papers not filed electronically must be filed with the clerk, not a judge.

(5) *Where to File.* Papers not filed electronically must be filed in the division where the case is pending, unless:

    (A) a person will be prejudiced if the paper is not filed the same day it is tendered; and

    (B) it includes an adequately sized envelope addressed to the clerk's office in the division where the case is pending and with adequate postage.

(6) *Return of File–Stamped Copies.* A party who wants a file-stamped copy of a paper must include with the filing an additional copy of the paper and a self-addressed envelope with adequate postage.

(7) *Recycled Paper.* The court encourages using recycled paper.

(8) *Form of Notices.* Parties manually filing a paper that requires the clerk to give others notice, must give the clerk:

    (A) sufficient copies of the notice; and

    (B) the name and address of each person entitled to receive the notice.

(c) Forms of Order. Parties filing a paper that requires the judge or clerk to enter a routine or uncontested order must include a suitable form of order.

(d) Notice by Publication. When published notice is required:

(1) the clerk must send the notice to the party originating the notice; and

(2) the party must deliver the notice to the appropriate newspapers for publication.

[Effective January 1, 2012.]

N.D. IND. L.R. 5.1–1 CONSTITUTIONAL QUESTIONS

(a) When to File the Notice. A party required to file a notice of constitutional question under Fed. R. Civ. P. 5.1 must do so by the later of:

(1) the day the parties tender their proposed case-management plan (if one is required); or

(2) 21 days after filing the pleading, written motion, or other paper questioning the constitutionality of a federal or state statute.

(b) Service on Government Officials. The party must also serve the notice and the pleading, written motion, or other paper questioning the constitutionality of a federal or state statute on:

(1) the Attorney General of the United States and the United States Attorney for the Northern District of Indiana, if a federal statute is challenged; or

(2) the Attorney General for the state if a state statute is challenged.

(c) Method of Service on Government Officials. Service required under subdivision (b) may be made either by certified or registered mail or by emailing it to an address designated by those officials for this purpose.

[Effective January 1, 2012.]

N.D. IND. L.R. 6–1. EXTENSIONS OF TIME

(a) By Motion. Ordinarily, requests for an extension of time not made in open court or at a conference must:

(1) be made by written motion;

(2) state the original deadline and the requested deadline; and

(3) either:

    (A) state that there is no objection to the extension; or

(B) describe the requesting party's efforts to get opposing attorneys to agree to the extension if there is an objection.

(b) Automatic Initial Extension. The deadline to respond to a pleading or a discovery request—including requests for admission—is automatically extended when an extension notice is filed with the court and:

(1) the deadline has not been extended before;

(2) the extension is for 28 or fewer days; and

(3) the notice states:

(A) the original deadline;

(B) the new deadline; and

(C) that all opposing attorneys the attorney could reach agreed to the extension; or that the party could not reach any other opposing attorneys despite due diligence.

(c) Pro Se Parties. The automatic initial extension does not apply to pro se parties.

[Effective January 1, 2012. Amended effective January 1, 2013.]

N.D. IND. L.R. 7–1. MOTION PRACTICE

(a) Motions Must Be Filed Separately. Motions must be filed separately, but alternative motions may be filed in a single paper if each is named in the title following the caption.

(b) Brief Required for Certain Motions. Parties must file a supporting brief with any motion under:

(1) Fed. R. Civ. P. 12;

(2) Fed. R. Civ. P. 37;

(3) Fed. R. Civ. P. 56; or

(4) Fed. R. Civ. P. 65(b).

(c) Rule 12 Defenses. The court will not rule on a defense under Fed. R. Civ. P. 12 until the party who raised it files a motion and brief.

(d) Response- and Reply–Brief Deadlines.

(1) *Summary–Judgment Motions.* Summary-judgment motions are subject to the deadlines in N.D. Ind. L.R. 56–1(b) and (c).

(2) *Other Motions.*

(A) Responses. A party must file any response brief to a motion within 14 days after the motion is served.

(B) Replies. The moving party must file any reply brief within seven days after the response brief is served.

(3) *Extensions.* The court may extend response- and reply-brief deadlines, but only for good cause.

(4) *Summary Rulings.* The court may rule on a motion summarily if an opposing party does not file a response before the deadline.

(e) Page Limits.

(1) *Rule.* Supporting and response briefs (excluding tables of contents, tables of authorities, and appendices) ordinarily must not exceed 25 pages. Reply briefs must not exceed 15 pages.

(2) *Exception.* The court may allow a party to file a brief exceeding these page limits for extraordinary and compelling reasons. But if the court permits a brief to exceed 25 pages, it must include:

(A) a table of contents with page references;

(B) an issue statement; and

(C) a table of authorities including:

(i) all cases (alphabetically arranged), statutes, and other authorities cited in the brief; and

(ii) references to where the authorities appear in the brief.

(f) Authority Not Available Electronically. A copy of any decision, statute, or regulation cited in a motion or brief must be attached to the paper if—and only if—it is not available on Westlaw or Lexis. But if a copy of a decision, statute, or regulation is only available electronically, a party must provide it to the court or another party upon request.

[Effective January 1, 2012.]

N.D. IND. L.R. 7–3. SOCIAL SECURITY APPEALS

(a) Answer. The Social Security Administration must respond to a complaint challenging an agency determination about Social Security benefits by filing either a motion to dismiss or the certified administrative record. The certified administrative record serves as the agency's answer to the complaint.

(b) Opening Brief. A person challenging an agency determination regarding entitlement to Social Security benefits must file an opening brief within 42 days after the administrative record is filed.

(c) Response Brief. Any response brief must be filed within 42 days after the opening brief.

(d) Reply Brief. Any reply brief must be filed within 14 days after the response brief.

[Effective January 1, 2012. Amended effective August 14, 2015.]

N.D. IND. L.R. 7–5. ORAL ARGUMENTS AND EVIDENTIARY HEARINGS

(a) Oral Argument.

(1) *How to Request.* A party may request oral argument on a motion by filing and serving a separate document explaining why oral argument is necessary and estimating how long the court should allow for the argument.

(2) *When to File Request.* The request must be filed and served with the party's supporting brief, response brief, or reply brief.

(3) *Additional Evidence Forbidden.* Parties may not present additional evidence at oral argument.

(b) Evidentiary Hearings.

(1) *How to Request.* A party may request an evidentiary hearing by filing and serving a separate document explaining why the hearing is necessary and estimating how long the court should allow for it.

(2) *Authorization Needed to Specify Hearing Date.* The party must not specify a hearing date in the notice of a motion or petition unless the court or the clerk has authorized it.

(c) Court's Authority. The court may:

(1) grant or deny a request for oral argument or an evidentiary hearing in its discretion;

(2) set oral argument or an evidentiary hearing without a request from a party; or

(3) order any oral argument or evidentiary hearing to be held anywhere within the district regardless of where the case will be tried.

[Effective January 1, 2012.]

N.D. IND. L.R. 8–1. PRO SE COMPLAINTS

Parties representing themselves must prepare the following types of complaints on clerk-supplied forms:

- Complaints alleging claims arising under The Civil Rights Act, 42 U.S.C. § 1983.
- Complaints alleging claims arising under The Social Security Act, 42 U.S.C. § 405(g).
- Complaints alleging employment discrimination under a federal statute.

[Effective January 1, 2012.]

N.D. IND. L.R. 9–2. REQUEST FOR THREE–JUDGE COURT

(a) Procedure. If a party believes the law requires a three-judge court in a case or proceeding, the party must:

(1) print "Three–Judge District Court Requested" or the equivalent immediately following the title on the first pleading asserting a claim requiring a three-judge court; and

(2) set forth the basis for the request in the pleading or in a short statement attached to the pleading, unless the basis is apparent from the pleading.

(b) Sufficiency of Request. The words "Three–Judge District Court Requested" or the equivalent on a pleading constitutes a "request" under 28 U.S.C. § 2284(b)(1).

[Effective January 1, 2012.]

N.D. IND. L.R. 10–1. RESPONSIVE PLEADINGS

(a) Rule. Responsive pleadings under Fed. R. Civ. P. 7(a) must:

(1) restate verbatim the paragraphs from the pleading they respond to; and

(2) immediately following each restated paragraph, state the response to that paragraph.

(b) Exception. This rule does not apply to pro se cases.

[Effective January 1, 2012.]

N.D. IND. L.R. 15–1. AMENDING PLEADINGS

(a) Supporting Documents. Motions to amend a pleading must include the original signed proposed amendment as an attachment.

(b) Form of Amended Pleading. Amendments to a pleading:

(1) must reproduce the entire pleading as amended, unless the court allows otherwise; and

(2) must not incorporate another pleading by reference.

(c) Failure to Comply. Failing to comply with this rule is not grounds to deny the motion.

[Effective January 1, 2012.]

N.D. IND. L.R. 16–1. PRETRIAL PROCEDURE

(a) Initial Pretrial Conference. In all cases not exempted under subsection (c) of this rule, the court may order the parties to appear for an initial pretrial conference.

(b) Notice from Clerk. A clerk-issued notice directing the parties to prepare for and appear at a pretrial conference is a court order for purposes of Fed. R. Civ. P. 16(a).

(c) Exemptions. The following cases are exempt from the requirements of Fed. R. Civ. P. 16(b):

(1) Actions to review an administrative record;

(2) Petitions for habeas corpus or other proceedings to challenge a criminal conviction or sentence;

(3) Civil forfeitures;

(4) Actions by the United States to recover benefit payments;

(5) Actions by the United States to collect on a student loan it guaranteed;

(6) Actions to enforce or quash an administrative summons or subpoena;

(7) Mortgage foreclosures if the United States is a party;

(8) Proceedings ancillary to proceedings in another court; and

(9) Actions to enforce, vacate, or modify an arbitration award.

(d) Planning–Meeting Report. When the court orders an initial pretrial conference, the parties must file a *Report of the Parties' Planning Meeting* following their Fed. R. Civ. P. 26(f) planning meeting. The report must be consistent with the form on the court's website (www.innd.uscourts.gov). The court may adopt all or some of the report as part of its scheduling order.

(e) Preparation for Pretrial Conferences. Parties must confer before each pretrial conference and must be prepared to address the following matters at the conference:

(1) case-management plan issues;

(2) alternative-dispute-resolution processes, including mediation, early neutral evaluation, and mini-trial;

(3) settlement, including their present positions on settlement;

(4) trial readiness; and

(5) any other matters specifically directed by the court.

(f) Settlement Negotiations.

(1) *Facilitation at Pretrial Conferences.* The court may facilitate settlement negotiations at any pretrial conference after an initial conference. Accordingly, attorneys attending a pretrial conference after the initial conference must:

(A) know their settlement authority; and

(B) be prepared to negotiate in good faith at the conference.

(2) *Attendance by Parties.* To assist settlement discussions, the court may require a party, a corporate party's agent, or an insurance-company representative to appear at a pretrial conference.

(3) *Disclosure Prohibited.* The court may not disclose the details of any negotiations at a pretrial conference in an order or docket entry.

(g) Settlement or Resolution. The parties must immediately notify the court if they reasonably expect to settle the case or resolve a pending motion.

[Effective January 1, 2012. Amended effective January 1, 2013.]

N.D. IND. L.R. 16–3. CONTINUANCES

(a) Court's Discretion. The court may continue proceedings in a civil case on its own or on the motion of one or more parties.

(b) Consultation with Clients. Attorneys must consult with their clients before asking the court to continue a trial.

(c) Unavailable Evidence. A party seeking to continue a trial because evidence is unavailable must include with the motion an affidavit showing:

(1) that the evidence is material;

(2) that the party has acted diligently to obtain it;

(3) where the evidence might be; and

(4) if the evidence is the testimony of an absent witness:

(A) the name and residence of the witness, if known;

(B) the likelihood of procuring the testimony within a reasonable time;

(C) that neither the party nor anyone at the party's request or with the party's knowledge procured the witness's absence;

(D) the facts the party believes the witness will truthfully testify to; and

(E) that the party cannot prove the facts by another witness whose testimony can be readily procured.

(d) Stipulation to Unavailable Evidence. The court may not continue a trial because evidence is unavailable if all parties stipulate to the content of the unavailable evidence. Despite the stipulation, the parties may contest the stipulated evidence as if it had been available at trial.

(e) Award of Costs. The court may order a party seeking a continuance to reimburse other parties for their actual expenses caused by the delay.

[Effective January 1, 2012.]

N.D. IND. L.R. 16–6. ALTERNATIVE DISPUTE RESOLUTION

(a) Report of Agreement. After they confer as required by Fed. R. Civ. P. 26(f), the parties must advise the court which, if any, alternative-dispute-resolution processes they expect to pursue and when they expect to undertake the process.

(b) Authority to Order Mediation or Evaluation. The court may order mediation or early neutral evaluation in any civil case.

(c) Rules. The Indiana Rules for Alternative Dispute Resolution (including the rules regarding privilege, confidentiality of communications, and disqualification of neutrals) apply to all alternative-dispute-resolution processes unless the court orders otherwise.

(d) Judicial Settlement Conference. A settlement conference conducted by a judge is not an alternative-dispute-resolution process.

(e) Immunity of Mediators. Mediators performing their duties under these rules have, to the extent the law allows, the same immunities a judge has.

(f) List of Neutrals. The clerk must maintain a list of neutrals available for mediation or early neutral evaluation. The list may be purchased from the clerk's office or accessed for free on the court's website.

[Effective January 1, 2012.]

N.D. IND. L.R. 23–1. CLASS ACTIONS

A party seeking to maintain a case as a class action (whether for or against a class) must include in the complaint, crossclaim, or counterclaim

(a) the words "Class Action" in the document's title; and

(b) a reference to each part of Fed. R. Civ. P. 23 that the party relies on in seeking to maintain the case as a class action.

[Effective January 1, 2012.]

N.D. IND. L.R. 26–1. FORM OF CERTAIN DISCOVERY DOCUMENTS

(a) Form of Requests. A party propounding written discovery under Fed. R. Civ. P. 33, 34, or 36 must number each interrogatory or request sequentially.

(b) Form of Responses. A party responding (by answer or objection) to written discovery must:

(1) fully quote each interrogatory or request immediately before the party's response; and

(2) number each response to correspond with the interrogatory or request being responded to.

(c) Limit on Requests for Admission. Ordinarily, a party may not serve more than 30 requests for admission on another party (not counting requests that relate to the authenticity of a document). A party wanting to serve more requests must file a motion setting forth the proposed additional requests and why they are necessary.

[Effective January 1, 2012.]

N.D. IND. L.R. 26–2. FILING OF DISCOVERY AND OTHER MATERIALS

(a) Generally.

(1) *Discovery Ordinarily Not Filed.* The party who serves a discovery request or notices a deposition is the custodian of the original discovery response or deposition transcript. Except as required under subdivision (a)(2), parties must not file:

(A) disclosures under Fed. R. Civ. P. 26(a)(1) or (2);

(B) deposition notices;

(C) deposition transcripts;

(D) interrogatories;

(E) requests for documents, to permit entry upon land, or for admission;

(F) answers to interrogatories;

(G) responses to requests for documents, to permit entry upon land, or for admission; or

(H) service-of-discovery notices.

(2) *Exceptions.*

(A) Pro Se Litigation. All discovery material in cases involving a pro se party must be filed.

(B) Specific Material. Discovery material must also be filed when:

(i) the court orders; or

(ii) the material is used in a proceeding.

(3) *Motions to Publish Not Required.* Motions to publish deposition transcripts are not required.

(b) Filing Materials with Motion for Relief. A party who files a motion for relief under Fed. R. Civ. P. 26(c) or 37 must file with the motion those parts of the discovery requests or responses that the motion pertains to.

(c) Materials Necessary for Motion. A party must file those portions of discovery requests or responses (including deposition transcripts) that the party relies on to support a motion that could result in a final order on an issue.

(d) Materials to be Used at Trial. A party who reasonably anticipates using discovery requests or responses—including deposition transcripts—at trial must file the relevant portions of the requests or responses with the clerk at the start of the trial.

[Effective January 1, 2012.]

N.D. IND. L.R. 30–1. SCHEDULING DEPOSITIONS

(a) **Avoiding Conflicts.** Attorneys must try in good faith to schedule depositions to avoid calendar conflicts.

(b) **Notice.** Attorneys must schedule depositions with at least 14–days' notice, unless opposing counsel agrees to shorter notice or the court orders otherwise.

[Effective January 1, 2012.]

N.D. IND. L.R. 37–1. RESOLVING DISCOVERY DISPUTES

(a) **Certification Required.** A party filing any discovery motion must file a separate certification that the party has conferred in good faith or attempted to confer with other affected parties in an effort to resolve the matter raised in the motion without court action. The certification must include:

(1) the date, time, and place of any conference or attempted conference; and

(2) the names of the parties participating in the conference.

(b) **Failure to File Certification.** The court may deny any motion described in subdivision (a)—except those motions brought by or against a person appearing pro se—if the required certification is not filed.

[Effective January 1, 2012.]

N.D. IND. L.R. 37–3. DEALING WITH OBJECTIONS DURING DEPOSITIONS

(a) **Attempt to Resolve Dispute.** Before contacting the court for a ruling on an objection during a deposition, all parties must confer in good faith or attempt to confer in an effort to resolve the matter without court action.

(b) **Raising Objections with the Court.** A party may recess a deposition to submit an objection by phone to a judge if:

(1) a judge is available and willing to address the objection; and

(2) the objection:

(A) could cause the deposition to be adjourned; and

(B) can be resolved without submitting written materials to the court.

[Effective January 1, 2012.]

N.D. IND. L.R. 40–1. CASE ASSIGNMENT

(a) **Assignment According to Court Order.** The clerk's office must assign cases to judges according to the court's general orders.

(b) **Assignment Sequence Is Confidential.** No one in the clerk's office may reveal to any person, other than a judge, the sequence in which cases are assigned.

(c) **Punishment for Tampering with Assignments.** The court may punish a person for contempt if the person, directly or indirectly, causes or attempts to cause a court employee to:

(1) reveal the sequence in which cases are assigned; or

(2) assign a case inconsistent with the court's order.

(d) **Notice of Related Action.** A party must file a notice of related action as soon as it appears that the party's case and another pending case:

(1) arise out of the same transaction or occurrence;

(2) involve the same property; or

(3) involve the validity or infringement of the same patent, trademark, or copyright.

(e) **Transfer of Related Cases.** When the court determines that two cases are related, the case filed later must be transferred to the judge handling the earlier-filed case. But a magistrate judge handling an earlier-filed case with consent under Fed. R. Civ. P. 73 must transfer the case to a district judge handling a later-filed case if the parties to the later case have not consented to a magistrate judge handling the entire case.

(f) **Reassignment of Cases.**

(1) *Workload.* The court may reassign cases among judges if workload and the speedy administration of justice so require.

(2) *Disqualification of District Judge.*

(A) Civil Cases. A civil case must be randomly reassigned to another district judge in the district if the presiding district judge is disqualified.

(B) Criminal Cases. If a district judge presiding over a criminal case is disqualified the case must be randomly assigned to another district judge in the same division if there is one. If there is no other district judge in the division, the case must be reassigned to another district judge by:

(i) the chief judge, if the chief judge is not disqualified; or

(ii) the district judge with the most seniority on the bench who is not disqualified.

(3) *Disqualification of Magistrate Judge.* If a magistrate judge handling a case with consent under Fed. R. Civ. P. 73 is disqualified, the district judge

most recently assigned to the case will reassign it to another magistrate judge within the district.

(g) Remands for New Trials. Cases remanded for a new trial under Seventh Circuit Rule 36 must be reassigned according to subdivision (f) unless:

(1) the remand order directs otherwise; or

(2) within 14 days after the mandate for a new trial is docketed, all parties in the case file a request that the judge previously assigned to the case retry it.

[Effective January 1, 2012.]

N.D. IND. L.R. 40–4. TIME–SENSITIVE MATTERS

If a matter needs to be heard quickly and the judge assigned to the case is unavailable, the clerk must notify the district judge in the same division with the most seniority on the bench. But if no district judge is available in that division, the clerk must notify the chief judge or—if the chief judge is unavailable—the district judge with the most seniority on the bench.

[Effective January 1, 2012.]

N.D. IND. L.R. 41–1. FAILURE TO PROSECUTE

The court may dismiss a civil case with judgment for costs if:

(a) no activity has occurred in the case for six months;

(b) the court or clerk has notified the parties that the case will be dismissed for failure to prosecute it; and

(c) at least 28 days have passed since the notice was given.

[Effective January 1, 2012.]

N.D. IND. L.R. 42–2. CONSOLIDATION

(a) Required Filings. A party seeking to consolidate two or more cases must file:

(1) a motion in the case with the earliest docket number; and

(2) a notice of the motion in all the other cases.

(b) Ruling. The judge assigned to the case in which the motion is filed will decide the motion.

[Effective January 1, 2012.]

N.D. IND. L.R. 47–1. VOIR DIRE

(a) Voir Dire Conducted by Court. Ordinarily, the court conducts voir dire in jury cases. But consis-

tent with Fed. R. Civ. P. 47, the court may allow attorneys to conduct voir dire.

(b) Requests to Cover Particular Subjects and Questions. At the time set by the court, parties may file with the clerk requests for the court to cover particular subjects or to ask particular questions during voir dire.

(c) Requests for Additional Questions after Initial Voir Dire. After the court completes its initial voir dire, parties may request that the court ask additional questions that are necessary and could not have been reasonably anticipated before trial.

[Effective January 1, 2012.]

N.D. IND. L.R. 47–2. COMMUNICATION WITH JURORS

(a) Communication Forbidden. Ordinarily, no party or attorney (or any of their employees or agents) may communicate off the record with:

(1) a member of the jury pool; or

(2) a juror during trial, during deliberations, or after a verdict.

(b) Exceptions. The court may allow a party or attorney to communicate with jurors if all other parties are given notice and if the court sets conditions on allowed communication.

[Effective January 1, 2012.]

N.D. IND. L.R. 47–3. ASSESSMENT OF JURY COSTS

(a) Authority of Court. The court may order any party or its counsel to pay juror costs (including marshal's fees, mileage, and per diem) if:

(1) prospective jurors have reported for voir dire;

(2) a trial does not start or resume as scheduled; and

(3) a settlement, change of plea, or other action by the party or its counsel causes the court to incur the costs.

(b) Safe Harbor. The court may not assess juror costs if at least one full business day before the trial is set to begin, the clerk is notified of the circumstances causing delay.

[Effective January 1, 2012.]

N.D. IND. L.R. 51–1. JURY INSTRUCTIONS

In jury cases, parties must use pattern jury instructions when possible.

[Effective January 1, 2012.]

N.D. IND. L.R. 54–1. TAXATION OF COSTS

(a) Process. To recover costs, a party must file and serve a completed AO Form 133 (available from the clerk or the court's website) within 14 days after final judgment is entered.

(b) Extensions. The court may extend the 14–day deadline for good cause if, before the original deadline, the party files a motion requesting an extension.

[Effective January 1, 2012.]

N.D. IND. L.R. 56–1. SUMMARY JUDGMENT PROCEDURE

(a) Moving Party's Obligations. The brief supporting a summary-judgment motion or the brief's appendix must include a section labeled "Statement of Material Facts" that identifies the facts that the moving party contends are not genuinely disputed.

(b) Opposing Party's Obligations.

(1) *Required Filings.* A party opposing the motion must, within 28 days after the movant serves the motion, file and serve

(A) a response brief; and

(B) any materials that the party contends raise a genuine dispute.

(2) *Content of Response Brief or Appendix.* The response brief or its appendix must include a section labeled "Statement of Genuine Disputes" that identifies the material facts that the party contends are genuinely disputed so as to make a trial necessary.

(c) Reply. The movant may file a reply brief within 14 days after a response is served.

(d) Oral Argument. The court will decide summary-judgment motions without oral argument unless a request under L.R. 7–5 is granted or the court directs otherwise.

(e) Disputes About Admissibility of Evidence. Any dispute regarding the admissibility of evidence should be addressed in a separate motion in accordance with L.R. 7–1.

(f) Notice Requirement for Pro Se Cases. A party seeking summary judgment against an unrepresented party must serve that party with the notice contained in Appendix C.

[Effective January 1, 2012.]

N.D. IND. L.R. 65–1. PRELIMINARY INJUNCTIONS AND TEMPORARY RESTRAINING ORDERS

(a) Preliminary Injunctions. The court will consider requests for preliminary injunctions only if the moving party files a separate motion for relief.

(b) Temporary Restraining Orders. The court will consider requests for temporary restraining orders only if the moving party:

(1) files a separate motion for relief;

(2) files a supporting brief; and

(3) complies with Fed. R. Civ. P. 65(b).

[Effective January 1, 2012.]

N.D. IND. L.R. 66–1. RECEIVERSHIPS

(a) Applicability. This rule applies to the administration of estates (excluding estates in bankruptcy) by court-appointed officers such as receivers.

(b) Officer's Duties.

(1) *Inventories.* Within 28 days after taking possession of an estate, the court-appointed officer must file:

(A) an inventory and appraisal of the estate's property and assets held by the officer or the officer's agent; and

(B) on a separate schedule, an inventory of the estate's property and assets held by others.

(2) *Regular Reports.* Within 28 days after the inventory is filed and every three months after that, the court-appointed officer must file a report:

(A) describing the acts and transactions the officer undertakes on the estate's behalf; and

(B) accounting for any monies received by or expended for the estate.

(c) Compensation of Receiver, Attorneys, and Other Officers.

(1) *Amount.* The court, in its discretion, will determine what to pay court-appointed officers, their attorneys, and others the court appoints to help administer an estate.

(2) *Procedures for Payment.* To get paid, persons seeking compensation must petition the court and notify:

(A) the estate's creditors; and

(B) any other interested parties the court requires to receive notice.

(d) Administration Generally. In all other respects the court-appointed officer must—to the extent it is reasonable to do so—administer the estate in the way that bankruptcy estates are typically administered unless the court authorizes a different practice.

(e) Deadlines. The court may alter any deadline imposed by this rule.

[Effective January 1, 2012.]

N.D. IND. L.R. 69–4. BODY ATTACHMENTS; HEARINGS

(a) Requirements for Body Attachments. The court may issue a body-attachment warrant against a judgment debtor only if:

(1) the debtor was served notice of a proceedings-supplemental hearing;

(2) the debtor failed to appear for the hearing;

(3) the judgment creditor filed a petition seeking a hearing for the debtor to show cause for failing to appear;

(4) the debtor was served notice of the show-cause hearing; and

(5) the debtor failed to appear at the show-cause hearing.

(b) Hearing after Arrest. When a judgment debtor is arrested on a body attachment, the court must conduct a hearing at its earliest convenience. The judgment-creditor's attorney will be notified of the hearing by telephone. Attorneys are deemed to have consented to telephonic notice by requesting the body attachment.

(c) Failure to Respond to Telephonic Notice. If the judgment-creditor's attorney fails to respond promptly to the telephonic notice, the court may release the judgment debtor or take other appropriate action.

(d) Appearance at Hearing by Creditor's Attorney. The judgment-creditor's attorney of record must personally appear at the hearing; neither clerical nor secretarial personnel may interrogate an attached judgment debtor.

[Effective January 1, 2012.]

N.D. IND. L.R. 72–1. UNITED STATES MAGISTRATE JUDGES

(a) Application. This rule applies to all United States magistrate judges, including full-time magistrate judges, part-time magistrate judges, and magistrate judges recalled under 28 U.S.C. § 636(h).

(b) Authority. Magistrate judges are judges. They are authorized—and specially designated—to perform all duties authorized by the United States Code and any rule governing proceedings in this court. Magistrate judges are authorized to perform the duties enumerated in these rules in cases assigned to the magistrate judge by rule, by court order, or by order or special designation of any of the court's district judges.

[Effective January 1, 2012.]

N.D. IND. L.R. 79–1. CUSTODY OF FILES AND EXHIBITS

(a) Evidence Placed in Clerk's Custody. Items offered into evidence during a case are placed in the clerk's custody.

(b) Claiming Items.

(1) *Procedure.* To claim items from the clerk, a party must give the clerk a detailed receipt. The clerk must file the receipt in the case.

(2) *Timing.* A party may claim an item from the clerk only after the case concludes unless the court orders otherwise.

(3) *Unclaimable Items.*

(A) Contraband Exhibits. Contraband exhibits (such as controlled substances, money, and weapons) must be released to the investigative agency responsible for them when the case concludes. The investigative agency must give the clerk a detailed receipt when the contraband exhibits are released.

(B) Original Papers. No one may claim an original paper filed in a case except as ordered by the court.

(c) When a Case Concludes. A case concludes when:

(1) the parties notify the court that they have settled the case; or

(2) the court has resolved all issues before it and:

(A) the deadline for appeal expires without an appeal being filed; or

(B) if an appeal is filed, the appellate court's final mandate is filed in the clerk's office.

(d) Unclaimed Items.

(1) *Authority.* The United States Marshal may dispose of any item that remains unclaimed for 28 days after the clerk notifies the party offering the item into evidence that it will be disposed of if it is not claimed.

(2) *Issuing Notice.* The clerk may issue the notice:

(A) 28 days after a case concludes, if the case was appealed; or

(B) 90 days after a case concludes otherwise.

(3) *Methods of Disposal.* Unclaimed items may be sold in a public or private sale or disposed of in any other manner the court directs. The net proceeds of a sale will be paid into the court's registry.

[Effective January 1, 2012.]

N.D. IND. L.R. 83–3. COURTROOM AND COURTHOUSE DECORUM

(a) Prohibited Activities. The following activities are prohibited anywhere on a floor where a courtroom, jury assembly room, grand-jury room, or clerk's office is located when they are done in connection with a judicial proceeding:

(1) taking photographs;

(2) making sound recordings (except by court reporters in the performance of their duties); and

(3) broadcasting by radio, television, or any other means.

(b) Exceptions.

(1) *Ceremonial Proceedings.* The court may permit these activities in connection with investiture, ceremonial, or naturalization proceedings.

(2) *U.S. Attorney's Office Space.* The U.S. Attorney may conduct press conferences and depositions within its office space.

(3) *Other Depositions.* If the court or clerk approves, a deposition may be taken and recorded by any means in another space in the courthouse.

(c) Cell Phones and PDAs.

(1) *Generally Prohibited.* Ordinarily, no one may have a cell phone or personal digital assistant ("PDA") in the courthouse.

(2) *Exceptions.*

(A) Attorneys. Members of the court's bar may have cell phones and PDAs.

(B) U.S. Marshals. The U.S. Marshal and all deputy marshals may have cell phones. But they may not have a cell phone in a courtroom unless it is set so that it cannot ring audibly.

(C) Building Personnel. Courthouse personnel may have cell phones, but not in a courtroom.

(D) Visiting Federal Law Enforcement Personnel. Visiting federal law-enforcement personnel may have cell phones if:

(i) the U.S. Marshal's Service approves them to carry cell phones;

(ii) they only carry the cell phones directly to and from the agency office they are visiting; and

(iii) they leave the cell phones in the office during their visit.

(3) *Restrictions on Use.* No one may use a cell phone or PDA in the courthouse for an improper purpose, including without limitation taking pictures or videos not permitted under subdivision (a). A judge may confiscate a cell phone or PDA or fine its user up to $1,500 (or both) if the cell phone or PDA makes an audible noise in the judge's courtroom while court is in session.

[Effective January 1, 2012.]

N.D. IND. L.R. 83–5. BAR ADMISSION

(a) Authority to Practice Before the Court.

(1) *Rule.* Only members of the court's bar may represent parties before the court.

(2) *Exceptions.*

(A) Pro Se. A nonmember may represent him or herself in a case.

(B) U.S. Government Attorneys. A nonmember who is an attorney may represent the United States, or an officer or agency of the United States.

(C) Pro Hac Vice. A nonmember who is an attorney may represent parties in a case if the nonmember:

(i) is admitted to practice as an attorney in another United States court or the highest court of any state;

(ii) is a member in good standing of the bar in every jurisdiction where the attorney is admitted to practice;

(iii) is not currently suspended from practice;

(iv) has certified that he or she will abide by the *Seventh Circuit Standards of Professional Conduct* and these rules;

(v) has paid the required filing fee; and

(vi) has applied for, and been granted by the court, leave to appear in the case.

(3) *Foreign Legal Consultants.* A person admitted as a foreign legal consultant is not "admitted to practice as an attorney" under this rule.

(b) Bar Membership. The bar consists of those persons who:

(1) are admitted by the court to practice; and

(2) have not resigned or been disbarred or suspended from the bar.

(c) Admission.

(1) *Who May Be Admitted.* An attorney admitted to practice by the United States Supreme Court or the highest court in any state may become a member of the court's bar on a member's motion.

(2) *Character.* An applicant will be admitted to the bar if the court is satisfied that the applicant:

(A) has good private and professional character; and

(B) is a member in good standing of the bar in every jurisdiction where the applicant is admitted to practice.

(3) *Entry on Court's Records.* The attorney's admission will be entered on the court's records and the court will issue a certificate to that effect only after the applicant:

(A) takes a prescribed oath or affirmation;

(B) certifies that he or she has read and will abide by:

    (i) the *Seventh Circuit Standards of Professional Conduct*; and

    (ii) the court's local rules;

(C) pays the required fees (law clerks to the court's judges are exempt from these fees);

(D) registers for electronic case filing;

(E) gives a current address; and

(F) agrees to notify the clerk promptly of any change in address.

(d) Local Counsel. The court may require an attorney residing outside the district to retain, as local counsel, a member of the court's bar who resides in the district.

(e) Standards. Indiana's Rules of Professional Conduct and the *Seventh Circuit Standards of Professional Conduct* (an appendix to these rules) govern the conduct of those practicing in the court.

[Effective January 1, 2012. Amended effective December 1, 2013; August 14, 2015.]

N.D. IND. L.R. 83–6.1 ATTORNEY DISCIPLINE

(a) Who Is Subject to Discipline. Any attorney authorized to represent a party before the court may be disciplined under N.D. Ind. L.R. 83–6.1 through 83–6.13.

(b) Scope of Discipline Rules. These discipline rules (N.D. Ind. L.R. 83–6.1 through 83–6.13) do not apply to or limit:

(1) sanctions or other disciplinary or remedial actions authorized by the Federal Rules of Civil or Criminal Procedure; or

(2) the court's inherent or statutory power to maintain control over the proceedings conducted before it, such as contempt proceedings under Title 18 United States Code or under Fed. R. Crim. P. 42.

[Effective January 1, 2012.]

N.D. IND. L.R. 83–6.2 GROUNDS FOR DISCIPLINE

(a) Court's Authority. The court may discipline an attorney who:

(1) engages in misconduct, even if the misconduct occurs outside an attorney-client relationship;

(2) is convicted of a serious crime; or

(3) is disciplined by any other court in the United States or its territories, commonwealths, or possessions.

(b) "Misconduct" Defined. "Misconduct" means a violation of the standards of professional conduct identified in N.D. Ind. L.R. 83–5(e).

(c) "Serious Crime" Defined. "Serious crime" includes

(1) any felony; and

(2) any lesser crime that under the law of the jurisdiction that entered the conviction has a necessary element involving:

- false swearing;
- misrepresentation;
- fraud;
- willful failure to file income-tax returns;
- deceit;
- bribery;
- extortion;
- misappropriation;
- theft;
- attempting to commit a serious crime; or
- conspiring with another or soliciting another to commit a serious crime

(d) Discipline. Discipline may include:

(1) a public or private reprimand;

(2) suspension from the court's bar;

(3) disbarment from the court; or

(4) other disciplinary action taken under the grievance process established in these rules.

[Effective January 1, 2012.]

N.D. IND. L.R. 83–6.3 GRIEVANCE COMMITTEE

(a) Members. The court will maintain a five-member grievance committee, which must include at least one attorney from each of the court's four divisions. The fifth member must also be an attorney.

(b) Appointment and Terms. The court's district judges will appoint committee members to five-year terms. Committee members will serve staggered terms so that the court replaces or reappoints one member each year.

(c) Replacement of Members. The court's district judges will promptly replace a committee member who is unable or unwilling to complete the member's term.

(d) Chairperson. The chief judge will designate one committee member as the chairperson to convene the committee.

(e) Secretary. The clerk must either serve, or designate a deputy clerk to serve, as the committee's secretary. The secretary may not vote, but must maintain the committee's records.

(f) Annual Report. By January 31, the committee must give the court a written report of its actions during the previous calendar year, including:

(1) the number of grievances filed;

(2) the number of pending investigations; and

(3) the disposition of grievances.

(g) Special Counsel. The court may appoint special counsel to:

(1) help the committee investigate a grievance; or

(2) prosecute a grievance at a hearing.

(h) Compensation and Expenses.

(1) *Committee Members.* Committee members serve without compensation. But when possible, the clerk must pay the committee members' necessary expenses from the library fund.

(2) *Special Counsel.* Special counsel is entitled to reasonable fees and expenses as the court determines. The clerk must pay approved fees and expenses from the library fund.

(i) Powers and Immunities. Members acting for the committee and any special counsel appointed by the court represent the court and act under its powers and immunities so long as they act in good faith in their official capacity.

(j) Quorum. Three or more members constitute a quorum. A quorum may act on the committee's behalf.

[Effective January 1, 2012.]

N.D. IND. L.R. 83–6.4 INITIATING GRIEVANCE PROCEEDINGS

(a) When the Proceeding Begins. A grievance proceeding begins when:

(1) the court, by order in a pending case, refers an instance of possible attorney misconduct to the grievance committee; or

(2) someone files a written allegation of attorney misconduct with the clerk that:

(A) identifies the attorney;

(B) briefly and plainly describes the alleged misconduct at issue; and

(C) is verified.

(b) Clerk's Duties. The clerk must:

(1) maintain a grievance form for making grievances; and

(2) promptly give each committee member a copy of any grievance.

(c) "Grievance" Defined. "Grievance" means:

(1) a written allegation of attorney misconduct filed with the clerk; or

(2) an order referring an instance of possible attorney misconduct to the grievance committee.

(d) Allegation to Remain Sealed. A written allegation of attorney misconduct must be filed under seal and remain sealed until the committee determines that there is a substantial question of misconduct.

[Effective January 1, 2012.]

N.D. IND. L.R. 83–6.5 CONDUCT OF GRIEVANCE PROCEEDINGS— GRIEVANCE COMMITTEE

(a) Initial Determination.

(1) *Generally.* Upon receiving a grievance, the committee must determine whether it raises a substantial question of misconduct.

(2) *If Substantial Question of Misconduct Does Not Exist.* If the committee determines that no substantial question of misconduct exists, the committee must:

(A) take no further action against the attorney;

(B) advise the clerk and the person or judge who filed the grievance that no further action or investigation is warranted;

(C) notify the attorney that a grievance was filed and that the committee decided to take no further action; and

(D) supply the attorney with a copy of the grievance.

(3) *If Substantial Question of Misconduct Exists.* If the committee determines that a substantial question of misconduct exists, the committee must either:

(A) investigate the misconduct alleged in the grievance; or

(B) refer the matters raised in the grievance to another disciplinary agency with jurisdiction over the attorney.

(b) Investigation.

(1) *Requirements of Investigation.* If the committee investigates, it must:

(A) notify the attorney of its investigation;

(B) give the attorney a copy of the grievance;

(C) direct the attorney to file a written response:

(i) with the clerk;

(ii) under seal (unless the attorney files a written request with the committee to have it unsealed); and

(iii) within 30 days; and

(D) otherwise decide how, and to what extent, it will investigate.

(2) *Investigative Powers.* During its investigation, the committee may:

(A) interview witnesses;

(B) subpoena witnesses or documents;

(C) depose witnesses;

(D) administer oaths; and

(E) otherwise exercise the powers necessary to properly and expeditiously investigate the grievance.

(c) Determinations After Investigation.

(1) *Generally.* After completing an investigation, the committee must determine whether a substantial question of misconduct exists.

(2) *If Substantial Question of Misconduct Does Not Exist.* If the committee determines that no substantial question of misconduct exists, the committee must:

(A) Take no further action against the attorney; and

(B) advise the clerk, the attorney, and the person or judge who filed the grievance that no further action is warranted.

(3) *If Substantial Question of Misconduct Exists.* If the committee determines that a substantial question of misconduct exists, the committee must promptly schedule a formal hearing.

(d) Hearing.

(1) *Conduct of Hearing.*

(A) Attorney's Rights. The attorney may:

(i) attend the hearing;

(ii) be represented by counsel;

(iii) present evidence; and

(iv) confront and cross-examine witnesses.

(B) Evidentiary Rules. The *Federal Rules of Evidence* will guide the committee on evidentiary issues.

(C) Record. The committee must make a record of the hearing.

(D) Delays. Delays in the hearing do not affect the committee's jurisdiction.

(2) *Determinations.* After the hearing, the committee must determine:

(A) whether the attorney committed misconduct; and

(B) if so, whether the misconduct merits discipline.

(3) *When No Misconduct Is Found.* If the committee determines that the attorney did not commit misconduct or that the attorney's misconduct does not merit disciplinary action, the committee must:

(A) take no further action against the attorney; and

(B) advise the clerk, the attorney, and the person or judge who filed the grievance that no further action is warranted.

(4) *When Misconduct Is Found.* If the committee determines that the attorney's misconduct merits discipline, it must:

(A) prepare a written report setting forth:

(i) the committee's findings and conclusions, including a finding that the attorney committed misconduct;

(ii) the facts that support the findings and conclusions;

(iii) recommended discipline; and

(iv) the reasons for the recommended discipline.

(B) forward the report to:

(i) the chief judge;

(ii) if the matter involved conduct before the bankruptcy court, the bankruptcy court's chief judge;

(iii) the attorney; and

(iv) the person or judge who filed the grievance.

(5) *Recommended Discipline.* The following are among the discipline the committee may recommend:

(A) private reprimand;

(B) public reprimand;

(C) suspension from the court's bar;

(D) disbarment from the court; and

(E) referral to another appropriate disciplinary agency for disciplinary action.

(e) Attorney's Proposed Discipline. The attorney may propose discipline any time before the committee gives the chief judge its report. If the proposed discipline is appropriate, the committee may cease further proceedings and recommend the proposed discipline to the chief judge.

(f) Confidentiality.

(1) *Generally.* The committee's investigations, deliberations, hearings, determinations, and other proceedings—including all materials presented to the committee—are confidential.

(2) *Exceptions.* The committee may disclose some or all aspects of its proceedings to:

(A) the court's judges;

(B) the person who filed the grievance; and

(C) other disciplinary committees.

(3) *Written Report.* The committee's written report to the chief judge must be filed as a miscellaneous case. Ordinarily, the report is a public record. But it must be—and remain—sealed if the committee recommends a private reprimand.

[Effective January 1, 2012.]

N.D. IND. L.R. 83–6.6   CONDUCT OF GRIEVANCE PROCEEDINGS— DISTRICT COURT

(a) Initial Proceedings.

(1) *Show–Cause Order.* Upon receiving the committee's written report recommending discipline, the chief judge must issue an order requiring the attorney to show cause, in writing, why the court should not adopt the committee's findings and recommendations.

(2) *Response.* Any response by the attorney must be filed with the clerk within 30 days after the show-cause order is served.

(3) *Vote of Judges.* The court's district judges— and the bankruptcy court's judges if the matter involves conduct before the bankruptcy court—must:

(A) consider the committee's report and any response from the attorney; and

(B) vote on:

(i) whether to adopt, modify, or reject the committee's findings and recommendations; or

(ii) set the matter for a hearing before a judge.

(4) *Decision of Chief Judge.* The chief judge must enter an order consistent with the judges' majority vote.

(b) Hearing.

(1) *Conduct of Hearing.* Any hearing the chief judge sets must be conducted promptly and use the *Federal Rules of Evidence* as a guide on evidentiary issues.

(2) *Report.* The judge who conducts the hearing must give the chief judge a report on the hearing that includes proposed findings of fact and a recommendation for disposition.

(3) *Vote of Judges.* The court's district judges— and the bankruptcy court's judges if the matter involves conduct before the bankruptcy court—must vote on whether to:

(A) adopt, modify, or reject the judge's findings and recommendations; or

(B) take other appropriate action.

(4) *Decision of Chief Judge.* The chief judge must enter an order consistent with the judges' majority vote.

(c) **Final Disposition.** The chief judge must notify the following people of the court's resolution:

(1) the person or judge who filed the grievance;

(2) the attorney; and

(3) the grievance-committee chairperson.

[Effective January 1, 2012.]

N.D. IND. L.R. 83–6.7   ATTORNEYS CONVICTED OF CRIMES

(a) Serious Crimes.

(1) *Immediate Suspension.* An attorney may be suspended immediately if a court in the United States or its territories, possessions, or commonwealths convicts the attorney of a serious crime.

(2) *Evidence of Conviction.* A certified copy of a judgment or order reflecting conviction of a serious crime is conclusive evidence that the crime was committed.

(3) *Suspension Process.* When conclusive evidence of conviction of a serious crime is filed with the court:

(A) the court must immediately:

(i) suspend the attorney; and

(ii) serve the attorney with the suspension order; and

(B) the chief judge may refer the matter to the grievance committee.

(4) *Authority to Set Aside Suspension.* The chief judge may lift the suspension for good cause.

(5) *Effect of Reversal.* If a certificate demonstrating that the conviction has been reversed is filed with the court, the court must immediately reinstate the attorney. But:

(A) any pending disciplinary proceedings against the attorney will continue; and

(B) the court may resolve the pending disciplinary proceedings based on all available evidence pertaining to the attorney's guilt.

(6) *Grievance Committee Proceedings.* If the chief judge refers the matter to the grievance committee, the committee must generally treat the matter as a grievance. But:

(A) the committee may not conduct a hearing until all appeals from the conviction are concluded; and

(B) if the conviction is not reversed, the only issue before the committee will be what discipline to recommend.

(7) *Effect of Appeals and Manner of Conviction.* The court and chief judge's obligations under this rule do not change:

(A) because there are pending appeals or other actions attacking the conviction; or

(B) due to the manner of conviction (for example, from a guilty plea, nolo contendere, or a verdict after trial).

(b) Other Convictions. The chief judge may refer a conviction for a non-serious crime to the grievance committee, which must treat the referral as if it were a grievance.

[Effective January 1, 2012. Amended effective January 1, 2013.]

N.D. IND. L.R. 83–6.8 IDENTICAL DISCIPLINE

(a) Discipline by Another Court. The court may discipline an attorney if another court in the United States or its territories, possessions, or commonwealths disciplines the attorney.

(b) Discipline Process. When a certified or exemplified copy of the judgment or order imposing the discipline is filed with this court, the chief judge must promptly order the disciplined attorney to show cause within 30 days after the order is served why the court should not impose identical discipline (other than a fine).

(c) Identical Discipline. The court must impose identical discipline (other than a fine) as the other court unless:

(1) the other court stays its order, in which case this court must defer any identical discipline until the stay expires;

(2) the chief judge refers the matter to the grievance committee:

(A) for disciplinary proceedings, in which case the committee must treat the referral as a grievance; or

(B) to recommend appropriate action in light of the other court's discipline; or

(3) the attorney demonstrates, or the court finds from the record's face, that:

(A) the other court's procedure lacked sufficient notice or opportunity to be heard to provide the attorney with due process;

(B) the proof supporting the misconduct is so lacking that this court cannot, consistent with its duty, accept the other court's order as final;

(C) imposing identical discipline would result in a grave injustice; or

(D) the misconduct warrants substantially different discipline.

[Effective January 1, 2012.]

N.D. IND. L.R. 83–6.9 DISBARMENT ON CONSENT OR RESIGNATION IN OTHER COURTS

Attorneys may no longer practice in this court if, while being investigated for misconduct, they consent to disbarment or resign from the bar of any other court in the United States or its territories, commonwealths, or possessions.

[Effective January 1, 2012.]

N.D. IND. L.R. 83–6.10 DISBARMENT ON CONSENT IN THIS COURT

(a) How to Consent to Disbarment. An attorney who is the subject of pending disciplinary proceedings in this court may consent to disbarment from the court's bar by delivering to the clerk an affidavit stating that the attorney:

(1) freely and voluntarily consents to disbarment;

(2) is not subject to coercion or duress;

(3) fully understands the implications of consenting to disbarment;

(4) knows that he or she is the subject of pending disciplinary proceedings;

(5) knows the alleged material facts—which must be set forth in the affidavit—that provide the grounds for discipline;

(6) acknowledges that the material facts are true; and

(7) consents to disbarment because if required to mount a defense in the disciplinary proceedings, the attorney could not do so successfully.

(b) Clerk's Duties. The clerk must submit the affidavit to the chief judge to enter an order disbarring the attorney.

(c) Access to Order and Affidavit. The order disbarring the attorney is a public record. But the affidavit may only be publicly disclosed or made available for use in another proceeding by court order.

[Effective January 1, 2012.]

N.D. IND. L.R. 83–6.11 REINSTATEMENT

(a) Court Order Required. A suspended or disbarred attorney must not resume practice until reinstated by court order.

(b) Reinstatement by Affidavit.

(1) *When Permitted.* The chief judge may—without a vote of the court's judges—reinstate a suspended attorney after receiving an affidavit of compliance if the suspension was:

(A) for three months or less; or

(B) because the attorney had been suspended from a state bar for failing to:

(i) pay bar dues on time; or

(ii) comply with continuing-legal-education requirements; **or**

(iii) comply with IOLTA program requirements.

(2) *How Raised.* To be reinstated without a vote of the court, an attorney must file:

(A) an affidavit of compliance; and

(B) a certified copy of the judgment or order reinstating the attorney to the state bar, if applicable.

(c) Reinstatement by Petition and Court Vote.

(1) *Initiating the Process.* An attorney seeking reinstatement from disbarment or any suspension not described in subdivision (b)(1) must file:

(A) a petition with the court; and

(B) if the attorney was suspended or disbarred because another court disciplined the attorney, a certified copy of the other court's reinstatement order.

(2) *Chief Judge's Duties.* The chief judge must promptly:

(A) consider whether the petition and any supporting materials—including any findings and conclusions from another court's reinstatement order—establish the attorney's fitness to practice law; and

(B) based on the review of the petition and supporting materials, recommend a course of action to the other judges.

(3) *Action by Judges.* After the chief judge's review, the court's district judges—and bankruptcy judges, if the matter involved an attorney's conduct before the bankruptcy court—may by a majority vote:

(A) reinstate the attorney, if they find that the petition and supporting materials establish the attorney's fitness to practice law; or

(B) request additional evidence or a hearing before voting on the petition.

(4) *Hearing.*

(A) Referral to Grievance Committee. If the judges request a hearing, the chief judge must promptly refer the petition to the grievance committee and the chairperson must promptly set a hearing.

(B) Attorney's Burden of Proof. At the hearing, the attorney must establish:

(i) by clear and convincing evidence, that he or she has the moral qualifications, competency, and learning in the law required for admission to the court's bar; and

(ii) that the attorney's reinstatement will not harm the bar's integrity and standing, the administration of justice, or the public interest.

(C) Post–Hearing Report. After the hearing, the committee must give the court a written report including its:

(i) findings of fact about the petitioner's fitness to resume practicing law; and

(ii) recommendations about whether to reinstate the attorney.

(5) *Court's Decision.* After considering the committee's report, the court's district judges—and bankruptcy judges, if the matter involved an attorney's conduct before the bankruptcy court—may by majority vote:

(A) deny the petition, if they find that the attorney is unfit to resume practicing law;

(B) reinstate the attorney unconditionally; or

(C) reinstate the attorney conditioned on the attorney:

(i) paying for all or part of the proceeding's cost;

(ii) making restitution to parties harmed by the conduct that led to the discipline;

(iii) providing certification from any jurisdiction's bar examiners that the attorney has successfully completed an admission examination after the suspension or disbarment took effect;

(iv) otherwise proving competency and learning in the law (if the suspension or disbarment was for five or more years); or

(v) meeting any other terms the judges deem appropriate.

(d) Timing of Petition.

(1) *After Disbarment.* A disbarred attorney may not file a reinstatement petition until five years after disbarment.

(2) *After Previous Unsuccessful Petition.* An attorney who has previously filed a reinstatement petition that was denied may not file another reinstatement petition on the same matter until one year after the denial.

(e) Fee. Any request for reinstatement, whether by affidavit or petition, must be accompanied by a fee in an amount equal to the filing fee for miscellaneous cases.

[Effective January 1, 2012. Amended effective August 15, 2014.]

N.D. IND. L.R. 83–6.12 SERVICE OF SHOW–CAUSE ORDER

A show-cause order related to formal disciplinary proceedings may be served by:

(a) CM/ECF if the attorney subject to the order is a registered electronic filer; or

(b) by regular mail addressed to the attorney at the attorney's last-known address.

[Effective January 1, 2012.]

N.D. IND. L.R. 83–6.13 OTHER DISCIPLINARY DUTIES

(a) **Attorneys' Duties.** Attorneys must promptly notify the clerk when they:

(1) are convicted of a serious crime;

(2) have been publicly disciplined by any court in the United States or its territories, commonwealths, or possessions; or

(3) consent to disbarment or resign from the bar of any court in the United States or its territories, commonwealths, or possessions while being investigated for misconduct.

(b) **Clerk's Duties.**

(1) *Conviction or Discipline in Another Court.* When the clerk learns that an attorney has been convicted of a crime or disciplined in another court, the clerk must promptly obtain the certificate of the conviction or a certified copy of the disciplinary order and file it with the court.

(2) *Conviction or Discipline in This Court.* When this court disciplines an attorney, the clerk must promptly notify:

(A) each appropriate disciplinary agency with jurisdiction over the attorney; and

(B) the American Bar Association's National Discipline Data Bank if the discipline was public.

[Effective January 1, 2012.]

N.D. IND. L.R. 83–7. DUTY OF ATTORNEYS TO ACCEPT APPOINTMENTS IN CERTAIN CIVIL ACTIONS

(a) **Duty.** Every bar member should be available to represent, or assist in representing, indigent parties whenever reasonably possible.

(b) **Procedure.** If the judge assigned to a case involving a party proceeding in forma pauperis determines that representation of the party by an attorney is warranted under 28 U.S.C. § 1915 (e)(1) or 42 U.S.C. § 2000e–5(f), the judge may direct the clerk to request that a bar member represent the indigent party.

(c) **Entry of Appearance.** An attorney who accepts a request to represent an indigent party must enter an appearance for the party within 14 days after accepting the request.

(d) **Representation, Relief, and Discharge.** The following are subject to the judge's discretion:

(1) whether the attorney should continue representing the party;

(2) whether to relieve the attorney from the appointment; and

(3) whether to discharge the attorney.

(e) **Expense Reimbursement.**

(1) *Petition.* Attorneys may seek reimbursement of reasonable expenses incurred representing an indigent party by filing a petition with the court either before the expenses are incurred, or within 90 days after they were incurred. The petition:

(A) may be made ex parte; and

(B) must be accompanied by documentation sufficient to permit the court to determine the request's appropriateness and reasonableness.

(2) *Type of Expenses.* The court may approve reimbursement of expenses necessary to prepare and present a civil action in this district. The court will not approve payment for appeal-related expenses or for costs or fees taxed as part of a judgment against the indigent party.

(3) *Source.* Approved reimbursements are paid from the Library and Court Administration Fund.

(4) *Repayment Upon Recovering Attorney's Fees.* An attorney who receives a fee award must promptly repay all reimbursements.

[Effective January 1, 2012.]

N.D. IND. L.R. 83–8. APPEARANCE AND WITHDRAWAL OF APPEARANCE

(a) **Appearances Required.** Attorneys not representing the United States or its agencies must file an appearance when they represent (either in person or by filing a paper) a party.

(b) **Removed and Transferred Cases.** Attorneys whose names are not on the court's docket after a case is removed or transferred must file either an appearance or a copy of the appearance they filed in the original court. Attorneys who are not bar members must comply with the court's admission policy (as described in N.D. Ind. L.R. 83–5) within 21 days of removal or transfer.

(c) **Withdrawal of Appearance.** To withdraw an appearance, attorneys must file a motion requesting leave to do so. Unless another attorney has appeared for the party, the motion must include:

(1) satisfactory evidence that the attorney gave the party written notice of the attorney's intent to withdraw at least seven days before filing the motion; and

(2) in civil cases, the party's last known contact information, including an address and telephone number.

[Effective January 1, 2012.]

N.D. IND. L.R. 83–9. STUDENT PRACTICE

(a) Generally. A law student or law-school graduate may represent parties (including by appearing for, negotiating on behalf of, and advising parties) in civil and criminal matters pending in this district if the student or graduate:

(1) is supervised by a bar member;

(2) is either:

(A) a staff member of a clinic:

(i) organized by a city or county bar association or an accredited law school; or

(ii) funded under the Legal Services Corporation Act; or

(B) participating in a legal-training program organized by:

(i) the United States Attorney's office; or

(ii) the Federal Community Defender's office; and

(3) in the case of a law student:

(A) is in good standing at an accredited law school;

(B) has completed the first year;

(C) meets the academic and moral standards established by the school's dean; and

(D) has been certified by the school as having met these requirements.

(b) Supervision. The supervising bar member must examine and sign all pleadings filed on a client's behalf. But the student or graduate may, without the supervisor present, negotiate on behalf of or advise a client.

(c) Appearance in Court. A student or graduate may appear in court under this rule subject to the following:

(1) the presiding judge must approve the appearance;

(2) if the case is a criminal or juvenile case carrying a penalty exceeding six months, the supervisor must be in the courtroom; and

(3) the judge may suspend a trial at any stage if the judge determines that:

(A) the representation is professionally inadequate; and

(B) substantial justice requires the suspension.

[Effective January 1, 2012.]

N.D. IND. L.R. 200–1. BANKRUPTCY CASES AND PROCEEDINGS

(a) Matters Determined by the Bankruptcy Judges.

(1) Subject to paragraph (a)(3)(B), all cases under Title 11 of the United States Code, and any or all proceedings arising under Title 11 or arising in or related to a case under Title 11 are referred to the bankruptcy judges. It is the intention of this court that the bankruptcy judges be given the broadest possible authority to administer cases properly within their jurisdiction, and this rule shall be interpreted to achieve this end.

(2) Pursuant to 28 U.S.C. § 157(b)(1), the bankruptcy judges shall hear and determine all cases under Title 11 and all core proceedings (including those delineated in 28 U.S.C. § 157(b)(2)) arising under Title 11, or arising in a case under Title 11, and shall enter appropriate orders and judgments, subject to review under 28 U.S.C. § 158.

(3) The bankruptcy judges shall hear all non-core proceedings related to a case under Title 11.

(A) By Consent. With the consent of the parties, a bankruptcy judge shall conduct hearings and enter appropriate orders or judgments in the proceeding, subject only to review under 28 U.S.C. § 158.

(B) Absent Consent. Absent consent of the parties, a bankruptcy judge shall conduct hearings and file proposed findings of fact and conclusions of law and a proposed order or judgment with the bankruptcy clerk. The bankruptcy judge may also file recommendations concerning whether the review of the proceedings should be expedited, and whether or not the basic bankruptcy case should be stayed pending district court termination of the non-core proceedings. The bankruptcy clerk shall serve copies of these documents upon the parties. Within 14 days of service, any party to the proceedings may file objections with the bankruptcy clerk. Any final order or judgment shall be issued by the district judge after considering the bankruptcy judge's proposed findings and conclusions and after reviewing de novo those matters to which any party has timely and specifically objected. (Review of interlocutory orders shall be had following the procedure specified in paragraph (d) of this rule.)

(C) Signifying Consent. At time of pre-trial, or earlier, upon motion of a party in interest, the parties shall:

(i) Stipulate in writing that the proceeding is a core proceeding:

(ii) Stipulate in writing that the proceeding is a non-core proceeding, but that the bankruptcy judge can determine the matter and enter a final order subject to review pursuant to 28 U.S.C. § 158;

(iii) Stipulate that the proceeding is a non-core proceeding, the bankruptcy judge finds the matter is a non-core proceeding and at least one party refuses to have the bankruptcy judge determine the matter; or

(iv) State that there is no agreement between the parties as to whether the proceeding is a core or non-core proceeding and at least one party refuses to have the bankruptcy judge determine the matter if it is determined to be a non-core proceeding;

Attached as an Appendix to this rule is an example of a stipulated order which may be used at the pretrial conference.

(b) Matters to be Determined or Tried by District Judges.

(1) *Motions to Withdraw Cases and Proceedings to the District Court.*

(A) The district judge shall hear and determine any motion to withdraw any case, contested matter, or adversary proceeding pursuant to 28 U.S.C. § 157(d).

(B) All such motions shall be accompanied by a separate supporting brief and any appropriate affidavits. The motion shall be filed with the bankruptcy court and served upon all appropriate parties in interest. Unless the bankruptcy court directs otherwise, any response and opposing affidavits shall be served and filed within the time required by L.R. 7–1 and the movant may serve and file any reply thereto within the time provided in that rule.

(C) Upon the expiration of the time for filing briefs concerning the motion, the motion and all materials submitted in support thereof and in opposition thereto will be transmitted to the district court for a determination. The bankruptcy judge may submit a written recommendation concerning the motion, the effect of withdrawal upon the disposition of the underlying bankruptcy case, and whether the disposition of the motion should be expedited. Any such recommendation shall be served upon the parties in accordance with the procedures set forth in subparagraph (a)(3)(B) of this rule.

(D) Should the district judge grant the motion to withdraw, the case, contested matter or adversary proceeding may be referred back to the bankruptcy judge for proposed findings of fact and conclusions of law and a proposed order or judgment in accordance with the procedures set forth in subparagraph (a)(3)(B) of this rule.

(2) *Personal Injury or Wrongful Death Tort Claims.*

(A) In proceedings involving an objection to a personal injury or wrongful death claim, the bankruptcy judge may hold a preliminary pre-trial or scheduling conference. At this conference, the parties may agree to the termination of the automatic stay to allow the claim to be determined in the state or federal court that would, absent bankruptcy, have jurisdiction over the action. In the absence of such an agreement, the bankruptcy judge, after consulting with the parties or their counsel, may issue a preliminary scheduling order. The matter shall then be transmitted to the clerk of the district court for such proceedings as may be appropriate.

(c) Jury Trial.

(1) *Jury Trial Before a Bankruptcy Judge*: Jury trials before a bankruptcy judge are not permitted. Issues arising under section 303 of Title 11 shall be tried by the bankruptcy judge without a jury.

(2) *Jury Trials Before a District Judge*:

(A) Where jury trials are not permitted before a bankruptcy judge, the party demanding a jury trial shall file a motion to withdraw the proceeding to the district court, in accordance with paragraph (b)(1) of this rule. The motion shall be filed at the same time as the demand for a jury trial. Unless excused by the district judge, the failure to file a timely motion to withdraw the proceeding shall constitute a waiver of any right to a trial by jury.

(B) In a personal injury or wrongful death tort claim, parties have the right to trial by jury. The demand for a jury trial must be properly made to preserve the right to a trial by jury.

(d) Appeals to the District Court. All appeals in core cases, in non-core cases heard by consent, and appeals of interlocutory orders entered by the bankruptcy judges in non-core cases heard by the bankruptcy court under subparagraph (a)(3)(B) of this rule shall be taken in the same manner as appeals in civil proceedings generally are taken to the courts of appeals from the district courts and in the time provided by the Bankruptcy Rules.

(e) Mandate Following a Decision on Appeal. The court's mandate following a decision on appeal from the bankruptcy court consists of a certified copy of the court's judgment and the court's written opinion, if any. Unless the court orders otherwise, the clerk will issue the mandate to the clerk of the bankruptcy court:

(1) immediately, when an appeal is dismissed voluntarily;

(2) seven days after the expiration of the deadline for filing any notice of appeal from this court's decision, unless a notice of appeal is filed; or

(3) if a notice of appeal is filed, seven days after the conclusion of any proceedings undertaken as a result of the Seventh Circuit's mandate to this court, unless those proceedings result in the entry of an order that could be the subject of a further appeal.

The mandate is effective when issued.

(f) Filing of Papers. While a case or proceeding is pending before a bankruptcy judge, or prior to the docketing of an appeal in the district court as set forth in the Bankruptcy Rules, all pleadings and other papers shall be filed with the bankruptcy clerk. After the case or non-core proceeding is assigned to a district judge, or after the district clerk has given notice to all parties of the date on which the appeal was docketed, all pleadings shall bear a civil case number in addition to the bankruptcy case number(s) and shall be filed only with the district court clerk.

(g) Submission of Files to the District Court; Assignment to District Judges. After the expiration of the time for filing objections under subparagraph (a)(3)(B), upon receipt of any order by a district judge pursuant to 28 U.S.C. § 157(d) or upon the docketing of an appeal in the district court as specified in paragraph (d), the bankruptcy clerk shall submit the file for the case or proceeding to the district court clerk. The district court clerk shall affix a civil number to each submission, and shall make the assignment to a district judge in accordance with the usual system for assigning civil cases.

(h) Local Bankruptcy Rules. The bankruptcy judges are authorized to make and amend rules governing the practice and procedure in all cases and proceedings within the district court's bankruptcy jurisdiction, in accordance with the requirements of Bankruptcy Rule 9029. Unless the district court orders otherwise, such rules shall also apply to any bankruptcy case or proceeding in which the order of reference has been withdrawn.

[Effective January 1, 2012.]

LOCAL CRIMINAL RULES

N.D. IND. L. CR. R. 6–1. GRAND JURIES

(a) Restricted Areas. While a grand jury is in session, no one may be in the hall leading to the rooms or areas used by the grand jury or anyplace where witnesses before the grand jury can be seen or heard. This subdivision does not apply to:

(1) grand jurors;

(2) witnesses;

(3) government attorneys, agents, and employees;

(4) court personnel involved with grand-jury proceedings;

(5) private attorneys whose clients have been called to appear before the grand jury; and

(6) others specifically authorized to be present.

(b) Numbering. The clerk must open a sealed miscellaneous case for each newly-impaneled grand jury. Motions, orders, and other filings pertaining to the grand jury must bear the case number.

(c) Motions to Seal Unnecessary. Motions and orders to seal are unnecessary.

(d) Challenges to Subpoenas.

(1) *Content of Challenges.* Pre-indictment challenges to grand-jury subpoenas or grand-jury proceedings must:

(A) be in writing;

(B) be filed with the clerk; and

(C) contain legal arguments and all pertinent facts, including:

(i) the grand-jury number;

(ii) the date the subpoena was served; and

(iii) the subpoena's appearance or production date.

(2) *Timing of Filing and Service.* Absent good cause, motions to quash or to limit a grand-jury subpoena must be filed and served on the United States at least seven days before the appearance or production date.

(3) *Timing of Ruling.* Except in unusual circumstances, the court will rule on motions to quash or to limit a grand-jury subpoena before the appearance or production date.

(4) *Magistrate Judges' Authority.* Magistrate judges may hear and determine motions to quash or to limit grand-jury subpoenas.

[Effective January 1, 2012.]

N.D. IND. L. CR. R. 12–1. PRETRIAL AUTHENTICATION AND FOUNDATION FOR EXHIBITS

(a) Procedure. Parties are strongly encouraged to authenticate exhibits under Fed. R. Evid. 901 or establish the foundation for admitting the records of a regularly conducted activity under Fed. R. Evid. 803(6) by serving the following on opposing parties at least 30 days before trial:

(1) a copy of each exhibit; and

(2) a statement of intent to proceed under this local rule.

(b) Objections. If the procedure in subdivision (a) is used, objections to an exhibit's authenticity or the foundation for admitting it will be waived, unless an opposing party files an objection at least 14 days before trial.

[Effective January 1, 2012.]

N.D. IND. L. CR. R. 13–1. ASSIGNMENT OF RELATED CASES

Any subsequent case or superseding indictment or information against a defendant must be assigned to the same judge presiding over a pending criminal case against that defendant.

[Effective January 1, 2012.]

N.D. IND. L. CR. R. 16–1. STANDARD ORDERS

The court may issue a standard order at the arraignment that contains provisions for:

(a) a trial date;

(b) pretrial discovery;

(c) deadlines for filing, and responding to, pretrial motions; and

(d) other matters.

[Effective January 1, 2012.]

N.D. IND. L. CR. R. 30–1. JURY INSTRUCTIONS

A party requesting that the court instruct the jury under Fed. R. Crim. P. 30(a):

(a) must file the request;

(b) must use the *Seventh Circuit Pattern Jury Instructions* whenever possible;

(c) must request the Seventh Circuit Pattern Jury Instructions by number only; and

(d) is encouraged, when requesting non-pattern instructions, to submit them to chambers in an electronic format compatible with the court's word-processing program.

[Effective January 1, 2012.]

N.D. IND. L. CR. R. 46–1. SURETIES

(a) Requirements on Sureties. A surety securing a person's appearance must:

(1) be a corporate surety that:

(A) holds a certificate of authority from the Secretary of the Treasury; and

(B) acts through a bondsman registered with the clerk; or

(2) own fee-simple title to real estate:

(A) in which the surety's equity has a fair-market value at least double that of the bond's penalty;

(B) that is unencumbered except for current taxes and a first-mortgage lien; and

(C) that is not subject to an existing appearance bond in any court in this district—whether federal, state, county, or municipal.

(b) Sureties on Appearance Bonds. Only a corporate surety may charge a fee for an appearance bond.

[Effective January 1, 2012.]

N.D. IND. L. CR. R. 47–1. CONTINUANCES

(a) Grounds. A motion to continue will be granted only if the moving party demonstrates that:

(1) the ends of justice served by a continuance outweigh the defendant's and the public's interests to a speedy trial as provided by the Speedy Trial Act; or

(2) the continuance will not violate the Speedy Trial Act's deadlines for some other reason.

(b) Proposed Entry Required. The moving party must submit with the motion a proposed entry with findings about the applicable ends of justice or any other reason the continuance will not violate the Speedy Trial Act.

[Effective January 1, 2012.]

N.D. IND. L. Cr. R. 47–2. BRIEFING DEADLINES

A party who files a petition under 28 U.S.C. § 2254 or a motion under 28 U.S.C. § 2255 must file any reply brief within 28 days after the answer brief is served.

[Effective January 1, 2012. Amended effective January 1, 2013.]

N.D. IND. L. Cr. R 47–3. SPECIAL NOTICE REQUIREMENTS IN 28 U.S.C. § 2254 DEATH PENALTY HABEAS CORPUS CASES

(a) Applicability. This rule applies to 28 U.S.C. § 2254 death-penalty habeas corpus cases.

(b) Required Notices. The clerk must notify those entitled to notice when:

(1) the case is opened;

(2) a stay of execution is granted or denied;

(3) a final order is issued; or

(4) a notice of appeal is filed.

(c) Entitlement to Notice. The following are entitled to notice:

(1) the respondent;

(2) the Indiana Attorney General;

(3) the Indiana Supreme Court; and

(4) the Seventh Circuit.

(d) How to Give Notice. The Clerk will coordinate how to notify those entitled to notice.

[Effective January 1, 2012. Amended effective January 1, 2013.]

N.D. IND. L. CR. R. 53–1. SPECIAL ORDERS

(a) Orders to Preserve Decorum and Maintain Integrity. The court may, on its own motion or a party's motion, issue special orders to preserve decorum and maintain the integrity of trials. These special orders may regulate such matters as the court deems appropriate, including:

(1) extrajudicial statements by trial participants (including lawyers and their staff, parties, witnesses, and jurors) that are likely to interfere with a party's right to a fair trial;

(2) clearing the courthouse's entrances and hallways so that witnesses and jurors cannot mingle with or be in close proximity to reporters, photographers, parties, lawyers, and others during recesses in the trial or as the jurors enter and exit the courtroom and courthouse;

(3) the seating and courtroom conduct of parties, attorneys (including their staff), spectators, and news-media representatives;

(4) maintaining the confidentiality of the jurors' names and addresses (unless a statute requires disclosure);

(5) forbidding anyone from photographing or sketching jurors within the courthouse;

(6) jury sequestration (but the identity of any party requesting sequestration must not be disclosed);

(7) forbidding jurors from reading, listening to, or watching news reports about the case;

(8) forbidding jurors from discussing the case with anyone during the trial and from communicating with others in any manner during their deliberations; and

(9) insulating witnesses from news interviews during trial.

(b) Preliminary Criminal Proceedings. Ordinarily, preliminary proceedings (including preliminary examinations and hearings on pretrial motions) must be held in open court, with the public permitted to attend and observe. But the court may close preliminary proceedings if:

(1) the law allows it; and

(2) the court cites for the record the specific findings that make doing so necessary.

[Effective January 1, 2012.]

N.D. IND. L. CR. R. 53–2. RELEASE OF INFORMATION

(a) Applicability. The following are subject to this rule when they are associated with a pending or imminent criminal case:

(1) government attorneys and their staffs;

(2) defense attorneys and their law firms; and

(3) law-enforcement agencies or investigators associated with either the prosecution or defense.

(b) General Prohibition on Release of Facts and Opinions. A person subject to this rule must not release, or authorize the release of, facts or opinions about the criminal case if:

(1) a reasonable person would expect them to be disseminated by any means of public communication; and

(2) the dissemination would pose a serious and imminent threat of interference with the fair administration of justice.

(c) Presumptions of Imminent Threat or Interference. Unless allowed under subdivision (d), the following are presumed to pose a serious and imminent threat of interference with the fair administration of justice:

(1) during an investigation, statements by a government lawyer or law-enforcement agent that go beyond the public record;

(2) during preliminary criminal proceedings, out-of-court statements about:

(A) the accused's character, reputation, or prior criminal record (including arrests, indictments, or other criminal charges);

(B) the existence or contents of a confession, admission, or statement given by the accused;

(C) the fact that the accused has refused or failed to make a statement;

(D) the accused's performance on any examinations or tests;

(E) the fact that the accused has refused or failed to submit to an examination or test;

(F) the identity, testimony, or credibility of prospective witnesses (but identifying the victim is permissible if it is not otherwise legally prohibited);

(G) the possibility of a guilty plea to either the charged offense or a lesser one; or

(H) any opinion concerning either the accused's guilt or innocence or the evidence in the case; or

(3) during trial, out-of-court statements or interviews about the trial or the parties or issues in the trial.

(d) Permitted Statements.

(1) *During Investigation.* During an investigation, government lawyers or law-enforcement agents may make statements that go beyond the public record if they are necessary to:

(A) inform the public:

(i) that an investigation is under way; or

(ii) about the investigation's general scope;

(B) ask for public help apprehending the suspect;

(C) warn the public of any dangers involved in the investigation; or

(D) otherwise aid the investigation.

(2) *During Preliminary Criminal Proceedings.* During preliminary criminal proceedings and while discharging their official or professional obligations, a person subject to this rule may:

(A) announce:

(i) accused's name, age, address, occupation, and family status;

(ii) that the accused has been arrested;

(iii) the circumstances of the arrest (including time and place of arrest, resistance, pursuit, and use of weapons);

(iv) the identity of the investigating and arresting officer or agency and the length of the investigation;

(v) that physical evidence (other than a confession, admission, or statement) has been seized (so long as the announcement is made when the seizure occurs and is limited to a description of the seized evidence);

(vi) nature, substance, or text of the charge, including a brief description of the offense charged;

(vii) the scheduling or result of any stage in the judicial process; or

(viii) without further comment or elaboration, that the accused denies the charges and the general nature of the defense;

(B) request assistance in obtaining evidence; or

(C) if the accused has not been apprehended, release information that is necessary to:

(i) help apprehend the accused; or

(ii) warn the public of any dangers the accused may present.

(3) *During Trial.* Persons subject to this rule may quote or refer without comment to the court's public records in the case during trial.

(e) Definitions.

(1) *Preliminary Criminal Proceedings.* For purposes of this rule, preliminary criminal proceedings:

(A) start when:

(i) the accused is arrested;

(ii) an arrest warrant is issued; or

(iii) a complaint, information, or indictment is filed; and

(B) end when:

(i) the accused's trial starts; or

(ii) the proceedings are resolved without a trial.

(2) *Trial Defined.* For purposes of this rule, a trial includes:

(A) jury selection;

(B) a criminal trial; and

(C) any other proceeding that could result in incarceration.

(f) Limits on the Rule's Scope. This rule does not preclude:

(1) lawyers or law enforcement agents from replying to public charges of misconduct;

(2) legislative, administrative, or investigative bodies from holding hearings and issuing reports; or

(3) the court from promulgating more restrictive rules on the release of information about juveniles or other offenders.

[Effective January 1, 2012.]

N.D. IND. L. CR. R. 58–1. FORFEITURE OF COLLATERAL IN LIEU OF APPEARANCE

(a) When Permitted. A person charged with a criminal offense under 18 U.S.C. § 13, may, in lieu of an appearance, post collateral with a magistrate judge and consent to forfeit that collateral. But the offense must be one for which:

(1) the penalty under state law is equal to, or less than, that of a misdemeanor; and

(2) an appearance is not mandatory.

(b) Schedule of Offenses. These offenses, and the collateral amounts to be posted (if applicable), must appear on a schedule available for public inspection in each of the clerk's divisional offices. The schedule will be effective until rescinded or superseded by court order. The clerk must furnish copies of the schedule to the legal publishing houses that publish and distribute, for commercial purposes, the court's rules. The schedule should be included in any subsequent publication containing these rules.

(c) Failure to Appear. The collateral will be forfeited if the person charged with an offense covered by this rule fails to appear before the magistrate judge. The forfeiture:

(1) signifies that the offender neither:

(A) contests the charge; nor

(B) requests a hearing before the magistrate judge; and

(2) constitutes a finding of guilt.

(d) When Forfeitures are Not Permitted. Forfeitures are not permitted for violations involving an accident that results in personal injury. Arresting officers must treat multiple and aggravated offenses as mandatory-appearance offenses, and must direct the accused to appear for a hearing.

(e) Discretion of Officers to Arrest. Nothing in this rule prohibits a law-enforcement officer from:

(1) arresting a person for committing an offense (including those for which collateral may be posted and forfeited); and

(2) either:

(A) requiring the accused to appear before a magistrate judge, or

(B) taking that person before a magistrate judge immediately after arrest.

[Effective January 1, 2012.]

LOCAL PATENT RULES

N.D. IND. L.P.R. 1–1. SCOPE

(a) Applicability. These rules govern cases in which jurisdiction is based, in whole or in part, on 28 U.S.C. § 1338. The court may depart from these rules in exceptional circumstances.

(b) Citation. The patent rules may be cited as "N.D. Ind. L.P.R. ___."

(c) Compliance. Litigants are expected to comply with these rules. They may not circumvent them by, for example, pursuing discovery into infringement and invalidity contentions by seeking discovery responses before completion of the preliminary contentions process outlined in N.D. Ind. L.P.R. 3–1.

[Effective January 1, 2013.]

N.D. IND. L.P.R. 2–1. SCHEDULING, DISCOVERY, AND ORDERS

(a) Scheduling Conference. The court will hold a scheduling conference within 30 days after the last answer is filed.

(b) Discovery Plan. The parties must comply with Fed. R. Civ. P. 26(f) before the conference. Their discovery plan must address these topics:

- Date/place of conference;
- Counsel present/parties represented;
- Case summary;
- Jurisdictional questions;
- Type of trial;
- Discovery needed;
- Electronic-information disclosures;
- Stipulation regarding privilege claims/protecting trial-preparation materials;
- Interrogatories;
- Requests for admission;
- Depositions;
- Joinder of additional parties;
- Amending pleadings; and
- Settlement possibilities/mediation.

(c) Protective Orders. The court strongly prefers jointly proposed protective orders. They should be filed with the discovery plan. If the parties are unable to agree on a protective order, they may submit competing proposed protective orders accompanied by memoranda explaining the differences between the proposed orders and the party's justification for its proposal. These memoranda may not exceed five pages.

(d) Discovery Order. The court will issue a discovery order promptly after the 16(b) conference and rule on any protective-order requests.

(e) Confidential Disclosures. Before a protective order is entered the parties may not delay making the disclosures these rules require—or responding to discovery—on confidentiality grounds. The producing party may designate confidential disclosures and discovery responses as "outside attorneys' eyes only" until a protective order is entered. Once entered, all information must be treated according to the order's terms.

[Effective January 1, 2013.]

N.D. IND. L.P.R. 3–1. PRELIMINARY DISCLOSURES

(a) Preliminary Infringement Contentions. Within 28 days after the last answer is filed, a party claiming patent infringement must serve on all parties its *preliminary infringement contentions*.

(b) Content. The preliminary infringement contentions must include an infringement-claim chart for each accused product or process (the *accused instrumentality*). If two or more accused instrumentalities have the same relevant characteristics, they may be grouped together in the same chart. Each claim chart must contain the following contentions:

(1) Each claim of each patent in suit that is allegedly infringed by the accused instrumentality;

(2) A specific identification of where each limitation of the claim is found within each accused instrumentality, including for each limitation that the party contends is governed by 35 U.S.C. § 112(f), the identity of the structures, acts, or materials in the accused instrumentality that performs the claimed function; and

(3) Whether each limitation of each asserted claim is literally present in the accused instrumentality or present under the doctrine of equivalents.

(c) Document Production. The party asserting patent infringement must produce to each party (or make available for inspection and copying) the following documents with its preliminary infringement contentions and identify—by production number—which documents correspond to each category:

(1) Documents demonstrating each disclosure, sale (or offer to sell), or any public use, of the claimed invention before the application date for each patent in suit or the priority date (whichever is earlier);

(2) All documents that were created on or before the application date for each patent in suit or the

priority date (whichever is earlier) that demonstrate each claimed invention's conception and earliest reduction to practice;

(3) A copy of the certified Patent Office-file history for each patent in suit; and

(4) All documents demonstrating ownership of the patent rights by the party asserting infringement.

(d) Safe Harbor. Producing documents under this rule is not an admission that the document is—or constitutes—prior art under 35 U.S.C. § 102.

(e) Preliminary Invalidity Contentions. Within 28 days after receiving the preliminary infringement contentions, each party opposing the patent-infringement claim must serve on all parties its *preliminary invalidity contentions*. These contentions must include a chart (or charts) identifying each allegedly invalid claim, and each item of prior art that anticipates or renders each claim obvious. Claim charts must contain the following contentions:

(1) How and under what statutory section the item qualifies as prior art,

(2) Whether the prior-art item anticipates or renders each allegedly invalid claim obvious,

(3) A specific identification of where in the prior-art item each limitation of each allegedly invalid claim is found, including for each limitation alleged to be governed by 35 U.S.C. § 112(f), where the corresponding structures, acts, or materials are found in the prior-art item that performs the claimed function, and

(4) Why, if obviousness is alleged, the prior art renders the allegedly invalid claims obvious, including why combining the identified items of prior art demonstrate obviousness, and explain why a person of skill in the art would find the allegedly invalid claims obvious in light of such combinations (e.g., reasons for combining references).

(5) A statement identifying with specificity any other asserted grounds of invalidity of any allegedly invalid claims, including contentions based on 35 U.S.C. §§ 101, 112, or 251.

(f) Document Production. The party opposing a patent-infringement claim must produce to all parties (or make available for inspection and copying) the following documents with its preliminary invalidity contentions. The producing party must separately identify by production number which documents correspond to which category.

(1) Documents sufficient to show the operation of any aspects or elements of an accused instrumentality identified by the patent claimant in its preliminary infringement contentions charts; and

(2) A copy or sample of the prior art identified under N.D. Ind. L.P.R. 3(e). If these items are not in English, an English translation of the portions relied upon must be produced.

(g) Declaratory-judgment Actions. The same disclosure process (including the same disclosure sequence) applies in declaratory-judgment actions in which the plaintiff is asserting non-infringement, invalidity, or unenforceability of the patent(s) in suit. For example, in such actions the defendant-patentee will assert preliminary infringement contentions under the schedule set out above. If infringement is not contested, the parties seeking a declaratory judgment must comply with N.D. Ind. L.P.R. 3–1(c) and 3–1(f) within 28 days after the last answer is filed.

[Effective January 1, 2013.]

N.D. IND. L.P.R. 4–1. CLAIM-CONSTRUCTION PROCEEDINGS

(a) Exchanging Terms. Within 14 days after receiving the preliminary invalidity contentions (or within 42 days after receiving the preliminary infringement contentions in those actions in which validity is not at issue), each party must serve on all other parties a list of claim terms that the party contends should be construed by the court (terms for construction), and identify any claim term that the party contends should be governed by 35 U.S.C. § 112(f).

(b) Exchanging Preliminary Claim Constructions and Extrinsic Evidence; Parties' Conference.

(1) Within 14 days after the proposed terms for construction are exchanged, the parties must exchange proposed constructions of each term (preliminary claim construction[s]). Each preliminary claim construction must also, for each term which any party contends is governed by 35 U.S.C. § 112(f), identify the function of that term and the structures, acts, or materials corresponding to that term's function.

(2) When the parties exchange their preliminary claim constructions, they must also identify all references from the specification or prosecution history that support its construction and designate any supporting extrinsic evidence including:

(A) dictionary definitions;

(B) citations to learned treatises and prior art, and

(C) testimony of percipient and expert witnesses.

(3) Within 14 days after the preliminary claim constructions are exchanged, the parties must meet and confer to limit the terms in dispute by narrowing or resolving differences and plan to prepare a *joint claim-construction and prehearing statement*. The parties must also jointly identify no more than ten disputed terms per patent in suit, unless the court grants more for inclusion in the joint claim-construction and prehearing statement. If a dispute arises as

to which terms to include in the joint claim-construction and prehearing statement, each side must be presumptively limited to five disputed terms per patent in suit. This limit may only be altered by leave of court.

(c) Joint Claim-construction and Prehearing Statement. Within 14 days after they meet and confer, the parties must complete and file a *joint claim-construction and prehearing statement*. This statement must address the disputed terms and contain the following information:

(1) The construction of those terms on which the parties agree;

(2) Each party's construction of each disputed term (with the identity of all references from the specification or prosecution history that support its construction) and the identity of any extrinsic evidence known to the party on which it intends to rely either to support its construction or to oppose another party's construction, including dictionary definitions, citations to learned treatises and prior art, and testimony of percipient and expert witnesses;

(3) The anticipated length of time necessary for the claim-construction hearing; and

(4) If witnesses are to be called at the claim-construction hearing, the identity of each such witness, and for each witness, a summary of his or her testimony including, for any expert witness, a report containing the expert's claim-construction opinions and the reasons for them.

(d) Completing Claim-construction Discovery. Within 21 days after the *joint claim-construction and prehearing statement* is filed, the parties must complete all discovery relating to claim construction, including witness depositions.

(e) Claim-construction Briefs.

(1) *Opening Briefs.* Within 14 days after completing claim-construction discovery, the parties must file their respective opening briefs and any evidence supporting their claim constructions.

(2) *Length.* Opening briefs may not exceed 30 pages without leave of court.

(3) *Response Briefs.* Within 21 days after receiving an opening brief, each opposing party must file any response briefs and supporting evidence.

(4) *Length.* Response briefs may not exceed 20 pages without leave of court.

(5) *Additional Briefs.* Reply and surreply briefs are not permitted without leave of court.

(f) Claim-construction Hearing. When necessary to construe the claims, the court will endeavor to conduct a claim-construction hearing within 63 days after briefing is complete.

(g) Tutorial Hearings. The court may order a tutorial hearing to occur before, or during, the claim-construction hearing.

(h) Orders. The court will work expeditiously to issue a prompt claim-construction order after the hearing.

[Effective January 1, 2013.]

N.D. IND. L.P.R. 5–1. FINAL PATENT DISCLOSURES

(a) Final Infringement Contentions.

(1) *Due Date.* Within 28 days after the court's claim-construction order is entered, any party asserting infringement must serve on all parties its final infringement contentions.

(2) *Contents.* Parties may not assert at trial any infringement contentions not set out in its final infringement contentions.

(3) *Amendments.* Final infringement contentions may not identify additional accused products or processes not contained in the preliminary infringement contentions without good cause (e.g., discovery of previously undiscovered information or an unanticipated claim-construction ruling). The party asserting infringement must include a separate statement outlining the specific grounds that it claims constitute good cause for the amendment.

(4) *Exclusion.* Accused infringers may seek to exclude amendments on grounds that good cause does not exist.

(5) *Due Date.* Motions to exclude must be filed within 14 days after receiving the final infringement contentions.

(6) *Failure to Object.* Unopposed amendments are deemed effective.

(b) Final Invalidity Contentions.

(1) *Due Date.* Within 21 days after receiving the final infringement contentions, each accused infringer must serve on all parties its final invalidity contentions.

(2) *Contents.* Final invalidity contentions must include that party's final statement of all contentions. The party may not assert at trial any invalidity contentions not contained in its final invalidity contentions.

(3) *Amendments.* If the final invalidity contentions identify additional prior art, the amendment must be supported by good cause (e.g., discovery of previously undiscovered information or an unanticipated claim-construction ruling) and the accused infringer must include a separate statement providing the specific grounds establishing good cause for the amendment.

(4) *Exclusion.* The party asserting infringement may seek to exclude the amendment on grounds that good cause does not exist.

(5) *Due Date.* Motions to exclude must be filed within 14 days after receiving the final invalidity contentions.

(6) *Failure to Object.* Unopposed amendments are deemed effective.

[Effective January 1, 2013.]

N.D. IND. L.P.R. 6–1. EXPERT DISCOVERY

(a) **Applicability.** This rule governs expert discovery in patent cases.

(b) **Exception.** This rule does not apply to claim construction.

(c) **Reports.**

(1) *Opening Reports.* Opening expert reports on issues the proponent will bear the burden of proof at trial are due within 28 days after receiving the final invalidity contentions or, in cases in which invalidity is not at issue, within 28 days after receiving the final infringement contentions.

(2) *Rebuttal Reports.* Rebuttal expert reports are due 28 days after receiving opening expert reports.

(d) **Depositions.** Expert depositions must be completed within 35 days after receiving an expert's rebuttal report.

[Effective January 1, 2013.]

APPENDICES
APPENDIX A.   SAMPLE PRE–TRIAL ORDER
IN THE UNITED STATES DISTRICT COURT
FOR THE
NORTHERN DISTRICT OF INDIANA
HAMMOND DIVISION

CLAUDE JONES,	)	
	)	
Plaintiff,	)	
	)	
v.	)	CIVIL NO. 2:99–CV–798–RL
	)	
WILBUR SMITH,	)	
	)	
Defendant.	)	

PRE–TRIAL ORDER

Pursuant to the order of the Court, the attorneys for the parties to this action appeared before the United States District Judge at Hammond, Indiana, at 2:00 P.M. on September 30, 2000 for a conference under Rule 16 of the Federal Rules of Civil Procedure.

Plaintiff was represented by Richard Roe of the firm of Roe and Roe. Defendant was represented by John Doe of the firm of Diamond & Doe.

Thereupon, the following proceedings were had and the following engagements and undertakings arrived at:

A.   Jurisdiction was conceded by counsel and found by the Court to be present. (If otherwise, so state).

B.   The case is at issue on plaintiff's complaint and the defendant's answer. The First Defense denies defendant's negligence. The Second Defense alleges comparative fault on the part of the driver of plaintiff's car. The plaintiff and driver were engaged in a joint enterprise, and the driver's negligence is imputed to the plaintiff.

C.   There are no pending motions.

D.   The plaintiff contends that on June 1, 1998, he was riding in the front seat of a 1997 Ford automobile which was being driven in a northerly direction on U.S. Highway No. 31 approaching the intersection of Pierce Road, a county road in St. Joseph County, Indiana. The defendant was driving a Chevrolet convertible west on Pierce Road. The defendant negligently operated his automobile in the following manner: (1) He failed to stop for a stop sign before entering the intersection, (2) he failed to keep a proper lookout for vehicles traveling on U.S. Highway No. 31, and (3) he failed to yield the right-of-way to the vehicle in which plaintiff was riding. The plaintiff further contends that as a result of defendant's negligence, his car collided with the car in which plaintiff was riding, causing plaintiff to be injured permanently. Plaintiff lost wages and income as a result of his injuries in the amount of $32,000 and will suffer loss of income in the future. He was required to expend $39,455 for medical and hospital care and will be required to expend further sums in the future. Plaintiff sustained property damage of $8,500 to his automobile.

E.   The defendant contends that he was not negligent in the operation of his automobile as contended by the plaintiff and further contends that the driver of the car in which the plaintiff was riding was negligent in that (1) he drove at a fast and unreasonable rate of speed, to-wit: 80 miles per hour, and (2) he failed to yield the right-of-way to the defendant, who was in the intersection and almost clear of the

318

northbound lanes when struck in the left rear by the plaintiff's driver. Defendant also contends that the plaintiff and the driver of the car in which he was riding were engaged in a joint enterprise in that they had jointly rented the car in which plaintiff was riding to go on a business trip for the mutual benefit of both and had shared the driving and expense incident to the trip.

F.   The following facts are established by admissions in the pleadings or by stipulation of counsel:

1.   A collision occurred between the car of the defendant and the car driven by William Jones, with whom plaintiff was riding, at the intersection of U.S. 31 and Pierce Road in St. Joseph County, Indiana, on June 1, 1998, at approximately 4:00 P.M.

2.   U.S. 31 is a paved, four-lane, north-to-south highway divided by a median curb approximately four inches high and three feet wide. Pierce Road is a two-land, paved, east-and-west highway, paved with black top. A stop sign, legally erected, was located at the northwest corner of the intersection facing westbound traffic on Pierce Road. Both roads are level for at least 500 feet in both directions, and there are no obstructions to view within 500 feet of the intersection.

3.   The pavement was dry and the weather was clear and warm.

4.   Plaintiff was traveling north in the northbound lanes of U.S. 31. Defendant was traveling west in the westbound lane of Pierce Road.

5.   The defendant was alone in his Chevrolet automobile. The plaintiff was riding in a rented car being driven by his brother, William Jones, who died as a result of injuries received in the collision. The plaintiff and his brother William had gone from South Bend to Plymouth to negotiate for the joint purchase of a grocery store. The plaintiff had driven from South Bend to Plymouth, and William was driving on the return trip. They were sharing the cost of renting the car and any other expenses of the trip.

G.   The contested issues of fact are:

1.   The negligence of the defendant which was a proximate cause of the collision.

2.   The negligence of William Jones which was a proximate cause of the collision.

3.   Whether plaintiff and his brother were engaged in a joint enterprise, and, if so, is the negligence, if any, of the driver William imputed to the plaintiff.

4.   Extent of plaintiff's damages.

H.   A contested issues of law not implicit in the foregoing issue of fact will be:

1.   Whether the common-law doctrine of imputed negligence between members of a joint enterprise survived the adoption of Indiana's Comparative Fault Act, I.C. §§ 34–51–2–1 et seq.

2.   The admissibility of expert testimony attempting to reconstruct the manner in which the accident occurred. In that regard, it is represented that the plaintiff has a complete loss of memory concerning the manner in which the accident occurred and the only living eyewitness is the defendant.

I.   There were received in evidence:

1.   Plaintiff's exhibits 1, 2, 3, 4, and 5, the same being pictures of the scene taken by State Policeman John Williams; 7 and 8, being pictures of the intersection taken by Commercial Photographer Sam Bigley; 9, Memorial Hospital bill; 10, Dr. Willard Raymond's bill; 11, bill from Medical Appliance Company for back brace; 12, plaintiff's hospital record compiled by Memorial Hospital; 13, Dr. Max Small's bill.

2.   Defendant's exhibits A, an engineer's drawing of the intersection; and B, photograph of defendant's car.

3.   Except as otherwise indicated, the authenticity of received exhibits has been stipulated, but they have been received subject to objections, if any, by the opposing part at the trial as to their relevance and materiality.   If other exhibits are to be offered, they may be done so only with leave of court.

Exhibits which can be obtained only by a subpoena duces tecum shall not be covered by this requirement, but counsel for party offering such exhibits shall advise opposing counsel of the nature of such exhibits at the pretrial conference or at least ten (10) days prior to trial.

J. Witnesses:

1.   Plaintiff's witnesses may include any or all of the following:

a.   The plaintiff.

b.   Dr. Willard Raymond, Room 304 Medical Arts Building, South Bend, Indiana, attending physician.

c.   Dr. Max Small, 923 Sherland Building, South Bend, Indiana, consultant.

d.   John Williams, state policeman who investigated the accident.

e.   Dr. George Bundage, 1069 High Street, Evanston, Illinois, expert who will reconstruct the accident.

f.   Mrs. Claude Jones, wife of plaintiff, who will testify as to plaintiff's condition before and following the accident.

2.   Defendant's witnesses may include any or all of the following persons:

a.   The defendant.

b.   John Williams, state policeman.

c.   Alex Nagy, 124 West Indiana Avenue, South Bend, Indiana, deputy sheriff, St. Joseph County, who investigated the accident.

d.   Bill Hill, 29694 U.S. 31 South, South Bend, Indiana, a neighbor who came to the scene of the accident.

e.   Bert McClellan, engineer who made the drawing of the intersection.

f.   Dr. James Hyde, examining physician.

3.   In the event there are other witnesses to be called at the trial, their names and addresses and the general subject matter of their testimony will be reported to opposing counsel, with copy to the Court, at least ten (10) days prior to trial. Such witnesses may be called at trial only upon leave of Court.   This restriction shall not apply to rebuttal or impeachment witnesses, the necessity of whose testimony cannot reasonably be anticipated before trial.

K.   It is directed that requests for special instructions must be submitted to the Court, in writing and on a computer disk (or in another electronic format), with supporting authorities, at or prior to the commencement of the trial, subject to the right of counsel to supplement such requests during the course of the trial on matters that cannot reasonably be anticipated.

L.   No amendments to the pleadings are anticipated.

M.   Trial briefs shall be filed with the Court and exchanged among counsel at least seven (7) days before trial, covering specifically:

1.   Questions raised under Section H of this order.

2.   Whether under the facts the negligence, if any, of William Jones should be imputed to the plaintiff.

N.   The following additional matters pertinent to the trial will be considered.

1. Plaintiff will request the Court to instruct the jury that a violation of I.C. § 9–21–8–32 constitutes negligence per se.

2. Defendant will request the Court to instruct the jury that a violation of I.C. § 9–21–8–31 constitutes negligence per se.

3. Plaintiff contends that as a result of the accident, he suffered a skull fracture and concussion resulting in partial loss of memory, headaches, and occasional blackouts; that he suffered a broken left leg about the knee resulting in a shortening of the leg, causing plaintiff to limp; injury to the lumbar spine, with a probable ruptured intervertebral disc which will require an operation; permanent pain in the spine radiating down the right leg; that he has suffered permanent impairment of 15% of the whole man; that he is 36 years of age and has a life expectancy of 34.76 years.

4. Plaintiff claims the following special damages:

a.	Dr. Willard Raymond	$ 7,500
b.	Dr. Max Small	$ 1,500
c.	Memorial Hospital	$17,680
d.	Medical Appliance Co. (back brace)	$ 275
e.	Cost of future back operation:	
	Surgeon's	$ 5,000
	Hospital bill	$ 7,500

5. Plaintiff claims he lost income as follows:

Fifteen months as manager of the A.B.C. Supermarket located at 1764 Portage Street, South Bend, at $2,000 per month. Time lost began June 1, 1998, with the plaintiff returning for light work August 1, 1999. Plaintiff has lost four weeks since returning to work on August 1, 1999 (one week in September 1999 and three weeks in November 1999) due to his back condition. It is expected that he will lose three or four more weeks due to his future operation to repair back injury. Plaintiff's supervisor is Paul Dill, District Manager, A.B.C. Grocery Co., 1764 Portage Street, South Bend, Indiana.

O. This pre-trial order has been formulated after conference at which counsel for the respective parties have appeared. Reasonable opportunity has been afforded counsel for corrections or additions prior to signing by the Court. Hereafter, this order will control the course of the trial and may not be amended except by consent of the parties and the Court or by order of the Court to prevent manifest injustice. The pleadings will be deemed merged herein.

P. The parties have discussed settlement, but have been unable to reach agreement. They will continue to negotiate and will advise the Court immediately if settlement is reached.

Q. The probable length of trial is two days. The case is set down for trial before a jury on November 5, 2000 at 9:30 A.M.

Entered this 15th day of October, 2000.

Judge, United States District Court

APPROVED:

Richard Roe,

Attorney for Plaintiff

APPROVED:

John Doe,

Attorney for Defendant

[Adopted effective January 1, 1994. Amended effective October 2, 2000; January 1, 2012.]

APPENDIX B.   STANDARDS FOR PROFESSIONAL CONDUCT WITHIN THE SEVENTH FEDERAL JUDICIAL CIRCUIT

Preamble

A lawyer's conduct should be characterized at all times by personal courtesy and professional integrity in the fullest sense of those terms.   In fulfilling our duty to represent a client vigorously as lawyers, we will be mindful of our obligations to the administration of justice, which is a truth-seeking process designed to resolve human and societal problems in a rational, peaceful, and efficient manner.

A judge's conduct should be characterized at all times by courtesy and patience toward all participants.   As judges we owe to all participants in a legal proceeding respect, diligence, punctuality, and protection against unjust and improper criticism or attack.

Conduct that may be characterized as uncivil, abrasive, abusive, hostile, or obstructive impedes the fundamental goal of resolving disputes rationally, peacefully, and efficiently.   Such conduct tends to delay and often to deny justice.

The following standards are designed to encourage us, judges and lawyers, to meet our obligations to each other, to litigants and to the system of justice, and thereby achieve the twin goals of civility and professionalism, both of which are hallmarks of a learned profession dedicated to public service.

We expect judges and lawyers will make a mutual and firm commitment to these standards.   Voluntary adherence is expected as part of a commitment by all participants to improve the administration of justice throughout this Circuit.

These standards shall not be used as a basis for litigation or for sanctions or penalties.   Nothing in these standards supersedes or detracts from exiting disciplinary codes or alters existing standards of conduct against which lawyer negligence may be determined.

These standards should be reviewed and followed by all judges and lawyers participating in any proceeding in this Circuit.   Copies may be made available to clients to reinforce our obligation to maintain and foster these standards.

Lawyers' Duties to Other Counsel

1.   We will practice our profession with a continuing awareness that our role is to advance the legitimate interests of our clients.   In our dealings with others we will not reflect the ill feelings of our clients.   We will treat all other counsel, parties, and witnesses in a civil and courteous manner, not only in court, but also in all other written and oral communications.

2.   We will not, even when called upon by a client to do so, abuse or indulge in offensive conduct directed to other counsel, parties, or witnesses.   We will abstain from disparaging personal remarks or acrimony toward other counsel, parties, or witnesses.   We will treat adverse witnesses and parties with fair consideration.

3.   We will not encourage or knowingly authorize any person under our control to engage in conduct that would be improper if we were to engage in such conduct.

4.   We will not, absent good cause, attribute bad motives or improper conduct to other counsel or bring the profession into disrepute by unfounded accusations of impropriety.

5.   We will not seek court sanctions without first conducting a reasonable investigation and unless fully justified by the circumstances and necessary to protect our client's lawful interests.

6.   We will adhere to all express promises and to agreements with other counsel, whether oral or in writing, and will adhere in good faith to all agreements implied by the circumstances or local customs.

7. When we reach an oral understanding on a proposed agreement or a stipulation and decide to commit it to writing, the drafter will endeavor in good faith to state the oral understanding accurately and completely. The drafter will provide the opportunity for review of the writing to other counsel. As drafts are exchanged between or among counsel, changes from prior drafts will be identified in the draft or otherwise explicitly brought to the attention of other counsel. We will not include in a draft matters to which there has been no agreement without explicitly advising other counsel in writing of the addition.

8. We will endeavor to confer early with other counsel to assess settlement possibilities. We will not falsely hold out the possibility of settlement as a means to adjourn discovery or to delay trial.

9. In civil actions, we will stipulate to relevant matters if they are undisputed and if no good faith advocacy basis exists for not stipulating.

10. We will not use any form of discovery or discovery scheduling as a means of harassment.

11. We will make good faith efforts to resolve by agreement our objections to matters contained in pleadings and discovery requests and objections.

12. We will not time the filing or service of motions or pleadings in any way that unfairly limits another party's opportunity to respond.

13. We will not request an extension of time solely for the purpose of unjustified delay or to obtain a tactical advantage.

14. We will consult other counsel regarding scheduling matters in a good faith effort to avoid scheduling conflicts.

15. We will endeavor to accommodate previously scheduled dates for hearings, depositions, meetings, conferences, vacations, seminars, or other functions that produce good faith calendar conflicts on the part of other counsel. If we have been given an accommodation because of a calendar conflict, we will notify those who have accommodated us as soon as the conflict has been removed.

16. We will notify other counsel and, if appropriate, the court or other persons, at the earliest possible time when hearings, depositions, meetings, or conferences are to be canceled or postponed. Early notice avoids unnecessary travel and expense of counsel and may enable the court to use the previously reserved time for other matters.

17. We will agree to reasonable requests for extensions of time and for waiver of procedural formalities, provided our clients' legitimate rights will not be materially or adversely affected.

18. We will not cause any default or dismissal to be entered without first notifying opposing counsel, when we know his or her identity.

19. We will take depositions only when actually needed to ascertain facts or information or to perpetuate testimony. We will not take depositions for the purposes of harassment or to increase litigation expenses.

20. We will not engage in any conduct during a deposition that would not be appropriate in the presence of a judge.

21. We will not obstruct questioning during a deposition or object to deposition questions unless necessary under the applicable rules to preserve an objection or privilege for resolution by the court.

22. During depositions we will ask only those questions we reasonably believe are necessary for the prosecution or defense of an action.

23. We will carefully craft document production requests so they are limited to those documents we reasonably believe are necessary for the prosecution or defense of any action. We will not design production requests to place an undue burden or expense on a party.

24. We will respond to document requests reasonably and not strain to interpret the request in an artificially restrictive manner to avoid disclosure of relevant and non-privileged documents. We will not produce documents in a manner designed to hide or obscure the existence of particular documents.

25. We will carefully craft interrogatories so they are limited to those matters we reasonably believe are necessary for the prosecution or defense of an action, and we will not design them to place an undue burden or expense on a party.

26. We will respond to interrogatories reasonably and will not strain to interpret them in an artificially restrictive manner to avoid disclosure of relevant and non-privileged information.

27. We will base our discovery objections on a good faith belief in their merit and will not object solely for the purpose of withholding or delaying the disclosure of relevant information.

28. When a draft order is to be prepared by counsel to reflect a court ruling, we will draft an order that accurately and completely reflects the court's ruling. We will promptly prepare and submit a proposed order to other counsel and attempt to reconcile any differences before the draft order is presented to the court.

29. We will not ascribe a position to another counsel that counsel has not taken or otherwise seek to create an unjustified inference based on counsel's statements or conduct.

30. Unless specifically permitted or invited by the court, we will not send copies of correspondence between counsel to the court.

Lawyers' Duties to the Court

1. We will speak and write civilly and respectfully in all communications with the court.

2. We will be punctual and prepared for all court appearances so that all hearings, conferences, and trials may commence on time; if delayed, we will notify the court and counsel, if possible.

3. We will be considerate of the time constraints and pressures on the court and court staff inherent in their efforts to administer justice.

4. We will not engage in any conduct that brings disorder or disruption to the courtroom. We will advise our clients and witnesses appearing in court of the proper conduct expected and required there and, to the best of our ability, prevent our clients and witnesses from creating disorder or disruption.

5. We will not knowingly misrepresent, mischaracterize, misquote, or miscite facts or authorities in any oral or written communication to the court.

6. We will not write letters to the court in connection with a pending action, unless invited or permitted by the court.

7. Before dates for hearings or trials are set, or if that is not feasible, immediately after such date has been set, we will attempt to verify the availability of necessary participants and witnesses so we can promptly notify the court of any likely problems.

8. We will act and speak civilly to court marshals, clerks, court reporters, secretaries, and law clerks with an awareness that they, too, are in integral part of the judicial system.

Courts' Duties to Lawyers

1. We will be courteous, respectful, and civil to lawyers, parties, and witnesses. We will maintain control of the proceedings, recognizing that judges have both the

obligation and the authority to insure that all litigation proceedings are conducted in a civil manner.

2. We will not employ hostile, demeaning, or humiliating words in opinions or in written or oral communications with lawyers, parties, or witnesses.

3. We will be punctual in convening all hearings, meetings, and conferences; if delayed, we will notify counsel, if possible.

4. In scheduling all hearings, meetings and conferences we will be considerate of time schedules of lawyers, parties, and witnesses.

5. We will make all reasonable efforts to decide promptly all matters presented to us for decision.

6. We will give the issues in controversy deliberate, impartial, and studied analysis and consideration.

7. While endeavoring to resolve disputes efficiently, we will be considerate of the time constraints and pressures imposed on lawyers by the exigencies of litigation practice.

8. We recognize that a lawyer has a right and a duty to present a cause fully and properly, and that a litigant has a right to a fair and impartial hearing. Within the practical limits of time, we will allow lawyers to present proper arguments and to make a complete and accurate record.

9. We will not impugn the integrity or professionalism of any lawyer on the basis of the clients whom or the causes which a lawyer represents.

10. We will do our best to insure that court personnel act civilly toward lawyers, parties, and witnesses.

11. We will not adopt procedures that needlessly increase litigation expense.

12. We will bring to lawyers' attention uncivil conduct which we observe.

[Amended effective January 1, 2012.]

APPENDIX C. NOTICE TO PRO SE LITIGANT

(This form may be downloaded from the Northern District of Indiana's internet website at www.innd.uscourts.gov)

UNITED STATES DISTRICT COURT
NORTHERN DISTRICT OF INDIANA
_____ DIVISION

_____,

Plaintiff

v.   Case No.

_____,

Defendant

Notice of Summary–Judgment Motion

A summary-judgment motion has been filed against you. Attached to this notice is a copy of the motion. The motion asks the court to decide all or part of your case without a trial. The party that filed this motion does not think that a full trial is necessary. The motion says that there should not be a full trial because you cannot win on some or all of your claims. The motion asks the court to enter judgment against you.

Rule 56 and Local Rule 56–1 are set forth below. You should read—and follow—all the rules carefully. The outcome of this case may depend on it. Following the rules does not guarantee that the summary-judgment motion will be denied. But if you do not follow the rules, you may lose this case.

Before the court rules on the motion, you have the right to file a response. If you do not respond to the summary-judgment motion, you may lose this case. If you need more time to respond, you must file a motion asking for more time before the deadline expires. The court may—but is not required to—give you more time.

Fed. Rule Civ. Proc. 56. Summary Judgment

(a) **Motion for Summary Judgment or Partial Summary Judgment.** A party may move for summary judgment, identifying each claim or defense—or the part of each claim or defense—on which summary judgment is sought. The court shall grant summary judgment if the movant shows that there is no genuine dispute as to any material fact and the movant is entitled to judgment as a matter of law. The court should state on the record the reasons for granting or denying the motion.

(b) **Time to File a Motion.** Unless a different time is set by local rule or the court orders otherwise, a party may file a motion for summary judgment at any time until 30 days after the close of all discovery.

(c) **Procedures.**

   (1) **Supporting Factual Positions.** A party asserting that a fact cannot be or is genuinely disputed must support the assertion by:

   (A) citing to particular parts of materials in the record, including depositions, documents, electronically stored information, affidavits or declarations, stipulations (including those made for purposes of the motion only), admissions, interrogatory answers, or other materials; or

(B) showing that the materials cited do not establish the absence or presence of a genuine dispute, or that an adverse party cannot produce admissible evidence to support the fact.

(2) **Objection That a Fact Is Not Supported by Admissible Evidence.** A party may object that the material cited to support or dispute a fact cannot be presented in a form that would be admissible in evidence.

(3) **Materials Not Cited.** The court need consider only the cited materials, but it may consider other materials in the record.

(4) **Affidavits or Declarations.** An affidavit or declaration used to support or oppose a motion must be made on personal knowledge, set out facts that would be admissible in evidence, and show that the affiant or declarant is competent to testify on the matters stated.

(d) **When Facts Are Unavailable to the Nonmovant.** If a nonmovant shows by affidavit or declaration that, for specified reasons, it cannot present facts essential to justify its opposition, the court may:

(1) defer considering the motion or deny it;

(2) allow time to obtain affidavits or declarations or to take discovery; or

(3) issue any other appropriate order.

(e) **Failing to Properly Support or Address a Fact.** If a party fails to properly support an assertion of fact or fails to properly address another party's assertion of fact as required by Rule 56(c), the court may:

(1) give an opportunity to properly support or address the fact;

(2) consider the fact undisputed for purposes of the motion;

(3) grant summary judgment if the motion and supporting materials—including the facts considered undisputed—show that the movant is entitled to it; or

(4) issue any other appropriate order.

(f) **Judgment Independent of the Motion.** After giving notice and a reasonable time to respond, the court may:

(1) grant summary judgment for a nonmovant;

(2) grant the motion on grounds not raised by a party; or

(3) consider summary judgment on its own after identifying for the parties material facts that may not be genuinely in dispute.

(g) **Failing to Grant All the Requested Relief.** If the court does not grant all the relief requested by the motion, it may enter an order stating any material fact—including an item of damages or other relief—that is not genuinely in dispute and treating the fact as established in the case.

(h) **Affidavit or Declaration Submitted in Bad Faith.** If satisfied that an affidavit or declaration under this rule is submitted in bad faith or solely for delay, the court—after notice and a reasonable time to respond—may order the submitting party to pay the other party the reasonable expenses, including attorney's fees, it incurred as a result. An offending party or attorney may also be held in contempt or subjected to other appropriate sanctions.

N.D. Ind. L.R. 56–1

(a) **Moving Party's Obligations.** The brief supporting a summary-judgment motion or the brief's appendix must include a section labeled "Statement of Material Facts" that identifies the facts that the moving party contends are not genuinely disputed.

(b) Opposing Party's Obligations.

(1) **Required Filings.** A party opposing the motion must, within 28 days after the movant serves the motion, file and serve

(A) a response brief; and

(B) any materials that the party contends raise a genuine dispute.

(2) **Content of Response Brief or Appendix.** The response brief or its appendix must include a section labeled "Statement of Genuine Disputes" that identifies the material facts that the party contends are genuinely disputed so as to make a trial necessary.

(c) Reply. The movant may file a reply brief within 14 days after a response is served.

(d) Oral Argument. The court will decide summary-judgment motions without oral argument unless a request under L.R. 7–5 is granted or the court directs otherwise.

(e) Disputes about Admissibility of Evidence. Any dispute regarding the admissibility of evidence should be addressed in a separate motion.

(f) Notice Requirement for Pro Se Cases. A party seeking summary judgment against an unrepresented party must serve that party with the notice contained in Appendix C.

Certificate of Service

On _____, 20 ___, I served a copy of this notice via U.S. mail on _____, a pro se party at _____.

_____
[Attorney]

[Amended effective August 18, 2008. Amended effective December 1, 2009; December 1, 2010; January 1, 2012.]

ELECTRONIC CASE FILING
NOTICE TO THE PUBLIC AND MEMBERS OF THE PRACTICING BAR

The United States District Court for the Northern District of Indiana implemented a Case Management/Electronic Case Filing (CM/ECF) System on November 1, 2003.

Effective January 1, 2005, the judges of this court will enforce the CM/ECF User Manual, which requires that *all* documents (other than those specifically excepted by the User Manual) shall be filed electronically in *all* cases.

Attorneys of record in pending cases within the Northern District of Indiana who are not yet registered to file documents electronically need to register before January 1, 2005. An Attorney Registration Form may be obtained at each Clerk's Office and on the Court's Internet website at www.innd.uscourts.gov. CM/ECF training courses are held regularly at the United States Courthouses in Fort Wayne, Hammond, South Bend and Lafayette and an be scheduled by contacting the Clerk's Office. Attorneys and law firm staff are encouraged to attend training prior to January 1, 2005.

Questions concerning this notice should be directed to:

Karen L. Brickner
CM/ECF Project Manager
U.S. District Court
204 South Main Street, Room 102
South Bend, IN 46601
574–246–8020
karen_brickner@innd.uscourts.gov

[DATE: November 17, 2004.]

CM/ECF CIVIL AND CRIMINAL USER MANUAL
Electronic Means for Filing, Signing and Verification of Documents
ADMINISTRATIVE PROCEDURES

INTRODUCTION

Welcome to Northern District of Indiana Case Management/Electronic Case Filing (CM/ECF), hereinafter referred to as the "System". The System permits attorneys to file documents with the court from any location over the Internet. While all parties, including those proceeding pro se, may register to receive "read only" PACER accounts, only registered attorneys, as officers of the court, are permitted to file electronically at this time.

I. REGISTRATION FOR THE ELECTRONIC FILING SYSTEM ("System")

A. Designation of Cases. On November 1, 2003, the U.S. District Court for the Northern District of Indiana began using the CM/ECF electronic filing system for all civil and criminal cases. "Electronic filing" means uploading a pleading or document directly from the registered user's computer, using the court's System, to file that pleading or document in the court's case file. **Sending a document or pleading to the court via e-mail or facsimile does not constitute "electronic filing."**

B. Registration.

1. Unless otherwise permitted by these procedures or otherwise authorized by the assigned judge, attorneys admitted to the bar of the Northern District of

Indiana and appearing in an active case in this district (including those appearing pro hac vice), must register to use the CM/ECF system. An application for CM/ECF Registration is available on the court's website at www.innd.uscourts.gov.

2. Each attorney registering for the System will receive an internet e-mail message after the application process is completed. This is to insure that the attorney's internet e-mail address has been entered correctly in the System. After the e-mail address has been confirmed, a separate internet e-mail message will be sent indicating that the registration has been approved.

3. An attorney's registration will constitute a waiver of conventional service of documents and the attorney agrees to accept service of notice on behalf of the client of the electronic filing by hand, facsimile or authorized email.

4. Attorneys are responsible for notifying the court when their name, mailing address or e-mail address changes, by filing in CM/ECF a Notice of Change of Address/Information in each pending case before this court. If no pending cases, send this court an e-mail or letter indicating attorney's bar number, and both the new name or address and the old name or address, as instructed on the court's website at www.innd.uscourts.gov. Email should be sent to attorney_maintenance@ innd.uscourts.gov or a letter should be sent to the court addressed to:

U.S. District Court
Attn: Attorney Maintenance
204 S. Main Street
South Bend, IN 46601

5. Registered attorneys who leave the employment of the United States Attorney for the Northern District of Indiana or of the Federal Community Defender for the Northern District of Indiana and who wish to continue in the practice of law in a different capacity in this district shall complete a new application for registration for a new account in the System. The application is available on the court's website at www.innd.uscourts.gov. Those attorneys' original accounts for the United States Attorney or the Federal Community Defender will remain intact with new passwords and will continue to be administered by staff in those offices.

C. Passwords. Each attorney admitted to practice in this Court pursuant to L.R. 83–5 (including those admitted pro hac vice) and currently in good standing shall be entitled to one System password to permit the attorney to participate in the electronic retrieval and filing of pleadings and other documents using the System. Applications for admission to practice in the Northern District of Indiana and CM/ECF registration are available on the court's website at www.innd.uscourts.gov. Attorneys registered to use the CM/ECF system will be able to change their own passwords. Registration for a password is governed by Paragraph I(B).

In order to allow electronic retrieval of filings by employees of the Social Security Administration, one read-only system login and password will be issued to the Social Security Administration in their role as a party in civil cases. This account will have read-only access and will not allow a user to file electronically in a case. Any filings on behalf of the Social Security Administration shall be made by attorneys of record for that agency using their court issued attorney logins and passwords. Other than this exception for the Social Security Administration, no system login and password will be issued to a party in a case without prior approval of a judge in the case.

Pursuant to Fed. R. Civ. P. 11, every pleading, motion, and other paper (except lists, schedules, statements or amendments thereto) shall be signed by at least one attorney of record or, if the party is not represented by an attorney, all papers shall be signed by the party. An attorney's/participant's password issued by the court combined with the user's identification, serves as and constitutes the attorney/participant's signature for Rule 11 and other purposes. Therefore, an attorney/participant must protect and secure the password issued by the court. If there is any reason to suspect the password has been compromised in any way, it is the duty and responsibility of the attorney/participant to immediately notify the court by calling the CM/ECF Help Line between 9:00 a.m. and 4:00 p.m. local time in order to prevent access to the System by use of the old password. (See Section V. below for help line numbers) In the event of the resignation or reassignment of the person with authority to use the password, the attorney/participant should change the password immediately.

No attorney shall knowingly permit his or her password to be utilized by anyone other than an authorized employee of his or her office. Once registered, the attorney shall be responsible for all documents filed with his or her password.

Attorneys/participants may be subject to sanctions for failure to comply with the above provisions.

Attorneys may reset forgotten passwords by using the **Reset CM/ECF Password** link available under the Attorneys tab on the court's website: www.innd.uscourts. gov.

II. ELECTRONIC FILING AND SERVICE OF DOCUMENTS

A. Filing.

1. Unless otherwise permitted by these procedures or otherwise authorized by the assigned judge, all documents[1] submitted for filing in this district in civil and criminal cases, no matter when a case was originally filed, shall be filed electronically using the System.[2]

2. Electronically filed documents must meet the same requirements of format and page limits as documents "conventionally filed" (as defined in Section III A) pursuant to the Federal Rules of Civil and Criminal Procedure and this court's Local Rules.

3. Electronically filed documents may contain hyperlink references to an external document as a convenient mechanism for accessing material cited in the document. A hyperlink reference is neither validated for content nor considered a part of the court's records. The court neither endorses the product or organization at the destination of a hyperlink reference, nor does the court exercise any responsibility over the content at the destination. In order to preserve the integrity of the court record, attorneys wishing to insert hyperlinks in court filings shall continue to use the traditional citation method for the cited authority, in addition to the hyperlink. A hyperlink contained in a filing is no more than a convenient mechanism for accessing material cited in the document and a hyperlink reference is extraneous to any filed document and is not part of the court's record.

4. All documents which form part of a single pleading and which are being filed at the same time and by the same party may be electronically filed together under one document number, e.g., the motion and a supporting affidavit, with the exception of memoranda in support. Memoranda in support shall be electronically filed separately and shown as a related document to the motion.

5. In order to file a document which requires leave of court such as an amended complaint or a document to be filed out of time, the proposed document shall be attached as an exhibit to a motion.

6. Filing users must submit in electronic form all documents referenced as exhibits or attachments, unless the court permits conventional filing. A filing user must submit as exhibits or attachments only those excerpts of the referenced documents that are directly germane to the matter under consideration by the court. Excerpted material must be clearly and prominently identified as such. Filing users who file excerpts of documents as exhibits or attachments do so without prejudice to their right to timely file additional excerpts or the complete document. Responding parties may timely file additional excerpts or the complete document that they believe are directly germane. The court may require parties to file additional excerpts or the complete document.

B. Filing a Civil Complaint. All new civil complaints must be filed electronically in CM/ECF, and should be accompanied by a Civil Cover Sheet (JS–44) and summons forms with the top portion completed. If the complaint alleges a violation of a patent, trademark or copyright, a completed AO 120 (Patent & Trademark) or AO 121 (Copyright) form should also be attached. The court may sign, seal and issue a summons on paper or electronically. However, a party may not electronically serve a summons and complaint. Service of a summons and complaint upon parties must be perfected according to Fed. R. Civ. P. 4.

C. Filing Criminal Charges. All criminal complaints, informations, and indictments shall be filed conventionally on paper with the court. The court may issue a warrant or summons electronically; however, they may only be served in accordance with Fed.R.Crim.P. 4(c).

D. Service of Filed Documents on Parties.

1. The System will generate a "Notice of Electronic Filing" when any document is filed. This notice represents service of the document on parties who are registered participants with the System. Except as provided in Paragraph III.B, the filing party shall not be required to serve any pleading [3] or other documents on any party receiving electronic notice.

2. The filing party shall also serve those parties not designated or able to receive electronic notice but nevertheless are entitled to notice of said pleading or other document in accordance with the Federal Rules of Civil Procedure and the Local Rules of the Northern District of Indiana. If such service of a paper copy is to be made, it shall be done in the manner provided in the Federal Rules of Civil Procedures and the Local Rules of the Northern District of Indiana.

3. A party may not electronically serve a summons and complaint, but instead must perfect service according to the Fed. R. Civ. P. 4.

E. Signatures.

1. *Civil cases.* Documents which must be filed and which must contain original signatures other than those of a participating attorney or which require either verification or an unsworn declaration under any rule or statute, shall be filed electronically, with originally executed copies maintained by the filer. The pleading or other document electronically filed shall contain "s/" signature(s), as noted in 3(b) below.

2. *Criminal cases.* All documents which must contain original signatures other than those of a participating attorney or which require either verification or an unsworn declaration under any rule or statute, shall first be filed electronically with a .pdf version of the document and shall then also be filed conventionally on paper in the Clerk's office. The electronically filed document shall be completed and shall contain an "s/" signature in all places in which the original document contains a signature, as noted in 3(b) below. The conventionally filed document shall contain original signatures and shall be accompanied by a copy of the Notice of Electronic Filing generated when the document was filed electronically. Plea agreements signed by a defendant are an example of this type of document.

3. In the case of a stipulation or other document to be signed by two or more attorneys, the following procedure should be used:

   (a) The filing attorney shall initially confirm that the content of the document is acceptable to all persons required to sign the document and shall obtain the physical signatures of all attorneys on the document.

   (b) The filing attorney then shall file the document electronically, indicating the signatories, e.g., "s/Jane Doe," "s/John Doe," etc.

   (c) The filing attorney shall retain the hard copy of the document containing the original signatures.

F. Orders. All orders issued by the court shall be filed electronically by either the office of the clerk or a judge. Any order or other court-issued document filed electronically without the original signature of a judge or clerk has the same force and effect as if the judge or clerk had signed a paper copy of the order and it had been entered on the docket in a conventional manner. The assigned judge or the clerk's office, if appropriate, may grant routine orders by a text-only entry upon the docket. In such cases, no .pdf document will issue. The text-only entry shall constitute the court's only order on the matter, is in fact an order from the judge and carries the same weight and authority as a written order signed by the judge. The System will generate a Notice of Electronic Filing for text-only entries as described in these procedures, which will contain language indicating that no document is attached. Immediately upon the entry of an order or judgment in an action assigned to the System, the clerk will transmit to filing users in the case, in electronic form, a Notice of Electronic Filing. Electronic transmission of the Notice of Electronic Filing constitutes the notice required by Fed.R.Civ.P. 77(d). The clerk will give notice in paper form to a person who has not consented to electronic service in accordance with the Federal Rules of Civil Procedure.

PROPOSED ORDERS PROCEDURE

Proposed orders shall not be filed electronically either as a separate document or as an attachment to the main pleading or other document. Instead, all proposed orders must be e-mailed to the chambers of the appropriate judicial officer for the case. The proposed order must be in WordPerfect Format or Rich Text Format (RTF).[4] Proposed orders should be attached to an e-mail and sent to the appropriate judicial officer at the address listed below. The subject line of the email message should indicate the case title, cause number and document number of the motion, e.g., *Smith v. Jones 1:02–cv–1234, motion#* ___

Chief Judge Robert L. Miller, Jr.	miller_chambers@innd.uscourts.gov
Judge William C. Lee	lee_chambers@innd.uscourts.gov
Judge James T. Moody	moody_chambers@innd.uscourts.gov
Judge Rudy Lozano	lozano_chambers@innd.uscourts.gov
Judge Philip P. Simon	simon_chambers@innd.uscourts.gov
Judge Theresa L. Springmann	springmann_chambers@innd.uscourts.gov
Judge Joseph S. Van Bokkelen	van_bokkelen_chambers@innd.uscourts.gov
Judge Jon E. DeGuilio	deguilio_chambers@innd.uscourts.gov
Magistrate Judge Andrew P. Rodovich	rodovich_chambers@innd.uscourts.gov
Magistrate Judge Susan L. Collins	collins_chambers@innd.uscourts.gov
Magistrate Judge Christopher A. Nuechterlein	nuechterlein_chambers@innd.uscourts.gov
Magistrate Judge Paul R. Cherry	cherry_chambers@innd.uscourts.gov
Magistrate Judge John E. Martin	martin_chambers@innd.uscourts.gov

PROPOSED DISCOVERY PLANS/SCHEDULING ORDERS AND FINAL PRETRIAL ORDERS

Unlike proposed orders, Proposed Discovery Plans/Scheduling Orders and proposed Final Pretrial Orders should not contain a signature line for the Judge. The attorney filing these documents shall initially confirm that the content of the document is acceptable to all persons required to sign the document and shall obtain the physical signatures of all attorneys on the document. The filing attorney then shall file the document electronically, indicating the signatories, e.g., "s/Jane Doe," "s/John Doe," etc. The filing attorney shall retain the hard copy of the document containing the original signatures.

G. Title of Documents. The person electronically filing a pleading or other document will be responsible for designating a title for the pleading or other document by using one of the categories contained in the events listed in the CM/ECF Menu.

H. Certificate of Service. A Certificate of Service is still a requirement when filing documents electronically. A sample **Certificate of Service** is attached as **Form 1**.

I. Filing Deadlines. Filing documents electronically does not alter any filing deadlines or any time computation pursuant to Fed. R. Civ. P. 6. The counties of Lake, Porter, LaPorte, Pulaski and Starke are located in the Central time zone and the remaining counties in the Northern District of Indiana are located in the Eastern time zone. Nevertheless, all electronic transmissions of documents must be completed (*i.e.*, received completely by the clerk's office) prior to **midnight Eastern Time**, (South Bend/Fort Wayne/Lafayette time) in order to be considered timely filed that day, **regardless of the local time in the division where the case is pending**. Although documents can be filed electronically 24 hours a day, filers are strongly encouraged to file all documents during hours when the CM/ECF Help Line is available, from 9:00 a.m. to 4:00 p.m. local time. (See Section V. below for help line numbers)

J. Consents to Proceed before a Magistrate Judge. All parties to a civil action will receive Magistrate Judge Consent Forms from the court by electronic means, or by United States Mail if the party is not registered to receive electronic notices. Completed Magistrate judge consent forms should be returned by e-mail OR by United States Mail to the appropriate clerk's office where the case is pending. Consent forms are also available on the court's website at www.innd.uscourts.gov, under Attorneys, Attorney Forms, Magistrate Judge Consent Forms.

Any party who wishes to consent to jurisdiction by a United States Magistrate Judge shall sign the form and file it with the Clerk as soon as practicable but in any event within twenty (20) days following the date the Preliminary Pretrial Conference is held or within 20 days of receipt of the form in cases where no Preliminary Pretrial Conference is held. Nothing in this paragraph shall be construed as a limitation of the assigned district judge to refer, in his or her discretion, the case to a magistrate judge upon consent of all parties even though untimely filed. See General Order 2007–10 on the court's website at www.innd.uscourts.gov, under Local Rules and General Orders.

Clerk's Office E-mail addresses:

Hammond—hmdclerks@innd.uscourts.gov
Fort Wayne—fwclerks@innd.uscourts.gov
South Bend—sbclerks@innd.uscourts.gov
Lafayette—lafclerks@innd.uscourts.gov

Mailing addresses:

District Court Clerk's Office
1300 S. Harrison St.
Fort Wayne, IN 46802

District Court Clerk's Office
5400 Federal Plaza
Hammond, IN 46320

District Court Clerk's Office
204 S. Main St. Room 102
South Bend, IN 46601

District Court Clerk's Office
230 North Fourth Street
P.O. Box 1498
Lafayette, IN 47901

K. Filing a Social Security Administrative Record.

1. The United States Attorney's Office will file the Administrative Record provided by the Social Security Administration electronically. The System will generate a "Notice of Electronic Filing" when the document is filed. This notice represents service of the document on parties who are registered participants with the System and the filing party shall not be required to serve the document on any party receiving electronic notice.

2. One (1) courtesy paper copy of the administrative record must be delivered to the Clerk's Office in the division where the case is filed for routing to the presiding Judge in the case. This paper copy will not be returned to the United States Attorney's Office. Failure to deliver a paper copy will constitute an improper filing.

3. The United States Attorney's Office shall also serve those parties not designated or able to receive electronic notice but nevertheless are entitled to notice of said document in accordance with the Federal Rules of Civil Procedure and the Local Rules of the Northern District of Indiana. If such service of a paper copy is to be made, it shall be done in the manner provided in the Federal Rules of Civil Procedures and the Local Rules of the Northern District of Indiana.

III. CONVENTIONAL FILING OF DOCUMENTS

A. Conventional Filings. As used in these procedures, a "conventionally" filed or submitted document or pleading is one presented to the Clerk or a party in paper or other non-electronic, tangible format. The following documents shall be filed conventionally and not electronically unless specifically authorized by the Court:

1. Exhibits and other documents which cannot be converted to a legible electronic form. Whenever possible, counsel is responsible for converting filings to an electronic form. However, if that is not physically possible, counsel shall electronically file a .pdf document titled *Notice of Manual Filing* as a notation on the docket sheet that filings are being held in the clerk's office in paper. A sample **Notice of Manual Filing** is attached as **Form 2**. If documents are filed in paper format, counsel must provide an original for the clerk's office, a copy for the judge and a copy must be served on all parties in the case. Large documents which do not exist in an electronic format shall be scanned into .pdf format by counsel, in small batches if necessary, and filed electronically as separate attachments in the System.

2. Certain documents which are listed in II. E. 2. above.

3. Documents filed by pro se litigants.

B. Service of Conventional Filings. Pleadings or other documents which are filed conventionally rather than electronically shall be served in the manner provided for in the Federal Rules of Civil Procedure and the Local Rules of the Northern District of Indiana, except as otherwise provided by order of the Court.

IV. FILING OF SEALED AND EX PARTE MATERIALS

A. Civil Cases.

1. New civil cases filed under seal shall be filed conventionally pursuant to II. B above and L.R. 5-3. Any distribution to parties must be made conventionally on paper. Attorneys will not have electronic access to file documents or receive electronic notices for sealed cases. All subsequent filings and service made by attorneys must be made conventionally

2. In instances where a civil case is not sealed, but a party wishes to file sealed motions or sealed documents, those documents shall be filed electronically in the CM/ECF system using the appropriate civil event, either "Sealed Motion" or "Sealed Document". These events will produce a publicly viewable docket entry but will not allow access to the attached pdf document. Any distribution to parties must be made conventionally on paper.

3. Ex parte motions and ex parte documents in non-sealed civil cases shall be filed electronically in the CM/ECF system using the appropriate civil event, either "Ex Parte Motion" or "Ex Parte Document". The docket entries and pdf documents for these events will be accessible only to authorized court staff and the filing party. Other parties and the general public will not see the docket entry or have access to the pdf document.

4. A civil motion event exists for a "Motion to Seal", which will not be treated as a sealed or restricted entry in the CM/ECF system. Filers selecting this event will be presented with a warning that sealed pdf documents should not be attached to

this event, but should, instead, be electronically filed separately as a "Sealed Motion" or "Sealed Document" pursuant to IV. A. 2. above.

B. Criminal Cases.

1. In instances where a criminal case is not sealed, but a party wishes to file sealed motions or sealed documents, those documents shall be filed electronically in the CM/ECF system using the appropriate criminal events. A party must file a "Motion to Seal" or a "Motion to Seal Document," prior to filing a "Sealed Motion" or a "Sealed Document." Failure to file a "Motion to Seal" or a "Motion to Seal Document" will result in the striking from the record any "Sealed Motion" or "Sealed Document" that has been filed. These events will produce a publicly viewable docket entry but will not allow access to the attached pdf document. Any distribution to parties must be made conventionally on paper.

2. Ex parte motions and ex parte documents in non-sealed criminal cases shall be filed electronically in the CM/ECF system using the appropriate event, "Ex Parte Motion." The docket entries and pdf documents for this event will be accessible only to authorized court staff and the filing party. Other parties and the general public will not see the docket entry or have access to the pdf document.

V. PUBLIC ACCESS TO THE SYSTEM DOCKET

A. Public Remote Access Through Pacer. Civil cases: Public remote access to the System for viewing purposes is limited to subscribers to the Public Access to Court Electronic Records ("PACER") system. The Judicial Conference of the United States has ruled that a user fee will be charged for remotely accessing certain detailed case information, such as docket sheets and filed documents. PACER users may access the System at the Court's Internet site at www.innd. uscourts.gov. Such access to the System through the Internet site will allow retrieval of the docket sheet and documents on a time delayed basis. Unless a user has a CM/ECF filing level account, access to the System will be on a "read only" basis.

Social Security cases: Until further order of the court, only attorneys of record and employees of the Social Security Administration with access to the login and password authorized in Paragraph (I)(C) above may remotely view records in social security cases. Public remote access will be limited to viewing docket sheets only.

Criminal cases: Public remote access to non-sealed documents in criminal cases will be limited to documents filed on or after January 1, 2005, pursuant to the Judicial Conference Policy on Privacy and Public Access to Electronic Criminal Case Files. Public remote access to documents filed prior to January 1, 2005 will be limited to viewing docket sheets only.

B. Public Access at the Court. The public will have electronic access to civil and criminal documents filed in the System and to the System dockets in the Office of the Clerk, for viewing during regular business hours, from 9:00 a.m. to 4:00 p.m. (local time) Monday through Friday. A copy fee for reproduction is still required in accordance with 28 U.S.C. § 1914.

C. Conventional Copies and Certified Copies. Conventional copies and certified copies of the electronically filed documents may be purchased at the Office of the Clerk, during business hours listed in Paragraph B above. A list of fees is available on the court's website at www.innd.uscourts.gov.

VI. TECHNICAL FAILURES

A. The Court's System. The Clerk shall deem the Public Web site for the Northern District of Indiana to be subject to a technical failure on a given day if the site is unable to accept filings continuously or intermittently over the course of any period of time greater than one hour after 12:00 noon that day, in which case filings due that day which were not filed due solely to such technical failures shall become due the next business day. Such delayed filings shall be rejected unless accompanied by a declaration or affidavit attesting to the filing person's failed attempts to file electronically at least two times after 12:00 p.m. separated by at least one hour on each day of delay due to such technical failure. Questions about CM/ECF may be directed to our Help Line at the one of the following numbers between 9:00 a.m. to 4:00 p.m. local time:

Fort Wayne	800–745–0265
Hammond	800–473–0293
South Bend	866–217–5925
Lafayette	877–377–1219

B. The Attorney's System. If the attorney is unable to file a document in a timely manner due to technical difficulties in the user's system, the attorney must file a document with the court as soon as possible notifying the court of the inability to file the document. A sample document entitled **Declaration that Party was Unable to File in a Timely Manner Due to Technical Difficulties** is attached hereto as **Form 5.**

VII. PRIVACY

Counsel should not include sensitive information in any document filed with the court unless such inclusion is necessary and relevant to the case. See Fed. R. Civ. P. 5.2 regarding protection of personal identifiers in civil cases and Fed. R. Cr. P. 49.1 regarding privacy protection in criminal cases.

SPECIAL NOTICE TO SOCIAL SECURITY ATTORNEYS

It is the responsibility of counsel for plaintiff to provide the U.S. Attorneys' office with the social security number of the plaintiff upon the filing of a new social security case.

SAMPLE FORMAT

Certificate of Service

I hereby certify that on __(Date)__ I electronically filed the foregoing with the Clerk of the Court using the CM/ECF system which sent notification of such filing to the following: _____ and I hereby certify that I have mailed by United States Postal Service the document to the following non CM/ECF participants: _____.

s/

Form 1

SAMPLE FORMAT

IN THE UNITED STATES DISTRICT COURT FOR THE NORTHERN DISTRICT OF INDIANA _____ DIVISION

_____,   )
)
              Plaintiff(s),   )
)

U.S. DISTRICT COURT

vs.) Case No. _____
)
_____,)
)
Defendant(s).)

NOTICE OF MANUAL FILING

_____

is in paper form only and is being maintained in the case file in the Clerk's office.

_____

Attorney for (Plaintiff or Defendant)

Address: _____

_____

_____

_____

Date: _____

Form 2

SAMPLE FORMAT

IN THE UNITED STATES DISTRICT COURT FOR THE
NORTHERN DISTRICT OF INDIANA
_____ DIVISION

_____,)
)
)
Plaintiff(s),)
vs.) Case No. _____
_____,)
)
)
Defendant(s).)

DECLARATION THAT PARTY WAS UNABLE
TO FILE IN A TIMELY MANNER

Please take notice that _____ was unable to file _____ in a timely manner due to technical difficulties. The deadline for filing the _____ was _____. The reason(s) that I was unable to file the _____ in a timely manner and the good faith efforts I made prior to the filing deadline to both file in a timely manner and to inform the court and the other parties that I could not do so are set forth below.

[Statement of reasons and good faith efforts to file and to inform]

I declare under penalty of perjury that the foregoing is true and correct.

Respectfully submitted,

s/[Name of Password Registrant]

Name of Password Registrant

Address

City, State, Zip Code

Phone: XXX–XXX–XXXX

Fax: XXX–XXX–XXXX

E-mail: XXX@XXX.XXX

Form 3

[Effective February 21, 2012. Amended effective November 1, 2012; April 22, 2013; June 13, 2013; January 31, 2014; March 12, 2015.]

[1]The requirement that "all documents" be filed electronically includes briefs, and attachments and exhibits used in support of motions.

[2]Documents filed in the CM/ECF must be in .pdf format. A document created with almost any word-processing program can be converted to .pdf format. The .pdf program in effect takes a picture of the original document and allows anyone to open the converted document across a broad range of hardware and software, with layout, format, links, and images intact. For information on .pdf, users may visit the websites of .pdf vendors, such as http://www.adobe.com/products/acrobat/ or http://www.fineprint.com/.

[3]The term "pleading" refers only to those documents listed in Federal Rules of Civil Procedure 7(a).

[4]MS Word will allow a document to be saved in WordPerfect format or Rich Text Format (RTF).

GENERAL ORDER 2004–19. FILING OF DOCUMENTS UNDER SEAL

(a) General Rule. No document will be maintained under seal in the absence of an authorizing statute, Court rule, or Court order.

(b) Filing of Cases Under Seal. Any new case submitted for filing under seal must be accompanied by a motion to seal and proposed order. Any case presented in this manner will be assigned a new case number, District Judge and Magistrate Judge. The Clerk will maintain the case under seal until a ruling granting the motion to seal is entered by the assigned District Judge. If the motion to seal is denied, the case will be immediately unsealed with or without prior notice to the filing party.

(c) Filing of Documents Under Seal. Materials presented as sealed documents shall be inside an envelope which allows them to remain flat. Affixed to the exterior of the envelope shall be an 8 ½ x 11" cover sheet containing:

(1) the case caption;

(2) the name of the document if it can be disclosed publicly, otherwise an appropriate title by which the document may be identified on the public docket;

(3) the name, address and telephone number of the person filing the document; and

(4) in the event the motion requesting the document be filed under seal does not accompany the document, the cover sheet must set forth the citation of the statute or rule or the date of the Court order authorizing filing under seal.

(d) Prohibition of Electronic Filing of Sealed Documents. Sealed documents will not be filed electronically, but rather manually on paper. The party filing a sealed document shall file electronically a Notice of Manual Filing (see Form in Electronic Case Filing Administrative Policies and Procedures Manual for the Northern District of Indiana.) The courtroom deputy to the District or Magistrate Judge should be contacted for instructions when filing certain *ex parte* documents which could not be disclosed by the electronic Notice of Manual Filing.

[Dated: November 8, 2004.]

GENERAL ORDER 2005–3.   IN RE: PRIVACY AND PUBLIC ACCESS TO CIVIL ELECTRONIC CASE FILES.

IT IS HEREBY ORDERED that in compliance with the policy of the Judicial Conference of the United States, and in order to promote public electronic access to case files while also protecting sensitive information and other legitimate interests, parties shall refrain from including, or shall partially redact where inclusion is necessary, the following personal data identifiers from all papers filed with the court, including exhibits thereto, whether filed electronically or in paper:

(1) **Social Security numbers.** If an individual's social security number must be included in a paper, only the last four digits of that number should be used.

(2) **Names of minor children.** If the involvement of a minor child must be mentioned, only the initials of that child should be used.

(3) **Dates of birth.** If an individual's date of birth must be included in a paper, only the year should be used.

(4) **Financial account numbers.** If financial account numbers are relevant, only the last four digits of these numbers should be used.

A party wishing to file a paper containing the personal data identifiers listed above may

(1) file an unredacted version of the document under seal, or

(2) file a reference list under seal. The reference list shall contain the complete personal data identifier(s) and the redacted identifier(s) used in its(their) place in the filing. All references in the case to the redacted identifiers included in the reference list will be construed to refer to the corresponding complete personal data identifier. The reference list must be filed under seal, and may be amended as of right.

The unredacted version of the document or the reference list shall be retained by the court under seal as part of the record. This paper shall be retained by the court as part of the record. The court may, however, still require the party to file a redacted copy for the public file.

In cases filed under the Social Security Act, 42 U.S.C. § 405(g), there is no need for redaction of any information from the documents filed in the case.

The responsibility for redacting these personal identifiers rests solely with counsel and the parties. The Clerk will not review each paper for compliance with this rule.

This policy shall go into effect after notice to the bar and public and will apply to all documents filed on or after the effective date.

[Dated: June 13, 2005.]

GENERAL ORDER 2005–4   IN RE: PRIVACY AND PUBLIC ACCESS TO CRIMINAL ELECTRONIC CASE FILES

IT IS HEREBY ORDERED that in compliance with the policy of the Judicial Conference of the United States, and in order to promote public electronic access to case files while also protecting sensitive information and other legitimate interests, parties shall refrain from including, or shall partially redact where inclusion is necessary, the following personal data identifiers from all documents filed with the court, including exhibits thereto, whether filed electronically or in paper, unless otherwise ordered by the court.

(1) **Social Security numbers.** If an individual's Social Security number must be included, only the last four digits of that number should be used.

(2) **Names of minor children.** If the involvement of a minor child must be mentioned, only the initials of that child should be used.

(3) **Dates of birth.** If an individual's date of birth must be included, only the year should be used.

(4) **Financial account numbers.** If financial account numbers are relevant, only the last four digits of these numbers should be used.

(5) **Home addresses.** If a home address must be included, only the city and state should be listed.

A party wishing to file a document containing the personal data identifiers listed above may

(1) file an unredacted version of the document under seal, or

(2) file a reference list under seal. The reference list shall contain the complete personal data identifier(s) and the redacted identifier(s) used in its(their) place in the filing. All references in the case to the redacted identifiers included in the reference list will be construed to refer to the corresponding complete personal data identifier. The reference list must be filed under seal, and may be amended as of right.

The unredacted version of the document or the reference list shall be retained by the court as part of the record. The court may, however, still require the party to file a redacted copy for the public file.

The responsibility for redacting these personal identifiers rests solely with counsel and the parties. The Clerk will not review each pleading for compliance with this rule.

The policy shall go into effect after notice to the bar and public and will apply to all documents filed on or after the effective date.

[Dated: June 13, 2005.]

SELECTED GENERAL ORDERS
GENERAL ORDER 1996–6. IN THE MATTER OF A
UNITED STATES DISTRICT COURT LIBRARY
AND COURT ADMINISTRATION FUND

WHEREAS, this Court has determined that a United States District Court Library and Court Administration Fund should be established, and

WHEREAS, said Fund shall consist of receipts from admission fees paid by admittees to practice before the Bar of this Court.

WHEREAS, PURSUANT TO 28 U.S.C. § 1914(b) IT IS THE PRESENT PRACTICE OF THE COURT to collect a $20.00 admission fee to practice before the bar of the Court, and

WHEREAS, the Judicial Conference of the United States, at its March 1993 meeting, agreed to increase the fee for admission of attorneys to practice to $50.00 each, in coordination with the enactment of the Courts Improvement Act of 1966, the same to be effective December 18, 1996, and

WHEREAS, it has now been concluded by the Judges of this Court that the fee should be increased to $60.00,

IT IS ORDERED that the said fee, be, and the same is hereby increased to a total sum of $60.00, and that the Clerk's miscellaneous fee of $50.00 be deposited to the credit of the Treasury of the United States, and the fee of $10.00 be deposited in the United States District Court Library and Court Administration Fund.

IT IS FURTHER ORDERED that pursuant to this Court's Local Rule 83.5(c) Pro Hac Vice appearance fees be increased to $30.00 or half of the regular admission fee which shall be deposited in the United States District Court Library and Court Administration Fund.

NOW, THEREFORE, IT IS FURTHER ORDERED that monies may be expended from said Fund on behalf of this Court and its Judges by mutual agreement of the Judges for the purchase of books, publications, educational materials, and such additional expenditures as shall contribute to or benefit the effective operation of this Court;

IT IS FURTHER ORDERED that funds shall be withdrawn from the Fund by checks and withdrawal orders signed by the Clerk of the Court and countersigned by the Chief Judge.

This order shall take effect December 18, 1996.

[Effective December 18, 1996.]

GENERAL ORDER 2001–1.   IN RE: PRESENTENCE PROCEDURES*

In order to provide for the effective, orderly and timely discharge of the court's responsibilities in sentencing matters, and to comply with Federal Rule of Criminal Procedure 32, effective December 1, 1994, the following procedures are hereby ordered and adjudged in cases governed in whole or in part by the Sentencing Guidelines promulgated by the United States Sentencing Commission:

1. Sentencing proceedings shall be scheduled by each district judge no earlier than seventy (70) days following adjudication of guilt by either plea or verdict.

2. The initial interview will take place no more than three working days after the referral to the probation department. Upon request defense counsel shall be provided notice and a reasonable opportunity to attend any interview of the defendant by a probation officer in the course of a presentence investigation.

3. The presentence investigation report, including guideline computations, shall be completed, typed, and disclosed to the parties at least thirty-five (35) days before the scheduled sentencing proceeding, unless the defendant waives this minimum period. This time period contemplates that the report will be disclosed to the parties on or before the thirty fifth (35th) day following the adjudication of guilt unless additional time was requested and granted at the time of the plea or verdict. The presentence report shall be deemed to have been disclosed upon the occurrence of any of the following events, or within the following times:

(A) when a copy of the document is physically presented to the attorneys and defendant;

(B) one (1) day after the report's availability for inspection is verbally communicated by the probation office to the parties; or

(C) three (3) days after the report or a notice of the report's availability is mailed to the attorneys for the parties.

4. Within ten (10) days after a verdict of guilty, counsel for both parties shall submit, in writing, any versions, stipulations, or statements regarding the facts pertaining to the instant offense to the probation officer of the court. The defendant's failure to submit such a statement shall not delay the acts called for in this order, except to the extent the district judge shall find that justice so requires. In addition, investigative reports and other relevant materials shall be made available to the probation officer of the court to ensure an independent review and assessment in determining calculations on (among other matters) relevant behavior, obstruction of justice, role in the offense, acceptance of responsibility, etc.

5. In the matter of pleas and the filing of a petition to enter a plea of guilty, or like proceedings, counsel for both parties shall, on the date the plea is entered, provide to the probation officer of the court such information as is noted in the preceding paragraph.

6. If the defendant is in custody, the probation office may release the defendant's copy of the presentence report to counsel for the defendant to satisfy the requirement of disclosure via review of the report in person with counsel. The U. S. Marshal and the U. S. Probation Office will coordinate efforts with the defense counsel to bring defendant(s) to a reasonably close location to facilitate the responsibility of defense counsel to review the presentence report with counsel's defendant(s).

7. Within fourteen (14) days following disclosure, counsel for the government and the defendant shall communicate to the probation officer and opposing counsel, in writing, any objections they may have as to any material information, criminal history, sentencing classifications, sentencing guideline ranges and policy statements contained in or omitted from the report. They shall also submit, in writing, their acknowledgment of no objections.

8. The probation officer may require both counsel for the government and the defendant to meet with the probation officer to discuss unresolved factual and legal issues. Such meeting, if necessary shall be held as early as possible within the fourteen (14) days following the period of time allowed to make objections. Attendance at any such meeting shall be mandatory by all parties, and failure to attend may be deemed a waiver of any objections.

9. After receiving either or both counsel's objections, the probation officer shall conduct any further investigation and make any necessary revisions to the report.

10. In the matter of undisputed reports, the probation officer shall submit the report to the court not less than ten (10) days before sentencing.

11. If any revisions to the report are required, the probation officer shall make the needed changes and provide a final, revised version to the court, and all parties, not less than ten (10) days before sentencing.

12. In reports where disputed matters remain, the probation officer shall prepare an addendum setting forth the unresolved objections or disputes of either or both counsel. The addendum shall also state any stipulations concerning the disputed matters by counsel, but shall not be deemed binding on the court in determining the facts relevant to sentencing. See Guidelines § 6B1.4(d). Finally, the probation officer may submit the results of additional investigation or make appropriate additional statements relative to final resolution of these matters and provide this information to the court not less than ten (10) days before sentencing.

13. At the direction of each sentencing judge, the recommendation may be released to the defendant, defense counsel and attorney for the government, separate from the presentence report and addendum. The recommendation shall be returned to the probation department at the end of the proceedings.

14. Except with regard to any timely filed notice of objections or disputes that remain unresolved (see Paragraphs 7 and 12, supra), the court may adopt the presentence report as accurate.

15. The court may, however, for good cause shown, allow a new objection to be raised at any time before the imposition of sentence.

16. The court, in its discretion, may choose to resolve disputed matters in any of the following ways, or in any other manner the court deems appropriate:

(A) by calling a hearing of all parties prior to the sentencing hearing to resolve disputed matters;

(B) by informing the parties in writing of its tentative findings and affording an opportunity for arguments to be heard before imposition of the sentence; or

(C) by hearing arguments on disputed matters at the sentencing hearing and making findings of fact on each disputed issue prior to sentencing.

In resolving disputed matters, the court may consider any reliable information presented by the probation officer, the defendant, or the government, including witness testimony, without regard to its admissibility under the Federal Rules of Evidence. See 18 U.S.C. § 3661.

17. Because Federal Rule of Criminal Procedure 35 now allows for a modification of a sentence only under very limited circumstances, the court may state its tentative sentence and allow any objections thereto.

18. After sentencing, a copy of the presentence report shall be sealed within the court records to be available for appeal purposes. Any confidential information and/or recommendation shall be sealed separately and shall not be made available to appellate counsel in the absence of an order by this court or the court of appeals.

19. The time frames set forth within this order may be modified by the court for good cause shown, except that the fourteen (14) day period prescribed in Paragraph 7, supra, may be shortened only with the defendant's consent.

20. Nothing in this order requires the disclosure of any portion or portions of the presentence report that are not disclosed under Rule 32 of the Federal Rules of Criminal Procedure.

21. These are procedures for the court's internal operations. The court may dispense with their use in particular cases. Counsel and litigants acquire no rights under these procedures.

SO ORDERED

[Dated: January 8, 2001.]

* [**Publisher's Note:** See also General Order 2010-8, post.]

GENERAL ORDER 2003–21. IN RE: A GENERAL ORDER OF THE COURT [ALTERNATIVE DISPUTE RESOLUTION]

The Court shall follow the provisions of Local Rule 16.6(b) in every case unless the case is exempt by operation of Local Rule 16.1(b). Accordingly, in every case in which a Fed. R. Civ. P. 26(f) report is submitted, the parties **and the Court** shall consider the use of an Alternative Dispute Resolution Process (hereafter "ADR Process"), such as mediation. A settlement conference conducted by a judicial officer is not an ADR Process. *See*, Local Rule 16.6(b).

Following the consideration of that proposed ADR Process which the parties wish to employ, if any, as well as when that process should be undertaken, the Court shall, if the Court approves, incorporate the process in the Court's scheduling order entered in accordance with Fed. R. Civ. P. 16 (b)(6) and (c)(9). If the Court disapproves of the ADR Process proposed by the parties, or upon consideration determines that no ADR Process is to be employed in the case, the Court shall make specific findings on the record establishing good cause therefore.

If Mediation is the ADR Process selected by the parties and approved by the Court, either the name of the Mediator or the date by which his or her name will be supplied to the Court shall be specified in the scheduling order.

This Order is also not to discourage or prevent the agreed adoption of an ADR Process in any case in which a Fed. R. Civ. P. 26(f) report is not required.

[Effective July 9, 2003.]

GENERAL ORDER NO. 2007–2. IN RE: UTILIZATION OF UNITED STATES MAGISTRATE IN ANCILLARY PROCEEDINGS

IT IS HEREBY ORDERED THAT at the time any miscellaneous case is filed, other than a disbarment or a grand jury proceeding, a Magistrate Judge will be assigned as presider.

IT IS FURTHER ORDERED THAT at the time an issue becomes contested in a miscellaneous case, a civil case will be opened. The filings from the miscellaneous case will be copied into the civil case. A District Judge will be assigned to the civil case as presider and it will be referred to the previously assigned Magistrate Judge.

[Dated: April 23, 2007.]

GENERAL ORDER 2007–5. IN RE: REFERRAL OF PROCEEDINGS SUPPLEMENTAL

Pursuant to the Federal Magistrate Act, 28 U.S.C. § 636(b)(3), and Local Rule 72.1(i), all proceedings supplemental in any civil case filed in this district are hereby referred to the magistrate judge assigned to the case to conduct such proceedings as are required and, when appropriate, enter into the record a written order setting forth the disposition of those proceedings.

[Dated: April 23, 2007.]

GENERAL ORDER 2007–9. IN RE: RELEASE OF PRETRIAL SERVICE REPORTS TO ATTORNEYS

IT IS HEREBY ORDERED THAT a copy of the Pretrial Services Report shall be provided to and may be retained by the attorneys for the accused and the government, and shall be used only for the purpose of fixing conditions of release, including bail determinations. In addition, all supplemental reports prepared prior to the defendant's initial release will be provided to and may be retained by counsel. When a copy is provided, it will have a header on the first page advising the attorneys that (a) the report is not to be copied, (b) the report is not a public record, and (c) that the content may not be disclosed to unauthorized individuals. Otherwise, the reports shall remain confidential, as provided in 18 U.S.C. § 3153, subject to the expectations provided therein.

[Dated: July 25, 2007.]

GENERAL ORDER 2007–10. IN RE: UTILIZATION OF UNITED STATES MAGISTRATE JUDGES

IT IS HEREBY ORDERED THAT at the time a case is filed, a United States District Judge shall be assigned to the case in the manner prescribed by Local Rule 40.1 and the Order(s) governing the assignment of cases.

IT IS FURTHER ORDERED THAT at the time a case is assigned to a United States District Judge, it shall also be assigned to a United States Magistrate Judge then resident in the Division in which the case is filed. In any Division in which more than one United States Magistrate Judge is resident, the Clerk of the Court shall assign cases to the Magistrate Judges on a random and equal basis.

For any time period during which a Division has no active United States Magistrate Judge resident, this Order shall not apply. Every case filed in a Division having no active United States Magistrate Judge shall be assigned to the active United States Magistrate Judges in the District in a manner prescribed by the Chief Judge at that time.

IT IS FURTHER ORDERED THAT all non-dispositive pretrial matters and motions in a case, other than as excepted by Local Rule 72.1(d), shall be hereafter automatically referred to the United States Magistrate Judge assigned to the case. The United States Magistrate Judge shall promptly hear and determine such matters and motions prescribed by Local Rule 72.1(c).

IT IS FURTHER ORDERED THAT for every civil case filed the Clerk shall notify the parties of the option to consent to jurisdiction by a United States Magistrate Judge pursuant to Local Rule 72.1(h), and, with that notification, provide a blank consent form. Any party who wishes to consent to jurisdiction by a United States Magistrate Judge shall sign the form and file it with the Clerk as soon as practicable but in any event within twenty (20) days after the initial Preliminary Pretrial Conference.

If the case became fully consented by not later than twenty (20) days after the initial preliminary pretrial conference, an entry shall be made on the docket including substantially the following: "The parties having consented pursuant to 28 U.S.C. § 636(c), this case is referred to Magistrate Judge _____ for all purposes, and is reassigned pursuant to General Order 2007–10 from District Judge _____ to Magistrate Judge _____."

If the case became fully consented more than 20 days after the initial preliminary pretrial conference, the Clerk either (a) comply with any directive from the presiding District Judge concerning the handling of such cases (*e.g.*, directing the parties to file a motion for leave to file a belated consent), or (b) prepare for the presiding Judge's consideration an order of full referral/reassignment to the designated Magistrate Judge, including within the order that the case "is reassigned from District Judge _____ to Magistrate Judge _____."

Nothing in this order shall be construed as a limitation of the assigned District Judge to refer, in his or her discretion, the case to a Magistrate Judge upon consent of all parties even though untimely filed.

IT IS FURTHER ORDERED THAT at the time all parties to any civil case consent to the exercise of jurisdiction by a United States Magistrate Judge pursuant to Local Rule 72.1(h), the Clerk shall automatically refer the case to the United States Magistrate Judge resident in the Division in which the case pends, and that Magistrate Judge shall then conduct all proceedings including the conduct of a jury or non-jury trial, and may order the entry of a final judgment. In any Division in which more than one United States Magistrate Judge is resident, cases shall be referred to the Magistrate Judges on a random and equal basis. Once all parties to a case consent to the jurisdiction of a United States Magistrate Judge, the United States District Judge previously assigned to the action shall exercise no further jurisdiction over the case unless it becomes no longer fully consented because of the addition of a party who fails to consent. The Chief Judge may, for good cause shown on his own motion, or under extraordinary circumstances shown by any party, vacate a reference of a civil case to a Magistrate Judge.

IT IS FURTHER ORDERED THAT in any Division with more than one United States Magistrate Judge resident, all task performed by Magistrate Judges consistent with their assigned duties in Local Rule 72.1 shall be assigned on a random and equal basis. This General Order supersedes General Order 2003–19.

[Dated: September 17, 2007.]

GENERAL ORDER 2008–7. IN RE: CELL PHONE POLICY FOR THE UNITED STATES COURTHOUSES IN THE NORTHERN DISTRICT OF INDIANA

It is hereby ORDERED that members of the bar of this Court are now permitted to bring into the courthouses in this district cellular telephones and personal digital assistants (PDAs). Local Rule 83.3 remains in full force and effect as to any other individual entering the courthouses of this district. Lawyers who choose to bring cellular telephones or PDAs into the courthouses pursuant to this General Order are strictly prohibited from using such devices for any improper purpose, including, but not limited to, the taking of any photographs or moving pictures.

Any lawyer or other personnel who is permitted by Local Rule 83.3 to bring cellular telephones or PDAs into the courthouses of this district are hereby specifically warned that if the cellular telephone or PDA creates an audible noise in the courtrooms of this district while court is in session such occurrence is subject to a fine of up to $1500 and/or confiscation of the offending device at the discretion of the judicial officer before whom the device creates the audible noise.

[Dated: June 27, 2008.]

GENERAL ORDER NO. 2009–2. IN RE: APPLICATION FOR ADMISSION TO PRACTICE AND APPLICATION FOR ADMISSION TO PRACTICE PRO HAC VICE

The Court now approves the following attorney admission forms which are attached to this General Order:

a) Application for Admission to Practice; and

b) Application for Admission to Practice Pro Hac Vice.

SO ORDERED.

[Entered: May 29, 2009.]

UNITED STATES DISTRICT COURT FOR THE NORTHERN DISTRICT OF INDIANA

APPLICATION FOR ADMISSION TO PRACTICE

Prefix (check one) ☐ Mr.   ☐ Ms.   ☐ Mrs.

Last Name: _____ First Name: _____ Middle Initial _____

Generation (Sr, Jr, etc.) _____

Firm Name: _____

Street Address: _____ Suite/Room No.: _____

City: _____ State: _____ Zip: _____ Zip + 4: _____

Office Telephone No.: _____ Fax No.: _____

Attorney Registration No.: _____ State: _____

E–Mail Address: _____

Education:

College: _____ Degree: _____ Year Completed: _____

Law School: _____ Year Graduated: _____

Other Post–Graduate Schooling: _____

Currently Admitted to Practice Before:

☐ U.S. Supreme Court   ☐ 7th Circuit Court of Appeals   ☐ Indiana Supreme Court   ☐ Other

Please list below all other courts to which you have been admitted to practice, excluding Pro Hac Vice admissions. _____

_____

Note: In accordance with Local Rule 83.5 you must attach a current Certificate of Good Standing (less than 60 days old) from the appropriate agency of each state in which you are admitted to practice.

Have you ever been subjected to public discipline by any court of the United States of the District of Columbia or by a court of any State, Territory, commonwealth or possession of the United States?

☐ Yes (If yes, please attach an explanation)   ☐ No

Appointments Under the Criminal Justice Act and the Civil Rights Act:

Are you willing to represent defendants determined to be eligible for representation under the Criminal Justice Act of 1964?
       ☐ Yes   ☐ No

Are you willing to be appointed to represent complainants under the Civil Rights Act of 1964?
       ☐ Yes   ☐ No

Applicant: I, _____, do solemnly swear or affirm that:

I am a member in good standing of the bar of every jurisdiction to which I am admitted to practice.

I will support and defend the Constitution and laws of the United States of America against all enemies, foreign and domestic; that I will bear true faith and allegiance to the same; that I take this obligation freely, without any mental reservation or purpose of evasion; and that I will demean myself as attorney, proctor and solicitor of the United States District Court for the Northern District of Indiana uprightly and according to law, so help me God.

I have read and will abide by the Local Rules of the United States District Court for the Northern District of Indiana, including Appendix B: Standards for Professional Conduct Within the Seventh Federal Judicial Circuit.

I declare under penalty of perjury that the statements in this application are true and correct.

Dated: _____   _____
                                              Signature of Applicant

Movant: I, _____, a member in good standing of the bar of this Court hereby certify that the above information is correct to the best of my knowledge and I now personally assure the Court that the Applicant's private and professional character is good and do now move for the admission of the application.

Dated: _____   _____
                                              Signature of Movant

                                     _____
                                     Movant's Attorney Registration No.

                                     _____
                                              State Registered

Considered and approved.
SO ORDERED.

Dated: _____   _____
                                     Judge, U.S. District Court

Form Adopted and Approved by General Order 2009–2

UNITED STATES DISTRICT COURT
FOR THE NORTHERN DISTRICT OF INDIANA

_____

                    v.
                                     Cause No. _____
_____

MOTION FOR ADMISSION TO PRACTICE PRO HAC VICE ON BEHALF OF

_____
                    Party(s) Represented

Prefix (check one) ☐ Mr.   ☐ Ms.   ☐ Mrs.

Last Name: _____   First Name: _____   Middle Initial _____

Generation (Sr, Jr, etc): _____

Firm Name: _____

Street Address: _____   Suite/Room No.:_____

City: _____   State: _____   Zip: _____   Zip + 4: _____

Office Telephone No.: _____   Fax No.: _____

Attorney Registration No.: _____   State: _____

E–Mail Address: _____

Education:

College: _____ Degree: _____ Year Completed: _____

Law School: _____ Year Graduated: _____

Other Post–Graduate Schooling: _____

Currently Admitted to Practice Before:

☐ U.S. Supreme Court　　☐ 7th Circuit Court of Appeals　　☐ Indiana Supreme Court　　☐ Other

Please list below all other courts to which you have been admitted to practice, excluding Pro Hac Vice admissions. _____

Note: In accordance with Local Rule 83.5 you must attach a current Certificate of Good Standing (less than 60 days old) from the appropriate agency of each state in which you are admitted to practice.

Have you ever been subjected to public discipline by any court of the United States of the District of Columbia or by a court of any State, Territory, commonwealth or possession of the United States?

☐ Yes (If yes, please attach an explanation)　☐ No

Applicant: I, _____, do solemnly swear or affirm that:

I am a member in good standing of the bar of every jurisdiction to which I am admitted to practice.

I have read and will abide by the Local Rules of the United States District Court for the Northern District of Indiana, including Appendix B: Standards for Professional Conduct Within the Seventh Federal Judicial Circuit.

I declare under penalty of perjury that the statements in this application are true and correct.

Dated: _____　　　_____
　　　　　　　　　　　　　　　　　　　　　　　Signature of Applicant

Considered and approved.

SO ORDERED.

Dated: _____　　　_____
　　　　　　　　　　　　　　　　　　　　　Judge, U. S. District Court

Form Adopted and Approved by General Order 2009–2.

GENERAL ORDER 2010–8.　IN RE: ADDITIONAL PRESENTENCE PROCEDURES

Supplement to General Order 2001–1

Any request for a sentence involving a departure under the United States Sentencing Guidelines, or for a variance above or below a Guidelines sentence pursuant to 18 U.S.C. § 3553(a), with the exception of matters raised pursuant to § 5K1.1 of the Guidelines, shall be communicated to the probation officer and opposing counsel, in writing, within fourteen (14) days following initial disclosure of the presentence report.

Any sentencing memorandum addressing these or any other issues, including requests for a departure based on § 5K1.1 of the Guidelines, shall be filed with the Court no later than seven (7) days prior to the sentencing hearing.

Any relief from this order must be sought by written motion.

This order supplements General Order 2001–1 entered January 8, 2001.

SO ORDERED.

[Dated: May 14, 2010.]

GENERAL ORDER 2011–13. IN RE: THE ESTABLISHMENT OF MAXIMUM RATES PER PAGE FOR TRANSCRIPTS

Pursuant to the approval of the Judicial Conference of the United States at its September 2011 session and as reflected in the memorandum dated November 8, 2011 from the Administrative Office of the United States Courts, this court now establishes that the maximum rates per page for transcripts are as follows:

	Original	First Copy to each party	Each Additional Copy to the Same Party
Ordinary Transcript (30 Day)	$3.65	$ .90	$ .60
14–Day Transcript	$4.25	$ .90	$ .60
Expedited Transcript (7 day)	$4.85	$ .90	$ .60
Daily Transcript	$6.05	$1.20	$ .90
Hourly Transcript	$7.25	$1.20	$ .90
Realtime Transcript	One feed, [1] $3.05 per page; two to four feeds, $2.10 per page; five or more feeds, $1.50 per page.		

[1] A realtime "feed" is the electronic data flow from the court reporter to the computer of each person or party ordering and receiving the realtime transcription in the courtroom.

The above rates are effective January 1, 2012. This order supercedes General Order 2007–16 entered October 22, 2007.

[Dated: January 12, 2012.]

GENERAL ORDER NO. 2012–8. IN RE: RULES FOR FILING DOCUMENTS UNDER SEAL IN CRIMINAL CASES

IT IS ORDERED that in criminal cases the following documents may be filed under seal without motion or further order of the court provided counsel has a good faith belief that sealing is required to ensure the safety, privacy or cooperation of a person or entity, or to otherwise protect a substantial public interest:

1. Documents filed pre-indictment;

2. Documents filed in a sealed case post-indictment and prior to the first defendant being arrested;

3. Requests for search warrants, including warrants for tracking devices;

4. Requests for interception of communications pursuant to 18 U.S.C. § 2516;

5. Requests for phone record information pursuant to 18 U.S.C. § 2703;

6. Requests for tax return information pursuant to 26 U.S.C. § 6103;

7. Motions for sentence variance or reduction based on substantial assistance pursuant to Fed. R. Crim. P. 35 or U.S.S.G. § 5K1.1, including supporting documents; and

8. Motions for competency exam.

IT IS FURTHER ORDERED that when the documents identified above are filed under seal pursuant to this Order, the documents must contain the words "under seal" in parentheses below the case number or below the area where the case number will be placed.

IT IS FURTHER ORDERED that other than the documents identified above, in all criminal cases, documents may be sealed only if they are subject to a prior protective order or are accompanied by a contemporaneous motion to seal, which motions may be filed under seal if necessary.

IT IS FURTHER ORDERED that sealed motions for sentence variance or reduction based upon substantial assistance pursuant to Fed. R. Crim. P. 35 or U.S.S.G. § 5K1.1, including supporting documents, shall be filed electronically by attorneys. The proper event should be selected when filing the sealed document. The PDF document should be attached to the event and the system will automatically seal the document. Once electronically filed, this sealed entry may only be viewed by authorized court users and authorized attorneys. This order exempts sealed motions for sentence variance or reduction based upon substantial assistance from the requirements of N.D.Ind.L.R. 5–3.

[Dated: June 5, 2012.]

GENERAL ORDER NO. 2012–12. IN RE:
FEE PAYMENT VIA PAY.GOV

Effective July 16, 2012, the United States District Court for the Northern District of Indiana will implement notice of appeal fee payments via Pay.gov. All electronic case filers will be required to use the Pay.gov internet payment module in CM/ECF. Users will be automatically directed through the Pay.gov payment process by CM/ECF at the time the notice of appeal event is filed. Attached herewith is a list of Pay.gov filing fee events in CM/ECF (Exhibit A) and a Notice of Refund Policy of Electronic Filing Fees (Exhibit B). Further information regarding Pay.gov may be obtained on the Court's website at www.innd.uscourts.gov.

EXHIBIT A

UNITED STATES DISTRICT COURT FOR
THE NORTHERN DISTRICT OF INDIANA

PAY.GOV FILING FEE EVENTS

CIVIL	CRIMINAL
Notice of Appeal	Notice of Appeal Interlocutory
Notice of Interlocutory Appeal	Notice of Appeal—Final Judgment
Notice of Cross Appeal	Notice of Appeal—Conditions of Release

EXHIBIT B

UNITED STATES DISTRICT COURT
NORTHERN DISTRICT OF INDIANA

NOTICE OF REFUND POLICY OF ELECTRONIC FILING FEES

This Notice establishes procedures for the refunding of duplicate or erroneously paid filing fees which are generated during the electronic filing of documents. The Judicial Conference of the United States has generally prohibited the refunding of filing fees (JCUS_MAR 49). However, in March of 2005, the Judicial Conference of the United States issued guidance endorsing limited refund authority by the courts as a result of the increased likelihood of inadvertent, erroneous or duplicate payments made by parties using the Case Management/Electronic Case Files (CM/ECF) system. It further advised courts that determining appropriate policies and procedures for refunding erroneously applied filing fee payments be left to the sound discretion of each court.

The Clerk of the United States District Court for the Northern District of Indiana, or his designee, is authorized to refund all fees erroneously paid through the Pay.gov electronic filing fee tool in CM/ECF:

1. If discovered by the court or Clerk's office that a fee has been paid erroneously;

2. If an attorney files a motion for a refund and it can be determined by the Clerk or his designee that the fee has been erroneously paid.

Attorneys seeking a refund must electronically file a motion and supporting documentation must be attached, including a copy of the electronic payment receipt and the Notice(s) of Electronic Filing generated from the court's electronic case management system. The motion must include the name, address and telephone number of the party requesting the refund.

Upon order of the court, the Finance Department shall process the refund to the same credit card from which the erroneous payment was made and will forward notice of such to the Operations Department for recording to the docket. Refund checks will be issued only in the event the erroneous payment was made electronically through the ACH (Automated Clearing House) process of the Pay.gov system. Refund checks for credit card payments will not be issued.

In the event that an attorney or law firm consistently errs when submitting fees and thereby repeatedly requests refunds, the court will consider remedial action and may issue an order to show cause as to why further requests for refunds should be considered.

[Effective July 16, 2012.]

GENERAL ORDER 2015–8.   IN RE: DEPOSIT AND INVESTMENT OF REGISTRY FUNDS

Having determined that it is necessary to adopt local procedures to ensure uniformity in the deposit and investment of funds in the Court's Registry,

IT IS ORDERED that the following shall govern the receipt, deposit, and investment of registry funds:

I. Receipt of Funds.

A. No money shall be sent to the Court or its officers for deposit in the Court's registry without a court order signed by a judge in the case or proceeding.

B. The party making the deposit or transferring funds to the Court's registry shall serve the order permitting the deposit or transfer on the Clerk of Court.

C. Unless provided for elsewhere in this Order, all monies ordered to be paid to the Court or received by its officers in any case pending or adjudicated shall be deposited with the Treasurer of the United States in the name and to the credit of this Court pursuant to 28 U.S.C. § 2041 through depositories designed by the Treasury to accept such deposit on its behalf.

II. Investment of Registry Funds.

A. Where, by order of the Court, funds on deposit with the Court are to be placed in some form of interest-bearing account, or invested in a court-approved, interest-bearing instrument in accordance with Rule 67 of the Federal Rules of Civil Procedure, the Court Registry Investment System ("CRIS"), administered by the

Administrative Office of the United States Courts under 28 U.S.C. § 2045, shall be the only investment mechanism authorized.

B. The Director of Administrative Office of the United States Courts is designated as custodian for CRIS. The Director of the Director's designee shall perform the duties of custodian. Funds held in the CRIS remain subject to the control and jurisdiction of the Court.

C. Money from each case deposited in the CRIS shall be "pooled" together with those on deposit with Treasury to the credit of other courts in the CRIS and used to purchase Government Account Series securities through the Bureau of Public Debt, which will be held at Treasury, in an account in the name and to the credit of the Director of Administrative Office of the United States Courts. The pooled funds will be invested in accordance with the principals of the CRIS Investment Policy as approved by the Registry Monitoring Group.

D. An account for each case will be established in the CRIS titled in the name of the case giving rise to the investment in the fund. Income generated from fund investments will be distributed to each case based on the ratio each account's principal and earnings has to the aggregate principal and income total in the fund. Reports showing the interest earned and the principal amounts contributed in each case will be prepared and distributed to each court participating in the CRIS and made available to litigants and/or their counsel.

III. Deductions of Fees.

A. The custodian is authorized and directed by this Order to deduct the investment services fee for the management of investments in the CRIS and the registry fee for maintaining accounts deposited with the Court.

B. The investment services fee is assessed from interest earnings to the pool according to the Court's Miscellaneous Fee Schedule and is to be assessed before a pro rata distribution of earnings to court cases.

C. The registry fee is assessed by the custodian from each case's pro rata distribution of the earnings and is to be determined on the basis of the rates published by the Director of the Administrative Office of the United States Courts as approved by the Judicial Conference of the United States.

IV. Transition from Former Investment Procedure.

A. The Clerk of Court is further directed to develop a systematic method of redemption of all existing investments and their transfer to the CRIS.

B. Parties not wishing to transfer certain existing registry deposits into the CRIS may seek leave to transfer them to the litigants or their designees on proper motion and approval of the judge assigned to the specific case.

C. The Order supersedes and abrogates all prior orders of this Court regarding the deposit and investment of registry funds.

[Dated: May 28, 2015.]

AMENDED JURY SELECTION PLAN
JURY SELECTION PLAN FOR GRAND AND PETIT JURORS
DEFINITIONS

Words in this Plan which are defined in Title 28, U.S.C. § 1869 of the Act, as amended, shall have the meaning therein specified.

A. "Master Jury Wheel" or "Master Wheel" is a figurative term designating all names being randomly selected directly from official source lists in a manner described in this Plan.

B. "Qualified Jury Wheel" or "Qualified Wheel" is composed of those jurors who, based solely on the information provided on the juror qualification questionnaire, have been deemed eligible for service.

C. "Petit jury" or "petit juror" shall mean a jury or juror summoned to serve at a civil or criminal trial proceeding.

D. "Grand jury" or "grand juror" shall mean a jury or juror summoned to serve at a grand jury proceeding.

E. "Clerk" shall mean the Clerk of Court, any authorized deputy clerk, and any other person authorized by the Court to assist the Clerk in the performance of functions under this Plan.

"Juror Selection Plan" of the United States District Court for the Northern District of Indiana.

Pursuant to the Jury Selection and Service Act of 1968, as amended (28 U.S.C. § 1861 et seq), the following plan is hereby adopted by this court, subject to approval by the Reviewing Panel for the Seventh Circuit and to such rules and regulations as may be adopted from time to time by the Judicial Conference of the United States.

1. *Applicability of the Plan.* The Northern District of Indiana is divided for jury selection purposes, pursuant to § 1869(e) of the Act, as follows:

Jurors serving in the South Bend Division at South Bend shall be selected from citizens residing in that division, which is comprised of the following counties:

Cass	LaPorte	St. Joseph
Elkhart	Marshall	Starke
Fulton	Miami	Wabash
Kosciusko	Pulaski	

Jurors serving in the Hammond Division at Hammond shall be selected from citizens residing in that division, which is comprised of the following counties:

Lake	Porter

Jurors serving in the Fort Wayne Division at Fort Wayne shall be selected from citizens residing in that division, which is comprised of the following counties:

Adams	Huntington	Steuben
Allen	Jay	Wells
Blackford	LaGrange	Whitley
DeKalb	Noble	
Grant		

Jurors serving in the Hammond Division at Lafayette shall be selected from citizens residing in that division, which is comprised of the following counties:

Benton   Newton   White
Carroll   Tippecanoe
Jasper   Warren

The provisions of this plan apply to all divisions in this District unless specifically indicated to the contrary.

2. *Declaration of Policy.* It is the policy of this court that all litigants entitled to trial by jury shall have the right to grand and petit jurors selected at random from a fair cross section of the community in the District or division wherein the Court convenes and that all citizens resident within the District shall have the opportunity to be considered for service on grand and petit juries and shall have an obligation to serve as jurors when summoned for that purpose.

3. *Discrimination Prohibited.* No citizen shall be excluded from service as a grand or petit juror in this Court on account of race, color, religion, sex, national origin or economic status.

4. *Management and Supervision of the Jury Selection Process.* The Clerk of Court shall manage the jury selection process under the supervision and control of the Chief Judge.

The Clerk may use computers and other automation technologies in implementing this Plan but shall maintain a procedures manual to govern such use. The Clerk also may hire, or contract with, persons or entities to perform the duties set forth in this Plan as long as the Clerk supervises the work of such persons or entities and they certify that work has been completed pursuant to the Clerk's instructions.

5. *Jury Selection Sources.* The Judges of this Court find that the sources from which the names of grand and petit jurors shall be selected at random shall be from the general election voter registration lists. The Judges do further find that such lists represent a fair cross section of the community in this District.

Accordingly, names of grand and petit jurors serving in this Court shall be selected by random procedure from the lists, as aforementioned, of registered voters of the counties within each division and who are of record as registered voters in each presidential general election as maintained in the books or lists at the Board of Elections in each county.

This plan's references to lists of registered voters shall be to voter registration lists.

If the Court, pursuant to § 1863(b)(2), should find it necessary, it may authorize the Clerk to draw names of prospective jurors from supplementary lists in addition to voter lists. The selection of names from such lists shall be done in a manner consistent with the selection procedures described in this plan.

6. *Initial Selection of Names for the Master Jury Wheel.* The Judges of the Court find that the initial selection of persons to be considered for service as grand or petit jurors from the lists of registered voters shall be made at random in such a total number as may be deemed sufficient for a minimum of one (1) year.

The number of names drawn from each county shall be substantially in the same proportion to the total number drawn from all counties within the division as the number of names on that county's list of registered voters bears to the total number of names on the lists of registered voters for all counties within the division. For example, if there are exactly 240,000 names on the list of registered voters of all counties within the division and there are 48,000 names on county A's list (twenty percent of the total), then the number of county A's names initially selected should be substantially twenty percent of the total number selected from all counties within the division.

For the purpose of calculating the total number of registered voters in the respective divisions within the District, the Clerk will add together the totals obtained for each county. The number taken as the total for each county may be based, at the Clerk's option, upon either a manual or automated count of the names on the county's list or upon such total number as is furnished by the Election Board for the county.

After first determining the total number of names needed for the master wheel and then the proportionate share of names to be drawn from the list of registered voters for each particular county, the Clerk shall proceed through the use of a properly programmed data computer to make the initial selection of names from the list of registered voters of each county.

7. *Method and Manner of Random Selection.* The selection of names from complete source list databases in electronic media for the master jury wheel shall be accomplished by a purely randomized process. The Jury Management System (JMS), shall be used to select names from the master wheel for the purpose of determining qualification for jury service, and from the qualified wheel for summoning persons to serve as grand or petit jurors. Such random selections of names from the source list for inclusion in the master wheel by data computer personnel must ensure that each county within the jury division is substantially proportionally represented in the master jury wheel in accordance with 28 U.S.C. § 1863 (b)(3). The selections of names from the source list, the master wheel, and the qualified wheel must also ensure that the mathematical odds of any single name being picked are substantially equal.

8. *Maintaining Master Jury Wheels.* The Clerk shall maintain a master jury wheel for each of the divisions within the District. The names and addresses of all persons randomly selected from the lists of registered voters at the last presidential general election shall be placed in the master jury wheel for that division.

The physical form of record on which names for the master wheel(s) are kept may include electronic data storage. Pursuant to § 1863(b)(4) of the Act, the minimum number of names to be placed in the master jury wheel(s) shall be at least ½ of 1% of the total number of names on all county voter lists.

The senior active judge in each of the divisions of this District may order additional names to be placed in the master jury wheel for said division from time to time as may be necessary in accordance with the formula herein described. The master jury wheels currently in full force and effect shall be emptied and refilled annually between June 30 and December 31 unless the Chief Judge shall otherwise direct.

9. *Drawing of Names from the Master Jury Wheels and Completion of Juror Qualification Forms.* The Clerk, either all at one time or at periodic intervals, shall draw at random from the master jury wheels the names of as many persons as may be required to maintain an adequate number of names in the qualified jury wheels. The number of names to be drawn shall be determined by the Clerk based upon anticipated juror demands by the Court plus a margin of extra names sufficient to compensate for the estimated number that will turn out to be unavailable or ineligible.

The Clerk may have prepared, by manual or computer means, alphabetized lists of names drawn. These lists shall not be exhibited to any person except as provided herein and in § 1867 and § 1868 of the Act, as amended. The Clerk shall, by manual or computer means, prepare and have mailed to every person whose name is so drawn a juror qualification questionnaire form accompanied by instructions to execute and return the questionnaire, duly signed and sworn, to the Clerk by mail, or through the Court's internet website, within ten (10) days, in accordance with § 1864(a) of the Act, as amended.

10. *Excuses on Individual Request.* The Judges of this Court hereby find that jury service by members of certain occupational classes or groups of persons would entail undue hardship or extreme inconvenience to members thereof and the excuse of such members will not be inconsistent with the Act. Accordingly, the Clerk, under supervision of the court, shall grant excuses pursuant to 28 U.S.C. § 1863(b)(5) upon individual request to:

(a) persons over 70 years of age;

(b) persons who have, within the past two years, served on a federal grand or petit jury panel;

(c) persons having active care and custody of a child or children under twelve years of age whose health and/or safety would be jeopardized by their absence for jury service, or a person who is essential to the care of aged or infirm persons;

(d) any person whose services are so essential to the operation of a business, commercial, or agricultural enterprise that said enterprise must close if such person were required to perform jury duty;

(e) volunteer safety personnel. Such personnel are defined as those who serve a public agency in an official capacity, without compensation, as firefighters or members of a rescue squad or ambulance crew.

The Clerk, under the supervision of the court, may grant excuses of a temporary or permanent nature only to persons for whom jury service would constitute an undue hardship or extreme inconvenience at the time the jurors are summoned for jury service on a case by case basis. Such excuses shall be limited to such a period as the hardship or inconvenience dictates, and the excuse of such members will not be inconsistent with the Act. Examples are as follows:

(a) a person who lives a great distance from the place of holding court;

(b) a person whose illness or in whose family there is grave illness or other emergency which outweighs in immediacy and urgency the obligation to serve as a juror when summoned;

(c) in situations where it is anticipated that a trial or grand jury proceeding may require more than thirty days of service, a person who is a key employee during the period of such service and whose absence from work for such time would result in severe economic hardship to his employer;

(d) a person who has established business or recreational travel plans before the receipt of the summons for jury service.

11. *Exemption from Jury Service.* Only those persons who are exempt from jury service under the provisions of § 1863(b)(6) of the Act, as amended, shall be exempt, and thus barred, from jury service under this plan:

(a) members of the Armed Forces on active duty, defined in 10 U.S.C. § 101(a)(4) as including only the Army, Navy, Air Force, Marine Corps and Coast Guard;

(b) members of professional fire and police departments of any State, the District of Columbia, any territory or possession of the United States, or any subdivision of a State, the District of Columbia, or such territory or possession; and

(c) "Public officers" of the United States, State or local governments, who are actively engaged in the performance of public duties. A public officer is a person who is either elected to public office or who is directly appointed by a person elected to public office—in the executive, legislative, or judicial branches of the Government of the United States, or of any State, the District of Columbia, any territory or possession of the United States, or any subdivision of a State, the District of Columbia, or such territory or possession, who are actively engaged in the performance of official duties. 28 U.S.C. § 1869(*l*).

(Note: As a result of the Judicial Improvements and Access to Justice Act of 1988, courts can no longer exempt other classes of persons from jury service except those listed above. Prospective jurors who are found to be exempt are barred from jury service and may not serve even if they indicate a desire to do so.)

12. *Qualifications for Jury Service.* The presiding Judges in each division, upon the Clerk's recommendation, or the clerk under supervision of the court, shall determine solely on the basis of the information provided on the juror qualification

questionnaire, and other competent evidence, whether a person is unqualified for or exempt or to be excused from jury service.

In making such determination, the District Judge or the Clerk shall deem any person qualified to serve on grand or petit juries in this District unless the person:

(a) is not a citizen of the United States, eighteen (18) years of age or older, who has resided for a period of at least one year within this Judicial District;

(b) is unable to read, write and understand the English language with a degree of proficiency sufficient to fill out satisfactorily the juror qualification form;

(c) is unable to speak the English language;

(d) is unable, by reason of mental or physical infirmity to render satisfactory jury service; or

(e) has a charge pending against him for the commission of, or has been convicted in a State or Federal court of, a crime punishable by imprisonment for more than one year and his civil rights have not been restored.

13. *Qualified Jury Wheel.* The Clerk shall maintain separate qualified jury wheels for each division and shall place in such wheels the names of all persons drawn from the master jury wheel and not disqualified, exempt, or excused pursuant to this plan. The Clerk shall ensure that at all times an adequate number of names are contained in each such jury wheel.

Unless otherwise ordered by the Court, names drawn from the qualified jury wheel shall not be made a part of the Court's public record, neither in paper nor electronic format. A request for disclosure of juror names to the media or public may be made of the judge to whom the case is assigned. The Clerk shall not release juror names to the media or public unless specifically authorized by the assigned judge.

As grand juries are required in the Fort Wayne Division, the clerk shall select, at random, prospective grand jurors from the qualified wheel of the statutory Fort Wayne Division which consists of the following counties:

Adams	Grant	Noble
Allen	Huntington	Steuben
Blackford	Jay	Wells
DeKalb	LaGrange	Whitley

As grand juries are required in the South Bend Division, the clerk shall select, at random, prospective grand jurors from the qualified wheel of the statutory South Bend Division which consists of the following counties:

Cass	LaPorte	St. Joseph
Elkhart	Marshall	Starke
Fulton	Miami	Wabash
Kosciusko	Pulaski	

As grand juries are required in the Hammond Division or the Hammond Division at Lafayette, the clerk shall select, at random a proportional number of prospective grand jurors from the qualified wheels of both divisions of the statutory Hammond Division which consist of the following counties:

Benton	Lake	Tippecanoe
Carroll	Newton	Warren
Jasper	Porter	White

Upon motion of the United States Attorney's Office and when determined by the court to be appropriate, a grand jury sitting in any division may be selected from the entire district. In such case, the clerk will draw at random from the qualified wheel of each division such number of prospective grand jurors as may be required in the same ratio that the number of registered voters in each division bears to the total number of registered voters in the district.

Names of grand jurors shall not be disclosed at any time, except by order by the court.

The court's data processing center will prepare an alphabetical list of persons summoned. These lists shall not be exhibited to any person except as provided herein and in § 1867 and § 1868 of the Act, as amended.

Summons forms, at the option of the Clerk of Court, may be mailed to jurors by the Clerk's office, by the court's data processing center, or by a commercial mailing service.

14. *Public Announcement of the Month, Day and Year of Automated Selection of Names by Court's Data Processing Center.* Drawings of names of prospective jurors by automated selection methods shall be made at the court's designated data processing center. Drawings shall be announced in a public place such as the court's website.

The office of the Clerk of Court shall retain the court's Jury Selection Plan and provide public access to the Plan.

15. *Impaneling Jurors.* Names of persons summoned and/or appearing for service may be inserted in a panel assignment wheel, from which separate trial panels will be selected by lot. The Clerk shall prepare for the use of the court and counsel a separate list of names of persons assigned to each petit jury panel.

On the day of trial, the names of persons impaneled for that trial drawn from the qualified jury wheel shall be made public, provided that any District Judge, in a case or cases where the interests of justice so require, may order that the names be kept confidential until the time of voir dire examination.

16. *Frequency of Service.* In any two-year period, no person shall be required to (1) serve or attend court for prospective service as a petit juror for a total of more than thirty (30) days except when necessary to complete service in a particular case, (2) serve more than one grand jury, or (3) serve as both a grand and petit juror.

17. *Penalty for Failure to Appear for Jury Summons 28 U.S.C. § 1864.* If any person fails to return a completed juror qualification form as instructed, the Clerk shall thereupon pursue the matters each and all in accordance with the provisions of § 1864 of the Act, as amended.

18. *Supplemental Attendance Fee for Petit Jurors Serving on Lengthy Trials 28 U.S.C. § 1871(b)(2).* The Court finds a petit juror required to attend more than ten (10) days in hearing one case shall be paid an additional attendance fee of $10 for each day in excess of ten (10) days on which the juror is required to hear such case.

19. *Penalty for Employers who Retaliate Against Employees Serving on Jury Duty 28 U.S.C. § 1875.* No employer shall discharge, threaten to discharge, intimidate, or coerce any permanent employee by reason of such employee's jury service, or the attendance or scheduled attendance in connection with such service, in any court of the United States. Any employer who violates the provisions of this section shall be subject to a civil penalty of not more that $5,000 for each violation as to each employee, and may be ordered to perform community service.

20. *Maintenance of Records.* After the master jury wheel is emptied and refilled pursuant to this Plan and after all persons selected to serve as jurors before the master wheel was emptied have completed service, the records and papers compiled and maintained by the Clerk with regard to the emptied master jury wheel, shall be preserved in the custody of the Clerk for four (4) years in accordance with 28 U.S.C. § 1868.

21. *Effective Date.* This amended jury selection plan shall become effective upon such date after approval by the Reviewing Panel (Judicial Council of the Seventh Circuit), as the Panel shall direct, and if no such specific date is designated by the

Panel, this plan shall become effective upon the date of its approval by the Panel. 28 U.S.C. § 1863(a).

The above final plan was adopted by the Court on October 31, 2014 pursuant to 28 U.S.C. § 1863(a) and approved by the reviewing panel on December 4, 2014, pursuant to 28 U.S.C. § 1863(a). This plan shall become effective December 4, 2014, and shall remain in effect thereafter until superseded or amended.

[Adopted February 15, 2012, effective July 16, 2012. Amended effective December 4, 2014.]

CRIMINAL JUSTICE ACT PLAN

I. AUTHORITY

Pursuant to the Criminal Justice Act of 1964 (CJA), as amended, Section 3006A of Title 18, United States Code, and the *Guidelines for the Administration of the Criminal Justice Act and Related Statutes (CJA Guidelines)*, Volume VII, *Guide to Judiciary Policies and Procedures*, the judges of the United States District court for the Northern District of Indiana adopt this Plan for furnishing representation in federal court for any person financially unable to obtain adequate representation in accordance with the CJA.

II. STATEMENT OF POLICY

A. Objectives.

1. The objective of this Plan is to attain the ideal of equality before the law for all persons. Therefore, this Plan shall be administered so that those accused of crime, or otherwise eligible for services pursuant to the CJA, will not be deprived, because they are financially unable to pay for adequate representation, of any element of representation necessary to an adequate defense.

2. The further objective of this Plan is to particularize the requirements of the CJA, the Anti–Drug Abuse Act of 1988 (codified in part at Section 3599 of Title 18, United States Code), and the *CJA Guidelines* in a way that meets the needs of this district.

B. Compliance.

1. The court, its clerk, the federal community defender organization, and private attorneys appointed under the CJA, shall comply with the *CJA Guidelines* approved by the Judicial Conference of the United States and/or its Committee on Defender Services and with this Plan.

2. Each private attorney shall be provided by the federal community defender with a then-current copy of this Plan upon the attorney's first appointment under the CJA or designation as a member of the panel of private attorneys under the Criminal Justice Act (CJA panel). The federal community defender shall also maintain a current copy of the *CJA Guidelines* for the use of members of the CJA panel and shall make known to such attorneys its availability. The clerk shall maintain a copy of the CJA plan and the *CJA Guidelines* online at the District Court's website at (http://www.innd.uscourts.gov).

III. DEFINITIONS

A. "Representation" includes counsel and investigative, expert and other services.

B. "Appointed attorney" includes private attorneys and the executive director (federal defender) and staff attorneys of the federal defender organization recognized under paragraph V of this Plan.

IV. PROVISION OF REPRESENTATION

A. Circumstances.

1. *Mandatory.* Representation shall be provided for any financially eligible person who:

    a. is charged with a felony or with a Class A misdemeanor;

b.   is a juvenile alleged to have committed an act of juvenile delinquency as defined in Section 5031 of Title 18, United States Code;

c.   is charged with a violation of probation, or faces a change of a term or condition of probation (unless the modification sought is favorable to the probationer and the government has not objected to the proposed change);

d.   is under arrest, when such representation is required by law;

e.   is entitled to appointment of counsel in parole proceedings;

f.   is charged with a violation of supervised release or faces modification, reduction, or enlargement of a condition, or extension or revocation of a term of supervised release;

g.   is subject to a mental condition hearing under Chapter 313 of Title 18, United States Code;

h.   is in custody as a material witness;

i.   is seeking to set aside or vacate a death sentence under Sections 2254 or 2255 of Title 28, United States Code;

j.   is entitled to appointment of counsel in verification of consent proceedings pursuant to a transfer of an offender to or from the United States for the execution of a penal sentence under Section 4109 of Title 18, United States Code;

k.   is entitled to appointment of counsel under the Sixth Amendment to the Constitution; or

l.   faces loss of liberty in a case and federal law requires the appointment of counsel.

2.   *Discretionary.*   Whenever a district court judge or magistrate judge determines that the interests of justice so require, representation <u>may</u> be provided for any financially eligible person who:

a.   is charged with a petty offense (Class B or C misdemeanor, or an infraction) for which a sentence to confinement is authorized;

b.   is seeking relief, other than to set aside or vacate a death sentence under Sections 2241, 2254, or 2255 of Title 28, United States Code;

c.   is charged with civil or criminal contempt and faces loss of liberty;

d.   has been called as a witness before a grand jury, a court, the Congress, or a federal agency or commission which has the power to compel testimony, and there is reason to believe, either prior to or during testimony, that the witness could be subject to a criminal prosecution, a civil or criminal contempt proceeding, or face loss of liberty;

e.   is proposed by the United States Attorney for processing under a pretrial diversion program;

f.   is held for international extradition under Chapter 209 of Title 18, United States Code.

Representation may also be furnished for financially eligible persons in ancillary matters appropriate to the proceedings pursuant to subsection (c) of the CJA.

B.   When Counsel Shall Be Provided.   Counsel shall be provided to eligible persons as soon as feasible after they are taken into custody, when they appear before a district court judge or magistrate judge, when they are formally charged or notified of charges if formal charges are sealed, or when a district court judge or magistrate judge otherwise considers appointment of counsel appropriate under the CJA, whichever occurs earliest.

C.   Number and Qualifications of Counsel.

1.   *Number.*   More than one attorney may be appointed in any case determined by the court to be extremely difficult.   In a capital case, the following applies:

a. Federal Capital Prosecutions. Pursuant to 18 U.S.C. § 3005, a person charged with a federal capital offense is entitled to the appointment of two attorneys, at least one of whom shall be learned in the law applicable to capital cases. Pursuant to 18 U.S.C. § 3599(a), if necessary for adequate representation, more than two attorneys may be appointed to represent a defendant in such a case.

b. Habeas Corpus Proceedings. Pursuant to 18 U.S.C. § 3599(a), a financially eligible person seeking to vacate or set aside a death sentence in proceedings under 28 U.S.C. § 2254 or 2255 is entitled to appointment of one or more qualified attorneys. Due to the complex, demanding, and protracted nature of death penalty proceedings, judicial officers should consider appointing at least two counsel.

2. *Qualifications.* Qualifications for appointed counsel shall be determined by the court. In capital cases, the following also applies:

a. Appointment of Counsel Prior to Judgment. Pursuant to 18 U.S.C. § 3599(b), at least one of the attorneys appointed must have been admitted to practice in the court in which the case will be prosecuted for not less than five years, and must have had not less than three years experience in the actual trial of felony prosecutions in that court. Pursuant to 18 U.S.C. § 3005, at least one of the attorneys appointed must be knowledgeable in the law applicable to capital cases.

Pursuant to 18 U.S.C. § 3005, in appointing counsel in federal capital prosecutions, the court shall consider the recommendation of the federal community defender.

b. Appointment of Counsel After Judgment. Pursuant to 18 U.S.C. § 3599(c), at least one of the attorneys appointed must have been admitted to practice in the court of appeals for not less than five years, and must have had not less than three years experience in the handling of appeals in felony cases in the court.

c. Attorney Qualification Waiver. Pursuant to 18 U.S.C. § 3599(d), the presiding judicial officer, for good cause, may appoint an attorney who may not qualify under 18 U.S.C. § 3599(b) or (c), but who has the background, knowledge, and experience necessary to represent the defendant properly in a capital case, giving due consideration to the seriousness of the possible penalty and the unique and complex nature of the litigation.

D. Eligibility for Representation.

1. *Fact-finding.* The determination of eligibility for representation under the CJA is a judicial function to be performed by a district court judge or magistrate judge after making appropriate inquiries concerning the person's financial condition.

2. *Disclosure of Change in Eligibility.* If, at any time after appointment, counsel obtains information that a client is financially able to make payment, in whole or in part, for legal or other services in connection with his or her representation, and the source of the attorney's information is not protected as a privileged communication, counsel shall advise the court.

V. FEDERAL DEFENDER ORGANIZATION

A. Recognition of Existing Organization. The Northern District of Indiana Federal Community Defenders, Inc., previously established in this district pursuant to the provisions of the CJA, is hereby recognized as the federal defender organization for this district.

B. Supervision of Defender Organization. The federal community defender shall be responsible for the supervision and management of the federal defender organization. Accordingly, the federal community defender shall be responsible for the assignment of cases to staff attorneys at the discretion of the federal defender.

C. Management of the Panel. The Federal Defender Office shall also be responsible for the systematic distribution of cases to and for the CJA Panel subject to the provisions of the Plan for the Composition, Administration, and Management of the Panel of Private Attorneys under the Criminal Justice Act, found in the Appendix of this CJA Plan.

VI. PRIVATE ATTORNEYS

A. Establishment of CJA Panel. The existing, previously established panel of attorneys (CJA panel) who are eligible and willing to be appointed to provide representation under the CJA is hereby recognized.

B. Organization. The Plan for the Composition, Administration, and Management of the Panel of Private Attorneys under the Criminal Justice Act is found in the Appendix of this CJA Plan.

C. Ratio of Appointments. Where practical and cost effective, private attorneys from the CJA Panel shall be appointed in a substantial proportion of the cases in which the accused is determined to be financially eligible for representation under the CJA. "Substantial" shall usually be defined as at least 25% of the appointments under the CJA annually throughout the district.

VII. REPRESENTATION IN STATE DEATH PENALTY HABEAS CORPUS PROCEEDINGS UNDER 28 U.S.C. § 2254

The court shall appoint a member or members of the Special Death Penalty Habeas Corpus Panel, or the federal defender with his or her consent, or a qualified attorney recommended by the federal defender, or other attorney who qualifies for appointment pursuant to Section 3599 of Title 18, United States Code to represent financially eligible persons seeking habeas corpus relief in state death penalty proceedings under Section 2254 of Title 28, United States Code.

VIII. DUTIES OF APPOINTED COUNSEL

A. Standards. The services to be rendered a person represented by appointed counsel shall be commensurate with those rendered if counsel were privately employed by the person.

B. Professional Conduct. Attorneys appointed pursuant to the CJA shall conform to the highest standards of professional conduct, including, but not limited to, the provisions of Local Rule 83.5(f).

C. No Receipt of Other Payment. Appointed counsel may not require, request, or accept any payment or promise of payment or any other valuable consideration for representation under the appointment, unless such payment is approved by order of the court.

D. Continuing Representation. Once counsel is appointed under the CJA, counsel shall continue the representation until the matter, including appeals or review by certiorari (as governed by the circuit CJA plan provisions concerning representation on appeal), is closed; until substitute counsel has filed a notice of appearance; until an order has been entered allowing or requiring the person represented to proceed pro se; or until the appointment is terminated by court order.

IX. [Reserved]

X. MISCELLANEOUS

A. Forms. Standard forms, pertaining to the CJA and approved by the Judicial Conference of the United States or its Committee on Defender Services, and prescribed and distributed by the Director of the Administrative Office of the United States Courts, shall be used, where applicable, in all proceedings under this Plan.

B. Claims. Claims for compensation of private attorneys providing representation under the CJA and the claims of experts hired by those attorneys pursuant to CJA Forms 20, 21, 30, & 31 shall be submitted to the Federal Community Defenders, 31 East Sibley Street, Hammond, Indiana 46320. The federal community defender shall review the claim forms in a timely manner for mathematical and technical accuracy, reasonableness, and for conformity with the *CJA Guidelines*. If correct, the federal community defender shall forward the claim forms for the timely consideration of the appropriate district court judge or magistrate judge. CJA Form 24 (transcript requests) claims shall be submitted directly to the Financial Office in the Clerk's Office located in the South Bend Division for direct processing.

C. Supersession. This Plan supersedes all prior Criminal Justice Act Plans of this court.

XI. EFFECTIVE DATE

This Plan shall become effective when approved by the Judicial Council of the Seventh Circuit.

APPENDIX

PLAN FOR THE COMPOSITION, ADMINISTRATION AND MANAGEMENT OF THE PANEL OF PRIVATE ATTORNEYS UNDER THE CRIMINAL JUSTICE ACT

I. COMPOSITION OF PANEL OF PRIVATE ATTORNEYS

A. CJA Panel.

1. *Approval.* The district court judges in each division of this district (excepting the Lafayette Division) shall establish a panel of private attorneys (hereinafter referred to as the "CJA panel") who are eligible and willing to be appointed to provide representation under the Criminal Justice Act in that division. The district court judges of the divisions shall approve attorneys for membership on the CJA panel after receiving recommendations from the CJA panel selection committee, of the division established pursuant to paragraph B of this Plan. Members of the CJA panel shall serve at the pleasure of the judges.

2. *Size.* The district court judges in each division shall fix, periodically, the size of the CJA panel for that division. Each division's CJA panel shall be large enough to provide a sufficient number of experienced attorneys to handle the CJA caseload in the division, yet small enough so that panel members will receive an adequate number of appointments to maintain their proficiency in federal criminal defense work, and thereby provide a high quality of representation.

3. *Eligibility.* Attorneys who serve on the CJA panel must be members in good standing of the federal bar of this district, and have demonstrated experience in, and knowledge of, the Federal Rules of Criminal Procedure, the Federal Rules of Evidence, and the Sentencing Guidelines.

Subsection (b) of the Act provides, in part, that:

Counsel furnishing representation under the plan shall be selected from a panel of attorneys designated or approved by the court, or from a bar association, legal aid agency, or defender organization furnishing representation pursuant to the plan.

Counsel furnishing representation under the plan shall be selected from a panel of attorneys designated or approved by the court, or from a bar association, legal aid agency, or defender organization furnishing representation pursuant to the plan.

However, when the district court judge presiding over the case, or the chief judge if a district court judge has not yet been assigned to the case, determines that the appointment of an attorney, who is not a member of the CJA panel, is in the interest of justice, judicial economy or continuity of representation, or there is some other compelling circumstance warranting his or her appointment, the attorney may be admitted to the CJA panel pro hac vice and appointed to represent the CJA defendant. Consideration for preserving the integrity of the panel selection process suggests that such appointments should be made only in exceptional circumstances. Further, the attorney, who may or may not maintain an office in the district, should possess such qualities as would qualify him or her for admission to the district's CJA panel in the ordinary course of panel selection.

4. *Equal Opportunity.* All qualified attorneys shall be encouraged to participate in the furnishing of representation in CJA cases, without regard to race, color, religion, sex, age, national origin or disabling condition.

5. *Terms.* Attorneys admitted to membership on the CJA panel will each serve for a term of three years. A member of the CJA panel may be removed from the panel at the member's request or by a majority vote of the district court judges after consultation with the CJA panel selection committee.

6. *Application Process.* Any attorney wishing to apply for consideration to the CJA panel should submit his/her resume to the Federal Defender Office, 31 East Sibley, Hammond, Indiana 46320. Upon receipt of all resumes, the Federal Defender Office shall submit said resumes to the CJA panel selection committee in each division prior to the annual meeting of the CJA panel selection committee.

B. CJA Panel Selection Committee.

1. *Membership.* A CJA panel selection committee shall be established by the district court judges in each division. The committee shall consist of the magistrate judge(s) of the division, one current member of the CJA panel from the division, and the federal defender. The committee shall be chaired by the magistrate judge.

2. *Duties.*

a. The CJA panel selection committee in each division shall meet at least once per year to consider applications for any vacancies on the panel. The committee shall review the qualifications of applicants and the performance of current members wishing to remain on the panel for another term, and recommend, for approval by the district court judges in the division, those applicants best qualified to fill the vacancies.

b. At its annual meeting, the committee shall also review the operation and administration of the panel over the preceding year, and recommend to the district court judges any changes deemed necessary or appropriate by the committee regarding the appointment process and panel management. The committee shall also inquire annually as to the continued availability and willingness of each panel member to accept appointments.

c. If, at any time during the course of a year, the number of vacancies due to resignation, removal, or death significantly decreases the size of the CJA panel, the CJA panel selection committee shall solicit applications for the vacancies, convene a special meeting to review the qualifications of the applicants, and select prospective members for recommendation to the judges for approval. Members approved by the judges to fill mid-term vacancies shall serve until the expiration of the term that was vacated.

d. When the committee submits the names of applicants for panel membership to the district court judges for approval, the committee shall furnish information regarding the recruitment efforts undertaken by the committee in furtherance of the Equal Opportunity statement in Paragraph I.A. 4 of this plan. At least once each year, the CJA panel selection committee shall provide the judges with information on the CJA panel in each of the categories listed in paragraph I.A.4. of this Plan.

f.* A CJA panel selection committee may choose to meet at any time to consider matters relating to the composition of the division's CJA panel and make recommendations concerning the same to the judges.

II. CJA TRAINING PANEL

The district court judges, in conjunction with the federal community defender, will oversee a pilot program wherein attorneys who do not have the requisite experience for membership on the regular CJA panel (see 18 U.S.C. § 3006A; *Guide*, Volume 7) will be eligible to assist members of the CJA panel in a "second chair" capacity in order to gain the necessary experience required to provide high quality representation to defendants in federal court cases.

A. Administration of the CJA Training Program. Management of the CJA Training Panel program will be centralized at the Federal Defender Office located at 31 East Sibley Street, Hammond, Indiana, 46320. The Federal Defender Office, with the help of the CJA panel members, will provide each CJA training panel member with individual training and supervision.

B. Training Panel Membership.

1. *Approval.* The district court judges, after considering the recommendation of the CJA panel selection committee, will appoint the members of the CJA training panel who will serve at the pleasure of the district court judges.

2. *Size of Training Panel.* The size of the CJA training panel will be no greater than, but may be less than, five members for each division.

3. *Eligibility.* Attorneys serving on the CJA training panel will be in good standing of the federal bar of this district. Each member should demonstrate a strong interest in providing criminal defense services for the indigent.

CJA training panel members will be expected to keep current with developments in federal criminal defense law, practice and procedure. Members will be expected to attend the CLE seminars (training sessions designated to keep members of the CJA panel current with criminal defense practice in the district) which are sponsored by the federal community defender.

4. *Recruitment.* Resumes for the CJA training panel should be submitted to and maintained by the Federal Defender Office. All qualified attorneys are encouraged to apply without regard to race, color, religion, gender, sexual orientation, age, national origin or disabling condition.

5. *The Selection Process.* The responsibility for reviewing resumes and making recommendations to the district court judges regarding the CJA training panel membership will reside with the CJA panel selection committee for each division.

6. *Terms.* Each member of the CJA training panel program will serve on the training panel for a period of three years. At the expiration of said term, the CJA panel selection committee for each division will make a recommendation to the district court judges as to whether the training member should remain on the training panel for further educational experience. Service on the CJA training panel will not guarantee a member admission to the CJA panel program. However, CJA training panel members may be considered for admission if an opening arises and the district court judges approve after considering the recommendations of the Committee.

7. *Removal.* Members of the CJA training panel may be removed from the training program at any time. The decision to remove a member will rest exclusively with the district court judges after receiving a recommendation from the Committee.

C. Assignment of Cases.

1. *Appointment Procedures.* Upon receipt of a new case and after a CJA panel member or an attorney from the Federal Defender Office has been assigned to a case, the Federal Defender Office will review the case and decide if a CJA training panel member should be appointed in a second chair capacity. If the Federal Defender Office has been appointed, the CJA training panel member will be assigned to assist an attorney in the Federal Defender Office. If a CJA panel member has been appointed, the Federal Defender Office will contact the appointed CJA panel member and inquire if he/she is willing to allow a CJA training panel member to assist with his/her case. After the "lead" attorney has consented, the Federal Defender Office will provide the CJA training panel member with the pertinent information about the case, as well as information regarding the "lead" attorney (federal defender or CJA panel member), i.e., name, address, phone and fax numbers, etc.

2. A CJA training panel member will not enter his/her appearance in any criminal case nor appear in court without the lead attorney.

D. Compensation and Expenses of Appointed Counsel.

1. *Hourly Rates.* Compensation to be paid to CJA training panel members will not exceed $23.00 per hour for both in court and out of court services.

2. *Expenses.* The only reimbursable expenses allowed by a CJA training panel member are travel related expenses, such as mileage and toll related expenses. Travel expenses will be reimbursed at the current mileage rate prescribed for federal judiciary employees at the time of the claim. Any expenses incurred relative to "toll expenses" must be accompanied by receipts (when available at the toll booths) when billed.

Any other expenses, such as expenses associated with experts of any kind, investigators, reproduction of transcripts/briefs, computer-assisted legal research, filing fees, etc. shall not be reimbursable to any CJA training panel member. Rather, it will be the responsibility of the "lead" attorney to bear these expenses and seek reimbursement when appropriate as described in pertinent portions of the *Guide to Judiciary Policies and Procedures* (See Chapter II, Part C—Compensation and Expenses of Appointed Counsel and Chapter III, Parts A & B—Authorization and Payment for Investigative, Expert or Other Services).

3. *Source of Payment.* All services rendered by CJA training panel members, including fees and travel related expenses, will be paid from the District Court's Library Fund. The clerk's office will track and send out any IRS 1099's in the event a trainee exceeds $600.00 in attendance and preparation fees.

4. *PACER.* CJA training panel members will be eligible to receive, free of charge, PACER services in CJA related matters. In order to take advantage of this service, the CJA training panel member will need to access the PACER website at: http://pacer.psc.uscourts.gov and complete the online registration form. CJA training panel members should, under "Firm Name," type in his/her name followed by **"CJA Panel Attorney."** Once the registration has been submitted, the CJA training panel member will receive his/her own ID number and password directly from PACER. CJA training panel members should be aware, however, that PACER services are monitored and that the use of the free service is for CJA related matters only. Any CJA training panel member who wishes to use PACER for non-related CJA matters must register under his/her own name and obtain a different account number.

5. *Forms to Be Used.* The forms and worksheets for compensation and reimbursement of travel expenses shall be submitted on documents prepared by the Federal Defender Office. CJA training panel members may obtain the appropriate forms and worksheets from the Federal Defender Office.

6. *Instructions for Use of Forms/Submission for Payment.*

a. A form entitled *"CJA Training Form"* will be generated by the Federal Defender Officer after a CJA training panel member has been assigned to a case. Once the *"CJA Training Form"* has been generated and signed by the federal defender, it will then be sent to the CJA training panel member who will retain the form until the case has been completed.

b. Upon final disposition of the case, the CJA training panel member will complete the *"CJA Training Form,"* and attach any required *"In Court, Out of Court and Travel Expense Worksheets"*. After completing the worksheets, the CJA training panel member will be required to send all documents relating to the claim to the "lead" attorney for his/her review and signature on the *CJA Training Form* (Line 22) and the *In Court, Out of Court, and Travel Expenses Worksheets* (at the top of each page). After the "lead" attorney has reviewed and signed the form and worksheets for accuracy, he/she will forward the properly executed forms to the Federal Defender Office with the lead CJA's voucher. NOTE: The CJA Training Voucher MUST be routed together with the lead CJA voucher to the Federal Defender Office for payment consideration.

c. When the Federal Defender Office receives the above-mentioned forms/worksheets, the federal defender will review same for mathematical errors and accuracy. If changes need to be made, the federal defender will make the necessary changes, contact the CJA training panel member and/or the "lead" attorney for clarification, if necessary, and then advise the CJA training panel member of any changes. Thereafter, a "CJA Training Voucher Review Form" will be generated, approved, and signed by the federal defender. All documents relating to the claim will be forwarded to the respective district court judge or magistrate judge for final approval.

d. After the district court judge or magistrate judge receives the *"CJA Training Voucher Review Form"* (with all necessary attachments), he/she will review same and either approve or deny final payment. If payment is approved, the district court judge or magistrate judge will sign the *"CJA Training Form— Appointment and Authority to Pay Training Attorney"* form in the appropriate space. Thereafter, the district court judge or magistrate judge will have the form (with attachments) sent to the Financial Office of the United States District Court, 204 South Main Street, South Bend, Indiana 46601, for payment.

If payment is approved, the clerk's office will send the CJA training panel member's check directly to the trainee. If payment is denied, the district court judge or magistrate judge will advise the CJA training panel member, as well as the federal defender, via phone or letter. If payment is denied due to a technical error, the Federal Defender Office will coordinate a resubmission of the claim.

7. *Time Limits.* The *"CJA Training Form—Appointment and Authority to Pay Training Attorney"* shall be submitted to the Federal Defender Office together with the lead CJA's voucher.

8. *Case Compensation Maximums.* CJA training panel members should adhere to the following case compensation maximums for each case to which he/she is assigned:

Felonies	– $3,500.00 (trial level)
Misdemeanors (Including petty offenses Class B or C misdemeanors or infractions)	– $1,000.00 (trial level)
Supervised Release	– $ 750.00
Proceedings under Sec. 4107 or 4108 or Title 18, U.S.C. proceeding (for counsel & guardians ad litem providing services in connection with prisoner transfer proceedings)	– $1,000.00 (for each

Pre–Trial Diversion — $3,500.00 (if offense alleged by US Attorney is a felony) $1,000.00 (if offense alleged by US Attorney is a misdemeanor)

Proceedings under Sec. 983 of Title 18, U.S.C. (for services provided by counsel appointed under 18 U.S.C. 983(b)(1) in connection with certain judicial civil forfeiture proceedings) — $3,500.00 (trial level)

Non-capital Post–Conviction Proceedings under Sec. 2241, 2254, or 2255 of Title 18, U.S.C. — $3,500.00 (trial level)

Proceedings to Protect Federal Jurors Employment under Sec. 1875 of Title 28 U.S.C. — $3,500.00 (trial level)

Other Representations (required or authorized by the CJA) — $ 750.00 (trial level)

"Other Representations" includes:

   a.   Probation Violation

   b.   Supervised Release Hearing

   c.   Parole Proceedings under Chapter 311 of Title 18 U.S.C.

   d.   Material Witness in Custody

   e.   Mental Condition Hearings Pursuant to Chapter 313 or Title 18 U.S.C. (with the exception of hearings pursuant to Sections 4241 and 4244 of Title 18, U.S.C., which are considered part of the case in chief with no separate compensation maximums applying.)

   f.   Civil or Criminal Contempt (where the person faces loss of liberty)

   g.   Witness (before a grand jury, a court, the Congress, or a federal agency or commission which has the power to compel testimony, where there is a reason to believe either prior to or during testimony, that the witness could be subject to a criminal prosecution, a civil or criminal contempt proceeding, or face loss of liberty.)

   h.   International Extradition (under Chapter 209 of Title 18, U.S.C.)

   i.   Ancillary Matters (representation in ancillary matters shall be compensable as part of the representation in the principal matter for which counsel has been appointed, and shall not be considered a separate appointment for which a separate compensation maximum would apply.

9. *Waiving Case Compensation Maximums.* Unlike a CJA panel member, a CJA training panel member will not be eligible for excess payments beyond the case compensation maximum as set out above.

10. *Record Keeping.* Appointed CJA training panel members must maintain contemporaneous time and attendance records for all work performed. Such records, which may be subject to audit, must be retained for three years after approval of the final voucher for an appointment.

III. SELECTION FOR APPOINTMENT

A. Maintenance of List and Distribution of Appointments. The clerk, with the assistance of the Federal Defender Office, shall maintain a current list of all attorneys included on the CJA panel, with current office addresses and telephone numbers, as well as a statement of qualifications and experience. The clerk shall furnish a copy of this list to each district court judge and magistrate judge.

B. Method of Selection. After a district court judge or a magistrate judge determines that a defendant qualifies for CJA legal services and grants the defendant's request for the appointment of counsel, the Federal Defender Office shall assign appointed counsel from the list of CJA panel attorneys on a rotational basis, subject to the nature and complexity of the case, the attorney's experience and general reputation in the legal community, and geographical considerations.

Upon determination of a need for the appointment of counsel, the district court judge or magistrate judge shall notify the Federal Defender Office of the appointment of counsel and the nature of the case. After the Federal Defender Office has assigned appointed counsel from the list of CJA panel attorneys, the clerk will be notified, via phone and/or e-mail, of such appointment. The clerk shall then make the appropriate entries on the court docket regarding said appointment.

The Federal Defender Office shall monitor the status of distribution of cases between the Federal Defender Office and the CJA panel. In the event of an emergency, i.e., weekends, holidays, or other non-working hours of the Federal Defender Office, the presiding judge or magistrate judge may directly appoint any CJA panel member. In all cases where members of the CJA panel are appointed out of sequence directly by the district court judge or magistrate judge, the appointing judge or magistrate judge shall notify the Federal Defender Office as to the name of the CJA panel member appointed and the date of the appointment.

IV. COMPENSATION—FILING OF VOUCHERS

Claims for compensation on CJA Forms 20, 21, 30 & 31 shall be submitted to the Federal Defender Office, who will review the claim form for mathematical and technical accuracy and for conformity with the Guidelines for the Administration of the Criminal Justice Act (Volume VII, *Guide to Judiciary Policies and Procedures*) and, if correct, shall forward the claim forms for the consideration and action of the presiding judge or magistrate judge. Claims for compensation submitted on CJA Form 24 (transcript requests) shall be submitted directly to the Financial Office in South Bend, Indiana, for processing.

V. ADMINISTRATION BY FEDERAL DEFENDER

It is hereby agreed, by and between the court and the federal defender that the Federal Defender Office will oversee the management of the CJA panel, said management including, but not limited to, assignment of appointed counsel for new cases, maintaining updated CJA panel lists, overseeing the CJA training program, and processing vouchers, etc., as outlined above. It is further agreed that CJA panel appointments for this district shall be made on a rotational basis, taking into consideration the type of cases, qualifications of the attorneys, and geography, and subject to the discretion of the judges in the division.

[Effective September 29, 2007.]

* So in original. No subdivision e. promulgated.

UNITED STATES BANKRUPTCY COURT FOR THE NORTHERN DISTRICT OF INDIANA

Including Amendments Received Through
November 1, 2015

B–9029–2. Limitation on Sanctions for Error as to Form.

B–9070–1. Custody of Files and Exhibits.

SELECTED FORMS

LBF–2. Notice of Objection to Claim.
LBF–3a. Notice of Motion and Opportunity to Object.
LBF–3b. Notice of Motion and Opportunity to Object.
LBF–4004–2. Verified Motion for Entry of Chapter 13 Discharge.
LBF B–7056–1.

ELECTRONIC CASE FILING

In Re: Electronic Case Filing.
Electronic Availability of Transcripts of Court Proceedings.

SELECTED GENERAL ORDERS

2000–01. In re: Motions for Admission Pro Hac Vice.
2001–02. In re: Alternative Dispute Resolution.
2001–03. In re: Expenses of Chapter 13 Trustees.
2013–01. In re: Notice of Trustee's Final Report in Chapter 7 Asset Cases.

B–1001–1. TITLE AND SCOPE OF RULES

(a) These rules shall be known as the Local Rules of the United States Bankruptcy Court for the Northern District of Indiana. They may be cited as "N.D. Ind. L.B.R. B–___."

(b) These rules become effective on January 1, 1994.

(c) These rules shall govern all cases and proceedings referred to bankruptcy judges pursuant to N.D. Ind. L.R. 200–1.

(d) These rules supersede all previous rules and general orders governing practice or procedure promulgated by this court. They shall apply to all proceedings initiated in this court after they take effect and to all cases and proceedings pending at the time they take effect.

(e) In a particular case, the court, upon its own motion or upon the motion of any party in interest, may suspend or modify any of these rules if the interests of justice so require.

[Adopted effective January 1, 1994. Renumbered effective September 1, 2000. Amended effective May 21, 2012.]

Historical and Regulatory Notes

This rule was amended for technical numbering revisions pursuant to Order Amending Local Bankruptcy Rules dated May 21, 2012.

B–1002–1. MINIMUM FILING REQUIREMENTS TO COMMENCE A CASE

(a) The minimum filing requirements necessary to initiate a voluntary case under title 11 of the United States Code are set forth in the Bankruptcy Code, the Federal Rules of Bankruptcy Procedure, and the Official Forms. At the time of the adoption of these rules they require:

(1) The petition and, if the debtor has issued publicly-traded securities and is filing for relief under Chapter 11, exhibit "A" to the voluntary petition (11 U.S.C. § 301, Fed. R. Bankr. P. 1002 and Official Form 1);

(2) The appropriate filing fee, or, in an individual case, an application to either pay the filing fee in installments or, if the case is filed under Chapter 7, to waive that fee. (Fed. R. Bankr. P. 1006);

(3) Any miscellaneous fee applicable to the case (28 U.S.C. § 1930(b) and Bankruptcy Court Fee Schedule);

(4) A list of all creditors or a schedule of liabilities or a motion, together with a notice of the motion, directed to the United States trustee, for an extension of time to file the required list (Fed. R. Bankr. P. 1007(a)); and

(5) In cases under Chapter 9 and Chapter 11 a list of the creditors holding the twenty largest unsecured claims (Fed. R. Bankr. P. 1007(d)).

(b) The clerk may refuse to accept any case for filing which does not comply with the minimum filing requirements established by the Bankruptcy Code, the Federal Rules of Bankruptcy Procedure, and the Official Forms in effect at the time the case is presented for filing. If such a case is accepted for filing, it may be stricken by the court, sua sponte, without notice.

(c) A case that has been terminated pursuant to the provisions of this rule shall not constitute a case for the purpose of determining the creation, existence, or duration of the automatic stay as a result of any future petition that might be filed concerning the debtor, including § 362(c)(3), (c)(4), and (n).

[Adopted effective January 1, 1994. Renumbered and amended effective September 1, 2000. Amended effective October 17, 2005; December 1, 2007; July 7, 2015.]

Historical And Regulatory Notes

By Order Making Technical Amendments to Local Bankruptcy Rules dated July 7, 2015, this rule was amended to delete the reference to Interim Bankruptcy Rule 1006(c).

Pursuant to Order Amending Local Bankruptcy Rules dated November 30, 2007, paragraph (c) was added to this rule.

Pursuant to Order Adopting Interim Bankruptcy Rules and Amending Local Bankruptcy Rules dated October 14, 2005, this rule was revised to better implement the provisions of the Bankruptcy Abuse Prevention and Consumer Protection Act of 2005.

B–1007–1. MATRIX OF CREDITORS

(a) The schedules and any list of creditors required by Rule 1007 of the Federal Rules of Bankruptcy Procedure shall be supplemented by a matrix of creditors and parties in interest, which shall be filed at the same time as the list required by Fed. R. Bankr. P. 1007(a).

(b) The matrix shall be prepared in such a form and manner as may, from time to time, be prescribed by the clerk and shall be verified by the debtor as to its correctness.

(c) It shall be the responsibility of the debtor to ensure that the matrix is complete and accurate. The clerk shall not be required to compare the names and addresses shown on the matrix with those shown on the schedules or other lists.

(d) In the event a petition is filed without a schedule of liabilities, a matrix prepared in accordance with this rule will serve as the list required by Fed. R. Bankr. P. 1007(a).

[Adopted effective January 1, 1994. Renumbered effective September 1, 2000.]

B–1007–2. STATEMENT CONCERNING STATUS OF FILING OF TAX RETURNS AND TAX REVIEW PROCEEDINGS [ABROGATED]

[Adopted effective January 1, 1994. Renumbered and amended effective September 1, 2000. Abrogated effective April 28, 2003.]

Historical and Regulatory Notes

Abrogated April 28, 2003, by General Order 2003–01.

B–1007–3. STATEMENT OF INSIDER COMPENSATION

(a) In any case under Chapter 11 or 12 in which the debtor is not a natural person, within fourteen (14) days after the order for relief the debtor shall file a "Statement of Insider Compensation." This statement shall be verified and shall disclose:

(1) the identity and duties of any insider who received compensation from the debtor or an affiliate of the debtor during the year prior to the order for relief and the amount, terms, and conditions of such compensation;

(2) whether the amount, terms, or conditions of any insider's compensation have been altered or changed, in any way, during the year prior to the case and, if so, the date and the precise nature of any such alteration or change; and

(3) the identity of any insider who will be compensated during the case, the duties such insider is expected to be performing and the amount, terms, and conditions of any compensation.

(b) The debtor shall serve a copy of the "Statement of Insider Compensation" upon the United States trustee, any trustee, any committee and/or the entities included on any list required by Fed. R. Bankr. P. 1007(d) and shall file proof thereof.

(c) As to any insider hired or employed by the debtor after the date of the petition, the debtor shall file and serve, in accordance with paragraph (b), a supplemental statement, disclosing the information required by paragraph (a)(3), within fourteen (14) days after such employment.

(d) The debtor shall not compensate any insider until the statements required by this rule have been filed.

(e) The court may, upon its own initiative or the motion of any party in interest, review the reasonableness of the amount, terms, and conditions of any compensation received by any insider during the administration of the estate, following notice and hearing.

(f) As used in this rule, the term "insider" is as defined in § 101 of title 11 of the United States Code.

[Adopted effective January 1, 1994. Renumbered and amended effective September 1, 2000. Amended effective December 1, 2009.]

Historical and Regulatory Notes

By Order Amending Local Bankruptcy Rules dated November 18, 2009, this rule was amended effective December 1, 2009, to conform with the time computation changes in the Federal Rules of Bankruptcy Procedure.

B–1007–4. SCHEDULE OF INCOME AND EXPENDITURES FOR CORPORATIONS AND PARTNERSHIPS

(a) A corporation or a partnership will not be required to file a schedule of income and expenditures unless ordered to do so.

(b) Upon the request of a trustee or the United States trustee and without notice or hearing, a corporation or a partnership will be ordered to file a schedule of income and expenditures within fourteen (14) days.

[Adopted effective January 1, 1994. Renumbered effective September 1, 2000. Amended effective December 1, 2009.]

Historical and Regulatory Notes

By Order Amending Local Bankruptcy Rules dated November 18, 2009, this rule was amended effective December 1, 2009, to conform with the time computation changes in the Federal Rules of Bankruptcy Procedure.

B–1007–5. SCHEDULING FEDERAL AND STATE GOVERNMENTAL UNITS

(a) If any federal or state governmental unit, department, agency or instrumentality is a creditor of the debtor or otherwise a party in interest, the schedules, statements, matrix/lists of creditors, or other document required to be filed with the court in which such indebtedness or interest is required to be disclosed shall identify the department, agency or instrumentality of the federal or state governmental unit through which the debtor became indebted, or which otherwise has an interest in the case.

(b) The address of any federal or state governmental unit, department, agency or instrumentality required to be stated in any schedule, statement of affairs, matrix/list of creditors or other document required to be filed with the court shall be the address for that governmental unit, department, agency or instrumentality as designated in the list maintained pursuant to Rule 5003(e) of the Federal Rules of Bankruptcy Procedure.

[Adopted effective January 1, 1994. Renumbered effective September 1, 2000; June 4, 2001.]

Historical and Regulatory Notes

By Order Amending Local Rules dated April 30, 2001, this rule was revised effective June 4, 2001, to apply to both Federal and State agencies.

B–1009–1. AMENDMENTS

(a)(1) An amendment to a voluntary petition, list, schedule or statement shall be made in accordance with Fed. R. Bankr. P. 1009 and shall be accompanied by a separate notice of amendment which shall identify the document amended, the general purpose of the amendment, and state the information added, deleted or changed by the amendment. Each amendment shall be verified and signed as in the original document. No amendments by interlineation shall be permitted. Except by leave of court, the entire document which the amendments affect shall be reproduced. In order to accommodate the possibility of multiple amendments, each amendment shall be numerically identified.

(2) To correct the address of a scheduled creditor, the BNC Bypass Notice may be used. The BNC Bypass Notice may not be used to add a previously unscheduled creditor.

(b) If a schedule of creditors (Schedule D, E, or F) is amended to add previously unscheduled creditors, the amendment shall also be accompanied by a supplement to the matrix of creditors. This supplement shall contain the name and address of the added creditor(s).

(c) Debtor shall serve a copy of the notice of amendment upon the United States trustee, any trustee, any committee and/or the entities included on any list required by Fed. R. Bankr. P. 1007(d), and all entities affected thereby, including any added creditors, and file proof thereof along with the amendment.

[Adopted effective January 1, 1994. Renumbered and amended effective September 1, 2000. Amended effective September 22, 2005; October 31, 2011.]

Historical and Regulatory Notes

By Order Amending Local Bankruptcy Rules dated October 31, 2011, this rule was amended to allow the use of the BNC Bypass Notice to correct the address of a previously scheduled creditor.

By General Order 2005–02 dated September 22, 2005, this rule was revised to change the way in which changed or added information is indicated when a document is amended.

B–1017–1. DISMISSALS FOR FAILURE TO FILE REQUIRED DOCUMENTS

(a) If an individual debtor in a voluntary case under Chapter 7 or Chapter 13 fails to file documents containing the information required by 11 U.S.C. § 521(a)(1)(A) and (B)(i–iii, v, vi) within 45 days following the date of the petition, unless that deadline has been extended or the trustee files an appropriate motion, the court will issue a notice reflecting the dismissal of the case pursuant to § 521(i)(1) on the 46th day after the date of the petition or as soon thereafter as may be practicable. A debtor or other party in interest who contends such a notice was issued in error may seek relief under Rule 9024(a) of the Federal Rules of Bankruptcy Procedure. In addition to the requirements of Local Bankruptcy Rule B–9023–1, any such motion shall:

(1) Specifically indicate where in the record documents containing the required information may be found;

(2) Describe how those documents provide all the information required; and

(3) State the date upon which they were filed.

(b) The absence of a notice reflecting dismissal of the case pursuant to § 521(i)(1) indicates that the court believes the debtor has filed the required information, and constitutes a presumption that such a dismissal has not occurred and that the case may continue to proceed. Notwithstanding the absence of such a notice, a party in interest that contends § 521(i)(1) requires dismissal of the case may file a motion for an order dismissing the case pursuant to § 521(i)(2). Such a motion must:

(1) Be filed electronically;

(2) Refer to § 521(i)(2) in both the title and the docket text entered by the movant; and

(3) Be accompanied by an affidavit from movant's counsel. A motion which fails to so refer to § 521(i)(2) will be deemed to be a motion to dismiss

for some other cause, a waiver of the court's need to act within seven days, and will be set for a hearing on notice to all creditors and parties in interest.

(c) The affidavit accompanying the motion for an order dismissing the case pursuant to § 521(i)(2) must:

(1) Indicate that counsel has personally reviewed the docket and every page of every document filed in the case;

(2) Specifically identify what information required by § 521(a)(1)(A) and (B)(i–iii, v, vi) the debtor has failed to file;

(3) Specifically describe how the information that has been filed by the debtor does not provide what is required; and

(4) State whether the debtor has sought an extension of time to file the required documents and whether the trustee has filed a motion asking the court to decline to dismiss the case.

[Effective January 1, 2010.]

Historical and Regulatory Notes

By Order Amending Local Bankruptcy Rules dated December 16, 2009, this new rule was adopted effective January 1, 2010. General Order 2006–01 is vacated effective with the adoption of this new rule.

B–1073–1. ASSIGNMENT OF CASES

(a) The administrative orders of the court may provide for the assignment of cases and proceedings to the various divisions within this district.

(b) Judges may be assigned to a division of this court, permanently and for trial sessions, as the court may from time to time order.

(c) The judge to whom a case has been assigned has the primary responsibility with respect to all proceedings in this district arising in, under, or related to that case.

(d) All judges have concurrent jurisdiction and may act in any matter in the absence of, or with the consent of, the judge to whom the case or proceeding is assigned.

[Adopted effective January 1, 1994. Renumbered effective September 1, 2000.]

B–2002–1. TREATMENT OF RETURNED NOTICES

(a) Envelopes containing notices of the § 341 meeting will bear the return address of debtor's counsel or the debtor if pro se. Debtor or debtor's counsel shall retain all such notices returned by the postal service for no less than one hundred eighty (180) days after the case is closed or dismissed.

(b) As to any notice which is not served by the clerk, the party responsible for serving the notice shall retain all notices returned by the postal service for no less than one-hundred eighty (180) days after the date the case is closed or dismissed.

[Adopted effective January 1, 1994. Renumbered and amended effective September 1, 2000. Amended effective June 23, 2004.]

Historical and Regulatory Notes

Pursuant to Order Amending Local Bankruptcy Rules dated June 23, 2004, paragraph (c) of Rule 2002–1 was deleted.

B–2002–2. NOTICE OF OPPORTUNITY TO OBJECT TO MOTIONS

(a) Except as otherwise ordered, the court will consider the following matters without holding a hearing, unless a party in interest files a timely objection to the relief requested:

(1) Motions to approve agreements relating to relief from the automatic stay; providing adequate protection; or prohibiting or conditioning the use, sale or lease of property.

(2) Motions to approve agreements relating to the use of cash collateral.

(3) Motions for authority to obtain credit.

(4) In cases pending under Chapter 7, motions for relief from the automatic stay.

(5) Motions to avoid liens on exempt property.

(6) Motions to redeem personal property from liens.

(7) Applications for administrative expenses, including compensation for services rendered and reimbursement of expenses.

(8) Motions to extend the time for filing claims.

(9) Motions to extend the exclusivity periods for filing a Chapter 11 plan.

(10) Motions to extend the time to assume or reject executory contracts and unexpired leases.

(11) Motions filed by a trustee or debtor-in-possession to assume or reject executory contracts and unexpired leases.

(12) Motions to approve a modification to a confirmed Chapter 11, Chapter 12 or Chapter 13 plan.

(13) Motions to approve a compromise or settlement.

(14) Motions to transfer a case to another district or to another division in this district.

(15) Motions to approve transactions outside the ordinary course of business, except motions for the sale or lease of personally identifiable information.

(16) Motions to sell property free and clear of liens and/or to distribute the proceeds of sale, except motions to sell or lease personally identifiable information.

(17) Motions to abandon property of the estate.

(18) Motions for relief from the co-debtor stay of 11 U.S.C. § 1201 or § 1301.

(19) Motions for the joint administration or substantive consolidation of cases.

(20) Motions to compel the debtor to turnover or deliver property to a trustee.

(21) In cases under Chapter 12 and 13, motions for a discharge prior to the completion of payments under a confirmed plan (motions for hardship discharge).

(22) Motion of a party in interest to enter a final decree in a case under Chapter 11.

(23) Trustees' Applications to Employ Professionals after Notice to Creditors filed pursuant to N.D. Ind. L.B.R. B–2014–2(b).

(24) Applications to employ professionals retroactively.

(25) Motions for discharge in individual Chapter 11 cases.

(26) Motions to determine final cure pursuant to FRBP Rule 3002.1(h).

(b) Except as otherwise ordered by the court:

(1) no less than fourteen (14) days notice shall be given of the opportunity to file objections to:

　(A) motions to approve agreements relating to relief from the automatic stay, providing adequate protection, prohibiting or conditioning the use, sale or lease of property;

　(B) motions to approve agreements relating to the use of cash collateral;

　(C) motions for authority to obtain credit;

　(D) motions for relief from the automatic stay in cases pending under Chapter 7; and

　(E) motions relating to abandonment of property from the estate.

(2) no less than twenty-one (21) days notice shall be given of the opportunity to file objections to the other motions subject to this rule.

In all cases, the time within which objections may be filed shall be measured from the date notice of the opportunity to object is served.

(c) Local Bankruptcy Form 3a (LBF–3a), Local Bankruptcy Form 3b (LBF–3b) or another form of notice substantially similar thereto shall be used to give creditors and parties in interest notice of the motion and the opportunity to object thereto. This notice **must** (1) identify the party seeking relief, (2) state the name of the motion and the date upon which it was filed, (3) briefly and specifically state what you are asking the court to do, (4) contain a brief summary of the ground for the motion or have a copy of the motion attached to it, (5) state the date by which objections to the motion are to be filed, where objections should be filed and upon whom copies should be served, (6) contain a statement to the effect that if no objections are filed by the date due the court may grant the relief requested without holding a hearing, (7) be dated as of the date it is served, and (8) be signed by counsel for the movant or the movant, if pro se, and contain the name, address and telephone number of the individual signing the notice.

(d) The moving party shall be responsible for properly completing the appropriate version of LBF–3 so that it contains the required information, serving it upon the entities required by the United States Bankruptcy Code, the applicable rules of bankruptcy procedure, the local rules of this court,[1] and/or any order of the court, and making due proof thereof. The failure to do so within seven (7) days of the date the motion was filed will be deemed to be a waiver of any time limits associated with ruling on the motion, including the time limits set forth in 11 U.S.C. § 362(e).

(e) The appropriate version of LBF–3 may also be adapted for use in those instances, not specifically covered by this rule, where the court directs that particular relief may be granted without a hearing following the expiration of notice to creditors. In those situations, in addition to complying with the other requirements of this rule, the notice shall be accompanied by a copy of the court's order authorizing notice to creditors and establishing the deadline for filing objections.

[Adopted April 28, 2003. Amended effective February 15, 2005; April 28, 2005; August 31, 2007; May 11, 2009; December 1, 2009; August 31, 2012; October 7, 2014; July 7, 2015; October 5, 2015.]

[1] Pursuant to Rule 5003(e) of the Federal Rules of Bankruptcy Procedure, the clerk maintains a list containing the addresses of various state and federal governmental units. The list is available at the clerk's office and on the court's web site.

Commentary

Certain motions and applications can be granted after notice and the opportunity for a hearing. This Rule standardizes the practice and procedure for dealing with these motions. Paragraph (a) identifies the applications and motions to which this Rule applies. Paragraph (b) identifies the minimum amount of time between the date of service of the notice and the last day for objecting to the relief requested. Paragraph (c) governs the form of notice. Compliance with this paragraph is mandatory. Because the party filing a motion is responsible for preparing and serving the notice to creditors, the failure to use a complete and proper form of notice may result in the court's refusal to rule on the motion until proper notice has been sent.

Paragraph (a)(24) has been amended to clarify its scope, by changing the phrase "nunc pro tunc" to the word "retroactively." The term "nunc pro tunc" has a precise meaning (*See In re IFC Credit Corporation*, 663 F.3d 315, 317–18 (7th Cir. 2011)), which relates to correcting a record to properly document an actual previous event, rather than to relate something back when the event did not previously occur. The notice requirement refers to a circumstance in which a professional has in fact rendered services or established a professional relationship prior to being approved as a professional by the court—the professional now seeks to authorize employment retroactively to the date upon which services were first performed or the professional relationship arose.

Paragraph (b) does not specify which creditors and parties in interest are entitled to receive notice. Not all types of relief require notice to all creditors. You should consult the Code, the Bankruptcy Rules, and the Local Rules and General Orders to determine which creditors and parties in interest are entitled to receive notice of a particular type of motion.

Local Forms LBF–3a and LBF–3b may be used to comply with paragraph (c) of the Rule. Form 3a is used if you intend to summarize the grounds for the motion; Form 3b is used if a copy of the motion or application is attached to the notice. In briefly stating the specific remedy or relief you want the court to grant, it is important to be both brief and specific. A Motion for Abandonment, for example, would be the name of the motion; the relief requested by the movant, briefly summarized, would be to abandon from the bankruptcy estate the debtor's 1995 Ford Tempo automobile. Or, for example, if the motion is to modify a confirmed Chapter 13 Plan, the relief requested might be to extend the plan payments from 36 months to 60 months. The requested relief should be stated with sufficient particularity in the notice that the reader can determine, from this statement alone, what it is that the movant is asking the court to do. Would your client be satisfied if the court granted the relief you request in this part of the notice, as worded? If the relief you mention is generic or ambiguous, an order granting that relief in those terms might be ineffectual. Specificity is needed, but brevity is also required. The statement of relief sought should be concise, clear, and informative.

If you will not be attaching the actual motion to the notice, then Form 3a should be used. In addition to the brief, particular statement of the relief you are asking the court to grant, you should provide a summary of the grounds for the motion. Here you should state, in summary form, the factual basis for seeking the relief. The statement of the grounds of the motion should not be argumentative; nor should it be generic. The purpose is to inform the creditor body of the essential facts supporting your motion or application.

Paragraph (d) of the Rule is a reminder that the moving party is responsible for preparing the notice to creditors, making certain it is in proper form, and serving the notice on the proper parties. In certain cases, parties who must receive the notice include all creditors and parties in interest; in other circumstances only particular creditors or parties are required to be served with the notice. The identity of the entities required to be served is beyond the scope of this Rule; the identity of parties required to be served is determined by the provisions of the Bankruptcy Code itself, applicable rules of bankruptcy procedure, the local rules of this court, or by any order of this court.

Paragraph (e) of the Rule provides for certain adaptations of the forms, in the event of circumstances not anticipated by the Rule for example, where the court independently orders notice to creditors with respect to motions, applications or relief, not specifically mentioned in paragraph (a) of the Rule.

Historical and Regulatory Notes

By Order Making Technical Amendments to Local Bankruptcy Rules dated July 7, 2015, this rule was amended to change the word "mailed" to "served" in paragraph (a) and in the commentary.

By Order Making Technical Amendments to Local Bankruptcy Rules dated July 7, 2015, LBF–3a and 3b were amended to change the phrase "mail a copy of your objection to" to "serve a copy of your objection upon" and the word "mailed" to "served."

Pursuant to Order Amending Local Bankruptcy Rules dated October 9, 2014, paragraph (a)(24) was amended by changing the phrase "nunc pro tunc" to the word "retroactively" for clarification and adding additional explanatory commentary.

By Order Amending Local Bankruptcy Rules dated August 31, 2012, this rule was amended to include motions to disburse sales proceeds.

By Order Amending Local Bankruptcy Rules dated November 18, 2009, this rule was amended effective December 1, 2009, to conform with the time computation changes in the Federal Rules of Bankruptcy Procedure.

Pursuant to Order Amending Local Bankruptcy Rules dated May 11, 2009, paragraph (a)(25) was added to include motions for discharge in individual Chapter 11 cases.

Pursuant to Order Amending Local Bankruptcy Rules dated May 11, 2009, paragraph (a)(19) was amended to make a technical change to clarify the rule.

Pursuant to Order Amending Local Bankruptcy Rules dated August 31, 2007, paragraph (b)(1)(B) was amended to make a technical change to clarify the rule.

Pursuant to Order Adopting Interim Bankruptcy Rules and Amending Local Bankruptcy Rules dated October 14, 2005, this rule was revised to better implement the provisions of the Bankruptcy Abuse Prevention and Consumer Protection Act of 2005.

Pursuant to General Order 2005–01 dated April 28, 2005, paragraph (a)(24) was added to include applications to employ professionals nunc pro tunc.

Pursuant to Order Amending Local Bankruptcy Rules dated February 15, 2005, paragraph (a)(23) was added to include motions filed pursuant to new Rule 2014–2.

Pursuant to General Order 2003–01 dated April 28, 2003, new Rule 2002–2 became effective immediately.

B–2002–3.   LIMITED NOTICE IN CHAPTER 7 CASES

In Chapter 7 cases, after all time periods for filing proofs of claim have expired, all notices required by Fed. R. Bankr. P. 2002(a), except for the notice of dismissal or denial of discharge, shall be served only upon the debtor, the attorney for debtor, the case trustee, the United States trustee, creditors who have filed claims, and creditors, if any, who are still permitted to file claims by reason of an extension granted under Fed. R. Bankr. P. 3002(c)(1) or (c)(2).

[Adopted effective August 29, 2008. Amended effective July 7, 2015.]

Historical and Regulatory Notes

By Order Making Technical Amendments to Local Bankruptcy Rules dated July 7, 2015, this rule was amended to change the phrase "mailed only to" to "served only upon."

This new rule was adopted by Order Amending Local Bankruptcy Rules dated August 29, 2008.

B–2014–1. EMPLOYMENT OF PROFESSIONALS BY DEBTOR-IN-POSSESSION

(a)(1) Except when employed for a special purpose under 11 U.S.C. § 327(e), to be eligible to be employed as counsel for the debtor-in-possession, an attorney must be a registered ECF user and shall make all filings in the case, including the application to employ, electronically.

(a)(2) All applications for employment of professionals by a debtor-in-possession, together with the accompanying affidavits and disclosures, including the disclosure of compensation required by Fed. R. Bankr. P. 2016, shall be served upon the United States trustee, any committee and/or the entities included on any list required by Fed. R. Bankr. P. 1007(d), and all secured creditors.

(b) In addition to the other disclosures and affidavits required by the Bankruptcy Code and applicable Federal Rules of Bankruptcy Procedure, where the debtor-in-possession is not a natural person, the affidavit of the proposed professional shall specifically state:

(1) whether or not the debtor has any affiliates, as defined by 11 U.S.C. § 101(2), and, if so, (a) whether the professional or a member of the professional's firm or business represented or was employed by any such affiliate during the twelve months prior to the petition, and (b) any position, other than legal counsel, the professional or a member of the professional's firm or business holds or held in any such affiliate during the two years prior to the petition;

(2) if the professional or a member of the professional's firm or business has represented or been employed by any affiliate of the debtor during the twelve months prior to the petition, the circumstances of such representation or employment, all payments received on account of such representation or employment during the twelve months prior to the petition, and any amount owed on account of such representation or employment on the date of the petition;

(3) whether or not the professional or a member of the professional's firm or business represented or was employed by the debtor during the twelve months

prior to the petition and, if so, the circumstances of such representation or employment, all payments received on account of such representation or employment during the twelve months prior to the petition, and any amount owed on account of such representation or employment on the date of the petition;

(4) any position, other than legal counsel, the professional or a member of the professional's firm or business holds or held in the debtor during the two years prior to the petition;

(5) whether or not the professional or a member of the professional's firm or business represented or was employed by an officer, director, shareholder, partner or limited partner of the debtor, or any entity that has guaranteed an obligation of the debtor or is liable on any obligation of the debtor or pledged property to secure an obligation of the debtor and, if so, the circumstances of such representation or employment; and

(6) whether or not the professional or a member of the professional's firm or business has represented any scheduled creditor within the year prior to the date of the petition and, if so, the circumstances of such representation or employment.

(c) Unless objections to the application are filed seven (7) days prior to the date first set for the § 341 meeting or within twenty-one (21) days following service of the application, whichever is later, the court may approve the application without further notice or hearing. Unless the court orders otherwise for good cause shown, the failure to file an objection to the application within the time required will be deemed a waiver of any objection to the professional's employment by the debtor-in-possession and to the allowance or payment of fees on account of such employment based upon the disclosures made pursuant to paragraph (b).

(d) In the event the court approves the application, unless otherwise requested following notice to all creditors, the approval will relate back to the date the application was filed.

Historical and Regulatory Notes

By Order Amending Local Bankruptcy Rules dated August 3, 2011, this rule was amended effective immediately, to add a requirement that counsel for the debtor-in-possession be a registered ECF user and make all filings electronically.

[Adopted effective January 1, 1994. Renumbered and amended effective September 1, 2000. Amended effective August 3, 2011.]

B–2014–2. EMPLOYMENT OF PROFESSIONALS BY TRUSTEES

(a) Except as otherwise requested, the court will consider and rule upon a bankruptcy trustee's application to employ a professional without notice or hearing.

(b)(1) If the trustee would like the court to defer ruling on an application to employ a professional until creditors have been given the opportunity to object to the application, the trustee shall file an "Application to Employ (Identify type of professional–attorney, accountant, etc.) After Notice to Creditors." In addition to the other disclosures and affidavits required by the Bankruptcy Code and the applicable Rules of Bankruptcy Procedure, the verified statement of the proposed professional shall also set forth the connections with any affiliates and/or insiders of the debtor and shall specifically state:

(A)(i) whether the professional or a member of the professional's firm or business represented or was employed by any affiliate or insider of the debtor during the twelve months prior to the petition, and (ii) any position the professional or a member of the professional's firm or business holds or held in any affiliate or insider of the debtor during the two years prior to the petition;

(B) if the professional or a member of the professional's firm or business has represented or been employed by any affiliate or insider of the debtor during the twelve months prior to the petition, the circumstances of such representation or employment, all payments received on account of such representation or employment, and any amount owed on account of such representation or employment on the date of the petition;

(C) whether or not the professional or a member of the professional's firm or business represented or was employed by the debtor during the twelve months prior to the petition and, if so, the circumstances of such representation or employment, all payments received on account of such representation or employment, and any amount owed on account of such representation or employment on the date of the petition;

(D) any position the professional or a member of the professional's firm or business holds or held in the debtor during the two years prior to the petition;

(E) whether or not the professional or a member of the professional's firm or business represented or was employed by an officer, director, shareholder, partner or limited partner of the debtor, or any entity that has guaranteed an obligation of the debtor or is liable on any obligation of the debtor or pledged property to secure an obligation of the debtor and, if so, the circumstances of such representation or employment; and

(F) whether or not the professional or a member of the professional's firm or business has represented any scheduled creditor within the year prior to

the date of the petition and, if so, the circumstances of such representation or employment.

(2) The application, together with the accompanying affidavits and disclosures, shall be served upon the United States trustee and all creditors and parties in interest, along with a notice of the application and the opportunity to object thereto prepared in accordance with local bankruptcy rule B–2002–2(c). Unless objections to the application are filed within twenty-one (21) days following service of the application and the notice of the opportunity to object thereto, the court may grant the application and approve the employment without further notice or hearing. Unless the court orders otherwise for good cause shown, the failure of any party served with notice of the opportunity to object to the application to file an objection within the time required will be deemed a waiver of any objection to the professional's employment by the trustee and to the allowance or payment of fees on account of such employment based upon the disclosures made in the application and the accompanying affidavits.

(c) Unless otherwise requested following notice to all creditors, the approval of a professional's employment will relate back to the date the application was filed.

[Adopted effective February 15, 2005. Amended effective December 1, 2009.]

Historical and Regulatory Notes

By Order Amending Local Bankruptcy Rules dated November 18, 2009, this rule was amended effective December 1, 2009, to conform with the time computation changes in the Federal Rules of Bankruptcy Procedure.

This new rule was adopted by Order Amending Local Bankruptcy Rules dated February 15, 2005.

B–2015–1. REPORT OF OPERATIONS

(a) Every trustee, Chapter 11 debtor in possession, or other debtor who operates a business under any chapter of the Bankruptcy Code shall file a monthly statement of the cash receipts and disbursements no later than twenty-one (21) days after the end of the calendar month. This report shall include:

(1) A summary of all income and expenses for the reporting period;

(2) A statement of the use of, reductions and additions to raw materials and inventory, crops, livestock or other items held or produced for sale;

(3) A statement of the collection of and addition to accounts receivable;

(4) A reconciliation of all income and expenses while operating under Title 11;

(5) An itemized statement of all unpaid post-petition obligations;

(6) A statement of insurance coverage;

(7) Proof or certification of payment of all post-petition taxes due, including taxes withheld or collected from others; and

(8) A statement identifying any federal or state tax returns filed during the reporting period, including verification of tax deposits. The report may be in any appropriate form or format containing the minimum information required.

(b) In addition to the electronic service automatically effected by the court's ECF System, the report shall be served upon the chair of any committee.

(c) The failure to comply with the reporting requirements of paragraph (a) may constitute cause for conversion, dismissal, or the appointment (or removal) of a trustee pursuant to 11 U.S.C. § 1112.

[Adopted effective January 1, 1994. Renumbered and amended effective September 1, 2000. Amended effective December 1, 2009; January 1, 2010.]

Historical and Regulatory Notes

By Order Amending Local Bankruptcy Rules dated December 16, 2009, this rule was amended effective January 1, 2010, to provide for substantive changes and delete paragraph (d).

By Order Amending Local Bankruptcy Rules dated November 18, 2009, this rule was amended effective December 1, 2009, to conform with the time computation changes in the Federal Rules of Bankruptcy Procedure.

B–2015–2. POST-PETITION TAXES AND TAX RETURNS

Every trustee or debtor who operates a business under any chapter of the United States Code shall:

(1) file all federal, state and local tax returns and shall pay all federal, state and local taxes on account of the operations of the estate as and when due; and

(2) segregate and pay as and when due any and all taxes withheld from employees or collected from others under any federal, state or local law.

[Adopted effective January 1, 1994. Renumbered effective September 1, 2000. Subsection (b) abrogated effective April 28, 2003.]

Historical and Regulatory Notes

Pursuant to General Order 2003–01 dated April 28, 2003, paragraph (b) of this rule was abrogated.

B–2090–1. STUDENT PRACTICE RULE

(a) Purpose. Effective legal service for each person in the Northern District of Indiana, regardless of that person's ability to pay, is important to the directly affected person, to our court system, and to our whole citizenry. Law students, under supervision by a member of the bar of the District Court for the Northern District of Indiana, may staff legal aid clinics organized under city or county bar associations or accred-

ited law schools, or which are funded pursuant to the Legal Service Corporation Act. Law students and graduates may participate in legal training programs organized in the offices of United States Attorneys.

(b) Procedure. A member of the legal aid clinic, in representation of clients of such clinic, shall be authorized to advise such persons and to negotiate and appear on their behalf. These activities shall be conducted under the supervision of a member of the bar of the District Court for the Northern District of Indiana. Supervision by a member of this bar shall include the duty to examine and sign all pleadings filed on behalf of a client. Supervision shall not require that any such member of the bar be present in the room while a student or law graduate is advising a client or negotiating on his or her behalf nor that the supervisor be present in the courtroom during a student's or graduate's appearance. In no case shall any such student or graduate appear without first having received the approval of the judge of that court for the student's appearance. Where such permission has been granted, the judge of any court may suspend the trial proceedings at any stage where the judge in his or her sole discretion determines that such student's or graduate's representation is professionally inadequate and substantial justice so requires. Law students or graduates serving in a United States Attorney's program may be authorized to perform comparable functions and duties as assigned by the United States Attorney subject to all the conditions and restrictions in this rule and the further restriction that they may not be appointed as Assistant United States Attorneys.

(c) Eligible Students. Any student in an accredited law school who has received a passing grade in law school courses and has completed the freshman year shall be eligible to participate in a legal aid clinic if (1) the student meets the academic and moral standards established by the dean of that school, and (2) the school certifies to the court that the student has met the eligibility requirements of this rule.

[Adopted effective September 1, 2000.]

B–3002–1. FILING AND ALLOWANCE OF § 503(B)(9) ADMINISTRATIVE CLAIMS

(a) A creditor whose claim may include amounts entitled to priority under 11 U.S.C. § 503(b)(9) (value of goods delivered during the 20 days prior to the commencement of the case) may file a proof of claim within the claims deadline established by the court. The amount of the claim entitled to priority, and the basis for the claimed priority, shall be stated on the proof of claim.

(b) Unless the Court orders otherwise, a motion for the allowance of a § 503(b)(9) administrative expense must be filed no later than the expiration of the claims deadline. This motion shall state, with particularity, the goods delivered to the debtor during the 20 days prior to the petition, the date or dates of delivery, and their value. Movant shall be responsible for serving all creditors and parties in interest with notice of the motion, in accordance with Local Bankruptcy Rule B–2002–2(a)(7), and making due proof thereof. Absent objection within the time required by that rule, *see*, N.D. Ind. L.B.R. B–2002–2(b), the court will consider the motion without a hearing.

[Adopted effective May 5, 2011.]

Commentary

Section 503(b)(9) administrative claims are something of a chimera. They have all the attributes of a prepetition claim, see, e.g., 11 U.S.C. §§ 101(5), 501, and as such are subject to the requirements for those claims. See, e.g., 11 U.S.C. § 502(a), (b). Yet, having been given administrative, not just priority, status, compare 11 U.S.C. § 507(a) with 11 U.S.C. § 503(b), they are also subject to the requirements of administrative claims, including allowing them "[a]fter notice and a hearing." The proposed rule tries to recognize both aspects of these claims and by doing so preserve the creditor's rights.

As a right to payment arising before the date of the petition, the Proof of Claim form (Official Form 10) may be used to assert a claim which might be entitled to administrative status under 11 U.S.C. § 503(b)(9). In doing so, the creditor should, in section 5 of that form regarding priority status, mark the box labeled "Other" and specify that the claim is filed pursuant to 11 U.S.C. § 507(a)(3) and § 503(b)(9), and then state the amount so claimed in the blanks provided. Among other things, using the claim form and following the usual claims process will preserve the creditor's rights to a general unsecured claim in the event any issue of administrative status would be resolved against it. To receive administrative status, the claimant must also satisfy the procedural requirements of 11 U.S.C. § 503(b) which require "notice and a hearing" before administrative claims — including § 503(b)(9) claims — can be allowed. This does not require an actual hearing, only the opportunity for one, 11 U.S.C. § 102(1), but it does require something more than whatever "notice" might come from simply filing something on the docket. The language of § 102(1)(B)(i) that no hearing is required if "a hearing is not timely requested" suggests that some type of formal notice of the deadline for requesting a hearing needs to be given.

This Rule also establishes a deadline for requesting the allowance of § 503(b)(9) administrative claims. See, 11 U.S.C. § 503(a). Unlike other administrative claims, which do not exist as of the date of the petition, a § 503(b)(9)claimant can determine the amount of its administrative claim early in the case, and so the rule establishes a deadline for it to do so and to file the required motion. Absent a timely motion for allowance, the claim may still be allowed as a general unsecured claim under 11 U.S.C. § 502(a).

Historical and Regulatory Notes

By Order Amending Local Bankruptcy Rules dated May 5, 2011, this new rule was adopted effective immediately.

B–3006–1. WITHDRAWAL OF CLAIM

(a) A request to withdraw a claim after it has been objected to, after the creditor has been named as a defendant in an adversary proceeding, or after the creditor has participated significantly in the case, shall be served upon the trustee or debtor-in-possession, any committee, all parties who objected to the claim, and the United States Trustee. In the absence of an objection or other response within twenty–one (21) days after the date the request to withdraw is filed with the court, the court may allow the claim to be withdrawn without further notice or hearing.

(b) A request to withdraw a claim does not extend or defer the deadline for filing a response to a claim objection and will not delay any proceeding concerning the claim or the court's ruling thereon.

[Adopted effective June 23, 2004. Amended effective December 1, 2009.]

Historical and Regulatory Notes

By Order Amending Local Bankruptcy Rules dated November 18, 2009, this rule was amended effective December 1, 2009, to conform with the time computation changes in the Federal Rules of Bankruptcy Procedure.

This new rule was adopted pursuant to Order Amending Local Bankruptcy Rules dated June 23, 2004.

B–3007–1. OBJECTIONS TO CLAIMS; DEFAULT

(a) Except as otherwise authorized by Rule 3007 of the Federal Rules of Bankruptcy Procedure regarding omnibus claim objections, an objection to a proof of claim shall be limited to the claim or claims filed by a single creditor, unless the objection is directed to a claim which has been filed jointly by more than one creditor.

(b) An objection to a proof of claim shall identify the creditor by name and the claim number as assigned by the court, and shall state with specificity the basis for disallowance or allowance in an amount or with a priority other than that claimed.

(c) Local Bankruptcy Form 2 (LBF–2) shall be used to give the claimant notice of the claim objection and the opportunity to respond thereto, instead of Official Bankruptcy Form 20(B).

(d) The objector shall be responsible for completing LBF–2 and serving it, along with the claim objection, and making due proof thereof, in accordance with Rule 7004 of the Federal Rules of Bankruptcy Procedure upon:

(1) the claimant, and claimant's attorney if an appearance has been filed;

(2) any trustee; and

(3) the debtor and debtor's counsel.

(e) Unless a response to the objection is filed within thirty (30) days following service of the notice of objection, the court may disallow or modify the claim in accordance with the objection, without further hearing.

[Adopted effective January 1, 1994. Renumbered and amended effective September 1, 2000. Amended effective December 1, 2007; May 5, 2011; July 7, 2015.]

Historical and Regulatory Notes

By Order Making Technical Amendments to Local Bankruptcy Rules dated July 7, 2015, LBF–2 was amended to change the phrase "mail a copy of your response to" to "serve a copy of your response upon" and the word "mailed" to "served."

By Order Amending Local Bankruptcy Rules dated May 5, 2011, this rule was amended to make technical corrections to clarify the rule.

Pursuant to Order Amending Local Bankruptcy Rules dated November 30, 2007, paragraph (a) of this rule was amended to conform to the provisions of the amended national rules.

Pursuant to General Order 2001–01 dated February 2, 2001, this rule was adopted along with LBF–2; General Order 98–1 was vacated.

B–3011–1. PAYMENT OF UNCLAIMED FUNDS

(a) A motion or other request for the payment of unclaimed funds, which have been deposited with the court pursuant to 11 U.S.C. § 347(a), Fed. R. Bankr. P. 3010 or Fed. R. Bankr. P. 3011, must be made through an attorney who is a member of the bar of this court, unless the entity entitled to receive payment is a natural person making the request on its own behalf and not as an agent or other representative of the claimant.

(b) The motion shall be accompanied by an affidavit, together with any appropriate supporting documentation, executed by the claimant demonstrating the claimant's present entitlement to the funds. If the claimant is the entity for whose benefit the funds were originally deposited, the affidavit shall contain a statement to the effect that the right to payment has not, in any way, been transferred or assigned to any other entity.

(c) If the claimant is not a natural person, the affidavit required by paragraph (b) shall be executed by an officer, director, general partner, or other individual authorized to do so and shall be accompanied by proof that the individual executing the affidavit has been authorized to do so on behalf of the claimant and of the capacity in which the individual acts.

(d) The motion and a notice of the motion shall be served upon the United States Attorney, in the manner required by Fed. R. Bankr. P. 7004, and shall be accompanied by a proof of service showing the address to which service was directed and the manner in which service was made.

(e) In the absence of an objection or other response from the United States Attorney, within thirty (30) days of the date the motion is filed, the court may determine the motion, without further notice or hearing.

(f) The failure to comply with the requirements of this rule may result in the motion being denied.

[Adopted effective January 1, 1994. Renumbered effective September 1, 2000.]

B–3017.1–1 CONSIDERATION OF DISCLOSURE STATEMENTS IN SMALL BUSINESS CASES AND CONFIRMATION DEADLINES

(a) If the proponent of a plan in a small business case would like the court to:

(1) determine that the plan itself provides adequate information and that a separate disclosure statement is not necessary;

(2) approve a disclosure statement submitted on an approved official form,

(3) conditionally approve a disclosure statement subject to final approval at hearing where the court will also consider confirmation of a proposed plan, or

(4) allow the proponent to defer filing of a proposed plan until after a disclosure statement has been approved,

it shall file an appropriate motion at the same time as the proposed plan or the proposed disclosure statement is filed. Such a motion shall state, with particularity, why a separate disclosure statement may be dispensed with, why a separate hearing to consider the adequacy of a disclosure statement is not necessary, or why the filing of a plan should be deferred.

(b) Absent an order granting a motion submitted in accordance with paragraph (a), the court will schedule the matter for such proceedings as it deems appropriate.

(c) At any hearing where the court is to consider the adequacy of a proposed disclosure statement, the court may also, either on its own initiative or at the request of any party in interest, consider whether any applicable deadlines for confirming a proposed plan should be extended.

[Adopted effective August 31, 2007.]

Historical and Regulatory Notes

This new rule was adopted pursuant to Order Amending Local Bankruptcy Rules dated August 31, 2007.

B-3018-1. CHAPTER 11 CONFIRMATION: BALLOTING

(a) Any entity entitled to accept or reject a proposed plan may do so by delivering an appropriate ballot to the proponent or other individual identified by the court on or before the date set by the court. Each ballot shall clearly indicate, either by designation or description, the class in which the entity is voting to accept or reject. An entity entitled to cast a ballot in more than one class shall submit a separate ballot for each class in which it desires to vote to accept or reject a proposed plan.

(b) Unless the court orders otherwise, the proponent of the plan shall prepare, file, and serve a verified report of the results of the balloting no later than fourteen (14) days before the date set for the hearing on confirmation. The report shall include the designation and description of each class provided for by the plan and whether or not any such class is impaired, the total number and amount of claims voting in each class and the number and amount of claims voting to accept and to reject the plan. The report shall also identify any material change from the disclosure statement's representations concerning the requirements for confirmation established by 11 U.S.C. § 1129(a) and shall indicate whether there are sufficient funds available with which to make the payments due upon the effective date of the plan. All ballots received shall be attached to the ballot report. A similar report on any ballots received after the last date fixed for delivering acceptances or rejections shall be made by the proponent of the plan at the hearing on confirmation and shall be accompanied by such ballots.

(c) The proponent shall serve copies of the first ballot report upon the United States trustee, any trustee, any committee and/or the entities included on any list required by Fed. R. Bankr. P. 1007(d). If the proponent is an entity other than the debtor, a copy shall also be served upon the debtor and debtor's counsel.

[Adopted effective January 1, 1994. Renumbered and amended effective September 1, 2000. Amended effective December 1, 2009.]

Historical and Regulatory Notes

By Order Amending Local Bankruptcy Rules dated November 18, 2009, this rule was amended effective December 1, 2009, to conform with the time computation changes in the Federal Rules of Bankruptcy Procedure.

B-3020-1. CHAPTER 11 CONFIRMATION: HEARING

(a) In a case under Chapter 11, if all the requirements for confirmation of 11 U.S.C. § 1129(a) are met other than those contained in paragraph (8) (acceptance or deemed acceptance of the plan by all classes),

should the proponent intend to seek confirmation over the rejection of any class pursuant to the requirements of 11 U.S.C. § 1129(b), the proponent shall file and serve a request to do so no later than fourteen (14) days before the date set for the confirmation hearing. The request shall identify the class or classes which have rejected the plan as to which the proponent contends the requirements of 11 U.S.C. § 1129(b) are fulfilled and shall state how those requirements have been fulfilled as to each such class, so that the plan may be confirmed notwithstanding the rejection of such class or classes. The request shall be served upon each entity which cast a ballot in any such rejecting class and upon the entities entitled to receive copies of the ballot report. At the initial confirmation hearing the court may determine that the proposed plan does not discriminate unfairly and is fair and equitable as to a rejecting class, based upon the information contained in the request, without further proof, unless at least one rejecting member of such class appears at the confirmation hearing.

(b) The proponent of the plan may be required to file an application to fix the amount of any confirmation deposit, no less than fourteen (14) days before the date set for the hearing on confirmation, which shall include the computations which were used in arriving at the amount of any deposit.

[Adopted effective January 1, 1994. Renumbered effective September 1, 2000. Amended effective December 1, 2009.]

Historical and Regulatory Notes

By Order Amending Local Bankruptcy Rules dated November 18, 2009, this rule was amended effective December 1, 2009, to conform with the time computation changes in the Federal Rules of Bankruptcy Procedure.

B-3022-1. FINAL DECREE IN CHAPTER 11 CASES

(a) Unless the confirmed plan or the order of confirmation otherwise provides, an estate under Chapter 11 may be deemed to be fully administered when:

(1) at least one-hundred eighty (180) days have passed after the date of the entry of the order of confirmation;

(2) all adversary proceedings, contested matters and other disputes, including appeals, have been resolved by a final, nonappealable order or dismissed; and

(3) no paper has been filed in the case for a least sixty (60) days.

(b) The court may, on its own motion and without notice or hearing, enter a final decree and close a case under Chapter 11 when the estate is deemed to be fully administered.

(c) Upon the motion of a party in interest, following notice to creditors, the court may enter a final decree and close a case under Chapter 11, without a hearing, in the absence of an objection thereto.

[Adopted effective January 1, 1994. Renumbered effective September 1, 2000.]

B–4001–1. RELIEF FROM STAY IN CHAPTER 13 CASES

(a) If a confirmed chapter 13 plan provides for the surrender of property in which a creditor has an interest, whether as a lienholder or as a lessor, the automatic stay is terminated upon confirmation, and without the need for a further order of the court, to allow the creditor to foreclose upon, repossess, or otherwise proceed in rem against that property. The surrendered property will, nonetheless, remain property of the estate until it has been disposed of pursuant to applicable non-bankruptcy law as a result of the creditor's proceedings unless the confirmed plan specifically provides for its abandonment or the court enters a separate order of abandonment, following an appropriate motion and notice to creditors.

(b) In a case under chapter 13, if the provisions of a plan provide for the surrender of property in which a creditor has an interest, the court will consider a motion for relief from stay and/or abandonment as to such property without holding a hearing, unless a party in interest files an objection to the relief requested, provided that:

(1) The motion is titled "Motion for Relief from Stay and/or Abandonment Because Plan Proposes to Surrender Property";

(2) Movant serves all creditors and parties in interest with a notice of the motion and the opportunity to object thereto, containing the information required by Local Bankruptcy Rule B–2002–2(c), and makes due proof thereof; and

(3) The deadline for filing objections to the motion is no less than fourteen (14) days after service of the notice and no sooner than seven (7) days after the first date set for the meeting of creditors held pursuant to section 341(a) of the United States Bankruptcy Code.

The failure to comply with the requirements of subparagraphs (b)(2) and (b)(3) will constitute a waiver of any time limits associated with ruling on the motion, including the time limits set forth in 11 U.S.C. § 362(e).

(c) In a case under Chapter 13, a motion for relief from stay and/or abandonment, other than a motion because a plan proposes to surrender property, will be set for such proceedings as the court deems appropriate, and must include the following information:

(1) Copies of documents upon which the claim is based, including loan documents and documents that evidence both the grant of the lien, security interest,

mortgage or other encumbrance, and its proper perfection or proper recordation;

(2) The balance owing as of the date the petition is filed, and the date and amount of any payments received since the filing;

(3) The total arrearage as of the petition date, the number of pre-petition payments in arrears, and the amount of each such payment;

(4) The movant's best estimate of the value of the collateral and the basis for that value;

(5) The identity of any person or entity claiming an interest in the property that is the subject of the motion and of which movant is aware; and

(6) If the motion is based upon a post-petition payment default, the motion and/or exhibits thereto shall also contain the following:

(A) A legible post-petition payment history that sets forth the date each post-petition payment was received, the amount of each post-petition payment, and how each post-petition payment was applied;

(B) An itemization of any other expenses or fees that are due post-petition including attorney fees, filing fees, late payment fees, and escrow advance;

(C) The total dollar amount necessary to cure the post-petition debt as of a date certain; and

(D) The address where the current monthly payment is to be mailed if the mailing address is not listed in the movant's filed proof of claim or if the mailing address has changed.

The failure to provide the documentation and/or information required by this paragraph may result in the motion being stricken or denied.

[Adopted effective May 11, 2009. Amended effective December 1, 2009; January 1, 2010.]

Historical and Regulatory Notes

By Order Amending Local Bankruptcy Rules dated December 16, 2009, this rule was amended effective January 1, 2010, to provide for substantive changes in paragraph (c).

By Order Amending Local Bankruptcy Rules dated November 18, 2009, this rule was amended effective December 1, 2009, to conform with the time computation changes in the Federal Rules of Bankruptcy Procedure.

Pursuant to Order Amending Local Bankruptcy Rules dated May 11, 2009, this new rule became effective immediately.

B–4002–1. DEBTOR'S DUTIES

(a) In addition to the other duties imposed upon a debtor by the Bankruptcy Code and Federal Rules of Bankruptcy Procedure, the debtor under any chapter shall:

(1) Cooperate with the United States trustee by furnishing such information as the United States trus-

tee may reasonably require in supervising the administration of the estate; and

(2) Immediately upon the entry of an order for relief, give written notice of the bankruptcy to any court or other tribunal where an action or other proceeding is being maintained against the debtor, whether or not the matter has proceeded to final judgment, and to all the parties involved in any such action or proceeding

(b) The payment advices or other evidence of payment referred to in 11 U.S.C. § 521(a)(1)(B)(iv) need not be filed with the court.

[Adopted effective January 1, 1994. Renumbered effective September 1, 2000. Amended effective January 1, 2010.]

Historical and Regulatory Notes

By Order Amending Local Bankruptcy Rules dated December 16, 2009, this rule was amended effective January 1, 2010, to provide for substantive changes including renumbering of paragraphs and adding paragraph (b). General Order 2005–03 is vacated with the amendment of this rule.

B-4002-2. PAYMENTS BY DEBTORS IN CHAPTER 13 CASES

Notwithstanding the provisions of 11 U.S.C. § 1326(a)(1)(B) and 1326(a)(1)(C), the debtor shall not reduce the payments to the Chapter 13 trustee, and any payments required by these sections shall be paid by the trustee following proper notice and order of the court.

[Effective January 1, 2010.]

Historical and Regulatory Notes

By Order Amending Local Bankruptcy Rules dated December 16, 2009, this new rule was adopted effective January 1, 2010. General Order 2005–03 is vacated with the adoption of this new rule.

B-4003-1. MANNER OF CLAIMING EXEMPTIONS

(a) Any property claimed as exempt shall be adequately described and itemized on the schedules required by Fed. R. Bankr. P. 1007. General terms (*i.e.*, "automobile," "personal property," "common stock," etc.) are not sufficiently descriptive and shall render any such claim ineffective. The section number of the statute under which such exemption is claimed shall be shown.

(b) The amount of a claimed exemption shall be limited by the dollar "Value of Claimed Exemption" listed on Schedule C regardless of the value of the asset. A debtor intending to claim an exemption which is not limited by a dollar amount shall indicate

on Schedule C that the "Value of Claimed Exemption" is "ALL."

[Adopted effective January 1, 1994. Renumbered effective September 1, 2000. Amended effective September 11, 2009.]

Historical and Regulatory Notes

Pursuant to Order Amending Local Bankruptcy Rules dated September 11, 2009, this rule was amended to add paragraph (b).

B-4004-1. EXTENSIONS OF TIME FOR FILING DISCHARGE OBJECTIONS AND DISCHARGEABILITY COMPLAINTS

(a) Motions for an extension of the time within which to file complaints objecting to a debtor's discharge, pursuant to 11 U.S.C. § 727, or to determine the dischargeability of debt, pursuant to 11 U.S.C. § 523, shall be combined with notice thereof, be filed prior to the expiration of the bar date to be extended and be served upon the United States trustee, any trustee, debtor and debtor's counsel, any committee and/or the entities included on any list required by Fed.R.Bankr.P. 1007(d).

(b) At a minimum, the motion shall state the cause for the requested extension, the date to which the time is to be extended, and contain a statement that any objections to the motion must be filed within fourteen (14) days of the date the motion was served.

(c) In the absence of an objection to the motion within fourteen (14) days after service the court may grant the motion without further notice or hearing.

[Adopted effective January 1, 1994. Renumbered and amended effective September 1, 2000. Amended effective February 15, 2004.]

Historical and Regulatory Notes

Pursuant to Order Amending Local Bankruptcy Rules dated February 15, 2005, paragraph (d) of this rule was deleted.

B-4004-2. DISCHARGE IN CHAPTER 13 CASES

(a) In any case filed on or after October 17, 2005, in order to receive a discharge after completing all the payments under a confirmed plan, the debtor shall file a Verified Motion for the Entry of a Chapter 13 Discharge. In a joint case a separate motion shall be filed by each debtor.

(b)(1) The Verified Motion for the Entry of a Chapter 13 Discharge shall separately affirm under penalties of perjury that the debtor has fulfilled each of the statutory requirements for a discharge. At the time of the adoption of this rule, those requirements are:

(A) that the debtor has completed all the payments required by the confirmed plan, whether made to the Chapter 13 trustee, or made directly to creditors (11 U.S.C. § 1328(a));

(B) if the debtor is required by any judicial or administrative order, or any statute, to pay a domestic support obligation, as defined by 11 U.S.C. § 101(14A), that the debtor has paid all amounts payable under such order or such statute that are due on or before the date of the certification (including amounts due before the petition was filed to the extent payment of such amounts was provided for by the plan (11 U.S.C. § 1328(a));

(C) that the debtor did not receive a discharge in a case filed under Chapter 7, 11, or 12 of the United States Bankruptcy Code during the four years prior to the date of the order for relief under Chapter 13 in the case (11 U.S.C. § 1328(f)(1));

(D) that the debtor did not receive a discharge in a case filed under Chapter 13 of the United States Bankruptcy Code during the two years prior to the date of the order for relief under Chapter 13 in the case (11 U.S.C. § 1328(f)(2));

(E) that, after filing the petition, the debtor completed a course concerning personal financial management, and that a copy of the certificate of completion of that course has been filed with the court, or that the court has exempted the debtor from completing such a course (11 U.S.C. § 1328(g)); and

(F) that there is no proceeding pending in which the debtor might be found guilty of a felony of the kind described in 11 U.S.C. § 522(q)(1)(A), or liable for a debt of the kind described in 11 U.S.C. § 522(q)(1)(B), and there is no reason to believe that 11 U.S.C. § 522(q)(1) might apply to the debtor (11 U.S.C. § 1328(h)).[1]

(2) In the event the debtor is required to pay a domestic support obligation, the verified motion shall also contain the name and address of the entity to whom such payments are to be made and the name and address of the debtor's employer. (See, 11 U.S.C. § 1302(d)(1)(C)).

(3) Local Bankruptcy Form LBF–4004–2 shall be used to file a motion for discharge, and any other form of motion may be subject to summary denial without notice or hearing. If the debtor is represented by counsel, the motion shall also be signed by debtor's counsel.

(c) The clerk will issue notice of a Motion for the Entry of a Chapter 13 Discharge and give all creditors and parties in interest at least thirty (30) days notice of the opportunity to object thereto. Absent timely objection, the motion may be granted and a discharge issued, without a hearing.

(d) If a Motion for the Entry of a Chapter 13 Discharge is not filed within thirty (30) days after the

filing of the trustee's final report, the court may close the case without issuing a discharge, but doing so shall not prejudice the debtor's right to file a motion to reopen under 11 U.S.C. § 350(b).

[Adopted effective June 15, 2008. Amended effective July 23, 2008; December 1, 2009.]

[1] This requirement is applicable to cases filed on or after April 20, 2005.

Historical and Regulatory Notes

Pursuant to Order Amending Local Bankruptcy Rules dated December 1, 2009, this rule and associated local form were amended to conform to the statutory provisions of 11 U.S.C. § 1328.

Pursuant to Order Amending Local Bankruptcy Rules dated July 23, 2008, this rule was amended to add a sentence to the end of paragraph (a).

Pursuant to Order Amending Local Bankruptcy Rules dated April 25, 2008, this new rule became effective June 15, 2008, along with LBF–4004–2.

B–4004–3.   DISCHARGE IN CHAPTER 11 CASES FOR INDIVIDUAL DEBTORS

(a) If the debtor is an individual, in order to receive a discharge in a case under Chapter 11 the debtor must file an appropriate motion. The motion may be filed either before or after confirmation of a plan in accordance with the provisions of this rule.

(b) Prior to confirmation, if the debtor would like the court to consider issuing a discharge upon confirmation of a proposed plan, it shall file a "Motion for Discharge Upon Confirmation." The motion shall state, with particularity, the reason or reasons for issuing a discharge before payments under the plan have been completed and shall be filed prior to the hearing to consider the adequacy of the disclosure statement or at the same time the debtor files a motion under local bankruptcy rule B–3017.1–1 to dispense with such a hearing. The court will hold a hearing on the debtor's motion for discharge, upon notice to all creditors and parties in interest, at the same time it considers confirmation of the proposed plan. Any objections to the motion must be filed within the time required by local bankruptcy rule B–9014–1(b) (no later than seven days prior to the hearing).

(c) After confirmation, when the debtor would like the court to consider issuing a discharge it shall file a "Motion for Discharge." The motion shall state how the debtor has satisfied the requirements for the entry of discharge, see, 11 U.S.C. § 1141(d)(5), by alleging, with particularity:

(1) that all the payments required by the confirmed plan have been completed; or,

(2) if all the payments required by the confirmed plan have not been completed, which payments have yet to be made, and

(A) the reason or reasons for issuing a discharge before payments have been completed; or

(B) how the distribution actually made on account of each allowed unsecured claim has satisfied the best interest of creditors test and why modification of the plan is not practicable.

The debtor shall serve all creditors and parties in interest with notice of a motion for discharge, in accordance with local bankruptcy rule B–2002–2, giving at least twenty–one (21) days notice of the opportunity to object thereto. Unless a creditor or other party in interest files a timely objection, the court will consider the motion and may issue a discharge without holding a hearing.

(d) In addition to satisfying the requirements of paragraph (b) or (c), any motion for discharge, whether filed before or after confirmation, must also state that there is no proceeding pending in which the debtor might be found guilty of a felony of the kind described in 11 U.S.C. § 522(q)(1)(A), or liable for a debt of the kind described in 11 U.S.C. § 522(q)(1)(B), and there is no reason to believe that 11 U.S.C. § 522(q)(1) might apply to the debtor (11 U.S.C. § 1141(d)(5)(C)).

(e) This rule applies only to cases filed on or after October 17, 2005.

[Adopted effective May 11, 2009. Amended effective December 1, 2009.]

Historical and Regulatory Notes

By Order Amending Local Bankruptcy Rules dated November 18, 2009, this rule was amended effective December 1, 2009, to conform with the time computation changes in the Federal Rules of Bankruptcy Procedure.

Pursuant to Order Amending Local Bankruptcy Rules dated May 11, 2009, this new rule became effective immediately.

B–4008–1. DISCHARGE AND REAFFIRMATION HEARINGS

(a) The court will not hold hearings concerning any reaffirmation agreement unless a motion to do so, signed by the debtor and, if the debtor is represented by counsel, debtor's counsel, is filed with the court.

(b) A motion for a hearing concerning any reaffirmation agreement shall be filed as a separate document and not incorporated into any other filing.

[Adopted effective January 1, 1994. Renumbered effective September 1, 2000. Amended effective October 17, 2005.]

Historical and Regulatory Notes

Pursuant to Order Adopting Interim Bankruptcy Rules and Amending Local Bankruptcy Rules dated October 14, 2005, this rule was revised to better implement the provisions of the Bankruptcy Abuse Prevention and Consumer Protection Act of 2005.

B–4008–2. RESCISSION OF REAFFIRMATION AGREEMENTS

(a) Court approval of the rescission of a reaffirmation agreement is not required.

(b) Should a debtor choose to rescind a reaffirmation agreement with any creditor, notice of rescission shall be given to the creditor at the address set forth in the reaffirmation agreement and, if known, to creditor's counsel within the time required and a copy thereof filed with the court.

(c) The failure to comply with paragraph (b) will not affect the validity of a rescission which otherwise complies with 11 U.S.C. § 524(c)(4).

[Adopted effective January 1, 1994. Renumbered effective September 1, 2000.]

B–5004–1. REASSIGNMENT UPON RECUSAL

If for any reason it should become necessary for a judge to be disqualified or recused from a case, contested matter or adversary proceeding assigned to that judge, the case, contested matter or adversary proceeding shall be sent to the Chief Bankruptcy Judge of the district for reassignment to any other judge who is not also disqualified. If the Chief Bankruptcy Judge is disqualified or recused from either deciding or reassigning such a case, contested matter or adversary proceeding, the case, contested matter or adversary proceeding shall be sent to the judge who is next senior in service on the bench and who is not also disqualified or recused for reassignment.

[Adopted effective January 1, 1994. Renumbered effective September 1, 2000.]

B–5005–1. MANDATORY ELECTRONIC CASE FILING (ECF)

(a) Effective July 1, 2005, any attorney who files any paper or appears in more than five (5) cases in a calendar year, regardless of when the case was originally commenced, shall file all documents electronically through the court's ECF system. The failure to do so may result in the noncomplying document being stricken and/or the imposition of other appropriate sanctions. For purposes of this rule, the calendar year will begin on January 1 of each year.

(b) All ECF Users shall maintain an active email address to which the court will electronically send notices and all ECF Users shall promptly advise the court of any change to that address.

[Adopted effective January 15, 2004. Amended effective April 28, 2005; August 20, 2013; July 7, 2015.]

Historical and Regulatory Notes

By Order Making Technical Amendments to Local Bankruptcy Rules dated July 7, 2015, this rule was amended to the word "document" to "paper."

Pursuant to Order Amending Local Bankruptcy Rule dated August 20, 2013, this rule was amended to include the requirement that all ECF users shall maintain an active email address with the court.

Pursuant to General Order 2005–01 dated April 28, 2005, this rule was amended to reflect the change in the threshold number from twenty-five (25) to five (5).

Pursuant to Order Amending Local Bankruptcy Rules dated January 15, 2004, this new rule was adopted, which renumbered then existing Rule B–5005–1 as B–5005–2; and renumbered then existing Rule B–5005–2 as B–5005–3.

B–5005–2. FORM AND STYLE REQUIREMENTS

(a) The following format requirements apply to all papers submitted for filing, whether in paper or electronic format:

(1) They shall be plainly typewritten or printed and double spaced, except for quoted material.

(2) The title must be set out on the first page.

(3) Each page shall be consecutively numbered.

(4) All papers must be clearly legible.

(b) For filings submitted in paper format:

(1) They shall be flat and unfolded.

(2) They shall be on white paper of good quality, 8½″ × 11″ in size, printed on one side of the paper only.

(3) They shall have no covers or backs and shall be fastened together at the top left corner and at no other place.

(4) If the filer wishes to receive a file-stamped copy of any paper document which is not presented for filing in person, they shall provide a self-addressed, stamped envelope of adequate size and postage.

(c) For filings submitted electronically:

(1) No paper submitted electronically may contain any watermarks, embedded links or hyperlinks relating to websites promoting commercial products except when relevant to the matter addressed in the filing. The failure to comply with this prohibition may result in the imposition of appropriate sanctions.

(2) All papers submitted electronically shall comply with the technical requirements of the court's Electronic Case Filing system.

(d) The originally signed paper copy of all documents submitted under oath or penalties of perjury shall be retained by the filing attorney for at least three years following the closing of the case by the court. Examples of such documents include, but are not limited to, affidavits, bankruptcy petitions, lists, schedules, statements, and amendments thereto. Such originally signed documents shall be produced upon request. The failure to do so may result in the imposition of sanctions, on the court's own initiative or upon the motion of the case trustee, United States trustee, United States Attorney, or other appropriate party.

(e) Fax and email filings are not permitted and will not be accepted. If such transmissions are received, they shall be of no effect and will be ignored.

[Adopted effective January 1, 1994. Renumbered and amended effective September 1, 2000. Amended June 4, 2001; August 27, 2002; September 24, 2002; October 28, 2003. Renumbered and amended effective January 15, 2004. Amended effective December 22, 2006; May 5, 2011.]

Historical and Regulatory Notes

By Order Amending Local Bankruptcy Rules dated May 5, 2011, this rule was amended to reorganize the rule to specify requirements relating to paper and electronic filings and to incorporate parts of abrogated Rule 5005–3.

By Order Amending Local Bankruptcy Rules dated December 22, 2006, this rule was amended to delete paragraph (b) which pertained to computer generated versions of Official Forms and paragraph (c) which pertained to the number of paper copies presented for filing; and to redesignate the remaining paragraph (d) as paragraph (b).

This rule was previously numbered as Rule 5005–1 until January 15, 2004, when a new Rule 5005–1 became effective, renumbering this rule as Rule 5005–2.

By Order Amending Local Bankruptcy Rules dated October 28, 2003, paragraph (c)(2) of this rule (then Rule 5005–1) was deleted, and paragraph (c)(1) was re-designated as paragraph (c).

By Second Order Amending Local Bankruptcy Rule B–5005–1 dated September 24, 2002, paragraph (a) and paragraph (c)(2) of this rule (then Rule 5005–1) were amended to conform procedures to electronic case filing requirements.

Pursuant to General Order 2002–01 dated August 27, 2002, this rule (then Rule 5005–1) was amended to conform procedures to electronic case filing requirements.

By Order Amending Local Rules dated April 30, 2001, this rule (then Rule 5005–1) was revised effective June 4, 2001.

B–5005–3. REQUIREMENTS AND PLACE OF FILING [ABROGATED]

[Adopted effective January 1, 1994. Renumbered and amended effective September 1, 2000; August 27, 2002; April 28, 2003; October 28, 2003. Renumbered effective January 15, 2004. Amended effective December 1, 2007. Abrogated effective May 5, 2011.]

B–5071–1. CONTINUANCES

(a) A request to continue, reschedule, postpone or cancel any matter scheduled before the court shall be made by motion, demonstrating good cause, or by stipulation of all parties involved. Whether the request or stipulation is granted, and upon what terms and conditions, if any, is in the discretion of the court.

(b) A request to continue, reschedule, postpone or cancel based upon a prior conflict shall specifically describe the conflict and must be filed no later than ten (10) days after the issuance of the notice or order scheduling the matter sought to be continued.

(c) Requests to continue, reschedule, or relocate a § 341 meeting shall be directed to the United States trustee or, if a trustee has been designated, to the trustee. Whether the request is granted is in the discretion of the United States trustee or the trustee.

(d) A motion to postpone an evidentiary hearing on account of the absence of evidence shall be made only upon affidavit, showing the materiality of the evidence expected to be obtained; that due diligence has been used to obtain it; where the evidence may be. If the motion is for an absent witness, the affidavit must show the name and residence of the witness, if known; the probability of procuring the testimony within a reasonable time and that the absence has not been procured by the act or connivance of the party, or by others at the party's request, or with his or her knowledge or consent, the facts that the party believes to be true, and that the party is unable to prove such facts by any other witness whose testimony can be as readily procured. If the adverse party will stipulate to the content of the evidence that would have been elicited at trial from the absent document or witness, the trial shall not be postponed. In the event of such a stipulation, the parties shall have the right to contest the stipulated evidence to the same extent as if the absent document or witness were available at trial.

[Adopted effective January 1, 1994. Renumbered effective September 1, 2000. Amended effective December 1, 2009; June 18, 2010.]

Historical and Regulatory Notes

By Order Amending Local Bankruptcy Rules dated June 18, 2010, this rule was amended to change the time computation in paragraph (b).

By Order Amending Local Bankruptcy Rules dated November 18, 2009, this rule was amended effective December 1, 2009, to conform with the time computation changes in the Federal Rules of Bankruptcy Procedure.

B–5072–1. COURTROOM AND COURT-HOUSE DECORUM [ABROGATED EFFECTIVE MAY 21, 2012]

[Adopted effective September 1, 2000. Abrogated effective May 21, 2012.]

B–5081–1. PAYMENT BY CHECK, CREDIT CARD AND RETURNED CHECKS

(a) No personal or business checks or credit cards will be accepted from debtors while the case is pending.

(b) In the event that any check or draft received by the clerk is returned for any reason, including but not limited to insufficient funds, closed account, etc., no further checks or drafts will be accepted from the maker unless the clerk is directed by the judge, after written application of the maker, to do so.

(c) Whenever a check or draft is returned for any reason, the returned check fee specified by the Judicial Conference shall be paid in full, in collected funds, in addition to the amount specified on the returned instrument, before the maker may apply for an order directing the clerk to accept checks or drafts.

[Adopted effective January 1, 1994. Renumbered and amended effective September 1, 2000.]

B–6004–1. SALES OUTSIDE THE ORDINARY COURSE OF BUSINESS

(a) A motion to sell property of the bankruptcy estate outside the ordinary course of business shall be served upon the United States trustee, any committee and/or the entities included on any list required by Fed. R. Bankr. P. 1007(d), and all entities that can be discovered through a reasonably diligent inquiry holding liens upon or having interests in the property to be sold.

(b) Notice of the motion must be given to all creditors and parties in interest, unless the court orders otherwise, in addition to service of the motion itself as required by paragraph (a).

(c) In the event the motion is granted, within seven (7) days following the sale the trustee or debtor-in-possession shall file or cause to be filed the report of sale required by Fed. R. Bankr. P. 6004(f)(1). The report of sale shall be served upon the parties identified in paragraph (a) and any objectors.

(d) The proceeds of the sale shall not be disbursed, except pursuant to court order following an appropriate motion upon notice to all creditors and parties in interest, in accordance with Local Bankruptcy Rule B–2002–2.

[Adopted effective January 1, 1994. Renumbered and amended effective September 1, 2000. Amended effective August 31, 2012.]

Historical and Regulatory Notes

By Order Amending Local Bankruptcy Rules dated August 31, 2012, this rule was amended to clarify that motions to disburse sale proceeds are subject to Local Bankruptcy Rule B–2002–2.

B–6006–1. EXTENSIONS OF TIME TO ASSUME OR REJECT EXECUTORY CONTRACTS

(a) Motions for an extension of the time within which to assume or reject an executory contract shall be filed prior to the expiration of the date to be extended and served upon all parties to the contract, the United States trustee, any trustee, the debtor and debtor's counsel, any committee and/or the entities included on any list required by Fed. R. Bankr. P. 1007(d).

(b) At a minimum, the motion shall identify the contract for which an extension is being requested and the identity of all parties thereto and shall also state the cause for the requested extension, and the date to which the time is to be extended.

[Adopted effective January 1, 1994. Renumbered and amended effective September 1, 2000. Amended effective January 1, 2002.]

Historical and Regulatory Notes

This rule was amended to conform with current practices pursuant to Order Amending Local Rules dated December 7, 2001, with an effective date of January 1, 2002.

B–6007–1. TRUSTEE'S NOTICE OF ABANDONMENT

(a) A trustee's or debtor-in-possession's notice of abandonment, served pursuant to 11 U.S.C. § 554(a) and Rule 6007(a), (not a motion to abandon filed by a party in interest pursuant to 11 U.S.C. § 554(b) and Rule 6007(b)) shall:

(1) identify the property to be abandoned;

(2) state the reason for the proposed abandonment; and

(3) state the date by which objections are to be filed, which shall be no less than 14 days from the date the notice is served, and where objections should be filed.

Except as authorized by local bankruptcy rule B–2002–3 or an order of the court, the notice shall be served upon all creditors and parties in interest and due proof thereof filed with the court.

(b) A no asset report is not a notice of abandonment.

[Adopted effective September 11, 2009.]

Historical and Regulatory Notes

Pursuant to Order Amending Local Bankruptcy Rules dated September 11, 2009, this new rule became effective immediately.

B–7007–1. MOTION PRACTICE; LENGTH AND FORM OF BRIEFS

(a) Any motion filed within a contested matter or an adversary proceeding (*e.g.*, motions filed pursuant to Fed. R. Bankr. P. 5011(b), 7012, 7037, and 7056) shall be accompanied by a separate supporting brief. Unless the court orders otherwise, the opposing party shall have thirty (30) days after service of the motion and initial brief within which to serve and file a response. The moving party shall have fourteen (14) days after service of any response within which to serve and file a reply. Time shall be computed as provided in Fed. R. Bankr. P. 9006. Extensions of time shall only be upon order of the court, for good cause shown. The failure to respond or reply within the time required will be deemed a waiver of the opportunity to do so and may subject the motion to a ruling without further submissions.

(b) Except by permission of the court, no brief shall exceed twenty-five (25) pages in length (exclusive of any pages containing a table of contents, table of authorities, and appendices), and no reply brief shall exceed fifteen (15) pages. Permission to file briefs in excess of these page limitations will be granted only upon motion supported by extraordinary and compelling reasons.

Briefs exceeding twenty-five (25) pages in length (exclusive of any pages containing the table of contents, table of authorities, and appendices) shall contain (a) a table of contents with page references; (b) a statement of issues; and (c) a table of cases (alphabetically arranged), statutes and other authorities cited, with reference to the pages of the brief where they are cited.

(c) A party citing a decision, statute, or regulation that is not available on Westlaw or Lexis/Nexis shall furnish a copy to the Court and other parties.

[Adopted effective January 1, 1994. Renumbered effective September 1, 2000. Amended effective June 4, 2001; December 1, 2009.]

Historical and Regulatory Notes

By Order Amending Local Bankruptcy Rules dated November 18, 2009, this rule was amended effective December 1, 2009, to conform with the time computation changes in the Federal Rules of Bankruptcy Procedure.

By Order Amending Local Rules dated April 30, 2001, this rule was revised to conform with current practices, effective June 4, 2001.

B–7007–2. ORAL ARGUMENT ON MOTIONS

(a) Any motion filed within an adversary proceeding or a contested matter may be determined by the court without argument or hearing, following the expiration of the time for any response or reply provided for by these rules.

(b) A request for oral argument shall be filed separately and served along with any brief, response, or reply. The request shall specifically identify the purpose of the request and estimate the time reasonably required for any argument. The granting of any request for oral argument shall be discretionary with the court.

(c) The court may, on its own initiative, schedule any motion for oral argument or a hearing.

[Adopted effective January 1, 1994. Renumbered effective September 1, 2000.]

B–7015–1. AMENDED PLEADINGS

(a) Except by leave of court, any amendment to a pleading in an adversary proceeding, whether submitted as a matter of course or in connection with a motion to amend, must reproduce the entire pleading and may not incorporate any prior pleading by reference or interlineation.

(b) A motion to amend any pleading filed in an adversary proceeding shall attach a copy of the proposed amended pleading to the motion. The original of the amended pleading shall be filed at the same time as the motion to amend.

[Adopted effective January 1, 1994. Renumbered and amended effective September 1, 2000.]

B–7016–1. PRE-TRIAL PROCEDURE

(a) The court, upon its own initiative or upon the request of a party in interest, may schedule any adversary proceeding, contested matter or other dispute for a pre-trial conference.

(b) The requirements of Fed. R. Bankr. P. 7016 shall apply to all adversary proceedings, contested matters and other disputes scheduled for a pre-trial conference.

(c) As a result of the pre-trial conference, the court may direct the parties to file a joint proposed pre-trial order, which, unless notified to the contrary, shall identify or contain:

(1) a statement concerning the court's subject matter jurisdiction which shall also state whether or not the matter before the court is a core or a non-core proceeding and, if non-core, whether or not the parties consent to the bankruptcy judge hearing and determining the matter and entering any final judgment or orders therein;

(2) a statement identifying the pleadings, motions, objections or other requests upon which the matter is at issue;

(3) the status of any pending motion filed within the adversary proceeding, contested matter, or other dispute;

(4) a separate statement by each party specifically identifying the theory of each claim or defense and a summary of the facts which each party will endeavor to prove in support thereof;

(5) stipulations as to any and all relevant and undisputed facts;

(6) a statement identifying the contested facts, if any;

(7) a statement identifying the contested legal issues, if any;

(8) a list of the exhibits which each party will offer into evidence at trial, except those to be used solely for impeachment or rebuttal, together with a stipulation concerning which, if any, exhibits may be received into evidence without further proof;

(9) a list of the names of the witnesses each party anticipates calling at trial, except those to be called solely for impeachment or rebuttal. The witness list shall specify the general qualifications of any witness who is to be called as an expert; and

(10) the estimated amount of time required for trial.

(d) The parties shall exchange copies of any exhibits listed in the pre-trial order on or before the date the pretrial order is filed with the court. If no pretrial order is required, exhibits shall be exchanged no later than fourteen (14) days prior to trial.

(e) In any non-core matter in which all parties have not consented to the bankruptcy judge hearing and determining the issue and entering any final judgment or orders thereon, each party shall file along with any joint proposed pre-trial order proposed findings of fact and conclusions of law, including citations for each conclusion of law, if available.

[Adopted effective January 1, 1994. Renumbered and amended effective September 1, 2000. Amended effective December 1, 2009.]

Historical and Regulatory Notes

By Order Amending Local Bankruptcy Rules dated November 18, 2009, this rule was amended effective December 1, 2009, to conform with the time computation changes in the Federal Rules of Bankruptcy Procedure.

B–7023–1. DESIGNATION OF "CLASS ACTION" IN CAPTION

(a) In any case sought to be maintained as a class action, the complaint shall bear next to its caption the legend "Complaint—Class Action." The complaint shall also contain a reference to the portion or portions of Rule 23, Federal Rules of Civil Procedure, under which it is claimed that the suit is properly maintained as a class action.

(b) Unless it is not practicable within the meaning of Rule 23(c)(1) of the Federal Rules of Civil Procedure to do so, a person seeking certification of a class action shall file a motion seeking class certification within ninety (90) days of the filing of a complaint brought as a class action. In ruling upon such a motion, the court may allow the action to be maintained as a class action, may disallow the action to be so maintained, or may order postponement of the determination pending discovery or other such preliminary procedures as appear to be appropriate and necessary in the circumstances. Whenever possible, where it is held that the determination should be postponed, a date will be fixed by the court for renewal of the motion.

(c) The provisions of this Rule shall apply, with appropriate adaptations, to any counterclaim or cross-claim alleged to be brought for or against a class.

[Adopted effective September 1, 2000.]

B–7024–1. PROCEDURE FOR NOTIFICATION OF ANY CLAIM OF UNCONSTITUTIONALITY [ABROGATED]

[Adopted effective September 1, 2000. Abrogated effective May 5, 2011.]

B–7026–1. FORM OF INTERROGATORIES, REQUESTS FOR PRODUCTION AND REQUESTS FOR ADMISSION

(a) The party propounding written interrogatories, requests for production of documents or things, or requests for admission, shall number each such interrogatory or request sequentially. The party answering, responding or objecting to such interrogatories or requests shall quote each such interrogatory or request in full immediately preceding the statement of any answer, response or objection thereto, and shall number each such response to correspond with the number assigned to the request.

(b) No party shall serve on any other party more than thirty (30) requests for admission without leave of court. Requests relating to the authenticity or genuineness of documents are not subject to this limitation. Any party desiring to serve additional requests for admission shall file a written motion setting forth the proposed additional requests for admission and the reason(s) for their use.

[Adopted effective September 1, 2000. Amended effective June 4, 2001.]

Historical and Regulatory Notes

By Order Amending Local Rules dated April 30, 2001, this rule was revised to conform with current practices, effective June 4, 2001.

B–7026–2. REQUESTS FOR FILING OF DISCOVERY MATERIALS

On its own motion or upon the request of a party in interest and for cause shown, the court may order that discovery materials in any adversary proceeding or contested matter which would not otherwise be filed, be filed, distributed or otherwise made available to parties in interest.

[Adopted effective January 1, 1994. Renumbered and amended effective September 1, 2000. Renumbered effective June 4, 2001.]

Historical and Regulatory Notes

By Order Amending Local Rules dated April 30, 2001, then existing Rule 7026–2 was abrogated and Rule 7026–3 was renumbered as Rule 7026–2.

B–7037–1. INFORMAL CONFERENCE TO SETTLE DISCOVERY DISPUTES

The court may deny any discovery motion (except those involving pro se litigants) unless the motion is accompanied by the certification required to be made under Rules 26(c)(1), 37(a)(1), and 37(d)(1)(B) of the Federal Rules of Civil Procedure. The certification shall be filed as a separate document and shall, in addition to the information required under the appropriate Federal Rule, also recite the date, time, and place of the conference or attempted conference and the names of all persons participating therein. If counsel for any party advises the court in writing that opposing counsel has refused or delayed meeting and discussing the problems covered in this Rule, the court may take such action as is appropriate to avoid unreasonable delay.

[Adopted effective September 1, 2000. Amended effective June 4, 2001; September 11, 2009.]

Historical and Regulatory Notes

By Order Amending Local Bankruptcy Rules dated September 11, 2009, this rule was amended to reflect updated Federal Rules of Civil Procedure.

By Order Amending Local Rules dated April 30, 2001, this rule was revised to conform with current practices, effective June 4, 2001.

B–7038–1. JURY TRIAL OF RIGHT

The provisions of Rule 38(b), (c), and (d) of the Federal Rules of Civil Procedure apply to adversary proceedings.

[Adopted effective January 1, 1994. Renumbered effective September 1, 2000.]

B–7041–1. FAILURE TO PROSECUTE

Any contested matter or adversary proceeding in which no action has been taken for a period of sixty (60) days may be dismissed due to the lack of prosecution, with judgment for costs, if any, following twenty-one (21) days notice given by the court to counsel of record or, in the case of a pro se party, to the party unless, for good cause shown, the court orders otherwise.

[Adopted effective January 1, 1994. Renumbered effective September 1, 2000.]

B–7041–2. DISMISSAL OF OBJECTIONS TO DISCHARGE

(a) A motion for the voluntary dismissal of a complaint containing an objection to a debtor's discharge, pursuant to 11 U.S.C. § 727, or a stipulation between the parties for the dismissal of such a complaint shall be served upon the United States trustee and any trustee.

(b) The motion or stipulation shall contain a recital concerning the consideration, if any, for the dismissal or the terms and conditions of any agreement concerning the dismissal.

(c) Unless the United States trustee, the trustee or another entity seeks to intervene or to be substituted for the plaintiff in the proceeding or objects to the dismissal within twenty-one (21) days following service of the motion, the court may grant the motion, upon such terms and conditions as it deems proper, without further notice or hearing.

[Adopted effective January 1, 1994. Renumbered and amended effective September 1, 2000.]

B–7054–1. COSTS

A party who has been allowed to recover costs pursuant to Fed. R. Bankr. P. 7054 shall have thirty (30) days from the entry of a final judgment to file requests for the taxation of costs. This time may be extended by the court for good cause shown. Failure to file such requests or to obtain leave of court for extensions of time within which to file shall be deemed a waiver of the right to make such requests.

[Adopted effective January 1, 1994. Renumbered effective September 1, 2000.]

B–7056–1. MOTIONS FOR SUMMARY JUDGMENT

(a) In addition to complying with the requirements of N.D. Ind. L.B.R. B–7007–1, all motions for summary judgment shall be accompanied by a "Statement of Material Facts" which shall either be filed separately or as part of the movant's initial brief. The "Statement of Material Facts" shall identify those facts as to which the moving party contends there is no genuine issue and shall be supported by appropriate citations to discovery responses, depositions, affidavits, and other admissible evidence. Any party opposing the motion shall, within thirty (30) days of the date the motion is served upon it, serve and file a "Statement of Genuine Issues" setting forth all material facts as to which it is contended there exists a genuine issue, supported with appropriate citations to discovery responses, affidavits, depositions or other admissible evidence, together with any affidavits or other documentary material controverting the movant's position. The "Statement of Genuine Issues" may either be filed separately or as part of the responsive brief. In determining the motion for summary judgment, the court will assume that the facts as claimed and supported by admissible evidence by the moving party are admitted to exist without controversy, except to the extent that such facts are controverted in the "Statement of Genuine Issues" filed in opposition to the motion, as supported by the depositions, discovery responses, affidavits and other admissible evidence on file.

(b) A party opposing a summary judgment motion may file a surreply brief only if the movant cites new evidence in the reply or objects to the admissibility of the evidence cited in the non-movant's response to the motion. The surreply must be filed within 7 days after the movant serves the reply and must be limited to the new evidence and objections.

(c) If a party is proceeding pro se and an opposing party files a motion for summary judgment, counsel for the moving party shall also simultaneously serve all unrepresented parties using Local Bankruptcy Form (LBF) B–7056–1. The failure to do so may result in denial of the motion for summary judgment, without prejudice to resubmission.

[Adopted effective January 1, 1994. Renumbered effective September 1, 2000. Amended effective December 18, 2012; July 7, 2015.]

Historical and Regulatory Notes

By Order Amending Local Bankruptcy Rules dated July 7, 2015, this rule was amended to add a new paragraph requiring the moving party to serve unrepresented parties and establishing a new form LBF B–7056–1.

By Order Amending Local Bankruptcy Rules dated December 18, 2012, this rule was amended to redesignate a paragraph and to add a new paragraph concerning surreply briefs.

B–7065–1. MOTIONS FOR PRELIMINARY INJUNCTIONS AND TEMPORARY RESTRAINING ORDERS

The court will consider a request for a preliminary injunction or a temporary restraining order only when:

(1) the party seeking the relief files a separate verified motion for such relief;

(2) the verified motion establishes the willingness of the moving party to provide security as the court might deem proper;

(3) the moving party files an accompanying brief in support of the requested relief; and

(4) in the case of a temporary restraining order, the further requirements of Federal Rule of Civil Procedure 65(b) are fully complied with.

[Adopted effective September 1, 2000.]

B–7067–1. DEPOSITS

(a) **Deposit into Registry Account and Other Interest-Bearing Accounts.** All funds deposited into the court pursuant to Rule 67 of the Federal Rules of Civil Procedure and 28 U.S.C. § 2041 shall be deposited into an interest-bearing Registry Account maintained by the Clerk. The Order of Deposit should direct the clerk, without further order of the court, to deduct from the income earned on the investment a fee not exceeding the fee authorized from time to time by the Judicial Conference of the United States, as soon as such fee becomes available for deduction from the investment income.

(b) **Orders Directing Investments of Funds by Clerk of Court.** A party may petition the court for an Order of Investment which directs the clerk to hold the funds in a form of interest-bearing account other than the Registry Account. Whenever a party seeks a court order for money to be invested by the clerk into an interest-bearing account, the party shall personally deliver a proposed order to the clerk, who will inspect the order for proper form, content, and compliance with this rule. The clerk shall immediately forward the proposed order to the judge for whom the order was prepared.

Any order which, pursuant to 28 U.S.C. § 2041, directs the clerk to invest funds in an interest-bearing account or instrument shall include the following:

(1) The amount to be invested;

(2) The name of the financial institution in which the money will be invested;

(3) The type of instrument or account;

(4) The term of the investment; and

(5) If the deposit and/or interest received during the time of investment will exceed the FDIC Insurance amount, then the petitioning party shall obtain a collateral pledge by the financial institution for the remainder of the investment. The collateral pledge shall be approved by the judge.

[Adopted effective September 1, 2000.]

B–7069–1. ENFORCEMENT OF JUDGMENTS [ABROGATED EFFECTIVE MAY 21, 2012]

[Adopted effective January 1, 1994. Renumbered effective September 1, 2000. Abrogated effective May 21, 2012.]

B–9002–1. MEANING OF WORDS IN LOCAL RULES

In construing any local rules of the district court made applicable to proceedings before the bankruptcy court, all references to the court shall be deemed to be a reference to the bankruptcy court, all references to the district judge or magistrate judge shall be deemed to be a reference to the bankruptcy judge, all references to the clerk shall be deemed to be a reference to the clerk of the bankruptcy court, and all references to the Federal Rules of Civil Procedure shall be deemed to be a reference to the corresponding Federal Rules of Bankruptcy Procedure.

[Adopted effective September 1, 2000.]

B–9006–1. INITIAL ENLARGEMENT OF TIME

(a) In any adversary proceeding in which a party wishes to obtain an initial enlargement of time, not exceeding thirty (30) days, within which to file a responsive pleading and in any adversary proceeding or contested matter in which a party wishes to obtain an initial enlargement of time, not exceeding thirty (30) days, within which to file a response to a written request for discovery or request for admission, the party shall contact counsel for the opposing party and solicit opposing counsel's agreement to the extension. In the event opposing counsel does not object to the extension, the party requesting the extension shall document the lack of objection and file notice of the extension. No further filings or action by the court shall be required for the extension.

(b) In the event the opposing party is not represented by counsel or opposing counsel objects to the request for extension, the party seeking the extension shall file a formal request for extension and, unless the opposing party is pro se, shall recite in the request the unsuccessful effort to obtain agreement.

(c) Any motion or notice filed pursuant to this rule shall state the date such response is due and the date to which time is to be enlarged.

[Adopted effective January 1, 1994. Renumbered effective September 1, 2000. Amended effective July 21, 2006.]

Historical and Regulatory Notes

By Order Amending Local Bankruptcy Rules dated July 21, 2006, this rule was amended to delete the requirement to document the lack of objection by letter to opposing counsel.

B–9010–1. ATTORNEYS

(a) The bar of this court shall consist of those persons admitted to practice by the District Court for the Northern District of Indiana.

(b) The chair of any committee established pursuant to 11 U.S.C. § 705 or § 1102 may appear and speak for the committee at any non-evidentiary hearing in a contested matter. Such a committee must be represented by an attorney at any evidentiary hearing and in all adversary proceedings.

(c) A person not a member of the bar of this court shall not be permitted to practice in this court or before any officer thereof as an attorney, unless (1) such person appears on his or her own behalf as a party, or (2) such person is admitted to practice in any other United States Court or the highest court of any state and is, on application to this court, granted leave to appear in a specific action pro hac vice and tenders the required fee (which is one-half of the fee required for admission to the bar of the United States District Court for the Northern District of Indiana) by a check payable to the "Clerk, United States District Court" or (3) such person appears as attorney for the United States.

(d) The provisions of N.D. Ind. L.R. 83–5(a)(3), (d), and (e) are applicable to all matters pending in the bankruptcy court.

(e) In all matters and proceedings before this court, only natural persons may appear and represent themselves. All other entities shall be represented by an attorney. For the purposes of filing a proof of claim, participating in a meeting conducted pursuant to 11 U.S.C. § 341 or a reaffirmation agreement, a creditor need not be represented by or appear through an attorney.

(f) Paraprofessionals may not appear at a § 341 meeting on behalf of a debtor but may appear and question a debtor on behalf of a creditor.

(g) Persons appearing pro hac vice pursuant to subsection (c) of this rule shall certify that they have read the Standards for Professional Conduct within the Seventh Federal Judicial Circuit and the local rules of this court and shall abide by them in all cases in this court. This certification shall accompany the motion to appear pro hac vice on the form available from the clerk of court. The failure to make the required certification may result in the motion being denied.

[Adopted effective January 1, 1994. Renumbered and amended effective September 1, 2000. Amended effective June 4, 2001; August 29, 2008; August 3, 2011; May 21, 2012.]

Historical and Regulatory Notes

This rule was amended for technical numbering revisions pursuant to Order Amending Local Bankruptcy Rules dated May 21, 2012.

By Order Amending Local Bankruptcy Rules dated August 3, 2011, this rule was amended, effective immediately, to make a technical correction to the rule.

By Order Amending Local Bankruptcy Rules dated August 29, 2008, this rule was revised to add a provision

relating to the procedure for obtaining pro hac vice admission to practice.

By Order Amending Local Rules dated April 30, 2001, this rule was revised to add language concerning the required fee to district court, effective June 4, 2001.

B–9010–2. APPEARANCE AND WITHDRAWAL

(a)(1) Each attorney representing a party in interest, except an attorney signing a voluntary petition for relief or a complaint in an adversary proceeding, shall first file a separate formal written appearance clearly identifying the party or parties such attorney is representing, and the name, mailing address, telephone number, and e-mail address of the attorney filing it.

(2) A single appearance submitted on behalf of multiple attorneys is not permitted. Each attorney must file his or her own appearance separately. General appearances by a law firm are not permitted.

(3) An appearance must be filed as a separate document and may not be incorporated into any other pleading, motion, or request. See Local Bankruptcy Rule B–9013–1. An appearance incorporating a request for some type of relief or other action, e.g., an appearance and a request for notice, will be treated only as an appearance. Any other request joined with an appearance may be ignored by all parties.

(b) An appearance shall remain effective until withdrawn by order of the court.

(c) Separate appearances must be filed by each attorney in the main case and in any adversary proceeding in which that attorney is participating.

(d) For purposes of this rule, the granting of a motion for admission pro hac vice constitutes a written appearance in the case or proceeding in which the motion is filed.

(e) Upon filing an appearance in the main case, the attorney will be added to the matrix of creditors and will be entitled to be served with the notices, orders, motions, and other papers that are to be served upon all creditors and parties in interest.

(f) Any attorney desiring to withdraw an appearance shall file a verified application and notice requesting leave to do so. The application and notice shall be served upon the client and, if filed in the main case, the United States trustee, any trustee, any committee and/or the entities included on any list required by Fed. R. Bankr. P. 1007(d), or, if filed in an adversary proceeding, all parties that have appeared in the matter. Unless accompanied or preceded by an appearance of other counsel, the application shall:

(1) specifically state the grounds or cause for withdrawal;

(2) be accompanied by satisfactory evidence that counsel has advised the client, in writing, of the

reasons for and the intention to seek permission to withdraw at least fourteen (14) days prior to its filing; and

(3) unless the client has terminated counsel's services, contain a statement that any response, objection, or comments to the application should be filed within fourteen (14) days.

Unless requested or ordered by the court, the court may rule upon the application without a hearing upon the expiration of the time for any response.

(g) Separate applications to withdraw must be filed for the main case and each adversary proceeding in which the attorney has appeared. The withdrawal of an appearance in the main case will not constitute an order withdrawing an appearance in any pending adversary proceeding and an order withdrawing an appearance in any adversary proceeding will not constitute an order withdrawing an appearance in the main case or any other pending adversary proceeding.

[Adopted effective January 1, 1994. Renumbered and amended effective September 1, 2000. Amended effective March 1, 2007; December 1, 2009; October 29, 2010.]

Historical and Regulatory Notes

By Order Amending Local Bankruptcy Rules dated October 29, 2010, this rule was amended effective immediately to require that each attorney file a separate individual appearance; to prohibit general appearances by a law firm; to clarify that any appearance incorporating any other request will be treated only as an appearance; and to clarify that the granting of a motion for admission pro hac vice satisfies the written appearance requirement.

By Order Amending Local Bankruptcy Rules dated November 18, 2009, this rule was amended effective December 1, 2009, to conform with the time computation changes in the Federal Rules of Bankruptcy Procedure.

By Order Amending Local Rules dated March 1, 2007, paragraph (a) of this rule was revised to delete the requirement that the appearance list the attorney's bar identification number and to add a requirement to list the attorney's e-mail address.

B–9011–1. SIGNING OF PAPERS [ABROGATED]

[Adopted effective January 1, 1994. Renumbered and amended effective September 1, 2000; abrogated effective October 28, 2003.]

Historical and Regulatory Notes

Pursuant to Order Amending Local Bankruptcy Rules dated October 28, 2003, this rule was abrogated.

B–9013–1. MOTIONS INITIATING CONTESTED MATTERS AND OTHER REQUESTS FOR RELIEF

(a) Except as otherwise authorized by Federal Rule of Bankruptcy Procedure 6006, every application, motion, or other request for an order from the court, including motions initiating contested matters, shall be filed separately from any other request, except that requests for alternative relief may be filed together. All such requests shall be named in the caption, shall state with particularity the order or relief sought and the grounds for the motion.

(b) Motions seeking relief from the automatic stay or adequate protection may not be joined with any other request or objection except abandonment.

(c) The application, motion, or other request should be accompanied by a proposed form of order.

[Adopted effective January 1, 1994. Renumbered effective September 1, 2000. Amended effective June 4, 2001; January 1, 2002; December 1, 2007; May 21, 2012.]

Commentary

Different types of relief can be subject to very different procedural requirements. Some must be set for hearing on notice to all creditors, others receive a hearing only if an objection is filed, and different deadlines apply to different requests. This rule avoids the confusion that will result if multiple requests for relief are combined in a single motion. It requires each request for relief to be filed separately from any other, unless alternative relief is sought.

In everyday life, choosing between alternatives often involves a choice between mutually exclusive options; you can go one way or the other, but not both. It is much the same with alternative relief. The court is asked to choose between available remedies; it may do one thing or the other, but not both. If both options could be selected, or if the court is asked to do more than one thing in a given situation, the relief sought is not alternative.

Requests for alternative relief will generally use the conjunction "or" in the motion's title or prayer, rather than the word "and," i.e., "motion to convert or dismiss," not "motion to dismiss and objection to confirmation." In the event a movant is not certain whether alternative relief is being sought, separate motions should be filed. There is no penalty for filing separately.

Pursuant to Rule 9014(c), certain provisions applicable to adversary proceedings are incorporated into contested matters. Absent from provisions incorporated by Rule 9014(c) are Fed. R. Bankr. P. 7018, 7019, and 7020, which respectively reference Fed. R. Civ. P. 18, 19, and 20. It is clear from this omission that joinder of claims, and joinder of parties, are not contemplated in a contested matter. A contested matter is essentially a discrete action seeking one form of relief as to a single party.

Historical and Regulatory Notes

Pursuant to Order Amending Local Bankruptcy Rules dated May 21, 2012, this rule was amended for clarification and to add a commentary.

Pursuant to Order Amending Local Bankruptcy Rules dated November 30, 2007, paragraph (a) of this rule was amended to conform to the provisions of the amended national rules.

This rule was amended to conform with current practices pursuant to Order Amending Local Rules dated December 7, 2001, with an effective date of January 1, 2002.

By Order Amending Local Rules dated April 30, 2001, this rule was revised effective June 4, 2001.

B–9013–2. SERVICE OF MOTIONS AND OBJECTIONS

(a) The party filing a motion, application or an objection is responsible for serving the motion, application or objection upon all entities entitled to receive it.

(b) Service of a motion or application upon the entities entitled to receive it is required in addition to service of any notice concerning the motion or application upon such entities.

(c) Except as provided in these rules or otherwise ordered by the court, all motions, applications, objections and other requests for relief shall be served upon the United States trustee, any trustee and counsel for the trustee, debtor and debtor's counsel, any committee and/or the entities included on any list required by Fed. R. Bankr. P. 1007(d), in addition to any other entity and its counsel upon whom the motion is required to be served by the Bankruptcy Code and the Federal Rules of Bankruptcy Procedure.

(d) With respect to service pursuant to Fed. R. Bankr. P. 7004(b)(4) and (5)—either in an adversary proceeding under Fed. R. Bankr. P. 7001 or a contested matter under Fed. R. Bankr. P. 9014—the addresses of the departments, agencies and instrumentalities of the United States of America shall be designated as those stated in the list filed by the Office of the United States Attorney pursuant to N.D. Ind. L.B.R. B–1007–5(b).

[Adopted effective January 1, 1994. Renumbered and amended effective September 1, 2000.]

B–9013–3. SERVICE UPON COMMITTEES

(a) Where the court has authorized a committee which has been elected or appointed to employ counsel, service upon the committee shall be made by serving counsel and, if known, the chair of the committee.

(b) Where the court has not authorized a committee which has been elected or appointed to employ counsel, service upon the committee shall be made by serving each member thereof and, if such a committee is a committee of unsecured creditors, service shall also be made upon the entities included on any list required by Fed. R. Bankr. P. 1007(d).

[Adopted effective January 1, 1994. Renumbered effective September 1, 2000.]

B–9013–4. PROOF OF SERVICE

(a) In addition to identifying the pleading, motion or other paper served and showing the date upon which service was made, every proof of service or certificate of service shall state the name of every entity served and the address to which service was directed, together with the manner in which service was made. Where service is made through the court's ECF System, the manner of service and the address to which service was directed may be provided by identifying the individuals so served and stating that they were electronically served through the court's ECF System.

(b)(1) Proof of service by facsimile machine may be made by the person causing the paper to be transmitted. Such proof of service shall indicate the telephone number to which the paper was transmitted and the method of confirmation that the transmission was received.

(2) Proof of service by email may be made by the person causing the paper to be transmitted. Such proof of service shall indicate the email address to which the paper was transmitted and the method of confirmation that the transmission was received.

(c) Proof of service of all papers required or permitted to be served may be made by certificate of the person serving the same or by written acknowledgment of service, unless some other method of proof is expressly required by these rules or by the Federal Rules of Bankruptcy Procedure.

(d) The court may take no action with regard to any pleading, objection, motion or other paper required to be served upon any other party, including motions initiating contested matters, unless accompanied by a proper proof or certificate of service. Any such pleading, objection, motion or paper may be stricken, sua sponte, following seven (7) days notice.

[Adopted effective January 1, 1994. Renumbered and amended effective September 1, 2000. Amended effective October 28, 2003; December 1, 2009; July 7, 2015.]

Commentary

This rule does not authorize service by any particular manner. That is done by other rules and orders of the court. The rule merely specifies how proof of that service is to be made. Paragraph (b)(2) is new and specifies how proof of service by email is to be made. It is modeled on the original paragraph (b) which did the same thing for fax service. That paragraph has been re-designated (b)(1) to accommodate the new provision.

Historical and Regulatory Notes

By Order Amending Local Bankruptcy Rules dated July 7, 2015, this rule was amended to add a new paragraph (b)(2) describing proof of service when service is made by email, re-designate the existing paragraph (b) as (b)(1), and add a commentary.

By Order Amending Local Bankruptcy Rules dated November 18, 2009, this rule was amended effective December 1, 2009, to conform with the time computation changes in the Federal Rules of Bankruptcy Procedure.

Pursuant to Order Amending Local Bankruptcy Rules dated October 28, 2003, paragraph (a) of this rule was amended to conform with electronic case filing requirements.

B–9014–1. OBJECTIONS AND RESPONS-ES TO MOTIONS INITIATING CON-TESTED MATTERS

(a) As to any matter in which the court may grant relief without a hearing in the absence of a timely objection, objections to the motion, application, or request shall contain a short, plain statement concerning the factual or legal basis for the objection. The failure to state a sufficient factual or legal basis for the objection may result in the objection being over-ruled without a hearing.

(b) Except as otherwise ordered by the court, as to any matter in which the court may grant relief only after a hearing, a party desiring to oppose the motion, application, or request shall, except for good cause shown, file and serve any objection no later than seven (7) days prior to the hearing. If such a hearing is scheduled upon less than fourteen (14) days notice, the objection or response shall be filed and served any time prior to or at the hearing. The objection or response shall be concise and direct, stating in short and plain terms the factual or legal basis for the objection and shall fairly meet the substance of the allegations contained in the motion, application, or request.

(c) The objections or responses required by para-graphs (a) and (b) above shall also be served upon the moving party or parties and the entities specified in N.D. Ind. L.B.R. B–9013–2(c).

[Adopted effective January 1, 1994. Renumbered and amended effective September 1, 2000. Amended effective December 1, 2009.]

Historical and Regulatory Notes

By Order Amending Local Bankruptcy Rules dated November 18, 2009, this rule was amended effective December 1, 2009, to conform with the time computation changes in the Federal Rules of Bankruptcy Procedure.

B–9014–2. APPLICABILITY OF CERTAIN RULES OF THE FEDERAL RULES OF CIVIL PROCEDURE TO CONTESTED MATTERS

(a) The provisions of Rule 5(d) of the Federal Rules of Civil Procedure concerning the filing of dis-covery matters shall apply to contested matters.

(b) The provisions of Rule 16(f) of the Federal Rules of Civil Procedure shall apply to all contested matters.

[Adopted effective September 1, 2000. Renumbered and amended effective June 4, 2001. Amended effective June 23, 2004; April 28, 2005; July 21, 2006.]

Historical and Regulatory Notes

By Order Amending Local Rules dated July 21, 2006, this rule was amended to make Rule 16(f) of the Federal Rules of Civil Procedure applicable to contested matters.

Pursuant to General Order 2005–01 dated April 28, 2005, paragraph (a) of this rule was deleted. The designation of the remaining paragraph as paragraph (b) was deleted.

This rule was amended pursuant to Order Amending Local Bankruptcy Rules dated June 23, 2004, which renamed the rule and added new paragraph (b).

This rule was amended pursuant to Order Amending Local Rules dated April 30, 2001, which renumbered then rule B–7026–4 to Rule B–9014–2 which opts out of disclosure requirements under FRCP 26.

B–9018–1. FILING UNDER SEAL

(a) A motion to file papers under seal shall be accompanied by a brief in support thereof. ECF Users shall file this motion electronically.

(b) If the motion is granted, the papers ordered to be placed under seal shall be filed on paper with the clerk, and not electronically, along with a paper copy of the order granting the motion. The papers to be sealed shall be placed in a sealed envelope with a prominently marked cover sheet containing the case or proceeding caption, title of the paper, and the legend "Filed Under Seal."

(c) The clerk will maintain sealed papers in accor-dance with the court's internal procedures.

[Dated: August 20, 2013.]

Historical and Regulatory Notes

By Order Amending Local Rule dated August 20, 2013, this new rule was adopted to provide more specific procedur-al instruction.

B–9019–1. STIPULATIONS AND SETTLEMENTS

When a case, adversary proceeding, contested mat-ter, dispute, claim or controversy is settled, the par-ties shall promptly notify the court of the settlement or stipulation and, within the time required by the court, file an agreed judgment or order and, where appropriate, a motion to compromise which will be considered following notice to creditors in accordance with N.D. Ind. L.B.R. B–2002–2. The court may extend this time upon a showing of good cause. Fail-ure to file the required judgment or stipulation may result in the dismissal of the pleading, motion, objec-tion, or application upon which the matter was at issue.

[Adopted effective January 1, 1994. Renumbered effective September 1, 2000. Amended effective February 15, 2005.]

Historical and Regulatory Notes

Pursuant to Order Amending Local Bankruptcy Rules dated February 15, 2005, this rule was amended in accordance with Rule B–2002–2.

B–9019–2. ARBITRATION/ALTERNATIVE DISPUTE RESOLUTION

The court may, upon its own initiative, or upon the motion of a party, set any appropriate adversary proceeding or contested matter for a non-binding method of alternative dispute resolution. The parties may, however, agree to be bound by the results of any such alternative method of dispute resolution.

[Adopted effective January 1, 1994. Renumbered effective September 1, 2000.]

B–9023–1. POST JUDGMENT MOTIONS

(a) Any motion filed after the entry of a final judgment or order, whether filed pursuant to Fed. R. Bankr. P. 9023 or Fed. R. Bankr. P. 9024, shall be accompanied by a separate supporting brief and any appropriate affidavits or other materials in support thereof. The failure to submit a supporting brief will be deemed a waiver of the opportunity to do so.

(b) Unless otherwise ordered by the court, no response to the motion is required.

(c) The provisions of N.D. Ind. L.B.R. B–7007–2 (oral argument on motions) apply to post judgment motions.

[Adopted effective January 1, 1994. Renumbered effective September 1, 2000.]

B–9027–1. REMAND OF REMOVED ACTIONS

(a) A motion to remand a claim or cause of action removed to the bankruptcy court, other than one based upon the lack of subject matter jurisdiction, shall be filed within the same time as a motion to remand actions which have been removed to the district court (*see e.g.*, 28 U.S.C. § 1447(c)) and shall be served upon all other parties to the removed action.

(b) The provisions of N.D. Ind. L.B.R. B–7007–1 (motion practice) and N.D. Ind. L.B.R. B–7007–2 (oral argument on motions) shall apply to motions to remand removed actions.

[Adopted effective January 1, 1994. Renumbered effective September 1, 2000.]

B–9029–2. LIMITATION ON SANCTIONS FOR ERROR AS TO FORM

The court may sanction any attorney or person appearing *pro se* for violation of any local rule governing the form of pleadings and other papers filed with the court by the imposition of a fine not to exceed $1,000.00, or by ordering stricken, after notice and opportunity to be heard or to cure the defect, a paper which does not comply with these Rules. Local rules governing the form of pleadings and other papers filed with the court include, but are not limited to, those local rules regulating the paper size, the number of copies filed with the court, and the requirement of a special designation in the caption.

[Adopted effective September 1, 2000.]

B–9070–1. CUSTODY OF FILES AND EXHIBITS

(a) **Custody During Pendency of Action.** After being marked for identification, models, diagrams, exhibits and material offered or admitted in evidence in any cause pending or tried in this court shall be placed in the custody of the clerk, unless otherwise ordered by the court, and shall not be withdrawn until after the time for appeal has run or the case is disposed of otherwise. Such items shall not be withdrawn until the final mandate of the reviewing court is filed in the office of the clerk and until the case is disposed of as to all issues, unless otherwise ordered.

(b) **Removal After Disposition of Action.** Subject to the provisions of subsections (a) and (d) hereof, unless otherwise ordered, all models, diagrams, exhibits or material placed in the custody of the clerk shall be removed from the clerk's office by the party offering them in evidence within ninety (90) days after the case is decided. In all cases in which an appeal is taken these items shall be removed within thirty (30) days after the mandate of the reviewing court is filed in the clerk's office and the case is disposed of as to all issues, unless otherwise ordered. At the time of removal a detailed receipt shall be given to the clerk and filed in the cause. No motion or order is required as a prerequisite to the removal of an exhibit pursuant to this rule.

(c) **Neglect to Remove.** Unless otherwise ordered by the court, if the parties or their attorneys shall neglect to remove models, diagrams, exhibits or material within thirty (30) days after notice from the clerk, the same shall be sold by the United States Marshal at public or private sale or otherwise disposed of as the court may direct. If sold, the proceeds, less the expense of sale, shall be paid into the registry of the court.

(d) **Withdrawal of Original Records and Papers.** Except as provided above with respect to the disposition of models and exhibits, no person shall withdraw any original pleading, paper, record, model or exhibit from the custody of the clerk or other officer of the court having custody thereof except upon order of a judge of this court.

[Adopted effective September 1, 2000. Amended effective December 22, 2006.]

Historical and Regulatory Notes

By Order Amending Local Bankruptcy Rules dated December 22, 2006, this rule was amended to delete paragraph (d) concerning custody of contraband exhibits; and to redesignate paragraph (e) as paragraph (d).

SELECTED FORMS
LBF–2. NOTICE OF OBJECTION TO CLAIM

UNITED STATES BANKRUPTCY COURT
NORTHERN DISTRICT OF INDIANA
———————— DIVISION

IN THE MATTER OF:)
)
    [name of Debtor]   )   CASE NO. *[case #]*
)
    DEBTOR(S)   )

NOTICE OF OBJECTION TO CLAIM

To: *[name of creditor]*

[Name of party objecting to claim] has filed an objection to your claim in this bankruptcy case. A copy of the objection accompanies this notice.

As a result of the objection, *your claim may be reduced, modified or eliminated*. You should read these papers carefully and discuss them with your attorney.

If you do not want the court to eliminate or change your claim, then **within thirty days (30)** of the date of this notice you or your attorney must:

1. File with the court a written response to the objection, explaining your position, at:

      [address of clerk's office for the division in which the case is pending]

If you mail your response to the court, you must mail it early enough so that it will be **received** within the time required.

2. You must also serve a copy of your response upon:

      [name and address of objector's attorney or the objector, if pro se]

      [name and address of the case trustee and the trustee's attorney, if any]

      *[in cases under Chapter 11, 12, or 13, name and address
of debtor's attorney or the debtor, if pro se]*

If you or your attorney do not take these steps, the court may decide that you do not oppose the objection to your claim.

Date: *[date notice is served]*   ———————— *[signature]*

                      Name:
                      Address:
                      Telephone:

[Amended effective September 1, 2000; August 4, 2010; July 7, 2015.]

LBF–3a. NOTICE OF MOTION AND OPPORTUNITY TO OBJECT

UNITED STATES BANKRUPTCY COURT
NORTHERN DISTRICT OF INDIANA
[division]

IN THE MATTER OF:

[name of debtor]	)	CASE NO. *[case number]*
	)	CHAPTER *[chapter number]*
DEBTOR(S)	)	

NOTICE OF MOTION AND OPPORTUNITY TO OBJECT

On *[date]*, *[name of moving party]*, filed *[name of motion]*, asking the court to *[briefly and specifically state what you are asking the court to do]*. In support of the relief requested, the motion states *[briefly summarize the motion]*. If you have not received a copy of the motion, you may get one by contacting the person who signed this notice or at the clerk's office.

Your rights may be affected. You should read these papers carefully and discuss them with your attorney. If you do not have an attorney, you may wish to consult one.

If you do not want the court to grant the motion, then **on or before** *[date]* you or your attorney must:

1. File a written objection to the motion, which should explain the reasons why you object, with the Clerk of the United States Bankruptcy Court at:

[address of the clerk's office for the division where the case is pending]

If you mail your objection, you must mail it early enough so that it will be **received** by the date it is due.

2. You must also serve a copy of your objection upon:

[name and address of movant's attorney or the movant, if pro se]

[name and address of any case trustee and the trustee's attorney, if any]

*[in cases under Chapter 11, 12, or 13, name and address
of debtor's attorney or the debtor, if pro se]*

[names and addresses of any others to be served]

If you do not file an objection by the date it is due, the court may grant the relief requested without holding a hearing. If you do file an objection, the court will set the motion for hearing, which you or your attorney will be expected to attend.

Date: *[date notice is served]* _____
[signed]

                                          Name:
                                          Title:
                                          Address:
                                          Telephone:

[Effective February 1, 2003; Revised August 4, 2010; July 7, 2015.]

LBF–3b. NOTICE OF MOTION AND OPPORTUNITY TO OBJECT

UNITED STATES BANKRUPTCY COURT
NORTHERN DISTRICT OF INDIANA
[*division*]

IN THE MATTER OF:

[*name of debtor*]	)	CASE NO. [*case number*]
	)	CHAPTER [*chapter number*]
DEBTOR(S)	)	

NOTICE OF MOTION AND OPPORTUNITY TO OBJECT

On [*date*], [*name of moving party*], filed [*name of motion*], asking the court to [*briefly and specifically state what you are asking the court to do*]. A copy of the motion is attached to this notice.

Your rights may be affected. You should read these papers carefully and discuss them with your attorney. If you do not have an attorney, you may wish to consult one.

If you do not want the court to grant the motion, then **on or before [*date*]** you or your attorney must:

1. File a written objection to the motion, which should explain the reasons why you object, with the Clerk of the United States Bankruptcy Court at:

[*address of the clerk's office for the division where the case is pending*]

If you mail your objection, you must mail it early enough so that it will be **received** by the date it is due.

2. You must also serve a copy of your objection upon:

[*name and address of movant's attorney or the movant, if pro se*]

[*name and address of any case trustee and the trustee's attorney, if any*]

[*in cases under Chapter 11, 12, or 13, name and address of debtor's attorney or the debtor, if pro se*]

[*names and addresses of any others to be served*]

If you do not file an objection by the date it is due, the court may grant the relief requested without holding a hearing. If you do file an objection, the court will set the motion for hearing, which you or your attorney will be expected to attend.

Date: [*date notice is served*]   _____
                                                   [*signed*]
                                                   Name:
                                                   Title:
                                                   Address:
                                                   Telephone:

[Effective February 1, 2003. Amended effective May 27, 2010; July 7, 2015.]

LBF–4004–2. VERIFIED MOTION FOR ENTRY
OF CHAPTER 13 DISCHARGE

UNITED STATES BANKRUPTCY COURT
NORTHERN DISTRICT OF INDIANA
_____ DIVISION

IN THE MATTER OF:)
)
)   CASE NO.
)
             DEBTOR)

VERIFIED MOTION FOR ENTRY OF CHAPTER 13 DISCHARGE

Comes now the debtor, _____, and, pursuant to 11 U.S.C. § 1328(a), moves the court for the entry of a discharge in this Chapter 13 case. In support of this request, I state the following:

1. All of the payments required by the confirmed plan, whether made to the Chapter 13 trustee or made directly to creditors, have been completed.

2. *NOTE: Please select one of the following paragraphs and delete the other.*

[*Option 1*] I am required to pay a domestic support obligation, as defined by 11 U.S.C. § 101(14A), to:

name of entity to whom support is paid—

mailing address—

and all such amounts that are due on or before the date of this motion have been paid. The name and address of my employer(s) is/are:

employer's name—

mailing address—

OR

[*Option 2*] I am not required to pay a domestic support obligation, as defined by 11 U.S.C. § 101(14A).

3. I did not receive a discharge in a case filed under Chapter 7, 11, or 12 of the United States Bankruptcy Code during the four years prior to the date of the order for relief under Chapter 13 in this case.

4. I did not receive a discharge in a case filed under Chapter 13 of the United States Bankruptcy Code during the two years prior to the date of the order for relief under Chapter 13 in this case.

5. *NOTE: Please select one of the following paragraphs and delete the other.*

[*Option 1*] After filing the petition in this case, I completed a course concerning personal financial management, and a copy of the certificate of completion of that course has been filed with the court.

OR

[*Option 2*] The court has exempted me from completing a course concerning personal financial management.

6. There is no proceeding pending in which I might be found guilty of a felony of the kind described in 11 U.S.C. § 522(q)(1)(A), or liable for a debt of the kind described in 11 U.S.C. § 522(q)(1)(B), and there is no reason to believe that 11 U.S.C. § 522(q)(1) might apply to me.

7.   [*Available for additional explanation or information.*]

Wherefore, I respectfully request that, following notice and the opportunity for a hearing, the court enter a discharge pursuant to 11 U.S.C. § 1328(a).

I certify under the penalty of perjury, that the foregoing statements are true and correct.

_____
Signature of Debtor

Date: _____

Respectfully submitted,

_____
Attorney for Debtor

Address:

Telephone:
Email:

[Effective June, 2008. Amended effective December 1, 2009; January 2013.]

LBF–7056–1. NOTICE OF MOTION FOR SUMMARY JUDGMENT

[INSERT APPROPRIATE CASE OR ADVERSARY PROCEEDING CAPTION]

NOTICE OF MOTION FOR SUMMARY JUDGMENT

A motion for summary judgment has been filed asking to have this matter decided against you, in whole or in part, without a trial. The motion claims there are no genuine issues of material fact and is based on the evidence presented in the affidavits and/or documents referenced in the motion or the argument that you are not able to offer admissible evidence in support of your position. The material facts set forth in the motion and accompanying affidavits/documents may be accepted as true unless you submit affidavits and/or other documentary evidence contradicting those assertions, along with a "statement of genuine issues" identifying the facts you dispute and any brief arguing your position.

Your response to the motion must be filed within thirty days from the date the motion was served [1] and comply with Rule 56 of the Federal Rules of Civil Procedure and local bankruptcy rule B–7056–1. Your response must include a "statement of genuine issues" identifying the facts you dispute and be accompanied by affidavits or other admissible evidence supporting your factual assertions. If you do not respond within the time required the court may rule against you. If you need more time to respond, you must file a motion asking the court for an extension of the deadline before it expires. The court may—but is not required to—give you more time.

Copies of Rule 56 of the Federal Rules of Civil Procedure and local bankruptcy rule B–7056–1 (N.D. Ind. L.B.R. B–7056–1) accompany this notice.

Date: _____   Signed: _____
                                  name:
                                  address:
                                  telephone:

[Effective July 7, 2015.]

[1] The date of service can be determined from the certificate of service accompanying the motion or by reviewing the docket at the clerk's office.

ELECTRONIC CASE FILING

REVISED SIXTH AMENDED ORDER AUTHORIZING ELECTRONIC CASE FILING

Pursuant to Rules 5(e) and 83 of the Federal Rules of Civil Procedure and Rules 5005(a)(2), 9011, 9029 and 9036 of the Federal Rules of Bankruptcy Procedure that authorize this court to establish practices and procedures for the filing, signing and verification of pleadings and papers, and sending of notices by electronic means, IT IS ORDERED that:

1. Electronic Filing Authorized. The court will accept the electronic filing of papers effective September 3, 2002, by way of the court's Electronic Case Filing System (ECF System).

2. Official Record. Except as otherwise ordered, the official record of the court for all papers filed on or after September 3, 2002, is the electronic record maintained by the clerk. Except for sealed papers, all papers submitted in a hard copy format by any person on or after September 3, 2002, will be imaged into an electronic form. All imaged papers will be destroyed in accordance with the procedure authorized by the court. Papers filed before September 3, 2002, will not be converted to an electronic format unless otherwise ordered by the court.

3. ECF Registered Users (ECF Users).

a. Attorneys admitted to the bar of this court (including those admitted pro hac vice under the applicable local rules) and others as the court deems appropriate, including creditors in a limited user status, may register as Users of the court's ECF System. Registrants will be issued a login and password upon fulfilling the following requirements:

i. Successful completion of a court-sponsored ECF training program;

ii. Completion of an ECF User application form;

The court may consider other factors or experience that demonstrate ECF proficiency in lieu of a court sponsored training program.

b. Registration as an ECF User constitutes:

i. The ECF User's consent to receive notice electronically and a waiver of the right to receive notice by first class mail, including notice of the entry of an order or judgment under Fed. R. Bankr. P. 9022;

ii. The ECF User's waiver of the right to personal service or service by first class mail and consent to electronic service, except with regard to service of a summons and complaint under Fed. R. Bankr. P. 7004 and subpoenas; and

iii. An affirmation that the ECF User will file all papers electronically.

c. A creditor, or others as the court may direct, may submit an application, available from the clerk's office, for a limited use password for the ECF System. Creditors with a limited use password may only electronically file proofs of claim and related papers.

4. Account Security. ECF Users should protect the security of their account and should immediately notify the clerk if they believe that the security of their account has been compromised.

5. Filing of Papers. Except as otherwise provided under this order, *e.g.*, paragraph 10.b, or other rules of this court, ECF Users are not permitted to electronically submit papers on behalf of another individual.

6. Exhibits and Attachments. Exhibits to an electronically filed paper, such as leases, notes, contracts, mortgages, etc., must be filed electronically as attachments to the paper.

7. Time of Electronic Filing. A paper filed electronically is filed as of the date and time stated on the "Notice of Electronic Filing" generated by the court's ECF System, which is the time the court's ECF server receives the electronic transmission. Filing in the Northern District of Indiana must be completed before midnight in South Bend, Indiana, where the court's ECF server is located, to be considered filed that day.

8. Effect of Electronic Filing. Electronic filing of a paper shall constitute entry of the paper on the docket of the case in which it was filed.

9. Signature Requirements.

a. *Signature of ECF Users.* The use of an ECF User's login and password for the electronic filing of any paper, including proofs of claim, constitutes that ECF User's signature for all purposes, including Rule 9011 of the Federal Rules of Bankruptcy Procedure.

Unless the electronically filed paper has been scanned and shows the individual's original signature, the signature of the ECF User shall also be indicated by "/s/ ECF User's Full Name" on the line where the signature would otherwise appear. Electronically filed papers must include a signature block that sets forth the name, complete mailing address, email address, and telephone number of the ECF User.

b. *Signatures on Jointly Signed or Filed Papers.* In the case of a stipulation, agreed order, joint motion or other paper which bears the signature of two or more persons, the signatures may be indicated by either:

i. Submitting a scanned copy of the originally signed paper, or its signature page(s); or

ii. Through the use of "/s/ Name" in the signature block where the signature(s) would otherwise appear. The use of "/s/ Name" constitutes the filer's representation that the filer has obtained the affirmative consent of all other signatories to the paper submitted.

c. *Debtor Signatures on Petitions, Statements, Schedules and Lists.* Debtor's signature upon any paper required to be signed under penalties of perjury, including, but not limited to, the bankruptcy petition, schedules, statements and lists, and any amendment thereto, may be indicated by any of the following methods:

i. Submitting a scanned copy of the originally signed paper(s);

ii. Attaching a scanned copy of the originally signed signature page(s) to the electronic paper; or

iii. Separately submitting a scanned copy of the originally signed signature pages(s) immediately after the electronic filing of the signed paper.

d. *Signatures on Other Papers Signed Under Oath.* Signatures upon affidavits or other papers signed under the penalties of perjury, other than the bankruptcy petition, schedules, statements and lists, and any amendment thereto, may be indicated by either:

i. Submitting a scanned copy of the originally signed paper; or

ii. Attaching a scanned copy of the signature page(s) to the electronic paper.

10. Service. The filer of an electronic paper is responsible for serving that paper on all entities entitled to receive it. Whenever a paper is filed electronically, a "Notice of Electronic Filing" will be transmitted automatically by email to all ECF Users who have appeared in the case or proceeding. Service of this email Notice shall constitute the service or notice of the paper filed. Any other entity entitled to be served with the paper shall be served with a hard copy of the paper in accordance with the Federal Rules of Bankruptcy Procedure.

11. Submission of Proposed Orders. Proposed orders shall be submitted electronically through the court's ECF System. Proposed orders submitted at the time an application, motion or other request for relief is filed (*see, e.g.,* N.D. Ind. L.B.R. B–9013–1(c)) should be attached to the request and identified as such.

Proposed orders submitted in response to directions from the court should be submitted as a separate paper, identified as a proposed order, and linked to the motion, objection, and/or directions to which it relates. Regardless of when they are electronically submitted, proposed orders should always be identified as such on the docket (*i.e.*, "Proposed Order regarding _____") and should never be dated or bear an indication of having been signed by the judge.

12. Entry of Orders. The clerk's electronic transmission of the "Notice of Electronic Filing" constitutes the notice required by Rule 9022, Federal Rules of Bankruptcy Procedure.

13. Technical Failures.

a. An ECF User who is unable to file a paper electronically due to circumstances beyond the ECF User's control, such as technical failures, may file the paper in a hard copy format. Such a filing shall be accompanied by a statement specifically explaining the reason for the paper filing.

b. If a filing is not timely as a result of a technical system failure, the ECF User may seek appropriate relief from the court, through Rule 9006 or Rule 9024 of the Federal Rules of Bankruptcy Procedure.

14. Electronic Paper Requirements.

a. File Format of Electronic Papers: All electronic filings, except the matrix of creditors and parties in interest required by local rule N.D. Ind. L.B.R. B–1007–1, must be submitted as portable document format (PDF) files and formatted in accordance with the requirement of local rule N.D. Ind. L.B.R. B–5005–2. PDF document images must be filed in black-and-white or text formats only. Grayscale or color PDF document images shall not be filed electronically. Papers should be scanned in black-and-white, and scanner resolution should be 300 dots per inch (DPI).

b. File Format of the Matrix of Creditors: The creditor matrix must be in an ASCII text format, a "*.TXT" file extension.

c. File Size of Papers Filed Electronically: Electronic filings, whether a paper, exhibit, or attachment thereto, should not exceed 3 megabytes (3Mb) in size, which is approximately 50 pages of black-and-white text. If a paper, exhibit or attachment exceeds 3Mb in size, it must be divided into parts no larger than 3Mb each.

15. Paper Retention Requirements.

a. *Petition, Schedules, and Statements.* Debtor's counsel shall retain the originally signed bankruptcy petition, schedules, statement and lists, and any amendments thereto for no less than three (3) years following the closing of the case by the bankruptcy court. Debtor's counsel shall produce the originally signed paper(s) upon request.

b. *Other Papers Signed Under Penalties of Perjury.* The ECF User filing any affidavit or other paper signed under penalties of perjury shall retain the original signed paper for no less than three (3) years following the closing of the case by the bankruptcy court and shall produce the originally signed paper upon request.

c. *Proofs of Claim.* The ECF User shall retain the originally signed proof of claim and all exhibits and attachments for no less than three (3) years following the closing of the case by the bankruptcy court and shall produce the originally signed paper upon request.

d. *Sanctions.* The failure to produce the originally signed paper upon request may result in the imposition of sanctions on the court's own initiative or appropriate motion.

16. Viewing Electronic Court Records. Persons wishing to view court records may do so at the clerk's office or through the Public Access to Court Electronic

Records (PACER) system. Information about the PACER system can be found at http://www.pacer.gov.

[Dated: July 7, 2015.]

ELECTRONIC AVAILABILITY OF TRANSCRIPTS OF COURT PROCEEDINGS

In accordance with the policy of the Judicial Conference of the United States (Judicial Conference) regarding the electronic availability of transcripts of court proceedings, effective March 9, 2009, the following procedures will apply to all transcripts filed on and after that date in the United States Bankruptcy Court for the Northern District of Indiana.

A. Access During the 90 Days After Filing.

1. *Limited Access at the Clerk's Office.* A transcript provided by a court reporter or transcriber will be available only for inspection and public viewing at public access terminals in the office of the clerk of court for a period of 90 days after it is delivered to the clerk. During this time, the original transcript may not be printed or copied by the clerk for any person.

2. *Obtaining Copies of Transcripts.* During the 90 days after a transcript has been filed with the court, a copy of the transcript may be obtained from the court reporter or transcriber at the rate established by the Judicial Conference. An attorney who purchases a transcript from the court reporter or transcriber will be allowed remote electronic access to the transcript through the court's CM/ECF system but will be assessed a PACER fee for all such access which will not be capped at 30 pages.

B. Redaction of Personal Identification Information.

1. *Review of Transcript.* It is the responsibility of attorneys and pro se parties who attended the hearing to review the transcript for redaction of personal identification information.

2. *Redaction Under Rule 9037(a).*

    a. Notice of Intent to Request Redaction. If a party wants to redact information contained in the transcript, that party must file a Notice of Intent to Request Redaction within 7 days after the original transcript is filed with the clerk. A copy of this Notice must be served on the court reporter or transcriber.

    b. Request for Redaction. After filing a Notice of Intent to Request Redaction, the filer has 21 days from the date of the filing of the original transcript to file a Request for Redaction. This Request must identify each personal identifier that is to be redacted and where that information appears in the transcript by listing the page and line number.

    c. Filing of Redacted Transcript. Once a Request for Redaction has been filed, the court reporter or transcriber has 31 days from the date of the filing of the original transcript to file a redacted version of the transcript.

3. *Redaction Under Rule 9037(d).* A person seeking to redact information that is not covered by Rule 9037(a) of the Federal Rules of Bankruptcy Procedure must file a Motion for Protective Order, together with a brief in support thereof, pursuant to Rule 9037(d).

C. Availability of Transcripts After 90 Days. After the 90–day period has ended, the filed transcript will be available for inspection and copying in the clerk's office and for downloading from the court's CM/ECF system through the judiciary's PACER system as described below. Charges for access to transcripts through PACER are not capped at 30 pages.

1. *No Redacted Transcript Filed.* If a redacted version of the transcript has not been filed, the unredacted transcript will be available for inspection and copying in

the clerk's office and for remote electronic access through the PACER system unless otherwise ordered by the court upon appropriate motion and for cause shown.

2. *Redacted Transcript Filed.* After a redacted version of the transcript has been filed, only the redacted transcript will be available for inspection and copying in the clerk's office and for remote electronic access through the PACER system. The unredacted version will not be available, either at the clerk's office or through PACER.

[Dated February 23, 2009, effective March 9, 2009.]

SELECTED GENERAL ORDERS
GENERAL ORDER 2000–01. IN RE: MOTIONS FOR ADMISSION PRO HAC VICE

In order to better implement the requirements of N.D.Ind.L.R. 83.5(c)(2), which, pursuant to N.D.Ind.L.B.R. B–9010.1(c), apply to proceedings in this bankruptcy court, the following procedures shall apply to motions to appear pro hac vice:

1. The court will not consider or act upon any motion to appear pro hac vice unless, in addition to complying with any other requirements that may govern admission pro hac vice, the motion is accompanied by:

a. A check payable to the "Clerk, United States District Court" in the amount required by N.D.Ind.L.R. 83.5(c)(2), "which is one-half of the fee required for admission to the bar of the [United States District Court for the Northern District of Indiana]," and

b. A proposed form of order granting the motion to appear.

2. If the motion to appear pro hac vice is granted, the clerk of the bankruptcy court shall forward movant's check to the clerk of the United States District Court for the Northern District of Indiana along with a copy of the order granting the motion. If the motion to appear pro hac vice is denied, the clerk of the bankruptcy court shall return the check to the movant along with a copy of the order denying the motion.

3. The court may refuse to consider or act upon any request for relief (other than a motion to appear pro hac vice) filed by any attorney who, pursuant to N.D.Ind.L.R. 83.5(c), is required to obtain leave to appear and has failed to do so.

[Dated: June 16, 2000. Amended February 2, 2001.]

GENERAL ORDER 2001–02. IN RE: ALTERNATIVE DISPUTE RESOLUTION
GENERAL ORDER REGARDING ALTERNATIVE DISPUTE RESOLUTION

The Court recognizes that a full, formal litigation may impose significant economic burdens on parties, and may delay resolutions of disputes for considerable periods. The Court also recognizes that sometimes an alternative dispute resolution procedure may enhance the quality of justice by improving the parties' clarity of understanding of their case, their access to evidence, and the satisfaction with the process and result. The Court deems it necessary to adopt local ADR procedures to make quicker, less expensive and potentially more satisfying alternatives to continuing litigation without impairing the quality of justice or the right to trial. *See N.D. Ind. L.B.R. B–9019–2.*

THEREFORE, in the interest of prompt, efficient and economical administration of bankruptcy cases, the Court ORDERS that the following procedures shall govern alternative dispute resolution effective June 4, 2001.

SECTION ONE. GENERAL PROVISIONS

Section 1.1 Purpose. Mediation under this section involves the confidential process by which a neutral, acting as a mediator, selected by the parties or appointed by the Court, assists the litigants in reaching a mutually acceptable agreement. The role of the mediator is to assist in identifying the issues, reducing misunderstanding, clarifying priorities, exploring areas of compromise, and finding points of agreement as well as legitimate points of disagreement. Any agreement reached by the parties is to be based on the voluntary decisions of the parties and not the decisions of the mediator. It is anticipated that an agreement may not resolve all of the disputed issues, but the process can reduce points of contention. Parties and their representatives are required to mediate in good faith, but are not compelled to reach an agreement.

Section 1.2 Immunity. All person serving as neutrals in any of the Court's ADR Programs are entitled to immunities and protections that the law accords to said persons, to the greatest extent possible while serving in such capacity.

Section 1.3 Jurisdiction of Proceeding. At all times during the course of any alternative dispute resolution proceeding, the case remains within the jurisdiction of the court. For good cause shown and upon hearing on this issue, the Court at any time may suspend or terminate the alternative dispute process.

Section 1.4 Other Methods of Dispute Resolution. These rules shall not preclude a court from ordering or the parties from agreeing upon any other reasonable method or technique to resolve disputes.

SECTION TWO. PROCEDURE

Section 2.1 Motion. Any contested matter or adversary proceeding ("controversy") may be referred to mediation ("mediation") by the Court upon its own motion, the agreement of parties, or upon the suggestion of any one party.

Section 2.2 Proposed Order. An agreement of the parties shall identify any filing deadlines or hearings that may need to be rescheduled to accommodate the mediation, shall propose such reasonable scheduling changes as are necessary to allow the mediation to proceed and shall be accompanied by a proposed order. If the parties have selected a mediator in accordance with Section 2.2 herein, the proposed order shall identify the mediator and provide for compensation in accordance with the requirements of Section 5.1 herein.

Section 2.3 Pendency of Matter. Unless otherwise ordered by the Court, the parties shall remain responsible for complying with all pleading, discovery, or Court imposed deadlines and any other applicable scheduling requirement established for the timely disposition of the controversy.

SECTION THREE. MEDIATORS

Section 3.1 Application and Qualification Requirements. Each applicant applying for inclusion on the Approved Mediators List ("List") must submit to the Clerk of the Court the Application Form prescribed by the Clerk. Except as otherwise determined by the court, to be included as a mediator in the List, each applicant must meet the following criteria:

(1) if the applicant is a lawyer, be a member in good standing of the bar of any state or the District of Columbia, with at least five years of practice;

(2) not have been suspended, or have had a professional license revoked, or have pending any proceeding to suspend or revoke such license;

(3) not have resigned from a professional organization while an investigation into allegations of misconduct which would warrant suspension, disbarment or professional license revocation was pending;

(4) not have been convicted of a felony;

(5) have completed appropriate mediation training, or have sufficient experience, in the mediation process; and

(6) be determined by the court to be competent to perform the duties of a mediator.

Section 3.2   Court Certification.

(1) The court in its sole discretion shall grant or deny an application submitted pursuant to subsection 3.1 of this General Order. If the court grants the application, the applicant's name shall be added to the List, subject to removal pursuant to Section 3.6 of this General Order. Said List shall be maintained by the Clerk of this Court.

(2) Each Applicant shall immediately notify the Court of any event that would be the basis for refusal of an application as set forth in Section 3.1. Failure to so inform the Court is in itself basis for removal.

Section 3.3   Reaffirmation of Qualifications.
Each applicant accepted for inclusion on the List shall reaffirm every five years the continued existence and accuracy of the qualifications, statements and representations made in the application. Failure to comply with this section shall be grounds for removal under Section 3.6.

Section 3.4   Mediator's Oath.
Before serving as a mediator, each person designated as a mediator shall take the oath or affirmation prescribed by 28 U.S.C. § 453, as if that person were a judge.

Section 3.5   Pro Bono Requirement.
Every Mediator shall agree to accept at least two appointments annually, if so appointed, to handle pro bono mediations in consideration for said mediator's inclusion on the List.

Section 3.6   Removal From Register.
A person shall be removed from the List either for the reasons as follows:

(1) Upon the person's request;

(2) Upon court order, after notice of hearing;

(3) On the first day of July following the third anniversary date of the person's inclusion on the list, unless said person refiles an Application pursuant to Section 3.3.

If removed by Court order, the person shall not be returned to the List absent a court order obtained on motion to the Chief Bankruptcy Judge supported by an affidavit sufficiently explaining the circumstances of such removal and the reasons justifying the return of the person to the List.

SECTION FOUR.   SELECTION

Section 4.1   Case Selection.
At any time no less than fifteen (15) days after the filing of the first responsive pleading is filed, or, thirty (30) days after filing the initial pleading in a controversy, whichever is longer, the court, on its own motion, by agreement of the parties, or the suggestion of a party, may refer a controversy to mediation.

Section 4.2   Appointment of Mediator.
Upon an order referring a case to mediation, the parties may, within seven (7) days:

(1) Choose a mediator from the List; or

(2) Agree upon a non-registered mediator who must be approved by the Court, and serves with leave of court.

In the event a mediator is not selected by the parties, the Court shall designate three (3) mediators from the List. Each side shall alternatively strike the name of one (1) mediator; the side initiating the controversy shall strike first. The mediator remaining after the striking process shall be deemed to be the selected mediator.

A person selected to serve as a mediator under this Rule may choose not to serve for any reason. At any time, a party may request the Court to replace the mediator for good cause shown. In the event a mediator chooses not to serve, or the Court decides to replace a mediator, the selection process shall be repeated.

Section 4.3   Disqualifying Events.
Any person selected as a mediator may be disqualified for bias or prejudice in the same manner that a judge may be

disqualified under 28 U.S.C. § 144. Any person selected as a mediator shall be disqualified in any matter where 28 U.S.C. § 455 would require disqualification if that person were a judge.

Section 4.4 Inquiry by Mediator; Disclosure. Promptly after receiving notice of appointment, the mediator shall make inquiry sufficient to determine whether there is a basis for disqualification under subsection 4.2 of this General Order. The inquiry shall include, but shall not be limited to, a search for conflicts of interest in the manner prescribed by the applicable rules of professional conduct for attorney mediators, and by the applicable rules pertaining to the mediator's profession for non-attorney mediators. Within seven calendar days after receiving notice of appointment, the mediator shall file with the court and serve on the parties to the mediation either (a) a statement that there is no basis for disqualification under subsection 4.3 and that the mediator has no actual or potential conflict of interest or (b) a notice of withdrawal.

(Note: Rejection is provided for in Section 4.2.)

SECTION FIVE. MEDIATION COSTS

Section 5.1 Mediation Costs. The parties and the mediator shall agree in writing upon the hourly rate for mediation which unless otherwise agreed shall be shared equally by the parties. The mediation costs shall be paid within thirty (30) days of the submission of the mediation invoice following the close of mediation.

Section 5.2 Party Unable to Afford Mediator. If the court determines that a party to a matter assigned to mediation cannot afford to pay the fees and costs of the mediator, the court may appoint a mediator to serve pro bono.

SECTION SIX. MEDIATION PROCEDURES

Section 6.1 Advisement of Participants.

The mediator shall:

(1) disclose to the parties or their attorneys any factual documentation revealed during the mediation if at the end of the mediation process the disclosure is agreed to by both parties; and

(2) advise the parties of all persons whose presence at mediation might facilitate settlement.

Section 6.2 Mediation Session.

(1) Mediation sessions shall not be open to the public.

(2) All mediation sessions shall be controlled by the written Agreement of the parties and the mediator. The Agreement may not conflict with the provisions of this Rule.

Section 6.3 Confidential Statement of Case. The attorney for each side may submit to the mediator and shall do so at the mediator's request, a confidential statement of the case, not to exceed ten (10) pages, prior to a mediation conference.

A confidential statement of the controversy may be supplemented by brochures, videos, and other exhibits or evidence. These supplemental materials shall be made available to opposing counsel at least five (5) days prior to the mediation. The confidential statement of the case shall at all times be held privileged and confidential from other parties unless an agreement to the contrary is provided to the mediator. In the mediation process, the mediator may meet jointly or separately with the parties and may express an evaluation of the case to one or more of the parties or their representatives. This evaluation may be expressed in the form of settlement ranges rather than exact amounts. The mediator may not share revealed settlement authority with other parties or their representatives without consent of said party.

Section 6.4   Termination of Mediation. The mediator may suspend or terminate mediation whenever the mediator believes that continuation of the process would harm or prejudice one or more of the parties or whenever the ability or willingness of any party to participate meaningfully in mediation is so lacking that a reasonable agreement is unlikely. At any time after two (2) sessions have been completed, any party may terminate mediation.

Section 6.5   Report of Mediation; Status.

(1) Within ten (10) days after the completion or termination of mediation, the mediator shall submit to the court, without comment or recommendation, a report of mediation status. The report shall indicate that an agreement was or was not reached in whole or in part. If the parties do not reach any agreement as to any matter as a result of the mediation, the mediator shall report the lack of any agreement to the court without comment or recommendation. With the consent of the parties, the mediator's report may also identify any pending motions or outstanding legal issues, discovery process, or other action by any party which, if resolved or completed, would facilitate the possibility of a settlement.

(2)(a) If an agreement is reached, in whole or in part, it shall be reduced to writing and signed by the parties and their counsel. If the agreement is complete on all issues, a joint stipulation of disposition shall be filed with the court. In all other matters the agreement shall be filed with the court only by agreement of the parties.

(b) Any settlement which requires notice pursuant to Bankruptcy Rule 2002(a) shall not be effective until approved by the Court after notice and hearing.

SECTION SEVEN.   CONFIDENTIALITY

Section 7.1   Protection of Information Disclosed at Mediation. The mediator and the participants in mediation are prohibited from divulging, outside of the mediation, any oral or written information disclosed by the parties or by witnesses in the course of the mediation. No person may rely on or introduce as evidence in any arbitral, judicial, or other proceedings, evidence pertaining to any aspect of the mediation effort, including but not limited to: (a) views expressed or suggestions made by a party with respect to a possible settlement of the controversy; (b) the fact that another party had or had not indicated willingness to accept a proposal for settlement made by the mediator; (c) proposals made or views expressed by the mediator; (d) statements or admissions made by a party in the course of the mediation; and (e) documents prepared for the purpose of, in the course of, or pursuant to the mediation. In addition, without limiting the foregoing, Rule 408 of the Federal Rules of Evidence and any applicable federal or state statute, rule, common law or judicial precedent relating to the privileged nature of settlement discussions, mediation or other alternative dispute resolution procedure shall apply. Information otherwise discoverable or admissible in evidence, however, does not become exempt from discovery, or inadmissible in evidence, merely by being used by a party in a mediation.

Section 7.2   Discovery from Mediator. The mediator may not be compelled to disclose to the court or to any person any of the records, reports, summaries, notes, communications, or other documents received or made by the mediator while serving in such capacity. The mediator shall not testify or be compelled to testify in regard to the mediation in connection with any arbitral, judicial, or other proceeding. The mediator shall not be a necessary party in any proceedings relating to the mediation. Nothing contained in this Section shall prevent the mediator from reporting the status, but not the substance, of the mediation effort to the court in writing, or from filing a final report as required by Section 6.5.

Section 7.3 Protection of Proprietary Information. The parties, the mediator, and all mediation participants shall not during or after the mediation conference disclose appropriately identified proprietary information.

Section 7.4 Preservation of Privileges. The disclosure by a party of privileged information to the mediator does not waive or otherwise adversely affect the privileged nature of the information.

SECTION EIGHT. SANCTIONS

Section 8.1 Sanctions. Upon motion by either party and hearing, the court may impose appropriate sanctions against any attorney, or party representative who fails to comply with these mediation rules.

[Dated: July 7, 2015.]

GENERAL ORDER 2001-03. IN RE: EXPENSES OF CHAPTER 13 TRUSTEES

The court has reviewed the amount of the administrative expenses of Chapter 13 Trustees at the request of the United States Trustee and the Chapter 13 Trustees. The court finds good cause has been shown to adjust the amount last set by the court in 2002.

Accordingly, the Chapter 13 Trustees shall be entitled to reimbursement of the following administrative expenses without the need for a motion, notice, hearing, or further order of the court:

1. Whenever the Chapter 13 Trustee is directed to serve a proposed Chapter 13 plan and an order fixing the deadline for filing objections thereto, the Trustee shall automatically be allowed an expense in the sum of $3.50 per notice served, per case, on account of the costs associated with the copying, mailing, and service of the plan and notice, and making proof thereof.

2. Whenever a Chapter 13 case is dismissed or converted prior to confirmation of a proposed plan, the Chapter 13 Trustee shall automatically be entitled to the reimbursement of costs in the sum of $50.00, in addition to the expenses set out in paragraph (1) above.

This order shall be effective as of October 1, 2012 as to all cases, whether filed before or after the date of this order. The court will periodically review the amount of these administrative expenses at the request of the United States Trustee.

[Amended: September 12, 2012.]

GENERAL ORDER 2013-01. IN RE: NOTICE OF TRUSTEE'S FINAL REPORT IN CHAPTER 7 ASSET CASES

The court notes that:

a. Procedures relating to closing chapter 7 asset cases have been set out in the Amended Memorandum of Understanding Between the Executive Office for United States Trustees and the Administrative Office of the United States Courts Regarding Case Closing and Post Confirmation Chapter 11 Monitoring, dated January 1999 (EOUST–AOUSC Memo).

b. Since April 1, 2009, 28 C.F.R. Part 58, § 58.7 requires trustees to use UST Form 101–7–NFR, Notice of Trustee's Final Report (NFR), to satisfy the notice requirements of Federal Rule of Bankruptcy Procedure 2002(f).

c. The court also notes that while the NFRs filed in this district set a 21–day period to file written objections to the NFR, the court has never formally established an objection period for the NFR.

d. Federal Rule of Bankruptcy Procedure 2002(f)(8) authorizes the court to direct someone other than the clerk to serve the summary of the trustee's final report.

Therefore, effective immediately, the court Orders

1. Pursuant to Federal Rule of Bankruptcy Procedure 2002(f)(8) the court authorizes the case trustee to serve the NFR on the debtor, all creditors, and parties in interest.

2. Any objections to the trustee's final report in a chapter 7 asset case shall be filed within 21–days from the service of the NFR by the trustee in the case as established by the EOUST–AOUSC Memo and the NFR.

3. Absent timely objections the NFR will be deemed approved and the trustee is authorized to make distributions in accord therewith without further order.

[Dated: December 2, 2013]

UNITED STATES DISTRICT COURT FOR THE SOUTHERN DISTRICT OF INDIANA

Including Amendments Received Through
November 1, 2015

GENERAL RULES

LOCAL RULE 1–1. SCOPE OF THE RULES

(a) Title and Citation. The local rules of the United States District Court for the Southern District of Indiana may be cited as "S.D. Ind. L.R."

(b) Effective Date and Scope of Rules. These rules, as amended from time to time, take effect February 1, 1992. They govern all civil and criminal cases on or after that date. However, in cases pending when the rules take effect, the court may apply the former local rules if it finds that applying these rules would not be feasible or would be unjust.

(c) Modification or Suspension of Rules. The court may, on its own motion or at the request of a party, suspend or modify any rule in a particular case in the interest of justice.

[Adopted effective February 1, 1992. Amended effective December 1, 2009; Former Rule 1.1 redesignated as Rule 1-1 and amended effective January 1, 2012; December 1, 2013.]

LOCAL RULE 1–2. ACCESS TO LOCAL RULES, ATTORNEY'S HANDBOOK, AND AMENDMENTS

(a) **Availability of Rules and Attorney's Handbook.** These rules and the *Attorney's Handbook* may be purchased from the clerk's office or accessed for free on the court's web site at www.insd.uscourts.gov.

(b) **Notice of Amendments.** These rules may not be amended without public notice and an opportunity for public comment. Notice will be submitted for publication in *Res Gestae*, the Indiana State Bar Association's monthly publication, and may also be published elsewhere.

[Adopted effective February 1, 1992. Amended effective January 1, 2000. Former Rule 1.2 redesignated as Rule 1-2 and amended effective January 1, 2012.]

LOCAL RULE 1–3. SANCTIONS FOR ERRORS AS TO FORM

The court may strike from the record any paper that does not comply with the rules governing the form of papers filed with the court, such as rules that regulate paper size or the number of copies to be filed or that require a special designation in the caption. The court may also sanction an attorney or party who files a non-compliant paper.

[Adopted effective February 1, 1992. Amended effective June 2, 1992; January 1, 2000. Former Rule 1.3 redesignated as Rule 1-3 and amended effective January 1, 2012.]

LOCAL RULE 4–6. REPRESENTATION OF INDIGENT LITIGANTS

(a) **Civil Trial Assistance Panel.** The court has established a civil trial assistance panel to help provide legal representation to indigent civil litigants who request it. The panel consists of attorneys, law school legal clinics, and law firms who have applied for membership and who are willing to represent litigants who cannot afford an attorney.

(b) **Requests for Representation.** If the court determines that a litigant is unable to afford an attorney and that one should be appointed under 28 U.S.C. § 1915(e), 42 U.S.C. § 2000e–5(f), or another statute, the court may:

(1) request that a specific member of the panel or of this court's bar represent the litigant; or

(2) direct the clerk to select an attorney from the panel at random and request that the attorney represent the litigant.

(c) **Right to Decline Request; Appearance upon Acceptance.** An attorney may decline a request to represent an indigent litigant. An attorney who accepts a request must file an appearance within 14 days of the request.

(d) **Duration of Representation.** An attorney who accepts a request must represent the litigant from the date the attorney enters an appearance until:

(1) the attorney withdraws as allowed under this rule;

(2) the attorney is discharged or removed from the case;

(3) the court enters final judgment (if reasonable collection and enforcement efforts are not appropriate); or

(4) the attorney undertakes reasonable collection and enforcement efforts after final judgment.

(e) **Withdrawal.** An attorney who accepts a request to represent an indigent litigant may not seek to withdraw from the litigant's case unless:

(1) the attorney and the litigant are personally incompatible;

(2) the attorney believes the litigant is pursuing the case for improper purposes;

(3) it appears that the litigant is able to afford a private attorney;

(4) another attorney appears for the litigant before or at the same time the attorney withdraws; or

(5) the attorney has, in writing, both

(A) asked the litigant for permission to withdraw, and

(B) informed the litigant that the court may choose not to replace the attorney should the attorney withdraw.

(f) **Discharge and Replacement Requests.** The litigant may ask the court to discharge or replace the attorney.

(g) **Discretion of Court to Remove Attorney.** The court has discretion to grant or deny requests to withdraw, discharge, or replace attorneys whom it has requested represent an indigent litigant.

(h) **Arrangements Between Litigant and Attorney.** An attorney who represents a litigant under this rule may:

(1) represent the litigant for pay if the litigant can afford a private attorney;

(2) represent the litigant for longer than is necessary to undertake reasonable collection or enforcement efforts; or

(3) negotiate and enter into a voluntary fee arrangement with the litigant.

(i) **Expenses.** The court will reimburse an attorney up to $500 for itemized copy, mail, telephone, travel, and expert-witness expenses that the attorney incurs while representing a litigant under this rule. But the court, in its discretion, may reimburse an attorney up to $1,000 for these expenses. To receive reimbursement, the attorney must file a petition and appropriately itemize the expenses. The court will not reimburse an attorney for expenses that the attorney could recover from a source other than the litigant.

(j) Award of Fees. Upon appropriate application, the court may award attorney's fees to a litigant who is represented by an attorney under this rule as if the litigant had retained a private attorney.

[Adopted effective February 1, 1992. Amended effective January 1, 1999; January 1, 2000; January 1, 2002; December 1, 2009; January 1, 2012.]

LOCAL RULE 5–1. FORMAT OF DOCUMENTS PRESENTED FOR FILING

(a) Filing. A paper or item submitted in relation to a matter within the court's jurisdiction is deemed filed upon delivery to the office of the clerk in a manner prescribed by these rules or the Federal Rules of Civil Procedure or authorized by the court. Any submission directed to the office of the clerk or any employee thereof in a manner that is not contemplated by this rule and without prior court authorization is prohibited.

(b) General. Any pleading, motion, brief, affidavit, notice, or proposed order filed with the court, whether electronically or with the clerk, must:

- be plainly typewritten, printed, or prepared by a clearly legible copying process;
- have at least 1–inch margins;
- use at least 12–point type in the body of the paper and at least 10–point type in footnotes;
- be double spaced (except for headings, footnotes, and quoted material);
- have consecutively numbered pages;
- include a title on the first page;
- if it has four or more exhibits, include a separate index that identifies and briefly describes each exhibit;
- if it is a form of order, include a statement of service, in the format required by S.D. Ind. L.R. 5–5(d) in the lower left corner of the paper; and
- in the case of pleadings, motions, legal briefs, and notices, include the name, complete address, telephone number, facsimile number (where available), and e-mail address (where available) of the pro se litigant or attorney who files it.

(c) Electronic Filings. Any paper submitted via the court's electronic case filing (ECF) system must be:

- in .pdf format;
- converted to a .pdf file directly from a word processing program, unless it exists only in paper

format (in which case it may be scanned to create a .pdf document);

- submitted as one or more .pdf files that do not exceed 10 megabytes each (consistent with the *CM/ECF Policies and Procedures Manual*); and
- otherwise prepared and filed in a manner consistent with the *CM/ECF Policies and Procedures Manual*.

(d) Non–Electronic Filings.

(1) *Form, Style, and Size of Papers.* Any paper that is not filed electronically must:

- be flat, unfolded, and on good-quality, 8.5″ × 11″ white paper;
- be single-sided;
- not have a cover or a back;
- be (if consisting of more than one page) fastened by paperclip or binder clip and may not be stapled;
- be two-hole punched at the top with the holes 2 ¾″ apart and appropriately centered; and
- include the original signature of the pro se litigant or attorney who files it.

(2) *Request for Nonconforming Fastening.* If a paper cannot be fastened or bound as required by this rule, a party may ask the clerk for permission to fasten it in another manner. The party must make such a request before attempting to file the paper with nonconforming fastening.

(e) Nonconforming Papers. The clerk will accept a paper that violates this rule, but the court may exclude the paper from the official record.

[Adopted effective February 1, 1992. Amended effective June 2, 1992; December 16, 1994; January 1, 2000; September 1, 2004; January 1, 2006; July 1, 2008; December 1, 2009. Former Rule 5.1 redesignated as Rule 5–1 and amended effective January 1, 2012; December 1, 2013; January 1, 2015.]

LOCAL RULE 5–2. FILING OF PAPERS ELECTRONICALLY REQUIRED

(a) Electronic Filing Required. All civil cases (other than those cases the court specifically exempts) must be maintained in the court's electronic case filing (ECF) system. Accordingly, as allowed by Fed. R. Civ. P. 5(d)(3), every paper filed in this court (including exhibits) must be transmitted to the clerk's office via the ECF system consistent with S.D. Ind. Local Rules 5–2 through 5–11 except:

(1) papers filed by pro se litigants;

(2) transcripts in cases filed by claimants under the Social Security Act (and related statutes);

(3) exhibits in a format that does not readily permit electronic filing (such as videos and large maps and charts);

(4) papers that are illegible when scanned into .pdf format;

(5) papers filed in cases not maintained on the ECF system; and

(6) any other papers that the court or these rules specifically allow to be filed directly with the clerk.

(b) Case Initiating Papers. The initial pleading and accompanying papers, including the complaint and issuance of the summons, may be filed either in paper form or electronically through the court's ECF system. Case initiating papers must be served in the traditional manner on paper. All subsequent papers must be filed electronically except as provided in these rules or as ordered by the court.

(c) Filing with the Clerk. Any paper that is exempt from electronic filing must be filed directly with the clerk and served on other parties in the case as required by those Federal Rules of Civil Procedure and these rules that apply to the service of non-electronic papers.

(d) Paper Filing by Non–Exempt Party. When a party who is not exempt from the electronic filing requirement files a paper directly with the clerk, the party must:

(1) electronically file a notice of manual filing that explains why the paper cannot be filed electronically;

(2) present the paper to the clerk within 1 business day after filing the notice of manual filing; and

(3) present the clerk with a copy of the notice of manual filing when the party files the paper with the clerk.

Note: Effective January 1, 2012, former Local Rule 5.6 is combined with former Local Rule 5.10 to create new Local Rule 5-2.

[Adopted effective January 1, 2012. Former Rules 5.6 and 5.10 redesignated in part as Rule 5–2 and Rule 5–10, and amended effective January 1, 2012.]

LOCAL RULE 5–3. ELIGIBILITY, REGISTRATION, PASSWORDS FOR ELECTRONIC FILING; EXEMPTION FROM ELECTRONIC FILING

(a) Mandatory Electronic Filing. Unless exempted pursuant to (e) below, attorneys admitted to the court's bar (including those admitted pro hac vice) or authorized to represent the United States must use the court's ECF system to file documents.

(b) Registration. To register to use the ECF system, an attorney must complete the registration form adopted by the clerk. The form must require:

(1) the attorney's name, address, and telephone number;

(2) the attorney's e-mail address; and

(3) a declaration that the attorney is admitted to this court's bar.

(c) Change in Information; Compromise of Password. An attorney who has registered to use the ECF system must notify the clerk:

(1) in writing within 30 days after the attorney's address, telephone number, or email address changes; and

(2) immediately upon learning that the attorney's password for the ECF system has been compromised.

(d) Consent to Electronic Service. By registering to use the ECF system, attorneys consent to electronic service of papers filed in cases maintained on the ECF system.

(e) Exemption from Participation. The court may exempt attorneys from using the ECF system in a particular case for good cause. An attorney must file a petition for ECF exemption and a CM/ECF technical requirements exemption questionnaire in each case in which the attorney seeks an exemption. (The CM/ECF technical requirements exemption questionnaire is available on the court's website, www.insd.uscourts.gov).

[Adopted effective July 1, 2002. Amended effective January 1, 2006. Former Rule 5.7 redesignated as Rule 5-3 and amended effective January 1, 2012. Amended effective January 1, 2013; January 1, 2015.]

LOCAL RULE 5–4. TIMING AND CONSEQUENCES OF ELECTRONIC FILING

(a) Deadlines. A paper due on a particular day must be filed before midnight local time of the division where the case is pending.

(b) When Electronic Filing Is Completed. Electronic transmission of a paper to the Electronic Case Filing System consistent with these rules, together with the transmission of a notice of Electronic Filing from the court, constitutes filing of the paper for all purposes of the Federal Rules of Civil Procedure and the court's local rules.

(c) Consequences of Electronic Filing. When a paper has been filed electronically:

(1) it is deemed entered on the clerk's docket under Fed. R. Civ. P. 58 and 79;

(2) the paper's electronic recording stored by the court is the official record of the paper;

(3) the paper, as filed, binds the filing party;

(4) the notice of electronic filing for the paper serves as the court's date-stamp and proof of filing;

(5) transmission of the notice of electronic filing generated by the ECF system to an attorney's e-mail address constitutes service of the paper on that attorney; and

(6) no other attempted service will constitute electronic service of the paper.

(d) Service on Exempt Parties. A filer must serve a copy of the paper consistent with Fed. R. Civ. P. 5 on any party or attorney who is exempt from participating in electronic filing.

Note: Effective January 1, 2012, former Local Rule 5.8 becomes Local Rule 5–4.

[Adopted effective July 1, 2002. Amended effective October 1, 2002; September 1, 2004; January 1, 2006. Former Rule 5.8 redesignated as Rule 5-4 and amended effective January 1, 2012.]

LOCAL RULE 5–5. ORDERS AND JUDGMENTS IN CASES FILED ELECTRONICALLY

(a) Court Will File Electronically. The court will file electronically any papers it issues. Doing so will constitute entry on the clerk's docket under Fed. R. Civ. P. 58 and 79.

(b) Notice of Order or Judgment.

(1) A notice of electronic filing will be generated and emailed to all ECF users who have appeared in a case immediately after an order or judgment is entered in that case. Issuance of the notice of electronic filing constitutes notice as required by Fed. R. Civ. P. 77(d)(1).

(2) If a party is represented by multiple attorneys from the same law firm and one or more is an ECF system user, notice of entry of an order or judgment in a case assigned to the ECF system will be transmitted only to the ECF system user. The clerk will send notice of the order or judgment to any party in the case that is not represented by at least one attorney using the ECF system. The clerk need not send any other notice of the order or judgment.

(c) Electronically Filed Orders. The court must file orders electronically. The court may issue orders signed electronically without an original signature or as "text-only" entries on the docket without an attached paper.

(d) Proposed Orders from Parties. A party must include a suitable form of order with any paper that requests the judge or the clerk to enter a routine or uncontested order. A party electronically filing a proposed order—whether voluntarily or because required by this rule—must convert the order directly from a word processing program and file it as an attachment to the paper it relates to. Proposed orders must include in the lower left-hand corner of the signature page a statement that service will be made electronically on all ECF–registered counsel of record via email generated by the court's ECF system, without listing all such counsel. A service list including the name and postal address of any pro se litigant or non-registered attorney of record must follow, stating that service on the listed individuals will be made in the traditional paper manner, via first-class U. S. Mail.

(e) Other Papers Requiring a Judge's Signature. A party electronically filing any other paper that requires a judge's signature must do so consistent with the *CM/ECF Policies and Procedures Manual.*

Note: Effective January 1, 2012, former Local Rule 5.9 is combined with former Local Rule 5.1(a)(5) and former Local Rule 5.12 to create new Local Rule 5–5.

[Adopted effective July 1, 2002; Amended effective September 1, 2004; January 1, 2006. Former Rules 5.9, 5.1(a)(5) and 5.12 combined and redesignated as Rule 5-5, and amended effective January 1, 2012. Amended effective January 1, 2013.]

LOCAL RULE 5–6. ATTACHMENTS AND EXHIBITS IN CASES FILED ELECTRONICALLY

(a) General Requirements. Each electronically filed exhibit to a main paper must be:

(1) created as a separate .pdf file;

(2) submitted as an attachment to the main paper and given a title which describes its content; and

(3) limited to excerpts that are directly germane to the main paper's subject matter.

(b) Excerpts. A party filing an exhibit that consists of excerpts from a larger document must clearly and prominently identify the exhibit as containing excerpted material. Either party will have the right to timely file additional excerpts or the complete document to the extent they are or become directly germane to the main paper's subject matter.

Note: Effective January 1, 2012, portions of former Local Rule 5.10 are incorporated into Local Rule 5–2 and the remainder of former Local Rule 5.10 becomes Local Rule 5–6.

[Former Rules 5.6 and 5.10 redesignated in part as Rule 5-2 and Rule 5-6, and amended effective January 1, 2012.]

LOCAL RULE 5–7. SIGNATURES IN CASES FILED ELECTRONICALLY

(a) Filing Certain Papers Signed by an Attorney. A pleading, motion, brief, or notice filed electronically under an attorney's ECF log-in and password must be signed by that attorney.

(b) Form of Electronic Signature. If a paper is converted directly from a word processing application to .pdf (as opposed to scanning), the name of the Filing User under whose log-in and password the paper is submitted must be preceded by a "s/" and typed on the signature line where the Filing User's handwritten signature would otherwise appear.

(c) Other Papers. A signature on a paper other than a paper filed as provided under subdivision (a) must be an original handwritten signature and must be scanned into .pdf format for electronic filing.

(d) Effect of Electronic Signature. Filing an electronically signed paper under an attorney's ECF log-in and password constitutes the attorney's signature on the paper under the Federal Rules of Civil Procedure, under these local rules, and for any other reason a signature is required in connection with the court's activities.

(e) Papers with Multiple Attorneys' Signatures. A paper signed by more than one attorney and electronically filed must:

(1) include a representation on the signature lines where the handwritten signatures of the non-filing attorneys would otherwise appear that the non-filing attorneys consent to the paper;

(2) identify in the signature block the non-filing attorneys whose signatures are required and be followed by notices of endorsement filed by the other attorneys within three business days after the original paper is filed; or

(3) include a scanned paper containing all necessary signatures.

(f) Unauthorized Use of ECF Log-in and Password. No one may knowingly allow anyone other than a filer's authorized agent to use the filer's ECF log-in and password.

Note: Effective January 1, 2012, former Local Rule 5.11 becomes Local Rule 5–7.

[Adopted effective July 1, 2002; Amended effective September 1, 2004; December 1, 2009. Former Rule 5.11 redesignated as Rule 5-7 and amended effective January 1, 2012.]

LOCAL RULE 5–8. PUBLIC ACCESS TO CASES FILED ELECTRONICALLY

Any person may review any unsealed paper that has been filed with the court:

(a) in person at the clerk's office; or

(b) via the court's internet site (www.insd.uscourts. gov) if they have a PACER log-in and password.

Note: Effective January 1, 2012, former Local Rule 5.13 becomes Local Rule 5–8.

[Adopted effective July 1, 2002; Amended effective January 1, 2006. Former Rule 5.13 redesignated as Rule 5-8 and amended effective January 1, 2012.]

LOCAL RULE 5–9. RETENTION OF PAPERS IN CASES FILED ELECTRONICALLY

A person who electronically files a paper that requires an original signature must maintain the original signed paper for two years after all deadlines for appeals in the case expire. On request of the court, the Filing User must provide original papers for review.

Note: Effective January 1, 2012, former Local Rule 5.14 becomes 5–9.

[Adopted effective July 1, 2002; Amended effective December 1, 2009. Former Rule 5.14 redesignated as Rule 5-9 and amended effective January 1, 2012.]

LOCAL RULE 5–10. NON–ELECTRONIC FILINGS

(a) When Completed. A paper or other item that is not required to be filed electronically is deemed filed:

(1) upon delivery in person, by courier, or via U.S. Mail or other mail delivery service to the clerk's office during business hours;

(2) when the courtroom deputy clerk accepts it, if the paper or item is filed in open court; or

(3) upon completion of any other manner of filing that the court authorizes.

(b) Return of File–Stamped Copies. To receive a file-stamped copy of a paper filed directly with the clerk, a party must include with the original paper an additional copy and a self-addressed envelope. The envelope must be big enough to hold the copy and have enough postage on it to send the copy via regular first-class mail.

(c) Form of Orders. A party must include a suitable form of order with any paper that requires the judge or the clerk to enter a routine or uncontested order.

(d) Form of Notices. If a party files a paper directly with the clerk that requires the clerk to give others notice, the party must provide the clerk with sufficient copies of the notice and the names and addresses of each person who is to receive the notice.

(e) Faxed Papers. The clerk may not file a faxed paper without court authorization. The court may not authorize the clerk to file faxed papers without finding that compelling circumstances justify it. A party must submit a copy of the paper that otherwise complies with this rule to replace the faxed copy within seven days after faxing the paper.

(f) Notice by Publication. The clerk must send notices required to be published to the party originating the notice. The party must deliver the notice to the appropriate newspapers for publication.

(g) Signature. The court will strike any paper filed directly with the clerk that is not signed by an attorney of record or the pro se litigant filing it, but the court may do so only after giving the attorney or pro se litigant notice of the omission and reasonable time to correct it. Rubber-stamp or facsimile signatures are not original signatures and the court will deem papers containing them to be unsigned for purposes of Fed. R. Civ. P. 11 and 26(g) and this rule.

Note: Effective January 1, 2012, provisions formerly contained in Local Rule 5.1(b) become Local Rule 5–10.

[Provisions of former Rule 5.1(b) redesignated as Rule 5-10 and amended effective January 1, 2012.]

LOCAL RULE 5–11. FILING UNDER SEAL—CIVIL CASES

(a) Filing Cases Under Seal. To seal a case, a party must file a motion requesting that the court seal the case with a proposed order at or before the time the party files its initial pleading. The clerk will seal the case until the court rules on the motion. If the court denies the motion, the clerk will unseal the case 14 days after service of the order, absent a Fed. R.Civ.P. 72(a) objection; motion to reconsider; or notice by a party of an intent to file an interlocutory appeal.

(b) Filing Documents Under Seal—General Rule. The clerk may not maintain under seal any document unless authorized to do so by statute, rule, or court order. Once a document is sealed, the clerk may not, without a court order, allow anyone to see it other than:

(1) the court and its staff;

(2) the clerk's staff; and

(3) the attorneys who have appeared and any pro se party in the case in which the document has been filed.

(c) Redaction in Lieu of Filing Under Seal.

(1) Documents redacted pursuant to Fed.R.Civ.P. 5.2(a) must not be filed under seal.

(2) When any of the confidential information in a document is irrelevant or immaterial to resolution of the matter at issue, the filing party may redact, by blacking out, the confidential information in lieu of filing under seal. Any party who files such a redacted document must serve an unredacted and complete version of the document upon all counsel and pro se parties.

(d) Filing Documents Under Seal—Procedure.

(1) To file a document under seal, a party must file it electronically as required under section 18 of the *ECF Policies and Procedures Manual* unless exempt from electronic filing under S.D. Ind. L.R. 5–2(a) or 5–3(e). In either case, the party must include a cover sheet as the first page for each document being filed under seal that must include:

(A) the case caption;

(B) the title of the document, or an appropriate name to identify it on the public docket if the title cannot be publicly disclosed;

(C) the name, address, and telephone number of the person filing the document; and

(D) if a motion requesting that it be sealed does not accompany the document, identification of the statute, rule, or court order authorizing the document to be sealed. A protective order does not authorize a party to file a document under seal.

(2) Unless the sealed filing is authorized by statute, rule, or prior court order (other than a protective order), a party filing a document under seal must contemporaneously:

(A) file a Motion to Maintain Document(s) Under Seal, and

(i) if the filing party designated the subject information confidential, a Brief in Support that complies with the requirements of subsection (e); and/or

(ii) if the filing party did not designate the subject information confidential, an identification of the designating party(ies); and

(B) file a redacted (confidential portions blacked out) public version of the document that is being filed under seal; and

(C) serve an unredacted and complete version of the document upon all counsel and pro se parties.

(3) The designating party(ies) identified according to subsection (2)(A)(ii) must, within 14 days of service of the Motion to Maintain Document(s) under Seal, file a Statement Authorizing Unsealing of Document (or specific portions thereof) and/or a Brief in Support that complies with the requirements of subsection (e). If the designating party fails to file such Statement or Brief, then the filing party must notify the court of that failure. Such failure will result in unsealing the document(s).

(e) Brief in Support. A Brief in Support must not exceed 10 pages in length, without prior leave of court, and must include:

(1) identification of each specific document or portion(s) thereof that the party contends should remain under seal;

(2) the reasons demonstrating good cause to maintain the document, or portion(s) thereof, under seal including:

(A) why less restrictive alternatives to sealing, such as redaction, will not afford adequate protection;

(B) how the document satisfies applicable authority to maintain it under seal; and

(C) why the document should be kept sealed from the public despite its relevance or materiality to resolution of the matter; and

(3) a statement as to whether maintenance of the document under seal is opposed by any party; and

(4) a proposed order as an attachment.

(f) Opposition to Maintenance Under Seal. Any opposition to a Motion to Maintain Document(s) Under Seal must be filed within 14 days of service of the Brief in Support. Any Brief in Opposition must not exceed 10 pages in length. A member of the public may challenge at any time the maintenance of a document filed under seal.

(g) Denial of Motion to Maintain Under Seal. If the court denies the motion, the clerk will unseal the document(s) after 14 days, absent Fed.R.Civ.P. 72(a) objection, motion to reconsider, appeal, or further court order.

[Adopted effective July 1, 2002. Amended effective January 1, 2006. Former Rule 5.3 redesignated as Rule 5–11 and amended effective January 1, 2012; January 1, 2015.]

Local Rules Advisory Committee Comments Re: 2015 Amendment

The 2015 revision includes a more detailed procedure for obtaining permission from the court to maintain filed documents under seal in civil matters. Filings under seal in criminal matters are the subject of new Local Criminal Rule 49.1–2. The parties are encouraged to consider and confer regarding redaction whenever practical and possible to avoid multiple filings of the same document and unnecessary motion practice. Parties should note that a protective order does not authorize a party to file or maintain a document under seal. In addition, the parties should follow Seventh Circuit guidance on the legal parameters for maintaining documents under seal enunciated in cases such as *City of Greenville, Illinois v. Syngenta Crop Protection, LLC*, 764 F.3d 695 (7th Cir. 2014); *Bond v. Utreas*, 585 F.3d 1061 (7th Cir. 2009); and *Baxter International, Inc. v. Abbott Laboratories*, 297 F.3d 544 (7th Cir. 2002).

Note: Adopted effective January 1, 2015.

LOCAL RULE 5.1–1. CONSTITUTIONAL CHALLENGE TO A STATUTE— NOTICE

(a) Time for Filing. A notice of constitutional challenge to a statute filed in accordance with Fed. R. Civ. P. 5.1 must be filed at the same time the parties tender their proposed case management plan, if one is required, or within 21 days of the filing drawing into question the constitutionality of a federal or state statute, whichever occurs later.

(b) Additional Service Requirements. If a federal statute is challenged, in addition to the service requirements of Fed. R. Civ. P. 5.1(a), the party filing the notice of constitutional challenge must serve the notice and paper on the United States Attorney for the Southern District of Indiana, either by certified or registered mail or by sending it to an electronic address designated for that purpose by that official.

[Adopted effective January 1, 2012.]

LOCAL RULE 6–1. EXTENSIONS OF TIME

(a) Motion Ordinarily Required. Ordinarily, a request for an extension of time not made in open court or at a conference must:

(1) be made by written motion;

(2) state the original deadline and the requested deadline;

(3) provide the reasons why an extension is requested; and

(4) if all parties are represented by counsel, either:

(A) state that there is no objection to the extension; or

(B) describe all attempts made to obtain an agreement to the extension and state whether opposing counsel objects to it.

(b) Automatic Initial Extension. The deadline for filing a response to a pleading or to any written request for discovery or admissions will automatically be extended upon filing a notice of the extension with the court that states:

(1) the deadline has not been previously extended;

(2) the extension is for 28 or fewer days;

(3) the extension does not interfere with the Case Management Plan, scheduled hearings, or other case deadlines;

(4) the original deadline and extended deadline;

(5) that all opposing counsel the filing attorney could reach agreed to the extension; or that the filing attorney could not reach any opposing counsel, and providing the dates, times and manner of all attempts to reach opposing counsel.

(c) Pro Se Parties. The automatic initial extension does not apply to pro se parties.

[Adopted effective February 1, 1992. Amended effective June 2, 1992; December 16, 1994; April 1, 1997; January 1, 2000. Amended effective July 1, 2008; December 1, 2009; January 1, 2012; January 1, 2013.]

LOCAL RULE 7–1. MOTION PRACTICE

(a) Motions Must Be Filed Separately. Motions must be filed separately, but alternative motions may be filed in a single paper if each is named in the title. A motion must not be contained within a brief, response, or reply to a previously filed motion, unless ordered by the court.

(b) Brief Required for Certain Motions. The following motions must also be accompanied by a supporting brief:

(1) a motion to dismiss, for judgment on the pleadings, or for more definite statement under Fed. R. Civ. P. 12.

(2) any motion made under Fed. R. Civ. P. 37.

(3) a motion for summary judgment under Fed. R. Civ. P. 56.

(4) a motion for a temporary restraining order under Fed. R. Civ. P. 65(b) and S.D. Ind. L.R. 65–2(b).

(c) Response and Reply Deadlines.

(1) *Summary Judgment Motions.* Summary judgment motions are subject to the deadlines in S.D. Ind. L.R. 56–1:

(2) *Other Motions.*

(A) Responses. Responsive briefs are due within 14 days after service of the supporting brief.

(B) Replies. Any reply briefs are due within 7 days after service of the response brief.

(3) *Extensions.* The court may extend response and reply deadlines, but only for good cause.

(4) *Summary Ruling on Failure to Respond.* The court may summarily rule on a motion if an opposing party does not file a response within the deadline.

(d) Routine or Uncontested Motions. A party filing a routine or uncontested motion must also file a suitable proposed order. The court may rule upon a routine or uncontested motion before the response deadline passes, unless:

(1) the motion indicates that an opposing party objects to it; or

(2) the court otherwise believes that a response will be filed.

(e) Page Limits.

(1) *Generally.* Supporting and response briefs (excluding tables of contents, tables of authorities, appendices, and certificates of service) may not exceed 35 pages. Reply briefs may not exceed 20 pages.

(2) *Permission to Exceed Limits.* The court may allow a party to file a brief exceeding these page limits for extraordinary and compelling reasons.

(3) *Supporting and Response Briefs Exceeding Limits.* If the court allows a party to file a brief or response exceeding 35 pages, the paper must include:

(A) a table of contents with page references;

(B) a statement of issues; and

(C) a table of authorities including

(i) all cases (alphabetically arranged), statutes, and other authorities cited in the brief; and

(ii) page numbers where the authorities are cited in the brief.

(f) Copies of Authority. Generally, copies of cited authorities may not be attached to court filings. However, a party must attach to the party's motion or brief a copy of any cited authority if it is not available on Westlaw or Lexis. Upon request, a party must provide copies of any cited authority that is only available through electronic means to the court or the other parties.

(g) Motions for Fees, Sanctions, and Disqualification.

(1) *Reasonable Efforts to Resolve Dispute.* The court may not grant the following motions unless the movant's attorney files with the motion a statement showing that the attorney made reasonable efforts to confer with opposing counsel and resolve the matters raised in the motion:

(A) motion for attorney's fees (other than post-judgment).

(B) motion for sanctions under Fed. R. Civ. P. 11.

(C) motion to disqualify an attorney (other than one brought by a pro se party).

(2) *Statement Regarding Efforts.* The statement required by subdivision (g)(1) must include:

(A) the date, time, and place of all conferences; and

(B) the names of all conference participants.

(3) *Refusal or Delay of Conference.* The court may take action appropriate to avoid unreasonable delay if any party's attorney advises the court in writing that any opposing counsel has refused to meet or otherwise delayed efforts to resolve the matters raised in the motion.

(h) Notice of Settlement or Resolution. The parties must immediately notify the court if they reasonably anticipate settling their case or resolving a pending motion.

[Adopted effective February 1, 1992. Amended effective June 2, 1992; December 16, 1994. Amended January 2, 1997; January 1, 1999; January 1, 2000; January 1, 2004; January 1, 2007; December 1, 2009; January 1, 2012. Amended effective January 1, 2013.]

LOCAL RULE 7–5. ORAL ARGUMENTS AND HEARINGS

(a) Request for Oral Argument. A party may request oral argument by filing a separate motion explaining why oral argument is necessary and estimating how long the court should allow for the argument. The request must be filed and served with the supporting brief, response brief, or reply brief.

(b) No Additional Evidence at Oral Argument. Parties may not present additional evidence at oral argument.

(c) Request for Evidentiary Hearing. A party may request an evidentiary hearing on a motion or petition by serving and filing a separate motion explaining why the hearing is necessary and estimating how long the court should allow for the hearing.

(d) Directed by the Court. The court may:

(1) grant or deny a request for oral argument or an evidentiary hearing in its sole discretion;

(2) set oral argument or an evidentiary hearing without a request from a party; and

(3) order any oral argument or evidentiary hearing to be held anywhere within the district regardless of where the case will be tried.

[Adopted effective February 1, 1992. Amended effective January 1, 2012.]

LOCAL RULE 8–1. PRO SE COMPLAINTS

Parties representing themselves must file the following types of complaints on forms that the clerk supplies:

- Complaints alleging claims under The Civil Rights Act, 42 U.S.C. § 1983.
- Complaints alleging claims under The Social Security Act, 42 U.S.C. § 405(g).
- Complaints alleging employment discrimination under a federal statute.

[Adopted effective February 1, 1992. Amended effective January 1, 2000; January 1, 2012.]

LOCAL RULE 9–2. REQUEST FOR THREE–JUDGE COURT

(a) Procedure. To request a three-judge court in a case, a party must:

(1) print "Three–Judge District Court Requested" or the equivalent immediately following the title on the first pleading the party files; and

(2) set forth the basis for the request in the pleading or in a brief statement attached to the pleading, unless the basis is apparent from the pleading.

(b) Sufficiency of Request. The words "Three–Judge District Court Requested" or the equivalent on a pleading is a sufficient request under 28 U.S.C. § 2284.

(c) Non–Electronic Filings. Parties in a case where a three-judge court has been requested must file an original and three copies of any paper filed directly with the clerk (instead of electronically) until the court:

(1) denies the request;

(2) dissolves the three-judge court; or

(3) allows the parties to file fewer copies.

[Adopted effective February 1, 1992. Amended effective January 1, 2012.]

LOCAL RULE 15–1. MOTIONS TO AMEND PLEADINGS

(a) Supporting Papers. A motion to amend a pleading must:

(1) if it is filed electronically, include as attachments the signed proposed amended pleading and a proposed order; or

(2) if it is filed directly with the clerk, be accompanied by a proposed order and one signed original and one copy of the proposed amended pleading.

(b) Form of Amended Pleading. Amendments to a pleading must reproduce the entire pleading as amended.

[Adopted effective January 1, 2012.]

LOCAL RULE 16–1. PRETRIAL PROCEDURES

(a) Initial Pretrial Conference. In all cases not exempted under subsection (f) of this rule, the court may order the parties to appear for an initial pretrial conference.

(b) Case Management Plan. Unless otherwise ordered or exempted under (f) of this rule, the parties in a civil case must confer, prepare, and file a joint case management plan:

(1) within 90 days after the case was either filed or removed to the court; and

(2) according to the instructions and form available on the court's website (www.insd.uscourts.gov/Attorney/default.htm).

(c) Parties' Responsibilities for Case Management Plan. The plaintiff must initiate and coordinate the efforts to confer about, prepare, and file the case management plan. If the plaintiff fails to do so, the defendant must appear at the initial pretrial conference with a proposed case-management plan.

If the parties cannot agree on all provisions of the case management plan the parties must file a joint plan that contains their respective positions in the disputed portions of the case management plan. The court will enter a case management plan that the court deems most appropriate with or without additional input from the parties.

(d) Additional Conferences. The court may set additional pretrial conferences. The parties must confer before each conference and must be prepared to address case-management plan issues, settlement, tri-

al readiness, and any other matters specifically directed by the court.

(e) Deadlines. Absent court order, deadlines established in any order or pretrial entry under this rule
may not be altered unless the parties and the court
agree, or for good cause shown.

(f) Exempted Cases. Unless otherwise ordered by
the court, the following types of cases will be exempted from the scheduling and planning requirements of
Fed. R. Civ. P. Rule 16(b):

(1) an action for review of an administrative record;

(2) a petition for habeas corpus or other proceeding
to challenge a criminal conviction or sentence;

(3) an action brought by a person in custody of the
United States, a State or a State subdivision;

(4) an action to enforce or quash an administrative
summons or subpoena;

(5) an action by the United States to recover benefit payments;

(6) an action by the United States to collect on a
student loan guaranteed by the United States;

(7) a proceeding ancillary to proceedings in another
court;

(8) an action to enforce, vacate or modify an arbitration award;

(9) mortgage foreclosures in which the United
States is a party; and

(10) civil forfeiture cases.

[Adopted effective February 1, 1992. Amended effective
June 2, 1992; December 17, 1993; December 16, 1994;
amended January 2, 1997; January 1, 2000; January 1, 2001;
January 1, 2002; January 1, 2005; December 1, 2009; January 1, 2012; January 1, 2013.]

LOCAL RULE 16–2. RESPONSIBILITIES FOR CASES REMANDED OR TRANSFERRED

Within 21 days after the court receives a case
remanded by the court of appeals for further proceedings or that is transferred from another district, each
party must file a statement of position as to what
action the court should take in the case.

[Adopted effective January 1, 2001. Amended effective January 1, 2012.]

LOCAL RULE 16–3. CONTINUANCES IN CIVIL CASES

(a) Court's Discretion. The court may continue
proceedings in a civil case on its own or on the motion
of one or more parties.

(b) Consultation with Clients. Attorneys must
consult with their clients before asking the court to
continue a trial.

(c) Continuance for Unavailable Evidence. A
party seeking to continue a trial because evidence is
unavailable must include with the motion an affidavit
showing:

(1) how the evidence is material;

(2) that the party has used due diligence to obtain
the evidence;

(3) where the party believes the evidence is; and

(4) if the evidence is the testimony of an absent
witness,

(A) the name and residence of the witness, if
known;

(B) the likelihood of procuring the testimony
within a reasonable time;

(C) that neither the party nor anyone at the
party's request or with the party's knowledge procured the witness's absence;

(D) the facts the party believes the witness will
truthfully testify to; and

(E) that the party cannot prove the facts by any
other witness whose testimony can be readily procured.

(d) Stipulation to Absent Evidence. The court
may not continue a trial because evidence is unavailable if all parties stipulate to the content of the
unavailable evidence. Despite the stipulation, the parties may contest the stipulated evidence as if it had
been available at trial.

(e) Award of Costs Due to Continuance. The
court may order a party seeking a continuance to
reimburse other parties for their actual expenses
caused by the delay.

[Adopted effective February 1, 1992. Amended effective
January 1, 2000; January 1, 2012.]

LOCAL RULE 23–1. DESIGNATION OF "CLASS ACTION" IN THE CAPTION

(a) Designation in Complaint. A party seeking
to maintain a case as a class action (whether for or
against a class) must include in the complaint, crossclaim, or counterclaim:

(1) the words "Class Action" in the paper's title;
and

(2) a reference to each part of Fed. R. Civ. P. 23
that the party relies on in seeking to maintain the case
as a class action.

(b) Counterclaims and Crossclaims. The provisions of the Rule will apply, with appropriate adapta-

tions, to any counterclaim or crossclaim alleged to be brought for or against a class.

Notes: Former subsection (b) was deleted from the rule on January 1, 2011, thereby removing the requirement that a separate motion seeking class certification be filed within 90 days of filing of a complaint in a class action, leaving the timing of such a motion to be determined within the Case Management Plan for each case.

[Adopted effective February 1, 1992. Amended effective January 1, 2000; December 1, 2009; January 1, 2011; January 1, 2012.]

LOCAL RULE 26–1. FORM OF CERTAIN DISCOVERY REQUESTS

(a) Form of Discovery Requests. A party propounding written discovery under Fed. R. Civ. P. 33, 34, or 36 must number each interrogatory or request sequentially and, upon request, supply the written discovery to the responding party in an editable word processing format.

(b) Form of Discovery Responses. A party responding (by answer or objection) to written discovery must fully quote each interrogatory or request immediately before each response and number each response to correspond with the interrogatory or request.

[Adopted effective February 1, 1992. Amended effective December 16, 1994; January 1, 2001; December 1, 2009; January 1, 2012.]

LOCAL RULE 26–2. FILING OF DISCOVERY MATERIALS

Discovery materials (whether discovery requests, responses, or deposition transcripts) may not be filed with the court except in the following circumstances:

(a) Relevant to Certain Motions. A party seeking relief under Fed. R. Civ. P. 26(c) or 37, or by way of a pretrial motion that could result in a final order on an issue, must file with the motion those parts of the discovery materials relevant to the motion.

(b) For Anticipated Use at Trial. When a party can reasonably anticipate using discovery materials at trial, the party must file the relevant portions at the start of the trial.

(c) Materials Necessary for Appeal. A party seeking for purposes of appeal to supplement the record with discovery materials not previously filed may do so by stipulation of the parties or by court order approving the filing.

[Adopted effective February 1, 1992. Amended effective December 16, 1994; January 1, 2001; January 1, 2012.]

LOCAL RULE 30–1. CONDUCT OF DEPOSITIONS

(a) Questions About an Asserted Privilege. An attorney may question a deponent who refuses to answer a question on the basis of privilege about information related to the appropriateness of the privilege, including whether:

(1) the privilege applies under the circumstances;

(2) the privilege has been waived; and

(3) circumstances exist to overcome a claim of qualified privilege.

(b) Private Conference Regarding a Pending Question. A deponent's attorney may not initiate a private conference with the deponent during the deposition about a pending question except to determine whether to assert a claim of privilege.

(c) Raising Objections with the Court. A party may recess a deposition to submit an objection by phone to a judicial officer if the objection:

(1) could cause the deposition to be terminated; and

(2) can be resolved without submitting written materials to the court.

(d) Scheduling Depositions. Under the Standards for Professional Conduct within the Seventh Federal Judicial Circuit, Lawyers Duty to Other Counsel, paragraph 14, attorneys will make a good faith effort to schedule depositions in a manner that avoids scheduling conflicts. Unless agreed by counsel or otherwise ordered by the court, no deposition will be scheduled on less than 14 days notice.

[Adopted effective June 2, 1992. Amended effective December 16, 1994; January 1, 2001; December 1, 2009; January 1, 2012.]

LOCAL RULE 36–1. REQUESTS FOR ADMISSIONS

No party may serve on any other party more than 25 requests for admission without leave of court. Requests relating to the authenticity or genuineness of documents are not subject to this limitation. Any party desiring to serve additional requests for admission must file a written motion setting forth the proposed additional requests for admission and the reason(s) for their use.

[Adopted effective January 1, 2001. Amended effective January 1, 2012.]

LOCAL RULE 37–1. DISCOVERY DISPUTES

(a) Required Actions Prior to Court Involvement. Prior to involving the court in any discovery dispute, including disputes involving depositions, counsel must confer in a good faith attempt to resolve the dispute. If any such dispute cannot be resolved in this manner, counsel are encouraged to contact the chambers of the assigned Magistrate Judge to determine whether the Magistrate Judge is available to resolve the discovery dispute by way of a telephone conference or other proceeding prior to counsel filing a formal discovery motion. When the dispute involves an objection raised during a deposition that threatens to prevent completion of the deposition, any party may recess the deposition to contact the Magistrate Judge's chambers.

(b) Requirements of Motion to Compel. In the event that the discovery dispute is not resolved at the conference, counsel may file a motion to compel or other motion raising the dispute. Any motion raising a discovery dispute must contain a statement setting forth the efforts taken to resolve the dispute, including the date, time, and place of any discovery conference and the names of all participating parties. The court may deny any motion raising a discovery dispute that does not contain such a statement.

(c) Pro Se Parties. Discovery disputes involving pro se parties are not subject to S.D. Ind. L.R. 37–1.

Notes: January 1, 2011—Local Rule 37.1 was amended and consolidated with Local Rule 37.3, to encourage informal resolution of discovery disputes, including disputes that might otherwise derail a deposition. More complex discovery disputes may benefit from full briefing, but the amended rule recognizes that most discovery disputes can be resolved or at least narrowed by good faith efforts of counsel and intervention by the Magistrate Judge as necessary. The amendment also deletes prior language in the rule suggesting parties were required to file a separate statement regarding efforts to resolve the discovery dispute. The amended rule provides that such a statement must be contained in the motion.

[Adopted effective February 1, 1992. Amended effective January 1, 2011; January 1, 2012.]

LOCAL RULE 38–1. JURY DEMAND

A party demanding a jury trial in a pleading as permitted by Fed. R. Civ. P. 38(b) must include the demand in the title by way of a notation placed on the front page of the pleading, immediately following the title of the pleading, stating "Demand for Jury Trial." Failure to do so will not result in a waiver under Rule 38(d) if a jury demand is otherwise properly filed and served under Rule 38(b).

[Adopted effective February 1, 1992. Amended effective January 1, 2012.]

LOCAL RULE 39–1. AUTHORIZATION OF BANKRUPTCY JUDGES TO CONDUCT JURY TRIALS

As allowed by 28 U.S.C. § 157(e), bankruptcy judges may, with the express consent of all parties, conduct jury trials in cases for which the law provides a right to a jury trial. Bankruptcy judges conducting jury trials under this rule may use the court's pool of prospective jurors.

[Adopted effective June 8, 1998. Amended effective January 1, 2012.]

LOCAL RULE 40–1. ASSIGNMENT OF CASES

(a) Assignment According to Court Order. The clerk must assign cases to judicial officers according to the method that the court orders from time to time.

(b) Assignment Sequence Is Confidential. No one in the clerk's office may reveal to any person, other than a judge, the sequence in which cases are assigned.

(c) Punishment for Tampering with Assignments. The court may punish a person for contempt if the person causes or attempts to cause a court employee to:

(1) reveal the sequence in which cases are assigned; or

(2) assign a case inconsistent with the court's order.

(d) Notice of Related Action. A party must file a notice of related action:

(1) upon filing an appeal from a bankruptcy case, if another appeal arising out of the same case (including from an adversary proceeding) has already been filed; or

(2) as soon as it appears that the party's case and another pending case:

(A) arise out of the same transaction or occurrence;

(B) involve the same property; or

(C) involve the validity or infringement or the same patent, trademark, or copyright.

(e) Transfer of Related Cases. When the court determines that two cases are related, the case filed later may, in the court's discretion, be transferred to the judicial officer handling the earlier-filed case.

(f) Reassignment of Cases. The court may reassign cases among judicial officers if workload and the speedy administration of justice so require. If it is necessary to reassign a case for reasons other than workload, the chief judge will refer the case to the clerk and the clerk must reassign the case using a system similar to that used when cases are first filed.

(g) Remands for New Trials. The clerk must assign cases remanded for a new trial under Seventh Circuit Rule 36 by random lot unless:

(1) the remand order directs otherwise; or

(2) within 15 days after the mandate for a new trial is docketed, all parties in the case file a request that the judge previously assigned to the case retry it.

[Adopted effective February 1, 1992. Amended effective December 16, 1994; January 1, 1999; January 1, 2000; March 1, 2004; December 1, 2009; January 1, 2012.]

LOCAL RULE 40–3. TRIAL START DATES

The court expects that cases will be tried within 18 months after the complaint is filed, unless the court determines that this deadline is unreasonable due to:

(a) the case's complexity;

(b) staging provided by the case management plan; or

(c) the demands of the court's docket.

[Adopted effective June 2, 1992. Amended effective December 1, 2009; January 1, 2012.]

LOCAL RULE 40–4. DIVISION OF BUSINESS AMONG DISTRICT JUDGES

(a) Assignment to Divisions. The court may assign a judge to any of the district's four divisions (Indianapolis, Evansville, New Albany, or Terre Haute) permanently or by cause number.

(b) Divisions with Permanent Judges. A division with at least one permanently assigned judge must remain in continuous session.

(c) Motions Judge. The court will designate a "motions judge" to hear:

(1) emergency matters in cases where the assigned judge is absent; and

(2) other matters in cases not yet assigned to a judge.

(d) Identity of Motions Judge. The clerk must identify the motions judge upon request.

[Adopted effective February 1, 1992. Amended effective March 25, 1998; January 1, 2012.]

LOCAL RULE 41–1. DISMISSAL OF ACTIONS FOR FAILURE TO PROSECUTE

The court may dismiss a civil case with judgment for costs if:

(a) the plaintiff has not taken any action for 6 months;

(b) the judicial officer assigned to the case or the clerk has given notice to the parties that the case will be dismissed for failure to prosecute it; and

(c) at least 28 days have passed since the notice was given.

[Adopted effective February 1, 1992. Amended effective January 1, 2000; December 1, 2009; January 1, 2012.]

LOCAL RULE 42–1. MOTIONS TO CONSOLIDATE

A party seeking to consolidate two or more civil cases must:

(a) file the motion in the case with the earliest docket number; and

(b) file a notice of the motion in all the other cases.

Note: Effective January 1, 2012, former Local Rule 42.2 becomes Local Rule 42–1.

[Adopted effective January 1, 2001. Former Rule 42.2 redesignated as Rule 42-1 and amended effective January 1, 2012.]

LOCAL RULE 45–1. SERVICE OF SUBPOENA ON NON-PARTIES– NOTICE REQUIREMENT

If a subpoena to produce or permit is to be served upon a nonparty, a copy of the proposed subpoena must be served on all other parties at least 7 days prior to service of the subpoena on the nonparty, unless the parties agree to a different time frame or the case management plan provides otherwise. Provided, however, that if such subpoena relates to a matter set for hearing within such 7 day period or arises out of a bona fide emergency, such subpoena may be served upon a nonparty 1 day after a notice and copy of the subpoena is served on each party.

[Adopted effective December 1, 2013.]

LOCAL RULE 47–1. VOIR DIRE OF JURORS

(a) Voir Dire Conducted by Court. The court will conduct the voir dire examination in jury cases. However, nothing in this rule is intended to preclude or otherwise limit the court from allowing attorneys to conduct voir dire examination in any manner permitted by Fed. R. Civ. P. 47.

(b) Requests to Cover Particular Subjects and Questions. Parties may file with the clerk requests for the court to cover particular subjects or to ask particular questions during voir dire. Requests must be filed at least 24 hours before the trial starts unless the court orders otherwise.

(c) Requests for Additional Questions after Initial Voir Dire. After the court completes its initial voir dire, parties may request that the court ask additional questions that are necessary and could not have been reasonably anticipated before trial.

[Adopted effective February 1, 1992. Amended effective December 16, 1994; January 1, 2012.]

LOCAL RULE 47–2. COMMUNICATION WITH JURORS

(a) Communication Not Allowed. No party or attorney (or any of their employees or agents) may communicate or attempt to communicate off the record:

(1) with a member of the venire from which the jury will be selected; or

(2) with a juror.

(b) Exceptions. The court may allow a party or attorney to communicate with jurors after the trial if all other parties are given notice. In criminal cases, a party or attorney must show good cause before the court will allow communication with a juror.

(c) Control by Court. Any juror contact permitted by the court will be subject to the control of the judge.

[Adopted effective February 1, 1992. Amended effective January 1, 2012.]

LOCAL RULE 47–3. JUROR COSTS

(a) Failure to Notify the Court of Settlement. The court may order the parties to pay juror costs (including marshal's fees, mileage, and per diem) in a case if:

(1) the parties settle or otherwise dispose of the case before trial; and

(2) the clerk's office is not notified at least 1 full business day before the trial is set to begin.

(b) Division of Juror Costs. The court may divide juror costs among the parties, their attorneys, or both in its discretion.

Note: Effective January 1, 2012, former Local Rule 42.1 becomes Local Rule 47–3.

[Adopted effective July 12, 1994. Amended effective December 1, 2009. Former Rule 42.1 redesignated as Rule 47–3 and amended effective January 1, 2012.]

LOCAL RULE 47–4. JURY; UNANIMOUS VERDICT

(a) Number of Jurors. Each civil jury must have at least 6 members, unless the law requires otherwise.

(b) Additional Jurors. The court in its discretion may impanel up to 4 additional jurors. If it impanels additional jurors, the court may allow the parties additional peremptory challenges.

(c) Unanimous Verdict Required. Regardless of the number of jurors, the jury's verdict must be unanimous and be rendered by at least six jurors.

[Adopted effective February 1, 1992. Amended effective December 16, 1994; January 1, 2012.]

LOCAL RULE 54–1. TAXATION OF COSTS AND ATTORNEY'S FEES

(a) Deadline for Requests for Costs and Attorney's Fees. A party cannot recover attorney's fees and costs unless the party files and serves a bill of costs and a motion for fees within 14 days after final judgment is entered. The court may extend this deadline for good cause if a motion requesting an extension is filed before the original deadline.

(b) Form for Bill of Costs. The court prefers that parties use AO form 133 (available from the clerk) for the bill of costs.

[Adopted effective February 1, 1992. Amended effective December 16, 1994; January 1, 2000; January 1, 2012.]

LOCAL RULE 56–1. SUMMARY JUDGMENT PROCEDURE

(a) Movant's Obligations. A party seeking summary judgment must file and serve a supporting brief and any evidence (that is not already in the record) that the party relies on to support the motion. The brief must include a section labeled "Statement of Material Facts Not in Dispute" containing the facts:

(1) that are potentially determinative of the motion; and

(2) as to which the movant contends there is no genuine issue.

(b) Non–Movant's Obligations. A party opposing a summary judgment motion must, within 28 days after the movant serves the motion, file and serve a response brief and any evidence (that is not already in the record) that the party relies on to oppose the motion. The response must include a section labeled "Statement of Material Facts in Dispute" that identifies the potentially determinative facts and factual disputes that the party contends demonstrate a dispute of fact precluding summary judgment.

(c) Reply. The movant may file a reply brief within 14 days after a response is served.

(d) Surreply. A party opposing a summary judgment motion may file a surreply brief only if the movant cites new evidence in the reply or objects to the admissibility of the evidence cited in the response. The surreply must be filed within 7 days after the movant serves the reply and must be limited to the new evidence and objections.

(e) Citations to Supporting Facts. A party must support each fact the party asserts in a brief with a citation to a discovery response, a deposition, an affidavit, or other admissible evidence. The evidence must be in the record or in an appendix to the brief. The citation must refer to a page or paragraph number or otherwise similarly specify where the relevant information can be found in the supporting evidence.

(f) Court's Assumptions About Facts. In deciding a summary judgment motion, the court will assume that:

(1) the facts as claimed and supported by admissible evidence by the movant are admitted without controversy except to the extent that:

(A) the non-movant specifically controverts the facts in that party's "Statement of Material Facts in Dispute" with admissible evidence; or

(B) it is shown that the movant's facts are not supported by admissible evidence; or

(C) the facts, alone or in conjunction with other admissible evidence, allow the court to draw reasonable inferences in the non-movant's favor sufficient to preclude summary judgment.

(2) facts that a non-movant asserts are true to the extent admissible evidence supports them.

(g) Stipulation to Facts. The parties may stipulate to facts in the summary judgment process, and may state that their stipulations are entered only for the purpose of the motion for summary judgment and are not intended to be otherwise binding.

(h) No Duty to Search Record. The court has no duty to search or consider any part of the record not specifically cited in the manner described in subdivision (e).

(i) Collateral Motions. The court disfavors collateral motions—such as motions to strike—in the summary judgment process. Any dispute over the admissibility or effect of evidence must be raised through an objection within a party's brief.

(j) Oral Argument or Hearing. The court will decide summary judgment motions without oral argument or hearing unless the court otherwise directs or grants a request under S.D. Ind. L.R. 7–5.

(k) Notice Requirement for Pro Se Cases. A party seeking summary judgment against an unrepresented party must file and serve the notice contained in Appendix A.

(*l*) Compliance. The court may, in the interest of justice or for good cause, excuse failure to comply strictly with this rule.

Local Rules Advisory Committee Comments

Re: 2002 Amendment

The 2002 revision completely replaces the former rule. It is designed to reduce the length of briefs related to motions for summary judgment, particularly the statement of undisputed material facts. In some cases, the statement of undisputed material facts has grown to an unmanageable level for the courts and for the parties. The parties have included facts which are not material to the legal issues to be resolved by summary judgment. Including the statement of undisputed material facts in the 35–page limit for initial briefs established by S.D. Ind. L. R. 7.1(b) will require the parties to discipline their presentation.

Note to subdivision (a). This provision sets forth the general requirements for all briefs to be submitted by the parties. It requires that the movant's brief contain a "Statement of Material Facts Not in Dispute." Emphasis is made that "material" facts are ones which are potentially determinative (former Rule 56.1(h)). The Statement should not contain mere background facts which a party feels puts the case in perspective—that can be done in an introduction or background section of the brief. Further, the Statement of asserted material facts is to state facts, not the party's argument which should be in the argument portion of the brief. Asserted material facts must be supported by specific citations to the admissible evidence in the record, which requires that any material not already in the Court's file be contained in an appendix. Although the strict formatting requirements of former Rule 56.1(h) are eliminated, separately numbering the facts is recommended for presentation clarity.

Note to subdivision (b). The specific rules for the non-movant's response are contained in this section. The brief shall contain a "Statement of Material Facts in Dispute" identifying: (1) the material facts which preclude summary judgment and/or (2) disputed material facts which do so. Like movant's Statement, the non-movant's Statement should not contain mere background facts or be argumentative.

Note to subdivision (d). A non-moving party may file a surreply brief in two limited circumstances. It is permitted only when: (1) the moving party submits in its reply brief evidence not previously cited; or (2) the moving party objects in its Reply to the admissibility of evidence cited by the non-movant.

Note to subdivision (e). This provision sets forth the effect of facts asserted. If supported by cited admissible evidence, a party's asserted material facts will be assumed admitted unless the opposing party submits admissible evidence of a genuine issue of material fact, demonstrates that the movant's assertions are not supported by admissible evidence or, through argument, shows that reasonable inferences can be drawn from admissible facts which preclude summary judgment. Obviously, the parties may, and are encouraged to, stipulate to undisputed material facts. Any such fact stipulations may be for purposes of the summary judgment motion only. The Court will not search the record to find admissible evidence to support an asserted material fact.

Note to subdivision (f). Motion practice about the admissibility of evidence cited in support of asserted material facts is strongly discouraged. Challenges to the evidence belong in the parties' briefs.

Cross Motions. If the parties anticipate cross-motions for summary judgment, the briefing schedule and format should be addressed in the case management plan.

[Adopted effective February 1, 1992. Amended effective January 1, 1999; April 30, 1999; January 1, 2000; July 1, 2002. Amended effective July 1, 2008; December 1, 2009; January 1, 2012; January 1, 2013; January 1, 2015.]

LOCAL RULE 65–2. MOTIONS FOR PRELIMINARY INJUNCTIONS AND TEMPORARY RESTRAINING ORDERS

(a) Preliminary Injunctions. The court will consider a request for preliminary injunction only if the movant files a separate motion for relief and complies with Fed. R. Civ. P. 65(a). Supporting and response briefs are not required, but the court may request them.

(b) Temporary Restraining Orders. The court will consider a request for temporary restraining order only if the movant files a separate motion for relief with a supporting brief. The movant must also comply with Fed. R. Civ. P. 65(b).

[Adopted effective January 1, 2000. Amended effective January 1, 2009; January 1, 2012.]

LOCAL RULE 66–1. RECEIVERSHIPS

(a) Applicability. This rule applies to the administration of estates (excluding estates in bankruptcy) by court-appointed officers such as receivers.

(b) Officer's Duties.

(1) *Inventories.* Within 28 days after taking possession of an estate, the court-appointed officer must file:

(A) an inventory and appraisal of the estate's property and assets held by the officer or the officer's agent; and

(B) on a separate schedule, an inventory of the estate's property and assets held by others.

(2) *Regular Reports.* Within 28 days after the inventory is filed and every three months after that, the court-appointed officer must file a report:

(A) describing the acts and transactions the officer has undertaken on the estate's behalf; and

(B) accounting for any monies received by or expended for the estate.

(c) Compensation of Receiver, Attorneys, and Other Officers.

(1) *Amount.* The court, in its discretion, will determine what to pay court-appointed officers, their attorneys, and others the court appoints to help administer an estate.

(2) *Procedures for Payment.* To get paid, persons seeking compensation must petition the court and notify:

(A) the estate's creditors; and

(B) any other interested parties the court requires to receive notice.

(d) Administration Generally. In all other respects the court-appointed officer must—to the extent it is reasonable to do so—administer the estate in the way that bankruptcy estates are typically administered unless the court authorizes a different practice.

(e) Deadlines. The court may alter any deadline imposed by this rule.

[Adopted effective February 1, 1992. Amended effective December 1, 2009; January 1, 2012.]

LOCAL RULE 69–1. EXECUTION

All procedures on execution must accord with Fed. R. Civ. P. 69 and applicable state law. This rule applies to proceedings supplementary to, and in aid of, a judgment and to procedures on, and in aid of, execution.

[Adopted effective February 1, 1992. Amended effective January 1, 2012.]

LOCAL RULE 69–2. INTERROGATORIES TO GARNISHEES

(a) Order to Answer Interrogatories Required. Garnishees may be ordered to answer interrogatories. An order requiring a garnishee to answer interrogatories must accompany each set of interrogatories served on the garnishee. The interrogatories may be part of another paper or pleading.

(b) Content of Order. The order to answer interrogatories must advise the garnishee:

(1) that the plaintiff has a judgment against the defendant;

(2) of the judgment amount;

(3) of the time, date and place of the hearing on a motion for proceedings supplemental;

(4) that if the garnishee has a claim or defense to a proceedings supplemental or a garnishment order, the garnishee must present the claim or defense at the hearing; and

(5) that the garnishee has the option to either:

(A) answer the interrogatories in writing on or before the date specified, or

(B) appear in court and answer the interrogatories in person.

(c) Motion for Proceedings Supplemental. A motion for proceedings supplemental must be served on the garnishee when the garnishee is served with the interrogatories and the order to answer them.

(d) Requirements for Hold on Depository Account. If the order to answer interrogatories is to operate as a hold on a judgment-debtor's depository account, the order must comply with Indiana law.

[Adopted effective February 1, 1992. Amended effective January 1, 2012.]

LOCAL RULE 69–3. FINAL ORDERS IN WAGE GARNISHMENT

All final orders garnishing wages must comply with Ind. Code § 24–4.5–5–105.

[Adopted effective February 1, 1992. Amended effective January 1, 2012.]

LOCAL RULE 69–4. BODY ATTACHMENTS; HEARINGS

(a) Failure to Appear. If a judgment debtor fails to appear for a hearing despite service and actual notice, the magistrate judge may recommend that the district judge issue a body attachment.

(b) Hearing after Arrest. When a judgment debtor is arrested on a body attachment, the court must conduct a hearing at its earliest convenience. The judgment-creditor's attorney will be notified of the hearing by telephone. Attorneys are deemed to have consented to telephonic notice by requesting the body attachment.

(c) Failure to Respond to Telephonic Notice. If the judgment-creditor's attorney fails to respond promptly to the telephonic notice, the court may release the judgment debtor or take other appropriate action.

(d) Appearance at Hearing by Creditor's Attorney. The judgment-creditor's attorney of record must personally appear at the hearing; neither clerical nor secretarial personnel may interrogate an attached judgment debtor.

[Adopted effective February 1, 1992. Amended effective January 1, 2012.]

LOCAL RULE 72–1. AUTHORITY OF UNITED STATES MAGISTRATE JUDGES

(a) Application to Rule. This rule applies to all United States magistrate judges, including full-time magistrate judges, part-time magistrate judges, and magistrate judges recalled pursuant to 28 U.S.C. § 636(h).

(b) Authority of Magistrate Judges. Magistrate judges are judicial officers. They are authorized and

specially designated to perform all duties authorized by the United States Code and any rule governing proceedings in this court. Magistrate judges are authorized to perform the duties enumerated in these rules in cases assigned to the magistrate judge by rule, by court order, or by order or special designation of any of the court's district judges.

[Repealed and replaced effective December 1, 2009. Amended effective January 1, 2012.]

LOCAL RULE 72–2. FORFEITURE OF COLLATERAL IN LIEU OF APPEARANCE

(a) Nature of Offense. A person charged with an offense made criminal pursuant 18 U.S.C. § 13, and for which the penalty provided by state law is equal to or less than that of a misdemeanor, other than an offense for which a mandatory appearance is required may, in lieu of appearance, post collateral before a United States Magistrate Judge and consent to forfeiture of collateral.

(b) Schedule of Offenses. These offenses, and the amounts of collateral to be posted (if applicable), will appear on a schedule and be available for public inspection in the clerk's office in each of the district's divisions. The schedule will be effective until rescinded or superseded by court order.

(c) Failure to Appear. Posted collateral will be forfeited if the person charged with an offense covered by this rule fails to appear before the magistrate judge. The forfeiture will signify that the offender does not contest the charge and does not request a hearing before the magistrate judge. The forfeiture is tantamount to a finding of guilt.

(d) When Forfeitures Are Not Permitted. Forfeitures are not permitted for violations involving an accident that results in personal injury. Arresting officers must treat multiple and aggravated offenses as mandatory-appearance offenses and must direct the accused to appear for a hearing.

(e) Discretion of Officers to Arrest. Nothing in this rule prohibits a law-enforcement officer from:

(1) arresting a person for the commission of an offense (including those for which collateral may be posted and forfeited); and

(2) either:

(A) requiring the person charged to appear before a magistrate judge, or

(B) taking that person before a magistrate judge immediately after arrest.

[Adopted effective February 1, 1992. Amended effective January 1, 2012.]

LOCAL RULE 76–1. DESIGNATING ADDITIONAL ITEMS FOR RECORD ON APPEAL

An appellant designating items for the record on appeal under Circuit Rule 10(a) must serve a proposed joint designation on the appellee with the notice of appeal. The parties must then confer and, if they agree, prepare a joint designation, highlighting those entries on the court's docket sheet if it is practical to do so. The joint designation must be filed with the clerk within 14 days after the notice of appeal is filed. If the parties cannot reach agreement on a joint designation, each party must submit a separate designation within 14 days after filing the notice of appeal.

[Adopted effective February 1, 1992. Amended July 21, 1995; January 1, 2002; December 1, 2009; January 1, 2012.]

LOCAL RULE 79–1. CUSTODY OF FILES AND EXHIBITS

(a) **Custody During Pendency of Action.** Any item offered into evidence in a case—other than contraband exhibits—will be placed in the clerk's custody. Unless the court orders otherwise, these items may not be claimed from the clerk until the case is disposed of as to all issues, including appeals.

(b) **Claiming Items After Disposition of Action.** The party that offered the items into evidence must claim them from the clerk:

(1) if the case is not appealed, within 90 days after the case is disposed of as to all issues;

(2) if the case is appealed, within 28 days after the mandate of the reviewing court is filed in the clerk's office and the case is disposed of as to all issues, unless otherwise ordered.

(c) **Procedure for Claiming Items.** No motion or order is necessary to claim the items. The party withdrawing them must give the clerk a detailed receipt when the items are withdrawn. The clerk must file the receipt in the cause.

(d) **Failure to Claim Items.** If the parties fail to claim the items within the deadline in subdivision (b), the United States Marshals Service may sell the items in a public or private sale or dispose of them in any manner directed by the court. If sold, the proceeds, less the expense of sale, will be paid into the court's registry.

(e) **Contraband Exhibits.** Contraband exhibits (such as controlled substances, money, and weapons) may not be placed in the clerk's custody. They must be released to the investigative agency when the case is concluded. The investigative agency must give the clerk a detailed receipt when the contraband exhibits are released.

(f) **Withdrawal of Original Records and Papers.** No one may withdraw an original pleading, paper, record, model or exhibit from the clerk's custody except as provided by this rule or by court order.

[Adopted effective February 1, 1992. Amended effective December 1, 2009; January 1, 2012.]

LOCAL RULE 80–1. OFFICIAL TRANSCRIPTS OF COURT PROCEEDINGS

(a) **Filing Official Transcripts.** Upon completion of an official transcript of any proceeding in this court, the court reporter or transcriber will file electronically a certified copy of the official transcript, in accordance with 28 U.S.C. § 753(b).

(b) **Access Restrictions for Official Transcripts.** Access to an official transcript of a court proceeding will be restricted for a period of 90 days after the transcript is filed by the court reporter or transcriber (the "Restriction Period"), unless otherwise provided by this rule or ordered by the court.

(1) *Availability During the Restriction Period.* During the Restriction Period, the official transcript will be available:

(A) for purchase from the court reporter or transcriber who prepared and filed the transcript;

(B) to attorneys of record who have purchased the transcript from the court reporter and requested electronic access via the ECF system through the court reporter;

(C) for inspection only, via the public computer terminals located in the clerk's office; and

(D) as directed by the court.

(2) *Availability After the Restriction Period.* After the Restriction Period has expired and any pending motions related to an official transcript have been resolved, the official transcript and any redacted version of the official transcript will be available as provided by subdivision (b)(1) and as follows:

(A) If the official transcript has not been redacted, it will be available:

(i) for inspection and purchase via the public computer terminals located in the clerk's office; and

(ii) for downloading from the court's ECF system through PACER.

(B) If the official transcript has been redacted pursuant to S.D. Ind. L. R. 80–2, only the redacted version of the official transcript will be available as described in subdivisions (b)(2)(A)(i) and (ii).

(3) *Sealed Matters.* Official transcripts of sealed proceedings, official transcripts filed in sealed cases, and official transcripts which have been sealed by the

court will not be publicly available, electronically or otherwise, unless ordered by the court.

(c) Official Transcript Fees. Access fees apply to official transcripts of court proceedings, whether purchased from a court reporter or transcriber, downloaded via PACER, or obtained through the clerk's office. Current schedules of official transcript fees, electronic public access (PACER) fees, and clerk's office printing fees are established by the Judicial Conference and maintained on file in the clerk's office.

[Adopted effective January 1, 2012.]

LOCAL RULE 80–2. REDACTION OF OFFICIAL TRANSCRIPTS OF COURT PROCEEDINGS

(a) Redaction of Personal Data Identifiers. Upon the filing of an official transcript of any court proceeding under S.D. Ind. L.R. 80–1, attorneys of record will review the transcript and determine whether redaction of personal data identifiers within the transcript is necessary to comply with Fed. R. Civ. P. 5.2 or Fed. R. Crim. P. 49.1. The requirements of this rule apply to pro se litigants.

(1) *Review of Transcript.* Unless otherwise ordered by the court, attorneys of record who represent a party or parties in a matter in which an official transcript has been filed must review the following portions of the official transcript:

(A) opening and closing statements made on the party's behalf;

(B) statements of the party;

(C) the testimony of any witnesses called by the party;

(D) sentencing proceedings; and

(E) any other portion of the transcript as ordered by the court.

An attorney serving as "standby" counsel appointed to be available to assist a pro se defendant in his or her defense in a criminal case must review the same portions of the transcript as if the pro se defendant were his or her client. If the transcript relates to a panel attorney representation pursuant to the Criminal Justice Act (CJA), including serving as standby counsel, the attorney conducting the review is entitled to compensation under the CJA for functions reasonably performed to fulfill the redaction obligation and for reimbursement for related reasonable expenses.

(2) *Notice of Intent to Request Redaction.* If any portion of an official transcript is subject to the requirements of Fed. R. Civ. P. 5.2 or Fed. R. Crim. P. 49.1, the attorneys of record will either jointly or individually file a "Notice of Intent to Request Redaction" within 7 days from the date on which the official

transcript was filed. If a Notice of Intent to Redact is not filed within the allotted 7 days, the court will assume redaction of personal data identifiers from the transcript is not necessary.

(3) *Redaction Statement.* If redaction of personal data identifiers within an official transcript is required by Fed. R. Civ. P. 5.2 or Fed. R. Crim. P. 49.1, attorneys of record will either jointly or individually file a "Redaction Statement" within 21 days from the date on which the official transcript was filed. The Redaction Statement will certify that the official transcript has been reviewed by counsel and identify the following information:

(A) the filed date and document number of the official transcript for which redaction is requested;

(B) a description of each type of personal data identifier to be redacted (*e.g.,* social-security number);

(C) transcript page number(s) and line number(s) identifying the location of each personal data identifier to be redacted; and

(D) the redacted version of each such personal data identifier (*e.g.,* social-security number to read as XXX–XX–1234).

The Redaction Statement must not disclose, in its unredacted form, any personal data identifier.

(b) Redaction of Information other than Personal Data Identifiers. Any party may request redaction of information other than the personal data identifiers set forth in Fed. R. Civ. P. 5.2 and Fed. R. Crim. P. 49.1 by filing a "Motion to Redact Transcript." Such motion must state the grounds for requesting redaction, set forth the information to be redacted in the format required by (a)(3), and be filed within 21 days from the date on which the official transcript was filed.

(c) Filing Redacted Transcripts. After the filing of a Redaction Statement or court order granting a party's Motion to Redact Transcript, the court reporter will prepare and file a redacted version of the official transcript within 31 days from the date on which the official transcript was filed.

[Adopted effective January 1, 2012. Amended effective January 1, 2013.]

LOCAL RULE 81–1. NOTICE OF REMOVAL AND RESPONSE IN DIVERSITY CASES

(a) Notice Requirement. Every notice of removal based, in part or in whole, on diversity jurisdiction pursuant to 28 U.S.C. § 1332(a) must include:

(1) a statement that the amount in controversy, exclusive of interest and costs at issue satisfies the jurisdictional amount requirement; and

(2) a listing of the citizenship of each party.

(b) Response. Within 30 days after the filing of the notice of removal, every plaintiff who has not filed a motion to remand must file a statement responding to the notice of removal's allegations as to the citizenship of the parties and the amount in controversy. If the plaintiff lacks sufficient information upon which to form a belief about those allegations despite meeting and conferring in good faith with the removing party about them, the plaintiff may so state.

(c) Burden of Proof. Nothing in this rule alters the burden of proof with respect to jurisdictional allegations.

[Former L.R. 81.3 adopted effective June 2, 1992. Renumbered L.R. 81.1 effective January 1, 2000. Amended effective December 1, 2009; January 1, 2012.]

LOCAL RULE 83–3. COURTROOM AND COURTHOUSE DECORUM

(a) Prohibited Activities. The following may not be done in connection with a judicial proceeding anywhere on a floor where a courtroom is located:

(1) taking photographs;

(2) making sound recordings (except by court reporters in the performance of their duties and Judicial Conference approved digital audio recordings made utilizing court-owned equipment); and

(3) broadcasting by radio, television, or any other means.

(b) Exceptions. The court may permit these activities when they are incidental to investitive, ceremonial, or naturalization proceedings.

[Adopted effective February 1, 1992. Amended effective January 1, 2012.]

LOCAL RULE 83–5. BAR ADMISSION

(a) Authority to Practice Before the Court.

(1) *Rule.* Only members of the court's bar may represent parties before the court.

(2) *Exceptions.*

(A) Pro Se. A nonmember may represent him or herself in a case.

(B) U.S. Government Attorneys. A nonmember who is an attorney may represent the United States, or an officer or agency of the United States.

(C) Pro Hac Vice. Attorneys admitted pro hac vice pursuant to Local Rule 83–6 may represent parties in a case.

(3) *Foreign Legal Consultants.* Foreign legal consultants may not be admitted to practice in the court (despite the provisions of Rule 5 of the Indiana Rules for the Admission to the Bar and the Discipline of Attorneys).

(b) Bar Membership. The bar consists of those persons who:

(1) have been admitted by the court to practice and have signed the roll of attorneys; and

(2) have not resigned or been disbarred or suspended from the bar.

(c) Admission.

(1) *Who May Be Admitted.* An attorney admitted to practice by the United States Supreme Court or the highest court in any state may become a member of the court's bar on a member's motion.

(2) *Character.* An applicant will be admitted to the bar if the court—after being assured by a member or by the report of a committee appointed by the court—is satisfied that the applicant:

(A) has good private and professional character; and

(B) is a member in good standing of the bar in every jurisdiction where the applicant is admitted to practice.

(3) *Entry on Court's Records.* The attorney's admission will be entered on the court's records and the court will issue a certificate to that effect only after the applicant:

(A) takes a prescribed oath or affirmation;

(B) certifies that he or she has read and will abide by the *Seventh Circuit Standards of Professional Conduct;*

(C) pays the required fees (law clerks to the court's judges and attorneys representing the United States are exempt from these fees);

(D) signs the roll of attorneys;

(E) registers for electronic case filing;

(F) gives a current address; and

(G) agrees to notify the clerk promptly of any change in address.

(d) Local Counsel. The court may require an attorney residing outside the district to retain, as local counsel, a member of the court's bar who resides in the district.

(e) Standards. The Indiana Rules of Professional Conduct and the *Seventh Circuit Standards of Professional Conduct* (an appendix to these rules) govern the conduct of those practicing in the court.

(f) Sanctions. Attorneys may be disbarred or suspended from practicing in the court for good cause, but only after having had an opportunity to be heard.

They may also be reprimanded as provided for in the court's Rules of Disciplinary Enforcement.

[Adopted effective February 1, 1992. Amended effective January 1, 1998; January 1, 2001; January 1, 2002; January 1, 2007; January 1, 2012; January 1, 2013.]

LOCAL RULE 83–6. PRO HAC VICE ADMISSION

(a) Authority to Represent Parties in a Case. An attorney who is not a member of the bar of the court may represent parties in a case if the nonmember has paid the required pro hac vice admission fee to the clerk of court and been granted leave by the court to appear pro hac vice in the case. A motion requesting pro hac vice admission must include the following information.

(1) *Admission Status.* The motion must include a statement indicating that the attorney requesting admission is admitted to practice, currently in active status, and in good standing as an attorney in another United States court or the highest court of any state.

(2) *Disciplinary History.* The motion must include a statement indicating whether the attorney requesting admission is currently or has ever been disbarred or suspended from practice before any court, department, bureau or commission of any state or the United States, or has ever received a reprimand or been subject to other disciplinary action from any such court, department, bureau or commission pertaining to conduct or fitness as a member of the bar.

(3) *Certification as to Standards of Conduct.* The attorney requesting admission must certify that he or she has reviewed the *Seventh Circuit Standards of Professional Conduct* and the Local Rules of the court, including the Rules of Disciplinary Enforcement, and will abide by these rules.

(b) Form of Filing Pro Hac Vice Motion. A motion requesting pro hac vice admission may be filed by:

(1) The attorney seeking admission. The motion must be filed electronically if the attorney seeking pro hac vice admission is already registered for electronic filing in this district as required by Rule 5–3. Otherwise, the pro hac vice motion must be filed in paper form.

(2) An admitted attorney of record in the case on behalf of the attorney seeking admission. When filed by an attorney of record on behalf of the attorney seeking admission, the motion must be filed electronically and be accompanied by a certification addressing requirements (a)(1) through (3) of this rule and bearing the original signature of the attorney seeking admission.

(c) Local Counsel. The court may require an attorney residing outside the district to retain, as local counsel, a member of the court's bar who resides in the district.

[Effective January 1, 2013. Amended effective December 1, 2013.]

LOCAL RULE 83–7. APPEARANCE AND WITHDRAWAL OF APPEARANCE

(a) General. Every attorney who represents a party or who files a paper on a party's behalf must file an appearance for that party. Only those attorneys who have filed an appearance in a pending action are entitled to be served with case papers under Fed. R. Civ. P. 5(a).

(b) Removed and Transferred Cases. Attorneys whose names do not appear on the court's docket after a case has been removed from state court must file an appearance or a copy of the appearance they previously filed in state court. An attorney of record who is not admitted to practice before the court must either comply with this court's admission policy (see S.D. Ind. L.R. 83–5), or withdraw his or her appearance (see subdivision (c) of this rule) within 21 days after the case is removed or transferred to the court.

(c) Withdrawal of Appearance.

(1) An attorney must file a written motion to withdraw his or her appearance.

(2) The motion must fix a date for the withdrawal and must contain satisfactory evidence that the attorney provided the client with written notice of his or her intent to withdraw at least 7 days before the withdrawal date.

(3) If an attorney's withdrawal will leave a party without counsel, the motion must also include the party's contact information, including a current address and telephone number.

(4) The requirements of subparagraphs (1)–(3) are waived when a notice of withdrawal is filed contemporaneously with another attorney's appearance for the client.

[Adopted effective February 1, 1992. Amended effective January 1, 2007; June 1, 2007; December 1, 2009; January 1, 2011; January 1, 2012; January 1, 2013.]

LOCAL RULE 83–8. REFERRAL OF CASES TO BANKRUPTCY COURT

(a) Cases Referred to Bankruptcy Court. Consistent with 28 U.S.C. § 157(a), all cases and proceedings arising under Title 11 of the United States Code, or relating to a case under Title 11 of the United States Code, are referred to the district's bankruptcy court. This includes all cases removed under 28 U.S.C. §§ 1441(a) or 1452.

(b) Papers Filed in Cases in Bankruptcy Court. Papers filed in these cases, including the original petition, must be filed with the bankruptcy-court clerk and be captioned "United States Bankruptcy Court for the Southern District of Indiana."

(c) Promulgation of Bankruptcy Rules. Bankruptcy judges may make and amend rules of practice and procedure that:

(1) comply with—but do not duplicate—Acts of Congress and the Federal Rules of Bankruptcy Procedure, and

(2) do not prohibit or limit the use of the official forms.

[Adopted effective January 1, 2004. Amended effective June 1, 2007; December 1, 2009; January 1, 2012.]

APPENDIX A. NOTICE REGARDING RIGHT TO RESPOND TO AND SUBMIT EVIDENCE IN OPPOSITION TO MOTION FOR SUMMARY JUDGMENT

S.D. Indiana—Appendix A

S.D. Indiana—Appendix A

UNITED STATES DISTRICT COURT SOUTHERN DISTRICT OF INDIANA

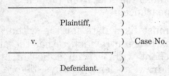

Plaintiff,

v.   Case No.

Defendant.

NOTICE REGARDING RIGHT TO RESPOND TO AND SUBMIT EVIDENCE IN OPPOSITION TO MOTION FOR SUMMARY JUDGMENT

[Moving party(ies)] has/have filed a motion seeking summary judgment. This means that the [moving party(ies)] seek(s) to have some part or all of this lawsuit decided against you without a trial. This motion is based on the evidence presented in the affidavits and documents attached to or referenced in the motion for summary judgment or based on the argument that you are unable to offer admissible evidence in support of your claim.

You have the right to file a response to the motion. Each of the facts stated in the "Statement of Material Facts Not in Dispute" which accompanies the motion for summary judgment will be accepted by the court as being true unless you submit your own affidavits or other admissible evidence disputing those facts. Your response may also dispute the admissibility of the evidence relied on in support of the motion for summary judgment. *However, a failure to properly respond will be the same as failing to present any evidence in your favor at a trial.*

You must file and serve a copy of your response to the motion for summary judgment by [date certain equal to 28 days after service of the motion, plus 3 days if served by mail] or by other such date ordered by the court. If you need more time to respond, you must file a motion with the court asking for more time before the deadline expires. The court may, but is not required to, give you more time.

Your response must also comply with all other portions of Federal Rule of Civil Procedure 56, and with Local Rule 56–1, copies of which are attached. Please note that for these rules you are considered a "party," the "non-moving party" and/or the "non-movant."

[Insert Federal Rule of Civil Procedure 56]

[Insert Local Rule 56–1]

Like other documents filed with the court, your response must comply with Southern District of Indiana Local Rule 5–1, which provides:

(a) Filing. A paper or item submitted in relation to a matter within the court's jurisdiction is deemed filed upon delivery to the office of the clerk in a manner prescribed by these rules or the Federal Rules of Civil Procedure or authorized by the court. Any submission directed to the office of the clerk or any employee thereof in a manner that is not contemplated by this rule and without prior court authorization is prohibited.

(b) General. Any pleading, motion, brief, affidavit, notice, or proposed order filed with the court, whether electronically or with the clerk, must:

- be plainly typewritten, printed, or prepared by a clearly legible copying process;
- have at least 1–inch margins;
- use at least 12–point type in the body of the paper and at least 10–point type in footnotes;
- be double spaced (except for headings, footnotes, and quoted material);
- have consecutively numbered pages;
- include a title on the first page;
- if it has four or more exhibits, include a separate index that identifies and briefly describes each exhibit;
- if it is a form of order, include a statement of service, in the format required by S.D. Ind. L.R. 5–5(d) in the lower left corner of the paper; and
- in the case of pleadings, motions, legal briefs, and notices, include the name, complete address, telephone number, facsimile number (where available), and email address (where available) of the pro se litigant or attorney who files it.

(c) Electronic Filings. Any paper submitted via the court's electronic case filing (ECF) system must be:

- in .pdf format;

- converted to a .pdf file directly from a word processing program, unless it exists only in paper format (in which case it may be scanned to create a .pdf document);

- submitted as one or more .pdf files that do not exceed 10 megabytes each (consistent with the *CM/ECF Policies and Procedures Manual*); and

- otherwise prepared and filed in a manner consistent with the *CM/ECF Policies and Procedures Manual*.

(d) Non–Electronic Filings.

(1) *Form, Style, and Size of Papers.* Any paper that is not filed electronically must:

- be flat, unfolded, and on good-quality, 8.5″ × 11″ white paper;

- be single-sided;

- not have a cover or a back;

- be (if consisting of more than one page) fastened by paperclip or binder clip and may not be stapled;

- be two-hole punched at the top with the holes 2 ¾′ apart and appropriately centered; and

- include the original signature of the pro se litigant or attorney who files it.

(2) *Request for Nonconforming Fastening.* If a paper cannot be fastened or bound as required by this rule, a party may ask the clerk for permission to fasten it in another manner. The party must make such a request before attempting to file the paper with nonconforming fastening.

(e) Nonconforming Papers. The clerk will accept a paper that violates this rule, but the court may exclude the paper from the official record.

APPENDIX B. STANDARDS FOR PROFESSIONAL CONDUCT WITHIN THE SEVENTH FEDERAL JUDICIAL CIRCUIT

Adopted by the United States District Court for the Southern District of Indiana Effective January 1, 1993

[*Publisher's Note: The Standards for Professional Conduct Within the Seventh Federal Judicial Circuit are set forth under the United States Court of Appeals for the Seventh Circuit.*]

CRIMINAL RULES

LOCAL CRIMINAL RULE 1–1. BAIL IN CRIMINAL CASES

(a) The conditions of release of defendants and material witnesses are set forth in 18 U.S.C. § 3141, et seq., and Rule 46, Federal Rules of Criminal Procedure.

(b) When the appearance of a person in a criminal case is required by the Court to be secured by a surety,

(1) every surety except a corporate surety must own fee simple title to real estate, unencumbered except for current taxes and the lien of a first mortgage. The surety's equity in such property shall have a fair market value at least double the penalty of said bond; provided, however, that a proposed surety whose real estate is then subject to an existing appearance bond in this Court or in any other Court in this district, including, state, county or municipal Courts, shall not be accepted as a surety; and

(2) a corporate surety must hold a certificate of authority from the Secretary of the Treasury and must act through a bondsman registered with the Clerk of this Court.

(c) No person who executes appearance bonds for a fee, price or other valuable consideration shall be eligible as a surety on any appearance bond unless such person be a corporate surety which is approved as provided by law.

[Former CR–1 adopted effective February 1, 1992; redesignated as C.R. 1.1 effective December 16, 1994.]

LOCAL CRIMINAL RULE 2–1. STANDARD ORDERS IN CRIMINAL CASES

The Court may issue a standard order in a criminal case which contains provisions for a plea of not guilty, a change of plea, trial date, attorney appearances, pretrial discovery, pretrial motions, plea agreement, and other matters. When such a standard order is issued, it shall be served on the defendant with the indictment or information. Copies of the form standard order are available from the Clerk of the Court.

[Former CR–2 adopted effective February 1, 1992; redesignated as C.R. 2.1 effective December 16, 1994.]

LOCAL CRIMINAL RULE 3–1. PROVISIONS FOR SPECIAL ORDERS IN APPROPRIATE CASES

(a) On motion of any party or on its own motion, when the Court deems it necessary, to preserve decorum and to maintain the integrity of the trial, the Court may issue a special order governing such matters as extra-judicial statements by parties and witnesses likely to interfere with the rights of any party to a fair trial, the seating and conduct in the Courtroom of parties, attorneys and their staff, spectators and news media representatives, the management and sequestration of jurors and witnesses, and any other matters which the Court may deem appropriate for inclusion in such an order. Such special order may be addressed to some or all, but not limited to the following subjects:

(1) A proscription of extra-judicial statements by participants in the trial, including lawyers and their staff, parties, witnesses, jurors, and Court officials, which might divulge prejudicial matter not of public record in the case.

(2) Specific directives regarding the clearing of entrances to and hallways in the Courthouse and respecting the management of the jury and witnesses during the course of the trial to avoid their mingling with or being in the proximity of reporters, photographers, parties, lawyers, and others, both in entering and leaving the Courtroom and Courthouse, and during recesses in the trial.

(3) A specific direction that the jurors refrain from reading, listening to, or watching news reports concerning the case, and that they similarly refrain from discussing the case with anyone during the trial and from communicating with others in any manner during their deliberations.

(4) Sequestration of the jury on motion of any party or the Court, without disclosure of the identity of the movant.

(5) Direction that the names and addresses of the jurors or prospective jurors not be publicly released except as required by statute, and that no photograph be taken or sketch made of any juror within the environs of the Court.

(6) Insulation of witnesses from news interviews during the trial period.

(7) Specific provisions regarding the seating of parties, attorneys and their staff, spectators and representatives of the news media.

(b) Unless otherwise permitted by law and ordered by the Court, all preliminary criminal proceedings, including preliminary examinations and hearings on pretrial motions, shall be held in open Court and shall be available for attendance and observation by the public.

If the Court orders closure of a pretrial hearing pursuant to this rule, it shall cite for the record its specific findings that compel the need for same.

[Former CR–3 adopted effective February 1, 1992; redesignated as C.R. 3.1 effective December 16, 1994.]

LOCAL CRIMINAL RULE 4–1. RELEASE OF INFORMATION BY COURT SUPPORTING PERSONNEL

All Court supporting personnel, including among others, Marshals, Deputy Marshals, Court Clerks, Deputy Court Clerks, Bailiffs, and Court or Grand Jury reporters and their employees or subcontractors, are prohibited from disclosing to any person, without authorization by the Court, information relating to a grand jury or pending criminal case that is not part of the public records of the Court. This Rule shall be applicable also to divulgence of information concerning grand jury proceedings, arguments, hearings held in chambers or otherwise outside the presence of the public.

[Former CR–4 adopted effective February 1, 1992; redesignated as C.R. 4.1 effective December 16, 1994.]

LOCAL CRIMINAL RULE 5–1. RELEASE OF INFORMATION BY ATTORNEYS IN CRIMINAL CASES

It is the duty of the attorneys for the government and the defense, including the law firm, not to release or authorize the release of information or opinion which a reasonable person would expect to be disseminated by any means of public communication, in connection with pending or imminent criminal litigation with which a lawyer or a law firm is associated, if such dissemination poses a serious and imminent threat of interference with the fair administration of justice.

The following actions will presumptively be deemed to pose a serious and imminent threat of interference with the fair administration of justice:

(a) With respect to a grand jury or other pending investigation of any criminal matter, the release, by a government lawyer participating in or associated with the investigation, of any extra-judicial statement, which a reasonable person would expect to be disseminated by any means of public communication, that goes beyond the public record or that is not necessary to inform the public that the investigation is under way, to describe the general scope of the investigation, to obtain assistance in the apprehension of a suspect, to warn the public of any dangers or otherwise to aid in the investigation.

(b) From the time of arrest, issuance of an arrest warrant or the filing of a complaint, information, or indictment in any criminal matter until the commencement of trial or disposition without a trial, the release

or giving of authority to release by a lawyer or law firm associated with the prosecution or defense, of any extra-judicial statement, which a reasonable person would expect to be disseminated, by any means of public communication, relating to that matter and concerning:

(1) the prior criminal record (including arrests, indictments, or other charges of crime), or the character or reputation of the accused, except a factual statement of the accused's name, age, residence, occupation, and family status, and if the accused has not been apprehended, the release by a lawyer associated with the prosecution of any information necessary to aid in the apprehension of the accused or to warn the public of any dangers he/she may present;

(2) the existence or contents of any confession, admission, or statement given by the accused, or the refusal or failure of the accused to make any statement;

(3) the performance of any examinations or tests or the accused's refusal or failure to submit to an examination or test;

(4) the identity, testimony, or credibility of prospective witnesses, except announcement of the identity of the victim if the announcement is not otherwise prohibited by law;

(5) the possibility of a plea of guilty to the offense charged or a lesser offense;

(6) any opinion as to the accused's guilt or innocence or the evidence in the case.

The foregoing shall not be construed to preclude the lawyer or law firm during this period, in the proper discharge of his/her or its official or professional obligations, from announcing the fact and circumstances of arrest (including time and place of arrest, resistance, pursuit, and use of weapons), the identity of the investigating and arresting officer or agency, and the length of the investigation; from making an announcement, at the time of seizure of any physical evidence other than a confession, admission or statement, which is limited to a description of the evidence seized; from disclosing the nature, substance, or text of the charge, including a brief description of the offense charged; from quoting or referring without comment to public records of the Court in the case; from announcing the scheduling or result of any stage in the judicial process; from requesting assistance in obtaining evidence; or from announcing without further comment that the accused denies the charges made against him/her and stating without elaboration the general nature of the defense.

(c) During a trial of any criminal matter, or any other proceeding that could result in incarceration, including a period of selection of the jury, the release or giving authority to release by a lawyer associated with the prosecution or defense, of any extra-judicial statement or interview, relating to the trial or the parties or issues in the trial, which a reasonable person would expect to be disseminated by any means of public communication, other than a quotation from or reference without comment to public records of the Court in the case.

Nothing in this Rule is intended to preclude the formulation or application of more restrictive Rules relating to the release of information about juvenile or other offenders, to preclude the holding of hearings or the lawful issuance of reports by legislative, administrative, or investigative bodies, or to preclude any lawyer from replying to charges of misconduct that are publicly made against him.

[Former CR–5 adopted effective February 1, 1992; redesignated as C.R. 5.1 effective December 16, 1994.]

LOCAL CRIMINAL RULE 6–0. PETITIONS FOR HABEAS CORPUS MOTIONS PURSUANT TO 28 U.S.C. SECTIONS 2254 AND 2255 BY PERSONS IN CUSTODY

Petitions for writs of habeas corpus and motions filed pursuant to 28 U.S.C. Sections 2254 and 2255 by persons in custody shall be in writing and signed under the penalty of perjury. Such petitions and motions shall be on the form contained in the Rules following 28 U.S.C. Section 2254, in the case of a person in state custody, or 28 U.S.C. Section 2255, in the case of a person in federal custody, or on forms adopted by general order of this Court, copies of which may be obtained from the Clerk of the Court.

[Former CR–6 adopted effective February 1, 1992; redesignated as C.R. 6.0 effective December 16, 1994.]

LOCAL CRIMINAL RULE 6–1. PETITIONS UNDER 28 U.S.C. SECTION 2254 OR 2255 IN CASES INVOLVING A SENTENCE OF CAPITAL PUNISHMENT

(a) Applicability. This Rule governs the procedures for a petition filed pursuant to 28 U.S.C. §§ 2254 or 2255, in which a prisoner seeks relief from a judgment imposing a sentence of death. The provisions of this Rule may, where appropriate, be determined to be applicable in any collateral challenge not authorized by §§ 2254 or 2255. The application of this Rule may be modified by the Judge to whom the petition is assigned.

(b) Clerk to Maintain the Records of Status of Cases; Request to Attorney General of Indiana. The clerk will request from the Indiana Attorney General, insofar as reasonably available, information pertaining to the movement of cases through the Indiana courts in which a prisoner is under sentence of death from an Indiana Court and as to which the judgment of conviction and sentence have been affirmed by the Supreme Court of Indiana. This information should include the following: defendant's name, court imposing sentence, date of affirmance on direct appeal by the Supreme Court of Indiana, date that denial of postconviction relief petition was affirmed by the Supreme Court of Indiana, and the execution date, if any.

(c) Clerk to Maintain the Records of Status of Cases; Request to United States Attorney. The clerk will request from the United States Attorney, insofar as reasonably available, information pertaining to the movement of cases through the federal courts in which a prisoner within the district is under sentence of death from a federal court and as to which the judgment of conviction and sentence are final. This information should include the following: defendant's name, court imposing sentence, date of affirmance on direct appeal by a Court of Appeals and the United States Supreme Court, date that denial of any postconviction relief petition was affirmed by a Court of Appeals or Supreme Court, and the execution date, if any.

(d) Notice of Intention to File Initial Petition. Whenever it is determined that a prisoner under sentence of death will file an initial petition for relief in this court, either counsel or the prisoner may file with the clerk a "Notice of Intention to File Initial Petition for a Writ of Habeas Corpus." Each such Notice will be on the form set out in Appendix A–Criminal to this Rule or in substantially similar terms. Forms will be available from the clerk. The failure to submit such a Notice will not preclude the filing of a petition.

(e) Action by Court Upon Filing of Notice. The clerk will forward copies of the Notice, together with copies of any motions or requests submitted therewith, and any rulings thereon, to the following: (i) the Indiana Attorney General if the prisoner is in state custody or the United States Attorney if the prisoner is in federal custody; (ii) the United States Marshal for the Southern District of Indiana; and (iii) the Warden or Superintendent of the institution where the prisoner is confined.

(f) Appointment of Counsel. Motions or requests for the appointment of counsel will be presented to, and counsel appointed by, the Judge to whom such action is assigned.

(g) Additional Required Materials. Within 14 days of filing the notice or petition, Petitioner or Movant must file a legible copy of the materials listed below. If a required document is not filed, the petitioner or movant must state the reason for the omission. The required documents are:

(1) listing of prior petitions, with docket numbers, filed in any state or federal court challenging the

conviction and sentence challenged in the current petition; and

(2) a copy of, or a citation to, each state or federal court opinion, memorandum decision, order, transcript of oral statement of reasons, or judgment involving an issue presented in the petition.

(h) Motions for Stay of Execution.

(1) The movant must attach to the motion for stay a legible copy of the documents listed in section (g) of this Rule, unless the documents have already been filed with the court. If the movant asserts that time does not permit the filing of a written motion, he or she must deliver to the clerk a legible copy of the listed documents as soon as possible. If a required document is not filed, the movant must state the reason for the omission.

(2) Parties must file motions with the clerk during the normal business hours of the clerk's office. The motion must contain a brief account of the prior actions of any court or Judge to which the motion or a substantially similar or related petition for relief has been submitted.

(3) The clerk will adopt procedures for filing of emergency motions or applications pursuant to this Rule when the clerk's office is closed.

(4) The clerk will maintain a separate list of all cases within the scope of this Rule.

Note: December 1, 2009, stylistic amendment. Technical amendment to (g) to achieve consistency in time counting format with the Federal Rules of Civil Procedure. Current Rule was formerly numbered 6.2, and was significantly amended effective January 1, 2007. Former Rule 6.1 was eliminated January 1, 2007.

[Adopted effective July 12, 1994. Amended effective January 1, 2000; January 1, 2007; December 1, 2009.]

LOCAL CRIMINAL RULE 7–1. CONTINUANCE IN CRIMINAL CASES

A motion for continuance in a criminal case will be granted only if the moving party demonstrates that the ends of justice served by a continuance outweigh the best interest of the public and the defendant to a speedy trial, as provided by 18 U.S.C. § 3161(h)(8), or that the continuance will not violate the Speedy Trial Act deadlines for trial because of some other reason. The moving party shall submit with the motion a proposed entry setting out the findings as to these ends of justice, or such other reason why the continuance will not violate the Speedy Trial Act, 18 U.S.C § 3151 et seq.

[Former CR–7 adopted effective February 1, 1992; redesignated as C.R. 7.1 effective December 16, 1994. Amended effective March 14, 2002.]

LOCAL CRIMINAL RULE 8–1. ASSIGNMENT OF RELATED CASES

When a pending indictment or information is superseded by an indictment or information charging one or more of the defendants charged in the pending indictment or information and charging one or more of the offenses charged in the original indictment or information growing out of one or more occurrences which gave rise to the original charge, the superseding indictment or information shall be assigned to the same Judge to whom the first case is assigned. When two or more indictments or criminal informations are filed against the same person or persons, corporation or corporations, charging like offenses or violations of the same statute, each of such cases shall be assigned to the Judge to whom the first of such cases is assigned. Further, when an indictment or information is pending against a defendant, all subsequent indictments or informations against the same defendant which may be returned or filed shall be assigned to the same Judge.

[Former CR–8 adopted effective February 1, 1992; redesignated as C.R. 8.1 effective December 16, 1994.]

LOCAL CRIMINAL RULE 9–1. PROCESSING OF CASES IN DIVISION WITHOUT A RESIDENT JUDGE

(a) In any criminal case presided over by a Judge to whom such case was not regularly assigned upon its filing, in which there is more than one defendant and in which one or more but not all of the defendants enter a plea of guilty, the Judge taking such plea shall retain control over the defendant or defendants making such plea and proceed toward final disposition of the case in so far as it concerns such defendants. The Judge may then elect to retain the case in his/her control for purposes of trial and final disposition as to the remaining defendants or may refer the case back to the Judge to whom such case was originally assigned.

(b) In any criminal case in which a defendant enters a plea of guilty or is found guilty upon trial, the Judge taking such plea or presiding at trial, as the case may be, shall retain control of such case for disposition and sentencing.

[Former CR–9 adopted effective February 1, 1992; redesignated as C.R. 9.1 effective December 16, 1994.]

LOCAL CRIMINAL RULE 10–1. THE GRAND JURY

(a) A regular session of the grand jury shall be called on the second Monday of February and August in each year, and shall serve for a six-month term.

Each Indianapolis-based Judge shall in rotation impanel the grand jury.

(b) A petition to extend the session of a grand jury impaneled pursuant to this Rule shall be made to and decided by the Judge who impaneled that grand jury, the Motions Judge, or the Chief Judge.

(c) Each newly impaneled grand jury shall be assigned a number on the miscellaneous docket. All motions, orders, and other filings pertaining to matters before that grand jury shall bear that particular docket number and shall be maintained by the Clerk under seal, without the necessity for a motion to seal or order.

(d) All pre-indictment challenges to grand jury subpoenas or grand jury proceedings shall be made in writing and filed with the Clerk, and shall recite all pertinent facts including the grand jury number, the date of service of the subpoena, the appearance or production date of the subpoena, and the law. Such matters shall be ruled on by the District Judge who impaneled the grand jury, or, in his/her absence, the Motions Judge or the Chief Judge.

(e) Motions to quash the appearance of a witness or the production of records commanded by grand jury subpoena shall be filed and served upon the United States no later than 48 hours prior to the appearance or production date unless good cause exists for a later filing.

(f) Upon the filing of any objection to a grand jury subpoena, the appropriate District Judge will endeavor to rule upon the motion on or prior to the return date of the subpoena.

[Former CR–10 adopted effective February 1, 1992; redesignated as C.R. 10.1 effective December 16, 1994.]

LOCAL CRIMINAL RULE 11–1. RECORDS RELATING TO PRESENTENCE REPORTS AND PROBATION SUPERVISION

(a) Records maintained by the Probation Office of this Court relating to the preparation of presentence investigation reports are considered to be confidential. Such information may be released only by Order of the Court. Requests for such information in a presentence report being released shall be by written petition establishing, with particularity, the need for specific information contained in such reports.

(b) When a demand by way of subpoena or other judicial process is made of the probation officer either for testimony concerning information contained in such presentence reports or for copies of the presentence reports, the probation officer may petition the Court for instructions. The probation officer shall neither disclose the information nor provide the presentence report or copies of the presentence report

except on Order of this Court or as provided in Rule 32(b)(3) of the Federal Rules of Criminal Procedure.

(c) Supervision records on persons under probation supervision are considered to be confidential. The occasional need to release information on probationers to governmental agencies is recognized as being conducive to the rehabilitative process. In those infrequent cases, the Chief U.S. Probation Officer has in his/her discretion the authority to release or not release the requested information.

Note: Subsection (d) deleted effective January 1, 2002.

[Former CR–11 adopted effective February 1, 1992. Amended October 28, 1994; redesignated as C.R. 11.1 effective December 16, 1994; subsection (d) deleted effective January 1, 2002.]

LOCAL CRIMINAL RULE 12–1. AUTHORITY OF UNITED STATES MAGISTRATE JUDGES IN CRIMINAL MATTERS

The authority of United States Magistrate Judges in criminal matters shall include, but is not necessarily limited to, those duties set forth in Local Rule 72.1—Authority of United States Magistrate Judges.

Note: Rule adopted effective January 1, 2002, to provide a cross-reference to applicable local civil rules.

[Effective January 1, 2002.]

LOCAL CRIMINAL RULE 13–1. SENTENCING PROCEDURE

(a) The sentencing hearing in each criminal case will be scheduled by the court in accordance with the following timetable, which commences with either the filing of a plea agreement, the entry of a guilty plea, or a verdict of guilty. In the event there is an intent on the part of the defendant to plead guilty, but no written plea agreement is filed, the parties shall file a petition to enter a plea of guilty.

(b) Within 14 days after the commencement of one of the actions in subsection (a) above, counsel for the government and counsel for the defendant must submit in writing their respective versions of the facts pertaining to the instant offense to the probation officer of the court for inclusion in the Presentence Investigation Report.

(c) The Presentence Investigation Report, including guideline computations, will be completed and disclosed to the parties as early as feasible. The presentence report will be deemed to have been disclosed when the document is electronically served upon counsel through the court's CM/ECF system or, if an attorney is not registered to receive electronic service, 3 days after a notice of the report's availability is mailed to the attorney. The probation office will also mail a disclosure letter to the defendant advising that the presentence report has been made available to both parties. The sentence recommendation provided to the court by the probation office will not be disclosed except to the court.

(d) Within 14 days following disclosure of the presentence report, unless the court determines otherwise, all counsel must file in writing with the probation officer and serve on each other all objections they may have as to any material information, sentencing classifications, sentencing guideline calculations, and policy statements contained in or omitted from the Report.

(e) After receiving counsels' objections, if any, the probation officer will conduct any further investigation and make any necessary revisions to the Presentence Investigation Report. The officer may require counsel for both parties to meet with the officer in person or by telephone to discuss unresolved factual and legal issues. It is the obligation of an objecting party to seek administrative resolution of disputed factors or facts through consultation with opposing counsel and the probation officer prior to the sentencing hearing.

(f) The probation officer will submit the Presentence Investigation Report to the sentencing judge immediately after the receipt and processing of objections but no later than 7 days before the sentencing date. The probation officer will notify the court immediately if additional time is necessary to investigate and resolve disputed issues raised by the attorneys and the defendant during the review period. The Report will be accompanied by an addendum setting forth any objections any counsel may have asserted that have not been resolved, together with the officer's comments thereon. The probation officer will certify that the contents of the Report, including any revisions thereof, have been disclosed to the defendant and to counsel for the defendant and counsel for the government, and that the addendum fairly summarizes any remaining objections.

(g) Any party objecting to the Presentence Investigation Report, the guidelines, computations, or commentary will have a reasonable opportunity, usually at the sentencing hearing, but in any event in advance of imposition of the sentence, to present evidence or argument to the court regarding disputed factors or facts. The court may consider any reliable information presented by the probation officer, the defendant, or the government. The manner and form of such presentations are committed to the discretion of each sentencing judge on a case by case basis.

(h) The presentence report will be disclosed to the defendant's counsel and the government's counsel by the probation officer. Defense counsel will be responsible for making the necessary arrangements for review of the report by defendants within the schedules set out by the sentencing court. The unauthorized disclosure of the information contained in the presentence report, statements, and other attachments may be considered a contempt and punished accordingly. The presentence report will be filed under seal with the clerk of court and retained as part of the case file for whatever further judicial purposes may occur or be necessary.

Note: August 7, 2015, amendment to (a) clarifies that the filing of a plea agreement can trigger the scheduling provisions of the rule. It also clarifies that if no plea agreement is filed, a petition to enter a plea of guilty must be filed. January 1, 2011, amendment to allow electronic service of presentence report and reflect previously adopted practice of defense counsel providing report to defendant rather than probation officer. December 1, 2009, stylistic amendment and technical amendment to (b) to achieve consistency in time counting format with the Federal Rules of Civil Procedure.

[Effective January 1, 2002. Amended effective December 1, 2009; January 1, 2011; August 7, 2015.]

LOCAL CRIMINAL RULE 49–1. FILING OF DOCUMENTS ELECTRONICALLY REQUIRED

(a) Electronic Filing Required. All criminal cases (other than those cases the court specifically exempts) must be maintained in the court's electronic case filing (ECF) system. Accordingly, as allowed by Fed. R. Crim. P. 49(e) every document filed in this court (including exhibits) must be transmitted to the clerk's office via the ECF system consistent with S.D. Ind. Local Rules 5–2 through 5–11 except:

(1) any case initiating document resulting in the assignment of a criminal, magistrate, or miscellaneous case number and any charging instrument, initiating or superseding, and accompanying documents;

(2) documents requiring the oath or affirmation of a law enforcement officer in the presence of a judge or magistrate;

(3) papers filed in open court;

(4) papers filed by pro se defendants;

(5) exhibits in a format that does not readily permit electronic filing (such as videos and large maps and charts);

(6) papers that are illegible when scanned into .pdf format;

(7) papers filed in cases not maintained on the ECF system; and

(8) any other papers that the court or these rules specifically allow to be filed directly with the clerk.

(b) Documents Requiring Hand Signatures. Waivers, plea agreements and other documents that require a defendant's signature or the signature of a person other than an attorney of record must be signed by hand and scanned into .pdf format for electronic filing, pursuant to Local Rule 5–7(c). All hand-signed documents that contain the signature of the defendant must be maintained in the custody of the filing attorney.

(c) Filing with the Clerk. Any paper that is exempt from electronic filing must be filed directly with the clerk and served on other parties in the case as required by Fed. R. Crim. P. 49(b) and Fed. R. Civ. P. 5(b) as they relate to the service of non-electronic papers. Original documents consisting of more than one page must be fastened by paperclip or binder clip and may not be stapled. Copies for service on other parties must be stapled in the top left corner.

[Effective January 1, 2013. Amended effective January 30, 2013.]

LOCAL CRIMINAL RULE 49.1–2 FILING UNDER SEAL

(a) Maintaining Cases Under Seal. There is a presumption upon the initial appearance of a defendant on a sealed charging instrument that the entire case, including a multi-defendant case in which the defendant is the first to appear, should be unsealed. To maintain a case under seal, no later than at the time of the initial appearance, a party must file a motion and brief in support establishing good cause why the court should maintain the case under seal following the procedures set forth in subsections (d) and (e). The clerk will maintain a seal on the case until the court rules on the motion. If the court denies the motion, the clerk will unseal the case 14 days after service of the Order, absent Fed.R.Crim.P. 59(a) objection, motion to reconsider, or notice by a party of an intent to file an interlocutory appeal.

(b) Filing Documents Under Seal—General Rule. Unless authorized in subsection (c), other rule, statute or court order, the clerk may not maintain under seal any document. Once a document is sealed, the clerk may not, without a court order, allow anyone to see it other than:

(1) the court and its staff;

(2) the clerk's staff; and

(3) the attorney(s) who has/have appeared in the individual defendant's case to which the document pertains.

(c) No Separate Motion Necessary. The following documents may be filed under seal without motion or further order of the court, provided counsel has a good faith belief that sealing is required to ensure the safety, privacy or cooperation of a person or entity, or to otherwise protect a substantial public interest:

(1) charging instruments (e.g., complaint, information, indictment) and accompanying documents (prior to the initial appearance of the defendant as set forth above in subsection (a);

(2) warrant-type applications (e.g., arrest warrants, search warrants, pen registers, trap and trace devices, tracking orders, cell site orders, and wiretaps under 18 U.S.C. §§ 2516 and 2703);

(3) motions for tax return information pursuant to 26 U.S.C. § 6103;

(4) documents filed in grand jury proceedings;

(5) documents filed in juvenile proceedings;

(6) plea agreements that reference a defendant's cooperation and related documents, whether filed by the government or the defendant;

(7) motions for sentence variance filed pursuant to Fed.R.Crim.P. 35(b) or U.S.S.G. § 5K1.1, and supporting or related documents, such as a motion for temporary custody;

(8) motions for competency evaluation and related documents, filed under the provisions of Fed. R.Crim.P. 12.2 and 18 U.S.C. § 4241.

With the exception of charging documents addressed in subsection (c)(1), such documents shall remain under seal subject to further order of the court.

(d) Separate Motion Necessary—Filing Documents Under Seal—Procedure.

(1) To file a document under seal, a party must file it electronically as required under section 18 of the *ECF Policies and Procedures Manual* unless excused from electronic filing under S.D. Ind. L.R. 5–2(a) and 5–3(e). In either case, the party must include a cover sheet as the first page for each document being filed under seal that must include:

(A) the case caption;

(B) the title of the document, or an appropriate name to identify it on the public docket if the title cannot be publicly disclosed; and

(C) the name, address, and telephone number of the person filing the document.

(2) Except as provided under subsection (c), a party filing a document under seal must contemporaneously:

(A) file a Motion to Maintain Document(s) Under Seal, and

(i) if the filing party designated the subject information confidential, *e.g.*, a trade secret, proprietary information, or a business practice or procedure, a Brief in Support that complies with the requirements of subsection (e); and/or

(ii) if the filing party did not designate the subject information confidential, an identification of the designating party(ies); and

(B) unless the motion is to be considered ex parte, in which case no service is required, serve an unredacted and complete version of the sealed document upon all counsel and pro se parties.

(3) The designating party(ies) identified according to subsection (2)(A)(ii) must, within 14 days of service of the Motion to Maintain Document(s) under Seal, file a Statement Authorizing Unsealing of Document (or specific portions thereof), or a Brief in Support that complies with the requirements of subsection (e). If the designating party fails to file such Statement or Brief, then the filing party must notify the court of that failure. Such failure will result in unsealing the document(s).

(e) Brief in Support. A Brief in Support must not exceed 10 pages in length and must include:

(1) identification of the case and/or each specific document or portion(s) thereof that the party contends should remain under seal;

(2) the reasons demonstrating good cause to maintain the case and/or document, or portion(s) thereof, under seal including:

(A) why less restrictive alternatives to sealing, such as redaction, will not afford adequate protection; and

(B) how the case and/or document satisfies applicable authority for it to be maintained under seal; and

(C) the time period for which the case and/or document should remain sealed; and

(3) a statement as to whether maintenance of the case and/or document under seal is opposed by any party or why such party's position is unknown; and

(4) a proposed order as an attachment.

(f) Opposition to Maintenance Under Seal. The filing of an Opposition to a Motion to Maintain Case or Document(s) Under Seal is governed by S.D. Ind. L.R. 7–1, but the time for response is triggered by the filing of the Brief in Support. Any Brief in Opposition must not exceed 10 pages in length.

(g) Denial of Motion to Maintain Under Seal. If the court denies the motion, the clerk will unseal the case 14 days after service of the Order, absent Fed. R.Crim.P. 59(a) objection, motion to reconsider, or notice by a party of an intent to file an interlocutory appeal.

[Adopted effective January 1, 2015.]

Local Rules Advisory Committee Comments Re: 2015 New Rule

New Local Criminal Rule 49.1–2 replaces Local Rule 5–11 for filing cases and/or documents under seal in criminal matters and includes a list of documents that may be filed under seal without a motion and a detailed procedure for obtaining permission from the court to maintain cases and filed documents under seal. Whenever practical, the parties should confer regarding redaction in lieu of filing sealed documents. In addition, the rule encourages the parties to follow Seventh Circuit guidance on the legal parameters for maintaining cases and documents under seal.

Note: Adopted effective January 1, 2015.

LOCAL CRIMINAL RULE 57–1. PUBLIC ACCESS TO CRIMINAL CASE INFORMATION [DELETED]

Note: The Local Rule was deleted effective December 1, 2007, as the enactment of Fed. R. Crim. P. 49.1, "Privacy Protection For Filings Made with the Court," rendered Local Criminal Rule 57.1 duplicative and/or inconsistent.

[Deleted effective December 1, 2007.]

APPENDIX A–CRIMINAL. NOTICE OF INTENTION TO FILE FIRST PETITION FOR WRIT OF HABEAS CORPUS BY PERSON IN STATE CUSTODY UNDER SENTENCE OF DEATH

The undersigned, being either counsel in the Indiana courts for a person under a sentence of death imposed by an Indiana court or such a person, hereby gives notice to the Clerk of the United States District Court for the Southern District of Indiana that such person will in the near future file a petition attacking such sentence or the underlying conviction or both.

The name of the person under sentence of death is _____, his inmate number within the Department of Correction is _____ and he is presently confined at the _____ (insert name of the institution where confined). In connection with this Notice the following representations are made:

1. The sentence of death was imposed by the _____ (insert name of court) in cause number _____;

2. The sentence and the underlying conviction have been appealed to the Indiana Supreme Court and the appeal and postconviction proceedings were concluded in that Court on _____ (insert dates of decision of the Indiana Supreme Court on direct appeal and, if applicable, on the denial of postconviction relief);

3. The person under sentence of death will/will not (select one) be represented by counsel when a petition for relief is presented to the United States District Court;

4. There is presently no date of execution set; or an execution date of _____ (insert date);

5. The person under sentence of death will/will not (select one) seek a stay of execution before/upon (select one) the filing of the petition for relief referred to in this Notice and will/will not (select one) be seeking the appointment of counsel to represent him in the proceeding.

6. This Notice is accompanied by the $30.00 docketing fee prescribed by 28 U.S.C. § 1914(a) or submitted by or on behalf of a person without sufficient funds to prepay the $20.00 docketing fee.

Date: _____   _____
                                         (Signature)

                        _____
                                         (Name)

[Adopted effective July 12, 1994.]

RULES OF DISCIPLINARY ENFORCEMENT

RULE I. ATTORNEYS CONVICTED OF CRIMES

A. Upon the filing with this Court of a certified copy of a judgment of conviction demonstrating that any attorney admitted to practice before the Court has been convicted in any court of the United States, or the District of Columbia, or of any state, territory, commonwealth or possession of the United States of a serious crime as hereinafter defined, the Court shall enter an order immediately suspending that attorney, whether the conviction resulted from a plea of guilty, or nolo contendere or from a verdict after trial or otherwise, and regardless of the pendency of any appeal, until final disposition of a disciplinary proceeding to be commenced upon such conviction. A copy of such order shall immediately be served upon the attorney. Upon good cause shown, the Court may set aside such order when it appears in the interest of justice to do so.

B. The term "serious crime" shall include any felony and any lesser crime a necessary element of which, as determined by the statutory or common law definition of such crime in the jurisdiction where the judgment was entered, involves false swearing, misrepresentation, fraud, willful failure to file income tax returns, deceit, bribery, extortion, misappropriation, theft, or an attempt or a conspiracy or solicitation of another to commit a "serious crime."

C. A certified copy of a judgment of conviction of an attorney for any crime shall be conclusive evidence of the commission of that crime in any disciplinary proceeding instituted against that attorney based upon the conviction.

D. Upon the filing of a certified copy of a judgment of conviction of an attorney for a serious crime, the Court shall in addition to suspending that attorney in accordance with the provisions of this Rule, also refer the matter to counsel for the institution of a disciplinary proceeding before the Court in which the sole issue to be determined shall be the extent of the final discipline to be imposed as a result of the conduct resulting in the conviction, provided that a disciplinary proceeding so instituted will not be brought to final hearing until all appeals from the conviction are concluded.

E. Upon the filing of a certified copy of a judgment of conviction of an attorney for a crime not constituting a "serious crime," the Court may refer the matter to counsel for whatever action counsel may deem warranted, including the institution of a disciplinary proceeding before the Court; provided, however, that the Court may in its discretion make no reference with respect to convictions for minor offenses.

F. An attorney suspended under the provisions of this Rule will be reinstated immediately upon the filing of a certificate demonstrating that the underlying conviction of a serious crime has been reversed but the reinstatement will not terminate any disciplinary proceeding then pending against the attorney, the disposition of which shall be determined by the Court on the basis of all available evidence pertaining to both guilt and the extent of discipline to be imposed.

[Effective January 1, 1979.]

RULE II. DISCIPLINE IMPOSED BY OTHER COURTS

A. Any attorney admitted to practice before this Court shall, upon being subjected to public discipline by any other court of the United States or the District of Columbia, or by a court of any state, territory, commonwealth or possession of the United States, promptly inform the Clerk of this Court of such action.

B. Upon the filing of a certified or exemplified copy of a judgment or order demonstrating that an attorney admitted to practice before this Court has been *publicly* disciplined by another court, *other than by censure or reprimand*, this Court shall forthwith issue a notice directed to the attorney containing:

1. a copy of the judgment or order from the other court; and

2. an order to show cause directing that the attorney inform this Court within 30 days after service of that order upon the attorney of any claim by the attorney predicated upon the grounds set forth in (D) hereof that the imposition of the identical discipline by the Court would be unwarranted and the reasons therefor. Service of an order to show cause why reciprocal discipline should not be imposed may be served on the attorney personally or by mailing a copy of the order to the attorney at the address he or she last provided to the court. Service by mail is complete upon mailing.

C. In the event the discipline imposed in the other jurisdiction has been stayed there, any reciprocal discipline imposed in this Court shall be deferred until such stay expires.

D. Upon the expiration of 30 days from service of the notice issued pursuant to the provisions of (B) above, this Court shall impose the identical discipline unless the respondent-attorney demonstrates, or this Court finds, that upon the face of the record upon which the discipline in another jurisdiction is predicated it clearly appears:

1. that the procedure was so lacking in notice or opportunity to be heard as to constitute a deprivation of due process; or

2. that there was such an infirmity of proof establishing the misconduct as to give rise to the clear conviction that this Court could not, consistent with its duty, accept as final the conclusion on that subject; or

3. that the imposition of the same discipline by this Court would result in grave injustice; or

4. that the misconduct established is deemed by this Court to warrant substantially different discipline.

Where this Court determines that any of said elements exist, it shall enter such other order as it deems appropriate.

E. In all other respects, a final adjudication in another court that an attorney has been guilty of misconduct shall establish conclusively the misconduct for purposes of a disciplinary proceeding in this Court.

F. This Court may at any stage appoint counsel to prosecute the disciplinary proceedings.

[Effective January 1, 1979. Amended effective July 1, 2008.]

RULE III. DISBARMENT ON CONSENT OR RESIGNATION IN OTHER COURTS

A. Any attorney admitted to practice before this Court who shall be disbarred on consent or resign from the bar of any other court of the United States or the District of Columbia, or from the bar of any state, territory, commonwealth or possession of the United States while an investigation into allegations of misconduct is pending, shall, upon the filing with this Court of a certified or exemplified copy of the judgment or order accepting such disbarment on consent or resignation, cease to be permitted to practice before this Court and be stricken from the roll of attorneys admitted to practice before this Court.

B. Any attorney admitted to practice before this Court shall, upon being disbarred on consent or resigning from the bar of any other court of the United States or the District of Columbia, or from the bar of any state, territory, commonwealth or possession of the United States while an investigation into allegations of misconduct is pending, promptly inform the Clerk of this Court of such disbarment on consent or resignation.

[Effective January 1, 1979.]

RULE IV. ADMINISTRATIVE SUSPENSION AND REINSTATEMENT

An attorney admitted to practice before this Court who is suspended from the bar of the State of Indiana for

A. nonpayment of the Annual Registration Fee required by Rule 23, Section 21, of the Indiana Rules for Admission to the Bar and the Discipline of Attorneys, Disciplinary Commission and Proceedings; or

B. failing to complete the yearly or Educational Period requirements required by Rule 29, Section 10, of the Indiana Rules for Admission to the Bar and the Discipline of Attorneys, Mandatory Continuing Legal Education will be automatically suspended from practice before this Court without any action by the Court other than written notice to the attorney. Upon receipt of notice that the attorney has been reinstated to the bar of the State of Indiana, the attorney will be automatically reinstated to the bar of this Court.

[Effective January 1, 2001.]

RULE V. STANDARDS FOR PROFESSIONAL CONDUCT

A. For misconduct defined in these Rules, and for good cause shown, and after notice and opportunity to be heard, any attorney admitted to practice before this Court may be disbarred, suspended from practice before this Court, reprimanded or subjected to such other disciplinary action as the circumstances may warrant.

B. Acts or omissions by an attorney admitted to practice before this Court, individually or in concert with any other person or persons, which violate the Code of Professional Responsibility adopted by this Court shall constitute misconduct and shall be grounds for discipline, whether or not the act or omission occurred in the course of an attorney-client relationship. The Rules of Professional Conduct adopted by this Court are the Rules of Professional Conduct adopted by the Supreme Court of the state of Indiana, as amended from time to time by that state court, except as otherwise provided by specific rule of this Court.

[Former Rule IV effective January 1, 1979. Amended effective April 22, 1988. Redesignated Rule V effective January 1, 2001.]

RULE VI. DISCIPLINARY PROCEEDINGS

A. When misconduct or allegations of misconduct which, if substantiated, would warrant discipline on the part of an attorney admitted to practice before this Court shall come to the attention of a judge of this Court, whether by complaint or otherwise, and the applicable procedure is not otherwise mandated by these Rules, the judge shall refer the matter to counsel for investigation and the prosecution of a formal disciplinary proceeding or the formulation of such other recommendation as may be appropriate.

B. Should counsel conclude after investigation and review that a formal disciplinary proceeding should not be initiated against the respondent-attorney because sufficient evidence is not present, or because there is pending another proceeding against the respondent-attorney, the disposition of which in the judgment of the counsel should be awaited before further action by this Court is considered or for any other valid reason, counsel shall file with the Court a recommendation for disposition of the matter, whether by dismissal, admonition, deferral, or otherwise setting forth the reasons therefor.

C. To initiate formal disciplinary proceedings, counsel shall obtain an order of this Court upon a showing of probable cause requiring the respondent-attorney to show cause within 30 days after service of that order upon that attorney, personally or by mail, why the attorney should not be disciplined.

D. Upon the respondent-attorney's answer to the order to show cause, if any issue of fact is raised or the respondent-attorney wishes to be heard in mitigation this Court shall set the matter for prompt hearing before one or more judges of this Court, provided, however, that if the disciplinary proceeding is predicated upon the complaint of a judge of this Court, the hearing shall be conducted before a panel of three other judges of this Court appointed by the Chief Judge.

[Former Rule V effective January 1, 1979. Redesignated Rule VI effective January 1, 2001.]

RULE VII. DISBARMENT ON CONSENT WHILE UNDER DISCIPLINARY INVESTIGATION OR PROSECUTION

A. Any attorney admitted to practice before this Court who is the subject of an investigation into, or a pending proceeding involving, allegations of misconduct may consent to disbarment, but only by delivering to this Court an affidavit stating that the attorney desires to consent to disbarment and that:

1. the attorney's consent is freely and voluntarily rendered; the attorney is not being subjected to coercion or duress; the attorney is fully aware of the implications of so consenting;

2. the attorney is aware that there is a presently pending investigation or proceeding involving allegations that there exist grounds for the attorney's discipline the nature of which the attorney shall specifically set forth;

3. the attorney acknowledges that the material facts so alleged are true; and

4. the attorney so consents because the attorney knows that if charges were predicated upon the matters under investigation, or if the proceeding were prosecuted, the attorney could not successfully defend himself.

B. Upon receipt of the required affidavit, this Court shall enter an order disbarring the attorney.

C. The order disbarring the attorney on consent shall be a matter of public record. However, the affidavit required under the provisions of this Rule shall not be publicly disclosed or made available for use in any other proceeding except upon order of this Court.

[Former Rule VI effective January 1, 1979. Redesignated Rule VII effective January 1, 2001.]

RULE VIII. REINSTATEMENT

A. Automatic Reinstatement. An attorney suspended for three months or less shall be automatically reinstated at the end of the period of suspension upon the filing with the court of an affidavit of compliance with the provisions of the order. An attorney suspended for more than three months or disbarred may not resume practice until reinstated by order of this Court.

B. Time of Application for Reinstatement Following Disbarment. A person who has been disbarred after hearing or by consent may not apply for reinstatement until the expiration of at least five years from the effective date of the disbarment.

C. Reinstatement Following Reciprocal Discipline. Petitions for reinstatement by a disbarred or suspended attorney under this Rule shall be filed with the Chief Judge of this Court.

An attorney, who has previously been the subject of reciprocal discipline and subsequent reinstatement by another court and also disbarred or suspended from practice in this court without provision for automatic reinstatement, may petition this Court for reinstatement by filing with the Chief Judge a petition for reinstatement together with a certified copy of the judgment or order of the other court granting reinstatement.

Upon receipt of the petition and certified reinstatement judgment or order, the Chief Judge shall promptly review the petition, as well as any findings and conclusions of another court, and recommend to the other judges of this court whether or not in his/her opinion the petition and/or findings of another court sufficiently establish the fitness of petitioner to practice law so that he should be reinstated to the roll of attorneys without further hearing. If, after receiving the recommendations of the Chief Judge, a majority of the judges of the court agree to reinstatement without further evidence or hearing, the Court shall enter a judgment accordingly and the petitioner shall be reinstated. If, on the other hand, after receiving and considering the recommendation of the Chief Judge a majority of the Judges of the Court request additional evidence or hearing prior to making a decision on the petition, a hearing shall be scheduled in accordance with Section D of this Rule.

D. Hearing on Application for Reinstatement. If evidence or argument is required in order to rule on a petition for reinstatement, the Chief Judge shall promptly refer the petition to the United States Attorney for this district, requesting that he/she or an Assistant United States Attorney serve as counsel for the Court in the reinstatement matter. The Chief Judge shall also assign the matter for prompt hearing before one or more judges of this Court, provided, however, that if the initial disciplinary proceeding which resulted in the attorney's suspension or disbarment was predicated upon the complaint of a judge of this Court the hearing shall be conducted before a panel of three other judges of this Court appointed by the Chief Judge. The judge or judges assigned to the matter shall, within thirty (30) days after referral, schedule a hearing at which the petitioner shall have the burden of demonstrating by clear and convincing evidence that he/she has the moral qualifications, competency and learning in the law required for admission to practice law before this Court and that his/her resumption of the practice of law will not be detrimental to the integrity and standing of the bar or to the administration of justice, or subversive of the public interest.

E. Duty of Counsel. In all proceedings upon a petition for reinstatement, cross-examination of the witnesses of the respondent-attorney and the submission of evidence, if any, in opposition to the petition shall be conducted by the United States Attorney or his assistant.

F. Deposit for Costs of Proceeding. Petitions for reinstatement under this Rule shall be accompanied by an advance cost deposit in an amount to be set from time to time by the Court to cover anticipated costs of the reinstatement proceeding.

G. Disposition of Petition for Reinstatement. If the petitioner is found unfit to resume the practice of law, the petition shall be dismissed. If the petitioner is found fit to resume the practice of law, the judgment shall reinstate him, provided that the judgment may make reinstatement conditional upon the payment of all or part of the costs of the proceedings, and upon the making of partial or complete restitution to parties harmed by the petitioner whose conduct led to the suspension or disbarment. Provided further, that if the petitioner has been suspended or disbarred for five years or more, reinstatement may be conditioned, in the discretion of the judge or judges before whom the matter is heard, upon the furnishing of proof of competency and learning in the law, which proof may include certification by the bar examiners of a state or other jurisdiction of the attorney's successful completion of an examination for admission to

practice subsequent to the date of suspension or disbarment.

H. Successive Petitions. No petition for reinstatement under this Rule shall be filed within one year following an adverse judgment upon a petition for reinstatement filed by or on behalf of the same person.

[Former Rule VII effective January 1, 1979. Amended effective March 11, 1988. Redesignated Rule VIII effective January 1, 2001. Amended effective July 1, 2008.]

RULE IX. ATTORNEYS SPECIALLY ADMITTED

Whenever an attorney applies to be admitted or is admitted to this Court for purposes of a particular proceeding (pro hac vice), the attorney shall be deemed thereby to have conferred disciplinary jurisdiction upon this Court for any alleged misconduct of that attorney arising in the course of or in the preparation for such proceeding.

[Former Rule VIII effective January 1, 1979. Redesignated Rule IX effective January 1, 2001.]

RULE X. SERVICE OF PAPERS AND OTHER NOTICES

A. Service of an order to show cause why reciprocal discipline should not be imposed shall be made by personal service or by mailing a copy of the order to the respondent/attorney at the address he or she last provided to the court. Service by mail of such an order is complete upon mailing.

B. Service of any order instituting an original formal disciplinary proceeding shall be made in accordance with Fed. R. Civ. P. 4(e).

[Former Rule IX effective January 1, 1997. Redesignated Rule X effective January 1, 2001. Amended effective July 1, 2008.]

RULE XI. APPOINTMENT OF COUNSEL

Whenever counsel is to be appointed pursuant to these Rules to investigate allegations of misconduct or prosecute disciplinary proceedings or in conjunction with a reinstatement petition filed by a disciplined attorney, this Court shall appoint as counsel the Executive Secretary and staff attorneys of the Indiana Supreme Court Disciplinary Commission. If such persons decline appointment, or such appointment is clearly inappropriate, this Court shall appoint as counsel one or more members of the bar of this Court to investigate allegations of misconduct or to prosecute disciplinary proceedings under these Rules; provided, however, that the respondent-attorney may move to disqualify an attorney so appointed who is or has been engaged as an adversary of the respondent-attorney in any matter. Counsel, once appointed, may not resign unless permission to do so is given by this Court.

[Former Rule X effective January 1, 1979. Amended effective December 3, 1982. Redesignated Rule XI effective January 1, 2001.]

RULE XII. DUTIES OF THE CLERK

A. Upon being informed that an attorney admitted to practice before this Court has been convicted of any crime, the Clerk of this Court shall determine whether the Clerk of the Court in which such conviction occurred has forwarded a certificate of such conviction to this Court. If a certificate has not been so forwarded, the Clerk of this Court shall promptly obtain a certificate and file it with this Court.

B. Upon being informed that an attorney admitted to practice before this Court has been subjected to discipline by another court, the Clerk of this Court shall determine whether a certified or exemplified copy of the disciplinary judgment or order has been filed with this Court, and, if not, the Clerk shall promptly obtain a certified or exemplified copy of the disciplinary judgment or order and file it with this Court.

C. Whenever it appears that any person convicted of any crime or disbarred or suspended or censured or disbarred on consent by this Court is admitted to practice law in any other jurisdiction or before any other court, the Clerk of this Court shall, within 10 days of that conviction, disbarment, suspension, censure, or disbarment on consent, transmit to the disciplinary authority in such other jurisdiction, or for such

other court, a certificate of the conviction or a certified exemplified copy of the judgment or order of disbarment, suspension, censure, or disbarment on consent, as well as the last known office and residence addresses of the defendant or respondent.

D. The Clerk of this Court shall, likewise, promptly notify the National Discipline Data Bank operated by the American Bar Association of any order imposing public discipline upon any attorney admitted to practice before this Court.

[Former Rule XI effective January 1, 1979. Redesignated Rule XII effective January 1, 2001.]

RULE XIII. JURISDICTION

Nothing contained in these rules shall be construed to deny this Court such powers as are necessary for the Court to maintain control over proceedings conducted before it, such as proceedings for contempt under Title 18 of the United States Code or under Rule 42 of the Federal Rules of Criminal Procedure.

[Former Rule XII effective January 1, 1979. Redesignated Rule XIII effective January 1, 2001.]

RULE XIV. EFFECTIVE DATE

These Rules shall become effective January 1, 1979, provided that any formal disciplinary proceeding then pending before this Court shall be concluded under the procedure existing prior to the effective date of these Rules.

[Former Rule XIII effective January 1, 1979. Redesignated Rule XIV effective January 1, 2001.]

LOCAL RULES OF ALTERNATIVE
DISPUTE RESOLUTION

PREAMBLE

These Rules have been adopted to provide uniform procedures for utilizing mediation in the resolution of certain cases in this Court, with the view that the interests of the parties before the Court may be better served by alternatives to the traditional adversarial litigation process. Mediation as provided under these Rules is a separate, alternative method of dispute resolution and does not preclude settlement conferences and mediation conducted by the District Judges or Magistrate Judges of the Court. The parties may also voluntarily pursue other forms of alternative dispute resolution not provided for under these Rules.

[Adopted effective December 1, 2000.]

RULE 1. GENERAL PROVISIONS

RULE 1.1 SCOPE OF THE RULES

(a) **Title and Citation**. These Rules shall be known as the Local Alternative Dispute Resolution Rules of the United States District Court for the Southern District of Indiana. They shall be cited as "S.D.Ind. Local A.D.R. Rule _____."

(b) **Scope of the Rules**. The alternative dispute resolution method governed by these Rules is mediation. Any individual who serves as the primary facilitator for mediation under these Rules is referred to herein as the Mediator.

Settlement conferences conducted by the Judges and Magistrate Judges of the Court are not governed by these Rules.

[Adopted effective December 1, 2000.]

RULE 1.2 APPLICATION OF ALTERNATIVE DISPUTE RESOLUTION

Unless limited by specific provisions, or unless there are other applicable specific statutory, common law, or constitutional procedures, these Rules shall apply in all civil litigation filed in the U.S. District Court for the Southern District of Indiana, except in the following cases and proceedings:

(a) Applications for writs of habeas corpus under 28 U.S.C. § 2254;

(b) Forfeiture cases;

(c) Non-adversary proceedings in bankruptcy;

(d) Social Security administrative review cases; and

(e) Such other matters as specified by order of the Court; for example, matters involving important public policy issues, constitutional law, or the establishment of new law.

[Adopted effective December 1, 2000.]

RULE 1.3 IMMUNITY FOR MEDIATORS ACTING UNDER THESE RULES

To the extent permitted under applicable law, each Mediator shall have immunity in the performance of his or her duties under these Rules, in the same manner, and to the same extent, as would a duly appointed Judge.

[Adopted effective December 1, 2000.]

RULE 1.4 JURISDICTION OF PROCEEDING

At all times during the course of mediation the case remains under the jurisdiction of the Judge to whom the case is assigned on the Court docket.

For good cause shown the assigned Judge at any time may terminate the mediation.

[Adopted effective December 1, 2000.]

RULE 1.5 OTHER METHODS OF DISPUTE RESOLUTION

These Rules shall not preclude the parties from utilizing any other reasonable method or technique of alternative dispute resolution to resolve disputes to which the parties agree. However, any use of arbitration by the parties will be governed by and comply with the requirements of 28 U.S.C. §§ 654–657.

[Adopted effective December 1, 2000.]

RULE 1.6 CONFIDENTIALITY OF PROCEEDINGS

Any written or oral communications made during the course of any processes or proceedings covered under these Rules are confidential unless otherwise agreed by the parties. The unauthorized disclosure of any confidential communications by any persons may result in the imposition of sanctions pursuant to Rule 2.9.

Mediation shall be regarded as settlement negotiations as governed by Fed. R. Evid. 408.

[Adopted effective December 1, 2000. Amended effective April 16, 2003.]

RULE 1.7   DISQUALIFICATION OF MEDIATORS

In any case in which a Mediator has been selected by the parties or appointed by the Court, the Mediator shall disqualify himself or herself from the proceeding if and when his or her impartiality might reasonably be questioned. In addition, each Mediator shall be subject to the disqualification rules found in 28 U.S.C. § 455.

In any case in which a party reasonably believes an appointed Mediator should be disqualified, a Request for Disqualification of Mediator, setting forth the grounds therefor, shall be filed with the Clerk for consideration by the Court.

[Adopted effective December 1, 2000.]

RULE 1.9   DESIGNATION OF ADMINISTRATOR

The Clerk and his/her designee shall serve as administrators of the processes covered under these Rules.

[Adopted effective December 1, 2000.]

RULE 2.   MEDIATION

RULE 2.1   PURPOSE

Mediation under this section involves the confidential process by which a person acting as a Mediator, selected by the parties or appointed by the Court, assists the litigants in reaching a mutually acceptable agreement. It is an informal and nonadversarial process. The role of the Mediator is to assist in identifying the issues, reducing misunderstandings, clarifying priorities, exploring areas of compromise, and finding points of agreement as well as legitimate points of disagreement. Final decision-making authority rests with the parties, not the Mediator.

It is anticipated that an agreement may not resolve all of the disputed issues, but the process, nonetheless, can reduce points of contention. Parties and their representatives are required to mediate in good faith, but are not compelled to reach an agreement.

[Adopted effective December 1, 2000.]

RULE 2.2   CASE SELECTION

The Court with the agreement of the parties may refer a civil case for mediation. Unless otherwise ordered or as specifically provided in Rule 2.8, referral to mediation does not abate or suspend the action, and no scheduled dates shall be delayed or deferred, including the date of trial.

[Adopted effective December 1, 2000. Amended effective January 1, 2002.]

RULE 2.3   LISTING OF MEDIATORS: COMMISSION REGISTRY OF MEDIATORS

Any person who wishes to serve as a Mediator pursuant to these Rules must be registered with and satisfy the requirements of the Indiana Supreme Court Commission for Continuing Legal Education (hereinafter "Commission").

[Adopted effective December 1, 2000.]

RULE 2.4   SELECTION OF MEDIATORS

Upon the issuance of an order referring a case to mediation, the parties may, within fifteen (15) days of referral: (1) choose a Mediator from the Commission's registry, or (2) agree upon a non-registered Mediator and notify the Court in writing of the agreement, providing the name and address of the selected Mediator. In the event a Mediator is not selected by agreement, the Court will designate three (3) registered Mediators from the Commission's registry who are willing to mediate within the Southern District of Indiana. Each side alternately shall strike the name of one Mediator. The side initiating the lawsuit will strike first. The Mediator remaining after the striking process will be deemed the selected Mediator.

A person selected to serve as a Mediator under this Rule may choose not to serve for any reason. At any time, a party may request that the Court replace the Mediator for good cause shown. In the event a Mediator chooses not to serve or the Court orders the replacement of the Mediator, the selection process will be repeated.

[Adopted effective December 1, 2000.]

RULE 2.5   MEDIATION COSTS

(a) **Mediation Fee.** Each Mediator to whom a civil action is referred shall be compensated at a rate agreed upon by the parties and the Mediator.

(b) **Prohibited Compensation.** A Mediator may not give or receive any commission, rebate, contingent fee, or similar remuneration for referring any person to mediation or for serving as a Mediator.

[Adopted effective December 1, 2000.]

RULE 2.6 MEDIATION PROCEDURE

(a) **Advisement of Participants**. The Mediator shall:

(1) advise the parties of all persons whose presence at the mediation might facilitate settlement; and

(2) disclose to the parties or their attorneys any factual documentation revealed during the mediation if, at the end of the mediation process, the disclosure is agreed upon by all parties.

(b) **Mediation Sessions.**

(1) The parties, their attorneys, and other persons with settlement authority shall be present at all mediation sessions unless otherwise agreed. At the discretion of the Mediator, non-parties to the dispute may also be present.

(2) Mediation sessions are not open to public.

(c) **Confidential Statement of Case.** The attorney for each side shall submit to the Mediator a confidential statement of the case, not to exceed ten (10) pages, prior to a mediation session, which shall include:

(1) the legal and factual contentions of the party as to both liability and damages;

(2) the factors considered in arriving at the current settlement posture; and

(3) the status of the settlement negotiations to date.

A confidential statement of the case may be supplemented by damage brochures, videos, and other exhibits or evidence. The supplemental materials shall be made available to opposing counsel at least five (5) days prior to the mediation session. The confidential statement of the case and its contents shall not be disclosed to opposing parties and shall at all times be held privileged and confidential to the extent provided by law, unless an agreement to the contrary is provided to the Mediator. In the mediation process, the Mediator may meet jointly or separately with the parties and may express an evaluation of the case to one or more of the parties or their representatives. If the mediation process does not result in settlement, any submitted confidential statement of the case shall be returned to the submitting attorney or party.

(d) **Termination of Mediation.** The Mediator shall terminate mediation whenever the Mediator believes that continuation of the process would harm or prejudice one or more of the parties, whenever the ability or willingness of any party to participate meaningfully in mediation is so lacking that a reasonable agreement is unlikely, or whenever the Mediator determines that continuing the mediation process would be futile. The Mediator shall not state the reason for termination to the Court except when the termination is due to conflict of interest or bias on the part of the Mediator, in which case another Mediator may be assigned by the Court. Either party may withdraw from and terminate mediation if it is determined that continuing the mediation process would be futile.

(e) **Report of Mediation: Status.**

(1) Within ten (10) days after the mediation, the Mediator shall submit to the Court under seal (unless the parties agree otherwise), without comment or recommendation, a report of mediation status. The report shall indicate whether an agreement was reached in whole or in part, or whether the mediation was continued by the parties.

(2) If an agreement is reached, in whole or in part, it shall be reduced to writing and signed by the parties and their counsel. Except with the consent of all parties, the agreement shall not be filed with the Court If the agreement is complete on all issues, a joint stipulation of disposition shall be filed with the Court.

(3) In the event of any breach or failure to perform under the agreement, upon motion and after hearing, the Court may impose sanctions, including entry of judgment consistent with the agreement.

[Adopted effective December 1, 2000.]

RULE 2.7 RULES OF EVIDENCE

With the exception of privileged communications, the rules of evidence do not apply in mediation, but factual information having a bearing on the question of damages should be supported by documentary evidence whenever possible.

[Adopted effective December 1, 2000.]

RULE 2.8 DISCOVERY

Whenever possible, parties are encouraged to limit discovery to the development of information necessary to facilitate the mediation process. Upon stipulation by the parties or as ordered by the Court, discovery may be deferred during mediation pursuant to FED. R. CIV. P. 26(c).

[Adopted effective December 1, 2000.]

RULE 2.9 SANCTIONS

Upon motion by either party, the Court may impose sanctions against any person who fails to comply with these Rules.

[Adopted effective December 1, 2000.]

RULE 2.10   MEDIATOR PRIVILEGE

Except as otherwise provided by law, Mediators shall not be subject to process requiring the disclosure of any matter discussed during the mediation, but rather, such matter shall be considered confidential and privileged in nature. The confidentially requirement may not be waived by the parties, and a party or the Mediator may object to any attempt to obtain testimony or physical evidence from mediation.

[Adopted effective December 1, 2000.]

RULE 3.   CONDUCT AND DISCIPLINE FOR PERSONS CONDUCTING MEDIATION

RULE 3.0   PURPOSE

This Rule establishes standards of conduct for persons conducting mediation pursuant to these Rules.

[Adopted effective December 1, 2000.]

RULE 3.1   ACCOUNTABILITY AND DISCIPLINE

A person who accepts appointment as a Mediator under these Rules consents to the jurisdiction of the Court in the enforcement of these standards.

[Adopted effective December 1, 2000.]

RULE 3.2   COMPETENCE

A Mediator shall decline appointment, request technical assistance, or withdraw from a dispute beyond the Mediator's competence.

[Adopted effective December 1, 2000.]

RULE 3.3   DISCLOSURE AND OTHER COMMUNICATIONS

(a) A Mediator has a continuing duty to communicate as follows:

(1) notify participants through their counsel of the date, time, and location of the process, at least ten (10) days in advance, unless a shorter time period is agreed upon by the parties;

(2) describe the mediation process, including the possibility that the Mediator may conduct private sessions;

(3) disclose the cost structure of the process;

(4) advise that the Mediator does not represent any of the parties or the Court;

(5) disclose any past, present or known future professional, business, or personal relationship with any party, insurer, or attorney involved in the process, and any other circumstances bearing on the perception of the Mediator's impartiality;

(6) explain the extent to which information obtained through the process from and about any participant is or is not privileged and may be subject to disclosure; and

(7) advise that any agreement signed by the parties constitutes evidence that may be introduced in litigation concerning enforcement of settlement.

(b) A Mediator may not misrepresent any material fact or circumstance nor promise a specific result or imply partiality.

(c) A Mediator shall preserve the confidentiality of all proceedings, except where otherwise provided by agreement of the parties or by law or order of the Court.

[Adopted effective December 1, 2000.]

RULE 3.4   DUTIES

(a) A Mediator shall observe all applicable statutes, administrative policies, rules of professional conduct, and rules of Court.

(b) A Mediator shall act in a timely and expeditious fashion.

(c) A Mediator shall be impartial and civil, and shall utilize an effective system to identify potential conflicts of interest at the time of appointment. After disclosure pursuant to S.D.Ind. Local A.D.R. Rule 3.3(A), to the extent provided under 28 U.S.C. § 455(e) a Mediator may serve with the consent of the parties, unless a conflict of interest arises or the Mediator believes the Mediator can no longer be impartial, in which case the Mediator shall withdraw.

(d) A Mediator shall avoid the appearance of impropriety.

(e) A Mediator shall display and promote mutual respect among the participants throughout the process.

[Adopted effective December 1, 2000.]

RULE 3.5   FAIR, REASONABLE AND VOLUNTARY AGREEMENTS

(a) A Mediator shall not coerce any party.

(b) A Mediator shall withdraw whenever a proposed resolution is unconscionable or unjust.

(c) A Mediator shall not make any substantive decision for any party.

[Adopted effective December 1, 2000.]

RULE 3.6 SUBSEQUENT PROCEEDINGS

(a) An individual may not serve as a Mediator in any dispute on which another Mediator already has been serving without first ascertaining that the current Mediator has been notified of the desired change.

(b) A person who has served as a Mediator in a proceeding may act as a Mediator in subsequent disputes between the parties, and the parties may provide for a review of the agreement with the Mediator on a periodic basis. However, the Mediator shall decline to act in any capacity except as a Mediator unless the subsequent association is clearly distinct from the issues involved in the alternative dispute resolution process. The Mediator may not subsequently act as an investigator for any court-ordered report or make any recommendations to the Court regarding the litigation.

[Adopted effective December 1, 2000.]

SELECTED FORMS
INSTRUCTIONS FOR PREPARING CASE MANAGEMENT PLAN

The following provisions apply to civil cases filed in the United States District Court for the Southern District of Indiana that are not exempt from filing a Case Management Plan ("CMP") under Local Rule 16–1.

Special Instructions For Pro Se Parties

Any party who is not represented by counsel (known as a pro se party) and who is not incarcerated may participate fully in the preparation of the CMP. Alternatively, however, non-incarcerated pro se parties may simply mail a letter containing that party's complete name, address, telephone number, and a summary of the case that includes only the main or major facts. This letter must be mailed to all opposing counsel (or parties, if unrepresented) within 70 days from the date that the case was filed or removed to this Court. Pro se parties may obtain the names and addresses of counsel for opposing parties by calling the clerk's office at 317–229–3700 or conducting a case search on the Court's webpage at www.insd.uscourts.gov. Counsel for opposing parties shall then incorporate the information from the pro se party's letter, timely sign and submit the CMP to the Court, and serve a copy on the pro se party.

General Instructions For All Cases

Unless the plaintiff is pro se, counsel for plaintiff shall be responsible for coordinating timely completion of the CMP. The deadline for filing the CMP is 90 days from the date the case was filed or removed. The deadline for filing the CMP shall not be extended without written motion which establishes good cause to extend the deadline. Regardless of the status of the CMP, the parties are free to engage in discovery in compliance with the Federal Rules of Civil Procedure and Local Rules of this Court.

The calculation of all deadlines for the CMP is based on the "Anchor Date," which means the date that the case was filed or removed to the Court. Because all CMP deadlines are linked to the Anchor Date, plaintiffs must promptly effectuate service on all defendants. The Court may entertain requests from defendants to modify/lengthen all CMP deadlines if service is not made promptly.

Depending on the type of case, the Anchor Date is used to calculate certain deadlines that will govern pretrial management. Please note, however, that the parties are encouraged to shorten these time frames in appropriate cases so that the case may be scheduled for trial more quickly than the outer deadlines otherwise applicable.

The use of the term "months" for calculating the dates (rather than counting days) is for ease of calculation. Thus, for example, if the Anchor Date is the 20th of the month, most of CMP deadlines will fall on the 20th of the respective months regardless of how many days comprise the intervening months.

District Judges and Magistrate Judges regularly receive documents filed by all parties. Therefore, parties shall not bring "courtesy copies" to any chambers unless specifically directed to do so by the Court. In accordance with Local Rule 26–2, discovery papers are not ordinarily filed with the Court.

In addition to those conferences required by Local Rule 37–1, counsel are encouraged to hold informal conferences in person or by phone to resolve any disputes involving non-dispositive issues that may otherwise require submission of a motion to the Court. This requirement does not apply to cases involving pro se parties. Therefore, prior to filing any non-dispositive motion (including motions for extension of time), the moving party must contact opposing counsel to determine whether there is an objection to any non-dispositive motion (including motions for extension of time), and state in the motion whether opposing counsel objects to the motion. If an objection cannot be resolved by counsel, the opposing counsel's position shall be stated within the motion. The motion should also indicate whether opposing counsel plans to file a written objection to the motion and the date by which the Court can expect to receive the objection (within the time limits set in Local Rule 7–1). If after a reasonable effort, opposing counsel cannot be reached, the moving party shall recite in the motion the dates and times that messages were left for opposing counsel.

Form date: November 2008 *(modified December 10, 2013)*

[INSERT CASE CAPTION]

CASE MANAGEMENT PLAN

I. Parties and Representatives

A. [Insert correct name of each party]

B. [Insert full name, address, telephone, fax number, and e-mail address of all counsel]

Counsel shall promptly file a notice with the Clerk if there is any change in this information.

II. Jurisdiction and Statement of Claims

A. The parties shall state the basis for subject matter jurisdiction. If there is disagreement, each party shall state its position.

B. [Insert a one paragraph statement of plaintiff's claims, including the legal theories and facts upon which the claims are based.]

C. [Insert a one paragraph responsive statement of defendant's claims or defenses, including the legal theories and facts upon which the claims are based.]

D. Within 14 days after the non-expert discovery deadline, and consistent with the certification provisions of Fed. R. Civ. Proc. 11(b) the party with the burden of proof shall file a statement of the claims or defenses it intends to prove at trial, stating specifically the legal theories upon which the claims or defenses are based.

III. Pretrial Pleadings and Disclosures

A. The parties shall serve their Fed. R. Civ. P. 26 initial disclosures on or before [no later than 4 months from Anchor Date]. [Note: Fed. R. Civ. P. 26(a)(1)(E) permits the parties to object to making initial disclosures or to stipulate to a different deadline for making such disclosures based upon the circumstances of the action. If any objection and/or stipulation is made to initial disclosures in the CMP, the parties shall briefly state the circumstances justifying their respective positions.

B. Plaintiff(s) shall file preliminary witness and exhibit lists on or before _____ [no later than 5 months from Anchor Date].

C. Defendant(s) shall file preliminary witness and exhibit lists on or before [no later than 6 months from Anchor Date].

D. All motions for leave to amend the pleadings and/or to join additional parties shall be filed on or before _____ [no later than 5 months from Anchor Date].

E. Plaintiff(s) shall serve Defendant(s) (but not file with the Court) a statement of special damages, if any, and make a settlement demand, on or before [no later than 5 months from the Anchor Date]. Defendant(s) shall serve on the Plaintiff(s) (but not file with the Court) a response thereto within 30 days after receipt of the demand.

F. Plaintiff(s) shall disclose the name, address, and vita of any expert witness, and shall serve the report required by Fed. R. Civ. P. 26(a)(2) on or before [no later than 13 months from Anchor Date]. Defendant(s) shall disclose the name, address, and vita of any expert witness, and shall serve the report required by Fed. R. Civ. P. 26(a)(2) on or before [30 days after Plaintiff(s) serves its expert witness disclosure]; or if Plaintiff has disclosed no experts, Defendant(s) shall make its expert disclosure on or before [no later than 14 months from Anchor Date].

G. If a party intends to use expert testimony in connection with a motion for summary judgment to be filed by that party, such expert disclosures must be served on opposing counsel no later than 90 days prior to the dispositive motion deadline. If such expert disclosures are served the parties shall confer within 7 days to stipulate to a date for responsive disclosures (if any) and completion of expert discovery necessary for efficient resolution of the anticipated motion for summary judgment. The parties shall make good faith efforts to avoid requesting enlargements of the dispositive motions deadline and related briefing deadlines. Any proposed modifications of the CMP deadlines or briefing schedule must be approved by the court.

H. Any party who wishes to limit or preclude expert testimony at trial shall file any such objections no later than _____ [60 days before trial]. Any party who wishes to preclude expert witness testimony at the summary judgment stage shall file any such objections with their responsive brief within the briefing schedule established by Local Rule 56–1.

I. All parties shall file and serve their final witness and exhibit lists on or before _____ [no later than 14 months from Anchor Date]. This list should reflect the specific potential witnesses the party may call at trial. It is not sufficient for a party to simply incorporate by reference "any witness listed in discovery" or such general statements. The list of final witnesses shall include a brief synopsis of the expected testimony.

J. Any party who believes that bifurcation of discovery and/or trial is appropriate with respect to any issue or claim shall notify the Court as soon as practicable.

K. Discovery of electronically stored information ("ESI"). If either party is seeking the production of a substantial volume of ESI, then complete the ESI Supplement to the Report of the Parties' Planning Meeting (also available in MS Word on the court's website at www.insd.uscourts.gov/Judges/CMP_info.htm.)

If the parties believe that a substantial volume of ESI will not be produced in the case, the parties should include herein a brief description of the information anticipated to be sought in discovery in the case and include (1) the parties' agreement regarding the format in which ESI will be produced (including whether the production will include metadata), (2) a description of any other issues the parties believe may be relevant to discovery in the case, and (3) either the following claw back provision or the language of any alternative provision being proposed:

In the event that a document protected by the attorney-client privilege, the attorney work product doctrine or other applicable privilege or protection is unintentionally produced by any party to this proceeding, the producing party may request that the document be returned. In the event that such a request is made, all parties to the litigation and their counsel shall promptly return all copies of the document in their possession, custody, or control to the producing party and shall not retain or make any copies of the document or any documents derived from such document. The producing party shall promptly identify the returned document on a privilege log. The unintentional disclosure of a privileged or otherwise protected document shall not constitute a waiver of the privilege or protection with respect to that document or any other documents involving the same or similar subject matter.

IV. Discovery[1] and Dispositive Motions.

Due to the time and expense involved in conducting expert witness depositions and other discovery, as well as preparing and resolving dispositive motions, the Court requires counsel to use the CMP as an opportunity to seriously explore whether this case is appropriate for such motions (including specifically motions for summary judgment), whether expert witnesses will be needed, and how long discovery should continue. To this end, counsel must select the track set forth below that they believe best suits this case. If the parties are unable to agree on a track, the parties must: (1) state this fact in the CMP where indicated below; (2) indicate which track each counsel believes is most appropriate; and (3) provide a brief statement supporting the reasons for the track each counsel believes is most appropriate. If the parties are unable to agree on a track, the Court will pick the track it finds most appropriate, based upon the contents of the CMP or, if necessary, after receiving additional input at an initial pretrial conference.

A. Does any party believe that this case may be appropriate for summary judgment or other dispositive motion? If yes, the party(ies) that expect to file such a motion must provide a brief statement of the factual and/or legal basis for such a motion. [Note: A statement such as, "Defendant will seek summary judgment because no material facts are in dispute," is insufficient. Such a statement does not indicate to the Court that the parties used the CMP as an opportunity to seriously explore whether this case is appropriate for summary judgment or other dispositive motion. However, the failure to set forth a basis for a dispositive motion in the CMP will not bar a party from raising this argument at the motions stage.]

B. Select the track that best suits this case:

____ Track 1: No dispositive motions are anticipated. All discovery shall be completed by _____ [no later than 16 months from Anchor Date]. [Note: Given that no dispositive motions are anticipated, the parties should consider accelerating discovery and other pretrial deadlines to the extent practicable and suggest a trial date (Section VI) substantially earlier than the presumptive trial date of 18 months from the Anchor Date. The Court encourages a track faster than the standard track in all cases in which dispositive motions are not anticipated].

____ Track 2: Dispositive motions are expected and shall be filed by [no later than 12 months from Anchor Date]; non–expert witness discovery and discovery relating to liability issues shall be completed by _____ [no later than 7–10 months from Anchor Date]; expert witness discovery and discovery relating to damages shall be completed by [no later than 12–16 months from Anchor Date]. [Note: The Court expects this will be the typical track when dispositive motions are anticipated.]

____ Track 3: Dispositive motions are expected and shall be filed no later than _____ [no later than 12 months from Anchor Date]; discovery relating to liability issues and expert witness discovery that may be necessary at the dispositive motions stage shall be completed by _____ [no later than 30 days prior to the dispositive motion deadline date]; all remaining discovery shall be completed by [no later than 12–16 months from Anchor Date]. [Note: The Court expects that this will not be the typical track when dispositive motions are anticipated.]

____ Track 4: Dispositive motions shall be filed by _____ [not later than 13 months from the Anchor Date]; non–expert discovery shall be completed by _____; expert witness discovery shall be completed by _____.

[Note: The Court provides Track 4 as an open option because it recognizes that there may be unusual cases for which special circumstances necessitate additional flexibility. However, the Court has found that Tracks 1–3 are appropriate in the large majority of cases, and therefore the parties must briefly state below the special circumstances justifying a departure from Tracks 1–3.]

Absent leave of court, and for good cause shown, all issues raised on summary judgment under Fed. R. Civ. P. 56 must be raised by a party in a single motion.

V. Pre–Trial/Settlement Conferences.

At any time, any party may call the Judge's Staff to request a conference, or the Court may sua sponte schedule a conference at any time. The presumptive time for a settlement conference is no later than 30 days before the close of non-expert discovery. **The parties are encouraged to request an earlier date if they believe the assistance of the Magistrate Judge would be helpful in achieving settlement. The parties recommend a settlement conference in _____ [month/ year].**

VI. Trial Date.

The presumptive trial date is 20 months from the Anchor Date. The parties request a trial date in month/year. The trial is by _____ [Court or jury] and is anticipated to take _____ hours/days. Counsel should indicate here the reasons that a shorter or longer track is appropriate. While all dates herein must be initially scheduled to match the presumptive trial date, if the Court agrees that a different track is appropriate, the case management order approving the CMP plan will indicate the number of months by which all or certain deadlines will be extended to match the track approved by the Court.

VII. Referral to Magistrate Judge

A. Case. At this time, all parties _____ [do/do not] consent to refer this matter to the currently assigned Magistrate Judge pursuant to 28 U.S.C. 636(b) and Federal Rules of Civil Procedure 73 for all further proceedings including trial. [This section should be marked in the affirmative only if all parties consent. Do not indicate if some parties consent and some do not. Indicating the parties' consent in this paragraph may result in this matter being referred to the currently assigned Magistrate Judge for all further proceedings, including trial. It is not necessary to file a separate consent. Should this case be reassigned to another Magistrate Judge, any attorney or party of record may object within 30 days of such reassignment. If no objection is filed, the consent will remain in effect.]

B. Motions. The parties may also consent to having the assigned Magistrate Judge rule on motions ordinarily handled by the District Judge, such as motions to dismiss, for summary judgment, or for remand. If all parties consent, they should file a joint stipulation to that effect. Partial consents are subject to the approval of the presiding district judge.

VIII. Required Pre–Trial Preparation

A. Two Weeks Before The Final Pretrial Conference, the parties shall:

1. File a list of trial witnesses, by name, who are actually expected to be called to testify at trial. This list may not include any witnesses not on a party's final witness list filed pursuant to section III.I.

2. Number in sequential order all exhibits, including graphs, charts and the like, that will be used during the trial. Provide the Court with a list of these exhibits, including a description of each exhibit and the identifying designation. Make the original exhibits available for inspection by opposing counsel. Stipulations as to the

authenticity and admissibility of exhibits are encouraged to the greatest extent possible.

3. Submit all stipulations of facts in writing to the Court. Stipulations are always encouraged so that at trial, counsel can concentrate on relevant contested facts.

4. A party who intends to offer any depositions into evidence during the party's case in chief shall prepare and file with the Court and copy to all opposing parties either:

    a. brief written summaries of the relevant facts in the depositions that will be offered. (Because such a summary will be used in lieu of the actual deposition testimony to eliminate time reading depositions in a question and answer format, this is strongly encouraged.); or

    b. if a summary is inappropriate, a document which lists the portions of the deposition(s), including the specific page and line numbers, that will be read, or, in the event of a video-taped deposition, the portions of the deposition that will be played, designated specifically by counter-numbers.

5. Provide all other parties and the Court with any trial briefs and motions in limine, along with all proposed jury instructions, voir dire questions, and areas of inquiry for voir dire (or, if the trial is to the Court, with proposed findings of fact and conclusions of law).

6. Notify the Court and opposing counsel of the anticipated use of any evidence presentation equipment.

B.   One Week Before The Final Pretrial Conference, the parties shall:

1. Notify opposing counsel in writing of any objections to the proposed exhibits. If the parties desire a ruling on the objection prior to trial, a motion should be filed noting the objection and a description and designation of the exhibit, the basis of the objection, and the legal authorities supporting the objection.

2. If a party has an objection to the deposition summary or to a designated portion of a deposition that will be offered at trial, or if a party intends to offer additional portions at trial in response to the opponent's designation, and the parties desire a ruling on the objection prior to trial, the party shall submit the objections and counter summaries or designations to the Court in writing. Any objections shall be made in the same manner as for proposed exhibits. However, in the case of objections to video-taped depositions, the objections shall be brought to the Court's immediate attention to allow adequate time for editing of the deposition prior to trial.

3. File objections to any motions in limine, proposed instructions, and voir dire questions submitted by the opposing parties.

4. Notify the Court and opposing counsel of requests for separation of witnesses at trial.

IX.   Other Matters.

[Insert any other matters any party believes should be brought to the Court's attention]

[INSERT SIGNATURE BLOCKS FOR ALL COUNSEL TO SIGN THE CMP HERE]

_____

PARTIES APPEARED IN PERSON/BY COUNSEL ON _____ FOR A PRETRIAL/STATUS CONFERENCE.
_____

_____ APPROVED AS SUBMITTED.

_____ APPROVED AS AMENDED.

_____ APPROVED AS AMENDED PER SEPARATE ORDER.

_____ APPROVED, BUT ALL OF THE FOREGOING DEADLINES ARE
SHORTENED/ LENGTHENED BY _____ MONTHS.

_____ APPROVED, BUT THE DEADLINES SET IN SECTION(S) _____ OF
THE PLAN IS/ARE SHORTENED/LENGTHENED BY _____
MONTHS.

_____ THIS MATTER IS SET FOR TRIAL BY _____ ON _____.
FINAL PRETRIAL CONFERENCE IS SCHEDULED FOR
_____ AT ___.M., ROOM _____.

_____ A SETTLEMENT/STATUS CONFERENCE IS SET IN THIS CASE FOR
_____ AT ___.M. COUNSEL SHALL APPEAR:

_____ IN PERSON IN ROOM _____; OR

_____ BY TELEPHONE, WITH COUNSEL FOR INITIAT-
ING THE CALL TO ALL OTHER PARTIES AND ADDING
THE COURT JUDGE AT (___) _____; OR

_____ BY TELEPHONE, WITH COUNSEL CALLING
THE JUDGE'S STAFF AT _____;

_____ DISPOSITIVE MOTIONS SHALL BE FILED NO LATER THAN
_____.

Upon approval, this Plan constitutes an Order of the Court. Failure to comply with an Order of the Court may result in sanctions for contempt, or as provided under Rule 16(f), to and including dismissal or default.

Approved and So Ordered.

_____   _____
Date   U.S. District Court
                                          Southern District of Indiana

[Effective March 14, 2012. Amended effective February 19, 2013; December 10, 2013.]

[1]The term "completed," as used in Section IV.B, means that counsel must serve their discovery requests in sufficient time to receive responses before this deadline. Counsel may not serve discovery requests within the 30-day period before this deadline unless they seek leave of Court to serve a belated request and show good cause for the same. In such event, the proposed belated discovery request shall be filed with the motion, and the opposing party will receive it with service of the motion but need not respond to the same until such time as the Court grants the motion.

INSTRUCTIONS FOR PREPARING PATENT
CASE MANAGEMENT PLAN "CMP"

The following provisions apply to patent cases filed in the United States District Court for the Southern District of Indiana.

General Instructions

Unless the plaintiff is pro se, counsel for plaintiff is responsible for coordinating timely completion of the CMP. The Court typically sets the deadline for filing a proposed CMP in the order setting the initial pretrial conference. Otherwise, the deadline for filing the CMP is 90 days from the date the case was filed or removed unless otherwise set by court order. The deadline for filing the CMP shall not be extended without written motion that establishes good cause to extend the deadline. Regardless of the status of the CMP, the parties are free to engage in discovery if in compliance with the Federal Rules of Civil Procedure and Local Rules of this Court.

The calculation of all deadlines for the CMP is based on the "Anchor Date," which means the date that the case was filed or removed to the Court. Because all CMP deadlines are linked to the Anchor Date, plaintiffs must promptly effectuate service on all defendants. The Court may entertain requests from defendants to use a modified Anchor Date if service is not made promptly.

The Anchor Date is used to calculate certain deadlines that will govern pretrial management. Please note, however, that the parties are encouraged to shorten these time frames in appropriate cases so that the case may be scheduled for trial more quickly than the outer deadlines otherwise applicable.

The use of the term "months" for calculating the dates (rather than counting days) is for ease of calculation. Thus, for example, if the Anchor Date is the 20th of the month, most of CMP deadlines will fall on the 20th of the respective months regardless of how many days comprise the intervening months.

[INSERT CASE CAPTION]

PATENT CASE MANAGEMENT PLAN

I. Parties and Representatives

A. [Insert correct name of each party]

B. [Insert full name, address, telephone, fax number, and e-mail address of all counsel]

Counsel must promptly file a notice with the Clerk if there is any change in this information.

II. Jurisdiction and Statement of Claims

A. The parties shall state the basis for subject matter jurisdiction. If there is disagreement, each party shall state its position.

B. [Insert a one paragraph synopsis of plaintiff's claims, including the legal theories and facts upon which the claims are based.]

C. [Insert a one paragraph responsive synopsis of defendant's claims or defenses, including the legal theories and facts upon which the claims are based.]

III. Early Filings and Disclosures

A. The parties must serve their Fed. R. Civ. P. 26 initial disclosures on or before [no later than 4 months from Anchor Date]. [Note: Fed. R. Civ. P. 26(a)(1)(E) permits the parties to object to making initial disclosures or to stipulate to a different deadline for making such disclosures based upon the circumstances of the action. If any objection and/or stipulation is made to initial disclosures in the CMP, the parties must briefly state the circumstances justifying their respective positions.]

B. Plaintiff(s) must file preliminary witness and exhibit lists on or before _____ [no later than 4 months from Anchor Date].

C. Defendant(s) must file preliminary witness and exhibit lists on or before [no later than 5 months from Anchor Date].

D. All motions for leave to amend the pleadings and/or to join additional parties must be filed on or before _____ [no later than 5 months from Anchor Date].

E. Plaintiff(s) must serve Defendant(s) (but not file with the Court) a preliminary statement of damages, if any, and make a settlement demand, on or before _____ [no later than 5 months from the Anchor Date]. Defendant(s) must serve on the Plaintiff(s) (but not file with the Court) a response thereto within 30 days after receipt of the demand.

F. Any party who believes that bifurcation of discovery and/or trial is appropriate with respect to any issue or claim must notify the Court as soon as practicable.

G. Any party who believes that the particular circumstances of the case warrant additional disclosures or briefing of critical issues different from that specified by the Court's uniform patent CMP should set out those matters in the proposed CMP and be prepared to present its position fully at the initial pretrial conference. By way of example, counsel should advise the court of any important claims construction disputes they anticipate or whether advice of counsel is expected or is likely to be asserted as a defense to allegations of willful infringement. Counsel are advised, however, that departures from the sequencing and timing included in the uniform plan will be the exception rather than the rule and that parties seeking departure must present compelling reasons.

IV. Discovery and Related Deadlines

A. All liability discovery—both fact and expert—must be completed[1] by _____ [12 months from the Anchor Date]. The parties should focus their early discovery in a manner that prepares them to respond timely to discovery requests concerning their preliminary infringement and invalidity contentions.

B. The parties must file and serve their infringement and invalidity contentions by _____ [8 months from the Anchor Date].

C. The party with the burden of proof as to any liability issue must disclose the name, address, and vita of any expert witness on liability, and shall serve the report required by Fed. R. Civ. P. 26(a)(2) on or before _____ [no later than 10 months from Anchor Date]. The responding party must disclose the name, address, and vita of any expert witness, and must serve the report required by Fed. R. Civ. P. 26(a)(2) on or before [30 days after the party with the burden serves its expert witness disclosure]. If the party with the burden has disclosed no experts, the responding party must make any expert disclosure on or before _____ [no later than 11 months from the Anchor Date].

D. Any dispositive motions must be filed no later than _____ [no later than 16 months from the Anchor Date]. **Absent leave of court, and for good cause shown, all issues raised on summary judgment under Fed. R. Civ. P. 56 must be raised by a party in a single motion. Issues of claims construction, infringement/non–infringement, and invalidity must be briefed at this time. Any motion to limit or preclude evidence (including expert testimony) in connection with dispositive motions must also be presented at this time.** The parties will proceed under a four-brief schedule. The plaintiff must file any dispositive motion by the above due date; the defendant must file any dispositive motion within twenty-eight days thereafter, along with a consolidated brief in support/brief in opposition to the plaintiff's motion; the plaintiff must file a consolidated brief in opposition/reply in support within 28 days thereafter; and the defendant may file any reply in support of its own motion within 14 days thereafter. If the plaintiff does not file a dispositive motion, any dispositive motion by the defendant is due [no later than 17 months from the Anchor Date], and briefing will proceed according to Local Rule 56–1. If the plaintiff files a dispositive motion and the defendant does not, briefing on the plaintiff's motion will proceed according to Local Rule 56–1. Counsel may confer and propose by motion a modified schedule and page limits different from those prescribed by Local Rule 7–1 so long as the briefing is completed within the time contemplated by this section.

E. The plaintiff must disclose the name, address, and vita of any expert witness on damages, and shall serve the report required by Fed. R. Civ. P. 26(a)(2) on or before _____ [no later than 18 months from Anchor Date]. The responding party must disclose the name, address, and vita of any expert witness, and must serve the report required by Fed. R. Civ. P. 26(a)(2) on or before [30 days after the party with the burden serves its expert witness disclosure]. If the party with the burden has disclosed no experts, the responding party must make any expert disclosure on or before _____ [no later than 19 months from the Anchor Date].

F. Damages discovery—both fact and expert—must be completed[2] by [3 months before the Trial Date].

G. Discovery of electronically stored information ("ESI"). If either party is seeking the production of a substantial volume of ESI, then complete the ESI Supplement to the Report of the Parties' Planning Meeting (also available in MS Word on the Court's website at www.insd.uscourts.gov/Judges/CMP_info.htm.)

If the parties believe that a substantial volume of ESI will not be produced in the case, the parties should include herein a brief description of the information anticipated to be sought in discovery in the case and include (1) the parties' agreement regarding the format in which ESI will be produced (including whether the production will include metadata), (2) a description of any other issues the parties believe may be relevant to discovery in the case, and (3) either the following claw back provision or the language of any alternative provision being proposed:

In the event that a document protected by the attorney-client privilege, the attorney work product doctrine or other applicable privilege or protection is unintentionally produced by any party to this proceeding, the producing party may request that the document be returned. In the event that such a request is made, all parties to the litigation and their counsel shall promptly return all copies of the document in their possession, custody, or control to the producing party and shall not retain or make any copies of the document or any documents derived from such document. The producing party shall promptly identify the returned document on a privilege log. The unintentional disclosure of a privileged or otherwise protected document shall not constitute a waiver of the privilege or protection with respect to that document or any other documents involving the same or similar subject matter.

V. Later Filings and Deadlines

A. Within 14 days after the liability discovery deadline, and consistent with the certification provisions of Fed. R. Civ. Proc. 11(b), the party with the burden of proof must file a statement of the claims or defenses it intends to prove at trial, stating specifically the legal theories upon which the claims or defenses are based.

B. To the extent requests to limit or preclude expert testimony were not raised and determined at the dispositive motions stage, any party who wishes to limit or preclude expert testimony at trial must file any such objections no later than [90 days before trial]. Any party who wishes to preclude expert witness testimony at the summary judgment stage shall file any such objections with their responsive brief within the briefing schedule established by Local Rule 56–1.

C. All parties must file and serve their final witness and exhibit lists on or before _____ [no later than 14 months from Anchor Date]. This list should reflect the specific potential witnesses the party may call at trial. It is not sufficient for a party to simply incorporate by reference "any witness listed in discovery" or such general statements. The list of final witnesses must include a brief synopsis of the expected testimony.

VI. Pre–Trial/Settlement Conferences

The Court will schedule regular status conferences following the initial pretrial conference. **Among the issues the parties must be prepared to address at every pretrial or status conference are settlement and the appropriate timing of a settlement conference with the magistrate judge.**

VII. Trial Date

The presumptive trial date is 24 months from the Anchor Date. The parties request a trial date in _____ [month/year]. The trial is by _____ [Court or jury] and is anticipated to take _____ hours/days. Counsel should indicate here the reasons that a shorter or longer schedule is appropriate. While all dates herein must be initially scheduled to match the presumptive trial date, if the Court agrees that a different schedule is appropriate, the case management order approving the CMP plan will indicate the number of months by which all or certain deadlines will be extended to match the schedule approved by the Court.

VIII. Referral to Magistrate Judge

A. Case. At this time, all parties _____ [do/do not] consent to refer this matter to the currently assigned Magistrate Judge pursuant to 28 U.S.C. 636(b) and Federal Rules of Civil Procedure 73 for all further proceedings including trial. [This section should be marked in the affirmative only if all parties consent. Do not indicate if some parties consent and some do not. Indicating the parties' consent in this paragraph may result in this matter being referred to the currently assigned Magistrate Judge for all further proceedings, including trial. It is not necessary to file a separate consent. Should this case be reassigned to another Magistrate Judge, any attorney or party of record may object within 30 days of such reassignment. If no objection is filed, the consent will remain in effect.]

B. Motions. The parties may also consent to having the assigned Magistrate Judge rule on motions ordinarily handled by the District Judge, such as motions to dismiss, for summary judgment, or for remand. If all parties consent, they should file a joint stipulation to that effect. Partial consents are subject to the approval of the presiding district judge.

IX. Required Pre–Trial Preparation

A. Three Weeks Before the Final Pretrial Conference, the parties must:

1. File a list of trial witnesses, by name, who are actually expected to be called to testify at trial. This list may not include any witnesses not on a party's final witness list filed pursuant to section III.I.

2. Number in sequential order all exhibits, including graphs, charts and the like, that will be used during the trial. Provide the Court with a list of these exhibits, including a description of each exhibit and the identifying designation. Make the original exhibits available for inspection by opposing counsel. Stipulations as to the authenticity and admissibility of exhibits are encouraged to the greatest extent possible.

3. Submit all stipulations of facts in writing to the Court. Stipulations are always encouraged so that at trial, counsel can concentrate on relevant contested facts.

4. A party who intends to offer any depositions into evidence during the party's case in chief must prepare and file with the Court and copy to all opposing parties a document that lists the portions of the deposition(s), including the specific page and

line numbers, that will be read, or, in the event of a video-taped deposition, the portions of the deposition that will be played, designated specifically by counter-numbers.

5. Provide all other parties and the Court with any motions in limine, along with all proposed jury instructions, voir dire questions, and areas of inquiry for voir dire (or, if the trial is to the Court, with proposed findings of fact and conclusions of law). If trial briefs are requested by the court or otherwise appropriate, they are to be filed at this time.

6. Notify the Court and opposing counsel of the anticipated use of any evidence presentation equipment and schedule training on the Court's Video Electronic Presentation System ("VEPS") with the judge's Courtroom Deputy.

B. Two Weeks Before the Final Pretrial Conference, the parties must:

1. Notify opposing counsel in writing of any objections to the proposed exhibits. If the parties desire a ruling on the objection prior to trial, a motion should be filed noting the objection and a description and designation of the exhibit, the basis of the objection, and the legal authorities supporting the objection.

2. If a party has an objection to the deposition summary or to a designated portion of a deposition that will be offered at trial, or if a party intends to offer additional portions at trial in response to the opponent's designation, and the parties desire a ruling on the objection prior to trial, the party must submit the objections and counter summaries or designations to the Court in writing. Any objections must be made in the same manner as for proposed exhibits. However, in the case of objections to video-taped depositions, the objections must be brought to the Court's immediate attention to allow adequate time for editing of the deposition prior to trial.

3. File objections to any motions in limine, proposed instructions, and voir dire questions submitted by the opposing parties.

4. Notify the Court and opposing counsel of requests for separation of witnesses at trial.

IX. Other Matters

[Insert any other matters any party believes should be brought to the Court's attention]

[INSERT SIGNATURE BLOCKS FOR ALL COUNSEL TO SIGN THE CMP HERE]

****

_____ PARTIES APPEARED IN PERSON/BY COUNSEL ON _____ FOR A PRETRIAL/STATUS CONFERENCE.

_____ APPROVED AS SUBMITTED.

_____ APPROVED AS AMENDED.

_____ APPROVED AS AMENDED PER SEPARATE ORDER.

_____ APPROVED, BUT ALL OF THE FOREGOING DEADLINES ARE SHORTENED/LENGTHENED BY _____ MONTHS.

APPROVED, BUT THE DEADLINES SET IN SECTION(S) _____ OF THE PLAN IS/ARE SHORTENED/LENGTHENED BY _____ MONTHS.

THIS MATTER IS SET FOR TRIAL BY _____ ON _____. FINAL PRETRIAL CONFERENCE IS SCHEDULED FOR _____ AT _____.M., ROOM _____.

A SETTLEMENT/STATUS CONFERENCE IS SET IN THIS CASE FOR _____ AT _____.M. COUNSEL SHALL APPEAR:

_____ IN PERSON IN ROOM _____; OR

_____ BY TELEPHONE, WITH COUNSEL FOR INITIATING THE CALL TO ALL OTHER PARTIES AND ADDING THE COURT JUDGE AT (_____) _____; OR

_____ BY TELEPHONE, WITH COUNSEL CALLING THE JUDGE'S STAFF AT (_____) _____;

DISPOSITIVE MOTIONS SHALL BE FILED NO LATER THAN _____

Upon approval, this Plan constitutes an Order of the Court. Failure to comply with an Order of the Court may result in sanctions for contempt, or as provided under Rule 16(f), to and including dismissal or default.

Approved and So Ordered.

_____   _____
Date   U.S. District Court
     Southern District of Indiana

[Effective December 10, 2013. Amended effective November 3, 2014.]

[1]The term "completed," as used in this section, means that counsel must serve their discovery requests in sufficient time to receive responses before this deadline. Counsel may not serve discovery requests within the 30–day period before this deadline unless they seek leave of Court to serve a belated request and show good cause for the same. In such event, the proposed belated discovery request must be filed with the motion, and the opposing party will receive it with service of the motion but need not respond to the discovery requests unless and until the Court grants the motion.

[2]See note 1.

UNIFORM STIPULATED PROTECTIVE ORDER–INSTRUCTIONS

In order to obtain a protective order, Movant must establish good cause and confer in good faith to specify the terms of discovery and its limits, particularly as to trade secrets and protectable information under Fed. R. Civ. P. 26(c). It is strongly recommended that counsel for all parties review the applicable rules to properly implement this form.

The Court has made this form available for the convenience of the parties and encourages them to consider using it because it is presumptively acceptable to the Court. These instructions should be deleted before filing the proposed protective order.

****

UNITED STATES DISTRICT COURT
SOUTHERN DISTRICT OF INDIANA

Plaintiff,	Case No.
vs.	
Defendant.	

UNIFORM STIPULATED PROTECTIVE ORDER

I. INTRODUCTION

The parties, by their undersigned counsel, pursuant to Fed. R. Civ. P. 26(c)(1), hereby stipulate to the following provisions of this Court's Uniform Stipulated Protective Order.

II. SCOPE OF PROTECTED INFORMATION

In the course of discovery in this action, the parties may be required to produce information that constitutes, in whole or in part, protected information such as trade secrets, non-public research and development, commercial or financial information, or other information that may cause harm to the producing party or a non-party. The parties anticipate production of the following categories of protected information: _____ [Here, the parties must define categories of protected information clearly and definitely so that the Court's burden of enforcement, if called upon, is minimized.]

III. DESIGNATION OF PROTECTED INFORMATION

A. Scope. This Order governs the production and handling of any protected information in this action. Any party or non-party who produces protected information in this action may designate it as "Confidential" or "Attorneys' Eyes Only" consistent with the terms of this Order. "Designating Party" means the party or non-party who so designates the protected information; "Receiving Party" means the party or non-party to whom such information was produced or disclosed. Whenever possible, the Designating Party must designate only those portions of a document, deposition, transcript, or other material that contain the protected information and refrain from designating entire documents. Regardless of any designations made hereunder, the Designating Party is not otherwise restricted from use or disclosure of its protected information outside of this action. In addition, any party may move to modify or seek other relief from any of the terms of this Order if it has first tried in writing and in good faith to resolve its needs or disputes with the other party(ies) pursuant to the terms of this Order and S.D. Ind. L.R. 37–1.

B. Application to Non–Parties. Before a non-party is given copies of designated information as permitted hereunder, it must first sign the acknowledgment to be bound to these terms that is attached hereto as <u>Exhibit A</u>; if it fails to do so, the parties to this action must resolve any such dispute before making disclosure of designated information as permitted hereunder to the non-party. If a non-party wishes to make designations hereunder, it must first sign the acknowledgment to be bound to these terms that is attached hereto as <u>Exhibit A</u>.

C. Timing and Provisional Protection. Designations may be made at any time. To avoid potential waiver of protection hereunder, the Designating Party should designate information at the time of production or disclosure, including on the record during the taking of any testimony. Deposition testimony will be deemed provisionally protected for a period of 30 days after the transcript is released to the parties by the court reporter, although the parties may agree at any time to different timelines of provisional protection of information as Confidential or Attorneys' Eyes Only as part of one or more specific depositions. To retain any designations beyond the provisional period, a Designating Party must designate specific pages and lines of deposition testimony before the provisional period has expired. Such designations must be made in writing so that all counsel and court reporters may append the designation to all copies of the transcripts.

D. Manner of Designation. Information may be designated hereunder in any reasonable manner or method that notifies the Receiving Party of the designation level and identifies with specificity the information to which the designation applies. If made verbally, the Designating Party must promptly confirm in writing the designation. Whenever possible, the Designating Party should stamp, affix, or embed a legend of "CONFIDENTIAL" or "ATTORNEYS' EYES ONLY" on each designated page of the document or electronic image.

IV.   CHALLENGES TO DESIGNATED INFORMATION

In the event that a Receiving Party disagrees at any time with any designation(s) made by the Designating Party, the Receiving Party must first try to resolve such challenge in good faith on an informal basis with the Designating Party pursuant to S.D. Ind. L.R. 37–1. The Receiving Party must provide written notice of the challenge and the grounds therefor to the Designating Party, who must respond in writing to the challenge within 15 days. At all times, the Designating Party carries the burden of establishing the propriety of the designation and protection level. Unless and until the challenge is resolved by the parties or ruled upon by the Court, the designated information will remain protected under this Order. The failure of any Receiving Party to challenge a designation does not constitute a concession that the designation is proper or an admission that the designated information is otherwise competent, relevant, or material.

V.   LIMITED ACCESS/USE OF PROTECTED INFORMATION

A. Restricted Use. Information that is produced or exchanged in the course of this action and designated under this Order may be used solely for the preparation, trial, and any appeal of this action, as well as related settlement negotiations, and for no other purpose, without the written consent of the Designating Party. No designated information may be disclosed to any person except in accordance with the terms of this Order. All persons in possession of designated information agree to exercise reasonable care with regard to the custody, use, or storage of such information to ensure that its confidentiality is maintained. This obligation includes, but is not limited to, the Receiving Party providing to the Designating Party prompt notice of the receipt of any subpoena that seeks production or disclosure of any designated information and consulting with the Designating Party before responding to the subpoena. Any use or disclosure of Confidential or Attorneys' Eyes Only information in violation of the terms of this Order may subject the disclosing person or party to sanctions.

B. Access to "Confidential" Information. The parties and all persons subject to this Order agree that information designated as "CONFIDENTIAL" may only be accessed or reviewed by the following:

1. The Court, its personnel, and court reporters;

2. Counsel of record for any party in this action and their employees who assist counsel of record in this action and are informed of the duties hereunder;

3. The parties, including their agents and employees who are assisting or have reason to know of this action, so long as each such agent or employee has signed the acknowledgment to be bound to these terms that is attached hereto as Exhibit A;

4. Experts or consultants employed by the parties or their counsel for purposes of this action, so long as each such expert or consultant has signed the acknowledgment to be bound to these terms that is attached hereto as Exhibit A; and

5. Other witnesses or persons with the Designating Party's consent or by court order.

C. [Instructions: Use only if Applicable. Because designation of information as "Attorneys' Eyes Only" is more restrictive on disclosure and may interfere with the discovery process, such designations should be used infrequently and minimally. Delete these instructions before submission.]

Access to "Attorneys' Eyes Only" Designations: The parties and all persons subject to this Order agree that information designated as "ATTORNEYS' EYES ONLY" may only be accessed or reviewed by the following:

1. The Court, its personnel, and court reporters;

2. Counsel of record for any party in this action and their employees who assist counsel of record in this action and are informed of the duties hereunder;

3. The following representatives for each party, who must also sign the acknowledgment to be bound to these terms that is attached hereto as Exhibit A:

   (a) For Plaintiff: _____;

   (b) For Defendant(s): _____;

4. Experts or consultants employed by the parties or their counsel for purposes of this action, so long as each such expert or consultant _____ [describe here, with particularity, the parameters for when "ATTORNEYS' EYES ONLY" information may be disclosed to experts or consultants who may have been associated with any party or non-party competitors without knowledge of the Designating Party; delete these instructions before submission]; and

5. Other witnesses or persons to whom the Designating Party agrees in advance of disclosure or by court order.

D. Review of Witness Acknowledgments. At any time and for any purpose, including to monitor compliance with the terms hereof, any Designating Party may demand to review all copies of Exhibit A in any Receiving Party's possession. The Receiving Party must, within 3 business days of the demand, provide all such copies to the Designating Party making the demand. Notwithstanding the foregoing, if the Receiving Party has retained an expert whose identity has not yet been disclosed to the Designating Party, the Receiving Party may generically identify how many acknowledgments that it has in its possession attributable to non-disclosed experts, whose acknowledgements must later be provided contemporaneously with any reports issued by one or more of said experts. If a Receiving Party is not required to disclose the identity of any consulting experts, it may not be compelled to produce any acknowledgments from those experts to the Designating Party. However, if the Designating Party provides to the Court evidence of breach of this Order via unauthorized leak of designated information, the Court may require an *in camera* production of all acknowledgments held by a Receiving Party in order to determine breach and consider enforcement of this Order.

E. Non–Waiver Effect of Designations. Neither the taking of, nor the failure to take, any action to enforce the provisions of this Order, nor the failure to object to any designation, will constitute a waiver of any party's claim or defense in this action or any other action or proceeding, including but not limited to a claim or defense that any designated information is or is not confidential, is or is not entitled to particular protection, or embodies or does not embody information protectable by law.

F. In–Court Use of Designated Information. If information designated pursuant to this Order will or may be offered in evidence at a hearing or trial, then the offering party must give advance notice to the party or non-party that designated prior to offering the information so that any use or disclosure may be addressed in accordance with the Court's case-management or other pre-trial order, or by a motion in limine.

Nothing in this Order shall be construed as a waiver by a party of any objections that may be raised as to the admissibility at trial of any evidentiary materials.

VI. CLAW–BACK REQUESTS

A. Failure to Make Designation. If, at any time, a party or non-party discovers that it produced or disclosed protected information without designation, it may promptly notify the Receiving Party and identify with particularity the information to be designated and the level of designation (the claw-back notification). The Receiving Party may then request substitute production of the newly-designated information. Within 30 days of receiving the claw-back notification, the Receiving Party must (1) certify to the Designating Party it has appropriately marked or, if substitute production has been requested, destroyed all unmarked copies that it received, made, and/or distributed; and (2) if it was practicably unable to mark or destroy any information because disclosures occurred while the Receiving Party was under no duty of confidentiality under the terms of this Order regarding that information, the Receiving Party must reasonably provide as much information as practicable to aid the Designating Party in protecting the information, consistently with the Receiving Party's attorney-client, work-product, and/or trial-preparation privileges.

B. Inadvertent Production of Privileged Information. If, at any time, a party discovers that it produced information that it reasonably believes is subject to protection under the attorney/client, work-product, or trial-preparation privileges, then it must promptly notify each Receiving Party of the claim for protection, the basis for it, amend its privilege log accordingly, and comply with Fed. R. Civ. P. 26(b)(5). Whenever possible, the producing party must produce substitute information that redacts the information subject to the claimed protection. The Receiving Party must thereupon comply with Fed. R. Civ. P. 26(b)(5) as to the information subject to the claimed protection. The parties must also comply with S.D. Ind. L.R. 37–1 before seeking Court intervention to resolve any related dispute.

VII. DURATION/CONTINUED RESTRICTIONS

A. Handling of Designated Information Upon Conclusion of Action. Upon conclusion of this action, including all appeals, the Designating Party(ies) is/are responsible for ensuring that any party or person to whom the party shared or disclosed designated information in this action returns or destroys all of its copies, regardless of the medium in which it was stored. Within 60 days after the later of dismissal of this action or expiration of all deadlines for appeal, the Receiving

Party(ies) must certify to each Designating Party that all designated information hereunder has been destroyed by all parties and witnesses for whom that party is responsible. No witness or party may retain designated information that it received from any other party or non-party under this Order; only counsel of record are the authorized agents who may retain one copy for their respective legal files, and who must also describe to the Designating Party the extra steps taken to seal its legal file containing paper and/or electronic copies of the designated information so that it is not accessed, used, or disclosed inconsistently with the obligations under this Order. This provision does not apply to the Court or Court staff.

    B. Continued Restrictions Under this Order. The restrictions on disclosure and use of confidential information survive the conclusion of this action.

VIII.   REQUESTS TO SEAL

This protective order does not authorize a party to file or maintain a document under seal. Any party that seeks to file any document, or any portion of a document, under seal, and any party that opposes its maintenance under seal, must comply with S.D. Ind. L.R. 5–11.

[Insert Date & Signature Block for the Parties]

[Insert Date & Signature Block for the Court]

EXHIBIT A

[INSERT CAPTION FOR CASE]

AGREEMENT TO BE BOUND BY PROTECTIVE ORDER

The undersigned acknowledges having been provided with and having read the "Uniform Stipulation Protective Order" in this matter ("Protective Order"). The undersigned further agrees he/she (i) is bound under the Protective Order, (ii) will comply with all of its provisions, and (iii) is subject to the jurisdiction of the Court for all purposes arising under the Protective Order, including enforcement of its terms.

[INSERT DATE & SIGNATURE BLOCK WITH WITNESS ATTEST]

[Effective January 15, 2015.]

ELECTRONIC CASE FILING
ELECTRONIC CASE FILING POLICIES AND PROCEDURES MANUAL
Revised December 30, 2014

Introduction

    The Court's Case Management/Electronic Case Filing system, CM/ECF, permits attorneys appearing in all pending civil and criminal cases to file documents with the Court via the Internet using the ECF (Electronic Case Filing) portion of the system. This ECF Policies and Procedures Manual governs electronic filing in all civil and criminal cases within the Southern District of Indiana. Attorneys, parties, and pro se litigants may view civil and criminal dockets as well as electronically filed documents via the Internet using the PACER (Public Access to Court Electronic Records) portion of the system.

    1. Authorization for Electronic Filing. Local Rule 5–2 and Local Criminal Rule 49–1 require electronic filing, as allowed by Federal Rule of Civil Procedure

5(d)(3) and Federal Rule of Criminal Procedure 49(e). The following policies and procedures govern electronic filing in this district unless, due to circumstances in a particular case, a judicial officer determines that these policies and procedures should be modified.

2. Definitions and Instructions. The following definitions and instructions shall apply to these Electronic Case Filing Policies and Procedures:

2.1 The term "document" shall include pleadings, motions, exhibits, declarations, affidavits, memoranda, papers, orders, notices, and any other filing by or to the Court.

2.2 The term "attorney" shall include counsel of record.

2.3 All hours stated shall be the local time of the division to which the case has been assigned (Local Rule 5–4).

2.4 The term "Notice of Electronic Filing" is used to refer to the email notice that is automatically generated by the Electronic Case Filing System at the time a document is filed by an attorney, or an order is entered by the Court. The Notice of Electronic Filing (NEF) will set forth the time of filing or issuance, the type of document, the text of the docket entry, the name of the attorney(s) receiving the notice, and an electronic link (hyperlink) to the document, which allows recipients to retrieve the document electronically.

2.5 The term "PDF" is used to refer to a document that exists in Portable Document Format. A document file created with a word processor or a paper document that has been scanned must first be converted to portable document format before the document can be electronically filed with the Court. Converted files contain the extension ".pdf".

2.6 The term "ECF" is used to refer to the Electronic Case Filing portion of the Court's CM/ECF System, which may be accessed by attorneys for the purpose of filing documents electronically in civil and criminal cases pending before the Court. Attorneys of record in pending cases may submit an ECF Registration Form in order to obtain an ECF login and password with which to file documents electronically. (See Appendix A).

2.7 The term "PACER" (Public Access to Court Electronic Records) is used to refer to the Public Access portion of the Court's CM/ECF System. PACER may be accessed by members of the public and attorneys for the purpose of viewing case dockets and electronically filed documents in cases pending before the Court. Individuals may obtain a PACER login and password at http://pacer.psc.uscourts.gov or (800) 676–6856.

3. Application of Rules and Orders. Unless modified by order of the Court, all Federal Rules of Civil and Criminal Procedure and Local Rules shall continue to apply to cases maintained in the Court's Case Management/Electronic Case Filing System (CM/ECF).

4. Cases Subject to Electronic Case Filing. Electronic filing by attorneys is <u>required</u> for eligible documents filed in civil and criminal cases pending with the Court, unless specifically exempted by Local Rule or Court Order. Attorneys may register for an ECF login and password with which to <u>file</u> documents electronically by visiting the Court's website at www.insd.uscourts.gov or by contacting the Clerk's Office.

         US District Court for the Southern District of Indiana,
         Office of the Clerk
Address: 46 East Ohio Street, Room 105
         Indianapolis, IN 46204
Phone: (317) 229–3700

Attorneys, parties, and pro se litigants may <u>view</u> dockets and electronically filed documents via the Internet through the use of the Court's PACER (Public Access to

Court Electronic Records) system. A login and password may be obtained by visiting the PACER website at www.pacer.psc.uscourts.gov or contacting the PACER Service Center at 1 (800) 676–6856.

5. **System Requirements.** The following hardware and software are needed to electronically file documents and receive electronic notice of case activity via the Electronic Case Filing system:

a. A computer running a Windows or a Macintosh operating system;

b. Software used to create PDF documents from a word processing application, such as Adobe Acrobat Professional® (links to free PDF creators can be found on the Court's website at www.insd.uscourts.gov);

c. A PDF viewer, such as Adobe Acrobat Reader® (free download available at www.adobe.com);

d. A PDF-compatible word processor like Macintosh or Windows-based versions of Microsoft Word®;

e. An Internet browser, such as Internet Explorer® or Firefox® (128–bit encryption is strongly recommended);

f. Internet access and an email address;

g. Access to a scanner may be necessary for paper exhibits which must be scanned into PDF pursuant to Local Rule 5–1(c); and

h. The filing attorney must have an ECF login and password assigned by the Clerk with which to access the Court's Electronic Case Filing system. (See Appendix A).

NOTE: To view dockets and electronically filed documents through the Court's PACER system, users must access the system through a PACER login and password. Attorneys and parties may register for a PACER account at www.pacer.psc.uscourts.gov or (800) 676–6856.

6. **Filing Case Initiating Documents.** A Civil Complaint or Notice of Removal may be filed, fee paid, and summons issued either in paper form or electronically through the CM/ECF system. Case initiating papers, including a civil cover sheet, must be served in the traditional manner on paper, rather than electronically. All subsequent papers must be filed electronically except as provided by Local Rule or Court Order. (Local Rule 5–2(b)).

A Criminal Complaint, Information, or Indictment shall be filed and served in the traditional manner on paper, rather than electronically.

7. **Filing Documents Electronically.** Electronic transmission of a document consistent with the procedures adopted by the Court shall, upon the complete receipt of the same by the Clerk of Court, constitute filing of the document for all purposes of the Federal Rules of Civil and Criminal Procedure and the Local Rules of this Court, and shall constitute entry of that document onto the docket maintained by the Clerk pursuant to Fed.R.Civ.P. 58 and 79.

A Notice of Electronic Filing (NEF) acknowledging that the document has been filed will immediately appear on the filer's screen after the document has been submitted. Attorneys are strongly encouraged to print or electronically save a copy of the NEF. Attorneys can also verify the filing of documents by inspecting the Court's electronic docket sheet through the use of a PACER login. The Court may, upon the motion of a party or upon its own motion, strike any inappropriately filed document.

Documents filed electronically must be submitted in PDF (Portable Document Format). Filing documents electronically does not alter filing deadlines. All electronic transmissions of documents must be completed (*i.e.* received completely by the Clerk's Office) prior to midnight of the local time of the division in which the case is pending in order to be considered timely filed that day (NOTE: time will be noted in Eastern Time on the Court's docket. If you have filed a document prior to midnight local time of the division in which the case is pending and the document is due that date, but the electronic receipt and docket reflect the following calendar day, please contact the Court). Although attorneys may file documents electronically 24 hours a day, 7 days a week, attorneys are encouraged to file all documents during the normal working hours of the Clerk's Office (Monday through Friday, 8:30 a.m. to 4:30 p.m.) when technical support is available.

8. Case Docket. Upon the electronic filing of a document, a docket entry will be automatically created by the CM/ECF System, using the information provided by the filing party. The Clerk of Court, where necessary and appropriate, will modify the docket entry description to comply with quality control standards.

9. System Availability. The Court's system is designed to provide service 24 hours a day, 7 days a week. Occasionally the CM/ECF system may be unavailable for brief scheduled maintenance. Notice of scheduled maintenance will be posted on the Court's website in advance. Attorneys are encouraged to file documents in advance of filing deadlines and during normal business hours. Questions regarding the electronic filing system and the registration process should be referred to the Clerk's Office, at (317) 229–3700. Technical difficulties should be referred to the Court's Help Desk, at (317) 229–3737. The Help Desk is staffed on business days from 8:30 a.m. to 4:30 p.m.

10. Registration. Attorneys seeking to file electronically must be admitted to practice in the U.S. District Court for the Southern District of Indiana, either via standard or pro hac vice admission, and must be in good standing. Each attorney seeking to file documents electronically must also submit a completed Electronic Case Filing Attorney Registration Form (Appendix A). Regardless of the division in which the attorney most frequently practices, completed registration forms should be returned to:

U.S. District Court, Southern District of Indiana
Attn: ECF Registration Processing
46 East Ohio Street, Room 105
Indianapolis, IN 46204

A registering attorney will receive an Internet e-mail message indicating his/her login and password have been assigned; this is to insure that the attorney's Internet e-mail address has been entered correctly in the ECF System. Use of the login and password when filing documents will serve in part as that attorney's signature for purposes of Fed.R.Civ.P. 11. Attorneys agree to protect the security of their passwords and immediately notify the Clerk of Court if they learn that their password has been compromised.

11. Service of Electronically Filed Documents. By participating in the Electronic Case Filing Program, attorneys consent to the electronic service of documents, and shall make available electronic mail addresses for service. Upon the filing of a document by a party, an e-mail message will be automatically generated by the electronic filing system and sent via electronic mail to the e-mail addresses of all registered attorneys who have appeared in the case. The Notice of Electronic Filing will contain a document hyperlink which will provide recipients with one "free look" at the electronically filed document. Recipients are encouraged to print and/or save a copy of the document during the "free look" to avoid incurring PACER charges for future viewings of the document. *It is the responsibility of the filing attorney to conventionally serve all parties who do not receive electronic service* (the identity of these parties will be indicated on the filing receipt generated by the ECF system). In addition to receiving e-mail notifications of filing activity, the parties are strongly encouraged to sign on to the PACER system at regular intervals to check the docket in their case.

Note: Although sealed documents are filed electronically, sealed documents must be served manually upon counsel pursuant to Fed.R.Civ.P. 5. *See* Local Rule 5–11 and Section 18 of this Policies and Procedures Manual.

A certificate of service must be included with all documents filed electronically. Such certificate shall indicate that service was accomplished pursuant to the Court's electronic filing procedures. With the exception of documents filed under seal, the party effectuates service on all registered attorneys by filing electronically. Service by electronic mail shall constitute service pursuant to Fed.R.Civ.P. 5(b)(2)(E) and shall entitle the party being served to the additional three (3) days provided by Fed.R.Civ.P. 6(d).

The following is a suggested format for a certificate of service for electronic filing:

Certificate of Service

I hereby certify that on [date], a copy of the foregoing [name of document] was filed electronically. Service of this filing will be made on all ECF–registered counsel by operation of the Court's electronic filing system. Parties may access this filing through the Court's system.

I further certify that on [date] a copy of the foregoing [name of document] was mailed, by first-class U.S. Mail, postage prepaid and properly addressed to the following:

[List parties receiving conventional service with law firm name (if applicable) and **postal** address]

> Name of Receiving party
> LAW FIRM NAME
> Postal Address
> City, State, ZIP Code

A service statement and/or list must be included on each proposed order, as required by Local Rule 5–5(d). Pursuant to Local Rule 5–5(b)(2), if a party is represented by multiple attorneys from the same law firm, and one or more is ECF–registered, notice of entry of an order or judgment in a case assigned to the Electronic Case Filing System will be transmitted only to the ECF–registered user(s).

A current distribution/service list for a case, may be obtained through the "Mailings" feature located under the "Utilities" menu in the Electronic Case Filing System.

12. Appearances. The filing of a Notice of Appearance shall act to establish the filing attorney as an attorney of record representing a designated party or parties in a particular cause of action. As a result, it is necessary for each attorney to file a separate Notice of Appearance when entering an appearance in a case. A joint appearance on behalf of multiple attorneys may be filed electronically only if it is filed separately for each attorney, using his/her ECF login.

A Notice of Appearance filed in a case which is maintained under seal must be filed in the traditional paper manner in order to establish the filing attorney as an attorney of record before access may be granted to the sealed case.

13. Format for Electronic Filings. Electronically filed documents must meet the requirements of Fed.R.Civ.P. 10 (Form of Pleadings), Local Rule 5–1 (Format of Papers Presented for Filing), and Fed.R.Civ.P. 5.2 and Fed.R.Crim.P. 49.1 (Privacy Protection for Filings Made with the Court), as if they had been submitted on paper. Documents filed electronically are also subject to any page limitations set forth by Court Order, by Local Rule 7–1 (Motion Practice), or Local Rule 56–1 (Summary Judgment Practice), as applicable.

A key objective of the electronic filing system is to ensure that as much of the case as possible is managed electronically. To facilitate electronic filing and retrieval, documents to be filed electronically are to be reasonably broken into their separate component parts. By way of example, most filings include a foundation document (*e.g.*, motion) and other supporting items (*e.g.*, exhibits, proposed orders, proposed amended pleadings). The foundation document, as well as the supporting items, are each separate components of the filing; supporting items must be filed as *attach-*

ments to the foundation document. These exhibits or attachments should include only those excerpts of the referenced documents that are directly germane to the matter under consideration.

When uploading attachments during the electronic filing process, exhibits must be uploaded in a logical sequence and a brief description must be entered for each individual PDF file. The description must include not only the exhibit number or letter, but also a brief description of the document. This information may be entered in CM/ECF using a combination of the *Category* drop-down menu, the *Description* text box, or both (see Figure 1 below). The information that is provided in each box will be combined to create a description of the document as it appears on the case docket (see Figure 2 below).

> **EXAMPLE:**   A *Motion for Continuance* is filed with the following three attachments:
> **Exhibit A—Affidavit of John Brown**
> Exhibit B—Letter from Bob Smith
> Proposed Order

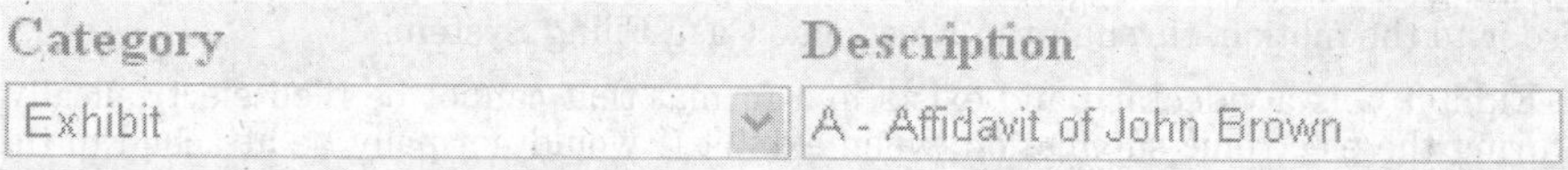

Category	Description
Exhibit	A - Affidavit of John Brown

Figure 1

09/1/2008   MOTION for Continuance, filed by Plaintiff XYZ CORPO-RATION. 7 (Attachments: # 1 **Exhibit A—Affidavit of John Brown**, # 2 Exhibit B—Letter from Bob Smith, 12/20/08, # 3 Text of Proposed Order)

Figure 2

To facilitate document retrieval for users who are accessing the system, components may not exceed an electronic file size of **10 megabytes**. (Local Rule 5–1). To electronically file a document or attachment that exceeds 10MB, the document must first be broken down into two or more smaller files. For example, if Exhibit A is a 12MB PDF file, it should be divided into 2 equal parts prior to electronic filing. Each component part of the exhibit would be filed as an attachment to the main document and described appropriately as "Exhibit A (part 1 of 2)" and "Exhibit A (part 2 of 2)."

The supporting items mentioned above should not be confused with memorandums or briefs in support of motions as outlined in Local Rule 7–1 or 56–1. These memorandums or briefs in support are to be filed as entirely separate documents pursuant to the appropriate rule. Additionally, no motion shall be embodied in the text of a response or reply brief/memorandum unless otherwise ordered by the Court.

All pleadings and other filings, including motions, briefs, and proposed orders must be converted to PDF format directly from a word processing program (*e.g.*, Microsoft® Word), rather than created from the scanned image of a paper document. An exhibit may be scanned into PDF format, at a recommended 300 dpi resolution or higher, only if it does not already exist in electronic format. The filing attorney is responsible for reviewing all PDF documents for legibility before submitting them through the Court's Electronic Case Filing system. For technical guidance in creating PDF documents, please contact the Clerk's Office at (317) 229–3700.

Where an individual component cannot be included in an electronic filing (*e.g.* the component cannot be converted to electronic format), the filer shall electronically file the prescribed Notice of Manual Filing in place of that component. A model form is provided as Appendix C.

Note: Sealed documents must be filed electronically as required by Local Rule 5–11 and Local Criminal Rule 49.1–2. *See* Section 18 of this Policies and Procedures Manual.

The following example illustrates the application of this section:

An attorney seeks to file a motion with three exhibits (A, B, and C), and a proposed order. The motion is a text document that was created with a word processing application and after conversion to PDF has a file size of 45kb. Exhibit A is a scanned image of a one-page document that after conversion to PDF has a size of 200kb. Exhibit B is a 100–page deposition transcript that exists on CD and after conversion to PDF it has a size of 5 MB. Exhibit C is an object that cannot be converted to digital format, such as a videotape. The proposed order is a text document that after conversion to PDF has a file size of 5kb.

In order to facilitate easy retrieval of any individual component, each document must be kept as a separate component (PDF file) rather than being merged together as one file. Each of the components should be filed electronically in one submission by filing the motion as the main document, and *attaching* the exhibits and proposed order to the motion, through the Electronic Case Filing System.

Exhibit C is a videotape and exists in a format that cannot be filed electronically. During the electronic submission, when exhibit C would normally be attached to the motion, it should instead be replaced by a Notice of Manual Filing (Appendix C) clearly stating what the exhibit is and why it cannot be filed electronically. Exhibit C should then be filed and served as it would if a traditional paper filing system were being used. When Exhibit C is presented to the Clerk for manual filing, it should be accompanied by a paper copy of the Notice of Manual Filing that was electronically filed in its place.

14. Signature Block. Use of the attorney's login and password when filing documents electronically serves in part as the attorney's signature for purposes of Fed.R.Civ.P. 11, the local rules of this Court, and any other purpose for which a signature is required in connection with proceedings before the Court. All documents filed electronically shall include a signature block and include the filing attorney's typewritten name, address, telephone number, facsimile number and e-mail address. In addition, the name of the filing attorney under whose ECF login the document will be filed should be preceded by a "s/" and typed in the space where the attorney's handwritten signature would otherwise appear. Documents signed by an attorney must be filed using that attorney's ECF log-in and password and may not be filed using a log-in and password belonging to another attorney.

s/ [Name of Filing Attorney]
Name of Filing Attorney
Law Firm Name
Address
City, State, ZIP Code
Phone: (xxx) xxx-xxxx
Fax: (xxx) xxx-xxxx
E-mail: xxx@xxx.xxx

Documents requiring signatures of more than one attorney shall be filed either by: (a) obtaining consent from the other attorney, then typing the "s/ [Name]" signature of the other attorney on the signature line where the other attorney's signature would otherwise appear; (b) identifying in the signature section the name of the other attorney whose signature is required and by the submission of a Notice of Endorsement (see Appendix B) by the other attorney no later than three business days after filing; (c) submitting a scanned document containing all handwritten signatures; or (d) in any other manner approved by the Court.

Documents requiring a signature other than that of an attorney must bear an original handwritten signature and must be scanned into PDF for electronic filing.

15. Manual Filings. Parties otherwise participating in the electronic filing system may be excused from filing a particular component electronically under certain limited circumstances, such as when the component cannot be reduced to an electronic format. Such components shall not be filed electronically, but instead shall be manually filed with the Clerk of Court and served upon the parties in accordance with the applicable Federal Rules of Civil and Criminal Procedure and the Local Rules for filing and service of non-electronic documents.

Before making a manual filing of a component, the filing party shall first electronically file a Notice of Manual Filing (See Appendix C). The filer shall initiate the electronic filing process as if filing the actual component but shall instead attach to the filing the Notice of Manual Filing setting forth the reason(s) why the component cannot be filed electronically. The manual filing should be accompanied by a copy of the previously filed Notice of Manual Filing. A party may seek to have a component excluded from electronic filing pursuant to applicable Federal and Local Rules (*e.g.* Fed.R.Civ.P. 26(c)).

16. Technical Difficulties. Parties are encouraged to file documents electronically during normal business hours, in case a problem is encountered. In the event a technical failure occurs and a document cannot be filed electronically despite the best efforts of the filing party, the party should print (if possible) a copy of the error message received. In addition, as soon as practically possible, the party should file a "Declaration that Party was Unable to File in a Timely Manner Due to Technical Difficulties." A model form is provided as Appendix D.

If a party is unable to file electronically and, as a result, may miss a filing deadline, the party must contact the Clerk's Office at (317) 229–3700 to inform the court's staff of the difficulty. If a party misses a filing deadline due to an inability to file electronically, the party may submit the untimely filed document, accompanied by a declaration stating the reason(s) for missing the deadline. Unless the Court orders otherwise, the document and declaration must be filed no later than 12:00 noon of the first day on which the Court is open for business following the original filing deadline.

17. Retention of Originals of Documents Requiring Scanning. Originals of documents filed electronically which require scanning (*e.g.* documents that contain signatures such as affidavits) must be retained for a period of two years following the expiration of all time periods for appeals (Local Rule 5–9) by the filing party and made available, upon request, to the Court and other parties.

18. Sealed Filings.

Criminal Matters. In criminal matters, which may include criminal, magistrate, or miscellaneous case types, documents may be filed under seal without motion or further order of the court pursuant to Local Criminal Rule 49.1–2(c), provided counsel has a good faith belief that sealing is required to ensure the safety, privacy or cooperation of a person or entity, or to otherwise protect a substantial public interest.

A document filed under seal in a criminal matter must be accompanied by a *Sealed Cover Sheet.* The contents of the *Sealed Cover Sheet* are set forth in Local Criminal Rule 49.1–2(d)(1).

Civil Matters. In civil matters, which may include civil or miscellaneous case types, a document may be filed under seal only if the document is subject to sealing by a prior order of the court, accompanied by a motion to seal pursuant to Local Rule 5–11, or filed under seal pursuant to Fed.R.Civ.P. 5.2.

Service of Sealed Filings. Documents filed electronically under seal are not served upon opposing counsel through the court's CM/ECF system. (See Local Rule 5–11(d)). A document filed electronically under seal must be served upon opposing counsel in the traditional paper manner, or by using any approved method listed under Fed.R.Civ.P. 5.

Sealed Filing Procedure. A sealed document must be filed electronically via the court's CM/ECF system, unless listed as an exception to the electronic filing requirement under Local Rule 5–2(a) or Local Criminal Rule 49–1(a). As with any electronically filed document, sealed filings must be submitted by an attorney of record in the case for which the document is being filed and must be filed on behalf of a party or parties for whom the filing attorney has previously appeared.

a) Filing a Document in a CASE That is Under Seal (Applies to Civil and Criminal Matters). Sealed cases as well as associated docket entries and documents are not available for public viewing via the court's PACER system. Therefore, documents filed electronically in a sealed case may be filed using any event from the CM/ECF civil or criminal events menu. It is not necessary to use one of the sealed filing events listed under subsection (b) when filing document in a sealed case. **Before counsel may electronically file a document in a sealed case, the attorney must first file a *Notice of Appearance* in the traditional paper manner to obtain access to the sealed case via CM/ECF.**

When a document is electronically filed in a sealed case, a *Notice of Electronic Filing* is not distributed via email to counsel of record in the case, including the filing attorney. For that reason, filers should print the *Notice of Electronic Filing* confirmation screen that appears at the conclusion of the filing as proof of the transmission to the court. A document filed electronically in a sealed case must be served upon opposing counsel in the traditional paper manner, or by using any approved method listed under Fed.R.Civ.P. 5.

NOTE: If a sealed case is later unsealed by order of the court, any or all of the documents previously filed in the case may also be unsealed. Prior to the unsealing of a case, counsel should bring to the court's attention any documents in the record which should remain under seal.

b) Filing a Sealed Document in a Case that is NOT under Seal. Sealed documents filed electronically in a case that is not under seal must be submitted using one of the sealed civil or criminal filing events listed below.

Civil Matters

Sealed Civil Filing Events

- SEALED Motion (Motion filed under Seal) (Sealed—doc)

- SEALED Response to Motion (Sealed—doc)

- SEALED Reply in Support of Motion (Sealed—doc)

- SEALED Document (Sealed—doc)

- Redaction Index (Sealed—doc)

Availability

PDF documents filed electronically using a sealed civil event are not accessible via the court's PACER system to the public and attorneys, including counsel of record in the case. *Docket text/entries* generated by the CM/ECF system or entered by the filer during the electronic filing process are displayed on the court's docket and available for public viewing via PACER.

Service

Each of the sealed civil events generates and distributes a *Notice of Electronic Filing* to ECF-registered counsel of record. The *Notice of Electronic Filing* provides recipients with the docket text and a description of the document(s) filed, but does not permit recipients to view any PDF document(s) filed under seal. Therefore, a document filed electronically under seal, must be served upon opposing counsel in the traditional paper manner, or by using any approved method listed under Fed.R.Civ.P. 5.

Criminal Matters

Sealed Criminal Filing Events

* Events that offer the filer the option to seal are designated as "optional Sealed"

- Plea Agreement (optional Sealed—entry)
- Petition to Enter a Plea of Guilty (optional Sealed—entry)
- Addendum to Plea Agreement (optional Sealed—entry)
- Stipulated Factual Basis (optional Sealed—entry)
- SEALED Motion—Motion filed under Seal (Sealed—entry)
- Motion for Temporary Custody (optional Sealed—entry)
- Motion for Writ of Garnishment (optional Sealed—entry)
- Response to Motion (Sealed—entry)
- Reply in Support of Motion (Sealed—entry)
- OBJECTION to Presentence Investigation Report (optional Sealed—entry)
- SEALED Document (Sealed—entry)
- Submission of Signature Requirement (optional Sealed—entry)

Availability

Docket text/entries and associated *PDF documents* filed electronically using a sealed <u>criminal</u> event are <u>not</u> displayed on the court's docket for public viewing via the court's PACER System.

Service

Sealed <u>criminal</u> events do <u>not</u> generate and distribute a *Notice of Electronic Filing* to ECF-registered counsel of record. A document filed electronically under seal, must be served upon opposing counsel in the traditional paper manner or by using any approved method listed under Fed.R.Civ.P. 5.

c) Split Filings; Filings in Which at Least one, but not all Documents are Sealed. Sealed exhibits or attachments filed in conjunction with a non-sealed foundation document (*e.g.*, motion, brief, response, reply) must be submitted in a separate transaction using the appropriate sealed event. For example, a non-sealed response might be filed with 10 exhibits, only 3 of which are sealed. In this situation, the foundation document (response) and any non-sealed exhibits must first be filed using the appropriate non-sealed filing event. Then, in a separate filing, using the *SEALED Document* event, the filer should submit the *Sealed Cover Sheet* as the main document and each of the 3 sealed exhibits as attachments.

26	RESPONSE in Opposition re 14 MOTION for Summary Judgment filed by ROBERT SMITH. (Attachments: #1 Exhibit 1 #2 Exhibit 2 #3 Exhibit 5 #4 Exhibit 6 #5 Exhibit 7 #6 Exhibit 9 #7 Exhibit 10)(Jones, Michael)
27	SEALED Exhibits in Support re 26 Response in Opposition to Motion filed by ROBERT SMITH. (Attachments: #1 Sealed Exhibit 3 #2 Sealed Exhibit 4 #3 Sealed Exhibit 8)(Jones, Michael)

---

d) Motions to Seal. A motion to seal is not filed under seal unless sealing is warranted because the content and the existence of the document to be sealed should not be revealed on the court's public docket. Whether filed under seal or not, a motion to seal is filed electronically and must be accompanied by a proposed order, which is required by Local Rule 7–1(d) and is filed as an attachment to the motion.

When filing a motion to seal a document, the document that is the object of the motion to seal must first be filed electronically using the appropriate sealed event listed under subsection (b). After filing under seal the document that is the object of the motion to seal, the motion may be filed and should be linked to the sealed filing.

If the motion to seal is granted, the object of the motion shall remain under seal. If the motion to seal is denied, the object of the motion will be unsealed immediately upon issuance of the order.

19. Restricted Access Filings—Submission of Sentencing Letters. Under appropriate circumstances, counsel may file documents and restrict access to only case parties and the court. This filing restriction can only be used under specific circumstances and for specific documents, and only when authorized by the court.

Counsel for each criminal defendant is encouraged to be the recipient of all letters in support of the defendant, and counsel for the government is encouraged to be the recipient of all victim impact letters. Counsel must file all defendant support and victim impact letters received, via CM/ECF, using the event listed below, which restricts access to these documents to case participants and the court. Submission of these letters via CM/ECF will allow the content of letters to become quickly accessible to the assigned Probation Officer, the Judge, and opposing counsel. Because access to the letters is restricted to case participants only, redaction under Fed.R.Crim.P. 49.1 is not required.

To restrict access to case participants, counsel will submit victim impact letters and letters in support of defendants through the court's CM/ECF system, using the following event, which is located under "Other Documents":

- Sentencing Letter (Case participants—entry)

20. Ex Parte Documents. Ex parte documents must be filed electronically, as required by Local Rule 5–1. All ex parte filings must be submitted using an appropriate "EX PARTE" filing event.

Ex Parte Civil and Criminal Filing Events

- EX PARTE Filing (ex parte—entry)
- EX PARTE Motion (ex parte-entry)

Docket text and PDF documents associated with an electronic filing created using an "EX PARTE" filing event are not posted on the Court's public docket and cannot be accessed via the Court's Counsel PACER System.

When a filing is submitted electronically using an "EX PARTE" filing event, a *Notice of Electronic Filing* is distributed via email only to counsel for the filing party. If the Motion remains *ex parte* at the time of the Court's ruling, any Order issued referencing the "EX PARTE" Motion will generate and distribute an NEF only to counsel for the applicable party.

21. Contact Information. Additional information about electronic filing may be obtained by visiting the court's website at www.insd.uscourts.gov or contacting the Clerk's Office at (317) 229–3700.

Appendix A

UNITED STATES DISTRICT COURT
FOR THE
SOUTHERN DISTRICT OF INDIANA

ELECTRONIC CASE FILING
Attorney Registration Form

This form shall be used to register for an account on the Court's Electronic Case Filing (ECF) system. Registered attorneys will have privileges both to electronically file documents, and to receive electronic notice of case activity for civil and criminal cases assigned to the Electronic Case Filing system. The following information is required for registration:

First/Middle/Last Name _____

Attorney Bar ID # _____ State _____

Firm Name _____

Firm Address _____

_____

Voice Phone Number _____

FAX Phone Number _____

Primary E–Mail Address: _____

Secondary E–Mail Address: _____

Basis under which attorney is permitted to practice law in the U.S.D.C. for Southern Indiana (check one):

☐ Admitted in INSD ☐ Pro Hac Vice ☐ Government Attorney

If Pro Hac Vice or Gov't Attorney, indicate the cause number for which admission is pending or has been granted:

Cause Number(s): _____

By submitting this registration form, the undersigned agrees to abide by all Court rules, orders and policies and procedures governing the use of the electronic filing system. The undersigned also consents to receiving notice of filings via the Court's electronic filing system.

1. This system is for use only in cases permitted by the *U.S. District Court for the Southern District of Indiana.* It may be used to file documents electronically for all pending civil and criminal cases in the Southern District of Indiana. Please contact the Clerk's Office at (317) 229–3700 to schedule training.

2. Pursuant to Federal Rule of Civil Procedure 11, every pleading, motion, and other paper (except lists, schedules, statements or amendments thereto) shall be signed by at least one attorney of record or, if the party is not represented by an attorney, all papers shall be signed by the party. An attorney's ECF login and password issued by the court serves in part as the attorney's signature per Local Rule 5–7. Therefore, an attorney must protect and secure the password issued by the court. If there is any reason to suspect the password has been compromised in any way, it is the duty and responsibility of the attorney to immediately notify the court. The Court will immediately delete that password from the electronic filing system and issue a new password.

3. An attorney's registration will not waive conventional service of a summons and complaint, subpoena, or other judicial process; submit the client to the jurisdiction of the Court; or operate as a consent to accept service of pleadings, documents, and orders in actions in which such attorney has not entered an appearance. An attorney's registration will constitute a waiver in law only of conventional service of other non-process pleadings, documents, and orders in the case. The attorney agrees to accept, on behalf of the client, service of notice of the electronic filing by hand, facsimile or authorized e-mail.

4. Attorneys must be active members of the bar of this Court to file pleadings electronically.

Please return this form
with <u>original</u> signature to:

U.S. District Court, Southern District of Indiana
Attn: ECF Registration Processing
46 East Ohio Street, Room 105
Indianapolis, IN 46204

***Photocopies and faxes <u>WILL NOT</u> be accepted.

_____

Attorney's Signature

_____

First Initial of First Name	Full Last Name	4 Digit Number (last 4 digits of SSN is suggested)

Appendix B

UNITED STATES DISTRICT COURT
SOUTHERN DISTRICT OF INDIANA

_____,)
    Plaintiff(s),)
)
   vs.)   Case No.
)
_____,)
    Defendant(s))

Notice of Endorsement

Please take notice that [Plaintiff/Defendant, Name of Party] electronically filed the following document on [Date of Filing]: [Title of Document]

[Plaintiff's/Defendant's] counsel now notifies the Court that [Plaintiff/Defendant, Name of Party] endorses the [Title of Document] filed by [Filing Party's Name] and would join in submitting said document for the Court's review.

s/ [Name of Filing Attorney]
Name of Filing Attorney
Law Firm Name
Address
City, State, ZIP Code
Phone: (xxx) xxx-xxxx
Fax: (xxx) xxx-xxxx
E-mail: xxx@xxx.xxx

Appendix C

UNITED STATES DISTRICT COURT
SOUTHERN DISTRICT OF INDIANA

_____,)
    Plaintiff(s),)
)
   vs.)   Case No.
)
_____,)
    Defendant(s))

Notice of Manual Filing

Please take notice that [Plaintiff/Defendant, Name of Party] has manually filed the following: [Title of Document or Object]

This exhibit has not been filed electronically because [it is an object and cannot be converted to an electronic format/the document exists only in paper form and is illegible when scanned to PDF].

The document or object has been manually served on all parties.

s/ [Name of Filing Attorney]
Name of Filing Attorney
Law Firm Name
Address
City, State, ZIP Code
Phone: (xxx) xxx-xxxx
Fax: (xxx) xxx-xxxx
E-mail: xxx@xxx.xxx

Appendix D

UNITED STATES DISTRICT COURT
SOUTHERN DISTRICT OF INDIANA

_____, Plaintiff(s),	)))
vs.	)) Case No.
_____, Defendant(s)	))))

Declaration that Party was Unable to File in a Timely Manner
Due to Technical Difficulties

Please take notice that [Plaintiff/Defendant, Name of Party] was unable to file his/her

[Title of Document] in a timely manner due to technical difficulties. The deadline for filing the [Title of Document] was [Filing Deadline Date]. The reason(s) that I was unable to file the [Title of Document] in a timely manner and the good faith efforts I made prior to the filing deadline to both file in a timely manner and to inform the Court and the other parties that I could not do so are set forth below.

[Statement of reasons and good faith efforts to file and to inform (including dates and times)]

I declare under penalty of perjury that the foregoing is true and correct.

s/ [Name of Filing Attorney]
Name of Filing Attorney
Law Firm Name
Address
City, State, ZIP Code
Phone: (xxx) xxx-xxxx
Fax: (xxx) xxx-xxxx
E-mail: xxx@xxx.xxx

[Adopted effective July 1, 2002; Amended effective January 1, 2006; September 1, 2006; February 1, 2008; September 30, 2008; March 16, 2009; July 17, 2009; January 1, 2012; January 3, 2013; May 23, 2013; October 21, 2013; November 19, 2013; December 30, 2014.]

SELECTED ORDERS
IN THE MATTER OF THE REFERENCE OF CASES AND PROCEEDINGS FILED UNDER TITLE 11, UNITED STATES CODE TO BANKRUPTCY JUDGES

Any and all cases and proceedings under Title 11, United States Code, and any and all proceedings arising in or related to a case under Title 11, United States Code, Bankruptcy Judges.

This Order shall be effective immediately.

[Dated: July 11, 1984.]

IN THE MATTER OF ADMISSION FEES OF ATTORNEYS

At its meeting on September 23, 1997, the Judicial Conference of the United States directed the Administrative Office of the United States Courts to inform courts that:

1) the $50 attorney admission fee prescribed in Item 11 of the District Court Miscellaneous Fee Schedule, promulgated pursuant to 28 U.S.C. section 1914, does not apply to pro hac vice requests or renewals of attorney admissions;

2) local courts may charge, at their option, a local fee above the $50 fee for original admission of attorneys to practice before this Court;

3) local courts may charge, at their option, a fee for pro hac vice admissions; and

4) revenues from such local fees may be deposited into a district court's Library Fund, which is used for projects which benefit the bar and the administration of justice.

Accordingly, to further the benefit the bar and the administration of justice, the Court has determined that the attorney admission fee in this District shall be $60, with $50 of that fee to be deposited into the U.S. Treasury and $10 to be deposited into this Court's Library Fund. The Court also has established a fee of $30 per request to be admitted *pro hac vice*, with such fee in its entirety to be deposited into the Court's Library Fund. The modification of fees as set forth herein shall be effective January 1, 1998.

[Dated: November 24, 1997.]

DEPOSIT OF FUNDS WITH THE COURT IN PENDING OR ADJUDICATED CASES PURSUANT TO 28 U.S.C. § 2041

WHEREAS, the Director of the Administrative Office of the United States Courts has established a Registry Fee to be assessed for administration of funds held in the registry of the Court pursuant to 28 U.S.C. § 2041 and placed in interest-bearing accounts or instruments;

WHEREAS such Registry Fee is authorized and set forth in the Judicial Conference Policy Notes appended to 28 U.S.C. § 1914, under the heading "Registry Fund Feeds–Item 13";

Accordingly, IT IS ORDERED that the Clerk of the Court shall deduct from income earned on registry funds invested in interest-bearing accounts or instruments, a fee not exceeding that authorized by the Judicial Conference of the United States and set by the Director of the Administrative Office in accordance with the schedule which shall be published periodically by the Director in the Federal Register. The fee shall be withdrawn whenever income earned becomes available for deduction and shall be deposited in the United States Treasury without further order of the Court. This assessment shall apply to all registry funds invested in interest-bearing accounts held outside the United States Treasury.

[Dated: March 17, 2005.]

ORDER RE: TRANSCRIPT FEE RATES*

At its March 2011 session, the Judicial Conference of the United States amended the maximum fees for realtime services. The amended fees are based on the number of realtime connections (feeds) provided by a certified realtime court reporter as follows:

- One feed, the ordering party pays $3.05 per page;
- Two to four feeds, each party receiving a feed pays $2.10 per page; or
- Five or more feeds, each party receiving a feed pays $1.50 per page.

Under the new maximum fees for realtime services, all parties to the case who receive a realtime feed pay the same amount for the services that are received. If a court reporter provides two or more feeds to the same party to the case, the reporter may charge for each feed provided based on the total number of feeds ordered.

Realtime services ordered prior to the date of this Order will be billed at the rates in effect at the time the realtime order was placed with the official court reporter.

This court voted to approve the amended maximum fees for realtime services; therefore,

IT IS HEREBY ORDERED that pursuant to Title 28, United States Code, Section 753, the following transcript rates per page are prescribed by the court and are effective, April 21, 2011.

TRANSCRIPT FEE RATES—ALL PARTIES PER PAGE

Transcript—Delivery Time Frame	Original	First Copy to Each Party	Each Add'l Copy to the Same Party
Ordinary Transcript: (30 days) A transcript to be delivered within thirty (30) calendar days after receipt of an order.	$3.65	$.90	$.60
14–Day Transcript: A transcript to be delivered within fourteen (14) calendar days after receipt of an order.	$4.25	$.90	$.60
Expedited Transcript: (7 days) A transcript to be delivered within seven (7) calendar days after receipt of an order.	$4.85	$.90	$.60
Daily Transcript: A transcript to be delivered following adjournment and prior to the normal opening hour of the court on the following morning whether or not it actually is a court day.	$6.05	$1.20	$.90
Hourly Transcript: A transcript of proceedings ordered under unusual circumstances to be delivered within two (2) hours.	$7.25	$1.20	$.90
Realtime Transcript:	One feed,[1]		

Transcript—Delivery Time Frame	Original	First Copy to Each Party	Each Add'l Copy to the Same Party
A draft unedited transcript produced by a certified realtime reporter as a byproduct of realtime to be delivered electronically during proceedings or immediately following adjournment.	$3.05 per page; two-to-four feeds, $2.10 per page; five or more feeds, $1.50 per page.		

1 A realtime "feed" is the electronic data flow from the court reporter to the computer of each person or party ordering and receiving the realtime transcription in the courtroom.

[Dated: April 21, 2011.]

    * Suggested title added by publisher.

GENERAL ORDER. IN THE MATTER OF CELLULAR PHONES AND ELECTRONIC DEVICES IN COURTROOMS

Rule 53 of the Federal Rules of Criminal Procedure and policy of the Judicial Conference of the United States provide that courtroom proceedings in civil and criminal cases in federal district courts may not be broadcast, televised, recorded, or photographed.

In an effort to increase compliance with Rule 53 and Judicial Conference policy, as well as to mitigate interference with sensitive courtroom sound equipment, the United States District Court for the Southern District of Indiana hereby **ORDERS** that cellular phones, electronic tablets, personal digital assistants, and all other electronic devices capable of audio or video recording be turned off (and not simply silenced) in all courtrooms of the United States District Court for the Southern District of Indiana.

Judges have the right to permit counsel and parties to turn such devices on, at the presiding judge's express verbal or written direction.

Specific exceptions to this Order are made for ceremonial proceedings, including naturalization ceremonies. The use of cellular phone and other electronic devices in courtrooms is allowed on these occasions.

Violation of this order may be punished as criminal contempt, and violators face possible sanction of confiscation of the device; fine; and/or imprisonment. This General Order does not apply to the United States Bankruptcy Court for the Southern District of Indiana.

SO ORDERED.

All of which is done at Indianapolis, Indiana, this 29th day of May, 2014.

[Dated: May 29, 2014.]

GENERAL ORDER. IN THE MATTER OF: SECURITY PROCEDURES

This order supersedes and replaces all prior orders of this Court on these subjects and establishes the security procedures applicable to all persons entering federal court facilities in the Southern District of Indiana, including the Birch Bayh Federal Building and U.S. Courthouse in Indianapolis; the United States Courthouse in Terre Haute; the United States Courthouse in Evansville; and the Lee H. Hamilton

Federal Building and Courthouse in New Albany (collectively referred to as "U.S. Courthouses in the Southern District" or "Courthouse Facilities").

SECURITY PROCEDURES

A.　Screening of Persons Entering the Building.

1.　The United States Marshals Service Court Security Officers shall operate X–ray machines and walk-through magnetometers at all public entrances to U.S. Courthouses in the Southern District for the purpose of screening persons entering the buildings. All persons and their belongings are subject to search by the United States Marshals Service while in these facilities.

2.　All employees and persons having business with the Courts or any other offices in a U.S. Courthouse in the Southern District shall pass through the walk-through magnetometers for the purpose of detection of firearms, explosives, pepper spray, incendiary devices, knives, or any other items prohibited by law, regulation or court order from introduction into these facilities. These persons shall submit to further screening by a United States Marshals Service Court Security Officer if the readings of the magnetometer indicate the presence of metallic substances. This further screening may encompass the removal of all metallic objects on their person and screening by a portable hand held metal detector or other screening procedures as necessary. Any person refusing to submit to this screening process shall be denied access to any of the Courthouses Facilities.

3.　All employees and persons having business with the Courts or any other offices in a U.S. Courthouse in the Southern District who are carrying, delivering or otherwise transporting any briefcase, suitcase, package, electronic device (including cell phones, pagers, electronic organizers or portable computers), or any other container (herein referred to as "carried item") shall surrender such carried item for screening through an X–ray device and/or personal inspection by a Court Security Officer. Any person refusing to submit his or her carried item(s) for screening through an X–ray device and/or personal inspection by a Court Security Officer shall be denied access to any Courthouse Facility. If a Court Security Officer concludes, after X–ray and/or personal inspection, that any item which the person seeks to bring into a Courthouse Facility may contain firearms, explosives, pepper spray, incendiary devices, knives, or any other dangerous item prohibited by law, regulation or court order, the individual is subject to arrest.

Exceptions. The following persons shall be exempt from the screening procedures set forth above (with appropriate official identification):

　　a.　Judges of the United States District Court for the Southern District of Indiana;

　　b.　Magistrate Judges of the United States District Court for the Southern District of Indiana;

　　c.　Judges of the United States Bankruptcy Court for the Southern District of Indiana;

　　d.　Employees of the United States Marshals Service and employees of contractors of the United States Marshals Service who serve as Court Security Officers who are authorized by law and agency regulations to carry firearms;

　　e.　Probation Officers who are employed by the United States Probation office who are authorized by law and agency regulations to carry firearms;

　　f.　Employees of the United States Federal Protective Service of the Department of Homeland Security who are authorized by law and agency regulations to carry firearms (this does not include private contract guards);

　　g.　Employees of the federal government (excluding contractors) who are assigned to a permanent duty station within one of the U.S. Courthouses within the Southern District;

h. Attorneys directly employed by the Office of the United States Attorney for the Southern District of Indiana, the Indiana Federal Community Defender for the Southern District of Indiana, the Office of the United States Trustee for the Southern District of Indiana, and the Internal Revenue Service for the Southern District of Indiana;

i. Standing Chapter 13 Trustees.

4. No person having authorized access to any Courthouse Facility, or a secured location therein, shall permit any unauthorized person access to any Courthouse Facility or to any elevator, locked stairwell door or any other locked door in a Courthouse Facility without proper authorization.

5. Only government employees authorized by their appropriate agency manager and possessing an official identification card may enter Courthouse Facilities through any secured entrance.

B. Cameras and Recording Devices. Except as specifically provided herein, no camera or recording device shall be permitted in any of the U.S. Courthouses in the Southern District.

Exceptions. Cameras and/or recording devices may be permitted in U.S. Courthouses in the Southern District under the following circumstances:

1. Cameras and recording devices are permitted if authorized for a specific occurrence by a Judge of the United States District Court, a Judge of the United States Bankruptcy Court, or the Clerk of the United States District or Bankruptcy Courts for the Southern District of Indiana or their authorized representatives. The permitting authority shall notify in writing the United States Marshals Service of such authorization.

2. Employees of the United States Courts and the tenant agencies in Courthouse Facilities may possess cameras and recording devices. No recording or pictures may be generated of the court, court hearings or other court functions without specific authorization by a court official (as listed above).

3. The General Services Administration Property Manager or his/her designee can authorize an individual or contract group to possess a camera or recording device for the purpose of maintaining or enhancing the Courthouse Facilities, to include repair and alterations.

C. Computers, Cellular Phones, Pagers and Related Electronic Equipment.

1. The use of portable computers and related electronic equipment in courtrooms and facilities adjacent to courtrooms is permitted, subject to specific restriction and direction by a judicial officer.

2. Cellular telephones that are not photo-enabled are permitted within Courthouse Facilities. Their use is prohibited within courtrooms (and these telephones may be confiscated upon entrance to any courtroom) and in any location where court proceedings may be disrupted by their use.

3. Cellular phones and pagers shall be set in a mode to emit no audible signals while on any of the courtroom floors of any Courthouse Facility.

4. No computers, cellular phones, pagers or related electronic equipment that are photo-enabled are permitted within any Courthouse Facility.

D. Weapons: Firearms, Knives, Explosives and other Dangerous Items. Except as specifically provided herein, no person shall possess a weapon in any U.S. Courthouse within the Southern District of Indiana. It is illegal to possess a firearm or other dangerous weapon in a federal building with or without the intent to commit a crime (Title 18, U.S.C. § 930), and any person possessing same is subject to arrest.

Firearms, knives, explosives, and other dangerous weapons shall be prohibited from Courthouse Facilities and are subject to confiscation by the United States Marshals Service.

This section of the policy covers only firearms and "Taser" type weapons. Local and federal law enforcement officers are permitted to maintain control of less than lethal weapons (including pepper spray, batons, etc.) throughout courthouses (including courtrooms) within the Southern District, with limited exceptions.

A. *Local Law Enforcement Officers.* When a local law enforcement officer arrives at a security control point ("SCP") and identifies himself/herself, the on-duty Court Security Officer ("CSO") shall question the law enforcement officer as to his/her business within the courthouse.

1. If the local law enforcement officer has official business inside the courthouse but not within a courtroom, the law enforcement officer shall fill out a "check-in" form that will be supplied by the USMS, and the law enforcement officer will be permitted to maintain control of his/her firearm(s). The screening CSO will instruct the law enforcement officer that he/she may not enter any courtroom while armed.

2. If the local law enforcement officer advises that he/she has business inside a courtroom, the officer must surrender any/all firearms (including "Taser" type weapons) at the SCP, except in the following circumstances:

a. Department of Corrections officers/guards and Sheriff's Deputies escorting prisoners inside a courtroom are permitted to carry their firearms inside the courtroom.

b. Local law enforcement officers assigned to a federal task force (e.g. DEA, ATF, USMS, etc.) are permitted to carry their firearm(s) into the courtroom as long as the firearm(s) are concealed. The officer should endeavor to make contact with the assigned Judge's courtroom deputy prior to entering the courtroom, so the courtroom deputy can apprise the Judge that a firearm will be present.

3. If the local law enforcement officer has appeared at the courthouse in conjunction with his/her status as a party or witness to any proceeding, criminal or civil—including as a debtor in a case before the bankruptcy court, the officer shall surrender all firearms and other weapons, including non-lethal, at the SCP.

B. *Federal Law Enforcement Officers.* Federal law enforcement officers are generally permitted to carry their firearms inside courthouses within the Southern District and also inside courtroom(s) as long as the firearms are concealed. Federal law enforcement officers that are not tenants of a courthouse shall fill out a "check-in" form that will be supplied by the USMS upon entering the building. If a federal law enforcement officer has appeared at the courthouse in conjunction with his/her status as a party or witness to any proceeding, criminal or civil—including as a debtor in a case before the bankruptcy court, the officer shall surrender all firearms and other weapons at the SCP.

Proposed Expansion of Policy Regarding Uniform Photo Identification for Courthouse Tenants in the Southern District of Indiana

Individuals possessing United States Courthouse issued photo identification cards will be permitted to bypass security screening upon entering any courthouse within the Southern District of Indiana. The Court Security Committee recommends that staff of the United States Attorneys Office and Federal Community Defender's Office be given the opportunity to participate in the program. The Office of the United States Trustee also maintains space in the courthouse and would like similar consideration.

This policy will be in effect unless authorized otherwise for a specific occurrence by the United Sates Marshal, Chief Deputy United Sates Marshal, or his designee.

Any person who refuses to abide by this order governing the possession of weapons will not be permitted access to Courthouse Facilities.

VIOLATIONS

A violation of this court order may be subject to arrest and a violation of a criminal code or contempt of court. Additionally, a violation may make the equipment subject to seizure and forfeiture as determined by the presiding Judicial Officer.

UNITED STATES MARSHALS SERVICE
SECURITY ALERT PLAN

The USMS SECURITY ALERT PLAN is divided into five levels. Escalating levels provide additional security requirements designed to supplement security procedures already mandated by USMS policy.

When the USMS Security Alert protocol is activated, the national policy guidelines directing security levels will supercede this court order.

IT IS SO ORDERED.

[Dated: April 16, 2015.]

PLAN FOR THE RANDOM SELECTION
OF GRAND AND PETIT JURORS

Pursuant to the Jury Selection and Service Act of 1968, as amended (28 U.S.C. § 1861, *et seq.*), the following Plan is hereby adopted by the Judges of the United States District Court for the Southern District of Indiana, subject to approval by the Reviewing Panel for the Judicial Council for the Seventh Circuit and to such rules and regulations as may be adopted from time to time by the Judicial Conference of the United States.

EFFECTIVE DATE AND DURATION

This Plan for Random Selection of Grand and Petit Jurors (the "Plan") will become effective <u>April 11, 2014</u>, as approved by the Reviewing Panel as provided in 28 U.S.C. § 1863 (a) and (c). It will remain in force and effect until modified by the court with the approval of the Reviewing Panel.

IT IS SO ORDERED.

s/<u>RICHARD L. YOUNG</u>
RICHARD L. YOUNG, Chief Judge
United States District Court

1. DEFINITIONS

A. "Plan" refers to this Plan for the Random Selection of Grand and Petit Jurors.

B. Words used in this Plan that are defined in 28 U.S.C. § 1869 of the Act, as amended, will have the meaning therein specified.

C. "Master jury wheel" is a figurative term designating all names selected directly from official source lists in a manner described in this Plan.

D. "Divisional jury wheel" is a term designating all names selected directly from official source lists in a manner described in this Plan, broken down by judicial division as defined in Section 2.A. of this Plan.

E. The "qualified jury wheel" is composed of those jurors who, based solely on the information provided on the juror qualification questionnaire, have been deemed eligible for service.

F. The "source lists" are comprised of the names and data provided by the Indiana Secretary of State, Election Division, and the Indiana Supreme Court (Statewide Jury List), as identified in Section 6.A. and B. of this Plan.

G. The term "petit jury" or "petit juror" means a jury or juror summoned to serve at a civil or criminal trial proceeding.

H. The term "grand jury" or "grand juror" means a jury or juror summoned to serve at a grand jury proceeding.

2. APPLICABILITY OF THE PLAN

A. The Southern District of Indiana is divided for jury selection purposes into four (4) divisions, which are identical with the statutory composition of the district as set forth in 28 U.S.C. § 94, and as referenced at 28 U.S.C. § 1869(e). Those divisions are:

(1) *Indianapolis*—Bartholomew, Boone, Brown, Clinton, Decatur, Delaware, Fayette, Fountain, Franklin, Hamilton, Hancock, Hendricks, Henry, Howard, Johnson, Madison, Marion, Monroe, Montgomery, Morgan, Randolph, Rush, Shelby, Tipton, Union, and Wayne counties.

(2) *Terre Haute*—Clay, Greene, Knox, Owen, Parke, Putnam, Sullivan, Vermillion, and Vigo counties.

(3) *Evansville*—Davies, Dubois, Gibson, Martin, Perry, Pike, Posey, Spencer, Vanderburgh, and Warrick counties.

(4) *New Albany*—Clark, Crawford, Dearborn, Floyd, Harrison, Jackson, Jefferson, Jennings, Lawrence, Ohio, Orange, Ripley, Scott, Switzerland, and Washington counties.

B. The provisions of this Plan apply to all divisions of the district unless otherwise indicated.

3. DECLARATION OF POLICY

A. The purpose of this Plan is to implement the policies of the United States as set forth in 28 U.S.C. § 1861:

(1) that all litigants in Federal courts entitled to trial by jury will have the right to grand and petit juries selected at random from a fair cross section of the community in the district or division wherein the court convenes.

(2) that all citizens will have the opportunity to be considered for service on grand and petit juries in the district courts of the United States, and

(3) that all citizens will have an obligation to serve as jurors when summoned for that purpose.

4. DISCRIMINATION PROHIBITED

A. No citizen will be excluded from service as a grand or petit juror on account of race, color, religion, sex, national origin, or economic status.

5. MANAGEMENT AND SUPERVISION OF THE JURY SELECTION PROCESS

A. The clerk, under the supervision and control of the Chief Judge and other Judges of this court, will manage the jury selection process. Such management will be consistent with this Plan and in accordance with 28 U.S.C. § 1863(b).

B. The clerk may use computers and other automation technologies in implementing this Plan but will maintain a procedure manual to govern such use. The clerk also may hire, or contract with, persons or entities to perform the duties set forth in this Plan as long as the clerk supervises the work of such persons or entities and such persons or entities certify that work has been completed pursuant to the clerk's instructions.

6. JURY SELECTION SOURCES

A. Voter Registration—Indiana law provides a uniform system of voter registration in all counties throughout the state of Indiana. The voter registration lists contain names which represent a fair cross section of the community in the Southern District of Indiana. Accordingly, the names of grand and petit jurors for each of the four (4) divisions will be selected at random from the Indiana master voter registration lists maintained by the Indiana Secretary of State, Election Division.

B. Indiana Supreme Court Statewide Jury List—As permitted by 28 U.S.C. § 1863 (b)(2), the court hereby authorizes the clerk to draw names of prospective jurors for each of the four (4) divisions from the Indiana Supreme Court Statewide Jury List in addition to voter registration lists. This supplemental source list is a combination of data maintained (or collected) by: (1) the Indiana State Bureau of Motor Vehicles, consisting of Indiana residents with state-issued identification cards, driver's licenses, and vehicle registration records, excluding individuals under the age of eighteen (18) and non-U.S. citizens; and (2) the Indiana Department of Revenue, which includes all Indiana state resident taxpayers.

C. The names and data provided by the Indiana Secretary of State, Election Division, and the Indiana Supreme Court (Statewide Jury List), as identified in 6.A. and B. above, will constitute the "source lists." The selection of names from such source lists will be done in a manner consistent with the selection procedures described within this Plan.

7. INITIAL SELECTION OF NAMES FOR THE MASTER JURY WHEEL

A. Pursuant to 28 U.S.C. § 1863(b)(4), the master jury wheel will be emptied and refilled each odd-numbered year (2011, 2013, *etc.*) unless the Chief Judge otherwise directs. The total number of names drawn for each division will be no less than one-half of 1% of the total number of persons on the source lists in that division. The Chief Judge may order additional names to be placed in any master jury wheel at any time.

8. MASTER JURY WHEEL

A. The names which are chosen through the methods listed above will be used to fill the master jury wheel.

B. A record of the names within the master jury wheel may be kept on paper and/or electronic media. Thereafter, the names drawn may be arranged alphabetically on a list, which will not be disclosed except as provided in 28 U.S.C. §§ 1867 and 1868, by order of this court, or as provided in Sections 17 and 18 of this Plan.

9. METHOD AND MANNER OF RANDOM SELECTION OF JURORS

A. At the clerk's option, and after consultation with the court, the selection of names from the source lists for the master jury wheel may be accomplished by a purely randomized process through a properly programmed electronic data processing system. Similarly, at the option of the clerk and after consultation with the court, a properly programmed electronic data processing system for pure randomized selection may be used to select names from the master wheel for the purpose of determining qualification for jury service, and from the qualified wheel for summoning persons to serve as grand or petit jurors. Such random selections of names from the source lists for inclusion in the master jury wheel by data computer personnel will ensure that names of persons residing in each of the counties within the judicial district or division are placed in the master jury wheel; and will ensure that each county within the district or division is substantially proportionally represented in the master jury wheel for that judicial district, division, or combination of divisions, in accordance with 28 U.S.C. § 1863(b)(3). The selections of names from the source lists, the master jury wheel, and the qualified jury wheel must insure that the mathematical odds of any single name being selected are substantially equal.

B. The Jury Management System (JMS), provided and supported by the Administrative Office of the U.S. Courts, will be used to select names from the master and qualified jury wheels of persons to be summoned to serve as grand or petit jurors.

10. DIVISIONAL JURY WHEELS

A. The clerk is required to maintain separate jury wheels for each of the divisions within the district, as defined in section 2.A. of this Plan. These separate jury wheels are referred to as "divisional jury wheels." The names and addresses of all persons randomly selected from the source lists from each division will be placed in the divisional jury wheel created for that division.

B. The clerk will maintain divisional jury wheels in electronic format, with backup media stored off-site and as directed in the court's Continuity of Operations Plan for emergency preparedness.

11. SCHEDULE FOR FILLING THE QUALIFIED JURY WHEELS: MAILING OF JUROR QUALIFICATION QUESTIONNAIRES

A. The clerk will determine the number of prospective jurors required for qualification to fill the qualified jury wheel in each division and will utilize JMS to select at random that number of names from each divisional jury wheel. The number of names to be drawn will be determined by the clerk based upon anticipated juror demands by the court plus a number of additional names sufficient to compensate for the estimated number of juror qualification questionnaires that will be undeliverable or not completed and returned. The clerk will post a general notice explaining the automated selection process. The qualified jury wheels will be emptied and refilled each odd-numbered year (2001, 2013, *etc.*).

B. The clerk may prepare an alphabetized list of names drawn from the master jury wheel and divisional jury wheels. These lists will not be exhibited to any person except as provided in Sections 1867 and 1868 of the Jury Act, as amended. The clerk will prepare and mail to every person whose name is so drawn a juror qualification questionnaire, in a form as prescribed by the Director of the Administrative Office of the United States Courts. The questionnaire will be accompanied by instructions to: (1) execute and submit the questionnaire duly signed and sworn, to the clerk by mail; or (2) complete the questionnaire via the court's Internet website. The instructions will specify that either must be completed within ten (10) days of receipt of the questionnaire. The foregoing steps shall be taken in accordance with 28 U.S.C. § 1864(a) of the Jury Act, as amended.

C. If a juror qualification questionnaire from the initial mailing is returned to the court as undeliverable, a substitute will be mailed to a person whose name has been drawn from the master jury wheel and whose address is within the same zip code to which the undeliverable juror qualification questionnaire was initially sent.

D. If a juror qualification questionnaire from the initial mailing is not returned or otherwise responded to, the clerk will mail follow-up letters to the prospective juror. If any such follow-up letter fails to garner a response from a prospective juror selected for an initial mailing, the clerk will mail a juror qualification questionnaire to a person whose name has been drawn from the master jury wheel and whose address is within the same zip code as the address of the person who has failed to respond to the questionnaire.

E. Once a year, the clerk may, but is not required to, submit the names on the master jury wheel to be updated and corrected through the national change of address system of the United States Postal Service.

F. In accordance with 28 U.S.C. § 1878, at the option of the district court, jurors may be summoned and qualified in a single procedure, in lieu of the two separate procedures otherwise provided for by the Jury Act and this Plan.

12. QUALIFICATIONS FOR JURY SERVICE

A. In accordance with 28 U.S.C. § 1865(a), the clerk, under the supervision of the Judges of this court, will determine solely on the basis of information provided on the juror qualification questionnaire and other competent evidence whether a person is unqualified for, or exempt, or to be excused from jury service and will record such determination(s) along with the reasons underlying them.

B. In accordance with 28 U.S.C. § 1865(b), the clerk, under the supervision of the Judges of this court, will deem any person qualified to serve on grand and petit juries in this district unless the person:

(1) is not a citizen of the United States, at least eighteen (18) years old, who has resided for a period of one (1) year within the judicial district;

(2) is unable to read, write, and understand the English language with a degree of proficiency sufficient to fill out satisfactorily the juror qualification questionnaire;

(3) is unable to speak the English language;

(4) is incapable, by reason of mental or physical infirmity, to render satisfactory jury service; or

(5) has a charge pending against him or her for the commission of, or has been convicted in a State or Federal court of record of, a crime punishable by imprisonment for more than one (1) year and that person's civil rights have not been restored.

13. PERSONS EXEMPT FROM JURY SERVICE

A. The Jury Act, at 28 U.S.C. § 1863(b)(6), provides that the following persons who are employed on a full time basis are exempt, and therefore barred, from jury service:

(1) Members in active service in the Armed Forces of the United States, as defined in 10 U.S.C. § 101(a)(4) as including only the Army, Navy, Air Force, Marine Corps and Coast Guard;

(2) Members of the fire or police departments of any State, the District of Columbia, any territory or possession of the United States, or any subdivision of a State, the District of Columbia, or such territory or possession;

(3) Public officers in the executive, legislative, or judicial branches of the Government of the United States, or of any State, the District of Columbia, any territory or possession of the United States, or any subdivision of a State, the District of Columbia, or such territory or possession, who are actively engaged in the performance of official duties.

14. PERSONS WHO MAY BE EXCUSED FROM SERVICE UPON REQUEST

A. Pursuant to 28 U.S.C. § 1863(b)(5), this court finds members of the following occupational classes or groups of persons would endure undue hardship or extreme inconvenience if required to perform jury service and, therefore, will be excused from such service upon individual request:

(1) a person over seventy (70) years of age;

(2) a person who has served as a federal grand or petit juror within the last two (2) years;

(3) volunteer safety personnel, such as firefighters or members of a rescue squad or ambulance crew, who serve without compensation for a public agency, as defined in the 1203(6) of title I of the Omnibus Crime Control and Safe Streets Act of 1968 (42 U.S.C. § 3796b). Public agency, for this purpose, means the United States, any state of the United States, or any unit of local government, department or instrumentality of any of the foregoing;

(4) a person having active care and custody of a child under ten (10) years of age whose health and/or safety would be jeopardized by any absence for jury service; or a person who is essential to the care of aged or infirm person(s);

(5) a person whose services are so essential to the operation of a business, commercial, or agricultural enterprise that it must close or cease to function if such person is required to perform jury duty.

15. TEMPORARY EXCUSES

A. Pursuant to 28 U.S.C. § 1866(c)(1), the Judges of this court, or the clerk under supervision of the court, upon showing of undue hardship or extreme inconvenience, may temporarily excuse a person for such a period as the court deems necessary, at the conclusion of which such person either will be summoned again for jury service or the name of such person will be reinserted into the qualified jury wheel for selection.

16. SUMMONS OF JURORS

A. Pursuant to 28 U.S.C. § 1866(a), the clerk will draw at random from the qualified jury wheel such number of names of persons as may be required for assignment to grand and petit jury panels. The clerk will post a general notice for public review in the clerk's office and on the court's website explaining the process by which names are periodically and randomly drawn. The clerk will prepare a separate list of grand and petit jury panels.

B. Each petit jury panel will be summoned on a division-wide basis and will sit at the place where court is conducted within the division.

C. Each grand jury panel will be summoned on either a district-wide basis or on a division-wide basis. The number of names drawn will be sufficient to fill the grand jury panel as may be directed by the court. If summoned on a district-wide basis the grand jury panel may sit wherever court is conducted within the district. The clerk will randomly draw a pro-rata number of names from the qualified jury wheel of each division to ensure that each division is proportionately represented to fill a district-wide grand jury panel. If a grand jury is summoned on a division-wide basis, the grand jury panel may sit where court is conducted within that division.

D. Pursuant to 28 U.S.C. § 1866(e), in any two (2) year period, no person will be required to:

(1) serve or attend court for prospective service as a petit juror for a total of more than thirty (30) days, except when necessary to complete service in a particular case, or

(2) serve on more than one grand jury, or

(3) serve as both a grand and petit juror.

17. RELEASE OF JUROR INFORMATION

A. In accordance with 28 U.S.C. § 1867(f), the contents of records or papers used by the clerk in connection with the jury selection process will not be disclosed or made available to the general public. However, redacted copies of petit juror questionnaires may be provided by the clerk to counsel before trial. Redacted copies of grand juror questionnaires may be provided to the United States Attorney's Office by the clerk prior to the convening of the grand jury. At the conclusion of jury selection during a trial or grand jury proceeding, counsel must return all copies of juror questionnaires to the clerk for secure and immediate disposal.

B. Upon request, and only after the jurors' service has concluded, the court may order the clerk to disclose to the media or public the names of individuals who have served as jurors. The court may order any list of juror names to be kept confidential when the interest of justice so requires.

C. Upon written request, the clerk may authorize the disclosure of juror names and addresses of individuals: (1) whose mailings have been returned and processed as not deliverable; (2) who are deceased; and (3) who are not residents in this district for one year; or (4) who moved out of this district—to the administrator of the Indiana Supreme Court Statewide Jury List or the Indiana Secretary of State, Election Division (see Section 6A and B of this Plan).

18. MAINTENANCE AND INSPECTION OF RECORDS

A. After the master jury wheel is emptied and refilled pursuant to this Plan and after all persons selected to serve as jurors before the master jury wheel was emptied have completed such service, the records and papers compiled and maintained by the clerk with regard to the emptied master jury wheel will be preserved in the custody of the clerk for four (4) years and will be available for public inspection for the purpose of determining the validity of the selection of any jury.

INCORPORATION OF AMENDMENTS

Incorporated herein by reference is 28 U.S.C. §§ 1861—1871, together with all amendments which may hereafter be made, and all laws hereafter enacted relating to grand and petit juries and trial by jury in the United States.

This Plan, as amended, supersedes any and all Plans heretofore adopted and will constitute the rule of this court and become effective upon the approval of the Seventh Circuit Judicial Council.

APPROVED BY THE JUDICIAL COUNCIL OF THE SEVENTH CIRCUIT this 11th day of April, 2014.

[Effective October 5, 2005. Amended effective October 4, 2010; November 8, 2011; August 14, 2012; April 11, 2014.]

CRIMINAL JUSTICE ACT PLAN

Pursuant to the Criminal Justice Act of 1964, as amended (section 3006A of Title 18, United States Code (the "CJA"), and the "Guidelines for the Administration of the Criminal Justice Act," contained in the Guide to Judicial Policies and Procedures (the "CJA Guidelines"), the United States District Court for the Southern District of Indiana adopts this Amended Criminal Justice Act Plan (the "Amended CJA Plan") to prescribe the procedures and requirements for furnishing representation in the United States District Court for the Southern District of Indiana to any person financially unable to obtain adequate representation in accordance with the CJA.

I. OBJECTIVES OF THE AMENDED CJA PLAN

A. Principal Objective. The objective of this Amended CJA Plan is to attain the ideal of equality before the law for all persons. Therefore, this Amended CJA Plan shall be administered so that those accused of a crime, or otherwise eligible for services pursuant to the CJA, will not be deprived of legal services because they are financially unable to pay for adequate representation, or any element of representation necessary to an adequate defense.

B. Further Objective. The further objective of this Amended CJA Plan is to particularize the requirements of the CJA, the USA Patriot Act Reauthorization (codified in part at Section 3599 of Title 18, United States Code) (formerly the Anti–Drug Abuse Act of 1988 (codified in part at Section 848(q) of Title 21, United States Code)), and the CJA Guidelines to meet the needs of this judicial district.

C. Compliance. The court, its Clerk, the Indiana Federal Community Defender, and private attorneys appointed under the CJA shall comply with the CJA Guidelines approved by the Judicial Conference of the United States and/or its Committee on Defender Services and with this Amended CJA Plan.

II. DEFINITIONS

A. "Appointed Attorney" includes private attorneys, the Executive Director of the Indiana Federal Community Defenders, Inc., and staff attorneys employed by the Community Defender.

B. "Clerk" means the Clerk of the United States District Court for the Southern District of Indiana.

C. "Community Defender" means the Indiana Federal Community Defenders, Inc., which has previously been established and recognized by the court as a community defender organization pursuant to the provisions of the CJA.

D. "Court" means the United States District Court for the Southern District of Indiana and includes any of the District Judges and Magistrate Judges assigned to this judicial district.

E. "Judicial Officer" includes a United States District Judge assigned to the court, a United States Magistrate Judge assigned to the court, a Judge of the United States Court of Appeals for the Seventh Judicial Circuit, or a Justice of the United States Supreme Court.

F. "Representation" includes counsel and investigative, expert and other services.

III. PROVISION OF REPRESENTATION

A. Circumstances.

509

1. *Mandatory.* Representation shall be provided for any financially eligible person who:

    a. is charged with a felony or with a Class A misdemeanor;

    b. is a juvenile alleged to have committed an act of juvenile delinquency as defined in Section 5031 of Title 18, United States Code;

    c. is charged with a violation of probation, or faces a change of a term of condition of probation (unless the modification sought is favorable to the probationer and the government has not objected to the proposed change);

    d. is under arrest, when such representation is required by law;

    e. is entitled to appointment of counsel in parole proceedings;

    f. is charged with a violation of supervised release or faces modification, reduction, or enlargement of a condition, or extension or revocation of a term of supervised release;

    g. is subject to a mental condition hearing under Chapter 313 of Title 18, United States Code;

    h. is in custody as a material witness;

    i. is seeking to set aside or vacate a death sentence under Sections 2254 or 2255 of Title 28, United States Code;

    j. faces loss of liberty in a case, and federal law requires the appointment of counsel;

    k. is entitled to appointment of counsel under section 4109 of Title 18, United States Code; or

    l. is entitled to appointment of counsel under the Sixth Amendment to the Constitution.

2. *Discretionary.* Whenever a Judicial Officer determines that the interests of justice so require, representation may be provided for any financially eligible person who:

    a. is charged with a petty offense (Class B or C misdemeanor, or an infraction), for which a sentence to confinement is authorized;

    b. is seeking relief, other than to set aside or vacate a death sentence under Sections 2241, 2254, or 2255 of Title 28, United States Code;

    c. is charged with civil or criminal contempt who faces loss of liberty;

    d. has been called as a witness before a grand jury, a court, the Congress, or a federal agency or commission which has the power to compel testimony, and there is reason to believe, either prior to or during testimony, that the witness could be subject to a criminal prosecution, a civil or criminal contempt proceedings, or face loss of liberty;

    e. is proposed by the United States Attorney for processing under a pretrial diversion program;

    f. is held for international extradition under Chapter 209 of Title 18, United States Code.

3. *Ancillary Matters.* Representation may also be furnished for financially eligible persons in ancillary matters appropriate to the proceedings pursuant to subsection (c) of the CJA.

B. When Counsel Shall Be Provided. Counsel shall be provided to financially eligible persons as soon as feasible after they are taken into custody, when they first appear before a Judicial Officer, when they are formally charged or notified of charges if formal charges are sealed, or when a Judicial Officer otherwise considers appointment of counsel appropriate under the CJA, whichever occurs earliest.

C. Number and Qualifications of Counsel.

1. *Number.*

a. General Provision. More than one attorney may be appointed in any case determined by the court to be extremely difficult by the court.

b. Defendants Charged With Crime Punishable By Death. In every criminal action in which a defendant is charged with a crime which may be punishable by death, a defendant who is or becomes financially unable to obtain adequate representation or investigative, expert, or other reasonably necessary services at any time either:

(i). before judgment, shall be entitled to two counsel, of whom at least one shall be learned in the law applicable to capital cases; or

(ii). after the entry of a judgment imposing a sentence of death but before the execution of that judgment, shall be entitled to the appointment of one or more attorneys and the furnishing of investigative, expert, or other reasonably necessary services as set forth in this subsection C. Due to the complex, demanding, and protracted nature of death penalty proceedings, the court should consider appointing at least two counsel.

c. Post Conviction Proceedings Seeking to Vacate or Set Aside Death Sentence. In any post conviction proceeding under section 2254 or 2255 of Title 28, United States Code, seeking to vacate or set aside a death sentence, any defendant who is or becomes financially unable to obtain adequate representation or investigative, expert, or other reasonably necessary services shall be entitled to the appointment of one or more attorneys and the furnishing of investigative, expert, or other reasonably necessary services as set forth in this subsection C.

2. *Qualifications.* If an appointment under subsection C(1)(b), is made before judgment, at least one attorney so appointed must have been admitted to practice in the court for not less than five years, and must have had not less than three years experience in the actual trial of felony prosecutions in the court. Pursuant to 18 U.S.C. § 3005, at least one of the attorneys appointed must be knowledgeable in the law applicable to capital cases.

Pursuant to 18 U.S.C. § 3005, in assigning counsel under this section, the court shall consider the recommendation of the Indiana Federal Community Defenders, Inc.

If an appointment under subsection C(1)(b), is made after judgment, at least one attorney so appointed must have been admitted to practice in a federal court of appeals for not less than five years, and must have had not less than three years experience in the handling of federal appeals in felony cases.

In appointing counsel in federal capital appeals and federal post conviction cases, the court should consider the recommendation of the Indiana Federal Community Defenders, Inc.

Counsel appointed in federal capital prosecutions, appeals, or post conviction cases shall comply with the American Bar Association's Guidelines for the Appointment and Performance of Defense Counsel in Death Penalty Cases.

With respect to this subsection, the court, for good cause, may appoint another attorney whose background, knowledge, or experience would otherwise enable him or her to represent, properly, the defendant, with due consideration to the seriousness of the possible penalty and to the unique and complex nature of the litigation.

D. Eligibility of Representation.

1. *Fact-finding.* The determination of eligibility for representation under the CJA is a judicial function to be performed by a Judicial Officer after making appropriate inquiries concerning the person's financial eligibility.

2. *Disclosure of Change in Eligibility.* If, at any time after appointment, counsel obtains information that a client is financially able to make payment, in whole or in part, for legal or other services in connection with his or her representa-

tion, and the source of the attorney's information is not protected as a privileged communication, counsel shall advise the court.

IV.   COMPOSITION OF PANEL OF PRIVATE ATTORNEYS

A.   Criminal Justice Act Panels.

1. *Approval.*   The court shall establish for each division of the court a panel of private attorneys (hereinafter referred to as the "CJA Panel" or "CJA Panels") who are eligible and willing to be appointed to provide representation under the CJA. The court shall approve attorneys for membership on the CJA Panels for each division of the court.

2. *Size.*   The court shall fix, periodically, the size of the CJA Panel for each division of the court.   The panel shall be large enough to provide a sufficient number of experienced attorneys to handle the CJA caseload, yet small enough so that panel members will receive an adequate number of appointments to maintain their proficiency in federal criminal defense work, and thereby provide a high quality of representation.

3. *Eligibility.*   Attorneys who serve on a CJA Panel must be members in good standing of the federal bar of this court and have demonstrated experience in, and knowledge of, the Federal Rules of Criminal Procedure, the Federal Rules of Evidence, and the Sentencing Guidelines.   Attorneys who serve on a CJA Panel will also be expected to have and maintain acceptable standards of competence, judgment, character and demeanor to provide their clients with all the benefits of high quality legal counsel.

4. *Equal Opportunity.*   All qualified attorneys shall be encouraged to participate in the furnishing of representation in CJA cases, without regard to race, color, religion, sex, age, national origin or disabling condition.

B.   Existing CJA Panels.

1. *Prior Establishment.*   The court previously established four panels of eligible private attorneys willing to provide representation to those persons eligible for services within the jurisdiction of the court pursuant to the CJA: the "Indianapolis CJA Panel", the "Terre Haute CJA Panel", the "Evansville CJA Panel" and the "New Albany CJA Panel".

2. *Confirmation of Existing CJA Panels.*   The existing previously established CJA Panels are recognized and confirmed.

C.   Application for Membership on a CJA Panel.

1. *Application.*   Application forms for CJA Panel membership shall be made available, upon request, by the Clerk.

2. *Submission of Application.*   Completed applications for CJA Panel membership shall be submitted to the Clerk as to the Evansville and New Albany CJA Panels, or the Community Defender as to the Indianapolis and Terre Haute CJA Panels.   Completed applications will be forwarded to the appropriate person(s) charged with review and decision making.

D.   Appointments to a CJA Panel.

1. *Indianapolis and Terre Haute CJA Panels.*

a.   Referral to Panel Selection Committee.   Applications for membership shall first be referred to the CJA Panel Selection Committee.

b.   Appointments to the CJA Panel.   Appointments to the CJA Panel shall be made after receiving recommendations from the Panel Selection Committee.

c.   The Panel Selection Committee.

(i).   Membership.   A Panel Selection Committee shall be established by the court.   The Committee shall be appointed by the Chief Judge of the court and shall consist of one District Judge assigned to the court, one Magistrate Judge assigned to the court, one attorney member of the Indianapolis or Terre Haute CJA Panels, and the Executive Director of the Community Defender. The Committee shall select its own Chairperson.

(ii). Duties. The Panel Selection Committee shall meet at least once a year or upon call of the Chairperson to consider applications for any vacancies on the panel. The Committee shall review the qualifications of applicants and recommend, for approval by the court, those applicants best qualified to fill vacancies.

The Panel Selection Committee shall be empowered to review the operation and administration of the Indianapolis and Terre Haute CJA Panels and recommend to the court any changes deemed necessary or appropriate regarding the appointment process and panel management.

2. *Evansville and New Albany CJA Panels.* Appointments to the Evansville and New Albany CJA Panels shall be made by the court.

E. Term of Appointment.

1. *Three–Year Term.* Members of CJA Panels shall serve three-year terms, except in those instances in which an attorney is appointed to fill an unexpired term.

2. *Presumption of Reappointment.* A private attorney who provides high quality representation as a member of a CJA Panel shall have a presumption of reappointment.

3. *Appointments Subject to the Pleasure of the Court.* Notwithstanding the provisions of paragraphs E(1) and 2 above, each member of a CJA Panel shall serve at the pleasure of the court.

F. Inquiry into Continued Service on a CJA Panel.

1. *Indianapolis and Terre Haute CJA Panels.* The Executive Director of the Community Defender shall, from time to time, inquire as to the continued availability and willingness of each member of the Indianapolis and Terre Haute CJA Panels to accept future appointments.

2. *Evansville CJA Panel.* The District Judge or Magistrate Judge assigned to the Evansville Division shall, from time to time, inquire as to the continued availability and willingness of each member of the Evansville CJA Panel to accept future appointments.

3. *New Albany CJA Panel.* The District Judge or Magistrate Judge assigned to the New Albany Division shall, from time to time, inquire as to the continued availability and willingness of each member of the New Albany CJA Panel to accept future appointments.

G. Maintenance of Lists of Members of CJA Panels.
The Clerk and the Community Defender shall maintain a current list of all attorneys on the Indianapolis and Terre Haute CJA Panels, and the Community Defender will maintain updated resumes detailing each member's experience in the field of criminal law. The Clerk shall maintain a current list of all attorneys on the Evansville and New Albany CJA Panels, as well as updated resumes detailing each member's experience in the field of criminal law. The membership lists must contain the current office addresses and telephone numbers for each panel attorney. The Clerk will provide a copy of these lists to each Judicial Officer in the district.

H. Management of the CJA Panels.

1. *The Indianapolis and Terre Haute CJA Panels.* The Community Defender shall be responsible for the systematic distribution of actions to and for the management of the Indianapolis and Terre Haute CJA Panels.

2. *The Evansville CJA Panel.* Any Magistrate Judge assigned to the Evansville Division, or if absent, any District Judge assigned to the Evansville Division, shall be responsible for the systematic distribution of actions to and management of the Evansville CJA Panel.

3. *The New Albany Division.* The part-time Magistrate Judge assigned to the New Albany Division, or if absent, any District Judge assigned to the New Albany Division, shall be responsible for the systematic distribution of actions to and management of the New Albany CJA Panel.

V. APPOINTMENT OF CJA ATTORNEYS

A. Indianapolis and Terre Haute Divisions.

1. *Appointment of the Community Defender.* Upon the determination by a Judicial Officer of a need for the appointment of counsel, the Judicial Officer shall notify the Community Defender of the need for counsel and the nature of the action, except as provide in subsection V(A)(4) below. The court will ordinarily appoint the Executive Director of the Community Defender or an attorney employed by the Community Defender.

2. *Unavailability of the Community Defender.* If the Community Defender, or designee, is unable to accept the appointment, the Executive Director of the Community Defender shall notify an available member of the Indianapolis or Terre Haute CJA Panel who has handled, or assisted in, an action of equal or greater complexity than the action for which appointment of counsel is required. The Executive Director shall provide the name of the selected panel member to the Judicial Officer.

3. *Inappropriateness of Appointment of the Community Defender.* When circumstances of an action indicate that it would be inappropriate for the Community Defender to be involved in the appointment of counsel, the court may appoint a member of the Indianapolis or Terre Haute CJA Panel without consulting the Community Defender, but shall advise the Community Defender of the appointment. When necessary, the court may appoint a qualified defense lawyer who is not a member of the Indianapolis or Terre Haute CJA Panel.

4. *Required Appointment of Private Attorneys.* Where practical and cost effective, the Community Defender shall insure that approximately twenty-five percent (25%) of the appointments in the Indianapolis and Terre Haute Divisions are assigned to members of the Indianapolis and Terre CJA Panels.

B. Evansville Division. Upon the determination of the need for the appointment of counsel, any District Judge or Magistrate Judge, assigned to or handling a case filed or pending in the Evansville Division, shall appoint an available member of the Evansville CJA Panel who has handled, or assisted in, an action of equal or greater complexity than the action for which appointment of counsel is required. When necessary, the court may appoint a qualified defense lawyer who is not a member of the Evansville CJA Panel.

C. New Albany Division. Upon the determination of the need for the appointment of counsel, any District Judge or Magistrate Judge, assigned to or handling a case filed or pending in the New Albany Division, shall appoint an available member of the New Albany CJA Panel who has handled, or assisted in, an action of equal or greater complexity than the action for which appointment of counsel is required. When necessary, the court may appoint a qualified defense lawyer who is not a member of the New Albany CJA Panel.

D. Emergency. In the event of an emergency, *i.e.*, weekends, holidays, or other non-working hours, a Judicial Officer may appoint any attorney from the appropriate CJA Panel. In all actions where members of the Indianapolis and Terre Haute CJA Panel are appointed out of sequence, the appointing Judicial Officer shall notify the Community Defender of the attorney's name and the appointment date.

E. Special Appointment. When a Judicial Officer presiding over a case, or the Chief Judge, if no Judicial Officer has been assigned to the case, determines that the appointment of a specific attorney is in the interest of justice, economy or continuity of representation, or there is some compelling circumstances warranting his or her appointment, the attorney may be admitted to a CJA Panel pro hac vice and appointed to represent the CJA defendant.

Consideration for preserving the effectiveness of the CJA Panel selection process suggests that such appointments should be made only in exceptional circumstances. Further, the attorney, who may or may not maintain an office in the district, should possess such qualities as would qualify him or her for admission to a CJA Panel in this judicial district in the ordinary course of Panel selection.

F. Rotation of CJA Panel Members. Appointments from the list of private Panel attorneys should be made on a rotational basis, subject to the court's discretion to make exceptions due to the nature and complexity of the case, an attorney's experience, and geographical considerations. This procedure should result in a balanced distribution of appointments and compensation among the members of the CJA Panels and quality representation for each CJA defendant.

G. Record of Assignments.

1. *Indianapolis and Terre Haute CJA Panels.* The Community Defender shall maintain a public record of assignments of private attorneys from the Indianapolis and Terre Haute CJA Panels, and, when appropriate, supporting statistical data.

2. *Evansville and New Albany CJA Panels.* The Clerk shall maintain a public record of assignments of private attorneys from the Evansville and New Albany CJA Panels, and, when appropriate, supporting statistical data.

H. Distribution of a Copy of This Plan. Each private attorney shall be provided a copy of this Amended CJA Plan by the Clerk upon the attorney's first appointment under the CJA or designation as a CJA Panel member. The Clerk shall maintain a current copy of the CJA Guidelines for the use of members of the CJA Panels and shall make known to such attorneys its availability.

VII.* DUTIES OF APPOINTED COUNSEL

A. Standards. Services rendered by an appointed attorney shall be commensurate with those rendered if counsel were privately employed by the person.

B. Professional Conduct. Appointed counsel shall conform to the highest standards of professional conduct, including but not limited to the provisions of the Rules of Professional Conduct adopted by the Supreme Court of the State of Indiana and other standards for professional conduct adopted by the court.

C. No Receipt of Other Payment. Appointed counsel may not require, request or accept any payment or promise of payment or any other valuable consideration for representation under the appointment, unless such payment is approved by Order of the court.

D. Continuing Representation. Once counsel is appointed under the CJA, counsel shall continue the representation until the matter, including appeals or review by *certiorari* is closed; until substitute counsel has filed a notice of appearance; until an order has been entered allowing or requiring the person represented to proceed pro se; or until the appointment is terminated by court order.

In cases involving a defendant charged with a crime punishable by death or post conviction proceedings seeking to vacate or set aside a death sentence, unless replaced by similarly qualified counsel upon the attorney's own motion or upon motion of the defendant, each appointed attorney shall represent the defendant throughout every subsequent stage of available judicial proceedings, including pretrial proceedings, trial, sentencing, motions for new trial, appeals, applications for writ of *certiorari* to the Supreme Court of the United States, and all available post-conviction process, together with applications for stays of execution and other appropriate motions and procedures, and shall also represent the defendant in such competency proceedings and proceedings for executive or other clemency as may be available to the defendant.

VIII. DUTIES OF LAW ENFORCEMENT AND RELATED AGENCIES

A. Pretrial Services Interview. When practicable, unless the right to counsel is waived or the defendant otherwise consents to a pretrial interview without counsel, financially eligible defendants will be furnished appointed counsel prior to being interviewed by a pretrial services officer.

When counsel has been appointed, the pretrial services officer will provide counsel notice and a reasonable opportunity to attend any interview of the defendant by the pretrial services officer prior to the initial pretrial release hearing (*see*, 18 U.S.C. § 3154(1)) or a detention hearing held under 18 U.S.C. § 3142(f).

B. Notice of Indictment or Criminal Information. Upon the return or unsealing of an indictment or the filing of a criminal information, the United States Attorney shall immediately mail or otherwise deliver a copy of the document to the defendant and defendant's appointed or retained counsel. If counsel for the defendant is unknown, for cases assigned to the Indianapolis or Terre Haute Divisions, a copy of the document shall be delivered to the Community Defender.

Upon the filing or unsealing of a petition to revoke or modify probation or supervised release, the Clerk shall immediately mail or otherwise deliver a copy of the document to the defendant and defendant's appointed or retained counsel. If counsel for the defendant is unknown and the case is assigned to the Indianapolis or Terre Haute Division, a copy of the document shall be delivered to the Community Defender. If counsel for the defendant is unknown and the case is assigned to the Evansville or New Albany Division, previously appointed or retained counsel shall be contacted to determine if continued representation will occur.

IX. MISCELLANEOUS

A. Forms. Standard forms pertaining to the CJA and approved by the Judicial Conference of the United States or its Committee on Defender Services and prescribed and distributed by the Director of the Administrative Office of the United States Courts shall be used, where applicable, in all proceedings under this Amended CJA Plan.

B. Claims.

1. *Indianapolis Division.* Absent conflicts of interest, claims for compensation of private attorneys providing representation in the Indianapolis Division under the CJA shall be submitted on the appropriate CJA form to the office of the Community Defender. That office shall review the claim form for mathematical and technical accuracy, for reasonableness, for recordation of statistical information, and for conformity with the CJA Guidelines. If correct, the Community Defender shall forward the claim form for consideration by the appropriate Judicial Officer. The court will exert its best effort to avoid delays in reviewing payment vouchers.

2. *Evansville, Terre Haute and New Albany Divisions.* Absent conflicts of interest, claims for compensation of private attorneys providing representation in the Evansville, Terre Haute and New Albany Divisions under the CJA shall be submitted on the appropriate CJA form to the office of the Clerk in the division where the case was assigned. The Clerk shall review the claim form for mathematical and technical accuracy, for reasonableness, for recordation of statistical information, and for conformity with the CJA Guidelines. If after review, the Clerk shall forward the claim form for consideration by the appropriate Judicial Officer. The court will exert its best effort to avoid delays in reviewing payment vouchers.

C. Limitation on Review of Claims. The CJA provides that the reviewing Judicial Officer shall fix the compensation and reimbursement to be paid to private counsel. If the court determines that a claim should be reduced, private counsel will be provided (a) prior notice of the proposed reduction with a brief statement of the reason(s), and (b) an opportunity to address the matter. However, notice need not be given to a private attorney where the reduction is based on mathematical or technical errors.

Nothing contained in this Plan or in the CJA Guidelines should be construed as requiring a hearing or as discouraging the court from communicating informally with counsel about questions or concerns in person, telephonically, or electronically, as deemed appropriate or necessary.

D. Supersession. This Plan supersedes all prior Criminal Justice Act Plans of this court.

X.   EFFECTIVE DATE

This Plan, as amended this 12th day of November 2009, shall take effect when approved by the Judicial Council of the Seventh Circuit.

[Effective May 26, 2006; amended effective December 2, 2009.]

* [**Publisher's Note:** So in original.   No section VI. promulgated.]

SPEEDY TRIAL PLAN

Pursuant to the requirements of Rule 50 of the Federal Rules of Criminal Procedure, the Speedy Trial Act of 1974 (18 U.S.C. § 3161 et seq., Chapter 208), the Speedy Trial Act Amendments Act of 1979 (Pub. L. 96–43, 93 Stat. 327), the Federal Juvenile Delinquency Act (18 U.S.C. §§ 5036 and 5037), and the Bail Reform Act of 1984 (18 U.S.C. §§ 3141–3156), the Judges of the United States District Court for the Southern District of Indiana have adopted the following Plan setting forth time limits and procedures to minimize undue delay and to further the prompt disposition of criminal cases and certain juvenile proceedings. This Plan shall take effect upon approval of the Judicial Council of the Seventh Circuit.

A. Applicability.

1. *Offenses.* The time limits set forth herein are applicable to all criminal offenses triable in this court, including cases triable by United States Magistrate Judges, except for petty offenses as defined in 18 U.S.C. § 1 (3). Except as specifically provided, the time limits are not applicable to proceedings under the Federal Juvenile Delinquency Act. (18 U.S.C. § 3172).

2. *Persons.* The time limits are applicable to persons accused who have been arrested or served with a summons but not indicted or informed against as well as those who have; and the word "defendant" includes such persons unless the context indicates otherwise.

B. Priorities in Scheduling Criminal Cases.
Preference shall be given to criminal proceedings as far as practicable as required by Rule 50 of the Federal Rules of Criminal Procedure. The trial or other disposition of cases involving a detained person who is being held in detention solely because he or she is awaiting trial, and a released person who is awaiting trial and has been designated by the attorney for the Government as being of high risk, shall be accorded priority. (18 U.S.C. § 3164(a)).

C. Time Limit Within Which an Indictment of Information Must Be Filed.

1. *Time Limits.* Any information or indictment charging an individual with the commission of an offense to be prosecuted in this district shall be filed within 30 days from the date on which such individual was arrested or served with a summons in connection with such charges. (18 U.S.C. § 3161(b)).

2. *Grand Jury Not in Session.* If an individual is charged with a felony to be prosecuted in this district, and no grand jury in the district has been in session during the 30–day period prescribed in paragraph C.1. above, the period of time for filing of the indictment shall be extended an additional 30 days. (18 U.S.C. § 3161(b)).

3. *Measurement of Time Periods.* If a person has not been arrested or served with a summons on a federal charge, an arrest shall be deemed to have been made at the earliest of such times as the person:

(a) is held in custody solely for the purpose of responding to a federal charge;

(b) is delivered to the custody of a federal official in connection with a federal charge; or

(c) appears before a judicial officer in connection with a federal charge.

4. *Related Procedures.*

(a) At the time of the earliest appearance before a judicial officer of a person who has been arrested for an offense not charged in an indictment or information, the judicial officer shall establish for the record the date on which the arrest took place.

(b) In the absence of a showing to the contrary, a summons shall be deemed to have been served on the date of service shown on the return thereof.

D. Time Within Which Trial Must Commence.

1. *Time Limits—General.* In any case in which a plea of not guilty is entered, the trial of a defendant charged in an information or indictment with commission of an offense shall commence within 70 days from the filing date (and making public) of the information or indictment, or from the date the defendant has appeared before a judicial officer of the court in which such charge is pending, whichever date last occurs. If a defendant consents in writing to be tried before a magistrate judge on a complaint, the trial shall commence within 70 days from the date of such consent. (18 U.S.C. § 3161(c)(1)).

2. *Superseding Charges.* If, after an indictment or information has been filed against a defendant, another complaint, indictment, or information is filed which charges the defendant with the same offense or with an offense required to be joined with the offense initially charged, the time limit applicable to the subsequent charge shall be determined as follows:

(a) If the original indictment or information was dismissed on motion of the defendant before the filing of the subsequent charge, the time limit shall be determined without regard to the existence of the original charge. (18 U.S.C. § 3161(d)(1)). A dismissal of the indictment on order of the judge with the consent of the defendant shall be considered dismissed on motion of the defendant.

(b) If the original indictment or information was dismissed on motion of the attorney for the Government and thereafter a charge is filed against the defendant for the same offense, or any offense required to be joined with that offense, the trial shall commence within the time limit for commencement of trial on the original indictment or information, but any period of delay from the date the charge was dismissed to the date the time limit would commence to run as to the subsequent charge shall be excluded from the computations (18 U.S.C. § 3161(h)(5)).

(c) If the original indictment or information remains pending at the time the subsequent charge is filed, the trial shall commence within the time limit for commencement of the trial on the original indictment or information.

(d) If the subsequent charge is contained in a complaint, the formal time limit within which an indictment or information shall be obtained on the charge shall be determined without regard to the existence of the original indictment or information, but earlier action may be required if the time limit for commencement of trial is to be satisfied.

3. *Withdrawal of Plea.* If a defendant enters a plea of guilty or nolo contendre to any or all charges in an indictment or information and is subsequently permitted to withdraw it, the time limit shall be determined for all counts as if the indictment or information were filed on the day the order permitting withdrawal of the plea became final. (18 U.S.C. § 3161(i)).

4. *Charges Reinstated Following Appeal.* If the defendant is to be tried upon an indictment or information dismissed by a trial court and reinstated following an appeal, the trial shall commence within 70 days from the date the action occasioning the trial becomes final, except that the court retrying the case may extend the period for trial not to exceed 180 days from the date the action occasioning the trial becomes final if the unavailability of witnesses or other factors resulting from the passage of time shall make trial within 70 days impractical. (18 U.S.C. § 3161(d)(2)).

5. *Charges Reinstated Following Mistrial or Order for Retrial.* If the defendant is to be tried again following a declaration by the trial judge of a mistrial or following an order of such judge for a new trial, the trial shall commence within 70 days from the date the action occasioning the retrial becomes final. If the defendant is to be tried again following an appeal or a collateral attack, the trial shall commence within 70 days from the date the action occasioning the retrial becomes final, except that the court retrying the case may extend the period for retrial not to exceed 180 days from the date the action occasioning the retrial becomes final if

unavailability of witnesses or other factors resulting from passage of time shall make trial within 70 days impractical.   (18 U.S.C. § 3161(e)).

6.   *Measurement of Time Periods.*   For purposes of this section:

(a) If a defendant signs a written consent to be tried before a magistrate judge on a complaint and no indictment or information charging the offense has been filed, the time limit shall run from the date of such consent.

(b) In the event of a transfer to this district under Rule 20 of the Federal Rules of Criminal Procedure, the indictment or information shall be deemed filed in this district when the papers in the proceeding, or certified copies thereof, are received by the clerk of the court.

(c) A trial in a jury case shall be deemed to commence at the beginning of voir dire.

(d) A trial in a non-jury case shall be deemed to commence on the day the case is called, provided that some substantial step in the trial procedure immediately follows.

7.   *Related Procedures.*

(a) At the time of a defendant's earliest appearance before a judicial officer of this district, the officer shall take appropriate steps to assure that the defendant is represented by counsel and shall appoint counsel when appropriate under the Criminal Justice Act and Rule 44 of the Federal Rules of Criminal Procedure.

(b) The court has sole responsibility for setting cases for trial after consultation with counsel for the defendant and the attorney for the Government.   At the earliest practicable time, each case shall be set for trial on a day certain or listed for trial on a weekly or other short-term trial calendar at a place within the judicial district.   (18 U.S.C. § 3161(a)).

(c) A conflict in schedules of the attorney for the Government or defense counsel shall be grounds for a continuance or delay in the setting of a trial date only if approved by the court after being called to its attention at the earliest practicable time.   To the extent practicable, the attorney for the Government shall assign or reassign cases in such manner that the Government shall be prepared to try cases on the date set pursuant to subparagraph (b) of this section.

(d) At or promptly after the time of the filing of a complaint, indictment, or information such as described in above subparagraphs D.2(b) or (c), the attorney for the Government shall inform the court of that circumstance and his or her position with respect to the computation of the time limits.

(e) Pre–trial hearings deemed necessary to assist counsel in the preparation or disposition of their case shall be conducted as soon after the arraignment as possible, consistent with the priorities of other matters on the court's criminal docket.

E.   Persons Detained or Designated as Being of High Risk.

1.   *Time Limits.*   Notwithstanding any longer time periods that may be permitted under sections C and D above, the trial or other disposition of cases involving:

(a) a detained person who is being held in detention solely because he or she is awaiting trial, and

(b) a released person who is awaiting trial and has been designated by the attorney for the Government as being of high risk

shall commence not later than 90 days following the beginning of such continuous custody or designation of high risk by the attorney for the Government.   (18 U.S.C. § 3164(b)).

2.   *Measurement of Time Periods.*   For purposes of this section:

(a) A defendant is deemed to be in detention awaiting trial when he or she is arrested on a federal charge.   Detention is deemed to be solely because the defendant is awaiting trial unless the person exercising custodial authority has an independent basis (not including a detainer) for continuing to hold the defendant.

(b) If a case is transferred pursuant to Rule 20 of the Federal Rules of Criminal Procedure and the defendant subsequently rejects disposition under Rule 20 or the court declines to accept the plea, a new period of continuous detention awaiting trial shall begin at that time.

(c) A trial shall be deemed to commence as provided in subparagraphs D.6(c) and (d).

3. *Related Procedures.*

(a) If a defendant is being held in custody solely for the purpose of awaiting trial, the attorney for the Government shall advise the court at the earliest practicable time of the date of the beginning of such custody.

(b) The attorney for the Government shall advise the court at the earliest practicable time (usually at the hearing with respect to bail) if the defendant is considered to be high risk.

(c) If the court finds that the filing of a high-risk designation as a public record may result in prejudice to the defendant, it may order the designation sealed for such period as is necessary to protect the defendant's right to a fair trial, but not beyond the time that the court's judgment in the case becomes final. During the time the designation is under seal, it shall be made known to the defendant and his counsel but shall not be made known to other persons without the permission of the court.

F. Minimum Period for Defense Preparation. Unless the defendant consents in writing to the contrary, the trial shall not commence less than 30 days from the date on which the defendant first appears through counsel or expressly waives counsel and elects to proceed pro se. (18 U.S.C. § 3161(c)(2)).

In circumstances in which the 70–day time limit for commencing trial on a charge in an indictment or information is determined by reference to an earlier indictment or information pursuant to subsection D.2, the 30–day minimum period shall also be determined by reference to the earlier indictment or information.

When prosecution is resumed on an original indictment or information following a mistrial, appeal, or withdrawal of a guilty plea, a new 30–day minimum period shall not begin to run. In all such cases the court will schedule trials so as to permit defense counsel adequate preparation time in the light of all circumstances.

G. Exclusion of Time from Computations.

1. *Applicability.* In computing any time limit under sections C, D, and E above, the periods of delay set forth in 18 U.S.C. § 3161(h) shall be excluded. Such periods of delay shall not be excluded in computing the minimum period for commencement of trial under section F above.

2. *Basis for Excludable Time.* At the time it orders time excluded from the computation of any time limit under 18 U.S.C. § 3161, the court shall set forth on the record, in writing or orally, the basis for the finding of excludable time. The clerk of court shall enter on the docket information with respect to excludable period(s) of time for each criminal defendant.

3. *Stipulations.*

(a) The attorney for the Government and the attorney for the defendant may at any time enter into stipulations with respect to excludable time and submit the same to the court for its review and approval.

(b) Once accepted by the court, a stipulation with respect to excludable time shall be conclusive as between the parties unless it has no basis in fact or law. To the extent consistent with law, it shall similarly be conclusive as to a codefendant for the limited purpose of determining, under 18 U.S.C. § 3161(h)(7), whether time has run against the defendant entering into the stipulation.

4. *Pre–Indictment Procedures.*

(a) In the event that the attorney for the Government anticipates that an indictment or information will not be filed within the time limit set forth in Section C of this Plan, the attorney for the Government shall file a written motion with the court for a determination of excludable time. In the event that the attorney for the Government seeks a continuance under 18 U.S.C. § 3161(h)(7), the attorney for the Government shall file a written motion with the court requesting such a continuance.

(b) The motion of the attorney for the Government seeking a determination of excludable time or continuance under subparagraph (a) above shall state:

(1) the period of time proposed for exclusion; and

(2) the basis of the proposed exclusion.

If the motion is for a continuance under 18 U.S.C. § 3161(h)(7), it shall also state whether or not the defendant is being held in custody on the basis of the complaint.

In appropriate circumstances, the motion may include a request that some or all of the supporting material be considered ex parte and in camera.

(c) The court may grant a continuance under 18 U.S.C. § 3161(h)(7) for either a specific period of time or a period to be determined by reference to an event (such as recovery from illness) not within the control of the government. If the continuance is to a date not certain, the court shall require one or both parties to inform the court promptly when and if the circumstances that justify the continuance no longer exist. In addition, the court shall require one or both parties to file periodic reports bearing on the continued existence of such circumstances. The court shall determine the frequency of such reports in light of the facts of the particular case.

5. *Post–Indictment Procedures.*

(a) In the event that the court extends the time for a trial beyond the time limit set forth in sections D, E, and E above, the court shall determine whether the limit may be recomputed by excluding time pursuant to 18 U.S.C. § 3161(h).

(b) If the court finds that an extension of the time for trial beyond the time limits set forth in paragraphs D, E, and E is justified, the court shall state for the record, either orally or in writing, the fact or facts on which such determination is made. If the extension is to a date not certain, the court shall require one or both parties to inform the court promptly when and if the circumstances that justify the continuance no longer exist and to file periodic reports bearing on the continued existence of such circumstances. The court shall determine the required frequency of such reports in light of all the relevant circumstances.

H. Time Limits Within Which Defendants Should Be Sentenced.

1. *Time Limit.* A defendant shall ordinarily be sentenced within 90 days of conviction.

2. *Related Procedures.* For good cause, the court may order a presentence investigation commenced prior to a plea of guilty or nolo contendere or conviction.

I. Special Time Limitations Applicable to Juvenile Proceedings.

(a) *Time Within Which Trial Must Commence.* An alleged delinquent who is in detention pending trial shall be brought to trial within 30 days of the date on which such detention was begun, unless the Attorney General shows that additional delay was caused by the juvenile or his counsel, or consented to by the juvenile and his counsel, or would be in the interest of justice in the particular case. Delays attributable solely to court calendar congestion may not be considered in the interest of justice (18 U.S.C. § 5036).

(b) *Time of Dispositional Hearing.* If a juvenile is adjudicated delinquent, a separate dispositional hearing shall be held no later than 20 court days after trial, unless the court has ordered further study of the juvenile in accordance with 18 U.S.C. § 5037(a) and (e). [Note: subsection (a) erroneously refers to (d) instead of (e) due to an amendment to 18 U.S.C. § 5037 that did not correct cross–references.]

J. Sanctions.

(a) *Dismissal or Release From Custody.* Failure to comply with the requirements of the Speedy Trial Act, 18 U.S.C. § 3161 et seq., may entitle the defendant to dismissal of the charges against him or release from pretrial custody. However, nothing in this Plan shall be construed to require that a case be dismissed or a defendant released from custody in circumstances in which such action would not be required by 18 U.S.C. § 3162 or 18 U.S.C. § 3164.[1]

(b) *Alleged Juvenile Delinquents.* If an alleged delinquent in detention pending trial is not brought to trial within 30 days from the date upon which such detention was begun, the information shall be dismissed on motion of the alleged delinquent or at the direction of the court, unless the Attorney General shows that additional delay was caused by the juvenile or his counsel, or consented to by the juvenile and his counsel, or would be in the interest of justice in the particular case. (18 U.S.C. § 5036).

(c) *High Risk Defendants.* With regard to a detainee detained or designated as of high risk whose trial has not commenced within the time limits set forth in 18 U.S.C. § 3164(b), failure to commence the trial of the detainee, through no fault of the accused or his counsel, or failure to commence trial of a designated releasee, through no fault of the attorney for the Government, shall result in the automatic review by the court of the conditions of release.

A designated releasee, as specified in 18 U.S.C. § 3164(a), who is found by the court to have intentionally delayed the trial of his or her case shall be subject to an order of the court modifying his or her nonfinancial conditions of release to ensure that he or she shall appear at trial as required. 18 U.S.C. § 3164(c).

(c)* *Discipline of Attorneys.* The court may punish counsel as provided in 18 U.S.C. § 3162(b) and (c) in any case in which counsel for the defendant or the attorney for the Government:

    (i) knowingly allows the case to be set for trial without disclosing the fact that a necessary witness would be unavailable for trial;

    (ii) files a motion solely for the purpose of delay which he or she knows is totally frivolous and without merit;

    (iii) makes a statement for the purpose of obtaining a continuance which he or she knows to be false and which is material to the granting of a continuance; or

    (iv) otherwise willfully fails to proceed to trial without justification consistent with 18 U.S.C. § 3161.

    (18 U.S.C. § 3162).

K. Persons Serving Terms of Imprisonment.
If the attorney for the Government knows that a person charged with an offense is serving a term of imprisonment in any penal institution, the attorney for the Government shall promptly seek to obtain the presence of the prisoner for trial, or cause a detainer to be filed, in accordance with the provisions of 18 U.S.C. § 3161(j).

L. Monitoring Compliance with Time Limits.

(a) *Responsibilities of Clerk.* The clerk shall maintain and compile such statistical data as is required to be maintained by statute or the Administrative Office of the United States Courts and make the same available to the judicial officers of this district.

(b) *Responsibilities of United States Marshal.* The United States Marshal shall, every two weeks, furnish the attorney for the Government with a statement of persons in federal custody and the date of such custody according to his records.

M. Conflict of Law. In the event of conflict between the provisions of this Plan and any provisions contained in the United States Code, the Federal Rules of Criminal Procedure, or applicable Federal Regulations, the provisions contained in the United States Code, Federal Rules of Criminal Procedure, or Federal Regulations shall superseded* this Plan.

This Plan, as adopted this 3rd day of September, 2013, supersedes any and all Plans heretofore adopted and shall constitute the rule of this court.

APPROVED BY THE JUDICIAL COUNCIL OF THE SEVENTH CIRCUIT this 27th day of September, 2013.

[Adopted September 3, 2013.]

1Dismissal may also be required in some cases under the Interstate Agreement on Detainers, 18 U.S.C., Appendix.

* So in original.

UNITED STATES BANKRUPTCY COURT FOR THE SOUTHERN DISTRICT OF INDIANA

Including Amendments Received Through
November 1, 2015

INTRODUCTION TO RULES EFFECTIVE JUNE 1, 2010

This newest version of the local rules focuses on capturing the procedural changes that have evolved since the arrival of electronic filing and BAPCPA. Many of the current general orders become new rules or are incorporated into existing rules. The rules join the Court's Procedures Manual and its ECF Administrative Policies and Procedures Manual as the third source of guidance on how bankruptcy cases and proceedings are handled.

The rules follow the national numbering system for local rules, which in turn closely parallels the numbering system for the Federal Rules of Bankruptcy Procedure. The rules are accompanied by an expanded table of contents, to make searching for a specific topic simpler.

[Effective June 1, 2010.]

INTRODUCTION TO AMENDMENTS EFFECTIVE JUNE 1, 2011

These Rules were amended effective June 1, 2011. The amendments were mostly technical, to correct errors and ambiguities identified after publication of the original rules in June 2010.

[Effective June 1, 2011.]

INTRODUCTION TO AMENDMENTS EFFECTIVE OCTOBER 11, 2011

These rules were further amended effective October 11, 2011. These amendments were required because of changes to the national rules. One substantive change was the replacement of three-day deadlines for initial case filing requirements with seven-day deadlines. Another was the requirement that applications to employ include the terms of employment.

[Effective October 11, 2011.]

INTRODUCTION TO AMENDMENTS EFFECTIVE OCTOBER 1, 2012

The amendments in October 2012 served multiple purposes. First, the practice of cross-referencing to the District Court's rules by number only had proven to be less than ideal because (a) the cross references required the reader to visit the District Court's rules to find guidance; and (b) occasional failure to track changes the District Court made to its rules resulted in erroneous references. Now, these local rules capture the specific language desired from the District Court's rules, except in those few instances where the subject matter of the District Court's rules rarely arose in bankruptcy cases and proceedings OR the District Court's rules were so voluminous cross-reference remained the most efficient option.

Second, the rules now capture the shifting of responsibility for distribution or service of various documents from the Clerk to parties. The most significant shift concerns Chapter 13 plans, amended plans, and motions to modify plans, which will now be distributed by the trustee, debtor's counsel, or the party seeking to modify the plan, depending on the circumstances.

Third, the edits bring uniformity to the language used in the Rules, particularly references to certificates of service and the distinction between 'serving' and 'distributing' or 'sending' documents.

The amendments include substantive changes as well, a few of which are as follows:

a. A completely revised rule on Motions to Sell, B–6004–1;

b. A new requirement of service on and notice to any domestic support obligation holder when a Chapter 13 debtor seeks discharge, B–4004–1; and

c. Clarification of the procedures for filing pleadings in jointly administered cases, B–1015–1.

[Effective October 1, 2012.]

INTRODUCTION TO AMENDMENTS EFFECTIVE DECEMBER 3, 2012

The Court added a new rule, B–3002.1–2, establishing a procedure for certain lenders to be excused from filing the Notice of Payment Change otherwise required by Fed.R.Bankr.P. 3002.1. The Court also added or edited rules to require parties to indicate their consent to the entry of final judgment by the Bankruptcy Judge [B–7008–1, B–7012–1, and B–9027–1] and added a rule establishing the procedure to be followed when the Judge determines that he or she cannot enter a final order or judgment under the U.S. Constitution and the parties have not consented to such entry.

INTRODUCTION TO AMENDMENTS EFFECTIVE FEBRUARY 19, 2013 AND MAY 1, 2013

The edits effective February 19th are minor, and match Rules B–3015–3, B–4001–3, and B–9019–1 to current procedures. New Rule B–4008–1, which has a delayed effective date of May 1, 2013, moves the requirement found in General Order 10–0007 concerning use of official forms into a local rule and also clarifies the duties of counsel in the reaffirmation agreement process.

INTRODUCTION TO AMENDMENTS EFFECTIVE SEPTEMBER 23, 2013

The amendments effective September 23, 2013, update existing rules so that they more accurately reflect current procedures and recent changes to CM/ECF; shift several general orders into local rules; and edit language for consistency.

[Amended effective October 27, 2014.]

INTRODUCTION TO AMENDMENTS EFFECTIVE FEBRUARY 10, 2014

The amendments effective February 10, 2014, made some technical changes to ensure the rules accurately reflect how CM/ECF operates and to capture some of the Court's requirements that were not clearly noted. The rule on pre-packaged Chapter 11s, which referred to a general order for guidance, has been updated and reference to the general order removed.

[Amended effective October 27, 2014.]

INTRODUCTION TO AMENDMENTS EFFECTIVE OCTOBER 27, 2014

The amendments effective October 27, 2014 made comprehensive changes to the rule on motions to sell pursuant to 11 U.S.C. Section 363—expanding that rule from one to five. The local rule on alternative dispute resolution was also revised extensively. A new rule requires that in a Chapter 13 case the request to avoid a mortgage as wholly unsecured must now be pursued as an adversary proceeding. The rule on withdrawal of the reference was changed to make clear that the Judge can ask the District Court to withdraw the reference. A new rule establishes the procedure for motions to assume or reject executory contracts or leases, and shifts noticing to the filer. Other minor changes were made to match the rules with actual procedures or with recent changes made by the District Court to its local rules.

Note: On December 4, 2014, Local Rule B–7026–1 was removed by vote of the Judges.

[Amended effective October 27, 2014.]

B–1000–1. ABBREVIATIONS AND DEFINITIONS

(a) Abbreviations Applicable to All Rules

(1) *Clerk:* the Clerk of the Court.

(2) *Court:* the United States Bankruptcy Court for the Southern District of Indiana.

(3) *"Fed.R.Bankr.P."* refers to the Federal Rules of Bankruptcy Procedure.

(4) *"S.D.Ind. B–___":* refers to a local rule of the United States Bankruptcy Court for the Southern District of Indiana.

(5) *"S.D.Ind. L.R. ___":* refers to a local rule of the United States District Court for the Southern District of Indiana.

(6) *Fed.R.Civ.P.:* refers to the Federal Rules of Civil Procedure.

(7) *UST:* the United States Trustee for Region 10.

(8) *U.S.C.:* refers to the United States Code.

(9) *SSN:* Social Security Number.

(10) *ITIN:* Individual Taxpayer Identification Number.

(b) Definitions Applicable to All Rules.

(1) *Debtor:* Includes both debtors in a joint case and a debtor-in-possession in a Chapter 11 case. Except as to official forms which must be signed by the debtor (or debtor's representative in a non-individual case), a requirement imposed upon the "Debtor" by these rules shall be performed by counsel for the debtor, if any.

(2) *Trustee or trustee:* Refers to the trustee appointed in a bankruptcy case under 11 U.S.C. §§ 701, 702, 1104, 1202, or 1302.

(3) *Notice List:* the Service List and parties required to receive notice pursuant to Fed.R.Bankr.P. 2002, unless the Debtor has obtained an order limiting notice.

(4) *Service List:* Debtor, Debtor's counsel, the twenty largest unsecured creditors in a Chapter 11 case or, if applicable, the unsecured creditors' committee, the UST, all secured creditors, any indenture trustee, any other committee appointed under 11 U.S.C. § 1102 or 1114, and any counsel or party that has filed an appearance pursuant to S.D.Ind. B–9010–1. If counsel appears for any party listed above, then such counsel shall be substituted for the party for purpose of this definition, absent a specific request by the party that it be retained on the Service List.

(5) Non-electronically in reference to filing means delivery of documents on paper, and includes CDs and diskettes.

(6) Non-electronically in reference to service means other than by electronic means and in accordance with Fed.R.Bankr.P. 7004.

(7) Court's website: refers to the Court's website located at http://www.insb.uscourts.gov.

[Effective June 1, 2010.]

B–1002–1. FILING REQUIREMENTS TO COMMENCE A VOLUNTARY CASE

(a) Initial Filing. A voluntary case is commenced by the filing of a voluntary petition along with the lists, schedules, statements and other documents required by Fed.R.Bankr.P. 1002, 1007 and 11 U.S.C. §§ 301 and 521 or by subparagraph (b) of this rule. Filings can be made either electronically or non-electronically in accordance with S.D.Ind. B–5005–1(c) and B–5005–4.

(b) Emergency Filing; Minimum Required. Any voluntary petition filed without the lists, schedules, statements and other documents required by Fed.R.Bankr.P. 1007 and 11 U.S.C. § 521 must be accompanied by:

(1) if the Debtor is an individual, Exhibit D (Official Form B1D) with a certificate of counseling from the course provider or, if the certificate is not filed, Exhibit D (Official Form B1D) and, if applicable, a motion seeking a deferral or waiver of the credit counseling requirement pursuant to 11 U.S.C. § 109(h);

(2) if the Debtor is an individual, a Statement of Social Security Number (Official Form B21);

(3) the appropriate filing fee, an Application to Pay Filing Fee in Installments (Official Form B3A) or, if a Chapter 7, an application requesting waiver of the filing fee (Official Form B3B);

(4) Uploaded creditor information necessary to provide proper notice to all scheduled creditors or, if filed non-electronically, the CD or diskette required by S.D.Ind. B–1007–1(b); and

(5) in a Chapter 11 case, the list of the twenty largest unsecured creditors and a list of creditors who have or claim to have a secured claim.

Failure to submit the above required items at the time of filing or within seven (7) days thereafter may result in dismissal of the case pursuant to S.D.Ind. B–1017–1(b). Any request for an extension of time to file the other documents required by this rule must comply with Fed.R.Bankr.P. 1007.

(c) Emergency Filing: Dismissal for Failure to Provide Required Documents. Failure to submit the above required items at the time of filing or within seven (7) days thereafter may result in dismissal of the case pursuant to S.D. Ind. B–1017–1(b). Any request for an extension of time to file the other documents required by this rule must comply with Fed. R.Bankr.P. 1007.

(d) Filing a Case Non–Electronically. For cases filed non-electronically, the filing party shall comply with the filing requirements in S.D.Ind. B–5005–1(c).

(e) Place of Filing. For cases filed non-electronically, all petitions, lists, schedules, statements and other documents required by the Bankruptcy Court to commence a case shall be filed with the office of the Clerk in the division where the principal place of business, domicile, residence, or principal assets of the Debtor have been located for such period of time as required by 28 U.S.C. § 1408. If the Court determines that a case has been filed in the incorrect division, the Court may transfer the case to the correct division without notice. All papers tendered for filing after the commencement of a case shall be filed with the office of the Clerk in the division where the case is pending.

[Effective June 1, 2010. Amended effective October 11, 2011; October 27, 2014.]

B–1006–1. PAYMENT OF FILING FEE IN INSTALLMENTS

(a) Application Form. The application shall substantially conform to Official Form B3A.

(b) Payment Schedule. A Debtor filing an application to pay initial filing fees in installments shall propose a payment plan in accordance with the installment fee schedule maintained by the Clerk and available on the Court's website.

(c) Payment Due Dates. Unless otherwise ordered by the Court, payments shall be due on the same day of the month on which the petition was filed. If the installment due date falls on a day when the Court is closed, payment is due no later than the next business day.

(d) Installment Fees in Chapter 13 Cases. Installment fees authorized in a Chapter 13 case shall be paid directly by the Debtor to the office of the Clerk in the division where the case is pending and not through the Chapter 13 plan.

(e) Requirement to Pay Installments Electronically. If the Debtor is represented by counsel, then all payments must be made by counsel and counsel shall pay electronically.

[Effective June 1, 2010. Amended effective September 23, 2013.]

B–1007–1. LISTS, SCHEDULES AND STATEMENTS; TIME LIMITS

(a) Additional Requirements. In addition to complying with the Federal Rules of Bankruptcy Procedure and Official Forms, all schedules and statements shall:

(1) contain a response to each request for information on the statement of affairs and the schedules, even if such response is, "no", "none", or "not applicable";

(2) specifically describe and itemize all property claimed as exempt, and state the statutory reference and section number of the statute under which such exemption is claimed;

(3) list the creditors on each schedule in alphabetical order, including the full mailing address and zip code for each listed creditor, or statement that the address is unknown; and

(4) provide on Schedule E the name and address of any entity holding a domestic support obligation, and identify that entity as the holder of a domestic support obligation, even if the Debtor is current on that obligation when the case is filed.

(b) Providing Creditor Information for Cases Filed Non–Electronically. All cases and any amendment that adds creditors, filed non-electronically, must be accompanied by a CD or diskette listing the complete names and addresses of the creditors listed in the filing. In Chapter 11 cases, the CD or diskette must include equity security holders, if applicable. An exception to the requirement will be considered by the Court if a request for waiver is filed with the petition.

(c) Extensions of Time.

(1) *Motions Generally.* The first motion for an extension of time to file the initial lists, schedules, statements and other documents required to commence a new case shall be treated by the Court as a request for an extension of thirty (30) days from the petition date and the Clerk will provide notice except as described in subparagraph (2). Any subsequent motion for an extension of time shall be served by the Debtor on the trustee, the UST, any examiner, and any committee, and such service shall constitute the notice required by Fed.R.Bankr.P. 1007(c).

(2) *Presumption of No Objection.* The UST and any trustee appointed in a case, any examiner, and any committee are deemed to have no objection to the first motion for extension of time within which to file schedules or related documents Given this subparagraph, the Clerk is not required to give any notice of the first motion for extension of time.

(3) *Debtor's Waiver of Objection to Timeliness of Notice of Presumed Abuse.* If the new date for filing documents is extended beyond the deadline in 11 U.S.C. § 704(b)(1), then the Debtor is deemed to have waived any objection to the timeliness of a notice of presumed abuse which is filed no later than fourteen (14) days after the missing documents are filed or

after the meeting of creditors has been concluded, whichever is later.

[Effective June 1, 2010.   Amended effective June 1, 2011; October 27, 2014.]

B–1007–2. NOTICING, BALLOTING AND CLAIMS AGENTS

(a) Noticing, Balloting, and Claims in Chapter 11 Cases with More than 300 Creditors.

(1) *Requirement.*   Unless excused by order of the Court, if the number of scheduled creditors in any Chapter 11 case exceeds 300, the Debtor or trustee in a Chapter 11 case shall propose the retention pursuant to 28 U.S.C. § 156(c) of an entity to handle noticing (the "Noticing Agent"), an entity to receive and process claims (the "Claims Agent"), and an entity to process plan ballots (the "Balloting Agent"). One entity may serve in all three capacities (the "Agent"). Prior to employment, the proposed Agent shall meet with the Clerk or the Clerk's designee and agree on terms establishing the interactions between the Agent and the Clerk, which shall be incorporated in the order authorizing the employment of the Agent ("the Employment Order") or in a written agreement between the Clerk and the Agent ("the Agreement") that shall be made part of the record.

(2) *Motion.*   The motion(s) to retain noticing, claims, and balloting agent(s), or a motion to be excused from compliance with this rule, or a motion for extension of time, shall be filed within 28 days after the filing of any document or creditor list that causes the number of creditors on the case to exceed 300.

(3) *Contact with Clerk.*   Prior to employment, the proposed Agent shall meet with the Clerk or the Clerk's designee and agree on terms establishing the interactions between the Agent and the Clerk, which shall be incorporated in the order authorizing the employment of the Agent ("the Employment Order") or in a written agreement between the Clerk and the Agent ("the Agreement") that shall be made part of the record.

(b) Noticing Agent.   A Noticing Agent shall distribute notices as directed by the Court and provide proof of service information to the Debtor. That information shall be filed as established by the Agreement or the Employment Order.

(c) Claims Agent.   If a Claims Agent is to be employed, then the Agreement or Employment Order shall address each of the following areas:

(1) *Delivery of Claims Received by the Court.*   The Agreement or the Employment Order should establish procedures for handling of claims filed with the Clerk prior to and after the employment of the Claims Agent.

(2) *Mailing of Proof of Claim Forms and Notice of Bar Date.*   Proofs of Claim with a notice of bar date should be mailed by the Claims Agent and should reflect the scheduled amount of the creditor's claim. Unless alterations are approved by the Court, after notice to any committee and the UST, the forms shall comply substantially with Official Form B10. The forms will instruct claimants to send claims to the Claims Agent and not the Court.

(3) *Handling of Claims and Transfers of Claims.*   Generally, upon receipt of a claim, the Claims Agent should promptly date-stamp it, assign a claim number, scan the original, retain originals in a fire-proof safe or vault, and return a date-stamped copy to the claimant (if a self-addressed, postage paid envelope was provided). The Claims Agent shall review the Court's docket periodically, identify notices transferring claims, and issue such notices as are required by Fed.R.Bankr.P. 3001(e).

(4) *Maintenance of the Claims Register.*   Usually, the Claims Register should be maintained by the Claims Agent.   The Claims Agent should list the claim on the register within three (3) days of receipt, in alphabetical order, according to the name of the claimant (last name for individuals) and include the claimant's address, claim number assigned, date received, dollar amount claimed, and classification of claim.

(5) *Audits of Claims Records.*   The Agreement or the Employment Order may provide for the periodic audit of claims information by the Clerk, a representative of the creditors' committee, or some other entity.

(6) *Transmission of Claims Register.*   The Agreement or Employment Order should provide the mechanism and timing for delivery of a final Claims Register to the Clerk.

(7) *Mailing List.*   In addition to the Claims Register, the Claims Agent should maintain a separate mailing list including the claimants' addresses, edited to reflect any notice of change of address.

(8) *Transfers of Claims.*   The Agreement or the Employment Order should establish responsibility and method for processing transfers of claims.

(9) *Retention/Destruction of Documents.*   The Agreement or Employment Order should provide for the retention or destruction of documents received by the Claims Agent.

(10) *Effect of Conversion.*   The Agreement or the Employment Order shall provide for treatment and disposition of Proofs of Claim if the case is converted to Chapter 7.

(d) Balloting Agent.   The Balloting Agent will receive, record and tabulate ballots. The Agreement or Employment Order should provide for filing of a declaration showing the results of balloting and provide for the retention or destruction of original ballots.

[Effective June 1, 2010. Amended effective June 1, 2011; February 10, 2014.]

B–1009–1. AMENDMENTS OF VOLUNTARY PETITIONS, LISTS, SCHEDULES, AND STATEMENTS OF FINANCIAL AFFAIRS

(a) **Form of Amendments.** All amendments to voluntary petitions, lists, schedules, statements and other documents shall comply with Fed.R.Bankr.P. 1009 and S.D.Ind. B–1007–1, and shall be accompanied by the appropriate filing fee. Any amendment which adds a creditor shall state the date the debt was incurred. Each amendment shall also be verified and signed by the Debtor under penalty of perjury. If an amendment changes the totals on any schedule, then the Debtor shall also file an Amended Summary of Schedules and an Amended Statistical Summary of Certain Liabilities. An amendment which adds creditors and is filed non-electronically shall be accompanied by a CD or diskette listing the added creditors only.

(b) **Amendments Adding or Changing Status of Creditors.** Notice Requirements.

(1) If an amendment adds creditors, the Debtor shall also upload creditor information at the time of filing or, if filed non-electronically, shall provide a new CD or diskette pursuant to S.D. Ind. B–1007–1(c).

(2) The Debtor shall give notice to added creditors and provide copies of notices and documents in the case as appropriate, including the notice of the meeting of creditors with full SSN or ITIN, notice of possible assets, the most recent plan or amended plan, and confirmation hearing notice and shall file a certificate of service that complies with S.D.Ind. B–9013–2. If the Debtor asserts that no notice is required, the Debtor shall file a statement in lieu of notice. A sample form is available on the Court's website.

(3) If a Chapter 11 Debtor amends the creditor schedules and changes the status of a claim not previously listed as contingent, disputed, or unliquidated to a status of contingent, disputed, or unliquidated, or changes the scheduled amount of a claim, the Debtor shall give notice to that creditor of the change in status or amount and of the bar date for filing claims or a deadline for filing claims that is thirty (30) days after the notice, whichever date is later. A sample form is available on the Court's website.

(c) **Amendments to Social Security Number or Individual Taxpayer Identification Number: Notice Requirements.** If a SSN or ITIN is incorrect and the notice of the creditors' meeting has not been issued, the Debtor shall alert the Clerk by telephone to determine the necessary steps to correct the error prior to issuance of the meeting notice. If the notice of the creditors' meeting was issued with an incorrect SSN or ITIN, the Debtor shall contact the Court and complete steps (1) through (4) below, as applicable.

(1) If the SSN or ITIN on any Statement of Social Security Number (Official Form B21) is incorrect, the Debtor shall submit an amended statement to the Clerk.

(2) If the last four digits of the SSN or ITIN listed on the first page of the voluntary petition are incorrect, the Debtor shall file an amended petition with the correct last four digits of the SSN or ITIN.

(3) The Debtor shall distribute notice of the corrected SSN or ITIN to all creditors, trustee, and the UST.

(4) The Debtor shall file a certificate of service that complies with S.D.Ind. B–9013–2.

(d) **Amendments Changing Debtor's Name: Notice Requirements.** If the Debtor's name is incorrect and the notice of the creditors' meeting has not been issued, the Debtor shall alert the Clerk by telephone to determine the necessary steps to correct the error prior to issuance of the meeting notice. If the notice of the creditors' meeting was issued with an incorrect Debtor name, the Debtor shall contact the Court and complete steps (1) through (4) below, as applicable.

(1) If the Debtor's name on the petition is incorrect, the Debtor shall submit an amended petition.

(2) If the Debtor's name used for any electronic signature is incorrect, the Debtor shall file a declaration under penalty of perjury affirming that the documents filed with the incorrect electronic signature were signed in the original by the debtor using the correct name, and that the documents are true and correct to the best of the debtor's knowledge, information, and belief. A sample declaration is available on the Court's website.

(3) The Debtor shall distribute notice of the corrected name to all creditors, trustee, and the UST.

(4) The Debtor shall file a certificate of service that complies with S.D.Ind. B–9013–2.

[Effective June 1, 2010. Amended effective October 1, 2012; October 27, 2014.]

B–1010–1. INVOLUNTARY CASES: CONSENT TO ORDER FOR RELIEF

At any time after the filing of an involuntary petition and before the adjudication of that petition, the alleged debtor can file a consent to the entry of an order for relief. The consent must be as to relief under the chapter proposed by the involuntary petition. After the filing of such consent, the Court may enter the order for relief without further notice or hearing.

[Effective October 27, 2014.]

B–1010–2. INVOLUNTARY PETITIONS COMMENCED BY NON–ATTORNEYS

(a) Seal Upon Initial Filing. If an involuntary petition is commenced by a party who is not represented by counsel, the Clerk shall assign a number to the case and seal the name, the petition, and any documents filed with the petition.

(b) Review of and Continuation or Termination of Seal. Within seven (7) days of the initial filing, the Court shall review the petition and supporting documents and determine whether the seal should be continued, lifted or modified and, if necessary, hold a hearing on same.

(c) Notice to UST. Immediately upon filing of any involuntary petition subject to this Rule the Clerk shall provide telephonic notice of the case to the UST.

[Effective June 1, 2010; Former Rule 1010–1 renumbered effective October 27, 2014.]

B–1015–1. CONSOLIDATION OR JOINT ADMINISTRATION OF CASES PENDING IN SAME COURT

(a) Joint Cases. Unless otherwise ordered by the Court, a joint case commenced pursuant to 11 U.S.C. § 302(a) shall be jointly administered. The separate estates of Debtors in a joint case will only be consolidated upon motion, after notice.

(b) Manner of Joint Administration. Unless otherwise ordered, jointly administered cases shall be administered as follows:

(1) *Designation of Lead Case.* The case with the lowest number shall be designated as the "Lead Case." The other jointly administered cases are known as "Member Cases."

(2) *Caption.* All documents, except those which are to be filed in the Member Case pursuant to subparagraphs (b)(4) and (5) of this rule, shall have the caption with the name and case number of the Lead Case followed by the words "Jointly Administered," except that if one of the Member Cases is for an individual Debtor then the caption shall include the Lead Case name and case number and the case name for any individual Debtor. The caption for any jointly administered case shall not include the word "Consolidated."

(3) *Docket.* Except for the documents listed in subparagraphs (4) and (5) below, a pleading or document filed in any of the jointly administered cases after the entry of the order for joint administration shall be docketed under the case number of the Lead Case. If joint administration is terminated, documents filed after the order terminating joint administration shall be filed and docketed in the separate cases.

(4) *Claims.* A separate claims register shall be maintained for each case. Claims shall be filed only in the name and case number of the Debtor against which the claim is asserted. Any pleading related to a claim filed in a Member Case shall also be filed in that Member Case, and its caption shall have the name and case number of the Member Case. A separate claim must be filed in each jointly administered case in which a claim is asserted.

(5) *Documents to be Filed in Member Cases Separately.* Even if filed after the entry of the order for joint administration, the following documents shall be filed on the dockets of the Member Case as to which the document applies, and the caption of these documents shall have the name and case number of the Member Case:

(A) schedules, statements of financial affairs, and amendments thereto;

(B) in Chapter 11 cases, plans and disclosure statements and objections or other pleadings related thereto, and ballot reports;

(C) trustee final reports and accounts and related notices.

(6) *Ballots.* Ballots shall be styled only in the name and case number of the Member Case for which the plan being voted on was filed.

(c) Substantive Consolidation. Unless otherwise ordered, substantively consolidated cases shall be administered as follows:

(1) *Designation of Lead Case.* The case with the lowest number shall be designated as the "Lead Case".

(2) *Caption.* All documents in substantively consolidated cases shall contain in the caption only the name and case number of the Lead Case, unless one of those cases is for an individual Debtor; then the caption shall include the Lead Case and the case name for any individual Debtor.

(3) *Docket.* A single case docket shall be maintained after the entry of the order for consolidation. If consolidation is later terminated, then documents filed after the order terminating consolidation shall be filed and docketed in the separate cases.

(4) *Claims.* After consolidation all claims shall be filed in the Lead Case. Any claim filed and docketed prior to the consolidation shall be considered as if filed in the substantively consolidated cases but shall remain on the claims register of the originally filed case.

[Effective June 1, 2010. Amended effective June 1, 2011; October 1, 2012; September 23, 2013.]

B–1017–1. CONVERSION AND DISMISSAL

(a) "Automatic" Dismissal.

(1) Notwithstanding 11 U.S.C. § 521(i)(1), no case shall be deemed dismissed except upon entry of an order of dismissal.

(2) If a party moves for dismissal pursuant to § 521(i)(2) and if such motion specifically requests dismissal within seven (7) days, the Court may dismiss the case without further notice or hearing if the docket is missing one of the items identified in 11 U.S.C. § 521(a)(1)(A) and (a)(1)(B)(i) through (v). If the docket contains a filing denominated as such but which the moving party contends fails to include all the required contents, the motion shall identify the alleged deficiency. The movant shall serve the motion on the Debtor, trustee, and UST along with a notice requiring a response to be filed within fourteen (14) days of service. If no such response is timely filed, the Court may dismiss the case without further notice or hearing. If a response is timely filed, the Court will either rule on the motion or set the matter for hearing.

(3) The Court may also dismiss a case pursuant to 11 U.S.C. § 521(i)(1) on its own motion.

(b) Dismissal for Failure to File Required Documents or Pay Filing Fee.

(1) In any case where the lists, schedules, statements and other documents described in Fed. R.Bankr.P. 1007(b)(1), (4), (5) and (6) are not filed with the voluntary petition, within fourteen (14) days thereafter or within such other period set by Court order, the Court shall enter an order of dismissal without further notice or hearing unless a motion for extension of time has been filed prior to the expiration of the period.

(2) The Court shall also enter an order of dismissal without further notice or hearing unless the documents required by Fed.R.Bankr.P. 1007(b)(3) (credit counseling documentation or request for waiver under 11 U.S.C. § 109(h)(4)) and by Fed.R.Bankr.P. 1007(f) (SSN statement, Official Form B21) are filed with the voluntary petition or within seven (7) days thereafter.

(3) In any case where the filing fee has not been paid at the time of filing or within seven (7) days thereafter, the Court shall enter an order of dismissal without further notice or hearing unless an application to pay the filing fee in installments, or, if a Chapter 7, an application to waive the filing fee, has been filed prior to the expiration of the period. If a Debtor fails to pay a fee installment when due, the Court shall dismiss the case without further notice or hearing.

(4) In any case where creditor information has not been provided at the time of filing or within seven (7) days thereafter, the Court shall enter an order of dismissal without further notice or hearing unless a motion for extension of time has been filed prior to the expiration of the period.

(c) Obtaining Relief from Dismissal Order.

(1) *Reopening Case.* If a dismissed case has been closed, any party seeking relief from the dismissal order must first file a motion to reopen and pay the required fee. Then the party shall file a motion for relief from the dismissal order pursuant to Fed. R.Bankr.P. 9024 as set out in (2). (That motion for relief can be filed contemporaneously with the motion to reopen.)

(2) *Requirement of Motion for Relief from Dismissal Order.* If the dismissed case has not been closed or it has been reopened, then the party shall file the motion for relief from dismissal order (unless it was filed with the motion to reopen). If the case was dismissed because of a failure to file required documents, contemporaneously with the motion(s), the movant must submit the documents required, or file a motion seeking an extension of time for submitting those documents. If the case was dismissed for failure to pay the filing fee or an installment, then the movant must, contemporaneously with the motion for relief from dismissal order, pay the filing fee or any missed fee installment, or file a motion seeking an extension of time to pay the fees. If the movant fails to comply with these requirements the motion for relief from dismissal order will not be considered.

(3) *Refund of Reopening Fee.* If the motion to reopen or for relief from the dismissal order is denied, the Court may direct the refund of the filing fee for the motion to reopen only.

(d) Conversion. A Debtor seeking to convert from Chapter 12 or 13 to Chapter 7 shall file a notice of conversion pursuant to Fed.R.Bankr.P. 1017(f)(3). A Debtor's motion to convert pursuant to Fed. R.Bankr.P. 1017(f)(2) shall be served on the trustee, if any, and the UST.

(e) Service of Motion to Dismiss. A Debtor's motion to dismiss pursuant to Fed.R.Bankr.P. 1017(f)(2) shall be served on the trustee, if any; the UST; and counsel of record.

[Effective June 1, 2010. Amended effective June 1, 2011; October 11, 2011.]

B–1017–3. EFFECT OF DISMISSAL ON ADVERSARY PROCEEDINGS

Whenever a case under the Bankruptcy Code is dismissed, any adversary proceeding arising under, arising in, or related to the case then pending will be dismissed without prejudice unless otherwise ordered by the Court either in the order dismissing the case or by separate order. Cases that have been removed to the Court shall be remanded to the Courts from which they were removed.

[Effective June 1, 2010.]

B–1019–1. CONVERSION OF CHAPTER 11, CHAPTER 12, OR CHAPTER 13 CASE TO CHAPTER 7 CASE

(a) **Schedule of Post–Petition Debts.** The schedule of post-petition debts required by Fed.R.Bankr.P. 1019 shall comply with the requirements of S.D.Ind. B–1007–1(a).

(b) **Distribution of Notice of Bar Dates and Meeting of Creditors; Certificate of Service.** The Debtor shall distribute to added creditors the following:

(1) A notice providing twenty-one (21) days for the filing of a motion for payment of an administrative expense and, unless a notice of insufficient assets to pay a dividend has been mailed in accordance with Fed.R.Bankr.P. 2002(e), the time for filing a claim of a kind specified in 11 U.S.C. § 348(d) (A form notice is available on the Court's website);

(2) Unless the schedule of post-petition debts was filed and creditors were added before issuance of the notice of the meeting of creditors under the new chapter, a copy of the notice of the meeting of creditors under the new chapter with the Debtor's full SSN or ITIN.

Debtor shall file a certificate of service as to these documents that complies with S.D.Ind. B–9013–2.

(c) **No Delay of First Meeting.** Failure of the trustee or the Debtor to comply with Fed.R.Bankr.P. 1019 shall not delay the scheduling of the 11 U.S.C. § 341 meeting for the Chapter 7 case.

(d) **Waiver of Conversion Fee for Chapter 13 Trustees.** The conversion fee is waived for any motion to convert filed by a Chapter 13 trustee in a case to which that trustee has been assigned.

[Effective June 1, 2010. Amended effective October 1, 2012.]

B–2002–1. NOTICES TO CREDITORS, EQUITY SECURITY HOLDERS, AND UNITED STATES TRUSTEE

(a) **Obtaining Service of Pleadings and/or Notices.** Interested parties or their counsel who wish to receive copies of pleadings and documents (other than proofs of claim) shall file with the Clerk and serve the Debtor with an appearance in accordance with S.D. Ind. B–9010–1. A 'Request for Notice' or similar pleading will be considered a request pursuant to Fed.R.Bankr.P. 2002(g) and will not entitle the filer to service of pleadings or of notices other than those to which the filer is already entitled, nor will the address

on the request be deemed the appropriate address for service of process unless the pleading so states.

(b) **Notices Prepared and Distributed by Parties.** A notice prepared and distributed by a party shall:

(1) be signed by the party, not the Clerk or the Judge, unless its form has been approved by a courtroom deputy; and

(2) instruct recipients to file pleadings with the Bankruptcy Clerk and provide the correct address of the division of the Bankruptcy Clerk's Office where pleadings should be delivered; and

(3) be docketed separately unless included in another pleading.

(c) **Limited Notice in Chapter 7 Cases.** In Chapter 7 cases, ninety (90) days after the first date set for the meeting of creditors or, if a report of possible assets has been filed, ninety (90) days after the issuance of the Notice of Possible Assets, all notices required by Fed.R.Bankr.P. 2002(a), except the notice of the final report and of dismissal or denial of discharge, shall be mailed only to the Debtor, the trustee, the UST, creditors who have filed claims and creditors, if any, who are still permitted to file claims by reason of an extension granted under Fed. R.Bankr.P. 3002(c)(1) or (2).

(d) **Authorization for Chapter 13 Trustee to Recover Noticing Costs from Estate.** If the Chapter 13 trustee uses the services of an independent contractor for noticing, the trustee may recover the actual costs of noticing charged by that contractor from each estate. If noticing is performed by the trustee, the trustee may recover from each estate the actual costs of postage plus $.18 (eighteen cents) for each notice or as otherwise ordered by the Court. These noticing fees can be recovered from the first and any subsequent monies received from the Debtor, whether before or after confirmation. The Chapter 13 trustee shall list expenses charged for noticing in each case and separately identify the notices sent in the final report.

(e) **Notice of Final Report with Notice of Applications for Compensation.** In Chapter 7 cases in which the amount of net proceeds realized exceeds the amount set forth in Fed.R.Bankr.P. 2002(f)(8), or the amount of any application for compensation exceeds the amount set forth in Fed.R.Bankr.P. 2002(a)(6), the Chapter 7 trustee shall provide notice of the trustee's final report and of the applications for compensation and reimbursement of expenses. That notice shall include a deadline of twenty-one (21) days from the date of the notice to file an objection to the final report or to any application for compensation and reimbursement of expenses.

(f) Returned and Undeliverable Mail.

(1) *Designation of Debtor as Return Addressee.* The Clerk may instruct the Bankruptcy Noticing Center ("BNC") to designate the Debtor as the return addressee for orders and notices, including the notice of the commencement of the case and meeting of creditors and any order confirming a plan, dismissing a case, or discharging a Debtor.

(2) *Duty to Provide Accurate Address.* The Debtor shall file a Notice of Change of Address for any creditor or party in interest whose address appears undeliverable based either on the Debtor's receipt of returned mail or information received from the BNC. In addition, the Debtor shall distribute the documents required by S.D.Ind. B–1009–1(b)(2) to any creditor with a revised address. If the Debtor is unable to determine a correct address for a creditor or party in interest, the Debtor shall file a Notice of Unavailable Address specifying the creditor's name and reporting that a correct address cannot be located.

(3) *Returned Mail Received by the Clerk, Undeliverable Addresses Identified by Clerk's Noticing Agent and Duty to Correct.* Unless otherwise ordered, the Clerk shall docket any returned notices of the meeting of creditors received by the Court in an open case. The Debtor shall file a Notice of Change of Address for any such creditor, if the correct address can be identified, shall distribute the documents required by S.D.Ind. B–1009–1(b) to any creditor with a revised address, and shall file a certificate of service that complies with S.D.Ind. B–9013–2. All other returned mail received by the Clerk shall be discarded.

[Effective June 1, 2010. Amended effective June 1, 2011; October 1, 2012; September 23, 2013; October 27, 2014.]

B–2003–1. NOTICE OF CONTINUED MEETING OF CREDITORS

(a) Notice When Meeting Continued Before Convened. A Debtor's request to continue a meeting of creditors should be directed to the trustee in a Chapter 7, 12, or 13 case, and to the UST in a Chapter 11 case. The request should not be filed with the Court. The Debtor shall seek a continuance when the cause necessitating the continuance becomes known to the Debtor. When the continuance is sought before the meeting has been convened, and the trustee grants the request, the trustee shall file notice of the continued meeting date. The Debtor shall distribute notice of the continued meeting to all creditors, parties in interest, the trustee and the UST, and shall file a certificate of service that complies with S.D.Ind. B–9013–2.

If a trustee, sua sponte, continues a meeting before it has been convened, then the trustee shall file notice of the continued meeting date, distribute notice of the continued meeting to all creditors, parties in interest and the UST, and shall file a certificate of service that complies with S.D.Ind. B–9013–2.

(b) Notice When Meeting Continued After Convened. When a meeting is continued after it has been convened, the trustee or UST shall provide oral notice of the continued date, time, and location of the first meeting, and shall file notice of the continued meeting date, time, and location with the Court. No further distribution of notice is required.

[Effective June 1, 2010. Amended effective October 11, 2011; October 1, 2012.]

B–2014–1. EMPLOYMENT OF PROFESSIONAL PERSONS AND TREATMENT OF RETAINERS IN CHAPTER 11 CASES

(a) Employment Applications Generally. Any person (the "Applicant") seeking Court approval of the employment of a professional person (the "Professional") pursuant to 11 U.S.C. §§ 327, 1103(a) or 1114 shall file with the Court an application and a supporting affidavit or verified statement of the professional complying with Fed.R.Bankr.P. 2014 (an "Employment Application"), and a proposed order on the Employment Application. The Employment Application shall describe the proposed terms of employment. If employment is to be at an hourly rate, the proposed hourly rates of all Professionals who will work on the case shall be provided. If employment is on a contingent fee basis, the percentages and triggering events shall be disclosed. Promptly after discovering any additional material information relating to such employment (such as additional potential or actual conflicts of interest) the Applicant and Professional shall file and serve a supplemental affidavit disclosing the additional information.

(b) Employment Applications in Chapter 11 Cases.

(1) *Service of Notice and Hearing.* The Employment Application (including supporting affidavit or verified statement of the Professional and any supplemental affidavit) shall be served on the Service List. Notice of the Employment Application, an objection deadline, and any hearing shall be distributed to the Notice List. Any creditor or other party in interest who wishes to resist the Employment Application must, on or before the objection deadline provided in the notice, file an objection and serve such objection upon the Applicant, the Professional, and the Service List. If no objection is filed by the objection deadline the Court may grant the Employment Application and approve the proposed employment without a hearing or further notice. If the Employment Application is granted the employment shall be effective as of the date the Employment Application was filed unless otherwise ordered by the Court.

(2) *Conflicts.* If a Professional seeks to resolve any potential conflict of interest concerning any other

client or former client, the Professional shall comply with applicable Rules of Professional Conduct. All consents or waivers of conflicts of interest ("waivers") shall be in writing. The Professional shall serve copies of all such waivers upon the Applicant and the Service List with the Employment Application or promptly following receipt by the Professional of a waiver.

(3) *Disclosure of Compensation and Retainers.* As part of the Employment Application, a Debtor and a proposed Professional shall obtain approval from the Court of an arrangement whereby a retainer paid by the Debtor to the Professional may be retained and applied to the satisfaction of such Professional's fees and expenses. Those financial arrangements may include provisions similar to the following:

(A) The retainer shall be applied to satisfy the Professional's fees and expenses as they are approved by the Court pursuant to 11 U.S.C. §§ 330 and 331;

(B) The Professional may hold the entire retainer without any application for payment of fees and expenses until final approval by the Court of such Professional's final application for fees and expenses, with such allowed interim fees and expenses paid periodically from other estate assets;

(C) Pursuant to subparagraph (b)(4) of this Rule, the Professional may draw against the retainer at specified intervals prior to the award of fees and expenses by the Court; and

(D) Any other arrangement approved by the Court.

(4) *Periodic Payment Procedure.* Subject to prior Court approval, the Professional and the Debtor may agree to a streamlined procedure for periodic payment of fees and costs prior to allowance by the Court. "Payment" includes any transfer of funds from the Debtor to the Professional after the filing date. Any proposed procedure shall provide for payment of no more than 80% of requested fees but may provide for payment of 100% of expenses.

(A) All such arrangements shall provide that prior to the fee draw the Professional must file with the Clerk a Notice of Draw which sets forth the amount of the proposed draw and contains, as an attachment, a copy of the periodic billing which supports the amount of the draw.

(B) A copy of the Notice of Draw shall be distributed to the Service List and, in addition, a copy of the relevant periodic billing shall be delivered to the UST. Failure of a party to object to the draw does not affect the party's right to object to the final allowance of fees and expenses. Court approval of the draw procedure is not approval of fees and expenses. All fees and expenses drawn are subject

to disgorgement until the Court allows the final fee application of the Professional.

[Effective June 1, 2010. Amended effective October 11, 2011; October 1, 2012.]

B–2015–1. REPORT OF OPERATIONS

(a) **Operating Reports.** For all Chapter 11 cases, and for Chapter 7 cases in which the trustee operates a business, the trustee or the Debtor shall file reports of operations, at intervals to be determined by the UST or any applicable rule, using forms approved by the UST. For all Chapter 12 cases, and for Chapter 13 cases in which the Debtor operates a business, the Debtor shall file reports of operations as required by the trustee, at intervals to be determined by the trustee or any applicable rule, using forms acceptable to the trustee.

(b) **Distribution.** The report shall be distributed to the UST, the Debtor, any trustee and counsel for the trustee, the Service List in a Chapter 11 case, and any party requesting service of the reports.

(c) **Penalties for Failure to File.** The failure to file operating reports may constitute cause for the conversion or dismissal of the case, or for the appointment (or removal) of a trustee.

[Effective June 1, 2010. Amended effective October 1, 2012.]

B–2015–3. TRUSTEES: REPORTS AND DISPOSITION OF RECORDS

Except as otherwise required by the United States Code, the UST, or other applicable law, six months after the filing of the trustee's final account, the entry of an order dismissing a Chapter 11 case following the sale of substantially all assets, or the entry of a final decree in a liquidating Chapter 11 case, the trustee or the Debtor may destroy or otherwise dispose of the books and records of the Debtor in the trustee's or the Debtor's possession, after advising the Debtor, taxing agencies, counsel for any committee, and any other entity designated by the Court, unless an earlier disposition is authorized by the Court after notice and a hearing.

[Effective June 1, 2010.]

B–2016–1. APPLICATIONS FOR COMPENSATION FOR SERVICES RENDERED AND REIMBURSEMENT OF EXPENSES

(a) **Generally.** Applications for compensation and reimbursement of expenses shall comply with the national fee guidelines promulgated by the Executive Office for United States Trustee pursuant to 28 U.S.C. § 586(a)(3)(A)(i) and any Policy of the United States Trustee for Region 10 for Implementation of Fee

Guidelines. Applications for compensation and reimbursement of expenses shall be filed separately for the trustee and each professional.

(b) Chapter 13 Cases. The following are guidelines for the circumstances under which the Court will, as part of the Chapter 13 plan confirmation process, approve fees of attorneys representing a Chapter 13 Debtor ("Counsel"). Counsel shall file a proof of claim both for fees awarded pursuant to these guidelines and for fees awarded after application.

Counsel may decline to seek approval of compensation pursuant to these guidelines. If Counsel so declines, compensation shall be disclosed, reviewed, and approved in accordance with applicable authority including, without limitation, 11 U.S.C. §§ 329 and 330 and Fed.R.Bankr.P. 2002, 2016 and 2017. This authority requires, at a minimum, that payments on account of post petition services be held in trust until the Court approves the fees and expenses of the attorney.

Alternatively, Counsel may have fees approved and paid as part of the Chapter 13 plan confirmation process if they comply with the following guidelines.

(1) Counsel may seek approval for fees up to the amounts set forth in section (2) without filing a detailed application if:

(A) Counsel has filed an executed copy of the "Rights and Responsibilities of Chapter 13 Debtors and Their Attorneys," available on the Court's website.

(B) No objection to the requested fees has been raised.

(C) A proof of claim has been filed with the Court by Counsel and served upon the trustee.

(2) The maximum fee which can be approved through the procedure described in section (1) is set by general order.*

(3) If Counsel does not wish to obtain approval of fees in accordance with these guidelines, if an executed copy of the "Rights and Responsibilities of Chapter 13 Debtors and Their Attorneys" is not filed, if Counsel requests fees in excess of the amounts in section (2), or if there is an objection to use of these guidelines, fees will not be automatically approved upon plan confirmation pursuant to these guidelines. In such cases, Counsel must deposit all advance payment of post petition fees in trust, must apply for all fees, and shall comply with 11 U.S.C. §§ 329 and 330 and Fed.R.Bankr.P. 2002, 2016 and 2017.

(4) If Counsel has filed an executed copy of the "Rights and Responsibilities of Chapter 13 Debtors and Their Attorneys," but the maximum fee in (b)(2) above is not sufficient to fully compensate counsel for the legal services rendered in the case, the attorney may apply for additional fees. The application shall be accompanied by time records supporting the additional fees or by an affidavit explaining why the standard fee is inadequate in the case.

(5) Except for pre-petition retainers, all fees shall be paid through the plan unless otherwise ordered. Absent Court authorization, Counsel may not receive fees directly from the Debtor other than the pre-petition retainer. After plan confirmation, the trustee shall pay Counsel until the fee is paid in full.

(6) If Counsel has elected to be compensated pursuant to these guidelines but the case is dismissed prior to confirmation of a plan, absent contrary orders, the trustee shall pay to the Counsel, to the extent funds are available and subject to the trustee's percentage fee, an administrative claim equal to 50% of the unpaid fee balance if a properly documented fee claim (for the entire fee balance) has been filed by Counsel and served upon the trustee. Under appropriate circumstances, Counsel may file an application (within fourteen [14] days of the dismissal) for allowance and payment of additional fees. The application shall be accompanied by an affidavit supporting award of the amount requested. Counsel shall not collect, receive, or demand additional fees from the Debtor for work already performed unless authorized by the Court, even after dismissal.

(7) On its own motion or the motion of any party in interest at any time prior to entry of a final decree, the Court may order a hearing to review any fee paid or to be paid.

[Effective June 1, 2010. Amended effective June 1, 2011; October 1, 2012; October 16, 2014; June 8, 2015.]

* **[Publisher's Note:** For maximum fee allowed under B–2016–1(b)(1), *see* General Order 14–005, *post.*]

B–2070–1. MOTIONS FOR TURNOVER: NOTICE

A trustee who files a motion for turnover against the Debtor shall provide the Debtor(s), counsel for the Debtor(s), if any, the UST, and any committee notice of the motion. That notice shall give twenty-one (21) days from the date of service for the filing of any objection. Along with the motion, the trustee shall file a copy of the notice and a certificate of service that complies with S.D.Ind. B–9013–2. The motion, notice, and certificate of service may be combined into one document. A sample combined motion for turnover, notice, and certificate of service is available on the Court's website.

[Effective October 1, 2012. Amended effective October 27, 2014.]

B–2081–2. PREPACKAGED CHAPTER 11 CASES

(a) Definition. A "Prepackaged Chapter 11 Case" is a Chapter 11 case in which the Debtor, substantially contemporaneously with the filing of the Chapter 11 petition, files a Prepackaged Scheduling Motion, a proposed plan, a disclosure statement (or other solicitation document), and a voting certification with respect to votes solicited pre-petition that the Debtor contends may be counted to achieve confirmation of the proposed plan pursuant to 11 U.S.C. § 1126(b).

(b) Scheduling Procedures. A Prepackaged Scheduling Motion shall be included under Local Rule B–9013–3(f) and treated as a First Day Motion under S.D. Ind. B–9013–3. If a Prepackaged Scheduling Motion is properly filed and served in accordance with Local Rule B–9013–3, the Court will consider expedited scheduling of a hearing on confirmation of a proposed "prepackaged plan" (without the prior approval of a disclosure statement) when confirmation of such a plan is supported by pre-petition acceptances of the proposed "prepackaged plan" in accordance with 11 U.S.C. § 1126(b) and Fed.R.Bankr.P. 3018(b). To obtain such expedited scheduling, counsel for the Debtor shall contact the courtroom deputy for the Chief Judge.

[Effective June 1, 2010. Amended effective February 10, 2014.]

B–3001–1. PROOF OF CLAIM

(a) Method of Filing. A Proof of Claim may be filed non-electronically or electronically and shall substantially conform to Official Form B10 available on the Court's website. Entities which are registered users of CM/ECF shall file claims electronically.

(b) Copies. Any entity filing a proof of claim non-electronically shall comply with S.D.Ind. B–5005–1(c).

(c) Redaction of Personal Identifiers. Any claimant shall redact, on the proof of claim and any attached documents filed with the Clerk, all personal identifiers as required by Fed.R.Bankr.P. 9037.

(d) Wage Claimant. A proof of claim for wages or salary shall include only the last four digits of the claimant's SSN or ITIN. The claimant shall provide the trustee or Debtor the full SSN or ITIN and a telephone number.

[Effective June 1, 2010. Amended effective October 11, 2011.]

B–3002.1–1 MOTIONS TO DEEM MORTGAGE CURRENT

After all payments have been made pursuant to the confirmed plan, a Chapter 13 Debtor may file a Motion to Deem Mortgage Current only as to any mortgage that is not subject to Fed.R.Bankr.P. 3002.1. The Chapter 13 Debtor shall provide the mortgage lender with a notice giving the lender twenty-one (21) days from the date of service to file an objection. Along with the motion, the Chapter 13 Debtor shall

file a copy of the notice and a certificate of service that complies with S.D.Ind. B–9013–2.

[Effective October 1, 2012.]

B–3002.1–2 NOTICE OF EXCEPTION TO FILING NOTICES OF PAYMENT CHANGE PURSUANT TO FED. R.BANKR.P. 3002.1(b)

(a) Eligibility for Use of Notice of Exception to Filing a Notice of Payment Change. A creditor may use the procedure provided for by this local rule if:

(1) the creditor asserts a claim secured by a security interest in the Debtor's real property;

(2) that claim is provided for in the plan under § 1322(b)(5); and

(3) the monthly amount due on the claim changes more than once every sixty (60) days because the creditor's agreement with the Debtor provides for a variable interest rate and/or a variable payment amount.

(b) Filing and Effect of Filing Notice of Exception to Filing a Notice of Payment Change. If a creditor is eligible pursuant to subparagraph (a) of this rule, then the creditor shall be excused from the requirements of Fed.R.Bankr.P. 3002.1(b), requiring filing of a notice of payment change twenty-one (21) days prior to the change, if the creditor files a Notice of Exception to Filing a Notice of Payment Change ("Notice of Exception") and serves that Notice of Exception on the trustee, the Debtor, and the United States Trustee. If no objection to the Notice of Exception is filed pursuant to subparagraph (c), or if the Court determines after objection that the exception should apply, then the creditor is excused from filing any Notice of Payment Change other than a change resulting from a variance in the interest rate.

(c) Objection. Any party may object to the Notice of Exception to Filing a Notice of Payment Change within twenty-one (21) days after the Notice is filed.

(d) Duty to Provide Information. A creditor subject to the exception shall provide to the Debtor and the trustee each month a statement in a customary form in accordance with applicable non-bankruptcy law that clearly identifies the payment amount due on the claim, and in addition shall provide to the trustee or the Debtor, upon request, an updated total amount due.

[Effective December 3, 2012.]

B–3002.1–3 MOTION FOR DETERMINATION OF FINAL CURE AND PAYMENT: HEARING DEEMED WAIVED

If the trustee or Debtor files a motion for determination of final cure and payment pursuant to Fed.

R.Bankr.P. 3002.1(h), and the holder of the claim has filed a response that agrees with the previously filed notice of final cure and payment, or the holder of the claim files a response that concurs in the motion for determination, then the holder of the claim is deemed to have waived further notice and the Court may enter an order on the motion immediately.

[Effective October 27, 2014.]

B–3007–1. OBJECTIONS TO CLAIMS: NOTICE

(a) Notice. Any objection to a claim and the notice of that objection shall be served by the movant on the claimant(s) to whom the objection is directed, the Debtor, any trustee, and the UST. The notice shall allow thirty (30) days from the date of service for parties to file a response to the objection.

(b) Service. The objection and notice shall be served as follows:

(1) on the claimant, by first-class mail addressed to the person most recently designated on the original or amended proof of claim as the person to receive notices, at the address so indicated; and

(A) if the objection is to a claim of the United States or any of its officers or agencies, in the manner provided for serving a summons and complaint by Fed.R.Bankr.P. 7004(b)(4) or (5); or

(B) if the objection is to a claim of an insured depository institution, according to Fed.R.Bankr.P. 7004(h); and

(2) on the debtor, the trustee, and the UST electronically, by first-class mail or by other permitted means.

(c) Filing; Certificate of Service. The moving party shall file a copy of the notice and a certificate of service that complies with S.D.Ind. B–9013–2. The objection, notice, and certificate of service may be combined into one document. A sample combined objection, notice, and certificate of service is available on the Court's website. If no proper response to the objection is filed, the Court may sustain the objection without further notice or hearing.

[Effective November 28, 2011. Amended effective October 1, 2012.]

B–3010–1. SMALL DIVIDENDS AND PAYMENTS

Trustees in Chapters 7, 12, and 13 cases are authorized to distribute dividends and payments to creditors in any amount, and need not hold such funds or deposit them with the Court.

[Effective June 1, 2010.]

B–3011–1. UNCLAIMED FUNDS

Applications for payment of unclaimed funds shall comply with instructions from and be submitted on forms made available by the Clerk.

[Effective June 1, 2010.]

B–3015–1. FILING AND DISTRIBUTION OF CHAPTER 13 PLANS

(a) Form of Plan. Chapter 13 plans and amended plans shall use the applicable Model Plan form approved by the Court. The Model Plan is available on the Court's website.

(b) Extension of Time to File Plan. A motion to extend the time to file a Chapter 13 plan must be filed within fourteen (14) days after the commencement of the case.

(c) Distribution of Plans and Amended Plans. The Chapter 13 trustee appointed in the case shall distribute the original plan, the first and second amended plans and any related notice, and file a certificate of service that complies with S.D.Ind. B–9013–2. Debtors shall distribute any third amended or subsequent plan and any related notice, and file a certificate of service that complies with S.D.Ind. B–9013–2.

[Effective June 1, 2010. Amended effective October 1, 2012.]

B–3015–2. DISTRIBUTION OF CHAPTER 12 PLANS

The Debtor in a Chapter 12 case shall distribute any plan, amended plan, or motion to modify a plan, and any related notice, and shall file a certificate of service that complies with S.D.Ind. B–9013–2.

[Effective October 1, 2012.]

B–3015–3. FILING AND DISTRIBUTION OF PRE–CONFIRMATION AND POST–CONFIRMATION MODIFICATIONS TO CHAPTER 13 PLANS

(a) Pre–Confirmation Modifications.

(1) *Agreed Modifications with Creditor: Filing and Notice.* If the Debtor, a creditor, and the trustee agree upon a modification to the plan before confirmation, and that modification only affects the treatment of the creditor agreeing to the change, then the parties shall file an agreed modification not requiring notice. Notice to creditors of the modification is not required. Any such agreement will not result in a separate order, as the subsequent confirmation order will be deemed an approval of the plan as modified by agreement.

(2) *Agreed Modifications with Trustee: Filing and Notice.* If the Debtor and the trustee agree upon a modification to the plan before confirmation that does not adversely affect the treatment of **any** creditor, then the parties shall file an agreed modification not requiring notice. Notice to creditors of the agreement is not required. Any such agreement will not result in a separate order, as the subsequent confirmation order will be deemed an approval of the plan as modified by agreement.

(3) *Other Pre–Confirmation Modifications.* Any pre-confirmation modification that affects the treatment of creditors that have not agreed to the modification requires the filing of an amended plan which shall be distributed by the trustee or the Debtor pursuant to S.D.Ind. B–3015–1.

(b) Post–Confirmation Modifications. A proposed modification of a confirmed plan shall be filed as a Motion to Modify Plan. The movant shall distribute notice of the filing and of any hearing or deadline for objections and shall file a certificate of service that complies with S.D.Ind. B–9013–2.

[Effective June 1, 2010. Amended effective October 1, 2012; February 19, 2013.]

B–3015–4. PRE–CONFIRMATION PAYMENTS AND CONFIR-MATION HEARINGS

(a) Pre-confirmation Payments as Adequate Protection. For all cases filed on or after October 17, 2005, "adequate protection" under 11 U.S.C. § 1326(a)(1)(C) shall be paid directly to the trustee, as a portion of the payment made under 11 U.S.C. § 1326(a)(1), in an amount equal to one percent (1%) of the secured creditor's allowed secured claim. Such amount shall be presumed to constitute adequate protection although that presumption may be rebutted. The trustee shall disburse adequate protection payments to the secured creditor as soon as practicable after receiving them from the Debtor. All adequate protection payments shall be subject to the trustee's percentage fee as set by the UST.

(b) Confirmation Hearings. Consistent with 11 U.S.C. § 1324(b), absent a contrary order or objection, the Court finds that it is in the best interests of creditors and the bankruptcy estate to hold a confirmation hearing, in cases filed on or after October 17, 2005, prior to twenty-one (21) days after the 11 U.S.C. § 341(a) meeting of creditors.

[Effective October 15, 2012.]

B–3017–2. CONSIDERATION OF DISCLO-SURE STATEMENTS IN SMALL BUSI-NESS CASES AND CONFIRMATION DEADLINES

(a) Expedited Processing of Disclosure Statement. If the proponent of a plan in a small business case would like the Court to:

(1) determine that the plan itself provides adequate information and that a separate disclosure statement is not necessary;

(2) approve a disclosure statement submitted on an approved official form; or

(3) conditionally approve a disclosure statement subject to final approval at a hearing where the Court will also consider confirmation of the proposed plan,

the proponent shall file a notice at the same time as the proposed plan or disclosure statement is filed. Such notice shall state, with particularity, why a separate disclosure statement is not needed, why a separate hearing to consider the adequacy of a disclosure statement is not necessary, or why the filing of the plan should be deferred. A sample notice form is available on the Court's website.

(b) Absence of Notice Results in Hearing. Absent a notice submitted in accordance with subparagraph (a), the Court will schedule the case for such proceedings as it deems appropriate.

(c) Deadlines. At any hearing where the Court is to consider the adequacy of a proposed disclosure statement the Court may also, either on its own initiative or at the request of a party in interest, consider whether any applicable deadline for confirming a proposed plan should be extended.

[Effective June 1, 2010.]

B–3018–1. BALLOTS; VOTING ON PLAN—CHAPTER 11

(a) Distribution of Plan. Upon the approval or conditional approval of the disclosure statement, unless otherwise ordered by the Court, within seven (7) days the party filing the plan (the "Plan Proponent") shall distribute copies of the plan, the disclosure statement (unless none is required under 11 U.S.C. § 1125(f)(1)), and ballot(s) to all creditors and parties in interest, along with the notice of the hearing on confirmation. The Plan Proponent shall file within fourteen (14) days after the approval or conditional approval of the disclosure statement a certificate of service that complies with S.D.Ind. B–9013–2.

(b) Submission of Ballots and Balloting Report.

(1) *Delivery and Retention of Ballots.* Except as otherwise ordered and as provided in S.D.Ind. B–1007–2, all ballots shall be delivered to the Plan Proponent. Any original ballots received by the Clerk shall be forwarded to the Plan Proponent. The Plan Proponent shall establish an appropriate method for noting the date the ballot was received. Unless otherwise ordered by the Court, the Plan Proponent shall retain copies of the ballots in accordance with the Electronic Case Filing Administrative Policies and Procedures Manual.

(2) *Tabulation; Report and Certification.* The Plan Proponent shall tabulate the ballots and prepare a balloting report. The tabulation shall list, for each class, the total number of claims voting, total dollar amount of claims accepting, and percentages of claims voting that accept the plan. The report shall also indicate, for each class, whether it is impaired or unimpaired and whether or not the requisite vote has been attained in each class. A sample report form is available on the Court's website. The balloting report form shall be certified by the plan proponent. A sample certification form is available on the Court's website.

(3) *Filing and Service.* The certification and the balloting report shall be filed with the Court at least three (3) days before the confirmation hearing. Copies of the report shall be distributed to the UST, the Service List, and parties filing objections to the plan.

(c) **Form of Ballot.** Unless a different ballot form has been approved by the Court, the Plan Proponent shall use the form of a ballot available on the Court's website. The ballot shall be distributed to creditors, shall include the address of the Plan Proponent or the party designated to receive ballots, and shall indicate that ballots should be received no later than the deadline established by order of the Court.

(d) **Rules for Tabulating Ballots.** In tabulating the ballots, the following rules shall apply:

(1) Ballots that are not signed will not be counted either as an acceptance or rejection.

(2) Where the amount shown as owed on the ballot differs from the schedules, the amount shown on the schedules or, if a proof of claim has been filed and allowed or deemed allowed, the amount shown on the proof of claim will be used for the purpose of determining the amount voting unless the Court orders otherwise.

(3) Unless the Court orders otherwise, ballots that do not show a choice of either acceptance or rejection will not be counted either as an acceptance or rejection.

(4) Unless the Court orders otherwise, ballots that are received after the last date set for filing ballots will not be counted as either an acceptance or rejection.

[Effective June 1, 2010. Amended effective October 1, 2012.]

B–3022–1. FINAL DECREE IN CHAPTER 11 CASES WHERE DEBTOR IS NOT AN INDIVIDUAL

After the estate has been fully administered, the Plan Proponent or other entity administering the confirmed plan shall file an application for a final decree. The application shall include the percentage paid or proposed to be paid to general unsecured creditors in the plan.

[Effective June 1, 2010. Amended effective October 1, 2012.]

B–3022–2. FINAL DECREE IN CHAPTER 11 CASES WHERE DEBTOR IS AN INDIVIDUAL

(a) **Application for Final Decree: Payments Completed.** If the Debtor in a Chapter 11 case is an individual, and has completed all plan payments, then the Debtor shall file an application for final decree. The application for final decree shall include the percentage paid to general unsecured creditors in the plan. If the Debtor is otherwise eligible, the Court shall issue a discharge as soon as practicable.

(b) **Request for Discharge under 11 U.S.C. § 1141(d)(5)(B).** If a discharge is sought under 11 U.S.C. § 1141(d)(5)(B), the Debtor shall request entry of discharge by filing a motion for discharge, which shall be a contested matter governed by Fed. R.Bankr.P. 9014. If the motion is granted, and if the Debtor is otherwise eligible, the Clerk shall issue the discharge and the final decree, and close the case.

(c) **Closing Case Before Plan Payments Completed.** If the Debtor proposes to close the case before plan payments have been completed, and intends to reopen the case after plan completion to obtain a discharge, then the Debtor shall file a motion to close the case and include in that motion a statement of the debtor's intent to reopen. If such documentation is provided, the Clerk shall not issue the Notice of No Discharge as required by Fed. R.Bankr.P. 4006 or the final decree at the time the case is closed. Upon the filing of a motion to reopen, the Debtor shall be required to pay any fees due for reopening the case. After reopening, the Debtor shall file the Application for Final Decree and supporting documentation as required in subparagraph (a).

[Effective June 1, 2010. Amended effective October 1, 2012.]

B–3070–1. WAGE ASSIGNMENT ORDERS IN CHAPTER 13 CASES

(a) **Trustee's Authority to Require Wage Assignment Order.** Under 11 USC § 1325(c), the Chapter 13 Trustee may, in any case in which he or she has been appointed, at any time request an order directing the Debtor's employer to remit funds needed to fund the plan.

(b) **Procedure.** The trustee may:

(1) Submit an order ("the Wage Assignment Order" or "Order to Pay") directing a Debtor's employer to remit to the trustee the payment stated in Debtor's plan (including amended plans and motions for post-confirmation modification) or in a confirmation order; or

(2) Notify the Debtor's counsel or, if pro se, the Debtor, that he or she is to submit the Wage Assignment Order. Such notice shall be provided in writing, or orally at the meeting of creditors.

(c) Effect of Failure to Provide Order. If the Chapter 13 Trustee proceeds under subparagraph (b)(2), then the Debtor's counsel or Debtor shall submit such an order to the Court within seven (7) days of the notice from the trustee. Failure to do so is, in itself, grounds for the trustee to move to dismiss the case.

(d) Service of Orders. The party who tendered the order shall serve a copy of the signed order on the entity to which the order is directed, the trustee, and the Debtor.

(e) Amended Orders Required. Debtor or Debtor's counsel must advise the Chapter 13 Trustee if the Debtor's employer changes before plan payments have been completed. If the Chapter 13 Trustee has given notice that the Debtor's counsel or pro se Debtor should submit a Wage Assignment Order, that obligation continues throughout the case, unless rescinded by the Chapter 13 Trustee. Debtor or Debtor's counsel must submit a new order whenever the Debtor's employer or the plan payment changes.

[Effective September 23, 2013.]

B–4001–1. MOTIONS FOR RELIEF FROM STAY AND MOTIONS TO EXTEND OR IMPOSE THE STAY

(a) Relief from Stay or Co–Debtor Stay.

(1) *Contents of Motion.* A motion for relief from the automatic stay or relief from the stay as to a co-debtor pursuant to 11 U.S.C. § 1301 shall include the following information to the extent applicable:

(A) a description of the property as to which stay relief is sought;

(B) the amount of principal and interest due as of the date of the motion;

(C) documents upon which the movant relies to establish its lien or security interest (or incorporate by reference the movant's proof of claim if documentation attached);

(D) evidence of perfection of the movant's lien or security interest (or incorporate by reference the movant's proof of claim if documentation attached);

(E) if the case is pending under Chapter 13 and a post-petition default is alleged, a post-petition payment history;

(F) if the motion seeks relief from the co-debtor stay, the name of the co-debtor.

(2) *Sample Form.* A sample form motion is available on the Court's website. The motion may be combined with the notice required by subparagraph (a)(4).

(3) *Waiver of 30–day Hearing Requirement.* The movant may include in the motion a waiver of the 30–day hearing requirement in 11 U.S.C. § 362(e), and shall note that waiver by including in the caption, the statement, "with 30–day waiver." Selection of the waiver option when filing the motion electronically also results in waiver of the 30–day hearing requirement in 11 U.S.C. § 362(e).

(4) *Notice; Disposition.*

(A) Chapters 7, 12, and 13. In cases pending under any chapter except Chapter 11, notice of the motion shall be distributed by the movant to the Debtor, parties that have entered an appearance, any trustee, and the UST, except as otherwise provided by S.D.Ind. B–2002–1(c). If the motion also seeks abandonment, notice must be distributed to all creditors and parties in interest. The notice shall allow fourteen (14) days from the date of service to file objections. Along with the notice, the moving party shall file a copy of the motion and a certificate of service that complies with S.D.Ind. B–9013–2. A sample notice is available on the Court's website. If no proper response to the motion is filed, the Court may grant relief from the stay without further notice or hearing. At any hearing on the motion the Debtor or objecting party has the burden of establishing any payment alleged to have been made but not set forth in the payment history.

(B) Chapter 11. In cases pending under Chapter 11, unless the Court has previously entered a case management order covering preparation and distribution of notices, movant should contact the Courtroom Deputy to discuss who will prepare and distribute the notice and determine if a hearing is needed. Hearing date and time will be provided by the Courtroom Deputy. Notice of the motion shall be distributed to the Debtor, parties that have entered an appearance, any creditors committee or if no committee has been appointed, the twenty largest unsecured creditors, any trustee, and the UST. If the motion also seeks abandonment, notice must be distributed to all creditors and parties in interest. After distribution, the movant shall file a certificate of service that complies with S.D.Ind. B–9013–2. The certificate of service must be filed prior to any hearing the Court has set on the motion.

(b) Extend or Impose the Stay.

(1) *Motion Filed Ten (10) Days or Less After Filing Date.*

(A) The Motion will be set for hearing, and notice of that hearing and the deadline for objections will be issued by the Court.

(B) If, by the deadline, the debtor has filed an affidavit with sufficient facts to support the motion and no objection has been filed, then the Court may, in its discretion, rule on the motion without hearing, conduct a telephonic hearing, or make such other arrangements as will be most efficient for the Court and the debtor, including but not limited to excusing the debtor from appearing in person.

(2) *Motion Filed More than Ten (10) Days After Filing Date.*

(A) The movant shall contact the Courtroom Deputy for the Judge assigned to the case and obtain a hearing date.

(B) The movant shall send notice of the Motion and the hearing to those creditors as to whom it is proposed that the stay be imposed or extended.

(C) The movant shall file a certificate of service that complies with S.D.Ind. B–9013–2 on or before the hearing date.

(D) Debtor's attendance at the hearing may be required, even if no objection is filed.

[Effective June 1, 2010. Amended effective June 1, 2011; October 11, 2011; October 1, 2012; October 27, 2014.]

B–4001–2. MOTIONS TO USE CASH COLLATERAL AND TO OBTAIN CREDIT

(a) Contents of Motion to Use Cash Collateral. In addition to the requirements of Fed.R.Bankr.P. 4001(b)(1)(B), motions to use cash collateral shall also comply with the requirements of Fed.R.Bankr.P. 4001(c)(1)(B) unless otherwise directed by the Court.

(b) Other Provisions to Be Disclosed. In addition to the provisions listed in Fed.R.Bankr.P. 4001(b)(1)(B) and (c)(1)(B), any motion to use cash collateral or motion to obtain credit (collectively "Financing Motions") must also disclose as a "material provision" any provision of the type indicated below:

(1) *Cross–Collateralization of Pre–Petition Debt.* Provisions that grant cross-collateralization protection (other than replacement liens or other adequate protection) to the pre-petition secured creditor, i.e., clauses that secure pre-petition debt by post-petition assets in which the secured creditor does not assert a valid, perfected security interest by virtue of its pre-petition security agreement or applicable non-bankruptcy law, and provisions that deem pre-petition secured debt to be post-petition debt or that use post-petition loans from a pre-petition secured lender to pay all or part of that lender's pre-petition claim, other than as provided in 11 U.S.C. § 552(b);

(2) *Professional Fee Provisions.* Provisions that provide disparate treatment for the professionals retained by a creditors' committee from that provided for the professionals retained by the Debtor with respect to a professional fee carve-out (payment from a secured creditor's collateral);

(3) *Priming of Existing Liens.* Provisions that prime any secured lien without the consent of the holder of that lien;

(4) *Loan Documentation Costs.* Provisions that call for the payment of fees or costs by the Debtor other than reasonable attorney's fees for loan documentation; and

(5) *Plan Restrictions.* Provisions that limit, restrict, or otherwise affect the terms of a proposed plan of reorganization.

(c) Summary of Essential Terms. All Financing Motions must also set forth, unless good cause is shown, the total dollar amount requested, the Debtor's proposed budget for the use of the funds, an estimate of the value of the collateral which secures the creditor's asserted interest, the maximum borrowing available on an interim and final basis, the borrowing conditions, interest rate, fees, costs or other expenses to be borne by the Debtor, maturity, limitations on the use of the funds, events of default and the protections afforded under 11 U.S.C. §§ 363 and 364.

(d) Interim Relief. When Financing Motions are filed as First Day Motions, the Court may grant interim relief pending review by the interested parties of the proposed arrangements. Such interim relief is intended to avoid immediate and irreparable harm to the estate pending a final hearing. Absent extraordinary circumstances, the Court may not enter interim orders that include any of the provisions identified in subparagraph (b), above, or any provision listed in Fed.R.Bankr.P. 4001(c)(1)(B)(ii)–(xi).

[Effective June 1, 2010.]

B–4001–3. OBTAINING CREDIT IN CHAPTER 13 CASES

(a) Dollar Limits.

(1) *$1000 or Less.* The Debtor may incur non-emergency consumer debt up to one thousand dollars ($1,000.00), including the refinancing of real property debt, without written approval of the trustee or order of the Court.

(2) *Greater than $1000.* The Debtor must seek approval of the trustee or an order from the Court before incurring non-emergency consumer debt of more than one thousand dollars ($1,000) using the procedures set out in subparagraphs (b) through (d) of this rule.

(b) Request Directed to Trustee. If the proposed debt is unsecured or to be secured by personal property, the Debtor shall first request approval to incur debt by written application to the trustee. Such request shall not be filed with the Clerk. If approved by the trustee, the Debtor may incur the debt in accordance with the terms and conditions approved by the trustee. If the trustee has not directed use of a specific form, the application shall include the following information:

(1) a statement in support of the feasibility of the request;

(2) a description of the item to be purchased or the collateral affected by the credit to be obtained;

(3) a description of the interest held by any other entity in any collateral affected by the credit;

(4) the reasons for which the Debtor has the need for the credit;

(5) the terms of any financing involved, including the interest rate;

(6) a description of any method or proposal by which the interest held by any other entity in the collateral affected by the credit may be protected; and

(7) copies of all documents by which the interest of all entities in the collateral affected by the credit was created or perfected, or, if any of those documents are unavailable, the reason for the unavailability.

(c) Filing Approved Request with the Court. If the Debtor seeks an order from the Court on a request that has been approved by the trustee, the Debtor may file the approved request with the Court and provide an order. If the pleading is filed without documentation showing the trustee's approval, it will be treated as a Motion to Incur Debt filed under subparagraph (d). The trustee's approval can be documented by reference to same within the motion or by attaching a document signed by the trustee.

(d) Motion Directed to Court. If the proposed debt is greater than $1000 and is to be secured by real property or if Debtor's request under subparagraph (b) is not approved by the trustee, the Debtor may file a motion to incur such debt. The motion shall contain all of the information required for the request by subparagraph (b) and be served on the trustee. The Court shall give the trustee 14 days' notice of the opportunity to object to the Motion to Incur Debt.

[Effective June 1, 2010. Amended effective June 1, 2011; February 19, 2013; October 27, 2014.]

B-4002-1. DEBTOR'S DUTIES

(a) Notice to Other Tribunals. Immediately upon the entry of an order for relief, the Debtor shall give written notice to any Court or tribunal where an action is pending against the Debtor and to the parties and counsel involved in that action. If an action is commenced subsequent to the date of the order for relief, the Debtor shall give similar written notice to the Court or tribunal and to all parties and counsel involved.

(b) Notice to Garnishing Creditor and Garnishee Defendants. Immediately upon the entry of an order for relief, the Debtor shall give written notice to any creditor with a garnishment order, any garnishee defendant other than the Debtor's employer, and to any creditor whom the Debtor anticipates may seek a garnishment order.

(c) Notice to Employer. If the Debtor has authorized deductions from the Debtor's employment compensation in repayment of an unsecured claim or if the Debtor's employment compensation is subject to an involuntary garnishment, then upon the entry of an order for relief, the Debtor shall notify the employer and the entity authorized to receive any voluntary deduction that such deduction shall cease as of the date of the entry of the order for relief. If the employer or the entity authorized to receive a voluntary deduction is notified orally, the Debtor shall send to the employer, within three (3) days thereafter, a written notice which includes copies of the petition and that portion of the schedules listing the creditor receiving the deductions. If the Debtor has authorized the deduction from the Debtor's compensation for repayment of a secured claim which the Debtor intends to reaffirm, or the withholding of income governed by 11 U.S.C. § 362(b)(19), or if the Debtor's compensation is subject to garnishment for a debt not dischargeable pursuant to 11 U.S.C. § 523(a)(5), then the Debtor may elect not to provide the notice required by this subsection.

(d) Production of Business Records. In Chapter 13 cases, if a Debtor is engaged in business, as defined in 11 U.S.C. § 1304, the Debtor must produce any documents concerning the business requested by the trustee at or before the meeting of creditors.

(e) Additional Documents Upon Request. In addition to the documents required by Fed.R.Bankr.P. 4002, the Debtor shall produce such other documents as the trustee or UST requests.

[Effective June 1, 2010.]

B-4003-2. LIEN AVOIDANCE MOTIONS PURSUANT TO § 522(f)

(a) Requirements. Any Debtor seeking to avoid a lien pursuant to 11 U.S.C. § 522(f) shall file a separate written motion as to each alleged lien holder. The motion may be combined with the notice required by subparagraph (d) and the certificate of service that complies with S.D.Ind. B-9013-2. A sample notice, motion, and certificate of service are available on the Court's website. The motion shall identify:

(1) the value of the subject collateral;

(2) the amount, listed separately, of all mortgages and other liens on the property which the Debtor will not seek to avoid, and a list of the liens on the property which the Debtor will seek to avoid;

(3) the amount of the exemption to which the Debtor would be entitled but for the lien;

(4) the lien to be avoided and its approximate amount; and

(5) if lien avoidance is sought as to real property, the common address and legal description of that property.

(b) Judicial Liens: Additional Requirements. In addition to the information required by subparagraph (a), motions to avoid judicial liens shall also include:

(1) the case number and the Court where the underlying judgment was entered; and

(2) the date of the judgment.

(c) Nonpossessory, Nonpurchase Money Security Interests in Household Goods: Additional Requirements. In addition to the information required by subparagraph (a), motions to avoid a nonpossessory, nonpurchase money security interest in household goods under 11 U.S.C. § 522(f)(1)(B) shall also:

(1) specifically identify the household goods that are subject to the security interest sought to be avoided, referring to the definition of "household goods" provided in 11 U.S.C. § 522(f)(4); and

(2) state the date the debt that the lien secures was incurred.

(d) Service and Notice. The Debtor shall serve the motion and notice thereof on the lien holder, in accordance with Fed.R.Bankr.P. 9014(b) and 7004. The notice shall allow twenty-one (21) days from the date of service to file objections.

(e) Filing and Certificate of Service. Along with the motion, the Debtor shall file with the Court a copy of the notice and a certificate of service that complies with S.D.Ind. B–9013–2.

(f) Orders. An order avoiding a lien on real estate shall include both the common address and a legal description of that real estate.

[Effective June 1, 2010. Amended effective June 1, 2011; October 1, 2012; October 27, 2014.]

B–4003–3. STRIPPING MORTGAGES IN CHAPTER 13 CASES

Any Debtor seeking to strip a mortgage in a Chapter 13 case shall file a separate adversary proceeding as to each lien holder. In addition to any other required allegations, the complaint shall identify:

(a) the mortgage to be avoided and its approximate amount;

(b) the other mortgages and liens on the property which the Debtor asserts have higher priority than the mortgage to be avoided, and the amount—listed separately—of those mortgages and liens;

(c) the value of the property; and

(d) the common address and legal description of the property.

A proposed judgment tendered by the Debtor shall include both the common address and the legal description of the property.

[Effective October 27, 2014.]

B–4004–1. DISCHARGE IN CHAPTER 12 INDIVIDUAL AND CHAPTER 13 CASES

(a) Trustee's Notice of Completion. For all individual Chapter 12 cases and all Chapter 13 cases filed on or after October 17, 2005, the Chapter 12 or 13 trustee shall file a Notice of Plan Completion after all payments have been received. Sample forms are available on the Court's website.

(b) Debtor's Required Pleadings. Within thirty (30) days after the trustee files the notice of completion, the Debtor shall file a Motion for Entry of Discharge and a Certification of Eligibility for Discharge. Each Debtor in a joint case shall file a separate Certification. Sample forms are available on the Court's website.

(c) Service and Notice. The Debtor shall serve a copy of the Motion for Entry of Discharge and a Certification of Eligibility for Discharge on the trustee and any entity to whom the Debtor owes a domestic support obligation. The trustee shall have twenty-one (21) days from the date of filing to object to the Motion or the Certification. If the Debtor owes a domestic support obligation, the Debtor shall distribute to the holder of that obligation a notice giving the holder twenty-one (21) days from the date of service to file an objection to the entry of discharge. A sample notice is available on the Court's website. The Debtor shall file a certificate of service as to the notice that complies with S.D.Ind. B–9013–2.

(d) Closing and Reopening. If no motion for entry of discharge is filed, the case may be closed without entry of a discharge after filing of the trustee's final report. If the motion for entry of discharge is filed after the case has been closed, the Debtor must also file a motion to reopen the case. A filing fee to reopen the case must be paid with the motion.

[Effective June 1, 2010. Amended effective October 1, 2012; July 7, 2015.]

B–4004–2. OBTAINING DISCHARGE AF-TER CASE CLOSED WITHOUT DIS-CHARGE FOR FAILURE TO FILE FI-NANCIAL MANAGEMENT REPORT

A debtor may file a motion to reopen a case in order to obtain a discharge after a Notice of No Discharge where the discharge was not entered solely because the debtor failed to file a statement regarding completion of a course in personal financial management pursuant to Fed.R.Bankr.P. 1007(b)(7) and (c). In order for the motion to reopen to be granted, the debtor must pay the fee due to reopen the case and, contemporaneously with the Motion to Reopen, file the required statement of completion using the appropriate Official Form B23.

[Effective June 1, 2010.]

B–4008–1. REAFFIRMATION

(a) Official Bankruptcy Forms Required. Reaffirmation agreements shall be filed using the Administrative Office of the U.S. Courts Director's Procedural Forms for reaffirmation agreements (240A or 240A/B Alt.), as well as the cover sheet (Official Form 27). Failure to use these required forms will result in a Notice of Deficient Filing and the Court will take no action on the reaffirmation agreement.

(b) Debtor's Appearance Required. If the court sets a hearing to consider a reaffirmation agreement, the debtor must appear at the hearing. The hearing will be evidentiary.

(c) Duties of Debtor's Counsel. Unless the attorney has withdrawn as attorney for the debtor pursuant to S.D.Ind. L.R. B–9010–1, an attorney who files a petition on behalf of a debtor (or an attorney in the same firm as the filing attorney) must represent the debtor during the negotiation and filing of any reaffirmation agreements, and appear at any hearings on reaffirmation agreements.

[Effective May 1, 2013.]

B–5005–1. FILING OF DOCUMENTS: GENERAL REQUIREMENTS

(a) Method of Filing. Except as provided by S.D. Ind. B–5005–4 and the Electronic Case Filing Administrative Policies and Procedures Manual (available on the Court's website), all attorneys, and any other entity that filed more than ten (10) documents on paper in the previous calendar year, are required to file electronically. All other parties may file documents on paper.

(b) Form. All petitions, pleadings and other documents submitted for filing shall meet the following requirements of form:

(1) *Legibility.* Documents shall be plainly and legibly typewritten, printed, or reproduced on one side of the paper only.

(2) *Caption: Official Forms.* The caption and form of all petitions, pleadings, schedules and other documents shall be in substantial compliance with the Federal Rules of Bankruptcy Procedure, Official Forms, or Local Rules for the Southern District of Indiana. Each document or set of documents filed shall bear the name of the Debtor and chapter of the case. Each document other than the original petition shall also have the case number.

(3) *Signature.* Every pleading, whether filed electronically or on paper, shall be signed. Any pleading lacking a signature shall be stricken from the record, if not corrected after notice to the filer.

(c) Filing Non–Electronically.

(1) *Over the Counter.* A party filing a document over the counter shall provide a signed original and a copy (or two originals). The file-marked original will be returned to the filer, and shall be retained by the filer as required by the Court's Electronic Case Filing Administrative Policies and Procedures Manual available on the Court's website.

(2) *Proof of Identification for Initial Pleadings.* A pro se party filing a voluntary petition, an involuntary petition, or an adversary proceeding over the counter must appear in person and shall be required to provide a valid photo driver's license or other government-issued photo identification before the petition or complaint will be accepted for filing. For pro se joint cases filed under 11 U.S.C. § 302, only one spouse need be present. An exception may be granted if the Debtor, creditor, or plaintiff has executed a power of attorney, and the holder of the power of attorney has presented that document and sufficient identification.

(3) *By Mail.* For documents submitted by mail, the filer shall provide a signed original, a copy (or two originals), and a self-addressed, stamped envelope. A file-marked original will be returned to the filer and shall be retained by the filer as required by the Electronic Case Filing Administrative Policies and Procedures Manual, available on the Court's website.

(4) *Failure to Provide Copy or Self–Addressed, Stamped Envelope.* A party who fails to provide a copy (or second original) or a self-addressed, stamped envelope for pleadings submitted by mail shall be presumed to have retained an original as required by the Electronic Case Filing Administrative Policies and Procedures Manual (available on the Court's website). The Clerk shall not return the original to the filer. Documents that are not returned to the filer will be discarded by the Clerk after scanning.

[Effective June 1, 2010. Amended effective September 23, 2013.]

B–5005–3. SIZE OF PAPERS

Papers submitted for filing shall be no larger than 8 ½″ by 11″ in size.

[Effective June 1, 2010.]

B–5005–4. ELECTRONIC FILING

The Court has adopted Electronic Case Filing Administrative Policies and Procedures to permit filing, signing, service, and verification of documents by electronic means. These Administrative Policies and Procedures, as described in the Manual available on the Court's website, are incorporated into this Local Rule.

[Effective June 1, 2010. Amended effective September 23, 2013.]

B–5011–1. WITHDRAWAL OF REFERENCE

(a) **Form of Request; Place of Filing.** A motion for withdrawal of a case or proceeding shall be filed in the Bankruptcy Court. In addition, all such motions shall clearly and conspicuously state that "relief is sought from a U.S. District Judge."

(b) **Recommendation by Bankruptcy Court.** The Bankruptcy Court, on its own motion, may recommend to the District Court that a case or proceeding be withdrawn under 28 U.S.C. § 157(d). Any such recommendation must be served on the parties to the case or proceeding and forwarded to the Clerk of the District Court for assignment to and resolution by a District Judge.

(c) **Stay.** The filing of a motion to withdraw the reference or the Bankruptcy Court's recommendation to withdraw the reference does not stay the proceedings in the Bankruptcy Court. Fed.R.Bankr.P. 8005 governs requests for a stay pending decision on withdrawal of reference.

(d) **Designation of Record.** The moving party shall serve and file, together with the motion to withdraw the reference, a designation of those portions of the record believed to be necessary or pertinent to the District Court's consideration of the motion. Within fourteen (14) days after service of such designation of record, any other party may serve and file a designation of additional portions of the record. All designated documents shall be identified by document number as noted on the docket. If the record designated by any party includes a transcript of any proceeding, that party shall file a written request for the transcript and include with the request the fee for preparation of the transcript.

(e) **Responses to Motions to Withdraw Reference; Reply.** Opposing parties shall file with the Clerk, and serve all parties to the matter, their written responses to the motion within fourteen (14) days after being served a copy of the motion. The moving party may serve and file a reply within fourteen (14) days after service of a response.

(f) **Transmittal of Record to District Court.** When the record is complete, the Clerk of the Bankruptcy Court shall transmit to the Clerk of the District Court the motion and the portions of the record designated. After the opening of the docket in the District Court, documents pertaining to the matter under review by the District Court shall be filed with the Clerk of the District Court.

[Effective June 1, 2010. Amended effective October 27, 2014.]

B–5071–1. CONTINUANCES

Unless otherwise ordered by the Court, all requests to continue a scheduled hearing, conference or trial must be made by written motion. The motion to continue shall indicate whether the opposing party consents to the continuance. If the movant has been unable to reach the opposing party, the motion shall recite what efforts were made to contact the opposing party.

[Effective October 1, 2012.]

B–5080–3. DEFERRAL OF FILING FEES DUE FROM TRUSTEE

In an adversary proceeding, if the trustee certifies to the Clerk that the estate lacks the funds necessary to pay a filing fee, the Clerk shall defer the filing fee without Court order and enter the deferral on the docket. If the estate later receives funds sufficient to pay the deferred fees, the trustee shall pay the fee no later than the date the trustee makes distribution to creditors.

[Effective June 1, 2010.]

B–6004–1. SALE OF ASSETS OUTSIDE THE ORDINARY COURSE PURSUANT TO 11 U.S.C. § 363: GENERALLY

(a) **Applicability of Local Rule.** This rule applies to any motion to approve the sale of assets, outside the ordinary course of business, pursuant to 11 U.S.C. § 363 (the "Motion to Sell"), including motions filed by a trustee or a Debtor. This rule, and B–6004–2 through B–6004–5, do not apply to sales proposed as part of a plan.

(b) **Employment and Compensation of Professionals.** Except as otherwise permitted by Local Rule 6004–3, the movant shall file a separate application to employ, and a separate application to compensate, any broker, auctioneer, or other professional to be retained to assist with any sale. The retention of liquidators, auctioneers, and appraisers is also governed by Local Rule B–6005–1. No payment shall be made to any professional before the Court has entered an order approving compensation and reimbursement of expenses.

(c) Procedure; Contents of Motion; Notice. Unless otherwise ordered, any motion to sell shall follow the procedures outlined in and provide the information required by Local Rules B–6004–2 through B–6004–5, depending on the type of sale.

[Effective October 27, 2014.]

B–6004–2. PRIVATE SALE

(a) "Private Sale" Defined. For the purpose of this rule, a "private sale" is defined as a sale to a specific entity on terms that are fixed at the time the motion to sell is filed, with no consideration of competing bids contemplated.

(b) Contents of Motion: All Chapters. Any Motion to Sell by private sale shall identify:

(1) the property to be sold;

(2) the prospective purchaser ("Prospective Purchaser");

(3) the sales price and an estimate of the net proceeds to be received by the estate (including a deduction for any exemption);

(4) a brief summary of all material contingencies to the sale, together with a copy of the agreement, if available;

(5) a description of the manner in which the property was marketed for sale, and a description of any other offer to purchase;

(6) a description of any known relationship between the Prospective Purchaser and its insiders and the Debtor and its insiders or the trustee;

(7) a statement setting forth any relationship or connection the trustee or the Debtor (including its insiders) will have with the Prospective Purchaser or its insiders after the consummation of the sale, assuming it is approved; and

(8) a disclosure if the property to be sold contains personally identifiable information and, if so, the measures that will be taken to comply with 11 U.S.C. § 363(b)(1).

(c) Contents of Motion: Additional Requirements in Chapter 11 Cases. Any Motion to Sell by private sale in a Chapter 11 case that proposes the sale of all or substantially all of the Debtor's assets shall include, in addition to the requirements in subparagraph (b), the following:

(1) if schedules have not been filed by the Debtor, a summary of the Debtor's debt structure, including the amount of the Debtor's secured debt, priority claims, and general unsecured claims; and

(2) if a creditors' committee, or its equivalent, existed pre-petition, the identity of the members of the committee and the companies with which they are affiliated and the identity of any counsel.

(d) Notice.

(1) *Distribution; Contents; Certificate of Service Generally.* Unless otherwise ordered by the Court, the movant shall distribute notice of any hearing or of any deadline to object to a Motion to Sell, as determined by subparagraphs (2) and (3) below. The notice shall contain all of the information required by subparagraph (b) and (c) of this rule. The movant shall file a certificate of service that complies with S.D.Ind. B–9013–2. The motion, notice, and certificate of service may be combined into one document. A sample combined motion to sell, notice, and certificate of service is available on the Court's website.

(2) *Chapter 7, 12, and 13 Cases.* Unless the Court by separate order shortens the notice period, in a Chapter 7, Chapter 12, or Chapter 13 case, the movant shall distribute notice that provides twenty-one (21) days after the date of service for objections to be filed.

(3) *Chapter 11 Case.* In a Chapter 11 case, the movant shall contact the courtroom deputy to obtain direction as to whether the Court desires a notice with opportunity to object to the motion or a notice of the hearing date. The movant shall distribute the notice and file a certificate of service.

(e) Report of Sale. No later than fourteen (14) days after a private sale has been completed, the movant shall file a report of sale pursuant to Fed. R.Bankr.P. 6004(f)(1).

[Effective October 27, 2014.]

B–6004–3. PRIVATE SALE BY AGENT

(a) "Private Sale by Agent" Defined. A "private sale by agent" is defined as the sale by the trustee or Debtor of estate property other than real estate using an agent that is in the business of selling such property in a commercially reasonable manner' that would satisfy Indiana Code § 26–1–9.1–610. At the time approval of the sale is sought, the trustee or Debtor has not identified the purchaser or the exact purchase price.

(b) Contents of Motion. Any Motion to Sell by private sale using an agent shall identify:

(1) the property to be sold;

(2) information to support the determination that the agent is in the business of selling similar property in a commercially reasonable manner;

(3) the amount of any exemption claimed in the property; and

(4) a disclosure if the property to be sold contains personally identifiable information and, if so, the measures that will be taken to comply with 11 U.S.C. § 363(b)(1).

(c) Combining Retention and Compensation of Agent with Motion. The trustee or Debtor may combine a request to retain and to compensate the agent with the motion to sell. Any such request shall provide the information required by Fed.R.Bankr.P. 2014, describe how compensation will be determined, and estimate the fees to be paid.

(d) Notice. Unless the Court by separate order shortens the notice period, the movant shall distribute notice that provides twenty-one (21) days after the date of service for objections to be filed. The notice shall include a description of the property to be sold; the name of and contact information for the agent; the proposed terms of compensation for the agent, if proposed retention has not been noticed separately; and the location of the property prior to sale. The movant shall also file a certificate of service that complies with S.D.Ind. B–9013–2. The motion, notice, and certificate of service may be combined into one document. A sample combined motion to sell, notice, and certificate of service is available on the Court's website.

(e) Report of Sale. No later than fourteen (14) days after a private sale by agent has been completed, the movant shall file a report of sale pursuant to Fed.R.Bankr.P. 6004(f)(1). If retention and compensation of the agent were authorized by the order granting the motion to sell, pursuant to subparagraph (c), the report of sale shall include the amount of compensation actually paid to the agent.

[Effective October 27, 2014.]

B–6004–4. SALE BY AUCTION

(a) "Sale by Auction" Defined. A "sale by auction" is any sale by public auction, with no previously identified initial bidder.

(b) Contents of Motion. Any Motion to Sell by auction shall identify:

(1) the property to be sold;

(2) the name of and contact information for the entity conducting the auction;

(3) the date, time and place of the sale, if known, or instructions on how that information can be obtained;

(4) any bid procedures proposed for the sale, even if those bid procedures were previously disclosed in an application to employ an auctioneer; and

(5) a disclosure if the property to be sold contains personally identifiable information and, if so, the measures that will be taken to comply with 11 U.S.C. § 363(b)(1).

(c) Notice. Unless the Court by separate order shortens the notice period, the movant shall distribute notice that provides twenty-one (21) days after the date of service for objections to be filed. The notice shall provide the information required by subparagraph (b) of this rule. The movant shall also file a certificate of service that complies with S.D.Ind. B–9013–2. The motion, notice, and certificate of service may be combined into one document. A sample combined motion to sell, notice, and certificate of service is available on the Court's website.

(d) Report of Sale. Unless otherwise ordered by the Court, no later than fourteen (14) days after an auction the auctioneer or the party that filed the application to employ the auctioneer shall file the report pursuant to Fed.R.Bankr.P. 6004(f)(1).

[Effective October 27, 2014.]

B–6004–5. SALE WITH PROSPECTIVE PURCHASER IDENTIFIED BUT BIDS CONSIDERED

(a) "Sale with Prospective Purchaser Identified but Bids Considered" Defined. A "sale with prospective purchaser identified but bids considered" is also known as a "sale with a stalking horse bidder," and is a proposed sale to a specific entity for a set price, including a credit bid from a secured creditor, with competitive bids to be considered.

(b) Contents of Motion to Sell With Bid Procedures. Any Motion to Sell to a prospective purchaser but with bids considered shall identify or include:

(1) the property to be sold;

(2) the prospective purchaser ("Prospective Purchaser");

(3) the sales price and an estimate of the net proceeds to be received by the estate (including a deduction for any exemption);

(4) a brief summary of all material contingencies to the sale, together with a copy of the agreement, if available;

(5) the executory contracts and leases proposed to be assumed or rejected as part of the sale, if any;

(6) a description of any known relationship between the Prospective Purchaser and its insiders and the Debtor and its insiders or the description of the manner in which the property was marketed for sale, and a description of any other offer to purchase;

(7) a description of any known relationship between the Prospective Purchaser and its insiders and the Debtor and its insiders or the trustee;

(8) a statement setting forth any relationship or connection the trustee or the Debtor (including its insiders) will have with the Prospective Purchaser

after the consummation of the sale, assuming it is approved;

(9) if a topping fee or break-up fee is proposed to be paid to the Prospective Purchaser if another bidder prevails at the sale, a statement of the conditions under which the topping fee or break-up fee would be payable and the factual basis on which the seller determined the provision was reasonable;

(10) the identities of any other entity that expressed to the movant an interest in the purchase of all or a material portion of the assets to be sold within ninety (90) days prior to the filing of the sale motion, the offers made by them (if any), and the nature of the offer;

(11) any bid procedures proposed for the sale;

(12) a disclosure if the property to be sold contains personally identifiable information and, if so, the measures that will be taken to comply with 11 U.S.C. § 363(b)(1); and

(13) if the case is pending under Chapter 11, and proposes the sale of all or substantially all of the Debtor's assets, the following:

(A) If schedules have not been filed by the Debtor, a summary of the Debtor's debt structure, including the amount of the Debtor's secured debt, priority claims, and general unsecured claims; and

(B) If a creditors' committee, or its equivalent, existed pre-petition, the identity of the members of the committee and the companies with which they are affiliated and the identity of any counsel.

(c) **Notice of Motion to Sell and to Approve Bid Procedures.** After obtaining direction from the Court as to the contents of the notice, the movant shall distribute notice of the motion to sell and of the proposed bid procedures. If a notice of the opportunity to object is directed, unless the Court by separate order has shortened the notice period, that notice shall provide twenty-one (21) days after the date of service for objections to be filed. The notice shall provide the information required by subparagraph (b) of this rule. The movant shall also file a certificate of service that complies with S.D.Ind. B–9013–2. The motion, notice, and certificate of service may be combined into one document. A sample combined motion to sell and to approve bid procedures, notice, and certificate of service is available on the Court's website.

(d) **Notice of Approval of Bid Procedures and of Sale Process.** If the Court enters an order approving the bid procedures and setting the sale process, then the movant shall distribute notice of that order. The notice shall include the bid procedures; the date, time, and place where bids will be considered; and the date, time, and place of the hearing to approve the sale. The movant shall also file a certificate of service that complies with S.D.Ind. B–9013–2. A sample combined

notice and certificate of service is available on the Court's website.

(e) **Order Approving Sale.**

(1) *Sale to Prospective Purchaser.* If the Prospective Purchaser prevails at the sale, then the Court shall enter an order approving that sale.

(2) *Sale to Different Entity: No Change in Terms Except Price.* If a sale pursuant to this rule results in a sale to a party other than the identified Prospective Purchaser, with no change in terms other than the purchase price, then at the hearing on approval of the sale the movant shall identify the successful purchaser and the change in price, and shall make any request for approval of a topping or break-up fee if one was disclosed in the motion to sell. The Court shall enter an order approving that sale.

(3) *Sale to Different Entity with Change in Terms.* If a sale pursuant to this rule results in a sale to a party other than the identified Prospective Purchaser, and the terms of that sale other than price have changed, including but not limited to the proposed assumption or rejection of leases and contracts, then the movant shall identify the successful purchaser and the change in terms and shall make any request for approval of a topping or break-up fee if one was disclosed in the motion to sell. The Court shall consider whether the change in terms requires additional notice to parties who may be affected by those changes. If no additional notice is required, the Court shall enter an order approving the sale. If additional notice is required, the Court shall enter the order approving the sale only after such additional notice period.

(f) **Report of Sale.** No later than fourteen (14) days after a sale pursuant to this rule has been completed, the movant shall file a report of sale pursuant to Fed.R.Bankr.P. 6004(f)(1).

[Effective October 27, 2014.]

B–6005–1. LIQUIDATORS/AUCTIONEERS AND APPRAISERS

(a) **Bond Required.** All liquidators/auctioneers retained by a trustee or Debtor in any case who will come into possession or control of the assets or proceeds of assets of an estate shall either participate in the bond program administered by the UST or post a bond with the United States as obligee for the full value of the assets in the possession or control of the liquidator/auctioneer, unless otherwise ordered by the Court.

(b) **Remittance of Gross Proceeds.** Unless otherwise ordered by the Court, all gross proceeds shall be remitted to the trustee or Debtor within fourteen (14) days of the sale. Upon motion of any party in interest and for good cause shown, the Court may authorize the liquidator/auctioneer to submit net proceeds or to turn over to a secured creditor the net proceeds realized from the sale of that creditor's collateral.

(c) Validity of Checks. The validity of any checks or bank drafts accepted by the liquidator/auctioneer shall be the sole responsibility of the liquidator/auctioneer.

(d) Separate Escrow Account. If the liquidator/auctioneer does not make an immediate settlement with the trustee or Debtor in any case, and the proceeds of the property sold are $50,000.00 or more, the auctioneer shall open a segregated escrow or trust account for deposit of the sale proceeds. This account shall be designated by the bankruptcy estate case name and shall require the co-signature of the trustee for any withdrawals. If the proceeds of the sale are less than $50,000.00, the proceeds may be deposited in the auctioneer's trust or client fund account.

(e) Appraiser Serving as Liquidator/Auctioneer. No appraiser, agent, or employee of an appraiser who has been employed in a bankruptcy case may serve as the liquidator/auctioneer in that same case without the approval of the Court.

(f) Liquidator/Auctioneer Purchasing at Sale. No liquidator/auctioneer, or any agent or employee of a liquidator/auctioneer employed in a case may purchase an asset from the estate.

[Effective June 1, 2010. Amended effective October 27, 2014.]

B–6006–1. ASSUMPTION, REJECTION, OR ASSIGNMENT OF EXECUTORY CONTRACTS OR UNEXPIRED LEASES: NOTICE

(a) Assumption, Rejection, or Assignment. A party seeking to assume, reject or assign an executory contract or unexpired lease shall give notice of the motion. Notice shall be given to the parties identified in Fed.R.Bankr.P. 6006(c) as well as to any sublessee. The notice shall allow fourteen (14) days from the date of service to file objections. Along with the motion, the moving party shall file a copy of the notice and a certificate of service that complies with S.D.Ind. B–9013–2. The motion, notice, and certificate of service may be combined into one document. A sample combined motion for assumption or rejection or assignment, notice, and certificate of service is available on the Court's website.

(b) Compelling Assumption or Rejection. A party seeking to compel the trustee or the Debtor to assume or reject an executory contract or lease shall give notice of the motion. Notice shall be given to the Debtor, any trustee, counsel of record, the United States Trustee, any other party to the contract or lease, and any sublessee identified on the Debtor's

schedules. The notice shall give fourteen (14) days from the date of service to file objections. Along with the motion, the moving party shall file a copy of the notice and certificate of service that complies with S.D.Ind. B–9013–2. The motion, notice, and certificate of service may be combined into one document. A sample combined motion to compel assumption or rejection, notice, and certificate of service is available on the Court's website.

[Effective October 27, 2014.]

B–6007–1. ABANDONMENT OF PROPERTY

(a) Trustee's Notice of Possible Assets and Abandonment. In Chapter 7 cases where the trustee files a notice of possible assets and abandonment, the Clerk shall give notice to all creditors and parties in interest of those assets which are not being abandoned by the trustee, and of the proposed abandonment of all other assets.

(b) Trustee's Notice of Abandonment. In Chapter 7 cases where the trustee files a notice of abandonment more than one day after filing a notice of possible assets, the trustee shall distribute the notice to parties in interest and all creditors, except as otherwise provided in S.D.Ind. B–2002–1(b). The notice shall allow at least fourteen (14) days from the date of service to file objections. Along with the notice, the trustee shall file a certificate of service that complies with S.D.Ind. B–9013–2. A sample notice is available on the Court's website.

(c) Motion to Abandon Filed by Party in Interest. A motion to abandon filed by a party in interest shall be served on the Debtor and parties in interest. Notice of the motion shall be distributed to the Debtor, parties in interest, and all creditors, except as otherwise provided by S.D.Ind. B–2002–1(b). The notice shall allow at least fourteen (14) days from the date of service to file objections. Along with the motion, the moving party shall file a copy of the notice and a certificate of service that complies with S.D.Ind. 9013–2. A sample notice is available on the Court's website.

[Effective June 1, 2010. Amended effective October 1, 2012.]

B–6008–1. REDEMPTION OF PROPERTY

(a) Service. The Debtor shall serve the motion and notice thereof on the lien holder, in accordance with Fed.R.Bankr.P. 9014(b) and 7004 The notice shall allow at least twenty-one (21) days from the date of service to file objections. The motion and notice may be combined in one document. A sample combined motion and notice is available on the Court's website.

(b) Filing and Certificate of Service. Along with the motion, the Debtor must file with the Court a copy of the notice and a certificate of service that complies with S.D.Ind. 9013–2.

[Effective June 1, 2010. Amended effective October 1, 2012.]

B–7001–1. ADVERSARY PROCEEDING COVER SHEET

(a) **Cover Sheet Required.** A party filing an adversary proceeding non-electronically shall also file a cover sheet using Official Form 104. Failure to provide the adversary proceeding cover sheet may result in dismissal of the complaint.

(b) **Addresses for Defendants Required.** A plaintiff filing an adversary proceeding without counsel is required to provide the addresses of all defendants, to facilitate service of the summons by the Clerk.

[Effective February 10, 2014.]

B–7005–2. FILING OF DISCOVERY MATERIALS

Discovery materials (whether discovery requests, responses, or deposition transcripts) may not be filed with the court except in the following circumstances:

(a) **Relevant to Certain Motions.** A party seeking relief under Fed. R. Civ. P. 26(c) or 37, or by way of a pretrial motion that could result in a final order on an issue, must file with the motion those parts of the discovery materials relevant to the motion.

(b) **For Anticipated Use at Trial.** When a party can reasonably anticipate using discovery materials at trial, the party must file the relevant portions at the start of the trial.

(c) **Materials Necessary for Appeal.** A party seeking for purposes of appeal to supplement the record with discovery materials not previously filed may do so by stipulation of the parties or by court order approving the filing.

[Effective June 1, 2010. Amended effective October 1, 2012.]

B–7006–1. EXTENSIONS OF TIME

(a) **Initial Extensions.** In every adversary proceeding pending in this Court in which a party wishes to obtain an initial extension of time not exceeding twenty-eight (28) days within which to file a responsive pleading or a response to a written request for discovery or request for admission, or response to a motion, the party shall contact counsel for the opposing party, or if the opposing party is not represented by counsel, the opposing party, and solicit that person's agreement to the extension. In the event that person does not object to the extension or cannot with due diligence be reached, the party requesting the extension shall file a notice with the Court reciting the lack of objection to the extension or the fact that the person could not with due diligence be reached. The

notice shall state the original due date and the date to which the time is extended. No further filings with the Court nor action by the Court shall be required for the extension.

(b) **Other Extensions.** Any other request for an extension of time, unless made in open Court or at a telephonic pre-trial conference, shall be made by written motion.

[Effective June 1, 2010. Amended effective June 1, 2011; October 1, 2012.]

B–7008–1. REQUIRED STATEMENT REGARDING CONSENT TO ENTRY OF ORDERS OR JUDGMENT IN CORE PROCEEDING

In an adversary proceeding, in addition to the statements required by Fed.R.Bankr.P. 7008(a), the complaint, counterclaim, cross-claim, or third party complaint shall contain a statement that the pleader does or does not consent to the entry of final orders or judgment by the Bankruptcy Judge.

[Effective December 3, 2012.]

B–7012–1. REQUIRED STATEMENT IN RESPONSIVE PLEADING REGARDING CONSENT TO ENTRY OF ORDERS OR JUDGMENT IN CORE PROCEEDING

In addition to statements required by Fed. R.Bankr.P. 7012(b), a responsive pleading shall include a statement that the party does or does not consent to the entry of final orders or judgment by the Bankruptcy Judge.

[Effective December 3, 2012.]

B–7016–1. PRE–TRIAL PROCEDURES IN ADVERSARY PROCEEDINGS

(a) **Use of Pre–Trial or Pre–Hearing Conferences.** The Court may conduct a pre-trial or a pre-hearing conference in any adversary proceeding, at the Court's discretion, upon notice to parties in interest.

(b) **Applicability of S.D.Ind. L.R. 16–1.** The Court may determine on its own motion or on the request of any party in interest which provisions of S.D.Ind. L.R. 16–1 shall apply to an adversary proceeding governed by Fed.R.Bankr.P. 7001, et seq.

(c) **Telephonic Pre–Hearing or Pre–Trial Conference.** No later than twenty-four (24) hours before the time scheduled for a pre-hearing or pretrial conference, any party to the conference may request that the conference be conducted by telephone or that the party be allowed to participate by telephone. Such request may be made in writing, directed to chambers, or by telephone. At the time of the request, the requesting party shall advise the Court whether any other party to the conference has objected to the request. The request may be granted or denied at the sole discretion of the Court.

[Effective June 1, 2010.]

B-7026-2. FORM OF CERTAIN DISCOVERY DOCUMENTS

(a) **Form of Discovery Requests.** A party propounding written discovery under Fed. R. Civ. P. 33, 34, or 36 must number each interrogatory or request sequentially and supply the written discovery to the responding party in an editable word processing format.

(b) **Form of Discovery Responses.** A party responding (by answer or objection) to written discovery must fully quote each interrogatory or request immediately before each response and number each response to correspond with the interrogatory or request.

[Effective June 1, 2010. Amended effective October 1, 2012.]

B-7030-1. CONDUCT OF DEPOSITIONS

(a) **Questions About an Asserted Privilege.** An attorney may question a deponent who refuses to answer a question on the basis of privilege about information related to the appropriateness of the privilege, including whether:

(1) the privilege applies under the circumstances;

(2) the privilege has been waived; and

(3) circumstances exist to overcome a claim of qualified privilege.

(b) **Private Conference Regarding a Pending Question.** A deponent's attorney may not initiate a private conference with the deponent during the deposition about a pending question except to determine whether to assert a claim of privilege.

(c) **Raising Objections with the Court.** A party may recess a deposition to submit an objection by phone to a judicial officer if the objection:

(1) could cause the deposition to be terminated; and

(2) can be resolved without submitting written materials to the court.

(d) **Scheduling Depositions.** Attorneys will make a good faith effort to schedule depositions in a manner that avoids scheduling conflicts. Unless agreed by counsel or otherwise ordered by the court, no deposition will be scheduled on less than fourteen (14) days' notice.

[Effective October 1, 2012.]

B-7036-1. REQUESTS FOR ADMISSIONS

No party may serve on any other party more than 25 requests for admission without leave of court. Requests relating to the authenticity or genuineness of documents are not subject to this limitation. Any party desiring to serve additional requests for admission must file a written motion setting forth the proposed additional requests for admission and the reason(s) for their use.

[Effective October 1, 2012.]

B-7037-1. DISCOVERY DISPUTES

(a) **Required Actions Prior to Court Involvement.** Prior to involving the court in any discovery dispute, including disputes involving depositions, counsel must confer in a good faith attempt to resolve the dispute. If any such dispute cannot be resolved in this manner, counsel are encouraged to contact the chambers of the assigned Judge to determine whether the Judge is available to resolve the discovery dispute by way of a telephone conference or other proceeding prior to counsel filing a formal discovery motion. When the dispute involves an objection raised during a deposition that threatens to prevent completion of the deposition, any party may recess the deposition to contact the Judge's chambers.

(b) **Requirements of Motion to Compel.** In the event that the discovery dispute is not resolved at the conference, counsel may file a motion to compel or other motion raising the dispute. Any motion raising a discovery dispute must contain a statement setting forth the efforts taken to resolve the dispute, including the date, time, and place of any discovery conference and the names of all participating parties. The court may deny any motion raising a discovery dispute that does not contain such a statement.

(c) **Pro Se Parties.** Discovery disputes involving pro se parties are not subject to this rule.

[Effective October 1, 2012.]

B-7041-1. DISMISSAL FOR FAILURE TO PROSECUTE

The court may dismiss an adversary proceeding if:

(a) the plaintiff has not taken any action for 6 months;

(b) the Judge assigned to the case or the Clerk has given notice to the parties that the case will be dismissed for failure to prosecute it; and

(c) at least twenty-eight (28) days have passed since the notice was given.

[Effective June 1, 2010. Amended effective October 1, 2012.]

B–7041–2. COMPLAINTS TO DENY OR REVOKE DISCHARGE: DISMISSAL OR SETTLEMENT

(a) Contents and Service of Notice of, Motion for, or Stipulation Regarding Voluntary Dismissal of Complaint to Deny or Revoke Discharge. Any dismissal, whether by notice, motion or stipulation, of a complaint to deny or revoke the Debtor's discharge pursuant to 11 U.S.C. § 727, shall be served upon the UST, any trustee, counsel of record, and any party that has intervened in the adversary proceeding pursuant to Fed.R.Bankr.P. 7024. The notice, motion or stipulation shall contain a recital concerning the consideration, if any, for the dismissal or the terms and conditions of any agreement concerning the dismissal.

(b) Objection to Dismissal. Unless the UST, the trustee, or another entity seeks to intervene or to be substituted for the plaintiff in the proceeding or objects to the dismissal within twenty-one (21) days following service of the motion, the Court may dismiss the complaint and/or close the adversary proceeding, upon such terms and conditions as it deems proper, without further notice or hearing.

[Effective June 1, 2010.]

B–7055–1. DEFAULT

(a) Application for Entry of Default. A party seeking an entry of default from the clerk pursuant to Fed.R.Bankr.P. 7055(a) must file an application seeking such relief. Such application must be accompanied by an affidavit indicating that the defendant(s) has failed to plead or otherwise defend and that the defendant(s) is not protected by the Servicemembers Civil Relief Act of 2003 and is not a minor or incompetent person.

(b) Motions for Default Judgment. Notwithstanding Fed.R.Bankr.P. 7055(b)(1), a party seeking a default judgment shall present a motion to the Judge, rather than to the Clerk, and shall also tender a proposed judgment. If the claim to which no response was made is for a "sum certain," then the motion shall be accompanied by an affidavit showing the principal amount due and owing, not exceeding the amount sought in the claim, plus interest, if any computed by the movant, with credit for all payments received to date clearly set forth, and costs, if any, pursuant to 28 U.S.C. § 1920. If the amount of the claim is not readily ascertainable or if the amount requested in the motion exceeds the amount stated in the claim, the Court may conduct a hearing on the motion for default judgment.

(c) Certificate of Service. Both the application for entry of default and motion for default judgment must be accompanied by a certificate of service that complies with S.D.Ind. B–9013–2.

[Effective June 1, 2010. Amended effective October 1, 2012; October 27, 2014.]

B–7056–1. SUMMARY JUDGMENT PROCEDURE

(a) Movant's Obligations. A party seeking summary judgment must file and serve a supporting brief and any evidence (that is not already in the record) that the party relies on to support the motion. Unless otherwise ordered by the Court, the supporting brief shall be no more than thirty-five (35) pages. The brief must include a section labeled "Statement of Material Facts Not in Dispute" containing the facts:

(1) that are potentially determinative of the motion; and

(2) as to which the movant contends there is no genuine issue.

(b) Non–Movant's Obligations. A party opposing a summary judgment motion must, within twenty-eight (28) days after the movant serves the motion, file and serve a response brief and any evidence (that is not already in the record) that the party relies on to oppose the motion. Unless otherwise ordered by the Court, the response brief shall be no more than thirty-five (35) pages. The response must include a section labeled "Statement of Material Facts in Dispute" that identifies the potentially determinative facts and factual disputes that the party contends demonstrate a dispute of fact precluding summary judgment.

(c) Reply. The movant may file and serve a reply brief within fourteen (14) days after a response is served. Unless otherwise ordered by the Court, the reply brief shall be no more than twenty (20) pages.

(d) Surreply. A party opposing a summary judgment motion may file a surreply brief only if the movant cites new evidence in the reply or objects to the admissibility of the evidence cited in the response. The surreply must be filed and served within seven (7) days after the movant serves the reply and must be limited to the new evidence and objections.

(e) Citations to Supporting Facts. A party must support each fact the party asserts in a brief with a citation to a discovery response, a deposition, an affidavit, or other admissible evidence. The evidence must be in the record or in an appendix to the brief. The citation must refer to a page or paragraph number or otherwise similarly specify where the relevant information can be found in the supporting evidence.

(f) Oral Argument or Hearing. Unless a party has requested a hearing, the court **may** decide summary judgment motions without oral argument or hearing.

(g) Notice Requirement for Pro Se Cases. A party seeking summary judgment against an unrepresented party must serve that party with a notice that:

(1) briefly and plainly states that a fact stated in the moving party's Statement of Material Facts and supported by admissible evidence will be accepted by the court as true unless the opposing party cites specific admissible evidence contradicting that statement of material fact; and

(2) sets forth the full text of Fed.R.Civ.P. 56 and this rule; and

(3) otherwise complies with applicable case law regarding required notice to pro se litigants opposing summary judgment motions.

(h) Compliance. The court may, in the interest of justice or for good cause, excuse failure to comply strictly with this rule.

[Effective June 1, 2010. Amended effective October 1, 2012; October 27, 2014.]

B-7065-2. MOTIONS FOR PRELIMINARY INJUNCTIONS AND TEMPORARY RESTRAINING ORDERS

(a) Adversary Proceeding Required. Prior to submitting a motion for a temporary restraining order or for a preliminary injunction, an adversary proceeding shall be initiated by the filing of a complaint pursuant to Fed.R.Bankr.P. 7001(7).

(b) Motion for Temporary Restraining Order or for Preliminary Injunction. A motion for a temporary restraining order or for preliminary injunction shall be made by a document separate from the complaint and shall be accompanied by:

(1) a separate memorandum in support of the motion;

(2) a declaration or affidavit by the movant or counsel for the movant showing compliance with Fed. R.Bankr.P. 7065 regarding notice to opposing parties; and

(3) a copy of the filed complaint.

(c) Proposed Order. Along with the motion for temporary restraining order or preliminary injunction, the movant shall upload an appropriate proposed order.

[Effective June 1, 2010. Amended effective October 1, 2012.]

B-7067-1. REGISTRY FUNDS

(a) Interpleader and Other Deposit Motions: Contents. Any action in interpleader or that seeks to deposit funds with the Clerk pursuant to Fed.R. Bankr.P. 7067 shall include the filer's certification that the proposed deposit has been discussed with the Clerk or the Clerk's financial supervisor and that the

filer understands the terms and conditions that will be imposed upon the deposit.

(b) Fees Charged Against Deposits. The Clerk shall deduct from income earned on registry funds invested in interest-bearing accounts or instruments a fee, not exceeding that authorized by the Judicial Conference of the United States and set by the Director of the Administrative Office of the U.S. Courts in accordance with the schedule which shall be published periodically by the Director in the Federal Register. The fee shall be withdrawn whenever income earned becomes available for deduction and shall be deposited in the United States Treasury without further order of the Court. This assessment shall apply to all registry funds invested in interest-bearing accounts held outside the United States Treasury. Funds deposited with the Court pursuant to 11 U.S.C. § 347(a) are not subject to this rule.

[Effective June 1, 2010.]

B-7069-1. EXECUTION/ENFORCEMENT OF JUDGMENTS

(a) Availability of Enforcement Remedies. A trustee or Debtor who seeks to enforce a judgment in an adversary proceeding or an order of turnover for the benefit of the bankruptcy estate may pursue collection in the Bankruptcy Court. The order of turnover must be for a sum certain or direct turnover of specific tangible property.

(b) Applicability of District Court Rules. S.D.Ind. L.R. 69–1 (Execution), S.D.Ind. L.R. 69–2 (Interrogatories to Garnishees), and S.D.Ind. L.R. 69–3 (Final Orders in Wage Garnishment) apply to adversary proceedings and to orders directing a Debtor to turn over property. Answers to Interrogatories should not be filed with the Court but should be sent to the trustee or Debtor only.

[Effective June 1, 2010. Amended effective October 27, 2014.]

B-8006-1. RECORD AND ISSUES ON APPEAL

(a) Designating Record on Appeal. If the parties fail to file a timely designation of record with the Clerk pursuant to Fed.R.Bankr.P. 8006, the Clerk shall forward a certification that no designation of record was filed.

(b) Copies of Record. The party filing the designation of items to be included in the record on appeal shall list the items with the Court's document numbers as displayed on the docket.

[Effective June 1, 2010.]

B–9006–1. PROCEDURE FOR OBTAINING SHORTENED AND/OR LIMITED NOTICE OF NON–FIRST DAY MOTIONS

(a) General Application. This provision shall govern the procedures to be followed for any matter as to which shortened notice or shortened notice and expedited hearing is requested pursuant to Fed.R.Bankr.P. 9006(c) (a "9006(c) Request") except for any First Day Motion as defined by S.D.Ind. B–9013–2. The 9006(c) Request shall be considered by the Court without a hearing. If granted, the Court will issue an Order Shortening Notice and/or Setting Expedited Hearing.

(b) Filing Requirements. A 9006(c) Request shall be made by separate written motion and shall clearly refer to the non-First Day Motion or the contested matter to which it pertains (the "Underlying Motion"), shall specifically state the nature of the emergency or why the need for expedited treatment, and shall state the time by which the notice is to be shortened or the requested expedited hearing is to be held. The movant shall notify the chambers of the Judge assigned to the case of the filing of the 9006(c) Request and shall upload or otherwise tender an Order Shortening Notice and/or Setting Expedited Hearing as described below.

(c) Content of Order Shortening Notice and/or Setting Expedited Hearing. The Order Shortening Notice and/or Setting Expedited Hearing shall provide:

(1) the date and time of the hearing, if any;

(2) a brief description of the relief requested in the Underlying Motion;

(3) the last date to object to the Underlying Motion, and if no objection date is established, that objections are due immediately before the hearing;

(4) that any objection must be in writing and filed with the Clerk,

(5) that a copy of the written objection must also be served upon counsel for the movant, or the movant if not represented by counsel; and

(6) the Clerk's address for the division in which the case is pending;

(7) if no hearing was set in the initial notice, a statement that if any objection is filed, a hearing will be scheduled on the Underlying Motion and objections thereto by separate notice;

(8) if objections are due immediately before the hearing, that telephonic notice of the filing of the objection shall be given to the chambers of the Judge to whom the case is assigned.

(d) Service and Distribution of 9006(c) Request, Underlying Motion and Order Shortening Notice and/or Setting Expedited Hearing.

(1) *General Requirements.* The movant shall serve, by fax, e-mail or hand delivery, the 9006(c) Request and the Underlying Motion, along with the Order Shortening Notice and/or Setting Expedited Hearing, on the Service List, any party that has, or claims to have, an interest in the property to be affected by the relief requested in the Underlying Motion, parties required to receive notice under the applicable Federal Rule of Bankruptcy Procedure, and any other party as directed by the Court. If the documents are more than three (3) pages in length, the movant may fax the first page of the motion with instructions for obtaining all documents on the movant's website or by email. If the matter is a contested matter within an adversary proceeding, service of the 9006(c) Request and the Underlying Motion shall be made in the manner described above but only upon the parties to the adversary proceeding and any other party as directed by the Court.

(2) *Permissibility of Service by Overnight Delivery.* Service by overnight delivery is acceptable if sent at least 48 hours before any deadline or hearing in the notice.

(e) Certificate of Service. Prior to the hearing on, or the deadline for filing objections to, the Underlying Motion, the movant shall file a certificate of service that complies with S.D.Ind. B–9013–2 certifying that copies of the 9006(c) Request, Underlying Motion and Order Setting Emergency Hearing and/or Expedited Notice were sent to all parties required to receive notice.

(f) Motion to Limit Notice. If expedited service on the parties required to receive under the Federal Rules of Bankruptcy Procedure is impractical or cost-prohibitive, the movant may also seek to limit notice by filing a separate Motion to Limit Notice. Unless otherwise directed, notice may be limited to the UST, Debtor, the Unsecured Creditors Committee or its counsel if applicable, or if there is no Committee, the List of 20 Largest Unsecured Creditors, the Chapter 7, 11 or 13 trustee if applicable, any party that has or claims to have an interest in the property to be affected by the Underlying Motion, and all other counsel of record.

[Effective June 1, 2010. Amended effective October 1, 2012.]

B–9006–2. PRESUMPTIVE OBJECTION PERIOD IN CHAPTER 11 CASES

In a Chapter 11 case, when the Court opts to set an objection period on a motion or application rather than a set a hearing, if no other time period is set by the Federal Rules of Bankruptcy Procedure or these local rules, objections shall be filed within twenty-one (21) days from the service of the motion or application. The Court on its own or on the motion of a party, filed pursuant to L.R. B–9006–1, may shorten the time period for objection.

[Effective October 27, 2014.]

B–9010–1. APPEARANCES

(a) Appearances

(1) *Requirement in Bankruptcy Cases.* Each attorney representing a party, whether in person or by filing any document (other than a proof of claim, a reaffirmation agreement, request pursuant to Fed. R.Bankr.P. 2002(g), or creditor change of address), must file a separate Appearance for such party. Only those attorneys who have filed an Appearance in a pending action shall be entitled to receive service of case documents. An attorney who files a case for a Debtor using the Court's electronic filing system and is designated as counsel for the Debtor in that process need not file a separate appearance for that case.

(2) *Requirement in Adversary Proceedings.* Counsel for the plaintiff, including Debtor's counsel, shall file an appearance with the complaint. Counsel for a defendant, including Debtor's counsel, shall file an appearance before filing any other pleading.

(3) *Content of Appearance; Service.* The appearance shall include the attorney's address, telephone number, fax number, and an e-mail address for electronic service. Any change to an appearance shall be filed with the Clerk and served upon all counsel of record and the Debtor if not represented by counsel.

(b) Removed and Transferred Cases. Any attorney of record whose name does not appear on this Court's docket following the removal of a case must file an Appearance or a copy of the appearance as previously filed in the other venue.

Within twenty-one (21) days of removal or transfer of a case to this Court, any attorney of record who is not admitted to practice before this Court must either comply with this Court's admission policy, as set forth in S.D.Ind. B–9010–2, or withdraw his/her appearance, as permitted under section (c) of this rule.

(c) Withdrawal of Appearance in a Bankruptcy Case.

(1) *Successor Counsel Has Not Appeared.*

(A) Counsel for a Debtor desiring to withdraw his/her appearance in any case shall file a motion requesting leave to do so. Such motion shall fix a date for such withdrawal and shall include satisfactory evidence of either a written request to withdraw by counsel's client or a written notice regarding the withdrawal from counsel to counsel's client at least seven (7) days in advance of the withdrawal date and shall provide the Court with the client's last known telephone number.

(B) Counsel for a creditor or other non-debtor party who no longer has any issue pending in the case may file a notice of withdrawal. If counsel is involved in a pending issue, then counsel shall file a motion requesting leave to do so, complying with the requirements for such motions in the preceding subparagraph.

(2) *Successor Counsel Has Appeared.* No advance notice to client is required if an appearance by co-counsel, who will remain in the case, or if an appearance by successor counsel, is filed prior to or concurrently with a motion to withdraw. However, the attorney being replaced must file a motion to withdraw pursuant to subparagraph (c)(1), before that attorney will be removed as a counsel of record in the case unless a substitution of appearance is filed by new counsel.

(d) Withdrawal of Appearance in an Adversary Proceeding

(1) *Successor Counsel Has Not Appeared.* Counsel for any plaintiff or defendant in an adversary proceeding desiring to withdraw his/her appearance shall file a motion requesting leave to do so. Such motion shall fix a date for such withdrawal and shall include satisfactory evidence of either a written request to withdraw by counsel's client or a written notice regarding the withdrawal from counsel to counsel's client at least seven (7) days in advance of the withdrawal date and shall provide the Court with the client's last known telephone number.

(2) *Successor Counsel Has Appeared.* No advance notice to client is required if an appearance by co-counsel, who will remain in the case, or if an appearance by successor counsel, is filed prior to or concurrently with a motion to withdraw. However, the attorney being replaced must file a motion to withdraw before that attorney will be removed as a counsel of record in the case unless a substitution of appearance is filed by new counsel.

[Effective June 1, 2010. Amended effective June 1, 2011; September 23, 2013; February 10, 2014; October 27, 2014.]

B–9010–2. BAR ADMISSION

(a) The bar of this Court shall consist of those persons admitted to practice in the Southern District of Indiana.

(b) In all matters and proceedings before this Court, a person not a member of the bar of the Southern District of Indiana shall not be permitted to practice in this Court or before any officer thereof as an attorney, unless

(1) such person appears on his or her own behalf as a party;

(2) such person is admitted to practice in any other United States Court or the highest Court of any state,

is not currently under suspension or subject to other disciplinary action, and is, on motion to this Court pursuant to subparagraph (c), granted leave to appear in a specific action; or

(3) such person appears as an attorney for the United States. However, for the purposes of filing any document as to which an appearance is not required under S.D.Ind. B–9010–1(a)(1) or participating in a meeting conducted pursuant to 11 U.S.C. § 341, a creditor need not be represented or appear by an attorney.

(c) In order to obtain leave of this Court to appear in a specific action, the attorney seeking to be admitted must file with the Court a Motion to Appear pro hac vice. A separate motion for each attorney shall be filed, shall be in a form that complies substantially with the form available on the Court's website, and shall be accompanied by:

(1) if not admitted to practice in the State of Indiana, an affidavit that substantially complies with the form available on the Court's website; and

(2) a proposed form of order granting the motion.

(d) The Court may refuse to consider or act upon any request for relief filed by an attorney who is required to obtain leave to appear and has failed to do so.

(e) Whenever necessary to facilitate the conduct of the case, the Court may require any attorney appearing in any action in this Court to retain as local counsel a member of the bar of the Southern District of Indiana who maintains an office in this district.

(f) The Rules of Professional Conduct, as adopted by the Indiana Supreme Court, shall provide the rules governing conduct for those practicing in this Court.

[Effective June 1, 2010. Amended effective June 1, 2011.]

B–9013–1. MOTION PRACTICE; OBJECTIONS TO MOTIONS

(a) **Separate Motions and Objections.** Every application, motion, or other request for an order from the Court, including motions initiating contested matters, shall be filed separately, except that requests for alternative relief may be filed together, subject to paragraphs (b) and (c). All such requests shall be named in the caption, shall state with particularity the order or relief sought, and contain a short and plain statement concerning the factual basis or grounds for the motion. If the alternative relief requested has varying requirements for notice, the notice must provide the longest of the alternative periods. Objections to separately filed motions must also be filed separately.

(b) **Stay Relief or Adequate Protection Motions.** Motions seeking relief from the automatic stay or adequate protection may not be joined with any other objection or request for relief except abandonment.

(c) **Motions Where Hearing Scheduled by "Block Scheduling".** Where the hearing for the relief sought in the motion is subject to the "block scheduling" procedure established by the Court, the motion shall request only that type of relief, and a request for alternative relief may not be sought in the motion.

(d) **Content of Objections.** As to any matter in which the Court may grant relief without a hearing in the absence of a timely objection, objections to the motion, application, or request shall contain a short, plain statement concerning the factual or legal basis for the objection. The failure to state a sufficient legal or factual basis for the objection may result in the objection being overruled without a hearing.

(e) **Duty to Confer.** If a motion is contested, the movant shall confer with the respondent prior to the hearing to determine whether a consent order may be entered disposing of the motion, or in the alternative, to stipulate on as many facts and issues as possible.

[Effective June 1, 2010.]

B–9013–2. CERTIFICATE OF SERVICE

(a) **Filing.** All pleadings and documents filed in a bankruptcy case pursuant to Fed.R.Bankr.P. 9013 or 9014 shall comply with Fed.R.Bankr.P. 7005(d).

(b) **Requirements.** In addition to identifying the pleading or document served, certificates of service shall conform substantially to the certificate of service form adopted with the Administrative Policies and Procedures Manual and available on the Court's website.

(c) **Failure to Comply.** On its own motion, the Court may refuse consideration of or strike any pleading or document for which a certificate of service has not been filed or which lacks the information required by the Court's forms.

[Effective June 1, 2010. Amended effective June 1, 2011; September 23, 2013.]

B–9013–3. FIRST DAY MOTIONS IN CHAPTER 11 CASES

(a) **Motions Included.** In order to qualify as a First Day Motion, the motion must be filed with the petition, or within two (2) days thereafter, state in its caption that it is a First Day Motion, and be one of the motions included on the list below. The First Day Motions listed in (f) below shall be scheduled for an expedited hearing without any formal request by the Debtor. Other motions will only be set for hearing on an expedited basis if accompanied by a request for expedited hearing which establishes sufficient cause for such treatment.

(b) Procedure Prior to Filing. Prior to filing, the Debtor shall attempt to confer with and provide copies of any First Day Motion to the UST. Counsel shall include in any First Day Motion, or in a separate pleading, a statement of efforts made to meet with the UST and affected parties prior to filing when possible. The Debtor shall also contact the courtroom deputy for the Chief Judge to advise that a case with First Day Motions will be filed.

(c) Procedure Upon Filing. Upon filing, the Debtor shall contact the courtroom deputy for the Judge assigned. The Judge assigned, or a designated replacement, shall schedule and conduct a hearing on the First Day Motions within two (2) days of their filing, if possible, unless the Debtor requests a later hearing date.

(d) Service of First Day Motions and Notice. The Debtor shall serve copies of all First Day Motions and notice of the hearing on the initial Service List, known counsel for any party, and named respondents. Notice of the hearing and copies of the First Day Motions shall be served by fax, e-mail, or hand delivery. If the documents are more than three (3) pages in length, the movant may fax the first page of the motion with a statement as to the total number of pages in the document and instructions for obtaining all documents on the movant's website or by e-mail. Prior to the hearing, the Debtor shall file a certificate of service that complies with S.D.Ind. 9013–2. Failure to give timely notice may result in relief being denied or the hearing continued.

(e) Contents of Notice. The notice of hearing on the First Day Motions shall provide:

(1) the date and time of the hearing;

(2) a list by title of the First Day Motions; and

(3) the correct mailing address, fax number, telephone number, and e-mail address of the Debtor's counsel.

(f) List of Included Motions. The following shall be treated by the Court as First Day Motions if filed with the petition or within two (2) days thereafter:

(1) motion for joint administration;

(2) motion for use of cash collateral (interim hearing only) (see S.D.Ind. B–4001–2);

(3) motion for post-petition financing (interim hearing only) (see S.D.Ind. B–4001–2);

(4) motion to pay pre-petition employee wage claims (to the limit provided by 11 U.S.C. § 507);

(5) motion to limit notice generally;

(6) motion to provide adequate assurance to utilities;

(7) motion to pay pre-petition trust fund taxes;

(8) motion to honor pre-petition obligations to customers (to the limit provided by 11 U.S.C. § 507);

(9) motion to vary UST financial requirements, such as motion to authorize maintenance of existing bank accounts, existing business forms, cash management system, investment procedures, etc.;

(10) motion for authority to pay pre-petition claims of alleged critical vendors;

(11) motion to reject leases and contracts;

(12) motion to not appoint a creditors' committee pursuant to 11 U.S.C. § 1102(a)(3); and

(13) a Prepackaged Scheduling Motion (see S.D.Ind. B–2081–2).

[Effective June 1, 2010. Amended effective October 1, 2012; October 27, 2014.]

B–9014–1. APPLICABILITY OF ADVERSARY PROCEEDING RULES TO CONTESTED MATTERS

Unless otherwise ordered by the Court, the following adversary proceeding rules apply in contested matters other than motions to dismiss or convert a case:

7026–1	Discovery Disclosures and Conferences
7026–2	Filing of Discovery Materials
7030–1	Depositions
7036–1	Requests for Admissions
7037–1	Discovery Disputes
7041–1	Dismissal for Failure to Prosecute
7056–1	Summary Judgment

[Effective June 1, 2010. Amended effective January 1, 2012; October 1, 2012.]

B–9015–1. JURY TRIALS

(a) Authorization. Pursuant to S.D.Ind. L.R. 39–1, the District Court has authorized the Bankruptcy Judges of this District to conduct jury trials with the express consent of all parties.

(b) Applicability of District Court Rules. The following District Court rules concerning jury trials apply unless otherwise ordered by the Court:

38–1	Notation of a jury demand in a pleading
47–1	Voir dire
47–2	Communication with jurors
47–3	Juror costs
47–4	Jury; unanimous verdict

(c) Time for Consent. Unless within thirty (30) days after the demand for jury trial is filed the other parties to the proceeding file a consent, the Bankruptcy Judge shall request that the District Court withdraw the reference of the matter. Even if all parties consent, the Bankruptcy Judge will determine whether the request for a jury trial is proper.

[Effective June 1, 2010. Amended effective January 1, 2012.]

B–9016–1. SUBPOENAS

If a subpoena to produce or permit is to be served upon a nonparty, a copy of the proposed subpoena must be served on all other parties at least seven (7) days prior to service of the subpoena on the nonparty, unless the parties agree to a different time frame or the case management plan provides otherwise. Provided, however, that if such subpoena relates to a matter set for hearing within such seven (7) day period or arises out of a bona fide emergency, such subpoena may be served upon a nonparty one (1) day after a notice and copy of the subpoena is served on each party.

[Effective October 27, 2014.]

B–9019–1. STIPULATIONS AND SETTLEMENTS

(a) Notice.

(1) *When a Hearing Has Been Set.* When parties reach a settlement in a matter that has been set for hearing, the parties shall promptly advise the Court of the settlement and, within the time promised or as required by the Court, shall file the appropriate pleadings and any proposed order concerning the settlement. The Court may extend the time for filing upon request. Failure to file the settlement pleading may result in dismissal of the matter at issue.

(2) *Objection Deadline.* When approval of a settlement or compromise is required by Fed.R.Bankr.P. 9019, the parties to the agreement shall file a motion to approve the settlement in the bankruptcy case. One of the parties to the agreement shall serve notice on creditors, any trustee, and the UST in accordance with Fed.R.Bankr.P. 2002 and to any other entity as the Court may direct. The notice shall allow twenty-one (21) days from the date of service to file objections to the settlement.

(3) *Filing; Certificate of Service.* The moving party shall file a copy of the notice and a certificate of service that complies with S.D.Ind. B–9013–2. The motion, notice, and certificate of service may be combined into one document. (A sample combination motion, notice, and certificate of service is available on the Court's website). If no proper objection is filed, the Court may approve the settlement without further notice or hearing.

(b) Adversary Proceedings.

(1) *Generally.* Except as set forth in (3) of this section, if an adversary proceeding is settled before an answer has been filed, the parties may file a stipula-

tion of dismissal. No Court order is entered on that stipulation. However, if the agreement of the parties resulting in dismissal contains conditions precedent or subsequent, then the parties shall file an agreed consent to judgment. The Court shall enter a separate order on that consent to judgment, after notice, if required.

(2) *Settlements Under Fed.R.Bankr.P. 9019(a) or (b).* When approval of a settlement or compromise is required by Fed.R.Bankr.P. 9019(a) or (b), the trustee or debtor-in-possession shall file a motion to approve the settlement in the bankruptcy case and shall serve notice. The trustee or debtor-in-possession shall file a copy of the notice and a certificate of service that complies with S.D.Ind. B–9013–2. Once the motion is granted, the parties to the adversary proceeding shall then dismiss the adversary proceeding or file an agreed consent to judgment so that the adversary may be closed.

(3) *Settlements of Complaints to Deny or Revoke Discharge.* Settlements of complaints to deny or revoke discharge are governed by S.D.Ind. B–7041–2.

[Effective June 1, 2010. Amended effective October 1, 2012; February 19, 2013.]

B–9019–2. ALTERNATIVE DISPUTE RESOLUTION

(a) Scope of the Rule. The alternative dispute resolution method governed by this rule is mediation. This rule does not preclude the parties from agreeing to the use of any other reasonable method of alternative dispute resolution. However, any use of arbitration by the parties will be governed by 28 U.S.C. §§ 654–647.

(b) Applicability of the Rule. This rule applies to all contested matters and adversary proceedings pending before a Bankruptcy Judge of this District.

(c) Referral to Mediation: Process.

(1) *Motion to Refer to Mediation.* Any party may file a motion to refer a matter to mediation ("Motion to Refer to Mediation"). If a party's Motion to Refer to Mediation certifies that all parties to the matter consent to mediation and have been served with the motion, and the Court finds the motion to be appropriate under the circumstances, the Court may enter an order referring the matter to mediation without further notice or hearing. If a motion does not so certify, the motion shall be set for hearing. The Bankruptcy Judge may decide not to grant a motion to refer a particular matter to mediation if the Court determines that the motion was filed to delay the case or proceeding or if the matter involved is not likely to be resolved by mediation, given the issue or the parties involved.

(2) *Court's Referral to Mediation.*

(A) Court's Notice of Status Conference to Discuss Mediation. The Court may refer a matter to mediation on its own by setting a status conference to consider the referral. At the status conference, the parties can oppose the referral or indicate consent. After the hearing, the Court may enter an order referring the matter to mediation.

(B) Court's Proposal During Other Scheduled Hearing or Status Conference. The Court may propose referral to mediation at any other hearing or status conference. The parties can oppose referral, indicate consent, or request a separate status conference on the proposal. The Court may enter an order referring the matter to mediation or may set a status conference for a later date.

(d) Jurisdiction and Pendency of Matter: Deadlines and Discovery. At all times during the course of mediation, the matter remains under the jurisdiction of the Judge to whom the matter is assigned. Referral to mediation does not abate or suspend the matter. As to discovery matters, absent court order or the agreement of the parties, no scheduled dates shall be deferred or delayed. Whenever possible, parties are encouraged to limit discovery to the development of information needed to facilitate mediation.

(e) Selection of the Mediator.

(1) *Selection by Agreement.* Any person may be selected to serve as a mediator. Parties are encouraged to consider those appearing on the Court's list of mediators maintained by the Clerk. If a proposed mediator has been agreed upon by the parties, then within fourteen (14) days after the order referring the matter to mediation, the parties shall file a Notice of Selection of Mediator. The notice shall designate the name of the proposed mediator.

(2) *Selection of Candidates by the Court.* If the parties cannot agree on a mediator within fourteen (14) days after entry of the order referring the matter to mediation, or if the parties elect to request the Court to name a panel for their consideration before expiration of the fourteen (14)–day period, a party to the mediation shall file a Motion to Select a Panel of Mediator Candidates. The fourteen (14)–day selection period may be extended upon motion of either party to the matter. The Court will issue a Notice of Designation of Mediator Candidates which designates three (3) potential mediators. Each side, alternately, shall strike the name of one (1) mediator. The side initiating the controversy will strike first, and shall do so no later than three (3) days after the filing of the Notice of Designation of Mediator Candidates. The parties shall complete the striking process within seven (7) days of the Court's designation and shall file a Notice of Selection of Mediator with the Court. During the striking process, the parties can agree on a mediator other than one named on the panel of candidates. If a party fails to strike from the list when

required to do so, then the first name on the list that has not previously been stricken is deemed stricken by the party with the duty to strike. The other party then exercises its right to strike or, if only one name remains, files the Notice of Selection of Mediator.

(3) *Qualification and Immunity.* A mediator becomes qualified upon the filing of the affidavit required by subparagraph (e)(5). To the extent permitted under applicable law, a qualified mediator shall have immunity in the same manner and to the same extent as would a duly appointed Judge.

(4) *Disqualification.* Any person selected to serve as a mediator shall disqualify himself or herself from the matter if impartiality might reasonably be questioned. A mediator is also subject to the disqualification rules found in 28 U.S.C. § 455. A party that reasonably believes the mediator should be disqualified may file a Request for Disqualification of Mediator.

(5) *Affidavit.* A person proposed for selection as a mediator shall prepare an affidavit disclosing any connections with the parties or counsel involved with the controversy which in any way could affect the neutrality or partiality of the mediator and setting forth any other reason which could result in disqualification under section (e)(2) of this rule. The affidavit shall summarize the anticipated rate of compensation and terms of payment of the proposed mediator. The affidavit shall be filed no later than seven (7) days after the notice specified in subparagraph (e)(1) and (2). The time period for filing the affidavit can be extended upon motion of any party to the matter.

(6) *Replacement of Mediator.* If at any time the mediator is disqualified or opts not to continue to serve, the parties may agree upon another mediator and file the appropriate notice, or they may request that the Court designate a panel of candidates pursuant to subparagraph (e)(2).

(f) Compensation. Unless otherwise agreed by the parties or ordered by the Court, the compensation and costs of the mediation shall be borne equally by the parties to the mediation. If one of the parties is a trustee or debtor-in-possession, the amount of compensation to be paid by that party shall be treated as an administrative expense and paid by the estate.

(g) The Mediation.

(1) *Control of the Mediation.* The mediator shall control all procedural aspects of the mediation, including but not limited to:

(A) setting dates, times, and places for conducting sessions of the mediation;

(B) requiring the submission of confidential statements;

(C) requiring the attendance of representatives of each party with sufficient authority to negotiate and settle all disputed issues and amounts;

(D) designing and conducting the mediation sessions; and

(E) establishing a deadline for the parties to act upon a settlement proposal.

(2) *Termination of the Mediation by Mediator.* The mediator may terminate the mediation whenever the mediator believes that continuation of the process would harm or prejudice one or more of the parties; whenever the ability or willingness of any party to participate meaningfully in the mediation is so lacking that a reasonable agreement is unlikely; or whenever the mediator determines that continuing the mediation process would be futile.

(3) *Termination of the Mediation by a Party.* Parties are required to appear for mediation and to participate in good faith. However, parties are not compelled to reach an agreement. Either party may withdraw from the mediation if the party determines that continuing the mediation would be futile.

(4) *Conclusion of the Mediation.*

(A) If the mediation results in a full settlement of the contested matter or adversary proceeding, the mediator or the party who requested the mediation shall within seven (7) days of the conclusion of the mediation file a Report of Mediation so advising the Court. Within a reasonable time thereafter, the parties shall submit to the Court an agreed entry, agreed consent to judgment or motion for approval of compromise or settlement and provide such notice as is required by the Federal Rules of Bankruptcy Procedure or as the Court may direct. If mediation results in a partial settlement, such that a motion to compromise and settle is not required, the parties shall file a notice of submission of any appropriate stipulation.

(B) If the mediation is terminated or does not result in a settlement, and the mediator, after appropriate consultation with the parties and their counsel, is reasonably satisfied that no further mediation effort is feasible at that time, then the mediator or the party who initiated the mediation shall file a Report of Mediation with the Court, serving all parties to the controversy, that states only that the mediation was concluded without a settlement.

(5) *Release of Mediator.* Upon the filing of the report under subparagraph (g)(4), the mediation shall be deemed concluded and the mediator shall be relieved of all further duties or responsibilities.

(h) Confidentiality.

(1) *Protection of Information Disclosed at Mediation.* Any written or oral communication made during the course of any process or proceeding covered under this rule is confidential unless otherwise agreed by the parties. The unauthorized disclosure of confidential communication by any person may result in the imposition of sanctions pursuant to subparagraph (i). In addition, without limiting the foregoing, Rule 408 of the Federal Rules of Evidence and any applicable federal or state statute, rule, common law, or judicial precedent relating to the privileged nature of settlement discussions, mediation, or other alternative dispute resolution procedure shall apply. Information otherwise discoverable or admissible in evidence, however, does not become exempt from discovery, or inadmissible in evidence, merely by being used by a party in mediation.

(2) *No Discovery from Mediator.* The mediator shall not be compelled to disclose to the Court or to any person outside the mediation conference any of the records, reports, summaries, notes, communications, or other documents received or made by a mediator while serving in such capacity. The mediator shall not testify or be compelled to testify in regard to the mediation in connection with any arbitral, judicial, or other proceeding. The mediator shall not be a necessary party in any proceeding relating to the mediation.

(3) *Protection of Proprietary Information.* The parties, the mediator, and all mediation participants shall protect proprietary information during and after the mediation.

(4) *Preservation of Privileges.* The disclosure by a party of privileged information to the mediator or to another party during the mediation process does not waive or otherwise adversely affect the privileged nature of the information.

(i) Sanctions. Upon motion by any party, the Court may impose sanctions against any person who fails to comply with this rule.

[Effective June 1, 2010. Amended effective October 27, 2014.]

B–9022–1. NOTICE OF ENTRY OF JUDGMENT

(a) Clerk's Duty to Provide Notice. The Clerk shall mail or deliver by electronic means to the contesting parties a copy of a judgment or order showing the date the judgment or order was entered. The certificate of notice docketed by the Bankruptcy Noticing Center or other agent qualifies as the notice required by Fed.R.Bankr.P. 9022.

(b) Notice to Electronic Filers. Immediately upon entry of an order or judgment in a case or adversary proceeding the Clerk shall transmit electronically to the registered users in the case or adversary proceeding a "Notice of Electronic Filing." Electronic transmission of that Notice of Electronic

Filing constitutes the notice required by Fed. R.Bankr.P. 9022.

(c) Notice to Other Parties. The Clerk shall give notice in paper form to contesting parties who have not consented, or are not permitted to consent, to electronic service.

[Effective February 10, 2014.]

B–9027–1. REMOVAL

(a) Claim or Cause of Action Filed or Pending in a State Court within the Jurisdiction of the Southern District of Indiana. If the bankruptcy case is filed or pending in the Southern District of Indiana, removal is accomplished by filing a notice of removal as an adversary proceeding in the bankruptcy case. If the bankruptcy case is filed or pending in another jurisdiction, contact the Clerk of the Bankruptcy Court to open a miscellaneous proceeding. (After the filing with the Bankruptcy Court, a copy of the notice of removal should be filed in the state court where the matter is pending.)

(b) Claim or Cause of Action Filed or Pending in the District Court for the Southern District of Indiana and the Bankruptcy Case is Pending in this District. . A motion for a directed reference to the Bankruptcy Court may be filed with the District Court.

(c) Required Statement in Notice of Removal Regarding Consent to Entry of Orders or Judgment in Core Proceeding. In addition to the statements required by Fed.R.Bankr.P. 9027(a), the notice of removal shall contain a statement that upon removal of the claim or cause of action the party filing the notice does or does not consent to the entry of final orders or judgment by the Bankruptcy Judge.

(d) Required Statement Regarding Consent to Entry of Orders or Judgment in Core Proceeding. The statement filed pursuant to Fed.R.Bankr.P. 9027(e)(3) by a party who files a pleading in connection with a removed claim or cause of action shall contain a statement that the party does or does not consent to the entry of final orders or judgment by the Bankruptcy Judge.

(e) Court Review of Removal. The Bankruptcy Court may set a hearing, upon notice to the parties, to determine the propriety of the removal and whether the Court should abstain or remand.

[Effective June 1, 2010. Amended effective June 1, 2011; December 3, 2012; December 17, 2013.]

B–9029–1. LOCAL RULES: GENERAL

(a) Title and Citation. These rules shall be known as the Local Rules of the United States Bankruptcy Court for the Southern District of Indiana, and may be cited as "S.D.Ind. B–___."

(b) Effective Date. These rules become effective on June 1, 2010.

(c) Scope of Rules. These rules shall govern all bankruptcy cases and proceedings pending or commenced in the Southern District of Indiana on or after that date.

(d) Relationship to Prior Rules; Actions Pending on Effective Date. These rules supersede all previous rules promulgated by this Court or any Judge of this Court. They shall govern all applicable proceedings brought in this Court after they take effect, and shall apply to all pending proceedings at the time they take effect, except to the extent that the Court determines that application thereof would not be feasible or would work injustice, in which event the former rules shall govern.

(e) Modification or Suspension of Rules. In individual cases or proceedings, the Court, upon its own motion or the motion of any party, may suspend or modify any of these rules if the interests of justice so require.

(f) Conflicts Between S.D.Ind. L.R., Local and National Bankruptcy Rules. To the extent that any provision of the Local Rules for the United States District Court for the Southern District of Indiana (S.D.Ind. L.R.) differs from any provision of the Local Rules of the United States Bankruptcy Court for the Southern District of Indiana or the Federal Rules of Bankruptcy Procedure, then that provision of the S.D.Ind. L.R. shall not apply.

[Effective June 1, 2010. Amended effective June 1, 2011.]

B–9033–1. PROPOSED FINDINGS OF FACT AND CONCLUSIONS OF LAW IN CERTAIN CORE PROCEEDINGS

If the Court hears a proceeding and determines that it cannot enter a final order or judgment consistent with Article III of the United States Constitution in a particular proceeding referred to the Court and designated as core under 28 U.S.C. § 157(b), and if the parties have not consented to entry of final orders or judgment, then Fed.R.Bankr.P. 9033(a), (b), and (c) shall apply as if it is a non-core proceeding.

[Effective December 3, 2012.]

B–9037–1. PRIVACY PROTECTION FOR FILINGS MADE WITH THE COURT

The Court may rule upon a motion for a protective order filed pursuant to Fed.R.Bankr.P. 9037(d) or a motion to remove a document without notice or hearing.

[Effective June 1, 2010. Amended effective June 1, 2011.]

B–9070–1. DISPOSITION OF EXHIBITS

(a) **Custody During Pendency of Action.** Any item offered into evidence in a case will be placed in the Clerk's custody. Unless the court orders otherwise, these items may not be claimed from the Clerk until the case is disposed of as to all issues, including appeals.

(b) **Claiming Items After Disposition of Action.** The party that offered the items into evidence must claim them from the Clerk:

(1) if the case is not appealed, within ninety (90) days after the case is disposed of as to all issues;

(2) if the case is appealed, within twenty-eight (28) days after the mandate of the reviewing court is filed in the Clerk's office and the case is disposed of as to all issues, unless otherwise ordered.

(c) **Procedure for Claiming Items.** No motion or order is necessary to claim the items. The party withdrawing them must give the Clerk a detailed receipt when the items are withdrawn. The Clerk must file the receipt in the cause.

(d) **Failure to Claim Items.** If the parties fail to claim the items within the deadline in subdivision (b), the Clerk may dispose of them in any manner directed by the court.

(e) **Withdrawal of Original Records and Papers.** No one may withdraw an original pleading, paper, record, model or exhibit from the Clerk's custody except as provided by this rule or by court order. [Effective June 1, 2010. Amended effective October 1, 2012.]

ELECTRONIC CASE FILING
STANDING ORDER 04–0005. STANDING ORDER RELATING TO ELECTRONIC CASE FILING

Federal Rule of Civil Procedure 5(e), Federal Rules of Bankruptcy Procedure 5005(a)(2) and 9011 and Local Rule B–5005–4 authorize this Court to establish practices and procedures for the filing, signing and verification of pleadings and papers by electronic means. The Court has reviewed the proposed Administrative Procedures Concerning Electronic Case Files.

IT IS, THEREFORE, ORDERED that:

(1) The Administrative Procedures Concerning Electronic Case Files in this Court, including the procedure for registration of attorneys and for distribution of passwords to permit electronic filing and notice of pleadings and other papers, are hereby **APPROVED**.

(2) The provisions of this Order shall apply to all electronically filed cases and proceedings that are filed in the United States Bankruptcy Court for the Southern District of Indiana.

(3) Amendments to this Order may be entered from time to time in keeping with the needs of the Court.

[Effective: September 9, 2004.]

ADMINISTRATIVE POLICIES AND PROCEDURES MANUAL FOR ELECTRONIC CASE FILING (ATTORNEY EDITION)
Revised February 6, 2015

Introduction. The United States Bankruptcy Court for the Southern District of Indiana implemented an Electronic Case Filing/Case Management System on 10/17/2004. The Court's system, CM/ECF, permits limited users and attorneys who appear in all bankruptcy cases and adversary proceedings to file documents with the Court via the Internet using the ECF (Electronic Case Filing) portion of the system. This Administrative Policies and Procedures Manual governs electronic filing in all cases and proceedings in the Southern District of Indiana Bankruptcy Courts. Attorneys, limited users, parties, and pro se litigants may view bankruptcy cases and adversary proceedings, as well as documents filed electronically, by utilizing the PACER (Public Access to Court Electronic Records) portion of the system via the Internet. On June 3, 2013, the Court made available an alternative method for filing, amending, and withdrawing proofs of claim electronically. That process is not the same as filing through CM/ECF. However, some of the requirements and restrictions on CM/ECF users apply to those using the electronic claims filing option. [See the section on Filing Claims Electronically.]

This Manual is not intended to provide comprehensive guidance on the mechanics of electronic filing. Interested parties should consult the Local Rules and the Court's Procedures Manual, both available on the Internet at www.insb.uscourts.gov.

Authorization for Electronic Filing. Local Rule B–5005–4 authorizes electronic filing in conjunction with Fed.R.Bankr.P. 5005(a)(2). The following policies and procedures govern electronic filing in the Bankruptcy Courts of this District unless a Bankruptcy Judge determines that these policies and procedures should be modified due to circumstances in a particular case.

Definitions. The following definitions shall apply to this Electronic Case Filing Administrative Policies and Procedures Manual:

2.1 "Cases" means all bankruptcy cases and adversary proceedings.

2.2 "Document" means pleadings, motions, exhibits, declarations, affidavits, memoranda, papers, orders, notices, and any other filing by or with the Court.

2.3 "ECF" means the Electronic Case Filing portion of the Court's CM/ECF System, which may be accessed by e-filers for the purpose of filing documents electronically in cases pending before the Court. [See section under Registration.]

2.4 "E-filer" means an attorney or limited user authorized to file documents electronically through CM/ECF or a person filing, amending, or withdrawing a proof of claim electronically using a program other than CM/ECF made available by the Court.

2.5 "Electronic filing" means the submission of electronic documents through CM/ECF or an alternative electronic program made available by the Court.

2.6 "Electronic signature" means the e-filer's name preceded by /s/ in the space where the e-filer's wet signature otherwise would appear. [See section under Electronic Signature and Signature Block.] Debtors are not authorized to file electronically. The e-filer may use this "electronic signature" format for debtors if the e-filer has possession of the documents with the debtors' wet signatures. [See section "Cases and Documents Subject to Electronic Filing" for more information on use of the "electronic signature" format.]

2.7 "Limited user" means a creditor, or party in interest other than a debtor, given limited rights to file electronically. Limited Users are only permitted to file certain documents electronically. Any other document should be filed on paper, or filed on behalf of the Limited User by an attorney who has full electronic filing rights. [See the Court's Procedures Manual for a listing of limited documents.]

2.8 "Notice of Electronic Filing" means the e-mail notice that is automatically generated by the Electronic CaseFiling System at the time a document is filed by an e-filer or an order is entered by the Court. The Notice of Electronic Filing (NEF) will set forth the date and time of filing or issuance, the type of document, the text of the docket entry, the name of the parties receiving the notice, and an electronic link (hyperlink) to the document, which allows recipients to retrieve the document electronically.

2.9 "PACER" (Public Access to Court Electronic Records) means the Public Access portion of the Court's CM/ECF System, which may be accessed by anyone with a PACER user ID and password for the purpose of viewing case dockets and electronically filed documents in cases pending before the Court.

2.10 "PDF" means a document that exists in Portable Document Format. A document file created with a word processor, or a paper document which has been scanned, must first be converted to a portable document format before it can be electronically filed with the Court. Converted files contain the extension ".pdf."

2.11 "Traditional service" or "traditionally serve" means service in accordance with Fed.R.Bankr.P. 7004.

2.12 "Wet signature" means the original signature on a document which results from signing with pen. When required, a wet signature must be obtained before the document is filed.

2.13 "Manual" means this document—the Electronic Case Filing Policies and Procedures Manual.

Application of Rules and Orders. Unless modified by Order of the Court, all Federal Rules of Bankruptcy Procedure and Local Rules shall continue to apply to cases maintained in the Court's Case Management/Electronic Case Filing System (CM/ECF).

Cases and Documents Subject to Electronic Case Filing.

Generally. Pursuant to Local Rule B–5005–1, all attorneys must file all documents electronically, and those entities who file more than 10 documents per year must either become limited users in CM/ECF, which allows electronic filing of only a specific set of documents, and/or become ePOC/eWOC users, which allows an alternative method for electronically filing, amending, or withdrawing only proofs of claims. All others shall file cases, pleadings and documents on paper, except that the creditor matrix for any case must be submitted on a diskette, CD, or other electronic media acceptable to the Clerk.

Attorneys, limited users, parties, and pro se litigants may <u>view</u> dockets and electronically filed documents via the Internet through the use of the Court's PACER (Public Access to Court Electronic Records) System.

Documents Signed by Debtors. Documents signed by debtors shall be filed electronically by the debtors' attorney. Debtors are not authorized to file electronically, and therefore are not authorized to use the electronic signature format. Documents filed by debtors' counsel may only use the electronic signature format for pleadings executed by debtors if counsel has the debtors' wet signatures on originals prior to filing. [See "Electronic signature" in the Definitions section.]

Joint or Agreed Pleadings. If the document is a joint or agreed filing with counsel for an opposing party, the e-filer may use the electronic signature format for opposing counsel *only* if:

    a) the filer has received consent of that counsel to use an electronic signature, and

    b) the opposing counsel is also authorized to file electronically.

If both conditions are satisfied, then the e-filer need only retain proof of consent from the opposing party and is not required to obtain or retain a wet signature. If the other party to the joint or agreed filing is not an attorney or is an attorney but is not authorized to file electronically, then the e-filer must have a wet signature on the original document. (Note: Reaffirmation Agreements are subject to this requirement.) The e-filer may then use the electronic signature format for the opposing counsel or party but such use constitutes a representation that the e-filer has possession of the original document with the required wet signatures prior to filing.

Tools Needed for Electronic Filing. In order to file documents electronically and/or receive electronic notification of case activity via the Electronic Case Filing System, one must have the following:

- An ECF user ID and password assigned by the Clerk (in order to access the Court's Electronic Case Filing System);

- A computer running a Windows or a Macintosh operating system;

- Software used to create PDF documents from a word processing application, such as Adobe Acrobat Professional®;

- A PDF viewer, such as Adobe Acrobat Reader® (free download available at www.adobe.com);

- A PDF–compatible word processor like Macintosh or Windows-based versions of WordPerfect® or Microsoft Word®;

- An Internet browser such as Internet Explorer® 8.0 or 9.0 or Mozilla Firefox. CM/ECF is NOT compatible with Internet Explorer 10.0 or higher. The use of Internet Explorer 10.0 or higher, Opera, Safari, or any other such browser, may result in intermittent errors when filing documents and in receiving Court e-mail notifications from within CM/ECF.

- Internet access and an e-mail address;

- Access to a scanner (may be necessary for paper exhibits which must be scanned into PDF).

E-filers are strongly encouraged to maintain an anti-virus program to protect not only their system but also CM/ECF.

Electronic Signature and Signature Block. For documents filed electronically through CM/ECF, use of the e-filer's user ID and password when filing documents electronically, combined with the use of the required signature format, serves as the e-filer's signature for purposes of Fed.R.Bankr.P. 9011, the Local Rules of this Court, and any other purpose for which a signature is required in connection with proceedings before the Court. All documents filed electronically (except proofs of claim filed using a Court program other than CM/ECF) shall include a signature block consisting of the e-filer's electronic signature (/s/ typewritten name where the e-filer's wet signature would otherwise appear); the e-filer's typewritten name below the electronic signature; address; telephone number; facsimile number and e-mail address. This required format appears below.

/s/ (Typewritten Name of E–Filer)
Name of E–Filer
Address
City, State, ZIP Code
Phone: (xxx) xxx-xxxx
Fax: (xxx) xxx-xxxx
E-mail: xxx@xxx.xxx

The "/s/ (typewritten name)" format is also acceptable as a substitute for the wet signature of a party, such as the debtor, on an electronically filed document **provided** that the e-filer retains the document with wet signature according to the section below, Retention of Documents with Original Signatures.

A scanned, wet signature of the e-filer is also acceptable on an electronically filed document. However, if for any reason the e-filer is filing a document non-electronically, then the document tendered to the Clerk must have a wet signature.

No e-filer or other person may knowingly permit or cause to permit an e-filer's user ID and password to be used by anyone other than an authorized agent of the person assigned the user ID and password. All documents filed with the e-filer's user ID and password will be presumed for all purposes, including Fed.R.Bankr.P. 9011, to have been filed by the person assigned the user ID and password. Furthermore, when a person places his/her electronic signature on a document but then uses another e-filer's user ID and password to file the document, that filing will be treated by the Court for all purposes, including Fed.R.Bankr.P. 9011, as a document 'signed' by both the person whose name is on the document and the e-filer whose user ID and password were used.

If the document is a joint or agreed filing, refer to "Joint or Agreed Pleadings" in Cases and Documents Subject to Electronic Case Filing.

NOTE: On Official Forms, such as a Proof of Claim, signature blocks are not required. An e-filer may use either a wet signature or the "/s/ (typewritten name)."

Registration.

Initial Registration. Attorneys are required to file documents electronically per Local Rule B–5005–1. Attorneys must be admitted to practice in the U.S. District Court for the Southern District of Indiana, either via standard admission or pro hac vice admission, and must be in good standing.

Registering as an e-filer is now done on line by logging onto www.insb.uscourts. gov. Under Electronic Case Filing, select Registration>CM/ECF. Access the e–Registration Program either as an attorney with full rights or as an attorney/limited user with limited rights. **The registration process will result in a reply email from the Court. Make sure your email program will accept emails from INSBdb_Courtmail@insb.uscourts.gov.**

The Court's electronic records are also accessible through PACER, which requires a separate user ID and password from the one used for ECF. Confusion often arises concerning these two user IDs and passwords. A PACER user ID and password is needed in order to *view* dockets or documents other than those the e-filer receives through a Notice of Electronic Filing. An ECF user ID and password is needed in order to *file* documents with the Court. Attorneys, limited users, and parties may register for a PACER account by visiting the PACER website at http://

pacer.psc.uscourts.gov or by contacting the PACER Service Center at (800) 676–6856.

Maintaining or Changing Registration. All e-filers are responsible for maintaining the accuracy of their account information, including accurate mailing and email addresses, using Utilities/Maintain User Account.

Attorneys who leave their current practices should update their user record and determine which cases, if any, should be updated with their new information. Contact the Court prior to making any changes if a large number of cases will remain with the current law firm. As a safety precaution, attorneys should also change their passwords if they change law firms.

Note: Any change in user ID or password will not remove an attorney from a case or proceeding. The appropriate pleading, such as a motion to withdraw, must be filed before an attorney will be removed from the case or proceeding and its distribution list.

Termination or Suspension of Electronic Filing Rights. The Court may terminate an e-filer's rights to continue participating in electronic filing under the following circumstances:

- If the e-filer is an attorney who dies, retires, resigns, is suspended or disbarred from practice by the U. S. District Court for the Southern District of Indiana, then the Clerk shall terminate or restrict access to CM/ECF and any alternative electronic program made available by the Court. (This change in access will not result in the removal of the attorney from any case or proceeding in which that attorney previously appeared.)

- If the Court determines that an attorney has changed firms and has failed to alert the Clerk, the Clerk shall immediately terminate access to CM/ECF for the user name and ID assigned the attorney at the original firm and any alternative electronic program made available by the Court. (This change in access will not result in the removal of the attorney from any case or proceeding in which that attorney previously appeared.)

- If any Judge determines, based on a review of the user's actions, that an e-filer has demonstrated the inability to use the system properly, then the Judge may (a) direct the e-filer to obtain additional training; or (b) direct the Clerk to suspend the e-filer's access, either permanently or pending the completion of additional training. Inability to use the system properly shall be determined by any of the following: (a) an above average number of notices of deficient filing; (b) repeated failure to respond to notices of deficient filing; (c) repeated failure to select correct events designed to collect statistical data; (d) unauthorized use of another e-filer's user ID and password; (e) failure to protect user ID and password from unauthorized use by others; (f) repeated failure to remit fees electronically; (g) any other persistent conduct that produces errors or inaccuracies requiring Court resources to rectify. The Judge may rely on the Clerk for information establishing an e-filer's inability to use the system properly. (This change in access will not result in the removal of an attorney from any case or proceeding in which that attorney previously appeared.)

- If the e-filer is an attorney and it is determined that the attorney is not admitted to practice in the Southern District of Indiana, including pro hac vice admission, OR that the attorney misrepresented material facts about either (a) the ability to be admitted to this District; or (b) prior training on CM/ECF, then a Judge may direct that access to electronic filing be terminated or suspended after notice has been given to the e-filer. (This change in access will not result in the removal of the attorney from any case or proceeding in which that attorney previously appeared.)

- After the Court determines that an e-filer has used another e-filer's user ID and password without authorization, then a Judge may direct that access to electronic filing be terminated or suspended after notice has been given to the e-filer. (This change in access will not result in the removal of an attorney from any case or proceeding in which that attorney previously appeared.)

Suspension or termination of rights under this section does not affect an attorney's admission to practice in this District. Suspension or termination does not excuse the e-filer from compliance with the requirement that all documents be filed electronically; thus, it does not give the e-filer the right to file documents non-electronically.

System Availability. The Court's system is designed to provide service 24 hours a day, 7 days a week. Occasionally, the CM/ECF System may be unavailable for brief, scheduled maintenance. Notice of scheduled maintenance will be posted on the Court's website in advance. E–filers are encouraged to file documents in advance of filing deadlines and during normal business hours. Questions regarding the Electronic Case Filing System and the registration process should be referred to the Clerk's Office at (317) 229–3800. Technical difficulties should be referred to the Court's Help Desk via e-mail to cmecf_tier2@insb.uscourts.gov. The Help Desk is staffed on business workdays from 8:00 a.m. to 4:30 p.m.

If the CM/ECF System becomes unavailable for any reason and that unavailability is likely to last beyond normal business hours, the Chief Judge will issue a general order extending deadlines that expire on the day the system outage began. Any general order will invoke Fed.R.Bankr.P. 9006(a)(3), concerning the inaccessibility of the Clerk's office, and deadlines will be extended to the first business day that system access is restored. Usually, this day will be the next business day. (Even if CM/ECF access is unavailable when the general order is issued, the Court retains the ability to send an e-mail blast to e-filing customers and will do so.)

System availability should not be confused with an e-filer's inability to file because of problems specific to the e-filer's computer or the e-filer's lack of access to a computer (perhaps because of bad weather). For these situations, consult the section entitled Problems with E–Filing.

Filing Documents Electronically. Electronic transmission of a document containing a proper electronic signature or a scanned image of a wet signature and submitted in accordance with the Federal Rules of Civil Procedure and the Local Rules of this Court shall constitute the filing thereof.

A Notice of Electronic Filing (NEF), acknowledging that the document has been filed, will immediately appear on the e-filer's screen after the document has been submitted. E-filers are strongly encouraged to print or electronically save a copy of the NEF. E–filers can also verify the filing of documents by viewing the Court's electronic docket sheet with PACER.

Documents filed electronically must be submitted in PDF (Portable Document Format). Filing documents electronically does not alter filing deadlines. All electronic transmissions of documents must be completed (*i.e.* received completely by the Clerk's Office) prior to midnight, Eastern Time, to be considered timely filed that day. Although e-filers can file documents electronically 24 hours a day, 7 days a week, e-filers are encouraged to file all documents during the normal working hours of the Clerk's Office (Monday through Friday, 8:00 a.m. to 4:30 p.m.) when technical support is available. [See also Format for Electronic Filings.]

E-filers shall be responsible for selecting the appropriate event from the list of docketing events in CM/ECF. If the e-filer has made a mistake (for example, attached an incorrect PDF document or chosen an incorrect filing event), the Clerk may issue a Notice of Deficient Filing ("NDF") which will require the e-filer to re-submit the document. Once a document is submitted and becomes part of the case docket, corrections to the docket can only be made by the Clerk of Court.

Filing Claims Electronically. Proofs of claim can be filed electronically using CM/ECF or by any alternative electronic program made available by the Court.

The following sections of the Manual apply to filers using the Court's alternative program for filing claims electronically:

• Definitions
• Application of Rules and Order

- Electronic Signature and Signature Block

- Termination or Suspension of Electronic Filing Rights

- System Availability

- Redacting Personal Identifiers

Format for Electronic Filings. Electronically filed documents must meet the requirements of Fed.R.Bankr.P. 9004 (General Requirements of Form); Fed. R.Bankr.P. 9009 (Forms); Fed.R.Bankr.P. 9013 (Motions: Form and Service); Fed.R.Bankr.P. 7003 (Commencement of Adversary Proceeding); and Local Rule B–5005–1 (Filing of Papers), as if they had been submitted on paper. Documents filed electronically are also subject to any page limitations set forth by Court Order or Local Rule as applicable.

To facilitate document retrieval for users who are accessing the system, documents may not exceed an electronic file size of **10.0 megabytes (MB)**. What is too big? To electronically file a document or attachment that exceeds 10.0 MB, the document must first be broken down into two or more smaller files. For example, if Exhibit A is an 11.0 MB PDF, it should be divided into two equal parts prior to electronic filing. What about memoranda or briefs in support of a motion?

Any document filed should fit on an 8.5 × 11 inch page (if printed), single-sided, so as to not adversely impact the noticing process of the Bankruptcy Noticing Center. All pleadings and other filings (including motions, briefs, and proposed orders) must be in PDF format. The e-filer is responsible for reviewing all PDF documents for legibility before submission.

Attaching Exhibits to Documents. Except as the presiding Judge in a case may otherwise direct, attachments to documents (including, but not limited to, leases, notes, etc.), which may not exist in electronic form, shall be electronically imaged (scanned) and filed as a PDF document. Many docket events provide e-filers an opportunity to attach exhibits as part of the filing process. Consult specific docket event information in the Procedures Manual.

All documents with attachments, capable of electronic imaging and filing, shall be filed electronically together under one entry number. E-filers shall submit as exhibits or attachments only those excerpts of the referenced documents that are germane to the matter under consideration by the Court. Excerpted material must be clearly and prominently identified as such. E-filers who file excerpts of documents as exhibits or attachments under this rule do so without prejudice to their right to timely file additional excerpts or to file the complete document. Responding parties may timely file in electronic format additional excerpts that they believe to be germane to the matter under consideration by the Court.

Orders.

- *Electronic Submission.* Except as the presiding Judge in a case may otherwise direct, an attorney submitting a proposed order to the Clerk of Court shall do so electronically (by uploading the order) via ECF. [See the Procedures Manual for guidance on uploading orders.] [See Appendix C for Order format.]

- *Non–Electronic Submission.* Parties who are not required or authorized to be e-filers shall provide one copy of the proposed order on paper [See Appendix C for Order format.]

- *Signed Orders.* All orders shall be signed electronically. Any docketed order or other court-issued document has the same force and effect as if the Judge or the Clerk had signed a paper copy.

- *Distribution.* Parties are responsible for ensuring that any order (even if distributed by the Clerk) is sent to the proper entities. Service of an order can be determined by looking at the Bankruptcy Noticing Center (BNC) Certificate of Service, which appears on the docket approximately three days after filing.

Service of Electronically Filed Documents. By participating in the Electronic Case Filing System, attorney e-filers consent to the electronic service of documents and agree to make e-mail addresses available for service. Upon the filing of a document, an e-mail message will be automatically generated by the Electronic Case Filing System and sent via electronic mail to the e-mail addresses of all attorneys who have appeared in the case. The Notice of Electronic Filing (NEF) will contain a document hyperlink which will provide recipients with one "free look" at the electronically filed document. Recipients are encouraged to print and/or save a copy of the document during the "free look" to avoid incurring PACER charges for future viewings of the document. *It is the responsibility of the e-filer to traditionally serve all parties who do not receive electronic service* (the identity of these parties will be indicated at the bottom of the NEF receipt generated by the ECF System). In addition to receiving e-mail notifications of filing activity, attorneys are strongly encouraged to sign onto the PACER System at regular intervals to check the dockets in their cases.

A certificate of service must be included with all documents filed electronically as to which service is required. Such certificate shall indicate that service was accomplished pursuant to the Court's electronic filing procedures. Although documents filed electronically are served on all attorney e-filers, parties served electronically should still be listed on the Certificate of Service. [See Sealed Cases and Documents for special instructions on service.] A form Certificate of Service is available at Appendix B.

Docket. Upon the electronic filing of a document, a docket entry will be automatically created by the CM/ECF System using the information provided by the e-filer. The Clerk of Court, where necessary and appropriate, will modify the docket entry description to comply with quality control standards.

Retention of Documents With Original Signatures. Documents with original signatures of persons other than the e-filer must be retained by the e-filer for a period of two years after the closing of the case by the Clerk unless the Court orders a different period. This retention period does not affect or replace any other retention periods required by other applicable laws or rules. Upon request by the Court, the United States Trustee, or the case trustee, the e-filer must provide documents with original signatures of persons other than the e-filer for review or proof of consent as to joint or agreed pleadings with another attorney authorized to file electronically.

Parties permitted or required to file documents non-electronically must file the original with wet signatures and also provide a copy. The original will be returned to the filer (if the filing occurred in person or a return mail envelope was provided), and must be retained by the filer for the same duration as a document filed electronically. If the filing party submits a document by mail and fails to provide a self-addressed, postage-paid envelope, the party is presumed to have retained an original. All submitted documents not returned to the filer will be retained by the Court for 30 days and then discarded.

Redacting Personal Identifiers. E-filers must ensure that the documents they file do not contain personal identifiers. [See Fed.R.Bankr.P. 9037 for a list of such identifiers.] If a document containing personal identifiers is filed inadvertently, the e-filer must file an amended, redacted document and a Motion to Remove Document or Motion for Protective Order, whichever is applicable. [See CM/ECF Procedures Manual.]

Problems With E–Filing. E-filers are encouraged to file documents electronically during normal business hours so that assistance can be obtained if a problem is encountered. Generally, if a technical failure occurs (that is not a system outage affecting all e-filers but affects only the individual e-filer) and a document cannot be filed electronically in a case despite the best efforts of the filing party, the e-filer should print (if possible) a copy of the error message received, if any. If no error message is received, the e-filer should indicate so in the "Declaration that Party Was Unable to File in a Timely Manner Due to Technical Difficulties" [the "Declaration"] and file this document with the Court as soon as practically possible. A model form is provided as Appendix A.

If the technical problems affect the filing of a new case and timing is critical, the e-filer should contact the Clerk's Office and seek permission to file the new case on paper. In this situation, the Declaration is not required.

If an e-filer is likely to miss a filing deadline as a result of a technical failure and not because of a system outage, the e-filer must contact the Clerk's Office by sending an email to cmecf_tier2@insb.uscourts.gov to inform the Clerk's staff of the difficulty. If problems persist but the deadline has not yet passed, the e-filer may submit non-electronically the required document, accompanied by the Declaration, which would have the wet signature of the e-filer. If electronic filing has become possible *after* the missed deadline but before the document has been filed on paper, then the e-filer should submit the Declaration and the untimely filed document electronically. The document and Declaration must be filed by the close of the next business day, following the original filing deadline that was missed. If in the meantime the Court has entered the order which the e-filer sought to oppose, the e-filer will have to file a motion for relief from judgment or order.

E-filers should presume that CM/ECF is available, and deadline are running, even if one or more of the Clerk's Office locations or the Courthouses are closed to the public on a normal business day, because of inclement weather or for some other reason. If deadlines are being extended, the Chief Judge will issue a general order to that effect or the Court will otherwise officially indicate that the Clerk's Office has been deemed inaccessible pursuant to Fed.R.Bankr.P 9006(a)(3). [See the section System Availability.]

Non–Electronic Filings. Refer to Problems with E–Filing for guidance on how to proceed if the filer is unable to file electronically. If that section does not apply, an attorney seeking to file a case nonelectronically should contact and receive permission from the Clerk. An attorney seeking to file a document in a case non-electronically should file a Motion for Authority and receive permission from the Judge before doing so. This situation may arise as to documents that cannot be reduced to an electronic format. Documents not filed electronically must contain wet signatures.

Filing a Miscellaneous Case. Currently, the opening document in all miscellaneous cases must be filed in paper and cannot be filed electronically. Document must contain wet signatures. The Clerk's Office should be contacted for further instructions prior to filing a miscellaneous case.

Once the case has been opened and given a case number, all documents thereafter must be filed electronically with an electronic signature. If a miscellaneous case is to be sealed, refer to Sealed Cases and Documents.

Sealed Cases and Documents.

1) *General Information.*

   a) A sealed case, including the docket and all documents, may only be viewed by certain court users and by the party who filed the sealed case. Access may be given to other users as needed; but once a user is given access, he/she will have access to the entire docket and all documents. The party who filed the case and any other party given access must then file subsequent documents electronically. All other filing parties must file all documents non-electronically with wet signatures, and the Clerk will scan and docket the documents.

   b) A sealed document filed in a non-sealed case may only be viewed by certain court users and by the party who filed the document. Access may be given to other users as needed. The docket entry for the sealed document will be available on the public docket.

2) *Filing a BANKRUPTCY CASE Under Seal.*

a) Option A: Sealing an Entire Bankruptcy Case *before* the Filing of the Bankruptcy Petition:

i) File a Motion to Seal a Case non-electronically with wet signatures. The bankruptcy petition must be submitted with this motion. The Chief Judge or designee is alerted to the filing and will consider and rule upon the motion.

ii) If the motion is granted, the Clerk opens a new case in ECF. If the motion is denied, the requesting attorney must file the case electronically. The Motion to Seal and Order are scanned by the Clerk and added to the docket.

b) Option B: Sealing an Entire Case *after* the Bankruptcy Petition has been filed:

i) File a Motion to Seal a Case electronically. That motion will be ruled upon by the Judge assigned to the case upon its filing.

ii) If the motion is granted, the bankruptcy petition and any previously filed document are sealed immediately upon issuance of the order sealing the case. If a sealed case is later unsealed by Order of the Court, the docket and all of the documents previously filed in the case will also be unsealed.

3) *Filing a MISCELLANEOUS CASE Under Seal.*

a) File a Motion to Seal a Case non-electronically with wet signatures. The opening document (or miscellaneous case) must be submitted with this motion. The Chief Judge or designee is alerted to the filing and will consider and rule upon the motion.

b) If the motion is granted, the Clerk opens a new miscellaneous case in ECF. The Motion to Seal and Order are scanned by the Clerk and added to the docket.

4) *Filing and Serving a Document in a BANKRUPTCY CASE or MISCELLA-NEOUS CASE Which is Under Seal.* Any attorney, other than the attorney who filed the sealed case or anyone given access to the sealed case, wishing to file a document in a case that has previously been sealed must do so **non-electronically** by submitting paper documents to the Clerk. This document must be served as required by Fed.R.Bankr.P. 7004.

5) *Filing and Serving a Sealed Document in a BANKRUPTCY CASE or MISCELLANEOUS CASE Which is NOT Under Seal.* Before submitting a sealed document, a Motion to Seal Document must be filed electronically and served as required by Fed.R.Bankr.P. 7004. The Motion to Seal Document must include a description of the document to be sealed and a date on which the document may be unsealed. If approved, the sealed *documents* must be filed electronically using the Sealed Document event.

Ex Parte Documents. All ex parte filings must be submitted using an appropriate ex parte filing event. Docket text and PDF documents associated with an electronic filing created using an ex parte filing event are not posted on the Court's public docket and cannot be accessed via the Court's PACER System.

When a filing is submitted electronically using an ex parte filing event, a Notice of Electronic Filing is distributed, via e-mail only, to counsel for the filing party. If the Motion remains ex parte at the time of the Court's ruling, any Order issued referencing the ex parte Motion will generate and distribute an NEF only to counsel for the applicable party.

Fees Payable to the Clerk of the Court.

On–Line Credit Card Payments: E-filers shall pay the appropriate filing fee using the on-line Credit Card Transaction module, which will allow the e-filer to pay after each transaction or make one payment at the end of all transactions. All required fees must be paid online via https://pay.gov at the time of the transaction or by the end of the day. Non–payment will result in the e-filer being locked out of the ECF System. This lockout may extend to all of the e-filer's accounts.

In the event of non-payment, an e-mail will be sent to the e-filer listing the payments due; and the "Internet Payment" option becomes the only ECF menu item available. Upon receipt of all payments due, the lockout will be automatically terminated. For additional information about credit card payments in CM/ECF, refer to the Internet Credit Card Payment Manual.

Refunds/Fees Not Due: To assert that a fee should not be charged, the attorney must send an e-mail to nofee@insb.uscourts.gov *before* paying the fee. To request a refund after the fee has been filed, the attorney must file a Motion for Refund. Refer to the Refund Policy located under Fees and Unclaimed Funds on the Court's website.

Contact Information. Additional information about electronic filing may be obtained by visiting the Court's website at www.insb.uscourts.gov or by contacting the Clerk's Office at (317) 229–3800.

Appendix A

UNITED STATES BANKRUPTCY COURT
SOUTHERN DISTRICT OF INDIANA

(Put caption of case or adversary proceeding here)

DECLARATION THAT PARTY WAS UNABLE TO FILE IN A TIMELY MANNER DUE TO TECHNICAL DIFFICULTIES

Please take notice that (plaintiff/defendant, name of party) was unable to file his/her (title of document) in a timely manner due to technical difficulties. The deadline for filing the document was (filing deadline date). The reason(s) that I was unable to file the document in a timely manner and the good faith efforts I made prior to the filing deadline to both file in a timely manner and to inform the Court and the other parties that I could not do so are set forth below.

[Statement of reasons and good faith efforts to file and to inform (including dates and times)]

I declare under penalty of perjury that the foregoing is true and correct.

/s/ (Typewritten Name of E–Filer)*
(Name of E–Filer)
(Address)
(City, State, ZIP Code)
(Phone: (xxx) xxx-xxxx)
(Fax: (xxx) xxx-xxxx)
(E-mail: xxx@xxx.xxx)

*(Note: Signature format acceptable if filed electronically; if not electronically, a wet signature is required.)

Appendix B

CERTIFICATE OF SERVICE

I hereby certify that on (date), a copy of the foregoing (name of document) was filed electronically. Notice of this filing will be sent to the following parties through the Court's Electronic Case Filing System. Parties may access this filing through the Court's system.

(List parties receiving service electronically with **e–mail** address)

(Name of receiving party)
(E-mail address)

I further certify that on (date), a copy of the foregoing (name of document) was mailed by first-class U.S. Mail, postage prepaid and properly addressed, to the following:

(List parties receiving traditional service with **postal** address)

(Name of receiving party)
(Postal address)
(City, state, ZIP code)

/s/(Typewritten Name of E–Filer)
(Name of E–Filer)*

*(Note: If Certificate is filed separately from main document, entire signature block of e-filer must be present.)

Appendix C

(Include a 4″ margin before caption for Judge's electronic signature.)

UNITED STATES BANKRUPTCY COURT
SOUTHERN DISTRICT OF INDIANA

In re:

                        (xxxxx), Debtor(s).   CASE NO. (xxxxx)

ORDER ON (xxxxx)

{insert B O D Y of O R D E R here*}*

(Note: Three pound signs must be present for Order signing program to work properly.)

(Note: Do *NOT* provide a distribution list. Orders should not contain "Submitted by" language or word processing document identifiers.)

[Effective October 1, 2004. Amended effective July 1, 2009; January 1, 2010; September 12, 2011; November 9, 2011; November 18, 2011; December 21, 2011; April 4, 2012; January 22, 2013; April 3, 2013; May 30, 2013; July 1, 2013; July 12, 2013; September 30, 2013; February 26, 2014; April 14, 2014; February 6, 2015.]

SELECTED FORMS
SECTION 1126 BALLOT FORM

IN THE UNITED STATES BANKRUPTCY COURT FOR THE
SOUTHERN DISTRICT OF INDIANA

CASE NAME ＿＿＿＿＿＿ CASE NUMBER ＿＿＿＿＿＿
CONFIRMATION HEARING DATE ＿＿＿＿＿＿

SECTION 1126 BALLOT FORM

	#BALLOTS CAST	#ACCEPTING	#REJECTING	$ACCEPTING	$REJECTING	CLASS ACCEPTING	CLASS REJECTS
CLASS I							
CLASS II							
CLASS III							
CLASS IV							

	YES	NO
PLAN ACCEPTED		

Please note the following provisions of Title 11, Section 1126 of the United States Code

(c) A class of claims has accepted a plan if such plan has been accepted by creditors other than any entity designated under subsection (e) of this section, that hold at least two-thirds in amount and more than one-half in number of the allowed claims of such class help by creditors, other than any entity designated under subsection (e) of this section, that have accepted or rejected such plan.

(d) A class of interests has accepted a plan if such plan has been accepted by holders of such interest, other than any entity designated under subsection (e) of this section, that hold at least two-thirds in amount of the allowed interests of such class held by holders of such interests, other than any entity designated under subsection (e) of this section, that have accepted or rejected such plan.

(e) On request of a party in interest, and after notice and a hearing, the court may designate any entity whose acceptance or rejection of such plan was not in good faith, or was not solicited or procured in good faith or in accordance with the provisions of this title.

CERTIFICATION OF BALLOTING REPORT

B–3018– (rev 10/1/12)

UNITED STATES BANKRUPTCY COURT
Southern District of Indiana

In re:)
)
[Name of Debtor(s)],) Case No. (xx-xxxxx)
Debtor(s).)

CERTIFICATION OF BALLOTING REPORT

The plan proponent, (name of plan proponent), hereby certifies that the tabulations recorded on the attached balloting report are true and correct and that all classes of creditors are accurately represented as to acceptances, rejections, and total amounts for each class of claims or interests.

/s/ Name of Plan Proponent
Name of Plan Proponent
(required signature block)

CERTIFICATE OF SERVICE

(See "Certificate of Service—Generic" on the Court's website under
"Forms/Local/Motions & Related Notices–Certificates of
Service–Orders/Certificates of Service/Generic.")

(Note: Attach B–3018–1 Balloting Report form.)

[Revised effective May 14, 2012; October 1, 2012.]

BALLOT FOR ACCEPTING OR REJECTING
PLAN OF REORGANIZATION

Official Form 14
(12/03)

Form 14.   CLASS *[ ]* BALLOT FOR ACCEPTING OR REJECTING
PLAN OF REORGANIZATION

[Caption as in Form 16A]

CLASS *[ ]* BALLOT FOR ACCEPTING OR REJECTING
PLAN OF REORGANIZATION

[Proponent] filed a plan of reorganization dated *[Date]* (the "Plan") for the Debtor in this case.   The Court has *[conditionally]* approved a disclosure statement with respect to the Plan (the "Disclosure Statement").   The Disclosure Statement provides information to assist you in deciding how to vote your ballot.   If you do not have a Disclosure Statement, you may obtain a copy from *[name, address, telephone number and telecopy number of proponent/proponent's attorney.]* Court approval of the disclosure statement does not indicate approval of the Plan by the Court.

You should review the Disclosure Statement and the Plan before you vote.   You may wish to seek legal advice concerning the Plan and your classification and treatment under the Plan.   Your *[claim] [equity interest]* has been placed in class *[ ]* under the Plan.   If you hold claims or equity interests in more than one class, you will receive a ballot for each class in which you are entitled to vote.

If your ballot is not received by *[name and address of proponent's attorney or other appropriate address]* on or before *[date]*, and such deadline is not extended, your vote will not count as either an acceptance or rejection of the Plan.

If the Plan is confirmed by the Bankruptcy Court it will be binding on you whether or not you vote.

ACCEPTANCE OR REJECTION OF THE PLAN

[At this point the ballot should provide for voting by the particular class of creditors or equity holders receiving the ballot using one of the following alternatives;]
[If the voter is the holder of a secured, priority, or unsecured nonpriority claim:]
The undersigned, the holder of a Class *[ ]* claim against the Debtor in the unpaid amount of Dollars ($)
[or, if the voter is the holder of a bond, debenture, or other debt security:]
The undersigned, the holder of a Class *[ ]* claim against the Debtor, consisting of Dollars ($) principal amount of *[describe bond, debenture, or other debt security]* of the Debtor (For purposes of this Ballot, it is not necessary and you should not adjust the principal amount for any accrued or unmatured interest.)
[or, if the voter is the holder of an equity interest:]
The undersigned, the holder of Class *[ ]* equity interest in the Debtor, consisting of _____ shares or other interests of *[describe equity interest]* in the Debtor
[In each case, the following language should be included:]

   (Check one box only)

   [ ] ACCEPTS THE PLAN   [ ] REJECTS THE PLAN

Dated: _____

        Print or type name: _____

        Signature: _____

        Title (if corporation or partnership) _____

        Address: _____

        _____

RETURN THIS BALLOT TO:
[Name and address of proponent's attorney or other appropriate address]
[Revised effective December 17, 2003.]

RIGHTS AND RESPONSIBILITIES OF CHAPTER 13 DEBTORS AND THEIR ATTORNEYS

It is important for debtors who file a bankruptcy case under Chapter 13 to understand their rights and responsibilities. It is also important that debtors know what their attorney's responsibilities are and understand the importance of communicating with their attorney to make the case successful. Debtors should also know that they may expect certain services to be performed by their attorney. In order to assure that debtors and attorneys understand their rights and responsibilities in the bankruptcy process, the following guidelines provided by the Court are hereby agreed to by the debtors and their attorney.

BEFORE THE CASE IS FILED

The debtor agrees to:

1. Provide the attorney with complete, accurate and current financial information.

2. Discuss with the attorney the debtor's objectives in filing the case.

3. Disclose any previous bankruptcies filed in the previous 8 years.

4. Unless excused under 11 U.S.C. § 109(h), receive a briefing from an approved nonprofit budget and credit counseling agency and provide the attorney with a copy of the certificate from the agency showing such attendance, as well as a copy of the debt repayment plan, if any, developed through the agency.

5. Disclose to the attorney any and all domestic support obligations.

The attorney agrees to:

1. Meet with the debtor to review the debtor's debts, assets, liabilities, income and expenses.

2. Counsel the debtor regarding the advisability of filing either a Chapter 7 or Chapter 13 case, provide debtor with the notice required under 11 U.S.C. § 342(b) if applicable, discuss both procedures with the debtor and answer the debtor's questions.

3. Explain what payments will be made to creditors directly by the debtor and what payments will be made through the Chapter 13 plan, with particular attention to mortgage and vehicle loan payments, any other debts that accrue interest, domestic support obligations and leases.

4. Explain to the debtor how, when and where to make payments, pursuant to the plan, to the Chapter 13 trustee and of the necessity to include the debtor's case number, name and current address on each payment item.

5. Explain to the debtor how the attorney and trustee's fees are paid and provide an executed copy of this document to the debtor.

6. Explain to the debtor that the first payment due under Chapter 13 must be made to the trustee within 30 days of filing of the bankruptcy petition.

7. Advise the debtor of the requirement to attend the Section 341 Meeting of Creditors and instruct the debtor as to the date, time and place of the meeting and of the necessity to bring both picture identification and proof of the debtor's social security number to the meeting.

8. Advise the debtor of the necessity of maintaining liability, collision and comprehensive insurance on leased vehicles or those securing loans, and of the obligation to bring copies of the declaration page(s) documenting such insurance to the Meeting of Creditors.

9. Advise debtors engaged in business of the necessity to maintain liability insurance, workers compensation insurance, if required, and any other insurance coverage required by law.

10.   Timely prepare and file the debtor's petition, plan, statements, schedules, and any other papers or documents required under the Bankruptcy Code.

AFTER THE CASE IS FILED

The debtor agrees to:

1.   Timely make all required payments to the Chapter 13 trustee that first become due 30 days after the case is filed. Also, if required, turn over any tax refunds, personal injury settlement proceeds or any other property as requested by the trustee.

2.   Timely make all post-petition payments due to mortgage lenders, holders of domestic support obligations, lessors, and any other creditor that debtor agreed or is obligated to pay directly.

3.   Cooperate with the attorney in the preparation of all pleadings and attend all hearings as required.

4.   Keep the trustee, attorney and Court informed of any changes to the debtor's address and telephone number.

5.   Prepare and file any and all federal, state and local tax returns within 30 days of filing the petition.

6.   Inform the attorney of any wage garnishments or attachments of assets which occur or continue to occur after the filing of the case.

7.   Contact the attorney promptly with any information regarding changes in employment, increases or decreases in income or other financial problems or changes.

8.   Contact the attorney promptly if the debtor acquires any property after the petition is filed. Such property might include, but is not limited to, personal injury proceeds, inheritances, lottery winnings, etc.

9.   Inform the attorney if the debtor is sued during the case.

10.   Inform the attorney if any tax refunds to which the debtors are entitled are seized or not returned to the debtor by the IRS, the Indiana Department of Revenue or any other taxing authority.

11.   Contact the attorney to determine whether court approval is required before buying, refinancing or selling real property or before entering into any long-term loan agreement.

12.   Pay any filing fees and courts costs directly to the attorney.

13.   If the requirements of 11 U.S.C. § 109(h) were waived by the Court when the case was first filed, receive a briefing from an approved nonprofit budget and credit counseling agency within 30 days of the case being filed (unless the Court, for cause, extends such time) and provide counsel with the certificate from the agency stating that the debtor attended such briefing.

14.   Unless such attendance is excused under 11 U.S.C. § 1328(f), complete an instructional course concerning personal financial management and shall promptly submit to the debtor's attorney a signed and completed Certification of Completion of Instruction Course Concerning Personal Financial Management.

15.   Cooperate fully with any audit conducted pursuant to 28 U.S.C. § 586(a).

16.   After all plan payments have been made, and if the debtor is eligible for a discharge, timely provide counsel with the information needed to complete any documents required by the Court before a discharge will be entered.

The attorney agrees to provide the following legal services:

1.   Appear at the Section 341 Meeting of Creditors with the debtor.

2.   Respond to objections to plan confirmation and, where necessary, prepare an amended plan.

3. Timely submit properly documented profit and loss statements, tax returns and proof of income when requested by the trustee.

4. Prepare, file and serve necessary modifications to the plan.

5. Prepare, file and serve necessary amended statements and schedules, in accordance with information provided by the debtor.

6. Prepare, file and serve necessary motions to buy, sell or refinance property when appropriate.

7. Object to improper or invalid claims, if necessary, based upon documentation provided by the debtor or trustee.

8. Represent the debtor in motions for relief from stay and motions to dismiss and/or convert.

9. Where appropriate, prepare, file, serve and notice motions to avoid liens on real or personal property.

10. Where appropriate, prepare, file and serve a summons and complaint to avoid a wholly unsecured mortgage.

11. Be available to respond to debtor's questions throughout the life of the plan.

12. Negotiate with any creditor holding a claim against the debtor that is potentially nondischargeable to determine if the matter can be resolved prior to litigation. Discuss with debtor the cost and advisability of litigating the dischargeability of the claim. The attorney is not required, however, to represent the debtor in any adversary proceeding to determine the nondischargeability of any debt pursuant to these Rights and Responsibilities.

13. Represent the debtor with respect to any audit conducted pursuant to 28 U.S.C. § 586(a).

14. Negotiate all reaffirmation agreements and appear with the debtor at any hearing on same.

15. After all plan payments have been made, and if the debtor is eligible for a discharge, prepare, file and serve any documents required by the Court before a discharge will be entered.

The total fee charged in this case is $ _____. If this fee later proves to be insufficient to compensate the attorney for the legal service rendered in the case, the attorney has the right to apply to the court for any additional attorney fees. Fees shall be paid through the plan unless otherwise ordered. The attorney may not receive additional fees directly from the debtor other than the initial retainer. If an attorney has elected to be compensated pursuant to these guidelines, but the case is dismissed prior to confirmation of the plan, absent contrary order, the trustee shall pay to the attorney, to the extent funds are available, an administrative claim equal to 50% of the unpaid fee balance if a properly documented fee claim (for the entire fee balance) has been filed by the attorney and served upon the trustee.

If the debtor disputes the legal services provided or the fees charged by the attorney, an objection must be filed with the Court.

Dated: _____   _____
                            Debtor

Dated: _____   _____
                            Debtor

Dated: _____   _____
                            Attorney for Debtor(s)

[Amended effective February 14, 2013; October 10, 2014; June 8, 2015.]

CHAPTER 13 PLAN

Ch 13 Model Plan (rev 1/14/13)

UNITED STATES BANKRUPTCY COURT
Southern District Of Indiana

In re:)

)

[Name of Debtor(s)],   )   Case No. (xx–xxxxx)

               Debtor(s).   )

CHAPTER 13 PLAN

Original _____

Amended Plan # __ (e.g. 1st, 2nd)

** *Must Be Designated***

1. GENERAL PROVISIONS:

(a) **YOUR RIGHTS MAY BE AFFECTED.** Read these papers carefully and discuss them with your attorney. If you oppose any provision of this plan, you must file a timely written objection. This plan may be confirmed without further notice or hearing unless a written objection is filed before the deadline stated on the separate Notice you received from the Bankruptcy Court. If you have a secured claim, this plan may modify your lien if you do not object to the plan.

(b) **PROOFS OF CLAIM:** This plan does not allow claims. You must file a proof of claim to receive pre-confirmation adequate protection payments and to receive distribution under a confirmed plan. The filed proof of claim shall control as to the claim amount for pre-petition arrearages, secured and priority tax liabilities, and any payment in full offers unless specifically objected to and determined otherwise by the Court. All claims that are secured by a security interest in real estate shall comply with the requirements of FRBP 3001(c) without regard to whether the real estate is the debtor's principal residence.

(c) **NOTICES RELATING TO MORTGAGES:** All creditors with claims secured by a security interest in real estate shall comply with the requirements of B.R. 3002.1 without regard to whether the real estate is the debtor's principal residence. In addition to the requirements of FRBP 3002.1, should there be a change in the mortgage servicer while the bankruptcy is pending, the mortgage holder shall file with the Bankruptcy Court and serve upon the debtor, debtor's counsel and the Chapter 13 Trustee ("Trustee") a Notice setting forth the change and providing the name of the servicer, the payment address, a contact phone number and a contact e-mail address.

(d) **NOTICES (OTHER THAN THOSE RELATING TO MORTGAGES):** Non–mortgage creditors in Section 7(c) (whose rights are not being modified) or in Section 10 (whose executory contracts/unexpired leases are being assumed) may continue to mail customary notices or coupons to the debtor or the Trustee notwithstanding the automatic stay.

(e) **ADEQUATE PROTECTION PAYMENTS:** In accordance with Local Rule B–3015–3, any adequate protection payment offers shall be based upon 1% of the proposed allowed secured claim, although that presumption may be rebutted. The Trustee shall disburse such payments to the secured creditor as soon as practicable after receiving plan payments from the debtor, and the allowable secured claim will be reduced accordingly. All adequate protection payments shall be subject to the

Trustee's percentage fee as set by the United States Trustee. No adequate protection payments will be made by the Debtor directly to the creditor.

(f) **EQUAL MONTHLY PAYMENTS:** The Trustee may increase the amount of any "Equal Monthly Amount" offered to appropriately amortize the claim. The Trustee shall be permitted to accelerate payments to any class of creditor for efficient administration of the case.

(g) **PAYMENTS FOLLOWING ENTRY OF ORDERS LIFTING STAY:** Upon entry of an order lifting the stay, no distributions shall be made on any secured claim relating to the subject collateral until such time as a timely amended deficiency claim is filed by such creditor and deemed allowed, or the automatic stay is re-imposed by further order of the Court.

2. **SUBMISSION OF INCOME:** Debtor submits to the supervision and control of the Trustee all or such portion of future earnings or other future income or specified property of the debtor as is necessary for the execution of this plan.

3. **PLAN TERMS:**

(a) **PAYMENT AND LENGTH OF PLAN:** Debtor shall pay $ ___ per ___ to the Trustee, starting not later than 30 days after the order for relief, for approximately ___ months, for a total amount of $ ___. Additional payments to Trustee:

_____

_____

(b) **INCREASED FUNDING:** If additional property comes into the estate pursuant to 11 U.S.C. § 1306(a)(1) or if the Trustee discovers undisclosed property of the estate, then the Trustee may obtain such property or its proceeds to increase the total amount to be paid under the plan. No motion to modify the plan will be required but the Trustee may file a report to court. However, if the Trustee elects to take less than 100% of the property to which the estate is entitled OR less than the amount necessary to pay all allowed claims in full, then a motion to compromise and settle will be filed, and appropriate notice given.

(c) **CURING DEFAULTS:** If Debtor falls behind on plan payments or if changes to the payments owed to secured lenders require additional funds from the Debtor's income, the Debtor and the Trustee may agree that the Debtor(s) will increase the payment amount each month or that the time period for making payments will be extended, not to exceed 60 months. Creditors will not receive notice of any such agreement unless the total amount that the Debtor(s) will pay to the Trustee decreases. Any party may request in writing, addressed to the Trustee at the address shown on the notice of the meeting of creditors, that the Trustee give that party notice of any such agreement. Agreements under this section cannot extend the term of the plan more than 6 additional months.

(d) **OTHER PLAN CHANGES:** Any other modification of the plan shall be proposed by motion pursuant to 11 U.S.C. § 1329. Service of any motion to modify this plan shall be made by the moving party as required by FRBP 2002(a)(5) and 3015(g), unless otherwise ordered by the Court.

4. **ADMINISTRATIVE CLAIMS (INCLUSIVE OF DEBTOR'S ATTORNEY FEES):**

All administrative claims will be paid in full by the Trustee unless creditor agrees otherwise:

Creditor	Type of Priority	Scheduled Amount
<Debtor's Attorney>		
<Other>		

5. DOMESTIC SUPPORT OBLIGATIONS: The following Domestic Support Obligations will be paid in the manner specified:

Creditor	Type of Claim	Estimated Arrears	Treatment

DEBTOR IS REQUIRED TO PAY ANY PAYMENTS FALLING DUE AFTER THE FILING OF THE CASE PURSUANT TO A DOMESTIC SUPPORT ORDER DIRECTLY TO THE PAYEE IN ORDER FOR THIS PLAN TO BE <u>CONFIRMED</u> AND FOR DEBTOR TO RECEIVE A <u>DISCHARGE</u> FROM THE COURT UPON COMPLETION OF PLAN PAYMENTS HEREIN.

6. SECURED CLAIMS RELATING SOLELY TO THE DEBTOR'S PRINCIPAL RESIDENCE–CURING DEFAULTS AND/OR MAINTAINING PAYMENTS (INCLUSIVE OF REAL ESTATE TAXES AND HOMEOWNER'S ASSOCIATION ARREARS): If there is a pre-petition arrearage claim on a mortgage secured by the Debtor's principal residence, then both the pre-petition arrearage and the post-petition mortgage installments shall be made through the Trustee. Initial post-petition payment arrears shall be paid with secured creditors. If there are no arrears, the Debtor may pay the secured creditor directly. Estimated Current Monthly Installment listed below shall be adjusted based on filed claim and/or notice.

				Select One for Mortgages ONLY:	
Creditor	Residential Address	Estimated Arrears	Estimated Current Monthly Installment	Trustee Pay	Direct Pay

No late charges, fees or other monetary amounts shall be assessed based on the timing of any payments made by the Trustee under the provisions of the Plan, unless allowed by Order of the Court.

7. SECURED CLAIMS OTHER THAN CLAIMS RELATING TO THE DEBTOR'S PRINCIPAL RESIDENCE: After confirmation of the plan, the Trustee will pay to the holder of each allowed secured claim the equal monthly amount in column (a)(6) or (b)(7) based upon the amount of the claim [(Para. 7(a), column (4)] or value offer [(Para. 7(b), column (5)] with interest at the rate stated in column (a)(5) or (b)(6).

(a) Secured Claims To Which 11 U.S.C. 506 Valuation Is Not Applicable:

(1) Creditor	(2) Collateral	(3) Purchase Date	(4) Estimated Claim Amount	(5) Interest Rate	(6) Equal Monthly Amount	(7) Adequate Protection Amount (1% of allowed secured claim)

Additional plan offer, if any, as relates to above claim(s): _____

(b) Secured Claims to Which 11 U.S.C. 506 Valuation is Applicable:

(1) Creditor	(2) Collateral	(3) Purchase Date	(4) Scheduled Debt	(5) Value	(6) Interest Rate	(7) Equal Monthly Amount	(8) Adequate Protection Amount (1% of allowed secured claim)

Additional plan offer, if any, as relates to above claim(s): _____

(c) Curing Defaults and/or Maintaining Payments: Trustee shall pay allowed claim for arrearage, and Debtor shall pay regular post-petition contract payments directly to the creditor:

Creditor	Collateral/Type of Debt	Estimated Arrears	Interest Rate (if any)

(d) Surrendered/Abandoned Collateral: The Debtor intends to surrender the following collateral. Upon confirmation, the Chapter 13 estate abandons any interest in, and the automatic stay pursuant to 11 U.S.C. § 362 is terminated as to, the listed collateral. Upon confirmation, the secured creditor is free to pursue its in rem rights in state court.

Creditor	Collateral Surren- dered/Abandoned	Scheduled Value of Property

8. SECURED TAX CLAIMS AND 11 U.S.C. 507 PRIORITY CLAIMS: All allowed secured tax obligations shall be paid in full by the Trustee, inclusive of statutory interest thereon (whether or not an interest factor is expressly offered by plan terms). All allowed priority claims shall be paid in full by the Trustee, exclusive of interest, unless the creditor agrees otherwise:

Creditor	Type of Priority or Secured Claim	Scheduled Debt	Treatment

9. NON–PRIORITY UNSECURED CLAIMS:
  (a) Separately Classified or Long-term Debts:

Creditor	Basis for Classification	Treatment	Amount	Interest (if any)

    (b) **General Unsecured Claims:**
___ **Pro rata distribution from any remaining funds; or**
___ **Other:** _____

10. EXECUTORY CONTRACTS AND UNEXPIRED LEASES: All executory contracts and unexpired leases are REJECTED, except the following, which are assumed:

Creditor	Property Description	Treatment

11. AVOIDANCE OF LIENS: Debtor will file a separate motion or adversary proceeding to avoid the following non-purchase money security interests, judicial liens, wholly unsecured mortgages or other liens that impair exemptions:

Creditor	Collateral/Property Description	Amount of Lien to be Avoided

12. LIEN RETENTION: With respect to each allowed secured claim provided for by the plan, the holder of such claim shall retain its lien securing such claim until the earlier of a) the payment of the underlying debt determined under non-bankruptcy law or b) a discharge order being entered under 11 U.S.C. § 1328.

13. VESTING OF PROPERTY OF THE ESTATE: Except as necessary to fund the plan or as expressly retained by the plan or confirmation order, the property of the estate shall revest in the Debtor upon confirmation of the Debtor's plan, subject to the rights of the Trustee, if any, to assert claim to any additional property of the estate acquired by the Debtor post-petition pursuant to operation of 11 U.S.C. § 1306.

14. MISCELLANEOUS PROVISIONS:

Date: _____

                    /s/ Debtor
                    Printed Name of Debtor

                    /s/ Joint Debtor
                    Printed Name of Joint Debtor

                    /s/ Counsel for Debtor(s)
                    Counsel for Debtor(s) (required signature block)

[April 11, 2011. Amended effective November 21, 2011; January 14, 2013; July 22, 2013.]

SELECTED ORDERS

GENERAL ORDER 09–0005. CURRENT MORTGAGE PAYMENTS IN CHAPTER 13 CASES

For all Chapter 13 cases filed on or after August 1, 2009, if there is a pre-petition arrearage claim on a mortgage secured by the debtor's residential real property, then both the pre-petition arrearage and the post-petition mortgage installments shall be made through the Trustee. Such disbursements shall be subject to the Trustee's percentage fee as set by the United States Trustee.

[Dated: August 1, 2009.]

GENERAL ORDER 11–0002. ORDER REGARDING DEPOSIT AND INVESTMENT OF REGISTRY FUNDS

ORDER

The Court has decided to use the Court Registry Investment System ("CRIS") for the deposit and investment of registry funds, Therefore, it is ORDERED effective immediately that the following shall govern the receipt, deposit, and investment of registry funds:

I. Receipt of Funds

A. No money shall be sent to the Court or its officers for deposit in the Court's registry absent compliance with Local Rule B–7067–1 and without a court order signed by the presiding judge in the case or proceeding.

B. Unless provided for elsewhere in this Order, all monies ordered to be paid to the Court or received by its officers in any case pending or adjudicated shall be deposited with the Treasurer of the United States in the name and to the credit of this Court pursuant to 28 U.S.C. § 2041 through depositories designated by the Treasury to accept such deposit on its behalf.

II. Investment of Registry Funds

A. Where, by order of the Court, funds on deposit are to be placed in some form of interest-bearing account, CRIS, administered by the Administrative Office of United States Courts, shall be the only investment mechanism authorized.

B. Money from each case deposited in CRIS shall be "pooled" together with funds on deposit with Treasury to the credit of other courts in CRIS and used to purchase Government Account Series securities through the Bureau of Public Debt, which will be held at Treasury, in an account in the name of and to the credit of the Director of Administrative Office of the United States Courts, hereby designated as custodian for CRIS.

C. An account for each case will be established in CRIS titled in the name of the case giving rise to the investment in the fund. Income generated from fund investments will be distributed to each case based on the ratio each account's principal and earnings has to the aggregate principal and income total in the fund. Reports showing the interest earned and the principal amounts contributed in each case will be prepared and distributed to each court participating in CRIS and made available to litigants and/or their counsel.

III. Fees

A. The custodian is authorized and directed by this Order to deduct, for managing accounts in CRIS, the investment services fee to be assessed from the CRIS interest earnings. The proper investment services fee is to be determined on the basis of the rates published by the Director of the Administrative Office of United States Courts as approved by the Judicial Conference.

B. The Clerk shall assess a charge for the handling of registry funds deposited with the court, to be assessed from interest earnings and in accordance with the detailed fee schedule issued by the Director of the Administrative Office of the United States Courts.

[Dated: June 1, 2011.]

GENERAL ORDER 12–0006. IN RE: AMENDED ORDER ADOPTING INTERIM RULE 1007–I

The Court previously entered General Order 10–0008, which adopted Interim Bankruptcy Rule 1007–I, implementing the National Guard and Reservists Debt Relief Act of 2008.

That Interim Rule has now been amended. Accordingly, the Court rescinds General Order 10–0008 and by this General Order adopts the amended version of Interim Bankruptcy Rule 1007–I, which can be found at the following link:

http://www.uscourts.gov/RulesAndPolicies/rules/current-rules.aspx

Interim Rule 1007–I.[1] Lists, Schedules, Statements, and Other Documents; Time Limits; Expiration of Temporary Means Testing Exclusion[2]

* * * * *

(b) Schedules, Statements, and other Documents Required.

* * * * *

(4) *Unless either*: (A) § 707(b)(2)(D)(I) applies, or (B) § 707(b)(2)(D)(ii) applies and the exclusion from means testing granted therein extends beyond the period specified by Rule 1017(e), an individual debtor in a chapter 7 case shall file a statement of current monthly income prepared as prescribed by the appropriate Official Form, and, if the current monthly income exceeds the median family income for the applicable state and household size, the information, including calculations, required by § 707(b), prepared as prescribed by the appropriate Official Form.

* * * * *

(c) Time Limits. In a voluntary case, the schedules, statements, and other documents required by subdivision (b)(1), (4), (5), and (6) shall be filed with the petition or within 14 days thereafter, except as otherwise provided in subdivisions (d), (e), (f), (h), and (n) of this rule. In an involuntary case, the schedules, statements, and other documents required by subdivision (b)(1) shall be filed by the debtor within 14 days of the entry of the order for relief. In a voluntary case, the documents required by paragraphs (A), (C), and (D) of subdivision (b)(3) shall be filed with the petition. Unless the court orders otherwise, a debtor who has filed a statement under subdivision (b)(3)(B), shall file the documents required by subdivision (b)(3)(A) within 14 days of the order for relief. In a chapter 7 case, the debtor shall file the statement required by subdivision (b)(7) within 60 days after the first date set for the meeting of creditors under § 341 of the Code, and in a chapter 11 or 13 case no later than the date when the last payment was made by the debtor as required by the plan or the filing of a motion for a discharge under § 1141(d)(5)(B) or § 1328(b) of the Code. The court may, at any time and in its discretion, enlarge the time to file the statement required by subdivision (b)(7). The debtor shall file the statement required by subdivision (b)(8) no earlier than the date of the last payment made under the plan or the date of the filing of a motion for a discharge under §§ 1141(d)(5)(B), 1228(b), or 1328(b) of the Code. Lists, schedules, statements, and other documents filed prior to the conversion of a case to another chapter shall be deemed filed in the converted case unless the court directs otherwise. Except as provided in § 1116(3), any extension of time to file schedules, statements, and other documents required under this rule may be granted only on motion for cause shown and on notice to the United States trustee, any committee elected under § 705 or appointed under § 1102 of the Code, trustee, examiner, or other party as the court may direct. Notice of an extension shall be given to the United States trustee and to any committee, trustee, or other party as the court may direct.

* * * * *

(n) Time Limits for, and Notice to, Debtors Temporarily Excluded From Means Testing.

(1) An individual debtor who is temporarily excluded from means testing pursuant to § 707(b)(2)(D)(ii) of the Code shall file any statement and calculations required by subdivision (b)(4) no later than14 days after the expiration of the temporary exclusion if the expiration occurs within the time specified by Rule 1017(e) for filing a motion pursuant to § 707(b)(2).

(2) If the temporary exclusion from means testing under § 707(b)(2)(D)(ii) terminates due to the circumstances specified in subdivision (n)(1), and if the debtor has not previously filed a statement and calculations required by subdivision (b)(4), the clerk shall promptly notify the debtor that the required statement and calculations must be filed within the time specified in subdivision (n)(1).

[Effective November 30, 2012.]

[1]Interim Rule 1007–I has been adopted by the bankruptcy courts to implement the National Guard and Reservists Debt Relief Act of 2008, Public Law No: 110–438, as amended by Public Law No. 112–64. The amended Act, which provides a temporary exclusion from the application of the means test for certain members of the National Guard and reserve components of the Armed Forces, applies to bankruptcy cases commenced in the seven-year period beginning December 19, 2008.

[2]Incorporates (1) time amendments to Rule 1007 which took effect on December 1, 2009, (2) an amendment, effective December 1, 2010, which extended the time to file the statement of completion of a course in personal financial management in a chapter 7 case filed by an individual debtor, and (3) a conforming amendment, effective December 1, 2012, which removed an inconsistency created by the 2010 amendment.

GENERAL ORDER 13–0003. IN RE: STATUS AND MAINTENANCE OF GENERAL ORDERS

Review of the Court's records reveals that many previously issued general orders have been implicitly rescinded or superseded by local rules or other general orders. Some general orders adopt changes to the local rules, but remain posted on the Court's website even after those local rules edits become effective. The posting of obsolete general orders on the Court's website makes review of those general orders difficult.

Accordingly, the Court now orders that:

1. The following general orders are still in effect as of this date:

- 03–0011: procedure for prepackaged Chapter 11 cases
- 09–0003: mandatory electronic filing for attorneys
- 09–0004: wage assignment orders in Chapter 13 cases
- 09–0005: treatment of current mortgage payments in Chapter 13 plans
- 09–0006: requiring proof of identification for pro se parties filing documents
- 09–0011: requiring electronic filing by non-attorneys
- 10–0001: informal dispute resolution requirement for New Albany Chapter 13 cases
- 11–0002: concerning the deposit and investment of registry funds
- 12–0001: setting the maximum counsel fee for Chapter 13 cases

- 12–0005: establishing the schedule for installment fees
- 12–0006: adopting the latest version of interim rule 1007–I

2.   General orders adopting changes to the local rules remain effective, but shall be archived and removed from view to the public 30 days after the effective date of the rules changes in those orders.   The current version of the local rules always supersedes any earlier general order.

3.   A general order rescinding another general order, and the order that is rescinded, shall both be archived and removed from view to the public 30 days after the issuance of the order rescinding.

4.   All other general orders are hereby rescinded, and shall be archived and removed from view to the public on the Court's website if posted there.   Any paper versions of these General Orders shall be retained by the Clerk after being marked "Rescinded."

[Dated: April 26, 2013.]

GENERAL ORDER 14–0003.   IN RE: INSTALLMENT FEES: PAYMENT SCHEDULE

This Order is entered to establish minimum requirements for payment of filing fees in installments **on and after June 1, 2014.**   This order becomes effective on June 1, 2014, and replaces General Order 12–0005 on that date.

Pursuant to Fed.R.Bankr.P. 1006(b)(2), the Court fixes the number and amount of the installments as follows:

Chapter	Payment at Filing	One Month After Filing	Two Months After Filing	Three Months After Filing
7	$84	$84	$84	$83
11	$430	$429	$429	$429
12	$69	$69	$69	$68
13	$78	$78	$77	$77

On and after June 1, 2014, parties filing Applications to Pay Filing Fee in Installments shall propose a payment plan in accordance with this schedule.

Payments shall be due, as shown, on the same day of the month as the date on which the petition was filed.   If that date falls on a day that the Court is closed, payment is due no later than the next business day.

The Application must substantially conform to Official Form #3A.   This form is available in the Office of the Bankruptcy Clerk or on the Court's website at www.insb.uscourts.gov.

[Dated: April 18, 2014.]

GENERAL ORDER 14–0005.   ORDER SETTING MAXIMUM FEE FOR CHAPTER 13 CASES UNDER LOCAL RULE B–2016–1(b)

Local Rule B–2016–1(b) establishes the procedure pursuant to which counsel for a Chapter 13 debtor is excused from compliance with the fee application process of Fed.R.Bankr.P. 2016.

For all cases filed on or after October 27, 2014, the maximum fee allowable under the Local Rule is $4000.   However, if the attorney's work in the case will include filing an adversary proceeding to strip a wholly unsecured mortgage, pursuant to new Local Rule B–4003–3, then the maximum fee allowable is an additional $500 per adversary proceeding, PROVIDED that counsel complies with the following requirements:

- Discloses the higher fee at the time of filing in the statement required by Fed.R.Bankr.P. 2016(b) or in an amended statement;

- Files the adversary proceeding <u>before</u> filing a proof of claim for the higher fee or files an amended proof of claim after the filing of the adversary proceeding.

If an attorney seeks the higher maximum fee for a case pending on October 27, 2014, in which an adversary proceeding to strip a wholly unsecured mortgage is filed on or after October 27, 2014, then counsel may file an amended proof of claim after the adversary proceeding to strip the wholly unsecured mortgage has been filed.

The Court's earlier general order, 12–0001, which previously set the maximum fee, is hereby rescinded.

[Dated: October 16, 2014.]

GENERAL ORDER 14–0006.   ORDER WAIVING FEE FOR MOTIONS FOR PROTECTIVE ORDER PURSUANT TO FED.R.BANKR.P. 9037

On and after December 1, 2014, the Bankruptcy Court Miscellaneous Fee Schedule requires payment of a fee for filing a motion to redact a record. The fee is $25 per case in which redaction is sought, and applies to both opened and closed cases.

This Court's CM/ECF Dictionary does not include a Motion to Redact event. Instead, parties are directed to two different events, depending on who filed the document sought to be redacted:

- If a party seeks to redact the party's own document, the party shall file a Motion to Remove Document Pursuant to Fed.R.Bankr.P. 9037.

- If a party seeks redaction of a document filed by a different party, then the party shall file a Motion for Protective Order Pursuant to Fed.R.Bankr.P. 9037.

The event Motion to Restrict Access is intended for use with requests pursuant to 11 U.S.C. § 107. That event should not be used when requesting redaction of personal identifiers.

This Court may waive the fee for a motion to redact in appropriate circumstances. The Court has determined that the fee should never be charged when a party seeks to redact a record filed by a different party. Therefore, the Court hereby ORDERS THAT the fee will apply ONLY to a Motion to Remove Document Pursuant to Fed.R.Bankr.P. 9037.

Any party seeking to redact records from multiple cases should consult with the Bankruptcy Clerk about streamlined procedures which may be available through use of a miscellaneous proceeding.

[Effective November 4, 2014.]

RULES OF PROCEDURE OF THE JUDICIAL PANEL ON MULTIDISTRICT LITIGATION

Renumbered and Amended Effective November 2, 1998

Including Amendments Effective
July 6, 2011

I. RULES FOR MULTIDISTRICT LITIGATION UNDER 28 U.S.C. § 1407

RULE 1.1 DEFINITIONS

(a) "Panel" means the members of the United States Judicial Panel on Multidistrict Litigation appointed by the Chief Justice of the United States pursuant to 28 U.S.C. § 1407.

(b) "Chair" means the Chair of the Panel appointed by the Chief Justice of the United States pursuant to Section 1407, or the member of the Panel properly designated to act as Chair.

(c) "Clerk of the Panel" means the official that the Panel appoints to that position. The Clerk of the Panel shall perform such duties that the Panel or the Panel Executive delegates.

(d) "Electronic Case Filing (ECF)" refers to the Panel's automated system that receives and stores documents filed in electronic form. All attorneys filing pleadings with the Panel must do so using ECF. All pro se individuals are non-ECF users, unless the Panel orders otherwise.

(e) "MDL" means a multidistrict litigation docket which the Panel is either considering or has created by transferring cases to a transferee district for coordinated or consolidated pretrial proceedings pursuant to Section 1407.

(f) "Panel Executive" means the official appointed to act as the Panel's Chief Executive and Legal Officer. The Panel Executive may appoint, with the approval of the Panel, necessary deputies, clerical assistants and other employees to perform or assist in the performance of the duties of the Panel Executive. The Panel Executive, with the approval of the Panel, may make such delegations of authority as are necessary for the Panel's efficient operation.

(g) "Pleadings" means all papers, motions, responses, or replies of any kind filed with the Panel, including exhibits attached thereto, as well as all orders and notices that the Panel issues.

(h) "Tag-along action" refers to a civil action pending in a district court which involves common questions of fact with either (1) actions on a pending motion to transfer to create an MDL or (2) actions previously transferred to an existing MDL, and which the Panel would consider transferring under Section 1407.

(i) "Transferee district" is the federal district court to which the Panel transfers an action pursuant to Section 1407, for inclusion in an MDL.

(j) "Transferor district" is the federal district court where an action was pending prior to its transfer pursuant to Section 1407, for inclusion in an MDL, and where the Panel may remand that action at or before the conclusion of pretrial proceedings.

[Former Rule 1 adopted May 3, 1993, effective July 1, 1993. Renumbered Rule 1.1 September 1, 1998, effective November 2, 1998. Amended September 8, 2010, effective October 4, 2010.]

RULE 2.1 RULES AND PRACTICE

(a) Customary Practice. The Panel's customary practice shall govern, unless otherwise fixed by statute or these Rules.

(b) Failure to Comply With Rules. When a pleading does not comply with these Rules, the Clerk of the Panel may advise counsel of the deficiencies and set a date for full compliance. If counsel does not fully comply within the established time, the Clerk of the Panel shall file the non-complying pleading, but the Chair may thereafter order it stricken.

(c) Admission to Practice Before the Panel. Every member in good standing of the Bar of any district court of the United States is entitled to practice before the Panel, provided, however, that he or she has established and maintains a CM/ECF account with any United States federal court. Any attorney of record in any action transferred under Section 1407 may continue to represent his or her client in any district court of the United States to which such action is transferred. Parties are not required to obtain local counsel.

(d) Pendency of Motion or Conditional Order. The pendency of a motion, order to show cause, conditional transfer order or conditional remand order before the Panel pursuant to 28 U.S.C. § 1407 does not affect or suspend orders and pretrial proceedings in any pending federal district court action and does not limit the pretrial jurisdiction of that court. An order to transfer or remand pursuant to 28 U.S.C. § 1407 shall be effective only upon its filing with the clerk of the transferee district court.

(e) Reassignment. If for any reason the transferee judge is unable to continue those responsibilities, the Panel shall make the reassignment of a new transferee judge.

[Former Rule 5 adopted May 3, 1993, effective July 1, 1993. Renumbered Rule 1.2 September 1, 1998, effective November 2, 1998. Former Rule 4 adopted May 3, 1993, effective July 1, 1993. Renumbered Rule 1.3 and amended September 1, 1998, effective November 2, 1998. Former Rule 6 adopted May 3, 1993, effective July 1, 1993. Renumbered Rule 1.4 September 1, 1998, effective November 2, 1998. Former Rule 18 adopted May 3, 1993, effective July 1, 1993. Renumbered Rule 1.5 September 1, 1998, effective November 2, 1998. Former Rules 1.2, 1.3, 1.4, and 1.5 redesignated and amended September 8, 2010, effective October 4, 2010.]

RULE 3.1 ELECTRONIC RECORDS AND FILES; COPY FEES

(a) Electronic Record. Effective October 4, 2010, the official Panel record shall be the electronic file maintained on the Panel's servers. This record includes, but is not limited to, Panel pleadings, documents filed in paper and then scanned and made part of the electronic record, and Panel orders and notices filed. The official record also includes any documents or exhibits that may be impractical to scan. These documents and exhibits shall be kept in the Panel offices.

(b) Maintaining Records. Records and files generated prior to October 4, 2010, may be (i) maintained at the Panel offices, (ii) temporarily or permanently removed to such places at such times as the Clerk of the Panel or the Chair shall direct, or (iii) transferred whenever appropriate to the Federal Records Center.

(c) Fees. The Clerk of the Panel may charge fees for duplicating records and files, as prescribed by the Judicial Conference of the United States.

[Former Rule 2 adopted May 3, 1993, effective July 1, 1993. Renumbered Rule 5.1 and amended September 1, 1998, effective November 2, 1998. Former Rule 5.1 redesignated and amended September 8, 2010, effective October 4, 2010.]

RULE 3.2 ECF USERS: FILING REQUIREMENTS

(a) Form of Pleadings. This Rule applies to pleadings that ECF users file with the Panel.

(i) Each pleading shall bear the heading "Before the United States Judicial Panel on Multidistrict Litigation," the identification "MDL No. ___" and the descriptive title designated by the Panel. If the Panel has not yet designated a title, counsel shall use an appropriate description.

(ii) The final page of each pleading shall contain the name, address, telephone number, fax number and email address of the attorney or party designated to receive service of pleadings in the case, and the name of each party represented.

(iii) Each brief submitted with a motion and any response to it shall not exceed 20 pages, exclusive of exhibits. Each reply shall not exceed 10 pages and shall address arguments raised in the response(s). Absent exceptional circumstances and those set forth in Rule 6.1(d), the Panel will not grant motions to exceed page limits.

(iv) Each pleading shall be typed in size 12 point font (for both text and footnotes), double spaced (text only), in a letter size document (8 ½ × 11 inch) with sequentially numbered pages.

(v) Each exhibit shall be separately numbered and clearly identified.

(vi) Proposed Panel orders shall not be submitted.

(b) Place of Filing. Counsel shall sign and verify all pleadings electronically in accordance with these Rules and the Panel's Administrative Policies and Procedures for Electronic Case Filing found at www. jpml.uscourts.gov. A pleading filed electronically constitutes a written document for the purpose of these Rules and the Federal Rules of Civil Procedure and is deemed the electronically signed original thereof. All pleadings, except by pro se litigants, shall conform with this Rule beginning on October 4, 2010.

(i)* Pleadings shall not be transmitted directly to any Panel member.

(c) Attorney Registration. Only attorneys identified, or to be identified, pursuant to Rule 4.1, shall file pleadings. Each of these attorneys must register as a Panel CM/ECF user through www.jpml.uscourts.gov. Registration/possession of a CM/ECF account with any United States federal court shall be deemed consent to receive electronic service of all Panel orders and notices as well as electronic service of pleadings from other parties before the Panel.

(d) Courtesy Copy of Specified Pleadings. Counsel shall serve the Clerk of the Panel, for delivery within 1 business day of filing, with a courtesy paper copy of any of the following pleadings: (i) a motion to transfer and its supporting brief; (ii) a response to a show cause order; (iii) a motion to vacate a conditional transfer order or a conditional remand order; (iv) any response, reply, supplemental information or interested party response related to the pleadings listed in (i), (ii) and (iii); and (v) a corporate disclosure statement. No courtesy copies of any other pleadings are required. Courtesy copies of pleadings totaling 10

pages or less (including any attachments) may be faxed to the Panel. The courtesy copy shall include all exhibits, shall be clearly marked "Courtesy Copy—Do Not File," shall contain the CM/ECF pleading number (if known), and shall be mailed or delivered to:

Clerk of the Panel
United States Judicial Panel on Multidistrict
  Litigation
Thurgood Marshall Federal Judiciary Building
One Columbus Circle, NE,
Room G–255, North Lobby
Washington, DC 20002–8041

(e) Privacy Protections. The privacy protections contained in Rule 5.2 of the Federal Rules of Civil Procedure shall apply to all Panel filings.

[Former Rule 3 adopted May 3, 1993, effective July 1, 1993. Renumbered Rule 5.11 and amended September 1, 1998, effective November 2, 1998; renumbered Rule 5.1.1 and amended March 25, 2010, effective April 1, 2010. Former Rule 7 adopted May 3, 1993, effective July 1, 1993. Renumbered Rule 5.12 and amended September 1, 1998, effective November 2, 1998. Amended April 2, 2001, effective April 2, 2001; paragraph (a) suspended in part by Order filed April 19, 2005; renumbered Rule 5.1.2 and amended March 25, 2010, effective April 1, 2010. Former Rule 9 adopted May 3, 1993, effective July 1, 1993. Renumbered Rule 7.1 and amended September 1, 1998, effective November 2, 1998. Amended April 2, 2001, effective April 2, 2001. Former Rules 5.1.1, 5.1.2, and 7.1 redesignated in part and amended September 8, 2010, effective October 4, 2010. Amended effective July 6, 2011.]

* So in original. No subdivision (ii) promulgated.

RULE 3.3   NON–ECF USERS: FILING REQUIREMENTS

(a) Definition of Non–ECF Users. Non–ECF users are all pro se individuals, unless the Panel orders otherwise. This Rule shall apply to all motions, responses and replies that non-ECF users file with the Panel.

(b) Form of Pleadings. Unless otherwise set forth in this Rule, the provisions of Rule 3.2 shall apply to non-ECF users.

(i) Each pleading shall be flat and unfolded; plainly written or typed in size 12 point font (for both text and footnotes), double spaced (text only), and printed single-sided on letter size (8 ½ × 11 inch) white paper with sequentially numbered pages; and fastened at the top-left corner without side binding or front or back covers.

(ii) Each exhibit shall be separately numbered and clearly identified. Any exhibits exceeding a cumulative total of 50 pages shall be bound separately.

(c) Place of Filing. File an original and one copy of all pleadings with the Clerk of the Panel by mailing or delivering to:

Clerk of the Panel
United States Judicial Panel on Multidistrict
  Litigation
Thurgood Marshall Federal Judiciary Building
One Columbus Circle, NE,
Room G–255, North Lobby
Washington, DC 20002–8041

(i) Pleadings not exceeding a total of 10 pages, including exhibits, may be faxed to the Panel office.

(ii) The Clerk of the Panel shall endorse the date for filing on all pleadings submitted for filing.

[Former Rule 3 adopted May 3, 1993, effective July 1, 1993. Renumbered Rule 5.11 and amended September 1, 1998, effective November 2, 1998; renumbered Rule 5.1.1 and amended March 25, 2010, effective April 1, 2010. Former Rule 7 adopted May 3, 1993, effective July 1, 1993. Renumbered Rule 5.12 and amended September 1, 1998, effective November 2, 1998. Amended April 2, 2001, effective April 2, 2001; paragraph (a) suspended in part by Order filed April 19, 2005; renumbered Rule 5.1.2 and amended March 25, 2010, effective April 1, 2010. Former Rule 9 adopted May 3, 1993, effective July 1, 1993. Renumbered Rule 7.1 and amended September 1, 1998, effective November 2, 1998. Amended April 2, 2001, effective April 2, 2001. Former Rules 5.1.1, 5.1.2, and 7.1 redesignated in part and amended September 8, 2010, effective October 4, 2010.]

RULE 4.1   SERVICE OF PLEADINGS

(a) **Proof of Service.** The Panel's notice of electronic filing shall constitute service of pleadings. Registration/possession by counsel of a CM/ECF account with any United States federal court shall be deemed consent to receive electronic service of all pleadings. All pleadings shall contain a proof of service on all other parties in all involved actions. The proof of service shall indicate the name and manner of service. If a party is not represented by counsel, the proof of service shall indicate the name of the party and the party's last known address. The proof of service shall indicate why any person named as a party in a constituent complaint was not served with the Section 1407 pleading.

(b) **Service Upon Transferor Court.** The proof of service pertaining to motions for a transfer or remand pursuant to 28 U.S.C. § 1407 shall certify that counsel has transmitted a copy of the motion for filing to the clerk of each district court where an affected action is pending.

(c) **Notice of Appearance.** Within 14 days after the issuance of a (i) notice of filing of a motion to initiate transfer under Rule 6.2, (ii) notice of filed opposition to a CTO under Rule 7.1, (iii) a show cause order under Rules* 8.1, (iv) notice of filed opposition to a CRO under Rule 10.2, or (v) notice of filing of a motion to remand under Rule 10.3, each party or designated attorney as required hereinafter shall file a Notice of Appearance notifying the Clerk of the Panel of the name, address and email address of the attorney designated to file and receive service of all pleadings. Each party shall designate only one attorney. Any party not represented by counsel shall be served by mailing such pleadings to the party's last known address. Except in extraordinary circumstances, the Panel will not grant requests for an extension of time to file the Notice of Appearance.

(d) **Liaison Counsel.** If the transferee district court appoints liaison counsel, this Rule shall be satisfied by serving each party in each affected action and all liaison counsel. Liaison counsel shall receive copies of all Panel orders concerning their particular litigation and shall be responsible for distribution to the parties for whom he or she serves as liaison counsel.

[Former Rule 8 adopted May 3, 1993, effective July 1, 1993. Renumbered Rule 5.2 and amended September 1, 1998, effective November 2, 1998; March 26, 2009, effective December 1, 2009. Former Rule 5.2 redesignated and amended September 8, 2010, effective October 4, 2010. Technical revisions effective July 6, 2011.]

* So in original.

RULE 5.1   CORPORATE DISCLOSURE STATEMENT

(a) **Requirements.** A nongovernmental corporate party must file a disclosure statement that: (1) identifies any parent corporation and any publicly held corporation owning 10% or more of its stock; or (2) states that there is no such corporation.

(b) **Deadline.** A party shall file the corporate disclosure statement within 14 days after issuance of a notice of the filing of a motion to transfer or remand, an order to show cause, or a motion to vacate a conditional transfer order or a conditional remand order.

(c) **Updating.** Each party must update its corporate disclosure statement to reflect any change in the information therein (i) until the matter before the Panel is decided, and (ii) within 14 days after issuance of a notice of the filing of any subsequent motion to transfer or remand, order to show cause, or motion to vacate a conditional transfer order or a conditional remand order in that docket.

[Former Rule 2 adopted May 3, 1993, effective July 1, 1993. Renumbered Rule 5.1 and amended September 1, 1998, effective November 2, 1998. Former Rule 5.3 redesignated and amended September 8, 2010, effective October 4, 2010. Amended effective July 6, 2011.]

RULE 5.1.3   FILING OF PAPERS: COMPUTER GENERATED DISK REQUIRED [DELETED SEPT. 8, 2010, EFF. OCT. 4, 2010]

[Added May 22, 2000, effective June 1, 2000. And amended July 30, 2007, effective July 30, 2007; renumbered Rule 5.1.3 and amended March 25, 2010, effective April 1, 2010. Deleted September 8, 2010, effective October 4, 2010.]

RULE 6.1 MOTION PRACTICE

(a) Application. This Rule governs all motions requesting Panel action generally. More specific provisions may apply to motions to transfer (Rule 6.2), miscellaneous motions (Rule 6.3), conditional transfer orders (Rule 7.1), show cause orders (Rule 8.1), conditional remand orders (Rule 10.2) and motions to remand (Rule 10.3).

(b) Form of Motions. All motions shall briefly describe the action or relief sought and shall include:

(i) a brief which concisely states the background of the litigation and movant's factual and legal contentions;

(ii) a numbered schedule providing

(A) the complete name of each action involved, listing the full name of each party included as such on the district court's docket sheet, not shortened by the use of references such as "et al." or "etc.";

(B) the district court and division where each action is pending;

(C) the civil action number of each action; and

(D) the name of the judge assigned each action, if known;

(iii) a proof of service providing

(A) a service list listing the full name of each party included on the district court's docket sheet and the complaint, including opt-in plaintiffs not listed on the docket sheet; and

(B) in actions where there are 25 or more plaintiffs listed on the docket sheet, list the first named plaintiff with the reference "et al." if all the plaintiffs are represented by the same attorney(s);

(iv) a copy of all complaints and docket sheets for all actions listed on the Schedule; and

(v) exhibits, if any, identified by number or letter and a descriptive title.

(c) Responses and Joinders. Any other party may file a response within 21 days after filing of a motion. Failure to respond to a motion shall be treated as that party's acquiescence to it. A joinder in a motion shall not add any action to that motion.

(d) Replies. The movant may file a reply within 7 days after the lapse of the time period for filing a response. Where a movant is replying to more than one response in opposition, the movant may file a consolidated reply with a limit of 20 pages.

(e) Alteration of Time Periods. The Clerk of the Panel has the discretion to shorten or enlarge the time periods set forth in this Rule as necessary.

(f) Notification of Developments. Counsel shall promptly notify the Clerk of the Panel of any development that would partially or completely moot any Panel matter.

[Former Rule 10 adopted May 3, 1993, effective July 1, 1993. Renumbered Rule 7.2 and amended September 1, 1998, effective November 2, 1998. Amended April 2, 2001, effective April 2, 2001; March 26, 2009, December 1, 2009. Former Rule 7.2 redesignated in part and amended September 8, 2010, effective October 4, 2010.]

RULE 6.2 MOTIONS TO TRANSFER FOR COORDINATED OR CONSOLIDATED PRETRIAL PROCEEDINGS

(a) Initiation of Transfer. A party to an action may initiate proceedings to transfer under Section 1407 by filing a motion in accordance with these Rules. A copy of the motion shall be filed in each district court where the motion affects a pending action.

(b) Notice of Filing of Motion to Transfer. Upon receipt of a motion, the Clerk of the Panel shall issue a "Notice of Filing of Motion to Transfer" to the service list recipients. The Notice shall contain the following: the filing date of the motion, caption, MDL docket number, briefing schedule and pertinent Panel policies. After a motion is filed, the Clerk of the Panel shall consider any other pleading to be a response unless the pleading adds an action. The Clerk of the Panel may designate such a pleading as a motion, and distribute a briefing schedule applicable to all or some of the parties, as appropriate.

(c) Notice of Appearance. Within 14 days of issuance of a "Notice of the Filing of a Motion to Transfer," each party or designated attorney shall file a Notice of Appearance in accordance with Rule 4.1(c).

(d) Notice of Potential Tag-along Actions. Any party or counsel in a new group of actions under consideration for transfer under Section 1407 shall promptly notify the Clerk of the Panel of any potential tag-along actions in which that party is also named or in which that counsel appears.

(e) Interested Party Responses. Any party or counsel in one or more potential tag-along actions as well as amicus curiae may file a response to a pending motion to transfer. Such a pleading shall be deemed an Interested Party Response.

(f) Amendment to a Motion. Before amending a motion to transfer, a party shall first contact the Clerk of the Panel to ascertain whether such amendment is feasible and permissible considering the Panel's hearing schedule. Any such amendment shall be entitled "Amendment to Motion for Transfer," and shall clearly and specifically identify and describe the nature of the amendment.

(i) Where the amended motion includes new civil actions, the amending party shall file a "Schedule of Additional Actions" and a revised Proof of Service.

(ii) The Proof of Service shall state (A) that all new counsel have been served with a copy of the amendment and all previously-filed motion papers, and (B) that all counsel previously served with the original motion have been served with a copy of the amendment.

(iii) The Clerk of the Panel may designate the amendment with a different denomination (*e.g.*, a notice of potential tag-along action(s)) and treatment.

(h) Oral Argument*. The Panel shall schedule oral arguments as needed and as set forth in Rule 11.1.

[Former Rule 10 adopted May 3, 1993, effective July 1, 1993. Renumbered Rule 7.2 and amended September 1, 1998, effective November 2, 1998. Amended April 2, 2001, effective April 2, 2001; March 26, 2009, December 1, 2009. Former Rule 15 adopted May 3, 1993, effective July 1, 1993. Renumbered Rule 6.2 and amended September 1, 1998, effective November 2, 1998. Former Rule 7.2 redesignated in part and amended September 8, 2010, effective October 4, 2010. Technical revisions effective July 6, 2011.]

* So in original.

RULE 6.3 MOTIONS FOR MISCELLANEOUS RELIEF

(a) Definition. Motions for miscellaneous relief include, but are not limited to, requests for extensions of time, exemption from ECF requirements, page limit extensions, or expedited consideration of any motion.

(b) Panel Action. The Panel, through the Clerk, may act upon any motion for miscellaneous relief, at any time, without waiting for a response. A motion for extension of time to file a pleading or perform an act under these Rules must state specifically the revised date sought and must be filed before the deadline for filing the pleading or performing the act. Any party aggrieved by the Clerk of the Panel's action may file objections for consideration. Absent exceptional circumstances, the Panel will not grant any extensions of time to file a notice of opposition to either a conditional transfer order or a conditional remand order.

[Former Rule 15 adopted May 3, 1993, effective July 1, 1993. Renumbered Rule 6.2 and amended September 1, 1998, effective November 2, 1998. Former Rule 6.2 redesignated and amended September 8, 2010, effective October 4, 2010.]

RULE 7.1 CONDITIONAL TRANSFER ORDERS (CTO) FOR TAG–ALONG ACTIONS

(a) Notice of Potential Tag-along Actions. Any party or counsel in actions previously transferred under Section 1407 shall promptly notify the Clerk of the Panel of any potential tag-along actions in which that party is also named or in which that counsel appears. The Panel has several options: (i) filing a CTO under Rule 7.1, (ii) filing a show cause order under Rule 8.1, or (iii) declining to act (Rule 7.1(b)(i)).

(b) Initiation of CTO. Upon learning of the pendency of a potential tag-along action, the Clerk of the Panel may enter a conditional order transferring that action to the previously designated transferee district court for the reasons expressed in the Panel's previous opinions and orders. The Clerk of the Panel shall serve this order on each party to the litigation but shall not send the order to the clerk of the transferee district court until 7 days after its entry.

(i)* If the Clerk of the Panel determines that a potential tag-along action is not appropriate for inclusion in an MDL proceeding and does not enter a CTO, an involved party may move for its transfer pursuant to Rule 6.1.

(c) Notice of Opposition to CTO. Any party opposing the transfer shall file a notice of opposition with the Clerk of the Panel within the 7–day period. In such event, the Clerk of the Panel shall not transmit the transfer order to the clerk of the transferee district court, but shall notify the parties of the briefing schedule.

(d) Failure to Respond. Failure to respond to a CTO shall be treated as that party's acquiescence to it.

(e) Notice of Appearance. Within 14 days after the issuance of a "Notice of Filed Opposition" to a CTO, each opposing party or designated attorney shall file a Notice of Appearance in accordance with Rule 4.1(c).

(f) Motion to Vacate CTO. Within 14 days of the filing of its notice of opposition, the party opposing transfer shall file a motion to vacate the CTO and brief in support thereof. The Clerk of the Panel shall set the motion for the next appropriate hearing session. Failure to file and serve a motion and brief shall be treated as withdrawal of the opposition and the Clerk of the Panel shall forthwith transmit the order to the clerk of the transferee district court.

(g) Notification of Developments. Parties to an action subject to a CTO shall notify the Clerk of the Panel if that action is no longer pending in its transferor district court.

(h) Effective Date of CTO. CTOs are effective when filed with the clerk of the transferee district court.

[Former Rule 12 adopted May 3, 1993, effective July 1, 1993. Renumbered Rule 7.4 and amended September 1, 1998, effective November 2, 1998. Amended April 2, 2001, effective April 2, 2001; March 26, 2009, December 1, 2009. Former Rule 7.4 redesignated and amended September 8, 2010, effective October 4, 2010. Technical revisions effective July 6, 2011.]

* So in original. No subdivision (ii) promulgated.

RULE 7.2 MISCELLANEOUS PROVISIONS CONCERNING TAG–ALONG ACTIONS

(a) Potential Tag-alongs in Transferee Court. Potential tag-along actions filed in the transferee district do not require Panel action. A party should request assignment of such actions to the Section 1407 transferee judge in accordance with applicable local rules.

(b) Failure to Serve. Failure to serve one or more of the defendants in a potential tag-along action with the complaint and summons as required by Rule 4 of the Federal Rules of Civil Procedure does not preclude transfer of such action under Section 1407. Such failure, however, may constitute grounds for denying the proposed transfer where prejudice can be shown. The failure of the Clerk of the Panel to serve a CTO on all plaintiffs or defendants or their counsel may constitute grounds for the Clerk to reinstate the CTO or for the aggrieved party to seek § 1407(c) remand.

[Former Rule 13 adopted May 3, 1993, effective July 1, 1993. Renumbered Rule 7.5 and amended September 1, 1998, effective November 2, 1998. Amended April 2, 2001, effective April 2, 2001. Former Rule 7.5 redesignated and amended September 8, 2010, effective October 4, 2010. Amended effective July 6, 2011.]

RULE 8.1 SHOW CAUSE ORDERS

(a) Entry of Show Cause Order. When transfer of multidistrict litigation is being considered on the initiative of the Panel pursuant to 28 U.S.C. § 1407(c)(i), the Clerk of the Panel may enter an order directing the parties to show cause why a certain civil action or actions should not be transferred for coordinated or consolidated pretrial proceedings. Any party shall also promptly notify the Clerk of the Panel whenever they learn of any other federal district court actions which are similar to those which the show cause order encompasses.

(b) Notice of Appearance. Within 14 days of the issuance of an order to show cause, each party or designated attorney shall file a Notice of Appearance in accordance with Rule 4.1(c).

(c) Responses. Unless otherwise provided by order, any party may file a response within 21 days of the filing of the show cause order. Failure to respond to a show cause order shall be treated as that party's acquiescence to the Panel action.

(d) Replies. Within 7 days after the lapse of the time period for filing a response, any party may file a reply.

(e) Notification of Developments. Counsel shall promptly notify the Clerk of the Panel of any development that would partially or completely moot any matter subject to a show cause order.

[Former Rule 7.3 adopted May 3, 1993, effective July 1, 1993. Renumbered Rule 7.3 and amended September 1, 1998, effective November 2, 1998; March 26, 2009, effective December 1, 2009. Former Rule 7.3 redesignated and amended September 8, 2010, effective October 4, 2010.]

RULE 9.1 TRANSFER OF FILES; NOTIFICATION REQUIREMENTS

(a) Notice to Transferee Court Clerk. The Clerk of the Panel, via a notice of electronic filing, will notify the clerk of the transferee district whenever a Panel transfer order should be filed in the transferee district court. Upon receipt of an electronically certified copy of a Panel transfer order from the clerk of the transferee district, the clerk of the transferor district shall transmit the record of each transferred action to the transferee district and then, unless Rule 9.1(b) applies, close the transferred action in the transferor district.

(b) Retention of Claims. If the transfer order provides for the separation and simultaneous remand of any claim, cross-claim, counterclaim, or third-party claim, the clerk of the transferor district shall retain jurisdiction over any such claim and shall not close the action.

(c) Notice to Clerk of Panel. The clerk of the transferee district shall promptly provide the Clerk of the Panel with the civil action numbers assigned to all transferred actions and the identity of liaison counsel, if or when designated. The clerk of the transferee district shall also promptly notify the Clerk of the Panel of any dispositive ruling that terminates a transferred action.

[Former Rule 19 adopted May 3, 1993, effective July 1, 1993. Renumbered Rule 1.6 and amended September 1, 1998, effective November 2, 1998. Former Rule 1.6 redesignated in part and amended September 8, 2010, effective October 4, 2010.]

RULE 10.1 TERMINATION AND REMAND

(a) Termination. Where the transferee district court terminates an action by valid order, including but not limited to summary judgment, judgment of dismissal and judgment upon stipulation, the transferee district court clerk shall transmit a copy of that order to the Clerk of the Panel. The terminated action shall not be remanded to the transferor court and the transferee court shall retain the original files and records unless the transferee judge or the Panel directs otherwise.

(b) Initiation of Remand. Typically, the transferee judge recommends remand of an action, or a part of it, to the transferor court at any time by filing a suggestion of remand with the Panel. However, the Panel may remand an action or any separable claim, cross-claim, counterclaim or third-party claim within it, upon

    (i) the transferee court's suggestion of remand,

    (ii) the Panel's own initiative by entry of an order to show cause, a conditional remand order or other appropriate order, or

    (iii) motion of any party.

[Former Rule 14 adopted May 3, 1993, effective July 1, 1993. Renumbered Rule 7.6 and amended September 1, 1998, effective November 2, 1998. Amended April 2, 2001, effective April 2, 2001; March 26, 2009, effective December 1, 2009. Former Rule 7.6 redesignated in part and amended September 8, 2010, effective October 4, 2010.]

RULE 10.2   CONDITIONAL REMAND ORDERS (CRO)

(a) Entering a CRO. Upon the suggestion of the transferee judge or the Panel's own initiative, the Clerk of the Panel shall enter a conditional order remanding the action or actions to the transferor district court. The Clerk of the Panel shall serve this order on each party to the litigation but shall not send the order to the clerk of the transferee district court for 7 days from the entry thereof.

    (i)* The Panel may, on its own initiative, also enter an order that the parties show cause why a matter should not be remanded. Rule 8.1 applies to responses and replies with respect to such a show cause order.

(b) Notice of Opposition. Any party opposing the CRO shall file a notice of opposition with the Clerk of the Panel within the 7–day period. In such event, the Clerk of the Panel shall not transmit the remand order to the clerk of the transferee district court and shall notify the parties of the briefing schedule.

(c) Failure to Respond. Failure to respond to a CRO shall be treated as that party's acquiescence to it.

(d) Notice of Appearance. Within 14 days after the issuance of a "Notice of Filed Opposition" to a CRO, each opposing party or designated attorney shall file a Notice of Appearance in accordance with Rule 4.1(c).

(e) Motion to Vacate CRO. Within 14 days of the filing of its notice of opposition, the party opposing remand shall file a motion to vacate the CRO and brief in support thereof. The Clerk of the Panel shall set the motion for the next appropriate Panel hearing session. Failure to file and serve a motion and brief shall be treated as a withdrawal of the opposition and the Clerk of the Panel shall forthwith transmit the order to the clerk of the transferee district court.

(f) Effective Date of CRO. CROs are not effective until filed with the clerk of the transferee district court.

[Former Rule 14 adopted May 3, 1993, effective July 1, 1993. Renumbered Rule 7.6 and amended September 1, 1998, effective November 2, 1998. Amended April 2, 2001, effective April 2, 2001; March 26, 2009, effective December 1, 2009. Former Rule 7.6 redesignated in part and amended September 8, 2010, effective October 4, 2010. Technical revisions effective July 6, 2011.]

  * So in original. No subdivision (ii) promulgated.

RULE 10.3   MOTION TO REMAND

(a) Requirements of the Motion. If the Clerk of the Panel does not enter a CRO, a party may file a motion to remand to the transferor court pursuant to these Rules. Because the Panel is reluctant to order a remand absent the suggestion of the transferee judge, the motion must include:

    (i) An affidavit reciting whether the movant has requested a suggestion of remand and the judge's response, whether the parties have completed common discovery and other pretrial proceedings, and whether the parties have complied with all transferee court orders.

    (ii) A copy of the transferee district court's final pretrial order, if entered.

(b) Filing Copy of Motion. Counsel shall file a copy of the motion to remand in the affected transferee district court.

(c) Notice of Appearance. Within 14 days of the issuance of a "Notice of Filing" of a motion to remand, each party or designated attorney shall file a Notice of Appearance in accordance with Rule 4.1(c).

[Former Rule 14 adopted May 3, 1993, effective July 1, 1993. Renumbered Rule 7.6 and amended September 1, 1998, effective November 2, 1998. Amended April 2, 2001, effective April 2, 2001; March 26, 2009, effective December 1, 2009. Former Rule 7.6 redesignated in part and amended September 8, 2010, effective October 4, 2010. Technical revisions effective July 6, 2011.]

RULE 10.4   TRANSFER OF FILES ON REMAND

(a) Designating the Record. Upon receipt of an order to remand from the Clerk of the Panel, the parties shall furnish forthwith to the transferee district clerk a stipulation or designation of the contents of the record or part thereof to be remanded.

(b) Transfer of Files. Upon receipt of an order to remand from the Clerk of the Panel, the transferee district shall transmit to the clerk of the transferor district the following concerning each remanded action:

    (i) a copy of the individual docket sheet for each action remanded;

(ii) a copy of the master docket sheet, if applicable;

(iii) the entire file for each action remanded, as originally received from the transferor district and augmented as set out in this Rule;

(iv) a copy of the final pretrial order, if applicable; and

(v) a "record on remand" as designated by the parties in accordance with 10.4(a).

[Former Rule 19 adopted May 3, 1993, effective July 1, 1993. Renumbered Rule 1.6 and amended September 1, 1998, effective November 2, 1998. Former Rule 1.6 redesignated in part and amended September 8, 2010, effective October 4, 2010.]

RULE 11.1 HEARING SESSIONS AND ORAL ARGUMENT

(a) **Schedule.** The Panel shall schedule sessions for oral argument and consideration of other matters as desirable or necessary. The Chair shall determine the time, place and agenda for each hearing session. The Clerk of the Panel shall give appropriate notice to counsel for all parties. The Panel may continue its consideration of any scheduled matters.

(b) **Oral Argument Statement.** Any party affected by a motion may file a separate statement setting forth reasons why oral argument should, or need not, be heard. Such statements shall be captioned "Reasons Why Oral Argument Should [Need Not] Be Heard" and shall be limited to 2 pages.

(i)* The parties affected by a motion to transfer may agree to waive oral argument. The Panel will take this into consideration in determining the need for oral argument.

(c) **Hearing Session.** The Panel shall not consider transfer or remand of any action pending in a federal district court when any party timely opposes such transfer or remand without first holding a hearing session for the presentation of oral argument. The Panel may dispense with oral argument if it determines that:

(i) the dispositive issue(s) have been authoritatively decided; or

(ii) the facts and legal arguments are adequately presented and oral argument would not significantly aid the decisional process.

Unless otherwise ordered, the Panel shall consider all other matters, such as a motion for reconsideration, upon the basis of the pleadings.

(d) **Notification of Oral Argument.** The Panel shall promptly notify counsel of those matters in which oral argument is scheduled, as well as those matters that the Panel will consider on the pleadings. The Clerk of the Panel shall require counsel to file and serve notice of their intent to either make or waive oral argument. Failure to do so shall be deemed a waiver of oral argument. If counsel does not attend oral argument, the matter shall not be rescheduled and that party's position shall be treated as submitted for decision on the basis of the pleadings filed.

(i) Absent Panel approval and for good cause shown, only those parties to actions who have filed a motion or written response to a motion or order shall be permitted to present oral argument.

(ii) The Panel will not receive oral testimony except upon notice, motion and an order expressly providing for it.

(e) **Duty to Confer.** Counsel in an action set for oral argument shall confer separately prior to that argument for the purpose of organizing their arguments and selecting representatives to present all views without duplication. Oral argument is a means for counsel to emphasize the key points of their arguments, and to update the Panel on any events since the conclusion of briefing.

(f) **Time Limit for Oral Argument.** Barring exceptional circumstances, the Panel shall allot a maximum of 20 minutes for oral argument in each matter. The time shall be divided among those with varying viewpoints. Counsel for the moving party or parties shall generally be heard first.

[Former Rule 16 adopted May 3, 1998, effective July 1, 1993. Renumbered Rule 16.1 and amended September 1, 1998, effective November 2, 1998. Amended April 2, 2001, effective April 2, 2001. Former Rule 16.1 redesignated and amended September 8, 2010, effective October 4, 2010.]

* So in original. No subdivision (ii) promulgated.

RULES 12 TO 15. [RESERVED]

II. RULES FOR MULTICIRCUIT PETITIONS FOR REVIEW UNDER 28 U.S.C. § 2112(a)(3)

RULE 25.1 DEFINITIONS

The Panel promulgates these Rules pursuant to its authority under 28 U.S.C. § 2112(a)(3) to provide a means for the random selection of one circuit court of

appeals to hear consolidated petitions for review of agency decisions.

An "Agency" means an agency, board, commission or officer of the United States government, that has received two or more petitions for review in a circuit court of appeals to enjoin, set aside, suspend, modify or otherwise review or enforce an action.

[Former Rule 20 adopted May 3, 1993, effective July 1, 1993. Renumbered Rule 25.1 and amended September 1, 1998, effective November 2, 1998. Amended September 8, 2010, effective October 4, 2010.]

RULE 25.2   FILING OF NOTICES

(a) Submitting Notice. An affected agency shall submit a notice of multicircuit petitions for review pursuant to 28 U.S.C. § 2112(a)(3) to the Clerk of the Panel by electronic means in the manner these Rules require and in accordance with the Panel's Administrative Policies and Procedures for Electronic Case Filing, except that the portion of Rule 3.2(d) requiring a courtesy copy is suspended in its entirety.

(b) Accompaniments to Notices. All notices of multicircuit petitions for review shall include:

(i) a copy of each involved petition for review as the petition for review is defined in 28 U.S.C. § 2112(a)(2);

(ii) a schedule giving

(A) the date of the relevant agency order;

(B) the case name of each petition for review involved;

(C) the circuit court of appeals in which each petition for review is pending;

(D) the appellate docket number of each petition for review;

(E) the date of filing by the court of appeals of each petition for review; and

(F) the date of receipt by the agency of each petition for review; and

(iii) proof of service (*see* Rule 25.3).

(c) Scope of Notice. All notices of multicircuit petitions for review shall embrace exclusively petitions for review filed in the courts of appeals within 10 days after issuance of an agency order and received by the affected agency from the petitioners within that 10–day period.

(d) Filing at the Panel. The Clerk of the Panel shall file the notice of multicircuit petitions for review and endorse thereon the date of filing.

(e) Filing With Each Circuit Clerk. The affected agency shall file copies of notices of multicircuit petitions for review with the clerk of each circuit court of appeals in which a petition for review is pending.

[Former Rule 21 adopted May 3, 1993, effective July 1, 1993. Renumbered Rule 25.2 and amended September 1, 1998, effective November 2, 1998. Amended September 8, 2010, effective October 4, 2010. Technical revisions effective July 6, 2011.]

RULE 25.3   SERVICE OF NOTICES

(a) Proof of Service. Notices of multicircuit petitions for review shall include proof of service on all other parties in the petitions for review included in the notice. Rule 25 of the Federal Rules of Appellate Procedure governs service and proof of service. The proof of service shall state the name, address and email address of each person served and shall indicate the party represented by each and the manner in which service was accomplished on each party. If a party is not represented by counsel, the proof of service shall indicate the name of the party and his or her last known address. The affected party shall submit proof of service for filing with the Clerk of the Panel and shall send copies thereof to each person included within the proof of service.

(b) Service on Clerk of Circuit. The proof of service pertaining to notices of multicircuit petitions for review shall certify the affected party has mailed or delivered copies of the notices to the clerk of each circuit court of appeals in which a petition for review is pending that is included in the notice. The Clerk shall file the notice with the circuit court.

[Former Rule 22 adopted May 3, 1993, effective July 1, 1993. Renumbered Rule 25.3 September 1, 1998, effective November 2, 1998. Amended September 8, 2010, effective October 4, 2010.]

RULE 25.4   FORM OF NOTICES; PLACE OF FILING

(a) Unless otherwise provided here, Rule 3.2 governs the form of a notice of multicircuit petitions for review. Each notice shall bear the heading "Notice to the United States Judicial Panel on Multidistrict Litigation of Multicircuit Petitions for Review," followed by a brief caption identifying the involved agency, the relevant agency order, and the date of the order.

(b) Rule 3.2(b) and (c) govern the manner of filing a notice of multicircuit petitions for review.

[Former Rule 23 adopted May 3, 1993, effective July 1, 1993. Renumbered Rule 25.4 and amended September 1, 1998, effective November 2, 1998. Amended September 8, 2010, effective October 4, 2010.]

RULE 25.5   RANDOM SELECTION

(a) Selection Process. Upon filing a notice of multicircuit petitions for review, the Clerk of the Panel shall randomly select a circuit court of appeals from a drum containing an entry for each circuit wherein a constituent petition for review is pending. Multiple petitions for review pending in a single circuit shall be allotted only a single entry in the drum. A designated deputy other than the random selector shall witness the random selection. Thereafter, an order on behalf of the Panel shall be issued, signed by the random selector and the witness,

(i) consolidating the petitions for review in the court of appeals for the circuit that was randomly selected; and

(ii) designating that circuit as the one in which the record is to be filed pursuant to Rules 16 and 17 of the Federal Rules of Appellate Procedure.

(b) Effective Date. A consolidation of petitions for review shall be effective when the Clerk of the Panel enters the consolidation order.

[Former Rule 24 adopted May 3, 1993, effective July 1, 1993. Renumbered Rule 17.1 September 1, 1998, effective November 2, 1998. Former Rule 17.1 redesignated and amended September 8, 2010, effective October 4, 2010.]

RULE 25.6 SERVICE OF PANEL CONSOLIDATION ORDER

(a) The Clerk of the Panel shall serve the Panel's consolidation order on the affected agency through the individual or individuals, as identified in Rule 25.2(a), who submitted the notice of multicircuit petitions for review on behalf of the agency.

(b) That individual or individuals, or anyone else designated by the agency, shall promptly serve the Panel's consolidation order on all other parties in all petitions for review included in the Panel's consolidation order, and shall promptly submit a proof of that service to the Clerk of the Panel. Rule 25.3 governs service.

(c) The Clerk of the Panel shall serve the Panel's consolidation order on the clerks of all circuit courts of appeals that were among the candidates for the Panel's random selection.

[Former Rule 25 adopted May 3, 1993, effective July 1, 1993. Renumbered Rule 25.5 and amended September 1, 1998, effective November 2, 1998. Former Rule 25.5 redesignated and amended September 8, 2010, effective October 4, 2010.]

III.   CONVERSION TABLE

New to Old:

New Rule / Previous Rule		New Rule / Previous Rule	
1.1	1.1	9.1	1.6
2.1	1.2, 1.3, 1.4, 1.5	10.1	7.6
3.1	5.1	10.2	7.6
3.2	5.1.1, 5.1.2, 7.1	10.3	7.6
3.3	5.1.1, 5.1.2, 7.1	10.4	1.6
4.1	5.2	11.1	16.1
5.1	5.3	25.1	25.1
6.1	7.2	25.2	25.1, 25.2
6.2	7.2	25.3	25.3
6.3	6.2	25.4	25.1, 25.4
7.1	7.4	25.5	17.1
7.2	7.5	25.6	25.5
8.1	7.3		

Old to New:

Previous Rule / New Rule		Previous Rule / New Rule	
1.1	1.1	7.1	3.2, 3.3
1.2	2.1	7.2	6.1
1.3	2.1	7.3	8.1
1.4	2.1	7.4	7.1
1.5	2.1	7.5	7.2
1.6	10.4	7.6	10.1
5.1	3.1	16.1	11.1
5.1.1	3.2, 3.3	17.1	25.5
5.1.2	3.2, 3.3	25.1	25.1, 25.2, 25.4
5.1.3	-	25.2	25.2
5.2	4.1	25.3	25.3
5.3	5.1	25.4	25.4
6.2	6.3	25.5	25.6

[October 2010.]

ELECTRONIC CASE FILING ADMINISTRATIVE POLICIES AND PROCEDURES

1. DEFINITIONS.

1.1 "ELECTRONIC FILING SYSTEM" (ECF) refers to the United States Judicial Panel on Multidistrict Litigation's (the Panel's) automated system that receives and stores documents filed in electronic form. The program is part of the CM/ECF (Case Management/Electronic Case Files) software which was developed for the Federal Judiciary by the Administrative Office of the United States Courts.

1.2 "CLERK OF THE PANEL" means the official appointed by the Panel to act as Clerk of the Panel and shall include those deputized by the Clerk of the Panel to perform or assist in the performance of the duties of the Clerk of the Panel.

1.3 "FILING USER" is an individual who has a Panel-issued login and password to file documents electronically. In accordance with Rule 1.4 of the Rules of Procedure of the United States Judicial Panel on Multidistrict Litigation (the Panel Rules), every member in good standing of the Bar of any district court of the United States is entitled to practice before the Judicial Panel on Multidistrict Litigation.

1.4 "NOTICE OF ELECTRONIC FILING" (NEF) is a notice automatically generated by the Electronic Filing System at the time a document is filed with the system, setting forth the time of filing, the date the document is entered on the docket, the name of the party and attorney filing the document, the type of document, the text of the docket entry, the name of the party and/or attorney receiving the notice, and an electronic link (hyperlink) to the filed document, which allows recipients to retrieve the document automatically. A document shall not be considered filed for the purposes of the Panel's Rules until the filing party receives a system generated Notice of Electronic Filing with a hyperlink to the electronically filed document.

1.5 "PACER" (Public Access to Court Electronic Records) is an automated system that allows an individual to view, print and download Panel docket information over the Internet.

1.6 "PDF" (Portable Document Format). A document file created with a word processor, or a paper document which has been scanned, must be converted to portable document format to be filed electronically with the Panel. Converted files contain the extension ".pdf".

1.7 "TECHNICAL FAILURE" is defined as a failure of Panel owned/leased hardware, software, and/or telecommunications facility which results in the inability of a Filing User to submit a filing electronically. Technical failure does not include malfunctioning of a Filing User's equipment.

2. SCOPE OF ELECTRONIC FILING.

(a) All multidistrict litigation matters (MDLs) brought before the Panel under 28 U.S.C. § 1407 shall be assigned to the Electronic Filing System. Effective October 1, 2010, all MDLs, proceedings, motions, memoranda of law and other pleadings or documents filed with the Panel in new and existing dockets must be filed using CM/ECF unless otherwise specified herein.

(b) The filing of all MDL papers shall be accomplished electronically under procedures outlined in the Panel's CM/ECF User Manual.

(c) A party proceeding pro se shall not file electronically, unless otherwise permitted by the Panel. Pro se filers shall file paper originals of all documents. The clerk's office will scan these original documents into the JPML's electronic system, unless otherwise sealed.

3. ELIGIBILITY, REGISTRATION, PASSWORDS.

(a) Any attorney admitted to the Bar of any United States district court is eligible to practice before the Panel. Unless otherwise exempt as set forth herein, to become a Filing User, an attorney must register as a Filing User by completing the prescribed registration form and submitting it to the Clerk of the Panel.

(b) Registration as a Filing User constitutes consent to electronic service of all documents filed with or issued by the Panel in accordance with the Panel Rules.

(c) By submitting the online registration form, the Filing Users certify that they have read and are familiar with the Panel Rules and these administrative policies and procedures governing electronic filing and the method of training in the System used prior to becoming a Filing User. Filing users must also have a PACER account. An individual may register more than one Internet email address. The clerk's office will email the login and password to the attorney.

(d) Once the registration is processed by the clerk, the Filing User shall protect the security of the User password and immediately notify the clerk if the Filing User learns that the password has been compromised. Filing Users may be subject to sanctions for failure to comply with this provision. After registering, attorneys may change their passwords. If an attorney comes to believe that the security of an existing password has been compromised and that a threat to the System exists, the attorney must change his or her password immediately.

(e) Exemptions from mandatory electronic filing may be granted upon submission of a written request to the clerk. The written request shall include a supporting affidavit showing a substantial undue hardship. Final authority to grant such request is vested in the Clerk of the Panel or his/her designee.

(f)(1) Each attorney is responsible for keeping his/her contact information up to date. If an attorney is leaving a law firm and is the attorney of record on an existing case and representation in the case will remain with the law firm, withdrawal and substitution of counsel must be made prior to the attorney's termination in the law firm, for the following reason:

The attorney leaving the firm has an email address with the law firm he or she is leaving on record with the Panel. This email address may be disabled by the law firm as soon as the attorney terminates his/her employment. The electronic notices in CM/ECF will continue to go to the terminated attorney's email address at the former firm. If the email address is disabled at the law firm, the attorney will not receive the electronic notice. If a withdrawal/substitution of counsel has not been filed prior to the attorney leaving the firm, the law firm should not disable the email account of the attorney leaving the firm until another attorney in the firm enters his/her appearance. The law firm should designate someone in the firm to check this email account for CM/ECF notices until substitution of counsel has been filed with the Panel.

(2) If the attorney leaving the firm is taking active cases from the firm, the attorney needs to change his/her email address as soon as possible, otherwise the attorney will not receive electronic notices from CM/ECF. The email will continue to be sent to the former law firm's email address still on record. Procedures for changing an email address may be found in the Panel's CM/ECF User Manual.

4. ELECTRONIC FILING AND SERVICE OF DOCUMENTS.

(a) Electronic transmission of a document to the Electronic Filing System in accordance with these procedures, together with the transmission of a (System) Notice of Electronic Filing from the Panel with a hyperlink to the electronically filed document, constitutes filing of the document for all purposes of the Panel Rules of Procedure.

(b) Emailing a document to the clerk's office does not constitute filing the document. A document shall not be considered filed until the System generates a Notice of Electronic Filing (NEF) with a hyperlink to the electronically filed document.

(c) Before filing a scanned document with the court, a Filing User must verify its legibility.

(d) When a document has been filed electronically, the official record of that document is the electronic recording as stored by the Panel and the filing party is bound by the document as filed. A document filed electronically is deemed filed on the date and time stated on the Notice of Electronic Filing (NEF) from the Panel.

(e) Filing a document electronically does not alter the filing deadline for that document. Filing must be completed before midnight, **EASTERN TIME**, in order to be considered timely filed that day. However, if time of day is of the essence, the Clerk of the Panel may order a document filed by a certain time.

(f) Upon the filing of a document, a docket entry will be created using the information provided by the Filing User. The clerk will, where necessary and appropriate, modify the docket entry description to comply with quality control standards. In the event a Filing User electronically files a document in the wrong MDL or associated civil action, or the incorrect PDF document is attached, the Clerk of the Panel, or his/her designee, shall be authorized to strike the document from the record. A notice of the action striking a document from the record shall be served on all parties in the case.

(g) By participating in the electronic filing process, the parties consent to the electronic service of all documents, and shall make available electronic mail addresses for service. Upon the filing of a document by a Filing User, a Notice of Electronic Filing (NEF), with a hyperlink to the electronic document and an email message will be automatically generated by the electronic filing system, and sent via electronic mail to the email addresses of all parties who have registered in the MDL. In addition to receiving email notifications of filing activity, the Filing User is strongly encouraged to sign on to the electronic filing system at regular intervals to check the docket in his/her MDL and/or civil action.

(h) If the filing of an electronically submitted document requires leave of the Panel, such as a request to file out-of-time, the attorney shall attach the proposed document as an attachment to the motion requesting leave to file. If the Clerk of the Panel grants the motion, the document will be electronically filed without further action by the Filing User.

(i) A certificate of service must be included with all documents filed electronically. Such certificate shall indicate that service was accomplished pursuant to the Panel's electronic filing procedures. Service by electronic mail shall constitute service pursuant to Panel Rule 5.2.

A party who is not a registered CM/ECF participant with any United States federal court is entitled to a paper copy of any electronically filed pleading, document, or order pursuant to Panel Rule 5.1.1.(b). The filing party must therefore provide the non-registered attorney or party, including a terminated party or attorney, if appropriate, with the pleading, document, or order pursuant to Panel Rule 5.2. Under the Rule, they can be served with a paper copy of the electronically filed document, or they can consent in writing to service by any other method, including other forms of electronic service such as fax or direct email.

The following is a suggested certificate of service for electronic filing:

CERTIFICATE OF SERVICE

On [Date], I electronically filed this document through the CM/ECF system, which will send a notice of electronic filing to: [Attorney Name (attach list if necessary)]; and I [mailed] [hand delivered] [faxed] this document and the notice of electronic filing to: [Attorney/Party Name], [Address], [Parties Represented], [Civil Action(s)] (attach list if necessary).

> /s/ [typed name of attorney]
>
> Attorney's name
>
> Law Firm Name (if applicable)
>
> Address
>
> Phone Number
>
> Fax Number
>
> Attorney's Email address
>
> Attorney for:

5. ENTRY OF PANEL DOCUMENTS.

(a) A document entered or issued by the Panel will be filed in accordance with these procedures and such filing shall constitute entry on the docket kept by the Clerk.

(b) All signed orders will be electronically filed or entered. An order containing the electronic signature of a Panel Judge or the Clerk of the Panel shall have the same force and effect as if the Panel Judge or Clerk of the Panel had affixed a signature to a paper copy of the order and the order had been entered on the docket in a conventional manner.

(c) Orders may also be issued as "text-only" entries on the docket, without an attached document. Such orders are official and binding.

6. NOTICE OF PANEL ORDERS AND NOTICES.

Immediately upon the entry of an order or notice by the Panel, the clerk will transmit to Filing Users in affected cases in the MDL, in electronic form, a Notice of Electronic Filing (NEF), with a hyperlink to the electronic document. Electronic transmission of the NEF, along with a hyperlink to the electronic document, constitutes the notice required by Panel Rule 5.2. The clerk must give notice in paper form to a pro se party or an attorney who is not a Filing User to the extent notice is required.

7. ATTACHMENTS AND EXHIBITS.

Documents referenced as exhibits or attachments shall be filed in accordance with these administrative policies and procedures and the Panel's CM/ECF User Manual, unless otherwise ordered by the Panel. A Filing User shall submit as exhibits or attachments only those excerpts of the referenced documents that are directly germane to the matter under consideration by the Panel. Excerpted material must be clearly and prominently identified as such. Filing Users who file excerpts of documents as exhibits or attachments under these procedures do so without prejudice to their right to file timely additional excerpts or the complete document. Responding parties may timely file additional excerpts or the complete document that they believe are directly germane. The Panel may require parties to file additional excerpts or the complete document.

8. SEALED DOCUMENTS.

To ensure proper storage of a document, a document subject to a sealing order must be filed with the Panel on paper in a sealed envelope marked "sealed", citing thereon the MDL docket number and title and the associated case caption and case number; or by attaching thereto a paper copy of the Panel's order sealing the document or a copy of the NEF citing the entry of the court's order sealing the document. The clerk may require the document to be accompanied by a disk or CD–ROM containing the document in .pdf format. Only a motion to file a document under seal may be filed electronically, unless prohibited by law. The order of the Panel authorizing the filing of documents under seal may be filed electronically, unless prohibited by law or otherwise directed by the Panel. If a document is filed under seal pursuant to the E–Government Act of 2002, the filing party is nevertheless required to file a redacted copy for the public record along with the unredacted sealed document.

9. SPECIAL FILING REQUIREMENTS AND EXCEPTIONS.

9.1   Special Filing Requirements

The documents listed below shall be presented for filing on paper. The clerk may require the document be accompanied by a disk or CD–ROM containing the document in .pdf format:

Sealed

MDL dockets involving Qui Tam Cases (under seal)

9.2 Exceptions

All documents shall be filed electronically unless otherwise ordered by the Panel or specifically exempt herein.

10. RETENTION REQUIREMENTS.

(a) A document that is electronically filed and requires an original signature other than that of the Filing User must be maintained in paper form by counsel and/or the firm representing the party on whose behalf the document was filed until one year after all periods for appeals expire. On request of the Panel, said counsel must provide the original document for review.

(b) The clerk's office may choose to discard certain documents brought to the clerk's office for filing in paper form after those documents are scanned and uploaded to the System (to include pro se filings). Therefore, counsel and pro se filers shall provide the Panel with a copy of the original documents with intrinsic value for scanning and maintain the original signature in accordance with 10(a).

11. SIGNATURES.

(a) The user login and password required to submit documents to the Electronic Filing System serve as the Filing User signature on all electronic documents filed with the court. They serve as a signature for purposes of the Panel Rules and any other purpose for which a signature is required in connection with proceedings before the Panel.

(b) Each document filed electronically must indicate in the caption that it has been electronically filed. An electronically filed document must include a signature block in compliance with Panel Rule 7.1(e), and must set forth the name, address, telephone number, fax number, and email address. In addition, the name of the Filing User under whose login and password the document is submitted must be preceded by an "/s/" and typed in the space where the signature would otherwise appear. No Filing User or other person may knowingly permit or cause to permit a Filing User password to be used by anyone other than an authorized agent of the Filing User.

(c) A document requiring signatures of more than one party must be filed either by:

(1) electronically filing a scanned document containing all necessary signatures; or

(2) representing the consent of the other parties on the document; or

(3) identifying on the document the party whose signature is required and by the submission of a notice of endorsement by the other parties no later than three (3) business days after filing; or

(4) any other manner approved by the Panel.

(d) A non-filing signatory or party who disputes the authenticity of an electronically filed document with a non-attorney signature, or the authenticity of the signature on that document; or the authenticity of an electronically filed document containing multiple signatures or the authenticity of the signature themselves, must file an objection to the document within fourteen (14) days of service of the document.

(e) Any party challenging the authenticity of an electronically filed document or the attorney's signature on that document must file an objection to the document within fourteen (14) days of service of the document.

(f) If a party wishes to challenge the authenticity of an electronically filed document or signature after the fourteen (14) day period, the party shall file a motion to seek a ruling from the Panel.

12. SERVICE OF DOCUMENTS BY ELECTRONIC MEANS.

12.1 Service

12.1.1 Filing User

Upon the electronic filing of a pleading or other document, the Panel's Electronic Case Filing System will automatically generate and send a Notice of Electronic Filing (NEF) to all Filing Users associated with that MDL and/or associated cases, along with a hyperlink to the electronic document. Transmission of the Notice of Electronic Filing with a hyperlink to the electronic document constitutes service of the filed document.

The NEF must include the time of filing, the date the document was entered on the docket, the name of the party and attorney filing the document, the type of document, the text of the docket entry, and an electronic link (hyperlink) to the filed document, allowing anyone receiving the notice by email to retrieve the document automatically. If the Filing User becomes aware that the NEF was not transmitted successfully to a party, or that the notice is deficient, *i.e.*, the electronic link to the document is defective, the filer shall serve the electronically filed document by email, hand, facsimile, or by first-class mail postage prepaid immediately upon notification of the NEF deficiency.

12.1.2 Individual who is not a Filing User

A non-registered participant is entitled to receive a paper copy of any electronically filed document from the party making such filing. Service of such paper copy must be made according to the Panel Rules.

13. **TECHNICAL FAILURES.**

(a) If the site is unable to accept filings continuously or intermittently for more than one (1) hour occurring after 12:00 noon Eastern Time that day, the Clerk of the Panel shall deem the Panel's Electronic Case Filing web site to be subject to a technical failure.

(b) If a Filing User experiences a technical failure as defined herein, the Filing User may submit the document to the Clerk of the Panel, provided that the document is accompanied by a certification, signed by the Filing User, that the Filing User has attempted to file the document electronically at least twice, with those unsuccessful attempts occurring at least one (1) hour apart after 12:00 noon Eastern Time that day. The Clerk may require the document to be accompanied by a disk or CD–ROM which contains the document in .pdf format.

(c) The initial point of contact for a Filing User experiencing technical difficulty filing a document electronically will be the Panel's CM/ECF Help Desk at the numbers listed on the Panel's web site and in the CM/ECF User Manual.

(d) A Filing User who suffers prejudice as a result of a technical failure as defined herein or a Filing User who cannot file a time-sensitive document electronically due to unforeseen technical difficulties, such as the malfunctioning of a Filing User's equipment, may seek relief from the Clerk of the Panel.

14. **PUBLIC ACCESS.**

14.1 (a) A person may receive information from the Electronic Filing System at the Panel's Internet site by obtaining a PACER login and password. A person who has PACER access may retrieve docket sheets and documents (unless otherwise sealed or restricted) in MDL dockets and associated civil cases. Any case or document under seal shall not be available electronically or through any other means.

(b) If a case or document has been restricted, a PACER user may retrieve the docket sheet over the Internet, but only a Filing User who is counsel of record may retrieve restricted documents electronically. However, a restricted case or document will be available for viewing by the public at the clerk's office.

(c) Electronic access to electronic docket sheets and all documents filed in the System, unless sealed, is available to the public for viewing at no charge during regular business hours at the clerk's office. A copy fee for an electronic reproduction is required in accordance with 28 U.S.C. § 1932.

(d) Conventional copies and certified copies of electronically filed documents may be purchased at the clerk's office. The fee for copying and certifying will be in accordance with 28 U.S.C. § 1932.

14.2 Sensitive Information

Since the public may access certain case information over the Internet through the Panel's Electronic Filing System, sensitive information should not be included in any document filed with the court unless such inclusion is necessary and relevant. In accordance with these Administrative Policies and Procedures, if sensitive information must be included, certain personal and identifying information such as Social Security numbers, financial account numbers, dates of birth and names of minor children shall be redacted from the pleading, whether it is filed electronically or on paper.

The Panel recognizes that parties may need to include in the record a document containing information such as driver's license number; medical records, treatment and diagnosis; employment history; individual financial information; and proprietary or trade secret information.

To avoid unnecessary disclosure of private, personal or financial information, a party may:

(a) **RESTRICTED MDL DOCKETS OR DOCUMENTS.**

File a "Motion to Seal" or "Motion to Seal Document". The motion must state the reason and show good cause for restricting remote access to the case. If the motion is granted, remote access to documents will be limited to Filing Users who are counsel of record. However, the MDL docket sheet and/or documents will be available for viewing by the public at the clerk's office.

(b) **EXHIBITS.**

File an exhibit containing private, personal or financial information as an attachment to a pleading entitled "Notice of Filing Restricted Exhibit". The notice and the attached exhibit shall be filed as a separate docket entry, rather than as an attachment to the pleading supported by the exhibit. Remote public access to the notice and exhibit will be limited to Filing Users who are counsel of record. The notice and exhibit will, however, be available for viewing by the public at the clerk's office.

(c) **DOCUMENTS UNDER SEAL.**

(1) File a redacted copy of a pleading or exhibit containing private, personal or financial infor-

mation, whether electronically or on paper, while concurrently filing an unredacted copy under seal. This document shall be retained by the Panel as part of the record.

OR

(2) File a reference list under seal. The reference list shall contain the complete personal data identifier(s) and the redacted identifier(s) used in its (their) place in the filing. All references in the case to the redacted identifier(s) included in the reference list will be construed to refer to the corresponding complete identifier. The reference list must be filed under seal, and may be amended as of right. It shall be retained by the Panel as part of the record.

(d) **MOTION TO SEAL.**

File a motion to seal the document or MDL associated case. The motion must state the reason and show good cause for sealing the document or MDL associated case. If the motion to seal is granted, the document or case under seal will not be available electronically or through any other means.

It is the sole responsibility of counsel and the parties to ensure that all documents filed with the Panel comply with these Administrative Policies and Procedures, regarding public access to electronic case files. The Clerk will not review any document for redaction.

Counsel are strongly urged to share this information with all clients so that an informed decision about the inclusion, redaction, and/or exclusion of certain materials may be made.

[Effective May 2010.]

FEDERAL COURTS MISCELLANEOUS FEE SCHEDULES

COURT OF APPEALS FEE SCHEDULE[1]

(Effective December 1, 2014)

The fees included in the Court of Appeals Miscellaneous Fee Schedule are to be charged for services provided by the courts of appeals.

- The United States should not be charged fees under this schedule, except as prescribed in Items 2, 4, and 5 when the information requested is available through remote electronic access.

- Federal agencies or programs that are funded from judiciary appropriations (agencies, organizations, and individuals providing services authorized by the Criminal Justice Act, 18 U.S.C. § 3006A, and bankruptcy administrators) should not be charged any fees under this schedule.

(1) For docketing a case on appeal or review, or docketing any other proceeding, $500.

- Each party filing a notice of appeal pays a separate fee to the district court, but parties filing a joint notice of appeal pay only one fee.

- There is no docketing fee for an application for an interlocutory appeal under 28 U.S.C. § 1292(b) or other petition for permission to appeal under Fed. R. App. P. 5, unless the appeal is allowed.

- There is no docketing fee for a direct bankruptcy appeal or a direct bankruptcy cross appeal, when the fee has been collected by the bankruptcy court in accordance with item 14 of the Bankruptcy Court Miscellaneous Fee Schedule.

- This fee is collected in addition to the statutory fee of $5 that is collected under 28 U.S.C. § 1917.

(2) For conducting a search of the court of appeals records, $30 per name or item searched. This fee applies to services rendered on behalf of the United States if the information requested is available through remote electronic access.

(3) For certification of any document, $11.

(4) For reproducing any document, $.50 per page. This fee applies to services rendered on behalf of the United States if the document requested is available through remote electronic access.

(5) For reproducing recordings of proceedings, regardless of the medium, $30, including the cost of materials. This fee applies to services rendered on behalf of the United States if the recording is available through remote electronic access.

(6) For reproducing the record in any appeal in which the court of appeals does not require an appendix pursuant to Fed. R. App. P. 30(f), $83.

(7) For retrieval of one box of records from a Federal Records Center, National Archives, or other storage location removed from the place of business of the court, $64. For retrievals involving multiple boxes, $39 for each additional box.

(8) For any payment returned or denied for insufficient funds, $53.

(9) For copies of opinions, a fee commensurate with the cost of printing, as fixed by each court.

(10) For copies of the local rules of court, a fee commensurate with the cost of distributing the copies. The court may also distribute copies of the local rules without charge.

(11) For filing:

- Any separate or joint notice of appeal or application for appeal from the Bankruptcy Appellate Panel, $5;

- A notice of the allowance of an appeal from the Bankruptcy Appellate Panel, $5.

(12) For counsel's requested use of the court's videoconferencing equipment in connection with each oral argument, the court may charge and collect a fee of $200 per remote location.

(13) For original admission of attorney to practice, including a certificate of admission, $176.

For a duplicate certificate of admission or certificate of good standing, $18.

1 Issued in accordance with 28 U.S.C. § 1913.

DISTRICT COURT FEE SCHEDULE[1]

(Effective December 1, 2014)

The fees included in the District Court Miscellaneous Fee Schedule are to be charged for services provided by the district courts.

- The United States should not be charged fees under this schedule, with the exception of those specifically prescribed in Items 2, 4 and 5, when the information requested is available through remote electronic access.

- Federal agencies or programs that are funded from judiciary appropriations (agencies, organizations, and individuals providing services authorized by the Criminal Justice Act, 18 U.S.C. § 3006 and bankruptcy administrators) should not be charged any fees under this schedule.

1. For filing any document that is not related to a pending case or proceeding, $46.

2. For conducting a search of the district court records, $30 per name or item searched. This fee applies to services rendered on behalf of the United States if the information requested is available through electronic access.

3. For certification of any document, $11. For exemplification of any document, $21.

4. For reproducing any record or paper, $.50 per page. This fee shall apply to paper copies made from either: (1) original documents; or (2) microfiche or microfilm reproductions of the original records. This fee shall apply to services rendered on behalf of the United States if the record or paper requested is available through electronic access.

5. For reproduction of an audio recording of a court proceeding, $30. This fee applies to services rendered on behalf of the United States, if the recording is available electronically.

6. For each microfiche sheet of film or microfilm jacket copy of any court record, where available, $6.

7. For retrieval of one box of records from a Federal Records Center, National Archives, or other storage location removed from the place of business of the court, $64. For retrievals involving multiple boxes, $39 for each additional box.

8. For any payment returned or denied for insufficient funds, $53.

9. For an appeal to a district judge from a judgment of conviction by a magistrate judge in a misdemeanor case, $37.

10. For original admission of attorneys to practice, $176 each, including a certificate of admission. For a duplicate certificate of admission or certificate of good standing, $18.

11. The court may charge and collect fees commensurate with the cost of providing copies of the local rules of court. The court may also distribute copies of the local rules without charge.

12. The clerk shall assess a charge for the handling of registry funds deposited with the court, to be assessed from interest earnings and in accordance with the detailed fee schedule issued by the Director of the Administrative Office of the United States Courts.

For management of registry funds invested through the Court Registry Investment System, a fee at a rate of 2.5 basis points shall be assessed from interest earnings.

13. For filing an action brought under Title III of the Cuban Liberty and Democratic Solidarity (LIBERTAD) Act of 1996, P.L. 104–114, 110 Stat. § 785

(1996), $6,355. (This fee is in addition to the filing fee prescribed in 28 U.S.C. § 1914(a) for instituting any civil action other than a writ of habeas corpus.)

14. Administrative fee for filing a civil action, suit, or proceeding in a district court, $50. This fee does not apply to applications for a writ of habeas corpus or to persons granted in forma pauperis status under 28 U.S.C. § 1915.

15. Processing fee for a petty offense charged on a federal violation notice, $25.

1 Issued in accordance with 28 U.S.C. § 1914.

BANKRUPTCY COURT MISCELLANEOUS FEE SCHEDULE[1]

(Effective December 1, 2014)

The fees included in the Bankruptcy Court Miscellaneous Fee Schedule are to be charged for services provided by the bankruptcy courts.

- The United States should not be charged fees under this schedule, with the exception of those specifically prescribed in Items 1, 3 and 5 when the information requested is available through remote electronic access.

- Federal agencies or programs that are funded from judiciary appropriations (agencies, organizations, and individuals providing services authorized by the Criminal Justice Act, 18 U.S.C. § 3006A, and bankruptcy administrators) should not be charged any fees under this schedule.

(1) For reproducing any document, $.50 per page. This fee applies to services rendered on behalf of the United States if the document requested is available through electronic access.

(2) For certification of any document, $11.
For exemplification of any document, $21.

(3) For reproduction of an audio recording of a court proceeding, $30. This fee applies to services rendered on behalf of the United States if the recording is available electronically.

(4) For filing an amendment to the debtor's schedules of creditors, lists of creditors, or mailing list, $30, except:

- The bankruptcy judge may, for good cause, waive the charge in any case.

- This fee must not be charged if—

  - the amendment is to change the address of a creditor or an attorney for a creditor listed on the schedules; or

  - the amendment is to add the name and address of an attorney for a creditor listed on the schedules.

(5) For conducting a search of the bankruptcy court records, $30 per name or item searched. This fee applies to services rendered on behalf of the United States if the information requested is available through electronic access.

(6) For filing a complaint, $350, except:

- If the trustee or debtor-in-possession files the complaint, the fee must be paid only by the estate, to the extent there is an estate.

- This fee must not be charged if—

  - the debtor is the plaintiff; or

  - a child support creditor or representative files the complaint and submits the form required by § 304(g) of the Bankruptcy Reform Act of 1994.

(7) For filing any document that is not related to a pending case or proceeding, $46.

(8) Administrative fee:

- For filing a petition under Chapter 7, 12, or 13, $75.

- For filing a petition under Chapter 9, 11, or 15, $550.

- When a motion to divide a joint case under Chapter 7, 12, or 13 is filed, $75.

- When a motion to divide a joint case under Chapter 11 is filed, $550.

(9) For payment to trustees pursuant to 11 U.S.C. § 330(b)(2), a $15 fee applies in the following circumstances:

- For filing a petition under Chapter 7.
- For filing a motion to reopen a Chapter 7 case.
- For filing a motion to divide a joint Chapter 7 case.
- For filing a motion to convert a case to a Chapter 7 case.
- For filing a notice of conversion to a Chapter 7 case.

(10) In addition to any fees imposed under Item 9, above, the following fees must be collected:

- For filing a motion to convert a Chapter 12 case to a Chapter 7 case or a notice of conversion pursuant to 11 U.S.C. § 1208(a), $45.
- For filing a motion to convert a Chapter 13 case to a Chapter 7 case or a notice of conversion pursuant to 11 U.S.C. § 1307(a), $10.

The fee amounts in this item are derived from the fees prescribed in 28 U.S.C. § 1930(a).

If the trustee files the motion to convert, the fee is payable only from the estate that exists prior to conversion.

If the filing fee for the chapter to which the case is requested to be converted is less than the fee paid at the commencement of the case, no refund may be provided.

(11) For filing a motion to reopen, the following fees apply:

- For filing a motion to reopen a Chapter 7 case, $245.
- For filing a motion to reopen a Chapter 9 case, $1167.
- For filing a motion to reopen a Chapter 11 case, $1167.
- For filing a motion to reopen a Chapter 12 case, $200.
- For filing a motion to reopen a Chapter 13 case, $235.
- For filing a motion to reopen a Chapter 15 case, $1167.

The fee amounts in this item are derived from the fees prescribed in 28 U.S.C. § 1930(a).

The reopening fee must be charged when a case has been closed without a discharge being entered.

The court may waive this fee under appropriate circumstances or may defer payment of the fee from trustees pending discovery of additional assets. If payment is deferred, the fee should be waived if no additional assets are discovered.

The reopening fee must not be charged in the following situations:

- to permit a party to file a complaint to obtain a determination under Rule 4007(b); or
- when a debtor files a motion to reopen a case based upon an alleged violation of the terms of the discharge under 11 U.S.C. § 524; or
- when the reopening is to correct an administrative error; or
- to redact a record already filed in a case, pursuant to Fed. R. Bankr. 9037, if redaction is the only reason for reopening.

(12) For retrieval of one box of records from a Federal Records Center, National Archives, or other storage location removed from the place of business of the court, $64. For retrievals involving multiple boxes, $39 for each additional box.

(13) For any payment returned or denied for insufficient funds, $53.

(14) For filing an appeal or cross appeal from a judgment, order, or decree, $293.

This fee is collected in addition to the statutory fee of $5 that is collected under 28 U.S.C. § 1930(c) when a notice of appeal is filed.

Parties filing a joint notice of appeal should pay only one fee.

If a trustee or debtor-in-possession is the appellant, the fee must be paid only by the estate, to the extent there is an estate.

Upon notice from the court of appeals that a direct appeal or direct cross-appeal has been authorized, an additional fee of $207 must be collected.

(15) For filing a case under Chapter 15 of the Bankruptcy Code, $1167.

This fee is derived from and equal to the fee prescribed in 28 U.S.C. § 1930(a)(3) for filing a case commenced under Chapter 11 of Title 11.

(16) The court may charge and collect fees commensurate with the cost of providing copies of the local rules of court. The court may also distribute copies of the local rules without charge.

(17) The clerk shall assess a charge for the handling of registry funds deposited with the court, to be assessed from interest earnings and in accordance with the detailed fee schedule issued by the Director of the Administrative Office of the United States Courts.

For management of registry funds invested through the Court Registry Investment System, a fee at a rate of 2.5 basis points shall be assessed from interest earnings.

(18) For a motion filed by the debtor to divide a joint case filed under 11 U.S.C. § 302, the following fees apply:

- For filing a motion to divide a joint Chapter 7 case, $245.
- For filing a motion to divide a joint Chapter 11 case, $1167.
- For filing a motion to divide a joint Chapter 12 case, $200.
- For filing a motion to divide a joint Chapter 13 case, $235.

These fees are derived from and equal to the filing fees prescribed in 28 U.S.C. § 1930(a).

(19) For filing the following motions, $176:

- To terminate, annul, modify or condition the automatic stay;
- To compel abandonment of property of the estate pursuant to Rule 6007(b) of the Federal Rules of Bankruptcy Procedure;
- To withdraw the reference of a case or proceeding under 28 U.S.C. § 157(d); or
- To sell property of the estate free and clear of liens under 11 U.S.C. § 363(f).

This fee must not be collected in the following situations:

- For a motion for relief from the co-debtor stay;
- For a stipulation for court approval of an agreement for relief from a stay; or
- For a motion filed by a child support creditor or its representative, if the form required by § 304(g) of the Bankruptcy Reform Act of 1994 is filed.

(20) For filing a transfer of claim, $25 per claim transferred.

(21) For filing a motion to redact a record, $25 per affected case. The court may waive this fee under appropriate circumstances.

1 Issued in accordance with 28 U.S.C. § 1930.

JUDICIAL PANEL ON MULTIDISTRICT LITIGATION FEE SCHEDULE[1]

(28 U.S.C. § 1932)

(Effective December 1, 2013)

Following are fees to be charged for services to be performed by the clerk of the Judicial Panel on Multidistrict Litigation. No fees are to be charged for services rendered on behalf of the United States, with the exception of those specifically prescribed in items 1 and 3. No fees under this schedule shall be charged to federal agencies or programs which are funded from judiciary appropriations, including, but not limited to, agencies, organizations, and individuals providing services authorized by the Criminal Justice Act, 18 U.S.C. § 3006A.

(1) For every search of the records of the court conducted by the clerk of the court or a deputy clerk, $30 per name or item searched. This fee shall apply to services rendered on behalf of the United States if the information requested is available through electronic access.

(2) For certification of any document or paper, whether the certification is made directly on the document or by separate instrument, $11.

(3) For reproducing any record or paper, $.50 per page. This fee shall apply to paper copies made from either: (1) original documents; or (2) microfiche or microfilm reproductions of the original records. This fee shall apply to services rendered on behalf of the United States if the record or paper requested is available through electronic access.

(4) For retrieval of one box of records from a Federal Records Center, National Archives, or other storage location removed from the place of business of the court, $64. For retrievals involving multiple boxes, $39 for each additional box.

(5) For any payment returned or denied for insufficient funds, $53.

1 Issued in accordance with 28 U.S.C. § 1932.

ELECTRONIC PUBLIC ACCESS FEE SCHEDULE

(Issued in accordance with 28 U.S.C. §§ 1913, 1914, 1926, 1930, 1932)

(Effective December 1, 2013)

The fees included in the Electronic Public Access Fee Schedule are to be charged for providing electronic public access to court records.

Fees for Public Access to Court Electronic Records (PACER)

(1) Except as provided below, for electronic access to any case document, docket sheet, or case-specific report via PACER: $0.10 per page, not to exceed the fee for thirty pages.

(2) For electronic access to transcripts and non-case specific reports via PACER (such as reports obtained from the PACER Case Locator or docket activity reports): $0.10 per page.

(3) For electronic access to an audio file of a court hearing via PACER: $2.40 per audio file.

Fees for Courthouse Electronic Access

(4) For printing copies of any record or document accessed electronically at a public terminal in a courthouse: $0.10 per page.

PACER Service Center Fees

(5) For every search of court records conducted by the PACER Service Center, $30 per name or item searched.

(6) For the PACER Service Center to reproduce on paper any record pertaining to a PACER account, if this information is remotely available through electronic access: $0.50 per page.

(7) For any payment returned or denied for insufficient funds, $53.

Free Access and Exemptions

(8) **Automatic Fee Exemptions.**

- No fee is owed for electronic access to court data or audio files via PACER until an account holder accrues charges of more than $15.00 in a quarterly billing cycle.

- Parties in a case (including pro se litigants) and attorneys of record receive one free electronic copy, via the notice of electronic filing or notice of docket activity, of all documents filed electronically, if receipt is required by law or directed by the filer.

- No fee is charged for access to judicial opinions.

- No fee is charged for viewing case information or documents at courthouse public access terminals.

(9) **Discretionary Fee Exemptions.**

- Courts may exempt certain persons or classes of persons from payment of the user access fee. Examples of individuals and groups that a court may consider exempting include: indigents, bankruptcy case trustees, pro bono attorneys, pro bono alternative dispute resolution neutrals, Section 501(c)(3) not-for-profit organizations, and individual researchers associated with educational institutions. Courts should not, however, exempt individuals or groups that have the ability to pay the statutorily established access fee. Examples of individuals and groups that a court should not exempt include: local, state or federal government agencies, members of the media, privately paid attorneys or others who have the ability to pay the fee.

- In considering granting an exemption, courts must find:

- that those seeking an exemption have demonstrated that an exemption is necessary in order to avoid unreasonable burdens and to promote public access to information;

- that individual researchers requesting an exemption have shown that the defined research project is intended for scholarly research, that it is limited in scope, and that it is not intended for redistribution on the internet or for commercial purposes.

- If the court grants an exemption:

  - the user receiving the exemption must agree not to sell the data obtained as a result, and must not transfer any data obtained as the result of a fee exemption, unless expressly authorized by the court; and

  - the exemption should be granted for a definite period of time, should be limited in scope, and may be revoked at the discretion of the court granting the exemption.

- Courts may provide local court information at no cost (e.g., local rules, court forms, news items, court calendars, and other information) to benefit the public.

Applicability to the United States and State and Local Governments

(10) Unless otherwise authorized by the Judicial Conference, these fees must be charged to the United States, except to federal agencies or programs that are funded from judiciary appropriations (including, but not limited to, agencies, organizations, and individuals providing services authorized by the Criminal Justice Act [18 U.S.C. § 3006A], and bankruptcy administrators).

(11) The fee for printing copies of any record or document accessed electronically at a public terminal ($0.10 per page) described in (4) above does not apply to services rendered on behalf of the United States if the record requested is not remotely available through electronic access.

(12) The fee for local, state, and federal government entities, shall be $0.08 per page until April 1, 2015, after which time, the fee shall be $0.10 per page.

JUDICIAL CONFERENCE POLICY NOTES

The Electronic Public Access (EPA) fee and its exemptions are directly related to the requirement that the judiciary charge user-based fees for the development and maintenance of electronic public access services. The fee schedule provides examples of users that may not be able to afford reasonable user fees (such as indigents, bankruptcy case trustees, individual researchers associated with educational institutions, 501(c)(3) not-for-profit organizations, and court-appointed pro bono attorneys), but requires those seeking an exemption to demonstrate that an exemption is limited in scope and is necessary in order to avoid an unreasonable burden. In addition, the fee schedule includes examples of other entities that courts should not exempt from the fee (such as local, state or federal government agencies, members of the media, and attorneys). The goal is to provide courts with guidance in evaluating a requestor's ability to pay the fee.

Judicial Conference policy also limits exemptions in other ways. First, it requires exempted users to agree not to sell the data they receive through an exemption (unless expressly authorized by the court). This prohibition is not intended to bar a quote or reference to information received as a result of a fee exemption in a scholarly or other similar work. Second, it permits courts to grant exemptions for a definite period of time, to limit the scope of the exemptions, and to revoke exemptions. Third, it cautions that exemptions should be granted as the exception, not the rule, and prohibits courts from exempting all users from EPA fees.